Format for Bank Reconciliation:

Cash balance according to bank statement		$XXX
Add: Additions by company not on bank statement	$XXX	
Bank errors	XXX	XXX
		$XXX
Deduct: Deductions by company not on bank statement	$XXX	
Bank errors	XXX	XXX
Adjusted balance		$XXX

Cash balance according to company's records		$XXX
Add: Additions by bank not recorded by company	$XXX	
Company errors	XXX	XXX
		$XXX
Deduct: Deductions by bank not recorded by company	$XXX	
Company errors	XXX	XXX
Adjusted balance		$XXX

Inventory Costing Methods:

- First-in, First-out (FIFO)
- Last-in, First-out (LIFO)
- Average Cost

Interest Computations:

Interest = Face Amount (or Principal) × Rate × Time

Methods of Determining Annual Depreciation:

Straight-Line: $\frac{\text{Cost} - \text{Estimated Residual Value}}{\text{Estimated Life}}$

Double-Declining-Balance: Rate* × Book Value at Beginning of Period

*Rate is commonly twice the straight-line rate (1 ÷ Estimated Life).

Adjustments to Net Income (Loss) Using the Indirect Method:

	Increase (Decrease)
Net income (loss)	$ XXX
Adjustments to reconcile net income to net cash flow from operating activities:	
Depreciation of fixed assets	XXX
Amortization of intangible assets	XXX
Losses on disposal of assets	XXX
Gains on disposal of assets	(XXX)
Changes in current operating assets and liabilities:	
Increases in noncash current operating assets	(XXX)
Decreases in noncash current operating assets	XXX
Increases in current operating liabilities	XXX
Decreases in current operating liabilities	(XXX)
Net cash flow from operating activities	$ XXX or $(XXX)

Contribution Margin Ratio = $\frac{\text{Sales} - \text{Variable Costs}}{\text{Sales}}$

Break-Even Sales (Units) = $\frac{\text{Fixed Costs}}{\text{Unit Contribution Margin}}$

Sales (Units) = $\frac{\text{Fixed Costs} + \text{Target Profit}}{\text{Unit Contribution Margin}}$

Margin of Safety = $\frac{\text{Sales} - \text{Sales at Break-Even Point}}{\text{Sales}}$

Operating Leverage = $\frac{\text{Contribution Margin}}{\text{Income from Operations}}$

Variances:

Direct Materials Price Variance = $\left(\text{Actual Price} - \text{Standard Price}\right) \times$ Actual Quantity

Direct Materials Quantity Variance = $\left(\text{Actual Quantity} - \text{Standard Quantity}\right) \times$ Standard Price

Direct Labor Rate Variance = $\left(\text{Actual Rate per Hour} - \text{Standard Rate per Hour}\right) \times$ Actual Hours

Direct Labor Time Variance = $\left(\text{Actual Direct Labor Hours} - \text{Standard Direct Labor Hours}\right) \times$ Standard Rate per Hour

Variable Factory Overhead Controllable Variance = Actual Variable Factory Overhead − Budgeted Variable Factory Overhead

Fixed Factory Overhead Volume Variance = $\left(\text{Standard Hours for 100\% of Normal Capacity} - \text{Standard Hours for Actual Units Produced}\right) \times$ Fixed Factory Overhead Rate

Rate of Return on Investment (ROI) = $\frac{\text{Income from Operations}}{\text{Invested Assets}}$

Alternative ROI Computation:

$$\text{ROI} = \frac{\text{Income from Operations}}{\text{Sales}} \times \frac{\text{Sales}}{\text{Invested Assets}}$$

Capital Investment Analysis Methods:

Methods That Ignore Present Values:

- Average Rate of Return Method
- Cash Payback Method

Methods That Use Present Values:

- Net Present Value Method
- Internal Rate of Return Method

Average Rate of Return = $\frac{\text{Estimated Average Annual Income}}{\text{Average Investment}}$

Present Value Index = $\frac{\text{Total Present Value of Net Cash Flow}}{\text{Amount to Be Invested}}$

Present Value Factor for an Annuity of \$1 = $\frac{\text{Amount to Be Invested}}{\text{Equal Annual Net Cash Flows}}$

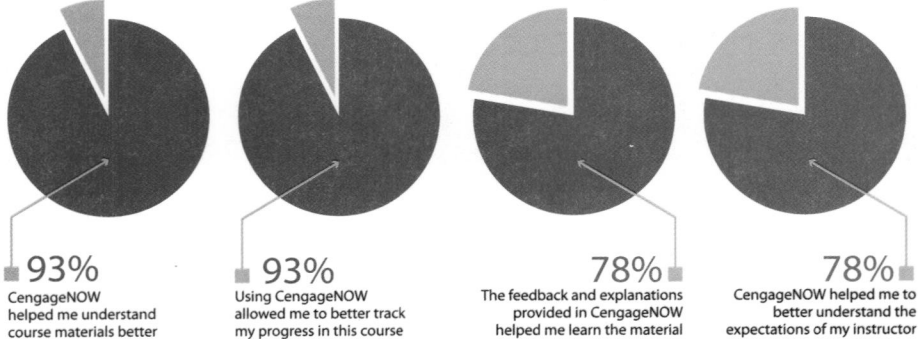

FINANCIAL ACCOUNTING

14e

Carl S. Warren
Professor Emeritus of Accounting
University of Georgia, Athens

James M. Reeve
Professor Emeritus of Accounting
University of Tennessee, Knoxville

Jonathan E. Duchac
Professor of Accounting
Wake Forest University

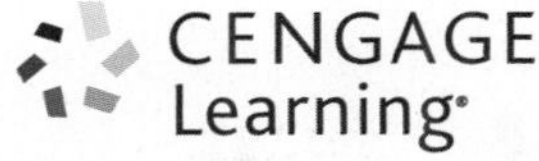

Australia • Brazil • Japan • Korea • Mexico • Singapore • Spain • United Kingdom • United States

Financial Accounting, 14e

Carl S. Warren
James M. Reeve
Jonathan E. Duchac

Vice President, General Manager, Science, Math, and Quantitative Business: Balraj Kalsi
Product Director: Mike Schenk
Sr. Product Manager: Matt Filimonov
Product Development Manager: Krista Kellman
Sr. Marketing Manager: Robin LeFevre
Sr. Marketing Coordinator: Eileen Corcoran
Managing Content Developer (Media): Scott Fidler
Content Developer (Media): Jessica Robbe
Software Development Manager: Phil Bower
Digital Content Designer: Peggy Hussey
Sr. Content Project Manager: Tim Bailey
Production Service: Cenveo Publisher Service
Manufacturing Planner: Doug Wilke
Sr. Art Director: Stacy Jenkins Shirley
Cover and Internal Designer: Red Hangar Design
Cover Image: © Design Pics Inc/Alamy
Intellectual Property:
Analyst: Christina Ciaramella
Project Manager: Betsy Hathaway

Library of Congress Control Number: 2014952912

ISBN-13: 978-1-305-08843-6
ISBN-10: 1-305-08843-3

Cengage Learning
20 Channel Center Street
Boston, MA 02210
USA

Cengage Learning is a leading provider of customized learning solutions with office locations around the globe, including Singapore, the United Kingdom, Australia, Mexico, Brazil, and Japan. Locate your local office at: **www.cengage.com/global**

Cengage Learning products are represented in Canada by Nelson Education, Ltd.

To learn more about Cengage Learning Solutions, visit **www.cengage.com**

Purchase any of our products at your local college store or at our preferred online store **www.cengagebrain.com**

Printed in the United States of America
Print Number: 01 Print Year: 2014

Warren/Reeve/Duchac Accounting & CengageNOWv2

An Integrated Learning System to Keep Students on Track and Progressing!

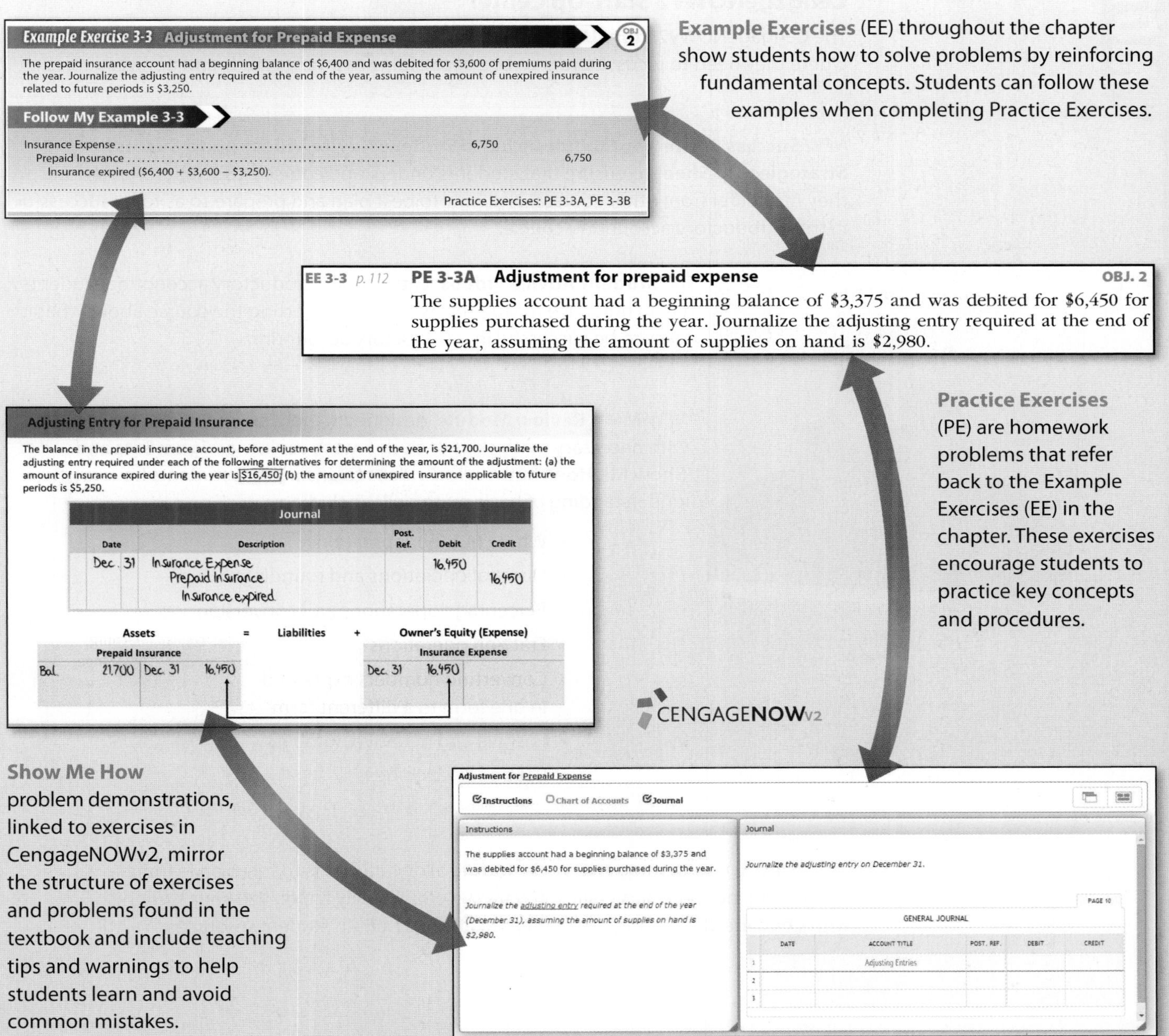

Example Exercise 3-3 Adjustment for Prepaid Expense
OBJ 2
The prepaid insurance account had a beginning balance of $6,400 and was debited for $3,600 of premiums paid during the year. Journalize the adjusting entry required at the end of the year, assuming the amount of unexpired insurance related to future periods is $3,250.
Follow My Example 3-3
Insurance Expense 6,750
Prepaid Insurance 6,750
Insurance expired ($6,400 + $3,600 – $3,250).
Practice Exercises: PE 3-3A, PE 3-3B
EE 3-3 p. 112 PE 3-3A Adjustment for prepaid expense OBJ. 2
The supplies account had a beginning balance of $3,375 and was debited for $6,450 for supplies purchased during the year. Journalize the adjusting entry required at the end of the year, assuming the amount of supplies on hand is $2,980.
Adjusting Entry for Prepaid Insurance
The balance in the prepaid insurance account, before adjustment at the end of the year, is $21,700. Journalize the adjusting entry required under each of the following alternatives for determining the amount of the adjustment: (a) the amount of insurance expired during the year is $16,450; (b) the amount of unexpired insurance applicable to future periods is $5,250.
Journal
Date Description Post. Ref. Debit Credit
Dec. 31 Insurance Expense 16,450
Prepaid Insurance 16,450
Insurance expired
Assets = Liabilities + Owner's Equity (Expense)
Prepaid Insurance
Bal. 21,700 Dec. 31 16,450
Insurance Expense
Dec. 31 16,450
CENGAGENOWv2
Adjustment for Prepaid Expense
Instructions Chart of Accounts Journal
Instructions
The supplies account had a beginning balance of $3,375 and was debited for $6,450 for supplies purchased during the year.
Journalize the adjusting entry required at the end of the year (December 31), assuming the amount of supplies on hand is $2,980.
Journal
Journalize the adjusting entry on December 31.
PAGE 10
GENERAL JOURNAL
DATE ACCOUNT TITLE POST. REF. DEBIT CREDIT
1 Adjusting Entries
2
3

Example Exercises (EE) throughout the chapter show students how to solve problems by reinforcing fundamental concepts. Students can follow these examples when completing Practice Exercises.

Practice Exercises (PE) are homework problems that refer back to the Example Exercises (EE) in the chapter. These exercises encourage students to practice key concepts and procedures.

Show Me How problem demonstrations, linked to exercises in CengageNOWv2, mirror the structure of exercises and problems found in the textbook and include teaching tips and warnings to help students learn and avoid common mistakes.

Practice Exercises are assignable in CengageNOWv2, which allows students to access helpful resources such as Check My Work and Show Me How problem demonstrations.

MOTIVATION

Set Course Expectations and Guide Students to Success!

Motivate students by reshaping their misconceptions about the introductory accounting course. Students are often surprised by both the approach to learning accounting and the necessary amount of time they need to spend outside of class working through homework assignments.

CengageNOWv2 Start-Up Center NEW!

The CengageNOWv2 **Start-Up Center** will help students identify what they need to do and where they need to focus in order to be successful with a variety of brand new resources.

NEW **Success Strategies Module** includes **Student Advice Videos** and a **Success Strategies Tip Sheet** to ensure that students understand course expectations (and how they may differ from other courses) and how to best plan and prepare so as to be successful in the introductory accounting course.

The **Student Advice Videos** feature real introductory accounting students giving guidance to students who are just starting the course about what it takes to be successful in introductory accounting.

NEW **Math Review Module**, designed to help students get up to speed with necessary math skills, includes **math review assignments** and **Show Me How** math review videos to ensure that students have an understanding of basic math skills, including:

- Whole number operations
- Decimal operations and rounding
- Percentage operations and conversion
- Fraction operations
- Converting numbers expressed in one form to a different form
- Positive and negative numbers
- Ratios and averages

NEW **How to Use CengageNOWv2 Module** allows students to focus on learning accounting, not on a particular software system. Quickly familiarize your students with CengageNOWv2 and direct them to all of its built-in student resources.

Expose Students to Concepts Before Class Begins!

With all the outside obligations accounting students have, finding time to read the textbook before class can be a struggle. Point students to the key concepts they need to know before they attend class.

Video: Animated Activities

Animated Activities are engaging animated scenarios that visually guide students through selected core topics in introductory accounting. Each activity uses a realistic company example to illustrate how the concepts relate to the everyday activities of a business. These activities include multiple-choice questions that gauge student understanding of the overarching chapter concepts.

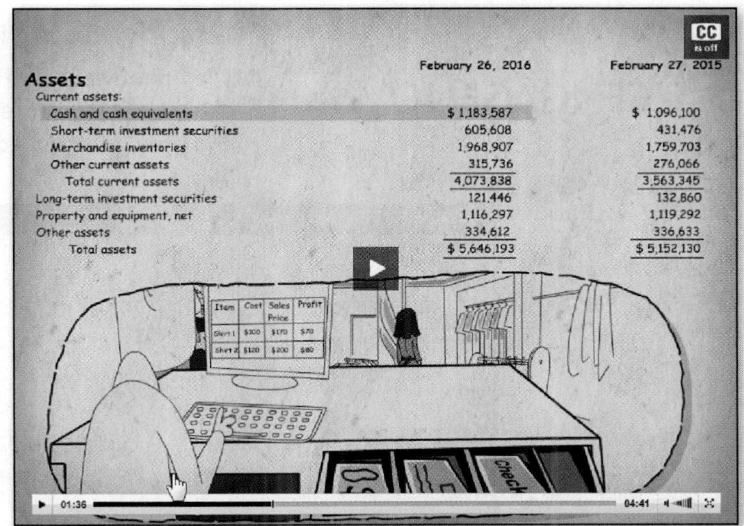

Animated Activities are assignable/gradable in CengageNOWv2 and available for self-study and review.

Prepaid Insurance

- The debit balance of $2,400 in NetSolutions' prepaid insurance account represents the December 1 prepayment of insurance for 12 months.

Dec.	31	Insurance Expense	55	200	
		Prepaid Insurance	15		200
		Insurance expired ($2,400 ÷ 12).			

Accounting Equation Impact

Assets = Liabilities + Owner's Equity (Expense)

Prepaid Insurance			15
Bal.	2,400	Dec. 31	200
Adj. Bal.	2,200		

decrease

increase

Insurance Expense			55
Dec. 31	200		

Tell Me More lecture activities for every Learning Objective are assignable/gradable in CengageNOWv2 and available for self-study and review.

Video: Tell Me More NEW!

Tell Me More lecture activities explain the core concepts of the chapter through an engaging auditory and visual presentation that is ideal for all class formats—flipped model, online, hybrid, face-to-face.

MOTIVATION

Expose Students to Concepts Before Class Begins!

Students don't want to waste time going over concepts that they have already mastered. With the NEW Adaptive Study Plan, they can focus on learning new topics and fully understanding difficult concepts.

Adaptive Study Plan NEW!

The Adaptive Study Plan in CengageNOWv2 is an assignable/gradable study center that adapts to each student's unique needs and provides a remediation pathway to keep students progressing.

The Adaptive Study Plan is assignable/gradable in CengageNOWv2 and available for self-study and review.

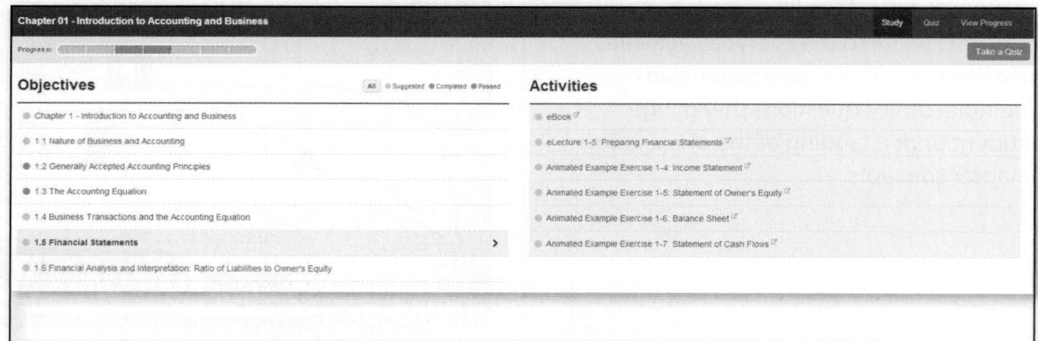

How does it work?

Step 1: Students take a chapter-level quiz consisting of randomized questions that cover both conceptual and procedural aspects of the chapter.

Step 2: Feedback is provided for each answer option explaining why the answer is right or wrong.

Step 3: Based on the quiz results, students are provided a remediation path that includes media assets and algorithmic practice problems to help them improve their understanding of the course material.

Instructors may use prerequisites that require students to achieve mastery in the Adaptive Study Plan before moving on to new material.

> *The new Adaptive Study Plan offers the benefit of customization coupled with remediation.*
>
> ***– Jennifer Schneider, professor at University of North Georgia***

Make Content Relatable!

Show students how the material they are learning matters in real life and help them connect accounting concepts to the world around them.

Pathways Commission "THIS is accounting!" 

Pathways Commission "THIS is accounting!" illustrates what students should understand as a result of their first exposure to accounting. Incorporated into Chapter 1, this graphic gives students a big picture view of how accounting can lead to a prosperous society.

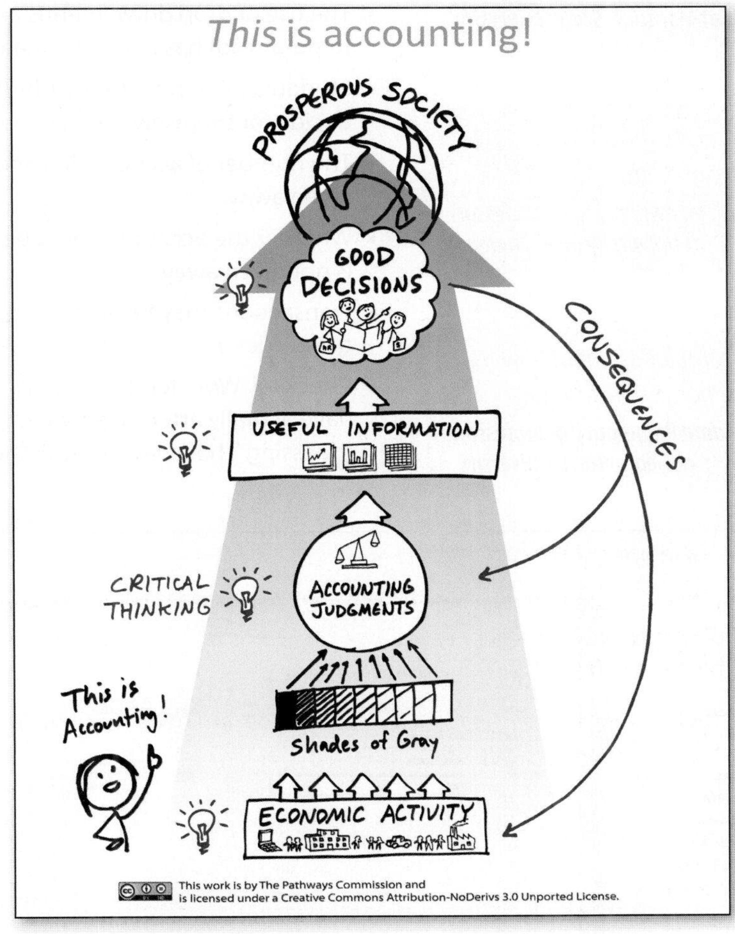

Source: ***Charting a National Strategy for the Next Generation of Accountants,*** **The Pathways Commission, July 2012.**

MOTIVATION

Close the Gap Between Homework and Exam Performance!

Many students perform well on homework but struggle when it comes to exams. Now, with the new Blank Sheet of Paper Experience, students must problem-solve on their own, just as they would if taking a test on a blank sheet of paper.

Good tool to make students understand concepts without overly relying on technology's help.
– Ramesh Narasimhan, professor at Montclair State University

I like it because it appears to bridge the gap between the homework and my exam.
– Lawrence Chui, professor at University of St. Thomas

This will minimize students' complaints about how the exam looks different from the homework format.
– Rama Ramamurthy, professor at Georgetown University

Blank Sheet of Paper Experience *NEW!*

A less-leading Blank Sheet of Paper Experience discourages overreliance on the system.

- The use of drop down menus and Smart Entry (type-ahead) has been eliminated.
- Students must refer to the Chart of Accounts and decide for themselves what account is impacted.
- The number of accounts in each transactions is not given away.
- Whether the account should be debited or credited is not given away.
- Transactions may be entered in any order (as long as the entries are correct).
- Check My Work feedback only reports on what students have actually attempted, which prevents students from "guessing" their way through the assignment.

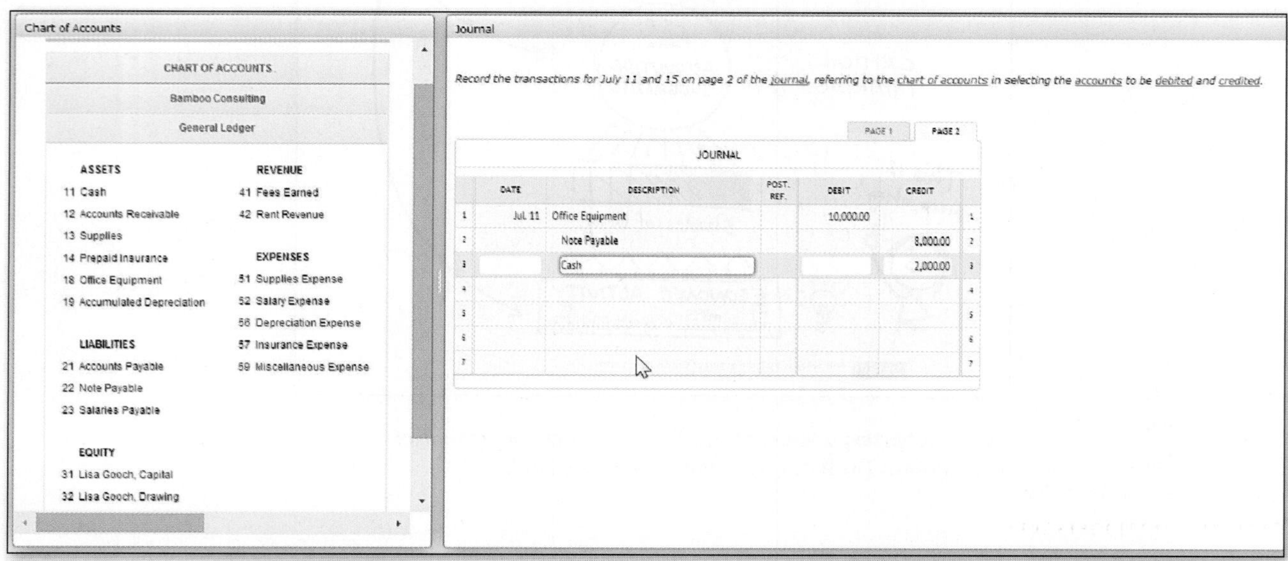

Check it out! Visit **cnowv2demo.cengage.com** for an interactive demo.

Help Students Make Connections and See the Big Picture!

Homework software should not get in the way of learning. One of the biggest complaints students have about online homework is the scrolling, which prevents students from seeing the big picture and understanding the accounting system. The new Multi-Panel View addresses this issue and enhances student learning.

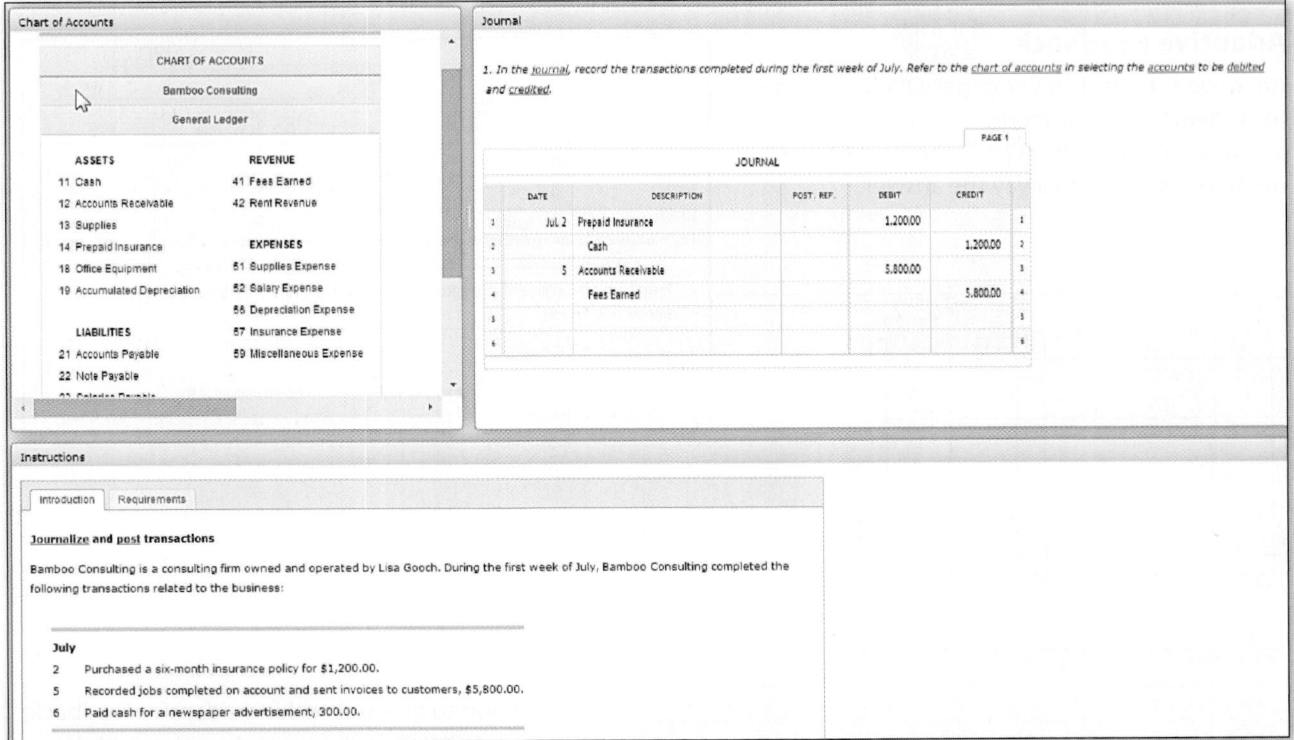

Multi-Panel View *NEW!*

The NEW Multi-Panel View in CengageNOWv2 enables students to see all the elements of a problem on one screen.

- Students make connections and see the tasks as connected components in the accounting process.
- Dramatically reduced scrolling eliminates student frustration.

With the ability to move and resize journals, ledgers, forms, and financial statements, it is easier to navigate the problem and understand the accounting system.

This is just a lot better and less confusing than scrolling up and down. … Having it like that would make it much easier —not so much scrolling and it wouldn't be so confusing.

– Tyler Mason, student at Northern Essex Community College

Multi-Panel View makes it much easier for students to see how each piece of the accounting cycle impacts the other pieces. Having it all in one view reduces student frustration and gives them a clearer picture of the complete accounting cycle.

– Kristen Quinn, professor at Northern Essex Community College

APPLICATION

Close the Gap Between Homework and Exam Performance!

Students often complete homework at odd times. And when they use CengageNOWv2, they get help right when they need it.

Adaptive Feedback NEW!

Adaptive Feedback in CengageNOWv2 responds to students based upon their unique answers and alerts them to the type of error they have made without giving away the answer.

PAGE 1 PAGE 2

JOURNAL Score: 33/138

	DATE	DESCRIPTION	POST. REF.	DEBIT	CREDIT	
1	Jul. 11	Office Equipment		10,000.00		1
2		Cash			8,000.00	2
3		Note Payaable			2,000.00	3

There is a minor spelling error in the account title. You will be graded as if you had entered "Note Payable."

Line

- The amount for this account is incorrect, although you've entered the amount in the correct column. [-2]

Points: 0.24 / 1

Feedback

▾ Check My Work

Identify which accounts are affected in each transaction. Keep in mind that every transaction involves at least two accounts. Determine whether the account increases or decreases and record each increase or decrease following the rules of debit and credit. Use the Posting Reference column to enter the corresponding account number from the general ledger account. Remember total debits should equal total credits in your entries.

Learning Objective 1
Learning Objective 2
Learning Objective 3

I like the adaptive feedback. It will reduce a number of errors that cause students to give up.

– Kevin Jones, professor at Drexel University

Excellent! Often learning from feedback is more powerful than learning from the instructor, text, etc.

– Lisa Brown, professor at Indiana Institute of Technology

In addition to groundbreaking, adaptive feedback, CengageNOWv2 continues to provide multiple layers of guidance to keep students on track and progressing.

- **Check My Work Feedback** provides general guidance and hints as students work through homework assignments.
- *NEW* **Check My Work Feedback** in CengageNOWv2 now only reports on what students have actually attempted, which prevents them from "guessing" their way through assignments.
- **Explanations** are available after the assignment has been submitted and provide a detailed description of how to arrive at the solution.

Check it out! Visit **cnowv2demo.cengage.com** for an interactive demo.

Help Students Make Connections and See the Big Picture!

The best way to learn accounting is through practice, but students often get stuck when attempting homework assignments on their own.

Video: Show Me How *NEW!*

Created for the most frequently assigned end-of-chapter items, hundreds of NEW Show Me How problem demonstration videos provide a step-by-step model of a similar problem. Embedded tips and warnings help students avoid common mistakes and pitfalls.

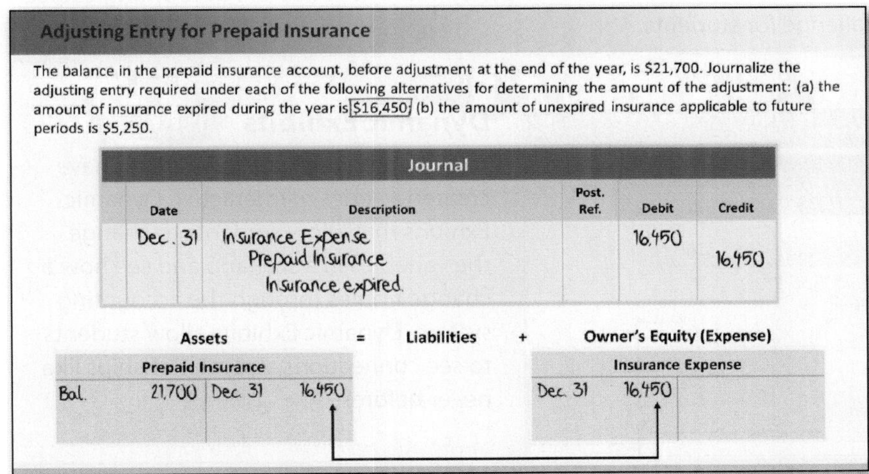

Adjusting Entry for Prepaid Insurance

The balance in the prepaid insurance account, before adjustment at the end of the year, is $21,700. Journalize the adjusting entry required under each of the following alternatives for determining the amount of the adjustment: (a) the amount of insurance expired during the year is $16,450; (b) the amount of unexpired insurance applicable to future periods is $5,250.

Journal

Date		Description	Post. Ref.	Debit	Credit
Dec.	31	Insurance Expense		16,450	
		Prepaid Insurance			16,450
		Insurance expired.			

Assets = Liabilities + Owner's Equity (Expense)

Prepaid Insurance			
Bal.	21,700	Dec. 31	16,450

Insurance Expense		
Dec. 31	16,450	

Identified by an icon in the text margins, Show Me How videos are linked to assignments in CengageNOWv2 and available for self-study and review.

Blueprint Problems

Blueprint Problems are teaching problems that walk students through a single accounting topic. These problems cover the primary learning objectives and are designed to help students understand foundational content and the associated building blocks versus memorizing the formulas or journal entries.

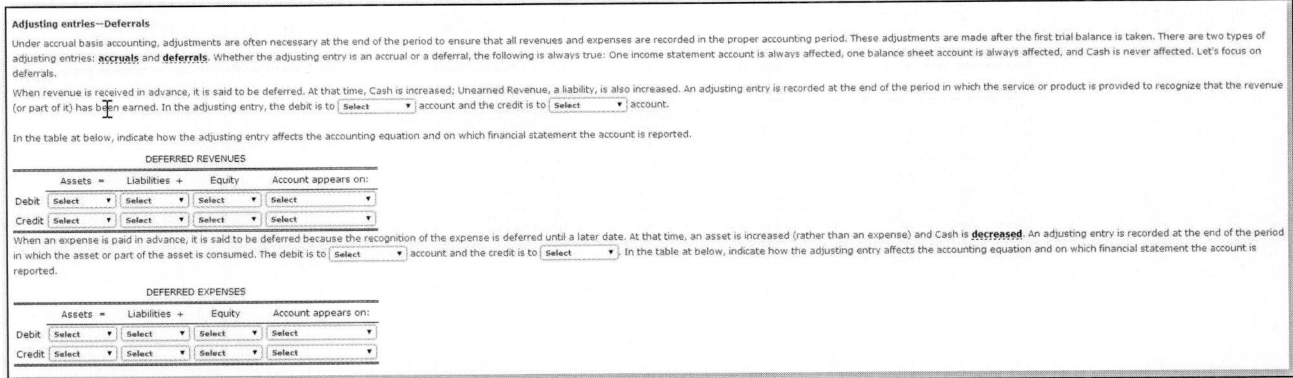

Adjusting entries—Deferrals

Under accrual basis accounting, adjustments are often necessary at the end of the period to ensure that all revenues and expenses are recorded in the proper accounting period. These adjustments are made after the first trial balance is taken. There are two types of adjusting entries: **accruals** and **deferrals**. Whether the adjusting entry is an accrual or a deferral, the following is always true: One income statement account is always affected, one balance sheet account is always affected, and Cash is never affected. Let's focus on deferrals.

When revenue is received in advance, it is said to be deferred. At that time, Cash is increased; Unearned Revenue, a liability, is also increased. An adjusting entry is recorded at the end of the period in which the service or product is provided to recognize that the revenue (or part of it) has been earned. In the adjusting entry, the debit is to [Select] account and the credit is to [Select] account.

In the table at below, indicate how the adjusting entry affects the accounting equation and on which financial statement the account is reported.

DEFERRED REVENUES

	Assets =	Liabilities +	Equity	Account appears on:
Debit	Select	Select	Select	Select
Credit	Select	Select	Select	Select

When an expense is paid in advance, it is said to be deferred because the recognition of the expense is deferred until a later date. At that time, an asset is increased (rather than an expense) and Cash is **decreased**. An adjusting entry is recorded at the end of the period in which the asset or part of the asset is consumed. The debit is to [Select] account and the credit is to [Select]. In the table at below, indicate how the adjusting entry affects the accounting equation and on which financial statement the account is reported.

DEFERRED EXPENSES

	Assets =	Liabilities +	Equity	Account appears on:
Debit	Select	Select	Select	Select
Credit	Select	Select	Select	Select

Blueprint Problems are assignable/gradable in CengageNOWv2.

NetSolutions Continuing Case Study

Students follow a fictitious company, **NetSolutions**, which demonstrates a rich variety of transactions. The continuity of presentation helps students master difficult concepts such as the accounting cycle.

APPLICATION

Help Students Go Beyond Memorization to True Understanding!

Students often struggle to understand how concepts relate to one another. For most students, an introductory accounting course is their first exposure to both *business transactions* and the *accounting system*. While these concepts are already difficult to master individually, their combination and interdependency in the introductory accounting course often pose a challenge for students.

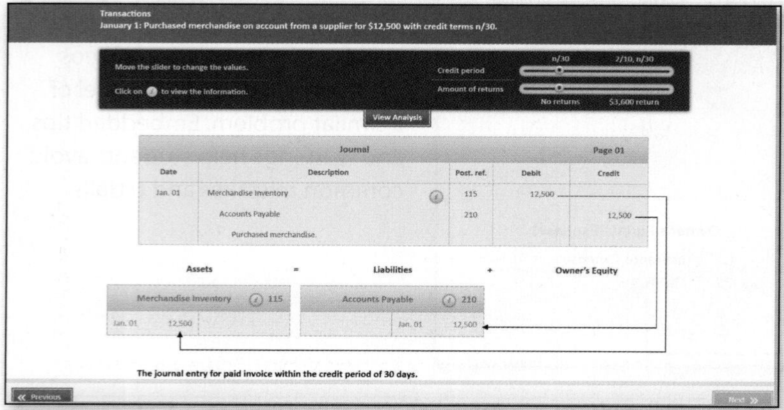

Identified by an icon in the text, Dynamic Exhibits are embedded within the MindTap eReader in CengageNOWv2. They are assignable/gradable in CengageNOWv2 and available for self-study and review.

Dynamic Exhibits NEW!

To overcome this gap, the authors have created a series of interactive Dynamic Exhibits that allow students to change the variables in a scenario and see how a change ripples through the accounting system. Dynamic Exhibits allow students to see connections and relationships like never before!

Blueprint Connections

Blueprint Connections are scenario-based teaching problems that solidify concepts and demonstrate their interrelationships, as well as promote critical thinking. Blueprint Connections combine multiple topics, allowing students to explore a larger concept more fully, and strengthen analytical skills.

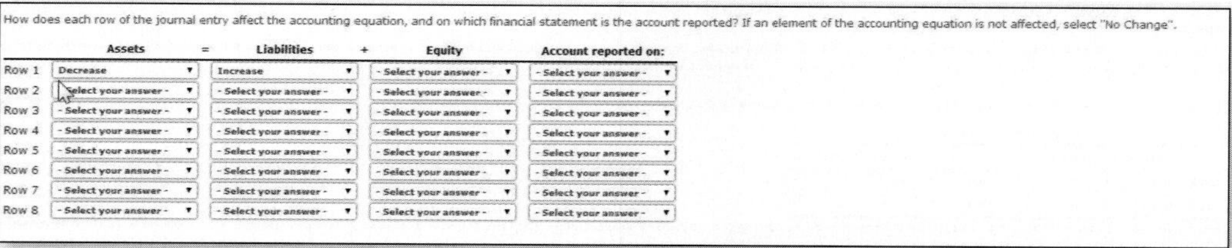

Blueprint Connections are assignable/gradable in CengageNOWv2.

Help Students Build Critical Thinking Skills!

Students often resort to memorization as a way to pass the course, but such surface learning does little to develop the critical thinking skills and deep understanding that are necessary for success in future business courses.

Activation Exercises

To overcome these challenges, the authors have created Activation Exercises to provide a learning system that focuses on developing a better understanding of:

- Key terms and definitions
- Economics of business transactions
- How transactions are recorded in the accounting system
- How transactions are ultimately reflected in the financial statements

These "what if" exercises help students understand relationships using interactive tools.

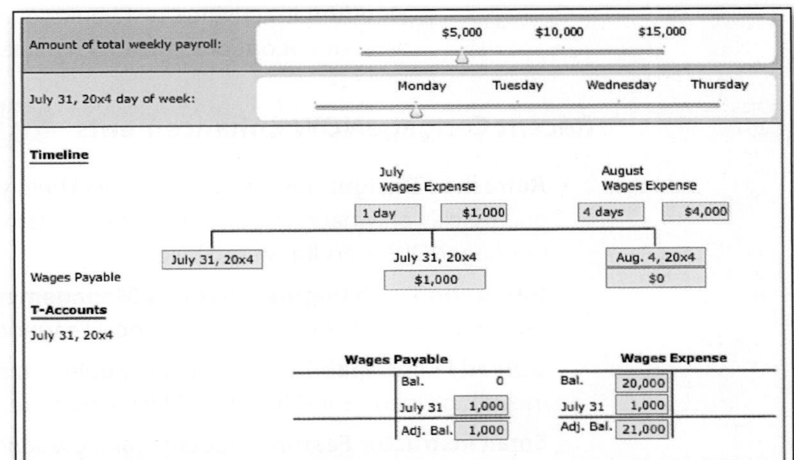

The Activation Exercises are assignable/gradable in CengageNOWv2.

> *These exercises are interactive and actually allow students to experiment with the data, visually viewing the impact when data is altered. The exercises show not only how a transaction looks in the journal and ledger accounts, but also the impact it ultimately has on financial statements. Finally, students are challenged to analyze the overall impact of a transaction by answering questions related to the topic. This is an excellent learning tool.*
>
> ***– Rita Mintz, professor at Calhoun Community College***

The Activation Exercises structure builds the critical thinking skills that are necessary for students to succeed in both introductory accounting and future accounting courses. Reviewers have enthusiastically praised the authors' online activities and indicated that they would be both ideal for pre-class activities and after-class assignments.

F·A·I

Financial Statement Analysis and Interpretation

The Financial Statement Analysis and Interpretation sections, at the end of financial accounting chapters, help students understand key ratios and how stakeholders interpret financial reports. These sections encourage students to go deeper into the material to analyze accounting information and improve critical thinking skills.

MASTERY

Online Solutions

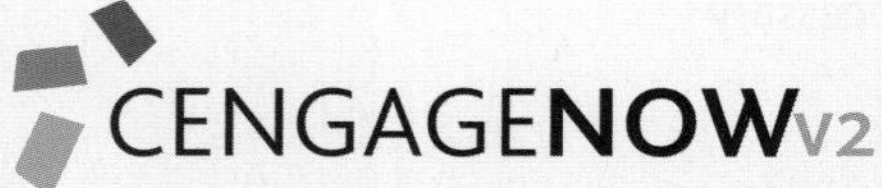

CengageNOWv2 is a powerful course management and online homework resource that provides control and customization to optimize the student learning experience. Included are many proven resources including algorithmic activities, test bank, course management tools, reporting and assessment options, and much more.

Recent CengageNOW Enhancements NEW!

- **Refreshed Design:** This refreshed look will help you and your students focus easily and quickly on what is important, while maintaining the same functionality that CengageNOW users know and love.
- **Integration with Popular Learning Management Systems:** Single login, deep linking, and grade return! (Check with your local Learning Consultant for more details!)
- **Upload Files Capability:** You can now upload files in CengageNOW for student use—including videos, Excel files, Word files, and more.
- **Email Instructor Feature**: Students can now send you a screenshot of the question they are working on directly through CengageNOW and ask specific questions about where they are stuck.
- **Better Date Management**: When modifying assignment due dates for a whole course, the system will now automatically adjust due dates based on a new start date, making it easier to reuse a course from one term to the next and adjust for snow days.
- **Streamlined Assignment Creation Process:** A simplified and streamlined Assignment Creation process allows instructors to quickly set up and manage assignments from a single page!
- **New Report Options:** New reporting options allow you to get better reports on your students' progress.
- **New Student Registration Process:** When you create a course, a URL will be generated that will automatically take students right into the instructor's course without them having to enter the course key!

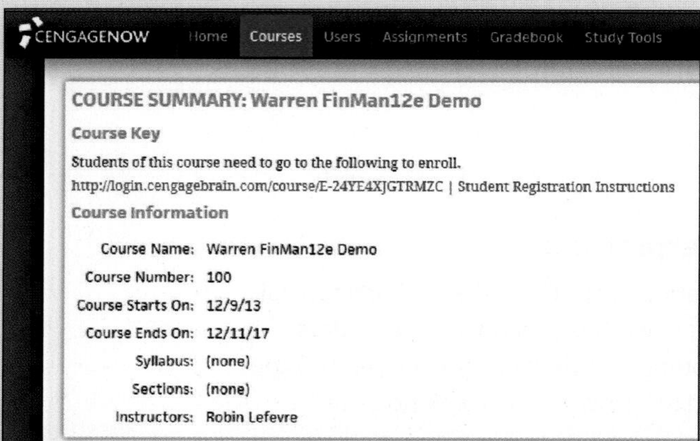

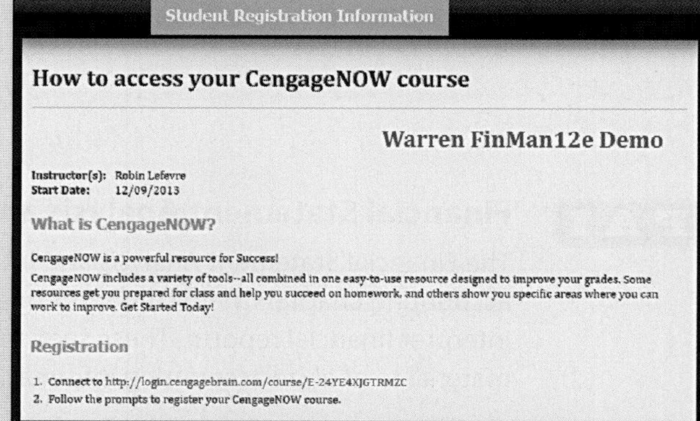

MindTap eReader

The MindTap eReader for Warren/Reeve/Duchac's *Financial Accounting* is the most robust digital reading experience available. Hallmark features include:

- Fully optimized for the iPad.
- Note taking, highlighting, and more.
- Embedded digital media such as Dynamic Exhibits.

The MindTap eReader also features ReadSpeaker®, an online text-to-speech application that vocalizes, or "speech-enables," online educational content. This feature is ideally suited for both instructors and learners who would like to listen to content instead of (or in addition to) reading it.

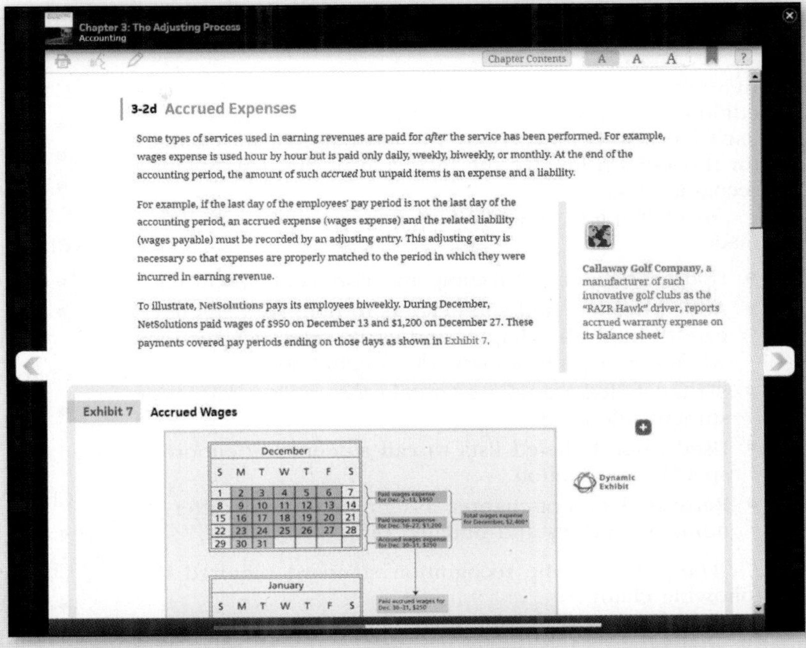

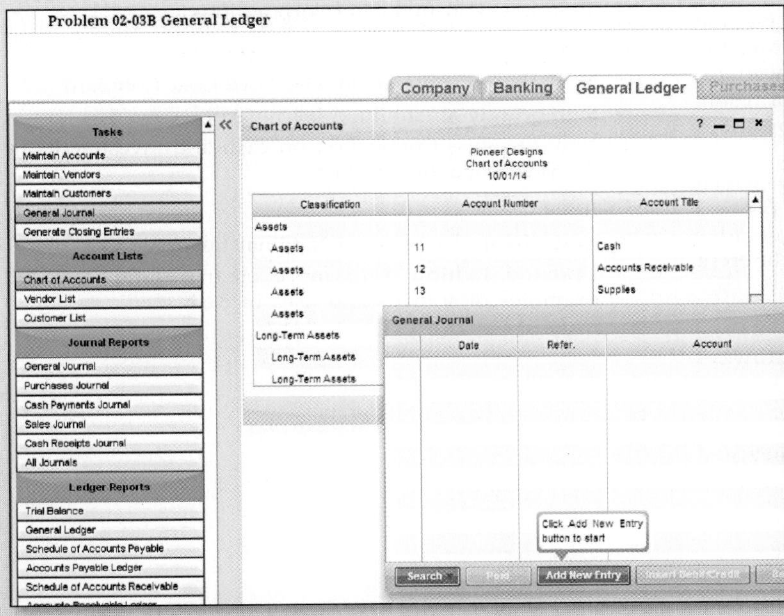

Cengage Learning General Ledger Software (CLGL)

CLGL exposes students to computerized accounting software without teaching the specifics of a certain software system—preparing students for *any* software program they might encounter in the real world.

- Now available in CengageNOWv2, CLGL allows students to work through end-of-chapter assignments and practice sets in a format that emulates commercial general ledger software, but in a manner that is more forgiving of errors.
- Assignments are automatically graded online.
- Selected problems that can be solved using CLGL are designated by an icon in the textbook and are listed in the assignment preparation grid in the Instructor's Manual.

New to This Edition

In addition to the many new digital assets created for this edition of *Financial Accounting*, the textbook content itself has also been revised. The most significant changes for this edition involve the inclusion of the new revenue recognition standard.

In all chapters, the following improvements have been made:

- Updated dates and real company information for currency
- Added headers and sub-headers to help students navigate through the chapter and easily reference sections when completing homework assignments
- Set unlabeled graphics as numbered exhibits for easier student reference
- Used more bulleted lists to call students' attention to specific information
- Refreshed end-of-chapter assignments with different numerical values and updated information

The new revenue recognition standard required the following changes:

- Revised the definitions of revenue and revenue recognition in Chapters 1–3, including the glossary. These revisions are consistent with the new revenue recognition standard, **Revenue from Contracts with Customers (Topic 606)**, FASB, May 2014.
- Revised Chapter 6, *Accounting for Merchandising Businesses*, to be consistent with the preceding standard. These revisions include using the net method for all purchase and sales discounts. In addition, the accounting for customer returns and allowances, including cash refunds, has been updated. As a result, sales discounts and sales return and allowances accounts are no longer used.
- Added new Appendix E, *Revenue Recognition*, which describes and illustrates the new Five-Step process for recognizing revenue. The illustration includes the accounting for a bundled product with different performance obligations.

Chapter 1

- New Business Connection includes The Pathways Commission definition of *accounting*

Chapter 2

- New Business Connection on Microsoft's unearned revenue

Chapter 3

- New chapter opener on Pandora
- Revised introduction to revenue recognition
- New Business Connection on Microsoft dealing with unearned revenue for support services

Chapter 4

- New chapter opener on Zynga
- Updated exposition of Appendix 1 showing end-of-period spreadsheet usage

Chapter 6

- Updated the Sales Discounts and Sales Returns and Allowances discussion for accuracy with the new revenue recognition standard

Chapter 10

- New chapter opener on McDonald's

Chapter 11

- New chapter opener on Starbucks
- Updated Exhibit 3 to reflect current wage withholding rates

Chapter 12

- New chapter opener on the Boston Celtics

Chapter 14

- Updated learning objective 1 to more clearly explain alternatives in financing corporations

Chapter 15

- New chapter opener on The Coca-Cola Company
- Significantly streamlined learning objective 5
- New Business Connection on cash and investments in the pharmaceutical industry

Chapter 16

- New chapter opener on National Beverage Co.
- Updated Exhibit 1 to more clearly detail specific examples of sources and uses of cash

Instructor Resources

Solutions Manual

Author-written and carefully verified multiple times to ensure accuracy and consistency with the text, the Solutions Manual contains answers to the Discussion Questions, Practice Exercises, Exercises, Problems (Series A and Series B), Cases, and Continuing Problems that appear in the text. These solutions help you easily plan, assign, and efficiently grade assignments.

Test Bank NEW!

NEW for this edition, Test Bank content is now delivered in an online platform. Cengage Learning Testing Powered by Cognero is a flexible, online system that allows you to:

- Author, edit, and manage test bank content from multiple Cengage Learning solutions
- Create multiple test versions in an instant
- Deliver tests from your LMS, your classroom, or wherever you want

Also *NEW* for this edition, 100 new Test Bank questions have been added (in addition to revising numeric values for approximately 20% of the existing questions).

Companion Website

This robust companion website provides immediate access to a rich array of teaching and learning resources–including the Instructor's Manual, PowerPoint slides, and Excel Template Solutions. Easily download the instructor resources you need from the password-protected, instructor-only section of the site.

Instructor's Manual Discover new ways to engage your students by utilizing the Instructor's Manual ideas for class discussion, group learning activities, writing exercises, and Internet activities. Moreover, simplify class preparation by reviewing a brief summary of each chapter, a detailed chapter synopsis (*NEW* for this edition), teaching tips regarding a suggested approach to the material, questions students frequently ask in the classroom, lecture aids, and demonstration problems in the Instructor's Manual. Transparency Masters and Handouts (with solutions) are also included. Quickly identify the assignments that best align with your course with the assignment preparation grid that includes information about learning objective coverage, difficulty level and Bloom's taxonomy categorization, time estimates, and accrediting standard alignment for business programs, AICPA, ACBSP, and IMA.

PowerPoint Slides Bring your lectures to life with slides designed to clarify difficult concepts for your students. The lecture PowerPoints include key terms and definitions, equations, examples, exhibits, and all Example Exercises (with solutions) from the textbook.

- *NEW* for this edition, descriptions for all graphics in the PowerPoints have been added to enhance PowerPoint usability for students with disabilities.
- Two separate PowerPoint decks that include just the Example Exercises (and solutions) and just the Exhibits from the textbook are ideal for instructors that create their own PowerPoint decks and just want to refresh them.

Excel Template Solutions Excel Templates are provided for selected long or complicated end-of-chapter exercises and problems to assist the student as they set up and work the problem. Certain cells are coded to display a red asterisk when an incorrect answer is entered, which helps students stay on track. Selected problems that can be solved using these templates are designated by an icon in the textbook and are listed in the assignment preparation grid in the Instructor's Manual. The Excel Template Solutions provide answers to these templates. *NEW* for this edition, 10 more Excel Templates have been added.

Practice Set Solutions Establish a fundamental understanding of the accounting cycle for your students with Practice Sets, which require students to complete one month of transactions for a fictional company. Brief descriptions of each Practice Set are provided in the Table of Contents. The Practice Set Solutions provide answers to these practice sets.

Student Resources

Study Guide

Now available free in CengageNOWv2, the Study Guide allows students to easily assess what they know with a "Do You Know" checklist covering the key points in each chapter. To further test their comprehension, students can work through Practice Exercises, which include a "strategy" hint and solution so they can continue to practice applying key accounting concepts.

Working Papers

Now available free in CengageNOWv2, students will find the tools they need to help work through end-of-chapter assignments with these working papers. The preformatted templates provide a starting point by giving students a basic structure for problems and journal entries. Working Papers are also available in a printed format as a bundle option.

Practice Sets

General**LEDGER**

For more in-depth application of accounting practices, instructors may choose from among six different Practice Sets for long-term assignments. Each Practice Set requires students to complete one month of transactions for a fictional company. Practice Sets can be solved manually or with the Cengage Learning General Ledger software.

Website

Designed specifically for your students' accounting needs, this website features student PowerPoint slides, Excel Templates, learning games, and flashcards.

- **PowerPoint Slides:** Students can easily take notes or review difficult concepts with the student version of this edition's PowerPoint slides.

- **Excel Templates:** These Excel Templates help students stay on track. If students enter an incorrect answer in certain cells, a red asterisk will appear to let them know something is wrong. Problems that can be solved using these templates are designated by an icon.
- **Crossword Puzzles:** Students can focus on learning the key terms and definitions for each chapter in a different way by completing these crossword puzzles.
- **Flashcards:** Students can prepare with these flashcards, which cover the key terms and definitions they need to know for each chapter.

Acknowledgements

The many enhancements to this edition of *Financial Accounting* are the direct result of one-on-one interviews, surveys, reviews, WebExes, and focus groups with over 300 instructors and students at institutions across the country over the past two years. We would like to take this opportunity to thank those who helped us better understand the challenges of the principles of accounting course and provided valuable feedback on our content and digital assets.

Instructors:
Aaron Pennington, York College of Pennsylvania
Adam Myers, Texas A&M University
Aileen Huang, Santa Monica College
Ajay Maindiratta, New York University
Alex Gialanella, Manhattanville College
Andrea Murowski, Brookdale Community College
Angelo Luciano, Columbia College, Chicago
Ann Gervais, Springfield Technical Comm College
Ann Gregory, South Plains College
Anna Boulware, St. Charles Community College
Anne Marie Anderson, Raritan Valley Community College
April Poe, University of the Incarnate Word
Barbara Kren, Marquette University
Bea Chiang, The College of New Jersey
Becky Hancock, El Paso Community College
Brenda McVey, Green River Community College
Bruce England, Massasoit Community College
Bruce L. Darling, University of Oregon
Bruce Leung, City College of San Francisco
Carol Dickerson, Chaffey College
Carol Graham, The University of San Francisco
Cassandra H. Catlett, Carson Newman University
Cecile Roberti, Community College of Rhode Island
Charles J.F. Leflar, University of Arkansas
Charles Lewis, Houston Community College
Chris Kinney, Mount Wachusett Community College
Chris McNamara, Finger Lakes Community College
Christopher Ashley, Everest College
Christopher Demaline, Central Arizona College
Cindy Bleasdal, Hilbert College
Colleen Chung, Miami Dade College
Cynthia Bolt, The Citadel
Cynthia J. Miller, University of Kentucky
Cynthia Johnson, University of Arkansas at Little Rock
Darlene Schnuck, Waukesha County Technical College
Dave Alldredge, Salt Lake Community College
David Centers, Grand Valley State University
David E. Laurel, South Texas College
Dawn Lopez, Johnson & Wales University
Dawn Peters, Southwestern Illinois College
Dawn W. Stevens, Northwest Mississippi Community College
Debbie Adkins, Remington College Online
Debbie Luna, El Paso Community College
Debbie Rose, Northeast Wisconsin Technical College
Debora Constable, Georgia Perimeter College
Denise Teixeira, Chemeketa Community College
Don Curfman, McHenry County College
Dori Danko, Grand Valley State University
Dorothy Davis, University of Louisiana, Monroe
Edwin Pagan, Passaic County Community College
Elizabeth Ammann, Lindenwood University
Emmanuel Danso, Palm Beach State College
Ercan Sinmaz, Houston Community College
Eric Blazer, Millersville University
Erik Lindquist, Lansing Community College
Esther S. Bunn, Stephen F Austin State University
Felicia R. Baldwin, Richard J. Daley College
Gary Bower, Community College of Rhode Island
Geoffrey D. Bartlett, Drake University
Gerald Smith, University of Northern Iowa
Glenn (Mel) McQueary, Houston Community College
Gloria Grayless, Sam Houston State University
Greg Lauer, North Iowa Area Community College
Gregory Brookins, Santa Monica College
Harold Little, Western Kentucky University
Jacqueline Burke, Hofstra University
James Lock, Northern Virginia Community College
James M. Emig, Villanova University
James Webb, University of the Pacific
Jamie O'Brien, South Dakota State University
Jan Barton, Emory University
Jana Hosmer, Blue Ridge Community College
Janice Akeo, Butler Community College
Jeanette Milius, Iowa Western Community College
Jeff Varblow, College of Lake County
Jeffrey T. Kunz, Carroll University
Jennifer LeSure, Ivy Tech Community College
Jennifer Mack, Lindenwood University
Jennifer Schneider, University of North Georgia
Jennifer Spring Sneed, Arkansas State University-Newport
Jenny Resnick, Santa Monica College
Jill Mitchell, Northern Virginia Community College
Jim Shelton, Harding University
Joel Strong, St. Cloud State University
Johh G. Ahmad, Northern Virginia Community College
John Babich, Kankakee Community College
John Nader, Davenport University
John Seilo, Irvine Valley College
John Verani, White Mountains Community College

Johnna Murray, University of Missouri-St. Louis
Joseph M. Nicassio, Westmoreland County Community College
Judith A. Toland, Bucks County Community College
Judith Zander, Grossmont College
Judy Patrick, Minnesota State Community and Technical College
Judy Smith, Parkland College
Julia M. Camp, Providence College
Julie Dawson, Carthage College
Julie Miller Millmann, Chippewa Valley Technical College
Karen C. Elsom, Fayetteville Technical Community College
Katherine Sue Hewitrt, Klamath Community College
Katy Long, Hill College
Keith Hallmark, Calhoun Community College
Kevin McNelis, New Mexico State University
Kimberly Franklin, St. Louis Community College
Kirk Canzano, Long Beach City College
Kristen Quinn, Northern Essex Community College
La Vonda Ramey, Schoolcraft College
Lana Tuss, Chemeketa Community College
Larry G. Stephens, Austin Community College
Lawrence A. Roman, Cuyahoga Community College
Lawrence Chui, University of St. Thomas
Leah Arrington, Northwest Mississippi Community College
Leah Russell, Holyoke Community College
Lee Smart, Southwest Tennessee Community College
Len Heritage, Tacoma Community College
Leonard Cronin, University Center Rochester
Linda Christiansen, Indiana University Southeast
Linda H. Tarrago, Hillsborough Community College
Linda Miller, Northeast Community College
Linda Muren, Cuyahoga Community College
Linda Tarrago, Hillsborough Community College
Lisa Busto, William Rainey Harper College
Lisa Novak, Mott Community College
Lori A. Grady, Bucks County Community College
Lori Johnson, Minnesota State University Moorhead
Louann Hofheins Cummings, The University of Findlay
Lucile Faurel, University of California Irvine
Lynn Almond, Virginia Tech
Lynn K. Saubert, Radford University
Lynn Krausse, Bakersfield College
Machiavelli W. Chao, University of California, Irvine
Magan Calhoun, Austin Peay State University
Marcela Raphael, Chippewa Valley Technical College
Marci Butterfield, University of Utah
Marianne James, California State University, Los Angeles
Marie Saunders, Dakota County Technical College
Marilyn Stansbury, Calvin College
Marina Grau, Houston Community College
Martin Hart, Manchester Comm College
Mary Zenner, College of Lake County
Meg Costello Lambert, Oakland Community College
Merrily Hoffman, San Jacinto College
Michael G. Schaefer, Blinn College
Michael Goeken, Northwest Vista College
Michael Gurevitz, Montgomery College
Michael J. Gallagher, DeSales University
Michael Lawrence, Mt. Hood Community College
Michael P. Dole, Marquette University
Michael P. Prockton, Finger Lakes Community College
Michele Martinez, Hillsborough Community College
Michelle Moshier, University at Albany
Ming Lu, Santa Monica College
Mon Sellers, Lone Star College-North Harris
Nancy Emerson, North Dakota State University
Nancy L. Snow, University of Toledo
Nino Gonzalez, El Paso Community College
Noel McKeon, Florida State College at Jacksonville
Odessa Jordan, Calhoun Community College
Pam Meyer, University of Louisiana at Lafayette
Pamela Knight, Columbus Technical College
Patricia Doherty, Boston University School of Management
Patricia Walczak, Lansing Community College
Patricia Worsham, Norco College
Patrick Rogan, Cosumnes River College
Perry Sellers, Lone Star College System
Rachel Pernia, Essex County College
Rebecca Grava Davis, East Mississippi Community College
Rebecca Hancock, El Paso Community College
Richard Lau, California State University, Los Angeles
Richard Mandau, Piedmont Technical College
Rick Andrews, Sinclair Community College
Rick Rinetti, Los Angeles City College
Rita Mintz, Calhoun Community College
Robert A. Pacheco, Massasoit Community College
Robert Almon, South Texas College
Robert E. (Reb) Beatty, Anne Arundel Community College
Robert Foster, Los Angeles Pierce College
Robert Urell, Irvine Valley College
Robin D'Agati, Palm Beach State College
Ron O'Brien, Fayetteville Technical Community College
Roy Carson, Anne Arundel Community College
Ryan Smith, Columbia College
Sandra Cohen, Columbia College Chicago
Sara Barritt, Northeast Community College
Saturnino (Nino) Gonzalez, El Paso Community College
Shani N. Robinson, Sam Houston State University
Sharif Soussi, Charter Oak State College
Sharon Agee, Rollins College
Sheila Ammons, Austin Community College
Sheila Guillot, Lamar State College-Port Arthur
Sol. Ahiarah, SUNY Buffalo State
Stacy Kline, Drexel University
Stani Kantcheva, Cincinnati State Technical and Community College
Steven J. LaFave, Augsburg College
Sue Cunningham, Rowan Cabarrus Community College
Suneel Maheshwari, Marshall University
Susan Cordes, Johnson County Community College

Suzanne Laudadio, Durham Technical Community College
Sy Pearlman, California State University, Long Beach
Tara Laken, Joliet Junior College
Taylor Klett, Sam Houston State University
Teresa Thompson, Chaffey Community College
Terri Walsh, Seminole State College
Thane Butt, Champlain College
Thomas Branton, Alvin Community College
Tim Green, North Georgia Technical College
Timothy Griffin, Hillsborough Community College
Timothy J. Moran, Aurora University
Timothy Swenson, Sullivan University
Tony Cioffi, Lorain County Community College
W. Jeff Knight, Flagler College
Wanda Wong, Chabot College

Students:
Allison Seaman, University of Findlay
Amber Bostick, Joliet Junior College
Amelia Lupis, Community College of Rhode Island
Andrew Buckley, Community College of Rhode Island
Andrew Mancini, Valparaiso University
Anita Jordan, Henry Ford Community College
Billie Ma, Middlesex County College
Blair Ericksen, The University of Findlay
Bonnie Eme, Ivy Tech Community College
Bradley "The Snowman" Koepke, Valparaiso University
Briana E Garrity, Community College of Rhode Island
Brittany Smothers, Ivy Tech Community College
Carly Butler, Sinclair Community College
Carmen Macvicar, Henry Ford Community College
Cassie Skal, University of Findlay
Charlene Resch, Ivy Tech Community College
Cheila Soares, Community College of Rhode Island
Christopher W. Gregory, Fayetteville Technical Community College
Colby Zachary, Austin Community College
Courtney Murphy, Sinclair Community College
Daniel Hart, Ivy Tech Community College
David Camargo, Fayetteville Technical Community College
Debborah Gideon, Ivy Tech Community College
Diana Contreras, Joliet Junior College
Dolores Velasquez, Ivy Tech Community College
Eleticia Feliciano, Henry Ford Community College
Eli Coulton, Sinclair Community College
Emilie Ferdelman, Sinclair Community College
Geoffrey Hlavach, Joliet Junior College
Jayme Thornley, Community College of Rhode Island
Jessie Laberge, Community College of Rhode Island
Joel Mondragon, Austin Community College
Jonathan Balsavich, Joliet Junior College
Jose Nieto, Austin Community College
J. Stoll, The University of Findlay
Karolina Tovpenec, The University of Findlay
Kathryn Shaw, Ivy Tech Community College
Kaylene Slayton, The University of Findlay
Kevin McMaster, Community College of Rhode island
Khadija Brikate, Erie Community College
Kimberlee Serrano, Middlesex County College
Kimberly Arruda, Community College of Rhode Island
Krista Jalette, Community College of Rhode Island
Leslie Bryant, Henry Ford Community College
Luke Fleming, Ivy Tech Community College
Malorie Masek, Valparaiso University
Marah Jammal, Henry Ford Community College
Marshall Miller, Valparaiso University
Matthew Vizzaccaro, Henry Ford Community College
Mayra Vargas, Austin Community College
Meghan Traster, Ivy Tech Community College
M. Lallier, Community College of Rhode Island
Michael L. Bardey, Sinclair Community College
Min Dou, Valparaiso University
Nicholas Johnson, Ivy Tech Community College
Nick L., Holyoke Community College
Nicholas Oliveira, Community College of Rhode island
Rachel Brown, Sinclair Community College
Ramona Hawkins, Ivy Tech Community College
Ryan Dvorak, Joliet Junior College
Ryan Truschke, Grand Valley State University
S.J. Cross, Ivy Tech Community College
Scott Nicol, Joliet Junior College
Sean Bingham, The University of Findlay
Sheila Diodonet, Holyoke Community College
Stephanie Theresa Plante, Community College of Rhode Island
Tasha Finley, Ivy Tech Community College
Trang Thi Vu, The University of Findlay
Tyler Philbin, Community College of Rhode Island
William Carter, The University of Findlay

About the Authors

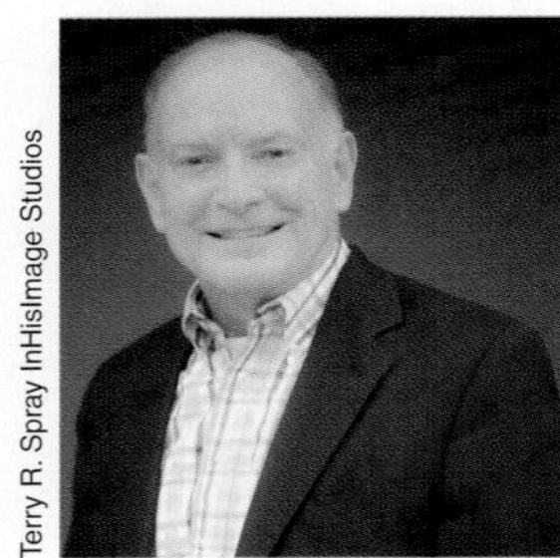
Terry R. Spray InHisImage Studios

Carl S. Warren

Dr. Carl S. Warren is Professor Emeritus of Accounting at the University of Georgia, Athens. Dr. Warren has taught classes at the University of Georgia, University of Iowa, Michigan State University, and University of Chicago. Professor Warren focused his teaching efforts on principles of accounting and auditing. He received his Ph.D. from Michigan State University and his B.B.A. and M.A. from the University of Iowa. During his career, Dr. Warren published numerous articles in professional journals, including *The Accounting Review, Journal of Accounting Research, Journal of Accountancy, The CPA Journal,* and *Auditing: A Journal of Practice & Theory*. Dr. Warren has served on numerous committees of the American Accounting Association, the American Institute of Certified Public Accountants, and the Institute of Internal Auditors. He has also consulted with numerous companies and public accounting firms. Professor Warren is an avid handball player and has played in the World Handball Championships in Portland, Oregon, and Dublin, Ireland. He enjoys backpacking and recently took an eleven-day, ten-night trip in the Thorofare area of Yellowstone National Park. He has rafted the Grand Canyon and backpacked rim-to-rim. Professor Warren also enjoys fly fishing, skiing, golfing, and motorcycling.

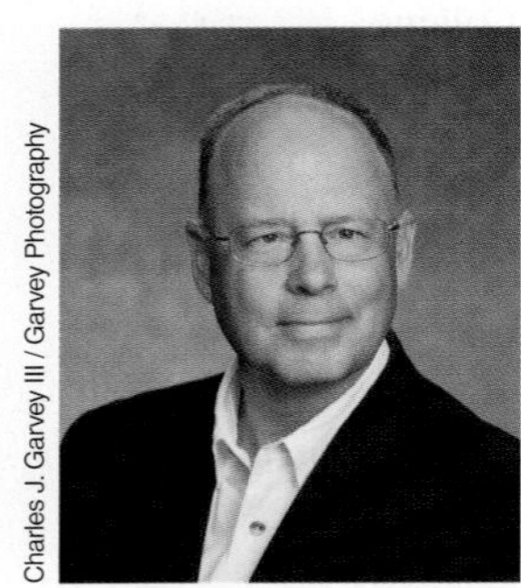
Charles J. Garvey III / Garvey Photography

James M. Reeve

Dr. James M. Reeve is Professor Emeritus of Accounting and Information Management at the University of Tennessee. Professor Reeve taught on the accounting faculty for 25 years, after graduating with his Ph.D. from Oklahoma State University. His teaching efforts focused on undergraduate accounting principles and graduate education in the Master of Accountancy and Senior Executive MBA programs. Beyond this, Professor Reeve is also very active in the Supply Chain Certification program, which is a major executive education and research effort of the College. His research interests are varied and include work in managerial accounting, supply chain management, lean manufacturing, and information management. He has published over 40 articles in academic and professional journals, including the *Journal of Cost Management, Journal of Management Accounting Research, Accounting Review, Management Accounting Quarterly, Supply Chain Management Review,* and *Accounting Horizons*. He has consulted or provided training around the world for a wide variety of organizations, including Boeing, Procter & Gamble, Norfolk Southern, Hershey Foods, Coca-Cola, and Sony. When not writing books, Professor Reeve plays golf and is involved in faith-based activities.

© Ken Bennett

Jonathan Duchac

Dr. Jonathan Duchac is the Merrill Lynch and Co. Professor of Accounting and Director of International Programs at Wake Forest University. He holds a joint appointment at the Vienna University of Business and Economics in Vienna, Austria. Dr. Duchac currently teaches introductory and advanced courses in financial accounting and has received a number of awards during his career, including the Wake Forest University Outstanding Graduate Professor Award, the T.B. Rose Award for Instructional Innovation, and the University of Georgia Outstanding Teaching Assistant Award. In addition to his teaching responsibilities, Dr. Duchac has served as Accounting Advisor to Merrill Lynch Equity Research, where he worked with research analysts in reviewing and evaluating the financial reporting practices of public companies. He has testified before the U.S. House of Representatives, the Financial Accounting Standards Board, and the Securities and Exchange Commission and has worked with a number of major public companies on financial reporting and accounting policy issues. In addition to his professional interests, Dr. Duchac has served on the Board of Directors of The Special Children's School of Winston-Salem, a private, nonprofit developmental day school serving children with special needs. Dr. Duchac is an avid long-distance runner, mountain biker, and snow skier. His recent events include the Grandfather Mountain Marathon, the Black Mountain Marathon, the Shut-In Ridge Trail run, and NO MAAM (Nocturnal Overnight Mountain Bike Assault on Mount Mitchell).

Brief Contents

Contents

Chapter 7 Inventories 321

Chapter 8 Sarbanes-Oxley, Internal Control, and Cash 369

Chapter 9 Receivables 415

Chapter 10 Fixed Assets and Intangible Assets 459

STUDY TIPS

What Successful Students Are Saying

In a recent survey of students who took financial and managerial accounting courses, students stated that, in order to be successful in these courses, students should (in order of importance):

- Complete assigned homework
- Attend class and pay attention during the lecture
- Study
- Ask for help or get a tutor
- Complete ungraded practice assignments or review exercises

- ❑ Did you read the chapter from the required textbook prior to attending class?
- ❑ Did you attend class?
- ❑ Did you take notes during class?
- ❑ Did you ask questions of the professor either during or after class when you did not understand a concept being taught?
- ❑ Did you complete all assigned homework?
- ❑ Did you complete ungraded practice assignments or review exercises to better learn and understand accounting concepts?
- ❑ Did you obtain an explanation from the professor for incorrect answers?
- ❑ Did you utilize additional resources provided such as demonstration videos & tutorials?

Successful students spent an average of 4 hours per week outside of class time studying, including completing assigned homework.

You just need to put in the effort. If you work through the homework problems and show up to class, you will do well.

—Brandy J. Gibson, Business Administration Major Ivy Tech Community College

Do not put off homework – it is more important than you know – and when in need – ASK FOR HELP!!

—Sally Cross, Accounting Major Ivy Tech Community College

You need to attend every class and pay attention. Take good notes and do all the homework.

—Melinda Lallier, Accounting Major Community College of Rhode Island

Come to class every day – if you miss a class, you miss a lot of notes and example problems. Homework is vital and so is studying for tests – you need to learn the different formulas and equations.

—Shannon Green, General Business Major Community College of Rhode Island

Anyone can succeed at learning & understanding accounting concepts!

<u>How?</u> Preparation, time management, & practice!

FINANCIAL ACCOUNTING

14e

© ANNETTE SHAFF/SHUTTERSTOCK.COM

CHAPTER 1

Introduction to Accounting and Business

Twitter

When two teams pair up for a game of football, there is often a lot of noise. The band plays, the fans cheer, and fireworks light up the scoreboard. Obviously, the fans are committed and care about the outcome of the game. Just like fans at a football game, the owners of a business want their business to "win" against their competitors in the marketplace. While having your football team win can be a source of pride, winning in the marketplace goes beyond pride and has many tangible benefits. Companies that are winners are better able to serve customers, provide good jobs for employees, and make money for their owners.

Twitter is one of the most visible companies on the Internet. It provides a real-time information network where members can post messages, called Tweets, of up to 140 characters for free. Millions post Tweets every day throughout the world.

Do you think Twitter is a successful company? Does it make money? How would you know? Accounting helps to answer these questions.

This textbook introduces you to accounting, the language of business. Chapter 1 begins by discussing what a business is, how it operates, and the role that accounting plays.

Learning Objectives

After studying this chapter, you should be able to: *Example Exercises*

OBJ	Objective	Example Exercises
1	**Describe the nature of a business and the role of accounting and ethics in business.**	
	Nature of Business and Accounting	
	Types of Businesses	
	Role of Accounting in Business	
	Role of Ethics in Accounting and Business	
	Opportunities for Accountants	
2	**Summarize the development of accounting principles and relate them to practice.**	
	Generally Accepted Accounting Principles	
	Business Entity Concept	
	Cost Concept	EE 1-1
3	**State the accounting equation and define each element of the equation.**	
	The Accounting Equation	EE 1-2
4	**Describe and illustrate how business transactions can be recorded in terms of the resulting change in the elements of the accounting equation.**	
	Business Transactions and the Accounting Equation	EE 1-3
5	**Describe the financial statements of a proprietorship and explain how they interrelate.**	
	Financial Statements	
	Income Statement	EE 1-4
	Statement of Owner's Equity	EE 1-5
	Balance Sheet	EE 1-6
	Statement of Cash Flows	EE 1-7
	Interrelationships Among Financial Statements	
6	**Describe and illustrate the use of the ratio of liabilities to owner's equity in evaluating a company's financial condition.**	
	Financial Analysis and Interpretation: Ratio of Liabilities to Owner's Equity	EE 1-8

At a Glance 1 Page 22

OBJ 1 Describe the nature of business and the role of accounting and ethics in business.

Nature of Business and Accounting

A **business**[1] is an organization in which basic resources (inputs), such as materials and labor, are assembled and processed to provide goods or services (outputs) to customers. Businesses come in all sizes, from a local coffee house to Starbucks, which sells over $10 billion of coffee and related products each year.

The objective of most businesses is to earn a profit. Profit is the difference between the amounts received from customers for goods or services and the amounts paid for the inputs used to provide the goods or services. This text focuses on businesses operating to earn a profit. However, many of the same concepts and principles also apply to not-for-profit organizations such as hospitals, churches, and government agencies.

Types of Businesses

Three types of businesses operating for profit include service, merchandising, and manufacturing businesses. Some examples of each type of business follow:

- **Service businesses** provide services rather than products to customers.
  - Delta Air Lines (transportation services)
  - The Walt Disney Company (entertainment services)
- **Merchandising businesses** sell products they purchase from other businesses to customers.
  - Walmart (general merchandise)
  - Amazon.com (Internet books, music, videos)

[1] A complete glossary of terms appears at the end of the text.

- **Manufacturing businesses** change basic inputs into products that are sold to customers.
  - Ford Motor Co. (cars, trucks, vans)
  - Dell Inc. (personal computers)

Role of Accounting in Business

The role of accounting in business is to provide information for managers to use in operating the business. In addition, accounting provides information to other users in assessing the economic performance and condition of the business.

Thus, **accounting** can be defined as an information system that provides reports to users about the economic activities and condition of a business. You could think of accounting as the "language of business." This is because accounting is the means by which businesses' financial information is communicated to users.

Note: Accounting is an information system that provides reports to users about the economic activities and condition of a business.

The process by which accounting provides information to users is as follows:

1. Identify users.
2. Assess users' information needs.
3. Design the accounting information system to meet users' needs.
4. Record economic data about business activities and events.
5. Prepare accounting reports for users.

As illustrated in Exhibit 1, users of accounting information can be divided into two groups: internal users and external users.

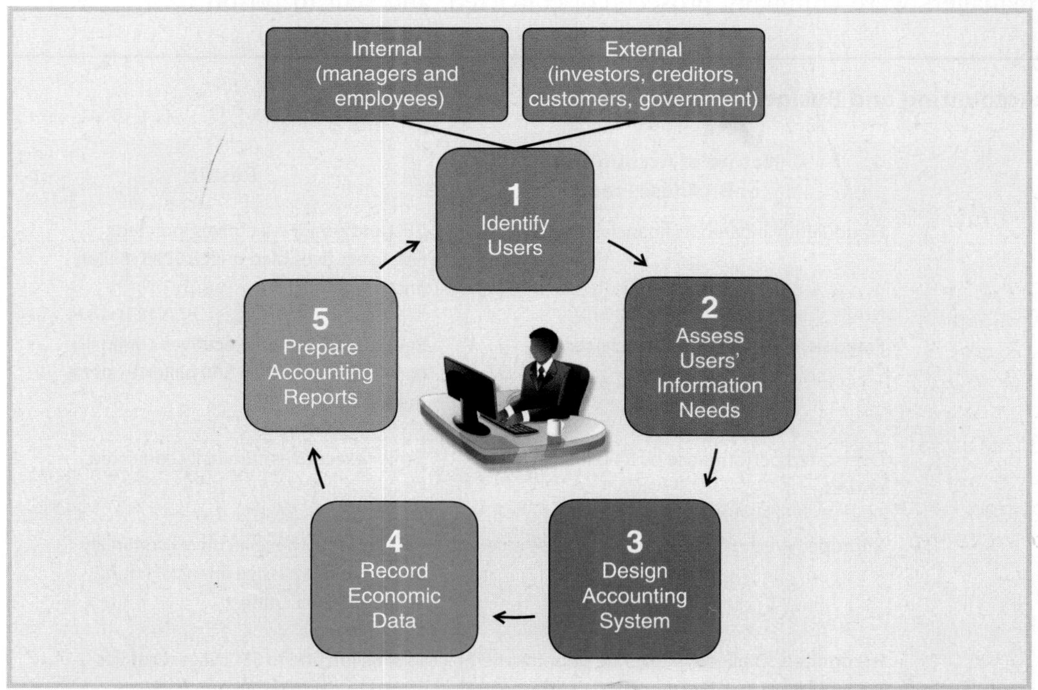

EXHIBIT 1

Accounting as an Information System

Managerial Accounting Internal users of accounting information include managers and employees. These users are directly involved in managing and operating the business. The area of accounting that provides internal users with information is called **managerial accounting**, or **management accounting**.

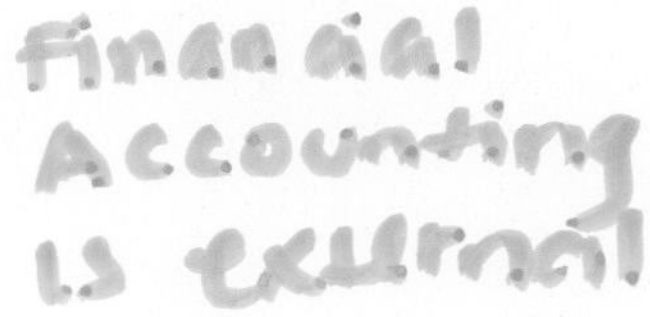

The objective of managerial accounting is to provide relevant and timely information for managers' and employees' decision-making needs. Oftentimes, such information is sensitive and is not distributed outside the business. Examples of sensitive information might include information about customers, prices, and plans to expand the business. Managerial accountants employed by a business are employed in **private accounting**.

Financial Accounting External users of accounting information include investors, creditors, customers, and the government. These users are not directly involved in managing and operating the business. The area of accounting that provides external users with information is called **financial accounting**.

The objective of financial accounting is to provide relevant and timely information for the decision-making needs of users outside of the business. For example, financial reports on the operations and condition of the business are useful for banks and other creditors in deciding whether to lend money to the business. **General-purpose financial statements** are one type of financial accounting report that is distributed to external users. The term *general-purpose* refers to the wide range of decision-making needs that these reports are designed to serve. Later in this chapter, general-purpose financial statements are described and illustrated.

Role of Ethics in Accounting and Business

The objective of accounting is to provide relevant, timely information for user decision making. Accountants must behave in an ethical manner so that the information they provide users will be trustworthy and, thus, useful for decision making. Managers and employees must also behave in an ethical manner in managing and operating a business. Otherwise, no one will be willing to invest in or loan money to the business.

Ethics are moral principles that guide the conduct of individuals. Unfortunately, business managers and accountants sometimes behave in an unethical manner. Many of the managers of the companies listed in Exhibit 2 engaged in accounting or business fraud. These ethical violations led to fines, firings, and lawsuits. In some cases, managers were criminally prosecuted, convicted, and sent to prison.

EXHIBIT 2 **Accounting and Business Frauds** 2002

Company	Nature of Accounting or Business Fraud	Result
Computer Associates International, Inc.	Fraudulently inflated its financial results.	CEO and senior executives indicted. Five executives pled guilty. $225 million fine.
Enron	Fraudulently inflated its financial results.	Bankrupcty. Senior executives criminally convicted. More than $60 billion in stock market losses.
HealthSouth	Overstated performance by $4 billion in false entries.	Senior executives criminally convicted.
Qwest Communications International, Inc.	Improperly recognized $3 billion in false receipts.	CEO and six other executives criminally convicted of "massive financial fraud." $250 million SEC fine.
Xerox Corporation	Recognized $3 billion in revenue prior to when it should have been recorded.	$10 million fine to SEC. Six executives forced to pay $22 million.

What went wrong for the managers and companies listed in Exhibit 2? The answer normally involved one or both of the following two factors:

- ***Failure of Individual Character.*** Ethical managers and accountants are honest and fair. However, managers and accountants often face pressures from supervisors to meet company and investor expectations. In many of the cases in Exhibit 2, managers and accountants justified small ethical violations to avoid such pressures. However, these small violations became big violations as the company's financial problems became worse.

- ***Culture of Greed and Ethical Indifference.*** By their behavior and attitude, senior managers set the company culture. In most of the companies listed in Exhibit 2, the senior managers created a culture of greed and indifference to the truth.

As a result of the accounting and business frauds shown in Exhibit 2, Congress passed laws to monitor the behavior of accounting and business. For example, the **Sarbanes-Oxley Act (SOX)** was enacted. SOX established a new oversight body for the accounting profession called the **Public Company Accounting Oversight Board (PCAOB).** In addition, SOX established standards for independence, corporate responsibility, and disclosure.

How does one behave ethically when faced with financial or other types of pressure? Guidelines for behaving ethically follow:[2]

1. Identify an ethical decision by using your personal ethical standards of honesty and fairness.
2. Identify the consequences of the decision and its effect on others.
3. Consider your obligations and responsibilities to those who will be affected by your decision.
4. Make a decision that is ethical and fair to those affected by it.

Integrity, Objectivity, and Ethics in Business

BERNIE MADOFF

In June 2009, Bernard L. "Bernie" Madoff was sentenced to 150 years in prison for defrauding thousands of investors in one of the biggest frauds in American history. Madoff's fraud started several decades earlier when he began a "Ponzi scheme" in his investment management firm, Bernard L. Madoff Investment Securities LLC.

In a Ponzi scheme, the investment manager uses funds received from new investors to pay a return to existing investors, rather than basing investment returns on the fund's actual performance. As long as the investment manager is able to attract new investors, he or she will have new funds to pay existing investors and continue the fraud. While most Ponzi schemes collapse quickly when the investment manager runs out of new investors, Madoff's reputation, popularity, and personal contacts provided a steady stream of investors, which allowed the fraud to survive for decades.

Opportunities for Accountants

Numerous career opportunities are available for students majoring in accounting. Currently, the demand for accountants exceeds the number of new graduates entering the job market. This is partly due to the increased regulation of business caused by the accounting and business frauds shown in Exhibit 2. Also, more and more businesses have come to recognize the importance and value of accounting information.

As indicated earlier, accountants employed by a business are employed in private accounting. Private accountants have a variety of possible career options within a company. Some of these career options are shown in Exhibit 3 along with their starting salaries. Accountants who provide audit services, called *auditors*, verify the accuracy of financial records, accounts, and systems. As shown in Exhibit 3, several private accounting careers have certification options.

Accountants and their staff who provide services on a fee basis are said to be employed in **public accounting**. In public accounting, an accountant may practice as an individual or as a member of a public accounting firm. Public accountants who have met a state's education, experience, and examination requirements may become **Certified Public Accountants (CPAs)**. CPAs typically perform general accounting,

[2] Many companies have ethical standards of conduct for managers and employees. In addition, the Institute of Management Accountants and the American Institute of Certified Public Accountants have professional codes of conduct, which can be obtained from their Web sites at www.imanet.org and www.aicpa.org, respectively.

EXHIBIT 3 **Accounting Career Paths and Salaries**

Accounting Career Track	Description	Career Options	Annual Starting Salaries*	Certification
Private Accounting	Accountants employed by companies, government, and not-for-profit entities.	Bookkeeper	$39,750	
		Payroll clerk	$38,250	Certified Payroll Professional (CPP)
		General accountant	$46,375	
		Budget analyst	$49,375	
		Cost accountant	$48,375	Certified Management Accountant (CMA)
		Internal auditor	$53,875	Certified Internal Auditor (CIA)
		Information technology auditor	$62,875	Certified Information Systems Auditor (CISA)
Public Accounting	Accountants employed individually or within a public accounting firm in tax or audit services.	Local firms	$48,500	Certified Public Accountant (CPA)
		National firms	$58,625	Certified Public Accountant (CPA)

*Mean salaries of a reported range. Private accounting salaries are reported for large companies. Salaries may vary by region.
Source: Robert Half *2013 U.S. Salary Guide (Finance and Accounting)*, Robert Half International, Inc. (http://www.rhi.com/salaryguides)

audit, or tax services. As can be seen in Exhibit 3, CPAs have slightly better starting salaries than private accountants. Career statistics indicate, however, that these salary differences tend to disappear over time.

Because all functions within a business use accounting information, experience in private or public accounting provides a solid foundation for a career. Many positions in industry and in government agencies are held by individuals with accounting backgrounds.

Business  Connection

PATHWAYS COMMISSION

The Pathway Commission recently issued its study titled *Charting a National Strategy for the Next Generation of Accountants*. The Commission was made up of diverse members and was jointly sponsored by the American Institute of Certified Public Accountants (AICPA) and the American Accounting Association (AAA). The Commission emphasized the importance of accounting for a prosperous society and good decision making. The Commission also emphasized that accountants must be critical thinkers who are comfortable addressing the shades of grey required by accounting judgments.

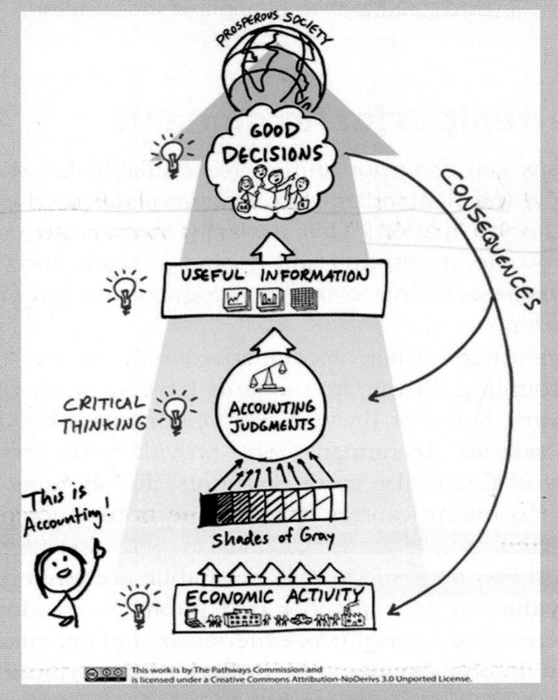

Sources: *Charting a National Strategy for the Next Generation of Accountants*, The Pathways Commission, July 2012.

Generally Accepted Accounting Principles

OBJ 2 Summarize the development of accounting principles and relate them to practice.

If a company's management could record and report financial data as it saw fit, comparisons among companies would be difficult, if not impossible. Thus, financial accountants follow **generally accepted accounting principles (GAAP)** in preparing reports. These reports allow investors and other users to compare one company to another.

Accounting principles and concepts develop from research, accepted accounting practices, and pronouncements of regulators. Within the United States, the **Financial Accounting Standards Board (FASB)** has the primary responsibility for developing accounting principles. The FASB publishes *Statements of Financial Accounting Standards* as well as *Interpretations* of these Standards. In addition, the **Securities and Exchange Commission (SEC),** an agency of the U.S. government, has authority over the accounting and financial disclosures for companies whose shares of ownership (stock) are traded and sold to the public. The SEC normally accepts the accounting principles set forth by the FASB. However, the SEC may issue *Staff Accounting Bulletins* on accounting matters that may not have been addressed by the FASB.

Many countries outside the United States use generally accepted accounting principles adopted by the **International Accounting Standards Board (IASB)**. The IASB issues *International Financial Reporting Standards (IFRSs)*. Differences currently exist between FASB and IASB accounting principles. However, the FASB and IASB are working together to reduce and eliminate these differences into a single set of accounting principles. Such a set of worldwide accounting principles would help facilitate investment and business in an increasingly global economy.

IFRS See Appendix D for more information.

In this chapter and text, accounting principles and concepts are emphasized. It is through this emphasis on the "why" as well as the "how" that you will gain an understanding of accounting.

International  Connection

IFRS INTERNATIONAL FINANCIAL REPORTING STANDARDS (IFRS)

IFRS are considered to be more "principles-based" than U.S. GAAP, which is considered to be more "rules-based." For example, U.S. GAAP consists of approximately 17,000 pages, which include numerous industry-specific accounting rules. In contrast, IFRS allow more judgment in deciding how business transactions are recorded. Many believe that the strong regulatory and litigation environment in the United States is the cause for the more rules-based GAAP approach. Regardless, IFRS and GAAP share many common principles.*

*Differences between U.S. GAAP and IFRS are further discussed and illustrated in Appendix D.

Business Entity Concept

The **business entity concept** limits the economic data in an accounting system to data related directly to the activities of the business. In other words, the business is viewed as an entity separate from its owners, creditors, or other businesses. For example, the accountant for a business with one owner would record the activities of the business only and would not record the personal activities, property, or debts of the owner.

Note: **Under the business entity concept, the activities of a business are recorded separately from the activities of its owners, creditors, or other businesses.**

A business entity may take the form of a proprietorship, partnership, corporation, or limited liability company (LLC). Each of these forms and their major characteristics are listed in Exhibit 4.

EXHIBIT 4 **Forms of Business Entities**

Form of Business Entity	Characteristics	Examples
Proprietorship is owned by one individual.	• 70% of business entities in the United States. • Easy and inexpensive to organize. • Resources are limited to those of the owner. • Used by small businesses.	• A & B Painting
Partnership is owned by two or more individuals.	• 10% of business organizations in the United States (combined with limited liability companies). • Combines the skills and resources of more than one person.	• Jones & Smith, Architects
Corporation is organized under state or federal statutes as a separate legal taxable entity.	• Generates 90% of business revenues. • 20% of the business organizations in the United States. • Ownership is divided into shares called stock. • Can obtain large amounts of resources by issuing stock. • Used by large businesses.	• Apple • Google • Ford Motor Company
Limited liability company (LLC) combines the attributes of a partnership and a corporation.	• 10% of business organizations in the United States (combined with partnerships). • Often used as an alternative to a partnership. • Has tax and legal liability advantages for owners.	• Mosel & Farmer, CPAs, LLC

The three types of businesses discussed earlier—service, merchandising, and manufacturing—may be organized as proprietorships, partnerships, corporations, or limited liability companies. Because of the large amount of resources required to operate a manufacturing business, most manufacturers such as **Ford Motor Company** are corporations. Most large retailers such as **Walmart** and **Home Depot** are also corporations.

Cost Concept

Under the **cost concept**, amounts are initially recorded in the accounting records at their cost or purchase price. To illustrate, assume that Aaron Publishers purchased the following building on February 20, 2014, for $150,000:

Price listed by seller on January 1, 2014	$160,000
Aaron Publishers' initial offer to buy on January 31, 2014	140,000
Purchase price on February 20, 2014	150,000
Estimated selling price on December 31, 2016	220,000
Assessed value for property taxes, December 31, 2016	190,000

Under the cost concept, Aaron Publishers records the purchase of the building on February 20, 2014, at the purchase price of $150,000. The other amounts listed have no effect on the accounting records.

The fact that the building has an estimated selling price of $220,000 on December 31, 2016, indicates that the building has increased in value. However, to use the $220,000 in the accounting records would be to record an illusory or unrealized profit. If Aaron Publishers sells the building on January 9, 2018, for $240,000, a profit of $90,000 ($240,000 − $150,000) is then realized and recorded. The new owner would record $240,000 as its cost of the building.

The cost concept also involves the objectivity and unit of measure concepts. The **objectivity concept** requires that the amounts recorded in the accounting records be based on objective evidence. In exchanges between a buyer and a seller, both try to get the best price. Only the final agreed-upon amount is objective enough to be recorded in the accounting records. If amounts in the accounting records were constantly being revised upward or downward based on offers, appraisals, and opinions, accounting reports could become unstable and unreliable.

- The **unit of measure concept** requires that economic data be recorded in dollars. Money is a common unit of measurement for reporting financial data and reports.

Example Exercise 1-1 Cost Concept (OBJ 2)

On August 25, Gallatin Repair Service extended an offer of $125,000 for land that had been priced for sale at $150,000. On September 3, Gallatin Repair Service accepted the seller's counteroffer of $137,000. On October 20, the land was assessed at a value of $98,000 for property tax purposes. On December 4, Gallatin Repair Service was offered $160,000 for the land by a national retail chain. At what value should the land be recorded in Gallatin Repair Service's records?

Follow My Example 1-1

$137,000. Under the cost concept, the land should be recorded at the cost to Gallatin Repair Service.

Practice Exercises: PE 1-1A, PE 1-1B

The Accounting Equation

OBJ 3 State the accounting equation and define each element of the equation.

The resources owned by a business are its **assets**. Examples of assets include cash, land, buildings, and equipment. The rights or claims to the assets are divided into two types: (1) the rights of creditors and (2) the rights of owners. The rights of creditors are the debts of the business and are called **liabilities**. The rights of the owners are called **owner's equity**. The following equation shows the relationship among assets, liabilities, and owner's equity:

Assets = Liabilities + Owner's Equity

This equation is called the **accounting equation**. Liabilities usually are shown before owner's equity in the accounting equation because creditors have first rights to the assets.

Given any two amounts, the accounting equation may be solved for the third unknown amount. To illustrate, if the assets owned by a business amount to $100,000 and the liabilities amount to $30,000, the owner's equity is equal to $70,000, computed as follows:

Assets	–	**Liabilities**	=	**Owner's Equity**
$100,000	–	$30,000	=	$70,000

Business Connection

THE ACCOUNTING EQUATION

The accounting equation serves as the basic foundation for the accounting systems of all companies. From the smallest business, such as the local convenience store, to the largest business, such as The Coca-Cola Company, companies use the accounting equation. Some examples taken from recent financial reports of well-known companies follow:

Company	Assets*	=	Liabilities	+	Owner's Equity
The Coca-Cola Company	$79,974	=	$48,339	+	$31,635
DuPont	$49,736	=	$39,648	+	$10,088
eBay	$37,074	=	$16,209	+	$20,865
Google	$93,798	=	$22,083	+	$71,715
McDonald's	$32,990	=	$18,600	+	$14,390
Microsoft Corporation	$121,271	=	$54,908	+	$66,363
Southwest Airlines	$18,596	=	$11,604	+	$6,992
Walmart	$193,406	=	$122,091	+	$71,315

*Amounts are shown in millions of dollars.

Example Exercise 1-2 Accounting Equation

OBJ 3

John Joos is the owner and operator of You're A Star, a motivational consulting business. At the end of its accounting period, December 31, 2015, You're A Star has assets of $800,000 and liabilities of $350,000. Using the accounting equation, determine the following amounts:

a. Owner's equity as of December 31, 2015.

b. Owner's equity as of December 31, 2016, assuming that assets increased by $130,000 and liabilities decreased by $25,000 during 2016.

Follow My Example 1-2

a. Assets = Liabilities + Owner's Equity

$800,000 = $350,000 + Owner's Equity

Owner's Equity = $450,000

b. First, determine the change in owner's equity during 2016 as follows:

Assets = Liabilities + Owner's Equity

$130,000 = −$25,000 + Owner's Equity

Owner's Equity = $155,000

Next, add the change in owner's equity during 2016 to the owner's equity on December 31, 2015 to arrive at owner's equity on December 31, 2016, as follows:

Owner's Equity on December 31, 2016 = $450,000 + $155,000 = $605,000

Practice Exercises: PE 1-2A, PE 1-2B

Describe and illustrate how business transactions can be recorded in terms of the resulting change in the elements of the accounting equation.

Business Transactions and the Accounting Equation

Paying a monthly bill, such as a telephone bill of $168, affects a business's financial condition because it now has less cash on hand. Such an economic event or condition that directly changes an entity's financial condition or its results of operations is a **business transaction**. For example, purchasing land for $50,000 is a business transaction. In contrast, a change in a business's credit rating does not directly affect cash or any other asset, liability, or owner's equity amount.

Note: **All business transactions can be stated in terms of changes in the elements of the accounting equation.**

All business transactions can be stated in terms of changes in the elements of the accounting equation. How business transactions affect the accounting equation can be illustrated by using some typical transactions. As a basis for illustration, a business organized by Chris Clark is used.

Assume that on November 1, 2015, Chris Clark begins a business that will be known as **NetSolutions**. The first phase of Chris's business plan is to operate NetSolutions as a service business assisting individuals and small businesses in developing Web pages and installing computer software. Chris expects this initial phase of the business to last one to two years. During this period, Chris plans on gathering information on the software and hardware needs of customers. During the second phase of the business plan, Chris plans to expand NetSolutions into a personalized retailer of software and hardware for individuals and small businesses.

Each transaction during NetSolutions' first month of operations is described in the following paragraphs. The effect of each transaction on the accounting equation is then shown.

Transaction A *Nov. 1, 2015 Chris Clark deposited $25,000 in a bank account in the name of NetSolutions.*

This transaction increases the asset cash (on the left side of the equation) by $25,000. To balance the equation, the owner's equity (on the right side of the equation) increases by the same amount. The equity of the owner is identified using the owner's name and "Capital," such as "Chris Clark, Capital."

The effect of this transaction on NetSolutions' accounting equation is as follows:

Assets	=	Owner's Equity
Cash	=	Chris Clark, Capital
a. 25,000		25,000

Since Chris Clark is the sole owner, NetSolutions is a proprietorship. Also, the preceding accounting equation is only for the business, NetSolutions. Under the business entity concept, Chris's personal assets, such as a home or personal bank account, and personal liabilities are excluded from the equation.

Nov. 5, 2015 NetSolutions paid $20,000 for the purchase of land as a future building site.

Transaction B

The land is located in a business park with access to transportation facilities. Chris Clark plans to rent office space and equipment during the first phase of the business plan. During the second phase, Chris plans to build an office and a warehouse on the land.

The purchase of the land changes the makeup of the assets, but it does not change the total assets. The items in the equation prior to this transaction and the effect of the transaction follow. The new amounts are called *balances.*

	Assets		=	Owner's Equity
	Cash	+ Land		Chris Clark, Capital
Bal.	25,000		=	25,000
b.	−20,000	+20,000		
Bal.	5,000	20,000		25,000

Nov. 10, 2015 NetSolutions purchased supplies for $1,350 and agreed to pay the supplier in the near future.

Transaction C

You have probably used a credit card to buy clothing or other merchandise. In this type of transaction, you received clothing for a promise to pay your credit card bill in the future. That is, you received an asset and incurred a liability to pay a future bill. NetSolutions entered into a similar transaction by purchasing supplies for $1,350 and agreeing to pay the supplier in the near future. This type of transaction is called a purchase *on account* and is often described as follows: *Purchased supplies on account, $1,350.*

The liability created by a purchase on account is called an **account payable.** Items such as supplies that will be used in the business in the future are called **prepaid expenses**, which are assets. Thus, the effect of this transaction is to increase assets (Supplies) and liabilities (Accounts Payable) by $1,350, as follows:

	Assets			=	Liabilities + Owner's Equity	
	Cash	+ Supplies +	Land		Accounts + Payable	Chris Clark, Capital
Bal.	5,000		20,000	=		25,000
c.		+1,350			+1,350	
Bal.	5,000	1,350	20,000		1,350	25,000

Nov. 18, 2015 NetSolutions received cash of $7,500 for providing services to customers.

Transaction D

You may have earned money by painting houses or mowing lawns. If so, you received money for rendering services to a customer. Likewise, a business earns money by selling goods or services to its customers. This amount is called **revenue**.

During its first month of operations, NetSolutions received cash of $7,500 for providing services to customers. The receipt of cash increases NetSolutions' assets and also increases Chris Clark's equity in the business. The revenues of $7,500 are recorded in a Fees Earned column to the right of Chris Clark, Capital. The effect of this transaction is to increase Cash and Fees Earned by $7,500, as follows:

	Assets			=	**Liabilities +**	**Owner's Equity**	
	Cash	+ Supplies +	Land	=	Accounts Payable +	Chris Clark, Capital +	Fees Earned
Bal.	5,000	1,350	20,000		1,350	25,000	
d.	+7,500						+7,500
Bal.	12,500	1,350	20,000		1,350	25,000	7,500

Different terms are used for the various types of revenues. As illustrated for NetSolutions, revenue from providing services is recorded as **fees earned**. Revenue from the sale of merchandise is recorded as **sales**. Other examples of revenue include rent, which is recorded as **rent revenue**, and interest, which is recorded as **interest revenue**.

Instead of receiving cash at the time services are provided or goods are sold, a business may accept payment at a later date. Such revenues are described as *fees earned on account* or *sales on account*. For example, if NetSolutions had provided services on account instead of for cash, transaction (d) would have been described as follows: *Fees earned on account, $7,500.*

In such cases, the firm has an **account receivable**, which is a claim against the customer. An account receivable is an asset, and the revenue is earned and recorded as if cash had been received. When customers pay their accounts, Cash increases, and Accounts Receivable decreases.

Transaction E *Nov. 30, 2015 NetSolutions paid the following expenses during the month: wages, $2,125; rent, $800; utilities, $450; and miscellaneous, $275.*

During the month, NetSolutions spent cash or used up other assets in earning revenue. Assets used in this process of earning revenue are called **expenses**. Expenses include supplies used and payments for employee wages, utilities, and other services.

NetSolutions paid the following expenses during the month: wages, $2,125; rent, $800; utilities, $450; and miscellaneous, $275. Miscellaneous expenses include small amounts paid for such items as postage, coffee, and newspapers. The effect of expenses is the opposite of revenues in that expenses reduce assets and owner's equity. Like fees earned, the expenses are recorded in columns to the right of Chris Clark, Capital. However, since expenses reduce owner's equity, the expenses are entered as negative amounts. The effect of this transaction is as follows:

	Assets			=	**Liabilities +**	**Owner's Equity**					
	Cash	+ Supplies +	Land	=	Accounts Payable +	Chris Clark, Capital	+ Fees Earned –	Wages Exp. –	Rent Exp. –	Utilities Exp. –	Misc. Exp.
Bal.	12,500	1,350	20,000		1,350	25,000	7,500				
e.	–3,650							–2,125	–800	–450	–275
Bal.	8,850	1,350	20,000		1,350	25,000	7,500	–2,125	–800	–450	–275

Businesses usually record each revenue and expense transaction as it occurs. However, to simplify, NetSolutions' revenues and expenses are summarized for the month in transactions (d) and (e).

Transaction F *Nov. 30, 2015 NetSolutions paid creditors on account, $950.*

When you pay your monthly credit card bill, you decrease the cash and decrease the amount you owe to the credit card company. Likewise, when NetSolutions pays $950 to creditors during the month, it reduces assets and liabilities, as follows:

	Assets			=	Liabilities +	Owner's Equity					
	Cash	+ Supplies +	Land		Accounts Payable +	Chris Clark, Capital	+ Fees Earned –	Wages Exp.	– Rent Exp. –	Utilities Exp.	– Misc. Exp.
Bal.	8,850	1,350	20,000	=	1,350	25,000	7,500	–2,125	–800	–450	–275
f.	–950				–950						
Bal.	7,900	1,350	20,000		400	25,000	7,500	–2,125	–800	–450	–275

Paying an amount on account is different from paying an expense. The paying of an expense reduces owner's equity, as illustrated in transaction (e). Paying an amount on account reduces the amount owed on a liability.

Nov. 30, 2015 Chris Clark determined that the cost of supplies on hand at the end of the month was $550. **Transaction G**

The cost of the supplies on hand (not yet used) at the end of the month is $550. Thus, $800 ($1,350 – $550) of supplies must have been used during the month. This decrease in supplies is recorded as an expense, as follows:

	Assets			=	Liabilities +	Owner's Equity						
	Cash	+ Supplies +	Land		Accounts Payable +	Chris Clark, Capital	+ Fees Earned –	Wages Exp.	– Rent Exp. –	Supplies Exp.	– Utilities Exp.	– Misc. Exp.
Bal.	7,900	1,350	20,000	=	400	25,000	7,500	–2,125	–800		–450	–275
g.		–800								–800		
Bal.	7,900	550	20,000		400	25,000	7,500	–2,125	–800	–800	–450	–275

Nov. 30, 2015 Chris Clark withdrew $2,000 from NetSolutions for personal use. **Transaction H**

At the end of the month, Chris Clark withdrew $2,000 in cash from the business for personal use. This transaction is the opposite of an investment in the business by the owner. Withdrawals by the owner should not be confused with expenses. Withdrawals *do not* represent assets or services used in the process of earning revenues. Instead, withdrawals are a distribution of capital to the owner. Owner withdrawals are identified by the owner's name and *Drawing*. For example, Chris's withdrawal is identified as Chris Clark, Drawing. Like expenses, withdrawals are recorded in a column to the right of Chris Clark, Capital. The effect of the $2,000 withdrawal is as follows:

	Assets			=	Liabilities +	Owner's Equity							
	Cash +	Supp.	+ Land		Accounts Payable +	Chris Clark, Capital	– Chris Clark, Drawing	+ Fees Earned	– Wages Exp.	– Rent Exp.	– Supplies Exp.	– Utilities Exp.	– Misc. Exp.
Bal.	7,900	550	20,000	=	400	25,000		7,500	–2,125	–800	–800	–450	–275
h.	–2,000						–2,000						
Bal.	5,900	550	20,000		400	25,000	–2,000	7,500	–2,125	–800	–800	–450	–275

Summary

The transactions of **NetSolutions** are summarized in Exhibit 5. Each transaction is identified by letter, and the balance of each accounting equation element is shown after every transaction.

You should note the following:

- The effect of every transaction *is an increase or a decrease in one or more of the accounting equation elements.*
- The two sides of the accounting equation are *always equal.*
- The owner's equity is *increased by amounts invested by the owner* and is *decreased by withdrawals by the owner.* In addition, the owner's equity is *increased by revenues* and is *decreased by expenses.*

EXHIBIT 5 Summary of Transaction for NetSolutions

	Assets			= Liabilities +	Owner's Equity							
	Cash	+ Supp. +	Land	= Accounts Payable +	Chris Clark, Capital	– Chris Clark, Drawing	+ Fees Earned	– Wages Exp.	– Rent Exp.	– Supplies Exp.	– Utilities Exp.	– Misc. Exp.
a.	+25,000				+25,000							
b.	−20,000		+20,000									
Bal.	5,000		20,000		25,000							
c.		+1,350		+1,350								
Bal.	5,000	+1,350	20,000	+1,350	25,000							
d.	+7,500						+7,500					
Bal.	12,500	1,350	20,000	1,350	25,000		7,500					
e.	−3,650							−2,125	−800		−450	−275
Bal.	8,850	1,350	20,000	1,350	25,000		7,500	−2,125	−800		−450	−275
f.	−950			−950								
Bal.	7,900	1,350	20,000	400	25,000		7,500	−2,125	−800		−450	−275
g.		−800								−800		
Bal.	7,900	550	20,000	400	25,000		7,500	−2,125	−800	−800	−450	−275
h.	−2,000					−2,000						
Bal.	5,900	550	20,000	400	25,000	−2,000	7,500	−2,125	−800	−800	−450	−275

Dynamic Exhibit

The four types of transactions affecting owner's equity are illustrated in Exhibit 6.

EXHIBIT 6

Types of Transactions Affecting Owner's Equity

Dynamic Exhibit

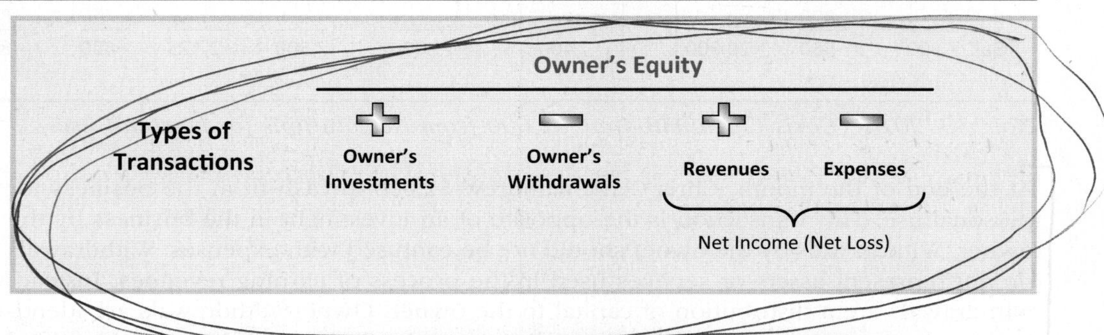

Example Exercise 1-3 Transactions

OBJ 4

Salvo Delivery Service is owned and operated by Joel Salvo. The following selected transactions were completed by Salvo Delivery Service during February:

1. Received cash from owner as additional investment, $35,000.
2. Paid creditors on account, $1,800.
3. Billed customers for delivery services on account, $11,250.
4. Received cash from customers on account, $6,740.
5. Paid cash to owner for personal use, $1,000.

Indicate the effect of each transaction on the accounting equation elements (Assets, Liabilities, Owner's Equity, Drawing, Revenue, and Expense). Also indicate the specific item within the accounting equation element that is affected. To illustrate, the answer to (1) follows:

(1) Asset (Cash) increases by $35,000; Owner's Equity (Joel Salvo, Capital) increases by $35,000.

Follow My Example 1-3

(2) Asset (Cash) decreases by $1,800; Liability (Accounts Payable) decreases by $1,800.
(3) Asset (Accounts Receivable) increases by $11,250; Revenue (Delivery Service Fees) increases by $11,250.
(4) Asset (Cash) increases by $6,740; Asset (Accounts Receivable) decreases by $6,740.
(5) Asset (Cash) decreases by $1,000; Drawing (Joel Salvo, Drawing) increases by $1,000.

Practice Exercises: PE 1-3A, PE 1-3B

Financial Statements

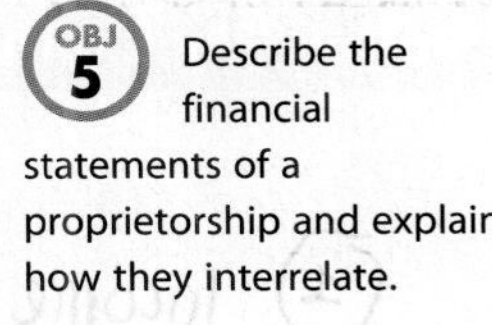

Describe the financial statements of a proprietorship and explain how they interrelate.

After transactions have been recorded and summarized, reports are prepared for users. The accounting reports providing this information are called **financial statements**. The primary financial statements of a proprietorship are the income statement, the statement of owner's equity, the balance sheet, and the statement of cash flows. The order in which the financial statements are prepared and the nature of each statement are described in Exhibit 7.

EXHIBIT 7

Financial Statements

Order Prepared	Financial Statement	Description of Statement
1.	**Income statement**	A summary of the revenue and expenses *for a specific period of time*, such as a month or a year.
2.	**Statement of owner's equity**	A summary of the changes in the owner's equity that have occurred *during a specific period of time*, such as a month or a year.
3.	**Balance sheet**	A list of the assets, liabilities, and owner's equity *as of a specific date*, usually at the close of the last day of a month or a year.
4.	**Statement of cash flows**	A summary of the cash receipts and cash payments for a *specific period of time*, such as a month or a year.

The four financial statements and their interrelationships are illustrated in Exhibit 8. The data for the statements are taken from the summary of **NetSolutions**' transactions in Exhibit 5.

All financial statements are identified by the name of the business, the title of the statement, and the *date* or *period of time*. The data presented in the income statement, the statement of owner's equity, and the statement of cash flows are for a period of time. The data presented in the balance sheet are for a specific date.

Income Statement

The income statement reports the revenues and expenses for a period of time, based on the **matching concept**. This concept is applied by *matching* the expenses incurred during a period with the revenue that those expenses generated. The excess of the revenue over the expenses is called **net income**, **net profit**, or **earnings**. If the expenses exceed the revenue, the excess is a **net loss**.

Note:
When revenues exceed expenses, it is referred to as *net income, net profit,* or *earnings*. When expenses exceed revenues, it is referred to as *net loss*.

The revenue and expenses for **NetSolutions** were shown in the equation as separate increases and decreases. Net income for a period increases the owner's equity (capital) for the period. A net loss decreases the owner's equity (capital) for the period.

The revenue, expenses, and the net income of $3,050 for NetSolutions are reported in the income statement in Exhibit 8. The order in which the expenses are listed in the income statement varies among businesses. Most businesses list expenses in order of size, beginning with the larger items. Miscellaneous expense is usually shown as the last item, regardless of the amount.

Example Exercise 1-4 Income Statement (OBJ 5)

The revenues and expenses of Chickadee Travel Service for the year ended April 30, 2016, follow:

Fees earned	$263,200
Miscellaneous expense	12,950
Office expense	63,000
Wages expense	131,700

Prepare an income statement for the year ended April 30, 2016.

(Continued)

Follow My Example 1-4

Chickadee Travel Service
Income Statement
For the Year Ended April 30, 2016

Fees earned		$263,200
Expenses:		
Wages expense	$131,700	
Office expense	63,000	
Miscellaneous expense	12,950	
Total expenses		207,650
Net income		$ 55,550

Practice Exercises: PE 1-4A, PE 1-4B

Statement of Owner's Equity

The statement of owner's equity reports the changes in the owner's equity for a period of time. It is prepared *after* the income statement because the net income or net loss for the period must be reported in this statement. Similarly, it is prepared *before* the balance sheet because the amount of owner's equity at the end of the period must be reported on the balance sheet. As a result, the statement of owner's equity is often viewed as the connecting link between the income statement and balance sheet.

Three types of transactions affected owner's equity of **NetSolutions** during November:

- the original investment of $25,000,
- the revenue and expenses that resulted in net income of $3,050 for the month, and
- a withdrawal of $2,000 by the owner.

The preceding information is summarized in the statement of owner's equity in Exhibit 8.

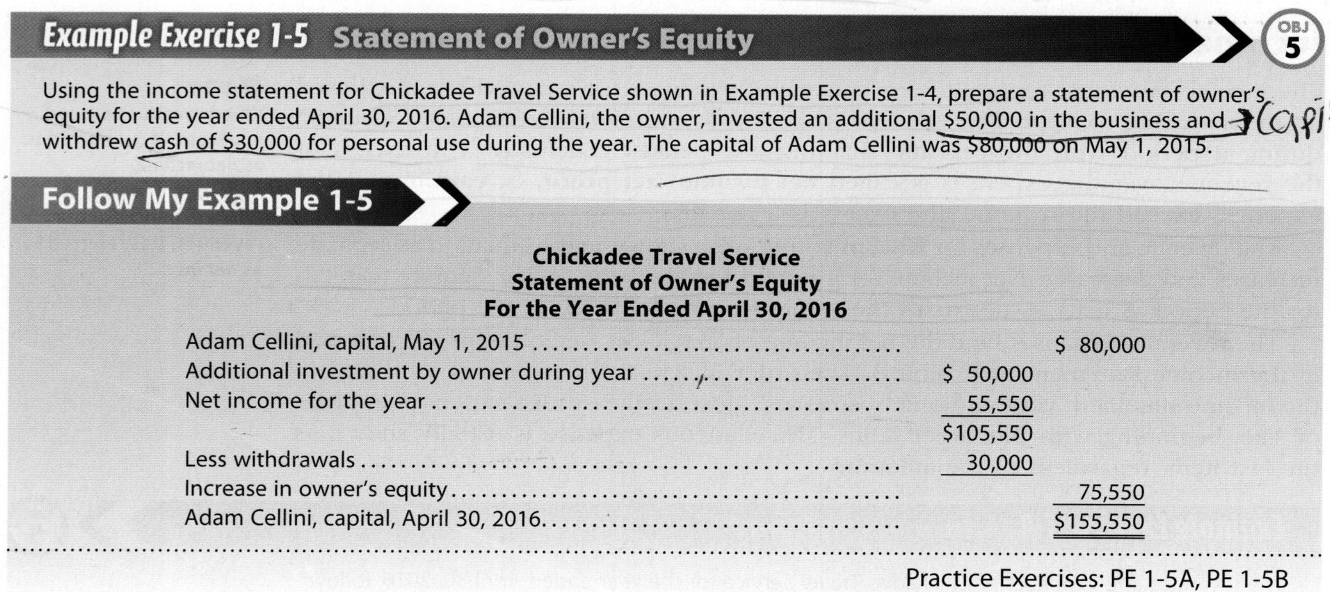

Example Exercise 1-5 Statement of Owner's Equity OBJ 5

Using the income statement for Chickadee Travel Service shown in Example Exercise 1-4, prepare a statement of owner's equity for the year ended April 30, 2016. Adam Cellini, the owner, invested an additional $50,000 in the business and withdrew cash of $30,000 for personal use during the year. The capital of Adam Cellini was $80,000 on May 1, 2015.

Follow My Example 1-5

Chickadee Travel Service
Statement of Owner's Equity
For the Year Ended April 30, 2016

Adam Cellini, capital, May 1, 2015		$ 80,000
Additional investment by owner during year	$ 50,000	
Net income for the year	55,550	
	$105,550	
Less withdrawals	30,000	
Increase in owner's equity		75,550
Adam Cellini, capital, April 30, 2016		$155,550

Practice Exercises: PE 1-5A, PE 1-5B

Balance Sheet

The balance sheet in Exhibit 8 reports the amounts of **NetSolutions**' assets, liabilities, and owner's equity as of November 30, 2015. The asset and liability amounts are taken from the last line of the summary of transactions in Exhibit 5. Chris Clark, Capital

EXHIBI

Financial Statements for NetSolutions

Dynamic Exhibit

NetSolutions
Income Statement
For the Month Ended November 30, 2015

Fees earned		$7,500
Expenses:		
Wages expense	$2,125	
Rent expense	800	
Supplies expense	800	
Utilities expense	450	
Miscellaneous expense	275	
Total expense		4,450
Net income		$3,050

NetSolutions
Statement of Owner's Equity
For the Month Ended November 30, 2015

Chris Clark, capital, November 1, 2015		$ 0
Investment on November 1, 2015	$25,000	
Net income for November	3,050	
	$28,050	
Less withdrawals	2,000	
Increase in owner's equity		26,050
Chris Clark, capital, November 30, 2015		$26,050

NetSolutions
Balance Sheet
November 30, 2015

Assets		Liabilities	
Cash	$ 5,900	Accounts payable	$ 400
Supplies	550	**Owner's Equity**	
Land	20,000	Chris Clark, capital	26,050
Total assets	$26,450	Total liabilities and owner's equity	$26,450

NetSolutions
Statement of Cash Flows
For the Month Ended November 30, 2015

Cash flows from operating activities:		
Cash received from customers	$ 7,500	
Deduct cash payments for expenses and payments to creditors	(4,600)	
Net cash flow from operating activities		$ 2,900
Cash flows used for investing activities:		
Cash payments for purchase of land		(20,000)
Cash flows from financing activities:		
Cash received as owner's investment	$25,000	
Deduct cash withdrawal by owner	(2,000)	
Net cash flows from financing activities		23,000
Net increase in cash and November 30, 2015, cash balance		$ 5,900

Bank loan officers use a business's financial statements in deciding whether to grant a loan to the business. Once the loan is granted, the borrower may be required to maintain a certain level of assets in excess of liabilities. The business's financial statements are used to monitor this level.

as of November 30, 2015, is taken from the statement of owner's equity. The form of balance sheet shown in Exhibit 8 is called the **account form**. This is because it resembles the basic format of the accounting equation, with assets on the left side and the liabilities and owner's equity sections on the right side.[3]

The assets section of the balance sheet presents assets in the order that they will be converted into cash or used in operations. Cash is presented first, followed by receivables, supplies, prepaid insurance, and other assets. The assets of a more permanent nature are shown next, such as land, buildings, and equipment.

In the liabilities section of the balance sheet in Exhibit 8, accounts payable is the only liability. When there are two or more liabilities, each should be listed and the total amount of liabilities presented as follows:

Liabilities		
Accounts payable	$12,900	
Wages payable	2,570	
Total liabilities		$15,470

Example Exercise 1-6 Balance Sheet

OBJ 5

Using the following data for Chickadee Travel Service as well as the statement of owner's equity shown in Example Exercise 1-5, prepare a balance sheet as of April 30, 2016.

Accounts payable	$12,200
Accounts receivable	31,350
Cash	53,050
Land	80,000
Supplies	3,350

Follow My Example 1-6

Chickadee Travel Service
Balance Sheet
April 30, 2016

Assets		**Liabilities**	
Cash	$ 53,050	Accounts payable	$ 12,200
Accounts receivable	31,350		
Supplies	3,350	**Owner's Equity**	
Land	80,000	Adam Cellini, capital	155,550
Total assets	$167,750	Total liabilities and owner's equity	$167,750

Practice Exercises: PE 1-6A, PE 1-6B

Statement of Cash Flows

The statement of cash flows consists of the following three sections, as shown in Exhibit 8:

1. operating activities
2. investing activities
3. financing activities

Each of these sections is briefly described in this section.

Cash Flows from Operating Activities This section reports a summary of cash receipts and cash payments from operations. The net cash flow from operating activities normally differs from the amount of net income for the period. In Exhibit 8, **NetSolutions** reported net cash flows from operating activities of $2,900 and net income

[3] An alternative form of balance sheet, called the *report form*, is illustrated in Chapter 6. It presents the liabilities and owner's equity sections below the assets section.

of $3,050. This difference occurs because revenues and expenses may not be recorded at the same time that cash is received from customers or paid to creditors.

Cash Flows from Investing Activities This section reports the cash transactions for the acquisition and sale of relatively permanent assets. Exhibit 8 reports that **NetSolutions** paid $20,000 for the purchase of land during November.

Cash Flows from Financing Activities This section reports the cash transactions related to cash investments by the owner, borrowings, and withdrawals by the owner. Exhibit 8 shows that Chris Clark invested $25,000 in **NetSolutions** and withdrew $2,000 during November.

Preparing NetSolutions' Statement of Cash Flows Preparing the statement of cash flows requires that each of the November cash transactions for **NetSolutions** be classified as an operating, investing, or financing activity. Using the summary of transactions shown in Exhibit 5, the November cash transactions for NetSolutions are classified as follows:

Transaction	Amount	Cash Flow Activity
a.	$25,000	Financing (Investment by Chris Clark)
b.	−20,000	Investing (Purchase of land)
d.	7,500	Operating (Fees earned)
e.	−3,650	Operating (Payment of expenses)
f.	−950	Operating (Payment of account payable)
h.	−2,000	Financing (Withdrawal by Chris Clark)

Transactions (c) and (g) are not listed since they did not involve a cash receipt or payment. In addition, the payment of accounts payable in transaction (f) is classified as an operating activity because the account payable arose from the purchase of supplies, which are used in operations. Using the preceding classifications of November cash transactions, the statement of cash flows is prepared as shown in Exhibit 8.[4]

The ending cash balance shown on the statement of cash flows is also reported on the balance sheet as of the end of the period. To illustrate, the ending cash of $5,900 reported on the November statement of cash flows in Exhibit 8 is also reported as the amount of cash on hand in the November 30, 2015, balance sheet.

Since November is NetSolutions' first period of operations, the net cash flow for November and the November 30, 2015, cash balance are the same amount, $5,900, as shown in Exhibit 8. In later periods, NetSolutions will report in its statement of cash flows a beginning cash balance, an increase or a decrease in cash for the period, and an ending cash balance. For example, assume that for December NetSolutions has a decrease in cash of $3,835. The last three lines of NetSolutions' statement of cash flows for December would be as follows:

Decrease in cash	$(3,835)
Cash as of December 1, 2015	5,900
Cash as of December 31, 2015	$ 2,065

Example Exercise 1-7 Statement of Cash Flows

OBJ 5

A summary of cash flows for Chickadee Travel Service for the year ended April 30, 2016, follows:

Cash receipts:	
Cash received from customers	$251,000
Cash received from additional investment of owner	50,000
Cash payments:	
Cash paid for expenses	210,000
Cash paid for land	80,000
Cash paid to owner for personal use	30,000

The cash balance as of May 1, 2015, was $72,050. Prepare a statement of cash flows for Chickadee Travel Service for the year ended April 30, 2016.

[4] This method of preparing the statement of cash flows is called the "direct method." This method and the indirect method are discussed further in Chapter 16.

(Continued)

Follow My Example 1-7

Chickadee Travel Service
Statement of Cash Flows
For the Year Ended April 30, 2016

Cash flows from operating activities:		
Cash received from customers	$ 251,000	
Deduct cash payments for expenses	(210,000)	
Net cash flows from operating activities		$ 41,000
Cash flows from investing activities:		
Cash payments for purchase of land		(80,000)
Cash flows from financing activities:		
Cash received from owner as investment	$ 50,000	
Deduct cash withdrawals by owner	(30,000)	
Net cash flows from financing activities		20,000
Net decrease in cash during year		$(19,000)
Cash as of May 1, 2015		72,050
Cash as of April 30, 2016		$ 53,050

Practice Exercises: PE 1-7A, PE 1-7B

Interrelationships Among Financial Statements

Financial statements are prepared in the order of the income statement, statement of owner's equity, balance sheet, and statement of cash flows. This order is important because the financial statements are interrelated. These interrelationships for **NetSolutions** are shown in Exhibit 8 and are described in Exhibit 9.[5]

EXHIBIT 9 **Financial Statement Interrelationships**

Financial Statements	Interrelationship	NetSolutions Example (Exhibit 8)
Income Statement *and* Statement of Owner's Equity	Net income or net loss reported on the income statement is also reported on the statement of owner's equity as either an addition (net income) to or deduction (net loss) from the beginning owner's equity and any additional investments by the owner during the period.	NetSolutions' net income of $3,050 for November is added to Chris Clark's investment of $25,000 on the statement of owner's equity.
Statement of Owner's Equity *and* Balance Sheet	Owner's capital at the end of the period reported on the statement of owner's equity is also reported on the balance sheet as owner's capital.	Chris Clark, Capital of $26,050 as of November 30, 2015, on the statement of owner's equity also appears on the November 30, 2015, balance sheet as Chris Clark, Capital.
Balance Sheet *and* Statement of Cash Flows	The cash reported on the balance sheet is also reported as the end-of-period cash on the statement of cash flows.	Cash of $5,900 reported on the balance sheet as of November 30, 2015, is also reported on the November statement of cash flows as the end-of-period cash.

The preceding interrelationships are important in analyzing financial statements and the impact of transactions on a business. In addition, these interrelationships serve as a check on whether the financial statements are prepared correctly. For example, if the ending cash on the statement of cash flows does not agree with the balance sheet cash, then an error has occurred.

[5] Depending on the method of preparing the cash flows from operating activities section of the statement of cash flows, net income (or net loss) may also appear on the statement of cash flows. This interrelationship or method of preparing the statement of cash flows, called the "indirect method," is described and illustrated in Chapter 16.

Financial Analysis and Interpretation: Ratio of Liabilities to Owner's Equity

 Describe and illustrate the use of the ratio of liabilities to owner's equity in evaluating a company's financial condition.

F·A·I

The basic financial statements illustrated in this chapter are useful to bankers, creditors, owners, and others in analyzing and interpreting the financial performance and condition of a company. Throughout this text, various tools and techniques that are often used to analyze and interpret a company's financial performance and condition are described and illustrated. The first such tool that is discussed is useful in analyzing the ability of a company to pay its creditors.

The relationship between liabilities and owner's equity, expressed as a **ratio of liabilities to owner's equity**, is computed as follows:

$$\text{Ratio of Liabilities to Owner's Equity} = \frac{\text{Total Liabilities}}{\text{Total Owner's Equity (or Total Stockholders' Equity)}}$$

NetSolutions' ratio of liabilities to owner's equity at the end of November is 0.015, computed as follows:

$$\text{Ratio of Liabilities to Owner's Equity} = \frac{\$400}{\$26{,}050} = 0.015 \text{ (Rounded)}$$

Corporations refer to total owner's equity as total stockholders' equity. Thus, total stockholders' equity is substituted for total owner's equity when computing this ratio.

To illustrate, recent balance sheet data (in millions) for **Google Inc.** and **McDonald's Corporation** follows:

	Recent Year	**Prior Year**
Google Inc.		
Total liabilities	$22,083	$14,429
Total stockholders' equity	71,715	58,145
McDonald's Corporation		
Total liabilities	$18,600	$17,341
Total stockholders' equity	14,390	14,634

The ratio of liabilities to stockholders' equity for Google and McDonald's for a recent year and the prior year is computed as follows:

	Recent Year*	**Prior Year***
Google Inc.		
Ratio of liabilities to stockholders' equity	0.31	0.25
	($22,083 ÷ $71,715)	($14,429 ÷ $58,145)
McDonald's Corporation		
Ratio of liabilities to stockholders' equity	1.29	1.18
	($18,600 ÷ $14,390)	($17,341 ÷ $14,634)

* Rounded to two decimal places.

The rights of creditors to a business's assets come before the rights of the owners or stockholders. Thus, the lower the ratio of liabilities to owner's equity, the better able the company is to withstand poor business conditions and to pay its obligations to creditors.

Google is unusual in that it has a very low amount of liabilities. Its ratio of liabilities to stockholders' equity of 0.31 in the recent year and 0.25 in the prior year is low. In contrast, McDonald's has more liabilities; its ratio of liabilities to stockholders' equity is 1.29 in the recent year and 1.18 in the prior year. Because McDonald's ratio of liabilities to stockholders' equity increased slightly, its creditors are slightly more at risk at the end of the recent year. Also, McDonald's creditors are more at risk than are Google's creditors. As well-established companies, however, the creditors of both companies are protected against the risk of nonpayment.

Example Exercise 1-8 Ratio of Liabilities to Owner's Equity

The following data were taken from Hawthorne Company's balance sheet:

	Dec. 31, 2016	Dec. 31, 2015
Total liabilities	$120,000	$105,000
Total owner's equity	80,000	75,000

a. Compute the ratio of liabilities to owner's equity.

b. Has the creditors' risk increased or decreased from December 31, 2015, to December 31, 2016?

Follow My Example 1-8

a.

	Dec. 31, 2016	Dec. 31, 2015
Total liabilities	$120,000	$105,000
Total owner's equity	80,000	75,000
Ratio of liabilities to owner's equity	1.50	1.40
	($120,000 ÷ $80,000)	($105,000 ÷ $75,000)

b. Increased

Practice Exercises: PE 1-8A, PE 1-8B

At a Glance 1

Describe the nature of a business and the role of accounting and ethics in business.

Key Points A business provides goods or services (outputs) to customers with the objective of earning a profit. Three types of businesses include service, merchandising, and manufacturing businesses.

Accounting is an information system that provides reports to users about the economic activities and condition of a business.

Ethics are moral principles that guide the conduct of individuals. Good ethical conduct depends on individual character and firm culture.

Accountants are engaged in private accounting or public accounting.

Learning Outcomes	Example Exercises	Practice Exercises
• Distinguish among service, merchandising, and manufacturing businesses.		
• Describe the role of accounting in business, and explain why accounting is called the "language of business."		
• Define ethics, and list two factors affecting ethical conduct.		
• Differentiate between private and public accounting.		

Summarize the development of accounting principles and relate them to practice.

Key Points Generally accepted accounting principles (GAAP) are used in preparing financial statements. Accounting principles and concepts develop from research, practice, and pronouncements of authoritative bodies.

The business entity concept views the business as an entity separate from its owners, creditors, or other businesses. Businesses may be organized as proprietorships, partnerships, corporations, and limited liability companies. The cost concept requires that purchases by a business be recorded in terms of actual cost. The objectivity concept requires that the accounting records and reports be based on objective evidence. The unit of measure concept requires that economic data be recorded in dollars.

Learning Outcomes	*Example Exercises*	*Practice Exercises*
• Explain what is meant by generally accepted accounting principles.		
• Describe how generally accepted accounting principles are developed.		
• Describe and give an example of what is meant by the business entity concept.		
• Describe the characteristics of a proprietorship, partnership, corporation, and limited liability company.		
• Describe and give an example of what is meant by the cost concept.	**EE1-1**	**PE1-1A, 1-1B**
• Describe and give an example of what is meant by the objectivity concept.		
• Describe and give an example of what is meant by the unit of measure concept.		

State the accounting equation and define each element of the equation.

Key Points The resources owned by a business and the rights or claims to these resources may be stated in the form of an equation, as follows: Assets = Liabilities + Owner's Equity

Learning Outcomes	*Example Exercises*	*Practice Exercises*
• State the accounting equation.		
• Define assets, liabilities, and owner's equity.		
• Given two elements of the accounting equation, solve for the third element.	**EE1-2**	**PE1-2A, 1-2B**

Describe and illustrate how business transactions can be recorded in terms of the resulting change in the elements of the accounting equation.

Key Points All business transactions can be stated in terms of the change in one or more of the three elements of the accounting equation.

Learning Outcomes	*Example Exercises*	*Practice Exercises*
• Define a business transaction.		
• Using the accounting equation as a framework, record transactions.	**EE1-3**	**PE1-3A, 1-3B**

Describe the financial statements of a proprietorship and explain how they interrelate.

Key Points The primary financial statements of a proprietorship are the income statement, the statement of owner's equity, the balance sheet, and the statement of cash flows. The income statement reports a period's net income or net loss, which is also reported on the statement of owner's equity. The ending owner's capital reported on the statement of owner's equity is also reported on the balance sheet. The ending cash balance is reported on the balance sheet and the statement of cash flows.

Learning Outcomes	Example Exercises	Practice Exercises
• List and describe the financial statements of a proprietorship.		
• Prepare an income statement.	**EE1-4**	**PE1-4A, 1-4B**
• Prepare a statement of owner's equity.	**EE1-5**	**PE1-5A, 1-5B**
• Prepare a balance sheet.	**EE1-6**	**PE1-6A, 1-6B**
• Prepare a statement of cash flows.	**EE1-7**	**PE1-7A, 1-7B**
• Explain how the financial statements of a proprietorship are interrelated.		

Describe and illustrate the use of the ratio of liabilities to owner's equity in evaluating a company's financial condition.

Key Points A ratio useful in analyzing the ability of a business to pay its creditors is the ratio of liabilities to owner's (stockholders') equity. The lower the ratio of liabilities to owner's equity, the better able the company is to withstand poor business conditions and to pay its obligations to creditors.

Learning Outcomes	Example Exercises	Practice Exercises
• Describe the usefulness of the ratio of liabilities to owner's (stockholders') equity.		
• Compute the ratio of liabilities to owner's (stockholders') equity.	**EE1-8**	**PE1-8A, 1-8B**

Key Terms

account form (18)
account payable (11)
account receivable (12)
accounting (3)
accounting equation (9)
assets (9)
balance sheet (15)
business (2)
business entity concept (7)
business transaction (10)
Certified Public Accountant (CPA) (5)
corporation (8)
cost concept (8)
earnings (15)
ethics (4)
expenses (12)
fees earned (12)
financial accounting (4)
Financial Accounting Standards Board (FASB) (7)
financial statements (15)
generally accepted accounting principles (GAAP) (7)
general-purpose financial statements (4)
income statement (15)
interest revenue (12)
International Accounting Standards Board (IASB) (7)
liabilities (9)
limited liability company (LLC) (8)
management (or managerial) accounting (3)
manufacturing business (3)
matching concept (15)

Illustrative Problem

Cecil Jameson, Attorney-at-Law, is a proprietorship owned and operated by Cecil Jameson. On July 1, 2015, the company has the following assets and liabilities: cash, $1,000; accounts receivable, $3,200; supplies, $850; land, $10,000; accounts payable, $1,530. Office space and office equipment are currently being rented, pending the construction of an office complex on land purchased last year. Business transactions during July are summarized as follows:

a. Received cash from clients for services, $3,928.
b. Paid creditors on account, $1,055.
c. Received cash from Cecil Jameson as an additional investment, $3,700.
d. Paid office rent for the month, $1,200.
e. Charged clients for legal services on account, $2,025.
f. Purchased supplies on account, $245.
g. Received cash from clients on account, $3,000.
h. Received invoice for paralegal services from Legal Aid Inc. for July (to be paid on August 10), $1,635.
i. Paid the following: wages expense, $850; utilities expense, $325; answering service expense, $250; and miscellaneous expense, $75.
j. Determined that the cost of supplies on hand was $980; therefore, the cost of supplies used during the month was $115.
k. Jameson withdrew $1,000 in cash from the business for personal use.

Instructions

1. Determine the amount of owner's equity (Cecil Jameson's capital) as of July 1, 2015.
2. State the assets, liabilities, and owner's equity as of July 1 in equation form similar to that shown in this chapter. In tabular form below the equation, indicate the increases and decreases resulting from each transaction and the new balances after each transaction.
3. Prepare an income statement for July, a statement of owner's equity for July, and a balance sheet as of July 31, 2015.
4. (Optional) Prepare a statement of cash flows for July.

Solution

1.

Assets – Liabilities = Owner's Equity (Cecil Jameson, capital)
($1,000 + $3,200 + $850 + $10,000) – $1,530 = Owner's Equity (Cecil Jameson, capital)
$15,050 – $1,530 = Owner's Equity (Cecil Jameson, capital)
$13,520 = Owner's Equity (Cecil Jameson, capital)

2.

	Assets				= Liabilities +				Owner's Equity						
	Cash +	Accts. Rec. +	Supp. +	Land =	Accts Pay. +	Cecil Jameson, Capital –	Cecil Jameson, Drawing +	Fees Earned –	Paralegal Exp. –	Rent Exp. –	Wages Exp. –	Utilities Exp. –	Answering Service Exp. –	Supp. Exp. –	Misc. Exp.
Bal.	1,000	3,200	850	10,000	1,530	13,520									
a.	+3,928							3,928							
Bal.	4,928	3,200	850	10,000	1,530	13,520		3,928							
b.	−1,055				−1,055										
Bal.	3,873	3,200	850	10,000	475	13,520		3,928							
c.	+3,700					+3,700									
Bal.	7,573	3,200	850	10,000	475	17,220		3,928							
d.	−1,200									−1,200					
Bal.	6,373	3,200	850	10,000	475	17,220		3,928		−1,200					
e.		+ 2,025						+ 2,025							
Bal.	6,373	5,225	850	10,000	475	17,220		5,953		−1,200					
f.			+245		+245										
Bal.	6,373	5,225	1,095	10,000	720	17,220		5,953		−1,200					
g.	+3,000	−3,000													
Bal.	9,373	2,225	1,095	10,000	720	17,220		5,953		−1,200					
h.					+1,635				−1,635						
Bal.	9,373	2,225	1,095	10,000	2,355	17,220		5,953	−1,635	−1,200					
i.	−1,500										−850	−325	−250		−75
Bal.	7,873	2,225	1,095	10,000	2,355	17,220		5,953	−1,635	−1,200	−850	−325	−250		−75
j.			−115											−115	
Bal.	7,873	2,225	980	10,000	2,355	17,220		5,953	−1,635	−1,200	−850	−325	−250	−115	−75
k.	−1,000						−1,000								
Bal.	6,873	2,225	980	10,000	2,355	17,220	−1,000	5,953	−1,635	−1,200	−850	−325	−250	−115	−75

3.

Cecil Jameson, Attorney-at-Law
Income Statement
For the Month Ended July 31, 2015

Fees earned		**$5,953**
Expenses:		
Paralegal expense	$1,635	
Rent expense	1,200	
Wages expense	850	
Utilities expense	325	
Answering service expense	250	
Supplies expense	115	
Miscellaneous expense	75	
Total expenses		4,450
Net income		$1,503

Cecil Jameson, Attorney-at-Law
Statement of Owner's Equity
For the Month Ended July 31, 2015

Cecil Jameson, capital, July 1, 2015		$13,520
Additional investment by owner	$3,700	
Net income for the month	1,503	
	$5,203	
Less withdrawals	1,000	
Increase in owner's equity		4,203
Cecil Jameson, capital, July 31, 2015		$17,723

(Continued)

Cecil Jameson, Attorney-at-Law
Balance Sheet
July 31, 2015

Assets		Liabilities	
Cash	$ 6,873	Accounts payable	$ 2,355
Accounts receivable	2,225	**Owner's Equity**	
Supplies	980	Cecil Jameson, capital	17,723
Land	10,000	Total liabilities and owner's	
Total assets	$20,078	equity	$20,078

4. (Optional)

Cecil Jameson, Attorney-at-Law
Statement of Cash Flows
For the Month Ended July 31, 2015

Cash flows from operating activities:		
Cash received from customers	$ 6,928*	
Deduct cash payments for operating expenses	(3,755)**	
Net cash flows from operating activities		$ 3,173
Cash flows from investing activities		—
Cash flows from financing activities:		
Cash received from owner as investment	$ 3,700	
Deduct cash withdrawals by owner	(1,000)	
Net cash flows from financing activities		2,700
Net increase in cash during year		$ 5,873
Cash as of July 1, 2015		1,000
Cash as of July 31, 2015		$ 6,873

*$6,928 = $3,928 + $3,000

**$3,755 = $1,055 + $1,200 + $1,500

Discussion Questions

1. Name some users of accounting information.
2. What is the role of accounting in business?
3. Why are most large companies like Microsoft, PepsiCo, Caterpillar, and AutoZone organized as corporations?
4. Josh Reilly is the owner of Dispatch Delivery Service. Recently Josh paid interest of $4,500 on a personal loan of $75,000 that he used to begin the business. Should Dispatch Delivery Service record the interest payment? Explain.
5. On July 12, Reliable Repair Service extended an offer of $150,000 for land that had been priced for sale at $185,000. On September 3, Reliable Repair Service accepted the seller's counteroffer of $167,500. Describe how Reliable Repair Service should record the land.
6. a. Land with an assessed value of $750,000 for property tax purposes is acquired by a business for $900,000. Ten years later, the plot of land has an assessed value of $1,200,000 and the business receives an offer of $2,000,000 for it. Should the monetary amount assigned to the land in the business records now be increased?

   b. Assuming that the land acquired in (a) was sold for $2,125,000, how would the various elements of the accounting equation be affected?
7. Describe the difference between an account receivable and an account payable.
8. A business had revenues of $679,000 and operating expenses of $588,000. Did the business (a) incur a net loss or (b) realize net income?

9. A business had revenues of $640,000 and operating expenses of $715,000. Did the business (a) incur a net loss or (b) realize net income?

10. The financial statements are interrelated. (a) What item of financial or operating data appears on both the income statement and the statement of owner's equity? (b) What item appears on both the balance sheet and the statement of owner's equity? (c) What item appears on both the balance sheet and the statement of cash flows?

Practice Exercises

EE 1-1 p. 9

PE 1-1A Cost concept — OBJ. 2

On February 22, Kountry Repair Service extended an offer of $200,000 for land that had been priced for sale at $250,000. On April 3, Kountry Repair Service accepted the seller's counteroffer of $230,000. On September 15, the land was assessed at a value of $185,000 for property tax purposes. On January 9 of the next year, Kountry Repair Service was offered $300,000 for the land by a national retail chain. At what value should the land be recorded in Kountry Repair Service's records?

EE 1-1 p. 9

PE 1-1B Cost concept — OBJ. 2

On March 31, Higgins Repair Service extended an offer of $415,000 for land that had been priced for sale at $460,000. On April 15, Higgins Repair Service accepted the seller's counteroffer of $437,500. On September 9, the land was assessed at a value of $375,000 for property tax purposes. On December 8, Higgins Repair Service was offered $475,000 for the land by a national retail chain. At what value should the land be recorded in Higgins Repair Service's records?

EE 1-2 p. 10

PE 1-2A Accounting equation — OBJ. 3

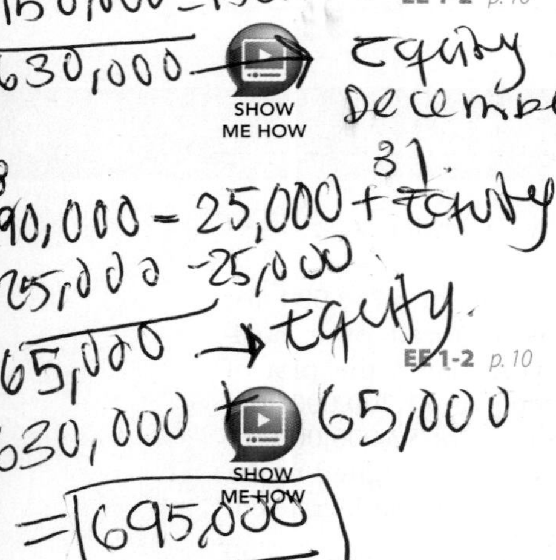

Brock Hahn is the owner and operator of Dream-It LLC, a motivational consulting business. At the end of its accounting period, December 31, 2015, Dream-It has assets of $780,000 and liabilities of $150,000. Using the accounting equation, determine the following amounts:

a. Owner's equity as of December 31, 2015.

b. Owner's equity as of December 31, 2016, assuming that assets increased by $90,000 and liabilities increased by $25,000 during 2016.

EE 1-2 p. 10

PE 1-2B Accounting equation — OBJ. 3

Fritz Evans is the owner and operator of Be-The-One, a motivational consulting business. At the end of its accounting period, December 31, 2015, Be-The-One has assets of $395,000 and liabilities of $97,000. Using the accounting equation, determine the following amounts:

a. Owner's equity as of December 31, 2015.

b. Owner's equity as of December 31, 2016, assuming that assets decreased by $65,000 and liabilities increased by $36,000 during 2016.

EE 1-3 p. 14

PE 1-3A Transactions — OBJ. 4

SHOW
ME HOW

Arrowhead Delivery Service is owned and operated by Gates Deeter. The following selected transactions were completed by Arrowhead Delivery Service during August:

1. Received cash from owner as additional investment, $25,000.
2. Paid creditors on account, $3,750.

3. Billed customers for delivery services on account, $22,400.
4. Received cash from customers on account, $11,300.
5. Paid cash to owner for personal use, $6,000.

Indicate the effect of each transaction on the accounting equation elements (Assets, Liabilities, Owner's Equity, Drawing, Revenue, and Expense). Also indicate the specific item within the accounting equation element that is affected. To illustrate, the answer to (1) follows:

> (1) Asset (Cash) increases by $25,000; Owner's Equity (Gates Deeter, Capital) increases by $25,000.

EE 1-3 p. 14

SHOW ME HOW

PE 1-3B Transactions — OBJ. 4

Interstate Delivery Service is owned and operated by Katie Wyer. The following selected transactions were completed by Interstate Delivery Service during May:

1. Received cash from owner as additional investment, $18,000.
2. Paid advertising expense, $4,850.
3. Purchased supplies on account, $2,100.
4. Billed customers for delivery services on account, $14,700.
5. Received cash from customers on account, $8,200.

Indicate the effect of each transaction on the accounting equation elements (Assets, Liabilities, Owner's Equity, Drawing, Revenue, and Expense). Also indicate the specific item within the accounting equation element that is affected. To illustrate, the answer to (1) follows:

> (1) Asset (Cash) increases by $18,000; Owner's Equity (Katie Wyer, Capital) increases by $18,000.

EE 1-4 p. 15

SHOW ME HOW

PE 1-4A Income statement — OBJ. 5

The revenues and expenses of Ousel Travel Service for the year ended November 30, 2016, follow:

Fees earned	$1,475,000
Office expense	320,000
Miscellaneous expense	28,000
Wages expense	885,000

Prepare an income statement for the year ended November 30, 2016.

EE 1-4 p. 15

SHOW ME HOW

PE 1-4B Income statement — OBJ. 5

The revenues and expenses of Sentinel Travel Service for the year ended August 31, 2016, follow:

Fees earned	$750,000
Office expense	295,000
Miscellaneous expense	12,000
Wages expense	450,000

Prepare an income statement for the year ended August 31, 2016.

EE 1-5 p. 16

SHOW ME HOW

PE 1-5A Statement of owner's equity — OBJ. 5

Using the income statement for Ousel Travel Service shown in Practice Exercise 1-4A, prepare a statement of owner's equity for the year ended November 30, 2016. Shane Ousel, the owner, invested an additional $50,000 in the business during the year and withdrew cash of $30,000 for personal use. Shane Ousel, capital as of December 1, 2015, was $666,000.

EE 1-5 p. 16

SHOW ME HOW

PE 1-5B Statement of owner's equity **OBJ. 5**

Using the income statement for Sentinel Travel Service shown in Practice Exercise 1-4B, prepare a statement of owner's equity for the year ended August 31, 2016. Barb Schroeder, the owner, invested an additional $36,000 in the business during the year and withdrew cash of $18,000 for personal use. Barb Schroeder, capital as of September 1, 2015, was $380,000.

EE 1-6 p. 18

SHOW ME HOW

PE 1-6A Balance sheet **OBJ. 5**

Using the following data for Ousel Travel Service as well as the statement of owner's equity shown in Practice Exercise 1-5A, prepare a balance sheet as of November 30, 2016:

Accounts payable	$ 62,500
Accounts receivable	186,000
Cash	308,000
Land	480,000
Supplies	16,500

EE 1-6 p. 18

SHOW ME HOW

PE 1-6B Balance sheet **OBJ. 5**

Using the following data for Sentinel Travel Service as well as the statement of owner's equity shown in Practice Exercise 1-5B, prepare a balance sheet as of August 31, 2016:

Accounts payable	$ 44,600
Accounts receivable	75,500
Cash	45,400
Land	310,000
Supplies	4,700

EE 1-7 p. 19

SHOW ME HOW

PE 1-7A Statement of cash flows **OBJ. 5**

A summary of cash flows for Ousel Travel Service for the year ended November 30, 2016, follows:

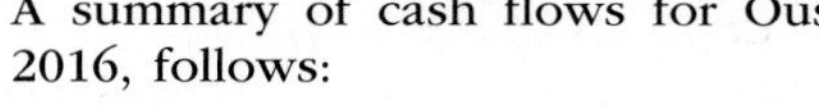

Cash receipts:	
Cash received from customers	$1,465,000
Cash received from additional investment of owner	50,000
Cash payments:	
Cash paid for operating expenses	1,230,000
Cash paid for land	150,000
Cash paid to owner for personal use	30,000

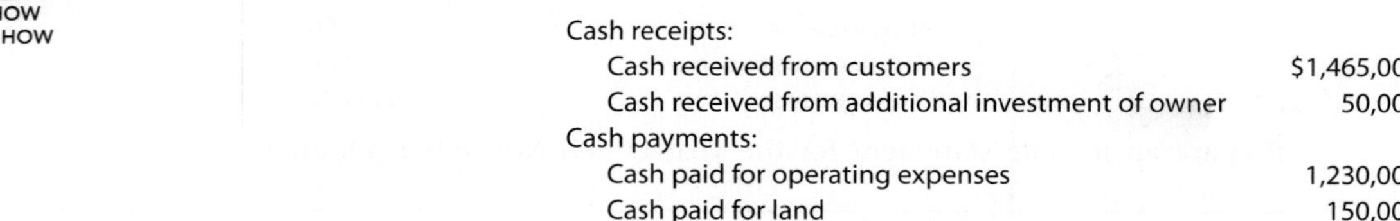

The cash balance as of December 1, 2015, was $203,000.

Prepare a statement of cash flows for Ousel Travel Service for the year ended November 30, 2016.

EE 1-7 p. 19

SHOW ME HOW

PE 1-7B Statement of cash flows **OBJ. 5**

A summary of cash flows for Sentinel Travel Service for the year ended August 31, 2016, follows:

Cash receipts:	
Cash received from customers	$734,000
Cash received from additional investment of owner	36,000
Cash payments:	
Cash paid for operating expenses	745,600
Cash paid for land	50,000
Cash paid to owner for personal use	18,000

The cash balance as of September 1, 2015, was $89,000.

Prepare a statement of cash flows for Sentinel Travel Service for the year ended August 31, 2016.

EE 1-8 *p. 22*

SHOW ME HOW

PE 1-8A Ratio of liabilities to owner's equity **OBJ. 6**

The following data were taken from Mesa Company's balance sheet:

	Dec. 31, 2016	Dec. 31, 2015
Total liabilities	$547,800	$518,000
Total owner's equity	415,000	370,000

a. Compute the ratio of liabilities to owner's equity.

b. Has the creditor's risk increased or decreased from December 31, 2015, to December 31, 2016?

EE 1-8 *p. 22*

SHOW ME HOW

PE 1-8B Ratio of liabilities to owner's equity **OBJ. 6**

The following data were taken from Alvarado Company's balance sheet:

	Dec. 31, 2016	Dec. 31, 2015
Total liabilities	$4,085,000	$2,880,000
Total owner's equity	4,300,000	3,600,000

a. Compute the ratio of liabilities to owner's equity.

b. Has the creditor's risk increased or decreased from December 31, 2015, to December 31, 2016?

Exercises

EX 1-1 Types of businesses **OBJ. 1**

The following is a list of well-known companies:

1. Alcoa Inc.
2. Boeing
3. Caterpillar
4. Citigroup Inc.
5. CVS
6. Dow Chemical Company
7. eBay Inc.
8. FedEx
9. Ford Motor Company
10. Gap Inc.
11. H&R Block
12. Hilton Hospitality, Inc.
13. Procter & Gamble
14. SunTrust
15. Walmart Stores, Inc.

a. Indicate whether each of these companies is primarily a service, merchandise, or manufacturing business. If you are unfamiliar with the company, use the Internet to locate the company's home page or use the finance Web site of Yahoo (finance.yahoo.com).

b. For which of the preceding companies is the accounting equation relevant?

EX 1-2 Professional ethics **OBJ. 1**

A fertilizer manufacturing company wants to relocate to Yellowstone County. A report from a fired researcher at the company indicates the company's product is releasing toxic by-products. The company suppressed that report. A later report commissioned by the company shows there is no problem with the fertilizer.

Should the company's chief executive officer reveal the content of the unfavorable report in discussions with Yellowstone County representatives? Discuss.

EX 1-3 Business entity concept

OBJ. 2

Ozark Sports sells hunting and fishing equipment and provides guided hunting and fishing trips. Ozark Sports is owned and operated by Eric Griffith, a well-known sports enthusiast and hunter. Eric's wife, Linda, owns and operates Lake Boutique, a women's clothing store. Eric and Linda have established a trust fund to finance their children's college education. The trust fund is maintained by Missouri State Bank in the name of the children, Mark and Steffy.

a. For each of the following transactions, identify which of the entities listed should record the transaction in its records:

Entities	
L	Lake Boutique
M	Missouri State Bank
O	Ozark Sports
X	None of the above

1. Linda authorized the trust fund to purchase mutual fund shares.
2. Linda purchased two dozen spring dresses from a St. Louis designer for a special spring sale.
3. Eric paid a breeder's fee for an English springer spaniel to be used as a hunting guide dog.
4. Linda deposited a $2,000 personal check in the trust fund at Missouri State Bank.
5. Eric paid a local doctor for his annual physical, which was required by the workmen's compensation insurance policy carried by Ozark Sports.
6. Eric received a cash advance from customers for a guided hunting trip.
7. Linda paid her dues to the YWCA.
8. Linda donated several dresses from inventory for a local charity auction for the benefit of a women's abuse shelter.
9. Eric paid for dinner and a movie to celebrate their twelfth wedding anniversary.
10. Eric paid for an advertisement in a hunters' magazine.

b. What is a business transaction?

EX 1-4 Accounting equation

OBJ. 3

✓ Starbucks, $5,109

The total assets and total liabilities (in millions) of **Green Mountain Coffee Roasters, Inc.** and **Starbucks Corporation** follow:

	Green Mountain	Starbucks
Assets	$3,616	$8,219
Liabilities	1,345	3,110

Determine the owners' equity of each company.

EX 1-5 Accounting equation

OBJ. 3

✓ Dollar Tree, $1,345

The total assets and total liabilities (in millions) of **Dollar Tree Inc.** and **Target Corporation** follow:

	Dollar Tree	Target Corporation
Assets	$2,329	$46,630
Liabilities	984	30,809

Determine the owners' equity of each company.

EX 1-6 Accounting equation

OBJ. 3

✓ a. $1,271,000

Determine the missing amount for each of the following:

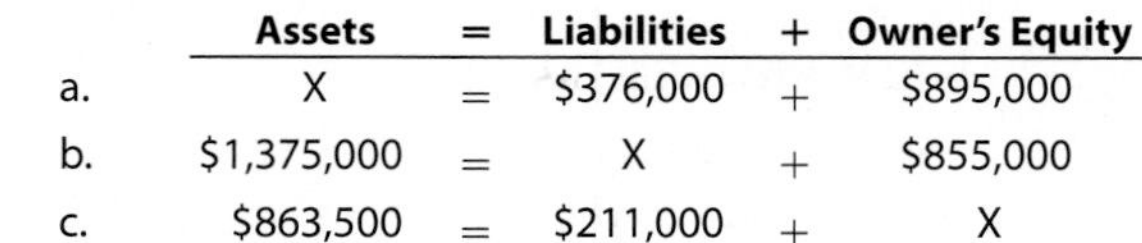

	Assets	=	Liabilities	+	Owner's Equity
a.	X	=	$376,000	+	$895,000
b.	$1,375,000	=	X	+	$855,000
c.	$863,500	=	$211,000	+	X

EX 1-7 Accounting equation

OBJ. 3, 4

✔ b. $606,500

SHOW ME HOW

Annie Rasmussen is the owner and operator of Go44, a motivational consulting business. At the end of its accounting period, December 31, 2015, Go44 has assets of $720,000 and liabilities of $180,000. Using the accounting equation and considering each case independently, determine the following amounts:

a. Annie Rasmussen, capital, as of December 31, 2015.

b. Annie Rasmussen, capital, as of December 31, 2016, assuming that assets increased by $96,500 and liabilities increased by $30,000 during 2016.

c. Annie Rasmussen, capital, as of December 31, 2016, assuming that assets decreased by $168,000 and liabilities increased by $15,000 during 2016.

d. Annie Rasmussen, capital, as of December 31, 2016, assuming that assets increased by $175,000 and liabilities decreased by $18,000 during 2016.

e. Net income (or net loss) during 2016, assuming that as of December 31, 2016, assets were $880,000, liabilities were $220,000, and there were no additional investments or withdrawals.

EX 1-8 Asset, liability, and owner's equity items

OBJ. 3

Indicate whether each of the following is identified with (1) an asset, (2) a liability, or (3) owner's equity:

a. accounts payable

b. cash

c. fees earned

d. land

e. supplies

f. wages expense

EX 1-9 Effect of transactions on accounting equation

OBJ. 4

Describe how the following business transactions affect the three elements of the accounting equation:

a. Invested cash in business.

b. Paid for utilities used in the business.

c. Purchased supplies for cash.

d. Purchased supplies on account.

e. Received cash for services performed.

EX 1-10 Effect of transactions on accounting equation

OBJ. 4

✔ a. (1) increase $183,000

SHOW ME HOW

a. A vacant lot acquired for $115,000 is sold for $298,000 in cash. What is the effect of the sale on the total amount of the seller's (1) assets, (2) liabilities, and (3) owner's equity?

b. Assume that the seller owes $80,000 on a loan for the land. After receiving the $298,000 cash in (a), the seller pays the $80,000 owed. What is the effect of the payment on the total amount of the seller's (1) assets, (2) liabilities, and (3) owner's equity?

c. Is it true that a transaction always affects at least two elements (Assets, Liabilities, or Owner's Equity) of the accounting equation? Explain.

EX 1-11 Effect of transactions on owner's equity

OBJ. 4

Indicate whether each of the following types of transactions will either (a) increase owner's equity or (b) decrease owner's equity:

1. expenses
2. owner's investments
3. owner's withdrawals
4. revenues

EX 1-12 Transactions **OBJ. 4**

The following selected transactions were completed by Cota Delivery Service during July:

1. Received cash from owner as additional investment, $35,000.
2. Purchased supplies for cash, $1,100.
3. Paid rent for October, $4,500.
4. Paid advertising expense, $900.
5. Received cash for providing delivery services, $33,000.
6. Billed customers for delivery services on account, $58,000.
7. Paid creditors on account, $2,900.
8. Received cash from customers on account, $27,500.
9. Determined that the cost of supplies on hand was $300 and $8,600 of supplies had been used during the month.
10. Paid cash to owner for personal use, $2,500.

Indicate the effect of each transaction on the accounting equation by listing the numbers identifying the transactions, (1) through (10), in a column, and inserting at the right of each number the appropriate letter from the following list:

a. Increase in an asset, decrease in another asset.
b. Increase in an asset, increase in a liability.
c. Increase in an asset, increase in owner's equity.
d. Decrease in an asset, decrease in a liability.
e. Decrease in an asset, decrease in owner's equity.

EX 1-13 Nature of transactions **OBJ. 4**

✔ d. $22,800

SHOW ME HOW

Teri West operates her own catering service. Summary financial data for July are presented in equation form as follows. Each line designated by a number indicates the effect of a transaction on the equation. Each increase and decrease in owner's equity, except transaction (5), affects net income.

	Assets			= Liabilities +	Owner's Equity			
	Cash	+ Supplies +	Land	= Accounts Payable +	Teri West, Capital	− Teri West, Drawing	+ Fees Earned	− Expenses
Bal.	40,000	3,000	82,000	7,500	117,500			
1.	+71,800						+71,800	
2.	−15,000		+15,000					
3.	−47,500							−47,500
4.		+1,100		+1,100				
5.	−5,000					−5,000		
6.	−4,000			−4,000				
7.		−1,500						−1,500
Bal.	40,300	2,600	97,000	4,600	117,500	−5,000	71,800	−49,000

a. Describe each transaction.
b. What is the amount of the net increase in cash during the month?
c. What is the amount of the net increase in owner's equity during the month?
d. What is the amount of the net income for the month?
e. How much of the net income for the month was retained in the business?

EX 1-14 Net income and owner's withdrawals **OBJ. 5**

The income statement of a proprietorship for the month of February indicates a net income of $17,500. During the same period, the owner withdrew $25,500 in cash from the business for personal use.

Would it be correct to say that the business incurred a net loss of $8,000 during the month? Discuss.

✔ Mars: Net income, $225,000

SHOW ME HOW

EX 1-15 Net income and owner's equity for four businesses **OBJ. 5**

Four different proprietorships, Jupiter, Mars, Saturn, and Venus, show the same balance sheet data at the beginning and end of a year. These data, exclusive of the amount of owner's equity, are summarized as follows:

	Total Assets	Total Liabilities
Beginning of the year	$550,000	$215,000
End of the year	844,000	320,000

On the basis of the preceding data and the following additional information for the year, determine the net income (or loss) of each company for the year. (*Hint:* First determine the amount of increase or decrease in owner's equity during the year.)

Jupiter: The owner had made no additional investments in the business and had made no withdrawals from the business.

Mars: The owner had made no additional investments in the business but had withdrawn $36,000.

Saturn: The owner had made an additional investment of $60,000 but had made no withdrawals.

Venus: The owner had made an additional investment of $60,000 and had withdrawn $36,000.

EX 1-16 Balance sheet items **OBJ. 5**

From the following list of selected items taken from the records of Bobcat Appliance Service as of a specific date, identify those that would appear on the balance sheet:

1. Accounts Receivable
2. Cash
3. Fees Earned
4. Land
5. Mary Bayern, Capital
6. Supplies
7. Supplies Expense
8. Utilities Expense
9. Wages Expense
10. Wages Payable

EX 1-17 Income statement items **OBJ. 5**

Based on the data presented in Exercise 1-16, identify those items that would appear on the income statement.

✔ Mark Kominksy, capital, April 30, 2016: $525,500

SHOW ME HOW

EX 1-18 Statement of owner's equity **OBJ. 5**

Financial information related to Udder Products Company, a proprietorship, for the month ended April 30, 2016, is as follows:

Net income for April	$166,000
Mark Kominksy's withdrawals during April	25,000
Mark Kominksy's capital, April 1, 2016	384,500

a. Prepare a statement of owner's equity for the month ended April 30, 2016.

b. Why is the statement of owner's equity prepared before the April 30, 2016, balance sheet?

✔ Net income: $178,100

SHOW ME HOW

EX 1-19 Income statement **OBJ. 5**

Dairy Services was organized on August 1, 2016. A summary of the revenue and expense transactions for August follows:

Fees earned	$783,000
Wages expense	550,000
Rent expense	35,000
Supplies expense	8,500
Miscellaneous expense	11,400

Prepare an income statement for the month ended August 31.

EX 1-20 Missing amounts from balance sheet and income statement data — OBJ. 5

✔ (a) $135,000

SHOW ME HOW

One item is omitted in each of the following summaries of balance sheet and income statement data for the following four different proprietorships:

	Freeman	Heyward	Jones	Ramirez
Beginning of the year:				
Assets	$ 900,000	$490,000	$115,000	(d)
Liabilities	360,000	260,000	81,000	$120,000
End of the year:				
Assets	1,260,000	675,000	100,000	270,000
Liabilities	330,000	220,000	80,000	136,000
During the year:				
Additional investment in the business	(a)	150,000	10,000	55,000
Withdrawals from the business	75,000	32,000	(c)	39,000
Revenue	570,000	(b)	115,000	115,000
Expenses	240,000	128,000	122,500	128,000

Determine the missing amounts, identifying them by letter. (*Hint:* First determine the amount of increase or decrease in owner's equity during the year.)

EX 1-21 Balance sheets, net income — OBJ. 5

✔ b. $135,000

SHOW ME HOW

Financial information related to the proprietorship of Ebony Interiors for February and March 2016 is as follows:

	February 29, 2016	March 31, 2016
Accounts payable	$310,000	$400,000
Accounts receivable	800,000	960,000
Cash	320,000	380,000
Justin Berk, capital	?	?
Supplies	30,000	35,000

a. Prepare balance sheets for Ebony Interiors as of February 29 and March 31, 2016.

b. Determine the amount of net income for March, assuming that the owner made no additional investments or withdrawals during the month.

c. Determine the amount of net income for March, assuming that the owner made no additional investments but withdrew $50,000 during the month.

EX 1-22 Financial statements — OBJ. 5

Each of the following items is shown in the financial statements of **Exxon Mobil Corporation**:

1. Accounts payable
2. Cash equivalents
3. Crude oil inventory
4. Equipment
5. Exploration expenses
6. Income taxes payable
7. Investments
8. Long-term debt
9. Marketable securities
10. Notes and loans payable
11. Notes receivable
12. Operating expenses
13. Prepaid taxes
14. Sales
15. Selling expenses

a. Identify the financial statement (balance sheet or income statement) in which each item would appear.

b. Can an item appear on more than one financial statement?

c. Is the accounting equation relevant for Exxon Mobil Corporation?

EX 1-23 Statement of cash flows — OBJ. 5

Indicate whether each of the following activities would be reported on the statement of cash flows as (a) an operating activity, (b) an investing activity, or (c) a financing activity:

1. Cash received from fees earned.
2. Cash paid for expenses.
3. Cash paid for land.
4. Cash paid to owner for personal use.

EX 1-24 Statement of cash flows **OBJ. 5**

SHOW ME HOW

A summary of cash flows for Ethos Consulting Group for the year ended May 31, 2016, follows:

Cash receipts:	
Cash received from customers	$637,500
Cash received from additional investment of owner	62,500
Cash payments:	
Cash paid for operating expenses	475,000
Cash paid for land	90,000
Cash paid to owner for personal use	17,500

The cash balance as of June 1, 2015, was $58,000.

Prepare a statement of cash flows for Ethos Consulting Group for the year ended May 31, 2016.

EX 1-25 Financial statements **OBJ. 5**

✔ **Correct amount of total assets is $51,500.**

We-Sell Realty, organized August 1, 2016, is owned and operated by Omar Farah. How many errors can you find in the following statements for We-Sell Realty, prepared after its first month of operations?

We-Sell Realty
Income Statement
August 31, 2016

Sales commissions		$140,000
Expenses:		
Office salaries expense	$87,000	
Rent expense	18,000	
Automobile expense	7,500	
Miscellaneous expense	2,200	
Supplies expense	1,150	
Total expenses		115,850
Net income		$ 25,000

Omar Farah
Statement of Owner's Equity
August 31, 2015

Omar Farah, capital, August 1, 2016	$ 0
Less withdrawals during August	10,000
	$(10,000)
Investment on August 1, 2016	15,000
	$ 5,000
Net income for August	25,000
Omar Farah, capital, August 31, 2016	$ 30,000

Balance Sheet
For the Month Ended August 31, 2016

Assets		**Liabilities**	
Cash	$ 8,900	Accounts receivable	$38,600
Accounts payable	22,350	Supplies	4,000
		Owner's Equity	
		Omar Farah, capital	30,000
Total assets	$31,250	Total liabilities and owner's equity	$72,600

EX 1-26 Ratio of liabilities to stockholders' equity — OBJ. 6

The Home Depot, Inc., is the world's largest home improvement retailer and one of the largest retailers in the United States based on net sales volume. The Home Depot operates over 2,200 Home Depot® stores that sell a wide assortment of building materials and home improvement and lawn and garden products.

The Home Depot recently reported the following balance sheet data (in millions):

	Year 2	Year 1
Total assets	$40,518	$40,125
Total stockholders' equity	22,620	21,236

a. Determine the total liabilities at the end of Years 2 and 1.

b. Determine the ratio of liabilities to stockholders' equity for Year 2 and Year 1. Round to two decimal places.

c. What conclusions regarding the margin of protection to the creditors can you draw from (b)?

EX 1-27 Ratio of liabilities to stockholders' equity — OBJ. 6

Lowe's Companies Inc., a major competitor of **The Home Depot** in the home improvement business, operates over 1,700 stores. Lowe's recently reported the following balance sheet data (in millions):

	Year 2	Year 1
Total assets	$33,559	$33,699
Total liabilities	17,026	15,587

a. Determine the total stockholders' equity at the end of Years 2 and 1.

b. Determine the ratio of liabilities to stockholders' equity for Year 2 and Year 1. Round to two decimal places.

c. What conclusions regarding the risk to the creditors can you draw from (b)?

d. Using the balance sheet data for The Home Depot in Exercise 1-26, how does the ratio of liabilities to stockholders' equity of Lowe's compare to that of The Home Depot?

Problems: Series A

PR 1-1A Transactions — OBJ. 4

✔ Cash bal. at end of April: $39,785

On April 1 of the current year, Andrea Byrd established a business to manage rental property. She completed the following transactions during April:

a. Opened a business bank account with a deposit of $45,000 from personal funds.

b. Purchased office supplies on account, $2,000.

c. Received cash from fees earned for managing rental property, $8,500.

d. Paid rent on office and equipment for the month, $5,000.

e. Paid creditors on account, $1,375.

f. Billed customers for fees earned for managing rental property, $11,250.

g. Paid automobile expenses (including rental charges) for month, $840, and miscellaneous expenses, $900.

h. Paid office salaries, $3,600.

i. Determined that the cost of supplies on hand was $550; therefore, the cost of supplies used was $1,450.

j. Withdrew cash for personal use, $2,000.

Instructions

1. Indicate the effect of each transaction and the balances after each transaction, using the following tabular headings:

Assets			= Liabilities +	Owner's Equity							
Cash +	Accounts Receivable +	Supplies =	Accounts Payable +	Andrea Byrd, Capital –	Andrea Byrd, Drawing +	Fees Earned –	Rent Expense –	Salaries Expense –	Supplies Expense –	Auto Expense –	Misc. Expense

2. Briefly explain why the owner's investment and revenues increased owner's equity, while withdrawals and expenses decreased owner's equity.
3. Determine the net income for April.
4. How much did April's transactions increase or decrease Andrea Byrd's capital?

PR 1-2A Financial statements **OBJ. 5**

✔ 1. Net income: $327,500

SHOW ME HOW

The amounts of the assets and liabilities of Nordic Travel Agency at December 31, 2016, the end of the year, and its revenue and expenses for the year follow. The capital of Ian Eisele, owner, was $670,000 on January 1, 2016, the beginning of the year. During the year, Ian withdrew $42,000.

Accounts payable	$ 69,500	Rent expense	$ 36,000
Accounts receivable	285,000	Supplies	5,500
Cash	190,500	Supplies expense	4,100
Fees earned	912,500	Utilities expense	28,500
Land	544,000	Wages expense	510,000
Miscellaneous expense	6,400		

Instructions

1. Prepare an income statement for the year ended December 31, 2016.
2. Prepare a statement of owner's equity for the year ended December 31, 2016.
3. Prepare a balance sheet as of December 31, 2016.
4. What item appears on both the statement of owner's equity and the balance sheet?

PR 1-3A Financial statements **OBJ. 5**

✔ 1. Net income: $31,200

Seth Feye established Reliance Financial Services on July 1, 2016. Reliance Financial Services offers financial planning advice to its clients. The effect of each transaction and the balances after each transaction for July follow:

	Assets			= Liabilities +	Owner's Equity							
	Cash +	Accounts Receivable +	Supplies =	Accounts Payable +	Seth Feye, Capital –	Seth Feye, Drawing +	Fees Earned –	Salaries Expense –	Rent Expense –	Auto Expense –	Supplies Expense –	Misc. Expense
a.	+50,000				+50,000							
b.			+7,000	+7,000								
Bal.	50,000		7,000	7,000	50,000							
c.	–3,600			–3,600								
Bal.	46,400		7,000	3,400	50,000							
d.	+110,000						+110,000					
Bal.	156,400		7,000	3,400	50,000		110,000					
e.	–33,000								–33,000			
Bal.	123,400		7,000	3,400	50,000		110,000		–33,000			
f.	–20,800									–16,000		–4,800
Bal.	102,600		7,000	3,400	50,000		110,000		–33,000	–16,000		–4,800
g.	–55,000							–55,000				
Bal.	47,600		7,000	3,400	50,000		110,000	–55,000	–33,000	–16,000		–4,800
h.			–4,500								–4,500	
Bal.	47,600		2,500	3,400	50,000		110,000	–55,000	–33,000	–16,000	–4,500	–4,800
i.		+34,500					+ 34,500					
Bal.	47,600	34,500	2,500	3,400	50,000		144,500	–55,000	–33,000	–16,000	–4,500	–4,800
j.	–15,000					–15,000						
Bal.	32,600	34,500	2,500	3,400	50,000	–15,000	144,500	–55,000	–33,000	–16,000	–4,500	–4,800

(Continued)

Instructions

1. Prepare an income statement for the month ended July 31, 2016.
2. Prepare a statement of owner's equity for the month ended July 31, 2016.
3. Prepare a balance sheet as of July 31, 2016.
4. *(Optional)* Prepare a statement of cash flows for the month ending July 31, 2016.

PR 1-4A Transactions; financial statements

OBJ. 4, 5

✔ 2. Net income: $27,350

On July 1, 2016, Pat Glenn established Half Moon Realty. Pat completed the following transactions during the month of July:

a. Opened a business bank account with a deposit of $25,000 from personal funds.
b. Purchased office supplies on account, $1,850.
c. Paid creditor on account, $1,200.
d. Earned sales commissions, receiving cash, $41,500.
e. Paid rent on office and equipment for the month, $3,600.
f. Withdrew cash for personal use, $4,000.
g. Paid automobile expenses (including rental charge) for month, $3,050, and miscellaneous expenses, $1,600.
h. Paid office salaries, $5,000.
i. Determined that the cost of supplies on hand was $950; therefore, the cost of supplies used was $900.

Instructions

1. Indicate the effect of each transaction and the balances after each transaction, using the following tabular headings:

Assets			= Liabilities +	Owner's Equity							
Cash	+ Supplies	=	Accounts Payable	+ Pat Glenn, Capital	− Pat Glenn, Drawing	+ Sales Commissions	− Salaries Expense	− Rent Expense	− Auto Expense	− Supplies Expense	− Misc. Expense

2. Prepare an income statement for July, a statement of owner's equity for July, and a balance sheet as of July 31.

PR 1-5A Transactions; financial statements

OBJ. 4, 5

✔ 3. Net income: $63,775

D'Lite Dry Cleaners is owned and operated by Joel Palk. A building and equipment are currently being rented, pending expansion to new facilities. The actual work of dry cleaning is done by another company at wholesale rates. The assets and the liabilities of the business on July 1, 2016, are as follows: Cash, $45,000; Accounts Receivable, $93,000; Supplies, $7,000; Land, $75,000; Accounts Payable, $40,000. Business transactions during July are summarized as follows:

a. Joel Palk invested additional cash in the business with a deposit of $35,000 in the business bank account.
b. Paid $50,000 for the purchase of land adjacent to land currently owned by D'Lite Dry Cleaners as a future building site.
c. Received cash from cash customers for dry cleaning revenue, $32,125.
d. Paid rent for the month, $6,000.
e. Purchased supplies on account, $2,500.
f. Paid creditors on account, $22,800.
g. Charged customers for dry cleaning revenue on account, $84,750.
h. Received monthly invoice for dry cleaning expense for July (to be paid on August 10), $29,500.

i. Paid the following: wages expense, \$7,500; truck expense, \$2,500; utilities expense, \$1,300; miscellaneous expense, \$2,700.

j. Received cash from customers on account, \$88,000.

k. Determined that the cost of supplies on hand was \$5,900; therefore, the cost of supplies used during the month was \$3,600.

l. Withdrew \$12,000 cash for personal use.

Instructions

1. Determine the amount of Joel Palk's capital as of July 1 of the current year.
2. State the assets, liabilities, and owner's equity as of July 1 in equation form similar to that shown in this chapter. In tabular form below the equation, indicate increases and decreases resulting from each transaction and the new balances after each transaction.
3. Prepare an income statement for July, a statement of owner's equity for July, and a balance sheet as of July 31.
4. *(Optional)* Prepare a statement of cash flows for July.

PR 1-6A Missing amounts from financial statements

OBJ. 5

✔ k. \$750,000

The financial statements at the end of Wolverine Realty's first month of operations are as follows:

Wolverine Realty
Income Statement
For the Month Ended April 30, 2016

Fees earned		\$ (a)
Expenses:		
Wages expense	\$300,000	
Rent expense	100,000	
Supplies expense	(b)	
Utilities expense	20,000	
Miscellaneous expense	25,000	
Total expenses		475,000
Net income		\$275,000

Wolverine Realty
Statement of Owner's Equity
For the Month Ended April 30, 2016

Dakota Rowe, capital, April 1, 2016		\$ (c)
Investment on April 1, 2016	\$375,000	
Net income for April	(d)	
	\$ (e)	
Less withdrawals	125,000	
Increase in owner's equity		(f)
Dakota Rowe, capital, April 30, 2016		\$ (g)

Wolverine Realty
Balance Sheet
April 30, 2016

Assets		Liabilities	
Cash	\$462,500	Accounts payable	\$100,000
Supplies	12,500	**Owner's Equity**	
Land	150,000	Dakota Rowe, capital	(i)
Total assets	\$ (h)	Total liabilities and owner's equity	\$ (j)

(Continued)

Wolverine Realty
Statement of Cash Flows
For the Month Ended April 30, 2016

Cash flows from operating activities:		
Cash received from customers	$ (k)	
Deduct cash payments for expenses and payments to creditors	(387,500)	
Net cash flows from operating activities		$ (l)
Cash flows from investing activities:		
Cash payments for acquisition of land		(m)
Cash flows from financing activities:		
Cash received as owner's investment	$ (n)	
Deduct cash withdrawal by owner	(o)	
Net cash flows from financing activities		(p)
Net increase (decrease) in cash and April 30, 2016, cash balance		$ (q)

Instructions

By analyzing the interrelationships among the four financial statements, determine the proper amounts for (a) through (q).

Problems: Series B

PR 1-1B Transactions

OBJ. 4

✔ Cash bal. at end of March: $48,650

SHOW ME HOW

Amy Austin established an insurance agency on March 1 of the current year and completed the following transactions during March:

a. Opened a business bank account with a deposit of $50,000 from personal funds.
b. Purchased supplies on account, $4,000.
c. Paid creditors on account, $2,300.
d. Received cash from fees earned on insurance commissions, $13,800.
e. Paid rent on office and equipment for the month, $5,000.
f. Paid automobile expenses for month, $1,150, and miscellaneous expenses, $300.
g. Paid office salaries, $2,500.
h. Determined that the cost of supplies on hand was $2,700; therefore, the cost of supplies used was $1,300.
i. Billed insurance companies for sales commissions earned, $12,500.
j. Withdrew cash for personal use, $3,900.

Instructions

1. Indicate the effect of each transaction and the balances after each transaction, using the following tabular headings:

Assets			= Liabilities +	Owner's Equity							
Cash +	Accounts Receivable +	Supplies =	Accounts Payable +	Amy Austin, Capital –	Amy Austin, Drawing +	Fees Earned –	Rent Expense –	Salaries Expense –	Supplies Expense –	Auto Expense –	Misc. Expense

2. Briefly explain why the owner's investment and revenues increased owner's equity, while withdrawals and expenses decreased owner's equity.
3. Determine the net income for March.
4. How much did March's transactions increase or decrease Amy Austin's capital?

✔ 1. Net income: $200,000

SHOW ME HOW

PR 1-2B Financial statements **OBJ. 5**

The amounts of the assets and liabilities of Wilderness Travel Service at April 30, 2016, the end of the year, and its revenue and expenses for the year follow. The capital of Harper Borg, owner, was $180,000 at May 1, 2015, the beginning of the year, and the owner withdrew $40,000 during the year.

Accounts payable	$ 25,000	Supplies	$ 9,000
Accounts receivable	210,000	Supplies expense	12,000
Cash	146,000	Taxes expense	10,000
Fees earned	875,000	Utilities expense	38,000
Miscellaneous expense	15,000	Wages expense	525,000
Rent expense	75,000		

Instructions

1. Prepare an income statement for the year ended April 30, 2016.
2. Prepare a statement of owner's equity for the year ended April 30, 2016.
3. Prepare a balance sheet as of April 30, 2016.
4. What item appears on both the income statement and statement of owner's equity?

✔ 1. Net income: $10,900

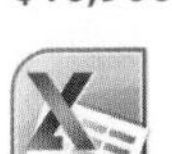

PR 1-3B Financial statements **OBJ. 5**

Jose Loder established Bronco Consulting on August 1, 2016. The effect of each transaction and the balances after each transaction for August follow:

	Assets			=Liabilities+	Owner's Equity							
	Cash	+ Accounts Receivable	+ Supplies	= Accounts Payable	+ Jose Loder, Capital	− Jose Loder, Drawing	+ Fees Earned	− Salaries Expense	− Rent Expense	− Auto Expense	− Supplies Expense	− Misc. Expense
a.	+75,000				+75,000							
b.			+9,000	+9,000								
Bal.	75,000		9,000	9,000	75,000							
c.	+92,000						+92,000					
Bal.	167,000		9,000	9,000	75,000		92,000					
d.	−27,000								−27,000			
Bal.	140,000		9,000	9,000	75,000		92,000		−27,000			
e.	−6,000			−6,000								
Bal.	134,000		9,000	3,000	75,000		92,000		−27,000			
f.		+33,000					+33,000					
Bal.	134,000	33,000	9,000	3,000	75,000		125,000		−27,000			
g.	−23,000									−15,500		−7,500
Bal.	111,000	33,000	9,000	3,000	75,000		125,000		−27,000	−15,500		−7,500
h.	−58,000							−58,000				
Bal.	53,000	33,000	9,000	3,000	75,000		125,000	−58,000	−27,000	−15,500		−7,500
i.			−6,100								−6,100	
Bal.	53,000	33,000	2,900	3,000	75,000		125,000	−58,000	−27,000	−15,500	−6,100	−7,500
j.	−15,000					−15,000						
Bal.	38,000	33,000	2,900	3,000	75,000	−15,000	125,000	−58,000	−27,000	−15,500	−6,100	−7,500

Instructions

1. Prepare an income statement for the month ended August 31, 2016.
2. Prepare a statement of owner's equity for the month ended August 31, 2016.
3. Prepare a balance sheet as of August 31, 2016.
4. *(Optional)* Prepare a statement of cash flows for the month ending August 31, 2016.

✔ 2. Net income: $10,850

PR 1-4B Transactions; financial statements **OBJ. 4, 5**

On April 1, 2016, Maria Adams established Custom Realty. Maria completed the following transactions during the month of April:

(Continued)

a. Opened a business bank account with a deposit of $24,000 from personal funds.
b. Paid rent on office and equipment for the month, $3,600.
c. Paid automobile expenses (including rental charge) for month, $1,350, and miscellaneous expenses, $600.
d. Purchased office supplies on account, $1,200.
e. Earned sales commissions, receiving cash, $19,800.
f. Paid creditor on account, $750.
g. Paid office salaries, $2,500.
h. Withdrew cash for personal use, $3,500.
i. Determined that the cost of supplies on hand was $300; therefore, the cost of supplies used was $900.

Instructions

1. Indicate the effect of each transaction and the balances after each transaction, using the following tabular headings:

Assets	= Liabilities +	Owner's Equity							
Cash + Supplies =	Accounts Payable +	Maria Adams, Capital −	Maria Adams, Drawing +	Sales Commissions −	Rent Expense −	Salaries Expense −	Auto Expense −	Supplies Expense −	Misc. Expense

2. Prepare an income statement for April, a statement of owner's equity for April, and a balance sheet as of April 30.

PR 1-5B Transactions; financial statements **OBJ. 4, 5**

✔ 3. Net income: $40,150

Bev's Dry Cleaners is owned and operated by Beverly Zahn. A building and equipment are currently being rented, pending expansion to new facilities. The actual work of dry cleaning is done by another company at wholesale rates. The assets and the liabilities of the business on November 1, 2016, are as follows: Cash, $39,000; Accounts Receivable, $80,000; Supplies, $11,000; Land, $50,000; Accounts Payable, $31,500. Business transactions during November are summarized as follows:

a. Beverly Zahn invested additional cash in the business with a deposit of $21,000 in the business bank account.
b. Purchased land adjacent to land currently owned by Bev's Dry Cleaners to use in the future as a parking lot, paying cash of $35,000.
c. Paid rent for the month, $4,000.
d. Charged customers for dry cleaning revenue on account, $72,000.
e. Paid creditors on account, $20,000.
f. Purchased supplies on account, $8,000.
g. Received cash from cash customers for dry cleaning revenue, $38,000.
h. Received cash from customers on account, $77,000.
i. Received monthly invoice for dry cleaning expense for November (to be paid on December 10), $29,450.
j. Paid the following: wages expense, $24,000; truck expense, $2,100; utilities expense, $1,800; miscellaneous expense, $1,300.
k. Determined that the cost of supplies on hand was $11,800; therefore, the cost of supplies used during the month was $7,200.
l. Withdrew $5,000 for personal use.

Instructions

1. Determine the amount of Beverly Zahn's capital as of November 1.
2. State the assets, liabilities, and owner's equity as of November 1 in equation form similar to that shown in this chapter. In tabular form below the equation, indicate increases and decreases resulting from each transaction and the new balances after each transaction.

3. Prepare an income statement for November, a statement of owner's equity for November, and a balance sheet as of November 30.
4. *(Optional)* Prepare a statement of cash flows for November.

✔ i. $208,000

PR 1-6B Missing amounts from financial statements

OBJ. 5

The financial statements at the end of Atlas Realty's first month of operations follow:

Atlas Realty
Income Statement
For the Month Ended May 31, 2016

Fees earned		$400,000
Expenses:		
Wages expense	$ (a)	
Rent expense	48,000	
Supplies expense	17,600	
Utilities expense	14,400	
Miscellaneous expense	4,800	
Total expenses		288,000
Net income		$ (b)

Atlas Realty
Statement of Owner's Equity
For the Month Ended May 31, 2016

LuAnn Martin, capital, May 1, 2016		$ (c)
Investment on May 1, 2016	$ (d)	
Net income for May	(e)	
	$ (f)	
Less withdrawals	(g)	
Increase in owner's equity		(h)
LuAnn Martin, capital, May 31, 2016		$ (i)

Atlas Realty
Balance Sheet
May 31, 2016

Assets		Liabilities	
Cash	$123,200	Accounts payable	$48,000
Supplies	12,800	**Owner's Equity**	
Land	(j)	LuAnn Martin, capital	(l)
Total assets	$ (k)	Total liabilities and owner's equity	$ (m)

Atlas Realty
Statement of Cash Flows
For the Month Ended May 31, 2016

Cash flows from operating activities:		
Cash received from customers	$ (n)	
Deduct cash payments for expenses and payments to creditors	(252,800)	
Net cash flows from operating activities		$ (o)
Cash flows from investing activities:		
Cash payments for acquisition of land		(120,000)
Cash flows from financing activities:		
Cash received as owner's investment	$ 160,000	
Deduct cash withdrawal by owner	(64,000)	
Net cash flows from financing activities		(p)
Net increase (decrease) in cash and May 31, 2016, cash balance		$ (q)

Instructions

By analyzing the interrelationships among the four financial statements, determine the proper amounts for (a) through (q).

Continuing Problem

✔ 2. Net income: $1,340

Peyton Smith enjoys listening to all types of music and owns countless CDs. Over the years, Peyton has gained a local reputation for knowledge of music from classical to rap and the ability to put together sets of recordings that appeal to all ages.

During the last several months, Peyton served as a guest disc jockey on a local radio station. In addition, Peyton has entertained at several friends' parties as the host deejay.

On June 1, 2016, Peyton established a proprietorship known as PS Music. Using an extensive collection of music MP3 files, Peyton will serve as a disc jockey on a fee basis for weddings, college parties, and other events. During June, Peyton entered into the following transactions:

June 1. Deposited $4,000 in a checking account in the name of PS Music.
2. Received $3,500 from a local radio station for serving as the guest disc jockey for June.
2. Agreed to share office space with a local real estate agency, Pinnacle Realty. PS Music will pay one-fourth of the rent. In addition, PS Music agreed to pay a portion of the wages of the receptionist and to pay one-fourth of the utilities. Paid $800 for the rent of the office.
4. Purchased supplies from City Office Supply Co. for $350. Agreed to pay $100 within 10 days and the remainder by July 5, 2016.
6. Paid $500 to a local radio station to advertise the services of PS Music twice daily for two weeks.
8. Paid $675 to a local electronics store for renting digital recording equipment.
12. Paid $350 (music expense) to Cool Music for the use of its current music demos to make various music sets.
13. Paid City Office Supply Co. $100 on account.
16. Received $300 from a dentist for providing two music sets for the dentist to play for her patients.
22. Served as disc jockey for a wedding party. The father of the bride agreed to pay $1,000 in July.
25. Received $500 for serving as the disc jockey for a cancer charity ball hosted by the local hospital.
29. Paid $240 (music expense) to Galaxy Music for the use of its library of music demos.
30. Received $900 for serving as PS disc jockey for a local club's monthly dance.
30. Paid Pinnacle Realty $400 for PS Music's share of the receptionist's wages for June.
30. Paid Pinnacle Realty $300 for PS Music's share of the utilities for June.
30. Determined that the cost of supplies on hand is $170. Therefore, the cost of supplies used during the month was $180.
30. Paid for miscellaneous expenses, $415.
30. Paid $1,000 royalties (music expense) to National Music Clearing for use of various artists' music during the month.
30. Withdrew $500 of cash from PS Music for personal use.

Instructions

1. Indicate the effect of each transaction and the balances after each transaction, using the following tabular headings:

Assets			=	Liabilities +	Owner's Equity										
Cash +	Accts. Rec. +	Supplies	=	Accounts Payable +	Peyton Smith, Capital –	Peyton Smith, Drawing +	Fees Earned –	Music Exp. –	Office Rent Exp. –	Equipment Rent Exp. –	Advertising Exp. –	Wages Exp. –	Utilities Exp. –	Supplies Exp. –	Misc. Exp.

2. Prepare an income statement for PS Music for the month ended June 30, 2016.
3. Prepare a statement of owner's equity for PS Music for the month ended June 30, 2016.
4. Prepare a balance sheet for PS Music as of June 30, 2016.

Cases & Projects

CP 1-1 Ethics and professional conduct in business

Group Project

Colleen Fernandez, president of Rhino Enterprises, applied for a $175,000 loan from First Federal Bank. The bank requested financial statements from Rhino Enterprises as a basis for granting the loan. Colleen has told her accountant to provide the bank with a balance sheet. Colleen has decided to omit the other financial statements because there was a net loss during the past year.

In groups of three or four, discuss the following questions:

1. Is Colleen behaving in a professional manner by omitting some of the financial statements?
2. a. What types of information about their businesses would owners be willing to provide bankers? What types of information would owners not be willing to provide?
   b. What types of information about a business would bankers want before extending a loan?
   c. What common interests are shared by bankers and business owners?

CP 1-2 Net income

On January 1, 2015, Dr. Marcie Cousins established Health-Wise Medical, a medical practice organized as a proprietorship. The following conversation occurred the following August between Dr. Cousins and a former medical school classmate, Dr. Avi Abu, at an American Medical Association convention in Seattle:

Dr. Abu: Marcie, good to see you again. Why didn't you call when you were in Miami? We could have had dinner together.

Dr. Cousins: Actually, I never made it to Miami this year. My husband and kids went up to our Vail condo twice, but I got stuck in Jacksonville. I opened a new consulting practice this January and haven't had any time for myself since.

Dr. Abu: I heard about it . . . Health . . . something . . . right?

Dr. Cousins: Yes, Health-Wise Medical. My husband chose the name.

Dr. Abu: I've thought about doing something like that. Are you making any money? I mean, is it worth your time?

Dr. Cousins: You wouldn't believe it. I started by opening a bank account with $25,000, and my July bank statement has a balance of $80,000. Not bad for six months—all pure profit.

Dr. Abu: Maybe I'll try it in Miami! Let's have breakfast together tomorrow and you can fill me in on the details.

Comment on Dr. Cousins' statement that the difference between the opening bank balance ($25,000) and the July statement balance ($80,000) is pure profit.

CP 1-3 Transactions and financial statements

Lisa Duncan, a junior in college, has been seeking ways to earn extra spending money. As an active sports enthusiast, Lisa plays tennis regularly at the Phoenix Tennis Club, where her family has a membership. The president of the club recently approached Lisa with the proposal that she manage the club's tennis courts. Lisa's primary duty would be to supervise the operation of the club's four indoor and 10 outdoor courts, including court reservations.

In return for her services, the club would pay Lisa $325 per week, plus Lisa could keep whatever she earned from lessons. The club and Lisa agreed to a one-month trial, after which both would consider an arrangement for the remaining two years of Lisa's college career. On this basis, Lisa organized Serve-N-Volley. During September 2016, Lisa managed the tennis courts and entered into the following transactions:

a. Opened a business account by depositing $950.

b. Paid $300 for tennis supplies (practice tennis balls, etc.).

(Continued)

c. Paid $275 for the rental of video equipment to be used in offering lessons during September.

d. Arranged for the rental of two ball machines during September for $250. Paid $100 in advance, with the remaining $150 due October 1.

e. Received $1,750 for lessons given during September.

f. Received $600 in fees from the use of the ball machines during September.

g. Paid $800 for salaries of part-time employees who answered the telephone and took reservations while Lisa was giving lessons.

h. Paid $290 for miscellaneous expenses.

i. Received $1,300 from the club for managing the tennis courts during September.

j. Determined that the cost of supplies on hand at the end of the month totaled $180; therefore, the cost of supplies used was $120.

k. Withdrew $400 for personal use on September 30.

As a friend and accounting student, you have been asked by Lisa to aid her in assessing the venture.

1. Indicate the effect of each transaction and the balances after each transaction, using the following tabular headings:

Assets	= Liabilities +			Owner's Equity				
Cash + Supplies =	Accounts Payable +	Lisa Duncan, Capital −	Lisa Duncan, Drawing +	Fees Earned −	Salaries Expense −	Rent Expense −	Supplies Expense −	Misc. Expense

2. Prepare an income statement for September.
3. Prepare a statement of owner's equity for September.
4. Prepare a balance sheet as of September 30.
5. a. Assume that Lisa Duncan could earn $10 per hour working 30 hours a week as a waitress. Evaluate which of the two alternatives, working as a waitress or operating Serve-N-Volley, would provide Lisa with the most income per month.

   b. Discuss any other factors that you believe Lisa should consider before discussing a long-term arrangement with the Phoenix Tennis Club.

CP 1-4 Certification requirements for accountants

Internet Project

By satisfying certain specific requirements, accountants may become certified as public accountants (CPAs), management accountants (CMAs), or internal auditors (CIAs). Find the certification requirements for one of these accounting groups by accessing one of the following Web sites:

Site	Description
www.ais-cpa.com	This site lists the address and/or Internet link for each state's board of accountancy. Find your state's requirements.
www.imanet.org	This site lists the requirements for becoming a CMA.
www.theiia.org	This site lists the requirements for becoming a CIA.

CP 1-5 Cash flows

Amazon.com, an Internet retailer, was incorporated and began operation in the mid-90s. On the statement of cash flows, would you expect Amazon.com's net cash flows from operating, investing, and financing activities to be positive or negative for its first three years of operations? Use the following format for your answers, and briefly explain your logic.

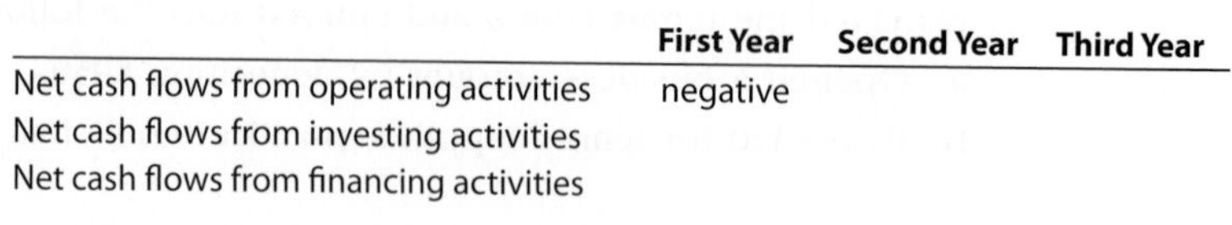

	First Year	Second Year	Third Year
Net cash flows from operating activities	negative		
Net cash flows from investing activities			
Net cash flows from financing activities			

CP 1-6 Financial analysis

Internet Project

The now defunct **Enron Corporation**, once headquartered in Houston, Texas, provided products and services for natural gas, electricity, and communications to wholesale and retail customers. Enron's operations were conducted through a variety of subsidiaries and affiliates that involved transporting gas through pipelines, transmitting electricity, and managing energy commodities. The following data were taken from Enron's financial statements:

	In millions
Total revenues	$100,789
Total costs and expenses	98,836
Operating income	1,953
Net income	979
Total assets	65,503
Total liabilities	54,033
Total owners' equity	11,470
Net cash flows from operating activities	4,779
Net cash flows from investing activities	(4,264)
Net cash flows from financing activities	571
Net increase in cash	1,086

The market price of Enron's stock was approximately $83 per share when the prior financial statement data were taken. Before it went bankrupt, Enron's stock sold for $0.22 per share.

Review the preceding financial statement data and search the Internet for articles on Enron Corporation. Briefly explain why Enron's stock dropped so dramatically.

CP 1-1 Financial analysis

The now-defunct Enron Corporation, once headquartered in Houston, Texas, provided products and services for natural gas, electricity, and communications to wholesale and retail customers. Enron's operations were conducted through a variety of subsidiaries and affiliates that involved transporting gas through pipelines, transmitting electricity, and managing energy commodities. The following data were taken from Enron's financial statements:

	In millions
Total revenues	$100,789
Total costs and expenses	98,836
Operating income	1,953
Net income	979
Total assets	65,503
Total liabilities	54,033
Total owners' equity	11,470
Net cash flows from operating activities	4,779
Net cash flows from investing activities	(4,264)
Net cash flows from financing activities	571
Net increase in cash	1,086

The market price of Enron's stock was approximately $83 per share when the prior financial statement data were taken. Before it went bankrupt, Enron's stock sold for $0.22 per share.

Review the preceding financial statement data and search the Internet for articles on Enron Corporation. Briefly explain why Enron's stock dropped so dramatically.

Analyzing Transactions

Apple Inc.™

Every day it seems like we get an incredible amount of incoming e-mail messages—from friends, relatives, subscribed e-mail lists, and even spammers! But how do you organize all of these messages? You might create folders to sort messages by sender, topic, or project. Perhaps you use keyword search utilities. You might even use filters or rules to automatically delete spam or send messages from your best friend to a special folder. In any case, you are organizing information so that it is simple to retrieve and allows you to understand, respond, or refer to the messages.

In the same way that you organize your e-mail, companies develop an organized method for processing, recording, and summarizing financial transactions. For example, **Apple Inc.** has a huge volume of financial transactions, resulting from sales of its innovative computers, digital media (iTunes), iPods, iPhones, and iPads. When Apple sells an iPad, a customer has the option of paying with credit card, a debit or check card, an Apple gift card, a financing arrangement, or cash. In order to analyze only the information related to Apple's cash transactions, the company must record or summarize all these similar sales using a single category or "cash" account. Similarly, Apple will record credit card payments for iPads and sales from financing arrangements in different accounts (records).

While Chapter 1 used the accounting equation (Assets = Liabilities + Owner's Equity) to analyze and record financial transactions, this chapter presents more practical and efficient recording methods that most companies use. In addition, this chapter discusses possible accounting errors that may occur, along with methods to detect and correct them.

Learning Objectives

After studying this chapter, you should be able to: *Example Exercises*

OBJ	Objective	Example Exercises
1	**Describe the characteristics of an account and a chart of accounts.** Using Accounts to Record Transactions Chart of Accounts	
2	**Describe and illustrate journalizing transactions using the double-entry accounting system.** Double-Entry Accounting System Balance Sheet Accounts Income Statement Accounts Owner Withdrawals Normal Balances Journalizing	 EE 2-1 EE 2-2
3	**Describe and illustrate the journalizing and posting of transactions to accounts.** Posting Journal Entries to Accounts	EE 2-3 EE 2-4 EE 2-5
4	**Prepare an unadjusted trial balance and explain how it can be used to discover errors.** Trial Balance Errors Affecting the Trial Balance Errors Not Affecting the Trial Balance	 EE 2-6 EE 2-7
5	**Describe and illustrate the use of horizontal analysis in evaluating a company's performance and financial condition.** Financial Analysis and Interpretation: Horizontal Analysis	EE 2-8

At a Glance 2 Page 75

OBJ 1 Describe the characteristics of an account and a chart of accounts.

Using Accounts to Record Transactions

In Chapter 1, the November transactions for **NetSolutions** were recorded using the accounting equation format shown in Exhibit 1. However, this format is not efficient or practical for companies that have to record thousands or millions of transactions daily. As a result, accounting systems are designed to show the increases and decreases in each accounting equation element as a separate record. This record is called an **account**.

To illustrate, the Cash column of Exhibit 1 records the increases and decreases in cash. Likewise, the other columns in Exhibit 1 record the increases and decreases in the other accounting equation elements. Each of these columns can be organized into a separate account.

An account, in its simplest form, has three parts.

- A title, which is the name of the accounting equation element recorded in the account
- A space for recording increases in the amount of the element
- A space for recording decreases in the amount of the element

The account form that follows is called a **T account** because it resembles the letter T. The left side of the account is called the *debit* side, and the right side is called the *credit* side:[1]

Title	
Left side *debit*	Right side *credit*

[1] The terms *debit* and *credit* are derived from the Latin *debere* and *credere*.

EXHIBIT 1 **NetSolutions' November Transactions**

	Assets			= Liabilities +	Owner's Equity							
	Cash	+ Supp.	+ Land	= Accounts Payable	+ Chris Clark, Capital	– Chris Clark, Drawing	+ Fees Earned	– Wages Exp.	– Rent Exp.	– Supplies Exp.	– Utilities Exp.	– Misc. Exp.
a.	+25,000				+25,000							
b.	–20,000		+20,000									
Bal.	5,000		20,000		25,000							
c.		+1,350		+1,350								
Bal.	5,000	1,350	20,000	1,350	25,000							
d.	+7,500						+7,500					
Bal.	12,500	1,350	20,000	1,350	25,000		7,500					
e.	–3,650							–2,125	–800		–450	–275
Bal.	8,850	1,350	20,000	1,350	25,000		7,500	–2,125	–800		–450	–275
f.	–950			–950								
Bal.	7,900	1,350	20,000	400	25,000		7,500	–2,125	–800		–450	–275
g.		–800								–800		
Bal.	7,900	550	20,000	400	25,000		7,500	–2,125	–800	–800	–450	–275
h.	–2,000					–2,000						
Bal.	5,900	550	20,000	400	25,000	–2,000	7,500	–2,125	–800	–800	–450	–275

The amounts shown in the Cash column of Exhibit 1 would be recorded in a cash account as follows:

Note:
Amounts entered on the left side of an account are debits, and amounts entered on the right side of an account are credits.

Cash

Debit Side of Account	(a)	25,000	(b)	20,000	Credit Side of Account
	(d)	7,500	(e)	3,650	
			(f)	950	
			(h)	2,000	
	Balance	5,900			

Balance of Account → 5,900

Recording transactions in accounts must follow certain rules. For example, increases in assets are recorded on the **debit** (left side) of an account. Likewise, decreases in assets are recorded on the **credit** (right side) of an account. The excess of the debits of an asset account over its credits is the **balance of the account**.

To illustrate, the receipt (increase in Cash) of $25,000 in transaction (a) is entered on the debit (left) side of the cash account. The letter or date of the transaction is also entered into the account. That way, if any questions later arise related to the entry, the entry can be traced back to the underlying transaction data. In contrast, the payment (decrease in Cash) of $20,000 to purchase land in transaction (b) is entered on the credit (right) side of the account.

The balance of the cash account of $5,900 is the excess of the debits over the credits, computed as follows:

Debits ($25,000 + $7,500)	$32,500
Less credits ($20,000 + $3,650 + $950 + $2,000)	26,600
Balance of Cash as of November 30, 2015	$ 5,900

The balance of the cash account is inserted in the account, in the Debit column. In this way, the balance is identified as a debit balance.[2] This balance represents NetSolutions' cash on hand as of November 30, 2015. This balance of $5,900 is reported on the November 30, 2015, balance sheet for NetSolutions as shown in Exhibit 8 of Chapter 1.

In an actual accounting system, a more formal account form replaces the T account. Later in this chapter, a four-column account is illustrated. The T account, however, is

[2] The totals of the debit and credit columns may be shown separately in an account. When this is done, these amounts should be identified in some way so that they are not mistaken for entries or the ending balance of the account.

a simple way to illustrate the effects of transactions on accounts and financial statements. For this reason, T accounts are often used in business to explain transactions.

Each of the columns in Exhibit 1 can be converted into an account form in a similar manner as was done for the Cash column of Exhibit 1. However, as mentioned earlier, recording increases and decreases in accounts must follow certain rules. These rules are discussed after the chart of accounts is described.

Chart of Accounts

A group of accounts for a business entity is called a **ledger**. A list of the accounts in the ledger is called a **chart of accounts**. The accounts are normally listed in the order in which they appear in the financial statements. The balance sheet accounts are listed first, in the order of assets, liabilities, and owner's equity. The income statement accounts are then listed in the order of revenues and expenses.

Assets

Assets are resources owned by the business entity. These resources can be physical items, such as cash and supplies, or intangibles that have value. Examples of intangible assets include patent rights, copyrights, and trademarks. Assets also include accounts receivable, prepaid expenses (such as insurance), buildings, equipment, and land.

Liabilities

Liabilities are debts owed to outsiders (creditors). Liabilities are often identified on the balance sheet by titles that include *payable*. Examples of liabilities include accounts payable, notes payable, and wages payable. Cash received before services are delivered creates a liability to perform the services. These future service commitments are called *unearned revenues*. Examples of unearned revenues include magazine subscriptions received by a publisher and tuition received at the beginning of a term by a college.

Owner's equity

Owner's equity is the owner's right to the assets of the business after all liabilities have been paid. For a proprietorship, the owner's equity is represented by the balance of the owner's **capital account**. A **drawing** account represents the amount of withdrawals made by the owner.

Revenues

Revenues are increases in assets and owner's equity as a result of selling services or products to customers. Examples of revenues include fees earned, fares earned, commissions revenue, and rent revenue.

Business  Connection

THE HIJACKING RECEIVABLE

A company's chart of accounts should reflect the basic nature of its operations. Occasionally, however, transactions take place that give rise to unusual accounts. The following is a story of one such account.

Before strict airport security was implemented across the United States, several airlines experienced hijacking incidents. One such incident occurred when a Southern Airways jet en route from Memphis to Miami was hijacked during a stopover in Birmingham, Alabama. The three hijackers boarded the plane in Birmingham armed with handguns and hand grenades. At gunpoint, the hijackers took the plane, the plane's crew, and the passengers to nine American cities, Toronto, and eventually to Havana, Cuba.

During the long flight, the hijackers demanded a ransom of $10 million. Southern Airways, however, was only able to come up with $2 million. Eventually, the pilot talked the hijackers into settling for the $2 million when the plane landed in Chattanooga for refueling.

Upon landing in Havana, the Cuban authorities arrested the hijackers and, after a brief delay, sent the plane, passengers, and crew back to the United States. The hijackers and the $2 million stayed in Cuba.

How did Southern Airways account for and report the hijacking payment in its subsequent financial statements? As you might have analyzed, the initial entry credited Cash for $2 million. The debit was to an account entitled "Hijacking Payment." This account was reported as a type of receivable under "other assets" on Southern Airways' balance sheet. The company maintained that it would be able to collect the cash from the Cuban government and that, therefore, a receivable existed. In fact, Southern Airways was later repaid $2 million by the Cuban government, which was, at that time, attempting to improve relations with the United States.

Expenses **Expenses** result from using up assets or consuming services in the process of generating revenues. Examples of expenses include wages expense, rent expense, utilities expense, supplies expense, and miscellaneous expense.

Illustration of Chart of Accounts A chart of accounts should meet the needs of a company's managers and other users of its financial statements. The accounts within the chart of accounts are numbered for use as references. A numbering system is normally used, so that new accounts can be added without affecting other account numbers.

Exhibit 2 is **NetSolutions**' chart of accounts that is used in this chapter. Additional accounts will be introduced in later chapters. In Exhibit 2, each account number has two digits. The first digit indicates the major account group of the ledger in which the account is located. Accounts beginning with 1 represent assets; 2, liabilities; 3, owner's equity; 4, revenue; and 5, expenses. The second digit indicates the location of the account within its group.

Procter & Gamble's account numbers have over 30 digits to reflect P&G's many different operations and regions.

EXHIBIT 2

Chart of Accounts for NetSolutions

Balance Sheet Accounts	Income Statement Accounts
1. Assets	**4. Revenue**
11 Cash	41 Fees Earned
12 Accounts Receivable	**5. Expenses**
14 Supplies	51 Wages Expense
15 Prepaid Insurance	52 Supplies Expense
17 Land	53 Rent Expense
18 Office Equipment	54 Utilities Expense
2. Liabilities	59 Miscellaneous Expense
21 Accounts Payable	
23 Unearned Rent	
3. Owner's Equity	
31 Chris Clark, Capital	
32 Chris Clark, Drawing	

Each of the columns in Exhibit 1 has been assigned an account number in the chart of accounts shown in Exhibit 2. In addition, Accounts Receivable, Prepaid Insurance, Office Equipment, and Unearned Rent have been added. These accounts will be used in recording NetSolutions' December transactions.

Double-Entry Accounting System

OBJ 2 Describe and illustrate journalizing transactions using the double-entry accounting system.

All businesses use what is called the **double-entry accounting system**. This system is based on the accounting equation and requires:

- Every business transaction to be recorded in at least two accounts.
- The total debits recorded for each transaction to be equal to the total credits recorded.

The double-entry accounting system also has specific **rules of debit and credit** for recording transactions in the accounts.

Balance Sheet Accounts

The debit and credit rules for balance sheet accounts are as follows:

Balance Sheet Accounts

ASSETS Asset Accounts		=	LIABILITIES Liability Accounts		+	OWNER'S EQUITY Owner's Equity Accounts	
Debit for increases (+)	Credit for decreases (–)		Debit for decreases (–)	Credit for increases (+)		Debit for decreases (–)	Credit for increases (+)

Income Statement Accounts

The debit and credit rules for income statement accounts are based on their relationship with owner's equity. As shown for balance sheet accounts, owner's equity accounts are increased by credits. Because revenues increase owner's equity, revenue accounts are increased by credits and decreased by debits. Because owner's equity accounts are decreased by debits, expense accounts are increased by debits and decreased by credits. Thus, the rules of debit and credit for revenue and expense accounts are as follows:

Income Statement Accounts			
Revenue Accounts		**Expense Accounts**	
Debit for decreases (–)	Credit for increases (+)	Debit for increases (+)	Credit for decreases (–)

Owner Withdrawals

The debit and credit rules for recording owner withdrawals are based on the effect of owner withdrawals on owner's equity. Because an owner's withdrawals decrease owner's equity, the owner's drawing account is increased by debits. Likewise, the owner's drawing account is decreased by credits. Thus, the rules of debit and credit for the owner's drawing account are as follows:

Drawing Account	
Debit for increases (+)	Credit for decreases (–)

Normal Balances

The sum of the increases in an account is usually equal to or greater than the sum of the decreases in the account. Thus, the **normal balance of an account** is either a debit or credit depending on whether increases in the account are recorded as debits or credits. For example, because asset accounts are increased with debits, asset accounts normally have debit balances. Likewise, liability accounts normally have credit balances.

The rules of debit and credit and the normal balances of the various types of accounts are summarized in Exhibit 3. Debits and credits are sometimes abbreviated as Dr. for debit and Cr. for credit.

EXHIBIT 3 **Rules of Debit and Credit, Normal Balances of Accounts**

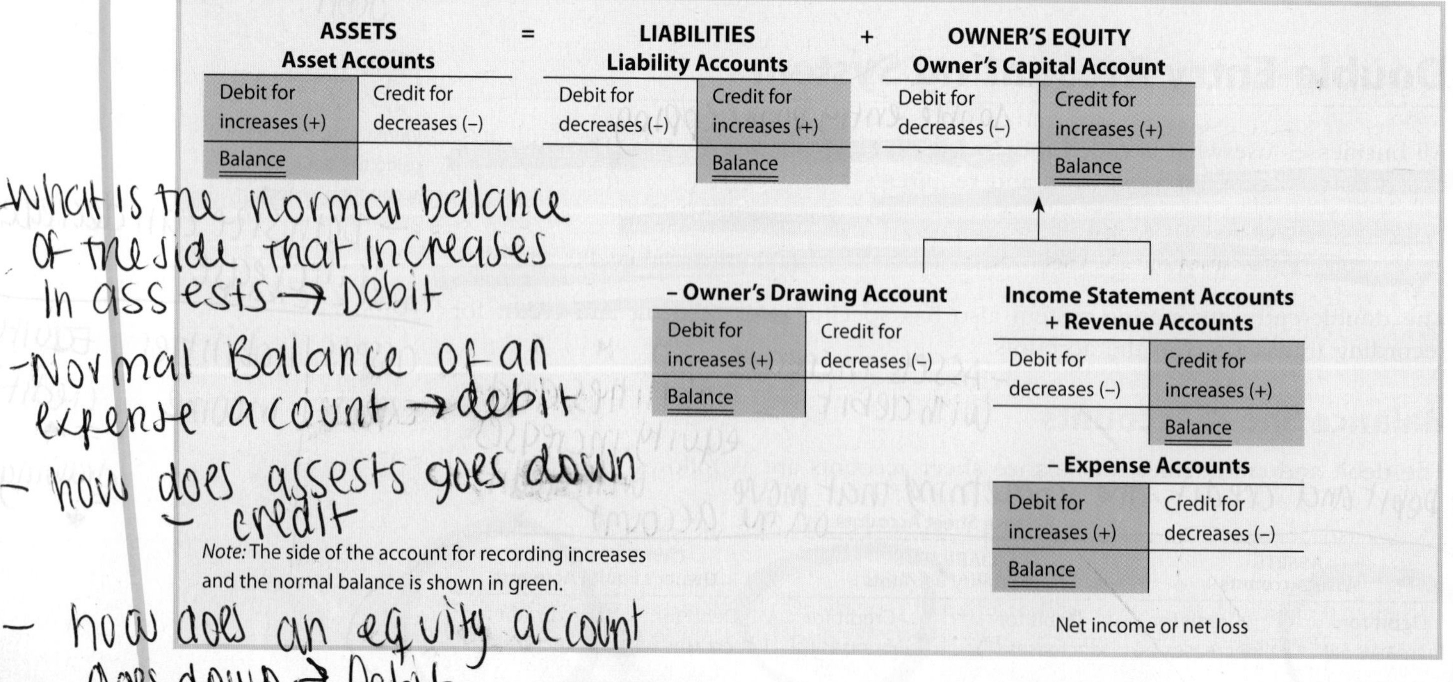

Note: The side of the account for recording increases and the normal balance is shown in green.

When an account normally having a debit balance has a credit balance, or vice versa, an error may have occurred or an unusual situation may exist. For example, a credit balance in the office equipment account could result only from an error. This is because a business cannot have more decreases than increases of office equipment. On the other hand, a debit balance in an accounts payable account could result from an overpayment.

Example Exercise 2-1 Rules of Debit and Credit and Normal Balances

OBJ 2

State for each account whether it is likely to have (a) debit entries only, (b) credit entries only, or (c) both debit and credit entries. Also, indicate its normal balance.

1. Amber Saunders, Drawing
2. Accounts Payable
3. Cash
4. Fees Earned
5. Supplies
6. Utilities Expense

Follow My Example 2-1

1. Debit entries only; normal debit balance
2. Debit and credit entries; normal credit balance
3. Debit and credit entries; normal debit balance
4. Credit entries only; normal credit balance
5. Debit and credit entries; normal debit balance
6. Debit entries only; normal debit balance

Practice Exercises: PE 2-1A, PE 2-1B

Journalizing

A journal can be thought of as being similar to an individual's diary of significant day-to-day life events.

Using the rules of debit and credit, transactions are initially entered in a record called **a journal**. In this way, the journal serves as a record of when transactions occurred and were recorded. To illustrate, the November transactions of **NetSolutions** from Chapter 1 are used.

Transaction A

Nov. 1 Chris Clark deposited $25,000 in a bank account in the name of NetSolutions.

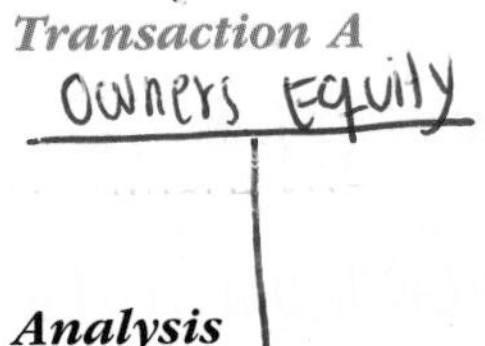

Analysis

This transaction increases an asset account and increases an owner's equity account. It is recorded in the journal as an increase (debit) to Cash and an increase (credit) to Chris Clark, Capital.

Journal Entry

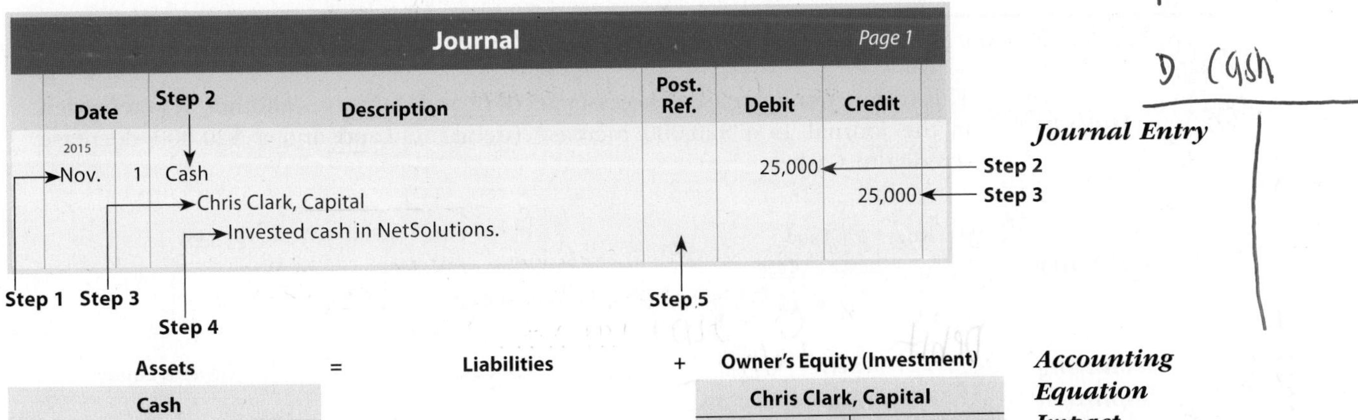

Journal Page 1

Date		Description	Post. Ref.	Debit	Credit
2015					
Nov.	1	Cash		25,000	
		Chris Clark, Capital			25,000
		Invested cash in NetSolutions.			

Accounting Equation Impact

Assets	=	Liabilities	+	Owner's Equity (Investment)
Cash				**Chris Clark, Capital**
Nov. 1 25,000				Nov. 1 25,000

The transaction is recorded in the journal using the following steps:

- Step 1. The date of the transaction is entered in the Date column.
- Step 2. The title of the account to be debited is recorded in the left-hand margin under the Description column, and the amount to be debited is entered in the Debit column.

- Step 3. The title of the account to be credited is listed below and to the right of the debited account title, and the amount to be credited is entered in the Credit column.
- Step 4. A brief description may be entered below the credited account.
- Step 5. The Post. Ref. (Posting Reference) column is left blank when the journal entry is initially recorded. This column is used later in this chapter when the journal entry amounts are transferred to the accounts in the ledger.

The process of recording a transaction in the journal is called **journalizing**. The entry in the journal is called a **journal entry**.

The following is a useful method for analyzing and journalizing transactions:

- Step 1. Carefully read the description of the transaction to determine whether an asset, a liability, an owner's equity, a revenue, an expense, or a drawing account is affected.
- Step 2. For each account affected by the transaction, determine whether the account increases or decreases.
- Step 3. Determine whether each increase or decrease should be recorded as a debit or a credit, following the rules of debit and credit shown in Exhibit 3.
- Step 4. Record the transaction using a journal entry.

Exhibit 4 summarizes terminology that is often used in describing a transaction along with the related accounts that would be debited and credited.

EXHIBIT 4

Transaction Terminology and Related Journal Entry Accounts

	Journal Entry Account	
Common Transaction Terminology	**Debit**	**Credit**
Received cash for services provided	Cash	Fees Earned
Services provided on account	Accounts Receivable	Fees Earned
Received cash on account	Cash	Accounts Receivable
Purchased on account	Asset account	Accounts Payable
Paid on account	Accounts Payable	Cash
Paid cash	Asset or expense account	Cash
Owner investments	Cash and/or other assets	(Owner's name), Capital
Owner withdrawals	(Owner's name), Drawing	Cash

The remaining transactions of **NetSolutions** for November are analyzed and journalized next.

Transaction B *Nov. 5* *NetSolutions paid $20,000 for the purchase of land as a future building site.*

Analysis

This transaction increases one asset account and decreases another. It is recorded in the journal as a $20,000 increase (debit) to Land and a $20,000 decrease (credit) to Cash.

Journal Entry

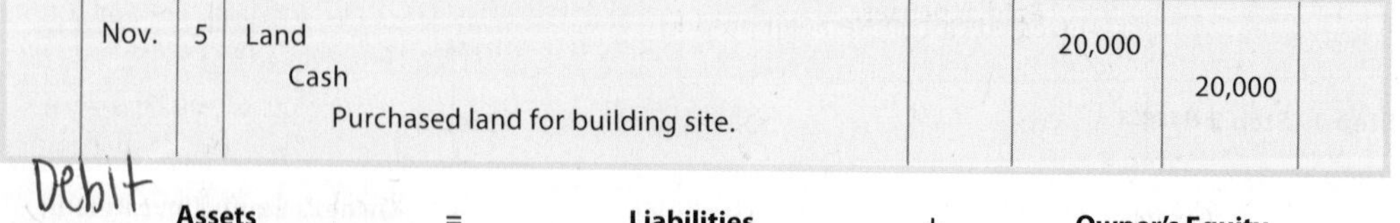

Nov.	5	Land		20,000	
		Cash			20,000
		Purchased land for building site.			

Accounting Equation Impact

Assets = **Liabilities** + **Owner's Equity**

Land

Nov. 5 20,000	

Cash

	Nov. 5 20,000

Nov. 10 NetSolutions purchased supplies on account for $1,350. — ***Transaction C***

Analysis

This transaction increases an asset account and increases a liability account. It is recorded in the journal as a $1,350 increase (debit) to Supplies and a $1,350 increase (credit) to Accounts Payable.

Journal Entry

	Nov.	10	Supplies		1,350	
			Accounts Payable			1,350
			Purchased supplies on account.			

Accounting Equation Impact

Assets = **Liabilities** + **Owner's Equity**

Supplies	
Nov. 10 1,350	

Accounts Payable	
	Nov. 10 1,350

Nov. 18 NetSolutions received cash of $7,500 from customers for services provided. — ***Transaction D***

Analysis

This transaction increases an asset account and increases a revenue account. It is recorded in the journal as a $7,500 increase (debit) to Cash and a $7,500 increase (credit) to Fees Earned.

Journal Entry

	Nov.	18	Cash		7,500	
			Fees Earned			7,500
			Received fees from customers.			

Accounting Equation Impact

Assets = **Liabilities** + **Owner's Equity (Revenue)**

Cash	
Nov. 18 7,500	

Fees Earned	
	Nov. 18 7,500

Nov. 30 NetSolutions incurred the following expenses: wages, $2,125; rent, $800; utilities, $450; and miscellaneous, $275. — ***Transaction E***

Analysis

This transaction increases various expense accounts and decreases an asset (Cash) account. You should note that regardless of the number of accounts, *the sum of the debits is always equal to the sum of the credits in a journal entry*. It is recorded in the journal with increases (debits) to the expense accounts (Wages Expense, $2,125; Rent Expense, $800; Utilities Expense, $450; and Miscellaneous Expense, $275) and a decrease (credit) to Cash, $3,650.

Journal Entry

	Nov.	30	Wages Expense		2,125	
			Rent Expense		800	
			Utilities Expense		450	
			Miscellaneous Expense		275	
			Cash			3,650
			Paid expenses.			

Accounting Equation Impact

Assets = **Liabilities** + **Owner's Equity (Expense)**

Cash	
	Nov. 30 3,650

Wages Expense	
Nov. 30 2,125	

Rent Expense	
Nov. 30 800	

Utilities Expense	
Nov. 30 450	

Miscellaneous Expense	
Nov. 30 275	

Transaction F *Nov. 30 NetSolutions paid creditors on account, $950.*

Analysis

This transaction decreases a liability account and decreases an asset account. It is recorded in the journal as a $950 decrease (debit) to Accounts Payable and a $950 decrease (credit) to Cash.

Journal Entry

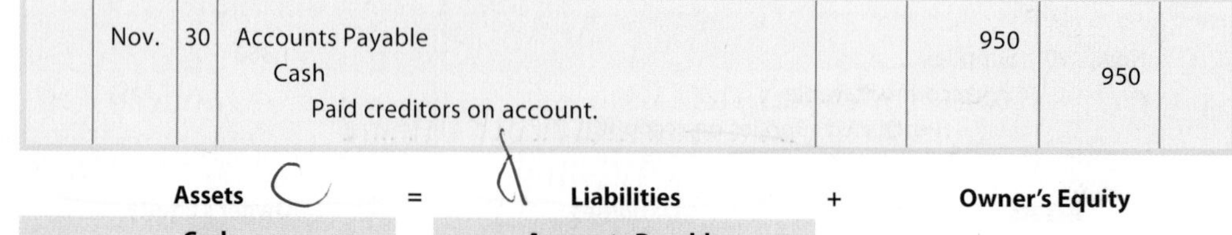

Nov.	30	Accounts Payable		950	
		Cash			950
		Paid creditors on account.			

Accounting Equation Impact

Assets = **Liabilities** + **Owner's Equity**

Cash		Accounts Payable	
	Nov. 30 950	Nov. 30 950	

Transaction G *Nov. 30 Chris Clark determined that the cost of supplies on hand at November 30 was $550.*

Analysis

NetSolutions purchased $1,350 of supplies on November 10. Thus, $800 ($1,350 – $550) of supplies must have been used during November. This transaction is recorded in the journal as an $800 increase (debit) to Supplies Expense and an $800 decrease (credit) to Supplies.

Journal Entry

Nov.	30	Supplies Expense		800	
		Supplies			800
		Supplies used during November.			

Accounting Equation Impact

Assets = **Liabilities** + **Owner's Equity (Expense)**

Supplies		Supplies Expense	
	Nov. 30 800	Nov. 30 800	

Transaction H *Nov. 30 Chris Clark withdrew $2,000 from NetSolutions for personal use.*

Analysis

This transaction decreases assets and owner's equity. This transaction is recorded in the journal as a $2,000 increase (debit) to Chris Clark, Drawing and a $2,000 decrease (credit) to Cash.

Journal Entry

Journal *Page 2*

Date		Description	Post. Ref.	Debit	Credit
2015					
Nov.	30	Chris Clark, Drawing		2,000	
		Cash			2,000
		Chris Clark withdrew cash for personal use.			

Accounting Equation Impact

Assets = **Liabilities** + **Owner's Equity (Drawing)**

Cash		Chris Clark, Drawing	
	Nov. 30 2,000	Nov. 30 2,000	

Integrity, Objectivity, and Ethics in Business

WILL JOURNALIZING PREVENT FRAUD?

While journalizing transactions reduces the possibility of fraud, it by no means eliminates it. For example, embezzlement can be hidden within the double-entry bookkeeping system by creating fictitious suppliers to whom checks are issued.

Example Exercise 2-2 Journal Entry for Asset Purchase OBJ 2

Prepare a journal entry for the purchase of a truck on June 3 for $42,500, paying $8,500 cash and the remainder on account.

Follow My Example 2-2

June 3	Truck	42,500	
	Cash		8,500
	Accounts Payable		34,000

Practice Exercises: PE 2-2A, PE 2-2B

Posting Journal Entries to Accounts

OBJ 3 Describe and illustrate the journalizing and posting of transactions to accounts.

As illustrated, a transaction is first recorded in a journal. Periodically, the journal entries are transferred to the accounts in the ledger. The process of transferring the debits and credits from the journal entries to the accounts is called **posting.**

The December transactions of **NetSolutions** are used to illustrate posting from the journal to the ledger. By using the December transactions, an additional review of analyzing and journalizing transactions is provided.

Transaction

Dec. 1 NetSolutions paid a premium of $2,400 for an insurance policy for liability, theft, and fire. The policy covers a one-year period.

Analysis

Advance payments of expenses, such as for insurance premiums, are called prepaid expenses. Prepaid expenses are assets. For NetSolutions, the asset purchased is insurance protection for 12 months. This transaction is recorded as a $2,400 increase (debit) to Prepaid Insurance and a $2,400 decrease (credit) to Cash.

Journal Entry

Accounting Equation Impact

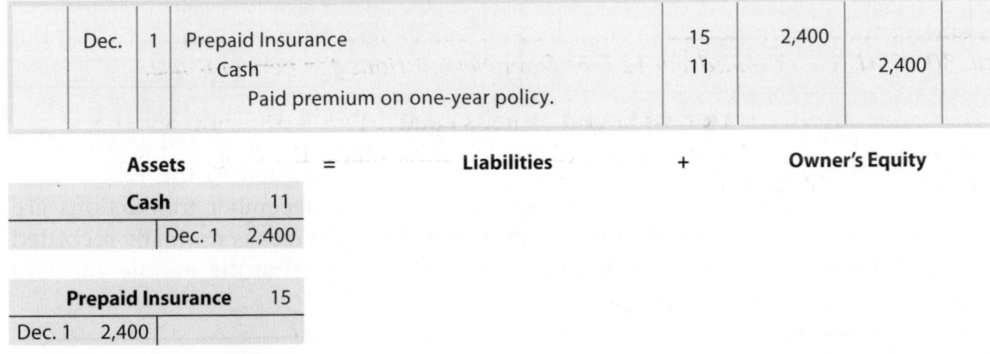

Dec.	1	Prepaid Insurance	15	2,400	
		Cash	11		2,400
		Paid premium on one-year policy.			

Assets = **Liabilities** + **Owner's Equity**

Cash		11
	Dec. 1	2,400

Prepaid Insurance		15
Dec. 1	2,400	

The posting of the preceding December 1 transaction is shown in Exhibit 5. Notice that the T account form is not used in Exhibit 5. In practice, the T account is usually replaced with a standard account form similar to that shown in Exhibit 5.

The debits and credits for each journal entry are posted to the accounts in the order in which they occur in the journal. To illustrate, the debit portion of the December 1 journal entry is posted to the prepaid account in Exhibit 5 using the following four steps:

- Step 1. The date (Dec. 1) of the journal entry is entered in the Date column of Prepaid Insurance.
- Step 2. The amount (2,400) is entered into the Debit column of Prepaid Insurance.
- Step 3. The journal page number (2) is entered in the Posting Reference (Post. Ref.) column of Prepaid Insurance.
- Step 4. The account number (15) is entered in the Posting Reference (Post. Ref.) column in the journal.

As shown in Exhibit 5, the credit portion of the December 1 journal entry is posted to the cash account in a similar manner.

EXHIBIT 5 **Diagram of the Recording and Posting of a Debit and a Credit**

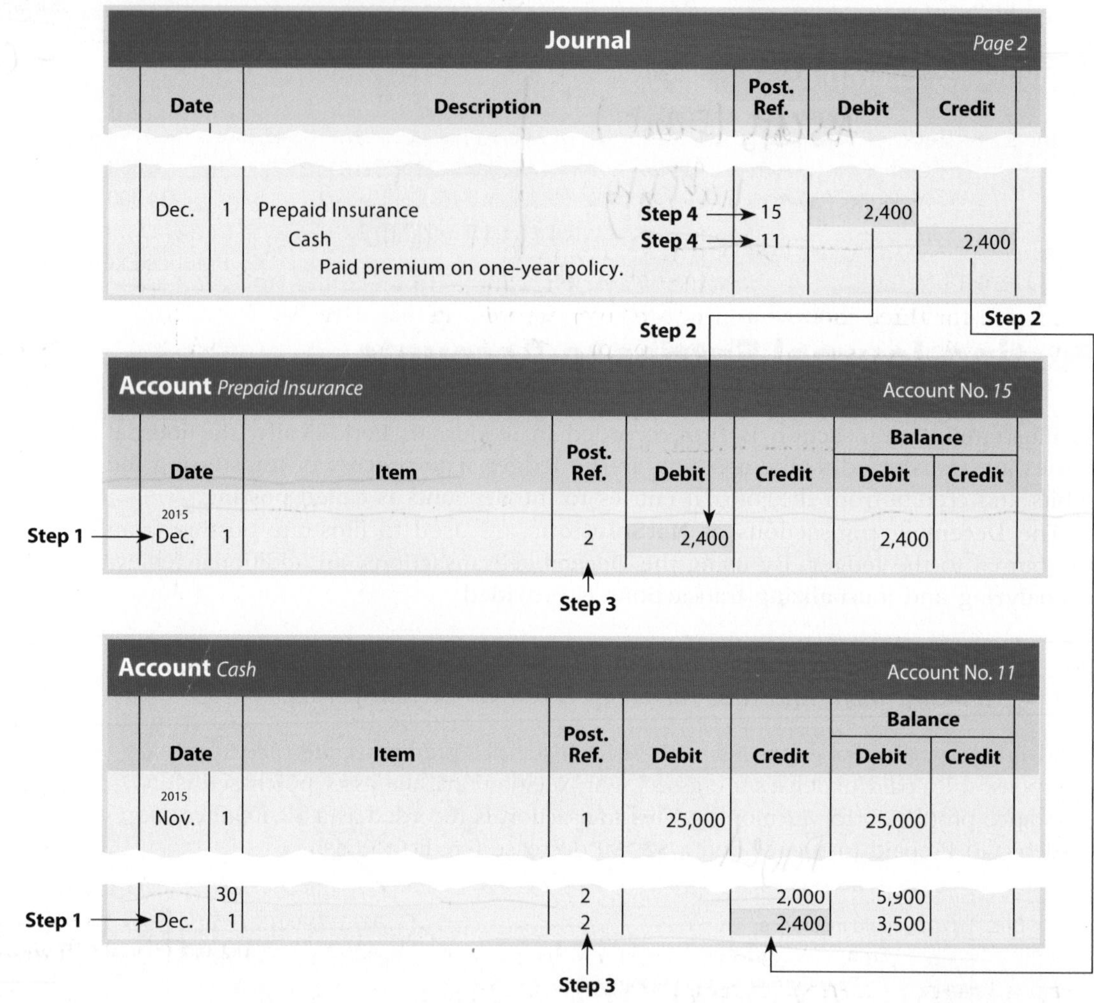

Journal — *Page 2*

Date		Description	Post. Ref.	Debit	Credit
Dec.	1	Prepaid Insurance	15	2,400	
		Cash	11		2,400
		Paid premium on one-year policy.			

Account *Prepaid Insurance* — Account No. *15*

Date		Item	Post. Ref.	Debit	Credit	Balance Debit	Balance Credit
2015 Dec.	1		2	2,400		2,400	

Account *Cash* — Account No. *11*

Date		Item	Post. Ref.	Debit	Credit	Balance Debit	Balance Credit
2015 Nov.	1		1	25,000		25,000	
	30		2		2,000	5,900	
Dec.	1		2		2,400	3,500	

The remaining December transactions for **NetSolutions** are analyzed and journalized in the following paragraphs. These transactions are posted to the ledger later in this chapter (see Exhibit 6). To simplify, some of the December transactions are stated in summary form. For example, cash received for services is normally recorded on a daily basis. However, only summary totals are recorded at the middle and end of the month for NetSolutions.

Transaction *Dec. 1* *NetSolutions paid rent for December, $800. The company from which NetSolutions is renting its office space now requires the payment of rent on the first of each month, rather than at the end of the month.*

Analysis The advance payment of rent is an asset, much like the advance payment of the insurance premium in the preceding transaction. However, unlike the insurance premium, this prepaid rent will expire in one month. When an asset is purchased with the expectation that it will be used up in a short period of time, such as a month, it is normal to debit an expense account initially. This avoids having to transfer the balance from an asset account (Prepaid Rent) to an expense account (Rent Expense) at the end of the month. Thus, this transaction is recorded as an $800 increase (debit) to Rent Expense and an $800 decrease (credit) to Cash.

Journal Entry

Date		Description	Post. Ref.	Debit	Credit
Dec.	1	Rent Expense	53	800	
		Cash	11		800
		Paid rent for December.			

Assets		=	Liabilities	+	Owner's Equity (Expense)	
Cash	11				Rent Expense	53
	Dec. 1 800				Dec. 1 800	

Accounting Equation Impact

Dec. 1 NetSolutions received an offer from a local retailer to rent the land purchased on November 5. The retailer plans to use the land as a parking lot for its employees and customers. NetSolutions agreed to rent the land to the retailer for three months, with the rent payable in advance. NetSolutions received $360 for three months' rent beginning December 1.

Transaction

By agreeing to rent the land and accepting the $360, NetSolutions has incurred an obligation (liability) to the retailer. This obligation is to make the land available for use for three months and not to interfere with its use. The liability created by receiving the cash in advance of providing the service is called **unearned revenue**. As time passes, the unearned rent liability will decrease and will become revenue. Thus, this transaction is recorded as a $360 increase (debit) to Cash and a $360 increase (credit) to Unearned Rent.

Analysis

Dec.	1	Cash	11	360	
		Unearned Rent	23		360
		Received advance payment for three months' rent on land.			

Journal Entry

Assets		=	Liabilities		+	Owner's Equity
Cash	11		Unearned Rent	23		
Dec. 1 360				Dec. 1 360		

Accounting Equation Impact

Business  Connection

MICROSOFT'S UNEARNED REVENUE

Microsoft Corporation develops, manufactures, licenses, and supports a wide range of computer software products, including Windows 7®, Windows 8®, Word®, Excel®, and the Xbox® gaming system. When Microsoft sells its products, it also provides technical support and periodic updates on those products for a period of time. Thus, at the time of sale a portion of the proceeds is unearned (deferred) for these services. As time passes and services are provided to customers, Microsoft records a portion of its unearned (deferred) revenue as revenue.[3]

To illustrate, the following excerpts were taken from recent financial statement of Microsoft:

> Unearned revenue comprises mainly unearned revenue from volume licensing programs, and payments for offerings for which we have been paid in advance and we earn the revenue when we provide the service or software or otherwise meet the revenue recognition criteria.... Also included in unearned revenue are payments for post-delivery support and consulting services to be performed in the future....
>
> Unearned revenue (in millions) by segment:

	June 30 current year	June 30 prior year
Windows Division	$ 2,086	$ 2,444
Server and Tools	8,639	7,445
Microsoft Business Division	10,142	9,015
Other segments	1,532	1,155
Total	$22,399	$20,059

During the year, Microsoft recognized $44.25 billion in unearned revenue as revenue. At the same time, Microsoft recorded additional unearned revenue from the current period of $41.92 billion. Out of $77.8 billion in total revenue, Microsoft recognized $44.2 billion from unearned revenue, or 56% of total revenues. Thus, unearned revenues are a significant reporting item for Microsoft.

Source: Microsoft Corp., Form 10-K for the Fiscal Year Ended June 30, 2013.

Dec. 4 NetSolutions purchased office equipment on account from Executive Supply Co. for $1,800.

Transaction

The asset (Office Equipment) and liability accounts (Accounts Payable) increase. This transaction is recorded as an $1,800 increase (debit) to Office Equipment and an $1,800 increase (credit) to Accounts Payable.

Analysis

[3] Separating unearned revenue from the initial sale of a product or service is consistent with FASB Exposure Draft, Revenue Recognition (Topic 605), June 24, 2010, paras. 23, 35-36.

Journal Entry

			Post. Ref.	Debit	Credit
Dec.	4	Office Equipment	18	1,800	
		Accounts Payable	21		1,800
		Purchased office equipment on account.			

Accounting Equation Impact

Assets = **Liabilities** + **Owner's Equity**

Office Equipment 18		Accounts Payable 21	
Dec. 4 1,800			Dec. 4 1,800

Transaction *Dec. 6 NetSolutions paid $180 for a newspaper advertisement.*

Analysis An expense increases, and an asset (Cash) decreases. Expense items that are expected to be minor in amount are normally included as part of the miscellaneous expense. This transaction is recorded as a $180 increase (debit) to Miscellaneous Expense and a $180 decrease (credit) to Cash.

Journal Entry

			Post. Ref.	Debit	Credit
Dec.	6	Miscellaneous Expense	59	180	
		Cash	11		180
		Paid for newspaper advertisement.			

Accounting Equation Impact

Assets = **Liabilities** + **Owner's Equity (Expense)**

Cash 11		Miscellaneous Exp. 59	
	Dec. 6 180	Dec. 6 180	

Transaction *Dec. 11 NetSolutions paid creditors $400.*

Analysis A liability (Accounts Payable) and an asset (Cash) decrease. This transaction is recorded as a $400 decrease (debit) to Accounts Payable and a $400 decrease (credit) to Cash.

Journal Entry

			Post. Ref.	Debit	Credit
Dec.	11	Accounts Payable	21	400	
		Cash	11		400
		Paid creditors on account.			

Accounting Equation Impact

Assets = **Liabilities** + **Owner's Equity**

Cash 11		Accounts Payable 21	
	Dec. 11 400	Dec. 11 400	

Transaction *Dec. 13 NetSolutions paid a receptionist and a part-time assistant $950 for two weeks' wages.*

Analysis This transaction is similar to the December 6 transaction, where an expense account is increased and Cash is decreased. This transaction is recorded as a $950 increase (debit) to Wages Expense and a $950 decrease (credit) to Cash.

Journal Entry

Journal *Page 3*

Date		Description	Post. Ref.	Debit	Credit
2015					
Dec.	13	Wages Expense	51	950	
		Cash	11		950
		Paid two weeks' wages.			

Accounting Equation Impact

Assets = **Liabilities** + **Owner's Equity (Expense)**

Cash 11		Wages Expense 51	
	Dec. 13 950	Dec. 13 950	

Business  Connection

COMPUTERIZED ACCOUNTING SYSTEMS

Computerized accounting systems are widely used by even the smallest companies. These systems simplify the record-keeping process in that transactions are recorded in electronic forms. Forms used to bill customers for services provided are often completed using drop-down menus that list services that are normally provided to customers. An auto-complete entry feature may also be used to fill in customer names. For example, type "ca" to display customers with names beginning with "Ca" (Caban, Cahill, Carey, and Caswell). And, to simplify data entry, entries are automatically posted to the ledger accounts when the electronic form is completed.

One popular accounting software package used by small- to medium-sized businesses is QuickBooks®. Some examples of using QuickBooks to record accounting transactions are illustrated and discussed in Chapter 5.

Dec. 16 NetSolutions received $3,100 from fees earned for the first half of December. — ***Transaction***

Analysis

An asset account (Cash) and a revenue account (Fees Earned) increase. This transaction is recorded as a $3,100 increase (debit) to Cash and a $3,100 increase (credit) to Fees Earned.

Journal Entry

Dec.	16	Cash	11	3,100	
		Fees Earned	41		3,100
		Received fees from customers.			

Accounting Equation Impact

Assets = **Liabilities** + **Owner's Equity (Revenue)**

Cash 11	
Dec. 16 3,100	

Fees Earned 41	
	Dec. 16 3,100

Dec. 16 Fees earned on account totaled $1,750 for the first half of December. — ***Transaction***

Analysis

When a business agrees that a customer may pay for services provided at a later date, an **account receivable** is created. An account receivable is a claim against the customer. An account receivable is an asset, and the revenue is earned even though no cash has been received. Thus, this transaction is recorded as a $1,750 increase (debit) to Accounts Receivable and a $1,750 increase (credit) to Fees Earned.

Journal Entry

Dec.	16	Accounts Receivable	12	1,750	
		Fees Earned	41		1,750
		Fees earned on account.			

Accounting Equation Impact

Assets = **Liabilities** + **Owner's Equity (Revenue)**

Accounts Receivable 12	
Dec. 16 1,750	

Fees Earned 41	
	Dec. 16 1,750

Example Exercise 2-3 Journal Entry for Fees Earned (OBJ 3)

Prepare a journal entry on August 7 for the fees earned on account, $115,000.

Follow My Example 2-3

Aug. 7	Accounts Receivable	115,000	
	Fees Earned		115,000

Practice Exercises: PE 2-3A, PE 2-3B

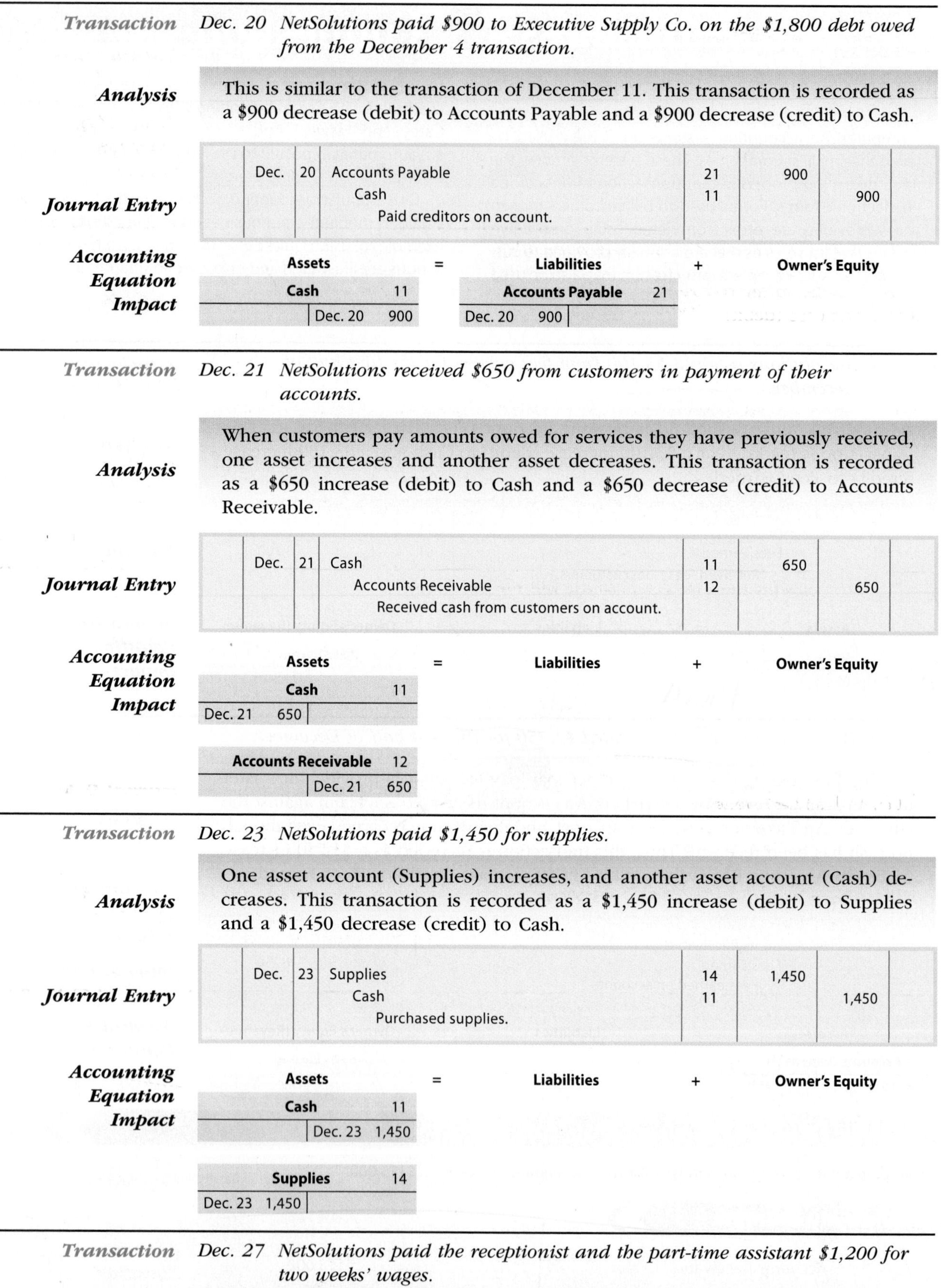

Transaction *Dec. 20 NetSolutions paid $900 to Executive Supply Co. on the $1,800 debt owed from the December 4 transaction.*

Analysis This is similar to the transaction of December 11. This transaction is recorded as a $900 decrease (debit) to Accounts Payable and a $900 decrease (credit) to Cash.

Journal Entry

Dec.	20	Accounts Payable	21	900	
		Cash	11		900
		Paid creditors on account.			

Accounting Equation Impact

Assets = **Liabilities** + **Owner's Equity**

Cash	11
	Dec. 20 900

Accounts Payable	21
Dec. 20 900	

Transaction *Dec. 21 NetSolutions received $650 from customers in payment of their accounts.*

Analysis When customers pay amounts owed for services they have previously received, one asset increases and another asset decreases. This transaction is recorded as a $650 increase (debit) to Cash and a $650 decrease (credit) to Accounts Receivable.

Journal Entry

Dec.	21	Cash	11	650	
		Accounts Receivable	12		650
		Received cash from customers on account.			

Accounting Equation Impact

Assets = **Liabilities** + **Owner's Equity**

Cash	11
Dec. 21 650	

Accounts Receivable	12
	Dec. 21 650

Transaction *Dec. 23 NetSolutions paid $1,450 for supplies.*

Analysis One asset account (Supplies) increases, and another asset account (Cash) decreases. This transaction is recorded as a $1,450 increase (debit) to Supplies and a $1,450 decrease (credit) to Cash.

Journal Entry

Dec.	23	Supplies	14	1,450	
		Cash	11		1,450
		Purchased supplies.			

Accounting Equation Impact

Assets = **Liabilities** + **Owner's Equity**

Cash	11
	Dec. 23 1,450

Supplies	14
Dec. 23 1,450	

Transaction *Dec. 27 NetSolutions paid the receptionist and the part-time assistant $1,200 for two weeks' wages.*

Analysis This transaction is similar to the transaction of December 13. This transaction is recorded as a $1,200 increase (debit) to Wages Expense and a $1,200 decrease (credit) to Cash.

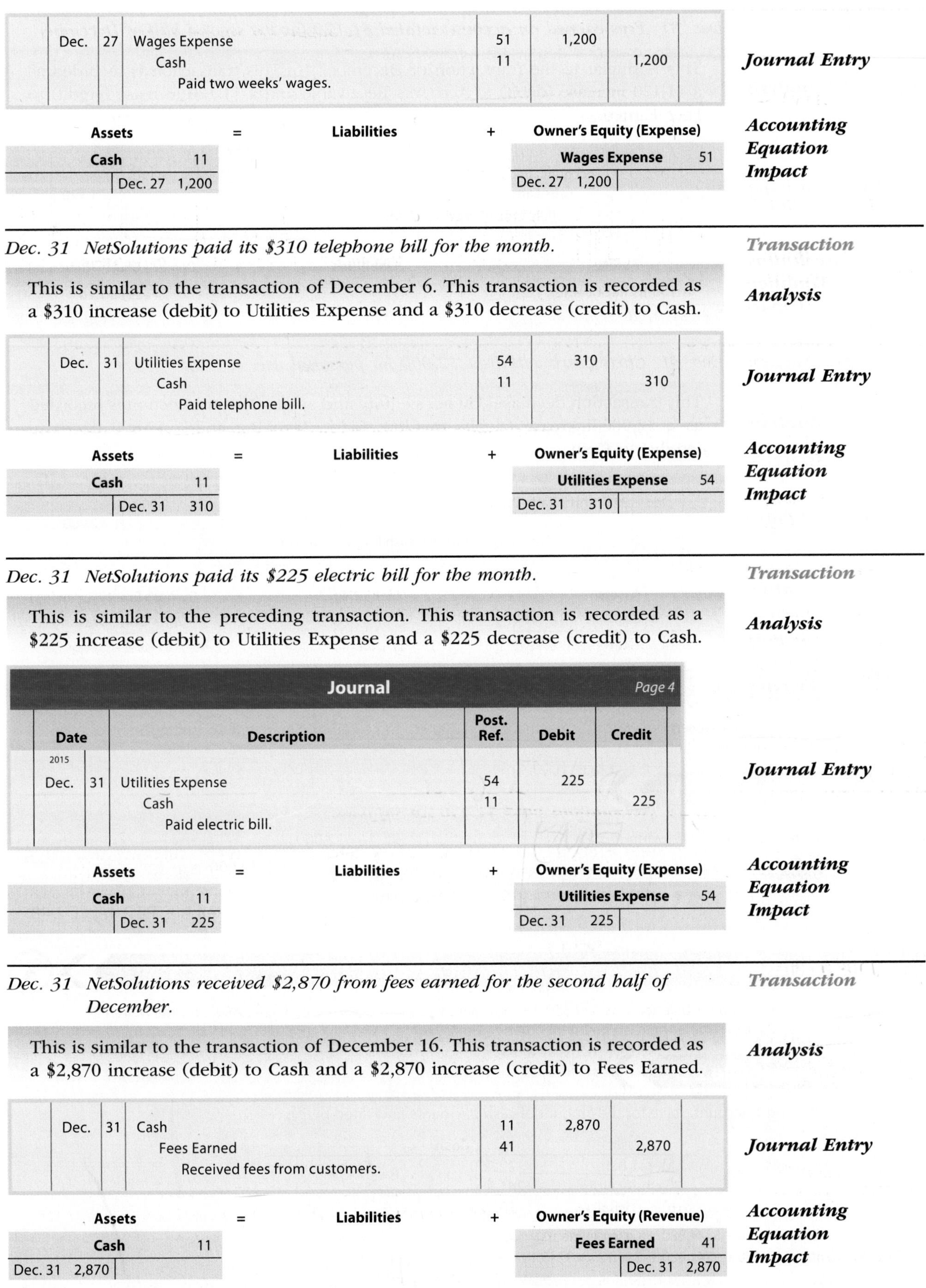

Dec.	27	Wages Expense	51	1,200	
		Cash	11		1,200
		Paid two weeks' wages.			

Journal Entry

Assets	=	Liabilities	+	Owner's Equity (Expense)
Cash 11				**Wages Expense** 51
Cr: Dec. 27 1,200				Dr: Dec. 27 1,200

Accounting Equation Impact

Dec. 31 NetSolutions paid its $310 telephone bill for the month.

Transaction

This is similar to the transaction of December 6. This transaction is recorded as a $310 increase (debit) to Utilities Expense and a $310 decrease (credit) to Cash.

Analysis

Dec.	31	Utilities Expense	54	310	
		Cash	11		310
		Paid telephone bill.			

Journal Entry

Assets	=	Liabilities	+	Owner's Equity (Expense)
Cash 11				**Utilities Expense** 54
Cr: Dec. 31 310				Dr: Dec. 31 310

Accounting Equation Impact

Dec. 31 NetSolutions paid its $225 electric bill for the month.

Transaction

This is similar to the preceding transaction. This transaction is recorded as a $225 increase (debit) to Utilities Expense and a $225 decrease (credit) to Cash.

Analysis

Journal *Page 4*

Date		Description	Post. Ref.	Debit	Credit
2015					
Dec.	31	Utilities Expense	54	225	
		Cash	11		225
		Paid electric bill.			

Journal Entry

Assets	=	Liabilities	+	Owner's Equity (Expense)
Cash 11				**Utilities Expense** 54
Cr: Dec. 31 225				Dr: Dec. 31 225

Accounting Equation Impact

Dec. 31 NetSolutions received $2,870 from fees earned for the second half of December.

Transaction

This is similar to the transaction of December 16. This transaction is recorded as a $2,870 increase (debit) to Cash and a $2,870 increase (credit) to Fees Earned.

Analysis

Dec.	31	Cash	11	2,870	
		Fees Earned	41		2,870
		Received fees from customers.			

Journal Entry

Assets	=	Liabilities	+	Owner's Equity (Revenue)
Cash 11				**Fees Earned** 41
Dr: Dec. 31 2,870				Cr: Dec. 31 2,870

Accounting Equation Impact

Transaction *Dec. 31 Fees earned on account totaled $1,120 for the second half of December.*

Analysis

This is similar to the transaction of December 16. This transaction is recorded as a $1,120 increase (debit) to Accounts Receivable and a $1,120 increase (credit) to Fees Earned.

Journal Entry

Dec.	31	Accounts Receivable	12	1,120	
		Fees Earned	41		1,120
		Fees earned on account.			

Accounting Equation Impact

Assets = **Liabilities** + **Owner's Equity (Revenue)**

Accounts Receivable	**12**
Dec. 31 1,120	

Fees Earned	**41**
	Dec. 31 1,120

Transaction *Dec. 31 Chris Clark withdrew $2,000 for personal use.*

Analysis

This transaction decreases owner's equity and assets. This transaction is recorded as a $2,000 increase (debit) to Chris Clark, Drawing and a $2,000 decrease (credit) to Cash.

Journal Entry

Dec.	31	Chris Clark, Drawing	32	2,000	
		Cash	11		2,000
		Chris Clark withdrew cash for personal use.			

Accounting Equation Impact

Assets = **Liabilities** + **Owner's Equity (Drawing)**

Cash	**11**
	Dec. 31 2,000

Chris Clark, Drawing	**32**
Dec. 31 2,000	

Example Exercise 2-4 Journal Entry for Owner's Withdrawal

OBJ 3

Prepare a journal entry on December 29 for the payment of $12,000 to the owner of Smartstaff Consulting Services, Dominique Walsh, for personal use.

Follow My Example 2-4

Dec. 29	Dominique Walsh, Drawing	12,000	
	Cash....................................		12,000

Practice Exercises: PE 2-4A, PE 2-4B

Example Exercise 2-5 Missing Amount from an Account

OBJ 3

On March 1, the cash account balance was $22,350. During March, cash receipts totaled $241,880, and the March 31 balance was $19,125. Determine the cash payments made during March.

Follow My Example 2-5

Using the following T account, solve for the amount of cash payments (indicated by ?):

Cash			
Mar. 1 Bal.	22,350	?	Cash payments
Cash receipts	241,880		
Mar. 31 Bal.	19,125		

$19,125 = $22,350 + $241,880 − Cash payments
Cash payments = $22,350 + $241,880 − $19,125 = $245,105

Practice Exercises: PE 2-5A, PE 2-5B

Exhibit 6 shows the ledger for **NetSolutions** after the transactions for both November and December have been posted.

EXHIBIT 6 **Cash Receipts Journal for a Merchandising Business**

Ledger

Account *Cash* — Account No. *11*

Date	Item	Post. Ref.	Debit	Credit	Balance Debit	Balance Credit
2015						
Nov. 1		1	25,000		25,000	
5		1		20,000	5,000	
18		1	7,500		12,500	
30		1		3,650	8,850	
30		1		950	7,900	
30		2		2,000	5,900	
Dec. 1		2		2,400	3,500	
1		2		800	2,700	
1		2	360		3,060	
6		2		180	2,880	
11		2		400	2,480	
13		3		950	1,530	
16		3	3,100		4,630	
20		3		900	3,730	
21		3	650		4,380	
23		3		1,450	2,930	
27		3		1,200	1,730	
31		3		310	1,420	
31		4		225	1,195	
31		4	2,870		4,065	
31		4		2,000	2,065	

Account *Accounts Receivable* — Account No. *12*

Date	Item	Post. Ref.	Debit	Credit	Balance Debit	Balance Credit
2015						
Dec. 16		3	1,750		1,750	
21		3		650	1,100	
31		4	1,120		2,220	

Account *Supplies* — Account No. *14*

Date	Item	Post. Ref.	Debit	Credit	Balance Debit	Balance Credit
2015						
Nov. 10		1	1,350		1,350	
30		1		800	550	
Dec. 23		3	1,450		2,000	

Account *Prepaid Insurance* — Account No. *15*

Date	Item	Post. Ref.	Debit	Credit	Balance Debit	Balance Credit
2015						
Dec. 1		2	2,400		2,400	

Account *Land* — Account No. *17*

Date	Item	Post. Ref.	Debit	Credit	Balance Debit	Balance Credit
2015						
Nov. 5		1	20,000		20,000	

Account *Office Equipment* — Account No. *18*

Date	Item	Post. Ref.	Debit	Credit	Balance Debit	Balance Credit
2015						
Dec. 4		2	1,800		1,800	

Account *Accounts Payable* — Account No. *21*

Date	Item	Post. Ref.	Debit	Credit	Balance Debit	Balance Credit
2015						
Nov. 10		1		1,350		1,350
30		1	950			400
Dec. 4		2		1,800		2,200
11		2	400			1,800
20		3	900			900

Account *Unearned Rent* — Account No. *23*

Date	Item	Post. Ref.	Debit	Credit	Balance Debit	Balance Credit
2015						
Dec. 1		2		360		360

Account *Chris Clark, Capital* — Account No. *31*

Date	Item	Post. Ref.	Debit	Credit	Balance Debit	Balance Credit
2015						
Nov. 1		1		25,000		25,000

Account *Chris Clark, Drawing* — Account No. *32*

Date	Item	Post. Ref.	Debit	Credit	Balance Debit	Balance Credit
2015						
Nov. 30		2	2,000		2,000	
Dec. 31		4	2,000		4,000	

(Continued)

EXHIBIT 6 **Cash Receipts Journal for a Merchandising Business (*Concluded*)**

Account *Fees Earned* Account No. *41*

Date	Item	Post. Ref.	Debit	Credit	Balance Debit	Balance Credit
2015						
Nov. 18		1		7,500		7,500
Dec. 16		3		3,100		10,600
16		3		1,750		12,350
31		4		2,870		15,220
31		4		1,120		16,340

Account *Wages Expense* Account No. *51*

Date	Item	Post. Ref.	Debit	Credit	Balance Debit	Balance Credit
2015						
Nov. 30		1	2,125		2,125	
Dec. 13		3	950		3,075	
27		3	1,200		4,275	

Account *Supplies Expense* Account No. *52*

Date	Item	Post. Ref.	Debit	Credit	Balance Debit	Balance Credit
2015						
Nov. 30		1	800		800	

Account *Rent Expense* Account No. *53*

Date	Item	Post. Ref.	Debit	Credit	Balance Debit	Balance Credit
2015						
Nov. 30		1	800		800	
Dec. 1		2	800		1,600	

Account *Utilities Expense* Account No. *54*

Date	Item	Post. Ref.	Debit	Credit	Balance Debit	Balance Credit
2015						
Nov. 30		1	450		450	
Dec. 31		3	310		760	
31		4	225		985	

Account *Miscellaneous Expense* Account No. *59*

Date	Item	Post. Ref.	Debit	Credit	Balance Debit	Balance Credit
2015						
Nov. 30		1	275		275	
Dec. 6		2	180		455	

Trial Balance

OBJ 4 Prepare an unadjusted trial balance and explain how it can be used to discover errors.

Errors may occur in posting debits and credits from the journal to the ledger. One way to detect such errors is by preparing a **trial balance.** Double-entry accounting requires that debits must always equal credits. The trial balance verifies this equality. The steps in preparing a trial balance are as follows:

- Step 1. List the name of the company, the title of the trial balance, and the date the trial balance is prepared.
- Step 2. List the accounts from the ledger, and enter their debit or credit balance in the Debit or Credit column of the trial balance.
- Step 3. Total the Debit and Credit columns of the trial balance.
- Step 4. Verify that the total of the Debit column equals the total of the Credit column.

The trial balance for **NetSolutions** as of December 31, 2015, is shown in Exhibit 7. The account balances in Exhibit 7 are taken from the ledger shown in Exhibit 6. Before a trial balance is prepared, each account balance in the ledger must be determined. When the standard account form is used as in Exhibit 6, the balance of each account appears in the balance column on the same line as the last posting to the account.

The trial balance shown in Exhibit 7 is titled an **unadjusted trial balance**. This is to distinguish it from other trial balances that will be prepared in later

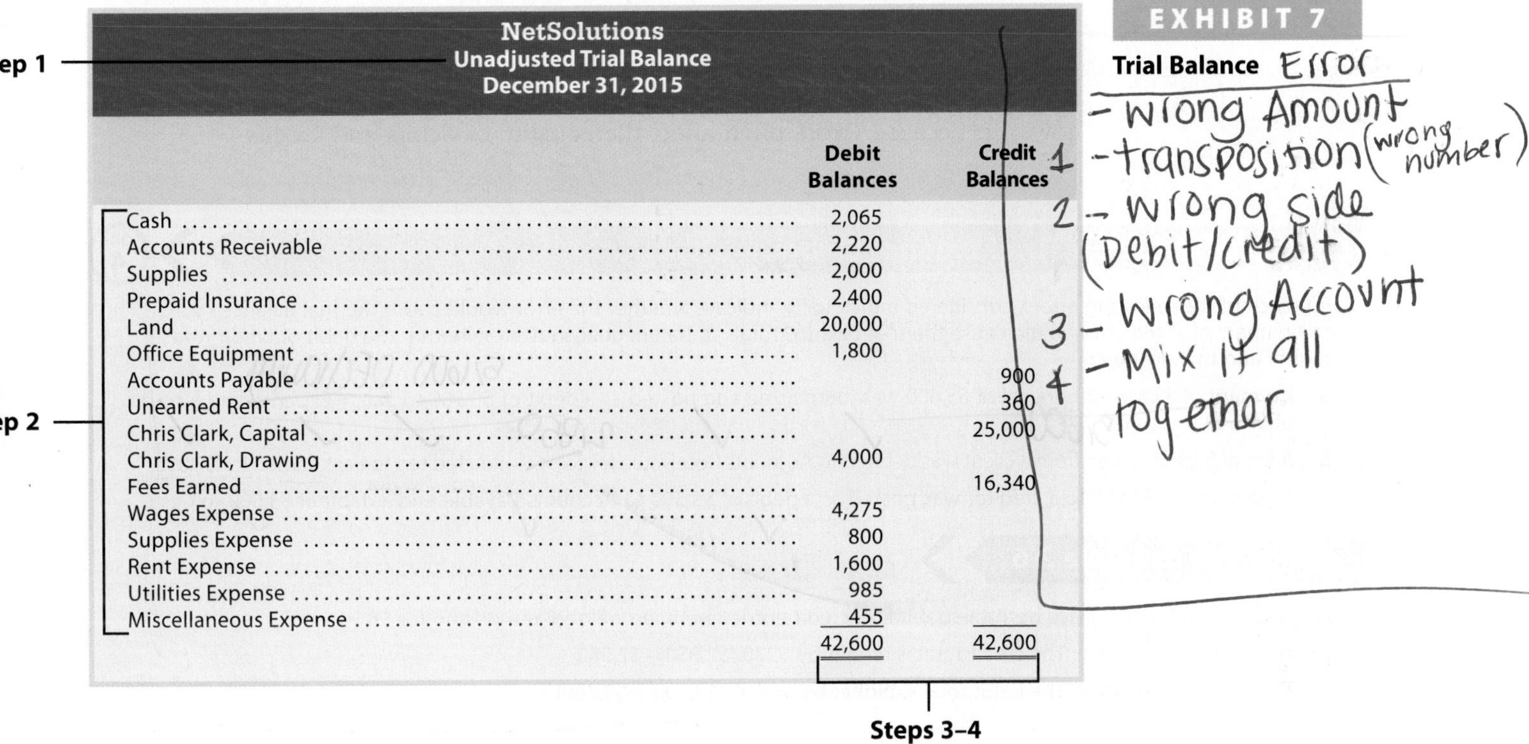

EXHIBIT 7

Trial Balance

NetSolutions
Unadjusted Trial Balance
December 31, 2015

	Debit Balances	Credit Balances
Cash	2,065	
Accounts Receivable	2,220	
Supplies	2,000	
Prepaid Insurance	2,400	
Land	20,000	
Office Equipment	1,800	
Accounts Payable		900
Unearned Rent		360
Chris Clark, Capital		25,000
Chris Clark, Drawing	4,000	
Fees Earned		16,340
Wages Expense	4,275	
Supplies Expense	800	
Rent Expense	1,600	
Utilities Expense	985	
Miscellaneous Expense	455	
	42,600	42,600

chapters. These other trial balances include an adjusted trial balance and a post-closing trial balance.[4]

Errors Affecting the Trial Balance

If the trial balance totals are not equal, an error has occurred. In this case, the error must be found and corrected. A method useful in discovering errors is as follows:

1. If the difference between the Debit and Credit column totals is 10, 100, or 1,000, an error in addition may have occurred. In this case, re-add the trial balance column totals. If the error still exists, recompute the account balances.
2. If the difference between the Debit and Credit column totals can be evenly divisible by 2, the error may be due to the entering of a debit balance as a credit balance, or vice versa. In this case, review the trial balance for account balances of one-half the difference that may have been entered in the wrong column. For example, if the Debit column total is $20,640 and the Credit column total is $20,236, the difference of $404 ($20,640 − $20,236) may be due to a credit account balance of $202 that was entered as a debit account balance.
3. If the difference between the Debit and Credit column totals is evenly divisible by 9, trace the account balances back to the ledger to see if an account balance was incorrectly copied from the ledger. Two common types of copying errors are transpositions and slides. A **transposition** occurs when the order of the digits is copied incorrectly, such as writing $542 as $452 or $524. In a **slide**, the entire number is copied incorrectly one or more spaces to the right or the left, such as writing $542.00 as $54.20 or $5,420.00. In both cases, the resulting error will be evenly divisible by 9.
4. If the difference between the Debit and Credit column totals is not evenly divisible by 2 or 9, review the ledger to see if an account balance in the amount of the error has been omitted from the trial balance. If the error is not discovered, review the journal postings to see if a posting of a debit or credit may have been omitted.

[4] The adjusted trial balance will be discussed in Chapter 3 and the post-closing trial balance in Chapter 4.

5. If an error is not discovered by the preceding steps, the accounting process must be retraced, beginning with the last journal entry.

The trial balance does not provide complete proof of the accuracy of the ledger. It indicates only that the debits and the credits are equal. This proof is of value, however, because errors often affect the equality of debits and credits.

Example Exercise 2-6 Trial Balance Errors

OBJ 4

For each of the following errors, considered individually, indicate whether the error would cause the trial balance totals to be unequal. If the error would cause the trial balance totals to be unequal, indicate whether the debit or credit total is higher and by how much.

a. Payment of a cash withdrawal of $5,600 was journalized and posted as a debit of $6,500 to Salary Expense and a credit of $6,500 to Cash.
b. A fee of $2,850 earned from a client was debited to Accounts Receivable for $2,580 and credited to Fees Earned for $2,850.
c. A payment of $3,500 to a creditor was posted as a debit of $3,500 to Accounts Payable and a debit of $3,500 to Cash.

Follow My Example 2-6

a. The totals are equal since both the debit and credit entries were journalized and posted for $6,500.
b. The totals are unequal. The credit total is higher by $270 ($2,850 – $2,580).
c. The totals are unequal. The debit total is higher by $7,000 ($3,500 + $3,500).

Practice Exercises: PE 2-6A, PE 2-6B

Errors Not Affecting the Trial Balance

An error may occur that does not cause the trial balance totals to be unequal. Such an error may be discovered when preparing the trial balance or may be indicated by an unusual account balance. For example, a credit balance in the supplies account indicates an error has occurred. This is because a business cannot have "negative" supplies. When such errors are discovered, they should be corrected. If the error has already been journalized and posted to the ledger, a **correcting journal entry** is normally prepared.

To illustrate, assume that on May 5 a $12,500 purchase of office equipment on account was incorrectly journalized and posted as a debit to Supplies and a credit to Accounts Payable for $12,500. This posting of the incorrect entry is shown in the following T accounts:

Incorrect:

Supplies	
12,500	

Accounts Payable	
	12,500

Before making a correcting journal entry, it is best to determine the debit(s) and credit(s) that should have been recorded. These are shown in the following T accounts:

Correct:

Office Equipment	
12,500	

Accounts Payable	
	12,500

Comparing the two sets of T accounts shows that the incorrect debit to Supplies may be corrected by debiting Office Equipment for $12,500 and crediting Supplies for $12,500. The following correcting entry is then journalized and posted:

Entry to Correct Error:

May	31	Office Equipment	18	12,500	
		Supplies	14		12,500
		To correct erroneous debit to Supplies on May 5. See invoice from Bell Office Equipment Co.			

Example Exercise 2-7 Correcting Entries

OBJ 4

The following errors took place in journalizing and posting transactions:

a. A withdrawal of $6,000 by Cheri Ramey, owner of the business, was recorded as a debit to Office Salaries Expense and a credit to Cash.

b. Utilities Expense of $4,500 paid for the current month was recorded as a debit to Miscellaneous Expense and a credit to Accounts Payable.

Journalize the entries to correct the errors. Omit explanations.

Follow My Example 2-7

a.	Cheri Ramey, Drawing	6,000	
	Office Salaries Expense		6,000
b.	Accounts Payable	4,500	
	Miscellaneous Expense		4,500
	Utilities Expense	4,500	
	Cash		4,500

Note: The first entry in (b) reverses the incorrect entry, and the second entry records the correct entry. These two entries could also be combined into one entry; however, preparing two entries will make it easier for someone later to understand what happened and why the entries were necessary.

Practice Exercises: PE 2-7A, PE 2-7B

Financial Analysis and Interpretation: Horizontal Analysis

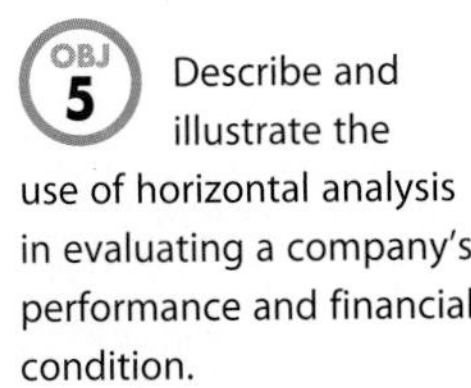
OBJ 5 Describe and illustrate the use of horizontal analysis in evaluating a company's performance and financial condition.

A single item in a financial statement, such as net income, is often useful in interpreting the financial performance of a company. However, a comparison with prior periods often makes the financial information even more useful. For example, comparing net income of the current period with the net income of the prior period will indicate whether the company's operating performance has improved.

In **horizontal analysis**, the amount of each item on a current financial statement is compared with the same item on an earlier statement. The increase or decrease in the *amount* of the item is computed together with the *percent* of increase or decrease. When two statements are being compared, the earlier statement is used as the base for computing the amount and the percent of change.

To illustrate, the horizontal analysis of two income statements for J. Holmes, Attorney-at-Law follows:

J. Holmes, Attorney-at-Law
Income Statements
For the Years Ended December 31

	Year 2	Year 1	Increase (Decrease) Amount	Percent
Fees earned	$187,500	$150,000	$37,500	25.0%*
Operating expenses:				
Wages expense	$ 60,000	$ 45,000	$15,000	33.3
Rent expense	15,000	12,000	3,000	25.0
Utilities expense	12,500	9,000	3,500	38.9
Supplies expense	2,700	3,000	(300)	(10.0)
Miscellaneous expense	2,300	1,800	500	27.8
Total operating expenses	$ 92,500	$ 70,800	$21,700	30.6
Net income	$ 95,000	$ 79,200	$15,800	19.9

*$37,500 ÷ $150,000

The horizontal analysis for J. Holmes, Attorney-at-Law, indicates both favorable and unfavorable trends. The increase in fees earned is a favorable trend, as is the decrease in supplies expense. Unfavorable trends include the increase in wages expense, utilities expense, and miscellaneous expense. These expenses increased the same as or faster than the increase in revenues, with total operating expenses increasing by 30.6%. Overall, net income increased by $15,800, or 19.9%, a favorable trend.

The significance of the various increases and decreases in the revenue and expense items should be investigated to see if operations could be further improved. For example, the increase in utilities expense of 38.9% was the result of renting additional office space for use by a part-time law student in performing paralegal services. This explains the increase in rent expense of 25.0% and the increase in wages expense of 33.3%. The increase in revenues of 25.0% reflects the fees generated by the new paralegal.

The preceding example illustrates how horizontal analysis can be useful in interpreting and analyzing the income statement. Horizontal analyses can also be performed for the balance sheet, the statement of owner's equity, and the statement of cash flows.

To illustrate, horizontal analysis for two recent years of **Apple Inc.**'s statements of cash flows (in millions) follows:

Apple Inc.
Statements of Cash Flows

	Year 2	Year 1	Increase (Decrease) Amount	Percent
Cash flows from operating activities	$ 50,856	$ 37,529	$13,327	35.5%
Cash flows used for investing activities	(48,227)	(40,419)	(7,808)	(19.3)
Cash flows from financing activities	(1,698)	1,444	(3,142)	(217.6)
Net increase (decrease) in cash	$ 931	$ (1,446)	$ 2,377	164.4
Beginning of the year balance of cash	9,815	11,261	(1,446)	(12.8)
End of the year balance of cash	$ 10,746	$ 9,815	$ 931	9.5

The horizontal analysis of cash flows for Apple Inc. indicates an increase in cash flows from operating activities of 35.5%, which is a favorable trend. At the same time, Apple increased the cash used in its investing activities by 19.3% and decreased the cash it received from financing activities by 217.6%. Overall, Apple had a 164.4% increase in cash for the year, which increased the end-of-the-year cash balance by 9.5%. In contrast, in the prior year Apple decreased its ending cash balance, which is the beginning cash balance of the current year, by 12.8%.

Example Exercise 2-8 Horizontal Analysis

OBJ 5

Two income statements for McCorkle Company follow:

McCorkle Company
Income Statements
For the Years Ended December 31

	2016	2015
Fees earned	$210,000	$175,000
Operating expenses	172,500	150,000
Net income	$ 37,500	$ 25,000

Prepare a horizontal analysis of McCorkle Company's income statements.

Follow My Example 2-8

McCorkle Company
Income Statements
For the Years Ended December 31

			Increase (Decrease)	
	2016	2015	Amount	Percent
Fees earned	$210,000	$175,000	$35,000	20%
Operating expenses	172,500	150,000	22,500	15
Net income	$ 37,500	$ 25,000	$12,500	50

Practice Exercises: PE 2-8A, PE 2-8B

At a Glance 2

Describe the characteristics of an account and a chart of accounts.

Key Points The simplest form of an account, a T account, has three parts: (1) a title, which is the name of the item recorded in the account; (2) a left side, called the debit side; and (3) a right side, called the credit side. Periodically, the debits in an account are added, the credits in the account are added, and the balance of the account is determined.

The system of accounts that make up a ledger is called a chart of accounts.

Learning Outcomes	Example Exercises	Practice Exercises
• Record transactions in T accounts.		
• Determine the balance of a T account.		
• Prepare a chart of accounts for a proprietorship.		

Describe and illustrate journalizing transactions using the double-entry accounting system.

Key Points Transactions are initially entered in a record called a journal. The rules of debit and credit for recording increases or decreases in accounts are shown in Exhibit 3. Each transaction is recorded so that the sum of the debits is always equal to the sum of the credits. The normal balance of an account is indicated by the side of the account (debit or credit) that receives the increases.

Learning Outcomes	Example Exercises	Practice Exercises
• Indicate the normal balance of an account.	EE2-1	PE2-1A, 2-1B
• Journalize transactions using the rules of debit and credit.	EE2-2	PE2-2A, 2-2B

Describe and illustrate the journalizing and posting of transactions to accounts.

Key Points Transactions are journalized and posted to the ledger using the rules of debit and credit. The debits and credits for each journal entry are posted to the accounts in the order in which they occur in the journal.

Learning Outcomes	Example Exercises	Practice Exercises
• Journalize transactions using the rules of debit and credit.	EE2-3	PE2-3A, 2-3B
• Given other account data, determine the missing amount of an account entry.	EE2-4	PE2-4A, 2-4B
• Post journal entries to a standard account.	EE2-5	PE2-5A, 2-5B
• Post journal entries to a T account.		

Prepare an unadjusted trial balance and explain how it can be used to discover errors.

Key Points A trial balance is prepared by listing the accounts from the ledger and their balances. The totals of the Debit column and Credit column of the trial balance must be equal. If the two totals are not equal, an error has occurred. Errors may occur even though the trial balance totals are equal. Such errors may require a correcting journal entry.

Learning Outcomes	Example Exercises	Practice Exercises
• Prepare an unadjusted trial balance.	EE2-6	PE2-6A, 2-6B
• Discover errors that cause unequal totals in the trial balance.	EE2-7	PE2-7A, 2-7B
• Prepare correcting journal entries for various errors.		

Describe and illustrate the use of horizontal analysis in evaluating a company's performance and financial condition.

Key Points In horizontal analysis, the amount of each item on a current financial statement is compared with the same item on an earlier statement. The increase or decrease in the *amount* of the item is computed, together with the *percent* of increase or decrease. When two statements are being compared, the earlier statement is used as the base for computing the amount and the percent of change.

Learning Outcomes	Example Exercises	Practice Exercises
• Describe horizontal analysis.		
• Prepare a horizontal analysis report of a financial statement.	EE2-8	PE2-8A, 2-8B

Key Terms

account (52)
account receivable (65)
assets (54)
balance of the account (53)
capital account (54)
chart of accounts (54)
correcting journal entry (72)
credit (53)
debit (53)
double-entry accounting system (55)
drawing (54)
expenses (55)
horizontal analysis (73)
journal (57)
journal entry (58)
journalizing (58)
ledger (54)
liabilities (54)
normal balance of an account (56)
owner's equity (54)
posting (61)
revenues (54)
rules of debit and credit (55)
slide (71)
T account (52)
transposition (71)
trial balance (70)
unadjusted trial balance (70)
unearned revenue (63)

Illustrative Problem

J. F. Outz, M.D., has been practicing as a cardiologist for three years. During April 2015, Outz completed the following transactions in her practice of cardiology:

Apr. 1. Paid office rent for April, $800.

3. Purchased equipment on account, $2,100.

5. Received cash on account from patients, $3,150.

8. Purchased X-ray film and other supplies on account, $245.

9. One of the items of equipment purchased on April 3 was defective. It was returned with the permission of the supplier, who agreed to reduce the account for the amount charged for the item, $325.

12. Paid cash to creditors on account, $1,250.

Apr. 17. Paid cash for renewal of a six-month property insurance policy, $370.

20. Discovered that the balances of the cash account and the accounts payable account as of April 1 were overstated by $200. A payment of that amount to a creditor in March had not been recorded. Journalize the $200 payment as of April 20.

24. Paid cash for laboratory analysis, $545.

27. Paid cash from business bank account for personal and family expenses, $1,250.

30. Recorded the cash received in payment of services (on a cash basis) to patients during April, $1,720.

30. Paid salaries of receptionist and nurses, $1,725.

30. Paid various utility expenses, $360.

30. Recorded fees charged to patients on account for services performed in April, $5,145.

30. Paid miscellaneous expenses, $132.

Outz's account titles, numbers, and balances as of April 1 (all normal balances) are listed as follows: Cash, 11, $4,123; Accounts Receivable, 12, $6,725; Supplies, 13, $290; Prepaid Insurance, 14, $465; Equipment, 18, $19,745; Accounts Payable, 22, $765; J. F. Outz, Capital, 31, $30,583; J. F. Outz, Drawing, 32, $0; Professional Fees, 41, $0; Salary Expense, 51, $0; Rent Expense, 53, $0; Laboratory Expense, 55, $0; Utilities Expense, 56, $0; Miscellaneous Expense, 59, $0.

Instructions

1. Open a ledger of standard four-column accounts for Dr. Outz as of April 1. Enter the balances in the appropriate balance columns and place a check mark (✓) in the Posting Reference column. (*Hint:* Verify the equality of the debit and credit balances in the ledger before proceeding with the next instruction.)
2. Journalize each transaction in a two-column journal.
3. Post the journal to the ledger, extending the month-end balances to the appropriate balance columns after each posting.
4. Prepare an unadjusted trial balance as of April 30.

Solution 1., 2., and 3.

Journal — Page *27*

Date	Description	Post. Ref.	Debit	Credit
2015				
Apr. 1	Rent Expense	53	800	
	Cash	11		800
	Paid office rent for April.			
3	Equipment	18	2,100	
	Accounts Payable	22		2,100
	Purchased equipment on account.			
5	Cash	11	3,150	
	Accounts Receivable	12		3,150
	Received cash on account.			
8	Supplies	13	245	
	Accounts Payable	22		245
	Purchased supplies.			
9	Accounts Payable	22	325	
	Equipment	18		325
	Returned defective equipment.			
12	Accounts Payable	22	1,250	
	Cash	11		1,250
	Paid creditors on account.			
17	Prepaid Insurance	14	370	
	Cash	11		370
	Renewed six-month property policy.			
20	Accounts Payable	22	200	
	Cash	11		200
	Recorded March payment to creditor.			

Journal — Page *28*

Date	Description	Post. Ref.	Debit	Credit
2015				
Apr. 24	Laboratory Expense	55	545	
	Cash	11		545
	Paid for laboratory analysis.			
27	J. F. Outz, Drawing	32	1,250	
	Cash	11		1,250
	J. F. Outz withdrew cash for personal use.			
30	Cash	11	1,720	
	Professional Fees	41		1,720
	Received fees from patients.			
30	Salary Expense	51	1,725	
	Cash	11		1,725
	Paid salaries.			
30	Utilities Expense	56	360	
	Cash	11		360
	Paid utilities.			
30	Accounts Receivable	12	5,145	
	Professional Fees	41		5,145
	Recorded fees earned on account.			
30	Miscellaneous Expense	59	132	
	Cash	11		132
	Paid expenses.			

Account *Cash* — Account No. *11*

Date	Item	Post. Ref.	Debit	Credit	Balance Debit	Balance Credit
2015						
Apr. 1	Balance	✓			4,123	
1		27		800	3,323	
5		27	3,150		6,473	
12		27		1,250	5,223	
17		27		370	4,853	
20		27		200	4,653	
24		28		545	4,108	
27		28		1,250	2,858	
30		28	1,720		4,578	
30		28		1,725	2,853	
30		28		360	2,493	
30		28		132	2,361	

Account *Accounts Receivable* — Account No. *12*

Date	Item	Post. Ref.	Debit	Credit	Balance Debit	Balance Credit
2015						
Apr. 1	Balance	✓			6,725	
5		27		3,150	3,575	
30		28	5,145		8,720	

Account *Supplies* — Account No. *13*

Date	Item	Post. Ref.	Debit	Credit	Balance Debit	Balance Credit
2015						
Apr. 1	Balance	✓			290	
8		27	245		535	

Account *Prepaid Insurance* — Account No. *14*

Date	Item	Post. Ref.	Debit	Credit	Balance Debit	Balance Credit
2015						
Apr. 1	Balance	✓			465	
17		27	370		835	

Account *Equipment* — Account No. *18*

Date	Item	Post. Ref.	Debit	Credit	Balance Debit	Balance Credit
2015						
Apr. 1	Balance	✓			19,745	
3		27	2,100		21,845	
9		27		325	21,520	

Account *Accounts Payable* — Account No. *22*

Date	Item	Post. Ref.	Debit	Credit	Balance Debit	Balance Credit
2015						
Apr. 1	Balance	✓				765
3		27		2,100		2,865
8		27		245		3,110
9		27	325			2,785
12		27	1,250			1,535
20		27	200			1,335

Account *J. F. Outz, Capital* — Account No. *31*

Date	Item	Post. Ref.	Debit	Credit	Balance Debit	Balance Credit
2015						
Apr. 1	Balance	✓				30,583

Account *J. F. Qutz, Drawing* — Account No. *32*

Date	Item	Post. Ref.	Debit	Credit	Balance Debit	Balance Credit
2015						
Apr. 27		28	1,250		1,250	

Account *Professional Fees* — Account No. *41*

Date	Item	Post. Ref.	Debit	Credit	Balance Debit	Balance Credit
2015						
Apr. 30		28		1,720		1,720
30		28		5,145		6,865

Account *Salary Expense* — Account No. *51*

Date	Item	Post. Ref.	Debit	Credit	Balance Debit	Balance Credit
2015						
Apr. 30		28	1,725		1,725	

Account *Rent Expense* — Account No. *53*

Date	Item	Post. Ref.	Debit	Credit	Balance Debit	Balance Credit
2015						
Apr. 1		27	800		800	

Account *Laboratory Expense* — Account No. *55*

Date	Item	Post. Ref.	Debit	Credit	Balance Debit	Balance Credit
2015						
Apr. 24		28	545		545	

Account *Utilities Expense* — Account No. *56*

Date	Item	Post. Ref.	Debit	Credit	Balance Debit	Balance Credit
2015						
Apr. 30		28	360		360	

Account *Miscellaneous Expense* — Account No. *59*

Date	Item	Post. Ref.	Debit	Credit	Balance Debit	Balance Credit
2015						
Apr. 30		28	132		132	

4.

J. F. Outz, M.D. Unadjusted Trial Balance April 30, 2015	Debit Balances	Credit Balances
Cash	2,361	
Accounts Receivable	8,720	
Supplies	535	
Prepaid Insurance	835	
Equipment	21,520	
Accounts Payable		1,335
J. F. Outz, Capital		30,583
J. F. Outz, Drawing	1,250	
Professional Fees		6,865
Salary Expense	1,725	
Rent Expense	800	
Laboratory Expense	545	
Utilities Expense	360	
Miscellaneous Expense	132	
	38,783	38,783

Discussion Questions

1. What is the difference between an account and a ledger?
2. Do the terms *debit* and *credit* signify increase or decrease or can they signify either? Explain.
3. McIntyre Company adheres to a policy of depositing all cash receipts in a bank account and making all payments by check. The cash account as of December 31 has a credit balance of $1,850, and there is no undeposited cash on hand. (a) Assuming no errors occurred during journalizing or posting, what caused this unusual balance? (b) Is the $1,850 credit balance in the cash account an asset, a liability, owner's equity, a revenue, or an expense?
4. eCatalog Services Company performed services in October for a specific customer, for a fee of $7,890. Payment was received the following November. (a) Was the revenue earned in October or November? (b) What accounts should be debited and credited in (1) October and (2) November?
5. If the two totals of a trial balance are equal, does it mean that there are no errors in the accounting records? Explain.
6. Assume that a trial balance is prepared with an account balance of $8,900 listed as $9,800 and an account balance of $1,000 listed as $100. Identify the transposition and the slide.
7. Assume that when a purchase of supplies of $2,650 for cash was recorded, both the debit and the credit were journalized and posted as $2,560. (a) Would this error cause the trial balance to be out of balance? (b) Would the trial balance be out of balance if the $2,650 entry had been journalized correctly but the credit to Cash had been posted as $2,560?
8. Assume that Muscular Consulting erroneously recorded the payment of $7,500 of owner withdrawals as a debit to Salary Expense. (a) How would this error affect the equality of the trial balance? (b) How would this error affect the income statement, statement of owner's equity, and balance sheet?
9. Assume that Sunshine Realty Co. borrowed $300,000 from Columbia First Bank and Trust. In recording the transaction, Sunshine erroneously recorded the receipt as a debit to Cash, $300,000, and a credit to Fees Earned, $300,000. (a) How would this error affect the equality of the trial balance? (b) How would this error affect the income statement, statement of owner's equity, and balance sheet?
10. Checking accounts are one of the most common forms of deposits for banks. Assume that Surety Storage has a checking account at Ada Savings Bank. What type of account (asset, liability, owner's equity, revenue, expense, drawing) does the account balance of $11,375 represent from the viewpoint of (a) Surety Storage and (b) Ada Savings Bank?

Practice Exercises

SHOW ME HOW

EE 2-1 p. 57

PE 2-1A Rules of debit and credit and normal balances **OBJ. 2**

State for each account whether it is likely to have (a) debit entries only, (b) credit entries only, or (c) both debit and credit entries. Also, indicate its normal balance.

1. Accounts Receivable
2. Commissions Earned
3. Notes Payable
4. Patricia Mayer, Capital
5. Rent Revenue
6. Wages Expense

SHOW ME HOW

EE 2-1 p. 57

PE 2-1B Rules of debit and credit and normal balances **OBJ. 2**

State for each account whether it is likely to have (a) debit entries only, (b) credit entries only, or (c) both debit and credit entries. Also, indicate its normal balance.

1. Accounts Payable
2. Cash
3. Del Robinson, Drawing
4. Miscellaneous Expense
5. Insurance Expense
6. Fees Earned

SHOW ME HOW

EE 2-2 p. 61

PE 2-2A Journal entry for asset purchase **OBJ. 2**

Prepare a journal entry for the purchase of office equipment on October 27 for $32,750, paying $6,550 cash and the remainder on account.

SHOW ME HOW

EE 2-2 p. 61

PE 2-2B Journal entry for asset purchase **OBJ. 2**

Prepare a journal entry for the purchase of office supplies on September 30 for $2,500, paying $800 cash and the remainder on account.

SHOW ME HOW

EE 2-3 p. 65

PE 2-3A Journal entry for fees earned **OBJ. 3**

Prepare a journal entry on March 16 for fees earned on account, $9,450.

SHOW ME HOW

EE 2-3 p. 65

PE 2-3B Journal entry for fees earned **OBJ. 3**

Prepare a journal entry on August 13 for cash received for services rendered, $9,000.

SHOW ME HOW

EE 2-4 p. 68

PE 2-4A Journal entry for owner's withdrawal **OBJ. 3**

Prepare a journal entry on December 23 for the withdrawal of $20,000 by Steve Buckley for personal use.

SHOW ME HOW

EE 2-4 p. 68

PE 2-4B Journal entry for owner's withdrawal **OBJ. 3**

Prepare a journal entry on June 30 for the withdrawal of $11,500 by Dawn Pierce for personal use.

EE 2-5 *p. 68*

PE 2-5A Missing amount from an account — OBJ. 3

On July 1, the cash account balance was $37,450. During July, cash payments totaled $115,860 and the July 31 balance was $29,600. Determine the cash receipts during July.

EE 2-5 *p. 68*

PE 2-5B Missing amount from an account — OBJ. 3

On August 1, the supplies account balance was $1,025. During August, supplies of $3,110 were purchased, and $1,324 of supplies were on hand as of August 31. Determine supplies expense for August.

EE 2-6 *p. 72*

PE 2-6A Trial balance errors — OBJ. 4

For each of the following errors, considered individually, indicate whether the error would cause the trial balance totals to be unequal. If the error would cause the trial balance totals to be unequal, indicate whether the debit or credit total is higher and by how much.

a. The payment of an insurance premium of $5,400 for a three-year policy was debited to Prepaid Insurance for $5,400 and credited to Cash for $4,500.

b. A payment of $270 on account was debited to Accounts Payable for $720 and credited to Cash for $720.

c. A purchase of supplies on account for $1,600 was debited to Supplies for $1,600 and debited to Accounts Payable for $1,600.

EE 2-6 *p. 72*

PE 2-6B Trial balance errors — OBJ. 4

For each of the following errors, considered individually, indicate whether the error would cause the trial balance totals to be unequal. If the error would cause the trial balance totals to be unequal, indicate whether the debit or credit total is higher and by how much.

a. The payment of cash for the purchase of office equipment of $12,900 was debited to Land for $12,900 and credited to Cash for $12,900.

b. The payment of $1,840 on account was debited to Accounts Payable for $184 and credited to Cash for $1,840.

c. The receipt of cash on account of $3,800 was recorded as a debit to Cash for $8,300 and a credit to Accounts Receivable for $3,800.

EE 2-7 *p. 73*

PE 2-7A Correcting entries — OBJ. 4

The following errors took place in journalizing and posting transactions:

a. Rent expense of $4,650 paid for the current month was recorded as a debit to Miscellaneous Expense and a credit to Rent Expense.

b. The payment of $3,700 from a customer on account was recorded as a debit to Cash and a credit to Accounts Payable.

Journalize the entries to correct the errors. Omit explanations.

EE 2-7 *p. 73*

PE 2-7B Correcting entries — OBJ. 4

The following errors took place in journalizing and posting transactions:

a. The receipt of $8,400 for services rendered was recorded as a debit to Accounts Receivable and a credit to Fees Earned.

b. The purchase of supplies of $2,500 on account was recorded as a debit to Office Equipment and a credit to Supplies.

Journalize the entries to correct the errors. Omit explanations.

EE 2-8 *p. 75*

PE 2-8A Horizontal analysis — OBJ. 5

Two income statements for Fuller Company follow:

(Continued)

SHOW ME HOW

Fuller Company Income Statements For Years Ended December 31		
	2016	2015
Fees earned	$680,000	$850,000
Operating expenses	541,875	637,500
Net income	$138,125	$212,500

Prepare a horizontal analysis of Fuller Company's income statements.

EE 2-8 p. 75

PE 2-8B Horizontal analysis OBJ. 5

SHOW ME HOW

Two income statements for Paragon Company follow:

Paragon Company Income Statements For Years Ended December 31		
	2016	2015
Fees earned	$1,416,000	$1,200,000
Operating expenses	1,044,000	900,000
Net income	$ 372,000	$ 300,000

Prepare a horizontal analysis of Paragon Company's income statements.

Exercises

EX 2-1 Chart of accounts OBJ. 1

The following accounts appeared in recent financial statements of **Delta Air Lines**:

Accounts Payable	Flight Equipment
Advanced Payments for Equipment	Frequent Flyer (Obligations)
Air Traffic Liability	Fuel Inventory
Aircraft Fuel (Expense)	Landing Fees (Expense)
Aircraft Maintenance (Expense)	Parts and Supplies Inventories
Aircraft Rent (Expense)	Passenger Commissions (Expense)
Cargo Revenue	Passenger Revenue
Cash	Prepaid Expenses
Contract Carrier Arrangements (Expense)	Taxes Payable

Identify each account as either a balance sheet account or an income statement account. For each balance sheet account, identify it as an asset, a liability, or owner's equity. For each income statement account, identify it as a revenue or an expense.

EX 2-2 Chart of accounts OBJ. 1

Innerscape Interiors is owned and operated by Jackie Vargo, an interior decorator. In the ledger of Innerscape Interiors, the first digit of the account number indicates its major account classification (1—assets, 2—liabilities, 3—owner's equity, 4—revenues, 5—expenses). The second digit of the account number indicates the specific account within each of the preceding major account classifications.

Match each account number with its most likely account in the list that follows. The account numbers are 11, 12, 13, 21, 31, 32, 41, 51, 52, and 53.

Accounts Payable	Jackie Vargo, Drawing
Accounts Receivable	Land
Cash	Miscellaneous Expense
Fees Earned	Supplies Expense
Jackie Vargo, Capital	Wages Expense

EX 2-3 Chart of accounts OBJ. 1

LeadCo School is a newly organized business that teaches people how to inspire and influence others. The list of accounts to be opened in the general ledger is as follows:

Accounts Payable	Miscellaneous Expense
Accounts Receivable	Prepaid Insurance
Cash	Rent Expense
Equipment	Supplies
Fees Earned	Supplies Expense
Ivy Bishop, Capital	Unearned Rent
Ivy Bishop, Drawing	Wages Expense

List the accounts in the order in which they should appear in the ledger of LeadCo School and assign account numbers. Each account number is to have two digits: the first digit is to indicate the major classification (1 for assets, etc.), and the second digit is to identify the specific account within each major classification (11 for Cash, etc.).

EX 2-4 Rules of debit and credit **OBJ. 1, 2**

The following table summarizes the rules of debit and credit. For each of the items (a) through (l), indicate whether the proper answer is a debit or a credit.

	Increase	Decrease	Normal Balance
Balance sheet accounts:			
Asset	(a)	(b)	Debit
Liability	(c)	Debit	(d)
Owner's equity:			
Capital	Credit	(e)	(f)
Drawing	(g)	(h)	(i)
Income statement accounts:			
Revenue	(j)	(k)	Credit
Expense	(l)	Credit	Debit

EX 2-5 Normal entries for accounts **OBJ. 2**

During the month, Gates Labs Co. has a substantial number of transactions affecting each of the following accounts. State for each account whether it is likely to have (a) debit entries only, (b) credit entries only, or (c) both debit and credit entries.

1. Accounts Payable
2. Accounts Receivable
3. Cash
4. Fees Earned
5. Insurance Expense
6. Miriam Ramsey, Drawing
7. Utilities Expense

EX 2-6 Normal balances of accounts **OBJ. 1, 2**

Identify each of the following accounts of Kaiser Services Co. as asset, liability, owner's equity, revenue, or expense, and state in each case whether the normal balance is a debit or a credit:

a. Accounts Payable
b. Accounts Receivable
c. Bobby Lund, Capital
d. Bobby Lund, Drawing
e. Cash
f. Fees Earned
g. Office Equipment
h. Rent Expense
i. Supplies
j. Wages Expense

EX 2-7 Transactions **OBJ. 2**

SHOW ME HOW

Jardine Consulting Co. has the following accounts in its ledger: Cash; Accounts Receivable; Supplies; Office Equipment; Accounts Payable; Cammy Jardine, Capital; Cammy Jardine, Drawing; Fees Earned; Rent Expense; Advertising Expense; Utilities Expense; Miscellaneous Expense.

Journalize the following selected transactions for March 2016 in a two-column journal. Journal entry explanations may be omitted.

(Continued)

Mar. 1. Paid rent for the month, $2,500.
3. Paid advertising expense, $675.
5. Paid cash for supplies, $1,250.
6. Purchased office equipment on account, $9,500.
10. Received cash from customers on account, $16,550.
15. Paid creditor on account, $3,180.
27. Paid cash for repairs to office equipment, $540.
30. Paid telephone bill for the month, $375.
31. Fees earned and billed to customers for the month, $49,770.
31. Paid electricity bill for the month, $830.
31. Withdrew cash for personal use, $1,750.

EX 2-8 Journalizing and posting **OBJ. 2, 3**

SHOW ME HOW

On January 7, 2016, Captec Company purchased $4,175 of supplies on account. In Captec Company's chart of accounts, the supplies account is No. 15, and the accounts payable account is No. 21.

a. Journalize the January 7, 2016, transaction on page 33 of Captec Company's two-column journal. Include an explanation of the entry.

b. Prepare a four-column account for Supplies. Enter a debit balance of $2,200 as of January 1, 2016. Place a check mark (✓) in the Posting Reference column.

c. Prepare a four-column account for Accounts Payable. Enter a credit balance of $18,430 as of January 1, 2016. Place a check mark (✓) in the Posting Reference column.

d. Post the January 7, 2016, transaction to the accounts.

e. Do the rules of debit and credit apply to all companies?

EX 2-9 Transactions and T accounts **OBJ. 2, 3**

SHOW ME HOW

The following selected transactions were completed during August of the current year:

1. Billed customers for fees earned, $73,900.
2. Purchased supplies on account, $1,960.
3. Received cash from customers on account, $62,770.
4. Paid creditors on account, $820.

a. Journalize these transactions in a two-column journal, using the appropriate number to identify the transactions. Journal entry explanations may be omitted.

b. Post the entries prepared in (a) to the following T accounts: Cash, Supplies, Accounts Receivable, Accounts Payable, Fees Earned. To the left of each amount posted in the accounts, place the appropriate number to identify the transactions.

c. Assume that the unadjusted trial balance on August 31 shows a credit balance for Accounts Receivable. Does this credit balance mean an error has occurred?

EX 2-10 Cash account balance **OBJ. 1, 2, 3**

During the month, Warwick Co. received $515,000 in cash and paid out $375,000 in cash.

a. Do the data indicate that Warwick Co. had net income of $140,000 during the month? Explain.

b. If the balance of the cash account is $200,000 at the end of the month, what was the cash balance at the beginning of the month?

EX 2-11 Account balances **OBJ. 1, 2, 3**

✓ c. $238,050

SHOW ME HOW

a. During February, $186,500 was paid to creditors on account, and purchases on account were $201,400. Assuming the February 28 balance of Accounts Payable was $59,900, determine the account balance on February 1.

b. On October 1, the accounts receivable account balance was $115,800. During October, $449,600 was collected from customers on account. Assuming the October 31 balance was $130,770 determine the fees billed to customers on account during October.

c. On April 1, the cash account balance was $46,220. During April, cash receipts totaled $248,600 and the April 30 balance was $56,770. Determine the cash payments made during April.

SHOW ME HOW

EX 2-12 Capital account balance — OBJ. 1, 2

As of January 1, Terrace Waters, Capital, had a credit balance of $314,000. During the year, withdrawals totaled $10,000, and the business incurred a net loss of $320,000.

a. Compute the balance of Terrace Waters, Capital, as of the end of the year.

b. Assuming that there have been no recording errors, will the balance sheet prepared at December 31 balance? Explain.

EX 2-13 Identifying transactions — OBJ. 1, 2

Wyoming Tours Co. is a travel agency. The nine transactions recorded by Wyoming Tours during June 2016, its first month of operations, are indicated in the following T accounts:

Cash

	Debit		Credit
(1)	40,000	(2)	2,500
(7)	8,700	(3)	4,000
		(4)	4,850
		(6)	5,500
		(9)	3,000

Equipment

	Debit		Credit
(3)	14,500		

Lorene Jones, Drawing

	Debit		Credit
(9)	3,000		

Accounts Receivable

	Debit		Credit
(5)	13,800	(7)	8,700

Accounts Payable

	Debit		Credit
(6)	5,500	(3)	10,500

Service Revenue

	Debit		Credit
		(5)	13,800

Supplies

	Debit		Credit
(2)	2,500	(8)	1,100

Lorene Jones, Capital

	Debit		Credit
		(1)	40,000

Operating Expenses

	Debit		Credit
(4)	4,850		
(8)	1,100		

Indicate for each debit and each credit: (a) whether an asset, liability, owner's equity, drawing, revenue, or expense account was affected and (b) whether the account was increased (+) or decreased (–). Present your answers in the following form, with transaction (1) given as an example:

	Account Debited		Account Credited	
Transaction	**Type**	**Effect**	**Type**	**Effect**
(1)	asset	+	owner's equity	+

EX 2-14 Journal entries — OBJ. 1, 2

Based upon the T accounts in Exercise 2-13, prepare the nine journal entries from which the postings were made. Journal entry explanations may be omitted.

✔ (a) Total of Debit column: $58,800

EX 2-15 Trial balance — OBJ. 4

Based upon the data presented in Exercise 2-13, (a) prepare an unadjusted trial balance, listing the accounts in their proper order. (b) Based upon the unadjusted trial balance, determine the net income or net loss.

✔ Total of Credit column: $925,000

EX 2-16 Trial balance — OBJ. 4

The accounts in the ledger of Hickory Furniture Company as of December 31, 2016, are listed in alphabetical order as follows. All accounts have normal balances. The balance of the cash account has been intentionally omitted.

(Continued)

Accounts Payable	$ 42,770	Notes Payable	$ 50,000
Accounts Receivable	116,900	Prepaid Insurance	21,600
Cash	?	Rent Expense	48,000
Elaine Wells, Capital	75,000	Supplies	4,275
Elaine Wells, Drawing	24,000	Supplies Expense	6,255
Fees Earned	745,230	Unearned Rent	12,000
Insurance Expense	3,600	Utilities Expense	26,850
Land	50,000	Wages Expense	580,700
Miscellaneous Expense	9,500		

Prepare an unadjusted trial balance, listing the accounts in their normal order and inserting the missing figure for cash.

EX 2-17 Effect of errors on trial balance **OBJ. 4**

Indicate which of the following errors, each considered individually, would cause the trial balance totals to be unequal:

a. A fee of $21,000 earned and due from a client was not debited to Accounts Receivable or credited to a revenue account, because the cash had not been received.

b. A receipt of $11,300 from an account receivable was journalized and posted as a debit of $11,300 to Cash and a credit of $11,300 to Fees Earned.

c. A payment of $4,950 to a creditor was posted as a debit of $4,950 to Accounts Payable and a debit of $4,950 to Cash.

d. A payment of $5,000 for equipment purchased was posted as a debit of $500 to Equipment and a credit of $500 to Cash.

e. Payment of a cash withdrawal of $19,000 was journalized and posted as a debit of $1,900 to Salary Expense and a credit of $19,000 to Cash.

Indicate which of the preceding errors would require a correcting entry.

EX 2-18 Errors in trial balance **OBJ. 4**

✔ Total of Credit column: $525,000

The following preliminary unadjusted trial balance of Ranger Co., a sports ticket agency, does not balance:

Ranger Co.
Unadjusted Trial Balance
August 31, 2016

	Debit Balances	Credit Balances
Cash	77,600	
Accounts Receivable	37,750	
Prepaid Insurance		12,000
Equipment	19,000	
Accounts Payable		29,100
Unearned Rent		10,800
Carmen Meeks, Capital	110,000	
Carmen Meeks, Drawing	13,000	
Service Revenue		385,000
Wages Expense		213,000
Advertising Expense	16,350	
Miscellaneous Expense		18,400
	273,700	668,300

When the ledger and other records are reviewed, you discover the following: (1) the debits and credits in the cash account total $77,600 and $62,100, respectively; (2) a billing of $9,000 to a customer on account was not posted to the accounts receivable account; (3) a payment of $4,500 made to a creditor on account was not posted to the accounts payable account; (4) the balance of the unearned rent account is $5,400; (5) the correct balance of the equipment account is $190,000; and (6) each account has a normal balance.

Prepare a corrected unadjusted trial balance.

EX 2-19 Effect of errors on trial balance **OBJ. 4**

The following errors occurred in posting from a two-column journal:

1. A credit of $6,000 to Accounts Payable was not posted.
2. An entry debiting Accounts Receivable and crediting Fees Earned for $5,300 was not posted.
3. A debit of $2,700 to Accounts Payable was posted as a credit.
4. A debit of $480 to Supplies was posted twice.
5. A debit of $3,600 to Cash was posted to Miscellaneous Expense.
6. A credit of $780 to Cash was posted as $870.
7. A debit of $12,620 to Wages Expense was posted as $12,260.

Considering each case individually (i.e., assuming that no other errors had occurred), indicate: (a) by "yes" or "no" whether the trial balance would be out of balance; (b) if answer to (a) is "yes," the amount by which the trial balance totals would differ; and (c) whether the Debit or Credit column of the trial balance would have the larger total. Answers should be presented in the following form, with error (1) given as an example:

Error	(a) Out of Balance	(b) Difference	(c) Larger Total
1.	yes	$6,000	debit

EX 2-20 Errors in trial balance **OBJ. 4**

✔ Total of Credit column: $1,040,000

SHOW ME HOW

Identify the errors in the following trial balance. All accounts have normal balances.

Mascot Co.
Unadjusted Trial Balance
For the Month Ending July 31, 2016

	Debit Balances	Credit Balances
Cash	36,000	
Accounts Receivable		112,600
Prepaid Insurance	18,000	
Equipment	375,000	
Accounts Payable	53,300	
Salaries Payable		7,500
Samuel Parson, Capital		297,200
Samuel Parson, Drawing		17,000
Service Revenue		682,000
Salary Expense	396,800	
Advertising Expense		73,000
Miscellaneous Expense	11,600	
	1,189,300	1,189,300

EX 2-21 Entries to correct errors **OBJ. 4**

SHOW ME HOW

The following errors took place in journalizing and posting transactions:

a. Insurance of $18,000 paid for the current year was recorded as a debit to Insurance Expense and a credit to Prepaid Insurance.

b. A withdrawal of $10,000 by Brian Phillips, owner of the business, was recorded as a debit to Wages Expense and a credit to Cash.

Journalize the entries to correct the errors. Omit explanations.

EX 2-22 Entries to correct errors **OBJ. 4**

SHOW ME HOW

The following errors took place in journalizing and posting transactions:

a. Cash of $8,800 received on account was recorded as a debit to Fees Earned and a credit to Cash.

b. A $1,760 purchase of supplies for cash was recorded as a debit to Supplies Expense and a credit to Accounts Payable.

Journalize the entries to correct the errors. Omit explanations.

SHOW ME HOW

EX 2-23 Horizontal analysis of income statement **OBJ. 5**

The following data (in millions) are taken from the financial statements of **Target Corporation**:

	Recent Year	Prior Year
Revenue	$69,865	$67,390
Operating expenses	64,543	62,138
Operating income	$ 5,322	$ 5,252

a. For Target Corporation, determine the amount of change in millions and the percent of change (round to one decimal place) from the prior year to the recent year for:

1. Revenue
2. Operating expenses
3. Operating income

b. What conclusions can you draw from your analysis of the revenue and the total operating expenses?

EX 2-24 Horizontal analysis of income statement **OBJ. 5**

The following data (in millions) were taken from the financial statements of **Walmart Stores, Inc**:

	Recent Year	Prior Year
Revenue	$446,950	$421,849
Operating expenses	420,392	396,307
Operating income	$ 26,558	$ 25,542

a. For Walmart Stores, Inc., determine the amount of change in millions and the percent of change (round to one decimal place) from the prior year to the recent year for:

1. Revenue
2. Operating expenses
3. Operating income

b. Comment on the results of your horizontal analysis in part (a).

c. Based upon Exercise 2-23, compare and comment on the operating results of Target and Walmart for the recent year.

Problems: Series A

PR 2-1A Entries into T accounts and trial balance **OBJ. 1, 2, 3, 4**

✔ 3. Total of Debit column: $80,650

Kimberly Manis, an architect, opened an office on January 1, 2016. During the month, she completed the following transactions connected with her professional practice:

a. Transferred cash from a personal bank account to an account to be used for the business, $18,000.
b. Paid January rent for office and workroom, $1,950.
c. Purchased used automobile for $28,500, paying $5,700 cash and giving a note payable for the remainder.
d. Purchased office and computer equipment on account, $4,500.
e. Paid cash for supplies, $1,875.
f. Paid cash for annual insurance policies, $3,600.
g. Received cash from client for plans delivered, $13,650.
h. Paid cash for miscellaneous expenses, $2,600.
i. Paid cash to creditors on account, $3,000.
j. Paid installment due on note payable, $950.
k. Received invoice for blueprint service, due in February, $3,750.
l. Recorded fees earned on plans delivered, payment to be received in February, $21,900.
m. Paid salary of assistants, $4,100.
n. Paid gas, oil, and repairs on automobile for January, $1,300.

Instructions

1. Record these transactions directly in the following T accounts, without journalizing: Cash; Accounts Receivable; Supplies; Prepaid Insurance; Automobiles; Equipment; Notes Payable; Accounts Payable; Kimberly Manis, Capital; Professional Fees; Salary Expense; Blueprint Expense; Rent Expense; Automobile Expense; Miscellaneous Expense. To the left of the amount entered in the accounts, place the appropriate letter to identify the transaction.
2. Determine account balances of the T accounts. Accounts containing a single entry only (such as Prepaid Insurance) do not need a balance.
3. Prepare an unadjusted trial balance for Kimberly Manis, Architect, as of January 31, 2016.
4. Determine the net income or net loss for January.

PR 2-2A Journal entries and trial balance

OBJ. 1, 2, 3, 4

✔ 4. c. $4,550

General Ledger

SHOW ME HOW

On August 1, 2016, Bill Hudson established Heritage Realty, which completed the following transactions during the month:

a. Bill Hudson transferred cash from a personal bank account to an account to be used for the business, $30,000.
b. Paid rent on office and equipment for the month, $3,250.
c. Purchased supplies on account, $2,150.
d. Paid creditor on account, $875.
e. Earned sales commissions, receiving cash, $14,440.
f. Paid automobile expenses (including rental charge) for month, $1,580, and miscellaneous expenses, $650.
g. Paid office salaries, $3,000.
h. Determined that the cost of supplies used was $1,300.
i. Withdrew cash for personal use, $2,500.

Instructions

1. Journalize entries for transactions (a) through (i), using the following account titles: Cash; Supplies; Accounts Payable; Bill Hudson, Capital; Bill Hudson, Drawing; Sales Commissions; Rent Expense; Office Salaries Expense; Automobile Expense; Supplies Expense; Miscellaneous Expense. Explanations may be omitted.
2. Prepare T accounts, using the account titles in (1). Post the journal entries to these accounts, placing the appropriate letter to the left of each amount to identify the transactions. Determine the account balances, after all posting is complete. Accounts containing only a single entry do not need a balance.
3. Prepare an unadjusted trial balance as of August 31, 2016.
4. Determine the following:
   a. Amount of total revenue recorded in the ledger.
   b. Amount of total expenses recorded in the ledger.
   c. Amount of net income for August.
5. Determine the increase or decrease in owner's equity for August.

PR 2-3A Journal entries and trial balance

OBJ. 1, 2, 3, 4

✔ 3. Total of Credit column: $81,450

General Ledger

SHOW ME HOW

On November 1, 2016, Patty Cosgrove established an interior decorating business, Classic Designs. During the month, Patty completed the following transactions related to the business:

Nov. 1. Patty transferred cash from a personal bank account to an account to be used for the business, $27,750.
1. Paid rent for period of November 1 to end of month, $4,000.
6. Purchased office equipment on account, $12,880.
8. Purchased a truck for $32,500 paying $6,500 cash and giving a note payable for the remainder.
10. Purchased supplies for cash, $1,860.
12. Received cash for job completed, $7,500.

(Continued)

Nov. 15. Paid annual premiums on property and casualty insurance, $2,400.

23. Recorded jobs completed on account and sent invoices to customers, $12,440.

24. Received an invoice for truck expenses, to be paid in November, $1,100.

Enter the following transactions on Page 2 of the two-column journal:

29. Paid utilities expense, $3,660.

29. Paid miscellaneous expenses, $1,700.

30. Received cash from customers on account, $8,000.

30. Paid wages of employees, $4,750.

30. Paid creditor a portion of the amount owed for equipment purchased on November 6, $6,220.

30. Withdrew cash for personal use, $2,000.

Instructions

1. Journalize each transaction in a two-column journal beginning on Page 1, referring to the following chart of accounts in selecting the accounts to be debited and credited. (Do not insert the account numbers in the journal at this time.) Explanations may be omitted.

11 Cash	31 Patty Cosgrove, Capital
12 Accounts Receivable	32 Patty Cosgrove, Drawing
13 Supplies	41 Fees Earned
14 Prepaid Insurance	51 Wages Expense
16 Equipment	53 Rent Expense
18 Truck	54 Utilities Expense
21 Notes Payable	55 Truck Expense
22 Accounts Payable	59 Miscellaneous Expense

2. Post the journal to a ledger of four-column accounts, inserting appropriate posting references as each item is posted. Extend the balances to the appropriate balance columns after each transaction is posted.
3. Prepare an unadjusted trial balance for Classic Designs as of November 30, 2016.
4. Determine the excess of revenues over expenses for November.
5. Can you think of any reason why the amount determined in (4) might not be the net income for November?

PR 2-4A Journal entries and trial balance

OBJ. 1, 2, 3, 4

✔ 4. Total of Debit column: $532,525

General Ledger

Elite Realty acts as an agent in buying, selling, renting, and managing real estate. The unadjusted trial balance on March 31, 2016, follows:

Elite Realty
Unadjusted Trial Balance
March 31, 2016

		Debit Balances	Credit Balances
11	Cash	26,300	
12	Accounts Receivable	61,500	
13	Prepaid Insurance	3,000	
14	Office Supplies	1,800	
16	Land	—	
21	Accounts Payable		14,000
22	Unearned Rent		—
23	Notes Payable		—
31	Lester Wagner, Capital		46,000
32	Lester Wagner, Drawing	2,000	
41	Fees Earned		240,000
51	Salary and Commission Expense	148,200	
52	Rent Expense	30,000	
53	Advertising Expense	17,800	
54	Automobile Expense	5,500	
59	Miscellaneous Expense	3,900	
		300,000	300,000

The following business transactions were completed by Elite Realty during April 2016:

Apr. 1. Paid rent on office for month, $6,500.
2. Purchased office supplies on account, $2,300.
5. Paid insurance premiums, $6,000.
10. Received cash from clients on account, $52,300.
15. Purchased land for a future building site for $200,000, paying $30,000 in cash and giving a note payable for the remainder.
17. Paid creditors on account, $6,450.
20. Returned a portion of the office supplies purchased on April 2, receiving full credit for their cost, $325.
23. Paid advertising expense, $4,300.

Enter the following transactions on Page 19 of the two-column journal:

27. Discovered an error in computing a commission; received cash from the salesperson for the overpayment, $2,500.
28. Paid automobile expense (including rental charges for an automobile), $1,500.
29. Paid miscellaneous expenses, $1,400.
30. Recorded revenue earned and billed to clients during the month, $57,000.
30. Paid salaries and commissions for the month, $11,900.
30. Withdrew cash for personal use, $4,000.
30. Rented land purchased on April 15 to local merchants association for use as a parking lot in May and June, during a street rebuilding program; received advance payment of $10,000.

Instructions

1. Record the April 1, 2016, balance of each account in the appropriate balance column of a four-column account, write *Balance* in the item section, and place a check mark (✓) in the Posting Reference column.
2. Journalize the transactions for April in a two-column journal beginning on Page 18. Journal entry explanations may be omitted.
3. Post to the ledger, extending the account balance to the appropriate balance column after each posting.
4. Prepare an unadjusted trial balance of the ledger as of April 30, 2016.
5. Assume that the April 30 transaction for salaries and commissions should have been $19,100. (a) Why did the unadjusted trial balance in (4) balance? (b) Journalize the correcting entry. (c) Is this error a transposition or slide?

PR 2-5A Corrected trial balance OBJ. 4

✓ 1. Total of Debit column: $725,000

The Colby Group has the following unadjusted trial balance as of August 31, 2016:

The Colby Group
Unadjusted Trial Balance
August 31, 2016

	Debit Balances	Credit Balances
Cash	17,300	
Accounts Receivable	37,000	
Supplies	7,400	
Prepaid Insurance	1,900	
Equipment	196,000	
Notes Payable		97,600
Accounts Payable		26,000
Terry Colby, Capital		129,150
Terry Colby, Drawing	56,000	
Fees Earned		454,450
Wages Expense	270,000	
Rent Expense	51,800	
Advertising Expense	25,200	
Miscellaneous Expense	5,100	
	667,700	707,200

(Continued)

The debit and credit totals are not equal as a result of the following errors:

a. The cash entered on the trial balance was understated by $6,000.

b. A cash receipt of $5,600 was posted as a debit to Cash of $6,500.

c. A debit of $11,000 to Accounts Receivable was not posted.

d. A return of $150 of defective supplies was erroneously posted as a $1,500 credit to Supplies.

e. An insurance policy acquired at a cost of $1,200 was posted as a credit to Prepaid Insurance.

f. The balance of Notes Payable was understated by $20,000.

g. A credit of $4,800 in Accounts Payable was overlooked when determining the balance of the account.

h. A debit of $7,000 for a withdrawal by the owner was posted as a credit to Terry Colby, Capital.

i. The balance of $58,100 in Rent Expense was entered as $51,800 in the trial balance.

j. Gas, Electricity, and Water Expense, with a balance of $24,150, was omitted from the trial balance.

Instructions

1. Prepare a corrected unadjusted trial balance as of August 31, 2016.
2. Does the fact that the unadjusted trial balance in (1) is balanced mean that there are no errors in the accounts? Explain.

Problems: Series B

PR 2-1B Entries into T accounts and trial balance **OBJ. 1, 2, 3, 4**

✔ 3. Total of Debit column: $69,550

Ken Jones, an architect, opened an office on April 1, 2016. During the month, he completed the following transactions connected with his professional practice:

a. Transferred cash from a personal bank account to an account to be used for the business, $18,000.

b. Purchased used automobile for $19,500, paying $2,500 cash and giving a note payable for the remainder.

c. Paid April rent for office and workroom, $3,150.

d. Paid cash for supplies, $1,450.

e. Purchased office and computer equipment on account, $6,500.

f. Paid cash for annual insurance policies on automobile and equipment, $2,400.

g. Received cash from a client for plans delivered, $12,000.

h. Paid cash to creditors on account, $1,800.

i. Paid cash for miscellaneous expenses, $375.

j. Received invoice for blueprint service, due in May, $2,500.

k. Recorded fees earned on plans delivered, payment to be received in May, $15,650.

l. Paid salary of assistant, $2,800.

m. Paid cash for miscellaneous expenses, $200.

n. Paid installment due on note payable, $300.

o. Paid gas, oil, and repairs on automobile for April, $550.

Instructions

1. Record these transactions directly in the following T accounts, without journalizing: Cash; Accounts Receivable; Supplies; Prepaid Insurance; Automobiles; Equipment; Notes Payable; Accounts Payable; Ken Jones, Capital; Professional Fees; Rent Expense; Salary Expense; Blueprint Expense; Automobile Expense; Miscellaneous Expense. To the left of each amount entered in the accounts, place the appropriate letter to identify the transaction.
2. Determine account balances of the T accounts. Accounts containing a single entry only (such as Prepaid Insurance) do not need a balance.

3. Prepare an unadjusted trial balance for Ken Jones, Architect, as of April 30, 2016.
4. Determine the net income or net loss for April.

PR 2-2B Journal entries and trial balance **OBJ. 1, 2, 3, 4**

✔ 4. c. $4,550

General Ledger

SHOW ME HOW

On August 1, 2016, Rafael Masey established Planet Realty, which completed the following transactions during the month:

a. Rafael Masey transferred cash from a personal bank account to an account to be used for the business, $17,500.
b. Purchased supplies on account, $2,300.
c. Earned sales commissions, receiving cash, $13,300.
d. Paid rent on office and equipment for the month, $3,000.
e. Paid creditor on account, $1,150.
f. Withdrew cash for personal use, $1,800.
g. Paid automobile expenses (including rental charge) for month, $1,500, and miscellaneous expenses, $400.
h. Paid office salaries, $2,800.
i. Determined that the cost of supplies used was $1,050.

Instructions

1. Journalize entries for transactions (a) through (i), using the following account titles: Cash; Supplies; Accounts Payable; Rafael Masey, Capital; Rafael Masey, Drawing; Sales Commissions; Rent Expense; Office Salaries Expense; Automobile Expense; Supplies Expense; Miscellaneous Expense. Journal entry explanations may be omitted.
2. Prepare T accounts, using the account titles in (1). Post the journal entries to these accounts, placing the appropriate letter to the left of each amount to identify the transactions. Determine the account balances, after all posting is complete. Accounts containing only a single entry do not need a balance.
3. Prepare an unadjusted trial balance as of August 31, 2016.
4. Determine the following:
   a. Amount of total revenue recorded in the ledger.
   b. Amount of total expenses recorded in the ledger.
   c. Amount of net income for August.
5. Determine the increase or decrease in owner's equity for August.

PR 2-3B Journal entries and trial balance **OBJ. 1, 2, 3, 4**

✔ 3. Total of Credit column: $70,300

General Ledger

SHOW ME HOW

On October 1, 2016, Jay Pryor established an interior decorating business, Pioneer Designs. During the month, Jay completed the following transactions related to the business:

Oct. 1. Jay transferred cash from a personal bank account to an account to be used for the business, $18,000.
4. Paid rent for period of October 4 to end of month, $3,000.
10. Purchased a used truck for $23,750, paying $3,750 cash and giving a note payable for the remainder.
13. Purchased equipment on account, $10,500.
14. Purchased supplies for cash, $2,100.
15. Paid annual premiums on property and casualty insurance, $3,600.
15. Received cash for job completed, $8,950.

Enter the following transactions on Page 2 of the two-column journal:

21. Paid creditor a portion of the amount owed for equipment purchased on October 13, $2,000.
24. Recorded jobs completed on account and sent invoices to customers, $14,150.
26. Received an invoice for truck expenses, to be paid in November, $700.
27. Paid utilities expense, $2,240.

(Continued)

Oct. 27. Paid miscellaneous expenses, $1,100.

29. Received cash from customers on account, $7,600.

30. Paid wages of employees, $4,800.

31. Withdrew cash for personal use, $3,500.

Instructions

1. Journalize each transaction in a two-column journal beginning on Page 1, referring to the following chart of accounts in selecting the accounts to be debited and credited. (Do not insert the account numbers in the journal at this time.) Journal entry explanations may be omitted.

11 Cash	31 Jay Pryor, Capital
12 Accounts Receivable	32 Jay Pryor, Drawing
13 Supplies	41 Fees Earned
14 Prepaid Insurance	51 Wages Expense
16 Equipment	53 Rent Expense
18 Truck	54 Utilities Expense
21 Notes Payable	55 Truck Expense
22 Accounts Payable	59 Miscellaneous Expense

2. Post the journal to a ledger of four-column accounts, inserting appropriate posting references as each item is posted. Extend the balances to the appropriate balance columns after each transaction is posted.
3. Prepare an unadjusted trial balance for Pioneer Designs as of October 31, 2016.
4. Determine the excess of revenues over expenses for October.
5. Can you think of any reason why the amount determined in (4) might not be the net income for October?

PR 2-4B Journal entries and trial balance

OBJ. 1, 2, 3, 4

✔ 4. Total of Debit column: $945,000

General Ledger

Valley Realty acts as an agent in buying, selling, renting, and managing real estate. The unadjusted trial balance on July 31, 2016, follows:

Valley Realty
Unadjusted Trial Balance
July 31, 2016

		Debit Balances	Credit Balances
11	Cash	52,500	
12	Accounts Receivable	100,100	
13	Prepaid Insurance	12,600	
14	Office Supplies	2,800	
16	Land	—	
21	Accounts Payable		21,000
22	Unearned Rent		—
23	Notes Payable		—
31	Cindy Getman, Capital		87,500
32	Cindy Getman, Drawing	44,800	
41	Fees Earned		591,500
51	Salary and Commission Expense	385,000	
52	Rent Expense	49,000	
53	Advertising Expense	32,200	
54	Automobile Expense	15,750	
59	Miscellaneous Expense	5,250	
		700,000	700,000

The following business transactions were completed by Valley Realty during August 2016:

Aug. 1. Purchased office supplies on account, $3,150.

2. Paid rent on office for month, $7,200.

3. Received cash from clients on account, $83,900.

Aug. 5. Paid insurance premiums, $12,000.

9. Returned a portion of the office supplies purchased on August 1, receiving full credit for their cost, $400.

17. Paid advertising expense, $8,000.

23. Paid creditors on account, $13,750.

Enter the following transactions on Page 19 of the two-column journal:

29. Paid miscellaneous expenses, $1,700.

30. Paid automobile expense (including rental charges for an automobile), $2,500.

31. Discovered an error in computing a commission during July; received cash from the salesperson for the overpayment, $2,000.

31. Paid salaries and commissions for the month, $53,000.

31. Recorded revenue earned and billed to clients during the month, $183,500.

31. Purchased land for a future building site for $75,000, paying $7,500 in cash and giving a note payable for the remainder.

31. Withdrew cash for personal use, $1,000.

31. Rented land purchased on August 31 to a local university for use as a parking lot during football season (September, October, and November); received advance payment of $5,000.

Instructions

1. Record the August 1 balance of each account in the appropriate balance column of a four-column account, write *Balance* in the item section, and place a check mark (✓) in the Posting Reference column.
2. Journalize the transactions for August in a two-column journal beginning on Page 18. Journal entry explanations may be omitted.
3. Post to the ledger, extending the account balance to the appropriate balance column after each posting.
4. Prepare an unadjusted trial balance of the ledger as of August 31, 2016.
5. Assume that the August 31 transaction for Cindy Getman's cash withdrawal should have been $10,000. (a) Why did the unadjusted trial balance in (4) balance? (b) Journalize the correcting entry. (c) Is this error a transposition or slide?

PR 2-5B Corrected trial balance

OBJ. 4

✓ 1. Total of Debit column: $712,500

Tech Support Services has the following unadjusted trial balance as of January 31, 2016:

Tech Support Services
Unadjusted Trial Balance
January 31, 2016

	Debit Balances	Credit Balances
Cash	25,550	
Accounts Receivable	44,050	
Supplies	6,660	
Prepaid Insurance	3,600	
Equipment	162,000	
Notes Payable		75,000
Accounts Payable		13,200
Thad Engelberg, Capital		101,850
Thad Engelberg, Drawing	33,000	
Fees Earned		534,000
Wages Expense	306,000	
Rent Expense	62,550	
Advertising Expense	23,850	
Gas, Electricity, and Water Expense	17,000	
	684,260	724,050

(Continued)

The debit and credit totals are not equal as a result of the following errors:

a. The cash entered on the trial balance was overstated by $8,000.

b. A cash receipt of $4,100 was posted as a debit to Cash of $1,400.

c. A debit of $12,350 to Accounts Receivable was not posted.

d. A return of $235 of defective supplies was erroneously posted as a $325 credit to Supplies.

e. An insurance policy acquired at a cost of $3,000 was posted as a credit to Prepaid Insurance.

f. The balance of Notes Payable was overstated by $21,000.

g. A credit of $3,450 in Accounts Payable was overlooked when the balance of the account was determined.

h. A debit of $6,000 for a withdrawal by the owner was posted as a debit to Thad Engelberg, Capital.

i. The balance of $28,350 in Advertising Expense was entered as $23,850 in the trial balance.

j. Miscellaneous Expense, with a balance of $4,600, was omitted from the trial balance.

Instructions

1. Prepare a corrected unadjusted trial balance as of January 31, 2016.
2. Does the fact that the unadjusted trial balance in (1) is balanced mean that there are no errors in the accounts? Explain.

Continuing Problem

✔ **4. Total of Debit column: $40,750**

General Ledger

The transactions completed by PS Music during June 2016 were described at the end of Chapter 1. The following transactions were completed during July, the second month of the business's operations:

July 1. Peyton Smith made an additional investment in PS Music by depositing $5,000 in PS Music's checking account.

1. Instead of continuing to share office space with a local real estate agency, Peyton decided to rent office space near a local music store. Paid rent for July, $1,750.

1. Paid a premium of $2,700 for a comprehensive insurance policy covering liability, theft, and fire. The policy covers a one-year period.

2. Received $1,000 on account.

3. On behalf of PS Music, Peyton signed a contract with a local radio station, KXMD, to provide guest spots for the next three months. The contract requires PS Music to provide a guest disc jockey for 80 hours per month for a monthly fee of $3,600. Any additional hours beyond 80 will be billed to KXMD at $40 per hour. In accordance with the contract, Peyton received $7,200 from KXMD as an advance payment for the first two months.

3. Paid $250 on account.

4. Paid an attorney $900 for reviewing the July 3 contract with KXMD. (Record as Miscellaneous Expense.)

5. Purchased office equipment on account from Office Mart, $7,500.

8. Paid for a newspaper advertisement, $200.

11. Received $1,000 for serving as a disc jockey for a party.

13. Paid $700 to a local audio electronics store for rental of digital recording equipment.

14. Paid wages of $1,200 to receptionist and part-time assistant.

Enter the following transactions on Page 2 of the two-column journal:

July 16. Received $2,000 for serving as a disc jockey for a wedding reception.

18. Purchased supplies on account, $850.

21. Paid $620 to Upload Music for use of its current music demos in making various music sets.

22. Paid $800 to a local radio station to advertise the services of PS Music twice daily for the remainder of July.

23. Served as disc jockey for a party for $2,500. Received $750, with the remainder due August 4, 2016.

27. Paid electric bill, $915.

28. Paid wages of $1,200 to receptionist and part-time assistant.

29. Paid miscellaneous expenses, $540.

30. Served as a disc jockey for a charity ball for $1,500. Received $500, with the remainder due on August 9, 2016.

31. Received $3,000 for serving as a disc jockey for a party.

31. Paid $1,400 royalties (music expense) to National Music Clearing for use of various artists' music during July.

31. Withdrew $1,250 cash from PS Music for personal use.

PS Music's chart of accounts and the balance of accounts as of July 1, 2016 (all normal balances), are as follows:

Account	Balance	Account	Balance
11 Cash	$3,920	41 Fees Earned	$6,200
12 Accounts Receivable	1,000	50 Wages Expense	400
14 Supplies	170	51 Office Rent Expense	800
15 Prepaid Insurance	—	52 Equipment Rent Expense	675
17 Office Equipment	—	53 Utilities Expense	300
21 Accounts Payable	250	54 Music Expense	1,590
23 Unearned Revenue	—	55 Advertising Expense	500
31 Peyton Smith, Capital	4,000	56 Supplies Expense	180
32 Peyton Smith, Drawing	500	59 Miscellaneous Expense	415

Instructions

1. Enter the July 1, 2016, account balances in the appropriate balance column of a four-column account. Write *Balance* in the Item column, and place a check mark (✓) in the Posting Reference column. (*Hint:* Verify the equality of the debit and credit balances in the ledger before proceeding with the next instruction.)
2. Analyze and journalize each transaction in a two-column journal beginning on Page 1, omitting journal entry explanations.
3. Post the journal to the ledger, extending the account balance to the appropriate balance column after each posting.
4. Prepare an unadjusted trial balance as of July 31, 2016.

Cases & Projects

CP 2-1 Ethics and professional conduct in business

At the end of the current month, Gil Frank prepared a trial balance for College App Services. The credit side of the trial balance exceeds the debit side by a significant amount. Gil has decided to add the difference to the balance of the miscellaneous expense account in order to complete the preparation of the current month's financial statements by a 5 o'clock deadline. Gil will look for the difference next week when he has more time. Discuss whether Gil is behaving in a professional manner.

CP 2-2 Account for revenue

Bozeman College requires students to pay tuition each term before classes begin. Students who have not paid their tuition are not allowed to enroll or to attend classes.

What journal entry do you think Bozeman College would use to record the receipt of the students' tuition payments? Describe the nature of each account in the entry.

CP 2-3 Record transactions

The following discussion took place between Tony Cork, the office manager of Hallmark Data Company, and a new accountant, Cassie Miles:

Cassie: I've been thinking about our method of recording entries. It seems that it's inefficient.

Tony: In what way?

Cassie: Well—correct me if I'm wrong—it seems like we have unnecessary steps in the process. We could easily develop a trial balance by posting our transactions directly into the ledger and bypassing the journal altogether. In this way, we could combine the recording and posting process into one step and save ourselves a lot of time. What do you think?

Tony: We need to have a talk.

What should Tony say to Cassie?

CP 2-4 Debits and credits

Group Project

The following excerpt is from a conversation between Kate Purvis, the president and chief operating officer of Light House Company, and her neighbor, Dot Evers:

Dot: Kate, I'm taking a course in night school, "Intro to Accounting." I was wondering—could you answer a couple of questions for me?

Kate: Well, I will if I can.

Dot: Okay, our instructor says that it's critical we understand the basic concepts of accounting, or we'll never get beyond the first test. My problem is with those rules of debit and credit . . . you know, assets increase with debits, decrease with credits, etc.

Kate: Yes, pretty basic stuff. You just have to memorize the rules. It shouldn't be too difficult.

Dot: Sure, I can memorize the rules, but my problem is I want to be sure I understand the basic concepts behind the rules. For example, why can't assets be increased with credits and decreased with debits like revenue? As long as everyone did it that way, why not? It would seem easier if we had the same rules for all increases and decreases in accounts. Also, why is the left side of an account called the debit side? Why couldn't it be called something simple . . . like the "LE" for Left Entry? The right side could be called just "RE" for Right Entry. Finally, why are there just two sides to an entry? Why can't there be three or four sides to an entry?

In a group of four or five, select one person to play the role of Kate and one person to play the role of Dot.

1. After listening to the conversation between Kate and Dot, help Kate answer Dot's questions.
2. What information (other than just debit and credit journal entries) could the accounting system gather that might be useful to Kate in managing Light House Company?

CP 2-5 Transactions and income statement

Cory Neece is planning to manage and operate Eagle Caddy Service at Canyon Lake Golf and Country Club during June through August 2016. Cory will rent a small maintenance building from the country club for $500 per month and will offer caddy services, including cart rentals, to golfers. Cory has had no formal training in record keeping.

Cory keeps notes of all receipts and expenses in a shoe box. An examination of Cory's shoe box records for June revealed the following:

June 1. Transferred $2,000 from personal bank account to be used to operate the caddy service.

1. Paid rent expense to Canyon Lake Golf and Country Club, $500.

2. Paid for golf supplies (practice balls, etc.), $750.

June 3. Arranged for the rental of 40 regular (pulling) golf carts and 20 gasoline-driven carts for $3,000 per month. Paid $600 in advance, with the remaining $2,400 due June 20.

7. Purchased supplies, including gasoline, for the golf carts on account, $1,000. Canyon Lake Golf and Country Club has agreed to allow Cory to store the gasoline in one of its fuel tanks at no cost.

15. Received cash for services from June 1–15, $5,400.

17. Paid cash to creditors on account, $1,000.

20. Paid remaining rental on golf carts, $2,400.

22. Purchased supplies, including gasoline, on account, $850.

25. Accepted IOUs from customers on account, $1,800.

28. Paid miscellaneous expenses, $395.

30. Received cash for services from June 16–30, $4,200.

30. Paid telephone and electricity (utilities) expenses, $340.

30. Paid wages of part-time employees, $850.

30. Received cash in payment of IOUs on account, $1,500.

30. Determined the amount of supplies on hand at the end of June, $675.

Cory has asked you several questions concerning his financial affairs to date, and he has asked you to assist with his record keeping and reporting of financial data.

a. To assist Cory with his record keeping, prepare a chart of accounts that would be appropriate for Eagle Caddy Service.

b. Prepare an income statement for June in order to help Cory assess the profitability of Eagle Caddy Service. For this purpose, the use of T accounts may be helpful in analyzing the effects of each June transaction.

c. Based on Cory's records of receipts and payments, compute the amount of cash on hand on June 30. For this purpose, a T account for cash may be useful.

d. A count of the cash on hand on June 30 totaled $6,175. Briefly discuss the possible causes of the difference between the amount of cash computed in (c) and the actual amount of cash on hand.

CP 2-6 Opportunities for accountants

Internet Project

The increasing complexity of the current business and regulatory environment has created an increased demand for accountants who can analyze business transactions and interpret their effects on the financial statements. In addition, a basic ability to analyze the effects of transactions is necessary to be successful in all fields of business as well as in other disciplines, such as law. To better understand the importance of accounting in today's environment, search the Internet or your local newspaper for job opportunities. One possible Internet site is www.careerbuilder.com. Then do one of the following:

1. Print a listing of one or two ads for accounting jobs. Alternatively, bring to class one or two newspaper ads for accounting jobs.
2. Print a listing of one or two ads for nonaccounting jobs for which some knowledge of accounting is preferred or necessary. Alternatively, bring to class one or two newspaper ads for such jobs.

©JORDAN SIEMENS/ICONICA/GETTY IMAGES

The Adjusting Process

Pandora

Do you use an Internet-based music service such as **Pandora**? Using playlist-generating algorithms, Pandora predicts a listener's music preferences based on their initial music selections. Pandora selects music they think the listener will enjoy, including music of new artists that match the listener's preferences. Recently, Pandora developed similar comedy-generating algorithms that match a listener's preferences for comedy with more than 1,000 comedians.

Most of Pandora's services are offered free to listeners with only 12.5% of its revenues generated from subscription services. So, where do most of Pandora's revenues come from?

Pandora generates more than 85% of its revenues from selling advertising banners that surround the video displays on its tuner. By analyzing its listener interactions, Pandora identifies listener age, gender, zip code, and content preferences. These attributes can then be matched with advertiser needs and desires.

When should Pandora record revenue from its advertisers and subscribers? Revenue should be recorded when earned. Advertising revenue is earned as ads are displayed, while subscriber revenue is earned when the service has been delivered to the listener. As a result, companies like Pandora must update their accounting records for such items as unearned advertising and subscription revenue before preparing financial statements.

This chapter describes and illustrates the process by which companies update their accounting records before preparing financial statements. This discussion includes the adjustments for unearned revenues that exist at the end of the accounting period.

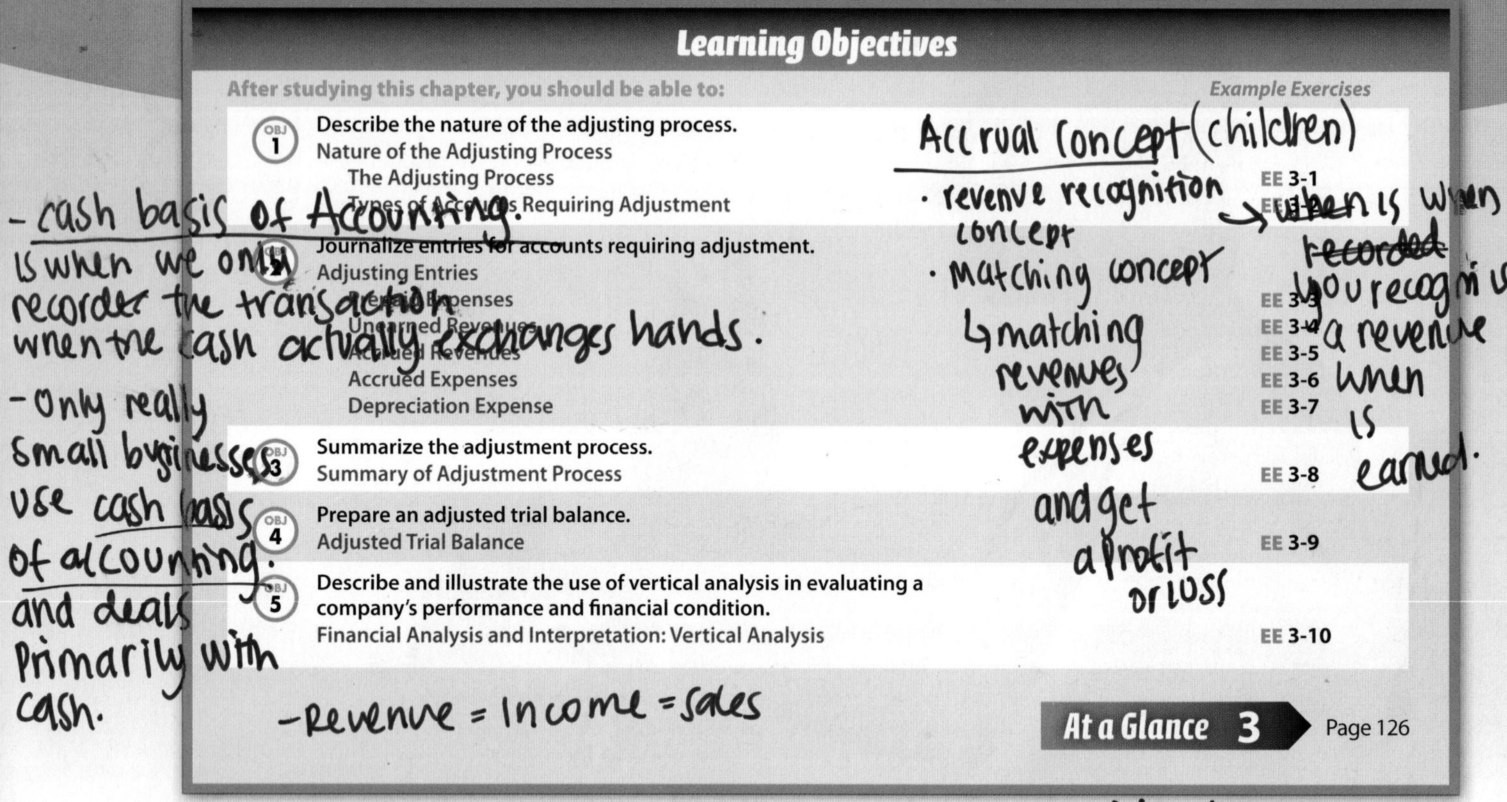

Learning Objectives

After studying this chapter, you should be able to: | Example Exercises

At a Glance 3 Page 126

OBJ 1 Describe the nature of the adjusting process.

Nature of the Adjusting Process

When preparing financial statements, the economic life of the business is divided into time periods. This **accounting period concept** requires that revenues and expenses be reported in the proper period. To determine the proper period, accountants use generally accepted accounting principles (GAAP), which requires the **accrual basis of accounting**.

Under the accrual basis of accounting, revenues are reported on the income statement in the period in which they are earned. For example, revenue is reported when the services are provided to customers. Cash may or may not be received from customers during this period. The accounting concept supporting this reporting of revenues is called the **revenue recognition concept**.

American Airlines uses the accrual basis of accounting. Revenues are recognized when passengers take flights, not when the passenger makes the reservation or pays for the ticket.

Under accrual accounting, revenues are recognized when services have been performed or products have been delivered to customers.[1] Revenue is measured as assets received, such as cash or accounts receivable, in exchange for a service or product. This process of recording revenues is called **revenue recognition**.

The accounting concept supporting reporting revenues and related expenses in the same period is called the **matching concept**. By matching revenues and expenses, net income or loss for the period is properly reported on the income statement.

Although GAAP requires the accrual basis of accounting, some businesses use the **cash basis of accounting**. Under the cash basis of accounting, revenues and expenses are reported on the income statement in the period in which cash is received or paid. For example, fees are recorded when cash is received from clients; likewise, wages are recorded when cash is paid to employees. The net income (or net loss) is the difference between the cash receipts (revenues) and the cash payments (expenses).

Small service businesses may use the cash basis because they have few receivables and payables. For example, attorneys, physicians, and real estate agents often use the cash basis. For them, the cash basis provides financial statements similar to those of the accrual basis. For most large businesses, however, the cash basis will not provide accurate financial statements for user needs. For this reason, the accrual basis is used in this text.

[1]Revenues may involve contracts with customers that have several elements or performance obligations. Recording of revenues under such contracts is described and illustrated in Appendix E Revenue Recognition.

The Adjusting Process

At the end of the accounting period, many of the account balances in the ledger are reported in the financial statements without change. For example, the balances of the cash and land accounts are normally the amounts reported on the balance sheet.

Some accounts, however, require updating for the following reasons:[2]

- Some expenses are not recorded daily. For example, the daily use of supplies would require many entries with small amounts. Also, the amount of supplies on hand on a day-to-day basis is normally not needed.
- Some revenues and expenses are incurred as time passes rather than as separate transactions. For example, rent received in advance (unearned rent) expires and becomes revenue with the passage of time. Likewise, prepaid insurance expires and becomes an expense with the passage of time.
- Some revenues and expenses may be unrecorded. For example, a company may have provided services to customers that it has not billed or recorded at the end of the accounting period. Likewise, a company may not pay its employees until the next accounting period even though the employees have earned their wages in the current period.

The analysis and updating of accounts at the end of the period before the financial statements are prepared is called the **adjusting process**. The journal entries that bring the accounts up to date at the end of the accounting period are called **adjusting entries**. All adjusting entries affect at least one income statement account and one balance sheet account. Thus, an adjusting entry will *always* involve a revenue or an expense account *and* an asset or a liability account.

Example Exercise 3-1 Accounts Requiring Adjustment

OBJ 1

Indicate with a *Yes* or *No* whether or not each of the following accounts normally requires an adjusting entry:

a. Cash	c. Wages Expense	e. Accounts Receivable
b. Prepaid Rent	d. Land	f. Unearned Rent

Follow My Example 3-1

a. No	c. Yes	e. Yes
b. Yes	d. No	f. Yes

Practice Exercises: PE 3-1A, PE 3-1B

Types of Accounts Requiring Adjustment

The following basic types of accounts require adjusting entries:

- Prepaid expenses
- Unearned revenues
- Accrued revenues
- Accrued expenses

Prepaid Expenses **Prepaid expenses** are the advance payment of *future* expenses and are recorded as assets when cash is paid. Prepaid expenses become expenses over time or during normal operations. To illustrate, the following transaction of **NetSolutions** from Chapter 2 is used:

Dec. 1	NetSolutions paid $2,400 as a premium on a one-year insurance policy.

On December 1, the cash payment of $2,400 was recorded as a debit to Prepaid Insurance and credit to Cash for $2,400. At the end of December, only $200 ($2,400 ÷ 12 months)

[2] Under the cash basis of accounting, accounts do not require adjusting. This is because transactions are recorded only when cash is received or paid. Thus, the matching concept is not used under the cash basis.

of the insurance premium is expired and has become an expense. The remaining $2,200 of prepaid insurance will become an expense in future months. Thus, the $200 is insurance expense of December and should be recorded with an adjusting entry.

Other examples of prepaid expenses include supplies, prepaid advertising, and prepaid interest.

Exhibit 1 summarizes the nature of prepaid expenses.

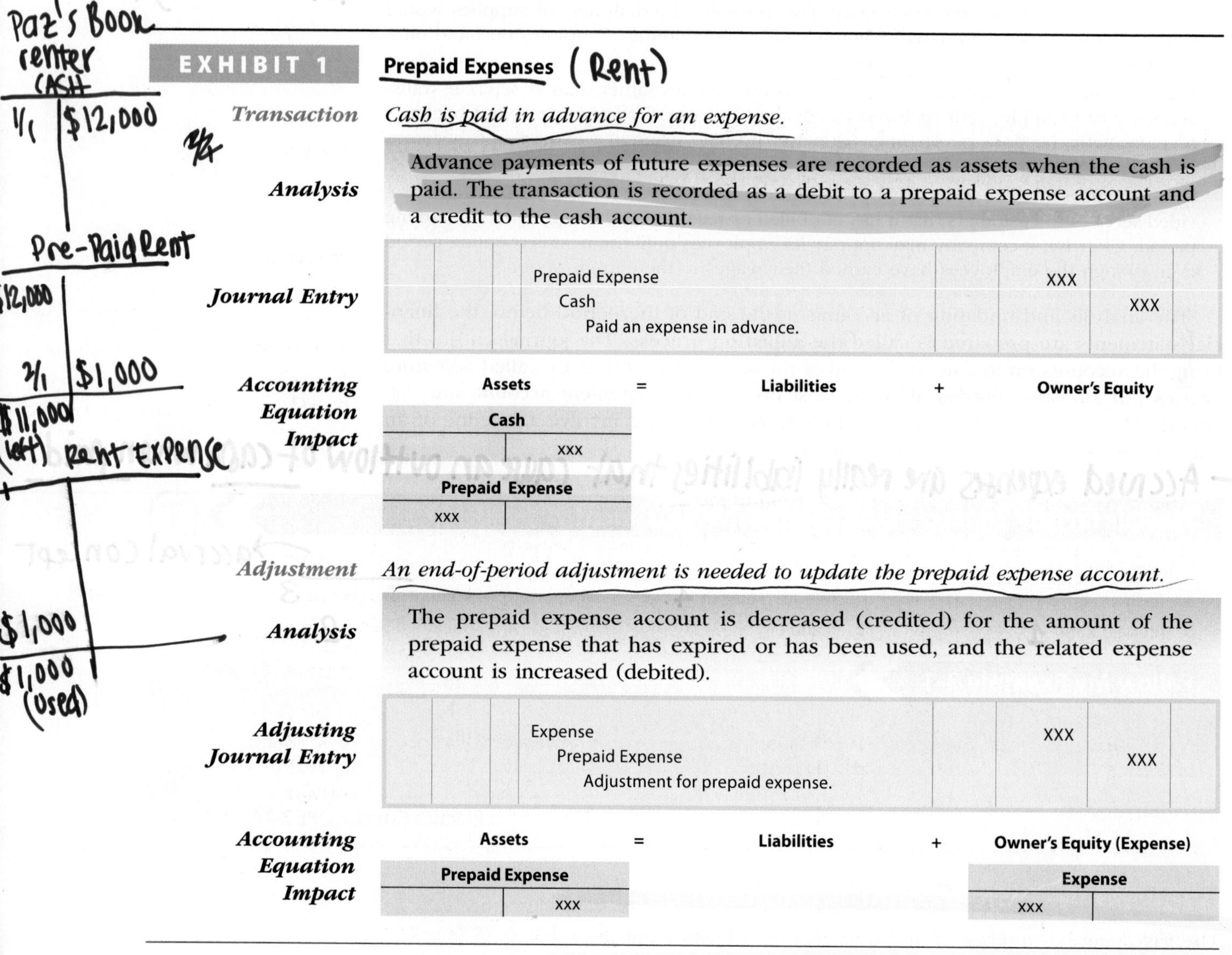

EXHIBIT 1 **Prepaid Expenses**

Transaction — *Cash is paid in advance for an expense.*

Analysis — Advance payments of future expenses are recorded as assets when the cash is paid. The transaction is recorded as a debit to a prepaid expense account and a credit to the cash account.

Journal Entry

			Account		Debit	Credit
			Prepaid Expense		XXX	
			Cash			XXX
			Paid an expense in advance.			

Accounting Equation Impact

Assets = Liabilities + Owner's Equity

Cash	
	XXX

Prepaid Expense	
XXX	

Adjustment — *An end-of-period adjustment is needed to update the prepaid expense account.*

Analysis — The prepaid expense account is decreased (credited) for the amount of the prepaid expense that has expired or has been used, and the related expense account is increased (debited).

Adjusting Journal Entry

			Account		Debit	Credit
			Expense		XXX	
			Prepaid Expense			XXX
			Adjustment for prepaid expense.			

Accounting Equation Impact

Assets = Liabilities + Owner's Equity (Expense)

Prepaid Expense	
	XXX

Expense	
XXX	

Unearned Revenues **Unearned revenues** are the advance receipt of *future* revenues and are recorded as liabilities when cash is received. Unearned revenues become earned revenues over time or during normal operations. To illustrate, the following December 1 transaction of **NetSolutions** is used:

Dec. 1	NetSolutions received $360 from a local retailer to rent land for three months.

On December 1, the cash receipt of $360 was recorded as a debit to Cash and a credit to Unearned Rent for $360. At the end of December, $120 ($360 divided by 3 months) of the unearned rent has been earned. The remaining $240 will become rent revenue in future months. Thus, the $120 is rent revenue of December and should be recorded with an adjusting entry.

Other examples of unearned revenues include tuition received in advance by a school, an annual retainer fee received by an attorney, premiums received in advance by an insurance company, and magazine subscriptions received in advance by a publisher.

Exhibit 2 summarizes the nature of unearned revenues.

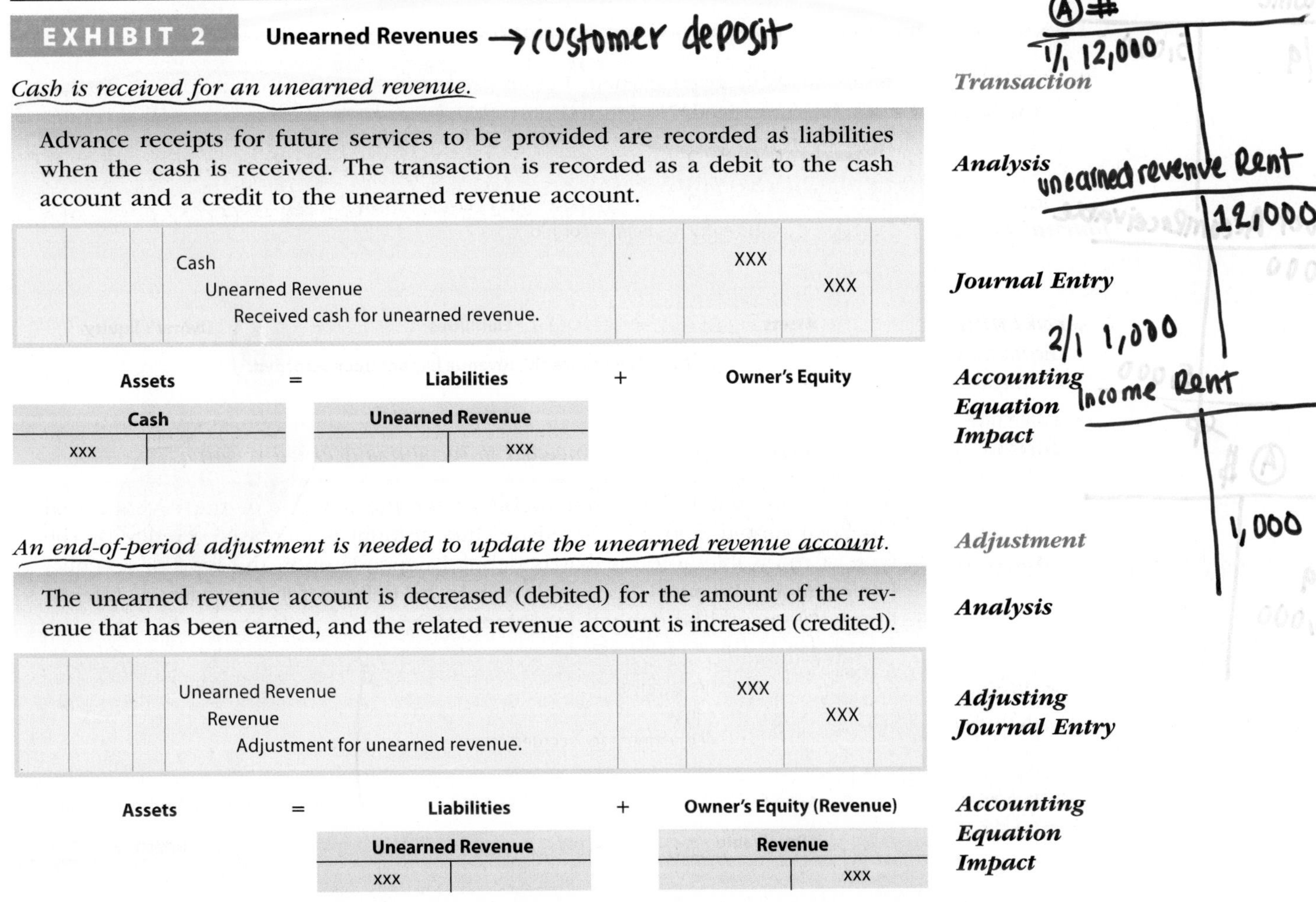

EXHIBIT 2 Unearned Revenues

Cash is received for an unearned revenue. — **Transaction**

Analysis: Advance receipts for future services to be provided are recorded as liabilities when the cash is received. The transaction is recorded as a debit to the cash account and a credit to the unearned revenue account.

Journal Entry

Cash	XXX	
Unearned Revenue		XXX
Received cash for unearned revenue.		

Accounting Equation Impact

Assets = Liabilities + Owner's Equity

Cash	
XXX	

Unearned Revenue	
	XXX

An end-of-period adjustment is needed to update the unearned revenue account. — **Adjustment**

Analysis: The unearned revenue account is decreased (debited) for the amount of the revenue that has been earned, and the related revenue account is increased (credited).

Adjusting Journal Entry

Unearned Revenue	XXX	
Revenue		XXX
Adjustment for unearned revenue.		

Accounting Equation Impact

Assets = Liabilities + Owner's Equity (Revenue)

Unearned Revenue	
XXX	

Revenue	
	XXX

Accrued Revenues

Accrued revenues are unrecorded revenues that have been earned and for which cash has yet to be received. Fees for services that an attorney or a doctor has provided but not yet billed are accrued revenues. To illustrate, the following example involving **NetSolutions** and one of its customers is used:

> Dec. 15 NetSolutions signed an agreement with Dankner Co. under which NetSolutions will bill Dankner Co. on the fifteenth of each month for services rendered at the rate of $20 per hour.

From December 16–31, NetSolutions provided 25 hours of service to Dankner Co. Although the revenue of $500 (25 hours × $20) has been earned, it will not be billed until January 15. Likewise, cash of $500 will not be received until Dankner pays its bill. Thus, the $500 of accrued revenue and the $500 of fees earned should be recorded with an adjusting entry on December 31.

Other examples of accrued revenues include accrued interest on notes receivable and accrued rent on property rented to others.

Exhibit 3 summarizes the nature of accrued revenues.

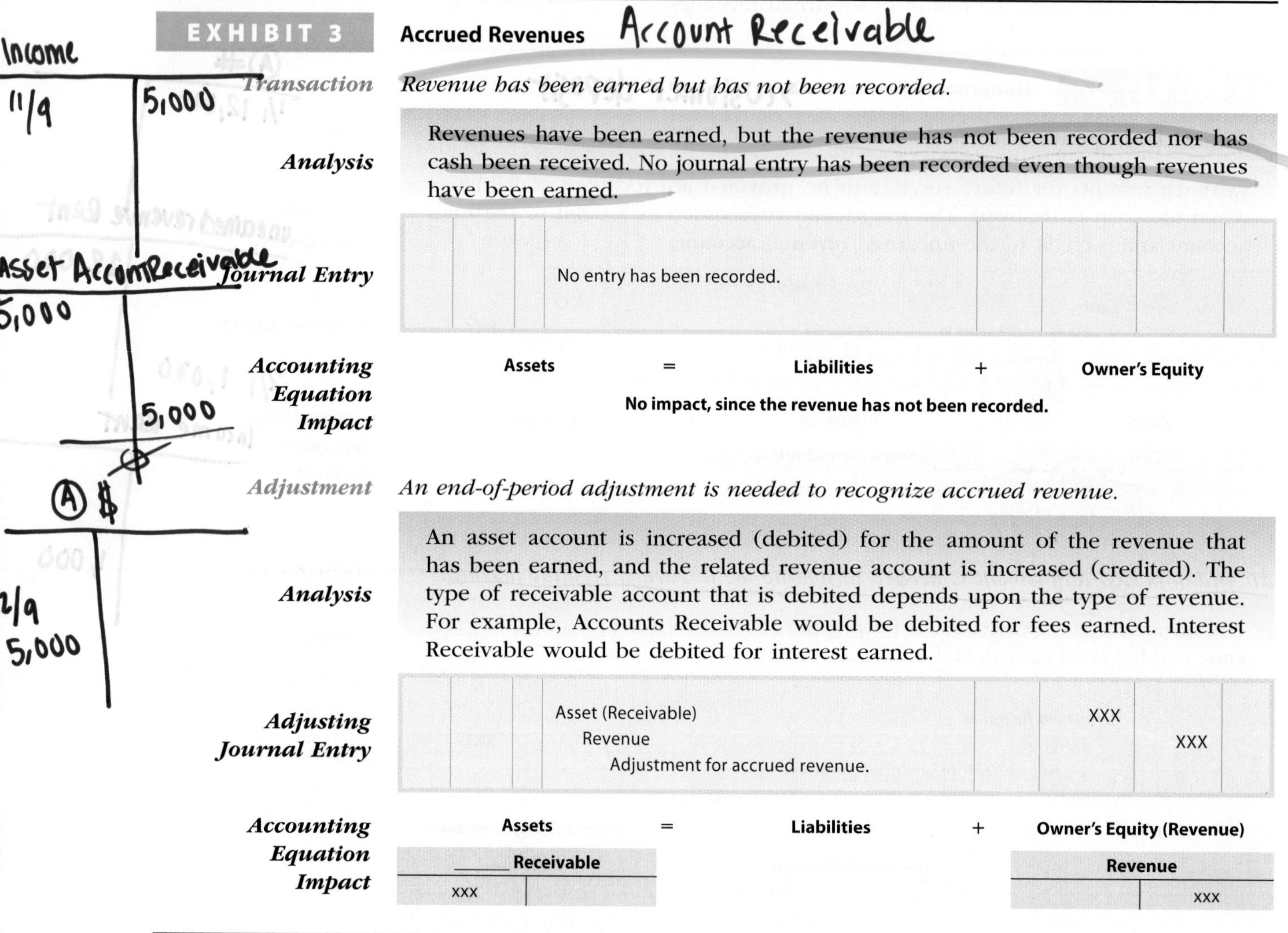

EXHIBIT 3 **Accrued Revenues**

Transaction *Revenue has been earned but has not been recorded.*

Analysis Revenues have been earned, but the revenue has not been recorded nor has cash been received. No journal entry has been recorded even though revenues have been earned.

Journal Entry No entry has been recorded.

Accounting Equation Impact

Assets	=	Liabilities	+	Owner's Equity

No impact, since the revenue has not been recorded.

Adjustment *An end-of-period adjustment is needed to recognize accrued revenue.*

Analysis An asset account is increased (debited) for the amount of the revenue that has been earned, and the related revenue account is increased (credited). The type of receivable account that is debited depends upon the type of revenue. For example, Accounts Receivable would be debited for fees earned. Interest Receivable would be debited for interest earned.

Adjusting Journal Entry

		Debit	Credit
Asset (Receivable)		XXX	
Revenue			XXX
Adjustment for accrued revenue.			

Accounting Equation Impact

Assets	=	Liabilities	+	Owner's Equity (Revenue)

_____ Receivable: XXX (debit)

Revenue: XXX (credit)

Accrued Expenses **Accrued expenses** are unrecorded expenses that have been incurred and for which cash has yet to be paid. Wages owed to employees at the end of a period but not yet paid are an accrued expense. To illustrate, the following example involving **NetSolutions** and its employees is used:

> Dec. 31 NetSolutions owes its employees wages of $250 for Monday and Tuesday, December 30 and 31.

NetSolutions paid wages of $950 on December 13 and $1,200 on December 27, 2015. These payments covered the biweekly pay periods that ended on those days. As of December 31, 2015, NetSolutions owes its employees wages of $250 for Monday and Tuesday, December 30 and 31. The wages of $250 will be paid on January 10, 2016; however, they are an expense of December. Thus, $250 of accrued wages should be recorded with an adjusting entry on December 31.

Other examples of accrued expenses include accrued interest on notes payable and accrued taxes.

Exhibit 4 summarizes the nature of accrued expenses.

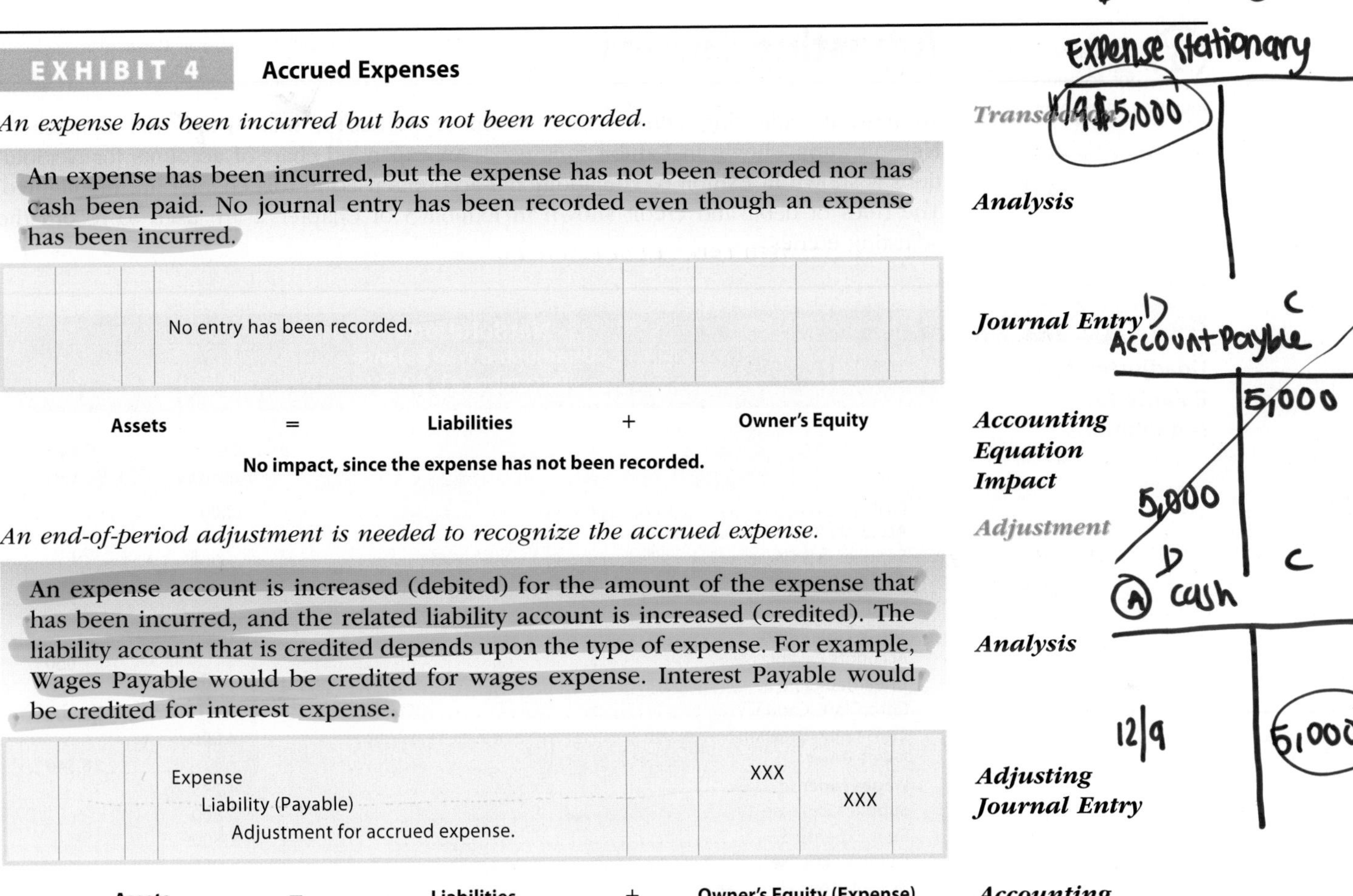

EXHIBIT 4 **Accrued Expenses**

An expense has been incurred but has not been recorded.

Transaction

Analysis

An expense has been incurred, but the expense has not been recorded nor has cash been paid. No journal entry has been recorded even though an expense has been incurred.

Journal Entry

No entry has been recorded.

Accounting Equation Impact

Assets	=	Liabilities	+	Owner's Equity

No impact, since the expense has not been recorded.

An end-of-period adjustment is needed to recognize the accrued expense.

Adjustment

Analysis

An expense account is increased (debited) for the amount of the expense that has been incurred, and the related liability account is increased (credited). The liability account that is credited depends upon the type of expense. For example, Wages Payable would be credited for wages expense. Interest Payable would be credited for interest expense.

Adjusting Journal Entry

	Debit	Credit
Expense	XXX	
Liability (Payable)		XXX
Adjustment for accrued expense.		

Accounting Equation Impact

Assets	=	Liabilities	+	Owner's Equity (Expense)
		______ Payable: XXX (credit)		Expense: XXX (debit)

Accruals Versus Deferrals As illustrated in Exhibit 3, accrued revenues are earned revenues that are unrecorded. The cash receipts for accrued revenues are normally received in the next accounting period. As illustrated in Exhibit 4, accrued expenses are expenses that have been incurred but are unrecorded. The cash payments for accrued expenses are normally paid in the next accounting period.

Prepaid expenses and unearned revenues are sometimes referred to as *deferrals*. This is because the recording of the related expense or revenue is deferred to a future period. Accrued revenues and accrued expenses are sometimes referred to as *accruals*. This is because the related revenue or expense should be recorded or accrued in the current period.

Example Exercise 3-2 Type of Adjustment

OBJ 1

Classify the following items as (1) prepaid expense, (2) unearned revenue, (3) accrued expense, or (4) accrued revenue:

a. Wages owed but not yet paid.
b. Supplies on hand.
c. Fees received but not yet earned.
d. Fees earned but not yet received.

Follow My Example 3-2

a. Accrued expense
b. Prepaid expense
c. Unearned revenue
d. Accrued revenue

Practice Exercises: PE 3-2A, PE 3-2B

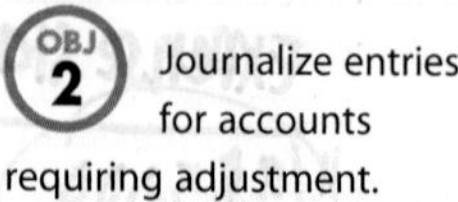
Journalize entries for accounts requiring adjustment.

Adjusting Entries

To illustrate adjusting entries, the December 31, 2015, unadjusted trial balance of **NetSolutions**, shown in Exhibit 5, is used. An expanded chart of accounts for NetSolutions is shown in Exhibit 6. The additional accounts used in this chapter are highlighted. The rules of debit and credit shown in Exhibit 3 of Chapter 2 are used to record the adjusting entries.

EXHIBIT 5

Unadjusted Trial Balance for NetSolutions

NetSolutions
Unadjusted Trial Balance
December 31, 2015

	Debit Balances	Credit Balances
Cash	2,065	
Accounts Receivable	2,220	
Supplies	2,000	
Prepaid Insurance	2,400	
Land	20,000	
Office Equipment	1,800	
Accounts Payable		900
Unearned Rent		360
Chris Clark, Capital		25,000
Chris Clark, Drawing	4,000	
Fees Earned		16,340
Wages Expense	4,275	
Supplies Expense	800	
Rent Expense	1,600	
Utilities Expense	985	
Miscellaneous Expense	455	
	42,600	42,600

EXHIBIT 6

Expanded Chart of Accounts for NetSolutions

Balance Sheet Accounts	Income Statement Accounts
1. Assets	**4. Revenue**
11 Cash	41 Fees Earned
12 Accounts Receivable	42 Rent Revenue
14 Supplies	**5. Expenses**
15 Prepaid Insurance	51 Wages Expense
17 Land	52 Supplies Expense
18 Office Equipment	53 Rent Expense
19 Accumulated Depreciation—Office Equipment	54 Utilities Expense
2. Liabilities	55 Insurance Expense
21 Accounts Payable	56 Depreciation Expense
22 Wages Payable	59 Miscellaneous Expense
23 Unearned Rent	
3. Owner's Equity	
31 Chris Clark, Capital	
32 Chris Clark, Drawing	

Prepaid Expenses

Supplies The December 31, 2015, unadjusted trial balance of **NetSolutions** indicates a balance in the supplies account of $2,000. In addition, the prepaid insurance account has a balance of $2,400. Each of these accounts requires an adjusting entry.

The balance in NetSolutions' supplies account on December 31 is $2,000. Some of these supplies (CDs, paper, envelopes, etc.) were used during December, and some are still on hand (not used). If either amount is known, the other can be determined. It is normally easier to determine the cost of the supplies on hand at the end of the month than to record daily supplies used.

Assuming that on December 31 the amount of supplies on hand is $760, the amount to be transferred from the asset account to the expense account is $1,240, computed as follows:

Supplies available during December (balance of account)	$2,000
Supplies on hand, December 31	760
Supplies used (amount of adjustment)	$1,240

At the end of December, the supplies expense account is increased (debited) for $1,240, and the supplies account is decreased (credited) for $1,240 to record the supplies used during December. The adjusting journal entry and T accounts for Supplies and Supplies Expense are as follows:

Journal *Page 5*

Date		Description	Post. Ref.	Debit	Credit
2015 Dec.	31	Supplies Expense	52	1,240	
		Supplies	14		1,240
		Supplies used ($2,000 – $760).			

Adjusting Journal Entry

Assets = Liabilities + Owner's Equity (Expense)

Supplies			14
Bal.	2,000	Dec. 31	1,240
Adj. Bal.	760		

Supplies Expense			52
Bal.	800		
Dec. 31	1,240		
Adj. Bal.	2,040		

Accounting Equation Impact

The adjusting entry is shown in color in the T accounts to separate it from other transactions. After the adjusting entry is recorded and posted, the supplies account has a debit balance of $760. This balance is an asset that will become an expense in a future period.

Prepaid Insurance The debit balance of $2,400 in **NetSolutions**' prepaid insurance account represents a December 1 prepayment of insurance for 12 months. At the end of December, the insurance expense account is increased (debited), and the prepaid insurance account is decreased (credited) by $200, the insurance for one month. The adjusting journal entry and T accounts for Prepaid Insurance and Insurance Expense are as follows:

Date		Description	Post. Ref.	Debit	Credit
Dec.	31	Insurance Expense	55	200	
		Prepaid Insurance	15		200
		Insurance expired ($2,400 ÷ 12).			

Adjusting Journal Entry

Assets = Liabilities + Owner's Equity (Expense)

Prepaid Insurance			15
Bal.	2,400	Dec. 31	200
Adj. Bal.	2,200		

Insurance Expense			55
Dec. 31	200		

Accounting Equation Impact

After the adjusting entry is recorded and posted, the prepaid insurance account has a debit balance of $2,200. This balance is an asset that will become an expense in future periods. The insurance expense account has a debit balance of $200, which is an expense of the current period.

If the preceding adjustments for supplies ($1,240) and insurance ($200) are not recorded, the financial statements prepared as of December 31 will be misstated. On the income statement, Supplies Expense and Insurance Expense will be understated

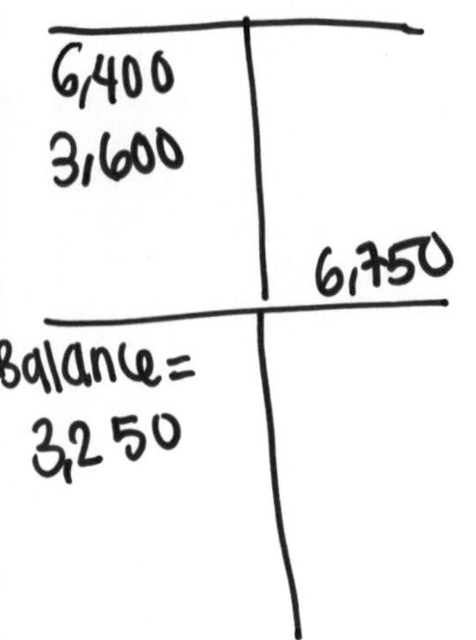

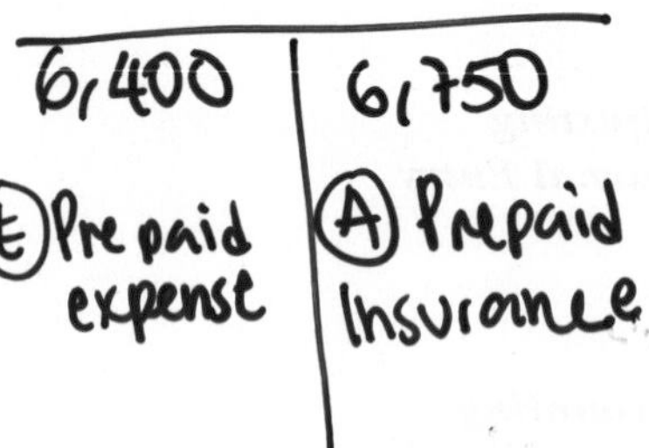

by a total of $1,440 ($1,240 + $200), and net income will be overstated by $1,440. On the balance sheet, Supplies and Prepaid Insurance will be overstated by a total of $1,440. Because net income increases owner's equity, Chris Clark, Capital will also be overstated by $1,440 on the balance sheet. The effects of omitting these adjusting entries on the income statement and balance sheet are as follows:

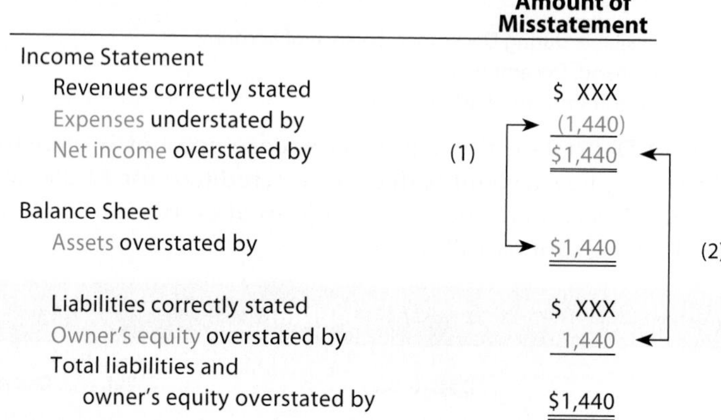

		Amount of Misstatement	
Income Statement			
Revenues correctly stated		$ XXX	
Expenses understated by		(1,440)	
Net income overstated by	(1)	$1,440	
Balance Sheet			
Assets overstated by		$1,440	(2)
Liabilities correctly stated		$ XXX	
Owner's equity overstated by		1,440	
Total liabilities and owner's equity overstated by		$1,440	

Arrow (1) indicates the effect of the understated expenses on assets. Arrow (2) indicates the effect of the overstated net income on owner's equity.

Payments for prepaid expenses are sometimes made at the beginning of the period in which they will be *entirely used or consumed*. To illustrate, the following December 1 transaction of NetSolutions is used:

Dec. 1	NetSolutions paid rent of $800 for the month.

On December 1, the rent payment of $800 represents Prepaid Rent. However, the Prepaid Rent expires daily, and at the end of December there will be no asset left. In such cases, the payment of $800 is recorded as Rent Expense rather than as Prepaid Rent. In this way, no adjusting entry is needed at the end of the period.[3]

Example Exercise 3-3 Adjustment for Prepaid Expense

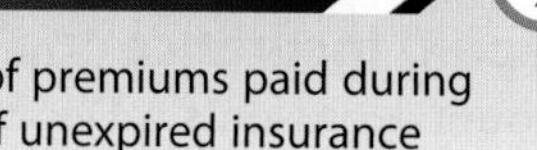

OBJ 2

The prepaid insurance account had a beginning balance of $6,400 and was debited for $3,600 of premiums paid during the year. Journalize the adjusting entry required at the end of the year, assuming the amount of unexpired insurance related to future periods is $3,250.

Follow My Example 3-3

Insurance Expense	6,750	
Prepaid Insurance		6,750
Insurance expired ($6,400 + $3,600 – $3,250).		

Practice Exercises: PE 3-3A, PE 3-3B

Integrity, Objectivity, and Ethics in Business

FREE ISSUE

Office supplies are often available to employees on a "free issue" basis. This means that employees do not have to "sign" for the release of office supplies but merely obtain the necessary supplies from a local storage area as needed. Just because supplies are easily available, however, doesn't mean they can be taken for personal use. There are many instances where employees have been terminated for taking supplies home for personal use.

[3] An alternative treatment of recording the cost of supplies, rent, and other prepayments of expenses is discussed in an appendix that can be downloaded from the book's companion Web site (www.cengagebrain.com).

Unearned Revenues

The December 31 unadjusted trial balance of **NetSolutions** indicates a balance in the unearned rent account of $360. This balance represents the receipt of three months' rent on December 1 for December, January, and February. At the end of December, one month's rent has been earned. Thus, the unearned rent account is decreased (debited) by $120, and the rent revenue account is increased (credited) by $120. The $120 represents the rental revenue for one month ($360 ÷ 3). The adjusting journal entry and T accounts are as follows:

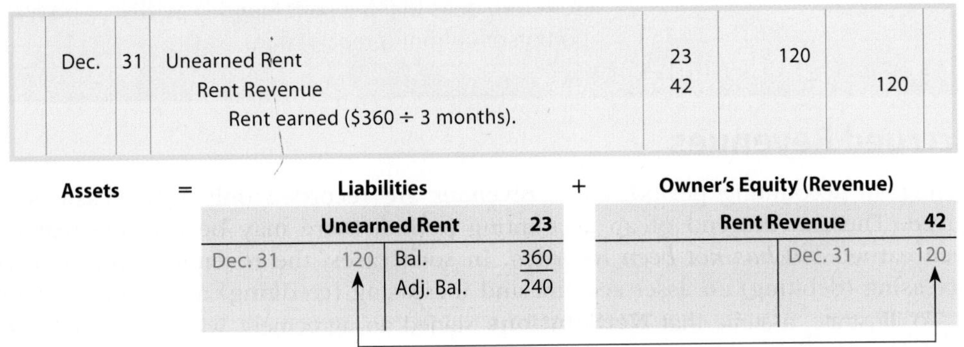

Dec.	31	Unearned Rent	23	120	
		Rent Revenue	42		120
		Rent earned ($360 ÷ 3 months).			

Assets = Liabilities + Owner's Equity (Revenue)

Unearned Rent			23
Dec. 31	120	Bal.	360
		Adj. Bal.	240

Rent Revenue			42
		Dec. 31	120

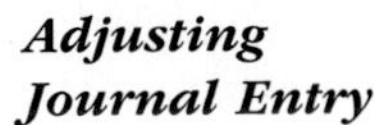

Adjusting Journal Entry

Accounting Equation Impact

After the adjusting entry is recorded and posted, the unearned rent account has a credit balance of $240. This balance is a liability that will become revenue in a future period. Rent Revenue has a balance of $120, which is revenue of the current period.[4]

If the preceding adjustment of unearned rent and rent revenue is not recorded, the financial statements prepared on December 31 will be misstated. On the income statement, Rent Revenue and the net income will be understated by $120. On the balance sheet, Unearned Rent will be overstated by $120, and Chris Clark, Capital will be understated by $120. The effects of omitting this adjusting entry are as follows:

Best Buy sells extended warranty contracts with terms between 12 and 36 months. The receipts from sales of these contracts are reported as unearned revenue on Best Buy's balance sheet. Revenue is recorded as the contracts expire.

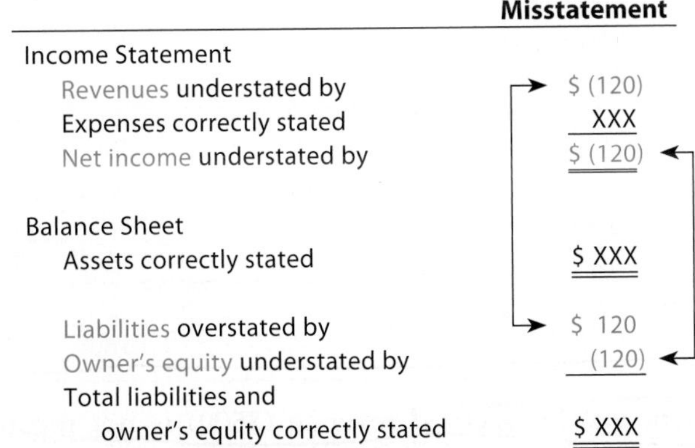

	Amount of Misstatement
Income Statement	
Revenues understated by	$ (120)
Expenses correctly stated	XXX
Net income understated by	$ (120)
Balance Sheet	
Assets correctly stated	$ XXX
Liabilities overstated by	$ 120
Owner's equity understated by	(120)
Total liabilities and owner's equity correctly stated	$ XXX

Example Exercise 3-4 Adjustment for Unearned Revenue

OBJ 2

The balance in the unearned fees account, before adjustment at the end of the year, is $44,900. Journalize the adjusting entry required if the amount of unearned fees at the end of the year is $22,300.

Follow My Example 3-4

Unearned Fees	22,600	
Fees Earned		22,600
Fees earned ($44,900 – $22,300).		

Practice Exercises: PE 3-4A, PE 3-4B

[4] An alternative treatment of recording revenues received in advance of their being earned is discussed in an appendix that can be downloaded from the book's companion Web site (www.cengagebrain.com).

Business  Connection

NATIONAL FITNESS CENTER: UPFRONT FEES

National Fitness Center imposes a nonrefundable upfront fee on some of its multiyear club memberships. Should the fee be recognized as revenue when the club receives the fee?

The upfront fee is like an advance payment made by customers for use of the club facilities. The company earns these fees over time as customers work out and use the facilities. Thus, the initial fee is unearned when received by the club and becomes earned revenue over time.[5] As a result, each month the club records revenue from club dues that are paid monthly as well as from a portion of upfront (prepaid) dues.

Accrued Revenues

RadioShack Corporation is engaged in consumer electronics retailing. RadioShack accrues revenue for finance charges and late payment charges related to its credit operations.

During an accounting period, some revenues are recorded only when cash is received. Thus, at the end of an accounting period, there may be revenue that has been earned *but has not been recorded*. In such cases, the revenue is recorded by increasing (debiting) an asset account and increasing (crediting) a revenue account.

To illustrate, assume that **NetSolutions** signed an agreement with Dankner Co. on December 15. The agreement provides that NetSolutions will answer computer questions and render assistance to Dankner Co.'s employees. The services will be billed to Dankner Co. on the fifteenth of each month at a rate of \$20 per hour. As of December 31, NetSolutions had provided 25 hours of assistance to Dankner Co. The revenue of \$500 (25 hours × \$20) will be billed on January 15. However, NetSolutions earned the revenue in December.

The claim against the customer for payment of the \$500 is an account receivable (*an asset*). Thus, the accounts receivable account is increased (debited) by \$500, and the fees earned account is increased (credited) by \$500. The adjusting journal entry and T accounts are as follows:

Adjusting Journal Entry

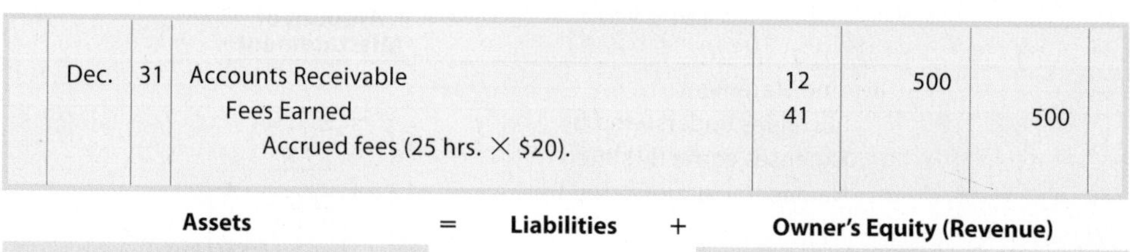

			Post. Ref.	Debit	Credit
Dec.	31	Accounts Receivable	12	500	
		Fees Earned	41		500
		Accrued fees (25 hrs. × \$20).			

Accounting Equation Impact

Assets = Liabilities + Owner's Equity (Revenue)

Accounts Receivable 12

	Debit	Credit
Bal.	2,220	
Dec. 31	500	
Adj. Bal.	2,720	

Fees Earned 41

Debit		Credit
	Bal.	16,340
	Dec. 31	500
	Adj. Bal.	16,840

If the adjustment for the accrued revenue (\$500) is not recorded, Fees Earned and the net income will be understated by \$500 on the income statement. On the balance sheet, Accounts Receivable and Chris Clark, Capital will be understated by \$500. The effects of omitting this adjusting entry are as follows:

	Amount of Misstatement
Income Statement	
Revenues understated by	\$ (500)
Expenses correctly stated	XXX
Net income understated by	\$ (500)
Balance Sheet	
Assets understated by	\$ (500)
Liabilities correctly stated	\$ XXX
Owner's equity understated by	(500)
Total liabilities and owner's equity understated by	\$ (500)

[5]FASB Exposure Draft, Revenue Recognition (Topic 605), June 24, 2010, para. IG29-IG32.

Example Exercise 3-5 Adjustment for Accrued Revenues

OBJ 2

At the end of the current year, $13,680 of fees have been earned but have not been billed to clients. Journalize the adjusting entry to record the accrued fees.

Follow My Example 3-5

Accounts Receivable	13,680	
Fees Earned		13,680
Accrued fees.		

Practice Exercises: PE 3-5A, PE 3-5B

Accrued Expenses

Some types of services used in earning revenues are paid for *after* the service has been performed. For example, wages expense is used hour by hour but is paid only daily, weekly, biweekly, or monthly. At the end of the accounting period, the amount of such *accrued* but unpaid items is an expense and a liability.

Callaway Golf Company, a manufacturer of such innovative golf clubs as the "RAZR Hawk" driver, reports accrued warranty expense on its balance sheet.

For example, if the last day of the employees' pay period is not the last day of the accounting period, an accrued expense (wages expense) and the related liability (wages payable) must be recorded by an adjusting entry. This adjusting entry is necessary so that expenses are properly matched to the period in which they were incurred in earning revenue.

To illustrate, **NetSolutions** pays its employees biweekly. During December, NetSolutions paid wages of $950 on December 13 and $1,200 on December 27. These payments covered pay periods ending on those days as shown in Exhibit 7.

EXHIBIT 7

Accrued Wages

Dynamic Exhibit

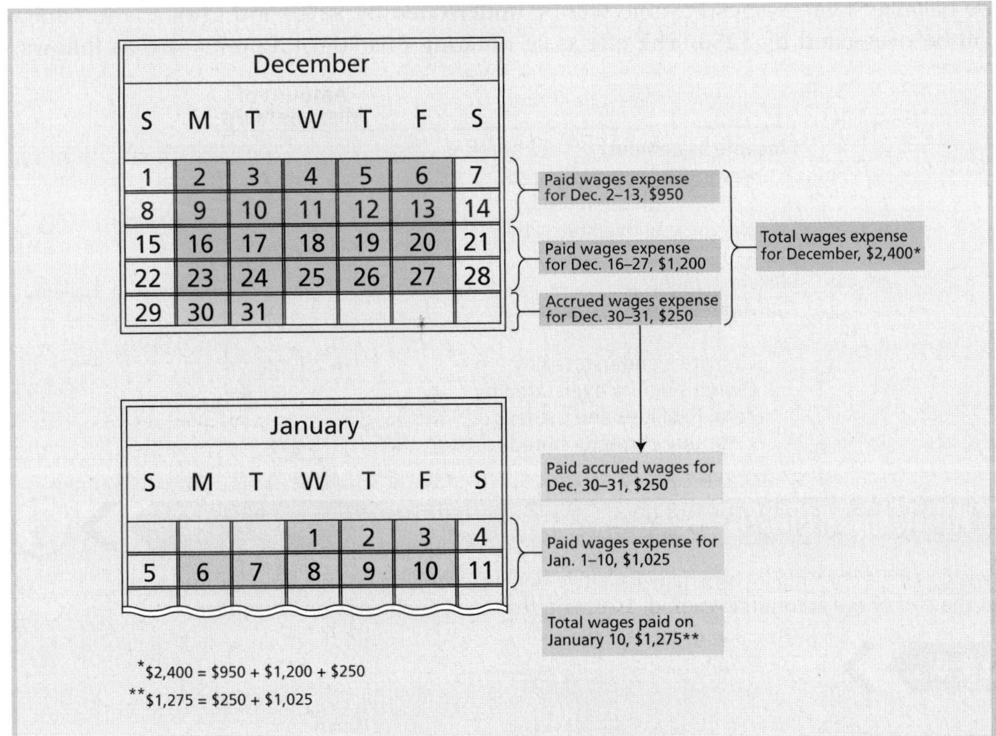

As of December 31, NetSolutions owes $250 of wages to employees for Monday and Tuesday, December 30 and 31. Thus, the wages expense account is increased (debited) by $250, and the wages payable account is increased (credited) by $250. The adjusting journal entry and T accounts are as follows:

Adjusting Journal Entry

Dec. 31	Wages Expense	51	250	
	Wages Payable	22		250
	Accrued wages.			

Accounting Equation Impact

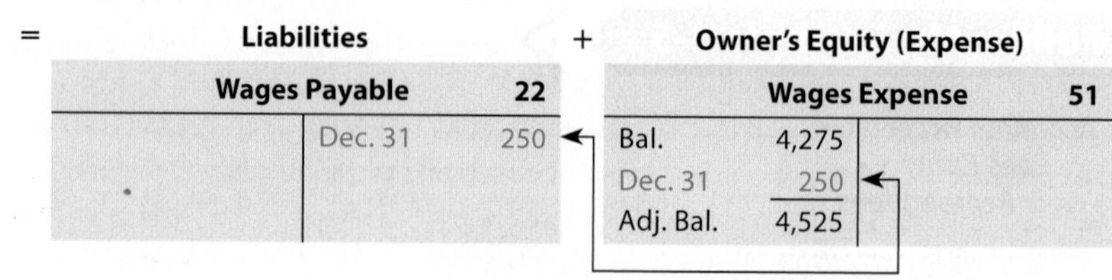

After the adjusting entry is recorded and posted, the debit balance of the wages expense account is $4,525. This balance of $4,525 is the wages expense for two months, November and December. The credit balance of $250 in Wages Payable is the liability for wages owed on December 31.

As shown in Exhibit 7, NetSolutions paid wages of $1,275 on January 10. This payment includes the $250 of accrued wages recorded on December 31. Thus, on January 10, the wages payable account is decreased (debited) by $250. Also, the wages expense account is increased (debited) by $1,025 ($1,275 – $250), which is the wages expense for January 1–10. Finally, the cash account is decreased (credited) by $1,275. The journal entry for the payment of wages on January 10 follows:[6]

Jan. 10	Wages Expense	51	1,025	
	Wages Payable	22	250	
	Cash	11		1,275

If the adjustment for wages ($250) is not recorded, Wages Expense will be understated by $250, and the net income will be overstated by $250 on the income statement. On the balance sheet, Wages Payable will be understated by $250, and Chris Clark, Capital will be overstated by $250. The effects of omitting this adjusting entry are as follows:

	Amount of Misstatement
Income Statement	
Revenues correctly stated	$ XXX
Expenses understated by	(250)
Net income overstated by	$ 250
Balance Sheet	
Assets correctly stated	$ XXX
Liabilities understated by	$ (250)
Owner's equity overstated by	250
Total liabilities and owner's equity correctly stated	$ XXX

Example Exercise 3-6 Adjustment for Accrued Expense

OBJ 2

Sanregret Realty Co. pays weekly salaries of $12,500 on Friday for a five-day week ending on that day. Journalize the necessary adjusting entry at the end of the accounting period, assuming that the period ends on Thursday.

Follow My Example 3-6

Salaries Expense	10,000	
Salaries Payable		10,000
Accrued salaries [($12,500 ÷ 5 days) × 4 days].		

Practice Exercises: PE 3-6A, PE 3-6B

[6] To simplify the subsequent recording of the following period's transactions, some accountants use what is known as reversing entries for certain types of adjustments. Reversing entries are discussed and illustrated in Appendix B at the end of the textbook.

Depreciation Expense

Fixed assets, or **plant assets**, are physical resources that are owned and used by a business and are permanent or have a long life. Examples of fixed assets include land, buildings, and equipment. In a sense, fixed assets are a type of *long-term* prepaid expense. However, because of their unique nature and long life, they are discussed separately from other prepaid expenses.

Fixed assets, such as office equipment, are used to generate revenue much like supplies are used to generate revenue. Unlike supplies, however, there is no visible reduction in the quantity of the equipment. Instead, as time passes, the equipment loses its ability to provide useful services. This decrease in usefulness is called **depreciation**.

All fixed assets, except land, lose their usefulness and, thus, are said to **depreciate**. As a fixed asset depreciates, a portion of its cost should be recorded as an expense. This periodic expense is called **depreciation expense**.

The adjusting entry to record depreciation expense is similar to the adjusting entry for supplies used. The depreciation expense account is increased (debited) for the amount of depreciation. However, the fixed asset account is not decreased (credited). This is because both the original cost of a fixed asset and the depreciation recorded since its purchase are reported on the balance sheet. Instead, an account entitled **Accumulated Depreciation** is increased (credited).

Accumulated depreciation accounts are called **contra accounts**, or **contra asset accounts**. This is because accumulated depreciation accounts are deducted from their related fixed asset accounts on the balance sheet. The normal balance of a contra account is opposite to the account from which it is deducted. Because the normal balance of a fixed asset account is a debit, the normal balance of an accumulated depreciation account is a credit.

Lowe's Companies, Inc., reported land, buildings, and store equipment at a cost of $34,332 million and accumulated depreciation of $12,362 million.

The normal titles for fixed asset accounts and their related contra asset accounts are as follows:

Fixed Asset Account	Contra Asset Account
Land	None—Land is not depreciated.
Buildings	Accumulated Depreciation—Buildings
Store Equipment	Accumulated Depreciation—Store Equipment
Office Equipment	Accumulated Depreciation—Office Equipment

The December 31, 2015, unadjusted trial balance of **NetSolutions** (Exhibit 5) indicates that NetSolutions owns two fixed assets: land and office equipment. Land does not depreciate; however, an adjusting entry is recorded for the depreciation of the office equipment for December. Assume that the office equipment depreciates $50 during December. The depreciation expense account is increased (debited) by $50, and the accumulated depreciation—office equipment account is increased (credited) by $50.[7] The adjusting journal entry and T accounts are as follows:

Dec.	31	Depreciation Expense	56	50	
		Accumulated Depreciation—Office Equip.	19		50
		Depreciation on office equipment.			

Adjusting Journal Entry

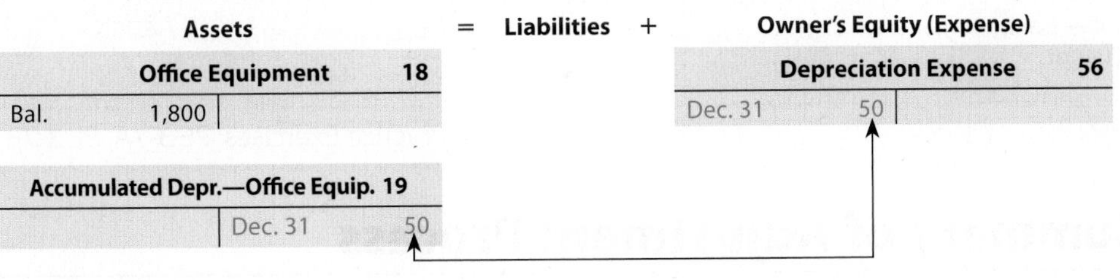

Accounting Equation Impact

After the adjusting journal entry is recorded and posted, the office equipment account still has a debit balance of $1,800. This is the original cost of the office equipment that

[7] Methods of computing depreciation expense are described and illustrated in Chapter 10.

was purchased on December 4. The accumulated depreciation—office equipment account has a credit balance of $50. The difference between these two balances is the cost of the office equipment that has not yet been depreciated. This amount, called the **book value of the asset** (or **net book value**), is computed as follows:

Book Value of Asset	= Cost of the Asset – Accumulated Depreciation of Asset
Book Value of Office Equipment	= Cost of Office Equipment – Accumulated Depr. of Office Equipment
	= $1,800 – $50
	= $1,750

The office equipment and its related accumulated depreciation are reported on the December 31, 2015, balance sheet as follows:

Office equipment	$1,800	
Less accumulated depreciation	50	$1,750

The market value of a fixed asset usually differs from its book value. This is because depreciation is an *allocation* method, not a *valuation* method. That is, depreciation allocates the cost of a fixed asset to expense over its estimated life. Depreciation does not measure changes in market values, which vary from year to year. Thus, on December 31, 2015, the market value of NetSolutions' office equipment could be more or less than $1,750.

If the adjustment for depreciation ($50) is not recorded, Depreciation Expense on the income statement will be understated by $50, and the net income will be overstated by $50. On the balance sheet, the book value of Office Equipment and Chris Clark, Capital will be overstated by $50. The effects of omitting the adjustment for depreciation are as follows:

	Amount of Misstatement
Income Statement	
Revenues correctly stated	$ XX
Expenses understated by	(50)
Net income overstated by	$ 50
Balance Sheet	
Assets overstated by	$ 50
Liabilities correctly stated	$ XX
Owner's equity overstated by	50
Total liabilities and owner's equity overstated by	$ 50

Example Exercise 3-7 Adjustment for Depreciation OBJ 2

The estimated amount of depreciation on equipment for the current year is $4,250. Journalize the adjusting entry to record the depreciation.

Follow My Example 3-7

Depreciation Expense	4,250	
Accumulated Depreciation—Equipment		4,250
Depreciation on equipment.		

Practice Exercises: PE 3-7A, PE 3-7B

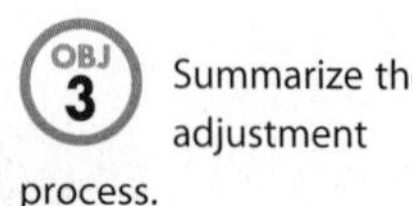
Summarize the adjustment process.

Summary of Adjustment Process

A summary of the basic types of adjusting entries is shown in Exhibit 8. The adjusting entries for **NetSolutions** are shown in Exhibit 9. The adjusting entries are dated as of the last day of the period. However, because collecting the adjustment data requires

EXHIBIT 8 **Summary of Adjustments**

Examples	Reason for Adjustment	Adjusting Entry	Examples from NetSolutions	Financial Statement Impact if Adjusting Entry Is Omitted
PREPAID EXPENSES				
Supplies, prepaid insurance	Prepaid expenses (assets) have been used or consumed in the business operations.	Expense Dr. Asset Cr.	Supplies Expense 1,240 Supplies 1,240 Insurance Expense 200 Prepaid Insurance 200	Income Statement: Revenues: No effect Expenses: Understated Net income: Overstated Balance Sheet: Assets: Overstated Liabilities: No effect Owner's equity (capital): Overstated
UNEARNED REVENUES				
Unearned rent, magazine subscriptions received in advance, fees received in advance of services	Cash received before the services have been provided is recorded as a liability. Some services have been provided to the customer before the end of the accounting period.	Liability Dr. Revenue Cr.	Unearned Rent 120 Rent Revenue 120	Income Statement: Revenues: Understated Expenses: No effect Net income: Understated Balance Sheet: Assets: No effect Liabilities: Overstated Owner's equity (capital): Understated
ACCRUED REVENUES				
Services performed but not billed, interest to be received	Services have been provided to the customer, but have not been billed or recorded. Interest has been earned, but has not been received or recorded.	Asset Dr. Revenue Cr.	Accounts Receivable 500 Fees Earned 500	Income Statement: Revenues: Understated Expenses: No effect Net income: Understated Balance Sheet: Assets: Understated Liabilities: No effect Owner's equity (capital): Understated
ACCRUED EXPENSES				
Wages or salaries incurred but not paid, interest incurred but not paid	Expenses have been incurred, but have not been paid or recorded.	Expense Dr. Liability Cr.	Wages Expense 250 Wages Payable 250	Income Statement: Revenues: No effect Expenses: Understated Net income: Overstated Balance Sheet: Assets: No effect Liabilities: Understated Owner's equity (capital): Overstated
DEPRECIATION				
Depreciation of equipment and buildings	Fixed assets depreciate as they are used or consumed in the business operations.	Expense Dr. Contra Asset Cr.	Depreciation Expense 50 Accum. Depreciation—Office Equipment 50	Income Statement: Revenues: No effect Expenses: Understated Net income: Overstated Balance Sheet: Assets: Overstated Liabilities: No effect Owner's equity (capital): Overstated

EXHIBIT 9

Adjusting Entries—NetSolutions

Journal Page 5

Date		Description	Post. Ref.	Debit	Credit
		Adjusting Entries			
2015 Dec.	31	Supplies Expense	52	1,240	
		Supplies	14		1,240
		Supplies used ($2,000 – $760).			
	31	Insurance Expense	55	200	
		Prepaid Insurance	15		200
		Insurance expired ($2,400 ÷ 12 months).			
	31	Unearned Rent	23	120	
		Rent Revenue	42		120
		Rent earned ($360 ÷ 3 months).			
	31	Accounts Receivable	12	500	
		Fees Earned	41		500
		Accrued fees (25 hrs. × $20).			
	31	Wages Expense	51	250	
		Wages Payable	22		250
		Accrued wages.			
	31	Depreciation Expense	56	50	
		Accum. Depreciation—Office Equipment	19		50
		Depreciation on office equipment.			

An accountant may check whether all adjustments have been made by comparing current period adjustments with those of the prior period.

Business  Connection

MICROSOFT CORPORATION

Microsoft Corporation develops, manufactures, licenses, and supports a wide range of computer software products, including Windows Vista®, Windows 7®, Windows XP®, Word®, Excel®, and the Xbox® gaming system. When Microsoft sells its products, it incurs an obligation to support its software with technical support and periodic updates. As a result, not all the revenue is earned on the date of sale; some of the revenue on the date of sale is unearned. The portion of revenue related to support services, such as updates and technical support, is earned as time passes and support is provided to customers. Thus, each year Microsoft makes adjusting entries transferring some of its unearned revenue to revenue. The following excerpts were taken from recent financial statements of Microsoft:

> The percentage of revenue recorded as unearned . . . ranges from approximately 15% to 25% of the sales price for Windows XP Home, approximately 5% to 15% of the sales price for Windows XP Professional, . . .
>
> Unearned Revenue:

	Recent Year	Prior Year
Unearned revenue (in millions)	$17,120	$14,830

During the next year, Microsoft expects to record more than $15,722 million of unearned revenue as revenue. At the same time, Microsoft will record additional unearned revenue from current period sales.

time, the entries are usually recorded at a later date. An explanation is normally included with each adjusting entry.

NetSolutions' adjusting entries are posted to the ledger shown in Exhibit 10. The adjustments are highlighted in Exhibit 10 to distinguish them from other transactions.

EXHIBIT 10 **Ledger with Adjusting Entries—NetSolutions**

Account *Cash* Account No. *11*

Date	Item	Post. Ref.	Debit	Credit	Balance Debit	Balance Credit
2015						
Nov. 1		1	25,000		25,000	
5		1		20,000	5,000	
18		1	7,500		12,500	
30		1		3,650	8,850	
30		1		950	7,900	
30		2		2,000	5,900	
Dec. 1		2		2,400	3,500	
1		2		800	2,700	
1		2	360		3,060	
6		2		180	2,880	
11		2		400	2,480	
13		3		950	1,530	
16		3	3,100		4,630	
20		3		900	3,730	
21		3	650		4,380	
23		3		1,450	2,930	
27		3		1,200	1,730	
31		3		310	1,420	
31		4		225	1,195	
31		4	2,870		4,065	
31		4		2,000	2,065	

Account *Accounts Receivable* Account No. *12*

Date	Item	Post. Ref.	Debit	Credit	Balance Debit	Balance Credit
2015						
Dec. 16		3	1,750		1,750	
21		3		650	1,100	
31		4	1,120		2,220	
31	Adjusting	5	500		2,720	

Account *Supplies* Account No. *14*

Date	Item	Post. Ref.	Debit	Credit	Balance Debit	Balance Credit
2015						
Nov. 10		1	1,350		1,350	
30		1		800	550	
Dec. 23		3	1,450		2,000	
31	Adjusting	5		1,240	760	

Account *Prepaid Insurance* Account No. *15*

Date	Item	Post. Ref.	Debit	Credit	Balance Debit	Balance Credit
2015						
Dec. 1		2	2,400		2,400	
31	Adjusting	5		200	2,200	

Account *Land* Account No. *17*

Date	Item	Post. Ref.	Debit	Credit	Balance Debit	Balance Credit
2015						
Nov. 5		1	20,000		20,000	

Account *Office Equipment* Account No. *18*

Date	Item	Post. Ref.	Debit	Credit	Balance Debit	Balance Credit
2015						
Dec. 4		2	1,800		1,800	

Account *Accum. Depr.—Office Equip.* Account No. *19*

Date	Item	Post. Ref.	Debit	Credit	Balance Debit	Balance Credit
2015						
Dec. 1	Adjusting	5		50		50

Account *Accounts Payable* Account No. *21*

Date	Item	Post. Ref.	Debit	Credit	Balance Debit	Balance Credit
2015						
Nov. 10		1		1,350		1,350
30		1	950			400
Dec. 4		2		1,800		2,200
11		2	400			1,800
20		3	900			900

Account *Wages Payable* Account No. *22*

Date	Item	Post. Ref.	Debit	Credit	Balance Debit	Balance Credit
2015						
Dec. 31	Adjusting	5		250		250

Account *Unearned Rent* Account No. *23*

Date	Item	Post. Ref.	Debit	Credit	Balance Debit	Balance Credit
2015						
Dec. 1		2		360		360
31	Adjusting	5	120			240

Account *Chris Clark, Capital* Account No. *31*

Date	Item	Post. Ref.	Debit	Credit	Balance Debit	Balance Credit
2015						
Nov. 1		1		25,000		25,000

(Continued)

EXHIBIT 10 **Ledger with Adjusting Entries—NetSolutions (*Concluded*)**

Account *Chris Clark, Drawing* — Account No. *32*

Date	Item	Post. Ref.	Debit	Credit	Balance Debit	Balance Credit
2015						
Nov. 30		2	2,000		2,000	
Dec. 31		4	2,000		4,000	

Account *Fees Earned* — Account No. *41*

Date	Item	Post. Ref.	Debit	Credit	Balance Debit	Balance Credit
2015						
Nov. 18		1		7,500		7,500
Dec. 16		3		3,100		10,600
16		3		1,750		12,350
31		4		2,870		15,220
31		4		1,120		16,340
31	Adjusting	5		500		16,840

Account *Rent Revenue* — Account No. *42*

Date	Item	Post. Ref.	Debit	Credit	Balance Debit	Balance Credit
2015						
Dec. 31	Adjusting	5		120		120

Account *Wages Expense* — Account No. *51*

Date	Item	Post. Ref.	Debit	Credit	Balance Debit	Balance Credit
2015						
Nov. 30		1	2,125		2,125	
Dec. 13		3	950		3,075	
27		3	1,200		4,275	
31	Adjusting	5	250		4,525	

Account *Supplies Expense* — Account No. *52*

Date	Item	Post. Ref.	Debit	Credit	Balance Debit	Balance Credit
2015						
Nov. 30		1	800		800	
Dec. 31	Adjusting	5	1,240		2,040	

Account *Rent Expense* — Account No. *53*

Date	Item	Post. Ref.	Debit	Credit	Balance Debit	Balance Credit
2015						
Nov. 30		1	800		800	
Dec. 1		2	800		1,600	

Account *Utilities Expense* — Account No. *54*

Date	Item	Post. Ref.	Debit	Credit	Balance Debit	Balance Credit
2015						
Nov. 30		1	450		450	
Dec. 31		3	310		760	
31		4	225		985	

Account *Insurance Expense* — Account No. *55*

Date	Item	Post. Ref.	Debit	Credit	Balance Debit	Balance Credit
2015						
Dec. 31	Adjusting	5	200		200	

Account *Depreciation Expense* — Account No. *56*

Date	Item	Post. Ref.	Debit	Credit	Balance Debit	Balance Credit
2015						
Dec. 31	Adjusting	5	50		50	

Account *Miscellaneous Expense* — Account No. *59*

Date	Item	Post. Ref.	Debit	Credit	Balance Debit	Balance Credit
2015						
Nov. 30		1	275		275	
Dec. 6		2	180		455	

Example Exercise 3-8 Effect of Omitting Adjustments

For the year ending December 31, 2016, Mann Medical Co. mistakenly omitted adjusting entries for (1) $8,600 of unearned revenue that was earned, (2) earned revenue of $12,500 that was not billed, and (3) accrued wages of $2,900. Indicate the combined effect of the errors on (a) revenues, (b) expenses, and (c) net income for the year ended December 31, 2016.

Follow My Example 3-8

a. Revenues were understated by $21,100 ($8,600 + $12,500).
b. Expenses were understated by $2,900.
c. Net income was understated by $18,200 ($8,600 + $12,500 − $2,900).

Practice Exercises: PE 3-8A, PE 3-8B

Adjusted Trial Balance

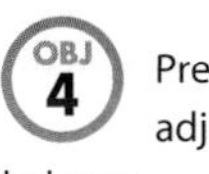

Prepare an adjusted trial balance.

After the adjusting entries are posted, an **adjusted trial balance** is prepared. The adjusted trial balance verifies the equality of the total debit and credit balances before the financial statements are prepared. If the adjusted trial balance does not balance, an error has occurred. However, as discussed in Chapter 2, errors may occur even though the adjusted trial balance totals agree. For example, if an adjusting entry were omitted, the adjusted trial balance totals would still agree.

Exhibit 11 shows the adjusted trial balance for **NetSolutions** as of December 31, 2015. Chapter 4 discusses how financial statements, including a classified balance sheet, are prepared from an adjusted trial balance.

EXHIBIT 11

Adjusted Trial Balance

NetSolutions
Adjusted Trial Balance
December 31, 2015

	Debit Balances	Credit Balances
Cash	2,065	
Accounts Receivable	2,720	
Supplies	760	
Prepaid Insurance	2,200	
Land	20,000	
Office Equipment	1,800	
Accumulated Depreciation—Office Equipment		50
Accounts Payable		900
Wages Payable		250
Unearned Rent		240
Chris Clark, Capital		25,000
Chris Clark, Drawing	4,000	
Fees Earned		16,840
Rent Revenue		120
Wages Expense	4,525	
Supplies Expense	2,040	
Rent Expense	1,600	
Utilities Expense	985	
Insurance Expense	200	
Depreciation Expense	50	
Miscellaneous Expense	455	
	43,400	43,400

Example Exercise 3-9 Effect of Errors on Adjusted Trial Balance

For each of the following errors, considered individually, indicate whether the error would cause the adjusted trial balance totals to be unequal. If the error would cause the adjusted trial balance totals to be unequal, indicate whether the debit or credit total is higher and by how much.

a. The adjustment for accrued fees of $5,340 was journalized as a debit to Accounts Payable for $5,340 and a credit to Fees Earned of $5,340.

b. The adjustment for depreciation of $3,260 was journalized as a debit to Depreciation Expense for $3,620 and a credit to Accumulated Depreciation for $3,260.

Follow My Example 3-9

a. The totals are equal even though the debit should have been to Accounts Receivable instead of Accounts Payable.

b. The totals are unequal. The debit total is higher by $360 ($3,620 – $3,260).

Practice Exercises: PE 3-9A, PE 3-9B

OBJ 5 Describe and illustrate the use of vertical analysis in evaluating a company's performance and financial condition.

Financial Analysis and Interpretation: Vertical Analysis

Comparing each item in a financial statement with a total amount from the same statement is useful in analyzing relationships within the financial statement. **Vertical analysis** is the term used to describe such comparisons.

In vertical analysis of a balance sheet, each asset item is stated as a percent of the total assets. Each liability and owner's equity item is stated as a percent of total liabilities and owner's equity. In vertical analysis of an income statement, each item is stated as a percent of revenues or fees earned.

Vertical analysis is also useful for analyzing changes in financial statements over time. To illustrate, a vertical analysis of two years of income statements for J. Holmes, Attorney-at-Law, follows:

J. Holmes, Attorney-at-Law
Income Statements
For the Years Ended December 31

	Year 2		Year 1	
	Amount	**Percent***	**Amount**	**Percent***
Fees earned	$187,500	100.0%	$150,000	100.0%
Operating expenses:				
Wages expense	$ 60,000	32.0%	$ 45,000	30.0%
Rent expense	15,000	8.0	12,000	8.0
Utilities expense	12,500	6.7	9,000	6.0
Supplies expense	2,700	1.4	3,000	2.0
Miscellaneous expense	2,300	1.2	1,800	1.2
Total operating expenses	$ 92,500	49.3%	$ 70,800	47.2%
Net income	$ 95,000	50.7%	$ 79,200	52.8%

*Rounded to one decimal place

The preceding vertical analysis indicates both favorable and unfavorable trends affecting the income statement of J. Holmes, Attorney-at-Law. The increase in wages expense of 2% (32.0% − 30.0%) is an unfavorable trend, as is the increase in utilities expense of 0.7% (6.7% − 6.0%). A favorable trend is the decrease in supplies expense of 0.6% (2.0% − 1.4%). Rent expense and miscellaneous expense as a percent of fees earned were constant. The net result of these trends is that net income decreased as a percent of fees earned from 52.8% to 50.7%.

The analysis of the various percentages shown for J. Holmes, Attorney-at-Law, can be enhanced by comparisons with industry averages. Such averages are published by trade associations and financial information services. Any major differences between industry averages should be investigated.

Vertical analysis of operating income taken from two recent years of income statements for **Pandora Media, Inc.** follows:

Pandora Media, Inc.
Income Statements
For the Years Ended January 31

	Year 2		Year 1	
	Amount*	**Percent****	**Amount***	**Percent****
Revenues:				
Advertising	$239,957	87.5%	$119,333	86.6%
Subscription services (other)	34,383	12.5	18,431	13.4
Total revenue	$274,340	100.0%	$137,764	100.0%
Expenses:				
Cost of revenues	22,759	8.3%	11,559	8.4%
Marketing and selling	65,010	23.7	36,250	26.3
General and administrative	35,428	12.9	14,183	10.3
Content acquisition	148,708	54.2	69,357	50.3
Product development	13,425	4.9	6,736	4.9
Total expenses	$285,330	104.0%	$138,085	100.2%
Operating income (loss)	$ (10,990)	(4.0)	$ (321)	(0.2)%

*In thousands
**Rounded to one decimal place

The preceding analysis illustrates the usefulness of vertical analysis. Since Year 2 revenues are almost twice those of Year 1, it is difficult to compare operating results using only dollar amounts. Vertical analysis, however, reveals that advertising revenue as a percent of total revenue in Year 2 increased 0.9% over that in Year 1, while subscription revenues fell by the same percent. In addition, expenses as a percent of total revenues increased 3.8% from Year 1 and to Year 2. Specifically, marketing and selling expenses declined from 26.3% to 23.7%, while general and administrative expenses increased from 10.3% to 12.9%. In addition, content acquisition costs, which include royalties paid to artists for playing their music, increased from 50.3% to 54.2%. As a result, the loss from operations increased from (0.2%) to (4.0%). There does not appear to be any major change in Pandora's overall operating performance from Year 1 to Year 2 except for increasing revenues and the related increase in expenses.

Example Exercise 3-10 Vertical Analysis

OBJ 5

Two income statements for Fortson Company follow:

Fortson Company
Income Statements
For the Years Ended December 31, 2016 and 2015

	2016	2015
Fees earned	$425,000	$375,000
Operating expenses	263,500	210,000
Operating income	$161,500	$165,000

a. Prepare a vertical analysis of Fortson Company's income statements.
b. Does the vertical analysis indicate a favorable or an unfavorable trend?

(Continued)

Follow My Example 3-10

a.

Fortson Company
Income Statements
For the Years Ended December 31, 2016 and 2015

	2016		2015	
	Amount	**Percent**	**Amount**	**Percent**
Fees earned	$425,000	100%	$375,000	100%
Operating expenses	263,500	62	210,000	56
Operating income	$161,500	38%	$165,000	44%

b. An unfavorable trend of increasing operating expenses and decreasing operating income is indicated.

Practice Exercises: PE 3-10A, PE 3-10B

At a Glance 3

Describe the nature of the adjusting process.

Key Points The accrual basis of accounting requires that revenues are reported in the period in which they are earned and expenses are matched with the revenues they generate. The updating of accounts at the end of the accounting period is called the adjusting process. Each adjusting entry affects an income statement and balance sheet account. The four types of accounts requiring adjusting entries are prepaid expenses, unearned revenues, accrued revenues, and accrued expenses.

Learning Outcomes	Example Exercises	Practice Exercises
• Explain why accrual accounting requires adjusting entries.		
• List accounts that do and do NOT require adjusting entries at the end of the accounting period.	**EE3-1**	**PE3-1A, 3-1B**
• Give an example of a prepaid expense, unearned revenue, accrued revenue, and accrued expense.	**EE3-2**	**PE3-2A, 3-2B**

Journalize entries for accounts requiring adjustment.

Key Points At the end of the period, adjusting entries are needed for prepaid expenses, unearned revenues, accrued revenues, and accrued expenses. In addition, an adjusting entry is necessary to record depreciation on fixed assets.

Learning Outcomes	Example Exercises	Practice Exercises
• Prepare an adjusting entry for a prepaid expense.	EE3-3	PE3-3A, 3-3B
• Prepare an adjusting entry for an unearned revenue.	EE3-4	PE3-4A, 3-4B
• Prepare an adjusting entry for an accrued revenue.	EE3-5	PE3-5A, 3-5B
• Prepare an adjusting entry for an accrued expense.	EE3-6	PE3-6A, 3-6B
• Prepare an adjusting entry for depreciation expense.	EE3-7	PE3-7A, 3-7B

Summarize the adjustment process.

Key Points A summary of adjustments, including the type of adjustment, reason for the adjustment, the adjusting entry, and the effect of omitting an adjustment on the financial statements, is shown in Exhibit 8.

Learning Outcomes	Example Exercises	Practice Exercises
• Determine the effect on the income statement and balance sheet of omitting an adjusting entry for prepaid expense, unearned revenue, accrued revenue, accrued expense, and depreciation.	EE3-8	PE3-8A, 3-8B

Prepare an adjusted trial balance.

Key Points After all the adjusting entries have been posted, the equality of the total debit balances and total credit balances is verified by an adjusted trial balance.

Learning Outcomes	Example Exercises	Practice Exercises
• Prepare an adjusted trial balance.		
• Determine the effect of errors on the equality of the adjusted trial balance.	EE3-9	PE3-9A, 3-9B

Describe and illustrate the use of vertical analysis in evaluating a company's performance and financial condition.

Key Points Comparing each item on a financial statement with a total amount from the same statement is called vertical analysis. On the balance sheet, each asset is expressed as a percent of total assets, and each liability and owner's equity is expressed as a percent of total liabilities and owner's equity. On the income statement, each revenue and expense is expressed as a percent of total revenues or fees earned.

Learning Outcomes	Example Exercises	Practice Exercises
• Describe vertical analysis.		
• Prepare a vertical analysis report of a financial statement.	EE3-10	PE3-10A, 3-10B

Key Terms

accounting period concept (104)
accrual basis of accounting (104)
accrued expenses (108)
accrued revenues (107)
Accumulated Depreciation (117)
adjusted trial balance (123)
adjusting entries (105)
adjusting process (105)
book value of the asset (or net book value) (118)
cash basis of accounting (104)
contra accounts (or contra asset accounts) (117)
depreciate (117)
depreciation (117)
depreciation expense (117)
fixed assets (or plant assets) (117)
matching concept (104)
prepaid expenses (105)
revenue recognition concept (104)
unearned revenues (106)
vertical analysis (124)

Illustrative Problem

Three years ago, T. Roderick organized Harbor Realty. At July 31, 2016, the end of the current year, the unadjusted trial balance of Harbor Realty follows:

Harbor Realty
Unadjusted Trial Balance
July 31, 2016

	Debit Balances	Credit Balances
Cash	3,425	
Accounts Receivable	7,000	
Supplies	1,270	
Prepaid Insurance	620	
Office Equipment	51,650	
Accumulated Depreciation—Office Equipment		9,700
Accounts Payable		925
Wages Payable		0
Unearned Fees		1,250
T. Roderick, Capital		29,000
T. Roderick, Drawing	5,200	
Fees Earned		59,125
Wages Expense	22,415	
Depreciation Expense	0	
Rent Expense	4,200	
Utilities Expense	2,715	
Supplies Expense	0	
Insurance Expense	0	
Miscellaneous Expense	1,505	
	100,000	100,000

The data needed to determine year-end adjustments are as follows:

a. Supplies on hand at July 31, 2016, $380.
b. Insurance premiums expired during the year, $315.
c. Depreciation of equipment during the year, $4,950.
d. Wages accrued but not paid at July 31, 2016, $440.
e. Accrued fees earned but not recorded at July 31, 2016, $1,000.
f. Unearned fees on July 31, 2016, $750.

Instructions

1. Prepare the necessary adjusting journal entries. Include journal entry explanations.
2. Determine the balance of the accounts affected by the adjusting entries, and prepare an adjusted trial balance.

Solution

1.

Journal

Date		Description	Post. Ref.	Debit	Credit
2016 July	31	Supplies Expense		890	
		Supplies			890
		Supplies used ($1,270 – $380).			
	31	Insurance Expense		315	
		Prepaid Insurance			315
		Insurance expired.			
	31	Depreciation Expense		4,950	
		Accumulated Depreciation—Office Equipment			4,950
		Depreciation expense.			
	31	Wages Expense		440	
		Wages Payable			440
		Accrued wages.			
	31	Accounts Receivable		1,000	
		Fees Earned			1,000
		Accrued fees.			
	31	Unearned Fees		500	
		Fees Earned			500
		Fees earned ($1,250 – $750).			

2.

Harbor Realty Adjusted Trial Balance July 31, 2016	Debit Balances	Credit Balances
Cash	3,425	
Accounts Receivable	8,000	
Supplies	380	
Prepaid Insurance	305	
Office Equipment	51,650	
Accumulated Depreciation—Office Equipment		14,650
Accounts Payable		925
Wages Payable		440
Unearned Fees		750
T. Roderick, Capital		29,000
T. Roderick, Drawing	5,200	
Fees Earned		60,625
Wages Expense	22,855	
Depreciation Expense	4,950	
Rent Expense	4,200	
Utilities Expense	2,715	
Supplies Expense	890	
Insurance Expense	315	
Miscellaneous Expense	1,505	
	106,390	106,390

Discussion Questions

1. How are revenues and expenses reported on the income statement under (a) the cash basis of accounting and (b) the accrual basis of accounting?
2. Is the matching concept related to (a) the cash basis of accounting or (b) the accrual basis of accounting?
3. Why are adjusting entries needed at the end of an accounting period?
4. What is the difference between *adjusting entries* and *correcting entries*?
5. Identify the four different categories of adjusting entries frequently required at the end of an accounting period.
6. If the effect of the debit portion of an adjusting entry is to increase the balance of an asset account, which of the following statements describes the effect of the credit portion of the entry?
   a. Increases the balance of a revenue account.
   b. Increases the balance of an expense account.
   c. Increases the balance of a liability account.
7. If the effect of the credit portion of an adjusting entry is to increase the balance of a liability account, which of the following statements describes the effect of the debit portion of the entry?
   a. Increases the balance of a revenue account.
   b. Increases the balance of an expense account.
   c. Increases the balance of an asset account.
8. Does every adjusting entry have an effect on determining the amount of net income for a period? Explain.
9. On November 1 of the current year, a business paid the November rent on the building that it occupies. (a) Do the rights acquired at November 1 represent an asset or an expense? (b) What is the justification for debiting Rent Expense at the time of payment?
10. (a) Explain the purpose of the two accounts: Depreciation Expense and Accumulated Depreciation. (b) What is the normal balance of each account? (c) Is it customary for the balances of the two accounts to be equal in amount? (d) In what financial statements, if any, will each account appear?

Practice Exercises

EE 3-1 *p. 105* **PE 3-1A Accounts requiring adjustment** **OBJ. 1**

SHOW ME HOW

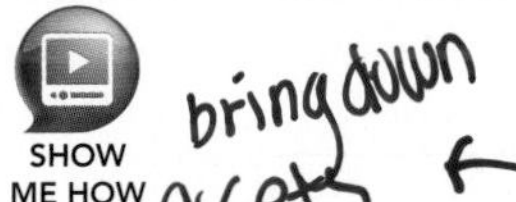

Indicate with a Yes or No whether or not each of the following accounts normally requires an adjusting entry:

a. Accumulated Depreciation
b. Frank Kent, Drawing
c. Land
d. Salaries Payable
e. Supplies
f. Unearned Rent

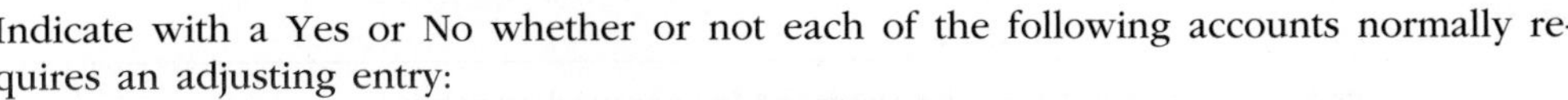

EE 3-1 *p. 105* **PE 3-1B Accounts requiring adjustment** **OBJ. 1**

SHOW ME HOW

Indicate with a Yes or No whether or not each of the following accounts normally requires an adjusting entry:

a. Building
b. Cash
c. Interest Expense
d. Miscellaneous Expense
e. Nancy Palmer, Capital
f. Prepaid Insurance

EE 3-2 *p. 109* **PE 3-2A Type of adjustment** **OBJ. 1**

SHOW ME HOW

Classify the following items as (1) prepaid expense, (2) unearned revenue, (3) accrued revenue, or (4) accrued expense:

a. Cash received for services not yet rendered
b. Insurance paid for the next year
c. Rent revenue earned but not received
d. Salaries owed but not yet paid

EE 3-2 *p. 109* **PE 3-2B Type of adjustment** **OBJ. 1**

SHOW ME HOW

Classify the following items as (1) prepaid expense, (2) unearned revenue, (3) accrued revenue, or (4) accrued expense:

a. Cash received for use of land next month
b. Fees earned but not received
c. Rent expense owed but not yet paid
d. Supplies on hand

EE 3-3 *p. 112* **PE 3-3A Adjustment for prepaid expense** **OBJ. 2**

SHOW ME HOW

The supplies account had a beginning balance of $3,375 and was debited for $6,450 for supplies purchased during the year. Journalize the adjusting entry required at the end of the year, assuming the amount of supplies on hand is $2,980.

EE 3-3 *p. 112* **PE 3-3B Adjustment for prepaid expense** **OBJ. 2**

SHOW ME HOW

The prepaid insurance account had a beginning balance of $9,600 and was debited for $12,900 of premiums paid during the year. Journalize the adjusting entry required at the end of the year, assuming the amount of unexpired insurance related to future periods is $7,360.

EE 3-4 *p. 113* **PE 3-4A Adjustment for unearned revenue** **OBJ. 2**

SHOW ME HOW

The balance in the unearned fees account, before adjustment at the end of the year, is $272,500. Journalize the adjusting entry required, assuming the amount of unearned fees at the end of the year is $189,750.

EE 3-4 *p. 113* **PE 3-4B Adjustment for unearned revenue** **OBJ. 2**

SHOW ME HOW

On June 1, 2016, Herbal Co. received $18,900 for the rent of land for 12 months. Journalize the adjusting entry required for unearned rent on December 31, 2016.

EE 3-5 p. 115

SHOW ME HOW

PE 3-5A Adjustment for accrued revenues **OBJ. 2**

At the end of the current year, $23,570 of fees have been earned but have not been billed to clients. Journalize the adjusting entry to record the accrued fees.

EE 3-5 p. 115

SHOW ME HOW

PE 3-5B Adjustment for accrued revenues **OBJ. 2**

At the end of the current year, $17,555 of fees have been earned but have not been billed to clients. Journalize the adjusting entry to record the accrued fees.

EE 3-6 p. 116

SHOW ME HOW

PE 3-6A Adjustment for accrued expense **OBJ. 2**

We-Sell Realty Co. pays weekly salaries of $11,800 on Friday for a five-day workweek ending on that day. Journalize the necessary adjusting entry at the end of the accounting period, assuming that the period ends on Wednesday.

EE 3-6 p. 116

SHOW ME HOW

PE 3-6B Adjustment for accrued expense **OBJ. 2**

Prospect Realty Co. pays weekly salaries of $27,600 on Monday for a six-day workweek ending the preceding Saturday. Journalize the necessary adjusting entry at the end of the accounting period, assuming that the period ends on Friday.

EE 3-7 p. 118

SHOW ME HOW

PE 3-7A Adjustment for depreciation **OBJ. 2**

The estimated amount of depreciation on equipment for the current year is $6,880. Journalize the adjusting entry to record the depreciation.

EE 3-7 p. 118

SHOW ME HOW

PE 3-7B Adjustment for depreciation **OBJ. 2**

The estimated amount of depreciation on equipment for the current year is $7,700. Journalize the adjusting entry to record the depreciation.

EE 3-8 p. 123

SHOW ME HOW

PE 3-8A Effect of omitting adjustments **OBJ. 3**

For the year ending August 31, 2016, Mammalia Medical Co. mistakenly omitted adjusting entries for (1) depreciation of $5,800, (2) fees earned that were not billed of $44,500, and (3) accrued wages of $7,300. Indicate the combined effect of the errors on (a) revenues, (b) expenses, and (c) net income for the year ended August 31, 2016.

EE 3-8 p. 123

SHOW ME HOW

PE 3-8B Effect of omitting adjustments **OBJ. 3**

For the year ending April 30, 2016, Urology Medical Services Co. mistakenly omitted adjusting entries for (1) $1,400 of supplies that were used, (2) unearned revenue of $6,600 that was earned, and (3) insurance of $9,000 that expired. Indicate the combined effect of the errors on (a) revenues, (b) expenses, and (c) net income for the year ended April 30, 2016.

EE 3-9 p. 124

SHOW ME HOW

PE 3-9A Effect of errors on adjusted trial balance **OBJ. 4**

For each of the following errors, considered individually, indicate whether the error would cause the adjusted trial balance totals to be unequal. If the error would cause the adjusted trial balance totals to be unequal, indicate whether the debit or credit total is higher and by how much.

a. The adjustment of $9,800 for accrued fees earned was journalized as a debit to Accounts Receivable for $9,800 and a credit to Fees Earned for $8,900.

b. The adjustment of depreciation of $3,600 was omitted from the end-of-period adjusting entries.

EE 3-9 p. 124

SHOW ME HOW

PE 3-9B Effect of errors on adjusted trial balance **OBJ. 4**

For each of the following errors, considered individually, indicate whether the error would cause the adjusted trial balance totals to be unequal. If the error would cause the adjusted trial balance totals to be unequal, indicate whether the debit or credit total is higher and by how much.

a. The adjustment for accrued wages of $5,200 was journalized as a debit to Wages Expense for $5,200 and a credit to Accounts Payable for $5,200.

b. The entry for $1,125 of supplies used during the period was journalized as a debit to Supplies Expense of $1,125 and a credit to Supplies of $1,152.

EE 3-10 p. 125

SHOW ME HOW

PE 3-10A Vertical analysis **OBJ. 5**

Two income statements for Hemlock Company follow:

Hemlock Company
Income Statements
For Years Ended December 31

	2016	2015
Fees earned	$725,000	$615,000
Operating expenses	435,000	356,700
Operating income	$290,000	$258,300

a. Prepare a vertical analysis of Hemlock Company's income statements.

b. Does the vertical analysis indicate a favorable or an unfavorable trend?

EE 3-10 p. 125

SHOW ME HOW

PE 3-10B Vertical analysis **OBJ. 5**

Two income statements for Cornea Company follow:

Cornea Company
Income Statements
For Years Ended December 31

	2016	2015
Fees earned	$1,640,000	$1,300,000
Operating expenses	869,200	715,000
Operating income	$ 770,800	$ 585,000

a. Prepare a vertical analysis of Cornea Company's income statements.

b. Does the vertical analysis indicate a favorable or an unfavorable trend?

Exercises

EX 3-1 Classifying types of adjustments **OBJ. 1**

Classify the following items as (a) prepaid expense, (b) unearned revenue, (c) accrued revenue, or (d) accrued expense:

1. A two-year premium paid on a fire insurance policy.
2. Fees earned but not yet received.
3. Fees received but not yet earned.
4. Salary owed but not yet paid.
5. Subscriptions received in advance by a magazine publisher.
6. Supplies on hand.
7. Taxes owed but payable in the following period.
8. Utilities owed but not yet paid.

EX 3-2 Classifying adjusting entries **OBJ. 1**

The following accounts were taken from the unadjusted trial balance of Orion Co., a congressional lobbying firm. Indicate whether or not each account would normally require an adjusting entry. If the account normally requires an adjusting entry, use the following notation to indicate the type of adjustment:

AE—Accrued Expense
AR—Accrued Revenue
PE—Prepaid Expense
UR—Unearned Revenue

To illustrate, the answer for the first account follows:

Account	Answer
Accounts Receivable	Normally requires adjustment (AR).
Cash	
Interest Expense	
Interest Receivable	
Johann Atkins, Capital	
Land	
Office Equipment	
Prepaid Rent	
Supplies	
Unearned Fees	
Wages Expense	

EX 3-3 Adjusting entry for supplies **OBJ. 2**

The balance in the supplies account, before adjustment at the end of the year, is $5,330. Journalize the adjusting entry required if the amount of supplies on hand at the end of the year is $1,875.

EX 3-4 Determining supplies purchased **OBJ. 2**

The supplies and supplies expense accounts at December 31, after adjusting entries have been posted at the end of the first year of operations, are shown in the following T accounts:

Supplies			Supplies Expense		
Bal.	2,550		Bal.	7,120	

Determine the amount of supplies purchased during the year.

EX 3-5 Effect of omitting adjusting entry **OBJ. 2, 3**

At March 31, the end of the first month of operations, the usual adjusting entry transferring prepaid insurance expired to an expense account is omitted. Which items will be incorrectly stated, because of the error, on (a) the income statement for March and (b) the balance sheet as of March 31? Also indicate whether the items in error will be overstated or understated.

EX 3-6 Adjusting entries for prepaid insurance **OBJ. 2**

The balance in the prepaid insurance account, before adjustment at the end of the year, is $18,630. Journalize the adjusting entry required under each of the following *alternatives* for determining the amount of the adjustment: (a) the amount of insurance expired during the year is $15,300; (b) the amount of unexpired insurance applicable to future periods is $3,330.

EX 3-7 Adjusting entries for prepaid insurance — OBJ. 2

The prepaid insurance account had a balance of $7,000 at the beginning of the year. The account was debited for $24,000 for premiums on policies purchased during the year. Journalize the adjusting entry required under each of the following *alternatives* for determining the amount of the adjustment: (a) the amount of unexpired insurance applicable to future periods is $8,500; (b) the amount of insurance expired during the year is $22,500.

EX 3-8 Adjusting entries for unearned fees — OBJ. 2

The balance in the unearned fees account, before adjustment at the end of the year, is $36,950. Journalize the adjusting entry required if the amount of unearned fees at the end of the year is $14,440.

EX 3-9 Effect of omitting adjusting entry — OBJ. 2, 3

At the end of July, the first month of the business year, the usual adjusting entry transferring rent earned to a revenue account from the unearned rent account was omitted. Indicate which items will be incorrectly stated, because of the error, on (a) the income statement for July and (b) the balance sheet as of July 31. Also indicate whether the items in error will be overstated or understated.

EX 3-10 Adjusting entry for accrued fees — OBJ. 2

At the end of the current year, $22,650 of fees have been earned but have not been billed to clients.

a. Journalize the adjusting entry to record the accrued fees.

b. If the cash basis rather than the accrual basis had been used, would an adjusting entry have been necessary? Explain.

EX 3-11 Adjusting entries for unearned and accrued fees — OBJ. 2

The balance in the unearned fees account, before adjustment at the end of the year, is $97,770. Of these fees, $82,220 have been earned. In addition, $34,250 of fees have been earned but have not been billed. Journalize the adjusting entries (a) to adjust the unearned fees account and (b) to record the accrued fees.

EX 3-12 Effect of omitting adjusting entry — OBJ. 2, 3

The adjusting entry for accrued fees was omitted at October 31, the end of the current year. Indicate which items will be in error, because of the omission, on (a) the income statement for the current year and (b) the balance sheet as of October 31. Also indicate whether the items in error will be overstated or understated.

EX 3-13 Adjusting entries for accrued salaries — OBJ. 2

Ocular Realty Co. pays weekly salaries of $16,600 on Friday for a five-day workweek ending on that day. Journalize the necessary adjusting entry at the end of the accounting period, assuming that the period ends (a) on Wednesday and (b) on Thursday.

EX 3-14 Determining wages paid — OBJ. 2

The wages payable and wages expense accounts at May 31, after adjusting entries have been posted at the end of the first month of operations, are shown in the following T accounts:

Wages Payable				Wages Expense			
		Bal.	7,175	Bal.	73,250		

Determine the amount of wages paid during the month.

EX 3-15 Effect of omitting adjusting entry **OBJ. 2, 3**

Accrued salaries owed to employees for October 30 and 31 are not considered in preparing the financial statements for the year ended October 31. Indicate which items will be erroneously stated, because of the error, on (a) the income statement for the year and (b) the balance sheet as of October 31. Also indicate whether the items in error will be overstated or understated.

EX 3-16 Effect of omitting adjusting entry **OBJ. 2, 3**

Assume that the error in Exercise 3-15 was not corrected and that the accrued salaries were included in the first salary payment in November. Indicate which items will be erroneously stated, because of failure to correct the initial error, on (a) the income statement for the month of November and (b) the balance sheet as of November 30.

EX 3-17 Adjusting entries for prepaid and accrued taxes **OBJ. 2**

✔ b. $67,000

SHOW ME HOW

Art Imaging Company was organized on April 1 of the current year. On April 2, Art Imaging Company prepaid $54,000 to the city for taxes (license fees) for the *next* 12 months and debited the prepaid taxes account. Art Imaging Company is also required to pay in January an annual tax (on property) for the *previous* calendar year. The estimated amount of the property tax for the current year (April 1 to December 31) is $26,500.

a. Journalize the two adjusting entries required to bring the accounts affected by the two taxes up to date as of December 31, the end of the current year.

b. What is the amount of tax expense for the current year?

EX 3-18 Adjustment for depreciation **OBJ. 2**

SHOW ME HOW

The estimated amount of depreciation on equipment for the current year is $10,650. Journalize the adjusting entry to record the depreciation.

EX 3-19 Determining fixed asset's book value **OBJ. 2**

SHOW ME HOW

The balance in the equipment account is $28,650,000, and the balance in the accumulated depreciation—equipment account is $16,430,000.

a. What is the book value of the equipment?

b. Does the balance in the accumulated depreciation account mean that the equipment's loss of value is $16,430,000? Explain.

EX 3-20 Book value of fixed assets **OBJ. 2**

In a recent balance sheet, **Microsoft Corporation** reported *Property, Plant, and Equipment* of $19,231 million and *Accumulated Depreciation* of $10,962 million.

a. What was the book value of the fixed assets?

b. Would the book value of Microsoft Corporation's fixed assets normally approximate their fair market values?

EX 3-21 Effects of errors on financial statements **OBJ. 2, 3**

For a recent period, the balance sheet for **Costco Wholesale Corporation** reported accrued expenses of $2,890 million. For the same period, Costco reported income before income taxes of $2,767 million. Assume that the adjusting entry for $2,890 million of accrued expenses was not recorded at the end of the current period. What would have been the income (loss) before income taxes?

EX 3-22 Effects of errors on financial statements OBJ. 2, 3

For a recent year, the balance sheet for **The Campbell Soup Company** includes accrued expenses of $598 million. The income before taxes for The Campbell Soup Company for the year was $1,106 million.

a. Assume the adjusting entry for $598 million of accrued expenses was not recorded at the end of the year. By how much would income before taxes have been misstated?

b. What is the percentage of the misstatement in (a) to the reported income of $1,106 million? Round to one decimal place.

EX 3-23 Effects of errors on financial statements OBJ. 2, 3

✔ 1. a. Revenue understated, $34,900

The accountant for Healthy Life Company, a medical services consulting firm, mistakenly omitted adjusting entries for (a) unearned revenue earned during the year ($34,900) and (b) accrued wages ($12,770). Indicate the effect of each error, considered individually, on the income statement for the current year ended July 31. Also indicate the effect of each error on the July 31 balance sheet. Set up a table similar to the following, and record your answers by inserting the dollar amount in the appropriate spaces. Insert a zero if the error does not affect the item.

	Error (a)		Error (b)	
	Over-stated	Under-stated	Over-stated	Under-stated
1. Revenue for the year would be	$____	$____	$____	$____
2. Expenses for the year would be	$____	$____	$____	$____
3. Net income for the year would be	$____	$____	$____	$____
4. Assets at July 31 would be	$____	$____	$____	$____
5. Liabilities at July 31 would be	$____	$____	$____	$____
6. Owner's equity at July 31 would be	$____	$____	$____	$____

EX 3-24 Effects of errors on financial statements OBJ. 2, 3

If the net income for the current year had been $196,400 in Exercise 3-23, what would have been the correct net income if the proper adjusting entries had been made?

EX 3-25 Adjusting entries for depreciation; effect of error OBJ. 2, 3

SHOW ME HOW

On December 31, a business estimates depreciation on equipment used during the first year of operations to be $13,900.

a. Journalize the adjusting entry required as of December 31.

b. If the adjusting entry in (a) were omitted, which items would be erroneously stated on (1) the income statement for the year and (2) the balance sheet as of December 31?

EX 3-26 Adjusting entries from trial balances OBJ. 4

SHOW ME HOW

The unadjusted and adjusted trial balances for American Leaf Company on October 31, 2016, follow:

(Continued)

American Leaf Company
Trial Balances
October 31, 2016

	Unadjusted		Adjusted	
	Debit Balances	**Credit Balances**	**Debit Balances**	**Credit Balances**
Cash	16		16	
Accounts Receivable	38		44	
Supplies	12		10	
Prepaid Insurance	20		8	
Land	26		26	
Equipment	40		40	
Accumulated Depreciation—Equipment		8		12
Accounts Payable		26		26
Wages Payable		0		2
Sloane Kissel, Capital		92		92
Sloane Kissel, Drawing	8		8	
Fees Earned		74		80
Wages Expense	24		26	
Rent Expense	8		8	
Insurance Expense	0		12	
Utilities Expense	4		4	
Depreciation Expense	0		4	
Supplies Expense	0		2	
Miscellaneous Expense	4		4	
	200	200	212	212

Journalize the five entries that adjusted the accounts at October 31, 2016. None of the accounts were affected by more than one adjusting entry.

EX 3-27 Adjusting entries from trial balances

OBJ. 4

✔ **Corrected trial balance totals, $369,000**

The accountant for Eva's Laundry prepared the following unadjusted and adjusted trial balances. Assume that all balances in the unadjusted trial balance and the amounts of the adjustments are correct. Identify the errors in the accountant's adjusting entries, assuming that none of the accounts were affected by more than one adjusting entry.

Eva's Laundry
Trial Balances
May 31, 2016

	Unadjusted		Adjusted	
	Debit Balances	**Credit Balances**	**Debit Balances**	**Credit Balances**
Cash	7,500		7,500	
Accounts Receivable	18,250		23,250	
Laundry Supplies	3,750		6,750	
Prepaid Insurance*	5,200		1,600	
Laundry Equipment	190,000		177,000	
Accumulated Depreciation—Laundry Equipment		48,000		48,000
Accounts Payable		9,600		9,600
Wages Payable				1,000
Eva Bruns, Capital		110,300		110,300
Eva Bruns, Drawing	28,775		28,775	
Laundry Revenue		182,100		182,100
Wages Expense	49,200		49,200	
Rent Expense	25,575		25,575	
Utilities Expense	18,500		18,500	
Depreciation Expense			13,000	
Laundry Supplies Expense			3,000	
Insurance Expense			600	
Miscellaneous Expense	3,250		3,250	
	350,000	350,000	358,000	351,000

* $3,600 of insurance expired during the year.

EX 3-28 Vertical analysis of income statement

OBJ. 5

The following data (in millions) are taken from recent financial statements of Nike Inc.:

	Year 2	Year 1
Net sales (revenues)	$24,128	$20,862
Net income	2,223	2,133

a. Determine the amount of change (in millions) and percent of change in net income for Year 2. Round to one decimal place.

b. Determine the percentage relationship between net income and net sales (net income divided by net sales) for Year 2 and Year 1. Round to one decimal place.

c. What conclusions can you draw from your analysis?

EX 3-29 Vertical analysis of income statement

OBJ. 5

The following income statement data (in millions) for Dell Inc. and Hewlett-Packard Company (HP) were taken from their recent annual reports:

	Dell	Hewlett-Packard
Net sales	$62,071	$120,357
Cost of goods sold (expense)	(48,260)	(92,385)
Operating expenses	(9,380)	(39,029)
Operating income (loss)	$ 4,431	$ (11,057)

a. Prepare a vertical analysis of the income statement for Dell. Round to one decimal place.

b. Prepare a vertical analysis of the income statement for HP. Round to one decimal place.

c. Based on (a) and (b), how does Dell compare to HP?

Problems: Series A

SHOW ME HOW

PR 3-1A Adjusting entries

OBJ. 2

On March 31, 2016, the following data were accumulated to assist the accountant in preparing the adjusting entries for Potomac Realty:

a. The supplies account balance on March 31 is $5,620 The supplies on hand on March 31 are $1,290.

b. The unearned rent account balance on March 31 is $5,000 representing the receipt of an advance payment on March 1 of four months' rent from tenants.

c. Wages accrued but not paid at March 31 are $2,290.

d. Fees accrued but unbilled at March 31 are $16,825.

e. Depreciation of office equipment is $4,600.

Instructions

1. Journalize the adjusting entries required at March 31, 2016.
2. Briefly explain the difference between adjusting entries and entries that would be made to correct errors.

SHOW ME HOW

PR 3-2A Adjusting entries

OBJ. 2, 3

Selected account balances before adjustment for Alantic Coast Realty at July 31, 2016, the end of the current year, are as follows:

(Continued)

	Debits	Credits
Accounts Receivable	$ 75,000	
Equipment	345,700	
Accumulated Depreciation—Equipment		$112,500
Prepaid Rent	9,000	
Supplies	3,350	
Wages Payable		—
Unearned Fees		12,000
Fees Earned		660,000
Wages Expense	325,000	
Rent Expense	—	
Depreciation Expense	—	
Supplies Expense	—	

Data needed for year-end adjustments are as follows:

a. Unbilled fees at July 31, $11,150.
b. Supplies on hand at July 31, $900.
c. Rent expired, $6,000.
d. Depreciation of equipment during year, $8,950.
e. Unearned fees at July 31, $2,000.
f. Wages accrued but not paid at July 31, $4,840.

Instructions

1. Journalize the six adjusting entries required at July 31, based on the data presented.
2. What would be the effect on the income statement if adjustments (a) and (f) were omitted at the end of the year?
3. What would be the effect on the balance sheet if adjustments (a) and (f) were omitted at the end of the year?
4. What would be the effect on the "Net increase or decrease in cash" on the statement of cash flows if adjustments (a) and (f) were omitted at the end of the year?

PR 3-3A Adjusting entries **OBJ. 2, 3**

General Ledger

Reliable Repairs & Service, an electronics repair store, prepared the following unadjusted trial balance at the end of its first year of operations:

Reliable Repairs & Service
Unadjusted Trial Balance
April 30, 2016

	Debit Balances	Credit Balances
Cash	10,350	
Accounts Receivable	67,500	
Supplies	16,200	
Equipment	116,100	
Accounts Payable		15,750
Unearned Fees		18,000
Karin Bickle, Capital		121,500
Karin Bickle, Drawing	13,500	
Fees Earned		294,750
Wages Expense	94,500	
Rent Expense	72,000	
Utilities Expense	51,750	
Miscellaneous Expense	8,100	
	450,000	450,000

For preparing the adjusting entries, the following data were assembled:

a. Fees earned but unbilled on April 30 were $9,850.

b. Supplies on hand on April 30 were $4,660.

c. Depreciation of equipment was estimated to be $6,470 for the year.

d. The balance in unearned fees represented the April 1 receipt in advance for services to be provided. During April, $15,000 of the services were provided.

e. Unpaid wages accrued on April 30 were $5,200.

Instructions

1. Journalize the adjusting entries necessary on April 30, 2016.
2. Determine the revenues, expenses, and net income of Reliable Service & Repairs before the adjusting entries.
3. Determine the revenues, expense, and net income of Reliable Service & Repairs after the adjusting entries.
4. Determine the effect of the adjusting entries on Karin Bickle, Capital.

PR 3-4A Adjusting entries

OBJ. 2, 3, 4

General Ledger

Good Note Company specializes in the repair of music equipment and is owned and operated by Robin Stahl. On November 30, 2016, the end of the current year, the accountant for Good Note Company prepared the following trial balances:

Good Note Company
Trial Balances
November 30, 2016

	Unadjusted		Adjusted	
	Debit Balances	**Credit Balances**	**Debit Balances**	**Credit Balances**
Cash	38,250		38,250	
Accounts Receivable	89,500		89,500	
Supplies	11,250		2,400	
Prepaid Insurance	14,250		3,850	
Equipment	290,450		290,450	
Accumulated Depreciation—Equipment		94,500		106,100
Automobiles	129,500		129,500	
Accumulated Depreciation—Automobiles		54,750		62,050
Accounts Payable		24,930		26,130
Salaries Payable		—		8,100
Unearned Service Fees		18,000		9,000
Robin Stahl, Capital		324,020		324,020
Robin Stahl, Drawing	75,000		75,000	
Service Fees Earned		733,800		742,800
Salary Expense	516,900		525,000	
Rent Expense	54,000		54,000	
Supplies Expense	—		8,850	
Depreciation Expense—Equipment	—		11,600	
Depreciation Expense—Automobiles	—		7,300	
Utilities Expense	12,900		14,100	
Taxes Expense	8,175		8,175	
Insurance Expense	—		10,400	
Miscellaneous Expense	9,825		9,825	
	1,250,000	1,250,000	1,278,200	1,278,200

Instructions

Journalize the seven entries that adjusted the accounts at November 30. None of the accounts were affected by more than one adjusting entry.

✔ 2. Total of Debit column: $776,180

General Ledger

PR 3-5A Adjusting entries and adjusted trial balances

OBJ. 2, 3, 4

Rowland Company is a small editorial services company owned and operated by Marlene Rowland. On August 31, 2016, the end of the current year, Rowland Company's accounting clerk prepared the following unadjusted trial balance:

Rowland Company
Unadjusted Trial Balance
August 31, 2016

	Debit Balances	Credit Balances
Cash	7,500	
Accounts Receivable	38,400	
Prepaid Insurance	7,200	
Supplies	1,980	
Land	112,500	
Building	150,250	
Accumulated Depreciation—Building		87,550
Equipment	135,300	
Accumulated Depreciation—Equipment		97,950
Accounts Payable		12,150
Unearned Rent		6,750
Marlene Rowland, Capital		221,000
Marlene Rowland, Drawing	15,000	
Fees Earned		324,600
Salaries and Wages Expense	193,370	
Utilities Expense	42,375	
Advertising Expense	22,800	
Repairs Expense	17,250	
Miscellaneous Expense	6,075	
	750,000	750,000

The data needed to determine year-end adjustments are as follows:

a. Unexpired insurance at August 31, $6,000.
b. Supplies on hand at August 31, $480.
c. Depreciation of building for the year, $7,500.
d. Depreciation of equipment for the year, $4,150.
e. Rent unearned at August 31, $1,550.
f. Accrued salaries and wages at August 31, $3,200.
g. Fees earned but unbilled on August 31, $11,330.

Instructions

1. Journalize the adjusting entries using the following additional accounts: Salaries and Wages Payable; Rent Revenue; Insurance Expense; Depreciation Expense—Building; Depreciation Expense—Equipment; and Supplies Expense.
2. Determine the balances of the accounts affected by the adjusting entries, and prepare an adjusted trial balance.

PR 3-6A Adjusting entries and errors

OBJ. 2, 3

✔ 2. Corrected net income: $137,750

At the end of April, the first month of operations, the following selected data were taken from the financial statements of Shelby Crawford, an attorney:

Net income for April	$120,000
Total assets at April 30	750,000
Total liabilities at April 30	300,000
Total owner's equity at April 30	450,000

In preparing the financial statements, adjustments for the following data were overlooked:

a. Supplies used during April, $2,750.
b. Unbilled fees earned at April 30, $23,700.
c. Depreciation of equipment for April, $1,800.
d. Accrued wages at April 30, $1,400.

Instructions

1. Journalize the entries to record the omitted adjustments.
2. Determine the correct amount of net income for April and the total assets, liabilities, and owner's equity at April 30. In addition to indicating the corrected amounts, indicate the effect of each omitted adjustment by setting up and completing a columnar table similar to the following. Adjustment (a) is presented as an example.

	Net Income	Total Assets	= Total Liabilities	+ Total Owner's Equity
Reported amounts	$120,000	$750,000	$300,000	$450,000
Corrections:				
Adjustment (a)	−2,750	−2,750	0	−2,750
Adjustment (b)				
Adjustment (c)				
Adjustment (d)				
Corrected amounts				

Problems: Series B

PR 3-1B Adjusting entries

OBJ. 2

SHOW ME HOW

On May 31, 2016, the following data were accumulated to assist the accountant in preparing the adjusting entries for Oceanside Realty:

a. Fees accrued but unbilled at May 31 are $19,750.

b. The supplies account balance on May 31 is $12,300. The supplies on hand at May 31 are $4,150.

c. Wages accrued but not paid at May 31 are $2,700.

d. The unearned rent account balance at May 31 is $9,000, representing the receipt of an advance payment on May 1 of three months' rent from tenants.

e. Depreciation of office equipment is $3,200.

Instructions

1. Journalize the adjusting entries required at May 31, 2016.
2. Briefly explain the difference between adjusting entries and entries that would be made to correct errors.

PR 3-2B Adjusting entries

OBJ. 2, 3

SHOW ME HOW

Selected account balances before adjustment for Intuit Realty at November 30, the end of the current year, follow:

	Debits	Credits
Accounts Receivable	$ 75,000	
Equipment	250,000	
Accumulated Depreciation—Equipment		$ 12,000
Prepaid Rent	12,000	
Supplies	3,170	
Wages Payable		—
Unearned Fees		10,000
Fees Earned		400,000
Wages Expense	140,000	
Rent Expense	—	
Depreciation Expense	—	
Supplies Expense	—	

Data needed for year-end adjustments are as follows:

a. Supplies on hand at November 30, $550.

b. Depreciation of equipment during year, $1,675.

(Continued)

c. Rent expired during year, $8,500.
d. Wages accrued but not paid at November 30, $2,000.
e. Unearned fees at November 30, $4,000.
f. Unbilled fees at November 30, $5,380.

Instructions

1. Journalize the six adjusting entries required at November 30, based on the data presented.
2. What would be the effect on the income statement if adjustments (b) and (e) were omitted at the end of the year?
3. What would be the effect on the balance sheet if adjustments (b) and (e) were omitted at the end of the year?
4. What would be the effect on the "Net increase or decrease in cash" on the statement of cash flows if adjustments (b) and (e) were omitted at the end of the year?

PR 3-3B Adjusting entries

OBJ. 2, 3

General Ledger

Crazy Mountain Outfitters Co., an outfitter store for fishing treks, prepared the following unadjusted trial balance at the end of its first year of operations:

Crazy Mountain Outfitters Co.
Unadjusted Trial Balance
April 30, 2016

	Debit Balances	Credit Balances
Cash	11,400	
Accounts Receivable	72,600	
Supplies	7,200	
Equipment	112,000	
Accounts Payable		12,200
Unearned Fees		19,200
Diana Keck, Capital		137,800
Diana Keck, Drawing	10,000	
Fees Earned		305,800
Wages Expense	157,800	
Rent Expense	55,000	
Utilities Expense	42,000	
Miscellaneous Expense	7,000	
	475,000	475,000

For preparing the adjusting entries, the following data were assembled:

a. Supplies on hand on April 30 were $1,380.
b. Fees earned but unbilled on April 30 were $3,900.
c. Depreciation of equipment was estimated to be $3,000 for the year.
d. Unpaid wages accrued on April 30 were $2,475.
e. The balance in unearned fees represented the April 1 receipt in advance for services to be provided. Only $14,140 of the services was provided between April 1 and April 30.

Instructions

1. Journalize the adjusting entries necessary on April 30, 2016.
2. Determine the revenues, expenses, and net income of Crazy Mountain Outfitters Co. before the adjusting entries.
3. Determine the revenues, expense, and net income of Crazy Mountain Outfitters Co. after the adjusting entries.
4. Determine the effect of the adjusting entries on Diana Keck, Capital.

PR 3-4B Adjusting entries

OBJ. 2, 3, 4

General Ledger

The Signage Company specializes in the maintenance and repair of signs, such as billboards. On March 31, 2016, the accountant for The Signage Company prepared the following trial balances:

The Signage Company
Trial Balances
March 31, 2016

	Unadjusted		Adjusted	
	Debit Balances	Credit Balances	Debit Balances	Credit Balances
Cash	4,750		4,750	
Accounts Receivable	17,400		17,400	
Supplies	6,200		2,175	
Prepaid Insurance	9,000		1,150	
Land	100,000		100,000	
Buildings	170,000		170,000	
Accumulated Depreciation—Buildings		51,500		61,000
Trucks	75,000		75,000	
Accumulated Depreciation—Trucks		12,000		17,000
Accounts Payable		6,920		8,750
Salaries Payable		—		1,400
Unearned Service Fees		10,500		3,850
Al Bosch, Capital		256,400		256,400
Al Bosch, Drawing	7,500		7,500	
Service Fees Earned		162,680		169,330
Salary Expense	80,000		81,400	
Depreciation Expense—Trucks	—		5,000	
Rent Expense	11,900		11,900	
Supplies Expense	—		4,025	
Utilities Expense	6,200		8,030	
Depreciation Expense—Buildings	—		9,500	
Taxes Expense	2,900		2,900	
Insurance Expense	—		7,850	
Miscellaneous Expense	9,150		9,150	
	500,000	500,000	517,730	517,730

Instructions

Journalize the seven entries that adjusted the accounts at March 31. None of the accounts were affected by more than one adjusting entry.

PR 3-5B Adjusting entries and adjusted trial balances

OBJ. 2, 3, 4

✔ 2. Total of Debit column: $420,300

General Ledger

Reece Financial Services Co., which specializes in appliance repair services, is owned and operated by Joni Reece. Reece Financial Services Co.'s accounting clerk prepared the following unadjusted trial balance at July 31, 2016:

Reece Financial Services Co.
Unadjusted Trial Balance
July 31, 2016

	Debit Balances	Credit Balances
Cash	10,200	
Accounts Receivable	34,750	
Prepaid Insurance	6,000	
Supplies	1,725	
Land	50,000	
Building	155,750	
Accumulated Depreciation—Building		62,850
Equipment	45,000	
Accumulated Depreciation—Equipment		17,650
Accounts Payable		3,750
Unearned Rent		3,600
Joni Reece, Capital		153,550
Joni Reece, Drawing	8,000	
Fees Earned		158,600
Salaries and Wages Expense	56,850	
Utilities Expense	14,100	
Advertising Expense	7,500	
Repairs Expense	6,100	
Miscellaneous Expense	4,025	
	400,000	400,000

(Continued)

The data needed to determine year-end adjustments are as follows:

a. Depreciation of building for the year, $6,400.
b. Depreciation of equipment for the year, $2,800.
c. Accrued salaries and wages at July 31, $900.
d. Unexpired insurance at July 31, $1,500.
e. Fees earned but unbilled on July 31, $10,200.
f. Supplies on hand at July 31, $615.
g. Rent unearned at July 31, $300.

Instructions

1. Journalize the adjusting entries using the following additional accounts: Salaries and Wages Payable; Rent Revenue; Insurance Expense; Depreciation Expense—Building; Depreciation Expense—Equipment; and Supplies Expense.
2. Determine the balances of the accounts affected by the adjusting entries and prepare an adjusted trial balance.

PR 3-6B Adjusting entries and errors

OBJ. 2, 3

✔ 2. Corrected net income: $128,700

At the end of August, the first month of operations, the following selected data were taken from the financial statements of Tucker Jacobs, an attorney:

Net income for August	$112,500
Total assets at August 31	650,000
Total liabilities at August 31	225,000
Total owner's equity at August 31	425,000

In preparing the financial statements, adjustments for the following data were overlooked:

a. Unbilled fees earned at August 31, $31,900.
b. Depreciation of equipment for August, $7,500.
c. Accrued wages at August 31, $5,200.
d. Supplies used during August, $3,000.

Instructions

1. Journalize the entries to record the omitted adjustments.
2. Determine the correct amount of net income for August and the total assets, liabilities, and owner's equity at August 31. In addition to indicating the corrected amounts, indicate the effect of each omitted adjustment by setting up and completing a columnar table similar to the following. Adjustment (a) is presented as an example.

	Net Income	Total Assets	= Total Liabilities	+ Total Owner's Equity
Reported amounts	$112,500	$650,000	$225,000	$425,000
Corrections:				
Adjustment (a)	+31,900	+31,900	0	+31,900
Adjustment (b)				
Adjustment (c)				
Adjustment (d)				
Corrected amounts				

Continuing Problem

✔ 3. Total of Debit column: $42,340

General Ledger

The unadjusted trial balance that you prepared for PS Music at the end of Chapter 2 should appear as follows:

PS Music
Unadjusted Trial Balance
July 31, 2016

	Debit Balances	Credit Balances
Cash	9,945	
Accounts Receivable	2,750	
Supplies	1,020	
Prepaid Insurance	2,700	
Office Equipment	7,500	
Accounts Payable		8,350
Unearned Revenue		7,200
Peyton Smith, Capital		9,000
Peyton Smith, Drawing	1,750	
Fees Earned		16,200
Music Expense	3,610	
Wages Expense	2,800	
Office Rent Expense	2,550	
Advertising Expense	1,500	
Equipment Rent Expense	1,375	
Utilities Expense	1,215	
Supplies Expense	180	
Miscellaneous Expense	1,855	
	40,750	40,750

The data needed to determine adjustments are as follows:

a. During July, PS Music provided guest disc jockeys for KXMD for a total of 115 hours. For information on the amount of the accrued revenue to be billed to KXMD, see the contract described in the July 3, 2016, transaction at the end of Chapter 2.

b. Supplies on hand at July 31, $275.

c. The balance of the prepaid insurance account relates to the July 1, 2016, transaction at the end of Chapter 2.

d. Depreciation of the office equipment is $50.

e. The balance of the unearned revenue account relates to the contract between PS Music and KXMD, described in the July 3, 2016, transaction at the end of Chapter 2.

f. Accrued wages as of July 31, 2016, were $140.

Instructions

1. Prepare adjusting journal entries. You will need the following additional accounts:

   18 Accumulated Depreciation—Office Equipment

   22 Wages Payable

   57 Insurance Expense

   58 Depreciation Expense

2. Post the adjusting entries, inserting balances in the accounts affected.
3. Prepare an adjusted trial balance.

Cases & Projects

CP 3-1 Ethics and professional conduct in business

Daryl Kirby opened Squid Realty Co. on January 1, 2015. At the end of the first year, the business needed additional capital. On behalf of Squid Realty Co., Daryl applied to Ocean National Bank for a loan of $375,000. Based on Squid Realty Co.'s financial statements, which had been prepared on a cash basis, the Ocean National Bank loan officer rejected the loan as too risky.

(Continued)

After receiving the rejection notice, Daryl instructed his accountant to prepare the financial statements on an accrual basis. These statements included $65,000 in accounts receivable and $25,000 in accounts payable. Daryl then instructed his accountant to record an additional $30,000 of accounts receivable for commissions on property for which a contract had been signed on December 28, 2015. The title to the property is to transfer on January 5, 2016, when an attorney formally records the transfer of the property to the buyer.

Daryl then applied for a $375,000 loan from Free Spirit Bank, using the revised financial statements. On this application, Daryl indicated that he had not previously been rejected for credit.

Discuss the ethical and professional conduct of Daryl Kirby in applying for the loan from Free Spirit Bank.

CP 3-2 Accrued revenue

The following is an excerpt from a conversation between Sonia Lopez and Pete Lemke just before they boarded a flight to Paris on **Delta Air Lines**. They are going to Paris to attend their company's annual sales conference.

Sonia: Pete, aren't you taking an introductory accounting course at college?

Pete: Yes, I decided it's about time I learned something about accounting. You know, our annual bonuses are based on the sales figures that come from the accounting department.

Sonia: I guess I never really thought about it.

Pete: You should think about it! Last year, I placed a $5,000,000 order on December 30. But when I got my bonus, the $5,000,000 sale wasn't included. They said it hadn't been shipped until January 9, so it would have to count in next year's bonus.

Sonia: A real bummer!

Pete: Right! I was counting on that bonus including the $5,000,000 sale.

Sonia: Did you complain?

Pete: Yes, but it didn't do any good. Julie, the head accountant, said something about matching revenues and expenses. Also, something about not recording revenues until the sale is final. I figure I'd take the accounting course and find out whether she's just messing with me.

Sonia: I never really thought about it. When do you think Delta Air Lines will record its revenues from this flight?

Pete: Hmmm . . . I guess it could record the revenue when it sells the ticket . . . or . . . when the boarding passes are scanned at the door . . . or . . . when we get off the plane . . . or when our company pays for the tickets . . . or . . . I don't know. I'll ask my accounting instructor.

Discuss when Delta Air Lines should recognize the revenue from ticket sales to properly match revenues and expenses.

CP 3-3 Adjustments and financial statements

Several years ago, your brother opened Magna Appliance Repairs. He made a small initial investment and added money from his personal bank account as needed. He withdrew money for living expenses at irregular intervals. As the business grew, he hired an assistant. He is now considering adding more employees, purchasing additional service trucks, and purchasing the building he now rents. To secure funds for the expansion, your brother submitted a loan application to the bank and included the most recent financial statements (which follow) prepared from accounts maintained by a part-time bookkeeper.

Magna Appliance Repairs
Income Statement
For the Year Ended October 31, 2016

Service revenue		$675,000
Less: Rent paid	$187,200	
Wages paid	148,500	
Supplies paid	42,000	
Utilities paid	39,000	
Insurance paid	21,600	
Miscellaneous payments	54,600	492,900
Net income		$ 182,100

Magna Appliance Repairs
Balance Sheet
October 31, 2016

Assets	
Cash	$ 95,400
Amounts due from customers	112,500
Truck	332,100
Total assets	$540,000
Equities	
Owner's capital	$540,000

After reviewing the financial statements, the loan officer at the bank asked your brother if he used the accrual basis of accounting for revenues and expenses. Your brother responded that he did and that is why he included an account for "Amounts Due from Customers." The loan officer then asked whether or not the accounts were adjusted prior to the preparation of the statements. Your brother answered that they had not been adjusted.

a. Why do you think the loan officer suspected that the accounts had not been adjusted prior to the preparation of the statements?

b. Indicate possible accounts that might need to be adjusted before an accurate set of financial statements could be prepared.

CP 3-4 Codes of ethics

Group Project

Internet Project

Obtain a copy of your college or university's student code of conduct. In groups of three or four, answer the following questions:

1. Compare this code of conduct with the Institute of Management Accountants' *Statement of Ethical Professional Practice*, which can be obtained from the IMA Web site at www.imanet.org, and the American Institute of Certified Public Accountants' *Code of Professional Conduct*, which can be obtained from the AICPA Web site at www.aicpa.org.
2. One of your classmates asks you for permission to copy your homework, which your instructor will be collecting and grading for part of your overall term grade. Although your instructor has not stated whether one student may or may not copy another student's homework, is it ethical for you to allow your classmate to copy your homework? Is it ethical for your classmate to copy your homework?

Magna Appliance Repairs
Income Statement
For the Year Ended October 31, 2016

Service revenue		[illegible]
Less cash paid:		
Rent paid	[illegible]	
Wages paid	[illegible]	
Supplies paid	[illegible]	
Utilities paid	[illegible]	
Insurance paid	[illegible]	
Miscellaneous payments	[illegible]	[illegible]
Net income		[illegible]

Magna Appliance Repairs
Balance Sheet
October 31, 2016

Assets	
Cash	[illegible]
Amounts due from customers	[illegible]
Truck	[illegible]
Total assets	[illegible]
Equity	
Owner's capital	[illegible]

After reviewing the financial statements, the loan officer at the bank asked your brother if he used the accrual basis of accounting for revenues and expenses. Your brother responded that he did and that is why he included an account for "Amounts Due from Customers." The loan officer then asked whether or not the accounts were adjusted prior to the preparation of the statements. Your brother answered that they had not been adjusted.

a. Why do you think the loan officer suspected that the accounts had not been adjusted prior to the preparation of the statements?

b. Indicate possible accounts that might need to be adjusted before an accurate set of financial statements could be prepared.

CP 3-[illegible] Codes of ethics

Obtain a copy of your college or university's student code of conduct. In groups of three or four, answer the following questions.

1. Compare this code of conduct with the Institute of Management Accountants' *Statement of Ethical Professional Practice*, which can be obtained from the IMA Web site at www.imanet.org, and the American Institute of Certified Public Accountants' *Code of Professional Conduct*, which can be obtained from the AICPA Web site at www.aicpa.org.
2. One of your classmates asks you for permission to copy your homework, which your instructor will be collecting and grading for part of your overall term grade. Although your instructor has not stated whether one student may or may not copy another student's homework, is it ethical for you to allow your classmate to copy your homework? Is it ethical for your classmate to copy your homework?

KEVIN BRITLAND/ALAMY

Completing the Accounting Cycle

Zynga

Zynga is a leading provider of social games with more than 240 million active players per month. Zynga's games, such as CityVille, FarmVille, CastleVille, and Café World, can be played on a variety of platforms including Facebook, Google Android, and Apple iOS.

Zynga was founded in 2007 and is named after CEO (Chief Executive Officer) Mark Pincus's dog. Zinga is an American Bulldog who is known for her human-like qualities, which include sitting on chairs and eating at the dinner table. Because she is playful, loyal, and lovable, Zinga is considered the guiding spirit of the company.

In developing its games, Zynga goes through a game development cycle that starts with the initial gaming concept, program development, and ends with testing and debugging errors. Businesses also go through a cycle of accounting activities that begins with recording transactions and ends with preparing financial statements and getting the accounting records ready for recording the next period's transactions.

In Chapter 1, the initial accounting cycle for **NetSolutions** began with Chris Clark's investment in the business on November 1,2015. The cycle continued with recording NetSolutions' transactions for November and December, as we discussed and illustrated in Chapters 1 and 2. In Chapter 3, the cycle continued when the adjusting entries for the two months ending December 31, 2015, were recorded. In this chapter, the cycle is completed for NetSolutions by preparing financial statements and getting the accounts ready for recording transactions of the next period.

Source: Zynga.com

Learning Objectives

ing this chapter, you should be able to:	Example Exercises
cribe the flow of accounting information from the unadjusted trial balance he adjusted trial balance and financial statements.	
ow of Accounting Information	EE 4-1
OBJ 2 Prepare financial statements from adjusted account balances.	
Financial Statements	
Income Statement	
Statement of Owner's Equity	EE 4-2
Balance Sheet	EE 4-3
OBJ 3 Prepare closing entries.	
Closing Entries	
Journalizing and Posting Closing Entries	EE 4-4
Post-Closing Trial Balance	
OBJ 4 Describe the accounting cycle.	
Accounting Cycle	EE 4-5
OBJ 5 Illustrate the accounting cycle for one period.	
Illustration of the Accounting Cycle	
OBJ 6 Explain what is meant by the fiscal year and the natural business year.	
Fiscal Year	
OBJ 7 Describe and illustrate the use of working capital and the current ratio in evaluating a company's financial condition.	
Financial Analysis and Interpretation: Working Capital and Current Ratio	EE 4-6

At a Glance 4 Page 184

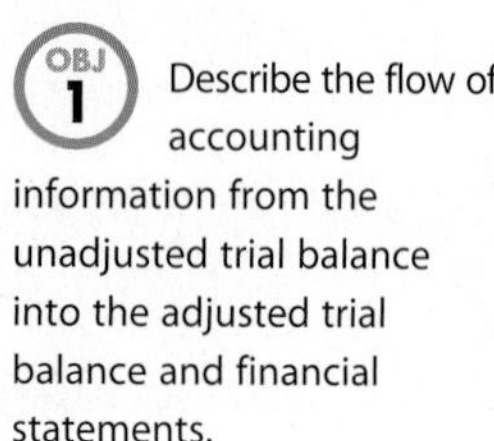

OBJ 1 Describe the flow of accounting information from the unadjusted trial balance into the adjusted trial balance and financial statements.

Flow of Accounting Information

The process of adjusting the accounts and preparing financial statements is one of the most important in accounting. Using the **NetSolutions** illustration from Chapters 1–3 and an end-of-period spreadsheet, the flow of accounting data in adjusting accounts and preparing financial statements are summarized in Exhibit 1.

The end-of-period spreadsheet in Exhibit 1 begins with the unadjusted trial balance. The unadjusted trial balance verifies that the total of the debit balances equals the total of the credit balances. If the trial balance totals are unequal, an error has occurred. Any errors must be found and corrected before the end-of-period process can continue.

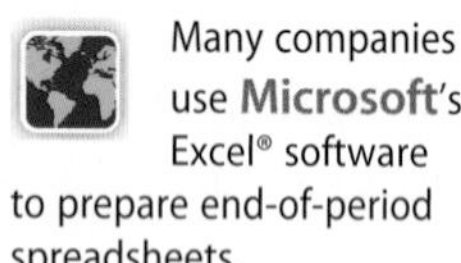

Many companies use **Microsoft's** Excel® software to prepare end-of-period spreadsheets.

The adjustments for NetSolutions from Chapter 3 are shown in the Adjustments columns of the spreadsheet. Cross-referencing (by letters) the debit and credit of each adjustment is useful in reviewing the effect of the adjustments on the unadjusted account balances. The adjustments are normally entered in the order in which the data are assembled. If the titles of the accounts to be adjusted do not appear in the unadjusted trial balance, the accounts are inserted in their proper order in the Account Title column. The total of the Adjustments columns verifies that the total debits equal the total credits for the adjusting entries. The total of the Debit column must equal the total of the Credit column.

The adjustments in the spreadsheet are added to or subtracted from the amounts in the Unadjusted Trial Balance columns to arrive at the amounts inserted in the Adjusted Trial Balance columns. In this way, the Adjusted Trial Balance columns of the spreadsheet illustrate the effect of the adjusting entries on the unadjusted accounts. The totals of the Adjusted Trial Balance columns verify that the totals of the debit and credit balances are equal after adjustment.

EXHIBIT 1

End-of-Period Spreadsheet and Flow of Accounting Data, NetSolutions

NetSolutions
Balance Sheet
December 31, 2015

Assets				Liabilities		
Current assets:				Current liabilities:		
Cash		$ 2,065		Accounts payable	$900	
Accounts receivable		2,720		Wages payable	250	
Supplies		760		Unearned rent	240	
Prepaid insurance		2,200		Total liabilities		$ 1,390
Total current assets			$ 7,745			
Property, plant, and equipment:						
Land		$20,000				
Office equipment	$1,800			Owner's Equity		
Less accum. depreciation	50	1,750		Chris Clark, capital		28,105
Total property, plant, and equipment			21,750	Total liabilities and owner's equity		$29,495
Total assets			$29,495			

	A	B	C	D	E	F	G
1			NetSolutions				
2			End-of-Period Spreadsheet				
3			For the Two Months Ended December 31, 2015				
4		Unadjusted				Adjusted	
5		Trial Balance		Adjustments		Trial Balance	
6	Account Title	Dr.	Cr.	Dr.	Cr.	Dr.	Cr.
7							
8	Cash	2,065				2,065	
9	Accounts Receivable	2,220		(d) 500		2,720	
10	Supplies	2,000			(a) 1,240	760	
11	Prepaid Insurance	2,400			(b) 200	2,200	
12	Land	20,000				20,000	
13	Office Equipment	1,800				1,800	
14	Accumulated Depreciation				(f) 50		50
15	Accounts Payable		900				900
16	Wages Payable				(e) 250		250
17	Unearned Rent		360	(c) 120			240
18	Chris Clark, Capital		25,000				25,000
19	Chris Clark, Drawing	4,000				4,000	
20	Fees Earned		16,340		(d) 500		16,840
21	Rent Revenue				(c) 120		120
22	Wages Expense	4,275		(e) 250		4,525	
23	Supplies Expense	800		(a) 1,240		2,040	
24	Rent Expense	1,600				1,600	
25	Utilities Expense	985				985	
26	Insurance Expense			(b) 200		200	
27	Depreciation Expense			(f) 50		50	
28	Miscellaneous Expense	455				455	
29		42,600	42,600	2,360	2,360	43,400	43,400
30							

NetSolutions
Statement of Owner's Equity
For the Two Months Ended December 31, 2015

Chris Clark, capital, November 1, 2015		$ 0
Investment on November 1, 2015	$25,000	
Net income for November and December	7,105	
	$32,105	
Less withdrawals	4,000	
Increase in owner's equity		28,105
Chris Clark, capital, December 31, 2015		$28,105

NetSolutions
Income Statement
For the Two Months Ended December 31, 2015

Revenues:		
Fees earned	$16,840	
Rent revenue	120	
Total revenues		$16,960
Expenses:		
Wages expense	$ 4,525	
Supplies expense	2,040	
Rent expense	1,600	
Utilities expense	985	
Insurance expense	200	
Depreciation expense	50	
Miscellaneous expense	455	
Total expenses		9,855
Net income		$ 7,105

Exhibit 1 illustrates the flow of accounts from the adjusted trial balance into the financial statements as follows:

1. The revenue and expense accounts (spreadsheet lines 20–28) flow into the income statement.
2. The owner's capital account, Chris Clark, Capital (spreadsheet line 18), and owner's drawing account, Chris Clark, Drawing (spreadsheet line 19), flow into the statement of owner's equity. The net income of $7,105 also flows into the statement of owner's equity from the income statement.
3. The asset and liability accounts (spreadsheet lines 8–17) flow into the balance sheet. The end-of-period owner's equity (Chris Clark, Capital of $28,105) also flows into the balance sheet from the statement of owner's equity.

To summarize, Exhibit 1 illustrates the process by which accounts are adjusted. In addition, Exhibit 1 illustrates how the adjusted accounts flow into the financial statements. The financial statements for NetSolutions can be prepared directly from Exhibit 1.

The spreadsheet in Exhibit 1 is not required. However, many accountants prepare such a spreadsheet, sometimes called a *work sheet*, as part of the normal end-of-period process. The primary advantage in doing so is that it allows managers and accountants to see the effect of adjustments on the financial statements. This is especially useful for adjustments that depend upon estimates. Such estimates and their effect on the financial statements are discussed in later chapters.[1]

Example Exercise 4-1 Flow of Accounts into Financial Statements (OBJ 1)

The balances for the accounts that follow appear in the Adjusted Trial Balance columns of the end-of-period spreadsheet. Indicate whether each account would flow into the income statement, statement of owner's equity, or balance sheet.

1. Office Equipment
2. Utilities Expense
3. Accumulated Depreciation—Equipment
4. Unearned Rent
5. Fees Earned
6. Doug Johnson, Drawing
7. Rent Revenue
8. Supplies

Follow My Example 4-1

1. Balance sheet
2. Income statement
3. Balance sheet
4. Balance sheet
5. Income statement
6. Statement of owner's equity
7. Income statement
8. Balance sheet

Practice Exercises: PE 4-1A, PE 4-1B

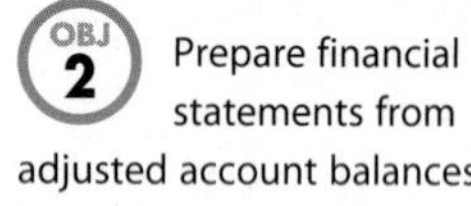
Prepare financial statements from adjusted account balances.

Financial Statements

Using the adjusted trial balance shown in Exhibit 1, the financial statements for **NetSolutions** can be prepared. The income statement, the statement of owner's equity, and the balance sheet are shown in Exhibit 2.

Income Statement

The income statement is prepared directly from the Adjusted Trial Balance columns of the Exhibit 1 spreadsheet, beginning with fees earned of $16,840. The expenses in the income statement in Exhibit 2 are listed in order of size, beginning with the larger items. Miscellaneous expense is the last item, regardless of its amount.

[1] The appendix to this chapter describes and illustrates how to prepare an end-of-period spreadsheet that includes financial statement columns.

EXHIBIT 2 **Financial Statements, NetSolutions**

NetSolutions
Income Statement
For the Two Months Ended December 31, 2015

Fees earned	$16,840	
Rent revenue	120	
Total revenues		$16,960
Expenses:		
Wages expense	$ 4,525	
Supplies expense	2,040	
Rent expense	1,600	
Utilities expense	985	
Insurance expense	200	
Depreciation expense	50	
Miscellaneous expense	455	
Total expenses		9,855
Net income		$ 7,105

NetSolutions
Statement of Owner's Equity
For the Two Months Ended December 31, 2015

Chris Clark, capital, November 1, 2015		$ 0
Investment on November 1, 2015	$25,000	
Net income for November and December	7,105	
	$32,105	
Less withdrawals	4,000	
Increase in owner's equity		28,105
Chris Clark, capital, December 31, 2015		$28,105

NetSolutions
Balance Sheet
December 31, 2015

Assets				**Liabilities**		
Current assets:				Current liabilities:		
Cash		$ 2,065		Accounts payable	$900	
Accounts receivable		2,720		Wages payable	250	
Supplies		760		Unearned rent	240	
Prepaid insurance		2,200		Total liabilities		$ 1,390
Total current assets			$ 7,745			
Property, plant, and equipment:						
Land		$20,000				
Office equipment	$1,800					
Less accum. depreciation	50	1,750		**Owner's Equity**		
Total property, plant, and equipment			21,750	Chris Clark, capital		28,105
Total assets			$29,495	Total liabilities and owner's equity		$29,495

Integrity, Objectivity, and Ethics in Business

CEO'S HEALTH?

How much and what information to disclose in financial statements and to investors presents a common ethical dilemma for managers and accountants. For example, Steve Jobs, co-founder and CEO of **Apple Inc.**, had been diagnosed and treated for pancreatic cancer. Apple Inc. had insisted that the status of Steve Jobs's health was a "private" matter and did not have to be disclosed to investors. Apple maintained this position even though Jobs was a driving force behind Apple's innovation and financial success.

However, in response to increasing investor concerns and speculation, Jobs released a letter on January 5, 2009, to investors on his health. The letter indicated that his recent weight loss was due to a hormone imbalance and not due to the recurrence of cancer. On October 5, 2011, Steve Jobs died at the age of 56.

Statement of Owner's Equity

The first item presented on the statement of owner's equity is the balance of the owner's capital account at the beginning of the period. The amount listed as owner's capital in the spreadsheet, however, is not always the account balance at the beginning of the period. The owner may have invested additional assets in the business during the period. For the beginning balance and any additional investments, it is necessary to refer to the owner's capital account in the ledger. These amounts, along with the net income (or net loss) and the drawing account balance, are used to determine the ending owner's capital account balance.

The basic form of the statement of owner's equity is shown in Exhibit 2. For NetSolutions, the amount of drawings by the owner was less than the net income. If the owner's withdrawals had exceeded the net income, the difference between the two items would then be deducted from the beginning capital account balance. Other factors, such as additional investments or a net loss, also require some change in the form, as follows:

Allan Johnson, capital, January 1, 2015		$39,000
Add: Investment during year	$ 6,000	
Less: Net loss for year	(5,600)	
Withdrawals	(9,500)	
Decrease in owner's equity		(9,100)
Allan Johnson, capital, December 31, 2015		$29,900

Example Exercise 4-2 Statement of Owner's Equity

Zack Gaddis owns and operates Gaddis Employment Services. On January 1, 2015, Zack Gaddis, Capital had a balance of $186,000. During the year, Zack invested an additional $40,000 and withdrew $25,000. For the year ended December 31, 2015, Gaddis Employment Services reported a net income of $18,750. Prepare a statement of owner's equity for the year ended December 31, 2015.

Follow My Example 4-2

Gaddis Employment Services
Statement of Owner's Equity
For the Year Ended December 31, 2015

Zack Gaddis, capital, January 1, 2015		$186,000
Add: Investment during 2015	$40,000	
Net income	18,750	
	$58,750	
Less: Withdrawals	25,000	
Increase in owner's equity		33,750
Zack Gaddis, capital, December 1, 2015		$219,750

Practice Exercises: PE 4-2A, PE 4-2B

Balance Sheet

The balance sheet is prepared directly from the Adjusted Trial Balance columns of the Exhibit 1 spreadsheet, beginning with Cash of $2,065. The asset and liability amounts are taken from the spreadsheet. The owner's equity amount, however, is taken from the statement of owner's equity, as illustrated in Exhibit 2.

The balance sheet in Exhibit 2 shows subsections for assets and liabilities. Such a balance sheet is a *classified balance sheet.* These subsections are described next.

Assets Assets are commonly divided into two sections on the balance sheet: (1) current assets and (2) property, plant, and equipment.

Note:
Two common classes of assets are current assets and property, plant, and equipment.

Current Assets Cash and other assets that are expected to be converted to cash or sold or used up usually within one year or less, through the normal operations of the business, are called **current assets**. In addition to cash, the current assets may include notes receivable, accounts receivable, supplies, and other prepaid expenses.

Notes receivable are amounts that customers owe. They are written promises to pay the amount of the note and interest. Accounts receivable are also amounts customers owe, but they are less formal than notes. Accounts receivable normally result from providing services or selling merchandise on account. Notes receivable and accounts receivable are current assets because they are usually converted to cash within one year or less.

Property, Plant, and Equipment The property, plant, and equipment section may also be described as **fixed assets** or **plant assets**. These assets include equipment, machinery, buildings, and land. With the exception of land, as discussed in Chapter 3, fixed assets depreciate over a period of time. The original cost, accumulated depreciation, and book value of each major type of fixed asset are normally reported on the balance sheet or in the notes to the financial statements.

Liabilities Liabilities are the amounts the business owes to creditors. Liabilities are commonly divided into two sections on the balance sheet: (1) current liabilities and (2) long-term liabilities.

Note:
Two common classes of liabilities are current liabilities and long-term liabilities.

Current Liabilities Liabilities that will be due within a short time (usually one year or less) and that are to be paid out of current assets are called **current liabilities**. The most common liabilities in this group are notes payable and accounts payable. Other current liabilities may include Wages Payable, Interest Payable, Taxes Payable, and Unearned Fees.

Long-Term Liabilities Liabilities that will not be due for a long time (usually more than one year) are called **long-term liabilities**. If NetSolutions had long-term liabilities, they would be reported below the current liabilities. As long-term liabilities come due and are to be paid within one year, they are reported as current liabilities. If they are to be renewed rather than paid, they would continue to be reported as long term. When an asset is pledged as security for a liability, the obligation may be called a *mortgage note payable* or a *mortgage payable.*

Owner's Equity The owner's right to the assets of the business is presented on the balance sheet below the liabilities section. The owner's equity is added to the total liabilities, and this total must be equal to the total assets.

Example Exercise 4-3 Classified Balance Sheet

OBJ 2

The following accounts appear in an adjusted trial balance of Hindsight Consulting. Indicate whether each account would be reported in the (a) current asset; (b) property, plant, and equipment; (c) current liability; (d) long-term liability; or (e) owner's equity section of the December 31, 2015, balance sheet of Hindsight Consulting.

1. Jason Corbin, Capital
2. Notes Receivable (due in six months)
3. Notes Payable (due in 10 years)
4. Land
5. Cash
6. Unearned Rent (three months)
7. Accumulated Depreciation—Equipment
8. Accounts Payable

(Continued)

Follow My Example 4-3

1. Owner's equity
2. Current asset
3. Long-term liability
4. Property, plant, and equipment
5. Current asset
6. Current liability
7. Property, plant, and equipment
8. Current liability

Practice Exercises: PE 4-3A, PE 4-3B

International  Connection

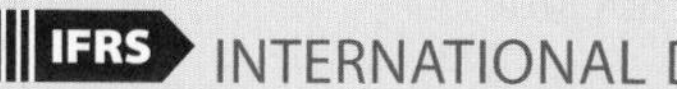

INTERNATIONAL DIFFERENCES

Financial statements prepared under accounting practices in other countries often differ from those prepared under generally accepted accounting principles in the United States. This is to be expected because cultures and market structures differ from country to country.

To illustrate, **BMW Group** prepares its financial statements under International Financial Reporting Standards as adopted by the European Union. In doing so, BMW's balance sheet reports fixed assets first, followed by current assets. It also reports owner's equity before the liabilities. In contrast, balance sheets prepared under U.S. accounting principles report current assets followed by fixed assets and current liabilities followed by long-term liabilities and owner's equity. The U.S. form of balance sheet is organized to emphasize creditor interpretation and analysis. For example, current assets and current liabilities are presented first to facilitate their interpretation and analysis by creditors. Likewise, to emphasize their importance, liabilities are reported before owner's equity.*

Regardless of these differences, the basic principles underlying the accounting equation and the double-entry accounting system are the same in Germany and the United States. Even though differences in recording and reporting exist, the accounting equation holds true: The total assets still equal the total liabilities and owner's equity.

*Examples of U.S. and IFRS financial statement reporting differences are further discussed and illustrated in Appendix D.

Prepare closing entries.

Closing Entries

As discussed in Chapter 3, the adjusting entries are recorded in the journal at the end of the accounting period. For **NetSolutions**, the adjusting entries are shown in Exhibit 9 of Chapter 3.

After the adjusting entries are posted to NetSolutions' ledger, shown in Exhibit 6, the ledger agrees with the data reported on the financial statements.

The balances of the accounts reported on the balance sheet are carried forward from year to year. Because they are relatively permanent, these accounts are called **permanent accounts** or **real accounts**. For example, Cash, Accounts Receivable, Equipment, Accumulated Depreciation, Accounts Payable, and Owner's Capital are permanent accounts.

The balances of the accounts reported on the income statement are not carried forward from year to year. Also, the balance of the owner's drawing account, which is reported on the statement of owner's equity, is not carried forward. Because these accounts report amounts for only one period, they are called **temporary accounts** or **nominal accounts**. Temporary accounts are not carried forward because they relate only to one period. For example, the Fees Earned of $16,840 and Wages Expense of $4,525 for NetSolutions shown in Exhibit 2 are for the two months ending December 31, 2015, and should not be carried forward to 2016.

Note:
Closing entries transfer the balances of temporary accounts to the owner's capital account.

At the beginning of the next period, temporary accounts should have zero balances. To achieve this, temporary account balances are transferred to permanent accounts at the end of the accounting period. The entries that transfer these balances are called **closing entries**. The transfer process is called the **closing process** and is sometimes referred to as **closing the books**.

The closing process involves the following four steps:

- Step 1. Revenue account balances are transferred to an account called Income Summary.
- Step 2. Expense account balances are transferred to an account called Income Summary.
- Step 3. The balance of Income Summary (net income or net loss) is transferred to the owner's capital account.
- Step 4. The balance of the owner's drawing account is transferred to the owner's capital account.

Exhibit 3 diagrams the closing process.

EXHIBIT 3

The Closing Process

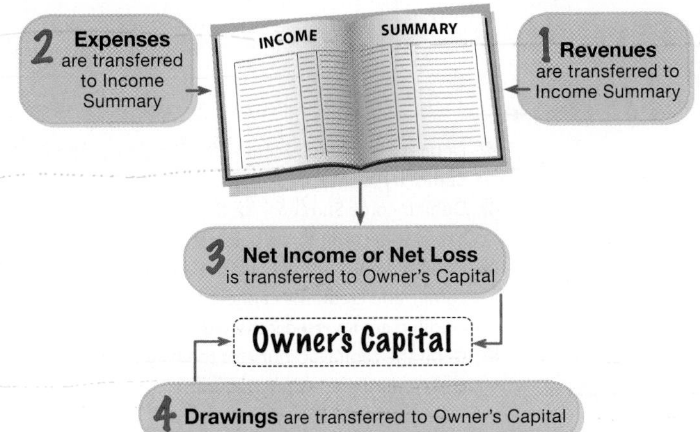

Income Summary is a temporary account that is only used during the closing process. At the beginning of the closing process, Income Summary has no balance. During the closing process, Income Summary will be debited and credited for various amounts. At the end of the closing process, Income Summary will again have no balance. Because Income Summary has the effect of clearing the revenue and expense accounts of their balances, it is sometimes called a **clearing account**. Other titles used for this account include Revenue and Expense Summary, Profit and Loss Summary, and Income and Expense Summary.

Note:
The income summary account does not appear on the financial statements.

The four closing entries required in the closing process are as follows:

1. Debit each revenue account for its balance and credit Income Summary for the total revenue.
2. Credit each expense account for its balance and debit Income Summary for the total expenses.
3. Debit Income Summary for its balance (net income) and credit the owner's capital account.
4. Debit the owner's capital account for the balance of the drawing account and credit the drawing account.

In the case of a net loss, Income Summary will have a debit balance after the first two closing entries. In this case, credit Income Summary for the amount of its balance and debit the owner's capital account for the amount of the net loss.

Closing entries are recorded in the journal and are dated as of the last day of the accounting period. In the journal, closing entries are recorded immediately following the adjusting entries. The caption, *Closing Entries*, is often inserted above the closing entries to separate them from the adjusting entries.

It is possible to close the temporary revenue and expense accounts without using a clearing account such as Income Summary. In this case, the balances of the revenue and expense accounts are closed directly to the owner's capital account.

Journalizing and Posting Closing Entries

A flowchart of the four closing entries for **NetSolutions** is shown in Exhibit 4. The balances in the accounts are those shown in the Adjusted Trial Balance columns of the end-of-period spreadsheet shown in Exhibit 1.

EXHIBIT 4 **Flowchart of Closing Entries for NetSolutions**

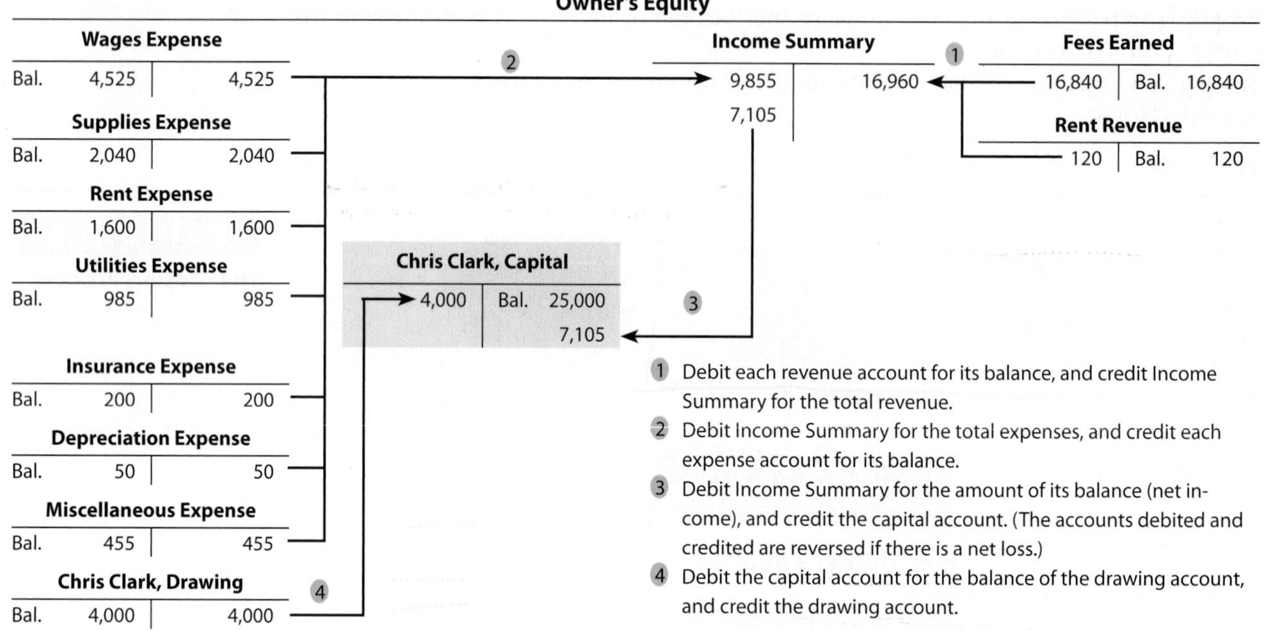

The closing entries for **NetSolutions** are shown in Exhibit 5. The account titles and balances for these entries may be obtained from the end-of-period spreadsheet, the adjusted trial balance, the income statement, the statement of owner's equity, or the ledger.

EXHIBIT 5

Closing Entries, NetSolutions

Journal *Page 6*

Date		Description	Post. Ref.	Debit	Credit
		Closing Entries			
2015					
Dec.	31	Fees Earned	41	16,840	
		Rent Revenue	42	120	
		Income Summary	33		16,960
	31	Income Summary	33	9,855	
		Wages Expense	51		4,525
		Supplies Expense	52		2,040
		Rent Expense	53		1,600
		Utilities Expense	54		985
		Insurance Expense	55		200
		Depreciation Expense	56		50
		Miscellaneous Expense	59		455
	31	Income Summary	33	7,105	
		Chris Clark, Capital	31		7,105
	31	Chris Clark, Capital	31	4,000	
		Chris Clark, Drawing	32		4,000

The closing entries are posted to NetSolutions' ledger as shown in Exhibit 6. Income Summary has been added to NetSolutions' ledger in Exhibit 6 as account number 33. After the closing entries are posted, NetSolutions' ledger has the following characteristics:

- The balance of Chris Clark, Capital of $28,105 agrees with the amount reported on the statement of owner's equity and the balance sheet.
- The revenue, expense, and drawing accounts will have zero balances.

As shown in Exhibit 6, the closing entries are normally identified in the ledger as "Closing." In addition, a line is often inserted in both balance columns after a closing entry is posted. This separates next period's revenue, expense, and withdrawal transactions from those of the current period. Next period's transactions will be posted directly below the closing entry.

Example Exercise 4-4 Closing Entries

OBJ 3

After the accounts have been adjusted at July 31, the end of the fiscal year, the following balances are taken from the ledger of Cabriolet Services Co.:

Terry Lambert, Capital	$615,850
Terry Lambert, Drawing	25,000
Fees Earned	380,450
Wages Expense	250,000
Rent Expense	65,000
Supplies Expense	18,250
Miscellaneous Expense	6,200

Journalize the four entries required to close the accounts.

Follow My Example 4-4

July	31	Fees Earned	380,450	
		Income Summary		380,450
	31	Income Summary	339,450	
		Wages Expense		250,000
		Rent Expense		65,000
		Supplies Expense		18,250
		Miscellaneous Expense		6,200
	31	Income Summary	41,000	
		Terry Lambert, Capital		41,000
	31	Terry Lambert, Capital	25,000	
		Terry Lambert, Drawing		25,000

Practice Exercises: PE 4-4A, PE 4-4B

Post-Closing Trial Balance

A post-closing trial balance is prepared after the closing entries have been posted. The purpose of the post-closing (after closing) trial balance is to verify that the ledger is in balance at the beginning of the next period. The accounts and amounts should agree exactly with the accounts and amounts listed on the balance sheet at the end of the period. The post-closing trial balance for **NetSolutions** is shown in Exhibit 7.

EXHIBIT 6 **Ledger, NetSolutions**

Account *Cash* — Account No. *11*

Date	Item	Post. Ref.	Debit	Credit	Balance Debit	Balance Credit
2015						
Nov. 1		1	25,000		25,000	
5		1		20,000	5,000	
18		1	7,500		12,500	
30		1		3,650	8,850	
30		1		950	7,900	
30		2		2,000	5,900	
Dec. 1		2		2,400	3,500	
1		2		800	2,700	
1		2	360		3,060	
6		2		180	2,880	
11		2		400	2,480	
13		3		950	1,530	
16		3	3,100		4,630	
20		3		900	3,730	
21		3	650		4,380	
23		3		1,450	2,930	
27		3		1,200	1,730	
31		3		310	1,420	
31		4		225	1,195	
31		4	2,870		4,065	
31		4		2,000	2,065	

Account *Accounts Receivable* — Account No. *12*

Date	Item	Post. Ref.	Debit	Credit	Balance Debit	Balance Credit
2015						
Dec. 16		3	1,750		1,750	
21		3		650	1,100	
31		4	1,120		2,220	
31	Adjusting	5	500		2,720	

Account *Supplies* — Account No. *14*

Date	Item	Post. Ref.	Debit	Credit	Balance Debit	Balance Credit
2015						
Nov. 10		1	1,350		1,350	
30		1		800	550	
Dec. 23		3	1,450		2,000	
31	Adjusting	5		1,240	760	

Account *Prepaid Insurance* — Account No. *15*

Date	Item	Post. Ref.	Debit	Credit	Balance Debit	Balance Credit
2015						
Dec. 1		2	2,400		2,400	
31	Adjusting	5		200	2,200	

Account *Land* — Account No. *17*

Date	Item	Post. Ref.	Debit	Credit	Balance Debit	Balance Credit
2015						
Nov. 5		1	20,000		20,000	

Account *Office Equipment* — Account No. *18*

Date	Item	Post. Ref.	Debit	Credit	Balance Debit	Balance Credit
2015						
Dec. 4		2	1,800		1,800	

Account *Accumulated Depreciation* — Account No. *19*

Date	Item	Post. Ref.	Debit	Credit	Balance Debit	Balance Credit
2015						
Dec. 31	Adjusting	5		50		50

Account *Accounts Payable* — Account No. *21*

Date	Item	Post. Ref.	Debit	Credit	Balance Debit	Balance Credit
2015						
Nov. 10		1		1,350		1,350
30		1	950			400
Dec. 4		2		1,800		2,200
11		2	400			1,800
20		3	900			900

Account *Wages Payable* — Account No. *22*

Date	Item	Post. Ref.	Debit	Credit	Balance Debit	Balance Credit
2015						
Dec. 31	Adjusting	5		250		250

Account *Unearned Rent* — Account No. *23*

Date	Item	Post. Ref.	Debit	Credit	Balance Debit	Balance Credit
2015						
Dec. 1		2		360		360
31	Adjusting	5	120			240

Account *Chris Clark, Capital* — Account No. *31*

Date	Item	Post. Ref.	Debit	Credit	Balance Debit	Balance Credit
2015						
Nov. 1		1		25,000		25,000
Dec. 31	Closing	6		7,105		32,105
31	Closing	6	4,000			28,105

EXHIBIT 6 **Ledger, NetSolutions (*Concluded*)**

Account *Chris Clark, Drawing* — Account No. *32*

Date	Item	Post. Ref.	Debit	Credit	Balance Debit	Balance Credit
2015						
Nov. 30		2	2,000		2,000	
Dec. 31		4	2,000		4,000	
31	Closing	6		4,000	—	—

Account *Income Summary* — Account No. *33*

Date	Item	Post. Ref.	Debit	Credit	Balance Debit	Balance Credit
2015						
Dec. 31	Closing	6		16,960		16,960
31	Closing	6	9,855			7,105
31	Closing	6	7,105		—	—

Account *Fees Earned* — Account No. *41*

Date	Item	Post. Ref.	Debit	Credit	Balance Debit	Balance Credit
2015						
Nov. 18		1		7,500		7,500
Dec. 16		3		3,100		10,600
16		3		1,750		12,350
31		4		2,870		15,220
31		4		1,120		16,340
31	Adjusting	5		500		16,840
31	Closing	6	16,840		—	—

Account *Rent Revenue* — Account No. *42*

Date	Item	Post. Ref.	Debit	Credit	Balance Debit	Balance Credit
2015						
Dec. 31	Adjusting	5		120		120
31	Closing	6	120		—	—

Account *Wages Expense* — Account No. *51*

Date	Item	Post. Ref.	Debit	Credit	Balance Debit	Balance Credit
2015						
Nov. 30		1	2,125		2,125	
Dec. 13		3	950		3,075	
27		3	1,200		4,275	
31	Adjusting	5	250		4,525	
31	Closing	6		4,525	—	—

Account *Supplies Expense* — Account No. *52*

Date	Item	Post. Ref.	Debit	Credit	Balance Debit	Balance Credit
2015						
Nov. 30		1	800		800	
Dec. 31	Adjusting	5	1,240		2,040	
31	Closing	6		2,040	—	—

Account *Rent Expense* — Account No. *53*

Date	Item	Post. Ref.	Debit	Credit	Balance Debit	Balance Credit
2015						
Nov. 30		1	800		800	
Dec. 1		2	800		1,600	
31	Closing	6		1,600	—	—

Account *Utilities Expense* — Account No. *54*

Date	Item	Post. Ref.	Debit	Credit	Balance Debit	Balance Credit
2015						
Nov. 30		1	450		450	
Dec. 31		3	310		760	
31		4	225		985	
31	Closing	6		985	—	—

Account *Insurance Expense* — Account No. *55*

Date	Item	Post. Ref.	Debit	Credit	Balance Debit	Balance Credit
2015						
Dec. 31	Adjusting	5	200		200	
31	Closing	6		200	—	—

Account *Depreciation Expense* — Account No. *56*

Date	Item	Post. Ref.	Debit	Credit	Balance Debit	Balance Credit
2015						
Dec. 31	Adjusting	5	50		50	
31	Closing	6		50	—	—

Account *Miscellaneous Expense* — Account No. *59*

Date	Item	Post. Ref.	Debit	Credit	Balance Debit	Balance Credit
2015						
Nov. 30		1	275		275	
Dec. 6		2	180		455	
31	Closing	6		455	—	—

EXHIBIT 7

Post-Closing Trial Balance, NetSolutions

NetSolutions
Post-Closing Trial Balance
December 31, 2015

	Debit Balances	Credit Balances
Cash	2,065	
Accounts Receivable	2,720	
Supplies	760	
Prepaid Insurance	2,200	
Land	20,000	
Office Equipment	1,800	
Accumulated Depreciation		50
Accounts Payable		900
Wages Payable		250
Unearned Rent		240
Chris Clark, Capital		28,105
	29,545	29,545

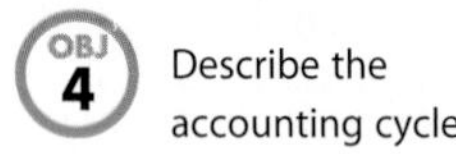

Describe the accounting cycle.

Accounting Cycle

The accounting process that begins with analyzing and journalizing transactions and ends with the post-closing trial balance is called the **accounting cycle**. The steps in the accounting cycle are as follows:

- Step 1. Transactions are analyzed and recorded in the journal.
- Step 2. Transactions are posted to the ledger.
- Step 3. An unadjusted trial balance is prepared.
- Step 4. Adjustment data are assembled and analyzed.
- Step 5. An optional end-of-period spreadsheet is prepared.
- Step 6. Adjusting entries are journalized and posted to the ledger.
- Step 7. An adjusted trial balance is prepared.
- Step 8. Financial statements are prepared.
- Step 9. Closing entries are journalized and posted to the ledger.
- Step 10. A post-closing trial balance is prepared.[2]

Example Exercise 4-5 Accounting Cycle

From the following list of steps in the accounting cycle, identify what two steps are missing:

a. Transactions are analyzed and recorded in the journal:
b. Transactions are posted to the ledger.
c. Adjustment data are assembled and analyzed.
d. An optional end-of-period spreadsheet is prepared.
e. Adjusting entries are journalized and posted to the ledger.
f. Financial statements are prepared.
g. Closing entries are journalized and posted to the ledger.
h. A post-closing trial balance is prepared.

Follow My Example 4-5

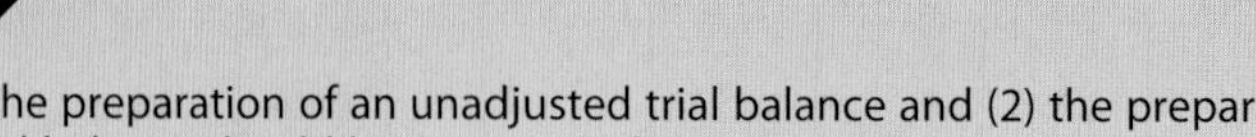

The following two steps are missing: (1) the preparation of an unadjusted trial balance and (2) the preparation of the adjusted trial balance. The unadjusted trial balance should be prepared after step (b). The adjusted trial balance should be prepared after step (e).

Practice Exercises: PE 4-5A, PE 4-5B

[2] Some accountants include the journalizing and posting of "reversing entries" as the last step in the accounting cycle. Because reversing entries are not required, they are described and illustrated in Appendix B at the end of the book.

Exhibit 8 illustrates the accounting cycle in graphic form. It also illustrates how the accounting cycle begins with the source documents for a transaction and flows through the accounting system and into the financial statements.

EXHIBIT 8

Accounting Cycle

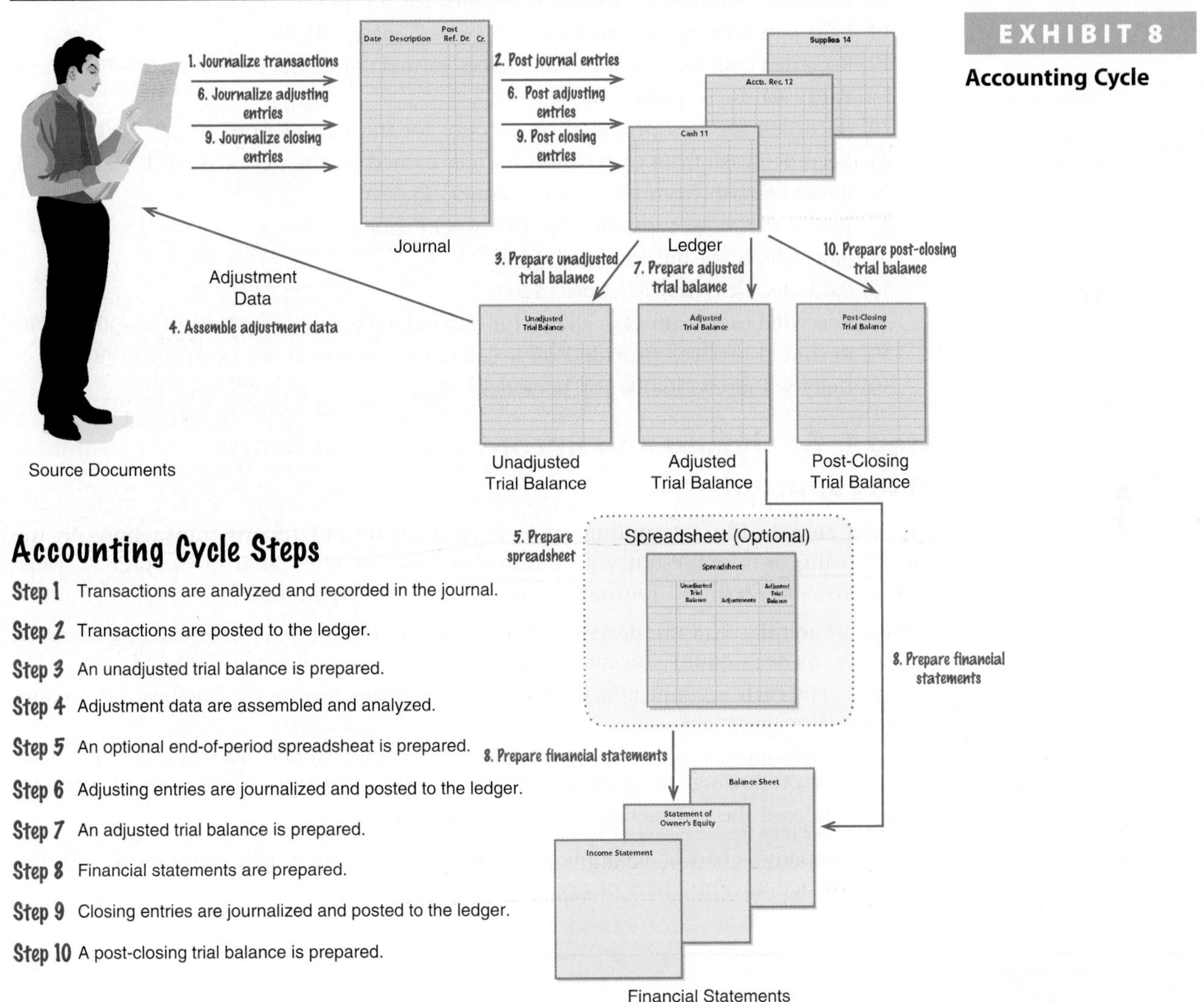

Illustration of the Accounting Cycle

OBJ 5 Illustrate the accounting cycle for one period.

In this section, the complete accounting cycle for one period is illustrated. Assume that for several years Kelly Pitney has operated a part-time consulting business from her home. As of April 1, 2016, Kelly decided to move to rented quarters and to operate the business on a full-time basis. The business will be known as Kelly Consulting. During April, Kelly Consulting entered into the following transactions:

Apr. 1. The following assets were received from Kelly Pitney: cash, $13,100; accounts receivable, $3,000; supplies, $1,400; and office equipment, $12,500. There were no liabilities received.

1. Paid three months' rent on a lease rental contract, $4,800.

2. Paid the premiums on property and casualty insurance policies, $1,800.

4. Received cash from clients as an advance payment for services to be provided and recorded it as unearned fees, $5,000.

Apr. 5. Purchased additional office equipment on account from Office Station Co., $2,000.
6. Received cash from clients on account, $1,800.
10. Paid cash for a newspaper advertisement, $120.
12. Paid Office Station Co. for part of the debt incurred on April 5, $1,200.
12. Recorded services provided on account for the period April 1–12, $4,200.
14. Paid part-time receptionist for two weeks' salary, $750.
17. Recorded cash from cash clients for fees earned during the period April 1–16, $6,250.
18. Paid cash for supplies, $800.
20. Recorded services provided on account for the period April 13–20, $2,100.
24. Recorded cash from cash clients for fees earned for the period April 17–24, $3,850.
26. Received cash from clients on account, $5,600.
27. Paid part-time receptionist for two weeks' salary, $750.
29. Paid telephone bill for April, $130.
30. Paid electricity bill for April, $200.
30. Recorded cash from cash clients for fees earned for the period April 25–30, $3,050.
30. Recorded services provided on account for the remainder of April, $1,500.
30. Kelly withdrew $6,000 for personal use.

Step 1. Analyzing and Recording Transactions in the Journal

The first step in the accounting cycle is to analyze and record transactions in the journal using the double-entry accounting system. As illustrated in Chapter 2, transactions are analyzed and journalized using the following steps:

- Step 1. Carefully read the description of the transaction to determine whether an asset, liability, owner's equity, revenue, expense, or drawing account is affected.
- Step 2. For each account affected by the transaction, determine whether the account increases or decreases.
- Step 3. Determine whether each increase or decrease should be recorded as a debit or a credit, following the rules of debit and credit shown in Exhibit 3 of Chapter 2.
- Step 4. Record the transaction using a journal entry.

The company's chart of accounts is useful in determining which accounts are affected by the transaction. The chart of accounts for Kelly Consulting is shown in Exhibit 9.

EXHIBIT 9

Chart of Accounts for Kelly Consulting

11 Cash	31 Kelly Pitney, Capital
12 Accounts Receivable	32 Kelly Pitney, Drawing
14 Supplies	33 Income Summary
15 Prepaid Rent	41 Fees Earned
16 Prepaid Insurance	51 Salary Expense
18 Office Equipment	52 Rent Expense
19 Accumulated Depreciation	53 Supplies Expense
21 Accounts Payable	54 Depreciation Expense
22 Salaries Payable	55 Insurance Expense
23 Unearned Fees	59 Miscellaneous Expense

After analyzing each of Kelly Consulting's transactions for April, the journal entries are recorded as shown in Exhibit 10.

Step 2. Posting Transactions to the Ledger

Periodically, the transactions recorded in the journal are posted to the accounts in the ledger. The debits and credits for each journal entry are posted to the accounts in the

EXHIBIT 10

Journal Entries for April, Kelly Consulting

Journal *Page 1*

Date		Description	Post. Ref.	Debit	Credit
2016 Apr.	1	Cash	11	13,100	
		Accounts Receivable	12	3,000	
		Supplies	14	1,400	
		Office Equipment	18	12,500	
		Kelly Pitney, Capital	31		30,000
	1	Prepaid Rent	15	4,800	
		Cash	11		4,800
	2	Prepaid Insurance	16	1,800	
		Cash	11		1,800
	4	Cash	11	5,000	
		Unearned Fees	23		5,000
	5	Office Equipment	18	2,000	
		Accounts Payable	21		2,000
	6	Cash	11	1,800	
		Accounts Receivable	12		1,800
	10	Miscellaneous Expense	59	120	
		Cash	11		120
	12	Accounts Payable	21	1,200	
		Cash	11		1,200
	12	Accounts Receivable	12	4,200	
		Fees Earned	41		4,200
	14	Salary Expense	51	750	
		Cash	11		750

Journal *Page 2*

Date		Description	Post. Ref.	Debit	Credit
2016 Apr.	17	Cash	11	6,250	
		Fees Earned	41		6,250
	18	Supplies	14	800	
		Cash	11		800
	20	Accounts Receivable	12	2,100	
		Fees Earned	41		2,100
	24	Cash	11	3,850	
		Fees Earned	41		3,850
	26	Cash	11	5,600	
		Accounts Receivable	12		5,600
	27	Salary Expense	51	750	
		Cash	11		750
	29	Miscellaneous Expense	59	130	
		Cash	11		130

(Continued)

EXHIBIT 10

Journal Entries for April, Kelly Consulting (*Concluded*)

Journal					Page 2
Date		Description	Post. Ref.	Debit	Credit
	30	Miscellaneous Expense	59	200	
		Cash	11		200
	30	Cash	11	3,050	
		Fees Earned	41		3,050
	30	Accounts Receivable	12	1,500	
		Fees Earned	41		1,500
	30	Kelly Pitney, Drawing	32	6,000	
		Cash	11		6,000

order in which they occur in the journal. As illustrated in Chapters 2 and 3, journal entries are posted to the accounts using the following four steps:

- Step 1. The date is entered in the Date column of the account.
- Step 2. The amount is entered into the Debit or Credit column of the account.
- Step 3. The journal page number is entered in the Posting Reference column.
- Step 4. The account number is entered in the Posting Reference (Post. Ref.) column in the journal.

The journal entries for Kelly Consulting have been posted to the ledger shown in Exhibit 18.

Step 3. Preparing an Unadjusted Trial Balance

An unadjusted trial balance is prepared to determine whether any errors have been made in posting the debits and credits to the ledger. The unadjusted trial balance shown in Exhibit 11 does not provide complete proof of the accuracy of the ledger. It indicates only that the debits and the credits are equal. This proof is of value, however, because errors often affect the equality of debits and credits. If the two totals of a trial balance are not equal, an error has occurred that must be discovered and corrected.

The unadjusted account balances shown in Exhibit 11 were taken from Kelly Consulting's ledger shown in Exhibit 18, before any adjusting entries were recorded.

Step 4. Assembling and Analyzing Adjustment Data

Before the financial statements can be prepared, the accounts must be updated. The four types of accounts that normally require adjustment include prepaid expenses, unearned revenue, accrued revenue, and accrued expenses. In addition, depreciation expense must be recorded for fixed assets other than land. The following data have been assembled on April 30, 2016, for analysis of possible adjustments for Kelly Consulting:

a. Insurance expired during April is $300.
b. Supplies on hand on April 30 are $1,350.
c. Depreciation of office equipment for April is $330.
d. Accrued receptionist salary on April 30 is $120.
e. Rent expired during April is $1,600.
f. Unearned fees on April 30 are $2,500.

EXHIBIT 11

Unadjusted Trial Balance, Kelly Consulting

Kelly Consulting Unadjusted Trial Balance April 30, 2016	Debit Balances	Credit Balances
Cash	22,100	
Accounts Receivable	3,400	
Supplies	2,200	
Prepaid Rent	4,800	
Prepaid Insurance	1,800	
Office Equipment	14,500	
Accumulated Depreciation		0
Accounts Payable		800
Salaries Payable		0
Unearned Fees		5,000
Kelly Pitney, Capital		30,000
Kelly Pitney, Drawing	6,000	
Fees Earned		20,950
Salary Expense	1,500	
Rent Expense	0	
Supplies Expense	0	
Depreciation Expense	0	
Insurance Expense	0	
Miscellaneous Expense	450	
	56,750	56,750

Step 5. Preparing an Optional End-of-Period Spreadsheet

Although an end-of-period spreadsheet is not required, it is useful in showing the flow of accounting information from the unadjusted trial balance to the adjusted trial balance. In addition, an end-of-period spreadsheet is useful in analyzing the impact of proposed adjustments on the financial statements. The end-of-period spreadsheet for Kelly Consulting is shown in Exhibit 12.

EXHIBIT 12

End-of-Period Spreadsheet, Kelly Consulting

	A	B	C	D	E	F	G
1		Kelly Consulting					
2		End-of-Period Spreadsheet					
3		For the Month Ended April 30, 2016					
4		Unadjusted				Adjusted	
5		Trial Balance		Adjustments		Trial Balance	
6	**Account Title**	**Dr.**	**Cr.**	**Dr.**	**Cr.**	**Dr.**	**Cr.**
7							
8	Cash	22,100				22,100	
9	Accounts Receivable	3,400				3,400	
10	Supplies	2,200			(b) 850	1,350	
11	Prepaid Rent	4,800			(e) 1,600	3,200	
12	Prepaid Insurance	1,800			(a) 300	1,500	
13	Office Equipment	14,500				14,500	
14	Accum. Depreciation				(c) 330		330
15	Accounts Payable		800				800
16	Salaries Payable				(d) 120		120
17	Unearned Fees		5,000	(f) 2,500			2,500
18	Kelly Pitney, Capital		30,000				30,000
19	Kelly Pitney, Drawing	6,000				6,000	
20	Fees Earned		20,950		(f) 2,500		23,450
21	Salary Expense	1,500		(d) 120		1,620	
22	Rent Expense			(e) 1,600		1,600	
23	Supplies Expense			(b) 850		850	
24	Depreciation Expense			(c) 330		330	
25	Insurance Expense			(a) 300		300	
26	Miscellaneous Expense	450				450	
27		56,750	56,750	5,700	5,700	57,200	57,200
28							

EXHIBIT 13

Adjusting Entries, Kelly Consulting

Journal — *Page 3*

Date		Description	Post. Ref.	Debit	Credit
		Adjusting Entries			
2016 Apr.	30	Insurance Expense	55	300	
		Prepaid Insurance	16		300
		Expired insurance.			
	30	Supplies Expense	53	850	
		Supplies	14		850
		Supplies used ($2,200 – $1,350).			
	30	Depreciation Expense	54	330	
		Accumulated Depreciation	19		330
		Depreciation of office equipment.			
	30	Salary Expense	51	120	
		Salaries Payable	22		120
		Accrued salary.			
	30	Rent Expense	52	1,600	
		Prepaid Rent	15		1,600
		Rent expired during April.			
	30	Unearned Fees	23	2,500	
		Fees Earned	41		2,500
		Fees earned ($5,000 – $2,500).			

Step 6. Journalizing and Posting Adjusting Entries

Based on the adjustment data shown in Step 4, adjusting entries for Kelly Consulting are prepared as shown in Exhibit 13. Each adjusting entry affects at least one income statement account and one balance sheet account. Explanations for each adjustment including any computations are normally included with each adjusting entry.

Each of the adjusting entries shown in Exhibit 13 is posted to Kelly Consulting's ledger shown in Exhibit 18. The adjusting entries are identified in the ledger as "Adjusting."

Step 7. Preparing an Adjusted Trial Balance

After the adjustments have been journalized and posted, an adjusted trial balance is prepared to verify the equality of the total of the debit and credit balances. This is the last step before preparing the financial statements. If the adjusted trial balance does not balance, an error has occurred and must be found and corrected. The adjusted trial balance for Kelly Consulting as of April 30, 2016, is shown in Exhibit 14.

Step 8. Preparing the Financial Statements

The most important outcome of the accounting cycle is the financial statements. The income statement is prepared first, followed by the statement of owner's equity and then the balance sheet. The statements can be prepared directly from the adjusted trial balance, the end-of-period spreadsheet, or the ledger. The net income or net loss shown on the income statement is reported on the statement of owner's equity along with any additional investments by the owner and any withdrawals. The ending owner's capital is reported on the balance sheet and is added with total liabilities to equal total assets.

The financial statements for Kelly Consulting are shown in Exhibit 15. Kelly Consulting earned net income of $18,300 for April. As of April 30, 2016, Kelly Consulting has total assets of $45,720, total liabilities of $3,420, and total owner's equity of $42,300.

EXHIBIT 14

Adjusted Trial Balance, Kelly Consulting

Kelly Consulting
Adjusted Trial Balance
April 30, 2016

	Debit Balances	Credit Balances
Cash	22,100	
Accounts Receivable	3,400	
Supplies	1,350	
Prepaid Rent	3,200	
Prepaid Insurance	1,500	
Office Equipment	14,500	
Accumulated Depreciation		330
Accounts Payable		800
Salaries Payable		120
Unearned Fees		2,500
Kelly Pitney, Capital		30,000
Kelly Pitney, Drawing	6,000	
Fees Earned		23,450
Salary Expense	1,620	
Rent Expense	1,600	
Supplies Expense	850	
Depreciation Expense	330	
Insurance Expense	300	
Miscellaneous Expense	450	
	57,200	57,200

EXHIBIT 15

Financial Statements, Kelly Consulting

Kelly Consulting
Income Statement
For the Month Ended April 30, 2016

Fees earned		$23,450
Expenses:		
Salary expense	$1,620	
Rent expense	1,600	
Supplies expense	850	
Depreciation expense	330	
Insurance expense	300	
Miscellaneous expense	450	
Total expenses		5,150
Net income		$18,300

Kelly Consulting
Statement of Owner's Equity
For the Month Ended April 30, 2016

Kelly Pitney, capital, April 1, 2016		$ 0
Investment during the month	$30,000	
Net income for the month	18,300	
	$48,300	
Less withdrawals	6,000	
Increase in owner's equity		42,300
Kelly Pitney, capital, April 30, 2016		$42,300

(Continued)

EXHIBIT 15 **Financial Statements, Kelly Consulting (*Concluded*)**

Kelly Consulting
Balance Sheet
April 30, 2016

Assets			Liabilities		
Current assets:			Current liabilities:		
Cash	$22,100		Accounts payable	$ 800	
Accounts receivable	3,400		Salaries payable	120	
Supplies	1,350		Unearned fees	2,500	
Prepaid rent	3,200		Total liabilities		$ 3,420
Prepaid insurance	1,500				
Total current assets		$31,550			
Property, plant, and equipment:					
Office equipment	$14,500				
Less accumulated depreciation	330		**Owner's Equity**		
Total property, plant, and equipment		14,170	Kelly Pitney, capital		42,300
Total assets		$45,720	Total liabilities and owner's equity		$45,720

Step 9. Journalizing and Posting Closing Entries

As described earlier in this chapter, four closing entries are required at the end of an accounting period. These four closing entries are as follows:

1. Debit each revenue account for its balance, and credit Income Summary for the total revenue.
2. Credit each expense account for its balance, and debit Income Summary for the total expenses.
3. Debit Income Summary for its balance, and credit the owner's capital account.
4. Debit the owner's capital account for the balance of the drawing account, and credit the drawing account.

The four closing entries for Kelly Consulting are shown in Exhibit 16. The closing entries are posted to Kelly Consulting's ledger as shown in Exhibit 18. After the closing entries are posted, Kelly Consulting's ledger has the following characteristics:

- The balance of Kelly Pitney, Capital of $42,300 agrees with the amount reported on the statement of owner's equity and the balance sheet.
- The revenue, expense, and drawing accounts will have zero balances.

The closing entries are normally identified in the ledger as "Closing." In addition, a line is often inserted in both balance columns after a closing entry is posted. This separates next period's revenue, expense, and withdrawal transactions from those of the current period.

Step 10. Preparing a Post-Closing Trial Balance

A post-closing trial balance is prepared after the closing entries have been posted. The purpose of the post-closing trial balance is to verify that the ledger is in balance at the beginning of the next period. The accounts and amounts in the post-closing trial balance should agree exactly with the accounts and amounts listed on the balance sheet at the end of the period.

EXHIBIT 16

Closing Entries, Kelly Consulting

Journal *Page 4*

Date		Description	Post. Ref.	Debit	Credit
		Closing Entries			
2016 Apr.	30	Fees Earned	41	23,450	
		Income Summary	33		23,450
	30	Income Summary	33	5,150	
		Salary Expense	51		1,620
		Rent Expense	52		1,600
		Supplies Expense	53		850
		Depreciation Expense	54		330
		Insurance Expense	55		300
		Miscellaneous Expense	59		450
	30	Income Summary	33	18,300	
		Kelly Pitney, Capital	31		18,300
	30	Kelly Pitney, Capital	31	6,000	
		Kelly Pitney, Drawing	32		6,000

The post-closing trial balance for Kelly Consulting is shown in Exhibit 17. The balances shown in the post-closing trial balance are taken from the ending balances in the ledger shown in Exhibit 18. These balances agree with the amounts shown on Kelly Consulting's balance sheet in Exhibit 15.

EXHIBIT 17

Post-Closing Trial Balance, Kelly Consulting

Kelly Consulting
Post-Closing Trial Balance
April 30, 2016

	Debit Balances	Credit Balances
Cash	22,100	
Accounts Receivable	3,400	
Supplies	1,350	
Prepaid Rent	3,200	
Prepaid Insurance	1,500	
Office Equipment	14,500	
Accumulated Depreciation		330
Accounts Payable		800
Salaries Payable		120
Unearned Fees		2,500
Kelly Pitney, Capital		42,300
	46,050	46,050

EXHIBIT 18 **Ledger, Kelly Consulting**

Ledger

Account *Cash* — Account No. *11*

Date	Item	Post. Ref.	Debit	Credit	Balance Debit	Balance Credit
2016						
Apr. 1		1	13,100		13,100	
1		1		4,800	8,300	
2		1		1,800	6,500	
4		1	5,000		11,500	
6		1	1,800		13,300	
10		1		120	13,180	
12		1		1,200	11,980	
14		1		750	11,230	
17		2	6,250		17,480	
18		2		800	16,680	
24		2	3,850		20,530	
26		2	5,600		26,130	
27		2		750	25,380	
29		2		130	25,250	
30		2		200	25,050	
30		2	3,050		28,100	
30		2		6,000	22,100	

Account *Accounts Receivable* — Account No. *12*

Date	Item	Post. Ref.	Debit	Credit	Balance Debit	Balance Credit
2016						
Apr. 1		1	3,000		3,000	
6		1		1,800	1,200	
12		1	4,200		5,400	
20		2	2,100		7,500	
26		2		5,600	1,900	
30		2	1,500		3,400	

Account *Supplies* — Account No. *14*

Date	Item	Post. Ref.	Debit	Credit	Balance Debit	Balance Credit
2016						
Apr. 1		1	1,400		1,400	
18		2	800		2,200	
30	Adjusting	3		850	1,350	

Account *Prepaid Rent* — Account No. *15*

Date	Item	Post. Ref.	Debit	Credit	Balance Debit	Balance Credit
2016						
Apr. 1		1	4,800		4,800	
30	Adjusting	3		1,600	3,200	

Account *Prepaid Insurance* — Account No. *16*

Date	Item	Post. Ref.	Debit	Credit	Balance Debit	Balance Credit
2016						
Apr. 2		1	1,800		1,800	
30	Adjusting	3		300	1,500	

Account *Office Equipment* — Account No. *18*

Date	Item	Post. Ref.	Debit	Credit	Balance Debit	Balance Credit
2016						
Apr. 1		1	12,500		12,500	
5		1	2,000		14,500	

Account *Accumulated Depreciation* — Account No. *19*

Date	Item	Post. Ref.	Debit	Credit	Balance Debit	Balance Credit
2016						
Apr. 30	Adjusting	3		330		330

Account *Accounts Payable* — Account No. *21*

Date	Item	Post. Ref.	Debit	Credit	Balance Debit	Balance Credit
2016						
Apr. 5		1		2,000		2,000
12		1	1,200			800

Account *Salaries Payable* — Account No. *22*

Date	Item	Post. Ref.	Debit	Credit	Balance Debit	Balance Credit
2016						
Apr. 30	Adjusting	3		120		120

Account *Unearned Fees* — Account No. *23*

Date	Item	Post. Ref.	Debit	Credit	Balance Debit	Balance Credit
2016						
Apr. 4		1		5,000		5,000
30	Adjusting	3	2,500			2,500

Account *Kelly Pitney, Capital* — Account No. *31*

Date	Item	Post. Ref.	Debit	Credit	Balance Debit	Balance Credit
2016						
Apr. 1		1		30,000		30,000
30	Closing	4		18,300		48,300
30	Closing	4	6,000			42,300

EXHIBIT 18 **Ledger, Kelly Consulting (*Concluded*)**

Account *Kelly Pitney, Drawing* — Account No. *32*

Date	Item	Post. Ref.	Debit	Credit	Balance	
					Debit	Credit
2016 Apr. 30		2	6,000		6,000	
30	Closing	4		6,000	—	—

Account *Income Summary* — Account No. *33*

Date	Item	Post. Ref.	Debit	Credit	Balance	
					Debit	Credit
2016 Apr. 30	Closing	4		23,450		23,450
30	Closing	4	5,150			18,300
30	Closing	4	18,300		—	—

Account *Fees Earned* — Account No. *41*

Date	Item	Post. Ref.	Debit	Credit	Balance	
					Debit	Credit
2016 Apr. 12		1		4,200		4,200
17		2		6,250		10,450
20		2		2,100		12,550
24		2		3,850		16,400
30		2		3,050		19,450
30		2		1,500		20,950
30	Adjusting	3		2,500		23,450
30	Closing	4	23,450		—	—

Account *Salary Expense* — Account No. *51*

Date	Item	Post. Ref.	Debit	Credit	Balance	
					Debit	Credit
2016 Apr. 14		1	750		750	
27		2	750		1,500	
30	Adjusting	3	120		1,620	
30	Closing	4		1,620	—	—

Account *Rent Expense* — Account No. *52*

Date	Item	Post. Ref.	Debit	Credit	Balance	
					Debit	Credit
2016 Apr. 30	Adjusting	3	1,600		1,600	
30	Closing	4		1,600	—	—

Account *Supplies Expense* — Account No. *53*

Date	Item	Post. Ref.	Debit	Credit	Balance	
					Debit	Credit
2016 Apr. 30	Adjusting	3	850		850	
30	Closing	4		850	—	—

Account *Depreciation Expense* — Account No. *54*

Date	Item	Post. Ref.	Debit	Credit	Balance	
					Debit	Credit
2016 Apr. 30	Adjusting	3	330		330	
30	Closing	4		330	—	—

Account *Insurance Expense* — Account No. *55*

Date	Item	Post. Ref.	Debit	Credit	Balance	
					Debit	Credit
2016 Apr. 30	Adjusting	3	300		300	
30	Closing	4		300	—	—

Account *Miscellaneous Expense* — Account No. *59*

Date	Item	Post. Ref.	Debit	Credit	Balance	
					Debit	Credit
2016 Apr. 10		1	120		120	
29		2	130		250	
30		2	200		450	
30	Closing	4		450	—	—

Fiscal Year

OBJ 6 Explain what is meant by the fiscal year and the natural business year.

The annual accounting period adopted by a business is known as its **fiscal year**. Fiscal years begin with the first day of the month selected and end on the last day of the following twelfth month. The period most commonly used is the calendar year. Other periods are not unusual, especially for businesses organized as corporations. For example, a corporation may adopt a fiscal year that ends when business activities have reached the lowest point in its annual operating cycle. Such a fiscal year is called the **natural business year**. At the low point in its operating cycle, a business has more time to analyze the results of operations and to prepare financial statements.

Because companies with fiscal years often have highly seasonal operations, investors and others should be careful in interpreting partial-year reports for such companies. That is, you should expect the results of operations for these companies to vary significantly throughout the fiscal year.

The financial history of a business may be shown by a series of balance sheets and income statements for several fiscal years. If the life of a business is expressed by a line moving from left to right, the series of balance sheets and income statements may be graphed as shown in Exhibit 19.

EXHIBIT 19 **Financial History of a Business**

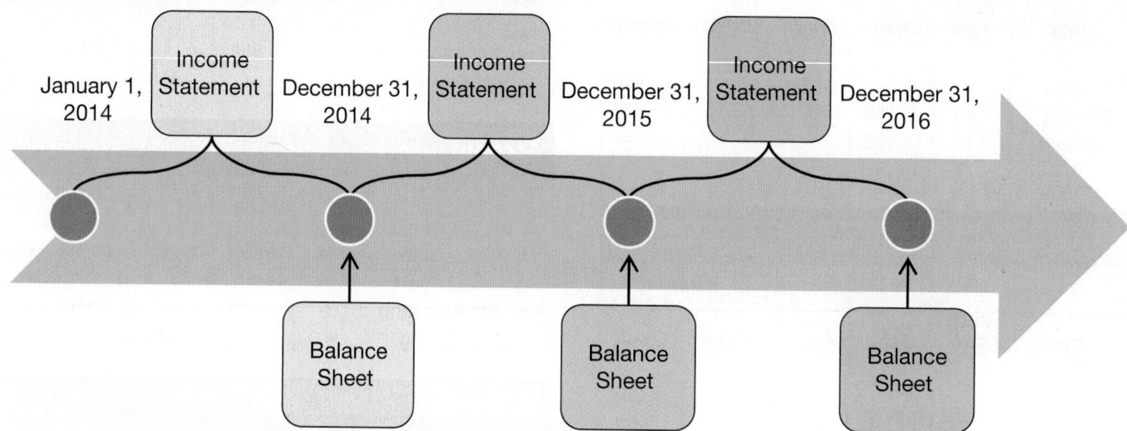

Business  **Connection**

CHOOSING A FISCAL YEAR

CVS Caremark Corporation (CVS) operates more than 7,000 pharmacies throughout the United States and fills more than one billion prescriptions annually. CVS recently chose December 31 as its fiscal year-end and described its decision as follows:

.... our Board of Directors approved a change in our fiscal year-end ... to December 31 of each year to better reflect our position in the health care ... industry.

In contrast, most large retailers such as Walmart and Target use fiscal years ending January 31, when their operations are the slowest following the December holidays.

OBJ 7 Describe and illustrate the use of working capital and the current ratio in evaluating a company's financial condition.

Financial Analysis and Interpretation: Working Capital and Current Ratio

The ability to convert assets into cash is called **liquidity**, while the ability of a business to pay its debts is called **solvency**. Two financial measures for evaluating a business's short-term liquidity and solvency are working capital and the current ratio.

Working capital is the excess of the current assets of a business over its current liabilities, computed as follows:

Working Capital = Current Assets − Current Liabilities

Current assets are more liquid than long-term assets. Thus, an increase in a company's current assets increases or improves its liquidity. An increase in working capital increases or improves liquidity in the sense that current assets are available for uses other than paying current liabilities.

A positive working capital implies that the business is able to pay its current liabilities and is solvent. Thus, an increase in working capital increases or improves a company's short-term solvency.

To illustrate, **NetSolutions**' working capital at the end of 2015 is $6,355 computed as follows:

Working Capital = Current Assets – Current Liabilities
= $7,745 – $1,390
= $6,355

This amount of working capital implies that NetSolutions is able to pay its current liabilities.

The **current ratio** is another means of expressing the relationship between current assets and current liabilities. The current ratio is computed by dividing current assets by current liabilities, as follows:

$$\text{Current Ratio} = \frac{\text{Current Assets}}{\text{Current Liabilities}}$$

To illustrate, the current ratio for **NetSolutions** at the end of 2015 is 5.6, computed as follows:

$$\text{Current Ratio} = \frac{\text{Current Assets}}{\text{Current Liabilities}}$$

$$= \frac{\$7{,}745}{\$1{,}390}$$

= 5.6 (Rounded)

The current ratio is more useful than working capital in making comparisons across companies or with industry averages. To illustrate, the following data (in millions) were taken from recent financial statements of **Electronic Arts Inc.**, **Take-Two Interactive Software, Inc.**, and **Zynga, Inc.**:

	Electronic Arts		**Take-Two**		**Zynga**	
	Year 2	**Year 1**	**Year 2**	**Year 1**	**Year 2**	**Year 1**
Current assets	$2,609	$3,032	$744	$567	$1,484	$2,024
Current liabilities	2,120	2,001	219	231	509	669
Working capital	$ 489	$1,031	$525	$336	$ 975	$1,355
Current ratio*	1.23	1.52	3.40	2.45	2.92	3.03
	($2,609 ÷ $2,120)	($3,032 ÷ $2,001)	($744 ÷ $219)	($567 ÷ $231)	($1,484 ÷ $509)	($2,024 ÷ $669)

* Rounded to two decimal places.

Electronic Arts has more than 3.5 times ($2,609 compared to $744) the current assets as does Take-Two and more than 1.7 times ($2,609 compared to $1,484) the current assets of Zynga. Such size differences makes meaningful comparisons difficult across companies. For this reason, ratios, such as the current ratio, are computed.

Although Electronic Arts is larger, Take-Two and Zynga have higher current ratios (3.40 and 2.45 for Take-Two; 2.92 and 3.03 for Zynga) than Electronic Arts. Overall, Take-Two and Zynga appear to be in a stronger short-term liquidity position than Electronic Arts. In addition, Electronics Arts' current ratio has decreased to 1.23 from 1.52, while Take-Two's current ratio has increased to 3.40 from 2.45 and Zynga's current ratio has decreased slightly to 2.92 from 3.03.

Example Exercise 4-6 Working Capital and Current Ratio OBJ 7

Current assets and current liabilities for Fortson Company follow:

	2016	2015
Current assets	$310,500	$262,500
Current liabilities	172,500	150,000

a. Determine the working capital and current ratio for 2016 and 2015.

b. Does the change in the current ratio from 2015 to 2016 indicate a favorable or an unfavorable trend?

Follow My Example 4-6

a.

	2016	2015
Current assets	$310,500	$262,500
Current liabilities	172,500	150,000
Working capital	$138,000	$112,500
Current ratio	1.80	1.75
	($310,500 ÷ $172,500)	($262,500 ÷ $150,000)

b. The change from 1.75 to 1.80 indicates a favorable trend.

Practice Exercises: PE 4-6A, PE 4-6B

APPENDIX 1

End-of-Period Spreadsheet

Accountants often use spreadsheets for analyzing and summarizing data. Such spreadsheets are not a formal part of the accounting records. This is in contrast to the chart of accounts, the journal, and the ledger, which are essential parts of an accounting system. Spreadsheets are usually prepared by using a computer program such as Microsoft's Excel.®

Exhibit 1 is an end-of-period spreadsheet used to summarize adjusting entries and their effects on the accounts. As illustrated in the chapter, the financial statements for NetSolutions can be prepared directly from the spreadsheet's Adjusted Trial Balance columns.

Some accountants prefer to expand the end-of-period spreadsheet shown in Exhibit 1 to include financial statement columns. Exhibits 20 through 24 illustrate the step-by-step process of how to prepare this expanded spreadsheet. As a basis for illustration, **NetSolutions** is used.

Step 1. Enter the Title

The spreadsheet is started by entering the following data:

1. Name of the business: *NetSolutions*
2. Type of spreadsheet: *End-of-Period Spreadsheet*
3. The period of time: *For the Two Months Ended December 31, 2015*

Exhibit 20 shows the preceding data entered for NetSolutions.

EXHIBIT 20 **Spreadsheet with Unadjusted Trial Balance Entered**

	A	B	C	D	E	F	G	H	I	J	K
1				NetSolutions							
2				End-of-Period Spreadsheet							
3				For the Two Months Ended December 31, 2015							
4		Unadjusted				Adjusted					
5		Trial Balance		Adjustments		Trial Balance		Income Statement		Balance Sheet	
6	Account Title	Dr.	Cr.	Dr.	Cr.	Dr.	Cr.	Dr.	Cr.	Dr.	Cr.
7											
8	Cash	2,065									
9	Accounts Receivable	2,220									
10	Supplies	2,000									
11	Prepaid Insurance	2,400									
12	Land	20,000									
13	Office Equipment	1,800									
14	Accumulated Depreciation										
15	Accounts Payable		900								
16	Wages Payable										
17	Unearned Rent		360								
18	Chris Clark, Capital		25,000								
19	Chris Clark, Drawing	4,000									
20	Fees Earned		16,340								
21	Rent Revenue										
22	Wages Expense	4,275									
23	Supplies Expense	800									
24	Rent Expense	1,600									
25	Utilities Expense	985									
26	Insurance Expense										
27	Depreciation Expense										
28	Miscellaneous Expense	455									
29		42,600	42,600								
30											

The spreadsheet is used for summarizing the effects of adjusting entries. It also aids in preparing financial statements.

Step 2. Enter the Unadjusted Trial Balance

Enter the unadjusted trial balance on the spreadsheet. The spreadsheet in Exhibit 20 shows the unadjusted trial balance for NetSolutions at December 31, 2015.

Step 3. Enter the Adjustments

The adjustments for NetSolutions from Chapter 3 are entered in the Adjustments columns, as shown in Exhibit 21. Cross-referencing (by letters) the debit and credit of each adjustment is useful in reviewing the spreadsheet. It is also helpful for identifying the adjusting entries that need to be recorded in the journal. This cross-referencing process is sometimes referred to as *keying* the adjustments.

The adjustments are normally entered in the order in which the data are assembled. If the titles of the accounts to be adjusted do not appear in the unadjusted trial balance, the accounts are inserted in their proper order in the Account Title column.

The adjusting entries for NetSolutions that are entered in the Adjustments columns are as follows:

(a) **Supplies.** The supplies account has a debit balance of $2,000. The cost of the supplies on hand at the end of the period is $760. The supplies expense for December is the difference between the two amounts, or $1,240 ($2,000 – $760). The adjustment is entered as (1) $1,240 in the Adjustments Debit column on the same line as Supplies Expense and (2) $1,240 in the Adjustments Credit column on the same line as Supplies.

(b) **Prepaid Insurance.** The prepaid insurance account has a debit balance of $2,400. This balance represents the prepayment of insurance for 12 months beginning December 1. Thus, the insurance expense for December is $200 ($2,400 ÷ 12). The adjustment is entered as (1) $200 in the Adjustments Debit column on the same line as Insurance Expense and (2) $200 in the Adjustments Credit column on the same line as Prepaid Insurance.

EXHIBIT 21 **Spreadsheet with Unadjusted Trial Balance and Adjustments**

	A	B	C	D	E	F	G	H	I	J	K
1		NetSolutions									
2		End-of-Period Spreadsheet									
3		For the Two Months Ended December 31, 2015									
4		Unadjusted				Adjusted					
5		Trial Balance		Adjustments		Trial Balance		Income Statement		Balance Sheet	
6	Account Title	Dr.	Cr.	Dr.	Cr.	Dr.	Cr.	Dr.	Cr.	Dr.	Cr.
7											
8	Cash	2,065									
9	Accounts Receivable	2,220		(d) 500							
10	Supplies	2,000			(a) 1,240						
11	Prepaid Insurance	2,400			(b) 200						
12	Land	20,000									
13	Office Equipment	1,800									
14	Accumulated Depreciation				(f) 50						
15	Accounts Payable		900								
16	Wages Payable				(e) 250						
17	Unearned Rent		360	(c) 120							
18	Chris Clark, Capital		25,000								
19	Chris Clark, Drawing	4,000									
20	Fees Earned		16,340		(d) 500						
21	Rent Revenue				(c) 120						
22	Wages Expense	4,275		(e) 250							
23	Supplies Expense	800		(a) 1,240							
24	Rent Expense	1,600									
25	Utilities Expense	985									
26	Insurance Expense			(b) 200							
27	Depreciation Expense			(f) 50							
28	Miscellaneous Expense	455									
29		42,600	42,600	2,360	2,360						
30											

The adjustments on the spreadsheet are used in preparing the adjusting journal entries.

(c) **Unearned Rent.** The unearned rent account has a credit balance of $360. This balance represents the receipt of three months' rent, beginning with December. Thus, the rent revenue for December is $120 ($360 ÷ 3). The adjustment is entered as (1) $120 in the Adjustments Debit column on the same line as Unearned Rent and (2) $120 in the Adjustments Credit column on the same line as Rent Revenue.

(d) **Accrued Fees.** Fees accrued at the end of December but not recorded total $500. This amount is an increase in an asset and an increase in revenue. The adjustment is entered as (1) $500 in the Adjustments Debit column on the same line as Accounts Receivable and (2) $500 in the Adjustments Credit column on the same line as Fees Earned.

(e) **Wages.** Wages accrued but not paid at the end of December total $250. This amount is an increase in expenses and an increase in liabilities. The adjustment is entered as (1) $250 in the Adjustments Debit column on the same line as Wages Expense and (2) $250 in the Adjustments Credit column on the same line as Wages Payable.

(f) **Depreciation.** Depreciation of the office equipment is $50 for December. The adjustment is entered as (1) $50 in the Adjustments Debit column on the same line as Depreciation Expense and (2) $50 in the Adjustments Credit column on the same line as Accumulated Depreciation.

After the adjustments have been entered, the Adjustments columns are totaled to verify the equality of the debits and credits. The total of the Debit column must equal the total of the Credit column.

Step 4. Enter the Adjusted Trial Balance

The adjusted trial balance is entered by combining the adjustments with the unadjusted balances for each account. The adjusted amounts are then extended to the Adjusted Trial Balance columns, as shown in Exhibit 22.

To illustrate, the cash amount of $2,065 is extended to the Adjusted Trial Balance Debit column since no adjustments affected Cash. Accounts Receivable has an initial

EXHIBIT 22 **Spreadsheet with Unadjusted Trial Balance, Adjustments, and Adjusted Trial Balance Entered**

	A	B	C	D	E	F	G	H	I	J	K
1				NetSolutions							
2				End-of-Period Spreadsheet							
3				For the Two Months Ended December 31, 2015							
4		Unadjusted				Adjusted					
5		Trial Balance		Adjustments		Trial Balance		Income Statement		Balance Sheet	
6	Account Title	Dr.	Cr.	Dr.	Cr.	Dr.	Cr.	Dr.	Cr.	Dr.	Cr.
7											
8	Cash	2,065				2,065					
9	Accounts Receivable	2,220		(d) 500		2,720					
10	Supplies	2,000			(a) 1,240	760					
11	Prepaid Insurance	2,400			(b) 200	2,200					
12	Land	20,000				20,000					
13	Office Equipment	1,800				1,800					
14	Accumulated Depreciation				(f) 50		50				
15	Accounts Payable		900				900				
16	Wages Payable				(e) 250		250				
17	Unearned Rent		360	(c) 120			240				
18	Chris Clark, Capital		25,000				25,000				
19	Chris Clark, Drawing	4,000				4,000					
20	Fees Earned		16,340		(d) 500		16,840				
21	Rent Revenue				(c) 120		120				
22	Wages Expense	4,275		(e) 250		4,525					
23	Supplies Expense	800		(a) 1,240		2,040					
24	Rent Expense	1,600				1,600					
25	Utilities Expense	985				985					
26	Insurance Expense			(b) 200		200					
27	Depreciation Expense			(f) 50		50					
28	Miscellaneous Expense	455				455					
29		42,600	42,600	2,360	2,360	43,400	43,400				
30											

The adjusted trial balance amounts are determined by adding the adjustments to or subtracting the adjustments from the trial balance amounts. For example, the Wages Expense debit of $4,525 is the trial balance amount of $4,275 plus the $250 adjustment debit.

balance of $2,220 and a debit adjustment of $500. Thus, $2,720 ($2,220 + $500) is entered in the Adjusted Trial Balance Debit column for Accounts Receivable. The same process continues until all account balances are extended to the Adjusted Trial Balance columns.

After the accounts and adjustments have been extended, the Adjusted Trial Balance columns are totaled to verify the equality of debits and credits. The total of the Debit column must equal the total of the Credit column.

Step 5. Extend the Accounts to the Income Statement and Balance Sheet Columns

The adjusted trial balance amounts are extended to the Income Statement and Balance Sheet columns. The amounts for revenues and expenses are extended to the Income Statement columns. The amounts for assets, liabilities, owner's capital, and drawings are extended to the Balance Sheet columns.[3]

The first account listed in the Adjusted Trial Balance columns is Cash with a debit balance of $2,065. Cash is an asset, is listed on the balance sheet, and has a debit balance. Therefore, $2,065 is extended to the Balance Sheet Debit column. The Fees Earned balance of $16,840 is extended to the Income Statement Credit column. The

[3] The balance of the dividends account is extended to the Balance Sheet columns because the spreadsheet does not have separate Statement of Owner's Equity columns.

EXHIBIT 23 **Spreadsheet with Amounts Extended to Income Statement and Balance Sheet Columns**

	A	B	C	D	E	F	G	H	I	J	K
1				NetSolutions							
2				End-of-Period Spreadsheet							
3				For the Two Months Ended December 31, 2015							
4		Unadjusted				Adjusted					
5		Trial Balance		Adjustments		Trial Balance		Income Statement		Balance Sheet	
6	Account Title	Dr.	Cr.	Dr.	Cr.	Dr.	Cr.	Dr.	Cr.	Dr.	Cr.
7											
8	Cash	2,065				2,065				2,065	
9	Accounts Receivable	2,220		(d) 500		2,720				2,720	
10	Supplies	2,000			(a) 1,240	760				760	
11	Prepaid Insurance	2,400			(b) 200	2,200				2,200	
12	Land	20,000				20,000				20,000	
13	Office Equipment	1,800				1,800				1,800	
14	Accumulated Depreciation				(f) 50		50				50
15	Accounts Payable		900				900				900
16	Wages Payable				(e) 250		250				250
17	Unearned Rent		360	(c) 120			240				240
18	Chris Clark, Capital		25,000				25,000				25,000
19	Chris Clark, Drawing	4,000				4,000				4,000	
20	Fees Earned		16,340		(d) 500		16,840		16,840		
21	Rent Revenue				(c) 120		120		120		
22	Wages Expense	4,275		(e) 250		4,525		4,525			
23	Supplies Expense	800		(a) 1,240		2,040		2,040			
24	Rent Expense	1,600				1,600		1,600			
25	Utilities Expense	985				985		985			
26	Insurance Expense			(b) 200		200		200			
27	Depreciation Expense			(f) 50		50		50			
28	Miscellaneous Expense	455				455		455			
29		42,600	42,600	2,360	2,360	43,400	43,400				
30											

The revenue and expense amounts are extended to (entered in) the Income Statement columns.

The asset, liability, owner's capital, and drawing amounts are extended to (entered in) the Balance Sheet columns.

same process continues until all account balances have been extended to the proper columns, as shown in Exhibit 23.

Step 6. Total the Income Statement and Balance Sheet Columns, Compute the Net Income or Net Loss, and Complete the Spreadsheet

After the account balances are extended to the Income Statement and Balance Sheet columns, each of the columns is totaled. The difference between the two Income Statement column totals is the amount of the net income or the net loss for the period. This difference (net income or net loss) will also be the difference between the two Balance Sheet column totals.

If the Income Statement Credit column total (total revenue) is greater than the Income Statement Debit column total (total expenses), the difference is the net income. If the Income Statement Debit column total is greater than the Income Statement Credit column total, the difference is a net loss.

As shown in Exhibit 24, the total of the Income Statement Credit column is $16,960, and the total of the Income Statement Debit column is $9,855. Thus, the net income for NetSolutions is $7,105, computed as follows:

Total of Income Statement Credit column (revenues)	$16,960
Total of Income Statement Debit column (expenses)	9,855
Net income (excess of revenues over expenses)	$ 7,105

The amount of the net income, $7,105, is entered in the Income Statement Debit column and the Balance Sheet Credit column. *Net income* is also entered in the Account Title column. Entering the net income of $7,105 in the Balance Sheet Credit column has the effect of transferring the net balance of the revenue and expense accounts to the retained earnings account.

If there was a net loss instead of net income, the amount of the net loss would be entered in the Income Statement Credit column and the Balance Sheet Debit column. *Net loss* would also be entered in the Account Title column.

EXHIBIT 24 **Completed Spreadsheet with Net Income Shown**

	A	B	C	D	E	F	G	H	I	J	K
1				NetSolutions							
2				End-of-Period Spreadsheet							
3				For the Two Months Ended December 31, 2015							
4		Unadjusted				Adjusted					
5		Trial Balance		Adjustments		Trial Balance		Income Statement		Balance Sheet	
6	Account Title	Dr.	Cr.	Dr.	Cr.	Dr.	Cr.	Dr.	Cr.	Dr.	Cr.
7											
8	Cash	2,065				2,065				2,065	
9	Accounts Receivable	2,220		(d) 500		2,720				2,720	
10	Supplies	2,000			(a) 1,240	760				760	
11	Prepaid Insurance	2,400			(b) 200	2,200				2,200	
12	Land	20,000				20,000				20,000	
13	Office Equipment	1,800				1,800				1,800	
14	Accumulated Depreciation				(f) 50		50				50
15	Accounts Payable		900				900				900
16	Wages Payable				(e) 250		250				250
17	Unearned Rent		360	(c) 120			240				240
18	Chris Clark, Capital		25,000				25,000				25,000
19	Chris Clark, Drawing	4,000				4,000				4,000	
20	Fees Earned		16,340		(d) 500		16,840		16,840		
21	Rent Revenue				(c) 120		120		120		
22	Wages Expense	4,275		(e) 250		4,525		4,525			
23	Supplies Expense	800		(a) 1,240		2,040		2,040			
24	Rent Expense	1,600				1,600		1,600			
25	Utilities Expense	985				985		985			
26	Insurance Expense			(b) 200		200		200			
27	Depreciation Expense			(f) 50		50		50			
28	Miscellaneous Expense	455				455		455			
29		42,600	42,600	2,360	2,360	43,400	43,400	9,855	16,960	33,545	26,440
30	Net income							7,105			7,105
31								16,960	16,960	33,545	33,545
32											

The difference between the Income Statement column totals is the net income (or net loss) for the period. The difference between the Balance Sheet column totals is also the net income (or net loss) for the period.

After the net income or net loss is entered on the spreadsheet, the Income Statement and Balance Sheet columns are totaled. The totals of the two Income Statement columns must now be equal. The totals of the two Balance Sheet columns must also be equal.

Preparing the Financial Statements from the Spreadsheet

The spreadsheet can be used to prepare the income statement, the statement of owner's equity, and the balance sheet shown in Exhibit 2. The income statement is normally prepared directly from the spreadsheet. The expenses are listed in the income statement in Exhibit 2 in order of size, beginning with the larger items. Miscellaneous expense is the last item, regardless of its amount.

The first item normally presented on the statement of owner's equity is the balance of the owner's capital account at the beginning of the period. The amount listed as owner's capital in the spreadsheet, however, is not always the account balance at the beginning of the period. The owner may have invested additional assets in the business during the period. Thus, for the beginning balance and any additional investments, it is necessary to refer to the capital account in the ledger. These amounts, along with the net income (or net loss) and the drawing amount shown in the spreadsheet, are used to determine the ending capital account balance.

The balance sheet can be prepared directly from the spreadsheet columns except for the ending balance of owner's capital. The ending balance of owner's capital is taken from the statement of owner's equity.

When a spreadsheet is used, the adjusting and closing entries are normally not journalized or posted until after the spreadsheet and financial statements have been prepared. The data for the adjusting entries are taken from the Adjustments columns of the spreadsheet. The data for the first two closing entries are taken from the Income Statement columns of the spreadsheet. The amount for the third closing entry is the net income or net loss appearing at the bottom of the spreadsheet. The amount for the fourth closing entry is the drawing account balance that appears in the Balance Sheet Debit column of the spreadsheet.

At a Glance 4

Describe the flow of accounting information from the unadjusted trial balance into the adjusted trial balance and financial statements.

Key Points Exhibit 1 illustrates the end-of-period process by which accounts are adjusted and how the adjusted accounts flow into the financial statements.

Learning Outcomes	Example Exercises	Practice Exercises
• Using an end-of-period spreadsheet, describe how the unadjusted trial balance accounts are affected by adjustments and how the adjusted trial balance accounts flow into the income statement and balance sheet.	EE4-1	PE4-1A, 4-1B

Prepare financial statements from adjusted account balances.

Key Points Using the end-of-period spreadsheet shown in Exhibit 1, the income statement and balance sheet for NetSolutions can be prepared. The statement of owner's equity is prepared by referring to transactions that have been posted to owner's capital accounts in the ledger. A classified balance sheet has sections for current assets; property, plant, and equipment; current liabilities; long-term liabilities; and owner's equity.

Learning Outcomes	Example Exercises	Practice Exercises
• Describe how the net income or net loss from the period can be determined from an end-of-period spreadsheet.		
• Prepare an income statement, a statement of owner's equity, and a balance sheet.	EE4-2	PE4-2A, 4-2B
• Indicate how accounts would be reported on a classified balance sheet.	EE4-3	PE4-3A, 4-3B

Prepare closing entries.

Key Points Four entries are required in closing the temporary accounts. The first entry closes the revenue accounts to Income Summary. The second entry closes the expense accounts to Income Summary. The third entry closes the balance of Income Summary (net income or net loss) to the owner's capital account. The fourth entry closes the drawing account to the owner's capital account.

After the closing entries have been posted to the ledger, the balance in the capital account agrees with the amount reported on the statement of owner's equity and balance sheet. In addition, the revenue, expense, and drawing accounts will have zero balances.

Learning Outcomes	Example Exercises	Practice Exercises
• Prepare the closing entry for revenues.	EE4-4	PE4-4A, 4-4B
• Prepare the closing entry for expenses.	EE4-4	PE4-4A, 4-4B
• Prepare the closing entry for transferring the balance of Income Summary to the owner's capital account.	EE4-4	PE4-4A, 4-4B
• Prepare the closing entry for the owner's drawing account.	EE4-4	PE4-4A, 4-4B

Describe the accounting cycle.

Key Points The 10 basic steps of the accounting cycle are as follows:

1. Transactions are analyzed and recorded in the journal.
2. Transactions are posted to the ledger.
3. An unadjusted trial balance is prepared.
4. Adjustment data are assembled and analyzed.
5. An optional end-of-period spreadsheet is prepared.
6. Adjusting entries are journalized and posted to the ledger.
7. An adjusted trial balance is prepared.
8. Financial statements are prepared.
9. Closing entries are journalized and posted to the ledger.
10. A post-closing trial balance is prepared.

Learning Outcomes	Example Exercises	Practice Exercises
• List the 10 steps of the accounting cycle.	EE4-5	PE4-5A, 4-5B
• Determine whether any steps are out of order in a listing of accounting cycle steps.		
• Determine whether there are any missing steps in a listing of accounting cycle steps.		

Illustrate the accounting cycle for one period.

Key Points The complete accounting cycle for Kelly Consulting for the month of April is described and illustrated in this chapter.

Learning Outcomes	Example Exercises	Practice Exercises
• Complete the accounting cycle for a period from beginning to end.		

Explain what is meant by the fiscal year and the natural business year.

Key Points The annual accounting period adopted by a business is its fiscal year. A company's fiscal year that ends when business activities have reached the lowest point in its annual operating cycle is called the natural business year.

Learning Outcomes	Example Exercises	Practice Exercises
• Explain why companies use a fiscal year that is different from the calendar year.		

Describe and illustrate the use of working capital and the current ratio in evaluating a company's financial condition.

Key Points The ability to convert assets into cash is called liquidity, while the ability of a business to pay its debts is called solvency. Two financial measures for evaluating a business's short-term liquidity and solvency are working capital and the current ratio. Working capital is computed by subtracting current liabilities from current assets. An excess of current assets over current liabilities implies that the business is able to pay its current liabilities. The current ratio is computed by dividing current assets by current liabilities. The current ratio is more useful than working capital in making comparisons across companies or with industry averages.

Learning Outcomes	Example Exercises	Practice Exercises
• Define liquidity and solvency.		
• Compute working capital.	**EE4-6**	**PE4-6A, 4-6B**
• Compute the current ratio.	**EE4-6**	**PE4-6A, 4-6B**

Key Terms

accounting cycle (164)
clearing account (159)
closing entries (158)
closing process (158)
closing the books (158)
current assets (157)
current liabilities (157)
current ratio (177)
fiscal year (175)
fixed (plant) assets (157)
Income Summary (159)
liquidity (176)
long-term liabilities (157)
natural business year (176)
notes receivable (157)
real (permanent) accounts (158)
solvency (176)
temporary (nominal) accounts (158)
working capital (176)

Illustrative Problem

Three years ago, T. Roderick organized Harbor Realty. At July 31, 2016, the end of the fiscal year, the following end-of-period spreadsheet was prepared:

	A	B	C	D	E	F	G
1		Harbor Realty					
2		End-of-Period Spreadsheet					
3		For the Year Ended July 31, 2016					
4		Unadjusted				Adjusted	
5		Trial Balance		Adjustments		Trial Balance	
6	**Account Title**	**Dr.**	**Cr.**	**Dr.**	**Cr.**	**Dr.**	**Cr.**
7							
8	Cash	3,425				3,425	
9	Accounts Receivable	7,000		(e) 1,000		8,000	
10	Supplies	1,270			(a) 890	380	
11	Prepaid Insurance	620			(b) 315	305	
12	Office Equipment	51,650				51,650	
13	Accum. Depreciation		9,700		(c) 4,950		14,650
14	Accounts Payable		925				925
15	Unearned Fees		1,250	(f) 500			750
16	Wages Payable				(d) 440		440
17	T. Roderick, Capital		29,000				29,000
18	T. Roderick, Drawing	5,200				5,200	
19	Fees Earned		59,125		(e) 1,000		60,625
20					(f) 500		
21	Wages Expense	22,415		(d) 440		22,855	
22	Depreciation Expense			(c) 4,950		4,950	
23	Rent Expense	4,200				4,200	
24	Utilities Expense	2,715				2,715	
25	Supplies Expense			(a) 890		890	
26	Insurance Expense			(b) 315		315	
27	Miscellaneous Expense	1,505				1,505	
28		100,000	100,000	8,095	8,095	106,390	106,390
29							

Instructions

1. Prepare an income statement, a statement of owner's equity (no additional investments were made during the year), and a balance sheet.
2. On the basis of the data in the end-of-period spreadsheet, journalize the closing entries.

Solution

1.

Harbor Realty Income Statement For the Year Ended July 31, 2016		
Fees earned		$60,625
Expenses:		
Wages expense	$22,855	
Depreciation expense	4,950	
Rent expense	4,200	
Utilities expense	2,715	
Supplies expense	890	
Insurance expense	315	
Miscellaneous expense	1,505	
Total expenses		37,430
Net income		$23,195

Harbor Realty Statement of Owner's Equity For the Year Ended July 31, 2016		
T. Roderick, capital, August 1, 2015		$29,000
Net income for the year	$23,195	
Less withdrawals	5,200	
Increase in owner's equity		17,995
T. Roderick, capital, July 31, 2016		$46,995

Harbor Realty Balance Sheet July 31, 2016					
Assets			**Liabilities**		
Current assets:			Current liabilities:		
Cash	$ 3,425		Accounts payable	$925	
Accounts receivable	8,000		Unearned fees	750	
Supplies	380		Wages payable	440	
Prepaid insurance	305		Total liabilities		$ 2,115
Total current assets		$12,110			
Property, plant, and equipment:					
Office equipment	$51,650				
Less accum. depreciation	14,650		**Owner's Equity**		
Total property, plant, and equipment		37,000	T. Roderick, capital		46,995
Total assets		$49,110	Total liabilities and owner's equity		$49,110

2.

Journal					Page
Date		Description	Post. Ref.	Debit	Credit
		Closing Entries			
2016 July	31	Fees Earned		60,625	
		Income Summary			60,625
	31	Income Summary		37,430	
		Wages Expense			22,855
		Depreciation Expense			4,950
		Rent Expense			4,200
		Utilities Expense			2,715
		Supplies Expense			890
		Insurance Expense			315
		Miscellaneous Expense			1,505
	31	Income Summary		23,195	
		T. Roderick, Capital			23,195
	31	T. Roderick, Capital		5,200	
		T. Roderick, Drawing			5,200

Discussion Questions

1. Why do some accountants prepare an end-of-period spreadsheet?

2. Describe the nature of the assets that compose the following sections of a balance sheet: (a) current assets, (b) property, plant, and equipment.

3. What is the difference between a current liability and a long-term liability?

4. What types of accounts are referred to as temporary accounts?

5. Why are closing entries required at the end of an accounting period?

6. What is the difference between adjusting entries and closing entries?

7. What is the purpose of the post-closing trial balance?

8. (a) What is the most important output of the accounting cycle? (b) Do all companies have an accounting cycle? Explain.

9. What is the natural business year?

10. Recent fiscal years for several well-known companies are as follows:

Company	Fiscal Year Ending
JCPenney	January 27
Limited Brands, Inc.	January 27
Sears	January 27
Target Corp.	January 27
Home Depot	January 28
Tiffany & Co.	January 30

What general characteristic shared by these companies explains why they do not have fiscal years ending December 31?

Practice Exercises

SHOW ME HOW

EE 4-1 p. 154

PE 4-1A Flow of accounts into financial statements

OBJ. 1

The balances for the accounts that follow appear in the Adjusted Trial Balance columns of the end-of-period spreadsheet. Indicate whether each account would flow into the income statement, statement of owner's equity, or balance sheet.

1. Accounts Receivable
2. Depreciation Expense—Equipment
3. Gene Cox, Capital (beginning of period)
4. Office Equipment
5. Rent Revenue
6. Supplies Expense
7. Unearned Revenue
8. Wages Payable

SHOW ME HOW

EE 4-1 p. 154

PE 4-1B Flow of accounts into financial statements

OBJ. 1

The balances for the accounts that follow appear in the Adjusted Trial Balance columns of the end-of-period spreadsheet. Indicate whether each account would flow into the income statement, statement of owner's equity, or balance sheet.

1. Accumulated Depreciation—Building
2. Cash
3. Fees Earned
4. Insurance Expense
5. Prepaid Rent
6. Supplies
7. Tina Greer, Drawing
8. Wages Expense

SHOW ME HOW

EE 4-2 p. 156

PE 4-2A Statement of owner's equity

OBJ. 2

Marcie Davies owns and operates Gemini Advertising Services. On January 1, 2015, Marcie Davies, Capital had a balance of $618,500. During the year, Marcie invested an additional $40,000 and withdrew $15,000. For the year ended December 31, 2015, Gemini Advertising Services reported a net income of $92,330. Prepare a statement of owner's equity for the year ended December 31, 2015.

SHOW ME HOW

EE 4-2 p. 156

PE 4-2B Statement of owner's equity

OBJ. 2

Blake Knudson owns and operates Grab Bag Delivery Services. On January 1, 2015, Blake Knudson, Capital had a balance of $918,000. During the year, Blake made no additional investments and withdrew $15,000. For the year ended December 31, 2015, Grab Bag Delivery Services reported a net loss of $43,500. Prepare a statement of owner's equity for the year ended December 31, 2015.

SHOW ME HOW

EE 4-3 p. 157

PE 4-3A Classified balance sheet

OBJ. 2

The following accounts appear in an adjusted trial balance of San Jose Consulting. Indicate whether each account would be reported in the (a) current asset; (b) property, plant, and equipment; (c) current liability; (d) long-term liability; or (e) owner's equity section of the December 31, 2015, balance sheet of San Jose Consulting.

1. Building
2. Nata Foust, Capital
3. Notes Payable (due in five years)
4. Prepaid Rent
5. Salaries Payable
6. Supplies
7. Taxes Payable
8. Unearned Service Fees

EE 4-3 p. 157

PE 4-3B Classified balance sheet — OBJ. 2

The following accounts appear in an adjusted trial balance of Kangaroo Consulting. Indicate whether each account would be reported in the (a) current asset; (b) property, plant, and equipment; (c) current liability; (d) long-term liability; or (e) owner's equity section of the December 31, 2015, balance sheet of Kangaroo Consulting.

1. Accounts Payable
2. Accounts Receivable
3. Accumulated Depreciation—Building
4. Cash
5. Lea Gabel, Capital
6. Note Payable (due in ten years)
7. Supplies
8. Wages Payable

EE 4-4 p. 161

PE 4-4A Closing entries — OBJ. 3

SHOW ME HOW

After the accounts have been adjusted at October 31, the end of the fiscal year, the following balances were taken from the ledger of Smart Delivery Services Co.:

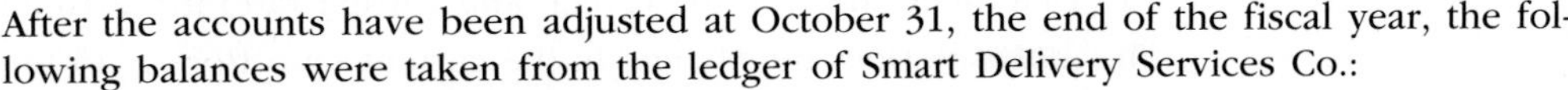

Fraser Smart, Capital	$3,550,000
Fraser Smart, Drawing	40,000
Fees Earned	1,145,000
Wages Expense	740,000
Rent Expense	65,000
Supplies Expense	14,750
Miscellaneous Expense	8,800

Journalize the four entries required to close the accounts.

EE 4-4 p. 161

PE 4-4B Closing entries — OBJ. 3

SHOW ME HOW

After the accounts have been adjusted at April 30, the end of the fiscal year, the following balances were taken from the ledger of Nuclear Landscaping Co.:

Felix Godwin, Capital	$643,600
Felix Godwin, Drawing	10,500
Fees Earned	356,500
Wages Expense	283,100
Rent Expense	56,000
Supplies Expense	11,500
Miscellaneous Expense	13,000

Journalize the four entries required to close the accounts.

EE 4-5 p. 164

PE 4-5A Accounting cycle — OBJ. 4

SHOW ME HOW

From the following list of steps in the accounting cycle, identify what two steps are missing:

a. Transactions are analyzed and recorded in the journal.
b. An unadjusted trial balance is prepared.
c. Adjustment data are assembled and analyzed.
d. An optional end-of-period spreadsheet is prepared.
e. Adjusting entries are journalized and posted to the ledger.
f. An adjusted trial balance is prepared.
g. Closing entries are journalized and posted to the ledger.
h. A post-closing trial balance is prepared.

EE 4-5 p. 164

PE 4-5B Accounting cycle — OBJ. 4

From the following list of steps in the accounting cycle, identify what two steps are missing:

a. Transactions are analyzed and recorded in the journal.
b. Transactions are posted to the ledger.
c. An unadjusted trial balance is prepared.

(Continued)

d. An optional end-of-period spreadsheet is prepared.
e. Adjusting entries are journalized and posted to the ledger.
f. An adjusted trial balance is prepared.
g. Financial statements are prepared.
h. A post-closing trial balance is prepared.

EE 4-6 p. 178

SHOW ME HOW

PE 4-6A Working capital and current ratio **OBJ. 7**

Balance sheet data for HQ Properties Company follows:

	2016	2015
Current assets	$2,175,000	$1,900,000
Current liabilities	1,500,000	1,250,000

a. Determine the working capital and current ratio for 2016 and 2015.
b. Does the change in the current ratio from 2015 to 2016 indicate a favorable or an unfavorable trend?

EE 4-6 p. 178

SHOW ME HOW

PE 4-6B Working capital and current ratio **OBJ. 7**

Balance sheet data for Brimstone Company follows:

	2016	2015
Current assets	$1,586,250	$1,210,000
Current liabilities	705,000	550,000

a. Determine the working capital and current ratio for 2016 and 2015.
b. Does the change in the current ratio from 2015 to 2016 indicate a favorable or an unfavorable trend?

Exercises

EX 4-1 Flow of accounts into financial statements **OBJ. 1, 2**

The balances for the accounts that follow appear in the Adjusted Trial Balance columns of the end-of-period spreadsheet. Indicate whether each account would flow into the income statement, statement of owner's equity, or balance sheet.

1. Accounts Payable
2. Accounts Receivable
3. Cash
4. Danny Reacher, Drawing
5. Fees Earned
6. Supplies
7. Unearned Rent
8. Utilities Expense
9. Wages Expense
10. Wages Payable

EX 4-2 Classifying accounts **OBJ. 1, 2**

Balances for each of the following accounts appear in an adjusted trial balance. Identify each as (a) asset, (b) liability, (c) revenue, or (d) expense.

1. Accounts Receivable
2. Equipment
3. Fees Earned
4. Insurance Expense
5. Prepaid Advertising
6. Prepaid Rent
7. Rent Revenue
8. Salary Expense
9. Salary Payable
10. Supplies
11. Supplies Expense
12. Unearned Rent

EX 4-3 Financial statements from the end-of-period spreadsheet

OBJ. 1, 2

SHOW ME HOW

Bamboo Consulting is a consulting firm owned and operated by Lisa Gooch. The following end-of-period spreadsheet was prepared for the year ended July 31, 2016:

	A	B	C	D	E	F	G
1		Bamboo Consulting					
2		End-of-Period Spreadsheet					
3		For the Year Ended July 31, 2016					
4		Unadjusted				Adjusted	
5		Trial Balance		Adjustments		Trial Balance	
6	Account Title	Dr.	Cr.	Dr.	Cr.	Dr.	Cr.
7							
8	Cash	58,000				58,000	
9	Accounts Receivable	106,200				106,200	
10	Supplies	11,900			(a) 7,500	4,400	
11	Office Equipment	515,000				515,000	
12	Accumulated Depreciation		28,000		(b) 5,600		33,600
13	Accounts Payable		20,500				20,500
14	Salaries Payable				(c) 2,500		2,500
15	Lisa Gooch, Capital		516,700				516,700
16	Lisa Gooch, Drawing	25,000				25,000	
17	Fees Earned		348,500				348,500
18	Salary Expense	186,500		(c) 2,500		189,000	
19	Supplies Expense			(a) 7,500		7,500	
20	Depreciation Expense			(b) 5,600		5,600	
21	Miscellaneous Expense	11,100				11,100	
22		913,700	913,700	15,600	15,600	921,800	921,800
23							

Based on the preceding spreadsheet, prepare an income statement, statement of owner's equity, and balance sheet for Bamboo Consulting.

EX 4-4 Financial statements from the end-of-period spreadsheet

OBJ. 1, 2

SHOW ME HOW

Elliptical Consulting is a consulting firm owned and operated by Jayson Neese. The following end-of-period spreadsheet was prepared for the year ended June 30, 2016:

	A	B	C	D	E	F	G
1		Elliptical Consulting					
2		End-of-Period Spreadsheet					
3		For the Year Ended June 30, 2016					
4		Unadjusted				Adjusted	
5		Trial Balance		Adjustments		Trial Balance	
6	Account Title	Dr.	Cr.	Dr.	Cr.	Dr.	Cr.
7							
8	Cash	27,000				27,000	
9	Accounts Receivable	53,500				53,500	
10	Supplies	3,000			(a) 2,100	900	
11	Office Equipment	30,500				30,500	
12	Accumulated Depreciation		4,500		(b) 1,500		6,000
13	Accounts Payable		3,300				3,300
14	Salaries Payable				(c) 375		375
15	Jayson Neese, Capital		82,200				82,200
16	Jayson Neese, Drawing	2,000				2,000	
17	Fees Earned		60,000				60,000
18	Salary Expense	32,000		(c) 375		32,375	
19	Supplies Expense			(a) 2,100		2,100	
20	Depreciation Expense			(b) 1,500		1,500	
21	Miscellaneous Expense	2,000				2,000	
22		150,000	150,000	3,975	3,975	151,875	151,875
23							

Based on the preceding spreadsheet, prepare an income statement, statement of owner's equity, and balance sheet for Elliptical Consulting.

EX 4-5 Income statement — OBJ. 2

✔ Net income, $218,000

SHOW ME HOW

The following account balances were taken from the adjusted trial balance for Laser Messenger Service, a delivery service firm, for the fiscal year ended April 30, 2016:

Depreciation Expense	$ 8,650	Rent Expense	$ 60,000
Fees Earned	674,000	Salaries Expense	336,900
Insurance Expense	1,500	Supplies Expense	4,100
Miscellaneous Expense	3,650	Utilities Expense	41,200

Prepare an income statement.

EX 4-6 Income statement; net loss — OBJ. 2

✔ Net loss, $20,900

SHOW ME HOW

The following revenue and expense account balances were taken from the ledger of Wholistic Health Services Co. after the accounts had been adjusted on February 29, 2016, the end of the fiscal year:

Depreciation Expense	$ 7,500	Service Revenue	$448,400
Insurance Expense	3,000	Supplies Expense	2,750
Miscellaneous Expense	8,150	Utilities Expense	33,900
Rent Expense	54,000	Wages Expense	360,000

Prepare an income statement.

EX 4-7 Income statement — OBJ. 2

Internet Project

✔ a. Net income: $2,032

FedEx Corporation had the following revenue and expense account balances (in millions) for a recent year ending May 31:

Depreciation Expense	$2,113	Purchased Transportation	$ 6,335
Fuel Expense	4,956	Rentals and Landing Fees	2,487
Maintenance and Repairs Expense	1,980	Revenues	42,680
Other Expense (Income) Net	5,569	Salaries and Employee Benefits	16,099
Provision for Income Taxes	1,109		

a. Prepare an income statement.

b. Compare your income statement with the income statement that is available at the FedEx Corporation Web site, (http://investors.fedex.com). Click on Annual Report and Download Annual Report. What similarities and differences do you see?

EX 4-8 Statement of owner's equity — OBJ. 2

✔ Bart Nesbit, capital, Dec. 31, 2016: $1,640,000

SHOW ME HOW

Apex Systems Co. offers its services to residents in the Seattle area. Selected accounts from the ledger of Apex Systems Co. for the fiscal year ended December 31, 2016, are as follows:

Bart Nesbit, Capital

Dec. 31	90,000	Jan. 1 (2016)	1,375,000
		Dec. 31	355,000

Bart Nesbit, Drawing

Mar. 31	22,500	Dec. 31	90,000
June 30	22,500		
Sept. 30	22,500		
Dec. 31	22,500		

Income Summary

Dec. 31	1,415,000	Dec. 31	1,770,000
31	355,000		

Prepare a statement of owner's equity for the year.

EX 4-9 Statement of owner's equity; net loss — OBJ. 2

✔ Doug Stone, capital, April 30, 2016: $439,300

Selected accounts from the ledger of Restoration Arts for the fiscal year ended April 30, 2016, are as follows:

Doug Stone, Capital

Apr. 30	31,200	May 1 (2015)	475,500
30	5,000		

Doug Stone, Drawing

Sept. 30	1,250	Apr. 30	5,000
Dec. 31	1,250		
March 31	1,250		
June 30	1,250		

Income Summary			
Apr. 30	197,000	Apr. 30	165,800
		30	31,200

Prepare a statement of owner's equity for the year.

EX 4-10 Classifying assets OBJ. 2

Identify each of the following as (a) a current asset or (b) property, plant, and equipment:

1. Accounts Receivable
2. Building
3. Cash
4. Equipment
5. Prepaid Insurance
6. Supplies

EX 4-11 Balance sheet classification OBJ. 2

At the balance sheet date, a business owes a mortgage note payable of $375,000, the terms of which provide for monthly payments of $1,250.

Explain how the liability should be classified on the balance sheet.

EX 4-12 Balance sheet OBJ. 2

✔ Total assets: $775,000

SHOW ME HOW

Optimum Weight Loss Co. offers personal weight reduction consulting services to individuals. After all the accounts have been closed on November 30, 2016, the end of the fiscal year, the balances of selected accounts from the ledger of Optimum Weight Loss Co. are as follows:

Accounts Payable	$ 37,700	Prepaid Insurance	$ 7,200
Accounts Receivable	116,750	Prepaid Rent	21,000
Accumulated Depreciation—Equipment	186,400	Salaries Payable	9,000
Cash	?	Cheryl Viers, Capital	710,300
Equipment	474,150	Supplies	4,800
Land	300,000	Unearned Fees	18,000

Prepare a classified balance sheet that includes the correct balance for Cash.

EX 4-13 Balance sheet OBJ. 2

✔ Corrected balance sheet, total assets: $625,000

List the errors you find in the following balance sheet. Prepare a corrected balance sheet.

Labyrinth Services Co.
Balance Sheet
For the Year Ended August 31, 2016

Assets			**Liabilities**		
Current assets:			Current liabilities:		
Cash	$ 18,500		Accounts receivable	$ 41,400	
Accounts payable	31,300		Accum. depr.—building	155,000	
Supplies	6,500		Accum. depr.—equipment	25,000	
Prepaid insurance	16,600		Net income	118,200	
Land	225,000		Total liabilities		$339,600
Total current assets		$297,900			
Property, plant, and equipment:			**Owner's Equity**		
Building	$400,000		Wages payable	$ 6,500	
Equipment	97,000		Ruben Daniel, capital	587,200	
Total property, plant, and equipment		635,400	Total owner's equity		593,700
Total assets		$933,300	Total liabilities and owner's equity		$933,300

EX 4-14 Identifying accounts to be closed OBJ. 3

From the list that follows, identify the accounts that should be closed to Income Summary at the end of the fiscal year:

(Continued)

a. Accounts Payable
b. Accumulated Depreciation—Equipment
c. Depreciation Expense—Equipment
d. Equipment
e. Ellen Drake, Capital
f. Ellen Drake, Drawing
g. Fees Earned
h. Land
i. Supplies
j. Supplies Expense
k. Wages Expense
l. Wages Payable

EX 4-15 Closing entries **OBJ. 3**

Prior to its closing, Income Summary had total debits of $1,190,500 and total credits of $1,476,300.

Briefly explain the purpose served by the income summary account and the nature of the entries that resulted in the $1,190,500 and the $1,476,300.

EX 4-16 Closing entries with net income **OBJ. 3**

SHOW ME HOW

After all revenue and expense accounts have been closed at the end of the fiscal year, Income Summary has a debit of $798,400 and a credit of $955,300. At the same date, Debra Allen, Capital has a credit balance of $1,439,000, and Debra Allen, Drawing has a balance of $36,000. (a) Journalize the entries required to complete the closing of the accounts. (b) Determine the amount of Debra Allen, Capital at the end of the period.

EX 4-17 Closing entries with net loss **OBJ. 3**

SHOW ME HOW

Mira Services Co. offers its services to individuals desiring to improve their personal images. After the accounts have been adjusted at October 31, the end of the fiscal year, the following balances were taken from the ledger of Mira Services Co.:

Bonnie Mira, Capital	$910,000	Rent Expense	$72,000
Bonnie Mira, Drawing	16,000	Supplies Expense	11,900
Fees Earned	519,300	Miscellaneous Expense	14,250
Wages Expense	488,000		

Journalize the four entries required to close the accounts.

EX 4-18 Identifying permanent accounts **OBJ. 3**

Which of the following accounts will usually appear in the post-closing trial balance?

a. Accounts Payable
b. Accumulated Depreciation
c. Ben Crayton, Capital
d. Ben Crayton, Drawing
e. Cash
f. Depreciation Expense
g. Fees Earned
h. Office Equipment
i. Salaries Expense
j. Salaries Payable
k. Supplies

EX 4-19 Post-closing trial balance **OBJ. 3**

✔ Correct column totals, $300,000

SHOW ME HOW

An accountant prepared the following post-closing trial balance:

La Casa Services Co.
Post-Closing Trial Balance
March 31, 2016

	Debit Balances	Credit Balances
Cash	46,540	
Accounts Receivable	122,260	
Supplies		4,000
Equipment		127,200
Accumulated Depreciation—Equipment	33,600	
Accounts Payable	52,100	
Salaries Payable		6,400
Unearned Rent	9,000	
Sonya Flynn, Capital	198,900	
	462,400	137,600

Prepare a corrected post-closing trial balance. Assume that all accounts have normal balances and that the amounts shown are correct.

EX 4-20 Steps in the accounting cycle **OBJ. 4**

Rearrange the following steps in the accounting cycle in proper sequence:

a. A post-closing trial balance is prepared.
b. Adjustment data are asssembled and analyzed.
c. Adjusting entries are journalized and posted to the ledger.
d. An adjusted trial balance is prepared.
e. An optional end-of-period spreadsheet is prepared.
f. An unadjusted trial balance is prepared.
g. Closing entries are journalized and posted to the ledger.
h. Financial statements are prepared.
i. Transactions are analyzed and recorded in the journal.
j. Transactions are posted to the ledger.

EX 4-21 Working capital and current ratio **OBJ. 7**

SHOW ME HOW

The following data (in thousands) were taken from recent financial statements of **Under Armour, Inc.**:

	December 31	
	Year 2	**Year 1**
Current assets	$689,663	$558,850
Current liabilities	183,607	149,147

a. Compute the working capital and the current ratio as of December 31, Year 2 and Year 1. Round to two decimal places.
b. What conclusions concerning the company's ability to meet its financial obligations can you draw from part (a)?

EX 4-22 Working capital and current ratio **OBJ. 7**

The following data (in thousands) were taken from recent financial statements of **Starbucks Corporation**:

	Year 2	**Year 1**
Current assets	$4,199,600	$3,794,900
Current liabilities	2,209,200	2,075,800

a. Compute the working capital and the current ratio for Year 2 and Year 1. Round to two decimal places.
b. What conclusions concerning the company's ability to meet its financial obligations can you draw from part (a)?

Appendix
EX 4-23 Completing an end-of-period spreadsheet

List (a) through (j) in the order they would be performed in preparing and completing an end-of-period spreadsheet.

a. Add the Debit and Credit columns of the Unadjusted Trial Balance columns of the spreadsheet to verify that the totals are equal.
b. Add the Debit and Credit columns of the Balance Sheet and Income Statement columns of the spreadsheet to verify that the totals are equal.

(Continued)

c. Add or deduct adjusting entry data to trial balance amounts, and extend amounts to the Adjusted Trial Balance columns.

d. Add the Debit and Credit columns of the Adjustments columns of the spreadsheet to verify that the totals are equal.

e. Add the Debit and Credit columns of the Balance Sheet and Income Statement columns of the spreadsheet to determine the amount of net income or net loss for the period.

f. Add the Debit and Credit columns of the Adjusted Trial Balance columns of the spreadsheet to verify that the totals are equal.

g. Enter the adjusting entries into the spreadsheet, based on the adjustment data.

h. Enter the amount of net income or net loss for the period in the proper Income Statement column and Balance Sheet column.

i. Enter the unadjusted account balances from the general ledger into the Unadjusted Trial Balance columns of the spreadsheet.

j. Extend the adjusted trial balance amounts to the Income Statement columns and the Balance Sheet columns.

Appendix

EX 4-24 Adjustment data on an end-of-period spreadsheet

✔ Total debits of Adjustments column: $31

Alert Security Services Co. offers security services to business clients. The trial balance for Alert Security Services Co. has been prepared on the following end-of-period spreadsheet for the year ended October 31, 2016:

Alert Security Services Co.
End-of-Period Spreadsheet
For the Year Ended October 31, 2016

	Unadjusted Trial Balance		Adjustments		Adjusted Trial Balance	
Account Title	**Dr.**	**Cr.**	**Dr.**	**Cr.**	**Dr.**	**Cr.**
Cash	12					
Accounts Receivable	90					
Supplies	8					
Prepaid Insurance	12					
Land	190					
Equipment	50					
Accum. Depr.—Equipment		4				
Accounts Payable		36				
Wages Payable		0				
Brenda Schultz, Capital		260				
Brenda Schultz, Drawing	8					
Fees Earned		200				
Wages Expense	110					
Rent Expense	12					
Insurance Expense	0					
Utilities Expense	6					
Supplies Expense	0					
Depreciation Expense	0					
Miscellaneous Expense	2					
	500	500				

The data for year-end adjustments are as follows:

a. Fees earned, but not yet billed, $13.

b. Supplies on hand, $4.

c. Insurance premiums expired, $10.

d. Depreciation expense, $3.
e. Wages accrued, but not paid, $1.
Enter the adjustment data, and place the balances in the Adjusted Trial Balance columns.

Appendix
EX 4-25 Completing an end-of-period spreadsheet

✔ **Net income: $65**

Alert Security Services Co. offers security services to business clients. Complete the following end-of-period spreadsheet for Alert Security Services Co.:

Alert Security Services Co.
End-of-Period Spreadsheet
For the Year Ended October 31, 2016

	Adjusted Trial Balance		Income Statement		Balance Sheet	
Account Title	**Dr.**	**Cr.**	**Dr.**	**Cr.**	**Dr.**	**Cr.**
Cash	12					
Accounts Receivable	103					
Supplies	4					
Prepaid Insurance	2					
Land	190					
Equipment	50					
Accum. Depr.—Equipment		7				
Accounts Payable		36				
Wages Payable		1				
Brenda Schultz, Capital		260				
Brenda Schultz, Drawing	8					
Fees Earned		213				
Wages Expense	111					
Rent Expense	12					
Insurance Expense	10					
Utilities Expense	6					
Supplies Expense	4					
Depreciation Expense	3					
Miscellaneous Expense	2					
	517	517				
Net income (loss)						

Appendix
EX 4-26 Financial statements from an end-of-period spreadsheet

✔ **Brenda Schultz, capital, October 31, 2016: $317**

Based on the data in Exercise 4-25, prepare an income statement, statement of owner's equity, and balance sheet for Alert Security Services Co.

Appendix
EX 4-27 Adjusting entries from an end-of-period spreadsheet

Based on the data in Exercise 4-24, prepare the adjusting entries for Alert Security Services Co.

Appendix
EX 4-28 Closing entries from an end-of-period spreadsheet

Based on the data in Exercise 4-25, prepare the closing entries for Alert Security Services Co.

Problems: Series A

✔ 3. Total assets: $354,500

General Ledger

SHOW ME HOW

PR 4-1A Financial statements and closing entries

OBJ. 1, 2, 3

Lamp Light Company maintains and repairs warning lights, such as those found on radio towers and lighthouses. Lamp Light Company prepared the following end-of-period spreadsheet at December 31, 2016, the end of the fiscal year:

	A	B	C	D	E	F	G
1				Lamp Light Company			
2				End-of-Period Spreadsheet			
3				For the Year Ended December 31, 2016			
4		Unadjusted				Adjusted	
5		Trial Balance		Adjustments		Trial Balance	
6	Account Title	Dr.	Cr.	Dr.	Cr.	Dr.	Cr.
7							
8	Cash	10,800				10,800	
9	Accounts Receivable	38,900		(a) 11,300		50,200	
10	Prepaid Insurance	4,200			(b) 3,000	1,200	
11	Supplies	2,730			(c) 2,250	480	
12	Land	98,000				98,000	
13	Building	400,000				400,000	
14	Accum. Depr.—Building		205,300		(d)10,100		215,400
15	Equipment	101,000				101,000	
16	Accum. Depr.—Equipment		85,100		(e) 6,680		91,780
17	Accounts Payable		15,700				15,700
18	Salaries & Wages Payable				(f) 4,900		4,900
19	Unearned Rent		2,100	(g) 1,300			800
20	Ted Hickman, Capital		203,100				203,100
21	Ted Hickman, Drawing	10,000				10,000	
22	Fees Earned		363,700		(a)11,300		375,000
23	Rent Revenue				(g) 1,300		1,300
24	Salaries & Wages Expense	163,100		(f) 4,900		168,000	
25	Advertising Expense	21,700				21,700	
26	Utilities Expense	11,400				11,400	
27	Depr. Exp.—Building			(d) 10,100		10,100	
28	Repairs Expense	8,850				8,850	
29	Depr. Exp.—Equipment			(e) 6,680		6,680	
30	Insurance Expense			(b) 3,000		3,000	
31	Supplies Expense			(c) 2,250		2,250	
32	Misc. Expense	4,320				4,320	
33		875,000	875,000	39,530	39,530	907,980	907,980
34							

Instructions

1. Prepare an income statement for the year ended December 31.
2. Prepare a statement of owner's equity for the year ended December 31. No additional investments were made during the year.
3. Prepare a balance sheet as of December 31.
4. Based upon the end-of-period spreadsheet, journalize the closing entries.
5. Prepare a post-closing trial balance.

PR 4-2A Financial statements and closing entries

OBJ. 2, 3

✔ 1. Stacy Tanner, capital, June 30: $483,300

Finders Investigative Services is an investigative services firm that is owned and operated by Stacy Tanner. On June 30, 2016, the end of the fiscal year, the accountant for Finders Investigative Services prepared an end-of-period spreadsheet, a part of which follows:

	A	F	G
1	Finders Investigative Services		
2	End-of-Period Spreadsheet		
3	For the Year Ended June 30, 2016		
4		Adjusted	
5		Trial Balance	
6	Account Title	Dr.	Cr.
7			
8	Cash	28,000	
9	Accounts Receivable	69,600	
10	Supplies	4,600	
11	Prepaid Insurance	2,500	
12	Building	439,500	
13	Accumulated Depreciation—Building		44,200
14	Accounts Payable		11,700
15	Salaries Payable		3,000
16	Unearned Rent		2,000
17	Stacy Tanner, Capital		373,800
18	Stacy Tanner, Drawing	12,000	
19	Service Fees		718,000
20	Rent Revenue		12,000
21	Salaries Expense	522,100	
22	Rent Expense	48,000	
23	Supplies Expense	10,800	
24	Depreciation Expense—Building	8,750	
25	Utilities Expense	7,150	
26	Repairs Expense	3,000	
27	Insurance Expense	2,500	
28	Miscellaneous Expense	6,200	
29		1,164,700	1,164,700

Instructions

1. Prepare an income statement, a statement of owner's equity (no additional investments were made during the year), and a balance sheet.
2. Journalize the entries that were required to close the accounts at June 30.
3. If Stacy Tanner, Capital has instead decreased $30,000 after the closing entries were posted, and the withdrawals remained the same, what would have been the amount of net income or net loss?

PR 4-3A T accounts, adjusting entries, financial statements, and closing entries; optional end-of-period spreadsheet **OBJ. 2, 3**

✔ 5. Net income: $10,700

General Ledger

The unadjusted trial balance of Epicenter Laundry at June 30, 2016, the end of the fiscal year, follows:

Epicenter Laundry
Unadjusted Trial Balance
June 30, 2016

	Debit Balances	Credit Balances
Cash	11,000	
Laundry Supplies	21,500	
Prepaid Insurance	9,600	
Laundry Equipment	232,600	
Accumulated Depreciation		125,400
Accounts Payable		11,800
Sophie Perez, Capital		105,600
Sophie Perez, Drawing	10,000	
Laundry Revenue		232,200
Wages Expense	125,200	
Rent Expense	40,000	
Utilities Expense	19,700	
Miscellaneous Expense	5,400	
	475,000	475,000

(Continued)

The data needed to determine year-end adjustments are as follows:

a. Laundry supplies on hand at June 30 are $3,600.

b. Insurance premiums expired during the year are $5,700.

c. Depreciation of laundry equipment during the year is $6,500.

d. Wages accrued but not paid at June 30 are $1,100.

Instructions

1. For each account listed in the unadjusted trial balance, enter the balance in a T account. Identify the balance as "June 30 Bal." In addition, add T accounts for Wages Payable, Depreciation Expense, Laundry Supplies Expense, Insurance Expense, and Income Summary.
2. *(Optional)* Enter the unadjusted trial balance on an end-of-period spreadsheet and complete the spreadsheet. Add the accounts listed in part (1) as needed.
3. Journalize and post the adjusting entries. Identify the adjustments by "Adj." and the new balances as "Adj. Bal."
4. Prepare an adjusted trial balance.
5. Prepare an income statement, a statement of owner's equity (no additional investments were made during the year), and a balance sheet.
6. Journalize and post the closing entries. Identify the closing entries by "Clos."
7. Prepare a post-closing trial balance.

PR 4-4A Ledger accounts, adjusting entries, financial statements, and closing entries; optional spreadsheet

OBJ. 2, 3

✔ 5. Net income: $51,150

The unadjusted trial balance of Lakota Freight Co. at March 31, 2016, the end of the year, follows:

Lakota Freight Co.
Unadjusted Trial Balance
March 31, 2016

		Debit Balances	Credit Balances
11	Cash	12,000	
13	Supplies	30,000	
14	Prepaid Insurance	3,600	
16	Equipment	110,000	
17	Accumulated Depreciation—Equipment		25,000
18	Trucks	60,000	
19	Accumulated Depreciation—Trucks		15,000
21	Accounts Payable		4,000
31	Kaya Tarango, Capital		96,000
32	Kaya Tarango, Drawing	15,000	
41	Service Revenue		160,000
51	Wages Expense	45,000	
53	Rent Expense	10,600	
54	Truck Expense	9,000	
59	Miscellaneous Expense	4,800	
		300,000	300,000

The data needed to determine year-end adjustments are as follows:

a. Supplies on hand at March 31 are $7,500.

b. Insurance premiums expired during year are $1,800.

c. Depreciation of equipment during year is $8,350.

d. Depreciation of trucks during year is $6,200.

e. Wages accrued but not paid at March 31 are $600.

Instructions

1. For each account listed in the trial balance, enter the balance in the appropriate Balance column of a four-column account and place a check mark (✓) in the Posting Reference column.
2. *(Optional)* Enter the unadjusted trial balance on an end-of-period spreadsheet and complete the spreadsheet. Add the accounts listed in part (3) as needed.
3. Journalize and post the adjusting entries, inserting balances in the accounts affected. Record the adjusting entries on Page 26 of the journal. The following additional accounts from Lakota Freight Co.'s chart of accounts should be used: Wages Payable, 22; Supplies Expense, 52; Depreciation Expense—Equipment, 55; Depreciation Expense—Trucks, 56; Insurance Expense, 57.
4. Prepare an adjusted trial balance.
5. Prepare an income statement, a statement of owner's equity (no additional investments were made during the year), and a balance sheet.
6. Journalize and post the closing entries. Record the closing entries on Page 27 of the journal. (Income Summary is account #33 in the chart of accounts.) Indicate closed accounts by inserting a line in both Balance columns opposite the closing entry.
7. Prepare a post-closing trial balance.

PR 4-5A Complete accounting cycle

OBJ. 4, 5

✓ 8. Net income: $33,475

For the past several years, Steffy Lopez has operated a part-time consulting business from his home. As of July 1, 2016, Steffy decided to move to rented quarters and to operate the business, which was to be known as Diamond Consulting, on a full-time basis. Diamond Consulting entered into the following transactions during July:

July 1. The following assets were received from Steffy Lopez: cash, $13,500; accounts receivable, $20,800; supplies, $3,200; and office equipment, $7,500. There were no liabilities received.

1. Paid two months' rent on a lease rental contract, $4,800.

2. Paid the premiums on property and casualty insurance policies, $4,500.

4. Received cash from clients as an advance payment for services to be provided, and recorded it as unearned fees, $5,500.

5. Purchased additional office equipment on account from Office Station Co., $6,500.

6. Received cash from clients on account, $15,300.

10. Paid cash for a newspaper advertisement, $400.

12. Paid Office Station Co. for part of the debt incurred on July 5, $5,200.

12. Recorded services provided on account for the period July 1–12, $13,300.

14. Paid receptionist for two weeks' salary, $1,750.

Record the following transactions on Page 2 of the journal:

17. Recorded cash from cash clients for fees earned during the period July 1–17, $9,450.

18. Paid cash for supplies, $600.

20. Recorded services provided on account for the period July 13–20, $6,650.

24. Recorded cash from cash clients for fees earned for the period July 17–24, $4,000.

26. Received cash from clients on account, $12,000.

27. Paid receptionist for two weeks' salary, $1,750.

29. Paid telephone bill for July, $325.

31. Paid electricity bill for July, $675.

31. Recorded cash from cash clients for fees earned for the period July 25–31, $5,200.

(Continued)

July 31. Recorded services provided on account for the remainder of July, $3,000.
31. Steffy withdrew $12,500 for personal use.

Instructions

1. Journalize each transaction in a two-column journal starting on Page 1, referring to the following chart of accounts in selecting the accounts to be debited and credited. (Do not insert the account numbers in the journal at this time.)

11	Cash	31	Steffy Lopez, Capital
12	Accounts Receivable	32	Steffy Lopez, Drawing
14	Supplies	41	Fees Earned
15	Prepaid Rent	51	Salary Expense
16	Prepaid Insurance	52	Rent Expense
18	Office Equipment	53	Supplies Expense
19	Accumulated Depreciation	54	Depreciation Expense
21	Accounts Payable	55	Insurance Expense
22	Salaries Payable	59	Miscellaneous Expense
23	Unearned Fees		

2. Post the journal to a ledger of four-column accounts.
3. Prepare an unadjusted trial balance.
4. At the end of July, the following adjustment data were assembled. Analyze and use these data to complete parts (5) and (6).
   a. Insurance expired during July is $375.
   b. Supplies on hand on July 31 are $1,525.
   c. Depreciation of office equipment for July is $750.
   d. Accrued receptionist salary on July 31 is $175.
   e. Rent expired during July is $2,400.
   f. Unearned fees on July 31 are $2,750.
5. *(Optional)* Enter the unadjusted trial balance on an end-of-period spreadsheet and complete the spreadsheet.
6. Journalize and post the adjusting entries. Record the adjusting entries on Page 3 of the journal.
7. Prepare an adjusted trial balance.
8. Prepare an income statement, a statement of owner's equity, and a balance sheet.
9. Prepare and post the closing entries. (Income Summary is account #33 in the chart of accounts.) Record the closing entries on Page 4 of the journal. Indicate closed accounts by inserting a line in both the Balance columns opposite the closing entry.
10. Prepare a post-closing trial balance.

Problems: Series B

PR 4-1B Financial statements and closing entries

OBJ. 1, 2, 3

✔ 3. Total assets: $342,425

General Ledger

Last Chance Company offers legal consulting advice to prison inmates. Last Chance Company prepared the end-of-period spreadsheet that follows at June 30, 2016, the end of the fiscal year.

Instructions

1. Prepare an income statement for the year ended June 30.
2. Prepare a statement of owner's equity for the year ended June 30. No additional investments were made during the year.
3. Prepare a balance sheet as of June 30.
4. On the basis of the end-of-period spreadsheet, journalize the closing entries.
5. Prepare a post-closing trial balance.

	A	B	C	D	E	F	G
1		Last Chance Company					
2		End-of-Period Spreadsheet					
3		For the Year Ended June 30, 2016					
4		Unadjusted				Adjusted	
5		Trial Balance		Adjustments		Trial Balance	
6	**Account Title**	Dr.	Cr.	Dr.	Cr.	Dr.	Cr.
7							
8	Cash	5,100				5,100	
9	Accounts Receivable	22,750		(a) 3,750		26,500	
10	Prepaid Insurance	3,600			(b) 1,300	2,300	
11	Supplies	2,025			(c) 1,500	525	
12	Land	80,000				80,000	
13	Building	340,000				340,000	
14	Accum. Depr.—Building		190,000		(d) 3,000		193,000
15	Equipment	140,000				140,000	
16	Accum. Depr.—Equipment		54,450		(e) 4,550		59,000
17	Accounts Payable		9,750				9,750
18	Salaries & Wages Payable				(f) 1,900		1,900
19	Unearned Rent		4,500	(g) 3,000			1,500
20	Tami Garrigan, Capital		361,300				361,300
21	Tami Garrigan, Drawing	20,000				20,000	
22	Fees Earned		280,000		(a) 3,750		283,750
23	Rent Revenue				(g) 3,000		3,000
24	Salaries & Wages Expense	145,100		(f) 1,900		147,000	
25	Advertising Expense	86,800				86,800	
26	Utilities Expense	30,000				30,000	
27	Travel Expense	18,750				18,750	
28	Depr. Exp.—Equipment			(e) 4,550		4,550	
29	Depr. Exp.—Building			(d) 3,000		3,000	
30	Supplies Expense			(c) 1,500		1,500	
31	Insurance Expense			(b) 1,300		1,300	
32	Misc. Expense	5,875				5,875	
33		900,000	900,000	19,000	19,000	913,200	913,200
34							

PR 4-2B Financial statements and closing entries

OBJ. 2, 3

✔ 1. Nicole Gorman, capital, October 31: $313,000

The Gorman Group is a financial planning services firm owned and operated by Nicole Gorman. As of October 31, 2016, the end of the fiscal year, the accountant for The Gorman Group prepared an end-of-period spreadsheet, part of which follows:

	A	F	G
1	The Gorman Group		
2	End-of-Period Spreadsheet		
3	For the Year Ended October 31, 2016		
4		Adjusted	
5		Trial Balance	
6	**Account Title**	Dr.	Cr.
7			
8	Cash	11,000	
9	Accounts Receivable	28,150	
10	Supplies	6,350	
11	Prepaid Insurance	9,500	
12	Land	75,000	
13	Buildings	250,000	
14	Accumulated Depreciation—Buildings		117,200
15	Equipment	240,000	
16	Accumulated Depreciation—Equipment		151,700
17	Accounts Payable		33,300
18	Salaries Payable		3,300
19	Unearned Rent		1,500
20	Nicole Gorman, Capital		220,000
21	Nicole Gorman, Drawing	20,000	
22	Service Fees		468,000
23	Rent Revenue		5,000
24	Salaries Expense	291,000	
25	Depreciation Expense—Equipment	17,500	
26	Rent Expense	15,500	
27	Supplies Expense	9,000	
28	Utilities Expense	8,500	
29	Depreciation Expense—Buildings	6,600	
30	Repairs Expense	3,450	
31	Insurance Expense	3,000	
32	Miscellaneous Expense	5,450	
33		1,000,000	1,000,000

(Continued)

Instructions

1. Prepare an income statement, a statement of owner's equity (no additional investments were made during the year), and a balance sheet.
2. Journalize the entries that were required to close the accounts at October 31.
3. If the balance of Nicole Gorman, Capital had instead increased $115,000 after the closing entries were posted, and the withdrawals remained the same, what would have been the amount of net income or net loss?

✔ 5. Net income: $27,350

General Ledger

PR 4-3B T accounts, adjusting entries, financial statements, and closing entries; optional end-of-period spreadsheet **OBJ. 2, 3**

The unadjusted trial balance of La Mesa Laundry at August 31, 2016, the end of the fiscal year, follows:

La Mesa Laundry
Unadjusted Trial Balance
August 31, 2016

	Debit Balances	Credit Balances
Cash	3,800	
Laundry Supplies	9,000	
Prepaid Insurance	6,000	
Laundry Equipment	180,800	
Accumulated Depreciation		49,200
Accounts Payable		7,800
Bobbi Downey, Capital		95,000
Bobbi Downey, Drawing	2,400	
Laundry Revenue		248,000
Wages Expense	135,800	
Rent Expense	43,200	
Utilities Expense	16,000	
Miscellaneous Expense	3,000	
	400,000	400,000

The data needed to determine year-end adjustments are as follows:

a. Wages accrued but not paid at August 31 are $2,200.
b. Depreciation of equipment during the year is $8,150.
c. Laundry supplies on hand at August 31 are $2,000.
d. Insurance premiums expired during the year are $5,300.

Instructions

1. For each account listed in the unadjusted trial balance, enter the balance in a T account. Identify the balance as "Aug. 31 Bal." In addition, add T accounts for Wages Payable, Depreciation Expense, Laundry Supplies Expense, Insurance Expense, and Income Summary.
2. *(Optional)* Enter the unadjusted trial balance on an end-of-period spreadsheet and complete the spreadsheet. Add the accounts listed in part (1) as needed.
3. Journalize and post the adjusting entries. Identify the adjustments by "Adj." and the new balances as "Adj. Bal."
4. Prepare an adjusted trial balance.
5. Prepare an income statement, a statement of owner's equity (no additional investments were made during the year), and a balance sheet.
6. Journalize and post the closing entries. Identify the closing entries by "Clos."
7. Prepare a post-closing trial balance.

PR 4-4B Ledger accounts, adjusting entries, financial statements, and closing entries; optional end-of-period spreadsheet

OBJ. 2, 3

✔ 5. Net income: $46,150

The unadjusted trial balance of Recessive Interiors at January 31, 2016, the end of the year, follows:

Recessive Interiors
Unadjusted Trial Balance
January 31, 2016

		Debit Balances	Credit Balances
11	Cash	13,100	
13	Supplies	8,000	
14	Prepaid Insurance	7,500	
16	Equipment	113,000	
17	Accumulated Depreciation—Equipment		12,000
18	Trucks	90,000	
19	Accumulated Depreciation—Trucks		27,100
21	Accounts Payable		4,500
31	Jeanne McQuay, Capital		126,400
32	Jeanne McQuay, Drawing	3,000	
41	Service Revenue		155,000
51	Wages Expense	72,000	
52	Rent Expense	7,600	
53	Truck Expense	5,350	
59	Miscellaneous Expense	5,450	
		325,000	325,000

The data needed to determine year-end adjustments are as follows:

a. Supplies on hand at January 31 are $2,850.
b. Insurance premiums expired during the year are $3,150.
c. Depreciation of equipment during the year is $5,250.
d. Depreciation of trucks during the year is $4,000.
e. Wages accrued but not paid at January 31 are $900.

Instructions

1. For each account listed in the unadjusted trial balance, enter the balance in the appropriate Balance column of a four-column account and place a check mark (✓) in the Posting Reference column.
2. *(Optional)* Enter the unadjusted trial balance on an end-of-period spreadsheet and complete the spreadsheet. Add the accounts listed in part (3) as needed.
3. Journalize and post the adjusting entries, inserting balances in the accounts affected. Record the adjusting entries on Page 26 of the journal. The following additional accounts from Recessive Interiors' chart of accounts should be used: Wages Payable, 22; Depreciation Expense—Equipment, 54; Supplies Expense, 55; Depreciation Expense—Trucks, 56; Insurance Expense, 57.
4. Prepare an adjusted trial balance.
5. Prepare an income statement, a statement of owner's equity (no additional investments were made during the year), and a balance sheet.
6. Journalize and post the closing entries. Record the closing entries on Page 27 of the journal. (Income Summary is account #33 in the chart of accounts.) Indicate closed accounts by inserting a line in both Balance columns opposite the closing entry.
7. Prepare a post-closing trial balance.

PR 4-5B Complete accounting cycle

OBJ. 4, 5

✔ 8. Net income: $53,775

For the past several years, Jeff Horton has operated a part-time consulting business from his home. As of April 1, 2016, Jeff decided to move to rented quarters and to operate the

(Continued)

business, which was to be known as Rosebud Consulting, on a full-time basis. Rosebud Consulting entered into the following transactions during April:

Apr. 1. The following assets were received from Jeff Horton: cash, $20,000; accounts receivable, $14,700; supplies, $3,300; and office equipment, $12,000. There were no liabilities received.

1. Paid three months' rent on a lease rental contract, $6,000.

2. Paid the premiums on property and casualty insurance policies, $4,200.

4. Received cash from clients as an advance payment for services to be provided and recorded it as unearned fees, $9,400.

5. Purchased additional office equipment on account from Smith Office Supply Co., $8,000.

6. Received cash from clients on account, $11,700.

10. Paid cash for a newspaper advertisement, $350.

12. Paid Smith Office Supply Co. for part of the debt incurred on April 5, $6,400.

12. Recorded services provided on account for the period April 1–12, $21,900.

14. Paid receptionist for two weeks' salary, $1,650.

Record the following transactions on Page 2 of the journal:

17. Recorded cash from cash clients for fees earned during the period April 1–16, $6,600.

18. Paid cash for supplies, $725.

20. Recorded services provided on account for the period April 13–20, $16,800.

24. Recorded cash from cash clients for fees earned for the period April 17–24, $4,450.

26. Received cash from clients on account, $26,500.

27. Paid receptionist for two weeks' salary, $1,650.

29. Paid telephone bill for April, $540.

30. Paid electricity bill for April, $760.

30. Recorded cash from cash clients for fees earned for the period April 25–30, $5,160.

30. Recorded services provided on account for the remainder of April, $2,590.

30. Jeff withdrew $18,000 for personal use.

Instructions

1. Journalize each transaction in a two-column journal starting on Page 1, referring to the following chart of accounts in selecting the accounts to be debited and credited. (Do not insert the account numbers in the journal at this time.)

11	Cash	31	Jeff Horton, Capital
12	Accounts Receivable	32	Jeff Horton, Drawing
14	Supplies	41	Fees Earned
15	Prepaid Rent	51	Salary Expense
16	Prepaid Insurance	52	Supplies Expense
18	Office Equipment	53	Rent Expense
19	Accumulated Depreciation	54	Depreciation Expense
21	Accounts Payable	55	Insurance Expense
22	Salaries Payable	59	Miscellaneous Expense
23	Unearned Fees		

2. Post the journal to a ledger of four-column accounts.
3. Prepare an unadjusted trial balance.
4. At the end of April, the following adjustment data were assembled. Analyze and use these data to complete parts (5) and (6).
   a. Insurance expired during April is $350.
   b. Supplies on hand on April 30 are $1,225.

c. Depreciation of office equipment for April is $400.

d. Accrued receptionist salary on April 30 is $275.

e. Rent expired during April is $2,000.

f. Unearned fees on April 30 are $2,350.

5. *(Optional)* Enter the unadjusted trial balance on an end-of-period spreadsheet and complete the spreadsheet.
6. Journalize and post the adjusting entries. Record the adjusting entries on Page 3 of the journal.
7. Prepare an adjusted trial balance.
8. Prepare an income statement, a statement of owner's equity, and a balance sheet.
9. Prepare and post the closing entries. Record the closing entries on Page 4 of the journal. (Income Summary is account #33 in the chart of accounts.) Indicate closed accounts by inserting a line in both the Balance columns opposite the closing entry.
10. Prepare a post-closing trial balance.

Continuing Problem

✔ 2. Net income: $4,955

General Ledger

The unadjusted trial balance of PS Music as of July 31, 2016, along with the adjustment data for the two months ended July 31, 2016, are shown in Chapter 3. Based upon the adjustment data, the following adjusted trial balance was prepared:

PS Music
Adjusted Trial Balance
July 31, 2016

	Debit Balances	Credit Balances
Cash	9,945	
Accounts Receivable	4,150	
Supplies	275	
Prepaid Insurance	2,475	
Office Equipment	7,500	
Accumulated Depreciation—Office Equipment		50
Accounts Payable		8,350
Wages Payable		140
Unearned Revenue		3,600
Peyton Smith, Capital		9,000
Peyton Smith, Drawing	1,750	
Fees Earned		21,200
Music Expense	3,610	
Wages Expense	2,940	
Office Rent Expense	2,550	
Advertising Expense	1,500	
Equipment Rent Expense	1,375	
Utilities Expense	1,215	
Supplies Expense	925	
Insurance Expense	225	
Depreciation Expense	50	
Miscellaneous Expense	1,855	
	42,340	42,340

Instructions

1. *(Optional)* Using the data from Chapter 3, prepare an end-of-period spreadsheet.
2. Prepare an income statement, a statement of owner's equity, and a balance sheet. (*Note:* Peyton Smith made investments in PS Music on June 1 and July 1, 2016.)

(Continued)

3. Journalize and post the closing entries. The income summary account is #33 in the ledger of PS Music. Indicate closed accounts by inserting a line in both Balance columns opposite the closing entry.
4. Prepare a post-closing trial balance.

Comprehensive Problem 1

✔ 8. Net income, $33,425

General Ledger

Kelly Pitney began her consulting business, Kelly Consulting, on April 1, 2016. The accounting cycle for Kelly Consulting for April, including financial statements, was illustrated in this chapter. During May, Kelly Consulting entered into the following transactions:

May 3. Received cash from clients as an advance payment for services to be provided and recorded it as unearned fees, $4,500.
5. Received cash from clients on account, $2,450.
9. Paid cash for a newspaper advertisement, $225.
13. Paid Office Station Co. for part of the debt incurred on April 5, $640.
15. Recorded services provided on account for the period May 1–15, $9,180.
16. Paid part-time receptionist for two weeks' salary including the amount owed on April 30, $750.
17. Recorded cash from cash clients for fees earned during the period May 1–16, $8,360.

Record the following transactions on Page 6 of the journal:

20. Purchased supplies on account, $735.
21. Recorded services provided on account for the period May 16–20, $4,820.
25. Recorded cash from cash clients for fees earned for the period May 17–23, $7,900.
27. Received cash from clients on account, $9,520.
28. Paid part-time receptionist for two weeks' salary, $750.
30. Paid telephone bill for May, $260.
31. Paid electricity bill for May, $810.
31. Recorded cash from cash clients for fees earned for the period May 26–31, $3,300.
31. Recorded services provided on account for the remainder of May, $2,650.
31. Kelly withdrew $10,500 for personal use.

Instructions

1. The chart of accounts for Kelly Consulting is shown in Exhibit 9, and the post-closing trial balance as of April 30, 2016, is shown in Exhibit 17. For each account in the post-closing trial balance, enter the balance in the appropriate Balance column of a four-column account. Date the balances May 1, 2016, and place a check mark (✓) in the Posting Reference column. Journalize each of the May transactions in a two-column journal starting on Page 5 of the journal and using Kelly Consulting's chart of accounts. (Do not insert the account numbers in the journal at this time.)
2. Post the journal to a ledger of four-column accounts.
3. Prepare an unadjusted trial balance.
4. At the end of May, the following adjustment data were assembled. Analyze and use these data to complete parts (5) and (6).
   a. Insurance expired during May is $275.
   b. Supplies on hand on May 31 are $715.
   c. Depreciation of office equipment for May is $330.
   d. Accrued receptionist salary on May 31 is $325.
   e. Rent expired during May is $1,600.
   f. Unearned fees on May 31 are $3,210.

5. *(Optional)* Enter the unadjusted trial balance on an end-of-period spreadsheet and complete the spreadsheet.
6. Journalize and post the adjusting entries. Record the adjusting entries on Page 7 of the journal.
7. Prepare an adjusted trial balance.
8. Prepare an income statement, a statement of owner's equity, and a balance sheet.
9. Prepare and post the closing entries. Record the closing entries on Page 8 of the journal. (Income Summary is account #33 in the chart of accounts.) Indicate closed accounts by inserting a line in both the Balance columns opposite the closing entry.
10. Prepare a post-closing trial balance.

Cases & Projects

CP 4-1 Ethics and professional conduct in business

Picasso Graphics is a graphics arts design consulting firm. Pablo Taylor, its treasurer and vice president of finance, has prepared a classified balance sheet as of July 31, 2016, the end of its fiscal year. This balance sheet will be submitted with Picasso Graphics' loan application to Paris Trust & Savings Bank.

In the Current Assets section of the balance sheet, Pablo reported a $56,000 receivable from Becky Holt, the president of Picasso Graphics, as a trade account receivable. Becky borrowed the money from Picasso Graphics in January 2014 for a down payment on a new home. She has orally assured Pablo that she will pay off the account receivable within the next year. Pablo reported the $56,000 in the same manner on the preceding year's balance sheet.

Evaluate whether it is acceptable for Pablo to prepare the July 31, 2016, balance sheet in this manner.

CP 4-2 Financial statements

The following is an excerpt from a telephone conversation between Ben Simpson, president of Main Street Co., and Tami Lundgren, owner of Reliable Employment Co.:

Ben: Tami, you're going to have to do a better job of finding me a new computer programmer. That last guy was great at programming, but he didn't have any common sense.

Tami: What do you mean? The guy had a master's degree with straight A's.

Ben: Yes, well, last month he developed a new financial reporting system. He said we could do away with manually preparing an end-of-period spreadsheet and financial statements. The computer would automatically generate our financial statements with "a push of a button."

Tami: So what's the big deal? Sounds to me like it would save you time and effort.

Ben: Right! The balance sheet showed a minus for supplies!

Tami: Minus supplies? How can that be?

Ben: That's what I asked.

Tami: So, what did he say?

Ben: Well, after he checked the program, he said that it must be right. The minuses were greater than the pluses....

Tami: Didn't he know that Supplies can't have a credit balance—it must have a debit balance?

Ben: He asked me what a debit and credit were.

Tami: I see your point.

1. Comment on (a) the desirability of computerizing Main Street Co.'s financial reporting system, (b) the elimination of the end-of-period spreadsheet in a computerized accounting system, and (c) the computer programmer's lack of accounting knowledge.
2. Explain to the programmer why Supplies could not have a credit balance.

CP 4-3 Financial statements

Assume that you recently accepted a position with Five Star National Bank & Trust as an assistant loan officer. As one of your first duties, you have been assigned the responsibility of evaluating a loan request for $300,000 from West Gate Auto Co., a small proprietorship. In support of the loan application, Joan Whalen, owner, submitted a "Statement of Accounts" (trial balance) for the first year of operations ended October 31, 2016.

West Gate Auto Co.
Statement of Accounts
October 31, 2016

Cash	5,000	
Billings Due from Others	40,000	
Supplies (chemicals, etc.)	7,500	
Building	222,300	
Equipment	50,000	
Amounts Owed to Others		31,000
Investment in Business		179,000
Service Revenue		215,000
Wages Expense	75,000	
Utilities Expense	10,000	
Rent Expense	8,000	
Insurance Expense	6,000	
Other Expenses	1,200	
	425,000	425,000

1. Explain to Joan Whalen why a set of financial statements (income statement, statement of owner's equity, and balance sheet) would be useful to you in evaluating the loan request.
2. In discussing the "Statement of Accounts" with Joan Whalen, you discovered that the accounts had not been adjusted at October 31. Analyze the "Statement of Accounts" and indicate possible adjusting entries that might be necessary before an accurate set of financial statements could be prepared.
3. Assuming that an accurate set of financial statements will be submitted by Joan Whalen in a few days, what other considerations or information would you require before making a decision on the loan request?

CP 4-4 Compare balance sheets

Internet Project

Group Project

In groups of three or four, compare the balance sheets of two different companies, and present to the class a summary of the similarities and differences of the two companies. You may obtain the balance sheets you need from one of the following sources:

1. Your school or local library.
2. The investor relations department of each company.
3. The company's Web site on the Internet.
4. EDGAR (Electronic Data Gathering, Analysis, and Retrieval), the electronic archives of financial statements filed with the Securities and Exchange Commission.

SEC documents can be retrieved using the EdgarScan™ service at http://sec.gov. To obtain annual report information, under Filings & Forms click on "Search for Company Filings," click on "Company or fund name, ticker symbol, ..." type in the company name, and then click on "Find Companies." Click on the CIK related to the company name, search for Form 10-K, and click on "Retrieve Selected Findings." Finally, click on the "html" for the latest period and the related document.

Accounting Systems

Intuit Inc.

Whether you realize it or not, you likely interact with accounting systems. For example, your bank statement is a type of accounting system. When you make a deposit, the bank records an addition to your cash; when you withdraw cash, the bank records a reduction in your cash. Such a simple accounting system works well for a person with just a few transactions per month. However, over time, you may find that your financial affairs will become more complex and involve many different types of transactions, including investments and loan payments. At this point, relying on your bank statement may not be sufficient for managing your financial affairs. Personal financial planning software, such as **Intuit**'s Quicken, can be useful when your financial affairs become more complex.

What happens if you decide to begin a small business? Transactions expand to include customers, vendors, and employees. As a result, the accounting system will need to adjust to this complexity. Thus, many small businesses will use small-business accounting software, such as Intuit's QuickBooks, as their first accounting system. As a business grows, more sophisticated accounting systems will be needed. Companies such as **SAP**, **Oracle**, **Microsoft**, and **Sage Software, Inc.**, offer accounting system solutions for businesses that become larger with more complex accounting needs.

Accounting systems used by large and small businesses employ the basic principles of the accounting cycle discussed in the previous chapters. However, these accounting systems include features that simplify the recording and summary process. In this chapter, we will discuss these simplifying procedures as they apply to both manual and computerized systems.

Learning Objectives

After studying this chapter, you should be able to: *Example Exercises*

OBJ	Objective	Example Exercises
1	**Define and describe an accounting system.** Basic Accounting Systems	
2	**Journalize and post transactions in a manual accounting system that uses subsidiary ledgers and special journals.** Manual Accounting Systems	
	Subsidiary Ledgers	
	Special Journals	
	Revenue Journal	EE 5-1
	Cash Receipts Journal	
	Accounts Receivable Control Account and Subsidiary Ledger	EE 5-2
	Purchases Journal	EE 5-3
	Cash Payments Journal	
	Accounts Payable Control Account and Subsidiary Ledger	EE 5-4
3	**Describe and illustrate the use of a computerized accounting system.** Computerized Accounting Systems	
4	**Describe the basic features of e-commerce.** E-Commerce	
5	**Use segment analysis in evaluating the operating performance of a company.** Financial Analysis and Interpretation: Segment Analysis	EE 5-5

At a Glance 5 Page 234

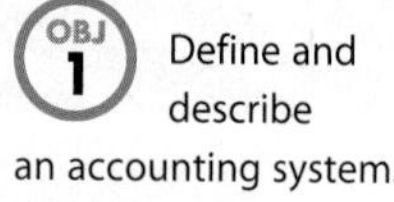

OBJ 1 Define and describe an accounting system.

Basic Accounting Systems

In Chapters 1–4, an accounting system for **NetSolutions** was described and illustrated. An **accounting system** is the methods and procedures for collecting, classifying, summarizing, and reporting a business's financial and operating information. Most accounting systems, however, are more complex than NetSolutions'. For example, **Southwest Airlines**'s accounting system not only records basic transaction data but also records data on such items as ticket reservations, credit card collections, frequent-flier mileage, and aircraft maintenance.

As a business grows and changes, its accounting system also changes in a three-step process. This three-step process is as follows:

- Step 1. *Analyze* user information needs.
- Step 2. *Design* the system to meet the user needs.
- Step 3. *Implement* the system.

For NetSolutions, our analysis determined that Chris Clark needed financial statements for the new business. We designed the system, using a basic manual system that included a chart of accounts, a two-column journal, and a general ledger. Finally, we implemented the system to record transactions and prepare financial statements.

Once a system has been implemented, input from users is used to analyze and improve the system. For example, in later chapters, NetSolutions expands its chart of accounts to record more complex transactions.

The accounting system design consists of:

- internal controls and
- information processing methods.

Internal controls are the policies and procedures that protect assets from misuse, ensure that business information is accurate, and ensure that laws and regulations are being followed. Internal controls are discussed in Chapter 8.

Processing methods are the means by which the accounting system collects, summarizes, and reports accounting information. These methods may be either *manual* or *computerized*. In the following sections, manual accounting systems that use special journals and subsidiary ledgers are described and illustrated. This is followed by a discussion of computerized accounting systems.

Manual Accounting Systems

OBJ 2 Journalize and post transactions in a manual accounting system that uses subsidiary ledgers and special journals.

Accounting systems are manual or computerized. Understanding a manual accounting system is useful in identifying relationships between accounting data and reports. Also, most computerized systems use principles from manual systems.

In prior chapters, the transactions for **NetSolutions** were manually recorded in an all-purpose (two-column) journal. The journal entries were then posted individually to the accounts in the ledger. Such a system is simple to use and easy to understand when there are a small number of transactions. However, when a business has a large number of *similar* transactions, using an all-purpose journal is inefficient and impractical. In such cases, subsidiary ledgers and special journals are useful.

Subsidiary Ledgers

A large number of individual accounts with a common characteristic can be grouped together in a separate ledger called a **subsidiary ledger**. The primary ledger, which contains all of the balance sheet and income statement accounts, is then called the **general ledger**. Each subsidiary ledger is represented in the general ledger by a summarizing account, called a **controlling account**. The sum of the balances of the accounts in a subsidiary ledger must equal the balance of the related controlling account. Thus, a subsidiary ledger is a secondary ledger that supports a controlling account in the general ledger.

Two of the most common subsidiary ledgers are as follows:

- Accounts receivable subsidiary ledger
- Accounts payable subsidiary ledger

The **accounts receivable subsidiary ledger**, or *customers ledger*, lists the individual customer accounts in alphabetical order. The controlling account in the general ledger that summarizes the debits and credits to the individual customer accounts is Accounts Receivable.

The **accounts payable subsidiary ledger**, or *creditors ledger*, lists individual creditor accounts in alphabetical order. The related controlling account in the general ledger is Accounts Payable.

The relationship between the general ledger and the accounts receivable and accounts payable subsidiary ledgers is illustrated in Exhibit 1.

Many businesses use subsidiary ledgers for other accounts in addition to Accounts Receivable and Accounts Payable. For example, businesses often use an equipment subsidiary ledger to keep track of each item of equipment purchased, its cost, location, and other data.

Special Journals

One method of processing transactions more efficiently in a manual system is to use special journals. **Special journals** are designed to record a single kind of transaction

EXHIBIT 1 **General Ledger and Subsidiary Ledgers**

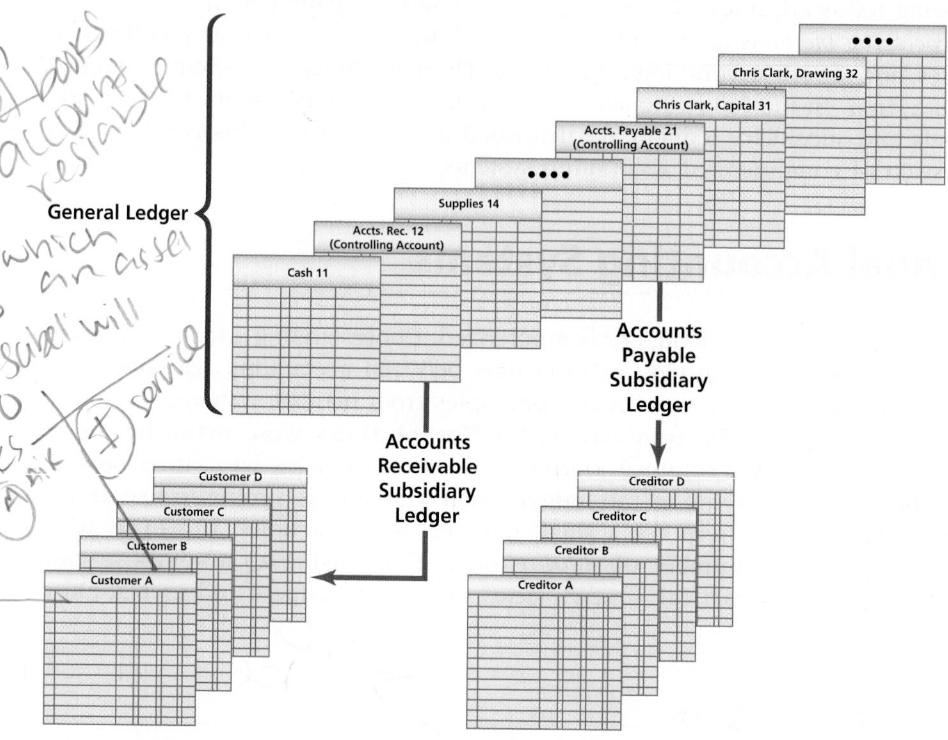

that occurs frequently. For example, since most businesses have many transactions in which cash is paid out, they will likely use a special journal for recording cash payments. Likewise, they will use another special journal for recording cash receipts.

The format and number of special journals that a business uses depends on the nature of the business. The common transactions and their related special journals used by small service businesses are as follows:

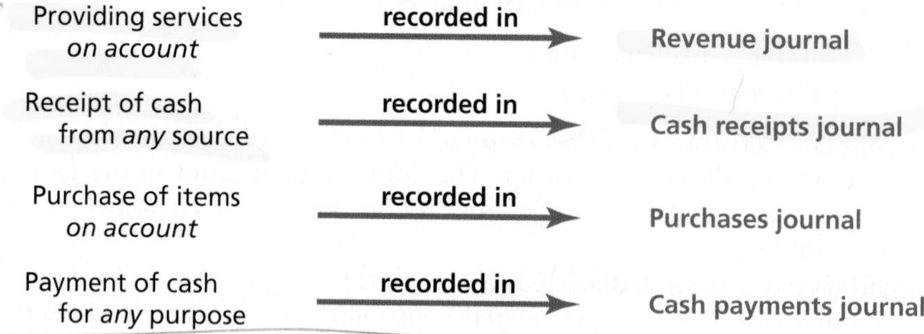

The all-purpose two-column journal, called the **general journal** or simply the *journal,* can be used for entries that do not fit into any of the special journals. For example, adjusting and closing entries are recorded in the general journal.

The following types of transactions, special journals, and subsidiary ledgers are described and illustrated for **NetSolutions**:

Transaction	Special Journal	Subsidiary Ledger
Fees earned on account	Revenue journal	Accounts receivable subsidiary ledger
Cash receipts	Cash receipts journal	Accounts receivable subsidiary ledger
Purchases on account	Purchases journal	Accounts payable subsidiary ledger
Cash payments	Cash payments journal	Accounts payable subsidiary ledger

As shown, transactions that are recorded in the revenue and cash receipts journals will affect the accounts receivable subsidiary ledger. Likewise, transactions that are recorded in the purchases and cash payments journals will affect the accounts payable subsidiary ledger.

We will assume that NetSolutions had the following selected general ledger balances on March 1, 2016:

Account Number	Account	Balance
11	Cash	$6,200
12	Accounts Receivable	3,400
14	Supplies	2,500
18	Office Equipment	2,500
21	Accounts Payable	1,230

Revenue Journal

Fees earned on account would be recorded in the **revenue journal**. *Cash fees earned* would be recorded in the cash receipts journal.

To illustrate the efficiency of using a revenue journal, an example for **NetSolutions** is used. Specifically, assume that NetSolutions recorded the following four revenue transactions for March in its general journal:

Date		Description	Post. Ref.	Debit	Credit
2016					
Mar.	2	Accounts Receivable—Accessories By Claire	12/✓	2,200	
		Fees Earned	41		2,200
	6	Accounts Receivable—RapZone	12/✓	1,750	
		Fees Earned	41		1,750
	18	Accounts Receivable—Web Cantina	12/✓	2,650	
		Fees Earned	41		2,650
	27	Accounts Receivable—Accessories By Claire	12/✓	3,000	
		Fees Earned	41		3,000

For the preceding entries, NetSolutions recorded eight accounts and eight amounts. In addition, NetSolutions made 12 postings to the ledgers—four to Accounts Receivable in the general ledger, four to the accounts receivable subsidiary ledger (indicated by each check mark), and four to Fees Earned in the general ledger.

The preceding revenue transactions could be recorded more efficiently in a revenue journal, as shown in Exhibit 2. In each revenue transaction, the amount of the debit to Accounts Receivable is the same as the amount of the credit to Fees Earned. Thus, only a single amount column is necessary. The date, invoice number, customer name, and amount are entered separately for each transaction.

Revenues are normally recorded in the revenue journal when the company sends an invoice to the customer. An **invoice** is the bill that is sent to the customer by the company. Each invoice is normally numbered in sequence for future reference.

To illustrate, assume that on March 2 NetSolutions issued Invoice No. 615 to Accessories By Claire for fees earned of $2,200. This transaction is entered in the revenue journal, shown in Exhibit 2, by entering the following items:

1. Date column: *Mar. 2*
2. Invoice No. column: *615*
3. Account Debited column: *Accessories By Claire*
4. Accts. Rec. Dr./Fees Earned Cr. column: *2,200*

EXHIBIT 2 **Revenue Journal**

Revenue Journal					Page 35
Date		Invoice No.	Account Debited	Post. Ref.	Accts. Rec. Dr. Fees Earned Cr.
2016					
Mar.	2	615	Accessories By Claire		2,200
	6	616	RapZone		1,750
	18	617	Web Cantina		2,650
	27	618	Accessories By Claire		3,000
	31				9,600

The process of posting from a revenue journal, shown in Exhibit 3, is as follows:

- Step 1. Each transaction is posted individually to a customer account in the accounts receivable subsidiary ledger. Postings to customer accounts should be made on a regular basis. In this way, the customer's account will show a current balance. Since the balances in the customer accounts are usually debit balances, the three-column account form is shown in Exhibit 3.

  To illustrate, Exhibit 3 shows the posting of the $2,200 debit to Accessories By Claire in the accounts receivable subsidiary ledger. After the posting, Accessories By Claire has a debit balance of $2,200.

- Step 2. To provide a trail of the entries posted to the subsidiary and general ledger, the source of these entries is indicated in the Posting Reference column of each account by inserting the letter R (for revenue journal) and the page number of the revenue journal.

  To illustrate, Exhibit 3 shows that after $2,200 is posted to Accessories By Claire's account, R35 is inserted into the Post. Ref. column of the account.

- Step 3. To indicate that the transaction has been posted to the accounts receivable subsidiary ledger, a check mark (✓) is inserted in the Post. Ref. column of the revenue journal, as shown in Exhibit 3.

  To illustrate, Exhibit 3 shows that a check mark (✓) has been inserted in the Post. Ref. column next to Accessories By Claire in the revenue journal to indicate that the $2,200 has been posted.

- Step 4. A single monthly total is posted to Accounts Receivable and Fees Earned in the general ledger. This total is equal to the sum of the month's debits to the individual accounts in the subsidiary ledger. It is posted in the general ledger as a debit to Accounts Receivable and a credit to Fees Earned, as shown in Exhibit 3. The accounts receivable account number (12) and the fees earned account number (41) are then inserted below the total in the revenue journal to indicate that the posting is completed.

  To illustrate, Exhibit 3 shows the monthly total of $9,600 was posted as a debit to Accounts Receivable (12) and as a credit to Fees Earned (41).

Exhibit 3 illustrates the efficiency gained by using the revenue journal rather than the general journal. Specifically, all of the transactions for fees earned during the month are posted to the general ledger only once—at the end of the month.

EXHIBIT 3 **Revenue Journal and Postings**

Revenue Journal *Page 35*

Date		Invoice No.	Account Debited	Post. Ref.	Accts. Rec. Dr. Fees Earned Cr.
2016					
Mar.	2	615	Accessories By Claire	✓	2,200
	6	616	RapZone	✓	1,750
	18	617	Web Cantina	✓	2,650
	27	618	Accessories By Claire	✓	3,000
	31				9,600
					(12) (41)

Step 3

General Ledger

Account *Accounts Receivable* Account No. *12*

Date		Item	Post. Ref.	Debit	Credit	Balance Debit	Balance Credit
2016							
Mar.	1	Balance	✓			3,400	
	31		R35	9,600		13,000	

Step 4

Account *Fees Earned* Account No. *41*

Date		Item	Post. Ref.	Debit	Credit	Balance Debit	Balance Credit
2016							
Mar.	31		R35		9,600		9,600

Step 4

Accounts Receivable Subsidiary Ledger

Name: *Accessories By Claire*

Date		Item	Post. Ref.	Debit	Credit	Balance
2016						
Mar.	2		R35	2,200		2,200
	27		R35	3,000		5,200

Step 2 Step 1

Name: *RapZone*

Date		Item	Post. Ref.	Debit	Credit	Balance
2016						
Mar.	6		R35	1,750		1,750

Name: *Web Cantina*

Date		Item	Post. Ref.	Debit	Credit	Balance
2016						
Mar.	1	Balance	✓			3,400
	18		R35	2,650		6,050

Example Exercise 5-1 Revenue Journal

The following revenue transactions occurred during December:

Dec. 5. Issued Invoice No. 302 to Butler Company for services provided on account, $5,000.
9. Issued Invoice No. 303 to JoJo Enterprises for services provided on account, $2,100.
15. Issued Invoice No. 304 to Salinas Inc. for services provided on account, $3,250.

Record these transactions in a revenue journal as illustrated in Exhibit 2.

Follow My Example 5-1

REVENUE JOURNAL

Date	Invoice No.	Account Debited	Post. Ref.	Accts. Rec. Dr. Fees Earned Cr.
Dec. 5	302	Butler Company		5,000
9	303	JoJo Enterprises		2,100
15	304	Salinas Inc.		3,250

Practice Exercises: PE 5-1A, PE 5-1B

Cash Receipts Journal

All transactions that involve the receipt of cash are recorded in a **cash receipts journal**. The cash receipts journal for **NetSolutions** is shown in Exhibit 4.

This journal has a Cash Dr. column. The types of cash receipt transactions and their frequency determine the titles of the other columns. For example, NetSolutions often receives cash from customers on account. Thus, the cash receipts journal in Exhibit 4 has an Accounts Receivable Cr. column.

To illustrate, on March 19 Web Cantina made a payment of $3,400 on its account. This transaction is recorded in the cash receipts journal, shown in Exhibit 4, by entering the following items:

1. Date column: *Mar. 19*
2. Account Credited column: *Web Cantina*

EXHIBIT 4 **Cash Receipts Journal and Postings**

Cash Receipts Journal *Page 14*

Date		Account Credited	Post. Ref.	Other Accounts Cr.	Accounts Receivable Cr.	Cash Dr.
2016						
Mar.	1	Rent Revenue	42	400		400
	19	Web Cantina	✓		3,400	3,400
	28	Accessories By Claire	✓		2,200	2,200
	30	RapZone	✓		1,750	1,750
	31			400	7,350	7,750
				(✓)	(12)	(11)

Step 3

General Ledger

Account *Cash* Account No. *11*

Date		Item	Post. Ref.	Debit	Credit	Balance Debit	Balance Credit
2016							
Mar.	1	Balance	✓			6,200	
	31		CR14	7,750		13,950	

Step 5

Account *Accounts Receivable* Account No. *12*

Date		Item	Post. Ref.	Debit	Credit	Balance Debit	Balance Credit
2016							
Mar.	1	Balance	✓			3,400	
	31		R35	9,600		13,000	
	31		CR14		7,350	5,650	

Step 4

Account *Rent Revenue* Account No. *42*

Date		Item	Post. Ref.	Debit	Credit	Balance Debit	Balance Credit
2016							
Mar.	1		CR14		400		400

Step 6

Accounts Receivable Subsidiary Ledger

Name: *Accessories By Claire*

Date		Item	Post. Ref.	Debit	Credit	Balance
2016						
Mar.	2		R35	2,200		2,200
	27		R35	3,000		5,200
	28		CR14		2,200	3,000

Name: *RapZone*

Date		Item	Post. Ref.	Debit	Credit	Balance
2016						
Mar.	6		R35	1,750		1,750
	30		CR14		1,750	—

Name: *Web Cantina*

Date		Item	Post. Ref.	Debit	Credit	Balance
2016						
Mar.	1	Balance	✓			3,400
	18		R35	2,650		6,050
	19		CR14		3,400	2,650

Step 2

Step 1

3. Accounts Receivable Cr. column: *3,400*
4. Cash Dr. column: *3,400*

The Other Accounts Cr. column in Exhibit 4 is used for recording credits to any account for which there is no special credit column. For example, NetSolutions received cash on March 1 for rent. Since no special column exists for Rent Revenue, Rent Revenue is entered in the Account Credited column. Thus, this transaction is recorded in the cash receipts journal, shown in Exhibit 4, by entering the following items:

1. Date column: *Mar. 1*
2. Account Credited column: *Rent Revenue*
3. Other Accounts Cr. column: *400*
4. Cash Dr. column: *400*

At the end of the month, all of the amount columns are totaled. The debits must equal the credits. If the debits do not equal the credits, an error has occurred. Before proceeding further, the error must be found and corrected.

The process of posting from the cash receipts journal, shown in Exhibit 4, is:

- Step 1. Each transaction involving the receipt of cash on account is posted individually to a customer account in the accounts receivable subsidiary ledger. Postings to customer accounts should be made on a regular basis. In this way, the customer's account will show a current balance.

  To illustrate, Exhibit 4 shows on March 19 the receipt of $3,400 on account from Web Cantina. The posting of the $3,400 credit to Web Cantina in the accounts receivable subsidiary ledger is also shown in Exhibit 4. After the posting, Web Cantina has a debit balance of $2,650. If a posting results in a customer's account with a credit balance, the credit balance is indicated by an asterisk or parentheses in the Balance column. If an account's balance is zero, a line may be drawn in the Balance column.

- Step 2. To provide a trail of the entries posted to the subsidiary ledger, the source of these entries is indicated in the Posting Reference column of each account by inserting the letters CR (for cash receipts journal) and the page number of the cash receipts journal.

  To illustrate, Exhibit 4 shows that after $3,400 is posted to Web Cantina's account in the accounts receivable subsidiary ledger, CR14 is inserted into the Post. Ref. column of the account.

- Step 3. To indicate that the transaction has been posted to the accounts receivable subsidiary ledger, a check mark (✓) is inserted in the Posting Reference column of the cash receipts journal.

  To illustrate, Exhibit 4 shows that a check mark (✓) has been inserted in the Post. Ref. column next to Web Cantina to indicate that the $3,400 has been posted.

- Step 4. A single monthly total of the Accounts Receivable Cr. column is posted to the accounts receivable general ledger account. This is the total cash received on account and is posted as a credit to Accounts Receivable. The accounts receivable account number (12) is then inserted below the Accounts Receivable Cr. column to indicate that the posting is complete.

  To illustrate, Exhibit 4 shows the monthly total of $7,350 was posted as a credit to Accounts Receivable (12).

- Step 5. A single monthly total of the Cash Dr. column is posted to the cash general ledger account. This is the total cash received during the month and is posted as a debit to Cash. The cash account number (11) is then inserted below the Cash Dr. column to indicate that the posting is complete.

  To illustrate, Exhibit 4 shows the monthly total of $7,750 was posted as a debit to Cash (11).

- Step 6. The accounts listed in the Other Accounts Cr. column are posted on a regular basis as a separate credit to each account. The account number is then inserted in the Post. Ref. column to indicate that the posting is complete. Because accounts in the Other Accounts Cr. column are posted individually, a check mark is placed below the column total at the end of the month to show that no further action is needed.

To illustrate, Exhibit 4 shows that $400 was posted as a credit to Rent Revenue in the general ledger, and the rent revenue account number (42) was entered in the Post. Ref. column of the cash receipts journal. Also, at the end of the month a check mark (✓) is entered below the Other Accounts Cr. column to indicate that no further action is needed.

Accounts Receivable Control Account and Subsidiary Ledger

After all posting has been completed for the month, the balances in the accounts receivable subsidiary ledger should be totaled. This total can be summarized in a separate schedule of customer balances. The total should then be compared with the balance of the accounts receivable controlling account in the general ledger. If the controlling account and the subsidiary ledger do not agree, an error has occurred and must be located and corrected.

The total of **NetSolutions'** accounts receivable customer balances is $5,650. This total agrees with the balance of its accounts receivable controlling account on March 31, 2016, as follows:

Accounts Receivable (Controlling)		**NetSolutions Accounts Receivable Customer Balances March 31, 2016**	
Balance, March 1, 2016	$ 3,400	Accessories By Claire	$3,000
Total debits (from revenue journal)	9,600	RapZone	0
Total credits (from cash receipts journal)	(7,350)	Web Cantina	2,650
Balance, March 31, 2016	$ 5,650	Total accounts receivable	$5,650

Equal debit balances

Example Exercise 5-2 Accounts Receivable Subsidiary Ledger

OBJ 2

The debits and credits from two transactions are presented in the following customer account:

NAME *Sweet Tooth Confections*
ADDRESS *1212 Lombard St.*

Date	Item	Post. Ref.	Debit	Credit	Balance
July 1	Balance				625
7	Invoice 35	R12	86		711
31	Invoice 31	CR4		122	589

Describe each transaction and the source of each posting.

Follow My Example 5-2

July 7. Provided $86 of services on account to Sweet Tooth Confections, itemized on Invoice No. 35. Amount posted from Page 12 of the revenue journal.

31. Collected cash of $122 from Sweet Tooth Confections (Invoice No. 31). Amount posted from Page 4 of the cash receipts journal.

Practice Exercises: PE 5-2A, PE 5-2B

Purchases Journal

All *purchases on account* are recorded in the **purchases journal**. *Cash purchases would be recorded in the cash payments journal.* The purchases journal for **NetSolutions** is shown in Exhibit 5.

The amounts purchased on account are recorded in the purchases journal in an Accounts Payable Cr. column. The items most often purchased on account determine the titles of the other columns. For example, NetSolutions often purchases supplies on account. Thus, the purchases journal in Exhibit 5 has a Supplies Dr. column.

EXHIBIT 5 **Purchases Journal and Postings**

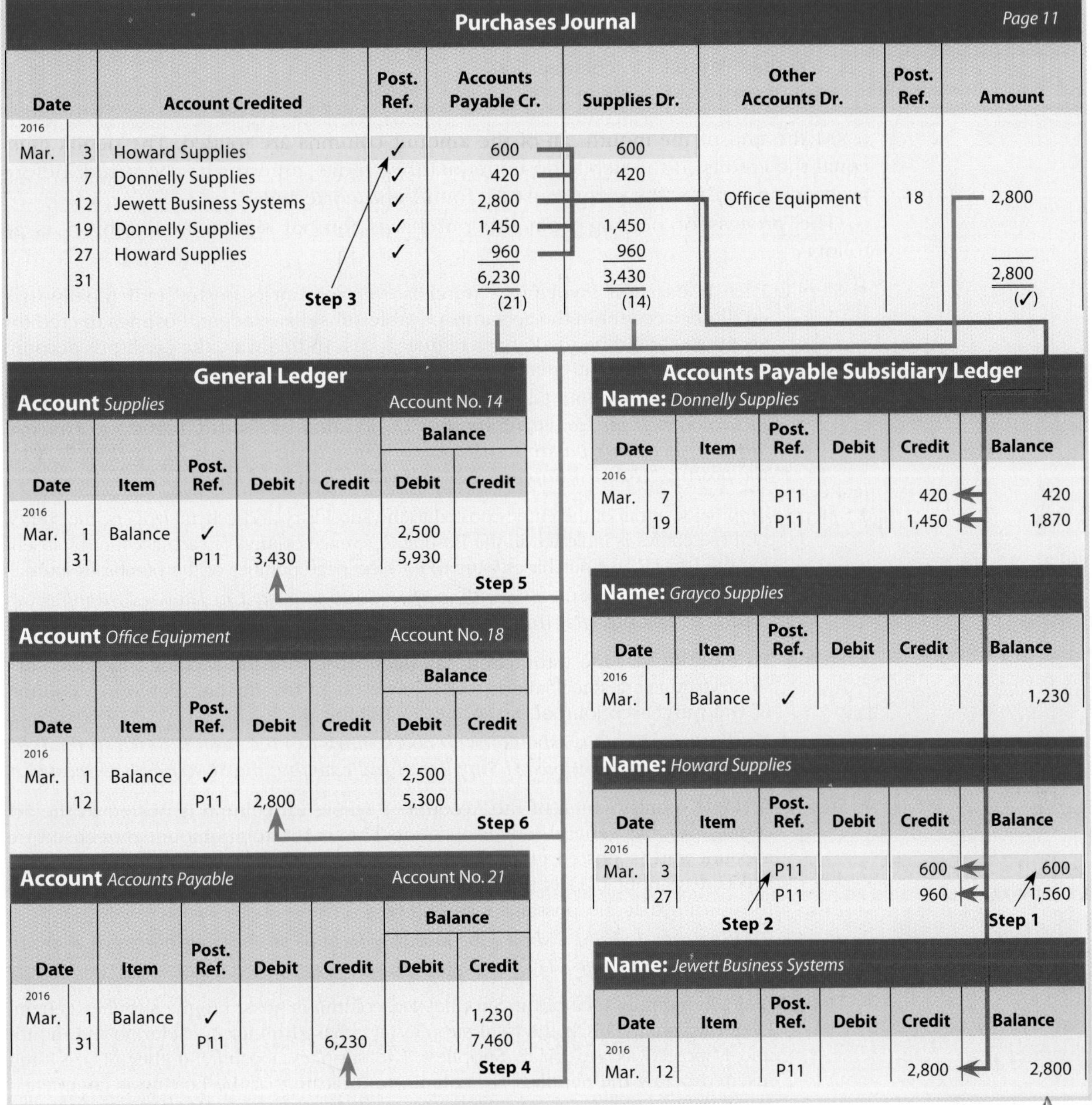

Purchases Journal *Page 11*

Date		Account Credited	Post. Ref.	Accounts Payable Cr.	Supplies Dr.	Other Accounts Dr.	Post. Ref.	Amount
2016								
Mar.	3	Howard Supplies	✓	600	600			
	7	Donnelly Supplies	✓	420	420			
	12	Jewett Business Systems	✓	2,800		Office Equipment	18	2,800
	19	Donnelly Supplies	✓	1,450	1,450			
	27	Howard Supplies	✓	960	960			
	31			6,230	3,430			2,800
				(21)	(14)			(✓)

General Ledger

Account *Supplies* Account No. *14*

Date		Item	Post. Ref.	Debit	Credit	Balance Debit	Balance Credit
2016							
Mar.	1	Balance	✓			2,500	
	31		P11	3,430		5,930	

Account *Office Equipment* Account No. *18*

Date		Item	Post. Ref.	Debit	Credit	Balance Debit	Balance Credit
2016							
Mar.	1	Balance	✓			2,500	
	12		P11	2,800		5,300	

Account *Accounts Payable* Account No. *21*

Date		Item	Post. Ref.	Debit	Credit	Balance Debit	Balance Credit
2016							
Mar.	1	Balance	✓				1,230
	31		P11		6,230		7,460

Accounts Payable Subsidiary Ledger

Name: *Donnelly Supplies*

Date		Item	Post. Ref.	Debit	Credit	Balance
2016						
Mar.	7		P11		420	420
	19		P11		1,450	1,870

Name: *Grayco Supplies*

Date		Item	Post. Ref.	Debit	Credit	Balance
2016						
Mar.	1	Balance	✓			1,230

Name: *Howard Supplies*

Date		Item	Post. Ref.	Debit	Credit	Balance
2016						
Mar.	3		P11		600	600
	27		P11		960	1,560

Name: *Jewett Business Systems*

Date		Item	Post. Ref.	Debit	Credit	Balance
2016						
Mar.	12		P11		2,800	2,800

To illustrate, on March 3 NetSolutions purchased $600 of supplies on account from Howard Supplies. This transaction is recorded in the purchases journal, shown in Exhibit 5, by entering the following items:

1. Date column: *Mar. 3*
2. Account Credited column: *Howard Supplies*
3. Accounts Payable Cr. column: *600*
4. Supplies Dr. column: *600*

The Other Accounts Dr. column in Exhibit 5 is used to record purchases on account of any item for which there is no special debit column. The title of the account to be debited is entered in the Other Accounts Dr. column, and the amount is entered in the Amount column.

Control Account: If you have a business employee goes on account payable and subsidiary ledger. Making sure that the sum on account payable is correct

To illustrate, on March 3 NetSolutions purchased supplies on account from Howard Supplies for $600. This transaction is recorded in the purchases journal shown in Exhibit 5 by entering the following items:

1. Date column: *Mar. 3*
2. Account Credited column: *Howard Supplies*
3. Accounts Payable Cr. column: *600*
4. Supplies Dr. column: *600*

At the end of the month, all of the amount columns are totaled. The debits must equal the credits. If the debits do not equal the credits, an error has occurred. Before proceeding further, the error must be found and corrected.

The process of posting from the purchases journal shown in Exhibit 5 is as follows:

- Step 1. Each transaction involving a purchase on account is posted individually to a creditor's account in the accounts payable subsidiary ledger. Postings to creditor accounts should be made on a regular basis. In this way, the creditor's account will show a current balance.

  To illustrate, Exhibit 5 shows on March 3 the purchase of supplies of $600 on account from Howard Supplies. The posting of the $600 credit to Howard Supplies accounts payable subsidiary ledger is also shown in Exhibit 5. After the posting, Howard Supplies has a credit balance of $600.

- Step 2. To provide a trail of the entries posted to the subsidiary and general ledgers, the source of these entries is indicated in the Posting Reference column of each account by inserting the letter P (for purchases journal) and the page number of the purchases journal.

  To illustrate, Exhibit 5 shows that after $600 is posted to Howard Supplies account, P11 is inserted into the Post. Ref. column of the account.

- Step 3. To indicate that the transaction has been posted to the accounts payable subsidiary ledger, a check mark (✓) is inserted in the Posting Reference column of the purchases journal, as shown in Exhibit 5.

  To illustrate, Exhibit 5 shows that a check mark (✓) has been inserted in the Post. Ref. column next to Howard Supplies to indicate that the $600 has been posted.

- Step 4. A single monthly total of the Accounts Payable Cr. column is posted to the accounts payable general ledger account. This is the total amount purchased on account and is posted as a credit to Accounts Payable. The accounts payable account number (21) is then inserted below the Accounts Payable Cr. column to indicate that the posting is complete.

  To illustrate, Exhibit 5 shows the monthly total of $6,230 was posted as a credit to Accounts Payable (21).

- Step 5. A single monthly total of the Supplies Dr. column is posted to the supplies general ledger account. This is the total supplies purchased on account during the month and is posted as a debit to Supplies. The supplies account number (14) is then inserted below the Supplies Dr. column to indicate that the posting is complete.

  To illustrate, Exhibit 5 shows the monthly total of $3,430 was posted as a debit to Supplies (14).

- Step 6. The accounts listed in the Other Accounts Dr. column are posted on a regular basis as a separate debit to each account. The account number is then inserted in the Post. Ref. column to indicate that the posting is complete. Because accounts in the Other Accounts Dr. column are posted individually, a check mark is placed below the column total at the end of the month to show that no further action is needed.

  To illustrate, Exhibit 5 shows that $2,800 was posted as a debit to Office Equipment in the general ledger, and the office equipment account number (18) was entered in the Post. Ref. column of the purchases journal. Also, at the end of the month, a check mark (✓) is entered below the Amount column to indicate no further action is needed.

Example Exercise 5-3 Purchases Journal

OBJ 2

The following purchase transactions occurred during October for Helping Hand Cleaners:

Oct. 11. Purchased cleaning supplies for $235, on account, from General Supplies.
19. Purchased cleaning supplies for $110, on account, from Hubble Supplies.
24. Purchased office equipment for $850, on account, from Office Warehouse.

Record these transactions in a purchases journal as illustrated at the top of Exhibit 5.

Follow My Example 5-3

PURCHASES JOURNAL

Date	Account Credited	Post. Ref.	Accounts Payable Cr.	Cleaning Supplies Dr.	Other Accounts Dr.	Post. Ref.	Amount
Oct. 11	General Supplies		235	235			
19	Hubble Supplies		110	110			
24	Office Warehouse		850		Office Equipment		850

Practice Exercises: PE 5-3A, PE 5-3B

Cash Payments Journal

All transactions that involve the payment of cash are recorded in a **cash payments journal**. The cash payments journal for **NetSolutions** is shown in Exhibit 6.

The cash payments journal shown in Exhibit 6 has a Cash Cr. column. The kinds of transactions in which cash is paid and how often they occur determine the titles of the other columns. For example, NetSolutions often pays cash to creditors on account. Thus, the cash payments journal in Exhibit 6 has an Accounts Payable Dr. column. In addition, NetSolutions makes all payments by check. Thus, a check number is entered for each payment in the Ck. No. (Check Number) column to the right of the Date column. The check numbers are helpful in controlling cash payments and provide a useful cross-reference.

To illustrate, on March 15 NetSolutions issued Check No. 151 for $1,230 to Grayco Supplies for payment on its account. This transaction is recorded in the cash payments journal shown in Exhibit 6 by entering the following items:

1. Date column: *Mar. 15*
2. Ck. No. column: *151*
3. Account Debited column: *Grayco Supplies*
4. Accounts Payable Dr. column: *1,230*
5. Cash Cr. column: *1,230*

The Other Accounts Dr. column in Exhibit 6 is used for recording debits to any account for which there is no special debit column. For example, NetSolutions issued Check No. 150 on March 2 for $1,600 in payment of March rent. This transaction is recorded in the cash payments journal, shown in Exhibit 6, by entering these items:

1. Date column: *Mar. 2*
2. Ck. No. column: *150*
3. Account Debited column: *Rent Expense*
4. Other Accounts Dr. column: *1,600*
5. Cash Cr. column: *1,600*

At the end of the month, all of the amount columns are totaled. The debits must equal the credits. If the debits do not equal the credits, an error has occurred. Before proceeding further, the error must be found and corrected.

The process of posting from the cash payments journal, Exhibit 6, is as follows:

- Step 1. Each transaction involving the payment of cash on account is posted individually to a creditor account in the accounts payable subsidiary ledger. Postings to

EXHIBIT 6 **Cash Payments Journal and Postings**

Cash Payments Journal — Page 7

Date		Ck. No.	Account Debited	Post. Ref.	Other Accounts Dr.	Accounts Payable Dr.	Cash Cr.
2016							
Mar.	2	150	Rent Expense	52	1,600		1,600
	15	151	Grayco Supplies	✓		1,230	1,230
	21	152	Jewett Business Systems	✓		2,800	2,800
	22	153	Donnelly Supplies	✓		420	420
	30	154	Utilities Expense	54	1,050		1,050
	31	155	Howard Supplies	✓		600	600
	31				2,650	5,050	7,700
					(✓)	(21)	(11)

Step 3

General Ledger

Account *Cash* — Account No. *11*

Date		Item	Post. Ref.	Debit	Credit	Balance Debit	Balance Credit
2016							
Mar.	1	Balance	✓			6,200	
	31		CR14	7,750		13,950	
	31		CP7		7,700	6,250	

Step 5

Account *Accounts Payable* — Account No. *21*

Date		Item	Post. Ref.	Debit	Credit	Balance Debit	Balance Credit
2016							
Mar.	1	Balance	✓				1,230
	31		P11		6,230		7,460
	31		CP7	5,050			2,410

Step 4

Account *Rent Expense* — Account No. *52*

Date		Item	Post. Ref.	Debit	Credit	Balance Debit	Balance Credit
2016							
Mar.	2		CP7	1,600		1,600	

Step 6

Account *Utilities Expense* — Account No. *54*

Date		Item	Post. Ref.	Debit	Credit	Balance Debit	Balance Credit
2016							
Mar.	30		CP7	1,050		1,050	

Step 6

Accounts Payable Subsidiary Ledger

Name: *Donnelly Supplies*

Date		Item	Post. Ref.	Debit	Credit	Balance
2016						
Mar.	7		P11		420	420
	19		P11		1,450	1,870
	22		CP7	420		1,450

Name: *Grayco Supplies*

Date		Item	Post. Ref.	Debit	Credit	Balance
2016						
Mar.	1	Balance	✓			1,230
	15		CP7	1,230		—

Step 1

Step 2

Name: *Howard Supplies*

Date		Item	Post. Ref.	Debit	Credit	Balance
2016						
Mar.	3		P11		600	600
	27		P11		960	1,560
	31		CP7	600		960

Name: *Jewett Business Systems*

Date		Item	Post. Ref.	Debit	Credit	Balance
2016						
Mar.	12		P11		2,800	2,800
	21		CP7	2,800		—

creditor accounts should be made on a regular basis. In this way, the creditor's account will show a current balance.

To illustrate, Exhibit 6 shows on March 15 the payment of $1,230 on account to Grayco Supplies. The posting of the $1,230 debit to Grayco Supplies in the accounts payable subsidiary ledger is also shown in Exhibit 6. After the posting, Grayco Supplies has a zero balance.

- Step 2. To provide a trail of the entries posted to the subsidiary and general ledgers, the source of these entries is indicated in the Posting Reference column of each account by inserting the letters CP (for cash payments journal) and the page number of the cash payments journal.

  To illustrate, Exhibit 6 shows that after $1,230 is posted to Grayco Supplies account, CP7 is inserted into the Post. Ref. column of the account.

- Step 3. To indicate that the transaction has been posted to the accounts payable subsidiary ledger, a check mark (✓) is inserted in the Posting Reference column of the cash payments journal.

  To illustrate, Exhibit 6 shows that a check mark (✓) has been inserted in the Post. Ref. column next to Grayco Supplies to indicate that the $1,230 has been posted.

- Step 4. A single monthly total of the Accounts Payable Dr. column is posted to the accounts payable general ledger account. This is the total cash paid on account and is posted as a debit to Accounts Payable. The accounts payable account number (21) is then inserted below the Accounts Payable Dr. column to indicate that the posting is complete.

  To illustrate, Exhibit 6 shows the monthly total of $5,050 was posted as a debit to Accounts Payable (21).

- Step 5. A single monthly total of the Cash Cr. column is posted to the cash general ledger account. This is the total cash payments during the month and is posted as a credit to Cash. The cash account number (11) is then inserted below the Cash Cr. column to indicate that the posting is complete.

  To illustrate, Exhibit 6 shows the monthly total of $7,700 was posted as a credit to Cash (11).

- Step 6. The accounts listed in the Other Accounts Dr. column are posted on a regular basis as a separate debit to each account. The account number is then inserted in the Post. Ref. column to indicate that the posting is complete. Because accounts in the Other Accounts Dr. column are posted individually, a check mark is placed below the column total at the end of the month to show that no further action is needed.

  To illustrate, Exhibit 6 shows that $1,600 was posted as a debit to Rent Expense (52) and $1,050 was posted as a debit to Utilities Expense (54) in the general ledger. The account numbers (52 and 54, respectively) were entered in the Post. Ref. column of the cash payments journal. Also, at the end of the month, a check mark (✓) is entered below the Other Accounts Dr. column to indicate that no further action is needed.

Accounts Payable Control Account and Subsidiary Ledger

After all posting has been completed for the month, the balances in the accounts payable subsidiary ledger should be totaled. This total can be summarized in a separate schedule of creditor balances. The total should then be compared with the balance of the accounts payable controlling account in the general ledger. If the controlling account and the subsidiary ledger do not agree, an error has occurred, and must be located and corrected.

The total of **NetSolutions'** accounts payable creditor balances is $2,410. This total agrees with the balance of its accounts payable controlling account on March 31, 2016, as follows:

Accounts Payable (Controlling)

Balance, March 1, 2016	$1,230
Total credits (from purchases journal)	6,230
Total debits (from cash payments journal)	(5,050)
Balance, March 31, 2016	$2,410

NetSolutions
Accounts Payable Creditor Balances
March 31, 2016

Donnelly Supplies	$1,450
Grayco Supplies	0
Howard Supplies	960
Jewett Business Systems	0
Total	$2,410

Equal credit balances

Example Exercise 5-4 Accounts Payable Subsidiary Ledger

OBJ 2

The debits and credits from two transactions are presented in the following creditor's (supplier's) account:

NAME *Lassiter Services Inc.*
ADDRESS *301 St. Bonaventure Ave.*

Date		Item	Post. Ref.	Debit	Credit	Balance
Aug.	1	Balance				320
	12	Invoice No. 101	CP36	200		120
	22	Invoice No. 106	P16		140	260

Describe each transaction and the source of each posting.

Follow My Example 5-4

Aug. 12. Paid $200 to Lassiter Services Inc. on account (Invoice No. 101). Amount posted from Page 36 of the cash payments journal.

22. Purchased $140 of services on account from Lassiter Services Inc. itemized on Invoice No. 106. Amount posted from Page 16 of the purchases journal.

Practice Exercises: PE 5-4A, PE 5-4B

Business  Connection

ACCOUNTING SYSTEMS AND PROFIT MEASUREMENT

A Greek restaurant owner in Canada had his own system of accounting. He kept his accounts payable in a cigar box on the left-hand side of his cash register, his daily cash returns in the cash register, and his receipts for paid bills in another cigar box on the right. A truly "manual" system.

When his youngest son graduated as an accountant, he was appalled by his father's primitive methods. "I don't know how you can run a business that way," he said. "How do you know what your profits are?"

"Well, son," the father replied, "when I got off the boat from Greece, I had nothing but the pants I was wearing. Today, your brother is a doctor. You are an accountant. Your sister is a speech therapist. Your mother and I have a nice car, a city house, and a country home. We have a good business, and everything is paid for. . . ."

"So, you add all that together, subtract the pants, and there's your profit!"

OBJ 3 Define and illustrate the use of a computerized accounting system.

Computerized Accounting Systems

Computerized accounting systems are widely used by even the smallest of companies. Computerized accounting systems have the following three main advantages over manual systems:

- Computerized systems simplify the record-keeping process by recording transactions in electronic journals or forms and, at the same time, posting them electronically to general and subsidiary ledger accounts.
- Computerized systems are generally more accurate than manual systems.
- Computerized systems provide management with current account balance information to support decision making, since account balances are posted as the transactions occur.

The popular QuickBooks accounting software for small- to medium-sized businesses is used to illustrate a computerized accounting system for **NetSolutions**. To simplify, the illustration is limited to transactions involving revenue earned on account and the subsequent recording of cash collections. Exhibit 7 illustrates the use of QuickBooks for NetSolutions to record transactions as follows:

Large companies have their accounting systems integrated within the automated business systems of the firm. Such integrated software is termed ERP, or enterprise resource planning.

- Step 1. Record fees by completing an electronic invoice form and sending to customer (print and mail, or e-mail).

  Sales transactions are entered onto the computer screen using an electronic invoice form. The electronic form appears like a paper form with spaces, or fields, to input transaction data. The data spaces may have pull-down lists to ease data entry. After the form is completed, it is printed out and mailed, or e-mailed, to the customer.

  To illustrate, on March 2, NetSolutions earned $2,200 on account from Accessories By Claire. As shown in Exhibit 7, Invoice No. 615 was created using an electronic form. Upon submitting the invoice form, QuickBooks automatically posts a $2,200 debit to the Accessories By Claire customer account and a credit to Fees Earned. An invoice is either e-mailed or printed for mailing to Accessories By Claire.

- Step 2. Record collection of payment by completing a "receive payment" form.

  Upon collection from the customer, a "receive payment" electronic form is opened and completed. As with the "invoice form," data are input into the various spaces directly or by using pull-down lists.

  To illustrate, a $2,200 payment was collected from Accessories By Claire on March 28. The $2,200 was applied to Invoice No. 615, as shown by the check mark (✓) next to the March 2 date at the bottom of the form in Exhibit 7. As shown at the bottom of the form, the March 27 invoice of $3,000 remains uncollected. When the screen is completed, a debit of $2,200 is automatically posted to the cash account, and a credit for $2,200 is posted to the Accessories By Claire account. This causes the balance of the Accessories By Claire account to be reduced from $5,200 to $3,000.

- Step 3. Prepare reports.

  At any time, managers may request reports from the software. Three such reports include the following:

  - "Accounts Receivable Customer Balances" lists as of a specific date the accounts receivable balances by customer.

    To illustrate, the Accounts Receivable Customer Balances report shown in Exhibit 7 for NetSolutions was generated as of March 31, 2016. The total of the balances of the Accounts Receivable Customer Balances report of $5,650 agrees with the accounts receivable subsidiary ledger balance total we illustrated using a manual system for NetSolutions in Exhibit 4.

  - "Fees Earned by Customer" lists revenue by customer for the month. It is created from the electronic invoice form used in step 1.

    To illustrate, the Fees Earned by Customer report shown in Exhibit 7 for NetSolutions is for the month of March 2016. The $9,600 of total fees earned by customer agree with the total of the revenue journal we illustrated using a manual system for NetSolutions in Exhibits 2 and 3.

  - "Cash Receipts" lists the cash receipts during the month.

    To illustrate, the Cash Receipts report shown in Exhibit 7 for NetSolutions is for the month of March 2016. The total cash receipts of $7,750 agree with the total of the Cash Dr. column of the cash receipts journal we illustrated using a manual system for NetSolutions in Exhibit 4.

Quickbooks and other computerized accounting systems use electronic forms. Alternatively, some computerized systems use electronic special journals. Such journals are designed similar to those illustrated in the text. Additionally, electronic general journals are found in all computerized systems.

EXHIBIT 7 **Revenue and Cash Receipts in QuickBooks**

1. **Record fees by completing an electronic invoice form and sending to customer (print and mail, or e-mail).**

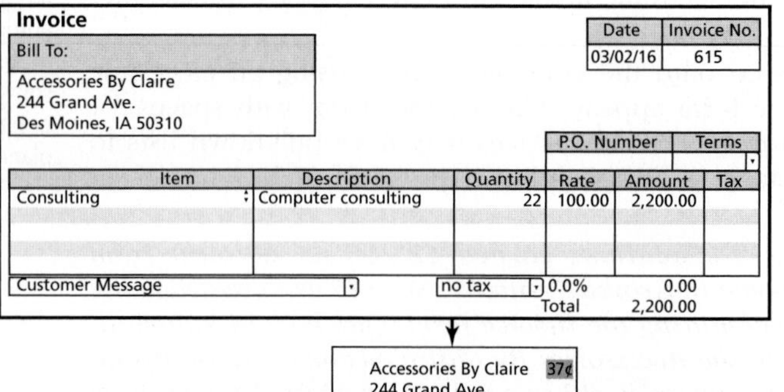

Invoice

Date	Invoice No.
03/02/16	615

Bill To:
Accessories By Claire
244 Grand Ave.
Des Moines, IA 50310

P.O. Number	Terms

Item	Description	Quantity	Rate	Amount	Tax
Consulting	Computer consulting	22	100.00	2,200.00	

Customer Message — no tax 0.0% 0.00
Total 2,200.00

Journal Entry Equivalent

	Dr.	Cr.
Accounts Receivable—Accessories By Claire	2,200	
Fees Earned		2,200

Accessories By Claire 37¢
244 Grand Ave.
Des Moines, IA 50310

Receive payment.

2. **Record collection of payment by completing a "receive payment" form.**

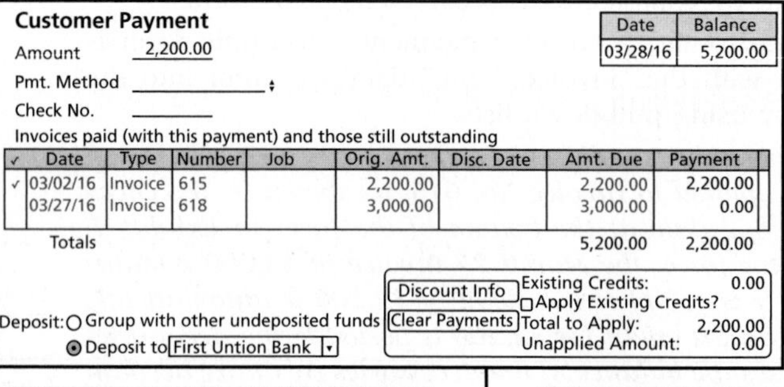

Customer Payment

Date	Balance
03/28/16	5,200.00

Amount 2,200.00
Pmt. Method
Check No.

Invoices paid (with this payment) and those still outstanding

✓	Date	Type	Number	Job	Orig. Amt.	Disc. Date	Amt. Due	Payment
✓	03/02/16	Invoice	615		2,200.00		2,200.00	2,200.00
	03/27/16	Invoice	618		3,000.00		3,000.00	0.00
	Totals						5,200.00	2,200.00

Discount Info — Existing Credits: 0.00
Apply Existing Credits?
Clear Payments — Total to Apply: 2,200.00
Unapplied Amount: 0.00

Deposit: Group with other undeposited funds
Deposit to First Untion Bank

Journal Entry Equivalent

	Dr.	Cr.
Cash	2,200	
Accounts Receivable—Accessories By Claire		2,200

3. **Prepare reports.**

Dates: Custom Dates From: 03/31/16 To: 03/31/16

NetSolutions
Accounts Receivable Customer Balances
March 31, 2016

	Mar 31,'16
Accessories By Claire	3,000.00
Web Cantina	2,650.00
TOTAL	5,650.00

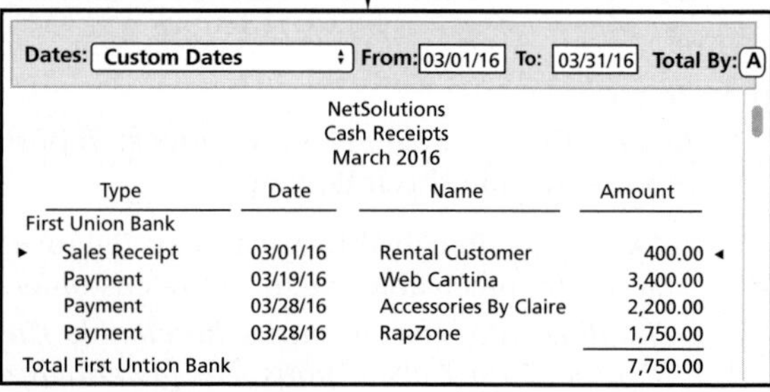

Dates: Custom Dates From: 03/01/16 To: 03/31/16 Total By:

NetSolutions
Cash Receipts
March 2016

Type	Date	Name	Amount
First Union Bank			
Sales Receipt	03/01/16	Rental Customer	400.00
Payment	03/19/16	Web Cantina	3,400.00
Payment	03/28/16	Accessories By Claire	2,200.00
Payment	03/28/16	RapZone	1,750.00
Total First Untion Bank			7,750.00

Dates: Custom Dates From: 03/01/16 To: 03/31/16 Hide Header Collapse

NetSolutions
Fees Earned by Customer
March 2016

Type	Date	Num	Name	Amount
Service				
Consulting				
Invoice	03/02/16	615	Accessories By Claire	2,200.00
Invoice	03/06/16	616	RapZone	1,750.00
Invoice	03/18/16	617	Web Cantina	2,650.00
Invoice	03/27/16	618	Accessories By Claire	3,000.00
Total Consulting				9,600.00

Business  Connection

TURBOTAX

Intuit sells TurboTax®, one of the most popular tax preparation software products for individuals. Using this product, the tax return is prepared using electronic tax forms. Thus, the familiar Form 1040 is presented as an electronic form with data-entry fields provided for the various line items. The advantage of this approach is that all the arithmetic and linking between forms is done automatically. A change in one field automatically updates all other linked fields.

In using these tools, the computer prevents transactions in which the total debits do not equal the total credits. In such cases, an error screen will notify the user to correct data inputs. Likewise, the computer will not make posting or mathematical errors.

In this section, revenue and cash receipt transactions are illustrated for NetSolutions using QuickBooks accounting software. Similar illustrations could be provided for purchases and cash payment transactions. A complete illustration of a computerized accounting system is beyond the scope of this text. However, this chapter provides a solid foundation for applying accounting system concepts in either a manual or a computerized system.

E-Commerce

Describe the basic features of e-commerce.

Using the Internet to perform business transactions is termed **e-commerce**. The U.S. Census Bureau indicates that e-commerce represents more than $225 billion in retail sales, or more than 5% of all retail sales.[1] When transactions are between a company and a consumer, it is termed *B2C (business-to-consumer) e-commerce.* Examples of companies engaged in B2C e-commerce include Amazon.com, priceline .com Incorporated, and Apple Inc. The B2C business allows consumers to shop and receive goods at home, rather than going to the store. For example, Apple Inc. allows consumers to use its Web site to select and purchase Apple products for direct shipment to the home.

When transactions are conducted between two companies, it is termed *B2B (business-to-business) e-commerce.* Examples of companies engaged in B2B e-commerce include Cisco Systems, Inc., an Internet equipment manufacturer, and Union Pacific Corporation, a railroad. Union Pacific, for example, allows their business customers to order freight transportation services from their Web site.

A new trend is toward "cloud" software solutions whereby the accounting system and data are stored and distributed over the Internet by a third party. Under this model, the software is "rented," while analysis, design, and implementation are largely provided by the software vendor.

The Internet creates opportunities for improving the speed and efficiency of transactions. As discussed, many companies are realizing these benefits of using e-commerce. Three additional areas where the Internet is being used for business purposes are as follows:

- **Supply chain management (SCM):** Internet applications to plan supply needs and coordinate them with suppliers.
- **Customer relationship management (CRM):** Internet applications to plan and coordinate marketing and sales effort.
- **Product life-cycle management (PLM):** Internet applications to plan and coordinate the product development and design process.

Many Web applications generate accounting transactions as they occur. For example, purchases using e-commerce shopping carts generate the accounting sales transaction.

Integrity, Objectivity, and Ethics in Business

ONLINE FRAUD

Fraud accounted for more than $3.4 billion in e-commerce losses in 2011, or approximately 1.0% of all online revenue. As a result, online retailers are using address verification and credit card security codes as additional security measures. Address verification matches the customer's address to the address on file with the credit card company, while the security code is the additional four-digit code designed to reduce fictitious credit card transactions. Online fraud has been decreasing the last several years as a result of these and other measures.

Source: 13th Annual CyberSource fraud survey, *CyberSource*, January 2012.

[1] Quarterly Retail E-commerce Sales, *U.S. Census Bureau News*, U.S. Department of Commerce, February 15, 2013, p. 1.

As the Internet continues to become the preferred method of conducting business, new applications will be developed. Many of these applications will be linked to the accounting system as transactions flow inside and outside the organization.

OBJ 5 Use segment analysis in evaluating the operating performance of a company.

F·A·I

Financial Analysis and Interpretation: Segment Analysis

Accounting systems often use computers to collect, classify, summarize, and report financial and operating information in a variety of ways. One way is to report revenue earned by different segments of business. Businesses may be segmented by region, by product or service, or by type of customer. Segment revenues are determined from the invoice data that are entered into the accounting system.

For example, **Intuit Inc.** uses invoice data from the accounting system to determine the amount of revenue earned by different products and services. Segment analysis uses horizontal and vertical comparisons to analyze the contributions of various segments to the total operating performance of a company. To illustrate, selected product and service segment revenue information from the notes to Intuit's financial statements for two recent fiscal years follows:

Segment	Recent Year (in millions)	Prior Year (in millions)
Financial Management Solutions	$ 691	$ 622
Employee Management Solutions	512	457
Payment Solutions	417	348
Consumer Tax	1,441	1,298
Accounting Professionals	423	399
Financial Institutions	362	346
Other Businesses	305	302
Total revenues	$4,151	$3,772

This segment information can be used to perform horizontal analysis using the prior year as the base year as follows:

Segment	Recent Year (in millions)	Prior Year (in millions)	Increase (Decrease)	
			Amount	Percent
Financial Management Solutions	$ 691	$ 622	$ 69	11.1%
Employee Management Solutions	512	457	55	12.0
Payment Solutions	417	348	69	19.8
Consumer Tax	1,441	1,298	143	11.0
Accounting Professionals	423	399	24	6.0
Financial Institutions	362	346	16	4.6
Other Businesses	305	302	3	1.0
Total revenues	$4,151	$3,772	$379	10.0

Intuit Inc. increased total revenue by 10% between the two years. This increase came from strong revenue gains in the Financial Management Solutions, Employee Management Solutions, Payment Solutions, and Consumer Tax segments.

In addition, vertical analysis could be performed on the segment disclosures as follows:

Segment	Recent Year Amount (in millions)	Recent Year Percent	Prior Year Amount (in millions)	Prior Year Percent
Financial Management Solutions	$ 691	16.6%	$ 622	16.5%
Employee Management Solutions	512	12.3	457	12.1
Payment Solutions	417	10.1	348	9.2
Consumer Tax	1,441	34.7	1,298	34.4
Accounting Professionals	423	10.2	399	10.6
Financial Institutions	362	8.7	346	9.2
Other Businesses	305	7.4	302	8.0
Total revenues	$4,151	100.0%	$3,772	100.0%

The preceding analysis shows that revenue in the Financial Management Solutions, Employee Management Solutions, Payment Solutions, and Consumer Tax segments increased as a percent of total revenues between the two years. The remaining segments all decreased as a percent of total revenues between the two years.

Both analyses together show that the largest segment, Consumer Tax, has increased revenues by 11% and has increased the segment's share of total revenues from 34.4% to 34.7% across the two years. In addition, the remaining segments are all showing strong revenue growth.

Example Exercise 5-5 Segment Analysis

Morse Company does business in two regional segments: East and West. The following annual revenue information was determined from the accounting system's invoice information:

Segment	2016	2015
East	$25,000	$20,000
West	50,000	60,000
Total revenues	$75,000	$80,000

Prepare horizontal and vertical analyses of the segments.

Follow My Example 5-5

Horizontal analysis:

Segment	2016	2015	Increase (Decrease) Amount	Increase (Decrease) Percent
East	$25,000	$20,000	$ 5,000	25.0%
West	50,000	60,000	(10,000)	(16.7)
Total revenues	$75,000	$80,000	$ (5,000)	(6.3)

Vertical analysis:

Segment	2016 Amount	2016 Percent	2015 Amount	2015 Percent
East	$25,000	33.3%	$20,000	25.0%
West	50,000	66.7	60,000	75.0
Total revenues	$75,000	100.0%	$80,000	100.0%

Practice Exercises: PE 5-5A, PE 5-5B

At a Glance 5

Define and describe an accounting system.

Key Points An accounting system is the methods and procedures for collecting, classifying, summarizing, and reporting a business's financial information. The three steps through which an accounting system evolves are: (1) analysis of information needs, (2) design of the system, and (3) implementation of the system design.

Learning Outcomes	Example Exercises	Practice Exercises
• Define an accounting system.		
• Describe the three steps for designing an accounting system: (1) analysis, (2) design, and (3) implementation.		

Journalize and post transactions in a manual accounting system that uses subsidiary ledgers and special journals.

Key Points Subsidiary ledgers may be used to maintain separate records for customers and creditors (vendors). A controlling account in the general ledger summarizes the subsidiary ledger accounts. The sum of the subsidiary ledger account balances must agree with the balance in the related controlling account.

Learning Outcomes	Example Exercises	Practice Exercises
• Prepare a revenue journal and post services provided on account to individual customer accounts and the column total to the corresponding general ledger accounts.	**EE5-1**	**PE5-1A, 5-1B**
• Prepare a cash receipts journal and post collections on account to individual customer accounts. Post Other Accounts column entries individually and special column totals to the corresponding general ledger accounts.	**EE5-2**	**PE5-2A, 5-2B**
• Prepare a purchases journal and post amounts owed to individual creditor accounts. Post Other Accounts column entries individually and special column totals to the corresponding general ledger accounts.	**EE5-3**	**PE5-3A, 5-3B**
• Prepare a cash payments journal and post the amounts paid to individual creditor accounts. Post Other Accounts column entries individually and special column totals to the corresponding general ledger accounts.	**EE5-4**	**PE5-4A, 5-4B**

OBJ 3 Describe and illustrate the use of a computerized accounting system.

Key Points Computerized accounting systems are similar to manual systems. The main advantages of a computerized accounting system are the simultaneous recording and posting of transactions, high degree of accuracy, and timeliness of reporting.

Learning Outcomes	Example Exercises	Practice Exercises
• Differentiate between a manual and a computerized accounting system.		
• Illustrate revenue and cash receipts transactions using QuickBooks.		

OBJ 4 Describe the basic features of e-commerce.

Key Points Using the Internet to perform business transactions is termed e-commerce. B2C e-commerce involves Internet transactions between a business and consumer, while B2B e-commerce involves Internet transactions between businesses. More elaborate e-commerce involves planning and coordinating suppliers, customers, and product design.

Learning Outcome	Example Exercises	Practice Exercises
• Define e-commerce and describe the major trends in e-commerce.		

OBJ 5 Use segment analysis in evaluating the operating performance of a company.

Key Points Businesses may be segmented by region, by product or service, or by type of customer. Segment revenues can be analyzed using horizontal and vertical analyses. Such analyses are useful to management for evaluating the causes of business performance.

Learning Outcome	Example Exercises	Practice Exercises
• Prepare horizontal and vertical analyses for business segments.	EE5-5	PE5-5A, 5-5B

Key Terms

accounting system (214)
accounts payable subsidiary ledger (215)
accounts receivable subsidiary ledger (215)
cash payments journal (225)
cash receipts journal (220)
controlling account (215)
e-commerce (231)
general journal (216)
general ledger (215)
internal controls (215)
invoice (217)
purchases journal (222)
revenue journal (217)
special journals (215)
subsidiary ledger (215)

Illustrative Problem

Selected transactions of O'Malley Co. for the month of May are as follows:

a.	May	1.	Issued Check No. 1001 in payment of rent for May, $1,200.
b.		2.	Purchased office supplies on account from McMillan Co., $3,600.
c.		4.	Issued Check No. 1003 in payment of freight charges on the supplies purchased on May 2, $320.
d.		8.	Provided services on account to Waller Co., Invoice No. 51, $4,500.
e.		9.	Issued Check No. 1005 for office supplies purchased, $450.
f.		10.	Received cash for office supplies sold to employees at cost, $120.
g.		11.	Purchased office equipment on account from Fender Office Products, $15,000.
h.		12.	Issued Check No. 1010 in payment of the supplies purchased from McMillan Co. on May 2, $3,600.
i.		16.	Provided services on account to Riese Co., Invoice No. 58, $8,000.
j.		18.	Received $4,500 from Waller Co. in payment of May 8 invoice.
k.		20.	Invested additional cash in the business, $10,000.
l.		25.	Provided services for cash, $15,900.
m.		30.	Issued Check No. 1040 for withdrawal of cash for personal use, $1,000.
n.		30.	Issued Check No. 1041 in payment of electricity and water invoices, $690.
o.		30.	Issued Check No. 1042 in payment of office and sales salaries for May, $15,800.
p.		31.	Journalized adjusting entries from the work sheet prepared for the fiscal year ended May 31.

O'Malley Co. maintains a revenue journal, a cash receipts journal, a purchases journal, a cash payments journal, and a general journal. In addition, accounts receivable and accounts payable subsidiary ledgers are used.

Instructions

1. Indicate the journal in which each of the preceding transactions, (a) through (p), would be recorded.
2. Indicate whether an account in the accounts receivable or accounts payable subsidiary ledgers would be affected for each of the preceding transactions.
3. Journalize transactions (b), (c), (d), (h), and (j) in the appropriate journals.

Solution

1. Journal	2. Subsidiary Ledger
a. Cash payments journal	
b. Purchases journal	Accounts payable ledger
c. Cash payments journal	
d. Revenue journal	Accounts receivable ledger
e. Cash payments journal	
f. Cash receipts journal	
g. Purchases journal	Accounts payable ledger
h. Cash payments journal	Accounts payable ledger
i. Revenue journal	Accounts receivable ledger
j. Cash receipts journal	Accounts receivable ledger
k. Cash receipts journal	
l. Cash receipts journal	
m. Cash payments journal	
n. Cash payments journal	
o. Cash payments journal	
p. General journal	

3.

Transaction (b):

Purchases Journal

Date		Account Credited	Post. Ref.	Accounts Payable Cr.	Office Supplies Dr.	Other Accounts Dr.	Post. Ref.	Amount
May	2	McMillan Co.		3,600	3,600			

Transactions (c) and (h):

Cash Payments Journal

Date		Ck. No.	Account Debited	Post. Ref.	Other Accounts Dr.	Accounts Payable Dr.	Cash Cr.
May	4	1003	Freight Expense		320		320
	12	1010	McMillan Co.			3,600	3,600

Transaction (d):

Revenue Journal

Date		Invoice No.	Account Debited	Post. Ref.	Accts. Rec. Dr. Fees Earned Cr.
May	8	51	Waller Co.		4,500

Transaction (j):

Cash Receipts Journal

Date		Account Credited	Post. Ref.	Other Accounts Cr.	Accounts Receivable Cr.	Cash Dr.
May	18	Waller Co.			4,500	4,500

Discussion Questions

1. Why would a company maintain separate accounts receivable ledgers for each customer, as opposed to maintaining a single accounts receivable ledger for all customers?
2. What are the major advantages of the use of special journals?
3. In recording 400 fees earned on account during a single month, how many times will it be necessary to write Fees Earned (a) if each transaction, including fees earned, is recorded individually in a two-column general journal; (b) if each transaction for fees earned is recorded in a revenue journal?

4. How many postings to Fees Earned for the month would be needed in Discussion Question 3 if the procedure described in (a) had been used; if the procedure described in (b) had been used?

5. During the current month, the following errors occurred in recording transactions in the purchases journal or in posting from it:

   a. An invoice for $1,875 of supplies from Kelly Co. was recorded as having been received from Kelley Co., another supplier.
   b. A credit of $420 to Blackstone Company was posted as $240 in the subsidiary ledger.
   c. An invoice for equipment of $4,800 was recorded as $4,000.
   d. The Accounts Payable column of the purchases journal was overstated by $3,600.

   How will each error come to the bookkeeper's attention, other than by chance discovery?

6. Assuming the use of a two-column general journal, a purchases journal, and a cash payments journal as illustrated in this chapter, indicate the journal in which each of the following transactions should be recorded:

   a. Purchase of office supplies on account.
   b. Purchase of supplies for cash.
   c. Purchase of store equipment on account.
   d. Payment of cash on account to creditor.
   e. Payment of cash for office supplies.

7. What is an electronic form, and how is it used in a computerized accounting system?

8. Do computerized systems use controlling accounts to verify the accuracy of the subsidiary accounts?

9. What happens to the special journal in a computerized accounting system that uses electronic forms?

10. How would e-commerce improve the revenue/collection cycle?

Practice Exercises

EE 5-1 p. 219

PE 5-1A Revenue journal

OBJ. 2

SHOW ME HOW

The following revenue transactions occurred during November:

Oct. 4. Issued Invoice No. 162 to Dawkins Co. for services provided on account, $320.
19. Issued Invoice No. 163 to City Electric Inc. for services provided on account, $245.
25. Issued Invoice No. 164 to Matthews Co. for services provided on account, $515.

Record these three transactions into the following revenue journal format:

REVENUE JOURNAL

Date	Invoice No.	Account Debited	Post. Ref.	Accts. Rec. Dr. Fees Earned Cr.

EE 5-1 p. 219

PE 5-1B Revenue journal

OBJ. 2

SHOW ME HOW

The following revenue transactions occurred during April:

Apr. 6. Issued Invoice No. 78 to Lemon Co. for services provided on account, $1,240.
11. Issued Invoice No. 79 to Hitchcock Inc. for services provided on account, $2,570.
19. Issued Invoice No. 80 to Fletcher Inc. for services provided on account, $990.

Record these three transactions into the following revenue journal format:

REVENUE JOURNAL

Date	Invoice No.	Account Debited	Post. Ref.	Accts. Rec. Dr. Fees Earned Cr.

SHOW ME HOW

EE 5-2 *p. 222*

PE 5-2A Accounts receivable subsidiary ledger

OBJ. 2

The debits and credits from two transactions are presented in the following customer account:

NAME *Horizon Entertainment*
ADDRESS *125 Wycoff Ave.*

Date	Item	Post. Ref.	Debit	Credit	Balance
Feb. 1	Balance	✓			280
22	Invoice 422	CR106		120	160
27	Invoice 445	R92	170		330

Describe each transaction and the source of each posting.

SHOW ME HOW

EE 5-2 *p. 222*

PE 5-2B Accounts receivable subsidiary ledger

OBJ. 2

The debits and credits from two transactions are presented in the following customer account:

NAME *Moravian Products Inc.*
ADDRESS *46 W. Main St.*

Date	Item	Post. Ref.	Debit	Credit	Balance
Aug. 1	Balance	✓			1,200
10	Invoice 119	R24	750		1,950
17	Invoice 106	CR46		610	1,340

Describe each transaction and the source of each posting.

EE 5-3 *p. 225*

PE 5-3A Purchases journal

OBJ. 2

The following purchase transactions occurred during March for Celebration Catering Service:

Mar. 11. Purchased party supplies for $610, on account from Party Hearty Supplies Inc.
16. Purchased party supplies for $312, on account from Fun 4 All Supplies Inc.
27. Purchased office furniture for $2,480, on account from Office Space Inc.

Record these transactions in the following purchases journal format:

PURCHASES JOURNAL

Date	Account Credited	Post. Ref.	Accounts Payable Cr.	Party Supplies Dr.	Other Accounts Dr.	Post. Ref.	Amount

EE 5-3 *p. 225*

PE 5-3B Purchases journal

OBJ. 2

The following purchase transactions occurred during November for Manheim Inc.:

Nov. 6. Purchased office supplies for $330, on account from Carry Out Supply Inc.
14. Purchased office equipment for $1,950, on account from Zell Computer Inc.
22. Purchased office supplies for $195, on account from Carry Out Supply Inc.

Record these transactions in the following purchases journal format:

PURCHASES JOURNAL

Date	Account Credited	Post. Ref.	Accounts Payable Cr.	Office Supplies Dr.	Other Accounts Dr.	Post. Ref.	Amount

EE 5-4 p. 228

PE 5-4A Accounts payable subsidiary ledger

OBJ. 2

SHOW ME HOW

The debits and credits from two transactions are presented in the following supplier's (creditor's) account:

NAME *Migrant Technology*
ADDRESS *2199 Commerce Place*

Date	Item	Post. Ref.	Debit	Credit	Balance
Nov. 1	Balance				9,400
11	Invoice 85	P8		1,845	11,245
22	Invoice 43	CP46	3,270		7,975

Describe each transaction and the source of each posting.

EE 5-4 p. 228

PE 5-4B Accounts payable subsidiary ledger

OBJ. 2

SHOW ME HOW

The debits and credits from two transactions are presented in the following supplier's (creditor's) account:

NAME *Colonial Inc.*
ADDRESS *5000 Grand Ave.*

Date	Item	Post. Ref.	Debit	Credit	Balance
Jan. 1	Balance				92
11	Invoice 122	CP71	64		28
26	Invoice 139	P55		72	100

Describe each transaction and the source of each posting.

EE 5-5 p. 233

PE 5-5A Segment analysis

OBJ. 5

SHOW ME HOW

McHale Company does business in two customer segments, Retail and Wholesale. The following annual revenue information was determined from the accounting system's invoice information:

	2016	2015
Retail	$126,000	$120,000
Wholesale	150,000	164,000
Total revenue	$276,000	$284,000

Prepare a horizontal and vertical analysis of the segments. Round to one decimal place.

EE 5-5 p. 233

PE 5-5B Segment analysis

OBJ. 5

SHOW ME HOW

Back Country Life, Inc., does business in two product segments, Camping and Fishing. The following annual revenue information was determined from the accounting system's invoice information:

	2016	2015
Camping	$280,000	$240,000
Fishing	140,000	160,000
Total revenue	$420,000	$400,000

Prepare a horizontal and vertical analysis of the segments. Round to one decimal place.

Exercises

EX 5-1 Identify postings from revenue journal — OBJ. 2

Using the following revenue journal for Zeta Services Inc., identify each of the posting references, indicated by a letter, as representing (1) posting to general ledger accounts or (2) posting to subsidiary ledger accounts:

REVENUE JOURNAL

Date	Invoice No.	Account Debited	Post. Ref.	Accounts Rec. Dr. Fees Earned Cr.
2016				
Mar. 1	112	Hazmat Safety Co.	(a)	$2,875
10	113	Masco Co.	(b)	980
20	114	Eco-Systems	(c)	1,700
27	115	Sunrise Enterprises	(d)	1,240
30				$6,795
				(e)

EX 5-2 Accounts receivable ledger — OBJ. 2

✔ d. Total accounts receivable, $7,275

SHOW ME HOW

Based on the data presented in Exercise 5-1, assume that the beginning balances for the customer accounts were zero, except for Sunrise Enterprises, which had a $480 beginning balance. In addition, there were no collections during the period.

a. Set up a T account for Accounts Receivable and T accounts for the four accounts needed in the customer ledger.
b. Post to the T accounts.
c. Determine the balance in the accounts.
d. Prepare a listing of the accounts receivable customer balances as of March 31, 2016.

EX 5-3 Identify journals — OBJ. 2

Assuming the use of a two-column (all-purpose) general journal, a revenue journal, and a cash receipts journal as illustrated in this chapter, indicate the journal in which each of the following transactions should be recorded:

a. Closing of drawing account at the end of the year.
b. Providing services for cash.
c. Sale of office supplies on account, at cost, to a neighboring business.
d. Receipt of cash from sale of office equipment.
e. Receipt of cash for rent.
f. Receipt of cash on account from a customer.
g. Providing services on account.
h. Investment of additional cash in the business by the owner.
i. Receipt of cash refund from overpayment of taxes.
j. Adjustment to record accrued salaries at the end of the year.

EX 5-4 Identify journals — OBJ. 2

Assuming the use of a two-column (all-purpose) general journal, a purchases journal, and a cash payments journal as illustrated in this chapter, indicate the journal in which each of the following transactions should be recorded:

a. Purchase of office supplies for cash.
b. Advance payment of a one-year fire insurance policy on the office.
c. Purchase of office equipment for cash.
d. Adjustment to prepaid insurance at the end of the month.

(Continued)

e. Adjustment to prepaid rent at the end of the month.
f. Adjustment to record accrued salaries at the end of the period.
g. Purchase of services on account.
h. Purchase of office supplies on account.
i. Adjustment to record depreciation at the end of the month.
j. Payment of six months' rent in advance.
k. Purchase of an office computer on account.

EX 5-5 Identify transactions in accounts receivable subsidiary ledger **OBJ. 2**

The debits and credits from three related transactions are presented in the following customer's account taken from the accounts receivable subsidiary ledger:

NAME *Mission Design*
ADDRESS *1319 Elm Street*

Date	Item	Post. Ref.	Debit	Credit	Balance
2016					
Apr. 3		R44	740		740
6		J11		60	680
24		CR81		680	—

Describe each transaction, and identify the source of each posting.

EX 5-6 Prepare journal entries in a revenue journal **OBJ. 2**

SHOW ME HOW

Global Services Company had the following transactions during the month of August:

Aug. 2. Issued Invoice No. 321 to Morgan Corp. for services rendered on account, $425.
3. Issued Invoice No. 322 to Mid States Inc. for services rendered on account, $260.
14. Issued Invoice No. 323 to Morgan Corp. for services rendered on account, $350.
22. Issued Invoice No. 324 to Rose Co. for services rendered on account, $690.
28. Collected Invoice No. 321 from Morgan Corp.

a. Record the August revenue transactions for Global Services Company into the following revenue journal format:

REVENUE JOURNAL

Date	Invoice No.	Account Debited	Post. Ref.	Accts. Rec. Dr. Fees Earned Cr.

b. What is the total amount posted to the accounts receivable and fees earned accounts from the revenue journal for August?

c. What is the August 31 balance of the Morgan Corp. customer account assuming a zero balance on August 1?

EX 5-7 Posting a revenue journal **OBJ. 2, 3**

SHOW ME HOW

The revenue journal for Sapling Consulting Inc. follows. The accounts receivable controlling account has a July 1, 2016, balance of $625 consisting of an amount due from Aladdin Co. There were no collections during July.

REVENUE JOURNAL **Page 12**

Date	Invoice No.	Account Debited	Post. Ref.	Accts. Rec. Dr. Fees Earned Cr.
2016				
July 4	355	Clearmark Co.		1,890
9	356	Life Star Inc.		3,410
18	357	Aladdin Co.		950
22	359	Clearmark Co.		3,660
31				9,910

a. Prepare a T account for the accounts receivable customer accounts.

b. Post the transactions from the revenue journal to the customer accounts, and determine their ending balances.

c. Prepare T accounts for the accounts receivable and fees earned accounts. Post control totals to the two accounts, and determine the ending balances.

d. Prepare a schedule of the customer account balances to verify the equality of the sum of the customer account balances and the accounts receivable controlling account balance.

e. How might a computerized system differ from a revenue journal in recording revenue transactions?

EX 5-8 Accounts receivable subsidiary ledger

OBJ. 2

✔ Accounts Receivable balance, August 31, $8,070

SHOW ME HOW

The revenue and cash receipts journals for Mirage Productions Inc. follow. The accounts receivable control account has a August 1, 2016, balance of $4,230 consisting of an amount due from Celestial Studios Inc.

REVENUE JOURNAL *Page 16*

Date	Invoice No.	Account Debited	Post. Ref.	Accts. Rec. Dr. Fees Earned Cr.
2016				
Aug. 6	1	Franklin Broadcasting Co.	✓	1,900
14	2	Gold Coast Media Inc.	✓	5,100
22	3	Franklin Broadcasting Co.	✓	2,350
25	4	Celestial Studios Inc.	✓	1,650
28	5	Amber Communications Inc.	✓	4,070
31				15,070
				(12) (41)

CASH RECEIPTS JOURNAL *Page 36*

Date	Account Credited	Post. Ref.	Fees Earned Cr.	Accts. Rec. Cr.	Cash Dr.
2016					
Aug. 6	Celestial Studios Inc.	✓	—	4,230	4,230
11	Fees Earned		3,200		3,200
18	Franklin Broadcasting Co.	✓	—	1,900	1,900
28	Gold Coast Media Inc.	✓	—	5,100	5,100
31			3,200	11,230	14,430
			(41)	(12)	(11)

Prepare a listing of the accounts receivable customer balances and verify that the total agrees with the ending balance of the accounts receivable controlling account.

EX 5-9 Revenue and cash receipts journals

OBJ. 2

SHOW ME HOW

Transactions related to revenue and cash receipts completed by Sycamore Inc. during the month of December 2016 are as follows:

Dec. 2. Issued Invoice No. 512 to Cadence Co., $775.
4. Received cash from CMI Inc., on account, for $230.
8. Issued Invoice No. 513 to Gabriel Co., $300.
12. Issued Invoice No. 514 to Ells Inc., $910.
19. Received cash from Ells Inc., on account, $605.
20. Issued Invoice No. 515 to Electronic Central Inc., $195.
28. Received cash from Marshall Inc. for services provided, $160.
29. Received cash from Cadence Co. for Invoice No. 512 of December 2.
31. Received cash from McCleary Co. for services provided, $110.

(Continued)

Prepare a single-column revenue journal and a cash receipts journal to record these transactions. Use the following column headings for the cash receipts journal: Fees Earned Cr., Accounts Receivable Cr., and Cash Dr. Place a check mark (✓) in the Post. Ref. column to indicate when the accounts receivable subsidiary ledger should be posted.

EX 5-10 Revenue and cash receipts journals **OBJ. 2**

✓ a. Revenue journal total, $8,700

Lasting Summer Inc. has $2,510 in the October 1 balance of the accounts receivable account consisting of $1,060 from Champion Co. and $1,450 from Wayfarer Co. Transactions related to revenue and cash receipts completed by Lasting Summer Inc. during the month of October 2016 are as follows:

Oct. 3. Issued Invoice No. 622 for services provided to Palace Corp., $2,890.
5. Received cash from Champion Co., on account, for $1,060.
8. Issued Invoice No. 623 for services provided to Sunny Style Inc., $1,940.
12. Received cash from Wayfarer Co., on account, for $1,450.
18. Issued Invoice No. 624 for services provided to Amex Services Inc., $2,970.
23. Received cash from Palace Corp. for Invoice No. 622 of October 3.
28. Issued Invoice No. 625 to Wayfarer Co., on account, for $900.
30. Received cash from Rogers Co. for services provided, $120.

a. Prepare a single-column revenue journal and a cash receipts journal to record these transactions. Use the following column headings for the cash receipts journal: Fees Earned Cr., Accounts Receivable Cr., and Cash Dr. Place a check mark (✓) in the Post. Ref. column to indicate when the accounts receivable subsidiary ledger should be posted.
b. Prepare a listing of the accounts receivable customer balances and verify that the total of the accounts receivable customer balances equals the balance of the accounts receivable controlling account on October 31, 2016.
c. Why does Lasting Summer Inc. use a subsidiary ledger for accounts receivable?

EX 5-11 Identify postings from purchases journal **OBJ. 2**

Using the following purchases journal, identify each of the posting references, indicated by a letter, as representing (1) a posting to a general ledger account, (2) a posting to a subsidiary ledger account, or (3) that no posting is required:

PURCHASES JOURNAL **Page 49**

Date		Account Credited	Post. Ref.	Accounts Payable Cr.	Store Supplies Dr.	Office Supplies Dr.	Other Accounts Dr.	Post. Ref.	Amount
2016									
Jan.	4	Coastal Equipment Co.	(a)	5,325			Warehouse Equipment	(g)	5,325
	6	Arrow Supply Co.	(b)	4,000		4,000			
	9	Thorton Products	(c)	1,875	1,600	275			
	14	Office Warehouse	(d)	2,200			Office Equipment	(h)	2,200
	20	Office Warehouse	(e)	6,000			Store Equipment	(i)	6,000
	25	Monroe Supply Co.	(f)	2,740	2,740				
	30			22,140	4,340	4,275			13,525
				(j)	(k)	(l)			(m)

EX 5-12 Identify postings from cash payments journal **OBJ. 2**

Using the following cash payments journal, identify each of the posting references, indicated by a letter, as representing (1) a posting to a general ledger account, (2) a posting to a subsidiary ledger account, or (3) that no posting is required.

CASH PAYMENTS JOURNAL — **Page 46**

Date	Ck. No.	Account Debited	Post. Ref.	Other Accounts Dr.	Accounts Payable Dr.	Cash Cr.
2016						
July 3	611	Energy Systems Co.	(a)		4,000	4,000
5	612	Utilities Expense	(b)	310		310
10	613	Prepaid Rent	(c)	3,200		3,200
16	614	Flowers to Go, Inc.	(d)		1,250	1,250
19	615	Advertising Expense	(e)	640		640
22	616	Office Equipment	(f)	3,600		3,600
25	617	Echo Co.	(g)		5,500	5,500
26	618	Office Supplies	(h)	250		250
31	619	Salaries Expense	(i)	1,750		1,750
31				9,750	10,750	20,500
				(j)	(k)	(l)

EX 5-13 Identify transactions in accounts payable subsidiary ledger — OBJ. 2

The debits and credits from three related transactions are presented in the following creditor's account taken from the accounts payable ledger:

NAME *Apex Performance Co.*
ADDRESS *101 W. Stratford Ave.*

Date	Item	Post. Ref.	Debit	Credit	Balance
2016					
May 6		P44		12,000	12,000
14		J12	150		11,850
16		CP23	11,850		—

Describe each transaction, and identify the source of each posting.

EX 5-14 Prepare journal entries in a purchases journal — OBJ. 2

SHOW ME HOW

Protection Services Inc. had the following transactions during the month of June:

June 4. Purchased office supplies from Office Universe Inc. on account, $490.
9. Purchased office equipment on account from Tek Village Inc., $2,790.
16. Purchased office supplies from Office Universe Inc. on account, $140.
21. Purchased office supplies from Paper-to-Go Inc. on account, $225.
27. Paid invoice on June 4 purchase from Office Universe Inc.

a. Record the June purchase transactions for Protection Services Inc. in the following purchases journal format:

PURCHASES JOURNAL

Date	Account Credited	Post. Ref.	Accts. Payable Cr.	Office Supplies Dr.	Other Accounts Dr.	Post. Ref.	Amount

b. What is the total amount posted to the accounts payable and office supplies accounts from the purchases journal for June?

c. What is the June 30 balance of the Office Universe Inc. creditor account assuming a zero balance on June 1?

EX 5-15 Posting a purchases journal — OBJ. 2, 3

✔ d. Total, $5,840

The purchases journal for Newmark Exterior Cleaners Inc. follows. The accounts payable account has a March 1, 2016, balance of $580 for an amount owed to Nicely Co. There were no payments made on creditor invoices during March.

(Continued)

PURCHASES JOURNAL — Page 16

Date		Account Credited	Post. Ref.	Accts. Payable Cr.	Cleaning Supplies Dr.	Other Accounts Dr.	Post. Ref.	Amount
2015								
Mar.	4	Enviro-Wash Supplies Inc.		690	690			
	15	Nicely Co.		325	325			
	20	Office Mate Inc.		3,860		Office Equipment		3,860
	26	Enviro-Wash Supplies Inc.		385	385			
	31			5,260	1,400			3,860

a. Prepare a T account for the accounts payable creditor accounts.
b. Post the transactions from the purchases journal to the creditor accounts, and determine their ending balances.
c. Prepare T accounts for the accounts payable control and cleaning supplies accounts. Post control totals to the two accounts, and determine their ending balances. Cleaning Supplies had a zero balance at the beginning of the month.
d. Prepare a schedule of the creditor account balances to verify the equality of the sum of the accounts payable creditor balances and the accounts payable controlling account balance.
e. How might a computerized accounting system differ from the use of a purchases journal in recording purchase transactions?

EX 5-16 Accounts payable subsidiary ledger

OBJ. 2

✔ Accts. Pay., June 30, $21,580

SHOW ME HOW

The cash payments and purchases journals for Outdoor Artisan Landscaping Co. follow. The accounts payable control account has an June 1, 2016, balance of $2,230, consisting of an amount owed to Augusta Sod Co.

CASH PAYMENTS JOURNAL — Page 31

Date		Ck. No.	Account Debited	Post. Ref.	Other Accounts Dr.	Accounts Payable Dr.	Cash Cr.
2015							
June	4	203	Augusta Sod Co.	✓		2,230	2,230
	5	204	Utilities Expense	54	440		440
	15	205	Home Centers Lumber Co.	✓		5,210	5,210
	24	206	Nu Lawn Fertilizer	✓		910	910
	30				440	8,350	8,790
					(✓)	(21)	(11)

PURCHASES JOURNAL — Page 22

Date		Account Credited	Post. Ref.	Accounts Payable Cr.	Landscaping Supplies Dr.	Other Accounts Dr.	Post. Ref.	Amount
2015								
June	3	Home Centers Lumber Co.	✓	5,210	5,210			
	7	Concrete Equipment Co.	✓	6,700		Equipment	18	6,700
	14	Nu Lawn Fertilizer	✓	910	910			
	24	Augusta Sod Co.	✓	6,450	6,450			
	29	Home Centers Lumber Co.	✓	8,430	8,430			
	30			27,700	21,000			6,700
				(21)	(14)			(✓)

Prepare a schedule of the accounts payable creditor balances, and determine that the total agrees with the ending balance of the accounts payable controlling account.

EX 5-17 Purchases and cash payments journals

OBJ. 2

✔ Purchases journal, Accts. Pay., Total, $1,045

SHOW ME HOW

Transactions related to purchases and cash payments completed by Brite Way Cleaning Services Inc. during the month of May 2016 are as follows:

May 1. Issued Check No. 57 to Liquid Klean Supplies Inc. in payment of account, $395.
3. Purchased cleaning supplies on account from Sani-Fresh Products Inc., $220.
8. Issued Check No. 58 to purchase equipment from Carson Equipment Sales, $3,150.

May 12. Purchased cleaning supplies on account from Porter Products Inc., $400.
15. Issued Check No. 59 to Bowman Electrical Service in payment of account, $165.
18. Purchased supplies on account from Liquid Klean Supplies Inc., $275.
20. Purchased electrical repair services from Bowman Electrical Service on account, $150.
26. Issued Check No. 60 to Sani-Fresh Products Inc. in payment of May 3 invoice.
31. Issued Check No. 61 in payment of salaries, $6,500.

Prepare a purchases journal and a cash payments journal to record these transactions. The forms of the journals are similar to those illustrated in the text. Place a check mark (✓) in the Post. Ref. column to indicate when the accounts payable subsidiary ledger should be posted. Brite Way Cleaning Services Inc. uses the following accounts:

Cash	11
Cleaning Supplies	14
Equipment	18
Accounts Payable	21
Salary Expense	51
Electrical Service Expense	53

EX 5-18 Purchases and cash payments journals **OBJ. 2**

Happy Tails Inc. has a June 1, 2016 accounts payable balance of $600, which consists of $360 due Labradore Inc. and $240 due Meow Mart Inc. Transactions related to purchases and cash payments completed by Happy Tails Inc. during the month of June 2016 are as follows:

June 4. Purchased pet supplies from Best Friend Supplies Inc. on account, $255.
6. Issued Check No. 345 to Labradore Inc. in payment of account, $360.
13. Purchased pet supplies from Poodle Pals Inc., $710.
18. Issued Check No. 346 to Meow Mart Inc. in payment of account, $240.
19. Purchased office equipment from Office Helper Inc. on account, $2,670.
23. Issued Check No. 347 to Best Friend Supplies Inc. in payment of account from purchase made on June 4.
27. Purchased pet supplies from Meow Mart Inc. on account, $400.
30. Issued Check No. 348 to Jennings Inc. for cleaning expenses, $65.

a. Prepare a purchases journal and a cash payments journal to record these transactions. The forms of the journals are similar to those used in the text. Place a check mark (✓) in the Post. Ref. column to indicate when the accounts payable subsidiary ledger should be posted. Happy Tails Inc. uses the following accounts:

Cash	11
Pet Supplies	14
Office Equipment	18
Accounts Payable	21
Cleaning Expense	54

b. Prepare a listing of accounts payable creditor balances on June 30, 2016. Verify that the total of the accounts payable creditor balances equals the balance of the accounts payable controlling account on June 30, 2016.
c. Why does Happy Tails Inc. use a subsidiary ledger for accounts payable?

EX 5-19 Error in accounts payable subsidiary ledger **OBJ. 2**

After Bunker Hill Assay Services Inc. had completed all postings for March in the current year (2016), the sum of the balances in the following accounts payable ledger did not agree with the $37,600 balance of the controlling account in the general ledger:

(*Continued*)

NAME *C. D. Greer and Son*
ADDRESS *972 S. Tenth Street*

Date	Item	Post. Ref.	Debit	Credit	Balance
2016					
Mar. 17		P30		3,750	3,750
27		P31		12,000	15,750

NAME *Carbon Supplies Inc.*
ADDRESS *1170 Mattis Avenue*

Date	Item	Post. Ref.	Debit	Credit	Balance
2016					
Mar. 1	Balance	✓			8,300
9		P30		7,000	14,000
12		J7	300		13,700
20		CP23	5,800		7,900

NAME *Cutler and Powell*
ADDRESS *717 Elm Street*

Date	Item	Post. Ref.	Debit	Credit	Balance
2016					
Mar. 1	Balance	✓			6,100
18		CP23	6,100		—
29		P31		7,800	7,800

NAME *Hudson Bay Minerals Co.*
ADDRESS *1240 W. Main Street*

Date	Item	Post. Ref.	Debit	Credit	Balance
2016					
Mar. 1	Balance	✓			4,750
10		CP22	4,750		—
17		P30		3,700	3,700
25		J7	3,000		1,700

NAME *Valley Power*
ADDRESS *915 E. Walnut Street*

Date	Item	Post. Ref.	Debit	Credit	Balance
2016					
Mar. 5		P30		3,150	3,150

Assuming that the controlling account balance of $36,600 has been verified as correct, (a) determine the error(s) in the preceding accounts and (b) prepare a listing of accounts payable creditor balances (from the corrected accounts payable subsidiary ledger).

EX 5-20 Identify postings from special journals **OBJ. 2**

Pinnacle Consulting Company makes most of its sales and purchases on credit. It uses the five journals described in this chapter (revenue, cash receipts, purchases, cash payments, and general journals). Identify the journal most likely used in recording the postings for selected transactions indicated by letter in the T accounts, as follows:

Cash

	Debit		Credit
a.	10,940	b.	6,500

Accounts Receivable

	Debit		Credit
c.	11,790	a.	10,940

Office Supplies

	Debit		Credit
d.	7,400		

Prepaid Rent

	Debit		Credit
		e.	1,200

Accounts Payable

	Debit		Credit
b.	6,500	d.	7,400

Fees Earned

	Debit		Credit
		c.	11,790

Rent Expense

	Debit		Credit
e.	1,200		

EX 5-21 Cash receipts journal **OBJ. 2**

The following cash receipts journal headings have been suggested for a small service firm. List the errors you find in the headings.

CASH RECEIPTS JOURNAL **Page 12**

Date	Account Credited	Post. Ref.	Fees Earned Cr.	Accts. Rec. Cr.	Cash Cr.	Other Accounts Dr.

EX 5-22 Computerized accounting systems **OBJ. 3**

Most computerized accounting systems use electronic forms to record transaction information, such as the invoice form illustrated at the top of Exhibit 7 in this chapter.

a. Identify the key input fields (spaces) in an electronic invoice form.

b. What accounts are posted from an electronic invoice form?

c. Why aren't special journal totals posted to control accounts at the end of the month in an electronic accounting system?

EX 5-23 Computerized accounting systems and e-commerce **OBJ. 3, 4**

Apple Inc.'s iTunes® provides digital products, such as music, video, and software, which can be downloaded to portable devices such as the iPhone® and iPad®. Purchases made on iTunes are made with credit cards that are on file with the credit card processing company. Such transactions are considered cash transactions. Once the purchases are made, consumers can download the requested digital products to their portable devices for their enjoyment and the charges will show up on their credit card bills.

a. What kind of e-commerce application is described by Apple iTunes?

b. Assume you purchased 12 songs for $1.25 each on iTunes. Provide the journal entry generated by Apple's e-commerce application.

c. If a special journal were used, what type of special journal would be used to record this sales transaction?

d. If an electronic form were used, what type of electronic form would be used to record this sales transaction?

e. Would it be appropriate for Apple to use either special journals or electronic forms for sales transactions from iTunes? Explain.

EX 5-24 E-commerce **OBJ. 4**

For each of the following companies, determine what they primarily sell, and whether their e-commerce strategy is primarily business-to-consumer (B2C), business-to-business (B2B), or both. Use the Internet to investigate each company's site in conducting your research.

a. Amazon.com

b. Dell Inc.

c. DuPont

d. Intuit Inc.

e. L.L. Bean, Inc.

f. W.W. Grainger, Inc.

EX 5-25 Segment revenue horizontal analysis **OBJ. 5**

Starbucks Corporation reported the following geographical segment revenues for a recent and a prior fiscal year:

	Recent Year (in millions, rounded)	Prior Year (in millions, rounded)
Americas	$ 9,936	$ 9,065
EMEA*	1,141	1,047
China/Asia Pacific	721	552
Channel Development**	1,292	860
Other	209	176
Total	$13,299	$11,700

* Europe, Middle East, and Africa
** Sells packaged coffee and teas globally

a. Prepare a horizontal analysis of the segment data using the prior year as the base year. Round whole percents to one decimal place.

b. Prepare a vertical analysis of the segment data. Round whole percents to one decimal place.

c. What conclusions can be drawn from your analyses?

EX 5-26 Segment revenue vertical analysis **OBJ. 5**

News Corporation is one of the world's largest entertainment companies that includes Twentieth Century Fox films, Fox Broadcasting, Fox News, the FX, and various satellite, cable, and publishing properties. The company provided revenue disclosures by its major product segments in the notes to its financial statements as follows:

Major Product Segments	For a Recent Year (in millions)
Cable Network Programming	$ 9,132
Filmed Entertainment	7,302
Television	4,734
Direct Broadcast Satellite Television	3,672
Publishing	8,248
Other	618
Total revenues	$33,706

a. Provide a vertical analysis of the product segment revenue. Round whole percents to one decimal place.

b. Are the revenues of News Corporation diversified or concentrated within a product segment? Explain.

EX 5-27 Segment revenue horizontal and vertical analyses **OBJ. 5**

The comparative regional segment revenues for **McDonald's Corporation** are as follows:

	Recent Year (in millions)	Prior Year (in millions)
United States	$ 8,814	$ 8,528
Europe	10,827	10,886
APMEA*	6,391	6,020
Other Countries & Corporate	1,535	1,572
Total revenues	$27,567	$27,006

* APMEA = Asia/Pacific, Middle East, Africa

a. Provide a horizontal analysis of the regional segment revenues using the prior year as the base year. Round whole percents to one decimal place.

b. Provide a vertical analysis of the regional segment revenues for both years. Round whole percents to one decimal place.

c. What conclusions can be drawn from your analyses?

Problems: Series A

PR 5-1A Revenue journal; accounts receivable subsidiary and general ledgers **OBJ. 2, 3**

✔ 1. Revenue journal, total fees earned, $1,170

Sage Learning Centers was established on July 20, 2016, to provide educational services. The services provided during the remainder of the month are as follows:

July 21. Issued Invoice No. 1 to J. Dunlop for $115 on account.
22. Issued Invoice No. 2 to K. Tisdale for $350 on account.
24. Issued Invoice No. 3 to T. Quinn for $85 on account.
25. Provided educational services, $300, to K. Tisdale in exchange for educational supplies.
27. Issued Invoice No. 4 to F. Mintz for $225 on account.
30. Issued Invoice No. 5 to D. Chase for $170 on account.
30. Issued Invoice No. 6 to K. Tisdale for $120 on account.
31. Issued Invoice No. 7 to T. Quinn for $105 on account.

Instructions

1. Journalize the transactions for July, using a single-column revenue journal and a two-column general journal. Post to the following customer accounts in the accounts receivable ledger, and insert the balance immediately after recording each entry: D. Chase; J. Dunlop; F. Mintz; T. Quinn; K. Tisdale.
2. Post the revenue journal and the general journal to the following accounts in the general ledger, inserting the account balances only after the last postings:

   12 Accounts Receivable
   13 Supplies
   41 Fees Earned

3. a. What is the sum of the balances of the customer accounts in the subsidiary ledger at July 31?
   b. What is the balance of the accounts receivable controlling account at July 31?
4. Assume Sage Learning Centers began using a computerized accounting system to record the sales transactions on August 1. What are some of the benefits of the computerized system over the manual system?

PR 5-2A Revenue and cash receipts journals; accounts receivable subsidiary and general ledgers **OBJ. 2, 3**

✔ 3. Total cash receipts, $37,600

General Ledger

SHOW ME HOW

Transactions related to revenue and cash receipts completed by Albany Architects Co. during the period November 2–30, 2016, are as follows:

Nov. 2. Issued Invoice No. 793 to Ohr Co., $5,650.
5. Received cash from Mendez Co. for the balance owed on its account.
6. Issued Invoice No. 794 to Rahal Co., $2,450.
13. Issued Invoice No. 795 to Shilo Co., $3,980.

Post revenue and collections to the accounts receivable subsidiary ledger.

15. Received cash from Rahal Co. for the balance owed on November 1.
16. Issued Invoice No. 796 to Rahal Co., $6,500.

Post revenue and collections to the accounts receivable subsidiary ledger.

19. Received cash from Ohr Co. for the balance due on invoice of November 2.
20. Received cash from Rahal Co. for balance due on invoice of November 6.
22. Issued Invoice No. 797 to Mendez Co., $8,040.
25. Received $3,000 note receivable in partial settlement of the balance due on the Shilo Co. account.
30. Recorded cash fees earned, $13,270.

Post revenue and collections to the accounts receivable subsidiary ledger.

(Continued)

Instructions

1. Insert the following balances in the general ledger as of November 1:

11	Cash	$11,350
12	Accounts Receivable	16,230
14	Notes Receivable	6,000
41	Fees Earned	—

2. Insert the following balances in the accounts receivable subsidiary ledger as of November 1:

Mendez Co.	$9,460
Ohr Co.	—
Rahal Co.	6,770
Shilo Co.	—

3. Prepare a single-column revenue journal (p. 40) and a cash receipts journal (p. 36). Use the following column headings for the cash receipts journal: Fees Earned Cr., Accounts Receivable Cr., and Cash Dr. The Fees Earned column is used to record cash fees. Insert a check mark (✓) in the Post. Ref. column when recording cash fees.
4. Using the two special journals and the two-column general journal (p. 1), journalize the transactions for November. Post to the accounts receivable subsidiary ledger, and insert the balances at the points indicated in the narrative of transactions. Determine the balance in the customer's account before recording a cash receipt.
5. Total each of the columns of the special journals, and post the individual entries and totals to the general ledger. Insert account balances after the last posting.
6. Determine that the sum of the customer balances agrees with the accounts receivable controlling account in the general ledger.
7. Why would an automated system omit postings to a controlling account as performed in step 5 for Accounts Receivable?

PR 5-3A Purchases, accounts payable subsidiary account, and accounts payable ledger

OBJ. 2, 4

✓ 5b. $18,110

General Ledger

SHOW ME HOW

Sterling Forest Landscaping designs and installs landscaping. The landscape designers and office staff use office supplies, while field supplies (rock, bark, etc.) are used in the actual landscaping. Purchases on account completed by Sterling Forest Landscaping during October 2016 are as follows:

Oct. 2. Purchased office supplies on account from Meade Co., $400.
5. Purchased office equipment on account from Peach Computers Co., $3,980.
9. Purchased office supplies on account from Executive Office Supply Co., $320.
13. Purchased field supplies on account from Yamura Co., $1,420.
14. Purchased field supplies on account from Omni Co., $2,940.
17. Purchased field supplies on account from Yamura Co., $1,890.
24. Purchased field supplies on account from Omni Co., $3,880.
29. Purchased office supplies on account from Executive Office Supply Co., $310.
31. Purchased field supplies on account from Omni Co., $1,800.

Instructions

1. Insert the following balances in the general ledger as of October 1:

14	Field Supplies	$ 5,920
15	Office Supplies	750
18	Office Equipment	12,300
21	Accounts Payable	1,170

2. Insert the following balances in the accounts payable subsidiary ledger as of October 1:

Executive Office Supply Co.	$390
Meade Co.	780
Omni Co.	—
Peach Computers Co.	—
Yamura Co.	—

3. Journalize the transactions for October, using a purchases journal (p. 30) similar to the one illustrated in this chapter. Prepare the purchases journal with columns for Accounts Payable, Field Supplies, Office Supplies, and Other Accounts. Post to the creditor accounts in the accounts payable subsidiary ledger immediately after each entry.
4. Post the purchases journal to the accounts in the general ledger.
5. a. What is the sum of the creditor balances in the subsidiary ledger at October 31?

   b. What is the balance of the accounts payable controlling account at October 31?
6. What type of e-commerce application would be used to plan and coordinate transactions with suppliers?

✔ 1. Total cash payments, $203,940

General Ledger

PR 5-4A Purchases and cash payments journals; accounts payable subsidiary and general ledgers **OBJ. 2**

AquaFresh Water Testing Service was established on April 16, 2016. AquaFresh uses field equipment and field supplies (chemicals and other supplies) to analyze water for unsafe contaminants in streams, lakes, and ponds. Transactions related to purchases and cash payments during the remainder of April are as follows:

April 16. Issued Check No. 1 in payment of rent for the remainder of April, $3,500.
16. Purchased field supplies on account from Hydro Supply Co., $5,340.
16. Purchased field equipment on account from Pure Equipment Co., $21,450.
17. Purchased office supplies on account from Best Office Supply Co., $510.
19. Issued Check No. 2 in payment of field supplies, $3,340, and office supplies, $400.

Post the journals to the accounts payable subsidiary ledger.

23. Purchased office supplies on account from Best Office Supply Co., $660.
23. Issued Check No. 3 to purchase land, $140,000.
24. Issued Check No. 4 to Hydro Supply Co. in payment of April 16 invoice, $5,340.
26. Issued Check No. 5 to Pure Equipment Co. in payment of April 16 invoice, $21,450.

Post the journals to the accounts payable subsidiary ledger.

30. Acquired land in exchange for field equipment having a cost of $12,000.
30. Purchased field supplies on account from Hydro Supply Co., $7,650.
30. Issued Check No. 6 to Best Office Supply Co. in payment of April 17 invoice, $510.
30. Purchased the following from Pure Equipment Co. on account: field supplies, $1,340, and field equipment, $4,700.
30. Issued Check No. 7 in payment of salaries, $29,400.

Post the journals to the accounts payable subsidiary ledger.

Instructions

1. Journalize the transactions for April. Use a purchases journal and a cash payments journal, similar to those illustrated in this chapter, and a two-column general journal. Use debit columns for Field Supplies, Office Supplies, and Other Accounts in the purchases journal. Refer to the following partial chart of accounts:

11	Cash	19	Land
14	Field Supplies	21	Accounts Payable
15	Office Supplies	61	Salary Expense
17	Field Equipment	71	Rent Expense

At the points indicated in the narrative of transactions, post to the following accounts in the accounts payable subsidiary ledger:

Best Office Supply Co.
Hydro Supply Co.
Pure Equipment Co.

(Continued)

2. Post the individual entries (Other Accounts columns of the purchases journal and the cash payments journal and both columns of the general journal) to the appropriate general ledger accounts.
3. Total each of the columns of the purchases journal and the cash payments journal, and post the appropriate totals to the general ledger. (Because the problem does not include transactions related to cash receipts, the cash account in the ledger will have a credit balance.)
4. Prepare a schedule of the accounts payable creditor balances.
5. Why might AquaFresh consider using a subsidiary ledger for the field equipment?

PR 5-5A All journals and general ledger; trial balance **OBJ. 2**

✔ 2. Total cash receipts, $57,430

General Ledger

The transactions completed by Revere Courier Company during December 2016, the first month of the fiscal year, were as follows:

Dec. 1. Issued Check No. 610 for December rent, $4,500.
2. Issued Invoice No. 940 to Capps Co., $1,980.
3. Received check for $5,100 from Trimble Co. in payment of account.
5. Purchased a vehicle on account from Boston Transportation, $39,500.
6. Purchased office equipment on account from Austin Computer Co., $4,800.
6. Issued Invoice No. 941 to Dawar Co., $5,680.
9. Issued Check No. 611 for fuel expense, $800.
10. Received check from Sing Co. in payment of $4,850 invoice.
10. Issued Check No. 612 for $360 to Office To Go Inc. in payment of invoice.
10. Issued Invoice No. 942 to Joy Co., $2,140.
11. Issued Check No. 613 for $3,240 to Essential Supply Co. in payment of account.
11. Issued Check No. 614 for $650 to Porter Co. in payment of account.
12. Received check from Capps Co. in payment of $1,980 invoice of December 2.
13. Issued Check No. 615 to Boston Transportation in payment of $39,500 balance of December 5.
16. Issued Check No. 616 for $40,900 for cash purchase of a vehicle.
16. Cash fees earned for December 1–16, $21,700.
17. Issued Check No. 617 for miscellaneous administrative expense, $600.
18. Purchased maintenance supplies on account from Essential Supply Co., $1,750.
19. Purchased the following on account from McClain Co.: maintenance supplies, $1,500; office supplies, $325.
20. Issued Check No. 618 in payment of advertising expense, $1,990.
20. Used $3,600 maintenance supplies to repair delivery vehicles.
23. Purchased office supplies on account from Office To Go Inc., $440.
24. Issued Invoice No. 943 to Sing Co., $6,400.
24. Issued Check No. 619 to S. Holmes as a personal withdrawal, $3,200.
25. Issued Invoice No. 944 to Dawar Co., $5,720.
25. Received check for $4,100 from Trimble Co. in payment of balance.
26. Issued Check No. 620 to Austin Computer Co. in payment of $4,800 invoice of December 6.
30. Issued Check No. 621 for monthly salaries as follows: driver salaries, $16,900; office salaries, $7,600.
31. Cash fees earned for December 17–31, $19,700.
31. Issued Check No. 622 in payment for office supplies, $310.

Instructions

1. Enter the following account balances in the general ledger as of December 1:

11	Cash	$160,900	32	S. Holmes, Drawing	—
12	Accounts Receivable	14,050	41	Fees Earned	—
14	Maintenance Supplies	10,850	51	Driver Salaries Expense	—
15	Office Supplies	4,900	52	Maintenance Supplies Exp.	—
16	Office Equipment	28,500	53	Fuel Expense	—
17	Accum. Depr.—Office Equip.	6,900	61	Office Salaries Expense	—
18	Vehicles	95,900	62	Rent Expense	—
19	Accum. Depr.—Vehicles	14,700	63	Advertising Expense	—
21	Accounts Payable	4,250	64	Miscellaneous Administrative Expense	—
31	S. Holmes, Capital	289,250			

2. Journalize the transactions for December 2016, using the following journals similar to those illustrated in this chapter: cash receipts journal (p. 31), purchases journal (p. 37, with columns for Accounts Payable, Maintenance Supplies, Office Supplies, and Other Accounts), single-column revenue journal (p. 35), cash payments journal (p. 34), and two-column general journal (p. 1). Assume that the daily postings to the individual accounts in the accounts payable subsidiary ledger and the accounts receivable subsidiary ledger have been made.
3. Post the appropriate individual entries to the general ledger.
4. Total each of the columns of the special journals, and post the appropriate totals to the general ledger; insert the account balances.
5. Prepare a trial balance.

Problems: Series B

PR 5-1B Revenue journal; accounts receivable subsidiary and general ledgers OBJ. 2, 3

✔ 1. Revenue journal, total fees earned, $2,875

Guardian Security Services was established on January 15, 2016, to provide security services. The services provided during the remainder of the month are as follows:

Jan. 18. Issued Invoice No. 1 to Murphy Co. for $490 on account.
20. Issued Invoice No. 2 to Qwik-Mart Co. for $340 on account.
24. Issued Invoice No. 3 to Hopkins Co. for $750 on account.
27. Issued Invoice No. 4 to Carson Co. for $680 on account.
28. Issued Invoice No. 5 to Amber Waves Co. for $120 on account.
28. Provided security services, $100, to Qwik-Mart Co. in exchange for supplies.
30. Issued Invoice No. 6 to Qwik-Mart Co. for $200 on account.
31. Issued Invoice No. 7 to Hopkins Co. for $295 on account.

Instructions

1. Journalize the transactions for January, using a single-column revenue journal and a two-column general journal. Post to the following customer accounts in the accounts receivable ledger, and insert the balance immediately after recording each entry: Amber Waves Co.; Carson Co.; Hopkins Co.; Murphy Co.; Qwik-Mart Co.
2. Post the revenue journal to the following accounts in the general ledger, inserting the account balances only after the last postings:

    12 Accounts Receivable
    14 Supplies
    41 Fees Earned

3. a. What is the sum of the balances of the customer accounts in the subsidiary ledger at January 31?
   b. What is the balance of the accounts receivable controlling account at January 31?

(Continued)

4. Assume Guardian Security Services began using a computerized accounting system to record the sales transactions on February 1. What are some of the benefits of the computerized system over the manual system?

PR 5-2B Revenue and cash receipts journals; accounts receivable subsidiary and general ledgers

OBJ. 2, 3

✔ 3. Total cash receipts, $9,270

General Ledger

SHOW ME HOW

Transactions related to revenue and cash receipts completed by Sterling Engineering Services during the period June 2–30, 2016, are as follows:

June 2. Issued Invoice No. 717 to Yee Co., $1,430.
3. Received cash from Auto-Flex Co. for the balance owed on its account.
7. Issued Invoice No. 718 to Cooper Development Co., $670.
10. Issued Invoice No. 719 to Ridge Communities, $2,840.
Post revenue and collections to the accounts receivable subsidiary ledger.
14. Received cash from Cooper Development Co. for the balance owed on June 1.
16. Issued Invoice No. 720 to Cooper Development Co., $400.
Post revenue and collections to the accounts receivable subsidiary ledger.
18. Received cash from Yee Co. for the balance due on invoice of June 2.
20. Received cash from Cooper Development Co. for invoice of June 7.
23. Issued Invoice No. 721 to Auto-Flex Co., $860.
30. Recorded cash fees earned, $4,520.
30. Received office equipment of $1,800 in partial settlement of balance due on the Ridge Communities account.
Post revenue and collections to the accounts receivable subsidiary ledger.

Instructions

1. Insert the following balances in the general ledger as of June 1:

11	Cash	$18,340
12	Accounts Receivable	2,650
18	Office Equipment	34,700
41	Fees Earned	—

2. Insert the following balances in the accounts receivable subsidiary ledger as of June 1:

Auto-Flex Co.	$1,670
Cooper Development Co.	980
Ridge Communities	—
Yee Co.	—

3. Prepare a single-column revenue journal (p. 40) and a cash receipts journal (p. 36). Use the following column headings for the cash receipts journal: Fees Earned Cr., Accounts Receivable Cr., and Cash Dr. The Fees Earned column is used to record cash fees. Insert a check mark (✓) in the Post. Ref. column when recording cash fees.
4. Using the two special journals and the two-column general journal (p. 1), journalize the transactions for June. Post to the accounts receivable subsidiary ledger, and insert the balances at the points indicated in the narrative of transactions. Determine the balance in the customer's account before recording a cash receipt.
5. Total each of the columns of the special journals, and post the individual entries and totals to the general ledger. Insert account balances after the last posting.
6. Determine that the sum of the customer accounts agrees with the accounts receivable controlling account in the general ledger.
7. Why would an automated system omit postings to a control account as performed in step 5 for Accounts Receivable?

PR 5-3B Purchases, accounts payable account, and accounts payable subsidiary ledger

OBJ. 2, 4

✔ 5a. $31,300

General Ledger

SHOW ME HOW

Plumb Line Surveyors provides survey work for construction projects. The office staff use office supplies, while surveying crews use field supplies. Purchases on account completed by Plumb Line Surveyors during May 2016 are as follows:

May 1. Purchased field supplies on account from Wendell Co., $3,240.
3. Purchased office supplies on account from Lassiter Co., $340.
8. Purchased field supplies on account from Tri Cities Supplies, $4,500.
12. Purchased field supplies on account from Wendell Co., $3,670.
15. Purchased office supplies on account from J-Mart Co., $500.
19. Purchased office equipment on account from Accu-Vision Supply Co., $8,150.
23. Purchased field supplies on account from Tri Cities Supplies, $2,450.
26. Purchased office supplies on account from J-Mart Co., $265.
30. Purchased field supplies on account from Tri Cities Supplies, $3,040.

Instructions

1. Insert the following balances in the general ledger as of May 1:

14	Field Supplies	$ 6,200
15	Office Supplies	1,490
18	Office Equipment	19,400
21	Accounts Payable	5,145

2. Insert the following balances in the accounts payable subsidiary ledger as of May 1:

Accu-Vision Supply Co.	$3,900
J-Mart Co.	730
Lassiter Co.	515
Tri Cities Supplies	—
Wendell Co.	—

3. Journalize the transactions for May, using a purchases journal (p. 30) similar to the one illustrated in this chapter. Prepare the purchases journal with columns for Accounts Payable, Field Supplies, Office Supplies, and Other Accounts. Post to the creditor accounts in the accounts payable subsidiary ledger immediately after each entry.
4. Post the purchases journal to the accounts in the general ledger.
5. a. What is the sum of the creditor balances in the subsidiary ledger at May 31?
   b. What is the balance of the accounts payable controlling account at May 31?
6. What type of e-commerce application would be used to plan and coordinate transactions with suppliers?

PR 5-4B Purchases and cash payments journals; accounts payable subsidiary and general ledgers

OBJ. 2

✔ 1. Total cash payments, $327,920

General Ledger

West Texas Exploration Co. was established on October 15, 2016, to provide oil-drilling services. West Texas uses field equipment (rigs and pipe) and field supplies (drill bits and lubricants) in its operations. Transactions related to purchases and cash payments during the remainder of October are as follows:

Oct. 16. Issued Check No. 1 in payment of rent for the remainder of October, $7,000.
16. Purchased field equipment on account from Petro Services Inc., $32,600.
17. Purchased field supplies on account from Midland Supply Co., $9,780.
18. Issued Check No. 2 in payment of field supplies, $4,570, and office supplies, $650.
20. Purchased office supplies on account from A-One Office Supply Co., $1,320.
Post the journals to the accounts payable subsidiary ledger.
24. Issued Check No. 3 to Petro Services Inc., in payment of October 16 invoice.

(*Continued*)

Oct. 26. Issued Check No. 4 to Midland Supply Co. in payment of October 17 invoice.
28. Issued Check No. 5 to purchase land, $240,000.
28. Purchased office supplies on account from A-One Office Supply Co., $3,670.
Post the journals to the accounts payable subsidiary ledger.
30. Purchased the following from Petro Services Inc. on account: field supplies, $25,300 and office equipment, $5,500.
30. Issued Check No. 6 to A-One Office Supply Co. in payment of October 20 invoice.
30. Purchased field supplies on account from Midland Supply Co., $12,450.
31. Issued Check No. 7 in payment of salaries, $32,000.
31. Rented building for one year in exchange for field equipment having a cost of $15,000.
Post the journals to the accounts payable subsidiary ledger.

Instructions

1. Journalize the transactions for October. Use a purchases journal and a cash payments journal, similar to those illustrated in this chapter, and a two-column general journal. Set debit columns for Field Supplies, Office Supplies, and Other Accounts in the purchases journal. Refer to the following partial chart of accounts:

11	Cash	18	Office Equipment
14	Field Supplies	19	Land
15	Office Supplies	21	Accounts Payable
16	Prepaid Rent	61	Salary Expense
17	Field Equipment	71	Rent Expense

   At the points indicated in the narrative of transactions, post to the following subsidiary accounts in the accounts payable ledger:

   A-One Office Supply Co.
   Midland Supply Co.
   Petro Services Inc.

2. Post the individual entries (Other Accounts columns of the purchases journal and the cash payments journal; both columns of the general journal) to the appropriate general ledger accounts.
3. Total each of the columns of the purchases journal and the cash payments journal, and post the appropriate totals to the general ledger. (Because the problem does not include transactions related to cash receipts, the cash account in the ledger will have a credit balance.)
4. Sum the balances of the accounts payable creditor balances.
5. Why might West Texas consider using a subsidiary ledger for the field equipment?

PR 5-5B All journals and general ledger; trial balance **OBJ. 2**

✔ 2. Total cash receipts, $96,050

General Ledger

The transactions completed by AM Express Company during March 2016, the first month of the fiscal year, were as follows:

Mar. 1. Issued Check No. 205 for March rent, $2,450.
2. Purchased a vehicle on account from McIntyre Sales Co., $26,900.
3. Purchased office equipment on account from Office Mate Inc., $1,570.
5. Issued Invoice No. 91 to Ellis Co., $7,000.
6. Received check for $7,950 from Chavez Co. in payment of invoice.
7. Issued Invoice No. 92 to Trent Co., $9,840.
9. Issued Check No. 206 for fuel expense, $820.
10. Received check for $10,000 from Sajeev Co. in payment of invoice.
10. Issued Check No. 207 to Office City in payment of $450 invoice.

Mar. 10. Issued Check No. 208 to Bastille Co. in payment of $1,890 invoice.

11. Issued Invoice No. 93 to Jarvis Co., $7,200.

11. Issued Check No. 209 to Porter Co. in payment of $415 invoice.

12. Received check for $7,000 from Ellis Co. in payment of March 5 invoice.

13. Issued Check No. 210 to McIntyre Sales Co. in payment of $26,900 invoice of March 2.

16. Cash fees earned for March 1–16, $26,800.

16. Issued Check No. 211 for purchase of a vehicle, $28,500.

17. Issued Check No. 212 for miscellaneous administrative expense, $4,680.

18. Purchased maintenance supplies on account from Bastille Co., $2,430.

18. Received check for rent revenue on office space, $900.

19. Purchased the following on account from Master Supply Co.: maintenance supplies, $2,640, and office supplies, $1,500.

20. Issued Check No. 213 in payment of advertising expense, $8,590.

20. Used maintenance supplies with a cost of $4,400 to repair vehicles.

21. Purchased office supplies on account from Office City, $990.

24. Issued Invoice No. 94 to Sajeev Co., $9,200.

25. Received check for $14,000 from Chavez Co. in payment of invoice.

25. Issued Invoice No. 95 to Trent Co., $6,300.

26. Issued Check No. 214 to Office Mate Inc. in payment of $1,570 invoice of March 3.

27. Issued Check No. 215 to J. Wu as a personal withdrawal, $4,000.

30. Issued Check No. 216 in payment of driver salaries, $33,300.

31. Issued Check No. 217 in payment of office salaries, $21,200.

31. Issued Check No. 218 for office supplies, $600.

31. Cash fees earned for March 17–31, $29,400.

Instructions

1. Enter the following account balances in the general ledger as of March 1:

11	Cash	$ 65,200	32	J. Wu, Drawing	—
12	Accounts Receivable	31,950	41	Fees Earned	—
14	Maintenance Supplies	7,240	42	Rent Revenue	—
15	Office Supplies	3,690	51	Driver Salaries Expense	—
16	Office Equipment	17,300	52	Maintenance Supplies Expense	—
17	Accum. Depr.—Office Equip.	4,250	53	Fuel Expense	—
18	Vehicles	62,400	61	Office Salaries Expense	—
19	Accum. Depr.—Vehicles	17,800	62	Rent Expense	—
21	Accounts Payable	2,755	63	Advertising Expense	—
31	J. Wu, Capital	162,975	64	Miscellaneous Administrative Exp.	—

2. Journalize the transactions for March 2016, using the following journals similar to those illustrated in this chapter: single-column revenue journal (p. 35), cash receipts journal (p. 31), purchases journal (p. 37, with columns for Accounts Payable, Maintenance Supplies, Office Supplies, and Other Accounts), cash payments journal (p. 34), and two-column general journal (p. 1). Assume that the daily postings to the individual accounts in the accounts payable subsidiary ledger and the accounts receivable subsidiary ledger have been made.
3. Post the appropriate individual entries to the general ledger.
4. Total each of the columns of the special journals, and post the appropriate totals to the general ledger; insert the account balances.
5. Prepare a trial balance.

Cases & Projects

CP 5-1 Ethics and professional conduct in business

Netbooks Inc. provides accounting applications for business customers on the Internet for a monthly subscription. Netbooks customers run their accounting system on the Internet; thus, the business data and accounting software reside on the servers of Netbooks Inc. The senior management of Netbooks believes that once a customer begins to use Netbooks, it would be very difficult to cancel the service. That is, customers are "locked in" because it would be difficult to move the business data from Netbooks to another accounting application, even though the customers own their own data. Therefore, Netbooks has decided to entice customers with an initial low monthly price that is half of the normal monthly rate for the first year of services. After a year, the price will be increased to the regular monthly rate. Netbooks management believes that customers will have to accept the full price because customers will be "locked in" after one year of use.

a. Discuss whether the half-price offer is an ethical business practice.

b. Discuss whether customer "lock in" is an ethical business practice.

CP 5-2 Manual vs. computerized accounting systems

The following conversation took place between Durable Construction Co.'s bookkeeper, Kyle Byers, and the accounting supervisor, Sarah Nelson:

Sarah: Kyle, I'm thinking about bringing in a new computerized accounting system to replace our manual system. I guess this will mean that you will need to learn how to do computerized accounting.

Kyle: What does computerized accounting mean?

Sarah: I'm not sure, but you'll need to prepare for this new way of doing business.

Kyle: I'm not so sure we need a computerized system. I've been looking at some of the sample reports from the software vendor. It looks to me as if the computer will not add much to what we are already doing.

Sarah: What do you mean?

Kyle: Well, look at these reports. This Sales by Customer Report looks like our revenue journal, and the Deposit Detail Report looks like our cash receipts journal. Granted, the computer types them, so they look much neater than my special journals, but I don't see that we're gaining much from this change.

Sarah: Well, surely there's more to it than nice-looking reports. I've got to believe that a computerized system will save us time and effort someplace.

Kyle: I don't see how. We still need to key in transactions into the computer. If anything, there may be more work when it's all said and done.

Do you agree with Kyle? Why might a computerized environment be preferred over the manual system?

CP 5-3 Accounts receivable and accounts payable

A subsidiary ledger is used for accounts receivable and accounts payable. Thus, transactions that are made "on account" are posted to the individual customer or creditor accounts.

a. Why do companies use subsidiary ledgers for accounts payable and accounts receivable?

b. Identify another account that may benefit from using a subsidiary ledger.

CP 5-4 Design of accounting systems

For the past few years, your client, Omni Care, has operated a small medical practice. Omni Care's current annual revenues are $945,000. Because the accountant has been spending more and more time each month recording all transactions in a two-column journal and preparing the financial statements, Omni Care is considering improving the accounting system by adding special journals and subsidiary ledgers. Omni Care has asked you to help with this project and has compiled the following information:

Type of Transaction	**Estimated Frequency per Month**
Fees earned on account	240
Purchase of medical supplies on account	190
Cash receipts from patients on account	175
Cash payments on account	160
Cash receipts from patients at time services provided	120
Purchase of office supplies on account	35
Purchase of magazine subscriptions on account	5
Purchase of medical equipment on account	4
Cash payments for office salaries	3
Cash payments for utilities expense	3

1. Briefly discuss the circumstances under which special journals would be used in place of a two-column (all-purpose) journal. Include in your answer your recommendations for Omni Care's medical practice.
2. Assume that Omni Care has decided to use a revenue journal and a purchases journal. Design the format for each journal, giving special consideration to the needs of the medical practice.
3. Which subsidiary ledgers would you recommend for the medical practice?

CP 5-5 Internet-based accounting systems

Internet Project

Internet-based accounting software is a recent trend in business computing. Major software firms such as Oracle, SAP, and NetSuite are running their core products on the Internet using cloud computing. NetSuite is one of the most popular small business Internet-based accounting systems.

Go to NetSuite Inc.'s Web site at www.netsuite.com. Read about the product from the site, and prepare a memo to management, defining Internet-based accounting. Also, outline the advantages and disadvantages of Internet-based accounting compared to running software on a company's internal computer network.

CP 5-6 SCM and CRM

Group Project

The two leading software application providers for supply chain management (SCM) and customer relationship management (CRM) software are JDA and Salesforce.com, respectively. In groups of two or three, go to the Web site for each company (www.jda.com and www.salesforce.com, respectively) and list the services provided by each company's software.

CHAPTER 6

Accounting for Merchandising Businesses

Dollar Tree Stores, Inc.

When you are low on cash but need to pick up party supplies, housewares, or other consumer items, where do you go? Many shoppers are turning to **Dollar Tree Stores, Inc.**, the nation's largest single price point dollar retailer with more than 4,000 stores in 48 states. For the fixed price of $1 on merchandise in its stores, Dollar Tree has worked hard providing "new treasures" every week for the entire family.

Despite the fact that items cost only $1, the accounting for a merchandiser, like Dollar Tree, is more complex than for a service company. This is because a service company sells only services and has no inventory. With Dollar Tree's locations and merchandise, the company must design its accounting system to not only record the receipt of goods for resale, but also to keep track of what merchandise is available for sale as well as where the merchandise is located. In addition, Dollar Tree must record the sales and costs of the goods sold for each of its stores. Finally, Dollar Tree must record such data as delivery costs, merchandise discounts, and merchandise returns.

This chapter focuses on the accounting principles and concepts for a merchandising business. In doing so, the basic differences between merchandiser and service company activities are highlighted. The financial statements of a merchandising business and accounting for merchandise transactions are also described and illustrated.

Learning Objectives

After studying this chapter, you should be able to: *Example Exercises*

OBJ 1 **Distinguish between the activities and financial statements of service and merchandising businesses.**

- Nature of Merchandising Businesses — EE 6-1
  - Operating Cycle
  - Financial Statements

OBJ 2 **Describe and illustrate the accounting for merchandise transactions.**

- Merchandising Transactions
  - Purchases Transactions — EE 6-2
  - Sales Transactions — EE 6-3
  - Freight — EE 6-4
  - Summary: Recording Merchandise Inventory Transactions
  - Dual Nature of Merchandise Transactions — EE 6-5
  - Chart of Accounts for a Merchandising Business
  - Sales Taxes and Trade Discounts

OBJ 3 **Describe and illustrate the financial statements of a merchandising business.**

- Financial Statements for a Merchandising Business
  - Multiple-Step Income Statement
  - Single-Step Income Statement
  - Statement of Owner's Equity
  - Balance Sheet

OBJ 4 **Describe the adjusting and closing process for a merchandising business.**

- The Adjusting and Closing Process
  - Adjusting Entry for Inventory Shrinkage — EE 6-6
  - Closing Entries

OBJ 5 **Describe and illustrate the use of the ratio of sales to assets in evaluating a company's operating performance.**

- Financial Analysis and Interpretation: Ratio of Sales to Assets — EE 6-7

At a Glance 6 Page 293

OBJ 1 Distinguish between the activities and financial statements of service and merchandising businesses.

Nature of Merchandising Businesses

The activities of a service business differ from those of a merchandising business. These differences are reflected in the operating cycles of a service and merchandising business as well as in their financial statements.

Operating Cycle

The **operating cycle** is the process by which a company spends cash, generates revenues, and receives cash either at the time the revenues are generated or later by collecting an accounts receivable. The operating cycle of a service and merchandising business differs in that a merchandising business must purchase merchandise for sale to customers. The operating cycle for a merchandise business is shown in Exhibit 1.

EXHIBIT 1

The Operating Cycle for a Merchandising Business

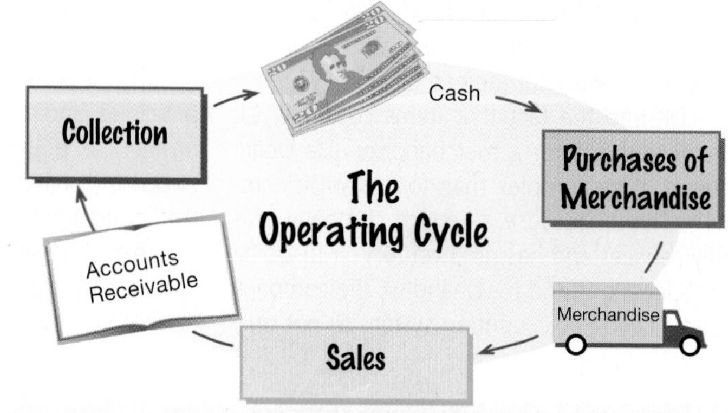

The time in days to complete an operating cycle differs significantly among merchandise businesses. Grocery stores normally have short operating cycles because of the nature of their merchandise. For example, many grocery items, such as milk, must be sold within their expiration dates of a week or two. In contrast, jewelry stores often carry expensive items that are often displayed months before being sold to customers.

Financial Statements

The differences between service and merchandising businesses are also reflected in their financial statements. For example, these differences are illustrated in the following condensed income statements:

Service Business		**Merchandising Business**	
Fees earned	$XXX	Sales	$XXX
Operating expenses	–XXX	Cost of merchandise sold	–XXX
Net income	$XXX	Gross profit	$XXX
		Operating expenses	–XXX
		Net income	$XXX

The revenue activities of a service business involve providing services to customers. On the income statement for a service business, the revenues from services are reported as *fees earned*. The operating expenses incurred in providing the services are subtracted from the fees earned to arrive at *net income*.

In contrast, the revenue activities of a merchandising business involve the buying and selling of merchandise. A merchandising business first purchases merchandise to sell to its customers. When this merchandise is sold, the revenue is reported as **sales**, and its cost is recognized as an expense. This expense is called the **cost of merchandise sold**. The cost of merchandise sold is subtracted from sales to arrive at gross profit. This amount is called **gross profit** because it is the profit *before* deducting operating expenses.

Merchandise on hand (not sold) at the end of an accounting period is called **merchandise inventory**. Merchandise inventory is reported as a current asset on the balance sheet.

Business  Connection

H&R BLOCK VERSUS THE HOME DEPOT

H&R Block is a service business that primarily offers tax planning and preparation to its customers. **The Home Depot** is a large home improvement retailer. The differences in the operations of a service and merchandise business are illustrated in their recent income statements, as shown.

H&R Block
Condensed Income Statement
(in millions)

Revenue	$2,794
Operating expenses	2,235
Operating income	$ 559
Other expense (net)	63
Income before taxes	$ 496
Income taxes	230
Net income	$ 266

As discussed in a later chapter, corporations are subject to income taxes. Thus, the income statements of H&R Block and The Home Depot report "income taxes" as a deduction from "income before income taxes" in arriving at net income. This is in contrast to a proprietorship, such as **NetSolutions**, which is not subject to income taxes.

The Home Depot
Condensed Income Statement
(in millions)

Sales	$70,395
Cost of merchandise sold	46,133
Gross profit	$24,262
Operating expenses	17,601
Operating income	$ 6,661
Other expense (net)	593
Income before taxes	$ 6,068
Income taxes	2,185
Net income	$ 3,883

Example Exercise 6-1 Gross Profit OBJ 1

During the current year, merchandise is sold for $250,000 cash and for $975,000 on account. The cost of the merchandise sold is $735,000. What is the amount of the gross profit?

Follow My Example 6-1

The gross profit is $490,000 ($250,000 + $975,000 – $735,000).

Practice Exercises: PE 6-1A, PE 6-1B

OBJ 2 Describe and illustrate the accounting for merchandise transactions.

Merchandising Transactions

This section illustrates merchandise transactions for **NetSolutions** after it becomes a retailer of computer hardware and software. During 2015, Chris Clark implemented the second phase of NetSolutions' business plan. In doing so, Chris notified clients that beginning July 1, 2016, NetSolutions would no longer offer consulting services. Instead, it would become a retailer.

NetSolutions' business strategy is to offer personalized service to individuals and small businesses that are upgrading or purchasing new computer systems. NetSolutions' personal service includes a no-obligation, on-site assessment of the customer's computer needs. By providing personalized service and follow-up, Chris feels that NetSolutions can compete effectively against such retailers as **Best Buy**, **Office Max**, **Office Depot**, and **Dell**.

Merchandise transactions are recorded in the accounts, using the rules of debit and credit that are described and illustrated in Chapter 2. Most merchandising companies use computerized accounting systems with reports that are similar to special journals and subsidiary ledgers. For example, a computerized merchandise accounting system would typically produce sales and inventory reports. However, for the sake of simplicity, the journal entries in this chapter will be illustrated using a two-column general journal.

Purchases Transactions

There are two systems for accounting for merchandise transactions: perpetual and periodic. In a **perpetual inventory system,** each purchase and sale of merchandise is recorded in the inventory account and related subsidiary ledger. In this way, the amount of merchandise available for sale and the amount sold are continuously (perpetually) updated in the inventory records. In a **periodic inventory system**, the inventory does not show the amount of merchandise available for sale and the amount sold. Instead, a listing of inventory on hand, called a **physical inventory**, is prepared at the end of the accounting period. This physical inventory is used to determine the cost of merchandise on hand at the end of the period and the cost of merchandise sold during the period.

Most merchandise companies use computerized perpetual inventory systems. Such systems use bar codes or radio frequency identification codes embedded in a product. An optical scanner or radio frequency identification device is then used to read the product codes and track inventory on hand and sold.

Because computerized perpetual inventory systems are widely used, this chapter illustrates merchandise transactions using a perpetual inventory system. The periodic system is described and illustrated in an appendix at the end of this chapter.

Retailers, such as **Best Buy**, **Sears Holding Corporation**, and **Walmart**, and grocery store chains, such as **Winn-Dixie Stores, Inc.**, and **Kroger**, use bar codes and optical scanners as part of their computerized inventory systems.

Under the perpetual inventory system, cash purchases of merchandise are recorded as follows:

Journal *Page 24*

Date		Description	Post. Ref.	Debit	Credit
2017 Jan.	3	Merchandise Inventory		2,510	
		Cash			2,510
		Purchased inventory from Bowen Co.			

Purchases of merchandise on account are recorded as follows:

Date		Description	Post. Ref.	Debit	Credit
Jan.	4	Merchandise Inventory		9,250	
		Accounts Payable—Thomas Corporation			9,250
		Purchased inventory on account.			

The terms of purchases on account are normally indicated on the **invoice** or bill that the seller sends the buyer. An example of an invoice sent to NetSolutions by Alpha Technologies is shown in Exhibit 2.

EXHIBIT 2

Invoice

Alpha Technologies
1000 Matrix Blvd.
San Jose, CA 95116-1000

Invoice
106-8

Made in U.S.A.

SOLD TO	CUSTOMER ORDER NO.	ORDER DATE	
NetSolutions 5101 Washington Ave. Cincinnati, OH 45227-5101	412	Jan. 3, 2017	
DATE SHIPPED	**HOW SHIPPED AND ROUTE**	**TERMS**	**INVOICE DATE**
Jan. 5, 2017	US Express Trucking Co.	2/10, n/30	Jan. 5, 2017
FROM	**F.O.B.**		
San Jose	Cincinnati		
QUANTITY	**DESCRIPTION**	**UNIT PRICE**	**AMOUNT**
20	HC9 Printer/Fax/Copiers	150.00	3,000.00

The terms for when payments for merchandise are to be made are called the **credit terms**. If payment is required on delivery, the terms are cash or net cash. Otherwise, the buyer is allowed an amount of time, known as the **credit period**, in which to pay. The credit period usually begins with the date of the sale as shown on the invoice.

If payment is due within a stated number of days after the invoice date, such as 30 days, the terms are net 30 days. These terms may be written as *n/30*.[1] If payment is due by the end of the month in which the sale was made, the terms are written as *n/eom*.

Purchases Discounts To encourage the buyer to pay before the end of the credit period, the seller may offer a discount. For example, a seller may offer a 2% discount if the buyer pays within 10 days of the invoice date. If the buyer does not take the

[1] The word *net* as used here does not have the usual meaning of a number after deductions have been subtracted, as in *net income*.

discount, the total invoice amount is due within 30 days. These terms are expressed as 2/10, n/30 and are read as "2% discount if paid within 10 days, net amount due within 30 days." The credit terms of 2/10, n/30 are summarized in Exhibit 3, using the invoice in Exhibit 2.

EXHIBIT 3 **Credit Terms**

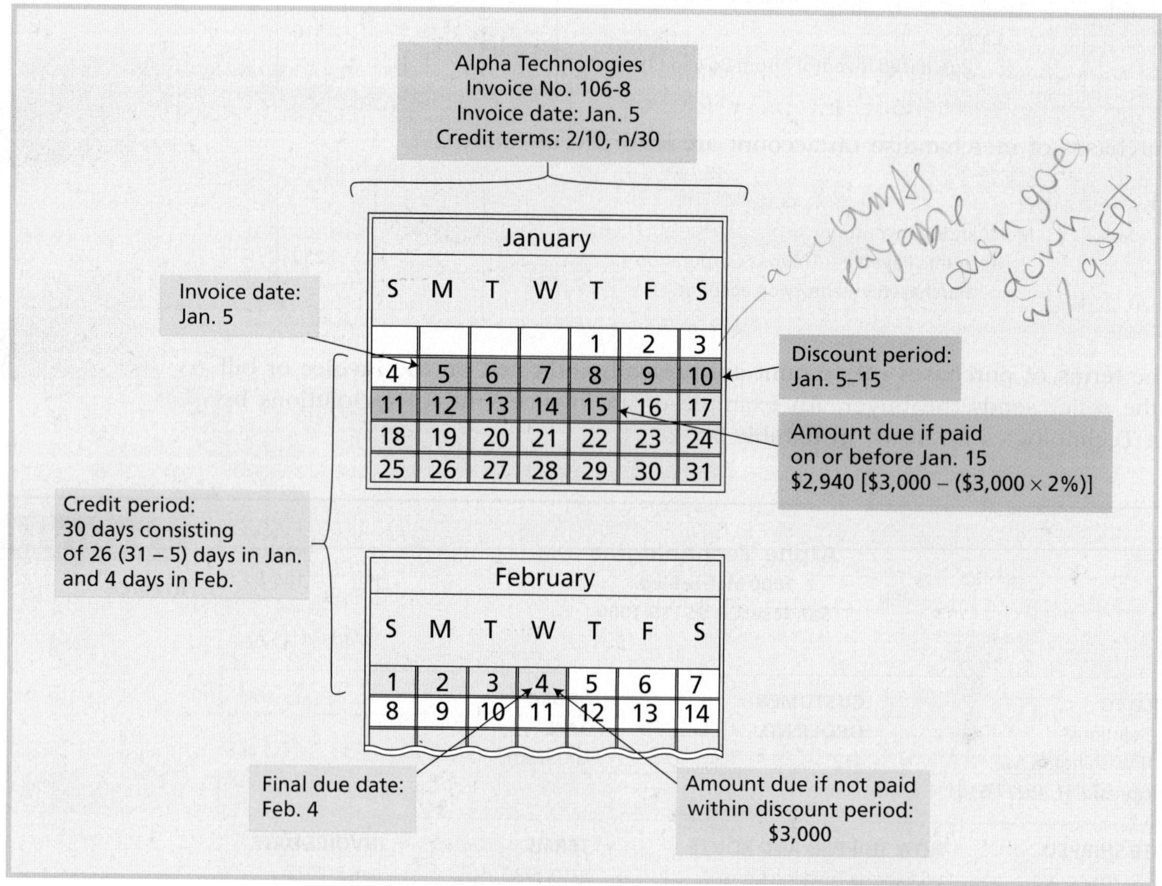

Discounts taken by the buyer for early payment of an invoice are called **purchases discounts**. Purchases discounts taken by a buyer reduce the cost of the merchandise purchased. Even if the buyer has to borrow to pay within a discount period, it is normally to the buyer's advantage to do so. For this reason, accounting systems are normally designed so that all available discounts are taken.

To illustrate, the invoice shown in Exhibit 2 is used. The last day of the discount period is January 15 (invoice date of January 5 plus 10 days). Assume that in order to pay the invoice on January 15, **NetSolutions** borrows $2,940, which is $3,000 less the discount of $60 ($3,000 × 2%). If an annual interest rate of 6% and a 360-day year is also assumed, the interest on the loan of $2,940 for the remaining 20 days of the credit period is $9.80 ($2,940 × 6% × 20 ÷ 360).[2]

The net savings to NetSolutions of taking the discount is $50.20, computed as follows:

Discount of 2% on $3,000	$60.00
Interest for 20 days at a rate of 6% on $2,940	9.80
Savings from taking the discount	$50.20

The savings can also be seen by comparing the interest rate on the money *saved* by taking the discount and the interest rate on the money *borrowed* to take the

[2] To simplify computations and rounding, we use a 360-day year rather than a 365-year.

discount. The interest rate on the money saved in the prior example is estimated by converting 2% for 20 days to a yearly rate, as follows:

$$2\% \times \frac{360 \text{ days}}{20 \text{ days}} = 2\% \times 18 = 36\%$$

NetSolutions borrowed $2,940 at 6% to take the discount. If NetSolutions does not take the discount, it *pays* an estimated interest rate of 36% for using the $2,940 for the remaining 20 days of the credit period. Thus, buyers should normally take all available purchase discounts.

Since buyers normally take all purchases discounts, Merchandise Inventory is debited for the net purchase price under the perpetual inventory system. That is, the buyer debits Merchandise Inventory for the amount of the invoice less the discount.[3]

To illustrate, NetSolutions would record the Alpha Technologies invoice and its payment as follows:

Jan.	5	Merchandise Inventory	2,940	
		Accounts Payable—Alpha Technologies		2,940
	15	Accounts Payable—Alpha Technologies	2,940	
		Cash		2,940

Purchases Returns and Allowances A buyer may request an allowance for merchandise that is returned (purchases return) or a price allowance (purchases allowance) for damaged or defective merchandise. From a buyer's perspective, such returns and allowances are called **purchases returns and allowances**. In both cases, the buyer normally sends the seller a debit memorandum to notify the seller of reasons for the return (purchase return) or to request a price reduction (purchase allowance).

A **debit memorandum**, often called a **debit memo**, is shown in Exhibit 4. A debit memo informs the seller of the amount the buyer proposes to *debit* to the account payable due the seller. It also states the reasons for the return or the request for the price allowance.

The buyer may use the debit memo as the basis for recording the return or allowance or wait for approval from the seller (creditor). In either case, the buyer debits Accounts Payable and credits Merchandise Inventory.

EXHIBIT 4

Debit Memo

NetSolutions No. 18
5101 Washington Ave.
Cincinnati, OH 45227-5101

DEBIT MEMO

TO
Maxim Systems
7519 East Wilson Ave.
Seattle, WA 98101-7519

DATE
March 7, 2017

WE DEBITED YOUR ACCOUNT AS FOLLOWS

10	Server Network Interface Cards, your invoice No. 7291, are being returned via parcel post. Our order specified No. 825X.	@90.00	900.00

[3] To simplify, we assume that all purchase discounts are taken.

To illustrate, **NetSolutions** records the return of the merchandise indicated in the debit memo in Exhibit 4 as follows:

Mar.	7	Accounts Payable—Maxim Systems	900	
		Merchandise Inventory		900
		Debit Memo No. 18.		

Before paying an invoice, a buyer may return merchandise or be granted a price allowance for an invoice with a purchase discount. In this case, the amount of the return is recorded at its invoice amount less the discount.

To illustrate, assume the following data concerning a purchase of merchandise by NetSolutions on May 2:

May 2. Purchased $5,000 of merchandise on account from Delta Data Link, terms 2/10, n/30.
4. Returned $1,000 of the merchandise purchased on May 2.
12. Paid for the purchase of May 2 less the return and discount.

NetSolutions would record these transactions as follows:

May	2	Merchandise Inventory	4,900	
		Accounts Payable—Delta Data Link		4,900
		Purchased merchandise.		
		[$5,000 – ($5,000 × 2%)]		
	4	Accounts Payable—Delta Data Link	980	
		Merchandise Inventory		980
		Returned portion of merch. purchased.		
		[$1,000 – ($1,000 × 2%)]		
	12	Accounts Payable—Delta Data Link	3,920	
		Cash		3,920
		($4,900 – $980)		

Example Exercise 6-2 Purchases Transactions

OBJ 2

Rofles Company purchased merchandise on account from a supplier for $11,500, terms 2/10, n/30. Rofles Company returned $2,500 of the merchandise and received full credit.

a. If Rofles Company pays the invoice within the discount period, what is the amount of cash required for the payment?

b. Under a perpetual inventory system, what account is credited by Rofles Company to record the return?

Follow My Example 6-2

a. $8,820. Purchase of $11,270 [$11,500 – ($11,500 × 2%)] less the return of $2,450 [$2,500 – ($2,500 × 2%)].

b. Merchandise Inventory

Practice Exercises: PE 6-2A, PE 6-2B

Sales Transactions

Revenue from merchandise sales is usually recorded as *Sales*. Sometimes a business may use the title *Sales of Merchandise.*

Cash Sales A business may sell merchandise for cash. Cash sales are normally entered on a cash register and recorded in the accounts. To illustrate, assume that on March 3, **NetSolutions** sells merchandise for $1,800. These cash sales are recorded as follows:

Journal *Page 25*

Date		Description	Post. Ref.	Debit	Credit
2017 Mar.	3	Cash		1,800	
		Sales			1,800
		To record cash sales.			

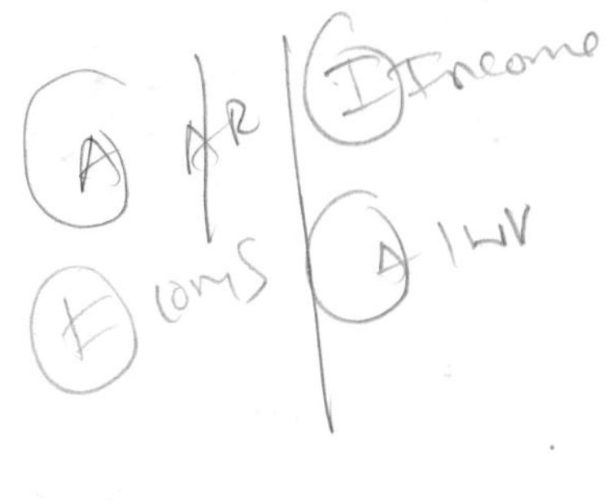

Using the perpetual inventory system, the cost of merchandise sold and the decrease in merchandise inventory are also recorded. In this way, the merchandise inventory account indicates the amount of merchandise on hand (not sold).

To illustrate, assume that the cost of merchandise sold on March 3 is $1,200. The entry to record the cost of merchandise sold and the decrease in the merchandise inventory is as follows:

Mar.	3	Cost of Merchandise Sold		1,200	
		Merchandise Inventory			1,200
		To record the cost of merchandise sold.			

Sales may be made to customers using credit cards such as **MasterCard** or **VISA**. Such sales are recorded as cash sales. This is because these sales are normally processed by a clearinghouse that contacts the bank that issued the card. The issuing bank then electronically transfers cash directly to the retailer's bank account.[4] Thus, the retailer normally receives cash within a few days of making the credit card sale.

If customers use MasterCards to pay for their purchases, the sales would be recorded exactly as shown in the first March 3 entry illustrated in this section. Any processing fees charged by the clearinghouse or issuing bank are periodically recorded as an expense. This expense is normally reported on the income statement as an administrative expense. To illustrate, assume that NetSolutions paid credit card processing fees of $4,150 on March 31. These fees would be recorded as follows:

Mar.	31	Credit Card Expense		4,150	
		Cash			4,150
		To record service charges on credit card sales for the month.			

A retailer may accept **MasterCard** or **VISA** but not **American Express**. Why? American Express Co.'s service fees are normally higher than MasterCard's or VISA's. As a result, some retailers choose not to accept American Express cards. The disadvantage of this practice is that the retailer may lose customers to competitors who do accept American Express cards.

Instead of using MasterCard or VISA, a customer may use a credit card that is not issued by a bank. For example, a customer might use an **American Express** card. If the seller uses a clearinghouse, the clearinghouse will collect the receivable and transfer the cash to the retailer's bank account, similar to the way it would have if the customer had used MasterCard or VISA. Large businesses, however, may not use a clearinghouse. In such cases, nonbank credit card sales must first be reported to the card company before cash is received. Thus, a receivable is created with the nonbank credit card company. However, because most retailers use clearinghouses to process both bank and nonbank credit cards, all credit card sales will be recorded as cash sales.

Sales on Account A business may sell merchandise on account. The seller records such sales as a debit to Accounts Receivable and a credit to Sales. An example of an entry for a **NetSolutions** sale on account of $18,000 follows. The cost of merchandise sold was $10,800.

[4] CyberSource is one of the major credit card clearinghouse. For a more detailed description of how credit card sales are processed, see the following CyberSource Web page: www.cybersource.com, click on Products & Services, click on Global Payment Services, and then click on Credit Card Processing.

Mar.	10	Accounts Receivable—Digital Technologies	18,000	
		Sales		18,000
		Invoice No. 7172.		
	10	Cost of Merchandise Sold	10,800	
		Merchandise Inventory		10,800
		Cost of merch. sold on Invoice No. 7172.		

Customer Discounts A seller may grant customers a variety of discounts, called **customer discounts**, as incentives to encourage customers to act in a way benefiting the seller. For example, a seller may offer customer discounts to encourage customers to purchase in volume or order early.

A common discount, called a **sales discount**, encourages customers to pay their invoice early. For example, a seller may offer credit terms of 2/10, n/30, which provides a 2% sales discount if the invoice is paid within 10 days. If not paid within 10 days, the total invoice amount is due within 30 days.[5]

To illustrate the accounting for sales discounts, assume that **NetSolutions** sold $18,000 of merchandise to Digital Technologies on March 10 with credit terms 2/10, n/30. The March 10 sale would be recorded as follows:[6]

Mar.	10	Accounts Receivable—Digital Technologies	17,640	
		Sales [$18,000 – ($18,000 × 2%)]		17,640

The sale to Digital Technologies is recorded by **NetSolutions** as $17,640, which is the invoice amount of $18,000 less the sales discount of $360 ($18,000 × 2%).[7] The payment by Digital Technologies on March 19 is recorded as follows:[8]

Mar.	19	Cash	17,640	
		Accounts Receivable—Digital Technologies		17,640

Customer Returns and Allowances Merchandise sold may be returned to the seller (returns). In other cases, the seller may reduce the initial selling price (allowances). This might occur if the merchandise is defective, damaged during shipment, or does not meet the buyer's expectations. From a seller's perspective, these are termed **customer returns and allowances**, sometimes called *sales returns and allowances*.

To illustrate the accounting for customer returns and allowances, assume Schafer Co. had sales of $2,000,000 and related cost of merchandise sold of $1,400,000 for its first year of operations ending December 31, 2016. Schafer Co. provides customers a refund for any returned or damaged merchandise. At the end of the year, Schafer Co. estimates that customers will request refunds for 2% of sales and estimates that merchandise costing $25,000 will be returned.

On December 31, 2016, the following two adjusting journal entries must be recorded.[9]

Dec.	31	Sales (2% × $2,000,000)	40,000	
		Customer Refunds Payable		40,000
	31	Estimated Returns Inventory	25,000	25,000
		Cost of Merchandise Sold		

[5] From the buyer's perspective, a sales discount is referred to as a purchases discount, which was discussed earlier in this chapter.
[6] The accounting for customer discounts other than sales discounts is discussed in advanced accounting courses.
[7] This is consistent with *Revenue from Contracts with Customers, Topic 606, FASB Accounting Standards Update*, Financial Accounting Standards Board, Norwalk, CT, May 2014.
[8] To simplify, we assume buyers take all sales discounts.
[9] The accounting illustrated is based upon *Revenue from Contracts with Customers, Topic 606, FASB Accounting Standards Update*, Financial Accounting Standards Board, Norwalk, CT, May 2014.

The first adjusting entry reduces 2016 Sales by the amount of estimated refunds that may occur in 2017. Since 2% refunds are expected, Sales is debited for $40,000 (2% × $2,000,000). In addition, a liability is recorded for $40,000 by crediting Customer Refunds Payable for the estimated refunds expected to be paid in 2017.

The second adjusting entry debits the asset Estimated Returns Inventory for the $25,000 cost of the merchandise that is expected to be returned in 2017. In addition, Cost of Merchandise Sold is credited for $25,000 for the original cost recorded at the time of sale. The Estimated Returns Inventory account is used since the type of merchandise returned will not be known until the returns actually occur.

The preceding two adjusting entries ensure that current period sales are matched with the related cost of merchandise sold on the income statement. In addition, an asset for estimated returned inventory and a liability for customer refunds is reported on the balance sheet.

To continue the illustration, on January 15, 2017, Baker Company returned merchandise with a selling price of $3,000 for cash refund. The merchandise originally cost Schafer Co. $2,100.

Schafer Co. would record the return and refund with the following two entries.

Jan.	15	Customer Refunds Payable		3,000	
		Cash			3,000
	15	Merchandise Inventory		2,100	
		Estimated Returns Inventory			2,100

The first entry records the cash refund paid Baker Company of $3,000. The cash paid Baker also reduces the estimated liability for customer refunds payable. The second entry records the cost of the merchandise that was returned of $2,100. Since the type of merchandise is now known, Merchandise Inventory is debited and Estimated Returns Inventory is credited for $2,100.[10]

In some cases, a customer that is due a refund has an outstanding account receivable balance. In this case, the seller may credit the customer's accounts receivable rather than pay cash. When this is done, the seller normally sends the buyer a credit memorandum or credit memo indicating its intent to credit the customer's accounts receivable.

To illustrate, assume that Schafer Company issued the credit memo shown in Exhibit 5 to Blake & Sons. Exhibit 5 indicates that Schafer Company intends to credit Blake & Sons account receivable for $900 as an allowance for merchandise that was damaged in shipment. Blake & Sons has agreed to keep the merchandise and make any necessary repairs.

EXHIBIT 5

Credit Memo

Schafer Co.
9004 Madison Road
Bozeman, MT 59715

No. 321

CREDIT MEMO

TO
Blake & Sons
7608 Melton Avenue
Los Angeles, CA 90025-3942

DATE
March 4, 2017

WE CREDIT YOUR ACCOUNT AS FOLLOWS
Allowance for merchandise damaged in shipment 900.00

[10] Because of wear, tear, and damage, companies may segregate returned items from normal inventory by using a separate returns inventory account.

Schafer Co. would record issuance of the credit memo as follows:

Mar.	4	Customer Refunds Payable	900	
		Accounts Receivable—Blake & Sons		900

The preceding entry reduces the estimated liability Customer Refunds Payable, but credits Blake & Sons' accounts receivable instead of Cash. Since the merchandise was not returned, there is no need to record a second entry for merchandise inventory.

Integrity, Objectivity, and Ethics in Business

THE CASE OF THE FRAUDULENT PRICE TAGS

One of the challenges for a retailer is policing its sales return policy. There are many ways in which customers can unethically or illegally abuse such policies. In one case, a couple was accused of attaching **Marshalls'** store price tags to cheaper merchandise bought or obtained elsewhere. The couple then returned the cheaper goods and received the substantially higher refund amount. Company security officials discovered the fraud and had the couple arrested after they had allegedly bilked the company for more than $1 million.

Example Exercise 6-3 Sales Transactions

Journalize the following merchandise transactions:

a. Sold merchandise on account, $7,500, with terms 2/10, n/30. The cost of the merchandise sold was $5,625.

b. Received payment less the discount.

Follow My Example 6-3

a.	Accounts Receivable [$7,500 – ($7,500 × 2%)]	7,350	
	Sales		7,350
	Cost of Merchandise Sold	5,625	
	Merchandise Inventory		5,625
b.	Cash	7,350	
	Accounts Receivable		7,350

Practice Exercises: PE 6-3A, PE 6-3B

Freight

Purchases and sales of merchandise often involve freight. The terms of a sale indicate when ownership (title and control) of the merchandise passes from the seller to the buyer. This point determines whether the buyer or the seller pays the freight costs.[11]

The ownership of the merchandise may pass to the buyer when the seller delivers the merchandise to the freight carrier. In this case, the terms are said to be **FOB (free on board) shipping point**. This term means that the buyer pays the freight costs from the shipping point to the final destination. Such costs are part of the buyer's total cost of purchasing inventory and are added to the cost of the inventory by debiting Merchandise Inventory.

Note:
The buyer bears the freight costs if the shipping terms are FOB shipping point.

[11] The passage of title also determines whether the buyer or seller must pay other costs, such as the cost of insurance, while the merchandise is in transit.

To illustrate, assume that on June 10, **NetSolutions** purchased merchandise as follows:

June 10. Purchased merchandise from Magna Data, $900, terms FOB shipping point.
10. Paid freight of $50 on June 10 purchase from Magna Data.

NetSolutions would record these two transactions as follows:

June	10	Merchandise Inventory		900	
		Accounts Payable—Magna Data			900
		Purchased merchandise, terms FOB shipping point.			
	10	Merchandise Inventory		50	
		Cash			50
		Paid shipping cost on merchandise purchased.			

The ownership of the merchandise may pass to the buyer when the buyer receives the merchandise. In this case, the terms are said to be **FOB (free on board) destination**. This term means that the seller pays the freight costs from the shipping point to the buyer's final destination. When the seller pays the delivery charges, the seller debits Delivery Expense or Freight Out. Delivery Expense is reported on the seller's income statement as a selling expense.

Note:
The seller bears the freight costs if the shipping terms are FOB destination.

Sometimes FOB shipping point and FOB destination are expressed in terms of a specific location at which the title to the merchandise passes to the buyer. For example, if **Toyota Motor Corporation**'s assembly plant in Osaka, Japan, sells automobiles to a dealer in Chicago, FOB shipping point is expressed as FOB Osaka. Likewise, FOB destination is expressed as FOB Chicago.

To illustrate, assume that **NetSolutions** sells merchandise as follows:

June 15. Sold merchandise to Kranz Company on account, $700, terms FOB destination. The cost of the merchandise sold is $480.
15. NetSolutions pays freight of $40 on the sale of June 15.

NetSolutions records the sale, the cost of the sale, and the freight cost as follows:

June	15	Accounts Receivable—Kranz Company		700	
		Sales			700
		Sold merchandise, terms FOB destination.			
	15	Cost of Merchandise Sold		480	
		Merchandise Inventory			480
		Recorded cost of merchandise sold to Kranz Company.			
	15	Delivery Expense		40	
		Cash			40
		Paid shipping cost on merchandise sold.			

The seller may prepay the freight, even though the terms are FOB shipping point. The seller will then add the freight to the invoice. The buyer debits Merchandise Inventory for the total amount of the invoice, including the freight. Any discount terms would not apply to the prepaid freight.

To illustrate, assume that **NetSolutions** sells merchandise as follows:

June 20. Sold merchandise to Planter Company on account, $800, terms FOB shipping point. NetSolutions paid freight of $45, which was added to the invoice. The cost of the merchandise sold is $360.

NetSolutions records the sale, the cost of the sale, and the freight as follows:

Date		Description	Post. Ref.	Debit	Credit
June	20	Accounts Receivable—Planter Company		800	
		Sales			800
		Sold merchandise, terms FOB shipping point.			
	20	Cost of Merchandise Sold		360	
		Merchandise Inventory			360
		Recorded cost of merchandise sold to Planter Company.			
	20	Accounts Receivable—Planter Company		45	
		Cash			45
		Prepaid shipping cost on merchandise sold.			

Shipping terms, the passage of title (control), and whether the buyer or seller is to pay the freight costs are summarized in Exhibit 6.

EXHIBIT 6 **Freight Terms**

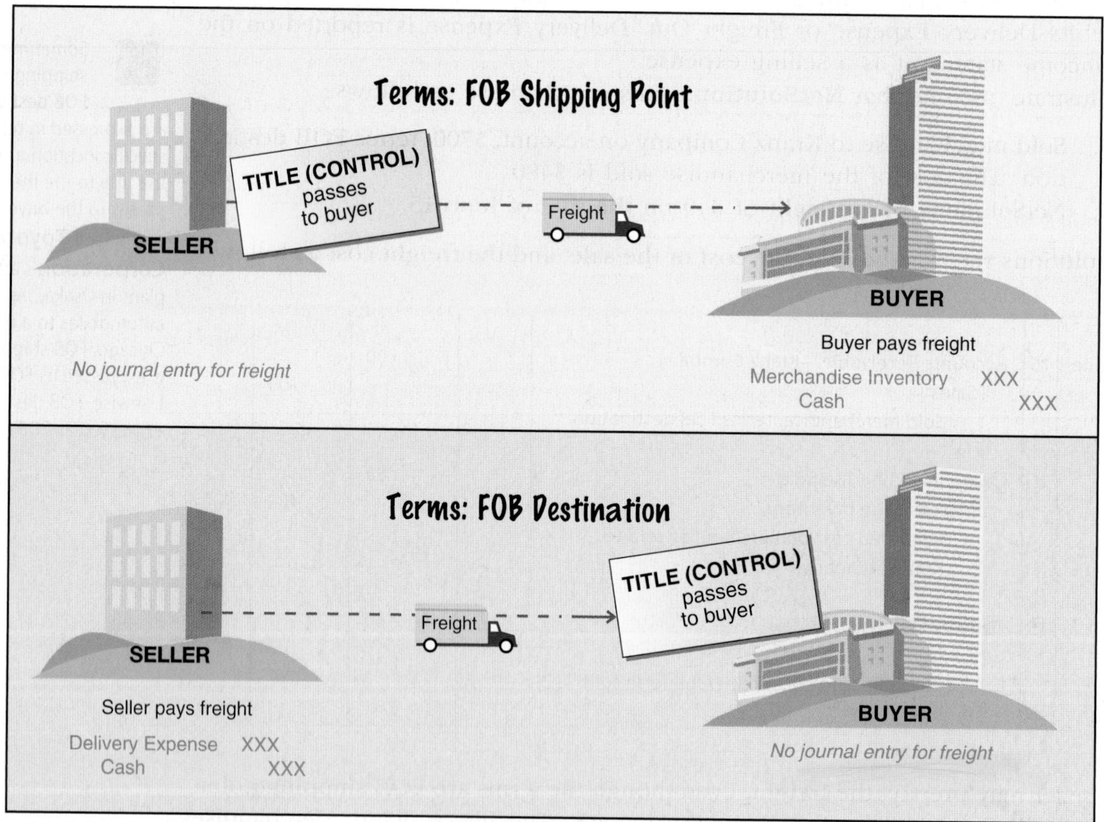

Example Exercise 6-4 Freight Terms

Determine the amount to be paid in full settlement of each of the two invoices, (a) and (b), assuming that credit for returns and allowances was received prior to payment and that all invoices were paid within the discount period.

	Merchandise	Freight Paid by Seller	Freight Terms	Returns and Allowances
a.	$4,500	$200	FOB shipping point, 1/10, n/30	$ 800
b.	5,000	60	FOB destination, 2/10, n/30	2,500

Follow My Example 6-4

a. $3,863. Purchase of $4,455 [$4,500 – ($4,500 × 1%)] less return of $792 [$800 – ($800 × 1%)] plus $200 of shipping.

b. $2,450. Purchase of $4,900 [$5,000 – ($5,000 × 2%)] less return of $2,450 [$2,500 – ($2,500 × 2%)].

Practice Exercises: PE 6-4A, PE 6-4B

Summary: Recording Merchandise Inventory Transactions

Recording merchandise inventory transactions under the perpetual inventory system has been described and illustrated in the preceding sections. These transactions involved purchases, purchases returns and allowances, freight, cost of merchandise sold (from sales), and customer returns. Exhibit 7 summarizes how these transactions are recorded in T account form.

EXHIBIT 7

Recording Merchandise Inventory Transactions

Merchandise Inventory

Debit		Credit	
Purchases (net of discounts)	XXX	Purchases returns and allowances (net of discounts)	XXX
Freight for merchandise purchased FOB shipping point	XXX	Cost of merchandise sold	XXX
Customer returns	XXX		

Estimated Returns Inventory

Debit		Credit	
Adjusting entry for estimated customer returns	XXX	Customer returns	XXX

Cost of Merchandise Sold

Debit		Credit	
Cost of merchandise sold	XXX	Adjusting entry for estimated customer returns	XXX

Dual Nature of Merchandise Transactions

Each merchandising transaction affects a buyer and a seller. In the illustration shown in Exhibit 8, the same transactions for a seller and buyer are recorded. In Exhibit 8, the seller is Scully Company and the buyer is Burton Co.

EXHIBIT 8 **Illustration of Merchandise Inventory Transactions for Seller and Buyer**

Transaction	Scully Company (Seller)			Burton Co. (Buyer)		
July 1. Scully Company sold merchandise on account to Burton Co., $7,500, terms FOB shipping point, n/45. The cost of the merchandise sold was $4,500.	Accounts Receivable—Burton Co.	7,500		Merchandise Inventory	7,500	
	Sales		7,500	Accounts Payable—Scully Co.		7,500
	Cost of Merchandise Sold	4,500				
	Merchandise Inventory		4,500			
July 2. Burton Co. paid freight of $150 on July 1 purchase from Scully Company.	No journal entry.			Merchandise Inventory	150	
				Cash		150
July 5. Scully Company sold merchandise on account to Burton Co., $5,000, terms FOB destination, n/30. The cost of the merchandise sold was $3,500.	Accounts Receivable—Burton Co.	5,000		Merchandise Inventory	5,000	
	Sales		5,000	Accounts Payable—Scully Co.		5,000
	Cost of Merchandise Sold	3,500				
	Merchandise Inventory		3,500			
July 7. Scully Company paid freight of $250 for delivery of merchandise sold to Burton Co. on July 5.	Delivery Expense	250		No journal entry.		
	Cash		250			
July 15. Scully Company received payment from Burton Co. for purchase of July 5.	Cash	5,000		Accounts Payable—Scully Co.	5,000	
	Accounts Receivable—Burton Co.		5,000	Cash		5,000
July 18. Scully Company sold merchandise on account to Burton Co.,$12,000, terms FOB shipping point, 2/10, n/eom. Scully Company prepaid freight of $500, which was added to the invoice. The cost of the merchandise sold was $7,200.	Accounts Receivable—Burton Co.	11,760		Merchandise Inventory	12,260	
	Sales		11,760	Accounts Payable—Scully Co.		12,260
	Accounts Receivable—Burton Co.	500				
	Cash		500			
	Cost of Merchandise Sold	7,200				
	Merchandise Inventory		7,200			
July 28. Scully Company received payment from Burton Co. for purchase of July 18.	Cash	12,260		Accounts Payable—Scully Co.	12,260	
	Accounts Receivable—Burton Co.		12,260	Cash		12,260

Example Exercise 6-5 Transactions for Buyer and Seller

Sievert Co. sold merchandise to Bray Co. on account, $11,500, terms 2/15, n/30. The cost of the merchandise sold is $6,900. Journalize the entries for Sievert Co. and Bray Co. for the sale, purchase, and payment of amount due.

Follow My Example 6-5

Sievert Co. journal entries:

Accounts Receivable [$11,500 – ($11,500 × 2%)]	11,270	
Sales		11,270
Cost of Merchandise Sold	6,900	
Merchandise Inventory		6,900
Cash	11,270	
Accounts Receivable—Bray Co.		11,270

Bray Co. journal entries:

Merchandise Inventory [$11,500 – ($11,500 × 2%)]	11,270	
Accounts Payable		11,270
Accounts Payable—Sievert Co.	11,270	
Cash		11,270

Practice Exercises: PE 6-5A, PE 6-5B

Chart of Accounts for a Merchandising Business

The chart of accounts for a merchandising business should reflect the types of merchandise transactions described and illustrated earlier in this chapter. The chart of accounts for **NetSolutions** is shown in Exhibit 9. The accounts related to merchandising transactions are highlighted.[12]

EXHIBIT 9

Chart of Accounts for NetSolutions, a Merchandising Business

Balance Sheet Accounts	Income Statement Accounts
100 Assets	400 Revenues
110 Cash	410 Sales
112 Accounts Receivable	500 Costs and Expenses
115 Merchandise Inventory	510 Cost of Merchandise Sold
116 Office Supplies	520 Sales Salaries Expense
117 Prepaid Insurance	521 Advertising Expense
120 Land	522 Depreciation Expense—Store Equipment
123 Store Equipment	523 Delivery Expense
124 Accumulated Depreciation—Store Equipment	529 Miscellaneous Selling Expense
125 Office Equipment	530 Office Salaries Expense
126 Accumulated Depreciation—Office Equipment	531 Rent Expense
200 Liabilities	532 Depreciation Expense—Office Equipment
210 Accounts Payable	533 Insurance Expense
211 Salaries Payable	534 Office Supplies Expense
212 Unearned Rent	539 Misc. Administrative Expense
215 Notes Payable	600 Other Income
300 Owner's Equity	610 Rent Revenue
310 Chris Clark, Capital	700 Other Expense
311 Chris Clark, Drawing	710 Interest Expense
312 Income Summary	

[12] To simplify, we assume NetSolutions does not accept customer returns and allowances.

As shown in Exhibit 9, NetSolutions' chart of accounts consists of three-digit account numbers. The first digit indicates the major financial statement classification (1 for assets, 2 for liabilities, and so on). The second digit indicates the subclassification (e.g., 11 for current assets, 12 for noncurrent assets, etc.). The third digit identifies the specific account (e.g., 110 for Cash, 123 for Store Equipment, etc.). Using a three-digit numbering system makes it easier to add new accounts as they are needed.

Sales Taxes and Trade Discounts

Sales of merchandise often involve sales taxes. Also, the seller may offer buyers trade discounts.

Sales Taxes Almost all states levy a tax on sales of merchandise.[13] The liability for the sales tax is incurred when the sale is made.

At the time of a cash sale, the seller collects the sales tax. When a sale is made on account, the seller charges the tax to the buyer by debiting Accounts Receivable. The seller credits the sales account for the amount of the sale and credits the tax to Sales Tax Payable. For example, the seller would record a sale of $100 on account, subject to a tax of 6%, as follows:

Aug.	12	Accounts Receivable—Lemon Co.		106	
		Sales			100
		Sales Tax Payable			6
		Invoice No. 339.			

On a regular basis, the seller pays to the taxing authority (state) the amount of the sales tax collected. The seller records such a payment as follows:

Sept.	15	Sales Tax Payable		2,900	
		Cash			2,900
		Payment for sales taxes collected during August.			

Business  **Connection**

SALES TAXES

While there is no federal sales tax, most states have enacted statewide sales taxes. In addition, many states allow counties and cities to collect a "local option" sales tax. Delaware, Montana, New Hampshire, and Oregon have no state or local sales taxes. Tennessee (9.45%), Washington (8.8%), and Louisiana (8.75%) have the highest average combined rates (including state and local option taxes). Several towns in Tuscaloosa County, Alabama, have the highest combined rates in the United States of 11%, while Chicago, Illinois, has the highest combined city rate of 10.25%.

What about companies that sell merchandise through the Internet? The general rule is that if the company ships merchandise to a customer in a state where the company does not have a physical location, no sales tax is due. For example, a customer in Montana who purchases merchandise online from a New York retailer (and no physical location in Montana) does not have to pay sales tax to either Montana or New York.

Source: The Sales Tax Clearinghouse at www.thestc.com/FAQ.stm.

Trade Discounts Wholesalers are companies that sell merchandise to other businesses rather than to the public. Many wholesalers publish sales catalogs. Rather than updating their catalogs, wholesalers may publish price updates. These updates may include large discounts from the catalog list prices. In addition, wholesalers often offer

[13] Businesses that purchase merchandise for resale to others are normally exempt from paying sales taxes on their purchases. Only final buyers of merchandise normally pay sales taxes.

special discounts to government agencies or businesses that order large quantities. Such discounts are called **trade discounts**.

Sellers and buyers do not normally record the list prices of merchandise and trade discounts in their accounts. For example, assume that an item has a list price of $1,000 and a 40% trade discount. The seller records the sale of the item at $600 [$1,000 less the trade discount of $400 ($1,000 × 40%)]. Likewise, the buyer records the purchase at $600.

Financial Statements for a Merchandising Business

OBJ 3 Describe and illustrate the financial statements of a merchandising business.

Although merchandising transactions affect the balance sheet in reporting inventory, they primarily affect the income statement. An income statement for a merchandising business is normally prepared using either a multiple-step or single-step format.

Multiple-Step Income Statement

The 2017 income statement for **NetSolutions** is shown in Exhibit 10.[14] This form of income statement, called a **multiple-step income statement**, contains several sections, subsections, and subtotals.

EXHIBIT 10

Multiple-Step Income Statement

NetSolutions Income Statement For the Year Ended December 31, 2017			
Sales			$708,255
Cost of merchandise sold			525,305
Gross profit			$182,950
Operating expenses:			
Selling expenses:			
Sales salaries expense	$53,430		
Advertising expense	10,860		
Depreciation expense—store equipment	3,100		
Delivery expense	2,800		
Miscellaneous selling expense	630		
Total selling expenses		$ 70,820	
Administrative expenses:			
Office salaries expense	$21,020		
Rent expense	8,100		
Depreciation expense—office equipment	2,490		
Insurance expense	1,910		
Office supplies expense	610		
Miscellaneous administrative expense	760		
Total administrative expenses		34,890	
Total operating expenses			105,710
Income from operations			$ 77,240
Other income and expense:			
Rent revenue		$ 600	
Interest expense		(2,440)	(1,840)
Net income			$ 75,400

[14] The NetSolutions income statement for 2017 is used because it allows a better illustration of the computation of the cost of merchandise sold in the appendix to this chapter.

Sales The total amount of sales to customers for cash and on account is reported in this section. NetSolutions reported sales of $708,255 for the year ended December 31, 2017.

Cost of Merchandise Sold As shown in Exhibit 10, NetSolutions reported cost of merchandise sold of $525,305 during 2017. This amount is the cost of merchandise sold to customers. Cost of merchandise sold may also be reported as *cost of goods sold* or *cost of sales*.

For many merchandising businesses, the cost of merchandise sold is usually the largest expense. For example, the approximate percentage of cost of merchandise sold to sales is 64% for **JCPenney** and 66% for **The Home Depot**.

Gross Profit The excess of sales over cost of merchandise sold is gross profit. As shown in Exhibit 10, NetSolutions reported gross profit of $182,950 in 2017.

Income from Operations **Income from operations**, sometimes called *operating income*, is determined by subtracting operating expenses from gross profit. Operating expenses are normally classified as either selling expenses or administrative expenses.

Selling expenses are incurred directly in the selling of merchandise. Examples of selling expenses include sales salaries, store supplies used, depreciation of store equipment, delivery expense, and advertising.

Administrative expenses, sometimes called **general expenses**, are incurred in the administration or general operations of the business. Examples of administrative expenses include office salaries, depreciation of office equipment, and office supplies used.

Each selling and administrative expense may be reported separately as shown in Exhibit 10. However, many companies report selling, administrative, and operating expenses as single line items, as follows for NetSolutions:

IFRS

See Appendix D for more information.

Gross profit		$182,950
Operating expenses:		
Selling expenses	$70,820	
Administrative expenses	34,890	
Total operating expenses		105,710
Income from operations		$ 77,240

Other Income and Expense Other income and expense items are not related to the primary operations of the business. **Other income** is revenue from sources other than the primary operating activity of a business. Examples of other income include income from interest, rent, and gains resulting from the sale of fixed assets. **Other expense** is an expense that cannot be traced directly to the normal operations of the business. Examples of other expenses include interest expense and losses from disposing of fixed assets.

Other income and other expense are offset against each other on the income statement. If the total of other income exceeds the total of other expense, the difference is added to income from operations to determine net income. If the reverse is true, the difference is subtracted from income from operations. The other income and expense items of NetSolutions are reported as follows and in Exhibit 10:

Income from operations		$77,240
Other income and expense:		
Rent revenue	$ 600	
Interest expense	(2,440)	(1,840)
Net income		$75,400

Single-Step Income Statement

An alternate form of income statement is the **single-step income statement.** As shown in Exhibit 11, the income statement for **NetSolutions** deducts the total of all expenses *in one step* from the total of all revenues.

The single-step form emphasizes total revenues and total expenses in determining net income. A criticism of the single-step form is that gross profit and income from operations are not reported.

EXHIBIT 11

Single-Step Income Statement

NetSolutions
Income Statement
For the Year Ended December 31, 2017

Revenues:		
Sales		$708,255
Rent revenue		600
Total revenues		$708,855
Expenses:		
Cost of merchandise sold	$525,305	
Selling expenses	70,820	
Administrative expenses	34,890	
Interest expense	2,440	
Total expenses		633,455
Net income		$ 75,400

Statement of Owner's Equity

The statement of owner's equity for **NetSolutions** is shown in Exhibit 12. This statement is prepared in the same manner as for a service business.

EXHIBIT 12

Statement of Owner's Equity for Merchandising Business

NetSolutions
Statement of Owner's Equity
For the Year Ended December 31, 2017

Chris Clark, capital, January 1, 2017		$153,800
Net income for the year	$75,400	
Less withdrawals	18,000	
Increase in owner's equity		57,400
Chris Clark, capital, December 31, 2017		$211,200

Balance Sheet

The balance sheet may be presented with assets on the left-hand side and the liabilities and owner's equity on the right-hand side. This form of the balance sheet is called the **account form.** The balance sheet may also be presented in a downward sequence in three sections. This form of balance sheet is called the **report form.** The report form of balance sheet for **NetSolutions** is shown in Exhibit 13. In Exhibit 13, merchandise inventory is reported as a current asset and the current portion of the note payable of $5,000 is reported as a current liability.

EXHIBIT 13

Report Form of Balance Sheet

NetSolutions Balance Sheet December 31, 2017			
Assets			
Current assets:			
Cash		$52,950	
Accounts receivable		91,080	
Merchandise inventory		62,150	
Office supplies		480	
Prepaid insurance		2,650	
Total current assets			$209,310
Property, plant, and equipment:			
Land		$20,000	
Store equipment	$27,100		
Less accumulated depreciation	5,700	21,400	
Office equipment	$15,570		
Less accumulated depreciation	4,720	10,850	
Total property, plant, and equipment			52,250
Total assets			$261,560
Liabilities			
Current liabilities:			
Accounts payable		$22,420	
Note payable (current portion)		5,000	
Salaries payable		1,140	
Unearned rent		1,800	
Total current liabilities			$ 30,360
Long-term liabilities:			
Note payable (final payment due in ten years)			20,000
Total liabilities			$ 50,360
Owner's Equity			
Chris Clark, capital			211,200
Total liabilities and owner's equity			$261,560

Describe the adjusting and closing process for a merchandising business.

The Adjusting and Closing Process

Thus far, the recording of transactions, chart of accounts, and financial statements for a merchandising business (NetSolutions) have been described and illustrated. In the remainder of this chapter, the adjusting and closing process for a merchandising business will be described. In this discussion, the focus will be on the elements of the accounting cycle that differ from those of a service business.

Adjusting Entry for Inventory Shrinkage

Under the perpetual inventory system, the merchandise inventory account is continually updated for purchase and sales transactions. As a result, the balance of the merchandise inventory account is the amount of merchandise available for sale at that point in time. However, retailers normally experience some loss of inventory due to shoplifting, employee theft, or errors. Thus, the physical inventory on hand at the end of the accounting period is usually less than the balance of Merchandise Inventory. This difference is called **inventory shrinkage** or **inventory shortage**.

To illustrate, **NetSolutions**' inventory records indicate the following on December 31, 2017:

Account balance of Merchandise Inventory	$63,950
Physical merchandise inventory on hand	62,150
Inventory shrinkage	$ 1,800

At the end of the accounting period, inventory shrinkage is recorded by the following adjusting entry:

		Adjusting Entry		
Dec.	31	Cost of Merchandise Sold	1,800	
		Merchandise Inventory		1,800
		Inventory shrinkage ($63,950 – $62,150).		

After the preceding entry is recorded, the balance of Merchandise Inventory agrees with the physical inventory on hand at the end of the period. Since inventory shrinkage cannot be totally eliminated, it is considered a normal cost of operations. If, however, the amount of the shrinkage is unusually large, it may be disclosed separately on the income statement. In such cases, the shrinkage may be recorded in a separate account, such as Loss from Merchandise Inventory Shrinkage.

Integrity, Objectivity, and Ethics in Business

THE COST OF EMPLOYEE THEFT

One survey reported that the 24 largest U.S. retail store chains have lost more than $6 billion to shoplifting and employee theft. The stores apprehended over 1 million shoplifters and dishonest employees and recovered more than $161 million from these thieves. Approximately 1 out of every 36 employees was apprehended for theft from his or her employer. Each dishonest employee stole approximately 6 times the amount stolen by shoplifters ($665.77 versus $113.30).

Source: Jack L. Hayes International, 24th Annual Retail Theft Survey, 2012.

Example Exercise 6-6 Inventory Shrinkage

Pulmonary Company's perpetual inventory records indicate that $382,800 of merchandise should be on hand on March 31, 2016. The physical inventory indicates that $371,250 of merchandise is actually on hand. Journalize the adjusting entry for the inventory shrinkage for Pulmonary Company for the year ended March 31, 2016. Assume that the inventory shrinkage is a normal amount.

Follow My Example 6-6

Mar. 31	Cost of Merchandise Sold	11,550	
	Merchandise Inventory..................................		11,550
	Inventory shrinkage ($382,800 – $371,250).		

Practice Exercises: PE 6-6A, PE 6-6B

Closing Entries

The closing entries for a merchandising business are similar to those for a service business. The four closing entries for a merchandising business are as follows:

1. Debit each temporary account with a credit balance, such as Sales, for its balance and credit Income Summary.
2. Credit each temporary account with a debit balance, such as the various expenses, and debit Income Summary. Since Cost of Merchandise Sold is a temporary account with a debit balance, it is credited for its balance.

3. Debit Income Summary for the amount of its balance (net income) and credit the owner's capital account. The accounts debited and credited are reversed if there is a net loss.
4. Debit the owner's capital account for the balance of the drawing account and credit the drawing account.

The four closing entries for **NetSolutions** follow:

Journal *Page 29*

Date		Item	Post. Ref.	Debit	Credit
2017		Closing Entries			
Dec.	31	Sales	410	708,255	
		Rent Revenue	610	600	
		Income Summary	312		708,855
	31	Income Summary	312	633,455	
		Cost of Merchandise Sold	510		525,305
		Sales Salaries Expense	520		53,430
		Advertising Expense	521		10,860
		Depr. Expense—Store Equipment	522		3,100
		Delivery Expense	523		2,800
		Miscellaneous Selling Expense	529		630
		Office Salaries Expense	530		21,020
		Rent Expense	531		8,100
		Depr. Expense—Office Equipment	532		2,490
		Insurance Expense	533		1,910
		Office Supplies Expense	534		610
		Misc. Administrative Expense	539		760
		Interest Expense	710		2,440
	31	Income Summary	312	75,400	
		Chris Clark, Capital	310		75,400
	31	Chris Clark, Capital	310	18,000	
		Chris Clark, Drawing	311		18,000

NetSolutions' income summary account after the closing entries have been posted is as follows:

Account *Income Summary* Account No. *312*

Date		Item	Post. Ref.	Debit	Credit	Balance Debit	Balance Credit
2017							
Dec.	31	Revenues	29		708,855		708,855
	31	Expenses	29	633,455			75,400
	31	Net income	29	75,400		—	—

After the closing entries are posted to the accounts, a post-closing trial balance is prepared. The only accounts that should appear on the post-closing trial balance are the asset, contra asset, liability, and owner's capital accounts with balances. These are the same accounts that appear on the end-of-period balance sheet. If the two totals of the trial balance columns are not equal, an error has occurred that must be found and corrected.

Financial Analysis and Interpretation: Ratio of Sales to Assets

OBJ 5 Describe and illustrate the use of the ratio of sales to assets in evaluating a company's operating performance.

The **ratio of sales to assets** measures how effectively a business is using its assets to generate sales. A high ratio indicates an effective use of assets. The assets used in computing the ratio may be the total assets at the end of the year, the average of the total assets at the beginning and end of the year, or the average of the monthly assets. For our purposes, the average of the total assets at the beginning and end of the year is used.

The ratio of sales to assets is computed as follows:

$$\text{Ratio of Sales to Assets} = \frac{\text{Sales}}{\text{Average Total Assets}}$$

To illustrate the use of this ratio, the following data (in millions) were taken from recent annual reports of **Dollar Tree, Inc.**:

	Year 2	Year 1
Total revenues (sales)	$6,631	$5,882
Total assets:		
Beginning of year	2,381	2,290
End of year	2,328	2,381

The ratios of sales to assets for each year are as follows:

	Year 2	Year 1
Ratio of sales to assets*	2.82	2.52
	$6,631 ÷ [($2,381 + $2,328) ÷ 2]	$5,882 ÷ [($2,290 + $2,381) ÷ 2]

*Rounded to two decimal places.

Based on the preceding ratios, Dollar Tree improved its ratio of sales to assets from 2.52 in Year 1 to 2.82 in Year 2. Thus, Dollar Tree improved the utilization of its assets to generate sales in Year 2.

Using the ratio of sales to assets for comparisons to competitors and with industry averages could also be beneficial in interpreting Dollar Tree's use of its assets. For example, the following data (in millions) were taken from recent annual reports of **Dollar General Corporation**:

	Year 2
Total revenues (sales)	$14,807
Total assets:	
Beginning of year	9,546
End of year	9,689

Dollar General's ratio of sales to assets for Year 2 is as follows:

	Year 2
Ratio of sales to assets*	1.54
	$14,807 ÷ [($9,546 + $9,689) ÷ 2]

*Rounded to two decimal places.

Comparing Dollar General's Year 2 ratio of 1.54 to Dollar Tree's Year 2 ratio of 2.82 implies that Dollar Tree is using its assets more efficiently than is Dollar General.

Example Exercise 6-7 Ratio of Sales to Assets

OBJ 5

Financial statement data for the years ending December 31, 2016 and 2015, for Gilbert Company follow:

	2016	2015
Sales	$1,305,000	$962,500
Total assets:		
Beginning of year	840,000	700,000
End of year	900,000	840,000

a. Determine the ratio of sales to assets for 2016 and 2015.

b. Does the change in the ratio of sales to assets from 2015 to 2016 indicate a favorable or an unfavorable trend?

Follow My Example 6-7

a.

	2016	2015
Ratio of sales to assets	1.50	1.25
	$1,305,000 ÷ [($840,000 + $900,000) ÷ 2]	$962,500 ÷ [($700,000 + $840,000) ÷ 2]

b. The change from 1.25 to 1.50 indicates a favorable trend in using assets to generate sales.

Practice Exercises: PE 6-7A, PE 6-7B

APPENDIX

The Periodic Inventory System

Throughout this chapter, the perpetual inventory system was used to record purchases and sales of merchandise. Not all merchandise businesses, however, use the perpetual inventory system. For example, small merchandise businesses, such as a local hardware store, may use a manual accounting system. A manual perpetual inventory system is time consuming and costly to maintain. In this case, the periodic inventory system may be used.

Under the periodic inventory system, purchases are normally recorded at their invoice amount. If the invoice is paid within the discount period, the discount is recorded in a separate account called Purchases Discounts. Likewise, purchases returns are recorded in a separate account called Purchases Returns and Allowances.

Chart of Accounts Under the Periodic Inventory System

The chart of accounts for **NetSolutions** under a periodic inventory system is shown in Exhibit 14. The accounts used to record transactions under the periodic inventory system are highlighted in Exhibit 14.

EXHIBIT 14

Chart of Accounts Under the Periodic Inventory System

Balance Sheet Accounts	Income Statement Accounts
100 Assets	400 Revenues
110 Cash	410 Sales
111 Notes Receivable	500 Costs and Expenses
112 Accounts Receivable	510 Purchases
115 Merchandise Inventory	511 Purchases Returns and Allowances
116 Office Supplies	512 Purchases Discounts
117 Prepaid Insurance	513 Freight In
120 Land	520 Sales Salaries Expense
123 Store Equipment	521 Advertising Expense
124 Accumulated Depreciation—Store Equipment	522 Depreciation Expense—Store Equipment
125 Office Equipment	523 Delivery Expense
126 Accumulated Depreciation—Office Equipment	529 Miscellaneous Selling Expense
200 Liabilities	530 Office Salaries Expense
210 Accounts Payable	531 Rent Expense
211 Salaries Payable	532 Depreciation Expense—Office Equipment
212 Unearned Rent	533 Insurance Expense
215 Notes Payable	534 Office Supplies Expense
300 Owner's Equity	539 Misc. Administrative Expense
310 Chris Clark, Capital	600 Other Income
311 Chris Clark, Drawing	610 Rent Revenue
312 Income Summary	700 Other Expense
	710 Interest Expense

Recording Merchandise Transactions Under the Periodic Inventory System

Using the periodic inventory system, purchases of inventory are not recorded in the merchandise inventory account. Instead, purchases, purchases discounts, and purchases returns and allowances accounts are used. In addition, the sales of merchandise are not recorded in the inventory account. Thus, there is no detailed record of the amount of inventory on hand at any given time. At the end of the period, a physical count of merchandise inventory on hand is taken. This physical count is used to determine the cost of merchandise sold as will be illustrated later.

The use of purchases, purchases discounts, purchases returns and allowances, and freight in accounts are described in this section.

Purchases Purchases of inventory are recorded in a purchases account rather than in the merchandise inventory account. Purchases is debited for the invoice amount of a purchase.

Purchases Discounts Purchases discounts are normally recorded in a separate purchases discounts account. The balance of the purchases discounts account is reported as a deduction from Purchases for the period. Thus, Purchases Discounts is a contra (or offsetting) account to Purchases.

Purchases Returns and Allowances Purchases returns and allowances are recorded in a similar manner as purchases discounts. A separate purchases returns and allowances account is used to record returns and allowances. Purchases returns and allowances are reported as a deduction from Purchases for the period. Thus, Purchases Returns and Allowances is a contra (or offsetting) account to Purchases.

Freight In When merchandise is purchased FOB shipping point, the buyer pays for the freight. Under the periodic inventory system, freight paid when purchasing merchandise FOB shipping point is debited to Freight In, Transportation In, or a similar account.

The preceding periodic inventory accounts and their effect on the cost of merchandise purchased are summarized as follows:

Account	Entry to Increase	Normal Balance	Effect on Cost of Merchandise Purchased
Purchases	Debit	Debit	Increases
Purchases Discounts	Credit	Credit	Decreases
Purchases Returns and Allowances	Credit	Credit	Decreases
Freight In	Debit	Debit	Increases

Exhibit 15 illustrates the recording of merchandise transactions using the periodic system.

Adjusting Process Under the Periodic Inventory System

The adjusting process is the same under the periodic and perpetual inventory systems except for the inventory shrinkage adjustment. The ending merchandise inventory is determined by a physical count under both systems.

Under the perpetual inventory system, the ending inventory physical count is compared to the balance of Merchandise Inventory. The difference is the amount of inventory shrinkage. The inventory shrinkage is then recorded as a debit to Cost of Merchandise Sold and a credit to Merchandise Inventory.

Under the periodic inventory system, the merchandise inventory account is not kept up to date for purchases and sales. As a result, the inventory shrinkage cannot be directly determined. Instead, any inventory shrinkage is included indirectly in the computation of the cost of merchandise sold as shown in Exhibit 14. This is a major disadvantage of the periodic inventory system. That is, under the periodic inventory system, inventory shrinkage is not separately determined.

When the periodic inventory system is used, the cost of merchandise sold is determined as shown in Exhibit 16.

EXHIBIT 15

Transactions Using the Periodic Inventory System

Transaction	Periodic Inventory System		
June 5. Purchased $30,000 of merchandise on account, terms 2/10, n/30.	Purchases	30,000	
	Accounts Payable..........		30,000
June 8. Returned merchandise purchased on account on June 5, $500.	Accounts Payable.............	500	
	Purchases Returns and Allowances..............		500
June 15. Paid for purchase of June 5, less return of $500 and discount of $590 [($30,000 – $500) × 2%].	Accounts Payable.............	29,500	
	Cash.......................		28,910
	Purchases Discounts		590
June 18. Sold merchandise on account, $12,500, 1/10, n/30. The cost of the merchandise sold was $9,000.	Accounts Receivable [$12,500 – ($12,500 × 1%)]	12,375	
	Sales		12,375
June 22. Purchased merchandise, $15,000, terms FOB shipping point, 2/15, n/30, with prepaid freight of $750 added to the invoice.	Purchases	15,000	
	Freight In.....................	750	
	Accounts Payable..........		15,750
June 28. Received payment on account from June 18 sale	Cash	12,375	
	Accounts Receivable.......		12,375
June 29. Received $19,600 from cash sales. The cost of the merchandise sold was $13,800.	Cash	19,600	
	Sales		19,600

Financial Statements Under the Periodic Inventory System

The financial statements are similar under the perpetual and periodic inventory systems. When the multiple-step format of income statement is used, the cost of merchandise sold may be reported as shown in Exhibit 16.

EXHIBIT 16

Determining Cost of Merchandise Sold Using the Periodic System

Merchandise inventory, January 1, 2017			$ 59,700
Purchases		$521,980	
Less: Purchases returns and allowances	$9,100		
Purchases discounts..................................	2,525	11,625	
Net purchases...		$510,355	
Add freight in		17,400	
Cost of merchandise purchased			527,755
Merchandise available for sale..............................			$587,455
Less merchandise inventory, December 31, 2017.............			62,150
Cost of merchandise sold..................................			$525,305

Closing Entries Under the Periodic Inventory System

The closing entries differ in the periodic inventory system in that there is no cost of merchandise sold account to close to Income Summary. Instead, the purchases,

purchases discounts, purchases returns and allowances, and freight in accounts are closed to Income Summary. In addition, the merchandise inventory account is adjusted to the end-of-period physical inventory count during the closing process.

The four closing entries under the periodic inventory system are as follows:

1. Debit each temporary account with a credit balance, such as Sales, for its balance and credit Income Summary. Since Purchases Discounts and Purchases Returns and Allowances are temporary accounts with credit balances, they are debited for their balances. In addition, Merchandise Inventory is debited for its end-of-period balance based on the end-of-period physical inventory.
2. Credit each temporary account with a debit balance, such as the various expenses, and debit Income Summary. Since Freight In is a temporary account with a debit balance, it is credited for its balance. In addition, Merchandise Inventory is credited for its balance as of the beginning of the period.
3. Debit Income Summary for the amount of its balance (net income) and credit the owner's capital account. The accounts debited and credited are reversed if there is a net loss.
4. Debit the owner's capital account for the balance of the drawing account and credit the drawing account.

The four closing entries for **NetSolutions** under the periodic inventory system follow:

Journal

Date		Item	Post. Ref.	Debit	Credit
2017		Closing Entries			
Dec.	31	Merchandise Inventory	115	62,150	
		Sales	410	708,255	
		Purchases Returns and Allowances	511	9,100	
		Purchases Discounts	512	2,525	
		Rent Revenue	610	600	
		Income Summary	312		782,630
	31	Income Summary	312	707,230	
		Merchandise Inventory	115		59,700
		Purchases	510		521,980
		Freight In	513		17,400
		Sales Salaries Expense	520		53,430
		Advertising Expense	521		10,860
		Depreciation Expense—Store Equipment	522		3,100
		Delivery Expense	523		2,800
		Miscellaneous Selling Expense	529		630
		Office Salaries Expense	530		21,020
		Rent Expense	531		8,100
		Depreciation Expense—Office Equipment	532		2,490
		Insurance Expense	533		1,910
		Office Supplies Expense	534		610
		Miscellaneous Administrative Expense	539		760
		Interest Expense	710		2,440
	31	Income Summary	312	75,400	
		Chris Clark, Capital	310		75,400
	31	Chris Clark, Capital	310	18,000	
		Chris Clark, Drawing	311		18,000

In the first closing entry, Merchandise Inventory is debited for $62,150. This is the ending physical inventory count on December 31, 2017. In the second closing entry, Merchandise Inventory is credited for its January 1, 2017, balance of $59,700. In this way, the closing entries highlight the importance of the beginning and ending balances of Merchandise Inventory in determining the cost of merchandise sold, as shown in Exhibit 16. After the closing entries are posted, Merchandise Inventory will have a balance of $62,150. This is the amount reported on the December 31, 2017, balance sheet.

In the preceding closing entries, the periodic accounts are highlighted. Under the perpetual inventory system, the highlighted periodic inventory accounts are replaced by the cost of merchandise sold account.

At a Glance 6

Distinguish between the activities and financial statements of service and merchandising businesses.

Key Points Merchandising businesses purchase merchandise for selling to customers. On a merchandising business's income statement, revenue from selling merchandise is reported as sales. The cost of the merchandise sold is subtracted from sales to arrive at gross profit. The operating expenses are subtracted from gross profit to arrive at net income. Merchandise inventory, which is merchandise not sold, is reported as a current asset on the balance sheet.

Learning Outcomes	Example Exercises	Practice Exercises
• Describe how the activities of a service and a merchandising business differ.		
• Describe the differences between the income statements of a service and a merchandising business.		
• Compute gross profit.	EE6-1	PE6-1A, 6-1B
• Describe how merchandise inventory is reported on the balance sheet.		

Describe and illustrate the accounting for merchandise transactions.

Key Points Purchases of merchandise for cash or on account are recorded as merchandise inventory. Discounts for early payment of purchases on account are purchases discounts. Purchases of merchandise inventory subject to purchase discounts are recorded net of the discount. Price adjustments or returned merchandise are purchases returns. Price adjustments or returned merchandise are recorded net of any purchase discount.

Sales of merchandise for cash or on account are recorded as sales. The cost of merchandise sold and the reduction in merchandise inventory are also recorded at the time of sale.

A seller may grant customers a variety of discounts, called customer discounts. A sales discount encourages customer to pay their invoice early. Sales subject to a sales discount are recorded net of the discount.

A seller may pay a customer a refund or grant a price allowance for returned or damaged merchandise, called customer returns and allowances. At the end of the accounting period, a seller must record two adjusting entries for expected returns and allowances. The first adjusting entry debits Sales and credits Customer Refunds Payable. The second entry debits Estimated Returns Inventory and credits Cost of Merchandise Sold. When merchandise is returned for a refund, Customer Refunds Payable is debited and Cash is credited for the amount of the refund. The returned merchandise is recorded as a debit to Merchandise Inventory and credit to Estimated Returns Inventory. When a customer doesn't return merchandise, but is granted an allowance Customer Refunds Payable is debited and either Cash, if the customer has already paid for the merchandise, or Account Receivable is credited.

When merchandise is shipped FOB shipping point, the buyer pays the freight and debits Merchandise Inventory. When merchandise is shipped FOB destination, the seller pays the freight and debits Delivery Expense or Freight Out. Merchandise transactions can be summarized in T account form as shown in Exhibit 7. Each merchandising transaction affects a buyer and a seller. The chart of accounts for a merchandising business (NetSolutions) is shown in Exhibit 9. The liability for sales tax is incurred when the sale is made and is recorded by the seller as a credit to the sales tax payable account. Trade discounts are discounts off the list price of merchandise.

Learning Outcomes	Example Exercises	Practice Exercises
• Prepare journal entries to record the purchases of merchandise for cash.		
• Prepare journal entries to record the purchases of merchandise on account.	EE6-2	PE6-2A, 6-2B
• Prepare journal entries to record purchases discounts and purchases returns and allowances.	EE6-2	PE6-2A, 6-2B
• Prepare journal entries to record sales of merchandise for cash or using a credit card.		
• Prepare journal entries to record sales of merchandise on account.	EE6-3	PE6-3A, 6-3B
• Prepare journal entries to record sales discounts and customer returns and allowances.	EE6-3	PE6-3A, 6-3B
• Prepare journal entries for freight from the point of view of the buyer and seller.		
• Determine the total cost of the purchase of merchandise under differing freight terms.	EE6-4	PE6-4A, 6-4B
• Record the same merchandise transactions for the buyer and seller.	EE6-5	PE6-5A, 6-5B
• Prepare a chart of accounts for a merchandising business.		
• Determine the cost of merchandise purchased when a trade discount is offered by the seller.		
• Record sales transactions involving sales taxes and trade discounts.		

Describe and illustrate the financial statements of a merchandising business.

Key Points The multiple-step income statement of a merchandiser reports sales. The cost of the merchandise sold is subtracted from sales to determine the gross profit. Operating income is determined by subtracting selling and administrative expenses from gross profit. Net income is determined by adding or subtracting the net of other income and expense. The income statement may also be reported in a single-step form.

The statement of owner's equity is similar to that for a service business.

The balance sheet reports merchandise inventory at the end of the period as a current asset.

Learning Outcomes	Example Exercises	Practice Exercises
• Prepare a multiple-step income statement for a merchandising business.		
• Prepare a single-step income statement.		
• Prepare a statement of owner's equity for a merchandising business.		
• Prepare a report form of balance sheet for a merchandising business.		

Describe the adjusting and closing process for a merchandising business.

Key Points The normal adjusting entry for inventory shrinkage is to debit Cost of Merchandise Sold and credit Merchandise Inventory.

The closing entries for a merchandising business are similar to those for a service business except that the cost of merchandise sold is also closed to Income Summary.

Learning Outcomes	Example Exercises	Practice Exercises
• Prepare the adjusting journal entry for inventory shrinkage.	EE6-6	PE6-6A, 6-6B
• Prepare the closing entries for a merchandising business.		

Describe and illustrate the use of the ratio of sales to assets in evaluating a company's operating performance.

Key Points The ratio of sales to assets measures how effectively a business is using its assets to generate sales. A high ratio indicates an effective use of assets. Using the average of the total assets at the beginning and end of the year, the ratio is computed as follows:

$$\text{Ratio of Sales to Assets} = \frac{\text{Sales}}{\text{Average Total Assets}}$$

Learning Outcomes	Example Exercises	Practice Exercises
• Interpret a high ratio of sales to assets.		
• Compute the ratio of sales to assets.	EE6-7	PE6-7A, 6-7B

Key Terms

account form (283)
administrative expenses (general expenses) (282)
cost of merchandise sold (265)
credit memorandum (credit memo) (273)
credit period (267)
credit terms (267)
customer discounts (272)
customer returns and allowances (272)
debit memorandum (debit memo) (269)
FOB (free on board) destination (275)
FOB (free on board) shipping point (274)
gross profit (265)
income from operations (operating income) (282)
inventory shrinkage (inventory shortage) (284)
invoice (267)
merchandise inventory (265)
multiple-step income statement (281)
operating cycle (264)
other expense (282)
other income (282)
periodic inventory system (266)
perpetual inventory system (266)
physical inventory (266)
purchases discounts (268)
purchases returns and allowances (269)
ratio of sales to assets (287)
report form (283)
sales (265)
sales discounts (272)
selling expenses (282)
single-step income statement (283)
trade discounts (281)

Illustrative Problem

The following transactions were completed by Montrose Company during May of the current year. Montrose Company uses a perpetual inventory system.

May 3. Purchased merchandise on account from Floyd Co., $4,000, terms FOB shipping point, 2/10, n/30, with prepaid freight of $120 added to the invoice.

5. Purchased merchandise on account from Kramer Co., $8,500, terms FOB destination, 1/10, n/30.

6. Sold merchandise on account to C. F. Howell Co., list price $4,000, trade discount 30%, terms 2/10, n/30. The cost of the merchandise sold was $1,125.

8. Purchased office supplies for cash, $150.

10. Returned merchandise purchased on May 5 from Kramer Co., $1,300.

13. Paid Floyd Co. on account for purchase of May 3.

14. Purchased merchandise for cash, $10,500.

15. Paid Kramer Co. on account for purchase of May 5, less return of May 10.

16. Received cash on account from sale of May 6 to C. F. Howell Co.

19. Sold merchandise on MasterCard credit cards, $2,450. The cost of the merchandise sold was $980.

22. Sold merchandise for cash to Comer Co., $3,480. The cost of the merchandise sold was $1,400.

24. Sold merchandise on account to Smith Co., $4,350. The cost of the merchandise sold was $1,750.

25. Refunded Comer Co. $1,480 for returned merchandise from sale on May 22. The cost of the returned merchandise was $600.

31. Paid a service processing fee of $140 for MasterCard sales.

Instructions

1. Journalize the preceding transactions.
2. Journalize the adjusting entry for merchandise inventory shrinkage, $3,750.

Solution

	Date		Account	Debit	Credit
1.	May	3	Merchandise Inventory [$4,000 – ($4,000 × 2%)] + $120	4,040	
			Accounts Payable—Floyd Co.		4,040
		5	Merchandise Inventory [$8,500 – ($8,500 × 1%)]	8,415	
			Accounts Payable—Kramer Co.		8,415
		6	Accounts Receivable—C. F. Howell Co.	2,744	
			Sales		2,744
			[$4,000 – (30% × $4,000)] = $2,800		
			[$2,800 – ($2,800 × 2%)] = $2,744		
		6	Cost of Merchandise Sold	1,125	
			Merchandise Inventory		1,125
		8	Office Supplies	150	
			Cash		150
		10	Accounts Payable—Kramer Co. [$1,300 – ($1,300 × 1%)]	1,287	
			Merchandise Inventory		1,300
		13	Accounts Payable—Floyd Co.	4,040	
			Cash		4,040
		14	Merchandise Inventory	10,500	
			Cash		10,500
		15	Accounts Payable—Kramer Co. ($8,415 – $1,287)	7,128	
			Cash		7,128
		16	Cash	2,744	
			Accounts Receivable—C. F. Howell Co.		2,744
		19	Cash	2,450	
			Sales		2,450
		19	Cost of Merchandise Sold	980	
			Merchandise Inventory		980
		22	Cash	3,480	
			Sales		3,480
		22	Cost of Merchandise Sold	1,400	
			Merchandise Inventory		1,400
		24	Accounts Receivable—Smith Co.	4,350	
			Sales		4,350
		24	Cost of Merchandise Sold	1,750	
			Merchandise Inventory		1,750
		25	Customers Refunds Payable	1,480	
			Cash		1,480
		25	Merchandise Inventory	600	
			Estimated Returns Inventory		600
		31	Credit Card Expense	140	
			Cash		140
2.	May	31	Cost of Merchandise Sold	3,750	
			Merchandise Inventory		3,750
			Inventory shrinkage.		

Discussion Questions

1. What distinguishes a merchandising business from a service business?
2. Can a business earn a gross profit but incur a net loss? Explain.
3. The credit period during which the buyer of merchandise is allowed to pay usually begins with what date?
4. What is the meaning of (a) 1/15, n/60; (b) n/30; (c) n/eom?
5. How are sales to customers using MasterCard and VISA recorded?
6. What is the nature of (a) a credit memo issued by the seller of merchandise, (b) a debit memo issued by the buyer of merchandise?
7. Who bears the freight when the terms of sale are (a) FOB shipping point, (b) FOB destination?
8. Name three accounts that would normally appear in the chart of accounts of a merchandising business but would not appear in the chart of accounts of a service business.
9. Audio Outfitter Inc., which uses a perpetual inventory system, experienced a normal inventory shrinkage of $13,675. What accounts would be debited and credited to record the adjustment for the inventory shrinkage at the end of the accounting period?
10. Assume that Audio Outfitter Inc. in Discussion Question 9 experienced an abnormal inventory shrinkage of $98,600. Audio Outfitter Inc. has decided to record the abnormal inventory shrinkage so that it would be separately disclosed on the income statement. What account would be debited for the abnormal inventory shrinkage?

Practice Exercises

EE 6-1 p. 266

SHOW ME HOW

PE 6-1A Gross profit

OBJ. 1

During the current year, merchandise is sold for $615,000 cash and $4,110,000 on account. The cost of the merchandise sold is $2,835,000. What is the amount of the gross profit?

EE 6-1 p. 266

SHOW ME HOW

PE 6-1B Gross profit

OBJ. 1

During the current year, merchandise is sold for $18,300 cash and $295,700 on account. The cost of the merchandise sold is $188,000. What is the amount of the gross profit?

EE 6-2 p. 270

SHOW ME HOW

PE 6-2A Purchases transactions

OBJ. 2

Halibut Company purchased merchandise on account from a supplier for $18,600, terms 2/10, n/30. Halibut Company returned $5,000 of the merchandise and received full credit.

a. If Halibut Company pays the invoice within the discount period, what is the amount of cash required for the payment?

b. What account is credited by Halibut Company to record the return?

EE 6-2 p. 270

SHOW ME HOW

PE 6-2B Purchases transactions

OBJ. 2

Hoffman Company purchased merchandise on account from a supplier for $65,000, terms 1/10, n/30. Hoffman Company returned $7,500 of the merchandise and received full credit.

a. If Hoffman Company pays the invoice within the discount period, what is the amount of cash required for the payment?

b. What account is debited by Hoffman Company to record the return?

EE 6-3 *p. 274*

SHOW ME HOW

PE 6-3A Sales transactions

OBJ. 2

Journalize the following merchandise transactions:

a. Sold merchandise on account, $72,500 with terms 2/10, n/30. The cost of the merchandise sold was $43,500.

b. Received payment less the discount.

EE 6-3 *p. 274*

SHOW ME HOW

PE 6-3B Sales transactions

OBJ. 2

Journalize the following merchandise transactions:

a. Sold merchandise on account, $92,500 with terms 1/10, n/30. The cost of the merchandise sold was $55,500.

b. Received payment less the discount.

EE 6-4 *p. 277*

SHOW ME HOW

PE 6-4A Freight terms

OBJ. 2

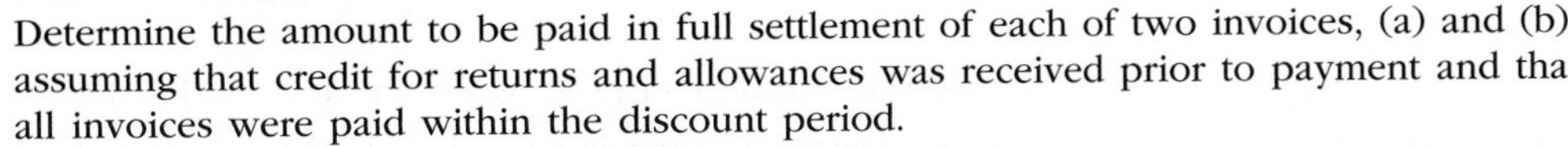

Determine the amount to be paid in full settlement of each of two invoices, (a) and (b), assuming that credit for returns and allowances was received prior to payment and that all invoices were paid within the discount period.

	Merchandise	Freight Paid by Seller	Freight Terms	Returns and Allowances
a.	$ 90,000	$1,000	FOB shipping point, 1/10, n/30	$15,000
b.	110,000	1,575	FOB destination, 2/10, n/30	8,500

EE 6-4 *p. 277*

SHOW ME HOW

PE 6-4B Freight terms

OBJ. 2

Determine the amount to be paid in full settlement of each of two invoices, (a) and (b), assuming that credit for returns and allowances was received prior to payment and that all invoices were paid within the discount period.

	Merchandise	Freight Paid by Seller	Freight Terms	Returns and Allowances
a.	$36,000	$800	FOB destination, 1/10, n/30	$4,000
b.	44,900	375	FOB shipping point, 2/10, n/30	2,400

EE 6-5 *p. 279*

SHOW ME HOW

PE 6-5A Transactions for buyer and seller

OBJ. 2

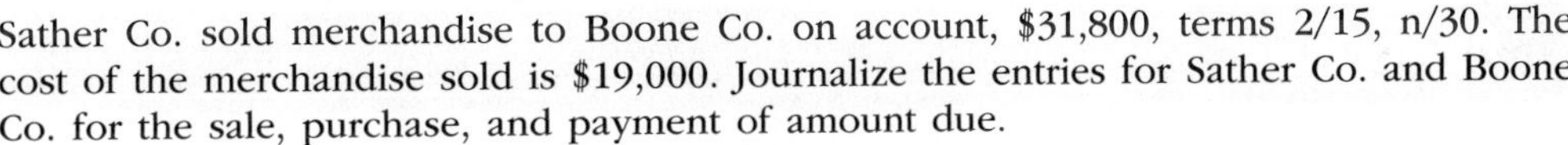

Sather Co. sold merchandise to Boone Co. on account, $31,800, terms 2/15, n/30. The cost of the merchandise sold is $19,000. Journalize the entries for Sather Co. and Boone Co. for the sale, purchase, and payment of amount due.

EE 6-5 *p. 279*

SHOW ME HOW

PE 6-5B Transactions for buyer and seller

OBJ. 2

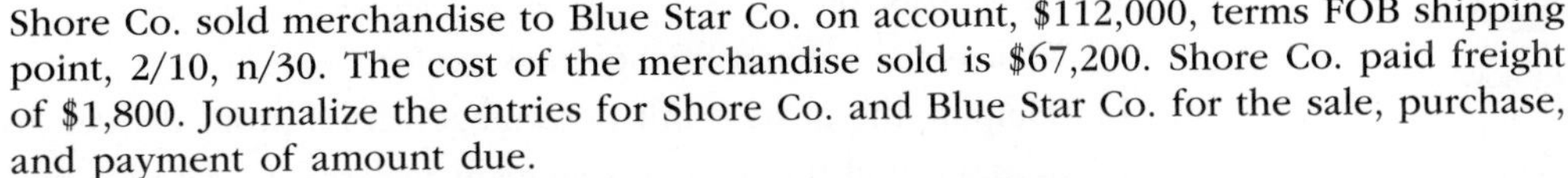

Shore Co. sold merchandise to Blue Star Co. on account, $112,000, terms FOB shipping point, 2/10, n/30. The cost of the merchandise sold is $67,200. Shore Co. paid freight of $1,800. Journalize the entries for Shore Co. and Blue Star Co. for the sale, purchase, and payment of amount due.

EE 6-6 *p. 285*

SHOW ME HOW

PE 6-6A Inventory shrinkage

OBJ. 4

Castle Furnishings Company's perpetual inventory records indicate that $675,400 of merchandise should be on hand on November 30, 2016. The physical inventory indicates that $663,800 of merchandise is actually on hand. Journalize the adjusting entry for the inventory shrinkage for Castle Furnishings Company for the year ended November 30, 2016. Assume that the inventory shrinkage is a normal amount.

EE 6-6 p. 285

PE 6-6B Inventory shrinkage

OBJ. 4

SHOW ME HOW

Hahn Flooring Company's perpetual inventory records indicate that $1,333,150 of merchandise should be on hand on December 31, 2016. The physical inventory indicates that $1,309,900 of merchandise is actually on hand. Journalize the adjusting entry for the inventory shrinkage for Hahn Flooring Company for the year ended December 31, 2016. Assume that the inventory shrinkage is a normal amount.

EE 6-7 p. 288

PE 6-7A Ratio of sales to assets

OBJ. 5

SHOW ME HOW

Financial statement data for years ending December 31 for Latchkey Company follows:

	2016	2015
Sales	$1,734,000	$1,645,000
Total assets:		
Beginning of year	480,000	460,000
End of year	540,000	480,000

a. Determine the ratio of sales to assets for 2016 and 2015.

b. Does the change in the ratio of sales to assets from 2015 to 2016 indicate a favorable or an unfavorable trend?

EE 6-7 p. 288

PE 6-7B Ratio of sales to assets

OBJ. 5

SHOW ME HOW

Financial statement data for years ending December 31 for Edison Company follows:

	2016	2015
Sales	$1,884,000	$1,562,000
Total assets:		
Beginning of year	770,000	650,000
End of year	800,000	770,000

a. Determine the ratio of sales to assets for 2016 and 2015.

b. Does the change in the ratio of sales to assets from 2015 to 2016 indicate a favorable or an unfavorable trend?

Exercises

EX 6-1 Determining gross profit

OBJ. 1

SHOW ME HOW

During the current year, merchandise is sold for $4,885,000. The cost of the merchandise sold is $3,028,700.

a. What is the amount of the gross profit?

b. Compute the gross profit percentage (gross profit divided by sales).

c. Will the income statement necessarily report a net income? Explain.

EX 6-2 Determining cost of merchandise sold

OBJ. 1

SHOW ME HOW

For a recent year, Best Buy reported sales of $50,705 million. Its gross profit was $12,573 million. What was the amount of Best Buy's cost of merchandise sold?

EX 6-3 Purchase-related transactions

OBJ. 2

SHOW ME HOW

The Stationery Company purchased merchandise on account from a supplier for $28,900, terms 1/10, n/30. The Stationery Company returned $6,100 of the merchandise and received full credit.

a. What is the amount of cash required for the payment?

b. Under a perpetual inventory system, what account is credited by The Stationery Company to record the return?

EX 6-4 Purchase-related transactions **OBJ. 2**

A retailer is considering the purchase of 250 units of a specific item from either of two suppliers. Their offers are as follows:

Supplier One: $400 a unit, total of $100,000, 1/10, n/30, no charge for freight.

Supplier Two: $399 a unit, total of $99,750, 2/10, n/30, plus freight of $975.

Which of the two offers, Supplier One or Supplier Two, yields the lower price?

EX 6-5 Purchase-related transactions **OBJ. 2**

The debits and credits from four related transactions are presented in the following T accounts. Describe each transaction.

Cash

		(2)	300
		(4)	16,660

Accounts Payable

(3)	3,920	(1)	20,580
(4)	16,660		

Merchandise Inventory

(1)	20,580	(3)	3,920
(2)	300		

✔ (c) Cash, cr. $64,680

SHOW ME HOW

EX 6-6 Purchase-related transactions **OBJ. 2**

Warwick's Co., a women's clothing store, purchased $75,000 of merchandise from a supplier on account, terms FOB destination, 2/10, n/30. Warwick's returned $9,000 of the merchandise, receiving a credit memo, and then paid the amount due within the discount period. Journalize Warwick's entries to record (a) the purchase, (b) the merchandise return, and (c) the payment.

✔ (e) Cash, dr. $1,425

SHOW ME HOW

EX 6-7 Purchase-related transactions **OBJ. 2**

Journalize entries for the following related transactions of South Coast Heating & Air Company:

a. Purchased $48,000 of merchandise from Atlas Co. on account, terms 1/10, n/30.

b. Paid the amount owed on the invoice within the discount period.

c. Discovered that $7,500 of the merchandise purchased in (a) was defective and returned items, receiving credit.

d. Purchased $6,000 of merchandise from Atlas Co. on account, terms n/30.

e. Received a refund from Atlas Co. for return in (c) less the purchase in (d).

SHOW ME HOW

EX 6-8 Sales-related transactions, including the use of credit cards **OBJ. 2**

Journalize the entries for the following transactions:

a. Sold merchandise for cash, $30,000. The cost of the merchandise sold was $18,000.

b. Sold merchandise on account, $258,000. The cost of the merchandise sold was $154,800.

c. Sold merchandise to customers who used MasterCard and VISA, $160,000. The cost of the merchandise sold was $96,000.

d. Sold merchandise to customers who used American Express, $72,000. The cost of the merchandise sold was $43,200.

e. Received an invoice from National Clearing House Credit Co. for $8,800, representing a service fee paid for processing MasterCard, VISA, and American Express sales.

EX 6-9 Customer returns and allowances

OBJ. 2

Zell Company had sales of $1,800,000 and related cost of merchandise sold of $1,150,000 for its first year of operations ending December 31, 2016. Zell Company provides customers a refund for any returned or damaged merchandise. At the end of the year, Zell Company estimates that customers will request refunds for 1.5% of sales and estimates that merchandise costing $16,000 will be returned. Assume that on February 3, 2017 Anderson Co. returned merchandise with a selling price of $5,000 for a cash refund. The returned merchandise originally cost Zell Company $3,100. (a) Journalize the adjusting entries on December 31, 2016 to record the expected customer returns. (b) Journalize the entries to record the returned merchandise and cash refund to Anderson Co.

EX 6-10 Sales-related transactions

OBJ. 2

SHOW ME HOW

After the amount due on a sale of $28,000, terms 2/10, n/eom, is received from a customer within the discount period, the seller consents to the return of the entire shipment for a cash refund. The cost of the merchandise returned was $16,800. (a) What is the amount of the refund owed to the customer? (b) Journalize the entries made by the seller to record the return and the refund.

EX 6-11 Sales-related transactions

OBJ. 2

The debits and credits for three related transactions are presented in the following T accounts. Describe each transaction.

Cash

(5)	39,200		

Accounts Receivable

(1)	41,160	(3)	1,960
		(5)	39,200

Merchandise Inventory

(4)	1,200	(2)	25,200

Estimated Returns Inventory

		(4)	1,200

Customer Refunds Payable

(3)	1,960		

Sales

		(1)	41,160

Cost of Merchandise Sold

(2)	25,200		

EX 6-12 Sales-related transactions

OBJ. 2

✔ c. $57,470

SHOW ME HOW

Merchandise is sold on account to a customer for $56,500, terms FOB shipping point, 2/10, n/30. The seller paid the freight of $2,100. Determine the following: (a) amount of the sale, (b) amount debited to Accounts Receivable, and (c) amount received within the discount period.

EX 6-13 Determining amounts to be paid on invoices

OBJ. 2

✔ a. $22,500

SHOW ME HOW

Determine the amount to be paid in full settlement of each of the following invoices, assuming that credit for returns and allowances was received prior to payment and that all invoices were paid within the discount period:

	Merchandise	Freight Paid by Seller		Customer Returns and Allowances
a.	$27,000	—	FOB destination, n/30	$4,500
b.	18,600	$475	FOB shipping point, 2/10, n/30	3,000
c.	8,400	—	FOB shipping point, 1/10, n/30	700
d.	48,300	900	FOB shipping point, 2/10, n/30	6,500
e.	33,000	—	FOB destination, 1/10, n/30	—

SHOW ME HOW

EX 6-14 Sales-related transactions OBJ. 2

Showcase Co., a furniture wholesaler, sells merchandise to Balboa Co. on account, $254,500, terms n/30. The cost of the merchandise sold is $152,700. Showcase Co. issues a credit memo for $30,000 for merchandise returned prior to Balboa Co. paying the original invoice. The cost of the merchandise returned is $17,500. Journalize Showcase Co.'s entries for (a) the sale, including the cost of the merchandise sold, (b) the credit memo, including the cost of the returned merchandise, and (c) the receipt of the check for the amount due from Balboa Co.

SHOW ME HOW

EX 6-15 Purchase-related transactions OBJ. 2

Based on the data presented in Exercise 6-14, journalize Balboa Co.'s entries for (a) the purchase, (b) the return of the merchandise for credit, and (c) the payment of the invoice.

EX 6-16 Chart of accounts OBJ. 2

Monet Paints Co. is a newly organized business with a list of accounts arranged in alphabetical order, as follows:

Accounts Payable	Merchandise Inventory
Accounts Receivable	Miscellaneous Administrative Expense
Accumulated Depreciation—Office Equipment	Miscellaneous Selling Expense
Accumulated Depreciation—Store Equipment	Notes Payable
Advertising Expense	Office Equipment
Cash	Office Salaries Expense
Cost of Merchandise Sold	Office Supplies
Delivery Expense	Office Supplies Expense
Depreciation Expense—Office Equipment	Prepaid Insurance
Depreciation Expense—Store Equipment	Rent Expense
Income Summary	Salaries Payable
Insurance Expense	Sales
Interest Expense	Sales Salaries Expense
Kailey Garner, Capital	Store Equipment
Kailey Garner, Drawing	Store Supplies
Land	Store Supplies Expense

Construct a chart of accounts, assigning account numbers and arranging the accounts in balance sheet and income statement order, as illustrated in Exhibit 9. Each account number is three digits: the first digit is to indicate the major classification (1 for assets, and so on); the second digit is to indicate the subclassification (11 for current assets, and so on); and the third digit is to identify the specific account (110 for Cash, 112 for Accounts Receivable, 114 for Merchandise Inventory, 115 for Store Supplies, and so on).

✔c. $38,880

SHOW ME HOW

EX 6-17 Sales tax OBJ. 2

A sale of merchandise on account for $36,000 is subject to an 8% sales tax. (a) Should the sales tax be recorded at the time of sale or when payment is received? (b) What is the amount of the sale? (c) What is the amount debited to Accounts Receivable? (d) What is the title of the account to which the $2,880 ($36,000 × 8%) is credited?

SHOW ME HOW

EX 6-18 Sales tax transactions OBJ. 2

Journalize the entries to record the following selected transactions:

a. Sold $62,800 of merchandise on account, subject to a sales tax of 5%. The cost of the merchandise sold was $37,500.

b. Paid $39,650 to the state sales tax department for taxes collected.

EX 6-19 Normal balances of merchandise accounts OBJ. 2

What is the normal balance of the following accounts: (a) Cost of Merchandise Sold, (b) Customer Refunds Payable, (c) Delivery Expense, (d) Estimated Returns Inventory, (e) Merchandise Inventory, (f) Sales, (g) Sales Tax Payable.

SHOW ME HOW

EX 6-20 Income statement and accounts for merchandiser **OBJ. 3**

For the fiscal year, sales were $25,565,000 and the cost of merchandise sold was $15,400,000.

a. What was the amount of gross profit?

b. If total operating expenses were $4,550,000, could you determine net income?

c. Is Customer Refunds Payable an asset, liability, or owner's equity account and what is its normal balance?

d. Is Estimated Returns Inventory an asset, liability, or owner's equity account and what is its normal balance?

EX 6-21 Income statement for merchandiser **OBJ. 3**

The following expenses were incurred by a merchandising business during the year. In which expense section of the income statement should each be reported: (a) selling, (b) administrative, or (c) other?

1. Advertising expense
2. Depreciation expense on store equipment
3. Insurance expense on office equipment
4. Interest expense on notes payable
5. Rent expense on office building
6. Salaries of office personnel
7. Salary of sales manager
8. Sales supplies used

SHOW ME HOW

EX 6-22 Determining amounts for items omitted from income statement **OBJ. 3**

Two items are omitted in each of the following four lists of income statement data. Determine the amounts of the missing items, identifying them by letter.

Sales	$463,400	(b)	$1,295,000	(d)
Cost of merchandise sold	(a)	410,000	(c)	900,000
Gross profit	83,500	$277,500	275,000	600,000

✔ a. Net income: $1,345,000

SHOW ME HOW

EX 6-23 Multiple-step income statement **OBJ. 3**

On October 31, 2016, the balances of the accounts appearing in the ledger of Prestige Furnishings Company, a furniture wholesaler, are as follows:

Accumulated Depreciation—Building	$ 750,000	Merchandise Inventory	$ 980,000
Administrative Expenses	540,000	Notes Payable	250,000
Building	2,500,000	Office Supplies	20,000
Cash	175,000	Salaries Payable	8,000
Cost of Merchandise Sold	3,800,000	Sales	6,410,000
Interest Expense	10,000	Selling Expenses	715,000
Jan Brown, Capital	1,587,000	Store Supplies	90,000
Jan Brown, Drawing	175,000		

a. Prepare a multiple-step income statement for the year ended October 31, 2016.

b. Compare the major advantages and disadvantages of the multiple-step and single-step forms of income statements.

EX 6-24 Multiple-step income statement

OBJ. 3

Identify the errors in the following income statement:

Curbstone Company
Income Statement
For the Year Ended August 31, 2016

Sales		$8,595,000
Cost of merchandise sold		6,110,000
Income from operations		$2,485,000
Expenses:		
Selling expenses	$ 800,000	
Administrative expenses	575,000	
Delivery expense	425,000	
Total expenses		1,800,000
		$ 685,000
Other expense:		
Interest revenue		45,000
Gross profit		$ 640,000

EX 6-25 Single-step income statement

OBJ. 3

✔ Net income: $1,277,500

SHOW ME HOW

Summary operating data for Custom Wire & Tubing Company during the year ended April 30, 2016, are as follows: cost of merchandise sold, $6,100,000; administrative expenses, $740,000; interest expense, $25,000; rent revenue, $60,000; sales, $9,332,500; and selling expenses, $1,250,000. Prepare a single-step income statement.

EX 6-26 Adjusting entry for merchandise inventory shrinkage

OBJ. 4

SHOW ME HOW

Paragon Tire Co.'s perpetual inventory records indicate that $2,780,000 of merchandise should be on hand on March 31, 2016. The physical inventory indicates that $2,734,800 of merchandise is actually on hand. Journalize the adjusting entry for the inventory shrinkage for Paragon Tire Co. for the year ended March 31, 2016.

EX 6-27 Closing the accounts of a merchandiser

OBJ. 4

From the following list, identify the accounts that should be closed to Income Summary at the end of the fiscal year under a perpetual inventory system: (a) Accounts Payable, (b) Advertising Expense, (c) Cost of Merchandise Sold, (d) Merchandise Inventory, (e) Sales, (f) Supplies, (g) Supplies Expense, (h) Valery Lavine, Drawing, (i) Wages Payable.

EX 6-28 Closing entries; net income

OBJ. 4

Based on the data presented in Exercise 6-23, journalize the closing entries.

EX 6-29 Closing entries

OBJ. 4

On July 31, 2016, the balances of the accounts appearing in the ledger of Serbian Interiors Company, a furniture wholesaler, are as follows:

Accumulated Depr.—Building	$365,000	Notes Payable	$ 100,000
Administrative Expenses	440,000	Sales	1,437,000
Building	810,000	Sales Tax Payable	4,500
Cash	78,000	Selling Expenses	160,000
Cost of Merchandise Sold	775,000	Store Supplies	16,000
Interest Expense	6,000	Store Supplies Expense	21,500
Peter Bronsky, Capital	530,000		
Peter Bronsky, Drawing	15,000		
Merchandise Inventory	115,000		

Prepare the July 31, 2016, closing entries for Serbian Interiors Company.

EX 6-30 Ratio of sales to assets

OBJ. 5

SHOW ME HOW

The Home Depot reported the following data (in millions) in its recent financial statements:

	Year 2	Year 1
Sales	$70,395	$67,997
Total assets at the end of the year	40,518	40,125
Total assets at the beginning of the year	40,125	40,877

a. Determine the ratio of sales to assets for The Home Depot for Year 2 and Year 1. Round to two decimal places.

b. What conclusions can be drawn from these ratios concerning the trend in the ability of The Home Depot to effectively use its assets to generate sales?

EX 6-31 Ratio of sales to assets

OBJ. 5

Kroger, a national supermarket chain, reported the following data (in millions) in its financial statements for a recent year:

Total revenue	$90,374
Total assets at end of year	23,476
Total assets at beginning of year	23,505

a. Compute the ratio of sales to assets. Round to two decimal places.

b. **Tiffany & Co.** is a large North American retailer of jewelry, with a ratio of sales to assets of 0.92. Why would Tiffany's ratio of sales to assets be lower than that of Kroger?

Appendix
EX 6-32 Rules of debit and credit for periodic inventory accounts

Complete the following table by indicating for (a) through (g) whether the proper answer is debit or credit:

Account	Increase	Decrease	Normal Balance
Purchases	debit	(a)	(b)
Purchases Discounts	credit	(c)	credit
Purchases Returns and Allowances	(d)	(e)	(f)
Freight In	debit	(g)	debit

Appendix
EX 6-33 Journal entries using the periodic inventory system

The following selected transactions were completed by Air Systems Company during January of the current year. Air Systems Company uses the periodic inventory system.

Jan. 2. Purchased $18,200 of merchandise on account, FOB shipping point, terms 2/15, n/30.
5. Paid freight of $190 on the January 2 purchase.
6. Returned $2,750 of the merchandise purchased on January 2.
13. Sold merchandise on account, $37,300, FOB destination, 1/10, n/30. The cost of merchandise sold was $22,400.
15. Paid freight of $215 for the merchandise sold on January 13.
17. Paid for the purchase of January 2 less the return and discount.
23. Received payment on account for the sale of January 13 less the discount.

Journalize the entries to record the transactions of Air Systems Company.

Appendix
EX 6-34 Identify items missing in determining cost of merchandise sold

For (a) through (d), identify the items designated by X and Y.

a. Purchases − (X + Y) = Net purchases.
b. Net purchases + X = Cost of merchandise purchased.
c. Merchandise inventory (beginning) + Cost of merchandise purchased = X.
d. Merchandise available for sale − X = Cost of merchandise sold.

Appendix
EX 6-35 Cost of merchandise sold and related items

✔ a. Cost of merchandise sold, $3,551,600

The following data were extracted from the accounting records of Harkins Company for the year ended April 30, 2016:

Merchandise inventory, May 1, 2015	$ 380,000
Merchandise inventory, April 30, 2016	415,000
Purchases	3,800,000
Purchases returns and allowances	150,000
Purchases discounts	80,000
Sales	5,850,000
Freight in	16,600

a. Prepare the cost of merchandise sold section of the income statement for the year ended April 30, 2016, using the periodic inventory system.
b. Determine the gross profit to be reported on the income statement for the year ended April 30, 2016.
c. Would gross profit be different if the perpetual inventory system was used instead of the periodic inventory system?

Appendix
EX 6-36 Cost of merchandise sold

Based on the following data, determine the cost of merchandise sold for November:

Merchandise inventory, November 1	$ 28,000
Merchandise inventory, November 30	31,500
Purchases	475,000
Purchases returns and allowances	15,000
Purchases discounts	9,000
Freight in	7,000

Appendix
EX 6-37 Cost of merchandise sold

Based on the following data, determine the cost of merchandise sold for July:

Merchandise inventory, July 1	$ 190,850
Merchandise inventory, July 31	160,450
Purchases	1,126,000
Purchases returns and allowances	46,000
Purchases discounts	23,000
Freight in	17,500

✔ Correct cost of merchandise sold, $1,033,300

Appendix
EX 6-38 Cost of merchandise sold

Identify the errors in the following schedule of the cost of merchandise sold for the year ended May 31, 2016:

Cost of merchandise sold:			
Merchandise inventory, May 31, 2016			$ 105,000
Purchases		$1,110,000	
Plus: Purchases returns and allowances	$55,000		
Purchases discounts	30,000	85,000	
Gross purchases		$1,195,000	
Less freight in		22,000	
Cost of merchandise purchased			1,173,000
Merchandise available for sale			$1,278,000
Less merchandise inventory, June 1, 2015			91,300
Cost of merchandise sold			$1,186,700

Appendix
Ex 6-39 Closing entries using periodic inventory system

United Rug Company is a small rug retailer owned and operated by Pat Kirwan. After the accounts have been adjusted on December 31, the following selected account balances were taken from the ledger:

Advertising Expense	$ 36,000
Depreciation Expense	13,000
Freight In	17,000
Merchandise Inventory, December 1	375,000
Merchandise Inventory, December 31	460,000
Miscellaneous Expense	9,000
Purchases	1,760,000
Purchases Discounts	35,000
Purchases Returns and Allowances	45,000
Pat Kirwan, Drawing	65,000
Salaries Expense	375,000
Sales	2,220,000

Journalize the closing entries on December 31.

Problems: Series A

PR 6-1A Purchase-related transactions using perpetual inventory system — OBJ. 2

General Ledger

The following selected transactions were completed by Capers Company during October of the current year:

Oct. 1. Purchased merchandise from UK Imports Co., $14,448, terms FOB destination, n/30.
3. Purchased merchandise from Hoagie Co., $9,950, terms FOB shipping point, 2/10, n/eom. Prepaid freight of $220 was added to the invoice.
4. Purchased merchandise from Taco Co., $13,650, terms FOB destination, 2/10, n/30.
6. Issued debit memo to Taco Co. for $4,550 of merchandise returned from purchase on October 4.
13. Paid Hoagie Co. for invoice of October 3.
14. Paid Taco Co. for invoice of October 4, less debit memo of October 6.
19. Purchased merchandise from Veggie Co., $27,300, terms FOB shipping point, n/eom.
19. Paid freight of $400 on October 19 purchase from Veggie Co.
20. Purchased merchandise from Caesar Salad Co., $22,000, terms FOB destination, 1/10, n/30.
30. Paid Caesar Salad Co. for invoice of October 20.
31. Paid UK Imports Co. for invoice of October 1.
31. Paid Veggie Co. for invoice of October 19.

Instructions

Journalize the entries to record the transactions of Capers Company for October.

PR 6-2A Sales-related transactions using perpetual inventory system — OBJ. 2

General Ledger

SHOW ME HOW

The following selected transactions were completed by Amsterdam Supply Co., which sells office supplies primarily to wholesalers and occasionally to retail customers:

Mar. 2. Sold merchandise on account to Equinox Co., $18,900, terms FOB destination, 1/10, n/30. The cost of the merchandise sold was $13,300.
3. Sold merchandise for $11,350 plus 6% sales tax to retail cash customers. The cost of merchandise sold was $7,000.
4. Sold merchandise on account to Empire Co., $55,400, terms FOB shipping point, n/eom. The cost of merchandise sold was $33,200.
5. Sold merchandise for $30,000 plus 6% sales tax to retail customers who used MasterCard. The cost of merchandise sold was $19,400.
12. Received check for amount due from Equinox Co. for sale on March 2.
14. Sold merchandise to customers who used American Express cards, $13,700. The cost of merchandise sold was $8,350.
16. Sold merchandise on account to Targhee Co., $27,500, terms FOB shipping point, 1/10, n/30. The cost of merchandise sold was $16,000.
18. Issued credit memo for $4,800 to Targhee Co. for merchandise returned from sale on March 16. The cost of the merchandise returned was $2,900.
19. Sold merchandise on account to Vista Co., $8,250, terms FOB shipping point, 2/10, n/30. Added $75 to the invoice for prepaid freight. The cost of merchandise sold was $5,000.
26. Received check for amount due from Targhee Co. for sale on March 16 less credit memo of March 18.

(Continued)

Mar. 28. Received check for amount due from Vista Co. for sale of March 19.

31. Received check for amount due from Empire Co. for sale of March 4.

31. Paid Fleetwood Delivery Service $5,600 for merchandise delivered during March to customers under shipping terms of FOB destination.

Apr. 3. Paid City Bank $940 for service fees for handling MasterCard and American Express sales during March.

15. Paid $6,544 to state sales tax division for taxes owed on sales.

Instructions

Journalize the entries to record the transactions of Amsterdam Supply Co.

PR 6-3A Sales-related and purchase-related transactions using perpetual inventory system **OBJ. 2**

General Ledger

SHOW ME HOW

The following were selected from among the transactions completed by Babcock Company during November of the current year:

Nov. 3. Purchased merchandise on account from Moonlight Co., list price $85,000, trade discount 25%, terms FOB destination, 2/10, n/30.

4. Sold merchandise for cash, $37,680. The cost of the merchandise sold was $22,600.

5. Purchased merchandise on account from Papoose Creek Co., $47,500, terms FOB shipping point, 2/10, n/30, with prepaid freight of $810 added to the invoice.

6. Returned $13,500 ($18,000 list price less trade discount of 25%) of merchandise purchased on November 3 from Moonlight Co.

8. Sold merchandise on account to Quinn Co., $15,600 with terms n/15. The cost of the merchandise sold was $9,400.

13. Paid Moonlight Co. on account for purchase of November 3, less return of November 6.

14. Sold merchandise on VISA, $236,000. The cost of the merchandise sold was $140,000.

15. Paid Papoose Creek Co. on account for purchase of November 5.

23. Received cash on account from sale of November 8 to Quinn Co.

24. Sold merchandise on account to Rabel Co., $56,900, terms 1/10, n/30. The cost of the merchandise sold was $34,000.

28. Paid VISA service fee of $3,540.

30. Paid Quinn Co. a cash refund of $6,000 for returned merchandise from sale of November 8. The cost of the returned merchandise was $3,300.

Instructions

Journalize the transactions.

PR 6-4A Sales-related and purchase-related transactions for seller and buyer using perpetual inventory system **OBJ. 2**

The following selected transactions were completed during August between Summit Company and Beartooth Co.:

Aug. 1. Summit Company sold merchandise on account to Beartooth Co., $48,000, terms FOB destination, 2/15, n/eom. The cost of the merchandise sold was $28,800.

2. Summit Company paid freight of $1,150 for delivery of merchandise sold to Beartooth Co. on August 1.

5. Summit Company sold merchandise on account to Beartooth Co., $66,000, terms FOB shipping point, n/eom. The cost of the merchandise sold was $40,000.

9. Beartooth Co. paid freight of $2,300 on August 5 purchase from Summit Company.

Aug. 15. Summit Company sold merchandise on account to Beartooth Co., $58,700, terms FOB shipping point, 1/10, n/30. Summit Company paid freight of $1,675, which was added to the invoice. The cost of the merchandise sold was $35,000.

16. Beartooth Co. paid Summit Company for purchase of August 1.

25. Beartooth Co. paid Summit Company on account for purchase of August 15.

31. Beartooth Co. paid Summit Company on account for purchase of August 5.

Instructions

Journalize the August transactions for (1) Summit Company and (2) Beartooth Co.

PR 6-5A Multiple-step income statement and report form of balance sheet — OBJ. 3

✔ 1. Net income $943,400

General Ledger

The following selected accounts and their current balances appear in the ledger of Clairemont Co. for the fiscal year ended May 31, 2016:

Cash	$ 240,000	Kristina Marble, Drawing	$ 100,000
Accounts Receivable	966,000	Sales	11,343,000
Merchandise Inventory	1,712,500	Cost of Merchandise Sold	7,850,000
Office Supplies	13,500	Sales Salaries Expense	916,000
Prepaid Insurance	8,000	Advertising Expense	550,000
Office Equipment	830,000	Depreciation Expense—Store Equipment	140,000
Accumulated Depreciation—Office Equipment	550,000	Miscellaneous Selling Expense	38,000
Store Equipment	3,600,000	Office Salaries Expense	650,000
Accumulated Depreciation—Store Equipment	1,820,000	Rent Expense	94,000
Accounts Payable	366,000	Depreciation Expense—Office Equipment	50,000
Salaries Payable	41,500	Insurance Expense	48,000
Note Payable (final payment due 2022)	300,000	Office Supplies Expense	28,100
Kristina Marble, Capital	3,449,100	Miscellaneous Administrative Exp.	14,500
		Interest Expense	21,000

Instructions

1. Prepare a multiple-step income statement.
2. Prepare a statement of owner's equity.
3. Prepare a report form of balance sheet, assuming that the current portion of the note payable is $50,000.
4. Briefly explain (a) how multiple-step and single-step income statements differ and (b) how report-form and account-form balance sheets differ.

PR 6-6A Single-step income statement and account form of balance sheet — OBJ. 3

✔ 3. Total assets: $5,000,000

Selected accounts and related amounts for Clairemont Co. for the fiscal year ended May 31, 2016, are presented in Problem 6-5A.

Instructions

1. Prepare a single-step income statement in the format shown in Exhibit 11.
2. Prepare a statement of owner's equity.
3. Prepare an account form of balance sheet, assuming that the current portion of the note payable is $50,000.
4. Prepare closing entries as of May 31, 2016.

Appendix
PR 6-7A Purchase-related transactions using periodic inventory system

Selected transactions for Capers Company during October of the current year are listed in Problem 6-1A.

Instructions

Journalize the entries to record the transactions of Capers Company for October using the periodic inventory system.

Appendix
PR 6-8A Sales-related and purchase-related transactions using periodic inventory system

Selected transactions for Babcock Company during November of the current year are listed in Problem 6-3A.

Instructions

Journalize the entries to record the transactions of Babcock Company for November using the periodic inventory system.

Appendix
PR 6-9A Sales-related and purchase-related transactions for buyer and seller using periodic inventory system

Selected transactions during August between Summit Company and Beartooth Co. are listed in Problem 6-4A.

Instructions

Journalize the entries to record the transactions for (1) Summit Company and (2) Beartooth Co., assuming that both companies use the periodic inventory system.

Appendix
PR 6-10A Periodic inventory accounts, multiple-step income statement, closing entries

✔ 2. Net income, $180,000

On December 31, 2016, the balances of the accounts appearing in the ledger of Wyman Company are as follows:

Cash	$ 13,500	Purchases	$2,650,000
Accounts Receivable	72,000	Purchases Returns and Allowances	93,000
Merchandise Inventory, January 1, 2016	257,000	Purchases Discounts	37,000
		Freight In	48,000
Office Supplies	3,000	Sales Salaries Expense	300,000
Prepaid Insurance	4,500	Advertising Expense	45,000
Land	150,000	Delivery Expense	9,000
Store Equipment	270,000	Depreciation Expense—Store Equipment	6,000
Accumulated Depreciation—Store Equipment	55,900	Miscellaneous Selling Expense	12,000
Office Equipment	78,500	Office Salaries Expense	175,000
Accumulated Depreciation—Office Equipment	16,000	Rent Expense	28,000
		Insurance Expense	3,000
Accounts Payable	27,800	Office Supplies Expense	2,000
Salaries Payable	3,000	Depreciation Expense—Office Equipment	1,500
Unearned Rent	8,300		
Notes Payable	50,000	Miscellaneous Administrative Expense	3,500
Shirley Wyman, Capital	580,500	Rent Revenue	7,000
Shirley Wyman, Drawing	25,000	Interest Expense	2,000
Sales	3,280,000		

Instructions

1. Does Wyman Company use a periodic or perpetual inventory system? Explain.
2. Prepare a multiple-step income statement for Wyman Company for the year ended December 31, 2016. The merchandise inventory as of December 31, 2016, was $305,000.
3. Prepare the closing entries for Wyman Company as of December 31, 2016.
4. What would be the net income if the perpetual inventory system had been used?

Problems: Series B

PR 6-1B Purchase-related transactions using perpetual inventory system OBJ. 2

General Ledger

The following selected transactions were completed by Niles Co. during March of the current year:

Mar. 1. Purchased merchandise from Haas Co., $43,250, terms FOB shipping point, 2/10, n/eom. Prepaid freight of $650 was added to the invoice.

5. Purchased merchandise from Whitman Co., $19,175, terms FOB destination, n/30.

10. Paid Haas Co. for invoice of March 1.

13. Purchased merchandise from Jost Co., $15,550, terms FOB destination, 2/10, n/30.

14. Issued debit memo to Jost Co. for $3,750 of merchandise returned from purchase on March 13.

18. Purchased merchandise from Fairhurst Company, $13,560, terms FOB shipping point, n/eom.

18. Paid freight of $140 on March 18 purchase from Fairhurst Company.

19. Purchased merchandise from Bickle Co., $6,500, terms FOB destination, 2/10, n/30.

23. Paid Jost Co. for invoice of March 13, less debit memo of March 14.

29. Paid Bickle Co. for invoice of March 19.

31. Paid Fairhurst Company for invoice of March 18.

31. Paid Whitman Co. for invoice of March 5.

Instructions

Journalize the entries to record the transactions of Niles Co. for March.

PR 6-2B Sales-related transactions using perpetual inventory system OBJ. 2

General Ledger

SHOW ME HOW

The following selected transactions were completed by Green Lawn Supplies Co., which sells irrigation supplies primarily to wholesalers and occasionally to retail customers:

July 1. Sold merchandise on account to Landscapes Co., $33,450, terms FOB shipping point, n/eom. The cost of merchandise sold was $20,000.

2. Sold merchandise for $86,000 plus 8% sales tax to retail cash customers. The cost of merchandise sold was $51,600.

5. Sold merchandise on account to Peacock Company, $17,500, terms FOB destination, 1/10, n/30. The cost of merchandise sold was $10,000.

8. Sold merchandise for $112,000 plus 8% sales tax to retail customers who used VISA cards. The cost of merchandise sold was $67,200.

13. Sold merchandise to customers who used MasterCard cards, $96,000. The cost of merchandise sold was $57,600.

14. Sold merchandise on account to Loeb Co., $16,000, terms FOB shipping point, 1/10, n/30. The cost of merchandise sold was $9,000.

15. Received check for amount due from Peacock Company for sale on July 5.

16. Issued credit memo for $3,000 to Loeb Co. for merchandise returned from sale on July 14. The cost of the merchandise returned was $1,800.

18. Sold merchandise on account to Jennings Company, $11,350, terms FOB shipping point, 2/10, n/30. Paid $475 for freight and added it to the invoice. The cost of merchandise sold was $6,800.

24. Received check for amount due from Loeb Co. for sale on July 14 less credit memo of July 16.

28. Received check for amount due from Jennings Company for sale of July 18.

31. Paid Black Lab Delivery Service $8,550 for merchandise delivered during July to customers under shipping terms of FOB destination.

(Continued)

July 31. Received check for amount due from Landscapes Co. for sale of July 1.

Aug. 3. Paid Hays Federal Bank $3,770 for service fees for handling MasterCard and VISA sales during July.

10. Paid $41,260 to state sales tax division for taxes owed on sales.

Instructions

Journalize the entries to record the transactions of Green Lawn Supplies Co.

PR 6-3B Sales-related and purchase-related transactions using perpetual inventory system **OBJ. 2**

General Ledger

SHOW ME HOW

The following were selected from among the transactions completed by Essex Company during July of the current year:

July 3. Purchased merchandise on account from Hamling Co., list price $72,000, trade discount 15%, terms FOB shipping point, 2/10, n/30, with prepaid freight of $1,450 added to the invoice.

5. Purchased merchandise on account from Kester Co., $33,450, terms FOB destination, 2/10, n/30.

6. Sold merchandise on account to Parsley Co., $36,000, terms n/15. The cost of the merchandise sold was $25,000.

7. Returned $6,850 of merchandise purchased on July 5 from Kester Co.

13. Paid Hamling Co. on account for purchase of July 3.

15. Paid Kester Co. on account for purchase of July 5, less return of July 7.

21. Received cash on account from sale of July 6 to Parsley Co.

21. Sold merchandise on MasterCard, $108,000. The cost of the merchandise sold was $64,800.

22. Sold merchandise on account to Tabor Co., $16,650, terms 2/10, n/30. The cost of the merchandise sold was $10,000.

23. Sold merchandise for cash, $91,200. The cost of the merchandise sold was $55,000.

28. Paid Parsley Co. a cash refund of $7,150 for returned merchandise from sale of July 6. The cost of the returned merchandise was $4,250.

31. Paid MasterCard service fee of $1,650.

Instructions

Journalize the transactions.

PR 6-4B Sales-related and purchase-related transactions for seller and buyer using perpetual inventory system **OBJ. 2**

The following selected transactions were completed during April between Swan Company and Bird Company:

Apr. 2. Swan Company sold merchandise on account to Bird Company, $32,000, terms FOB shipping point, 2/10, n/30. Swan Company paid freight of $330, which was added to the invoice. The cost of the merchandise sold was $19,200.

8. Swan Company sold merchandise on account to Bird Company, $49,500, terms FOB destination, 1/15, n/eom. The cost of the merchandise sold was $29,700.

8. Swan Company paid freight of $710 for delivery of merchandise sold to Bird Company on April 8.

12. Bird Company paid Swan Company for purchase of April 2.

23. Bird Company paid Swan Company for purchase of April 8.

24. Swan Company sold merchandise on account to Bird Company, $67,350, terms FOB shipping point, n/eom. The cost of the merchandise sold was $40,400.

Apr. 26. Bird Company paid freight of $875 on April 24 purchase from Swan Company.
30. Bird Company paid Swan Company on account for purchase of April 24.

Instructions

Journalize the April transactions for (1) Swan Company and (2) Bird Company.

✔ 1. Net income: $1,340,000

General Ledger

PR 6-5B Multiple-step income statement and report form of balance sheet — OBJ. 3

The following selected accounts and their current balances appear in the ledger of Kanpur Co. for the fiscal year ended June 30, 2016:

Cash	$ 92,000	Gerri Faber, Drawing	$ 300,000
Accounts Receivable	450,000	Sales	8,925,000
Merchandise Inventory	375,000	Cost of Merchandise Sold	5,620,000
Office Supplies	10,000	Sales Salaries Expense	850,000
Prepaid Insurance	12,000	Advertising Expense	420,000
Office Equipment	220,000	Depreciation Expense—	
Accumulated Depreciation—		Store Equipment	33,000
Office Equipment	58,000	Miscellaneous Selling Expense	18,000
Store Equipment	650,000	Office Salaries Expense	540,000
Accumulated Depreciation—		Rent Expense	48,000
Store Equipment	87,500	Insurance Expense	24,000
Accounts Payable	48,500	Depreciation Expense—	
Salaries Payable	4,000	Office Equipment	10,000
Note Payable		Office Supplies Expense	4,000
(final payment due 2032)	140,000	Miscellaneous Administrative Exp.	6,000
Gerri Faber, Capital	431,000	Interest Expense	12,000

Instructions

1. Prepare a multiple-step income statement.
2. Prepare a statement of owner's equity.
3. Prepare a report form of balance sheet, assuming that the current portion of the note payable is $7,000.
4. Briefly explain (a) how multiple-step and single-step income statements differ and (b) how report-form and account-form balance sheets differ.

✔ 3. Total assets: $1,663,500

PR 6-6B Single-step income statement and account form of balance sheet — OBJ. 3

Selected accounts and related amounts for Kanpur Co. for the fiscal year ended June 30, 2016, are presented in Problem 6-5B.

Instructions

1. Prepare a single-step income statement in the format shown in Exhibit 11.
2. Prepare a statement of owner's equity.
3. Prepare an account form of balance sheet, assuming that the current portion of the note payable is $7,000.
4. Prepare closing entries as of June 30, 2016.

Appendix
PR 6-7B Purchase-related transactions using periodic inventory system

Selected transactions for Niles Co. during March of the current year are listed in Problem 6-1B.

Instructions

Journalize the entries to record the transactions of Niles Co. for March using the periodic inventory system.

Appendix

PR 6-8B Sales-related and purchase-related transactions using periodic inventory system

Selected transactions for Essex Company during July of the current year are listed in Problem 6-3B.

Instructions

Journalize the entries to record the transactions of Essex Company for July using the periodic inventory system.

Appendix

PR 6-9B Sales-related and purchase-related transactions for buyer and seller using periodic inventory system

Selected transactions during April between Swan Company and Bird Company are listed in Problem 6-4B.

Instructions

Journalize the entries to record the transactions for (1) Swan Company and (2) Bird Company assuming that both companies use the periodic inventory system.

Appendix

PR 6-10B Periodic inventory accounts, multiple-step income statement, closing entries

✔ 2. Net income, $1,200,000

On June 30, 2016, the balances of the accounts appearing in the ledger of Simkins Company are as follows:

Cash	$ 125,000	Purchases	$4,100,000
Accounts Receivable	340,000	Purchases Returns and Allowances	32,000
Merchandise Inventory, July 1, 2015	415,000	Purchases Discounts	13,000
Office Supplies	9,000	Freight In	45,000
Prepaid Insurance	18,000	Sales Salaries Expense	580,000
Land	300,000	Advertising Expense	315,000
Store Equipment	550,000	Delivery Expense	18,000
Accumulated Depreciation— Store Equipment	190,000	Depreciation Expense— Store Equipment	12,000
Office Equipment	250,000	Miscellaneous Selling Expense	28,000
Accumulated Depreciation— Office Equipment	110,000	Office Salaries Expense	375,000
		Rent Expense	43,000
Accounts Payable	85,000	Insurance Expense	17,000
Salaries Payable	9,000	Office Supplies Expense	5,000
Unearned Rent	6,000	Depreciation Expense— Office Equipment	4,000
Notes Payable	50,000		
Amy Gant, Capital	825,000	Miscellaneous Administrative Expense	16,000
Amy Gant, Drawing	275,000	Rent Revenue	32,500
Sales	6,590,000	Interest Expense	2,500

Instructions

1. Does Simkins Company use a periodic or perpetual inventory system? Explain.
2. Prepare a multiple-step income statement for Simkins Company for the year ended June 30, 2016. The merchandise inventory as of June 30, 2016, was $508,000.
3. Prepare the closing entries for Simkins Company as of June 30, 2016.
4. What would be the net income if the perpetual inventory system had been used?

Continuing Problem

✔ **8. Net income: $741,855**

Palisade Creek Co. is a merchandising business that uses the perpetual inventory system. The account balances for Palisade Creek Co. as of May 1, 2016 (unless otherwise indicated), are as follows:

110	Cash	$ 83,600
112	Accounts Receivable	233,900
115	Merchandise Inventory	624,400
116	Estimated Returns Inventory	28,000
117	Prepaid Insurance	16,800
118	Store Supplies	11,400
123	Store Equipment	569,500
124	Accumulated Depreciation—Store Equipment	56,700
210	Accounts Payable	96,600
211	Salaries Payable	—
212	Customers Refunds Payable	50,000
310	Lynn Tolley, Capital, June 1, 2015	685,300
311	Lynn Tolley, Drawing	135,000
312	Income Summary	—
410	Sales	5,069,000
510	Cost of Merchandise Sold	2,823,000
520	Sales Salaries Expense	664,800
521	Advertising Expense	281,000
522	Depreciation Expense	—
523	Store Supplies Expense	—
529	Miscellaneous Selling Expense	12,600
530	Office Salaries Expense	382,100
531	Rent Expense	83,700
532	Insurance Expense	—
539	Miscellaneous Administrative Expense	7,800

During May, the last month of the fiscal year, the following transactions were completed:

May 1. Paid rent for May, $5,000.

3. Purchased merchandise on account from Martin Co., terms 2/10, n/30, FOB shipping point, $36,000.

4. Paid freight on purchase of May 3, $600.

6. Sold merchandise on account to Korman Co., terms 2/10, n/30, FOB shipping point, $68,500. The cost of the merchandise sold was $41,000.

7. Received $22,300 cash from Halstad Co. on account.

10. Sold merchandise for cash, $54,000. The cost of the merchandise sold was $32,000.

13. Paid for merchandise purchased on May 3.

15. Paid advertising expense for last half of May, $11,000.

16. Received cash from sale of May 6.

19. Purchased merchandise for cash, $18,700.

19. Paid $33,450 to Buttons Co. on account.

20. Paid Korman Co. a cash refund of $13,230 for returned merchandise from sale of May 6. The invoice amount of the returned merchandise was $13,500 and the cost of the returned merchandise was $8,000.

Record the following transactions on Page 21 of the journal:

20. Sold merchandise on account to Crescent Co., terms 1/10, n/30, FOB shipping point, $110,000. The cost of the merchandise sold was $70,000.

21. For the convenience of Crescent Co., paid freight on sale of May 20, $2,300.

21. Received $42,900 cash from Gee Co. on account.

(Continued)

May 21. Purchased merchandise on account from Osterman Co., terms 1/10, n/30, FOB destination, $88,000.

24. Returned of damaged merchandise purchased on May 21, receiving a credit memo from the seller for $5,000.

26. Refunded cash on sales made for cash, $7,500. The cost of the merchandise returned was $4,800.

28. Paid sales salaries of $56,000 and office salaries of $29,000.

29. Purchased store supplies for cash, $2,400.

30. Sold merchandise on account to Turner Co., terms 2/10, n/30, FOB shipping point, $78,750. The cost of the merchandise sold was $47,000.

30. Received cash from sale of May 20 plus freight paid on May 21.

31. Paid for purchase of May 21, less return of May 24.

Instructions

1. Enter the balances of each of the accounts in the appropriate balance column of a four-column account. Write *Balance* in the item section, and place a check mark (✓) in the Posting Reference column. Journalize the transactions for July, starting on Page 20 of the journal.
2. Post the journal to the general ledger, extending the month-end balances to the appropriate balance columns after all posting is completed. In this problem, you are not required to update or post to the accounts receivable and accounts payable subsidiary ledgers.
3. Prepare an unadjusted trial balance.
4. At the end of May, the following adjustment data were assembled. Analyze and use these data to complete (5) and (6).

a.	Merchandise inventory on May 31		$570,000
b.	Insurance expired during the year		12,000
c.	Store supplies on hand on May 31		4,000
d.	Depreciation for the current year		14,000
e.	Accrued salaries on May 31:		
	Sales salaries	$7,000	
	Office salaries	6,600	13,600

f. The adjustment for customer returns and allowances is $60,000 for sales and $35,000 for cost of merchandise sold.

5. *(Optional)* Enter the unadjusted trial balance on a 10-column end-of-period spreadsheet (work sheet), and complete the spreadsheet.
6. Journalize and post the adjusting entries. Record the adjusting entries on Page 22 of the journal.
7. Prepare an adjusted trial balance.
8. Prepare an income statement, a statement of owner's equity, and a balance sheet.
9. Prepare and post the closing entries. Record the closing entries on Page 23 of the journal. Indicate closed accounts by inserting a line in both the Balance columns opposite the closing entry. Insert the new balance in the owner's capital account.
10. Prepare a post-closing trial balance.

Cases & Projects

CP 6-1 Ethics and professional conduct in business

On April 18, 2016, Bontanica Company, a garden retailer, purchased $9,800 of seed, terms 2/10, n/30, from Whitetail Seed Co. Even though the discount period had expired, Shelby Davey subtracted the discount of $196 when he processed the documents for payment on May 1, 2016.

Discuss whether Shelby Davey behaved in a professional manner by subtracting the discount, even though the discount period had expired.

CP 6-2 Purchases discounts and accounts payable

Rustic Furniture Co. is owned and operated by Cam Pfeifer. The following is an excerpt from a conversation between Cam Pfeifer and Mitzi Wheeler, the chief accountant for Rustic Furniture Co:

Cam: Mitzi, I've got a question about this recent balance sheet.

Mitzi: Sure, what's your question?

Cam: Well, as you know, I'm applying for a bank loan to finance our new store in Garden Grove, and I noticed that the accounts payable are listed as $320,000.

Mitzi: That's right. Approximately $275,000 of that represents amounts due our suppliers, and the remainder is miscellaneous payables to creditors for utilities, office equipment, supplies, etc.

Cam: That's what I thought. But as you know, we normally receive a 2% discount from our suppliers for earlier payment, and we always try to take the discount.

Mitzi: That's right. I can't remember the last time we missed a discount.

Cam: Well, in that case, it seems to me the accounts payable should be listed minus the 2% discount. Let's list the accounts payable due suppliers as $314,500, rather than $320,000. Every little bit helps. You never know. It might make the difference between getting the loan and not.

How would you respond to Cam Pfeifer's request?

CP 6-3 Determining cost of purchase

The following is an excerpt from a conversation between Mark Loomis and Krista Huff. Mark is debating whether to buy a stereo system from Tru-Sound Systems, a locally owned electronics store, or Wholesale Stereo, an online electronics company.

Mark: Krista, I don't know what to do about buying my new stereo.

Krista: What's the problem?

Mark: Well, I can buy it locally at Tru-Sound Systems for $1,175.00. However, Wholesale Stereo has the same system listed for $1,200.00.

Krista: What's the big deal? Buy it from Tru-Sound Systems.

Mark: It's not quite that simple. Wholesale Stereo charges $49.99 for shipping and handling. If I have them send it next-day air, it'll cost $89.99 for shipping and handling.

Krista: So?

Mark: But, that's not all. Tru-Sound Systems will give an additional 2% discount if I pay cash. Otherwise, they will let me use my VISA, or I can pay it off in three monthly installments. In addition, if I buy it from Tru-Sound Systems, I have to pay 9% sales tax. I won't have to pay sales tax if I buy it from Wholesale Stereo, since they are out of state.

Krista: Anything else???

Mark: Well . . . Wholesale Stereo says I have to charge it on my VISA. They don't accept checks.

Krista: I am not surprised. Many online stores don't accept checks.

Mark: I give up. What would you do?

1. Assuming that Wholesale Stereo doesn't charge sales tax on the sale to Mark, which company is offering the best buy?
2. What might be some considerations other than price that might influence Mark's decision on where to buy the stereo system?

CP 6-4 Sales discounts

Your sister operates Watercraft Supply Company, an online boat parts distributorship that is in its third year of operation. The following income statement was recently prepared for the year ended October 31, 2016:

Watercraft Supply Company
Income Statement
For the Year Ended October 31, 2016

Revenues:		
Sales		$1,350,000
Interest revenue		15,000
Total revenues		$1,365,000
Expenses:		
Cost of merchandise sold	$810,000	
Selling expenses	140,000	
Administrative expenses	90,000	
Interest expense	4,000	
Total expenses		1,044,000
Net income		$ 321,000

Your sister is considering a proposal to increase net income by offering sales discounts of 2/15, n/30, and by shipping all merchandise FOB shipping point. Currently, no sales discounts are allowed and merchandise is shipped FOB destination. It is estimated that these credit terms will increase sales by 10%. The ratio of the cost of merchandise sold to sales is expected to be 60%. All selling and administrative expenses are expected to remain unchanged, except for store supplies, miscellaneous selling, office supplies, and miscellaneous administrative expenses, which are expected to increase proportionately with increased sales. The amounts of these preceding items for the year ended October 31, 2016, were as follows:

Store supplies expense	$12,000
Miscellaneous selling expense	6,000
Office supplies expense	3,000
Miscellaneous administrative expense	2,500

The other income and other expense items will remain unchanged. The shipment of all merchandise FOB shipping point will eliminate all delivery expenses, which for the year ended October 31, 2016, were $12,000.

1. Prepare a projected single-step income statement for the year ending October 31, 2017, based on the proposal. Assume all sales are collected within the discount period.
2. a. Based on the projected income statement in (1), would you recommend the implementation of the proposed changes?

   b. Describe any possible concerns you may have related to the proposed changes described in (1).

CP 6-5 Shopping for a television

Group Project

Assume that you are planning to purchase a 55-inch LED, LCD flat-screen television. In groups of three or four, determine the lowest cost for the television, considering the available alternatives and the advantages and disadvantages of each alternative. For example, you could purchase locally, through mail order, or through an Internet shopping service. Consider such factors as delivery charges, interest-free financing, discounts, coupons, and availability of warranty services. Prepare a report for presentation to the class.

CHAD BAKER/JASON REED/PHOTODISC/GETTY IMAGES

CHAPTER 7

Inventories

Best Buy

Assume that in September you purchased a Sony HDTV from **Best Buy**. At the same time, you purchased a Denon surround sound system for $399.99. You liked your surround sound so well that in November you purchased an identical Denon system on sale for $349.99 for your bedroom TV. Over the holidays, you moved to a new apartment and in the process of unpacking discovered that one of the Denon surround sound systems was missing. Luckily, your renters or homeowners insurance policy will cover the theft; but the insurance company needs to know the cost of the system that was stolen.

The Denon systems were identical. However, to respond to the insurance company, you will need to identify which system was stolen. Was it the first system, which cost $399.99, or was it the second system, which cost $349.99? Whichever assumption you make may determine the amount that you receive from the insurance company.

Merchandising businesses such as Best Buy make similar assumptions when identical merchandise is purchased at different costs. For example, Best Buy may have purchased thousands of Denon surround sound systems over the past year at different costs. At the end of a period, some of the Denon systems will still be in inventory, and some will have been sold. But which costs relate to the sold systems, and which costs relate to the Denon systems still in inventory? Best Buy's assumption about inventory costs can involve large dollar amounts and, thus, can have a significant impact on the financial statements. For example, Best Buy reported $5,731 million of inventory and net loss of $1,231 million for a recent year.

This chapter discusses such issues as how to determine the cost of merchandise in inventory and the cost of merchandise sold. However, this chapter begins by discussing the importance of control over inventory.

Learning Objectives

After studying this chapter, you should be able to: | Example Exercises

OBJ	Objective	Example Exercises
1	**Describe the importance of control over inventory.** Control of Inventory Safeguarding Inventory Reporting Inventory	
2	**Describe three inventory cost flow assumptions and how they impact the income statement and balance sheet.** Inventory Cost Flow Assumptions	EE 7-1
3	**Determine the cost of inventory under the perpetual inventory system, using the FIFO, LIFO, and weighted average cost methods.** Inventory Costing Methods Under a Perpetual Inventory System First-In, First-Out Method Last-In, First-Out Method Weighted Average Cost Method Computerized Perpetual Inventory Systems	 EE 7-2 EE 7-3 EE 7-4
4	**Determine the cost of inventory under the periodic inventory system, using the FIFO, LIFO, and weighted average cost methods.** Inventory Costing Methods Under a Periodic Inventory System First-In, First-Out Method Last-In, First-Out Method Weighted Average Cost Method	 EE 7-5 EE 7-5 EE 7-5
5	**Compare and contrast the use of the three inventory costing methods.** Comparing Inventory Costing Methods	
6	**Describe and illustrate the reporting of merchandise inventory in the financial statements.** Reporting Merchandise Inventory in the Financial Statements Valuation at Lower of Cost or Market Merchandise Inventory on the Balance Sheet Effect of Inventory Errors on the Financial Statements	 EE 7-6 EE 7-7
7	**Describe and illustrate the inventory turnover and the number of days' sales in inventory in analyzing the efficiency and effectiveness of inventory management.** Financial Analysis and Interpretation: Inventory Turnover and Number of Days' Sales in Inventory	EE 7-8

At a Glance 7 Page 344

OBJ 1 Describe the importance of control over inventory.

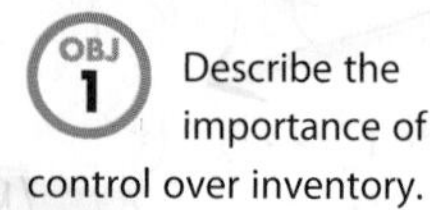

Control of Inventory

Two primary objectives of control over inventory are as follows:[1]

- Safeguarding the inventory from damage or theft.
- Reporting inventory in the financial statements.

Safeguarding Inventory

Controls for safeguarding inventory begin as soon as the inventory is ordered. The following documents are often used for inventory control:

- Purchase order
- Receiving report
- Vendor's invoice

The **purchase order** authorizes the purchase of the inventory from an approved vendor. As soon as the inventory is received, a receiving report is completed. The **receiving report** establishes an initial record of the receipt of the inventory. To make sure the inventory received is what was ordered, the receiving report is compared

[1] Additional controls used by businesses are described and illustrated in Chapter 8, "Sarbanes-Oxley, Internal Control, and Cash."

with the purchase order. The price, quantity, and description of the item on the purchase order and receiving report are then compared to the vendor's invoice. If the receiving report, purchase order, and vendor's invoice agree, the inventory is recorded in the accounting records. If any differences exist, they should be investigated and reconciled.

Recording inventory using a perpetual inventory system is also an effective means of control. The amount of inventory is always available in the **subsidiary inventory ledger**. This helps keep inventory quantities at proper levels. For example, comparing inventory quantities with maximum and minimum levels allows for the timely reordering of inventory and prevents ordering excess inventory.

Best Buy uses scanners to screen customers as they leave the store for merchandise that has not been purchased. In addition, Best Buy stations greeters at the store's entrance to keep customers from bringing in bags that can be used to shoplift merchandise.

Finally, controls for safeguarding inventory should include security measures to prevent damage and customer or employee theft. Some examples of security measures include the following:

- Storing inventory in areas that are restricted to only authorized employees
- Locking high-priced inventory in cabinets
- Using two-way mirrors, cameras, security tags, and guards

Reporting Inventory

A **physical inventory** or *count of inventory* should be taken near year-end to make sure that the quantity of inventory reported in the financial statements is accurate. After the quantity of inventory on hand is determined, the cost of the inventory is assigned for reporting in the financial statements. Most companies assign costs to inventory using one of three inventory cost flow assumptions. If a physical count is not possible or inventory records are not available, the inventory cost may be estimated as described in the appendix at the end of this chapter.

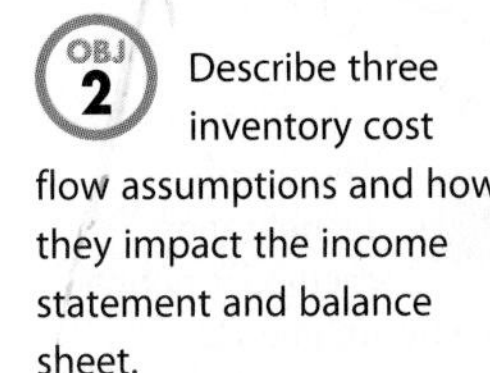

Describe three inventory cost flow assumptions and how they impact the income statement and balance sheet.

Inventory Cost Flow Assumptions

An accounting issue arises when identical units of merchandise are acquired at different unit costs during a period. In such cases, when an item is sold, it is necessary to determine its cost using a cost flow assumption and related inventory costing method. Three common cost flow assumptions and related inventory costing methods are shown in Exhibit 1.

EXHIBIT 1 **Cost Flow Assumptions**

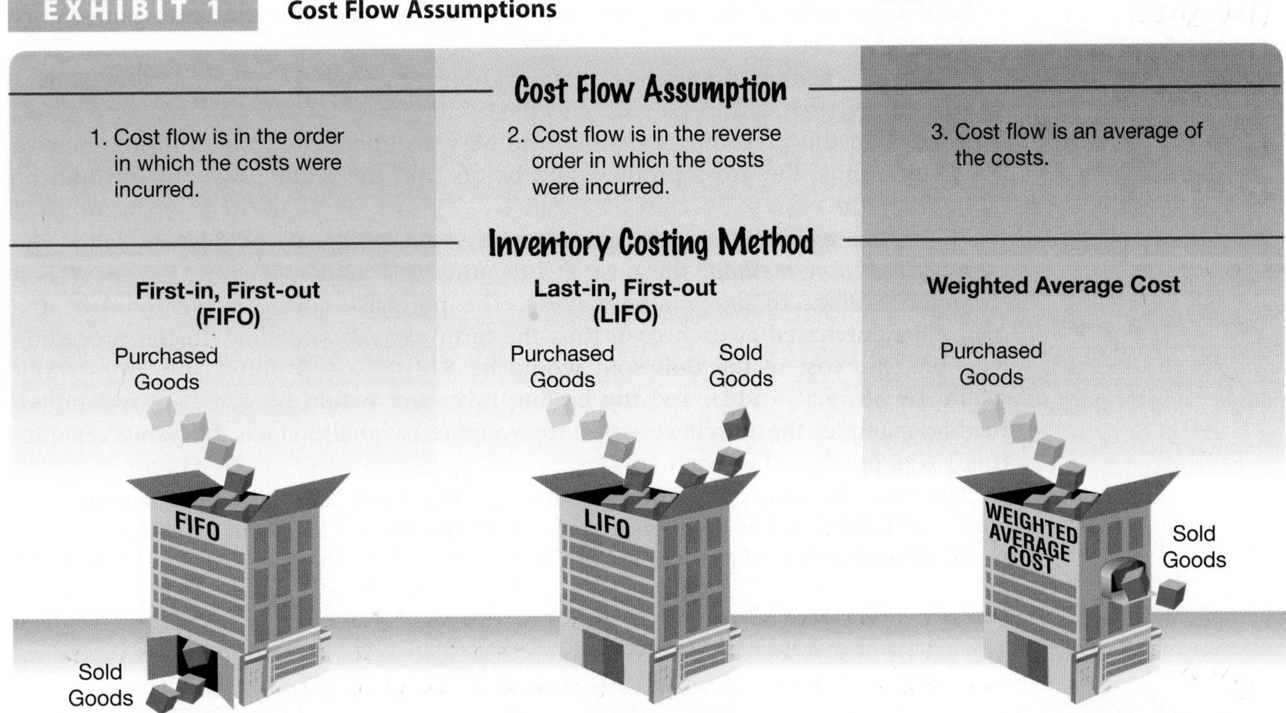

To illustrate, assume that three identical units of merchandise are purchased during May, as follows:

			Units	Cost
May	10	Purchase	1	$ 9
	18	Purchase	1	13
	24	Purchase	1	14
Total			3	$36

Average cost per unit: $12 ($36 ÷ 3 units)

Assume that one unit is sold on May 30 for $20. Depending upon which unit was sold, the gross profit varies from $11 to $6, computed as follows:

	May 10 Unit Sold	May 18 Unit Sold	May 24 Unit Sold
Sales	$20	$20	$20
Cost of merchandise sold	9	13	14
Gross profit	$11	$ 7	$ 6
Ending inventory	$27	$23	$22
	($13 + $14)	($9 + $14)	($9 + $13)

The specific identification method is normally used by automobile dealerships, jewelry stores, and art galleries.

Under the **specific identification inventory cost flow method**, the unit sold is identified with a specific purchase. The ending inventory is made up of the remaining units on hand. Thus, the gross profit, cost of merchandise sold, and ending inventory can vary as illustrated. For example, if the May 18 unit was sold, the cost of merchandise sold is $13, the gross profit is $7, and the ending inventory is $23.

The specific identification method is not practical unless each inventory unit can be separately identified. For example, an automobile dealer may use the specific identification method because each automobile has a unique serial number. However, most businesses cannot identify each inventory unit separately. In such cases, one of the following three inventory cost flow methods is used.

Under the **first-in, first-out (FIFO) inventory cost flow method**, the first units purchased are assumed to be sold and the ending inventory is made up of the most recent purchases. In the preceding example, the May 10 unit would be assumed to have been sold. Thus, the gross profit would be $11, and the ending inventory would be $27 ($13 + $14).

Under the **last-in, first-out (LIFO) inventory cost flow method**, the last units purchased are assumed to be sold and the ending inventory is made up of the first purchases. In the preceding example, the May 24 unit would be assumed to have been sold. Thus, the gross profit would be $6, and the ending inventory would be $22 ($9 + $13).

Under the **weighted average inventory cost flow method**, sometimes called the *average cost flow method*, the cost of the units sold and in ending inventory is a weighted average of the purchase costs. The purchase costs are weighted by the quantities purchased at each cost, thus the term *weighted average*. In the preceding example, the cost of the unit sold would be $12 ($36 ÷ 3 units), the gross profit would be $8 ($20 − $12), and the ending inventory would be $24 ($12 × 2 units). In this example, the purchase costs are weighted equally, since the same quantity (one) was purchased at each cost.

The three inventory cost flow methods, FIFO, LIFO, and weighted average, are shown in Exhibit 2. The frequency with which the FIFO, LIFO, and weighted average methods are used is shown in Exhibit 3.

EXHIBIT 2 **Inventory Costing Methods**

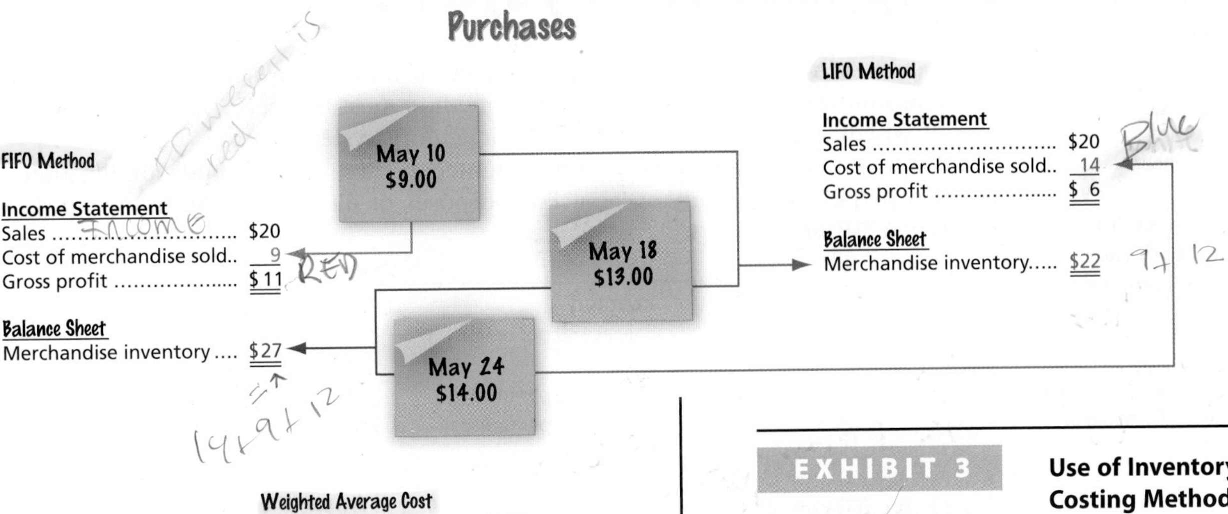

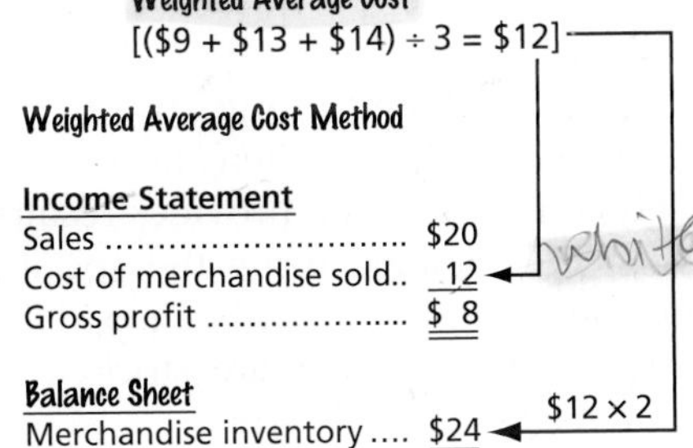

Weighted Average Cost
[($9 + $13 + $14) ÷ 3 = $12]
Weighted Average Cost Method
Income Statement
Sales $20
Cost of merchandise sold.. 12
Gross profit .... $ 8
Balance Sheet
Merchandise inventory $24
$12 × 2

EXHIBIT 3 **Use of Inventory Costing Methods***

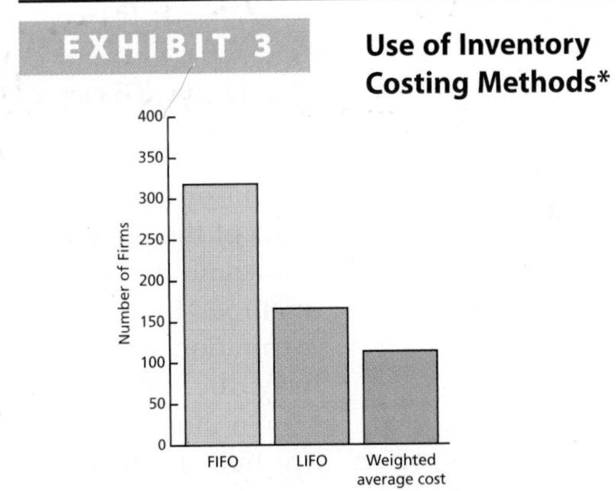

*Firms may be counted more than once for using multiple methods.
Source: *Accounting Trends and Techniques*, 66th edition, 2012 (New York: American Institute of Certified Public Accountants).

Example Exercise 7-1 Cost Flow Methods

OBJ 2

The following three identical units of Item QBM are purchased during February:

		Item QBM	Units	Cost
Feb.	8	Purchase	1	$ 45
	15	Purchase	1	48
	26	Purchase	1	51
	Total		3	$144
	Average cost per unit			$ 48 ($144 ÷ 3 units)

Assume that one unit is sold on February 27 for $70.

Determine the gross profit for February and ending inventory on February 28 using the (a) first-in, first-out (FIFO); (b) last-in, first-out (LIFO); and (c) weighted average cost methods.

Follow My Example 7-1

	Gross Profit	Ending Inventory
a. First-in, first-out (FIFO)...............	$25 ($70 – $45)	$99 ($48 + $51)
b. Last-in, first-out (LIFO)...............	$19 ($70 – $51)	$93 ($45 + $48)
c. Weighted average cost	$22 ($70 – $48)	$96 ($48 × 2)

Practice Exercises: PE 7-1A, PE 7-1B

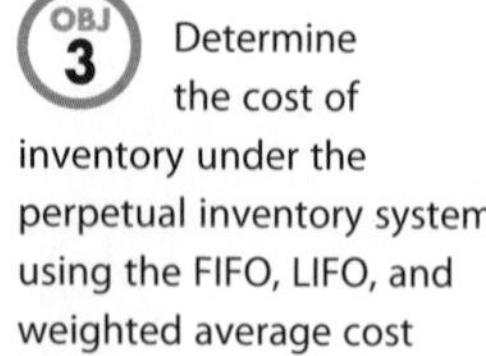

OBJ 3 Determine the cost of inventory under the perpetual inventory system, using the FIFO, LIFO, and weighted average cost methods.

Although e-tailers, such as **eToys Direct, Inc.**, **Amazon.com**, and **Furniture.com, Inc.**, don't have retail stores, they still take possession of inventory in warehouses. Thus, they must account for inventory as illustrated in this chapter.

Inventory Costing Methods Under a Perpetual Inventory System

As illustrated in the prior section, when identical units of an item are purchased at different unit costs, an inventory cost flow method must be used. This is true regardless of whether the perpetual or periodic inventory system is used.

In this section, the FIFO, LIFO, and weighted average cost methods are illustrated under a perpetual inventory system. For purposes of illustration, the following data for Item 127B are used:

	Item 127B	Units	Cost
Jan. 1	Inventory	1,000	$20.00
4	Sale at $30 per unit	700	
10	Purchase	500	22.40
22	Sale at $30 per unit	360	
28	Sale at $30 per unit	240	
30	Purchase	600	23.30

First-In, First-Out Method

When the FIFO method is used, costs are included in the cost of merchandise sold in the order in which they were purchased. This is often the same as the physical flow of the merchandise. Thus, the FIFO method often provides results that are about the same as those that would have been obtained using the specific identification method. For example, grocery stores shelve milk and other perishable products by expiration dates. Products with early expiration dates are stocked in front. In this way, the oldest products (earliest purchases) are sold first.

To illustrate, Exhibit 4 shows the use of FIFO under a perpetual inventory system for Item 127B. The journal entries and the subsidiary inventory ledger for Item 127B are shown in Exhibit 4 as follows:

1. The beginning balance on January 1 is $20,000 (1,000 units at a unit cost of $20).
2. On January 4, 700 units were sold at a price of $30 each for sales of $21,000 (700 units at a selling price of $30 per unit). The cost of merchandise sold is $14,000 (700 units at a unit cost of $20). After the sale, there remains $6,000 of inventory (300 units at a unit cost of $20).

EXHIBIT 4 **Entries and Perpetual Inventory Account (FIFO)**

Date	Account	Debit	Credit
Jan. 4	Accounts Receivable	21,000	
	Sales		21,000
4	Cost of Merchandise Sold	14,000	
	Merchandise Inventory		14,000
10	Merchandise Inventory	11,200	
	Accounts Payable		11,200
22	Accounts Receivable	10,800	
	Sales		10,800
22	Cost of Merchandise Sold	7,344	
	Merchandise Inventory		7,344
28	Accounts Receivable	7,200	
	Sales		7,200
28	Cost of Merchandise Sold	5,376	
	Merchandise Inventory		5,376
30	Merchandise Inventory	13,980	
	Accounts Payable		13,980

Item 127B

	Purchases			Cost of Merchandise Sold			Inventory		
Date	**Quantity**	**Unit Cost**	**Total Cost**	**Quantity**	**Unit Cost**	**Total Cost**	**Quantity**	**Unit Cost**	**Total Cost**
Jan. 1							1,000	20.00	20,000
4				700	20.00	14,000	300	20.00	6,000
10	500	22.40	11,200				300	20.00	6,000
							500	22.40	11,200
22				300	20.00	6,000			
				60	22.40	1,344	440	22.40	9,856
28				240	22.40	5,376	200	22.40	4,480
30	600	23.30	13,980				200	22.40	4,480
							600	23.30	13,980
31	Balances					26,720			18,460

Cost of merchandise sold ↑ 26,720 — **January 31 inventory** ↑ 18,460

3. On January 10, $11,200 is purchased (500 units at a unit cost of $22.40). After the purchase, the inventory is reported on two lines, $6,000 (300 units at a unit cost of $20.00) from the beginning inventory and $11,200 (500 units at a unit cost of $22.40) from the January 10 purchase.
4. On January 22, 360 units are sold at a price of $30 each for sales of $10,800 (360 units at a selling price of $30 per unit). Using FIFO, the cost of merchandise sold of $7,344 consists of $6,000 (300 units at a unit cost of $20.00) from the beginning inventory plus $1,344 (60 units at a unit cost of $22.40) from the January 10 purchase. After the sale, there remains $9,856 of inventory (440 units at a unit cost of $22.40) from the January 10 purchase.
5. The January 28 sale and January 30 purchase are recorded in a similar manner.
6. The ending balance on January 31 is $18,460. This balance is made up of two layers of inventory as follows:

	Date of Purchase	Quantity	Unit Cost	Total Cost
Layer 1:	Jan. 10	200	$22.40	$ 4,480
Layer 2:	Jan. 30	600	23.30	13,980
Total		800		$18,460

Example Exercise 7-2 Perpetual Inventory Using FIFO OBJ 3

Dynamic Exhibit

Beginning inventory, purchases, and sales for Item ER27 are as follows:

Nov. 1	Inventory	40 units at $5
5	Sale	30 units
11	Purchase	70 units at $7
21	Sale	36 units

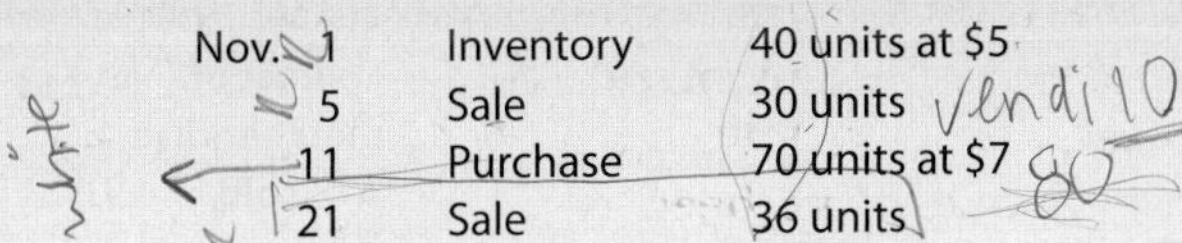

Assuming a perpetual inventory system and using the first-in, first-out (FIFO) method, determine (a) the cost of merchandise sold on November 21 and (b) the inventory on November 30.

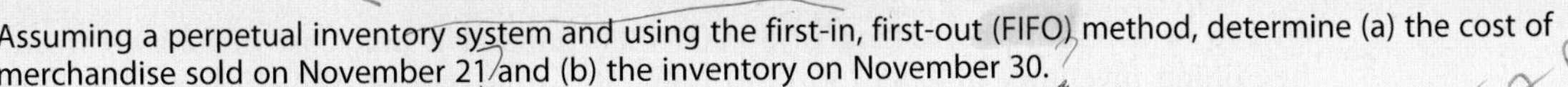

Follow My Example 7-2

a. Cost of merchandise sold (November 21):

10 units at $5	$ 50
26 units at $7	182
36 units	$232

b. Inventory, November 30:
$308 (44 units × $7)

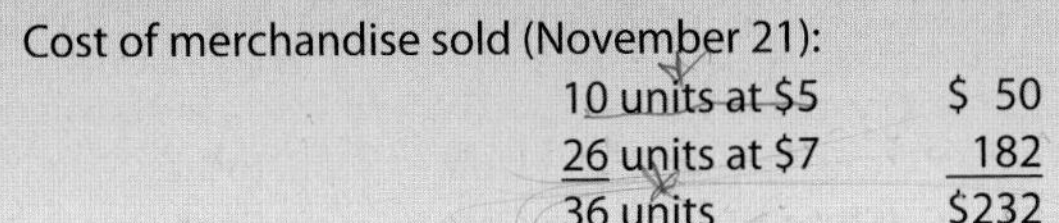

Practice Exercises: PE 7-2A, PE 7-2B

Last-In, First-Out Method

When the LIFO method is used, the cost of the units sold is the cost of the most recent purchases. The LIFO method was originally used in those rare cases where the units sold were taken from the most recently purchased units. However, for tax purposes, LIFO is now widely used even when it does not represent the physical flow of units. The tax impact of LIFO is discussed later in this chapter.

IFRS See Appendix D for more information.

To illustrate, Exhibit 5 shows the use of LIFO under a perpetual inventory system for Item 127B. The journal entries and the subsidiary inventory ledger for Item 127B are shown in Exhibit 5 as follows:

1. The beginning balance on January 1 is $20,000 (1,000 units at a unit of cost of $20.00).
2. On January 4, 700 units were sold at a price of $30 each for sales of $21,000 (700 units at a selling price of $30 per unit). The cost of merchandise sold is $14,000 (700 units at a unit cost of $20). After the sale, there remains $6,000 of inventory (300 units at a unit cost of $20).
3. On January 10, $11,200 is purchased (500 units at a unit cost of $22.40). After the purchase, the inventory is reported on two lines, $6,000 (300 units at a unit cost of $20.00) from the beginning inventory and $11,200 (500 units at $22.40 per unit) from the January 10 purchase.
4. On January 22, 360 units are sold at a price of $30 each for sales of $10,800 (360 units at a selling price of $30 per unit). Using LIFO, the cost of merchandise sold is $8,064 (360 units at unit cost of $22.40) from the January 10 purchase. After the sale, there remains

EXHIBIT 5 **Entries and Perpetual Inventory Account (LIFO)**

Jan. 4 Accounts Receivable	21,000	
Sales		21,000
4 Cost of Merchandise Sold	14,000	
Merchandise Inventory		14,000
10 Merchandise Inventory	11,200	
Accounts Payable		11,200
22 Accounts Receivable	10,800	
Sales		10,800
22 Cost of Merchandise Sold	8,064	
Merchandise Inventory		8,064
28 Accounts Receivable	7,200	
Sales		7,200
28 Cost of Merchandise Sold	5,136	
Merchandise Inventory		5,136
30 Merchandise Inventory	13,980	
Accounts Payable		13,980

Item 127B

	Purchases			Cost of Merchandise Sold			Inventory		
Date	Quantity	Unit Cost	Total Cost	Quantity	Unit Cost	Total Cost	Quantity	Unit Cost	Total Cost
Jan. 1							1,000	20.00	20,000
4				700	20.00	14,000	300	20.00	6,000
10	500	22.40	11,200				300	20.00	6,000
							500	22.40	11,200
22				360	22.40	8,064	300	20.00	6,000
							140	22.40	3,136
28				140	22.40	3,136	200	20.00	4,000
				100	20.00	2,000			
30	600	23.30	13,980				200	20.00	4,000
							600	23.30	13,980
31	Balances					27,200			17,980

Cost of merchandise sold ↑ 27,200 — **January 31 inventory** ↑ 17,980

$9,136 of inventory consisting of $6,000 (300 units at a unit cost of $20.00) from the beginning inventory and $3,136 (140 units at a unit cost of $22.40) from the January 10 purchase.

5. The January 28 sale and January 30 purchase are recorded in a similar manner.
6. The ending balance on January 31 is $17,980. This balance is made up of two layers of inventory as follows:

	Date of Purchase	Quantity	Unit Cost	Total Cost
Layer 1:	Beg. inv. (Jan. 1)	200	$20.00	$ 4,000
Layer 2:	Jan. 30	600	23.30	13,980
Total		800		$17,980

When the LIFO method is used, the subsidiary inventory ledger is sometimes maintained in units only. The units are converted to dollars when the financial statements are prepared at the end of the period.

Example Exercise 7-3 Perpetual Inventory Using LIFO

OBJ 3

Beginning inventory, purchases, and sales for Item ER27 are as follows:

Nov.	1	Inventory	40 units at $5
	5	Sale	30 units
	11	Purchase	70 units at $7
	21	Sale	36 units

Assuming a perpetual inventory system and using the last-in, first-out (LIFO) method, determine (a) the cost of the merchandise sold on November 21 and (b) the inventory on November 30.

Follow My Example 7-3

a. Cost of merchandise sold (November 21):
$252 (36 units × $7)

b. Inventory, November 30:

10 units at $5	$ 50
34 units at $7	238
44 units	$288

Practice Exercises: PE 7-3A, PE 7-3B

International Connection

IFRS INTERNATIONAL FINANCIAL REPORTING STANDARDS (IFRS)

IFRS permit the first-in, first-out and weighted average cost methods but prohibit the last-in, first-out (LIFO) method for determining inventory costs. Since LIFO is used in the United States, adoption of IFRS could have a significant impact on many U.S. companies. For example, **Caterpillar Inc.** uses LIFO. For a recent year, Caterpillar reported that its inventories would have been $2,750 million higher if FIFO had been used. Since Caterpillar reported profits of $5,681 million for the year, the adoption of IFRS would have significantly affected net income if IFRS and FIFO had been used.*

*Differences between U.S. GAAP and IFRS are further discussed and illustrated in Appendix D.

Weighted Average Cost Method

When the weighted average cost method is used in a perpetual inventory system, a weighted average unit cost for each item is computed each time a purchase is made. This unit cost is used to determine the cost of each sale until another purchase is made and a new average is computed. This technique is called a *moving average*.

To illustrate, Exhibit 6 shows the use of weighted average under a perpetual inventory system for Item 127B.

EXHIBIT 6 Entries and Perpetual Inventory Account (Weighted Average)

Date	Account	Debit	Credit
Jan. 4	Accounts Receivable	21,000	
	Sales		21,000
4	Cost of Merchandise Sold	14,000	
	Merchandise Inventory		14,000
10	Merchandise Inventory	11,200	
	Accounts Payable		11,200
22	Accounts Receivable	10,800	
	Sales		10,800
22	Cost of Merchandise Sold	7,740	
	Merchandise Inventory		7,740
28	Accounts Receivable	7,200	
	Sales		7,200
28	Cost of Merchandise Sold	5,160	
	Merchandise Inventory		5,160
30	Merchandise Inventory	13,980	
	Accounts Payable		13,980

Item 127B

	Purchases			Cost of Merchandise Sold			Inventory		
Date	Quantity	Unit Cost	Total Cost	Quantity	Unit Cost	Total Cost	Quantity	Unit Cost	Total Cost
Jan. 1							1,000	20.00	20,000
4				700	20.00	14,000	300	20.00	6,000
10	500	22.40	11,200				800	21.50	17,200
22				360	21.50	7,740	440	21.50	9,460
28				240	21.50	5,160	200	21.50	4,300
30	600	23.30	13,980				800	22.85	18,280
31	Balances					26,900	800	22.85	18,280

Cost of merchandise sold (26,900)

January 31 inventory (18,280)

The journal entries and the subsidiary inventory ledger for Item 127B are shown in Exhibit 6 as follows:

1. The beginning balance on January 1 is $20,000 (1,000 units at a unit cost of $20).
2. On January 4, 700 units were sold at a price of $30 each for sales of $21,000 (700 units at a selling price of $30 per unit). The cost of merchandise sold is $14,000 (700 units at a unit cost of $20.00). After the sale, there remains $6,000 of inventory (300 units at a unit cost of $20.00).
3. On January 10, $11,200 is purchased (500 units at a unit cost of $22.40). After the purchase, the weighted average unit cost of $21.50 is determined by dividing the total

cost of the inventory on hand of $17,200 ($6,000 + $11,200) by the total quantity of inventory on hand of 800 (300 + 500) units. Thus, after the purchase, the inventory consists of 800 units at $21.50 per unit for a total cost of $17,200.

4. On January 22, 360 units are sold at a price of $30 each for sales of $10,800 (360 units at a selling price of $30 per unit). Using weighted average, the cost of merchandise sold is $7,740 (360 units × $21.50 per unit). After the sale, there remains $9,460 of inventory (440 units × $21.50 per unit).
5. The January 28 sale and January 30 purchase are recorded in a similar manner.
6. The ending balance on January 31 is $18,280 (800 units × $22.85 per unit).

Example Exercise 7-4 Perpetual Inventory Using Weighted Average

OBJ 3

Beginning inventory, purchases, and sales for ER27 are as follows:

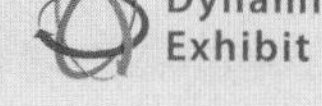

Nov.	1	Inventory	40 units at $5
	5	Sale	30 units
	11	Purchase	70 units at $7
	21	Sale	36 units

Assuming a perpetual inventory system using the weighted average method, determine (a) the weighted average unit cost after the November 11 purchase, (b) the cost of the merchandise sold on November 21, and (c) the inventory on November 30.

Follow My Example 7-4

a. Weighted average unit cost: $6.75
Inventory total cost after purchase on November 21:

	Cost
10 units at $5	$ 50
70 units at $7	490
80 units	$540

Weighted average unit cost = $6.75 ($540 ÷ 80 units)

b. Cost of merchandise sold (November 21):
$243 (36 units × $6.75)

c. Inventory, November 30:
$297 (44 units at $6.75)

Practice Exercises: PE 7-4A, PE 7-4B

Computerized Perpetual Inventory Systems

A perpetual inventory system may be used in a manual accounting system. However, if there are many inventory transactions, such a system is costly and time consuming. In almost all cases, perpetual inventory systems are computerized.

Computerized perpetual inventory systems are useful to managers in controlling and managing inventory. For example, fast-selling items can be reordered before the stock runs out. Sales patterns can also be analyzed to determine when to mark down merchandise or when to restock seasonal merchandise. Finally, inventory data can be used in evaluating advertising campaigns and sales promotions.

OBJ 4 Determine the cost of inventory under the periodic inventory system, using the FIFO, LIFO, and weighted average cost methods.

Inventory Costing Methods Under a Periodic Inventory System

When the periodic inventory system is used, only revenue is recorded each time a sale is made. No entry is made at the time of the sale to record the cost of the merchandise sold. At the end of the accounting period, a physical inventory is taken to determine the cost of the inventory and the cost of the merchandise sold.[2]

[2] Determining the cost of merchandise sold using the periodic system was illustrated in the appendix to Chapter 6.

Like the perpetual inventory system, a cost flow assumption must be made when identical units are acquired at different unit costs during a period. In such cases, the FIFO, LIFO, or weighted average cost method is used.

First-In, First-Out Method

To illustrate the use of the FIFO method in a periodic inventory system, we use the same data for Item 127B as in the perpetual inventory example. The beginning inventory and purchases of Item 127B in January are as follows:

Jan. 1	Inventory	1,000 units at	$20.00	$20,000
10	Purchase	500 units at	22.40	11,200
30	Purchase	600 units at	23.30	13,980
Available for sale during month		2,100		$45,180

The physical count on January 31 shows that 800 units are on hand. Using the FIFO method, the cost of the merchandise on hand at the end of the period is made up of the most recent costs. The cost of the 800 units in the ending inventory on January 31 is determined as follows:

Most recent costs, January 30 purchase	600 units at	$23.30	$13,980
Next most recent costs, January 10 purchase	200 units at	$22.40	4,480
Inventory, January 31	800 units		$18,460

Deducting the cost of the January 31 inventory of $18,460 from the cost of merchandise available for sale of $45,180 yields the cost of merchandise sold of $26,720, computed as follows:

Beginning inventory, January 1	$20,000
Purchases ($11,200 + $13,980)	25,180
Cost of merchandise available for sale in January	$45,180
Less ending inventory, January 31	18,460
Cost of merchandise sold	$26,720

The $18,460 cost of the ending merchandise inventory on January 31 is made up of the most recent costs. The $26,720 cost of merchandise sold is made up of the beginning inventory and the earliest costs. Exhibit 7 shows the relationship of the cost of merchandise sold for January and the ending inventory on January 31.

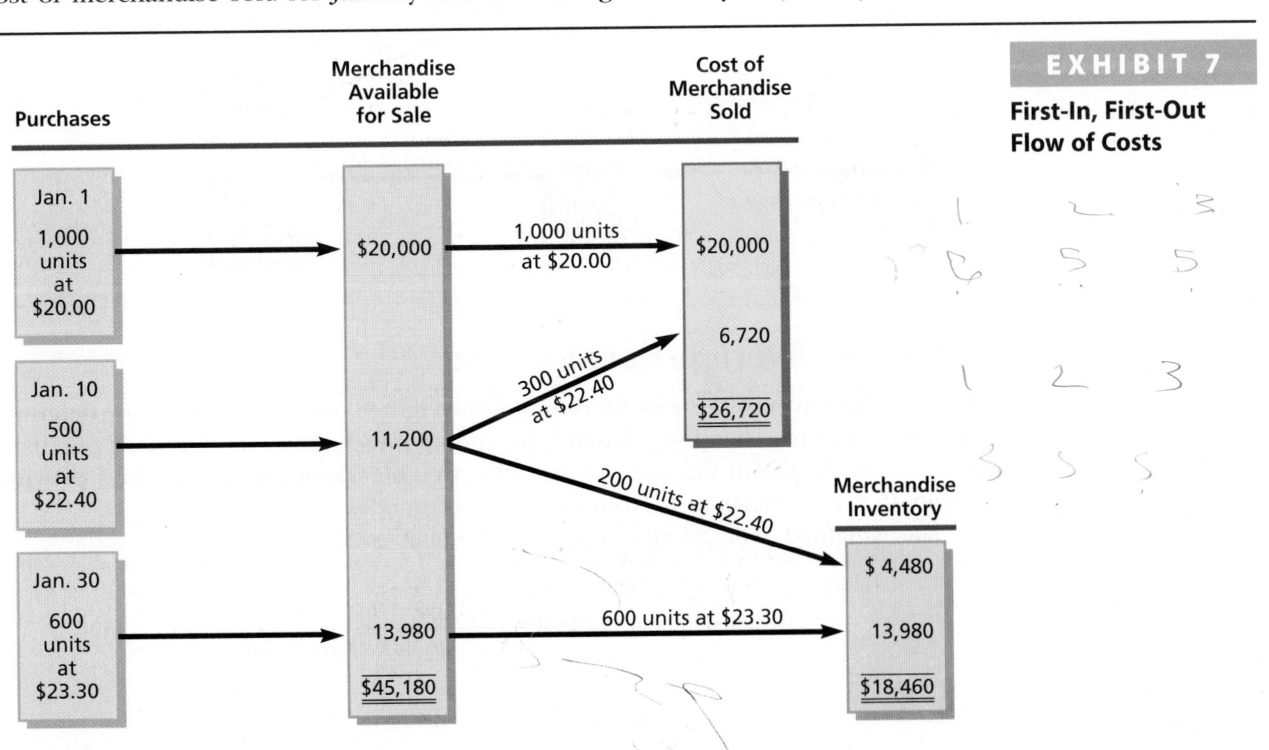

EXHIBIT 7

First-In, First-Out Flow of Costs

Last-In, First-Out Method

IFRS

See Appendix D for more information.

When the LIFO method is used, the cost of merchandise on hand at the end of the period is made up of the earliest costs. Based on the same data as in the FIFO example, the cost of the 800 units in ending inventory on January 31 is $16,000, which consists of 800 units from the beginning inventory at a cost of $20.00 per unit.

Deducting the cost of the January 31 inventory of $16,000 from the cost of merchandise available for sale of $45,180 yields the cost of merchandise sold of $29,180, computed as follows:

Beginning inventory, January 1	$20,000
Purchases ($11,200 + $13,980)	25,180
Cost of merchandise available for sale in January	$45,180
Less ending inventory, January 31	16,000
Cost of merchandise sold	$29,180

The $16,000 cost of the ending merchandise inventory on January 31 is made up of the earliest costs. The $29,180 cost of merchandise sold is made up of the most recent costs. Exhibit 8 shows the relationship of the cost of merchandise sold for January and the ending inventory on January 31.

EXHIBIT 8

Last-In, First-Out Flow of Costs

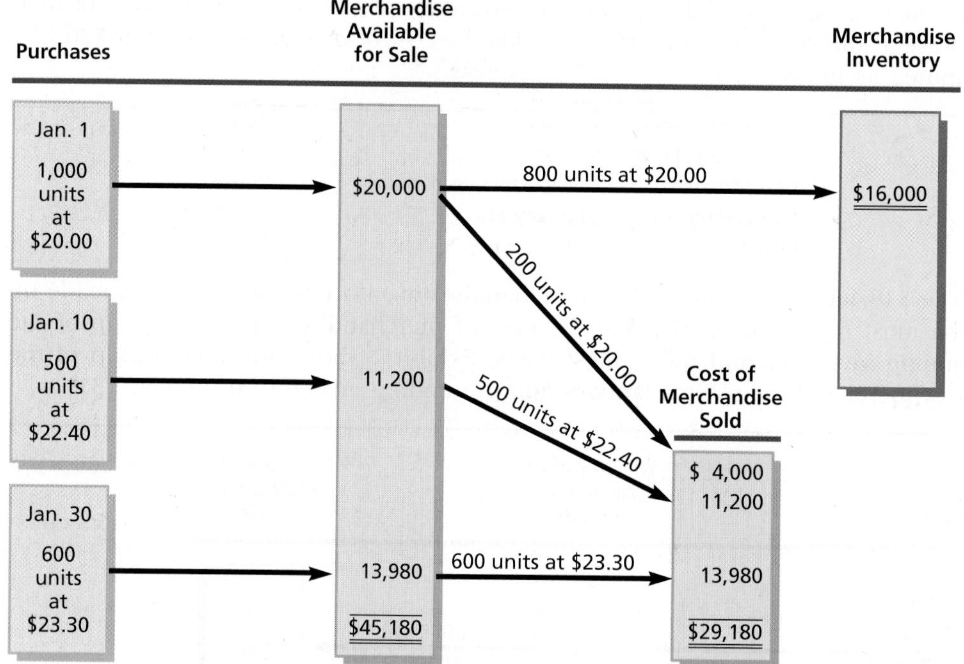

Weighted Average Cost Method

The weighted average cost method uses the weighted average unit cost for determining the cost of merchandise sold and the ending merchandise inventory. If purchases are relatively uniform during a period, the weighted average cost method provides results that are similar to the physical flow of goods.

The weighted average unit cost is determined as follows:

$$\text{Weighted Average Unit Cost} = \frac{\text{Total Cost of Units Available for Sale}}{\text{Units Available for Sale}}$$

To illustrate, the data for Item 127B is used as follows:

$$\text{Weighted Average Unit Cost} = \frac{\text{Total Cost of Units Available for Sale}}{\text{Units Available for Sale}} = \frac{\$45{,}180}{2{,}100 \text{ units}}$$

$$= \$21.51 \text{ per unit (Rounded)}$$

The cost of the January 31 ending inventory is as follows:

Inventory, January 31: $17,208 (800 units × $21.51)

Deducting the cost of the January 31 inventory of $17,208 from the cost of merchandise available for sale of $45,180 yields the cost of merchandise sold of $27,972, computed as follows:

Beginning inventory, January 1	$20,000
Purchases ($11,200 + $13,980)	25,180
Cost of merchandise available for sale in January	$45,180
Less ending inventory, January 31	17,208
Cost of merchandise sold	$27,972

Example Exercise 7-5 Periodic Inventory Using FIFO, LIFO, and Weighted Average Cost Methods

OBJ 4

The units of an item available for sale during the year were as follows:

Jan. 1	Inventory	6 units at $50	$ 300
Mar. 20	Purchase	14 units at $55	770
Oct. 30	Purchase	20 units at $62	1,240
Available for sale		40 units	$2,310

There are 16 units of the item in the physical inventory at December 31. The periodic inventory system is used. Determine the inventory cost using (a) the first-in, first-out (FIFO) method; (b) the last-in, first-out (LIFO) method; and (c) the weighted average cost method.

Follow My Example 7-5

a. First-in, first-out (FIFO) method: $992 = (16 units × $62)
b. Last-in, first-out (LIFO) method: $850 = (6 units × $50) + (10 units × $55)
c. Weighted average cost method: $924 (16 units × $57.75), where average cost = $57.75 = $2,310 ÷ 40 units

Practice Exercises: PE 7-5A, PE 7-5B

Comparing Inventory Costing Methods

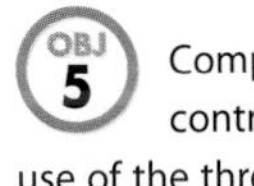

OBJ 5 Compare and contrast the use of the three inventory costing methods.

A different cost flow is assumed for the FIFO, LIFO, and weighted average inventory cost flow methods. As a result, the three methods normally yield different amounts for the following:

- Cost of merchandise sold
- Gross profit
- Net income
- Ending merchandise inventory

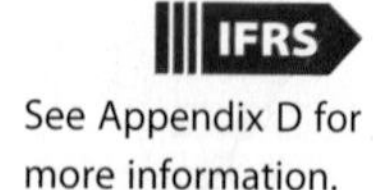

See Appendix D for more information.

Using the perpetual inventory system illustration with sales of $39,000 (1,300 units × $30), the following differences are apparent:[3]

Partial Income Statements

	First-In, First-Out	Weighted Average Cost	Last-In, First-Out
Sales	$39,000	$39,000	$39,000
Cost of merchandise sold:	26,720	26,900	27,200
Gross profit	$12,280	$12,100	$11,800
Merchandise Inventory, Jan. 31	$18,460	$18,280	$17,980

The preceding differences show the effect of increasing costs (prices). If costs (prices) remain the same, all three methods would yield the same results. However, costs (prices) normally do change. The effects of changing costs (prices) on the FIFO and LIFO methods are summarized in Exhibit 9. The weighted average cost method will always yield results between those of FIFO and LIFO.

EXHIBIT 9

Effects of Changing Costs (Prices): FIFO and LIFO Cost Methods

	+ Increasing Costs (Prices)		− Decreasing Costs (Prices)	
	↑ Highest Amount	↓ Lowest Amount	↑ Highest Amount	↓ Lowest Amount
Cost of merchandise sold	LIFO	FIFO	FIFO	LIFO
Gross profit	FIFO	LIFO	LIFO	FIFO
Net income	FIFO	LIFO	LIFO	FIFO
Ending merchandise inventory	FIFO	LIFO	LIFO	FIFO

FIFO reports higher gross profit and net income than the LIFO method when costs (prices) are increasing, as shown in Exhibit 9. However, in periods of rapidly rising costs, the inventory that is sold must be replaced at increasingly higher costs. In such cases, the larger FIFO gross profit and net income are sometimes called *inventory profits* or *illusory profits*.

During a period of increasing costs, LIFO matches more recent costs against sales on the income statement. Thus, it can be argued that the LIFO method more nearly matches current costs with current revenues. LIFO also offers an income tax savings during periods of increasing costs. This is because LIFO reports the lowest amount of gross profit and, thus, taxable net income.[4] However, under LIFO, the ending inventory on the balance sheet may be quite different from its current replacement cost. In such cases, the financial statements normally include a note that estimates what the inventory would have been if FIFO had been used.

The weighted average cost method is, in a sense, a compromise between FIFO and LIFO. The effect of cost (price) trends is averaged in determining the cost of merchandise sold and the ending inventory.

[3] Similar results would also occur when comparing inventory costing methods under a periodic inventory system.
[4] A proposal currently exists to not allow the use of LIFO for tax purposes.

Integrity, Objectivity, and Ethics in Business

WHERE'S THE BONUS?

Managers are often given bonuses based on reported earnings numbers. This can create a conflict. LIFO can improve the value of the company through lower taxes. However, in periods of rising costs (prices), LIFO also produces a lower earnings number and, therefore, lower management bonuses. Ethically, managers should select accounting procedures that will maximize the value of the firm, rather than their own compensation. Compensation specialists can help avoid this ethical dilemma by adjusting the bonus plan for the accounting procedure differences.

Reporting Merchandise Inventory in the Financial Statements

OBJ 6 Describe and illustrate the reporting of merchandise inventory in the financial statements.

Cost is the primary basis for valuing and reporting inventories in the financial statements. However, inventory may be valued at other than cost in the following cases:

1. The cost of replacing items in inventory is below the recorded cost.
2. The inventory cannot be sold at normal prices due to imperfections, style changes, spoilage, damage, obsolescence, or other causes.

Valuation at Lower of Cost or Market

If the market is lower than the purchase cost, the **lower-of-cost-or-market (LCM) method** is used to value the inventory. *Market,* as used in *lower of cost or market,* is the **net realizable value** of the merchandise.[5] Net realizable value is determined as follows:

IFRS See Appendix D for more information.

Net Realizable Value = Estimated Selling Price – Direct Costs of Disposal

Direct costs of disposal include selling expenses such as special advertising or sales commissions.

To illustrate, assume the following data about an item of damaged merchandise:

Original cost	$1,000
Estimated selling price	800
Estimated selling expenses	150

In applying LCM, the market value of the merchandise is $650, computed as follows:

Market Value (Net Realizable Value) = $800 – $150 = $650

Thus, the merchandise would be valued at $650, which is the lower of its cost of $1,000 and its market value of $650.

The lower-of-cost-or-market method can be applied in one of three ways. The cost, market price, and any declines could be determined for the following:

- Each item in the inventory
- Each major class or category of inventory
- Total inventory as a whole

The amount of any price decline is included in the cost of merchandise sold. This, in turn, reduces gross profit and net income in the period in which the price declines occur. This matching of price declines to the period in which they occur is the primary advantage of using the lower-of-cost-or-market method.

[5] The FASB has issued a Proposed Accounting Standards Update that uses net realizable value as market. Proposed Accounting Standards Update, *Inventory (Topic 3330): Simplifying the Measurement of Inventory,* July 15, 2014, FASB.

To illustrate, assume the following data for 400 identical units of Item A in inventory on December 31, 2016:

Cost per unit	$10.25
Market value (net realizable value) per unit	9.50

Since the market value of Item A is $9.50 per unit, $9.50 is used under the lower-of-cost-or-market method.

Exhibit 10 illustrates applying the lower-of-cost-or-market method to each inventory item (Echo, Foxtrot, Sierra, Tango). As applied on an item-by-item basis, the total lower-of-cost-or-market is $15,070, which is a market decline of $450 ($15,520 – $15,070). This market decline of $450 is included in the cost of merchandise sold.

In Exhibit 10, Items Echo, Foxtrot, Sierra, and Tango could be viewed as a class of inventory items. If the lower-of-cost-or-market method is applied to the class, the inventory would be valued at $15,472, which is a market decline of $48 ($15,520 – $15,472). Likewise, if Items Echo, Foxtrot, Sierra, and Tango make up the total inventory, the lower-of-cost-or-market method as applied to the total inventory would be the same amount, $15,472.

EXHIBIT 10

Determining Inventory at Lower of Cost or Market (LCM)

	A	B	C	D	E	F	G
1				Market Value			
2		Inventory	Cost per	per Unit		Total	
3	Item	Quantity	Unit	(Net Realizable Value)	Cost	Market	LCM
4	Echo	400	$10.25	$ 9.50	$ 4,100	$ 3,800	$ 3,800
5	Foxtrot	120	22.50	24.10	2,700	2,892	2,700
6	Sierra	600	8.00	7.75	4,800	4,650	4,650
7	Tango	280	14.00	14.75	3,920	4,130	3,920
8	Total				$15,520	$15,472	$15,070
9							

Example Exercise 7-6 Lower-of-Cost-or-Market Method

On the basis of the following data, determine the value of the inventory at the lower of cost or market. Apply lower of cost or market to each inventory item as shown in Exhibit 10.

Item	Inventory Quantity	Cost per Unit	Market Value per Unit (Net Realizable Value)
C17Y	10	$ 39	$40
B563	7	110	98

Follow My Example 7-6

	A	B	C	D	E	F	G
1				Market Value			
2		Inventory	Cost per	per Unit		Total	
3	Item	Quantity	Unit	(Net Realizable Value)	Cost	Market	LCM
4	C17Y	10	$ 39	$40	$ 390	$ 400	$ 390
5	B563	7	110	98	770	686	686
6	Total				$1,160	$1,086	$1,076
7							

Practice Exercises: PE 7-6A, PE 7-6B

Business Connection

INVENTORY WRITE-DOWNS

Worthington Industries, Inc., is a diversified metal processing company that manufactures metal products, such as metal framing and pressure cylinders. One year, the company experienced rapidly changing business conditions. Due to the global financial crisis and recession, steel prices underwent a severe and rapid decline. As a result, the company recorded an inventory write-down of $105 million and an overall net loss of $108 million for the year.

Merchandise Inventory on the Balance Sheet

Merchandise inventory is usually reported in the Current Assets section of the balance sheet. In addition to this amount, the following are reported:

See Appendix D for more information.

- The method of determining the cost of the inventory (FIFO, LIFO, or weighted average)
- The method of valuing the inventory (cost or the lower of cost or market)

The financial statement reporting for the topics covered in Chapters 7–15 are illustrated using excerpts from the financial statements of **Mornin' Joe**. Mornin' Joe is a fictitious company that offers drip and espresso coffee in a coffeehouse setting. The complete financial statements of Mornin' Joe are illustrated at the end of Chapter 15. The balance sheet presentation for merchandise inventory for Mornin' Joe is as follows:

Mornin' Joe
Balance Sheet
December 31, 2016

Current assets:		
Cash and cash equivalents		$235,000
Trading investments (at cost)	$420,000	
Plus valuation allowance on trading investments	45,000	465,000
Accounts receivable	$305,000	
Less allowance for doubtful accounts	12,300	292,700
Merchandise inventory—at lower of cost (first-in, first-out method) or market		120,000

It is not unusual for a large business to use different costing methods for segments of its inventories. Also, a business may change its inventory costing method. In such cases, the effect of the change and the reason for the change are disclosed in the financial statements.

Effect of Inventory Errors on the Financial Statements

Any errors in merchandise inventory will affect the balance sheet and income statement. Some reasons that inventory errors may occur include the following:

- Physical inventory on hand was miscounted.
- Costs were incorrectly assigned to inventory. For example, the FIFO, LIFO, or weighted average cost method was incorrectly applied.
- Inventory in transit was incorrectly included or excluded from inventory.
- Consigned inventory was incorrectly included or excluded from inventory.

Inventory errors often arise from merchandise that is in transit at year-end. As discussed in Chapter 6, shipping terms determine when the title to merchandise passes. When goods are purchased or sold *FOB shipping point*, title passes to the buyer when the goods are shipped. When the terms are *FOB destination*, title passes to the buyer when the goods are received.

To illustrate, assume that SysExpress ordered the following merchandise from American Products:

Date ordered:	December 27, 2015
Amount:	$10,000
Terms:	FOB shipping point, 2/10, n/30
Date shipped by seller:	December 30
Date delivered:	January 3, 2016

When SysExpress counts its physical inventory on December 31, 2015, the merchandise is still in transit. In such cases, it would be easy for SysExpress to not include the $10,000 of merchandise in its December 31 physical inventory. However, since the merchandise was purchased *FOB shipping point*, SysExpress owns the merchandise. Thus, it should be included in the December 31 inventory, even though it is not on hand. Likewise, any merchandise *sold* by SysExpress *FOB destination* is still SysExpress's inventory, even if it is in transit to the buyer on December 31.

Inventory errors often arise from **consigned inventory**. Manufacturers sometimes ship merchandise to retailers who act as the manufacturer's selling agent. The manufacturer, called the **consignor**, retains title until the goods are sold. Such merchandise is said to be shipped *on consignment* to the retailer, called the **consignee**. Any unsold merchandise at year-end is a part of the manufacturer's (consignor's) inventory, even though the merchandise is in the hands of the retailer (consignee). At year-end, it would be easy for the retailer (consignee) to incorrectly include the consigned merchandise in its physical inventory. Likewise, the manufacturer (consignor) should include consigned inventory in its physical inventory, even though the inventory is not on hand.

Income Statement Effects Inventory errors will misstate the income statement amounts for cost of merchandise sold, gross profit, and net income. The effects of inventory errors on the current period's income statement are summarized in Exhibit 11.

EXHIBIT 11

Effect of Inventory Errors on Current Period's Income Statement

	Income Statement Effect		
Inventory Error	**Cost of Merchandise Sold**	**Gross Profit**	**Net Income**
Beginning inventory is:			
Understated ↓	Understated ↓	↑ Overstated	↑ Overstated
↑ Overstated	↑ Overstated	Understated ↓	Understated ↓
Ending inventory is:			
Understated ↓	↑ Overstated	Understated ↓	Understated ↓
↑ Overstated	Understated ↓	↑ Overstated	↑ Overstated

To illustrate, the income statements of SysExpress shown in Exhibit 12 are used.[6] On December 31, 2015, assume that SysExpress incorrectly records its physical inventory as $50,000 instead of the correct amount of $60,000. Thus, the December 31, 2015, inventory is understated by $10,000 ($60,000 – $50,000). As a result, the cost of merchandise sold is overstated by $10,000. The gross profit and the net income for the year will also be understated by $10,000.

The December 31, 2015, merchandise inventory becomes the January 1, 2016, inventory. Thus, the beginning inventory for 2016 is understated by $10,000. As a result, the cost of merchandise sold is understated by $10,000 for 2016. The gross profit and net income for 2016 will be overstated by $10,000.

As shown in Exhibit 12, because the ending inventory of one period is the beginning inventory of the next period, the effects of inventory errors carry forward to the next period. Specifically, if uncorrected, the effects of inventory errors reverse themselves in the next period. In Exhibit 12, the combined net income for the two years of $525,000 is correct, even though the 2015 and 2016 income statements were incorrect.

[6] The effect of inventory errors will be illustrated using the periodic system. This is because it is easier to see the impact of inventory errors on the income statement using the periodic system. The effect of inventory errors would be the same under the perpetual inventory system.

EXHIBIT 12 **Effects of Inventory Errors on Two Years' Income Statements**

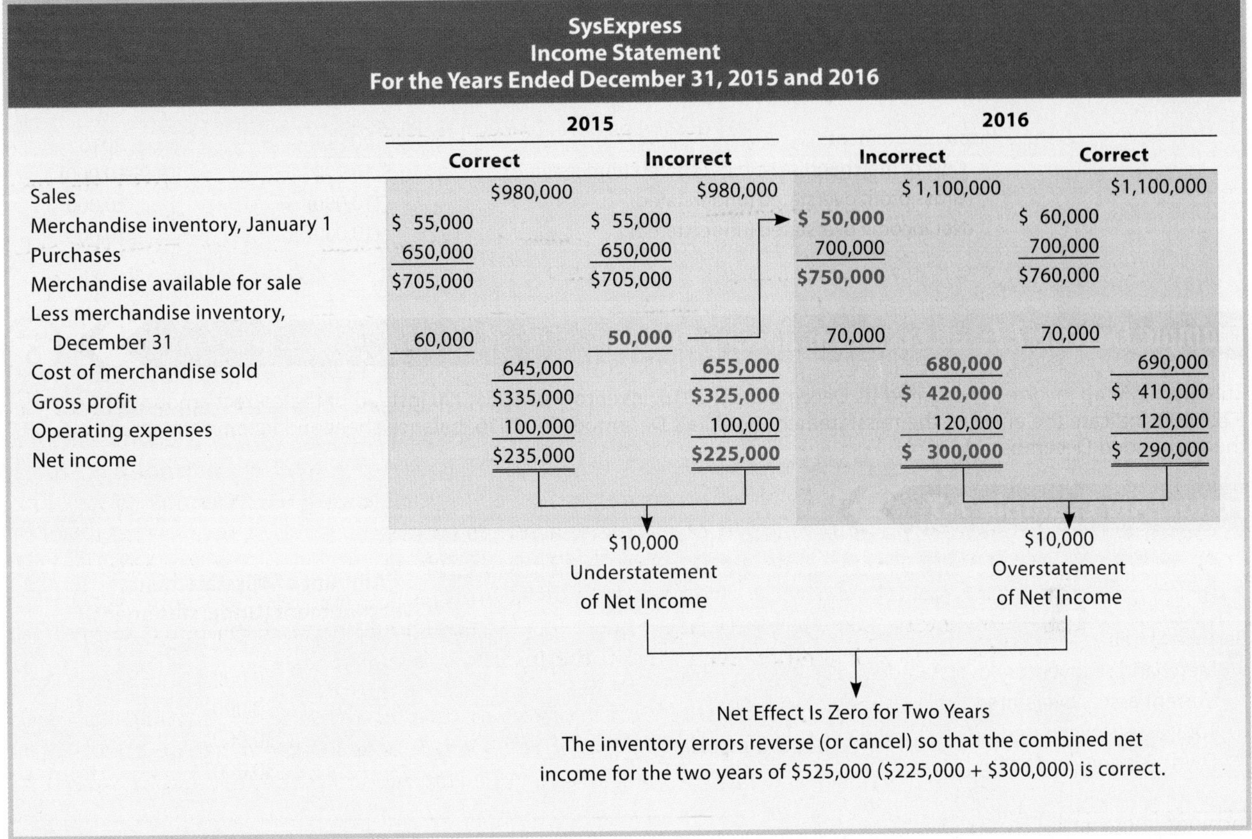

SysExpress
Income Statement
For the Years Ended December 31, 2015 and 2016

	2015				2016			
	Correct		Incorrect		Incorrect		Correct	
Sales		$980,000		$980,000		$ 1,100,000		$1,100,000
Merchandise inventory, January 1	$ 55,000		$ 55,000		$ 50,000		$ 60,000	
Purchases	650,000		650,000		700,000		700,000	
Merchandise available for sale	$705,000		$705,000		$750,000		$760,000	
Less merchandise inventory, December 31	60,000		50,000		70,000		70,000	
Cost of merchandise sold		645,000		655,000		680,000		690,000
Gross profit		$335,000		$325,000		$ 420,000		$ 410,000
Operating expenses		100,000		100,000		120,000		120,000
Net income		$235,000		$225,000		$ 300,000		$ 290,000

$10,000
Understatement
of Net Income
$10,000
Overstatement
of Net Income
Net Effect Is Zero for Two Years
The inventory errors reverse (or cancel) so that the combined net income for the two years of $525,000 ($225,000 + $300,000) is correct.

Balance Sheet Effects Inventory errors misstate the merchandise inventory, current assets, total assets, and owner's equity on the balance sheet. The effects of inventory errors on the current period's balance sheet are summarized in Exhibit 13.

EXHIBIT 13

Effect of Inventory Errors on Current Period's Balance Sheet

	Balance Sheet Effect			
Ending Inventory Error	**Merchandise Inventory**	**Current Assets**	**Total Assets**	**Owner's Equity (Capital)**
Understated ↓	Understated ↓	Understated ↓	Understated ↓	Understated ↓
↑ Overstated	↑ Overstated	↑ Overstated	↑ Overstated	↑ Overstated

For the SysExpress illustration shown in Exhibit 12, the December 31, 2015, ending inventory was understated by $10,000. As a result, the merchandise inventory, current assets, and total assets would be understated by $10,000 on the December 31, 2015, balance sheet. Because the ending physical inventory is understated, the cost of merchandise sold for 2015 will be overstated by $10,000. Thus, the gross profit and the net income for 2015 are understated by $10,000. Because the net income is closed to owner's equity (capital) at the end of the period, the owner's equity on the December 31, 2015, balance sheet is also understated by $10,000.

Inventory errors reverse themselves within two years. As a result, the balance sheet will be correct as of December 31, 2016. Using the SysExpress illustration from Exhibit 12, these effects are summarized as follows:

	Amount of Misstatement	
Balance Sheet:	December 31, 2015	December 31, 2016
Merchandise inventory overstated (understated)	$(10,000)	Correct
Current assets overstated (understated)	(10,000)	Correct
Total assets overstated (understated)	(10,000)	Correct
Owner's equity overstated (understated)	(10,000)	Correct
Income Statement:	2015	2016
Cost of merchandise sold overstated (understated)	$ 10,000	$(10,000)
Gross profit overstated (understated)	(10,000)	10,000
Net income overstated (understated)	(10,000)	10,000

Example Exercise 7-7 Effect of Inventory Errors

OBJ 6

Zula Repair Shop incorrectly counted its December 31, 2016, inventory as $250,000 instead of the correct amount of $220,000. Indicate the effect of the misstatement on Zula's December 31, 2016, balance sheet and income statement for the year ended December 31, 2016.

Follow My Example 7-7

	Amount of Misstatement Overstatement (Understatement)
Balance Sheet:	
Merchandise inventory overstated	$ 30,000
Current assets overstated	30,000
Total assets overstated	30,000
Owner's equity overstated	30,000
Income Statement:	
Cost of merchandise sold understated	$(30,000)
Gross profit overstated	30,000
Net income overstated	30,000

Practice Exercises: PE 7-7A, PE 7-7B

OBJ 7 Describe and illustrate the inventory turnover and the number of days' sales in inventory in analyzing the efficiency and effectiveness of inventory management.

Financial Analysis and Interpretation: Inventory Turnover and Number of Days' Sales in Inventory

A merchandising business should keep enough inventory on hand to meet its customers' needs. A failure to do so may result in lost sales. However, too much inventory ties up funds that could be used to improve operations. Also, excess inventory increases expenses such as storage and property taxes. Finally, excess inventory increases the risk of losses due to price declines, damage, or changes in customer tastes.

Two measures to analyze the efficiency and effectiveness of inventory management are:

- inventory turnover and
- number of days' sales in inventory.

Inventory turnover measures the relationship between the cost of merchandise sold and the amount of inventory carried during the period. It is computed as follows:

$$\text{Inventory Turnover} = \frac{\text{Cost of Merchandise Sold}}{\text{Average Inventory}}$$

Business  Connection

RAPID INVENTORY AT COSTCO

Costco Wholesale Corporation operates more than 500 membership warehouses that offer members low prices on a limited selection of nationally branded and selected private label products. Costco emphasizes high sales volumes and rapid inventory turnover. This enables Costco to operate profitably at lower gross margins than traditional wholesalers, discount retailers, and supermarkets.

In addition, Costco's rapid inventory turnover allows it to conserve its working capital, described as follows:

Because of our high sales volume and rapid inventory turnover, we generally have the opportunity to sell and be paid for inventory before we are required to pay . . . our merchandise vendors. . . . As sales increase and inventory turnover becomes more rapid, a greater percentage of inventory is financed through payment terms provided by suppliers rather than by our working capital.

Source: Costco Wholesale Corporation, *Form 10-K For the Fiscal Year Ended September 1, 2013.*

To illustrate, inventory turnover for Best Buy is computed from the following data (in millions) taken from two recent annual reports:

	For the Year Ended	
	Year 2	**Year 1**
Cost of merchandise sold	$38,132	$37,206
Inventories:		
Beginning of year	5,897	5,486
End of year	5,731	5,897
Average inventory:*		
($5,897 + $5,731) ÷ 2	5,814.0	
($5,486 + $5,897) ÷ 2		5,691.5
Inventory turnover:*		
$38,132 ÷ $5,814.0	6.6	
$37,206 ÷ $5,691.5		6.5

* Rounded to one decimal place.

Generally, the larger the inventory turnover the more efficient and effective the company is in managing inventory. In the preceding example, inventory turnover increased slightly from 6.5 to 6.6 during Year 2, and thus Best Buy's inventory efficiency increased during Year 2.

The **number of days' sales in inventory** measures the length of time it takes to acquire, sell, and replace the inventory. It is computed as follows:

$$\text{Number of Days' Sales in Inventory} = \frac{\text{Average Inventory}}{\text{Average Daily Cost of Merchandise Sold}}$$

The average daily cost of merchandise sold is determined by dividing the cost of merchandise sold by 365.[6] Based upon the preceding data, the number of days' sales in inventory for Best Buy is computed as follows:

	For the Year Ended	
	Year 2	**Year 1**
Cost of merchandise sold	$38,132	$37,206
Average daily cost of merchandise sold:*		
$38,132 ÷ 365 days	104.5	
$37,206 ÷ 365 days		101.9
Average inventory:*		
($5,897 + $5,731) ÷ 2	5,814.0	
($5,486 + $5,897) ÷ 2		5,691.5
Number of days' sales in inventory:*		
$5,814.0 ÷ $104.5	55.6 days	
$5,691.5 ÷ $101.9		55.9 days

* Rounded to one decimal place.

[6] We use 365 days for all computations involving real world companies and data. We do this to highlight differences among companies and because computations using real world data normally require rounding.

Generally, the lower the number of days' sales in inventory, the more efficient and effective the company is in managing inventory. As shown previously, the number of days' sales in inventory decreased slightly from 55.9 to 55.6 during Year 2, and thus Best Buy's inventory management improved. This is consistent with the increase in inventory turnover during the year.

As with most financial ratios, differences exist among industries. To illustrate, **Zale Corporation** is a large retailer of fine jewelry in the United States. Because jewelry doesn't sell as rapidly as Best Buy's consumer electronics, Zale's inventory turnover and number of days' sales in inventory should be significantly different than Best Buy's. For a recent year, this is confirmed as follows:

	Best Buy	Zale
Inventory turnover	6.6	1.2
Number of days' sales in inventory	55.6 days	294.7 days

Example Exercise 7-8 Inventory Turnover and Number of Days' Sales in Inventory

OBJ 7

Financial statement data for years ending December 31 for Beadle Company follows:

	2016	2015
Cost of merchandise sold	$877,500	$615,000
Inventories:		
Beginning of year	225,000	185,000
End of year	315,000	225,000

a. Determine the inventory turnover for 2016 and 2015.
b. Determine the number of days' sales in inventory for 2016 and 2015, using 365 days.
c. Does the change in the inventory turnover and the number of days' sales in inventory from 2015 to 2016 indicate a favorable or an unfavorable trend?

Follow My Example 7-8

a. Inventory turnover:

	2016	2015
Average inventory:		
($225,000 + $315,000) ÷ 2	$270,000	
($185,000 + $225,000) ÷ 2		$205,000
Inventory turnover:		
$877,500 ÷ $270,000	3.25	
$615,000 ÷ $205,000		3.00

b. Number of days' sales in inventory:

Average daily cost of merchandise sold:		
$877,500 ÷ 365 days	$2,404	
$615,000 ÷ 365 days		$1,685
Average inventory:		
($225,000 + $315,000) ÷ 2	$270,000	
($185,000 + $225,000) ÷ 2		$205,000
Number of days' sales in inventory:		
$270,000 ÷ $2,404	112.3 days	
$205,000 ÷ $1,685		121.7 days

c. The increase in the inventory turnover from 3.00 to 3.25 and the decrease in the number of days' sales in inventory from 121.7 days to 112.3 days indicate favorable trends in managing inventory.

Practice Exercises: PE 7-8A, PE 7-8B

APPENDIX

Estimating Inventory Cost

A business may need to estimate the amount of inventory for the following reasons:

- Perpetual inventory records are not maintained.
- A disaster such as a fire or flood has destroyed the inventory records and the inventory.
- Monthly or quarterly financial statements are needed, but a physical inventory is taken only once a year.

This appendix describes and illustrates two widely used methods of estimating inventory cost.

Retail Method of Inventory Costing

The **retail inventory method** of estimating inventory cost requires costs and retail prices to be maintained for the merchandise available for sale. A ratio of cost to retail price is then used to convert ending inventory at retail to estimate the ending inventory cost.

The retail inventory method is applied as follows:

- Step 1. Determine the total merchandise available for sale at cost and retail.
- Step 2. Determine the ratio of the cost to retail of the merchandise available for sale.
- Step 3. Determine the ending inventory at retail by deducting the sales from the merchandise available for sale at retail.
- Step 4. Estimate the ending inventory cost by multiplying the ending inventory at retail by the cost to retail ratio.

Exhibit 14 illustrates the retail inventory method.

EXHIBIT 14

Determining Inventory by the Retail Method

		A	B	C
	1		Cost	Retail
	2	Merchandise inventory, January 1	$19,400	$ 36,000
	3	Purchases in January (net)	42,600	64,000
Step 1 →	4	Merchandise available for sale	$62,000	$100,000
Step 2 →	5	Ratio of cost to retail price: $\frac{\$62,000}{\$100,000} = 62\%$		
	6	Sales for January		70,000
Step 3 →	7	Merchandise inventory, January 31, at retail		$ 30,000
Step 4 →	8	Merchandise inventory, January 31, at estimated cost		
	9	($30,000 × 62%)		$ 18,600
	10			

When estimating the cost to retail ratio, the mix of items in the ending inventory is assumed to be the same as the merchandise available for sale. If the ending inventory is made up of different classes of merchandise, cost to retail ratios may be developed for each class of inventory.

An advantage of the retail method is that it provides inventory figures for preparing monthly statements. Department stores and similar retailers often determine gross profit and operating income each month but may take a physical inventory only once or twice a year. Thus, the retail method allows management to monitor operations more closely.

The retail method may also be used as an aid in taking a physical inventory. In this case, the items are counted and recorded at their retail (selling) prices instead of their costs. The physical inventory at retail is then converted to cost by using the cost to retail ratio.

Gross Profit Method of Inventory Costing

The **gross profit method** uses the estimated gross profit for the period to estimate the inventory at the end of the period. The gross profit is estimated from the preceding year, adjusted for any current-period changes in the cost and sales prices.

The gross profit method is applied as follows:

- Step 1. Determine the merchandise available for sale at cost.
- Step 2. Determine the estimated gross profit by multiplying the sales by the gross profit percentage.
- Step 3. Determine the estimated cost of merchandise sold by deducting the estimated gross profit from the sales.
- Step 4. Estimate the ending inventory cost by deducting the estimated cost of merchandise sold from the merchandise available for sale.

Exhibit 15 illustrates the gross profit method.

EXHIBIT 15

Estimating Inventory by Gross Profit Method

		A	B	C
	1			**Cost**
	2	Merchandise inventory, January 1		$ 57,000
	3	Purchases in January (net)		180,000
Step 1 →	4	Merchandise available for sale		$237,000
	5	Sales for January	$250,000	
Step 2 →	6	Less estimated gross profit ($250,000 × 30%)	75,000	
Step 3 →	7	Estimated cost of merchandise sold		175,000
Step 4 →	8	Estimated merchandise inventory, January 31		$ 62,000
	9			

The gross profit method is useful for estimating inventories for monthly or quarterly financial statements. It is also useful in estimating the cost of merchandise destroyed by fire or other disasters.

At a Glance 7

Describe the importance of control over inventory.

Key Points Two objectives of inventory control are safeguarding the inventory and properly reporting it in the financial statements. The perpetual inventory system and physical count enhance control over inventory.

Learning Outcomes	Example Exercises	Practice Exercises
• Describe controls for safeguarding inventory.		
• Describe how a perpetual inventory system enhances control over inventory.		
• Describe why taking a physical inventory enhances control over inventory.		

Describe three inventory cost flow assumptions and how they impact the income statement and balance sheet.

Key Points The three common inventory cost flow assumptions used in business are the (1) first-in, first-out method (FIFO); (2) last-in, first-out method (LIFO); and (3) weighted average cost method. The cost flow assumption affects the income statement and balance sheet.

Learning Outcomes	Example Exercises	Practice Exercises
• Describe the FIFO, LIFO, and weighted average cost flow methods.		
• Describe how the choice of a cost flow method affects the income statement and balance sheet.	EE7-1	PE7-1A, 7-1B

Determine the cost of inventory under the perpetual inventory system, using the FIFO, LIFO, and weighted average cost methods.

Key Points In a perpetual inventory system, the number of units and the cost of each type of merchandise are recorded in a subsidiary inventory ledger, with a separate account for each type of merchandise.

Learning Outcomes	Example Exercises	Practice Exercises
• Determine the cost of inventory and the cost of merchandise sold, using a perpetual inventory system under the FIFO method.	EE7-2	PE7-2A, 7-2B
• Determine the cost of inventory and the cost of merchandise sold, using a perpetual inventory system under the LIFO method.	EE7-3	PE7-3A, 7-3B
• Determine the cost of inventory and the cost of merchandise sold, using a perpetual inventory system under the weighted average cost method.	EE7-4	PE7-4A, 7-4B

Determine the cost of inventory under the periodic inventory system, using the FIFO, LIFO, and weighted average cost methods.

Key Points In a periodic inventory system, a physical inventory is taken to determine the cost of the inventory and the cost of merchandise sold.

Learning Outcomes	Example Exercises	Practice Exercises
• Determine the cost of inventory and the cost of merchandise sold, using a periodic inventory system under the FIFO method.	EE7-5	PE7-5A, 7-5B
• Determine the cost of inventory and the cost of merchandise sold, using a periodic inventory system under the LIFO method.	EE7-5	PE7-5A, 7-5B
• Determine the cost of inventory and the cost of merchandise sold, using a periodic inventory system under the weighted average cost method.	EE7-5	PE7-5A, 7-5B

Compare and contrast the use of the three inventory costing methods.

Key Points The three inventory costing methods will normally yield different amounts for (1) the ending inventory, (2) the cost of merchandise sold for the period, and (3) the gross profit (and net income) for the period.

Learning Outcomes	Example Exercises	Practice Exercises
• Indicate which inventory cost flow method will yield the highest and lowest ending inventory and net income during periods of increasing prices.		
• Indicate which inventory cost flow method will yield the highest and lowest ending inventory and net income during periods of decreasing prices.		

Describe and illustrate the reporting of merchandise inventory in the financial statements.

Key Points The lower of cost or market is used to value inventory. The market value is the net realizable value of the merchandise.

Merchandise inventory is usually presented in the Current Assets section of the balance sheet, following receivables. The method of determining the cost and valuing the inventory is reported.

Errors in reporting inventory based on the physical inventory will affect the balance sheet and income statement.

Learning Outcomes	Example Exercises	Practice Exercises
• Determine inventory using lower of cost or market.	EE7-6	PE7-6A, 7-6B
• Prepare the Current Assets section of the balance sheet that includes inventory.		
• Determine the effect of inventory errors on the balance sheet and income statement.	EE7-7	PE7-7A, 7-7B

Describe and illustrate the inventory turnover and the number of days' sales in inventory in analyzing the efficiency and effectiveness of inventory management.

Key Points Two measures to analyze the efficiency and effectiveness of inventory management are (1) inventory turnover and (2) number of days' sales in inventory

Learning Outcomes	Example Exercises	Practice Exercises
• Describe the use of inventory turnover and number of days' sales in inventory in analyzing how well a company manages inventory.		
• Compute the inventory turnover.	EE7-8	PE7-8A, 7-8B
• Compute the number of days' sales in inventory.	EE7-8	PE7-8A, 7-8B

Key Terms

consigned inventory (338)
consignee (338)
consignor (338)
first-in, first-out (FIFO) inventory cost flow method (324)
gross profit method (344)
inventory turnover (340)
last-in, first-out (LIFO) inventory cost flow method (324)
lower-of-cost-or-market (LCM) method (335)
net realizable value (336)
number of days' sales in inventory (341)
physical inventory (323)
purchase order (322)
receiving report (322)
retail inventory method (343)
specific identification inventory cost flow method (324)
subsidiary inventory ledger (323)
weighted average inventory cost flow method (324)

Illustrative Problem

Stewart Co.'s beginning inventory and purchases during the year ended December 31, 2016, were as follows:

		Unit	Units Cost	Total Cost
January 1	Inventory	1,000	$50.00	$ 50,000
March 10	Purchase	3,000	52.00	156,000
June 25	Sold 1,600 units			
August 30	Purchase	2,600	55.00	143,000
October 5	Sold 4,000 units			
November 26	Purchase	1,000	57.68	57,680
December 31	Sold 800 units			
Total		7,600		$406,680

Instructions

1. Determine the cost of inventory on December 31, 2016, using the perpetual inventory system and each of the following inventory costing methods:
   a. first-in, first-out
   b. last-in, first-out
   c. weighted average
2. Determine the cost of inventory on December 31, 2016, using the periodic inventory system and each of the following inventory costing methods:
   a. first-in, first-out
   b. last-in, first-out
   c. weighted average cost
3. (Appendix) Assume that during the fiscal year ended December 31, 2016, sales were $530,000 and the estimated gross profit rate was 36%. Estimate the ending inventory at December 31, 2016, using the gross profit method.

Solution

1. The perpetual inventory ledgers follow:
   a. First-in, first-out method: $68,680 ($11,000 + $57,680)
   b. Last-in, first-out method: $61,536 ($50,000 + $11,536)
   c. Weighted average cost method: $66,600 (1,200 units × $55.50)
2. a. First-in, first-out method:

1,000 units at $57.68	$57,680
200 units at $55.00	11,000
1,200 units	$68,680

   b. Last-in, first-out method:

1,000 units at $50.00	$50,000
200 units at $52.00	10,400
1,200 units	$60,400

   c. Weighted average cost method:
   Weighted average cost per unit: ($406,680 ÷ 7,600 units = $53.51 (Rounded)
   Inventory, December 31, 2016: 1,200 units at $53.51 = $64,212

1. a. First-in, first-out method: $68,680 ($11,000 + $57,680)

Date	Purchases			Cost of Merchandise Sold			Inventory		
	Quantity	Unit Cost	Total Cost	Quantity	Unit Cost	Total Cost	Quantity	Unit Cost	Total Cost
2016									
Jan. 1							1,000	50.00	50,000
Mar. 10	3,000	52.00	156,000				1,000	50.00	50,000
							3,000	52.00	156,000
June 25				1,000	50.00	50,000	2,400	52.00	124,800
				600	52.00	31,200			
Aug. 30	2,600	55.00	143,000				2,400	52.00	124,800
							2,600	55.00	143,000
Oct. 5				2,400	52.00	124,800	1,000	55.00	55,000
				1,600	55.00	88,000			
Nov. 26	1,000	57.68	57,680				1,000	55.00	55,000
							1,000	57.68	57,680
Dec. 31				800	55.00	44,000	200	55.00	11,000
							1,000	57.68	57,680
31	Balances					338,000			68,680

b. Last-in, first-out method: $61,536 ($50,000 + $11,536)

Date	Purchases			Cost of Merchandise Sold			Inventory		
	Quantity	Unit Cost	Total Cost	Quantity	Unit Cost	Total Cost	Quantity	Unit Cost	Total Cost
2016									
Jan. 1							1,000	50.00	50,000
Mar. 10	3,000	52.00	156,000				1,000	50.00	50,000
							3,000	52.00	156,000
June 25				1,600	52.00	83,200	1,000	50.00	50,000
							1,400	52.00	72,800
Aug. 30	2,600	55.00	143,000				1,000	50.00	50,000
							1,400	52.00	72,800
							2,600	55.00	143,000
Oct. 5				2,600	55.00	143,000	1,000	50.00	50,000
				1,400	52.00	72,800			
Nov. 26	1,000	57.68	57,680				1,000	50.00	50,000
							1,000	57.68	57,680
Dec. 31				800	57.68	46,144	1,000	50.00	50,000
							200	57.68	11,536
31	Balances					345,144			61,536

c. Weighted average cost method: $66,600 (1,200 units × $55.50)

Date	Purchases			Cost of Merchandise Sold			Inventory		
	Quantity	Unit Cost	Total Cost	Quantity	Unit Cost	Total Cost	Quantity	Unit Cost	Total Cost
Jan. 1							1,000	50.00	50,000
Mar. 10	3,000	52.00	156,000				4,000	51.50	206,000
June 25				1,600	51.50	82,400	2,400	51.50	123,600
Aug. 30	2,600	55.00	143,000				5,000	53.32	266,600
Oct. 5				4,000	53.32	213,280	1,000	53.32	53,320
Nov. 26	1,000	57.68	57,680				2,000	55.50	111,000
Dec. 31				800	55.50	44,400	1,200	55.50	66,600
31	Balances					340,080	1,200	55.50	66,600

3. (Appendix)

Merchandise inventory, January 1, 2016		$ 50,000
Purchases (net)		356,680
Merchandise available for sale		$406,680
Sales	$530,000	
Less estimated gross profit ($530,000 × 36%)	190,800	
Estimated cost of merchandise sold		339,200
Estimated merchandise inventory, December 31, 2016		$ 67,480

Discussion Questions

1. Before inventory purchases are recorded, the receiving report should be reconciled to what documents?
2. Why is it important to periodically take a physical inventory when using a perpetual inventory system?
3. Do the terms *FIFO, LIFO, and weighted average* refer to techniques used in determining quantities of the various classes of merchandise on hand? Explain.
4. If merchandise inventory is being valued at cost and the price level is decreasing, which of the three methods of costing—FIFO, LIFO, or weighted average cost—will yield (a) the highest inventory cost, (b) the lowest inventory cost, (c) the highest gross profit, and (d) the lowest gross profit?
5. Which of the three methods of inventory costing—FIFO, LIFO, or weighted average cost—will in general yield an inventory cost most nearly approximating current replacement cost?
6. If inventory is being valued at cost and the price level is steadily rising, which of the three methods of costing—FIFO, LIFO, or weighted average cost—will yield the lowest annual income tax expense? Explain.
7. Using the following data, how should the merchandise be valued under lower of cost or market?

Original cost	$1,350
Estimated selling price	1,475
Selling expenses	180

8. The inventory at the end of the year was understated by $14,750. (a) Did the error cause an overstatement or an understatement of the gross profit for the year? (b) Which items on the balance sheet at the end of the year were overstated or understated as a result of the error?
9. Hutch Co. sold merchandise to Bibbins Company on May 31, FOB shipping point. If the merchandise is in transit on May 31, the end of the fiscal year, which company would report it in its financial statements? Explain.
10. A manufacturer shipped merchandise to a retailer on a consignment basis. If the merchandise is unsold at the end of the period, in whose inventory should the merchandise be included?

Practice Exercises

EE 7-1 *p. 325*

PE 7-1A Cost flow methods

OBJ. 2

The following three identical units of Item BZ1810 are purchased during November:

		Item BZ1810	Units	Cost	
Nov.	2	Purchase	1	$ 55	
	14	Purchase	1	57	
	28	Purchase	1	62	
	Total		3	$174	
	Average cost per unit			$ 58	($174 ÷ 3 units)

Assume that one unit is sold on November 30 for $90.

Determine the gross profit for November and ending inventory on November 30 using the (a) first-in, first-out (FIFO); (b) last-in, first-out (LIFO); and (c) weighted average cost methods.

(Continued)

EE 7-1 p. 325

SHOW ME HOW

PE 7-1B Cost flow methods

OBJ. 2

The following three identical units of Item Beta are purchased during June:

		Item Beta	Units	Cost	
June	2	Purchase	1	$ 50	
	12	Purchase	1	60	
	23	Purchase	1	70	
	Total		3	$180	
	Average cost per unit			$ 60	($180 ÷ 3 units)

Assume that one unit is sold on June 27 for $110.

Determine the gross profit for June and ending inventory on June 30 using the (a) first-in, first-out (FIFO); (b) last-in, first-out (LIFO); and (c) weighted average cost methods.

EE 7-2 p. 327

SHOW ME HOW

PE 7-2A Perpetual inventory using FIFO

OBJ. 3

Beginning inventory, purchases, and sales for Item ProX2 are as follows:

Jan.	1	Inventory	60 units at $100
	9	Sale	35 units
	13	Purchase	50 units at $110
	25	Sale	48 units

Assuming a perpetual inventory system and using the first-in, first-out (FIFO) method, determine (a) the cost of merchandise sold on January 25 and (b) the inventory on January 31.

EE 7-2 p. 327

SHOW ME HOW

PE 7-2B Perpetual inventory using FIFO

OBJ. 3

Beginning inventory, purchases, and sales for Item Delta are as follows:

July	1	Inventory	50 units at $15
	7	Sale	44 units
	15	Purchase	90 units at $18
	24	Sale	40 units

Assuming a perpetual inventory system and using the first-in, first-out (FIFO) method, determine (a) the cost of merchandise sold on July 24 and (b) the inventory on July 31.

EE 7-3 p. 328

SHOW ME HOW

PE 7-3A Perpetual inventory using LIFO

OBJ. 3

Beginning inventory, purchases, and sales for Item Zebra 9x are as follows:

April	1	Inventory	420 units at $8
	10	Sale	300 units
	18	Purchase	280 units at $9
	27	Sale	250 units

Assuming a perpetual inventory system and using the last-in, first-out (LIFO) method, determine (a) the cost of merchandise sold on April 27 and (b) the inventory on April 30.

EE 7-3 p. 328

SHOW ME HOW

PE 7-3B Perpetual inventory using LIFO

OBJ. 3

Beginning inventory, purchases, and sales for Item Foxtrot are as follows:

Mar.	1	Inventory	270 units at $18
	8	Sale	225 units
	15	Purchase	375 units at $20
	27	Sale	240 units

Assuming a perpetual inventory system and using the last-in, first-out (LIFO) method, determine (a) the cost of merchandise sold on March 27 and (b) the inventory on March 31.

EE 7-4 p. 330

PE 7-4A Perpetual inventory using weighted average — OBJ. 3

SHOW ME HOW

Beginning inventory, purchases, and sales for 30xT are as follows:

May 1	Inventory	50 units at $80
12	Sale	35 units
23	Purchase	60 units at $90
26	Sale	55 units

Assuming a perpetual inventory system and using the weighted average method, determine (a) the weighted average unit cost after the May 23 purchase, (b) the cost of the merchandise sold on May 26, and (c) the inventory on May 31.

EE 7-4 p. 330

PE 7-4B Perpetual inventory using weighted average — OBJ. 3

SHOW ME HOW

Beginning inventory, purchases, and sales for WCS12 are as follows:

Oct. 1	Inventory	300 units at $8
13	Sale	175 units
22	Purchase	375 units at $10
29	Sale	280 units

Assuming a perpetual inventory system and using the weighted average method, determine (a) the weighted average unit cost after the October 22 purchase, (b) the cost of the merchandise sold on October 29, and (c) the inventory on October 31.

EE 7-5 p. 333

PE 7-5A Periodic inventory using FIFO, LIFO, and weighted average cost methods — OBJ. 4

SHOW ME HOW

The units of an item available for sale during the year were as follows:

Jan. 1	Inventory	12 units at $5,400	$ 64,800
Aug. 7	Purchase	18 units at $6,000	108,000
Dec. 11	Purchase	15 units at $6,480	97,200
Available for sale		45 units	$270,000

There are 14 units of the item in the physical inventory at December 31. The periodic inventory system is used. Determine the inventory cost using (a) the first-in, first-out (FIFO) method; (b) the last-in, first-out (LIFO) method; and (c) the weighted average cost method.

EE 7-5 p. 333

PE 7-5B Periodic inventory using FIFO, LIFO, and weighted average cost methods — OBJ. 4

SHOW ME HOW

The units of an item available for sale during the year were as follows:

Jan. 1	Inventory	20 units at $360	$ 7,200
Aug. 13	Purchase	260 units at $342	88,920
Nov. 30	Purchase	40 units at $357	14,280
Available for sale		320 units	$110,400

There are 57 units of the item in the physical inventory at December 31. The periodic inventory system is used. Determine the inventory cost using (a) the first-in, first-out (FIFO) method; (b) the last-in, first-out (LIFO) method; and (c) the weighted average cost method.

EE 7-6 p. 336

PE 7-6A Lower-of-cost-or-market method — OBJ. 6

SHOW ME HOW

On the basis of the following data, determine the value of the inventory at the lower of cost or market. Apply lower of cost or market to each inventory item, as shown in Exhibit 10.

Item	Inventory Quantity	Cost per Unit	Market Value per Unit (Net Realizable Value)
Raven 10	1,200	$115	$112
Dove 23	6,500	17	22

SHOW ME HOW

EE 7-6 p. 336

PE 7-6B Lower-of-cost-or-market method **OBJ. 6**

On the basis of the following data, determine the value of the inventory at the lower of cost or market. Apply lower of cost or market to each inventory item, as shown in Exhibit 10.

Item	Inventory Quantity	Cost per Unit	Market Value per Unit (Net Realizable Value)
JFW1	6,330	$10	$11
SAW9	1,140	36	34

SHOW ME HOW

EE 7-7 p. 340

PE 7-7A Effect of inventory errors **OBJ. 6**

During the taking of its physical inventory on August 31, 2016, Kate Interiors Company incorrectly counted its inventory as $366,900 instead of the correct amount of $378,500. Indicate the effect of the misstatement on Kate Interiors' August 31, 2016, balance sheet and income statement for the year ended August 31, 2016.

SHOW ME HOW

EE 7-7 p. 340

PE 7-7B Effect of inventory errors **OBJ. 6**

During the taking of its physical inventory on December 31, 2016, Waterjet Bath Company incorrectly counted its inventory as $728,660 instead of the correct amount of $719,880. Indicate the effect of the misstatement on Waterjet Bath's December 31, 2016, balance sheet and income statement for the year ended December 31, 2016.

SHOW ME HOW

EE 7-8 p. 342

PE 7-8A Inventory turnover and number of days' sales in inventory **OBJ. 7**

Financial statement data for years ending December 31 for Holland Company follows:

	2016	2015
Cost of merchandise sold	$4,504,500	$3,715,200
Inventories:		
Beginning of year	788,000	760,000
End of year	850,000	788,000

a. Determine the inventory turnover for 2016 and 2015.

b. Determine the number of days' sales in inventory for 2016 and 2015. Use 365 days and round to one decimal place.

c. Does the change in inventory turnover and the number of days' sales in inventory from 2015 to 2016 indicate a favorable or an unfavorable trend?

SHOW ME HOW

EE 7-8 p. 342

PE 7-8B Inventory turnover and number of days' sales in inventory **OBJ. 7**

Financial statement data for years ending December 31 for Tango Company follows:

	2016	2015
Cost of merchandise sold	$3,864,000	$4,001,500
Inventories:		
Beginning of year	770,000	740,000
End of year	840,000	770,000

a. Determine the inventory turnover for 2016 and 2015.

b. Determine the number of days' sales in inventory for 2016 and 2015. Use 365 days and round to one decimal place.

c. Does the change in inventory turnover and the number of days' sales in inventory from 2015 to 2016 indicate a favorable or an unfavorable trend?

Exercises

EX 7-1 Control of inventories

OBJ. 1

Triple Creek Hardware Store currently uses a periodic inventory system. Kevin Carlton, the owner, is considering the purchase of a computer system that would make it feasible to switch to a perpetual inventory system.

Kevin is unhappy with the periodic inventory system because it does not provide timely information on inventory levels. Kevin has noticed on several occasions that the store runs out of good-selling items, while too many poor-selling items are on hand.

Kevin is also concerned about lost sales while a physical inventory is being taken. Triple Creek Hardware currently takes a physical inventory twice a year. To minimize distractions, the store is closed on the day inventory is taken. Kevin believes that closing the store is the only way to get an accurate inventory count.

Will switching to a perpetual inventory system strengthen Triple Creek Hardware's control over inventory items? Will switching to a perpetual inventory system eliminate the need for a physical inventory count? Explain.

EX 7-2 Control of inventories

OBJ. 1

Hardcase Luggage Shop is a small retail establishment located in a large shopping mall. This shop has implemented the following procedures regarding inventory items:

a. Because the shop carries mostly high-quality, designer luggage, all inventory items are tagged with a control device that activates an alarm if a tagged item is removed from the store.

b. Because the display area of the store is limited, only a sample of each piece of luggage is kept on the selling floor. Whenever a customer selects a piece of luggage, the salesclerk gets the appropriate piece from the store's stockroom. Because all salesclerks need access to the stockroom, it is not locked. The stockroom is adjacent to the break room used by all mall employees.

c. Whenever Hardcase Luggage Shop receives a shipment of new inventory, the items are taken directly to the stockroom. Hardcase's accountant uses the vendor's invoice to record the amount of inventory received.

State whether each of these procedures is appropriate or inappropriate. If it is inappropriate, state why.

EX 7-3 Perpetual inventory using FIFO

OBJ. 2, 3

✔ Inventory balance, June 30, $29,920

SHOW ME HOW

Beginning inventory, purchases, and sales data for portable DVD players are as follows:

June	1	Inventory	240 units at $78
	10	Sale	180 units
	15	Purchase	280 units at $80
	20	Sale	220 units
	24	Sale	90 units
	30	Purchase	320 units at $86

The business maintains a perpetual inventory system, costing by the first-in, first-out method.

a. Determine the cost of the merchandise sold for each sale and the inventory balance after each sale, presenting the data in the form illustrated in Exhibit 4.

b. Based upon the preceding data, would you expect the inventory to be higher or lower using the last-in, first-out method?

EX 7-4 Perpetual inventory using LIFO

OBJ. 2, 3

✔ Inventory balance, June 30, $29,860

SHOW ME HOW

Assume that the business in Exercise 7-3 maintains a perpetual inventory system, costing by the last-in, first-out method. Determine the cost of merchandise sold for each sale and the inventory balance after each sale, presenting the data in the form illustrated in Exhibit 5.

✔ Inventory balance, May 31, $20,160

SHOW ME HOW

EX 7-5 Perpetual inventory using LIFO **OBJ. 2, 3**

Beginning inventory, purchases, and sales data for prepaid cell phones for May are as follows:

Inventory		Purchases		Sales	
May 1	1,550 units at $44	May 10	720 units at $45	May 12	1,200 units
		20	1,200 units at $48	14	830 units
				31	1,000 units

a. Assuming that the perpetual inventory system is used, costing by the LIFO method, determine the cost of merchandise sold for each sale and the inventory balance after each sale, presenting the data in the form illustrated in Exhibit 5.

b. Based upon the preceding data, would you expect the inventory to be higher or lower using the first-in, first-out method?

✔ Inventory balance, May 31, $21,120

SHOW ME HOW

EX 7-6 Perpetual inventory using FIFO **OBJ. 2, 3**

Assume that the business in Exercise 7-5 maintains a perpetual inventory system, costing by the first-in, first-out method. Determine the cost of merchandise sold for each sale and the inventory balance after each sale, presenting the data in the form illustrated in Exhibit 4.

✔ b. $22,000

SHOW ME HOW

EX 7-7 FIFO and LIFO costs under perpetual inventory system **OBJ. 2, 3**

The following units of an item were available for sale during the year:

Beginning inventory	3,600 units at $4.00
Sale	2,400 units at $8.00
First purchase	8,000 units at $4.20
Sale	6,000 units at $8.00
Second purchase	7,500 units at $4.40
Sale	5,500 units at $8.00

The firm uses the perpetual inventory system, and there are 5,200 units of the item on hand at the end of the year. What is the total cost of the ending inventory according to (a) FIFO, (b) LIFO?

✔ Total Cost of Merchandise Sold, $1,758,750

SHOW ME HOW

EX 7-8 Weighted average cost flow method under perpetual inventory system **OBJ. 3**

The following units of a particular item were available for sale during the calendar year:

Jan. 1	Inventory	10,000 units at $75.00
Mar. 18	Sale	8,000 units
May 2	Purchase	18,000 units at $77.50
Aug. 9	Sale	15,000 units
Oct. 20	Purchase	7,000 units at $80.25

The firm uses the weighted average cost method with a perpetual inventory system. Determine the cost of merchandise sold for each sale and the inventory balance after each sale. Present the data in the form illustrated in Exhibit 6.

✔ Total Cost of Merchandise Sold, $154,400

EX 7-9 Weighted average cost flow method under perpetual inventory system **OBJ. 3**

The following units of a particular item were available for sale during the calendar year:

Jan. 1	Inventory	4,000 units at $20
Apr. 19	Sale	2,500 units
June 30	Purchase	6,000 units at $24
Sept. 2	Sale	4,500 units
Nov. 15	Purchase	1,000 units at $25

The firm uses the weighted average cost method with a perpetual inventory system. Determine the cost of merchandise sold for each sale and the inventory balance after each sale. Present the data in the form illustrated in Exhibit 6.

EX 7-10 Perpetual inventory using FIFO OBJ. 3

✔ Total Cost of Merchandise Sold, $152,000

Assume that the business in Exercise 7-9 maintains a perpetual inventory system. Determine the cost of merchandise sold for each sale and the inventory balance after each sale, assuming the first-in, first-out method. Present the data in the form illustrated in Exhibit 4.

EX 7-11 Perpetual inventory using LIFO OBJ. 3

✔ Total Cost of Merchandise Sold, $158,000

Assume that the business in Exercise 7-9 maintains a perpetual inventory system. Determine the cost of merchandise sold for each sale and the inventory balance after each sale, assuming the last-in, first-out method. Present the data in the form illustrated in Exhibit 5.

EX 7-12 Periodic inventory by three methods OBJ. 2, 4

✔ b. $13,280

The units of an item available for sale during the year were as follows:

Jan.	1	Inventory	200 units at $60
Feb.	17	Purchase	275 units at $64
July	21	Purchase	300 units at $68
Nov.	23	Purchase	225 units at $70

There are 220 units of the item in the physical inventory at December 31. The periodic inventory system is used. Determine the inventory cost by (a) the first-in, first-out method, (b) the last-in, first-out method, and (c) the weighted average cost method.

EX 7-13 Periodic inventory by three methods; cost of merchandise sold OBJ. 2, 4

✔ a. Inventory, $6,228

The units of an item available for sale during the year were as follows:

Jan.	1	Inventory	90 units at $54
Mar.	10	Purchase	112 units at $55
Aug.	30	Purchase	100 units at $58
Dec.	12	Purchase	98 units at $60

There are 104 units of the item in the physical inventory at December 31. The periodic inventory system is used. Determine the inventory cost and the cost of merchandise sold by three methods, presenting your answers in the following form:

	Cost	
Inventory Method	**Merchandise Inventory**	**Merchandise Sold**
a. First-in, first-out	$	$
b. Last-in, first-out		
c. Weighted average cost		

EX 7-14 Comparing inventory methods OBJ. 5

Assume that a firm separately determined inventory under FIFO and LIFO and then compared the results.

a. In each space that follows, place the correct sign [less than (<), greater than (>), or equal (=)] for each comparison, assuming periods of rising prices.

1. FIFO inventory	________	LIFO inventory
2. FIFO cost of goods sold	________	LIFO cost of goods sold
3. FIFO net income	________	LIFO net income
4. FIFO income taxes	________	LIFO income taxes

b. Why would management prefer to use LIFO over FIFO in periods of rising prices?

✔ LCM: $37,870

EX 7-15 Lower-of-cost-or-market inventory **OBJ. 6**

On the basis of the following data, determine the value of the inventory at the lower of cost or market. Assemble the data in the form illustrated in Exhibit 10.

Commodity	Inventory Quantity	Cost per Unit	Market Value per Unit (Net Realizable Value)
Ash	80	$140	$125
Aspen	120	90	112
Beech	30	75	74
Maple	75	88	86
Oak	60	140	145

EX 7-16 Merchandise inventory on the balance sheet **OBJ. 6**

Based on the data in Exercise 7-15 and assuming that cost was determined by the FIFO method, show how the merchandise inventory would appear on the balance sheet.

EX 7-17 Effect of errors in physical inventory **OBJ. 6**

Missouri River Supply Co. sells canoes, kayaks, whitewater rafts, and other boating supplies. During the taking of its physical inventory on December 31, 2016, Missouri River Supply incorrectly counted its inventory as $233,400 instead of the correct amount of $238,600.

a. State the effect of the error on the December 31, 2016, balance sheet of Missouri River Supply.

b. State the effect of the error on the income statement of Missouri River Supply for the year ended December 31, 2016.

c. If uncorrected, what would be the effect of the error on the 2017 income statement?

d. If uncorrected, what would be the effect of the error on the December 31, 2017, balance sheet?

EX 7-18 Effect of errors in physical inventory **OBJ. 6**

Fonda Motorcycle Shop sells motorcycles, ATVs, and other related supplies and accessories. During the taking of its physical inventory on December 31, 2016, Fonda Motorcycle Shop incorrectly counted its inventory as $337,500 instead of the correct amount of $328,850.

a. State the effect of the error on the December 31, 2016, balance sheet of Fonda Motorcycle Shop.

b. State the effect of the error on the income statement of Fonda Motorcycle Shop for the year ended December 31, 2016.

c. If uncorrected, what would be the effect of the error on the 2017 income statement?

d. If uncorrected, what would be the effect of the error on the December 31, 2017, balance sheet?

EX 7-19 Error in inventory **OBJ. 6**

During 2016, the accountant discovered that the physical inventory at the end of 2015 had been understated by $42,750. Instead of correcting the error, however, the accountant assumed that the error would balance out (correct itself) in 2016.

➡ Are there any flaws in the accountant's assumption? Explain.

EX 7-20 Inventory turnover **OBJ. 7**

The following data (in thousands) were taken from recent annual reports of **Apple Inc.**, a manufacturer of personal computers and related products, and **American Greetings Corporation**, a manufacturer and distributor of greeting cards and related products:

	Apple	American Greetings
Cost of goods sold	$87,846,000	$741,645
Inventory, end of year	791,000	208,945
Inventory, beginning of the year	776,000	179,730

a. Determine the inventory turnover for Apple and American Greetings. Round to one decimal place.

b. Would you expect American Greetings' inventory turnover to be higher or lower than Apple's? Why?

EX 7-21 Inventory turnover and number of days' sales in inventory **OBJ. 7**

✔ a. Kroger, 26 days' sales in inventory

SHOW ME HOW

Kroger, Safeway Inc., and Whole Foods Markets, Inc. are three grocery chains in the United States. Inventory management is an important aspect of the grocery retail business. Recent balance sheets for these three companies indicated the following merchandise inventory information:

	Merchandise Inventory	
	End of Year (in millions)	Beginning of Year (in millions)
Kroger	$5,114	$4,966
Safeway	2,470	2,623
Whole Foods	374	337

The cost of goods sold for each company was:

	Cost of Goods Sold (in millions)
Kroger	$71,494
Safeway	31,837
Whole Foods	11,699

a. Determine the number of days' sales in inventory (use 365 days and round to the nearest day) and the inventory turnover (round to one decimal place) for the three companies.

b. Interpret your results in part (a).

c. If Kroger had Whole Foods' number of days' sales in inventory, how much additional cash flow (rounded to nearest million) would have been generated from the smaller inventory relative to its actual average inventory position?

Appendix
EX 7-22 Retail method

A business using the retail method of inventory costing determines that merchandise inventory at retail is $1,235,000. If the ratio of cost to retail price is 54%, what is the amount of inventory to be reported on the financial statements?

Appendix
EX 7-23 Retail method

A business using the retail method of inventory costing determines that merchandise inventory at retail is $396,400. If the ratio of cost to retail price is 61%, what is the amount of inventory to be reported on the financial statements?

Appendix
EX 7-24 Retail method

A business using the retail method of inventory costing determines that merchandise inventory at retail is $775,000. If the ratio of cost to retail price is 66%, what is the amount of inventory to be reported on the financial statements?

Appendix
EX 7-25 Retail method

On the basis of the following data, estimate the cost of the merchandise inventory at June 30 by the retail method:

		Cost	Retail
June 1	Merchandise inventory	$ 165,000	$ 275,000
June 1–30	Purchases (net)	2,361,500	3,800,000
June 1–30	Sales		3,550,000

Appendix
EX 7-26 Gross profit method

✓ a. Merchandise destroyed: $414,000

The merchandise inventory was destroyed by fire on December 13. The following data were obtained from the accounting records:

Jan. 1	Merchandise inventory	$ 350,000
Jan. 1–Dec. 13	Purchases (net)	2,950,000
	Sales	4,440,000
	Estimated gross profit rate	35%

a. Estimate the cost of the merchandise destroyed.

b. Briefly describe the situations in which the gross profit method is useful.

Appendix
EX 7-27 Gross profit method

Based on the following data, estimate the cost of the ending merchandise inventory:

Sales	$9,250,000
Estimated gross profit rate	36%
Beginning merchandise inventory	$ 180,000
Purchases (net)	5,945,000
Merchandise available for sale	$6,125,000

Appendix
EX 7-28 Gross profit method

Based on the following data, estimate the cost of the ending merchandise inventory:

Sales	$1,450,000
Estimated gross profit rate	42%
Beginning merchandise inventory	$ 100,000
Purchases (net)	860,000
Merchandise available for sale	$ 960,000

Problems: Series A

PR 7-1A FIFO perpetual inventory OBJ. 2, 3

✓ 3. $2,286,750

The beginning inventory at Funky Party Supplies and data on purchases and sales for a three-month period ending March 31, 2016, are as follows:

Date		Transaction	Number of Units	Per Unit	Total
Jan.	1	Inventory	2,500	$60.00	$150,000
	10	Purchase	7,500	68.00	510,000
	28	Sale	3,750	120.00	450,000
	30	Sale	1,250	120.00	150,000

Date	Transaction	Number of Units	Per Unit	Total
Feb. 5	Sale	500	$120.00	$ 60,000
10	Purchase	18,000	70.00	1,260,000
16	Sale	9,000	125.00	1,125,000
28	Sale	8,500	125.00	1,062,500
Mar. 5	Purchase	15,000	71.60	1,074,000
14	Sale	10,000	125.00	1,250,000
25	Purchase	2,500	72.00	180,000
30	Sale	8,750	125.00	1,093,750

Instructions

1. Record the inventory, purchases, and cost of merchandise sold data in a perpetual inventory record similar to the one illustrated in Exhibit 4, using the first-in, first-out method.
2. Determine the total sales and the total cost of merchandise sold for the period. Journalize the entries in the sales and cost of merchandise sold accounts. Assume that all sales were on account.
3. Determine the gross profit from sales for the period.
4. Determine the ending inventory cost as of March 31, 2016.
5. Based upon the preceding data, would you expect the inventory using the last-in, first-out method to be higher or lower?

✔ 2. Gross profit, $2,252,250

PR 7-2A LIFO perpetual inventory **OBJ. 2, 3**

The beginning inventory at Funky Party Supplies and data on purchases and sales for a three-month period are shown in Problem 7-1A.

Instructions

1. Record the inventory, purchases, and cost of merchandise sold data in a perpetual inventory record similar to the one illustrated in Exhibit 5, using the last-in, first-out method.
2. Determine the total sales, the total cost of merchandise sold, and the gross profit from sales for the period.
3. Determine the ending inventory cost as of March 31, 2016.

✔ 2. Gross profit, $2,284,250

PR 7-3A Weighted average cost method with perpetual inventory **OBJ. 2, 3**

The beginning inventory for Funky Party Supplies and data on purchases and sales for a three-month period are shown in Problem 7-1A.

Instructions

1. Record the inventory, purchases, and cost of merchandise sold data in a perpetual inventory record similar to the one illustrated in Exhibit 6, using the weighted average cost method.
2. Determine the total sales, the total cost of merchandise sold, and the gross profit from sales for the period.
3. Determine the ending inventory cost as of March 31, 2016.

✔ 2. Inventory, $235,000

PR 7-4A Periodic inventory by three methods **OBJ. 2, 3**

The beginning inventory for Funky Party Supplies and data on purchases and sales for a three-month period are shown in Problem 7-1A.

Instructions

1. Determine the inventory on March 31, 2016, and the cost of goods sold for the three-month period, using the first-in, first-out method and the periodic inventory system.
2. Determine the inventory on March 31, 2016, and the cost of goods sold for the three-month period, using the last-in, first-out method and the periodic inventory system.

(Continued)

3. Determine the inventory on March 31, 2016, and the cost of goods sold for the three-month period, using the weighted average cost method and the periodic inventory system. Round the weighted average unit cost to the nearest cent.
4. Compare the gross profit and the March 31, 2016, inventories, using the following column headings:

	FIFO	LIFO	Weighted Average
Sales			
Cost of merchandise sold			
Gross profit			
Inventory, March 31, 2016			

PR 7-5A Periodic inventory by three methods

OBJ. 2, 4

✔ 1. $10,700

Dymac Appliances uses the periodic inventory system. Details regarding the inventory of appliances at November 1, 2015, purchases invoices during the next 12 months, and the inventory count at October 31, 2016, are summarized as follows:

		Purchases Invoices			
Model	**Inventory, November 1**	**1st**	**2nd**	**3rd**	**Inventory Count, October 31**
A10	—	4 at $ 64	4 at $ 70	4 at $ 76	6
B15	8 at $176	4 at 158	3 at 170	6 at 184	8
E60	3 at 75	3 at 65	15 at 68	9 at 70	5
G83	7 at 242	6 at 250	5 at 260	10 at 259	9
J34	12 at 240	10 at 246	16 at 267	16 at 270	15
M90	2 at 108	2 at 110	3 at 128	3 at 130	5
Q70	5 at 160	4 at 170	4 at 175	7 at 180	8

Instructions

1. Determine the cost of the inventory on October 31, 2016, by the first-in, first-out method. Present data in columnar form, using the following headings:

Model	Quantity	Unit Cost	Total Cost

   If the inventory of a particular model comprises one entire purchase plus a portion of another purchase acquired at a different unit cost, use a separate line for each purchase.
2. Determine the cost of the inventory on October 31, 2016, by the last-in, first-out method, following the procedures indicated in (1).
3. Determine the cost of the inventory on October 31, 2016, by the weighted average cost method, using the columnar headings indicated in (1).
4. Discuss which method (FIFO or LIFO) would be preferred for income tax purposes in periods of (a) rising prices and (b) declining prices.

PR 7-6A Lower-of-cost-or-market inventory

OBJ. 6

✔ Total LCM, $39,873

Data on the physical inventory of Ashwood Products Company as of December 31, 2016, follows:

Description	Inventory Quantity	Market Value per Unit (Net Realizable Value)
B12	38	$ 57
E41	18	180
G19	33	126
L88	18	550
N94	400	7
P24	90	18
R66	8	250
T33	140	20
Z16	15	752

Quantity and cost data from the last purchases invoice of the year and the next-to-the-last purchases invoice are summarized as follows:

	Last Purchases Invoice		Next-to-the-Last Purchases Invoice	
Description	**Quantity Purchased**	**Unit Cost**	**Quantity Purchased**	**Unit Cost**
B12	30	$ 60	30	$ 59
E41	35	178	20	180
G19	20	128	25	129
L88	10	563	10	560
N94	500	8	500	7
P24	80	22	50	21
R66	5	248	4	260
T33	100	21	100	19
Z16	10	750	9	745

Instructions

Determine the inventory at cost and also at the lower of cost or market, using the first-in, first-out method. Record the appropriate unit costs on the inventory sheet, and complete the pricing of the inventory. When there are two different unit costs applicable to an item, proceed as follows:

1. Draw a line through the quantity, and insert the quantity and unit cost of the last purchase.
2. On the following line, insert the quantity and unit cost of the next-to-the-last purchase.
3. Total the cost and market columns and insert the lower of the two totals in the Lower of C or M column. The first item on the inventory sheet has been completed as an example.

Inventory Sheet
December 31, 2016

				Total		
Description	**Inventory Quantity**	**Cost per Unit**	**Market Value per Unit (Net Realizable Value)**	**Cost**	**Market**	**Lower of C or M**
B12	~~38~~ 30	$60	$57	$1,800	$1,710	
	8	59	57	472	456	
				$2,272	$2,166	$2,166

Appendix
PR 7-7A Retail method; gross profit method

✔ 1. $483,600

Selected data on merchandise inventory, purchases, and sales for Celebrity Tan Co. and Ranchworks Co. are as follows:

	Cost	Retail
Celebrity Tan		
Merchandise inventory, August 1	$ 300,000	$ 575,000
Transactions during August:		
Purchases (net)	2,149,000	3,375,000
Sales		3,170,000
Ranchworks Co.		
Merchandise inventory, March 1	$ 880,000	
Transactions during March through November:		
Purchases (net)	9,500,000	
Sales	15,800,000	
Estimated gross profit rate	38%	

(Continued)

Instructions

1. Determine the estimated cost of the merchandise inventory of Celebrity Tan Co. on August 31 by the retail method, presenting details of the computations.
2. a. Estimate the cost of the merchandise inventory of Ranchworks Co. on November 30 by the gross profit method, presenting details of the computations.
   b. Assume that Ranchworks Co. took a physical inventory on November 30 and discovered that $369,750 of merchandise was on hand. What was the estimated loss of inventory due to theft or damage during March through November?

Problems: Series B

PR 7-1B FIFO perpetual inventory

OBJ. 2, 3

✔ 3. $214,474

SHOW ME HOW

The beginning inventory of merchandise at Dunne Co. and data on purchases and sales for a three-month period ending June 30, 2016, are as follows:

Date	Transaction	Number of Units	Per Unit	Total
Apr. 3	Inventory	25	$1,200	$ 30,000
8	Purchase	75	1,240	93,000
11	Sale	40	2,000	80,000
30	Sale	30	2,000	60,000
May 8	Purchase	60	1,260	75,600
10	Sale	50	2,000	100,000
19	Sale	20	2,000	40,000
28	Purchase	80	1,260	100,800
June 5	Sale	40	2,250	90,000
16	Sale	25	2,250	56,250
21	Purchase	35	1,264	44,240
28	Sale	44	2,250	99,000

Instructions

1. Record the inventory, purchases, and cost of merchandise sold data in a perpetual inventory record similar to the one illustrated in Exhibit 4, using the first-in, first-out method.
2. Determine the total sales and the total cost of merchandise sold for the period. Journalize the entries in the sales and cost of merchandise sold accounts. Assume that all sales were on account.
3. Determine the gross profit from sales for the period.
4. Determine the ending inventory cost on June 30, 2016.
5. Based upon the preceding data, would you expect the inventory using the last-in, first-out method to be higher or lower?

PR 7-2B LIFO perpetual inventory

OBJ. 2, 3

✔ 2. Gross profit, $213,170

SHOW ME HOW

The beginning inventory for Dunne Co. and data on purchases and sales for a three-month period are shown in Problem 7-1B.

Instructions

1. Record the inventory, purchases, and cost of merchandise sold data in a perpetual inventory record similar to the one illustrated in Exhibit 5, using the last-in, first-out method.
2. Determine the total sales, the total cost of merchandise sold, and the gross profit from sales for the period.
3. Determine the ending inventory cost on June 30, 2016.

✔ 2. Gross profit, $214,396

PR 7-3B Weighted average cost method with perpetual inventory

OBJ. 2, 3

The beginning inventory for Dunne Co. and data on purchases and sales for a three-month period are shown in Problem 7-1B.

Instructions

1. Record the inventory, purchases, and cost of merchandise sold data in a perpetual inventory record similar to the one illustrated in Exhibit 6, using the weighted average cost method.
2. Determine the total sales, the total cost of merchandise sold, and the gross profit from sales for the period.
3. Determine the ending inventory cost on June 30, 2016.

✔ 2. Inventory, $31,240

PR 7-4B Periodic inventory by three methods

OBJ. 2, 3

The beginning inventory for Dunne Co. and data on purchases and sales for a three-month period are shown in Problem 7-1B.

Instructions

1. Determine the inventory on June 30, 2016, and the cost of goods sold for the three-month period, using the first-in, first-out method and the periodic inventory system.
2. Determine the inventory on June 30, 2016, and the cost of goods sold for the three-month period, using the last-in, first-out method and the periodic inventory system.
3. Determine the inventory on June 30, 2016, and the cost of goods sold for the three-month period, using the weighted average cost method and the periodic inventory system. Round the weighted average unit cost to the dollar.
4. Compare the gross profit and June 30, 2016, inventories using the following column headings:

	FIFO	LIFO	Weighted Average
Sales			
Cost of merchandise sold			
Gross profit			
Inventory, June 30, 2016			

✔ 1. $18,545

PR 7-5B Periodic inventory by three methods

OBJ. 2, 4

Pappa's Appliances uses the periodic inventory system. Details regarding the inventory of appliances at January 1, 2016, purchases invoices during the year, and the inventory count at December 31, 2016, are summarized as follows:

		Purchases Invoices			
Model	Inventory, January 1	1st	2nd	3rd	Inventory Count, December 31
C55	3 at $1,040	3 at $1,054	3 at $1,060	3 at $1,070	4
D11	9 at 639	7 at 645	6 at 666	6 at 675	11
F32	5 at 240	3 at 260	1 at 260	1 at 280	2
H29	6 at 305	3 at 310	3 at 316	4 at 317	4
K47	6 at 520	8 at 531	4 at 549	6 at 542	8
S33	—	4 at 222	4 at 232	—	2
X74	4 at 35	6 at 36	8 at 37	7 at 39	7

Instructions

1. Determine the cost of the inventory on December 31, 2016, by the first-in, first-out method. Present data in columnar form, using the following headings:

Model	Quantity	Unit Cost	Total Cost

(Continued)

If the inventory of a particular model comprises one entire purchase plus a portion of another purchase acquired at a different unit cost, use a separate line for each purchase.

2. Determine the cost of the inventory on December 31, 2016, by the last-in, first-out method, following the procedures indicated in (1).
3. Determine the cost of the inventory on December 31, 2016, by the weighted average cost method, using the columnar headings indicated in (1).
4. Discuss which method (FIFO or LIFO) would be preferred for income tax purposes in periods of (a) rising prices and (b) declining prices.

PR 7-6B Lower-of-cost-or-market inventory

OBJ. 6

✔ Total LCM, $41,873

Data on the physical inventory of Katus Products Co. as of December 31, 2016, follows:

Description	Inventory Quantity	Market Value per Unit (Net Realizable Value)
A54	37	$ 56
C77	24	178
F66	30	132
H83	21	545
K12	375	5
Q58	90	18
S36	8	235
V97	140	20
Y88	17	744

Quantity and cost data from the last purchases invoice of the year and the next-to-the-last purchases invoice are summarized as follows:

	Last Purchases Invoice		Next-to-the-Last Purchases Invoice	
Description	Quantity Purchased	Unit Cost	Quantity Purchased	Unit Cost
A54	30	$ 60	40	$ 58
C77	25	174	15	180
F66	20	130	15	128
H83	6	547	15	540
K12	500	6	500	7
Q58	75	25	80	26
S36	5	256	4	260
V97	100	17	115	16
Y88	10	750	8	740

Instructions

Determine the inventory at cost and also at the lower of cost or market, using the first-in, first-out method. Record the appropriate unit costs on the inventory sheet, and complete the pricing of the inventory. When there are two different unit costs applicable to an item:

1. Draw a line through the quantity, and insert the quantity and unit cost of the last purchase.
2. On the following line, insert the quantity and unit cost of the next-to-the-last purchase.
3. Total the cost and market columns and insert the lower of the two totals in the Lower of C or M column. The first item on the inventory sheet has been completed as an example.

Inventory Sheet

December 31, 2016

Description	Unit Inventory Quantity	Cost per Unit	Market Value per Unit (Net Realizable Value)	Total Cost	Total Market	Total LCM
A54	~~37~~ 30	60	$56	$1,800	$1,680	
	7	58	56	406	392	
				$2,206	$2,072	$2,072

Appendix
PR 7-7B Retail method; gross profit method

✔ 1. $630,000

Selected data on merchandise inventory, purchases, and sales for Jaffe Co. and Coronado Co. are as follows:

	Cost	Retail
Jaffe Co.		
Merchandise inventory, February 1	$ 400,000	$ 615,000
Transactions during February:		
Purchases (net)	4,055,000	5,325,000
Sales		5,100,000
Coronado Co.		
Merchandise inventory, May 1	$ 400,000	
Transactions during May thru October:		
Purchases (net)	3,150,000	
Sales	4,750,000	
Estimated gross profit rate	35%	

Instructions

1. Determine the estimated cost of the merchandise inventory of Jaffe Co. on February 28 by the retail method, presenting details of the computations.
2. a. Estimate the cost of the merchandise inventory of Coronado Co. on October 31 by the gross profit method, presenting details of the computations.

   b. Assume that Coronado Co. took a physical inventory on October 31 and discovered that $366,500 of merchandise was on hand. What was the estimated loss of inventory due to theft or damage during May thru October?

Cases & Projects

CP 7-1 Ethics and professional conduct in business

Anstead Co. is experiencing a decrease in sales and operating income for the fiscal year ending October 31, 2016. Ryan Frazier, controller of Anstead Co., has suggested that all orders received before the end of the fiscal year be shipped by midnight, October 31, 2016, even if the shipping department must work overtime. Because Anstead Co. ships all merchandise FOB shipping point, it would record all such shipments as sales for the year ending October 31, 2016, thereby offsetting some of the decreases in sales and operating income.

Discuss whether Ryan Frazier is behaving in a professional manner.

CP 7-2 LIFO and inventory flow

The following is an excerpt from a conversation between Paula Marlo, the warehouse manager for Musick Foods Wholesale Co., and its accountant, Mike Hayes. Musick Foods operates a large regional warehouse that supplies produce and other grocery products to grocery stores in smaller communities.

Paula: Mike, can you explain what's going on here with these monthly statements?

Mike: Sure, Paula. How can I help you?

Paula: I don't understand this last-in, first-out inventory procedure. It just doesn't make sense.

Mike: Well, what it means is that we assume that the last goods we receive are the first ones sold. So the inventory consists of the items we purchased first.

Paula: Yes, but that's my problem. It doesn't work that way! We always distribute the oldest produce first. Some of that produce is perishable! We can't keep any of it very long or it'll spoil.

(Continued)

Mike: Paula, you don't understand. We only *assume* that the products we distribute are the last ones received. We don't actually have to distribute the goods in this way.

Paula: I always thought that accounting was supposed to show what really happened. It all sounds like "make believe" to me! Why not report what really happens?

Respond to Paula's concerns.

CP 7-3 Costing inventory

Golden Eagle Company began operations in 2016 by selling a single product. Data on purchases and sales for the year were as follows:

Purchases:

Date	Units Purchased	Unit Cost	Total Cost
April 6	31,000	$36.60	$1,134,600
May 18	33,000	39.00	1,287,000
June 6	40,000	39.60	1,584,000
July 10	40,000	42.00	1,680,000
August 10	27,200	42.75	1,162,800
October 25	12,800	43.50	556,800
November 4	8,000	44.85	358,800
December 10	8,000	48.00	384,000
	200,000		$8,148,000

Sales:

April	16,000 units
May	16,000
June	20,000
July	24,000
August	28,000
September	28,000
October	18,000
November	10,000
December	8,000
Total units	168,000
Total sales	$10,000,000

On January 4, 2017, the president of the company, Connie Kilmer, asked for your advice on costing the 32,000-unit physical inventory that was taken on December 31, 2016. Moreover, since the firm plans to expand its product line, she asked for your advice on the use of a perpetual inventory system in the future.

1. Determine the cost of the December 31, 2016, inventory under the periodic system, using the (a) first-in, first-out method, (b) last-in, first-out method, and (c) weighted average cost method.
2. Determine the gross profit for the year under each of the three methods in (1).
3. a. Explain varying viewpoints why each of the three inventory costing methods may best reflect the results of operations for 2016.

   b. Which of the three inventory costing methods may best reflect the replacement cost of the inventory on the balance sheet as of December 31, 2016?

   c. Which inventory costing method would you choose to use for income tax purposes? Why?

   d. Discuss the advantages and disadvantages of using a perpetual inventory system. From the data presented in this case, is there any indication of the adequacy of inventory levels during the year?

CP 7-4 Inventory ratios for Dell and HP

F·A·I

Dell Inc. and **Hewlett-Packard Development Company, L.P. (HP)** are both manufacturers of computer equipment and peripherals. However, the two companies follow two different strategies. Dell follows primarily a build-to-order strategy, where the consumer orders the computer from a Web page. The order is then manufactured and shipped to the customer within days of the order. In contrast, HP follows a build-to-stock strategy, where the computer is first built for inventory, then sold from inventory to retailers, such as Best Buy. The two strategies can be seen in the difference between the inventory turnover and number of days' sales in inventory ratios for the two companies. The following financial statement information is provided for Dell and HP for a recent fiscal year (in millions):

	Dell	HP
Inventory, beginning of period	$ 1,301	$ 7,490
Inventory, end of period	1,404	6,317
Cost of goods sold	48,260	92,385

a. Determine the inventory turnover ratio and the number of days' sales in inventory ratio for each company. Use 365 days and round to one decimal place.

b. Interpret the difference between the ratios for the two companies.

CP 7-5 Comparing inventory ratios for two companies

Tiffany Co. is a high-end jewelry retailer, while Amazon.com uses its e-commerce services, features, and technologies to sell its products through the Internet. Recent balance sheet inventory disclosures for Tiffany and Amazon.com (in millons) are as follows:

	End-of-Period Inventory	Beginning-of-Period Inventory
Tiffany Co.	$2,073	$1,625
Amazon.com	6,031	4,992

The cost of merchandise sold reported by each company was as follows:

	Tiffany Co.	Amazon.com
Cost of merchandise sold	$1,492	$45,971

a. Determine the inventory turnover and number of days' sales in inventory for Tiffany and Amazon.com. Use 365 days and round to two decimal places.

b. Interpret your results.

CP 7-6 Comparing inventory ratios for three companies

The general merchandise retail industry has a number of segments represented by the following companies:

Company Name	Merchandise Concept
Costco Wholesale Corporation	Membership warehouse
Walmart	Discount general merchandise
JCPenney	Department store

For a recent year, the following cost of merchandise sold and beginning and ending inventories have been provided from corporate annual reports (in millions) for these three companies:

	Costco	Walmart	JCPenney
Cost of merchandise sold	$86,823	$335,127	$11,042
Merchandise inventory, beginning	6,638	36,437	3,213
Merchandise inventory, ending	7,096	40,714	2,916

a. Determine the inventory turnover ratio for all three companies. Round to one decimal place.

b. Determine the number of days' sales in inventory for all three companies. Use 365 days and round to one decimal place.

c. Interpret these results based on each company's merchandise concept.

within days of the order. In contrast, HP follows a build-to-stock strategy, where the computer is first built for inventory, then sold from inventory to retailers such as Best Buy. The two strategies can be seen in the difference between the inventory turnover and number of days' sales in inventory ratios for the two companies. The following financial statement information is provided for Dell and HP for a recent fiscal year (in millions):

	Dell	HP
Inventory, beginning of period	[illegible]	[illegible]
Inventory, end of period	[illegible]	[illegible]
Cost of goods sold	[illegible]	[illegible]

a. Determine the inventory turnover ratio and the number of days' sales in inventory ratio for each company. Use 365 days and round to one decimal place.

b. Interpret the difference between the ratios for the two companies.

CP 7-5 Comparing inventory ratios for two companies

Tiffany Co. is a high-end jewelry retailer, while Amazon.com uses its e-commerce services, features, and technologies to sell its products through the Internet. Recent balance sheet inventory disclosures for Tiffany and Amazon.com (in millions) are as follows:

	End-of-Period Inventory	Beginning-of-Period Inventory
Tiffany Co.	[illegible]	[illegible]
Amazon.com	6,031	4,992

The cost of merchandise sold reported by each company was as follows:

	Tiffany Co.	Amazon.com
Cost of merchandise sold	[illegible]	[illegible]

a. Determine the inventory turnover and number of days' sales in inventory for Tiffany and Amazon.com. Use 365 days and round to two decimal places.

b. Interpret your results.

CP 7-6 Comparing inventory ratios for three companies

The general merchandise retail industry has a number of segments represented by the following companies:

Company Name	Merchandise Concept
Costco Wholesale Corporation	Membership warehouse
Walmart	Discount general merchandise
JCPenney	Department store

For a recent year, the following cost of merchandise sold and beginning and ending inventories have been provided from corporate annual reports (in millions) for these three companies:

	Costco	Walmart	JCPenney
Cost of merchandise sold	[illegible]	[illegible]	[illegible]
Merchandise inventory, beginning	[illegible]	[illegible]	[illegible]
Merchandise inventory, ending	[illegible]	[illegible]	[illegible]

a. Determine the inventory turnover ratio for all three companies. Round to one decimal place.

b. Determine the number of days' sales in inventory for all three companies. Use 365 days and round to one decimal place.

c. Interpret these results based on each company's merchandise concept.

CHAPTER 8

Sarbanes-Oxley, Internal Control, and Cash

eBay Inc.

Controls are a part of your everyday life. At one extreme, laws are used to limit your behavior. For example, speed limits are designed to control your driving for traffic safety. In addition, you may also use many nonlegal controls. For example, you can keep credit card receipts in order to compare your transactions to the monthly credit card statement. Comparing receipts to the monthly statement is a control designed to catch mistakes made by the credit card company. In addition, banks give you a personal identification number (PIN) as a control against unauthorized access to your cash if you lose your automated teller machine (ATM) card. Dairies use freshness dating on their milk containers as a control to prevent the purchase or sale of soured milk. As you can see, you use and encounter controls every day.

Just as there are many examples of controls throughout society, businesses must also implement controls to help guide the behavior of their managers, employees, and customers. For example, **eBay Inc.** maintains an Internet-based marketplace for the sale of goods and services. Using eBay's online platform, buyers and sellers can browse, buy, and sell a wide variety of items including antiques and used cars. However, in order to maintain the integrity and trust of its buyers and sellers, eBay must have controls to ensure that buyers pay for their items and sellers don't misrepresent their items or fail to deliver sales. One such control eBay uses is a feedback forum that establishes buyer and seller reputations. A prospective buyer or seller can view the member's reputation and feedback comments before completing a transaction. Dishonest or unfair trading can lead to a negative reputation and even suspension or cancellation of the member's ability to trade on eBay.

This chapter discusses controls that can be included in accounting systems to provide reasonable assurance that the financial statements are reliable. Controls to discover and prevent errors to a bank account are also discussed. This chapter begins by discussing the Sarbanes-Oxley Act and its impact on controls and financial reporting.

Learning Objectives

After studying this chapter, you should be able to:	Example Exercises
OBJ 1 Describe the Sarbanes-Oxley Act and its impact on internal controls and financial reporting.	
Sarbanes-Oxley Act	
OBJ 2 Describe and illustrate the objectives and elements of internal control.	
Internal Control	
Objectives of Internal Control	
Elements of Internal Control	
Control Environment	EE 8-1
Risk Assessment	EE 8-1
Control Procedures	EE 8-1
Monitoring	EE 8-1
Information and Communication	EE 8-1
Limitations of Internal Control	
OBJ 3 Describe and illustrate the application of internal controls to cash.	
Cash Controls Over Receipts and Payments	
Control of Cash Receipts	
Control of Cash Payments	
OBJ 4 Describe the nature of a bank account and its use in controlling cash.	
Bank Accounts	
Bank Statement	EE 8-2
Using the Bank Statement as a Control Over Cash	
OBJ 5 Describe and illustrate the use of a bank reconciliation in controlling cash.	
Bank Reconciliation	EE 8-3
OBJ 6 Describe the accounting for special-purpose cash funds.	
Special-Purpose Cash Funds	EE 8-4
OBJ 7 Describe and illustrate the reporting of cash and cash equivalents in the financial statements.	
Financial Statement Reporting of Cash	
OBJ 8 Describe and illustrate the use of the ratio of cash to monthly cash expenses to assess the ability of a company to continue in business.	
Financial Analysis and Interpretation: Ratio of Cash to Monthly Cash Expenses	EE 8-5

At a Glance 8 Page 392

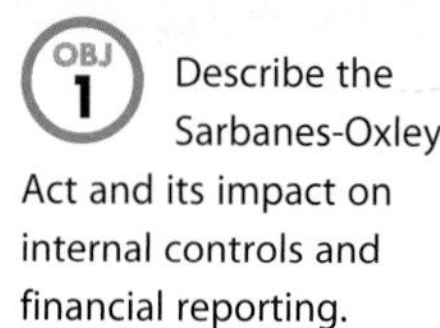

OBJ 1 Describe the Sarbanes-Oxley Act and its impact on internal controls and financial reporting.

Sarbanes-Oxley Act

During recent financial scandals, stockholders, creditors, and other investors lost billions of dollars.[1] As a result, the U.S. Congress passed the **Sarbanes-Oxley Act**. This act is one of the most important laws affecting U.S. companies in recent history. The purpose of Sarbanes-Oxley is to maintain public confidence and trust in the financial reporting of companies.

Sarbanes-Oxley applies only to companies whose stock is traded on public exchanges, referred to as *publicly held companies*. However, Sarbanes-Oxley highlighted the importance of assessing the financial controls and reporting of all companies. As a result, companies of all sizes have been influenced by Sarbanes-Oxley.

Sarbanes-Oxley emphasizes the importance of effective internal control.[2] **Internal control** is defined as the procedures and processes used by a company to:

- Safeguard its assets.
- Process information accurately.
- Ensure compliance with laws and regulations.

Sarbanes-Oxley requires companies to maintain effective internal controls over the recording of transactions and the preparing of financial statements. Such controls

[1] Exhibit 2 in Chapter 1 briefly summarizes these scandals.

[2] Sarbanes-Oxley also has important implications for corporate governance and the regulation of the public accounting profession. This chapter, however, focuses on the internal control implications of Sarbanes-Oxley.

are important because they deter fraud and prevent misleading financial statements as shown in Exhibit 1.

EXHIBIT 1

Effect of Sarbanes-Oxley

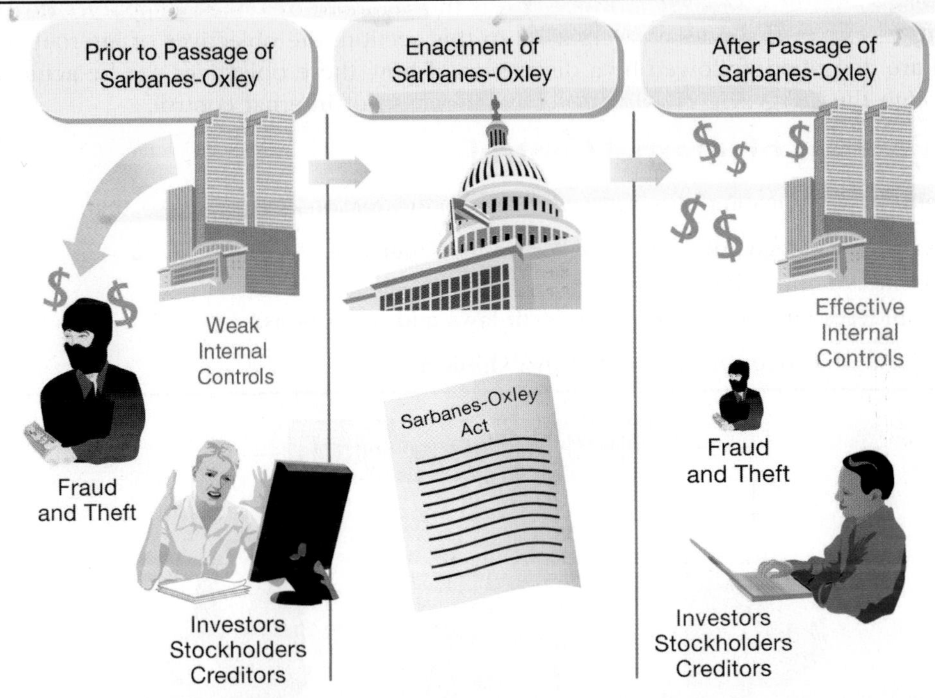

Sarbanes-Oxley also requires companies and their independent accountants to report on the effectiveness of the company's internal controls.[3] These reports are required to be filed with the company's annual 10-K report with the Securities and Exchange Commission. Companies are also encouraged to include these reports in their annual reports to stockholders. An example of such a report by the management of Nike is shown in Exhibit 2.

EXHIBIT 2

Sarbanes-Oxley Report of Nike

Management's Annual Report on Internal Control Over Financial Reporting

Management is responsible for establishing and maintaining adequate internal control over financial reporting. . . .

Under the supervision and with the participation of our Chief Executive Officer and Chief Financial Officer, our management conducted an evaluation of the effectiveness of our internal control over financial reporting based upon the framework in *Internal Control—Integrated Framework* issued by the Committee of Sponsoring Organizations of the Treadway Commission. Based on that evaluation, our management concluded that our internal control over financial reporting is effective. . . .

PricewaterhouseCoopers LLP, an independent registered public accounting firm, has audited . . . the effectiveness of our internal control over financial reporting . . . as stated in their report. . . .

MARK G. PARKER
Chief Executive Officer and President

DONALD W. BLAIR
Chief Financial Officer

Source: Nike, *Form 10-K For the Fiscal Year Ended May 31, 2013.*

Exhibit 2 indicates that Nike based its evaluation of internal controls on *Internal Control—Integrated Framework*, which was issued by the Committee of Sponsoring Organizations (COSO) of the Treadway Commission. This framework is the standard by which companies design, analyze, and evaluate internal controls. For this reason, this framework is used as the basis for discussing internal controls.

Information on *Internal Control—Integrated Framework* can be found on COSO's Web site at http://www.coso.org/.

[3] These reporting requirements are required under Section 404 of the act. As a result, these requirements and reports are often referred to as 404 requirements and 404 reports.

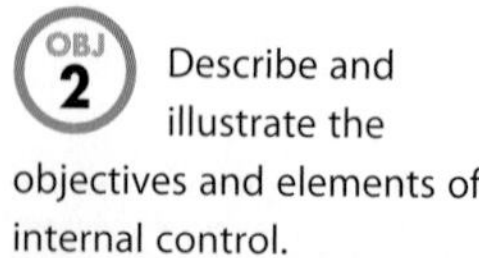
Describe and illustrate the objectives and elements of internal control.

Internal Control

Internal Control—Integrated Framework is the standard by which companies design, analyze, and evaluate internal control.[4] In this section, the objectives of internal control are described, followed by a discussion of how these objectives can be achieved through the *Integrated Framework's* five elements of internal control.

Objectives of Internal Control

The objectives of internal control are to provide reasonable assurance that:

- Assets are safeguarded and used for business purposes.
- Business information is accurate.
- Employees and managers comply with laws and regulations.

These objectives are illustrated in Exhibit 3.

EXHIBIT 3

Objectives of Internal Control

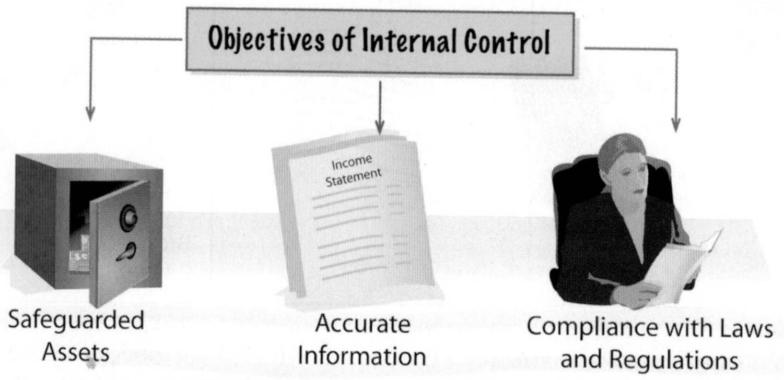

Internal control can safeguard assets by preventing theft, fraud, misuse, or misplacement. A serious concern of internal control is preventing employee fraud. **Employee fraud** is the intentional act of deceiving an employer for personal gain. Such fraud may range from minor overstating of a travel expense report to stealing millions of dollars. Employees stealing from a business often adjust the accounting records in order to hide their fraud. Thus, employee fraud usually affects the accuracy of business information.

Accurate information is necessary to successfully operate a business. Businesses must also comply with laws, regulations, and financial reporting standards. Examples of such standards include environmental regulations, safety regulations, and generally accepted accounting principles (GAAP).

Business  **Connection**

EMPLOYEE FRAUD

The Association of Fraud Examiners estimates that 5% of annual revenues worldwide or more than $3.5 trillion is lost to employee fraud. A common cash receipts employee fraud can occur when employees accept cash payments from customers, do not record the sale, and then pocket the cash. A common cash payments employee fraud can occur when employees bill their employer for false services or personal items.

Source: *2012 Report to the Nation on Occupational Fraud and Abuse*, Association of Fraud Examiners.

Elements of Internal Control

The three internal control objectives can be achieved by applying the five **elements of internal control** set forth by the *Integrated Framework*.[5] These elements are as follows:

- Control environment
- Risk assessment

[4] *Internal Control—Integrated Framework* by the Committee of Sponsoring Organizations of the Treadway Commission, 2013.
[5] Ibid., pp. 12–14.

- Control procedures
- Monitoring
- Information and communication

The elements of internal control are illustrated in Exhibit 4.

EXHIBIT 4

Elements of Internal Control

In Exhibit 4, the elements of internal control form an umbrella over the business to protect it from control threats. The control environment is the size of the umbrella. Risk assessment, control procedures, and monitoring are the fabric of the umbrella, which keep it from leaking. Information and communication connect the umbrella to management.

Control Environment

The **control environment** is the overall attitude of management and employees about the importance of controls. Three factors influencing a company's control environment include the following, as shown in Exhibit 5:

- Management's philosophy and operating style
- The company's organizational structure
- The company's personnel policies

EXHIBIT 5 **Control Environment**

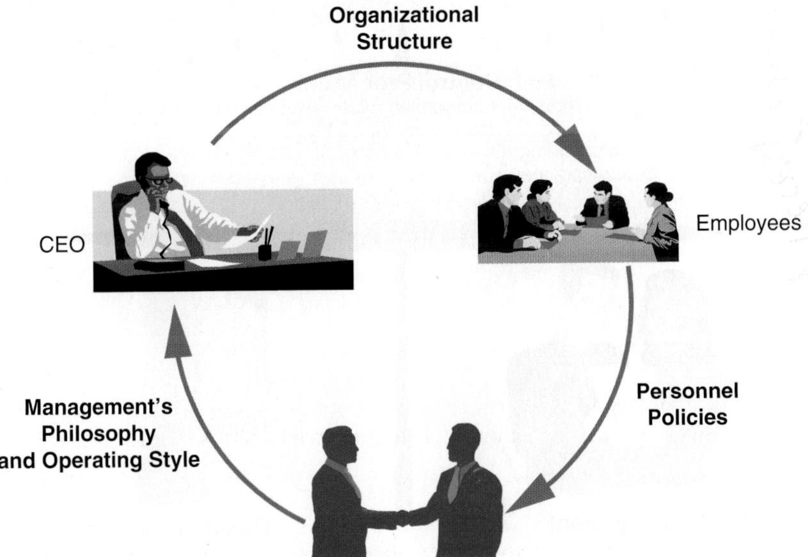

Management's philosophy and operating style relates to whether management emphasizes the importance of internal controls. An emphasis on controls and adherence to control policies creates an effective control environment. In contrast, overemphasizing operating goals and tolerating deviations from control policies creates an ineffective control environment.

The business's organizational structure is the framework for planning and controlling operations. For example, a retail store chain might organize each of its stores as separate business units. Each store manager has full authority over pricing and other operating activities. In such a structure, each store manager has the responsibility for establishing an effective control environment.

The business's personnel policies involve the hiring, training, evaluation, compensation, and promotion of employees. In addition, job descriptions, employee codes of ethics, and conflict-of-interest policies are part of the personnel policies. Such policies can enhance the internal control environment if they provide reasonable assurance that only competent, honest employees are hired and retained.

Risk Assessment

All businesses face risks such as changes in customer requirements, competitive threats, regulatory changes, and changes in economic factors. Management should identify such risks, analyze their significance, assess their likelihood of occurring, and take any necessary actions to minimize them.

Control Procedures

Control procedures provide reasonable assurance that business goals will be achieved, including the prevention of fraud. Control procedures, which constitute one of the most important elements of internal control, include the following as shown in Exhibit 6:

- Competent personnel, rotating duties, and mandatory vacations
- Separating responsibilities for related operations
- Separating operations, custody of assets, and accounting
- Proofs and security measures

EXHIBIT 6

Internal Control Procedures

Competent Personnel, Rotating Duties, and Mandatory Vacations A successful company needs competent employees who are able to perform the duties that they are assigned. Procedures should be established for properly training and supervising employees. It is also advisable to rotate duties of accounting personnel and mandate vacations for all employees. In this way, employees are encouraged to adhere to procedures. Cases of employee fraud are often discovered when a long-term employee, who never took vacations, missed work because of an illness or another unavoidable reason.

Separating Responsibilities for Related Operations The responsibility for related operations should be divided among two or more people. This decreases the possibility of errors and fraud. For example, if the same person orders supplies, verifies the receipt of the supplies, and pays the supplier, the following abuses may occur:

- Orders may be placed on the basis of friendship with a supplier, rather than on price, quality, and other objective factors.
- The quantity and quality of supplies received may not be verified; thus, the company may pay for supplies not received or that are of poor quality.
- Supplies may be stolen by the employee.
- The validity and accuracy of invoices may not be verified; hence, the company may pay false or inaccurate invoices.

For the preceding reasons, the responsibilities for purchasing, receiving, and paying for supplies should be divided among three persons or departments.

Separating Operations, Custody of Assets, and Accounting The responsibilities for operations, custody of assets, and accounting should be separated. In this way, the accounting records serve as an independent check on the operating managers and the employees who have custody of assets.

To illustrate, employees who handle cash receipts should not record cash receipts in the accounting records. To do so would allow employees to borrow or steal cash and hide the theft in the accounting records. Likewise, operating managers should not also record the results of operations. To do so would allow the managers to distort the accounting reports to show favorable results, which might allow them to receive larger bonuses.

Proofs and Security Measures Proofs and security measures are used to safeguard assets and ensure reliable accounting data. Proofs involve procedures such as authorization, approval, and reconciliation. For example, an employee planning to travel on company business may be required to complete a "travel request" form for a manager's authorization and approval.

Integrity, Objectivity, and Ethics in Business

TIPS ON PREVENTING EMPLOYEE FRAUD IN SMALL COMPANIES

- Do not have the same employee write company checks and keep the books. Look for payments to vendors you don't know or payments to vendors whose names appear to be misspelled.
- If your business has a computer system, restrict access to accounting files as much as possible. Also, keep a backup copy of your accounting files and store it at an off-site location.
- Be wary of anybody working in finance who declines to take vacations. They may be afraid that a replacement will uncover fraud.
- Require and monitor supporting documentation (such as vendor invoices) before signing checks.
- Track the number of credit card bills you sign monthly.
- Limit and monitor access to important documents and supplies, such as blank checks and signature stamps.
- Check W-2 forms against your payroll annually to make sure you're not carrying any fictitious employees.
- Rely on yourself, not on your accountant, to spot fraud.

Source: Steve Kaufman, "Embezzlement Common at Small Companies," Knight-Ridder Newspapers, reported in *Athens Daily News/Athens Banner-Herald*, March 10, 1996, p. 4D.

Documents used for authorization and approval should be prenumbered, accounted for, and safeguarded. Prenumbering of documents helps prevent transactions from being recorded more than once or not at all. In addition, accounting for and safeguarding prenumbered documents helps prevent fraudulent transactions from being recorded. For example, blank checks are prenumbered and safeguarded. Once a payment has been properly authorized and approved, the checks are filled out and issued.

Reconciliations are also an important control. Later in this chapter, the use of bank reconciliations as an aid in controlling cash is described and illustrated.

Security measures involve measures to safeguard assets. For example, cash on hand should be kept in a cash register or safe. Inventory not on display should be stored in a locked storeroom or warehouse. Accounting records such as the accounts receivable subsidiary ledger should also be safeguarded to prevent their loss. For example, electronically maintained accounting records should be safeguarded with access codes and backed up so that any lost or damaged files could be recovered if necessary.

Monitoring

Monitoring the internal control system is used to locate weaknesses and improve controls. Monitoring often includes observing employee behavior and the accounting system for indicators of control problems. Some such indicators are shown in Exhibit 7.[6]

EXHIBIT 7

Warning Signs of Internal Control Problems

Warning signs with regard to people	**Warning signs from the accounting system**
• Abrupt change in lifestyle (without winning the lottery). • Close social relationships with suppliers. • Refusing to take a vacation. • Frequent borrowing from other employees. • Excessive use of alcohol or drugs.	• Missing documents or gaps in transaction numbers (could mean documents are being used for fraudulent transactions). • An unusual increase in customer refunds (refunds may be phony). • Differences between daily cash receipts and bank deposits (could mean receipts are being pocketed before being deposited). • Sudden increase in slow payments (employee may be pocketing the payments). • Backlog in recording transactions (possibly an attempt to delay detection of fraud).

Evaluations of controls are often performed when there are major changes in strategy, senior management, business structure, or operations. Internal auditors, who are independent of operations, usually perform such evaluations. Internal auditors are also responsible for day-to-day monitoring of controls. External auditors also evaluate and report on internal control as part of their annual financial statement audit.

Information and Communication

Information and communication is an essential element of internal control. Information about the control environment, risk assessment, control procedures, and monitoring is used by management for guiding operations and ensuring compliance with reporting, legal, and regulatory requirements. Management also uses external

[6] Edwin C. Bliss, "Employee Theft," *Boardroom Reports*, July 15, 1994, pp. 5–6.

information to assess events and conditions that impact decision making and external reporting. For example, management uses pronouncements of the Financial Accounting Standards Board (FASB) to assess the impact of changes in reporting standards on the financial statements.

Example Exercise 8-1 Internal Control Elements (OBJ 2)

Identify each of the following as relating to (a) the control environment, (b) risk assessment, or (c) control procedures:

1. Mandatory vacations
2. Personnel policies
3. Report of outside consultants on future market changes

Follow My Example 8-1

1. (c) control procedures
2. (a) the control environment
3. (b) risk assessment

Practice Exercises: PE 8-1A, PE 8-1B

Limitations of Internal Control

Internal control systems can provide only reasonable assurance for safeguarding assets, processing accurate information, and compliance with laws and regulations. In other words, internal controls are not a guarantee. This is due to the following factors:

- The human element of controls
- Cost-benefit considerations

The *human element* recognizes that controls are applied and used by humans. As a result, human errors can occur because of fatigue, carelessness, confusion, or misjudgment. For example, an employee may unintentionally shortchange a customer or miscount the amount of inventory received from a supplier. In addition, two or more employees may collude together to defeat or circumvent internal controls. This latter case often involves fraud and the theft of assets. For example, the cashier and the accounts receivable clerk might collude to steal customer payments on account.

Cost-benefit considerations recognize that the cost of internal controls should not exceed their benefits. For example, retail stores could eliminate shoplifting by searching all customers before they leave the store. However, such a control procedure would upset customers and result in lost sales. Instead, retailers use cameras or signs saying, "*We prosecute all shoplifters.*"

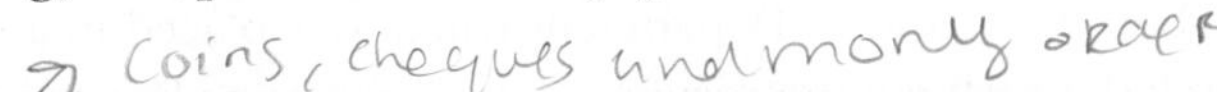

Cash Controls over Receipts and Payments

OBJ 3 Describe and illustrate the application of internal controls to cash.

Cash includes coins, currency (paper money), checks, and money orders. Money on deposit with a bank or other financial institution that is available for withdrawal is also considered cash. Normally, you can think of cash as anything that a bank would accept for deposit in your account. For example, a check made payable to you could normally be deposited in a bank and, thus, is considered cash.

Businesses usually have several bank accounts. For example, a business might have one bank account for general cash payments and another for payroll. A separate ledger account is normally used for each bank account. For example, a bank account at City Bank could be identified in the ledger as *Cash in Bank—City Bank*. To simplify, this chapter assumes that a company has only *one* bank account, which is identified in the ledger as *Cash*.

Cash is the asset most likely to be stolen or used improperly in a business. For this reason, businesses must carefully control cash and cash transactions.

Control of Cash Receipts

To protect cash from theft and misuse, a business must control cash from the time it is received until it is deposited in a bank. Businesses normally receive cash from two main sources.

- Customers purchasing products or services
- Customers making payments on account

Cash Received from Cash Sales An important control to protect cash received in over-the-counter sales is a cash register. The use of a cash register to control cash is shown in Exhibit 8.

EXHIBIT 8

Cash Register as a Control

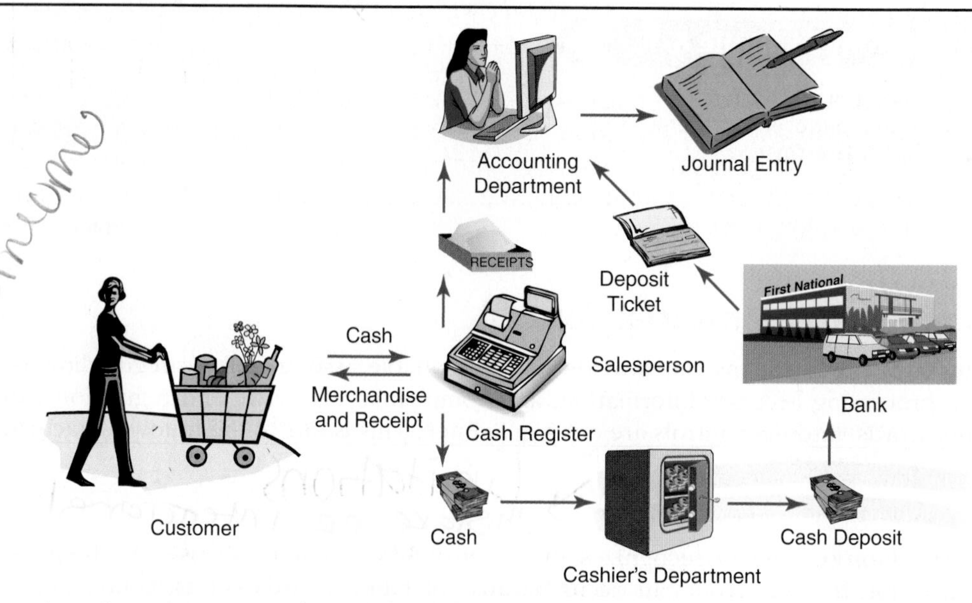

A cash register controls cash as follows:

1. At the beginning of every work shift, each cash register clerk is given a cash drawer containing a predetermined amount of cash. This amount is used for making change for customers and is sometimes called a *change fund*.
2. When a salesperson enters the amount of a sale, the cash register displays the amount to the customer. This allows the customer to verify that the clerk has charged the correct amount. The customer also receives a cash receipt.
3. At the end of the shift, the clerk and the supervisor count the cash in the clerk's cash drawer. The amount of cash in each drawer should equal the beginning amount of cash plus the cash sales for the day.
4. The supervisor takes the cash to the Cashier's Department where it is placed in a safe.
5. The supervisor forwards the clerk's cash register receipts to the Accounting Department.
6. The cashier prepares a bank deposit ticket.
7. The cashier deposits the cash in the bank, or the cash is picked up by an armored car service, such as **Wells Fargo**.
8. The Accounting Department summarizes the cash receipts and records the day's cash sales.
9. When cash is deposited in the bank, the bank normally stamps a duplicate copy of the deposit ticket with the amount received. This bank receipt is returned to the Accounting Department, where it is compared to the total amount that should have been deposited. This control helps ensure that all the cash is deposited and that no cash is lost or stolen on the way to the bank. Any shortages are thus promptly detected.

Salespersons may make errors in making change for customers or in ringing up cash sales. As a result, the amount of cash on hand may differ from the amount of cash sales. Such differences are recorded in a **cash short and over account**.

To illustrate, assume the following cash register data for May 3:

Cash register total for cash sales	$35,690
Cash receipts from cash sales	35,668

The cash sales, receipts, and shortage of $22 ($35,690 – $35,668) would be recorded as follows:

Date		Account	Post. Ref.	Debit	Credit
May	3	Cash		35,668	
		Cash Short and Over		22	
		Sales			35,690

If there had been cash over, Cash Short and Over would have been credited for the overage. At the end of the accounting period, a debit balance in Cash Short and Over is included in miscellaneous expense on the income statement. A credit balance is included in the Other Income section. If a salesperson consistently has large cash short and over amounts, the supervisor may require the clerk to take additional training.

Cash Received in the Mail Cash is received in the mail when customers pay their bills. This cash is usually in the form of checks and money orders. Most companies design their invoices so that customers return a portion of the invoice, called a *remittance advice*, with their payment. Remittance advices may be used to control cash received in the mail as follows:

1. An employee opens the incoming mail and compares the amount of cash received with the amount shown on the remittance advice. If a customer does not return a remittance advice, the employee prepares one. The remittance advice serves as a record of the cash initially received. It also helps ensure that the posting to the customer's account is for the amount of cash received.
2. The employee opening the mail stamps checks and money orders "For Deposit Only" in the bank account of the business.
3. The remittance advices and their summary totals are delivered to the Accounting Department.
4. All cash and money orders are delivered to the Cashier's Department.
5. The cashier prepares a bank deposit ticket.
6. The cashier deposits the cash in the bank, or the cash is picked up by an armored car service, such as **Wells Fargo**.
7. An accounting clerk records the cash received and posts the amounts to the customer accounts.
8. When cash is deposited in the bank, the bank normally stamps a duplicate copy of the deposit ticket with the amount received. This bank receipt is returned to the Accounting Department, where it is compared to the total amount that should have been deposited. This control helps ensure that all cash is deposited and that no cash is lost or stolen on the way to the bank. Any shortages are thus promptly detected.

Separating the duties of the Cashier's Department, which handles cash, and the Accounting Department, which records cash, is a control. If Accounting Department employees both handle and record cash, an employee could steal cash and change the accounting records to hide the theft.

Cash Received by EFT Cash may also be received from customers through **electronic funds transfer (EFT)**. For example, customers may authorize automatic electronic transfers from their checking accounts to pay monthly bills for such items as cell phone, Internet, and electric services. In such cases, the company sends the customer's bank a signed form from the customer authorizing the monthly electronic transfers. Each month, the company notifies the customer's bank of the amount of the transfer and the date the transfer should take place. On the due date, the company records the electronic transfer as a receipt of cash to its bank account and posts the amount paid to the customer's account.

Companies encourage customers to use EFT for the following reasons:

- EFTs cost less than receiving cash payments through the mail.
- EFTs enhance internal controls over cash, since the cash is received directly by the bank without any employees handling cash.
- EFTs reduce late payments from customers and speed up the processing of cash receipts.

Control of Cash Payments

Howard Schultz & Associates (HS&A) specializes in reviewing cash payments for its clients. HS&A searches for errors, such as duplicate payments, failures to take discounts, and inaccurate computations. Amounts recovered for clients range from thousands to millions of dollars.

The control of cash payments should provide reasonable assurance that:

- Payments are made for only authorized transactions.
- Cash is used effectively and efficiently. For example, controls should ensure that all available purchase discounts are taken.

In a small business, an owner/manager may authorize payments based on personal knowledge. In a large business, however, purchasing goods, inspecting the goods received, and verifying the invoices are usually performed by different employees. These duties must be coordinated to ensure that proper payments are made to creditors. One system used for this purpose is the voucher system.

Voucher System A **voucher system** is a set of procedures for authorizing and recording liabilities and cash payments. A **voucher** is any document that serves as proof of authority to pay cash or issue an electronic funds transfer. An invoice that has been approved for payment could be considered a voucher. In many businesses, however, a voucher is a special form used to record data about a liability and the details of its payment.

In a manual system, a voucher is normally prepared after all necessary supporting documents have been received. For the purchase of goods, a voucher is supported by the supplier's invoice, a purchase order, and a receiving report. After a voucher is prepared, it is submitted for approval. Once approved, the voucher is recorded in the accounts and filed by due date. Upon payment, the voucher is recorded in the same manner as the payment of an account payable.

In a computerized system, data from the supporting documents (such as purchase orders, receiving reports, and suppliers' invoices) are entered directly into computer files. At the due date, the checks are automatically generated and mailed to creditors. At that time, the voucher is electronically transferred to a paid voucher file.

Cash Paid by EFT Cash can also be paid by electronic funds transfer (EFT) systems. For example, you can withdraw cash from your bank account using an ATM machine. Your withdrawal is a type of EFT transfer.

Companies also use EFT transfers. For example, many companies pay their employees via EFT. Under such a system, employees authorize the deposit of their payroll checks directly into their checking accounts. Each pay period, the company transfers the employees' net pay to their checking accounts through the use of EFT. Many companies also use EFT systems to pay their suppliers and other vendors.

Bank Accounts

OBJ 4 Describe the nature of a bank account and its use in controlling cash.

A major reason that companies use bank accounts is for internal control. Some of the control advantages of using bank accounts are as follows:

- Bank accounts reduce the amount of cash on hand.
- Bank accounts provide an independent recording of cash transactions. Reconciling the balance of the cash account in the company's records with the cash balance according to the bank is an important control.
- Use of bank accounts facilitates the transfer of funds using EFT systems.

Bank Statement

Banks usually maintain a record of all checking account transactions. A summary of all transactions, called a **bank statement**, is mailed, usually each month, to the company (depositor) or made available online. The bank statement shows the beginning balance, additions, deductions, and the ending balance. A typical bank statement is shown in Exhibit 9.

Checks or copies of the checks listed in the order that they were paid by the bank may accompany the bank statement. If paid checks are returned, they are stamped "Paid," together with the date of payment. Many banks no longer return checks or check copies. Instead, the check payment information is available online.

EXHIBIT 9

Bank Statement

MEMBER FDIC

VALLEY NATIONAL BANK OF LOS ANGELES

LOS ANGELES, CA 90020-4253 (310)555-5151

PAGE 1
ACCOUNT NUMBER 1627042
FROM 6/30/15 TO 7/31/15
BALANCE 4,218.60
22 DEPOSITS 13,749.75
52 WITHDRAWALS 14,698.57
3 OTHER DEBITS AND CREDITS 90.00CR
NEW BALANCE 3,359.78

POWER NETWORKING
1000 Belkin Street
Los Angeles, CA 90014-1000

CHECKS AND OTHER DEBITS				DEPOSITS	DATE	BALANCE
No. 850	819.40	No. 852	122.54	585.75	07/01	3,862.41
No. 854	369.50	No. 853	20.15	421.53	07/02	3,894.29
No. 851	600.00	No. 856	190.70	781.30	07/03	3,884.89
No. 855	25.93	No. 857	52.50		07/04	3,806.46
No. 860	921.20	No. 858	160.00	662.50	07/05	3,387.76
No. 862	91.07	NSF	300.00	503.18	07/07	3,499.87
No. 880	32.26	No. 877	535.09	ACH 932.00	07/29	4,136.66
No. 881	21.10	No. 879	732.26	705.21	07/30	4,088.51
No. 882	126.20	SC	18.00	MS 408.00	07/30	4,352.31
No. 874	26.12	ACH	1,615.13	648.72	07/31	3,359.78

EC — ERROR CORRECTION
MS — MISCELLANEOUS
NSF — NOT SUFFICIENT FUNDS
ACH — AUTOMATED CLEARING HOUSE
SC — SERVICE CHARGE

* * * * * * * * *

THE RECONCILEMENT OF THIS STATEMENT WITH YOUR RECORDS IS ESSENTIAL.
ANY ERROR OR EXCEPTION SHOULD BE REPORTED IMMEDIATELY.

The company's checking account balance *in the bank records* is a liability. Thus, in the bank's records, the company's account has a credit balance. Because the bank statement is prepared from the bank's point of view, a credit memo entry on the bank statement indicates an increase (a credit) to the company's account. Likewise, a debit memo entry on the bank statement indicates a decrease (a debit) in the company's account. This relationship is shown in Exhibit 10.

EXHIBIT 10

Checking Account: Company and Bank Perspectives

A bank makes credit entries (issues credit memos) for the following:

- Deposits made by electronic funds transfer (EFT)
- Collections of notes receivable for the company
- Proceeds for a loan made to the company by the bank
- Interest earned on the company's account
- Correction (if any) of bank errors

A bank makes debit entries (issues debit memos) for the following:

- Payments made by electronic funds transfer (EFT)
- Service charges
- Customer checks returned for not sufficient funds
- Correction (if any) of bank errors

Customers' checks returned for not sufficient funds, called *NSF checks*, are customer checks that were initially deposited but were not paid by the customer's bank. Because the company's bank credited the customer's check to the company's account when it was deposited, the bank debits the company's account (issues a debit memo) when the check is returned without payment.

The reason for a credit or debit memo entry is indicated on the bank statement. Exhibit 9 identifies the following types of credit and debit memo entries:

- EC: Error correction to correct bank error
- NSF: Not sufficient funds check
- SC: Service charge
- ACH: Automated clearing house entry for electronic funds transfer
- MS: Miscellaneous item such as collection of a note receivable on behalf of the company or receipt of a loan by the company from the bank

The preceding list includes the notation "ACH" for electronic funds transfers. ACH is a network for clearing electronic funds transfers among individuals, companies, and banks.[7] Because electronic funds transfers may be either deposits or payments, ACH entries may indicate either a debit or credit entry to the company's account. Likewise, entries to correct bank errors and miscellaneous items may indicate a debit or credit entry to the company's account.

Example Exercise 8-2 Items on Company's Bank Statement

OBJ 4

The following items may appear on a bank statement:

1. NSF check
2. EFT deposit
3. Service charge
4. Bank correction of an error from recording a $400 check as $40

Using the following format, indicate whether the item would appear as a debit or credit memo on the bank statement and whether the item would increase or decrease the balance of the company's account:

Item No.	Appears on the Bank Statement as a Debit or Credit Memo	Increases or Decreases the Balance of the Company's Bank Account

Follow My Example 8-2

Item No.	Appears on the Bank Statement as a Debit or Credit Memo	Increases or Decreases the Balance of the Company's Bank Account
1	debit memo	decreases
2	credit memo	increases
3	debit memo	decreases
4	debit memo	decreases

Practice Exercises: PE 8-2A, PE 8-2B

[7] For further information on ACH, go to www.nacha.org/. Click on "ACH Network" and then click on "Intro to the ACH Network."

Using the Bank Statement as a Control over Cash

The bank statement is a primary control that a company uses over cash. A company uses the bank's statement by comparing the company's recording of cash transactions to those recorded by the bank.

The cash balance shown by a bank statement is usually different from the company's cash balance, as shown in Exhibit 11.

EXHIBIT 11

Power Networking's Records and Bank Statement

Bank Statement		
Beginning balance		$ 4,218.60
Additions:		
Deposits	$13,749.75	
Miscellaneous	408.00	14,157.75
Deductions:		
Checks	$14,698.57	
NSF check	300.00	
Service charge	18.00	(15,016.57)
Ending balance		$ 3,359.78

Power Networking Records	
Beginning balance	$ 4,227.60
Deposits	14,565.95
Checks	(16,243.56)
Ending balance	$ 2,549.99

Power Networking should determine the reason for the difference in these two amounts.

Differences between the company and bank balance may arise because of a delay by either the company or bank in recording transactions. For example, there is normally a time lag of one or more days between the date a check is written and the date that it is paid by the bank. Likewise, there is normally a time lag between when the company mails a deposit to the bank (or uses the night depository) and when the bank receives and records the deposit.

Differences may also arise because the bank has debited or credited the company's account for transactions that the company will not know about until the bank statement is received. Finally, differences may arise from errors made by either the company or the bank. For example, the company may incorrectly post to Cash a check written for $4,500 as $450. Likewise, a bank may incorrectly record the amount of a check.

Bank Reconciliation

OBJ 5 Describe and illustrate the use of a bank reconciliation in controlling cash.

A **bank reconciliation** is an analysis of the items and amounts that result in the cash balance reported in the bank statement to differ from the balance of the cash account in the ledger. The adjusted cash balance determined in the bank reconciliation is reported on the balance sheet.

A bank reconciliation is usually divided into two sections as follows:

1. The *bank section* begins with the cash balance according to the bank statement and ends with the *adjusted balance*.
2. The *company section* begins with the cash balance according to the company's records and ends with the *adjusted balance*.

The *adjusted balance* from bank and company sections must be equal. The format of the bank reconciliation follows:

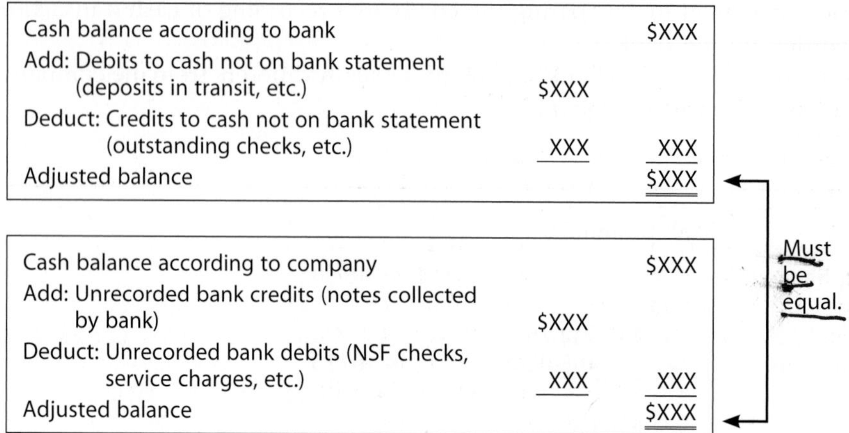

Cash balance according to bank		$XXX
Add: Debits to cash not on bank statement (deposits in transit, etc.)	$XXX	
Deduct: Credits to cash not on bank statement (outstanding checks, etc.)	XXX	XXX
Adjusted balance		$XXX

Cash balance according to company		$XXX
Add: Unrecorded bank credits (notes collected by bank)	$XXX	
Deduct: Unrecorded bank debits (NSF checks, service charges, etc.)	XXX	XXX
Adjusted balance		$XXX

Must be equal.

A bank reconciliation is prepared using steps illustrated in Exhibit 12.

EXHIBIT 12

How to Prepare a Bank Reconcilation

Bank Section of Reconciliation

- Step 1. Enter the *Cash balance according to bank* from the ending cash balance according to the bank statement.
- Step 2. *Add deposits not recorded by the bank.*
  Identify deposits not recorded by the bank by comparing each deposit listed on the bank statement with unrecorded deposits appearing in the preceding period's reconciliation and with the current period's deposits.
  Examples: Deposits in transit at the end of the period.
- Step 3. *Deduct outstanding checks that have not been paid by the bank.*
  Identify outstanding checks by comparing paid checks with outstanding checks appearing on the preceding period's reconciliation and with recorded checks.
  Examples: Outstanding checks at the end of the period.
- Step 4. Determine the *Adjusted balance* by adding Step 2 and deducting Step 3.

Company Section of Reconciliation

- Step 5. Enter the *Cash balance according to company* from the ending cash balance in the ledger.
- Step 6. *Add credit memos that have not been recorded.*
  Identify the bank credit memos that have not been recorded by comparing the bank statement credit memos to entries in the journal.
  Examples: A note receivable and interest that the bank has collected for the company.
- Step 7. *Deduct debit memos that have not been recorded.*
  Identify the bank debit memos that have not been recorded by comparing the bank statement debit memos to entries in the journal.
  Examples: Customers' not sufficient funds (NSF) checks; bank service charges.
- Step 8. Determine the *Adjusted balance* by adding Step 6 and deducting Step 7.

Verify That Adjusted Balances Are Equal

- Step 9. Verify that the adjusted balances determined in Steps 4 and 8 are equal.

The adjusted balances in the bank and company sections of the reconciliation must be equal. If the balances are not equal, an item has been overlooked and must be found.

Sometimes, the adjusted balances are not equal because either the company or the bank has made an error. In such cases, the error is often discovered by comparing the amount of each item (deposit and check) on the bank statement with that in the company's records.

Any bank or company errors discovered should be added to or deducted from the bank or company section of the reconciliation, depending on the nature of the error. For example, assume that the bank incorrectly recorded a company check for $50 as $500. This bank error of $450 ($500 – $50) would be added to the bank balance in the bank section of the reconciliation. In addition, the bank would be notified of the error so that it could be corrected. On the other hand, assume that the company recorded a deposit of $1,200 as $2,100. This company error of $900 ($2,100 – $1,200) would be deducted from the cash balance in the company section of the bank reconciliation. The company would later correct the error using a journal entry.

To illustrate, the bank statement for Power Networking in Exhibit 9 is used. This bank statement shows a balance of $3,359.78 as of July 31. The cash balance in Power Networking's ledger on the same date is $2,549.99. Using the preceding steps, the following reconciling items were identified:

Step 2. Deposit of July 31, not recorded on bank statement: $816.20
Step 3. Outstanding checks:

Check No. 812	$1,061.00
Check No. 878	435.39
Check No. 883	48.60
Total	$1,544.99

Step 6. Note receivable of $400 plus interest of $8 collected by bank not recorded in the journal as indicated by a credit memo of $408.
Step 7. Check from customer (Thomas Ivey) for $300 returned by bank because of insufficient funds (NSF) as indicated by a debit memo of $300.00.
Bank service charges of $18, not recorded in the journal as indicated by a debit memo of $18.00.

In addition, an error of $9 was discovered. This error occurred when Check No. 879 for $732.26 to Taylor Co., on account, was recorded in the company's journal as $723.26.

The bank reconciliation, based on the Exhibit 9 bank statement and the preceding reconciling items, is shown in Exhibit 13.

EXHIBIT 13 **Bank Reconciliation for Power Networking**

Power Networking
Bank Reconciliation
July 31, 2015

Step 1 →	Cash balance according to bank statement		$3,359.78
Step 2 →	Add deposit of July 31, not recorded by bank		816.20
			$4,175.98
Step 3 →	Deduct outstanding checks:		
	No. 812	$1,061.00	
	No. 878	435.39	
	No. 883	48.60	1,544.99
Step 4 →	Adjusted balance		$2,630.99 ←
Step 5 →	Cash balance according to Power Networking		$2,549.99
Step 6 →	Add note and interest collected by bank		408.00
			$2,957.99 Step 9
Step 7 →	Deduct: Check returned because of insufficient funds	$ 300.00	
	Bank service charge	18.00	
	Error in recording Check No. 879	9.00	327.00
Step 8 →	Adjusted balance		$2,630.99 ←

The company's records do not need to be updated for any items in the *bank section* of the reconciliation. This section begins with the cash balance according to the bank statement. However, the bank should be notified of any errors that need to be corrected.

The company's records do need to be updated for any items in the *company section* of the bank reconciliation. The company's records are updated using journal entries. For example, journal entries should be made for any unrecorded bank memos and any company errors.

The journal entries for Power Networking, based on the bank reconciliation shown in Exhibit 13, are as follows:

July	31	Cash	408	
		Notes Receivable		400
		Interest Revenue		8
	31	Accounts Receivable—Thomas Ivey	300	
		Miscellaneous Expense	18	
		Accounts Payable—Taylor Co.	9	
		Cash		327

After the preceding journal entries are recorded and posted, the cash account will have a debit balance of $2,630.99. This cash balance agrees with the adjusted balance shown on the bank reconciliation. This is the amount of cash on July 31 and is the amount that is reported on Power Networking's July 31 balance sheet.

Businesses may reconcile their bank accounts in a slightly different format from that shown in Exhibit 13. Regardless, the objective is to control cash by reconciling the company's records with the bank statement. In doing so, any errors or misuse of cash may be detected.

To enhance internal control, the bank reconciliation should be prepared by an employee who does not take part in or record cash transactions. Otherwise, mistakes may occur, and it is more likely that cash will be stolen or misapplied. For example, an employee who handles cash and also reconciles the bank statement could steal a cash deposit, omit the deposit from the accounts, and omit it from the reconciliation.

Bank reconciliations are also an important part of computerized systems where deposits and checks are stored in electronic files and records. Some systems use computer software to determine the difference between the bank statement and company cash balances. The software then adjusts for deposits in transit and outstanding checks. Any remaining differences are reported for further analysis.

Example Exercise 8-3 Bank Reconciliation

OBJ 5

The following data were gathered to use in reconciling the bank account of Photo Op:

Balance per bank	$14,500
Balance per company records	13,875
Bank service charges	75
Deposit in transit	3,750
NSF check	800
Outstanding checks	5,250

a. What is the adjusted balance on the bank reconciliation?

b. Journalize any necessary entries for Photo Op based on the bank reconciliation.

(Continued)

Follow My Example 8-3

a. $13,000, computed as follows:

Bank section of reconciliation: $14,500 + $3,750 – $5,250 = $13,000
Company section of reconciliation: $13,875 – $75 – $800 = $13,000

b.

Accounts Receivable	800	
Miscellaneous Expense	75	
Cash		875

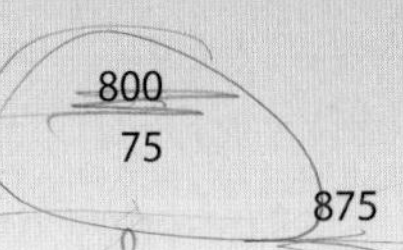

Practice Exercises: PE 8-3A, PE 8-3B

Integrity, Objectivity, and Ethics in Business

BANK ERROR IN YOUR FAVOR

It is possible that you may have a bank error in your favor, such as a misposted deposit. Such errors are not a case of "found money," as in the Monopoly® game. Bank control systems quickly discover most errors and make automatic adjustments. Even so, you have a legal responsibility to report the error and return the money to the bank.

Special-Purpose Cash Funds

OBJ 6 Describe the accounting for special-purpose cash funds.

A company often has to pay small amounts for such items as postage, office supplies, or minor repairs. Although small, such payments may occur often enough to total a significant amount. Thus, it is desirable to control such payments. However, writing a check for each small payment is not practical. Instead, a special cash fund, called a **petty cash fund**, is used.

A petty cash fund is established by estimating the amount of payments needed from the fund during a period, such as a week or a month. A check is then written and cashed for this amount. The money obtained from cashing the check is then given to an employee, called the *petty cash custodian*. The petty cash custodian disburses monies from the fund as needed. For control purposes, the company may place restrictions on the maximum amount and the types of payments that can be made from the fund. Each time money is paid from petty cash, the custodian records the details on a petty cash receipts form.

The petty cash fund is normally replenished at periodic intervals, when it is depleted, or reaches a minimum amount. When a petty cash fund is replenished, the accounts debited are determined by summarizing the petty cash receipts. A check is then written for this amount, payable to Petty Cash.

To illustrate, assume that a petty cash fund of $500 is established on August 1. The entry to record this transaction is as follows:

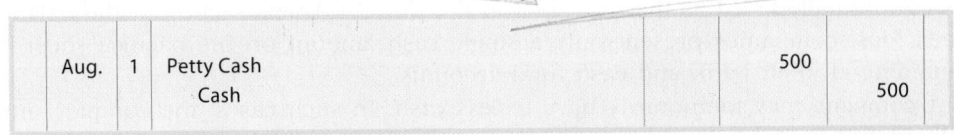

Aug.	1	Petty Cash		500	
		Cash			500

The only time Petty Cash is debited is when the fund is initially established, as shown in the preceding entry, or when the fund is being increased. The only time Petty Cash is credited is when the fund is being decreased.

At the end of August, the petty cash receipts indicate expenditures for the following items:

Office supplies	$380
Postage (debit Office Supplies)	22
Store supplies	35
Miscellaneous administrative expense	30
Total	$467

The entry to replenish the petty cash fund on August 31 is as follows:

Aug.	31	Office Supplies	402	
		Store Supplies	35	
		Miscellaneous Administrative Expense	30	
		Cash		467

Petty Cash is not debited when the fund is replenished. Instead, the accounts affected by the petty cash disbursements are debited, as shown in the preceding entry. Replenishing the petty cash fund restores the fund to its original amount of $500.

Companies often use other cash funds for special needs, such as payroll or travel expenses. Such funds are called **special-purpose funds**. For example, each salesperson might be given $1,000 for travel-related expenses. Periodically, each salesperson submits an expense report, and the fund is replenished. Special-purpose funds are established and controlled in a manner similar to that of the petty cash fund.

Example Exercise 8-4 Petty Cash Fund

OBJ 6

Prepare journal entries for each of the following:

a. Issued a check to establish a petty cash fund of $500.

b. The amount of cash in the petty cash fund is $120. Issued a check to replenish the fund, based on the following summary of petty cash receipts: office supplies, $300, and miscellaneous administrative expense, $75. Record any missing funds in the cash short and over account.

Follow My Example 8-4

a.	Petty Cash	500	
	Cash		500
b.	Office Supplies	300	
	Miscellaneous Administrative Expense	75	
	Cash Short and Over	5	
	Cash		380

Practice Exercises: PE 8-4A, PE 8-4B

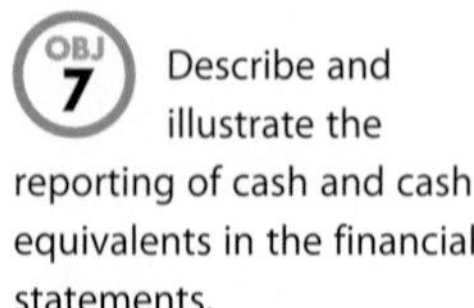

Describe and illustrate the reporting of cash and cash equivalents in the financial statements.

Financial Statement Reporting of Cash

Cash is normally listed as the first asset in the Current Assets section of the balance sheet. Most companies present only a single cash amount on the balance sheet by combining all their bank and cash fund accounts.

A company may temporarily have excess cash. In such cases, the company normally invests in highly liquid investments in order to earn interest. These investments are called **cash equivalents**.[8] Examples of cash equivalents include U.S. Treasury bills, notes issued by major corporations (referred to as *commercial paper*), and money

[8] To be classified as a cash equivalent, according to FASB *Accounting Standards Codification*, Section 305.10, the investment is expected to be converted to cash within three months.

market funds. In such cases, companies usually report *Cash and cash equivalents* as one amount on the balance sheet.

The balance sheet presentation for cash for **Mornin' Joe** follows:

Mornin' Joe Balance Sheet December 31, 2016	
Assets	
Current assets:	
Cash and cash equivalents	$235,000

Banks may require that companies maintain minimum cash balances in their bank accounts. Such a balance is called a **compensating balance**. This is often required by the bank as part of a loan agreement or line of credit. A *line of credit* is a preapproved amount the bank is willing to lend to a customer upon request. Compensating balance requirements are normally disclosed in notes to the financial statements.

Financial Analysis and Interpretation: Ratio of Cash to Monthly Cash Expenses

OBJ 8 Describe and illustrate the use of the ratio of cash to monthly cash expenses to assess the ability of a company to continue in business.

For startup companies or companies in financial distress, cash is critical for survival. In their first few years, startup companies often report losses and negative net cash flows from operations. Moreover, companies in financial distress can also report losses and negative cash flows from operations. In such cases, the **ratio of cash to monthly cash expenses** is useful for assessing how long a company can continue to operate without:

- Additional financing, or
- Generating positive cash flows from operations

The ratio of cash to monthly cash expenses is computed as follows:

$$\text{Ratio of Cash to Monthly Cash Expenses} = \frac{\text{Cash as of Year-End}}{\text{Monthly Cash Expenses}}$$

The cash, including any cash equivalents, is taken from the balance sheet as of year-end. The monthly cash expenses, sometimes called *cash burn*, are estimated from the operating activities section of the statement of cash flows as follows:

$$\text{Monthly Cash Expenses} = \frac{\text{Negative Cash Flow from Operations}}{12}$$

To illustrate, **Ocean Power Technologies, Inc.**, develops and markets systems that generate electricity from the rising and falling of ocean waves. The following data (in thousands) were taken from recent financial statements of Ocean Power Technologies:

	For Years Ended April 29			
	Year 4	**Year 3**	**Year 2**	**Year 1**
Cash and cash equivalents at year-end	$ 9,353	$4,376	$4,237	$ 12,268
Cash flow from operations	(13,915)	(18,770)	(15,771)	(16,708)

Based on the preceding data, the monthly cash expenses and ratio of cash to monthly cash expenses are computed as follows:

	For Years Ended April 29			
	Year 4	Year 3	Year 2	Year 1
Monthly cash expenses:*				
$13,915 ÷ 12	$1,160			
$18,770 ÷ 12		$1,564		
$15,771 ÷ 12			$1,314	
$16,708 ÷ 12				$1,392
Ratio of cash to monthly cash expenses:**				
$9,353 ÷ $1,160	8.1 months			
$4,376 ÷ $1,564		2.8 months		
$4,237 ÷ $1,314			3.2 months	
$12,268 ÷ $1,392				8.8 months

*Rounded to nearest dollar.

**Rounded to one decimal place.

The preceding computations indicate that Ocean Power had 8.8 months of cash available at the end of Year 1 to continue its operations. However, at the end of Year 1 Ocean Power also had short-term investments totaling almost $29 million. These investments had maturities greater than three months and, thus, were not included as cash equivalents. In addition, Ocean Power had more than $40 million of long-term investments at the end of Year 1. These short- and long-term investments were generated from issuing stock of almost $91 million two years earlier.

At the end of Year 2, Ocean Power had 3.2 months of cash available to continue its operations. During Year 2, Ocean Power sold short-term investments of almost $8 million to continue its operations. At the end of Year 3, Ocean Power had 2.8 months of cash available to continue its operations. During Year 3, Ocean Power sold short-term investments of $19 million to continue its operations. At the end of Year 4, Ocean Power had 8.1 months of cash available to continue its operations. During Year 4, Ocean Power sold short-term investments of almost $20 million to continue its operations.

The preceding analysis indicates that Ocean Power has generated negative cash flows from operations in each of the last four years. During each of the last four years, Ocean Power has been selling short-term investments, which were purchased from funds received by issuing stock, to finance its operations. At the end of Year 4, Ocean Power had no long-term investments and a little more than $22 million left in short-term investments. Unless Ocean Power can generate positive cash flows from operations in the next several years, it will have to raise additional funds from borrowing or issuing stock. On a favorable note, negative cash flows from operations decreased from $1,564 in Year 3 to $1,160 in Year 4.

Example Exercise 8-5 Ratio of Cash to Monthly Cash Expenses

OBJ 8

Financial data for Chapman Company follows:

	For Year Ended December 31, 2016
Cash on December 31, 2016	$ 102,000
Cash flow from operations	(144,000)

a. Compute the ratio of cash to monthly cash expenses.

b. Interpret the results computed in (a).

(Continued)

Follow My Example 8-5

a. $$\text{Monthly Cash Expenses} = \frac{\text{Negative Cash Flow from Operations}}{12} = \frac{\$144{,}000}{12} = \$12{,}000 \text{ per month}$$

$$\text{Ratio of Cash to Monthly Cash Expenses} = \frac{\text{Cash as of Year-End}}{\text{Monthly Cash Expenses}} = \frac{\$102{,}000}{\$12{,}000 \text{ per month}} = 8.5 \text{ months}$$

b. The preceding computations indicate that Chapman Company has 8.5 months of cash remaining as of December 31, 2016. To continue operations beyond 8.5 months, Chapman Company will need to generate positive cash flows from operations or raise additional financing from its owners or by issuing debt.

Practice Exercises: PE 8-5A, PE 8-5B

Business  Connection

MICROSOFT CORPORATION

Microsoft Corporation develops, manufactures, licenses, and supports software products for computing devices. Microsoft software products include computer operating systems, such as Windows®, and application software, such as Microsoft Word® and Excel®. Microsoft is actively involved in the video game market through its Xbox® and is also involved in online products and services.

Microsoft is known for its strong cash position. The following recent balance sheet of Microsoft reported more than $63 billion of cash and short-term investments:

Balance Sheet
(In millions)

Assets	
Current assets:	
Cash and equivalents	$ 6,938
Short-term investments	56,102
Total cash and short-term investments	$63,040

The cash and cash equivalents of $6,938 million are further described in the notes to the financial statements, as follows:

Cash and equivalents:	
Cash	$2,019
Mutual funds	820
Commercial paper	96
U.S. government and agency securities	561
Foreign government bonds	575
Certificates of deposit	342
Corporate notes and bonds	2,525
Total cash and equivalents	$6,938

Source: Microsoft Corporation, *Form 10-K For the Fiscal Year Ended June 30, 2012.*

At a Glance 8

Describe the Sarbanes-Oxley Act and its impact on internal controls and financial reporting.

Key Points Sarbanes-Oxley requires companies to maintain strong and effective internal controls and to report on the effectiveness of the internal controls.

Learning Outcomes	Example Exercises	Practice Exercises
• Describe why Congress passed Sarbanes-Oxley.		
• Describe the purpose of Sarbanes-Oxley.		
• Define internal control.		

Describe and illustrate the objectives and elements of internal control.

Key Points The objectives of internal control are to provide reasonable assurance that (1) assets are safeguarded and used for business purposes, (2) business information is accurate, and (3) the company is complying with laws and regulations. The elements of internal control are the control environment, risk assessment, control procedures, monitoring, and information and communication.

Learning Outcomes	Example Exercises	Practice Exercises
• List the objectives of internal control.		
• List the elements of internal control.		
• Describe each element of internal control and factors influencing each element.	EE8-1	PE8-1A, 8-1B

Describe and illustrate the application of internal controls to cash.

Key Points A cash register is a control for protecting cash received in over-the-counter sales. A remittance advice is a control for cash received through the mail. Separating the duties of handling cash and recording cash is also a control. A voucher system is a control system for cash payments. Many companies use electronic funds transfers for cash receipts and cash payments.

Learning Outcomes	Example Exercises	Practice Exercises
• Describe and give examples of controls for cash received from cash sales, cash received in the mail, and cash received by EFT.		
• Describe and give examples of controls for cash payments made using a voucher system and cash payments made by EFT.		

Describe the nature of a bank account and its use in controlling cash.

Key Points Bank accounts control cash by reducing the amount of cash on hand and facilitating the transfer of cash between businesses and locations. In addition, the bank statement allows a business to reconcile the cash transactions recorded in the accounting records to those recorded by the bank.

Learning Outcomes	*Example Exercises*	*Practice Exercises*
• Describe how the use of bank accounts helps control cash.	**EE8-2**	**PE8-2A, 8-2B**
• Describe a bank statement and provide examples of items that appear on a bank statement as debit and credit memos.		

Describe and illustrate the use of a bank reconciliation in controlling cash.

Key Points A bank reconciliation is prepared using the nine steps as summarized in Exhibit 12. The items in the company section of a bank reconciliation must be journalized on the company's records.

Learning Outcomes	*Example Exercises*	*Practice Exercises*
• Describe a bank reconciliation.		
• Prepare a bank reconciliation.	**EE8-3**	**PE8-3A, 8-3B**
• Journalize any necessary entries on the company's records, based on the bank reconciliation.	**EE8-3**	**PE8-3A, 8-3B**

Describe the accounting for special-purpose cash funds.

Key Points Special-purpose cash funds, such as a petty cash fund or travel funds, are used by businesses to meet specific needs. Each fund is established by cashing a check for the amount of cash needed. At periodic intervals, the fund is replenished and the disbursements recorded.

Learning Outcomes	*Example Exercises*	*Practice Exercises*
• Describe the use of special-purpose cash funds.		
• Journalize the entry to establish a petty cash fund.	**EE8-4**	**PE8-4A, 8-4B**
• Journalize the entry to replenish a petty cash fund.	**EE8-4**	**PE8-4A, 8-4B**

Describe and illustrate the reporting of cash and cash equivalents in the financial statements.

Key Points Cash is listed as the first asset in the Current assets section of the balance sheet. Companies that have invested excess cash in highly liquid investments usually report *Cash and cash equivalents* on the balance sheet.

Learning Outcomes	*Example Exercises*	*Practice Exercises*
• Describe the reporting of cash and cash equivalents in the financial statements.		
• Illustrate the reporting of cash and cash equivalents in the financial statements.		

Describe and illustrate the use of the ratio of cash to monthly cash expenses to assess the ability of a company to continue in business.

Key Points The ratio of cash to monthly cash expenses is useful for assessing how long a company can continue to operate without (1) additional financing or (2) generating positive cash flows from operations.

Learning Outcomes	*Example Exercises*	*Practice Exercises*
• Describe the use of the ratio of cash to monthly cash expenses.		
• Compute the ratio of cash to monthly cash expenses.	**EE8-5**	**PE8-5A, 8-5B**

Key Terms

bank reconciliation (383)
bank statement (380)
cash (377)
cash equivalents (388)
cash short and over account (378)
compensating balance (389)
control environment (373)
electronic funds transfer (EFT) (379)
elements of internal control (372)
employee fraud (372)
internal control (370)
petty cash fund (387)
ratio of cash to monthly cash expenses (389)
Sarbanes-Oxley Act (370)
special-purpose funds (388)
voucher (380)
voucher system (380)

Illustrative Problem

The bank statement for Urethane Company for June 30, 2015, indicates a balance of $9,293.11. All cash receipts are deposited each evening in a night depository, after banking hours. The accounting records indicate the following summary data for cash receipts and payments for June:

Cash balance as of June 1	$ 3,943.50
Total cash receipts for June	28,971.60
Total amount of checks issued in June	28,388.85

Comparing the bank statement and the accompanying canceled checks and memos with the records reveals the following reconciling items:

a. The bank had collected for Urethane Company $1,030 on a note left for collection. The face amount of the note was $1,000.

b. A deposit of $1,852.21, representing receipts of June 30, had been made too late to appear on the bank statement.

c. Checks outstanding totaled $5,265.27.

d. A check drawn for $139 had been incorrectly charged by the bank as $157.

e. A check for $370 returned with the statement had been recorded in the company's records as $730. The check was for the payment of an obligation to Avery Equipment Company for the purchase of office supplies on account.

f. Bank service charges for June amounted to $18.20.

Instructions

1. Prepare a bank reconciliation for June.
2. Journalize the entries that should be made by Urethane Company.

Solution

1.

Urethane Company
Bank Reconciliation
June 30, 2015

Cash balance according to bank statement		$ 9,293.11
Add: Deposit of June 30 not recorded by bank	$1,852.21	
Bank error in charging check as $157 instead of $139	18.00	1,870.21
		$11,163.32
Deduct: Outstanding checks		5,265.27
Adjusted balance		$ 5,898.05
Cash balance according to company's records		$ 4,526.25*
Add: Proceeds of note collected by bank, including $30 interest	$1,030.00	
Error in recording check	360.00	1,390.00
		$ 5,916.25
Deduct: Bank service charges		18.20
Adjusted balance		$ 5,898.05

*$3,943.50 + $28,971.60 – $28,388.85

2.

June	30	Cash		1,390.00	
		Notes Receivable			1,000.00
		Interest Revenue			30.00
		Accounts Payable—Avery Equipment Company			360.00
	30	Miscellaneous Administrative Expense		18.20	
		Cash			18.20

Discussion Questions

1. (a) Name and describe the five elements of internal control. (b) Is any one element of internal control more important than another?
2. Why should the employee who handles cash receipts not have the responsibility for maintaining the accounts receivable records? Explain.
3. The ticket seller at a movie theater doubles as a ticket taker for a few minutes each day while the ticket taker is on a break. Which control procedure of a business's system of internal control is violated in this situation?
4. Why should the responsibility for maintaining the accounting records be separated from the responsibility for operations? Explain.
5. Assume that Brooke Miles, accounts payable clerk for West Coast Design Inc., stole $48,350 by paying fictitious invoices for goods that were never received. The clerk set up accounts in the names of the fictitious companies and cashed the checks at a local bank. Describe a control procedure that would have prevented or detected the fraud.

6. Before a voucher for the purchase of merchandise is approved for payment, supporting documents should be compared to verify the accuracy of the liability. Give an example of supporting documents for the purchase of merchandise.
7. The balance of Cash is likely to differ from the bank statement balance. What two factors are likely to be responsible for the difference?
8. What is the purpose of preparing a bank reconciliation?
9. Knott Inc. has a petty cash fund of $750. (a) Since the petty cash fund is only $750, should Knott Inc. implement controls over petty cash? (b) What controls, if any, could be used for the petty cash fund?
10. (a) How are cash equivalents reported in the financial statements? (b) What are some examples of cash equivalents?

Practice Exercises

SHOW ME HOW

EE 8-1 p. 377

PE 8-1A Internal control elements

OBJ. 2

Identify each of the following as relating to (a) the control environment, (b) control procedures, or (c) information and communication:

1. Organizational structure 
2. Report of company's conformity with environmental laws and regulations
3. Proofs and security measures 

SHOW ME HOW

EE 8-1 p. 377

PE 8-1B Internal control elements

OBJ. 2

Identify each of the following as relating to (a) the control environment, (b) control procedures, or (c) monitoring:

1. Hiring of external auditors to review the adequacy of controls
2. Personnel policies
3. Safeguarding inventory in a locked warehouse

SHOW ME HOW

EE 8-2 p. 382

PE 8-2A Items on company's bank statement

OBJ. 4

The following items may appear on a bank statement:

1. Bank correction of an error from recording a $6,200 deposit as $2,600
2. EFT payment
3. Note collected for company
4. Service charge

Using the following format, indicate whether each item would appear as a debit or credit memo on the bank statement and whether the item would increase or decrease the balance of the company's account:

Item No.	Appears on the Bank Statement as a Debit or Credit Memo	Increases or Decreases the Balance of the Company's Bank Account

SHOW ME HOW

EE 8-2 *p. 382*

PE 8-2B Items on company's bank statement

OBJ. 4

The following items may appear on a bank statement:

1. Bank correction of an error from posting another customer's check (disbursement) to the company's account
2. EFT deposit
3. Loan proceeds
4. NSF check

Using the following format, indicate whether each item would appear as a debit or credit memo on the bank statement and whether the item would increase or decrease the balance of the company's account:

Item No.	Appears on the Bank Statement as a Debit or Credit Memo	Increases or Decreases the Balance of the Company's Bank Account

SHOW ME HOW

EE 8-3 *p. 386*

PE 8-3A Bank reconciliation

OBJ. 5

The following data were gathered to use in reconciling the bank account of Eves Company:

Balance per bank	$9,350
Balance per company records	8,510
Bank service charges	35
Deposit in transit	2,350
NSF check	1,875
Outstanding checks	5,100

a. What is the adjusted balance on the bank reconciliation?

b. Journalize any necessary entries for Eves Company based on the bank reconciliation.

SHOW ME HOW

EE 8-3 *p. 387*

PE 8-3B Bank reconciliation

OBJ. 5

The following data were gathered to use in reconciling the bank account of Conway Company:

Balance per bank	$23,900
Balance per company records	8,700
Bank service charges	50
Deposit in transit	5,500
Note collected by bank with $450 interest	9,450
Outstanding checks	11,300

a. What is the adjusted balance on the bank reconciliation?

b. Journalize any necessary entries for Conway Company based on the bank reconciliation.

SHOW ME HOW

EE 8-4 *p. 388*

PE 8-4A Petty cash fund

OBJ. 6

Prepare journal entries for each of the following:

a. Issued a check to establish a petty cash fund of $750.

b. The amount of cash in the petty cash fund is $115. Issued a check to replenish the fund, based on the following summary of petty cash receipts: repair expense, $515 and miscellaneous selling expense, $88. Record any missing funds in the cash short and over account.

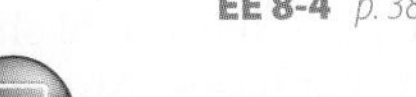

SHOW ME HOW

EE 8-4 *p. 388*

PE 8-4B Petty cash fund

OBJ. 6

Prepare journal entries for each of the following:

a. Issued a check to establish a petty cash fund of $900.

b. The amount of cash in the petty cash fund is $115. Issued a check to replenish the fund, based on the following summary of petty cash receipts: store supplies, $550 and miscellaneous selling expense, $200. Record any missing funds in the cash short and over account.

EE 8-5 p. 390

PE 8-5A Ratio of cash to monthly cash expenses **OBJ. 8**

SHOW ME HOW

Financial data for Otto Company follows:

	For Year Ended December 31, 2016
Cash on December 31, 2016	$ 69,350
Cash flow from operations	(114,000)

a. Compute the ratio of cash to monthly cash expenses.

b. Interpret the results computed in (a).

EE 8-5 p. 391

PE 8-5B Ratio of cash to monthly cash expenses **OBJ. 8**

SHOW ME HOW

Financial data for Bonita Company follows:

	For Year Ended December 31, 2016
Cash on December 31, 2016	$ 187,180
Cash flow from operations	(458,400)

a. Compute the ratio of cash to monthly cash expenses.

b. Interpret the results computed in (a).

Exercises

EX 8-1 Sarbanes-Oxley internal control report **OBJ. 1**

Internet Project

Using Wikipedia (www.wikipedia.com), look up the entry for Sarbanes-Oxley Act. Look over the table of contents and find the section that describes Section 404.

What does Section 404 require of management's internal control report?

EX 8-2 Internal controls **OBJ. 2, 3**

Faith Cassen has recently been hired as the manager of Gibraltar Coffee Shop. Gibraltar Coffee Shop is a national chain of franchised coffee shops. During her first month as store manager, Faith encountered the following internal control situations:

a. Faith caught an employee putting a case of 1,000 single-serving tea bags in his car. Not wanting to create a scene, Faith smiled and said, "I don't think you're putting those tea bags on the right shelf. Don't they belong inside the coffee shop?" The employee returned the tea bags to the stockroom.

b. Gibraltar Coffee Shop has one cash register. Prior to Faith's joining the coffee shop, each employee working on a shift would take a customer order, accept payment, and then prepare the order. Faith made one employee on each shift responsible for taking orders and accepting the customer's payment. Other employees prepare the orders.

c. Because only one employee uses the cash register, that employee is responsible for counting the cash at the end of the shift and verifying that the cash in the drawer matches the amount of cash sales recorded by the cash register. Faith expects each cashier to balance the drawer to the penny *every* time—no exceptions.

State whether you agree or disagree with Faith's method of handling each situation and explain your answer.

EX 8-3 Internal controls **OBJ. 2, 3**

Ramona's Clothing is a retail store specializing in women's clothing. The store has established a liberal return policy for the holiday season in order to encourage gift purchases. Any item purchased during November and December may be returned through January 31, with a receipt, for cash or exchange. If the customer does not have a receipt, cash will still be refunded for any item under $75. If the item is more than $75, a check is mailed to the customer.

Whenever an item is returned, a store clerk completes a return slip, which the customer signs. The return slip is placed in a special box. The store manager visits the return counter approximately once every two hours to authorize the return slips. Clerks are instructed to place the returned merchandise on the proper rack on the selling floor as soon as possible.

This year, returns at Ramona's Clothing have reached an all-time high. There are a large number of returns under $75 without receipts.

a. ➤ How can sales clerks employed at Ramona's Clothing use the store's return policy to steal money from the cash register?

b. ➤ What internal control weaknesses do you see in the return policy that make cash thefts easier?

c. ➤ Would issuing a store credit in place of a cash refund for all merchandise returned without a receipt reduce the possibility of theft? List some advantages and disadvantages of issuing a store credit in place of a cash refund.

d. ➤ Assume that Ramona's Clothing is committed to the current policy of issuing cash refunds without a receipt. What changes could be made in the store's procedures regarding customer refunds in order to improve internal control?

EX 8-4 Internal controls for bank lending **OBJ. 2, 3**

Pacific Bank provides loans to businesses in the community through its Commercial Lending Department. Small loans (less than $100,000) may be approved by an individual loan officer, while larger loans (greater than $100,000) must be approved by a board of loan officers. Once a loan is approved, the funds are made available to the loan applicant under agreed-upon terms. Pacific Bank has instituted a policy whereby its president has the individual authority to approve loans up to $5,000,000. The president believes that this policy will allow flexibility to approve loans to valued clients much quicker than under the previous policy.

➤ As an internal auditor of Pacific Bank, how would you respond to this change in policy?

EX 8-5 Internal controls **OBJ. 2, 3**

One of the largest losses in history from unauthorized securities trading involved a securities trader for the French bank, Societe Generale. The trader was able to circumvent internal controls and create more than $7 billion in trading losses in six months. The trader apparently escaped detection by using knowledge of the bank's internal control systems learned from a previous back-office monitoring job. Much of this monitoring involved the use of software to monitor trades. In addition, traders were usually kept to tight trading limits. Apparently, these controls failed in this case.

➤ What general weaknesses in Societe Generale's internal controls contributed to the occurrence and size of the losses?

EX 8-6 Internal controls **OBJ. 2, 3**

An employee of JHT Holdings, Inc., a trucking company, was responsible for resolving roadway accident claims under $25,000. The employee created fake accident claims and wrote settlement checks of between $5,000 and $25,000 to friends or acquaintances acting as phony "victims." One friend recruited subordinates at his place of work to cash some of the checks. Beyond this, the JHT employee also recruited lawyers, whom he paid to represent both the trucking company and the fake victims in the bogus accident settlements. When the lawyers cashed the checks, they allegedly split the money with the corrupt JHT employee. This fraud went undetected for two years.

➤ Why would it take so long to discover such a fraud?

EX 8-7 Internal controls **OBJ. 2, 3**

All-Around Sound Co. discovered a fraud whereby one of its front office administrative employees used company funds to purchase goods, such as computers, digital cameras, and other electronic items for her own use. The fraud was discovered when employees noticed an increase in delivery frequency from vendors and the use of unusual vendors. After some investigation, it was discovered that the employee would alter the description or change the quantity on an invoice in order to explain the cost on the bill.

➤ What general internal control weaknesses contributed to this fraud?

EX 8-8 Financial statement fraud

OBJ. 2, 3

A former chairman, CFO, and controller of Donnkenny, Inc., an apparel company that makes sportswear for Pierre Cardin and Victoria Jones, pleaded guilty to financial statement fraud. These managers used false journal entries to record fictitious sales, hid inventory in public warehouses so that it could be recorded as "sold," and required sales orders to be backdated so that the sale could be moved back to an earlier period. The combined effect of these actions caused $25 million out of $40 million in quarterly sales to be phony.

a. Why might control procedures listed in this chapter be insufficient in stopping this type of fraud?

b. How could this type of fraud be stopped?

EX 8-9 Internal control of cash receipts

OBJ. 2, 3

The procedures used for over-the-counter receipts are as follows. At the close of each day's business, the sales clerks count the cash in their respective cash drawers, after which they determine the amount recorded by the cash register and prepare the memo cash form, noting any discrepancies. An employee from the cashier's office counts the cash, compares the total with the memo, and takes the cash to the cashier's office.

a. Indicate the weak link in internal control.

b. How can the weakness be corrected?

EX 8-10 Internal control of cash receipts

OBJ. 2, 3

Sergio Flores works at the drive-through window of Big & Bad Burgers. Occasionally, when a drive-through customer orders, Sergio fills the order and pockets the customer's money. He does not ring up the order on the cash register.

Identify the internal control weaknesses that exist at Big & Bad Burgers, and discuss what can be done to prevent this theft.

EX 8-11 Internal control of cash receipts

OBJ. 2, 3

The mailroom employees send all remittances and remittance advices to the cashier. The cashier deposits the cash in the bank and forwards the remittance advices and duplicate deposit slips to the Accounting Department.

a. Indicate the weak link in internal control in the handling of cash receipts.

b. How can the weakness be corrected?

EX 8-12 Entry for cash sales; cash short

OBJ. 2, 3

SHOW ME HOW

The actual cash received from cash sales was $33,854 and the amount indicated by the cash register total was $33,866. Journalize the entry to record the cash receipts and cash sales.

EX 8-13 Entry for cash sales; cash over

OBJ. 2, 3

SHOW ME HOW

The actual cash received from cash sales was $51,175 and the amount indicated by the cash register total was $50,997. Journalize the entry to record the cash receipts and cash sales.

EX 8-14 Internal control of cash payments

OBJ. 2, 3

Abbe Co. is a small merchandising company with a manual accounting system. An investigation revealed that in spite of a sufficient bank balance, a significant amount of available cash discounts had been lost because of failure to make timely payments. In addition, it was discovered that the invoices for several purchases had been paid twice.

Outline procedures for the payment of vendors' invoices so that the possibilities of losing available cash discounts and of paying an invoice a second time will be minimized.

EX 8-15 Internal control of cash payments OBJ. 2, 3

Paragon Tech Company, a communications equipment manufacturer, recently fell victim to a fraud scheme developed by one of its employees. To understand the scheme, it is necessary to review Paragon Tech's procedures for the purchase of services.

The purchasing agent is responsible for ordering services (such as repairs to a photocopy machine or office cleaning) after receiving a service requisition from an authorized manager. However, because no tangible goods are delivered, a receiving report is not prepared. When the Accounting Department receives an invoice billing Paragon Tech for a service call, the accounts payable clerk calls the manager who requested the service in order to verify that it was performed.

The fraud scheme involves Mae Jansma, the manager of plant and facilities. Mae arranged for her uncle's company, Radiate Systems, to be placed on Paragon Tech's approved vendor list. Mae did not disclose the family relationship.

On several occasions, Mae would submit a requisition for services to be provided by Radiate Systems. However, the service requested was really not needed, and it was never performed. Radiate Systems would bill Paragon Tech for the service and then split the cash payment with Mae.

Explain what changes should be made to Paragon Tech's procedures for ordering and paying for services in order to prevent such occurrences in the future.

EX 8-16 Bank reconciliation OBJ. 5

Identify each of the following reconciling items as: (a) an addition to the cash balance according to the bank statement, (b) a deduction from the cash balance according to the bank statement, (c) an addition to the cash balance according to the company's records, or (d) a deduction from the cash balance according to the company's records. (None of the transactions reported by bank debit and credit memos have been recorded by the company.)

1. Bank service charges, $75.
2. Check of a customer returned by bank to company because of insufficient funds, $880.
3. Check for $275 incorrectly recorded by the company as $725.
4. Check for $100 incorrectly charged by bank as $1,000.
5. Deposit in transit, $5,550.
6. Outstanding checks, $10,350.
7. Note collected by bank, $12,720.

EX 8-17 Entries based on bank reconciliation OBJ. 5

Which of the reconciling items listed in Exercise 8-16 require an entry in the company's accounts?

EX 8-18 Bank reconciliation OBJ. 5

✔ Adjusted balance: $22,545

SHOW ME HOW

The following data were accumulated for use in reconciling the bank account of Zek's Co. for May 2016:

1. Cash balance according to the company's records at May 31, 2016, $22,110.
2. Cash balance according to the bank statement at May 31, 2016, $29,650.
3. Checks outstanding, $13,875.
4. Deposit in transit, not recorded by bank, $6,770.
5. A check for $50 in payment of an account was erroneously recorded in the check register as $500.
6. Bank debit memo for service charges, $15.

a. Prepare a bank reconciliation, using the format shown in Exhibit 13.
b. If the balance sheet were prepared for Zek's Co. on May 31, 2016, what amount should be reported for cash?
c. Must a bank reconciliation always balance (reconcile)?

SHOW ME HOW

EX 8-19 Entries for bank reconciliation **OBJ. 5**

Using the data presented in Exercise 8-18, journalize the entry or entries that should be made by the company.

SHOW ME HOW

EX 8-20 Entries for note collected by bank **OBJ. 5**

Accompanying a bank statement for Santee Company is a credit memo for $15,120 representing the principal ($14,000) and interest ($1,120) on a note that had been collected by the bank. The company had been notified by the bank at the time of the collection but had made no entries. Journalize the entry that should be made by the company to bring the accounting records up to date.

SHOW ME HOW

EX 8-21 Bank reconciliation **OBJ. 5**

An accounting clerk for Chesner Co. prepared the following bank reconciliation:

Chesner Co.
Bank Reconciliation
July 31, 2016

Cash balance according to company's records		$11,100
Add: Outstanding checks	$ 3,585	
Error by Chesner Co. in recording Check No. 1056 as $950 instead of $590	360	
Note for $12,000 collected by bank, including interest	12,480	16,425
		$27,525
Deduct: Deposit in transit on July 31	$ 7,200	
Bank service charges	25	7,225
Cash balance according to bank statement		$20,300

a. From the data in this bank reconciliation, prepare a new bank reconciliation for Chesner Co., using the format shown in the illustrative problem.

b. If a balance sheet were prepared for Chesner Co. on July 31, 2016, what amount should be reported for cash?

EX 8-22 Bank reconciliation **OBJ. 5**

✔ Corrected adjusted balance: $19,780

Identify the errors in the following bank reconciliation:

Poway Co.
Bank Reconciliation
For the Month Ended June 30, 2016

Cash balance according to bank statement			$16,185
Add outstanding checks:			
No. 1067		$ 575	
1106		470	
1110		1,050	
1113		910	3,005
			$19,190
Deduct deposit of June 30, not recorded by bank			6,600
Adjusted balance			$12,590
Cash balance according to company's records			$ 8,985
Add: Proceeds of note collected by bank:			
Principal	$6,000		
Interest	300	$6,300	
Service charges		15	6,315
			$15,300
Deduct: Check returned because of insufficient funds		$ 890	
Error in recording June 17 deposit of $7,150 as $1,750		5,400	6,290
Adjusted balance			$ 9,010

SHOW ME HOW

EX 8-23 Using bank reconciliation to determine cash receipts stolen **OBJ. 2, 3, 5**

Alaska Impressions Co. records all cash receipts on the basis of its cash register tapes. Alaska Impressions Co. discovered during October 2016 that one of its sales clerks had stolen an undetermined amount of cash receipts by taking the daily deposits to the bank. The following data have been gathered for October:

Cash in bank according to the general ledger	$11,680
Cash according to the October 31, 2016, bank statement	13,275
Outstanding checks as of October 31, 2016	3,670
Bank service charge for October	40
Note receivable, including interest collected by bank in October	2,100

No deposits were in transit on October 31.

a. Determine the amount of cash receipts stolen by the sales clerk.

b. What accounting controls would have prevented or detected this theft?

SHOW ME HOW

EX 8-24 Petty cash fund entries **OBJ. 6**

Journalize the entries to record the following:

a. Check No. 245-13 is issued to establish a petty cash fund of $1,100.

b. The amount of cash in the petty cash fund is now $115. Check No. 271-13 is issued to replenish the fund, based on the following summary of petty cash receipts: office supplies, $614; miscellaneous selling expense, $200; miscellaneous administrative expense, $145. (Because the amount of the check to replenish the fund plus the balance in the fund do not equal $1,100, record the discrepancy in the cash short and over account.)

EX 8-25 Variation in cash flows **OBJ. 7**

Mattel, Inc., designs, manufactures, and markets toy products worldwide. Mattel's toys include Barbie™ fashion dolls and accessories, Hot Wheels™, and Fisher-Price brands. For a recent year, Mattel reported the following net cash flows from operating activities (in thousands):

First quarter ending March 30	$ 171,506
Second quarter ending June 29	(232,557)
Third quarter ending September 29	(40,109)
Fourth quarter ending December 30	986,778

Explain why Mattel reported negative net cash flows from operating activities during the second and third quarters and a large positive cash flow for the fourth quarter, with overall net positive cash flow for the year.

SHOW ME HOW

EX 8-26 Cash to monthly cash expenses ratio **OBJ. 8**

During 2016, El Dorado Inc. has monthly cash expenses of $168,500. On December 31, 2016, the cash balance is $1,415,400.

a. Compute the ratio of cash to monthly cash expenses.

b. Based on (a), what are the implications for El Dorado Inc.?

SHOW ME HOW

F·A·I

EX 8-27 Cash to monthly cash expenses ratio **OBJ. 8**

Capstone Turbine Corporation produces and sells turbine generators for such applications as charging electric, hybrid vehicles. Capstone Turbine reported the following financial data for a recent year (in thousands):

Net cash flows from operating activities	$(21,438)
Cash and cash equivalents	49,952

a. Determine the monthly cash expenses. Round to one decimal place.

b. Determine the ratio of cash to monthly cash expenses. Round to one decimal place.

c. Based on your analysis, do you believe that Capstone Turbine will remain in business?

EX 8-28 Cash to monthly cash expenses ratio OBJ. 8

SHOW ME HOW

Amicus Therapeutics, Inc., is a biopharmaceutical company that develops drugs for the treatment of various diseases, including Parkinson's disease. Amicus Therapeutics reported the following financial data (in thousands) for three recent years:

	For Years Ended December 31		
	Year 3	Year 2	Year 1
Cash and cash equivalents	$ 25,668	$29,572	$ 19,339
Net cash flows from operations	(49,422)	(13,983)	(43,371)

a. Determine the monthly cash expenses for Year 3, Year 2, and Year 1. Round to one decimal place.

b. Determine the ratio of cash to monthly cash expenses for Year 3, Year 2, and Year 1 as of December 31. Round to one decimal place.

c. Based on (a) and (b), comment on Amicus Therapeutics' ratio of cash to monthly operating expenses for Year 3, Year 2, and Year 1.

Problems: Series A

PR 8-1A Evaluating internal control of cash OBJ. 2, 3

The following procedures were recently installed by Raspberry Creek Company:

a. After necessary approvals have been obtained for the payment of a voucher, the treasurer signs and mails the check. The treasurer then stamps the voucher and supporting documentation as paid and returns the voucher and supporting documentation to the accounts payable clerk for filing.

b. The accounts payable clerk prepares a voucher for each disbursement. The voucher along with the supporting documentation is forwarded to the treasurer's office for approval.

c. Along with petty cash expense receipts for postage, office supplies, etc., several post-dated employee checks are in the petty cash fund.

d. At the end of the day, cash register clerks are required to use their own funds to make up any cash shortages in their registers.

e. At the end of each day, all cash receipts are placed in the bank's night depository.

f. At the end of each day, an accounting clerk compares the duplicate copy of the daily cash deposit slip with the deposit receipt obtained from the bank.

g. All mail is opened by the mail clerk, who forwards all cash remittances to the cashier. The cashier prepares a listing of the cash receipts and forwards a copy of the list to the accounts receivable clerk for recording in the accounts.

h. The bank reconciliation is prepared by the cashier, who works under the supervision of the treasurer.

Instructions

Indicate whether each of the procedures of internal control over cash represents (1) a strength or (2) a weakness. For each weakness, indicate why it exists.

PR 8-2A Transactions for petty cash, cash short and over OBJ. 3, 6

Cactus Restoration Company completed the following selected transactions during May 2016:

SHOW ME HOW

Oct. 1. Established a petty cash fund of $750.

12. The cash sales for the day, according to the cash register records, totaled $12,440 The actual cash received from cash sales was $12,465.

31. Petty cash on hand was $157. Replenished the petty cash fund for the following disbursements, each evidenced by a petty cash receipt:

Oct. 3. Store supplies, $390.
7. Express charges on merchandise sold, $35 (Delivery Expense).
9. Office supplies, $16.
13. Office supplies, $22.
19. Postage stamps, $12 (Office Supplies).
21. Repair to office file cabinet lock, $15 (Miscellaneous Administrative Expense).
22. Postage due on special delivery letter, $27 (Miscellaneous Administrative Expense).
24. Express charges on merchandise sold, $55 (Delivery Expense).
30. Office supplies, $6.

Oct. 31. The cash sales for the day, according to the cash register records, totaled $18,820. The actual cash received from cash sales was $18,780.
31. Decreased the petty cash fund by $100.

Instructions

Journalize the transactions.

PR 8-3A Bank reconciliation and entries **OBJ. 5**

✓ 1. Adjusted balance: $114,960

General Ledger

SHOW ME HOW

The cash account for Capstone Medical Co. at November 30, 2016, indicated a balance of $89,620. The bank statement indicated a balance of $128,660 on November 30, 2016. Comparing the bank statement and the accompanying canceled checks and memos with the records revealed the following reconciling items:

a. Checks outstanding totaled $32,700.
b. A deposit of $18,550, representing receipts of November 30, had been made too late to appear on the bank statement.
c. The bank collected $26,750 on a $25,000 note, including interest of $1,750.
d. A check for $1,500 returned with the statement had been incorrectly recorded by Capstone Medical Co. as $150. The check was for the payment of an obligation to ABC Supply Co. for a purchase on account.
e. A check drawn for $490 had been erroneously charged by the bank as $940.
f. Bank service charges for November amounted to $60.

Instructions

1. Prepare a bank reconciliation.
2. Journalize the necessary entries. The accounts have not been closed.
3. If a balance sheet were prepared for Capstone Medical Co. on November 30, 2016, what amount should be reported as cash?

PR 8-4A Bank reconciliation and entries **OBJ. 5**

✓ 1. Adjusted balance: $39,475

General Ledger

SHOW ME HOW

The cash account for Brentwood Bike Co. at May 1, 2016, indicated a balance of $34,250. During May, the total cash deposited was $140,300, and checks written totaled $138,880. The bank statement indicated a balance of $43,525 on May 31. Comparing the bank statement, the canceled checks, and the accompanying memos with the records revealed the following reconciling items:

a. Checks outstanding totaled $6,440.
b. A deposit of $1,850 representing receipts of May 31, had been made too late to appear on the bank statement.
c. The bank had collected for Brentwood Bike Co. $5,250 on a note left for collection. The face of the note was $5,000.
d. A check for $390 returned with the statement had been incorrectly charged by the bank as $930.

(Continued)

e. A check for $210 returned with the statement had been recorded by Brentwood Bike Co. as $120. The check was for the payment of an obligation to Adkins Co. on account.

f. Bank service charges for May amounted to $30.

g. A check for $1,325 from Jennings Co. was returned by the bank due to insufficient funds.

Instructions

1. Prepare a bank reconciliation as of May 31.
2. Journalize the necessary entries. The accounts have not been closed.
3. If a balance sheet were prepared for Brentwood Bike Co. on May 31, 2016, what amount should be reported as cash?

PR 8-5A Bank reconciliation and entries

OBJ. 5

✔ 1. Adjusted balance: $13,216

Beeler Furniture Company deposits all cash receipts each Wednesday and Friday in a night depository, after banking hours. The data required to reconcile the bank statement as of June 30 have been taken from various documents and records and are reproduced as follows. The sources of the data are printed in capital letters. All checks were written for payments on account.

CASH ACCOUNT:

Balance as of June 1	$9,317.40
CASH RECEIPTS FOR MONTH OF JUNE	$9,223.76

DUPLICATE DEPOSIT TICKETS:

Date and amount of each deposit in June:

Date	Amount	Date	Amount	Date	Amount
June 1	$1,080.50	June 10	$ 996.61	June 22	$ 897.34
3	854.17	15	882.95	24	947.21
8	840.50	17	1,606.74	30	1,117.74

CHECKS WRITTEN:

Number and amount of each check issued in June:

Check No.	Amount	Check No.	Amount	Check No.	Amount
740	$237.50	747	Void	754	$ 449.75
741	495.15	748	$450.90	755	272.75
742	501.90	749	640.13	756	113.95
743	761.30	750	276.77	757	407.95
744	506.88	751	299.37	758	259.60
745	117.25	752	537.01	759	901.50
746	298.66	753	380.95	760	486.39
Total amount of checks issued in June					$8,395.66

BANK RECONCILIATION FOR PRECEDING MONTH:

Beeler Furniture Company
Bank Reconciliation
May 31, 2016

Cash balance according to bank statement		$ 9,447.20
Add deposit for May 31, not recorded by bank		690.25
		$10,137.45
Deduct outstanding checks:		
No. 731	$162.15	
736	345.95	
738	251.40	
739	60.55	820.05
Adjusted balance		$ 9,317.40
Cash balance according to company's records		$ 9,352.50
Deduct service charges		35.10
Adjusted balance		$ 9,317.40

Instructions

1. Prepare a bank reconciliation as of June 30. If errors in recording deposits or checks are discovered, assume that the errors were made by the company. Assume that all deposits are from cash sales. All checks are written to satisfy accounts payable.
2. Journalize the necessary entries. The accounts have not been closed.
3. What is the amount of Cash that should appear on the balance sheet as of June 30?
4. Assume that a canceled check for $390 has been incorrectly recorded by the bank as $930. Briefly explain how the error would be included in a bank reconciliation and how it should be corrected.

JUNE BANK STATEMENT:

MEMBER FDIC

AMERICAN NATIONAL BANK OF CHICAGO

CHICAGO, IL 60603 (312) 441-1239

PAGE 1

ACCOUNT NUMBER

FROM 6/01/2016 TO 6/30/2016

BEELER FURNITURE COMPANY

	BALANCE	9,447.20
9	DEPOSITS	8,691.77
20	WITHDRAWALS	7,599.26
4	OTHER DEBITS AND CREDITS	3,085.00CR
	NEW BALANCE	13,624.71

CHECKS AND OTHER DEBITS				DEPOSITS	DATE	BALANCE
No.731	162.15	No.736	345.95	690.25	6/01	9,629.35
No.739	60.55	No.740	237.50	1,080.50	6/02	10,411.80
No.741	495.15	No.742	501.90	854.17	6/04	10,268.92
No.743	671.30	No.744	506.88	840.50	6/09	9,931.24
No.745	117.25	No.746	298.66	MS 3,500.00	6/09	13,015.33
No.748	450.90	No.749	640.13	MS 210.00	6/09	12,134.30
No.750	276.77	No.751	299.37	896.61	6/11	12,454.77
No.752	537.01	No.753	380.95	882.95	6/16	12,419.76
No.754	449.75	No.755	272.75	1,606.74	6/18	13,304.00
No.757	407.95	No.760	486.39	897.34	6/23	13,307.00
				942.71	6/25	14,249.71
		NSF	550.00		6/28	13,699.71
		SC	75.00		6/30	13,624.71

EC — ERROR CORRECTION
MS — MISCELLANEOUS
NSF — NOT SUFFICIENT FUNDS

OD — OVERDRAFT
PS — PAYMENT STOPPED
SC — SERVICE CHARGE

* * * * * * * * *

THE RECONCILEMENT OF THIS STATEMENT WITH YOUR RECORDS IS ESSENTIAL.
ANY ERROR OR EXCEPTION SHOULD BE REPORTED IMMEDIATELY.

Problems: Series B

PR 8-1B Evaluating internal control of cash

OBJ. 2, 3

The following procedures were recently installed by The China Shop:

a. All sales are rung up on the cash register, and a receipt is given to the customer. All sales are recorded on a record locked inside the cash register.

b. Each cashier is assigned a separate cash register drawer to which no other cashier has access.

c. At the end of a shift, each cashier counts the cash in his or her cash register, unlocks the cash register record, and compares the amount of cash with the amount on the record to determine cash shortages and overages.

(Continued)

d. Checks received through the mail are given daily to the accounts receivable clerk for recording collections on account and for depositing in the bank.

e. Vouchers and all supporting documents are perforated with a PAID designation after being paid by the treasurer.

f. Disbursements are made from the petty cash fund only after a petty cash receipt has been completed and signed by the payee.

g. The bank reconciliation is prepared by the cashier.

Instructions

Indicate whether each of the procedures of internal control over cash represents (1) a strength or (2) a weakness. For each weakness, indicate why it exists.

PR 8-2B Transactions for petty cash, cash short and over — OBJ. 3, 6

SHOW ME HOW

Cedar Springs Company completed the following selected transactions during June 2016:

June 1. Established a petty cash fund of $1,000.

12. The cash sales for the day, according to the cash register records, totaled $9,440. The actual cash received from cash sales was $9,506.

30. Petty cash on hand was $46. Replenished the petty cash fund for the following disbursements, each evidenced by a petty cash receipt:

    June 2. Store supplies, $375.

    10. Express charges on merchandise purchased, $105 (Merchandise Inventory).

    14. Office supplies, $85.

    15. Office supplies, $90.

    18. Postage stamps, $33 (Office Supplies).

    20. Repair to fax, $100 (Miscellaneous Administrative Expense).

    21. Repair to office door lock, $25 (Miscellaneous Administrative Expense).

    22. Postage due on special delivery letter, $9 (Miscellaneous Administrative Expense).

    28. Express charges on merchandise purchased, $110 (Merchandise Inventory).

30. The cash sales for the day, according to the cash register records, totaled $13,390. The actual cash received from cash sales was $13,350.

30. Increased the petty cash fund by $200.

Instructions

Journalize the transactions.

PR 8-3B Bank reconciliation and entries — OBJ. 5

✔ 1. Adjusted balance: $24,305

General Ledger

SHOW ME HOW

The cash account for Stone Systems at July 31, 2016, indicated a balance of $17,750. The bank statement indicated a balance of $33,650 on July 31, 2016. Comparing the bank statement and the accompanying canceled checks and memos with the records reveals the following reconciling items:

a. Checks outstanding totaled $17,865.

b. A deposit of $9,150, representing receipts of July 31, had been made too late to appear on the bank statement.

c. The bank had collected $6,095 on a note left for collection. The face of the note was $5,750.

d. A check for $390 returned with the statement had been incorrectly recorded by Stone Systems as $930. The check was for the payment of an obligation to Holland Co. for the purchase of office supplies on account.

e. A check drawn for $1,810 had been incorrectly charged by the bank as $1,180.

f. Bank service charges for July amounted to $80.

Instructions

1. Prepare a bank reconciliation.
2. Journalize the necessary entries. The accounts have not been closed.
3. If a balance sheet were prepared for Stone Systems on July 31, 2014, what amount should be reported as cash?

PR 8-4B Bank reconciliation and entries

OBJ. 5

✔ 1. Adjusted balance: $78,535

General Ledger

SHOW ME HOW

The cash account for Collegiate Sports Co. on November 1, 2016, indicated a balance of $81,145. During November, the total cash deposited was $293,150, and checks written totaled $307,360. The bank statement indicated a balance of $112,675 on November 30, 2016. Comparing the bank statement, the canceled checks, and the accompanying memos with the records revealed the following reconciling items:

a. Checks outstanding totaled $41,840.

b. A deposit of $12,200, representing receipts of November 30, had been made too late to appear on the bank statement.

c. A check for $7,250 had been incorrectly charged by the bank as $2,750.

d. A check for $760 returned with the statement had been recorded by Collegiate Sports Co. as $7,600. The check was for the payment of an obligation to Ramirez Co. on account.

e. The bank had collected for Collegiate Sports Co. $7,385 on a note left for collection. The face of the note was $7,000.

f. Bank service charges for November amounted to $125.

g. A check for $2,500 from Hallen Academy was returned by the bank because of insufficient funds.

Instructions

1. Prepare a bank reconciliation as of November 30.
2. Journalize the necessary entries. The accounts have not been closed.
3. If a balance sheet were prepared for Collegiate Sports Co. on November 30, 2014, what amount should be reported as cash?

PR 8-5B Bank reconciliation and entries

OBJ. 5

✔ 1. Adjusted balance: $11,494

Sunshine Interiors deposits all cash receipts each Wednesday and Friday in a night depository, after banking hours. The data required to reconcile the bank statement as of July 31 have been taken from various documents and records and are reproduced as follows. The sources of the data are printed in capital letters. All checks were written for payments on account.

BANK RECONCILIATION FOR PRECEDING MONTH (DATED JUNE 30):

Cash balance according to bank statement		$ 9,422.80
Add deposit of June 30, not recorded by bank		780.80
		$10,203.60
Deduct outstanding checks:		
No. 580	$310.10	
No. 602	85.50	
No. 612	92.50	
No. 613	137.50	625.60
Adjusted balance		$ 9,578.00
Cash balance according to company's records		$ 9,605.70
Deduct service charges		27.70
Adjusted balance		$ 9,578.00
CASH ACCOUNT:		
Balance as of July 1		$ 9,578.00
CASH RECEIPTS FOR MONTH OF JULY		6,465.42

DUPLICATE DEPOSIT TICKETS:

Date and amount of each deposit in July:

Date	Amount	Date	Amount	Date	Amount
July 2	$569.50	July 12	$580.70	July 23	$ 713.45
5	701.80	16	600.10	26	601.50
9	819.24	19	701.26	31	1,177.87

(Continued)

CHECKS WRITTEN:

Number and amount of each check issued in July:

Check No.	Amount	Check No.	Amount	Check No.	Amount
614	$243.50	621	$309.50	628	$ 837.70
615	350.10	622	Void	629	329.90
616	279.90	623	Void	630	882.80
617	395.50	624	707.01	631	1,081.56
618	435.40	625	158.63	632	325.40
619	320.10	626	550.03	633	310.08
620	238.87	627	381.73	634	241.71
Total amount of checks issued in July					$8,379.42

JULY BANK STATEMENT:

MEMBER FDIC

AMERICAN NATIONAL BANK OF DETROIT

DETROIT, MI 48201-2500 (313) 933-8547

SUNSHINE INTERIORS

PAGE 1

ACCOUNT NUMBER

FROM 7/01/2016 TO 7/31/2016

	BALANCE	9,422.80
9	DEPOSITS	6,086.35
20	WITHDRAWALS	7,656.74
4	OTHER DEBITS AND CREDITS	3,749.00CR
	NEW BALANCE	11,601.41

CHECKS AND OTHER DEBITS					DEPOSITS	DATE	BALANCE
No.580	310.10	No.612	92.50		780.80	07/01	9,801.00
No.602	85.50	No.614	243.50		569.50	07/03	10,041.50
No.615	350.10	No.616	279.90		701.80	07/06	10,113.30
No.617	395.50	No.618	435.40		819.24	07/11	10,101.64
No.619	320.10	No.620	238.87		580.70	07/13	10,123.37
No.621	309.50	No.624	707.01		MS 4,000.00	07/14	13,106.86
No.625	158.63	No.626	550.03		MS 160.00	07/14	12,558.20
No.627	318.73	No.629	329.90		600.10	07/17	12,509.67
No.630	882.80	No.631	1,081.56	NSF 375.00		07/20	10,170.31
No.632	325.40	No.634	241.71		701.26	07/21	10,304.46
					731.45	07/24	11,035.91
					601.50	07/28	11,637.41
		SC	36.00			07/31	11,601.41

EC — ERROR CORRECTION
MS — MISCELLANEOUS
NSF — NOT SUFFICIENT FUNDS

OD — OVERDRAFT
PS — PAYMENT STOPPED
SC — SERVICE CHARGE

* * *

THE RECONCILEMENT OF THIS STATEMENT WITH YOUR RECORDS IS ESSENTIAL.
ANY ERROR OR EXCEPTION SHOULD BE REPORTED IMMEDIATELY.

Instructions

1. Prepare a bank reconciliation as of July 31. If errors in recording deposits or checks are discovered, assume that the errors were made by the company. Assume that all deposits are from cash sales. All checks are written to satisfy accounts payable.
2. Journalize the necessary entries. The accounts have not been closed.
3. What is the amount of Cash that should appear on the balance sheet as of July 31?
4. Assume that a canceled check for $180 has been incorrectly recorded by the bank as $1,800. Briefly explain how the error would be included in a bank reconciliation and how it should be corrected.

Cases & Projects

CP 8-1 Ethics and professional conduct in business

During the preparation of the bank reconciliation for Building Concepts Co., Joel Kimmel, the assistant controller, discovered that Lone Peak National Bank incorrectly recorded a $3,290 check written by Building Concepts Co. as $329. Joel has decided not to notify the bank but wait for the bank to detect the error. Joel plans to record the $2,961 error as Other Income if the bank fails to detect the error within the next three months.

Discuss whether Joel is behaving in a professional manner.

CP 8-2 Internal controls

The following is an excerpt from a conversation between two sales clerks, Jean Moen and Sara Cheney. Jean and Sara are employed by Turpin Meadows Electronics, a locally owned and operated electronics retail store.

Jean: Did you hear the news?

Sara: What news?

Jean: Neal and Linda were both arrested this morning.

Sara: What? Arrested? You're putting me on!

Jean: No, really! The police arrested them first thing this morning. Put them in handcuffs, read them their rights—the whole works. It was unreal!

Sara: What did they do?

Jean: Well, apparently they were filling out merchandise refund forms for fictitious customers and then taking the cash.

Sara: I guess I never thought of that. How did they catch them?

Jean: The store manager noticed that returns were twice that of last year and seemed to be increasing. When he confronted Neal, he became flustered and admitted to taking the cash, apparently more than $9,000 in just three months. They're going over the last six months' transactions to try to determine how much Linda stole. She apparently started stealing first.

Suggest appropriate control procedures that would have prevented or detected the theft of cash.

CP 8-3 Internal controls

The following is an excerpt from a conversation between the store manager of Wholesome Grocery Stores, Kara Dahl, and Lynn Shutes, president of Wholesome Grocery Stores:

Lynn: Kara, I'm concerned about this new scanning system.

Kara: What's the problem?

Lynn: Well, how do we know the clerks are ringing up all the merchandise?

Kara: That's one of the strong points about the system. The scanner automatically rings up each item, based on its bar code. We update the prices daily, so we're sure that the sale is rung up for the right price.

Lynn: That's not my concern. What keeps a clerk from pretending to scan items and then simply not charging his friends? If his friends were buying 10–15 items, it would be easy for the clerk to pass through several items with his finger over the bar code or just pass the merchandise through the scanner with the wrong side showing. It would look normal for anyone observing. In the old days, we at least could hear the cash register ringing up each sale.

Kara: I see your point.

Suggest ways that Wholesome Grocery Stores could prevent or detect the theft of merchandise as described.

CP 8-4 Ethics and professional conduct in business

Doris Tidwell and Jo Yost are both cash register clerks for Fuller's Organic Markets. Tom Ward is the store manager for Fuller's Organic Markets. The following is an excerpt of a conversation between Doris and Jo:

Doris: Jo, how long have you been working for Fuller's Organic Markets?

Jo: Almost five years this April. You just started two weeks ago . . . right?

Doris: Yes. Do you mind if I ask you a question?

Jo: No, go ahead.

Doris: What I want to know is, have they always had this rule that if your cash register is short at the end of the day, you have to make up the shortage out of your own pocket?

Jo: Yes, as long as I've been working here.

Doris: Well, it's the pits. Last week I had to pay in almost $40.

Jo: It's not that big a deal. I just make sure that I'm not short at the end of the day.

Doris: How do you do that?

Jo: I just shortchange a few customers early in the day. There are a few jerks that deserve it anyway. Most of the time, their attention is elsewhere, and they don't think to check their change.

Doris: What happens if you're over at the end of the day?

Jo: Tom lets me keep it as long as it doesn't get to be too large. I've not been short in over a year. I usually clear about $20 to $30 extra per day.

Discuss this case from the viewpoint of proper controls and professional behavior.

CP 8-5 Bank reconciliation and internal control

The records of Parker Company indicate a July 31, 2016 cash balance of $10,400, which includes undeposited receipts for July 30 and 31. The cash balance on the bank statement as of July 31 is $10,575. This balance includes a note of $2,250 plus $150 interest collected by the bank but not recorded in the journal. Checks outstanding on July 31 were as follows: No. 2670, $1,050; No. 3679, $675; No. 3690, $1,650; No. 5148, $225; No. 5149, $750; and No. 5151, $800.

On July 25, the cashier resigned, effective at the end of the month. Before leaving on July 31, the cashier prepared the following bank reconciliation:

Cash balance per books, July 31		$10,400
Add outstanding checks:		
No. 5148	$225	
5149	750	
5151	800	1,675
		$12,075
Less undeposited receipts		1,500
Cash balance per bank, July 31		$10,575
Deduct unrecorded note with interest		2,400
True cash, July 31		$ 8,175

Calculator Tape of Outstanding Checks:

0*
225+
750+
800+
1,675*

Subsequently, the owner of Parker Company discovered that the cashier had stolen an unknown amount of undeposited receipts, leaving only $1,500 to be deposited on July 31. The owner, a close family friend, has asked your help in determining the amount that the former cashier has stolen.

1. Determine the amount the cashier stole from Parker Company. Show your computations in good form.
2. How did the cashier attempt to conceal the theft?
3. a. Identify two major weaknesses in internal controls that allowed the cashier to steal the undeposited cash receipts.
   b. Recommend improvements in internal controls so that similar types of thefts of undeposited cash receipts can be prevented.

CP 8-6 Observe internal controls over cash

Group Project

Select a business in your community and observe its internal controls over cash receipts and cash payments. The business could be a bank or a bookstore, restaurant, department store, or other retailer. In groups of three or four, identify and discuss the similarities and differences in each business's cash internal controls.

CP 8-7 Cash to monthly cash expenses ratio

F·A·I

TearLab Corp. is a health care company that specializes in developing diagnostic devices for eye disease. TearLab reported the following data (in thousands) for three recent years:

	For Years Ended December 31		
	Year 3	**Year 2**	**Year 1**
Cash and cash equivalents	$ 2,807	$ 2,726	$ 106
Net cash flows from operations	(5,974)	(4,540)	(4,098)

1. Determine the monthly cash expenses for Year 3, Year 2, and Year 1. Round to one decimal place.
2. Determine the ratio of cash to monthly cash expenses as of December 31, for Year 3, Year 2, and Year 1. Round to one decimal place.
3. Based on (1) and (2), comment on TearLab's ratio of cash to monthly operating expenses for Year 3, Year 2, and Year 1.

CHAPTER 9

Receivables

Oakley, Inc.

The sale and purchase of merchandise involves the exchange of goods for cash. However, the point at which cash actually changes hands varies with the transaction. Consider transactions by **Oakley, Inc.**, a worldwide leader in the design, development, manufacture, and distribution of premium sunglasses, goggles, prescription eyewear, apparel, footwear, and accessories. Not only does the company sell its products through three different company-owned retail chains, but it also has approximately 10,000 independent distributors.

If you were to buy a pair of sunglasses at an Oakley Vault, which is one of the company's retail outlet stores, you would have to pay cash or use a credit card to pay for the glasses before you left the store. However, Oakley allows its distributors to purchase sunglasses "on account." These sales on account are recorded as receivables due from the distributors.

As an individual, you also might build up a trusted financial history with a local company or department store that would allow you to purchase merchandise on account. Like Oakley's distributors, your purchase on account would be recorded as an account receivable. Such credit transactions facilitate sales and are a significant current asset for many businesses.

This chapter describes common classifications of receivables, illustrates how to account for uncollectible receivables, and demonstrates the reporting of receivables on the balance sheet.

Learning Objectives

After studying this chapter, you should be able to:

OBJ		Example Exercises
1	**Describe the common classes of receivables.** Classification of Receivables Accounts Receivable Notes Receivable Other Receivables	
2	**Describe the accounting for uncollectible receivables.** Uncollectible Receivables	
3	**Describe the direct write-off method of accounting for uncollectible receivables.** Direct Write-Off Method for Uncollectible Accounts	EE 9-1
4	**Describe the allowance method of accounting for uncollectible receivables.** Allowance Method for Uncollectible Accounts Write-Offs to the Allowance Account Estimating Uncollectibles	EE 9-2 EE 9-3 EE 9-4
5	**Compare the direct write-off and allowance methods of accounting for uncollectible accounts.** Comparing Direct Write-Off and Allowance Methods	
6	**Describe the accounting for notes receivable.** Notes Receivable Characteristics of Notes Receivable Accounting for Notes Receivable	EE 9-5
7	**Describe the reporting of receivables on the balance sheet.** Reporting Receivables on the Balance Sheet	
8	**Describe and illustrate the use of accounts receivable turnover and number of days' sales in receivables to evaluate a company's efficiency in collecting its receivables.** Financial Analysis and Interpretation: Accounts Receivable Turnover and Number of Days' Sales in Receivables	EE 9-6

At a Glance 9 Page 433

OBJ 1 Describe the common classes of receivables.

Classification of Receivables

The receivables that result from sales on account are normally accounts receivable or notes receivable. The term **receivables** includes all money claims against other entities, including people, companies, and other organizations. Receivables are usually a significant portion of the total current assets.

Accounts Receivable

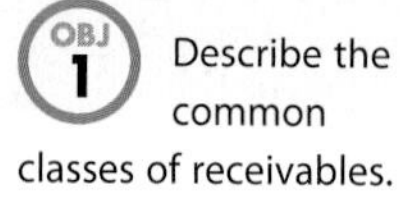

A recent balance sheet of **Caterpillar Inc.** reported that receivables made up more than 56% of its current assets.

The most common transaction creating a receivable is selling merchandise or services on account (on credit). The receivable is recorded as a debit to Accounts Receivable. Such **accounts receivable** are normally collected within a short period, such as 30 or 60 days. They are classified on the balance sheet as a current asset.

Notes Receivable

Notes receivable are amounts that customers owe for which a formal, written instrument of credit has been issued. If notes receivable are expected to be collected within a year, they are classified on the balance sheet as a current asset.

Notes are often used for credit periods of more than 60 days. For example, an automobile dealer may require a down payment at the time of sale and accept a note or a series of notes for the remainder. Such notes usually provide for monthly payments.

Notes may also be used to settle a customer's account receivable. Notes and accounts receivable that result from sales transactions are sometimes called *trade receivables*. In this chapter, all notes and accounts receivable are from sales transactions.

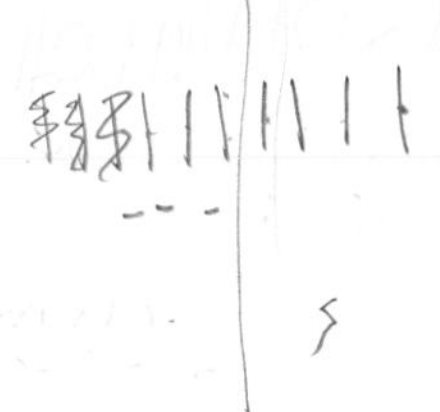

Other Receivables

Other receivables include interest receivable, taxes receivable, and receivables from officers or employees. Other receivables are normally reported separately on the balance sheet. If they are expected to be collected within one year, they are classified as current assets. If collection is expected beyond one year, they are classified as noncurrent assets and reported under the caption *Investments.*

Uncollectible Receivables

Describe the accounting for uncollectible receivables.

In prior chapters, the accounting for sales of merchandise or services on account (on credit) was described and illustrated. A major issue that has not yet been discussed is that some customers will not pay their accounts. That is, some accounts receivable will be uncollectible.

Companies may shift the risk of uncollectible receivables to other companies. For example, some retailers do not accept sales on account but will only accept cash or credit cards. Such policies shift the risk to the credit card companies.

Companies may also sell their receivables. This is often the case when a company issues its own credit card. For example, Macy's and JCPenney issue their own credit cards. Selling receivables is called *factoring* the receivables. The buyer of the receivables is called a *factor.* An advantage of factoring is that the company selling its receivables immediately receives cash for operating and other needs. Also, depending on the factoring agreement, some of the risk of uncollectible accounts is shifted to the factor.

Regardless of how careful a company is in granting credit, some credit sales will be uncollectible. The operating expense recorded from uncollectible receivables is called **bad debt expense**, *uncollectible accounts expense*, or *doubtful accounts expense.*

There is no general rule for when an account becomes uncollectible. Some indications that an account may be uncollectible include the following:

- The receivable is past due.
- The customer does not respond to the company's attempts to collect.
- The customer files for bankruptcy.
- The customer closes its business.
- The company cannot locate the customer.

If a customer doesn't pay, a company may turn the account over to a collection agency. After the collection agency attempts to collect payment, any remaining balance in the account is considered worthless.

Adams, Stevens & Bradley, Ltd. is a collection agency that operates on a contingency basis. That is, its fees are based on what it collects.

The two methods of accounting for uncollectible receivables are as follows:

- The **direct write-off method** records bad debt expense only when an account is determined to be worthless.
- The **allowance method** records bad debt expense by estimating uncollectible accounts at the end of the accounting period.

The direct write-off method is often used by small companies and companies with few receivables.[1] Generally accepted accounting principles (GAAP), however, require companies with a large amount of receivables to use the allowance method. As a result, most well-known companies such as General Electric, Pepsi, Intel, and FedEx use the allowance method.

Direct Write-Off Method for Uncollectible Accounts

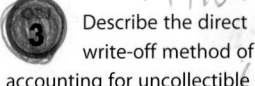

Describe the direct write-off method of accounting for uncollectible receivables.

Under the direct write-off method, Bad Debt Expense is not recorded until the customer's account is determined to be worthless. At that time, the customer's account receivable is written off.

[1] The direct write-off method is also required for federal income tax purposes.

To illustrate, assume that a $4,200 account receivable from D. L. Ross has been determined to be uncollectible. The entry to write off the account is as follows:

May	10	Bad Debt Expense		4,200	
		Accounts Receivable—D. L. Ross			4,200

An account receivable that has been written off may be collected later. In such cases, the account is reinstated by an entry that reverses the write-off entry. The cash received in payment is then recorded as a receipt on account.

To illustrate, assume that the D. L. Ross account of $4,200 written off on May 10 is later collected on November 21. The reinstatement and receipt of cash is recorded as follows:

Nov.	21	Accounts Receivable—D. L. Ross		4,200	
		Bad Debt Expense			4,200
	21	Cash		4,200	
		Accounts Receivable—D. L. Ross			4,200

The direct write-off method is used by businesses that sell most of their goods or services for cash or through the acceptance of **MasterCard** or **VISA**, which are recorded as cash sales. In such cases, receivables are a small part of the current assets and any bad debt expense is small. Examples of such businesses are a restaurant, a convenience store, and a small retail store.

Example Exercise 9-1 Direct Write-Off Method OBJ 3

Journalize the following transactions, using the direct write-off method of accounting for uncollectible receivables:

July 9. Received $1,200 from Jay Burke and wrote off the remainder owed of $3,900 as uncollectible.
Oct. 11. Reinstated the account of Jay Burke and received $3,900 cash in full payment.

Follow My Example 9-1

July 9	Cash	1,200	
	Bad Debt Expense	3,900	
	Accounts Receivable—Jay Burke		5,100
Oct. 11	Accounts Receivable—Jay Burke	3,900	
	Bad Debt Expense		3,900
11	Cash	3,900	
	Accounts Receivable—Jay Burke		3,900

Practice Exercises: PE 9-1A, PE 9-1B

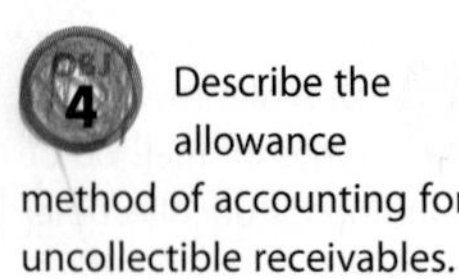

Describe the allowance method of accounting for uncollectible receivables.

Allowance Method for Uncollectible Accounts

The allowance method estimates the uncollectible accounts receivable at the end of the accounting period. Based on this estimate, Bad Debt Expense is recorded by an adjusting entry.

To illustrate, assume that **ExTone Company** began operations August 1. As of the end of its accounting period on December 31, 2015, ExTone has an accounts receivable balance of $200,000. This balance includes some past due accounts. Based on industry averages, ExTone estimates that $30,000 of the December 31 accounts receivable will be uncollectible. However, on December 31, ExTone doesn't know which customer accounts will be uncollectible. Thus, specific customer accounts cannot be decreased or credited. Instead, a contra asset account, **Allowance for Doubtful Accounts**, is credited for the estimated bad debts.

Using the $30,000 estimate, the following adjusting entry is made on December 31:

2015 Dec.	31	Bad Debt Expense		30,000	
		Allowance for Doubtful Accounts			30,000
		Uncollectible accounts estimate.			

The preceding adjusting entry affects the income statement and balance sheet. On the income statement, the $30,000 of Bad Debt Expense will be matched against the related revenues of the period. On the balance sheet, the value of the receivables is reduced to the amount that is expected to be collected or realized. This amount, $170,000 ($200,000 – $30,000), is called the **net realizable value** of the receivables.

Note:
The adjusting entry reduces receivables to their net realizable value and matches the uncollectible expense with revenues.

After the preceding adjusting entry is recorded, Accounts Receivable still has a debit balance of $200,000. This balance is the total amount owed by customers on account on December 31 as supported by the accounts receivable subsidiary ledger. The accounts receivable contra account, Allowance for Doubtful Accounts, has a credit balance of $30,000.

Integrity, Objectivity, and Ethics in Business

SELLER BEWARE

A company in financial distress will still try to purchase goods and services on account. In these cases, rather than "buyer beware," it is more like "seller beware." Sellers must be careful in advancing credit to such companies because trade creditors have low priority for cash payments in the event of bankruptcy. To help suppliers, third-party services specialize in evaluating court actions and payment decisions of financially distressed companies.

Write-Offs to the Allowance Account

When a customer's account is identified as uncollectible, it is written off against the allowance account. This requires the company to remove the specific accounts receivable and an equal amount from the allowance account.

To illustrate, on January 21, 2016, John Parker's account of $6,000 with **ExTone Company** is written off as follows:

2016 Jan.	21	Allowance for Doubtful Accounts		6,000	
		Accounts Receivable—John Parker			6,000

At the end of a period, Allowance for Doubtful Accounts will normally have a balance. This is because Allowance for Doubtful Accounts is based on an estimate. As a result, the total write-offs to the allowance account during the period will rarely equal the balance of the account at the beginning of the period. The allowance account will have a credit balance at the end of the period if the write-offs during the period are less than the beginning balance. It will have a debit balance if the write-offs exceed the beginning balance.

Exhibit 1 illustrates the allowance method where the adjusting entry increases the Allowance for Doubtful Accounts (fills the bucket) while writing off accounts decreases the Allowance for Doubtful Accounts (empties the bucket).

EXHIBIT 1 **The Allowance Method**

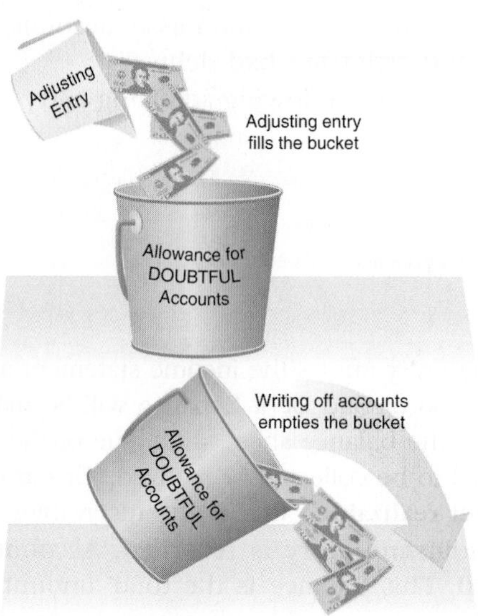

To illustrate, assume that during 2016 **ExTone Company** writes off $26,750 of uncollectible accounts, including the $6,000 account of John Parker recorded on January 21. Allowance for Doubtful Accounts will have a credit balance of $3,250 ($30,000 – $26,750), computed as follows:

ALLOWANCE FOR DOUBTFUL ACCOUNTS

				Jan. 1	Balance	30,000
Total accounts	Jan.	21	6,000			
written off $26,750	Feb.	2	3,900			
	⋮		⋮			
				Dec. 31	Unadjusted balance	3,250

If ExTone had written off $32,100 in accounts receivable during 2016, Allowance for Doubtful Accounts would have a debit balance of $2,100, computed as follows:

ALLOWANCE FOR DOUBTFUL ACCOUNTS

				Jan. 1	Balance	30,000
Total accounts	Jan.	21	6,000			
written off $32,100	Feb.	2	3,900			
	⋮		⋮			
Dec. 31	Unadjusted balance		2,100			

The allowance account balances (credit balance of $3,250 and debit balance of $2,100) in the preceding illustrations are *before* the end-of-period adjusting entry. After the end-of-period adjusting entry is recorded, Allowance for Doubtful Accounts should always have a credit balance.

An account receivable that has been written off against the allowance account may be collected later. Like the direct write-off method, the account is reinstated by an entry that reverses the write-off entry. The cash received in payment is then recorded as a receipt on account.

To illustrate, assume that Nancy Smith's account of $5,000, which was written off on April 2, is collected later on June 10. **ExTone Company** records the reinstatement and the collection as follows:

June	10	Accounts Receivable—Nancy Smith		5,000	
		Allowance for Doubtful Accounts			5,000
	10	Cash		5,000	
		Accounts Receivable—Nancy Smith			5,000

Example Exercise 9-2 Allowance Method

Journalize the following transactions, using the allowance method of accounting for uncollectible receivables:

July 9. Received $1,200 from Jay Burke and wrote off the remainder owed of $3,900 as uncollectible.
Oct. 11. Reinstated the account of Jay Burke and received $3,900 cash in full payment.

Follow My Example 9-2

July 9	Cash	1,200	
	Allowance for Doubtful Accounts	3,900	
	Accounts Receivable—Jay Burke		5,100
Oct. 11	Accounts Receivable—Jay Burke	3,900	
	Allowance for Doubtful Accounts		3,900
11	Cash	3,900	
	Accounts Receivable—Jay Burke		3,900

Practice Exercises: PE 9-2A, PE 9-2B

Estimating Uncollectibles

The allowance method requires an estimate of uncollectible accounts at the end of the period. This estimate is normally based on past experience, industry averages, and forecasts of the future.

The two methods used to estimate uncollectible accounts are as follows:

- Percent of sales method.
- Analysis of receivables method.

Percent of Sales Method Since accounts receivable are created by credit sales, uncollectible accounts can be estimated as a percent of credit sales. If the portion of credit sales to sales is relatively constant, the percent may be applied to total sales.

Business  Connection

ALLOWANCE PERCENTAGES ACROSS COMPANIES

The percent of the allowance for doubtful accounts to total accounts receivable will vary across companies and industries. For example, the following percentages were computed from recent annual reports:

Company	Industry	Percent of Allowance for Doubtful Accounts to Total Accounts Receivable
Apple Inc.	Computer and technology products	1.0%
Boeing	Aerospace and airplanes	1.0
Delta Air Lines	Transportation services	2.1
HCA Inc.	Health services	50.9
Sears	Retail	3.9

HCA's higher percentage of allowance for doubtful accounts to total accounts receivable is due in part because Medicare reimbursements are often less than the amounts billed patients.

To illustrate, assume the following data for **ExTone Company** on December 31, 2016, before any adjustments:

Balance of Accounts Receivable	$ 240,000
Balance of Allowance for Doubtful Accounts	3,250 (Cr.)
Total credit sales	3,000,000
Bad debt as a percent of credit sales	¾%

Bad Debt Expense of $22,500 is estimated as follows:

Bad Debt Expense = Credit Sales × Bad Debt as a Percent of Credit Sales
Bad Debt Expense = $3,000,000 × ¾% = $22,500

The adjusting entry for uncollectible accounts on December 31, 2016, is as follows:

Dec.	31	Bad Debt Expense	22,500	
		Allowance for Doubtful Accounts		22,500
		Uncollectible accounts estimate ($3,000,000 × ¾% = $22,500).		

After the adjusting entry is posted to the ledger, Bad Debt Expense will have an adjusted balance of $22,500. Allowance for Doubtful Accounts will have an adjusted balance of $25,750 ($3,250 + $22,500). Both T accounts follow:

BAD DEBT EXPENSE

Dec. 31	Adjusting entry	22,500	
Dec. 31	Adjusted balance	22,500	

ALLOWANCE FOR DOUBTFUL ACCOUNTS

			Jan. 1	Balance	30,000
Total accounts written off $26,750	Jan. 21	6,000			
	Feb. 2	3,900			
	⋮	⋮			
			Dec. 31	Unadjusted balance	3,250
			Dec. 31	Adjusting entry	22,500
			Dec. 31	Adjusted balance	25,750

Under the percent of sales method, the amount of the adjusting entry is the amount estimated for Bad Debt Expense. This estimate is credited to whatever the unadjusted balance is for Allowance for Doubtful Accounts.

Note:
The estimate based on sales is added to any balance in Allowance for Doubtful Accounts.

To illustrate, assume that in the preceding example the unadjusted balance of Allowance for Doubtful Accounts on December 31, 2016, had been a $2,100 debit balance instead of a $3,250 credit balance. The adjustment would still have been $22,500. However, the December 31, 2016, ending adjusted balance of Allowance for Doubtful Accounts would have been $20,400 ($22,500 − $2,100).

Example Exercise 9-3 Percent of Sales Method

OBJ 4

At the end of the current year, Accounts Receivable has a balance of $800,000; Allowance for Doubtful Accounts has a credit balance of $7,500; and sales for the year total $3,500,000. Bad debt expense is estimated at ½ of 1% of sales.

Determine (a) the amount of the adjusting entry for uncollectible accounts; (b) the adjusted balances of Accounts Receivable, Allowance for Doubtful Accounts, and Bad Debt Expense; and (c) the net realizable value of accounts receivable.

Follow My Example 9-3

Dynamic Exhibit

a. $17,500 ($3,500,000 × 0.005)

	Adjusted Balance
b. Accounts Receivable	$800,000
Allowance for Doubtful Accounts ($7,500 + $17,500)	25,000
Bad Debt Expense	17,500

c. $775,000 ($800,000 − $25,000)

Practice Exercises: PE 9-3A, PE 9-3B

Analysis of Receivables Method The analysis of receivables method is based on the assumption that the longer an account receivable is outstanding, the less likely that it will be collected. The analysis of receivables method is applied as follows:

- Step 1. The due date of each account receivable is determined.
- Step 2. The number of days each account is past due is determined. This is the number of days between the due date of the account and the date of the analysis.
- Step 3. Each account is placed in an aged class according to its days past due. Typical aged classes include the following:
  Not past due
  1–30 days past due
  31–60 days past due
  61–90 days past due
  91–180 days past due
  181–365 days past due
  Over 365 days past due
- Step 4. The totals for each aged class are determined.
- Step 5. The total for each aged class is multiplied by an estimated percentage of uncollectible accounts for that class.
- Step 6. The estimated total of uncollectible accounts is determined as the sum of the uncollectible accounts for each aged class.

The preceding steps are summarized in an aging schedule, and this overall process is called **aging the receivables**.

To illustrate, assume that **ExTone Company** uses the analysis of receivables method instead of the percent of sales method. ExTone prepared an aging schedule for its accounts receivable of $240,000 as of December 31, 2016, as shown in Exhibit 2.

EXHIBIT 2 **Aging of Receivables Schedule, December 31, 2016**

		A	B	C	D	E	F	G	H	I
	1			Not	Days Past Due					
	2			Past						Over
Steps 1–3	3	Customer	Balance	Due	1–30	31–60	61–90	91–180	181–365	365
	4	Ashby & Co.	1,500			1,500				
	5	B. T. Barr	6,100					3,500	2,600	
	6	Brock Co.	4,700	4,700						
	21									
	22	Saxon Woods Co.	600					600		
Step 4 →	23	Total	240,000	125,000	64,000	13,100	8,900	5,000	10,000	14,000
Step 5 →	24	Percent uncollectible		2%	5%	10%	20%	30%	50%	80%
Step 6 →	25	Estimate of uncollectible accounts	26,490	2,500	3,200	1,310	1,780	1,500	5,000	11,200

Assume that ExTone sold merchandise to Saxon Woods Co. on August 29 with terms 2/10, n/30. Thus, the due date (Step 1) of Saxon Woods' account is September 28, computed as follows:

Credit terms, net	30 days
Less: Aug. 29 to Aug. 31	2 days
Days in September	28 days

As of December 31, Saxon Woods' account is 94 days past due (Step 2), computed as follows:

Number of days past due in September	2 days (30 – 28)
Number of days past due in October	31 days
Number of days past due in November	30 days
Number of days past due in December	31 days
Total number of days past due	94 days

Exhibit 2 shows that the $600 account receivable for Saxon Woods Co. was placed in the 91–180 days past due class (Step 3).

The total for each of the aged classes is determined (Step 4). Exhibit 2 shows that $125,000 of the accounts receivable are not past due, while $64,000 are 1–30 days past due. ExTone applies a different estimated percentage of uncollectible accounts to the totals of each of the aged classes (Step 5). As shown in Exhibit 2, the percent is 2% for accounts not past due, while the percent is 80% for accounts over 365 days past due.

The sum of the estimated uncollectible accounts for each aged class (Step 6) is the estimated uncollectible accounts on December 31, 2016. This is the desired adjusted balance for Allowance for Doubtful Accounts. For ExTone, this amount is $26,490, as shown in Exhibit 2.

Note:
The estimate based on receivables is compared to the balance in the allowance account to determine the amount of the adjusting entry.

Comparing the estimate of $26,490 with the unadjusted balance of the allowance account determines the amount of the adjustment for Bad Debt Expense. For ExTone, the unadjusted balance of the allowance account is a credit balance of $3,250. The amount to be added to this balance is therefore $23,240 ($26,490 – $3,250). The adjusting entry is as follows:

Dec.	31	Bad Debt Expense	23,240	
		Allowance for Doubtful Accounts		23,240
		Uncollectible accounts estimate ($26,490 – $3,250).		

After the preceding adjusting entry is posted to the ledger, Bad Debt Expense will have an adjusted balance of $23,240. Allowance for Doubtful Accounts will have an adjusted balance of $26,490, and the net realizable value of the receivables is $213,510 ($240,000 – $26,490). Both T accounts follow:

BAD DEBT EXPENSE

Dec. 31	Adjusting entry	23,240			
Dec. 31	Adjusted balance	23,240			

ALLOWANCE FOR DOUBTFUL ACCOUNTS

			Dec. 31	Unadjusted balance	3,250
			Dec. 31	Adjusting entry	23,240
			Dec. 31	Adjusted balance	26,490

Under the analysis of receivables method, the amount of the adjusting entry is the amount that will yield an adjusted balance for Allowance for Doubtful Accounts equal to that estimated by the aging schedule.

To illustrate, if the unadjusted balance of the allowance account had been a debit balance of $2,100, the amount of the adjustment would have been $28,590 ($26,490 + $2,100). In this case, Bad Debt Expense would have an adjusted balance of $28,590. However, the adjusted balance of Allowance for Doubtful Accounts would still have been $26,490. After the adjusting entry is posted, both T accounts follow:

BAD DEBT EXPENSE

Dec. 31	Adjusting entry	28,590			
Dec. 31	Adjusted balance	28,590			

ALLOWANCE FOR DOUBTFUL ACCOUNTS

Dec. 31	Unadjusted balance	2,100			
			Dec. 31	Adjusting entry	28,590
			Dec. 31	Adjusted balance	26,490

Example Exercise 9-4 Analysis of Receivables Method

OBJ 4

At the end of the current year, Accounts Receivable has a balance of $800,000; Allowance for Doubtful Accounts has a credit balance of $7,500; and sales for the year total $3,500,000. Using the aging method, the balance of Allowance for Doubtful Accounts is estimated as $30,000.

Determine (a) the amount of the adjusting entry for uncollectible accounts; (b) the adjusted balances of Accounts Receivable, Allowance for Doubtful Accounts, and Bad Debt Expense; and (c) the net realizable value of accounts receivable.

Follow My Example 9-4

a. $22,500 ($30,000 – $7,500)

	Adjusted Balance
b. Accounts Receivable	$800,000
Allowance for Doubtful Accounts......	30,000
Bad Debt Expense......	22,500

c. $770,000 ($800,000 – $30,000)

Practice Exercises: PE 9-4A, PE 9-4B

Comparing Estimation Methods Both the percent of sales and analysis of receivables methods estimate uncollectible accounts. However, each method has a slightly different focus and financial statement emphasis.

Under the percent of sales method, Bad Debt Expense is the focus of the estimation process. The percent of sales method places more emphasis on matching revenues and expenses and, thus, emphasizes the income statement. That is, the amount of the adjusting entry is based on the estimate of Bad Debt Expense for the period. Allowance for Doubtful Accounts is then credited for this amount.

Under the analysis of receivables method, Allowance for Doubtful Accounts is the focus of the estimation process. The analysis of receivables method places more emphasis on the net realizable value of the receivables and, thus, emphasizes the balance sheet. That is, the amount of the adjusting entry is the amount that will yield an adjusted balance for Allowance for Doubtful Accounts equal to that estimated by the aging schedule. Bad Debt Expense is then debited for this amount.

Exhibit 3 summarizes these differences between the percent of sales and the analysis of receivables methods. Exhibit 3 also shows the results of the **ExTone Company** illustration for the percent of sales and analysis of receivables methods. The amounts shown in Exhibit 3 assume an unadjusted credit balance of $3,250 for Allowance for

EXHIBIT 3

Difference Between Estimation Methods

PERCENT OF SALES METHOD

Estimate emphasizes income statement (Bad Debt Expense adjustment)

Bad Debt Expense		Allowance for Doubtful Accounts	
Dec. 31 Adj. entry 22,500			Dec. 31 Unadj. bal. 3,250
			Dec. 31 Adj. entry 22,500
			Dec. 31 Adj. bal. 25,750

Allowance for Doubtful Accounts balance derived from Bad Debts Expense estimate

ANALYSIS OF RECEIVABLES METHOD

Estimate emphasizes balance sheet (Allowance for Doubtful Accounts balance)

Bad Debt Expense		Allowance for Doubtful Accounts	
Dec. 31 Adj. entry 23,240			Dec. 31 Unadj. bal. 3,250
			Dec. 31 Adj. entry 23,240
			Dec. 31 Adj. bal. 26,490

Bad Debt Expense adjustment (balance) derived from Allowance for Doubtful Accounts estimate

Doubtful Accounts. While the methods normally yield different amounts for any one period, over several periods the amounts should be similar.

OBJ 5 Compare the direct write-off and allowance methods of accounting for uncollectible accounts.

Comparing Direct Write-Off and Allowance Methods

Journal entries for the direct write-off and allowance methods are illustrated and compared in this section. As a basis for illustration, the following transactions, taken from the records of Hobbs Company for the year ending December 31, 2015, are used:

Mar. 1. Wrote off account of C. York, $3,650.

Apr. 12. Received $2,250 as partial payment on the $5,500 account of Cary Bradshaw. Wrote off the remaining balance as uncollectible.

June 22. Received the $3,650 from C. York, which had been written off on March 1. Reinstated the account and recorded the cash receipt.

Sept. 7. Wrote off the following accounts as uncollectible (record as one journal entry):

Jason Bigg	$1,100	Stanford Noonan	$1,360
Steve Bradey	2,220	Aiden Wyman	990
Samantha Neeley	775		

Dec. 31. Hobbs Company uses the percent of credit sales method of estimating uncollectible expenses. Based on past history and industry averages, 1.25% of credit sales are expected to be uncollectible. Hobbs recorded $3,400,000 of credit sales during 2015.

Exhibit 4 illustrates the journal entries for Hobbs using the direct write-off and allowance methods. Using the direct write-off method, there is no adjusting entry on December 31 for uncollectible accounts. In contrast, the allowance method records an adjusting entry for estimated uncollectible accounts of $42,500.

EXHIBIT 4 Comparing Direct Write-Off and Allowance Methods

		Direct Write-Off Method			Allowance Method		
2015 Mar.	1	Bad Debt Expense	3,650		Allowance for Doubtful Accounts	3,650	
		Accounts Receivable—C. York		3,650	Accounts Receivable—C. York		3,650
Apr.	12	Cash	2,250		Cash	2,250	
		Bad Debt Expense	3,250		Allowance for Doubtful Accounts	3,250	
		Accounts Receivable—Cary Bradshaw		5,500	Accounts Receivable—Cary Bradshaw		5,500
June	22	Accounts Receivable—C. York	3,650		Accounts Receivable—C. York	3,650	
		Bad Debt Expense		3,650	Allowance for Doubtful Accounts		3,650
	22	Cash	3,650		Cash	3,650	
		Accounts Receivable—C. York		3,650	Accounts Receivable—C. York		3,650
Sept.	7	Bad Debt Expense	6,445		Allowance for Doubtful Accounts	6,445	
		Accounts Receivable—Jason Bigg		1,100	Accounts Receivable—Jason Bigg		1,100
		Accounts Receivable—Steve Bradey		2,220	Accounts Receivable—Steve Bradey		2,220
		Accounts Receivable—Samantha Neeley		775	Accounts Receivable—Samantha Neeley		775
		Accounts Receivable—Stanford Noonan		1,360	Accounts Receivable—Stanford Noonan		1,360
		Accounts Receivable—Aiden Wyman		990	Accounts Receivable—Aiden Wyman		990
Dec.	31	No Entry			Bad Debt Expense	42,500	
					Allowance for Doubtful Accounts		42,500
					Uncollectible accounts estimate ($3,400,000 × 0.0125 = $42,500).		

The primary differences between the direct write-off and allowance methods are summarized in Exhibit 5.

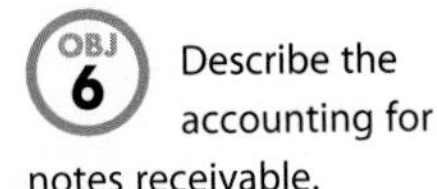

Direct Write-Off and Allowance Methods

	Direct Write-Off Method	**Allowance Method**
Bad debt expense is recorded	When the specific customer accounts are determined to be uncollectible.	Using estimate based on (1) a percent of sales or (2) an analysis of receivables.
Allowance account	No allowance account is used.	The allowance account is used.
Primary users	Small companies and companies with few receivables.	Large companies and those with a large amount of receivables.

Notes Receivable

OBJ 6 Describe the accounting for notes receivable.

A note has some advantages over an account receivable. By signing a note, the debtor recognizes the debt and agrees to pay it according to its terms. Thus, a note is a stronger legal claim.

Characteristics of Notes Receivable

A promissory note is a written promise to pay the face amount, usually with interest, on demand or at a date in the future.[2] Characteristics of a promissory note are as follows:

1. The *maker* is the party making the promise to pay.
2. The *payee* is the party to whom the note is payable.
3. The *face amount* is the amount for which the note is written on its face.
4. The *issuance date* is the date a note is issued.
5. The *due date* or *maturity date* is the date the note is to be paid.
6. The *term* of a note is the amount of time between the issuance and due dates.
7. The *interest rate* is that rate of interest that must be paid on the face amount for the term of the note.

Exhibit 6 illustrates a promissory note. The maker of the note is Selig Company, and the payee is Pearland Company. The face value of the note is $2,000, the interest rate is 10%, and the issuance date is March 16, 2015. The term of the note is 90 days, which results in a due date of June 14, 2015, computed as follows and shown in Exhibit 7:

Days in March	31 days
Minus issuance date of note	16
Days remaining in March	15 days
Add days in April	30
Add days in May	31
Add days in June (due date of June 14)	14
Term of note	90 days

The interest on a note is computed as follows:

Interest = Face Amount × Interest Rate × (Term ÷ 360 days)

The interest rate is stated on an annual (yearly) basis, while the term is expressed as days. Thus, the interest on the note in Exhibit 6 is computed as follows:

Interest = $2,000 × 10% × (90 ÷ 360) = $50

To simplify, 360 days per year will be used. In practice, companies such as banks and mortgage companies use the exact number of days in a year, 365.

[2] You may see references to non-interest-bearing notes. Such notes are not widely used and carry an assumed or implicit interest rate.

EXHIBIT 6 **Promissory Note**

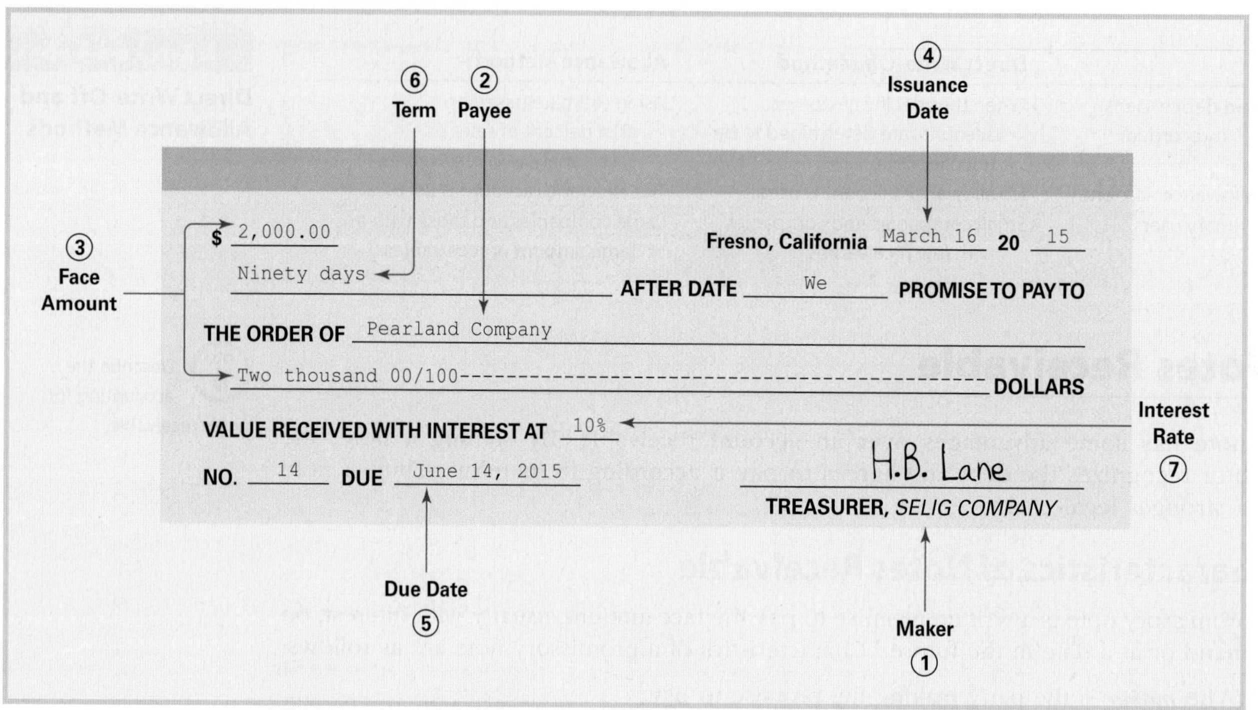

EXHIBIT 7 **Determining Due Date of Promissory Note**

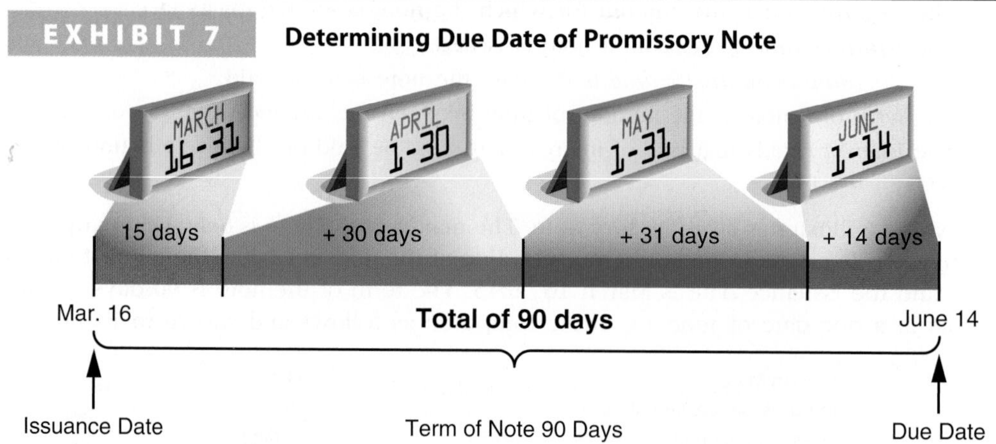

The **maturity value** is the amount that must be paid at the due date of the note, which is the sum of the face amount and the interest. The maturity value of the note in Exhibit 6 is $2,050 ($2,000 + $50).

Accounting for Notes Receivable

A promissory note may be received by a company from a customer to replace an account receivable. In such cases, the promissory note is recorded as a note receivable.[3]

To illustrate, assume that a company accepts a 30-day, 12% note dated November 21, 2016, in settlement of the account of W. A. Bunn Co., which is past due and has a balance of $6,000. The company records the receipt of the note as follows:

	Nov.	21	Notes Receivable—W. A. Bunn Co.		6,000	
			Accounts Receivable—W. A. Bunn Co.			6,000

[3] The accounting for notes payable is described and illustrated in Chapter 14.

At the due date, the company records the receipt of $6,060 ($6,000 face amount plus $60 interest) as follows:

Dec.	21	Cash	6,060	
		Notes Receivable—W. A. Bunn Co.		6,000
		Interest Revenue		60
		[$6,060 = $6,000 + ($6,000 × 12% × 30 ÷ 360)].		

If the maker of a note fails to pay the note on the due date, the note is a **dishonored note receivable**. A company that holds a dishonored note transfers the face amount of the note plus any interest due back to an accounts receivable account. For example, assume that the $6,000, 30-day, 12% note received from W. A. Bunn Co. and recorded on November 21 is dishonored. The company holding the note transfers the note and interest back to the customer's account as follows:

Dec.	21	Accounts Receivable—W. A. Bunn Co.	6,060	
		Notes Receivable—W. A. Bunn Co.		6,000
		Interest Revenue		60

The company has earned the interest of $60, even though the note is dishonored. If the account receivable is uncollectible, the company will write off $6,060 against Allowance for Doubtful Accounts.

A company receiving a note should record an adjusting entry for any accrued interest at the end of the period. For example, assume that Crawford Company issues a $4,000, 90-day, 12% note dated December 1, 2016, to settle its account receivable. If the accounting period ends on December 31, the company receiving the note would record the following entries:

2016 Dec.	1	Notes Receivable—Crawford Company	4,000	
		Accounts Receivable—Crawford Company		4,000
	31	Interest Receivable	40	
		Interest Revenue		40
		Accrued interest		
		($4,000 × 12% × 30 ÷ 360).		
2017 Mar.	1	Cash	4,120	
		Notes Receivable—Crawford Company		4,000
		Interest Receivable		40
		Interest Revenue		80
		Total interest of $120		
		($4,000 × 12% × 90 ÷ 360).		

The interest revenue account is closed at the end of each accounting period. The amount of interest revenue is normally reported in the Other Income section of the income statement.

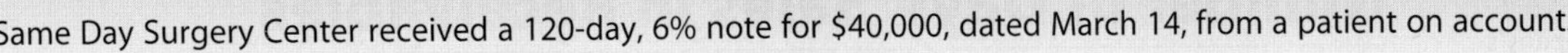

Example Exercise 9-5 Note Receivable OBJ 6

Same Day Surgery Center received a 120-day, 6% note for $40,000, dated March 14, from a patient on account.

a. Determine the due date of the note.

b. Determine the maturity value of the note.

c. Journalize the entry to record the receipt of the payment of the note at maturity.

(Continued)

Follow My Example 9-5

a. The due date of the note is July 12, determined as follows:

March		17 days (31 – 14)
April		30 days
May		31 days
June		30 days
July		12 days
	Total	120 days

b. $40,800 [$40,000 + ($40,000 × 6% × 120 ÷ 360)]

c. July 12	Cash	40,800	
	Notes Receivable		40,000
	Interest Revenue		800

Practice Exercises: PE 9-5A, PE 9-5B

OBJ 7 Describe the reporting of receivables on the balance sheet.

Reporting Receivables on the Balance Sheet

All receivables that are expected to be realized in cash within a year are reported in the Current assets section of the balance sheet. Current assets are normally reported in the order of their liquidity, beginning with cash and cash equivalents.

The balance sheet presentation for receivables for **Mornin' Joe** follows:

Mornin' Joe Balance Sheet December 31, 2016		
Assets		
Current assets:		
Cash and cash equivalents		$235,000
Trading investments (at cost)	$420,000	
Plus valuation allowance for trading investments	45,000	465,000
Accounts receivable	$305,000	
Less allowance for doubtful accounts	12,300	292,700

In Mornin' Joe's financial statements, the allowance for doubtful accounts is subtracted from accounts receivable. Some companies report receivables at their net realizable value with a note showing the amount of the allowance.

Other disclosures related to receivables are reported either on the face of the financial statements or in the financial statement notes. Such disclosures include the market (fair) value of the receivables. In addition, if unusual credit risks exist within the receivables, the nature of the risks are disclosed. For example, if the majority of the receivables are due from one customer or are due from customers located in one area of the country or one industry, these facts are disclosed.[4]

OBJ 8 Describe and illustrate the use of accounts receivable turnover and number of days' sales in receivables to evaluate a company's efficiency in collecting its receivables.

F·A·I

Financial Analysis and Interpretation: Accounts Receivable Turnover and Number of Days' Sales in Receivables

Two financial measures that are especially useful in evaluating efficiency in collecting receivables are the following:

- the accounts receivable turnover
- the number of days' sales in receivables

[4] *FASB Accounting Standards Codification*, Section 210-10-50.

The **accounts receivable turnover** measures how frequently during the year the accounts receivable are being converted to cash. For example, with credit terms of n/30, the accounts receivable should turn over about 12 times per year.

The accounts receivable turnover is computed as follows:[5]

$$\text{Accounts Receivable Turnover} = \frac{\text{Sales}}{\text{Average Accounts Receivable}}$$

The average accounts receivable can be determined by using monthly data or by simply adding the beginning and ending accounts receivable balances and dividing by two. For example, using the following financial data (in millions) for FedEx, the Year 2 and Year 1 accounts receivable turnover is 8.2 in Year 2 and 8.0 in Year 1, computed as follows:

	Year 2	Year 1
Sales	$42,680	$39,304
Accounts receivable:		
Beginning of year	5,191	4,692
End of year	5,237	5,191
Average accounts receivable:*		
($5,191 + $5,237) ÷ 2	5,214.0	
($4,692 + $5,191) ÷ 2		4,941.5
Accounts receivable turnover:*		
$42,680 ÷ $5,214	8.2	
$39,304 ÷ $4,941.5		8.0

* Rounded to one decimal place.

The **number of days' sales in receivables** is an estimate of the length of time the accounts receivable have been outstanding. With credit terms of n/30, the number of days' sales in receivables should be about 30 days. It is computed as follows:

$$\text{Number of Days' Sales in Receivables} = \frac{\text{Average Accounts Receivable}}{\text{Average Daily Sales}}$$

Average daily sales are determined by dividing sales by 365 days.[6] For example, using the preceding data for FedEx, the number of days' sales in receivables is 44.6 and 45.9 for Year 2 and Year 1, computed as follows:

	Year 2	Year 1
Average daily sales:*		
$42,680 ÷ 365	116.9	
$39,304 ÷ 365		107.7
Number of days' sales in receivables:*		
$5,214.0 ÷ 116.9	44.6	
$4,941.5 ÷ 107.7		45.9

* Rounded to one decimal place.

The number of days' sales in receivables confirms that FedEx's efficiency in collecting accounts receivable increased from Year 1 to Year 2. Generally, the efficiency in collecting accounts receivable has improved when the accounts receivable turnover increases or the number of days' sales in receivables decreases.

Example Exercise 9-6 Accounts Receivable Turnover and Number of Days' Sales in Receivables

OBJ 8

Financial statement data for years ending December 31 for Osterman Company follows:

	2016	2015
Sales	$4,284,000	$3,040,000
Accounts receivable:		
Beginning of year	550,000	400,000
End of year	640,000	550,000

(Continued)

[5] If known, credit sales can be used in the numerator. However, because credit sales are not normally disclosed to external users, most analysts use sales in the numerator.

[6] We use 365 days for all computations involving real world companies and data. We do this to highlight differences among companies and because computations using real world data normally require rounding.

Follow My Example 9-6

a. Determine the accounts receivable turnover for 2016 and 2015.

b. Determine the number of days' sales in receivables for 2016 and 2015. Use 365 days and round to one decimal place.

c. Does the change in accounts receivable turnover and the number of days' sales in receivable from 2015 to 2016 indicate a favorable or an unfavorable trend?

a. Accounts receivable turnover:

	2016	2015
Average accounts receivable:		
($550,000 + $640,000) ÷ 2	$595,000	
($400,000 + $550,000) ÷ 2		$475,000
Accounts receivable turnover:		
$4,284,000 ÷ $595,000	7.2	
$3,040,000 ÷ $475,000		6.4

b. Number of days' sales in receivables:

	2016	2015
Average daily sales:		
$4,284,000 ÷ 365 days	$11,737.0	
$3,040,000 ÷ 365 days		$8,328.8
Number of days' sales in receivables:		
$595,000 ÷ $11,737.0	50.7 days	
$475,000 ÷ $8,328.8		57.0 days

c. The increase in the accounts receivable turnover from 6.4 to 7.2 and the decrease in the number of days' sales in receivables from 57.0 days to 50.7 days indicate favorable trends in the efficiency of collecting accounts receivable.

Practice Exercises: PE 9-6A, PE 9-6B

Business  Connection

DELTA AIR LINES

Delta Air Lines is a major air carrier that services cities throughout the United States and the world. In its operations, Delta generates accounts receivable as reported in the following note to its financial statements:

Our accounts receivable are generated largely from the sale of passenger airline tickets and cargo transportation services. The majority of these sales are processed through major credit card companies, resulting in accounts receivable. . . .

We also have receivables from the sale of mileage credits under our SkyMiles Program to participating airlines and non-airline businesses such as credit card companies, hotels, and car rental agencies. The credit risk associated with our receivables is minimal.

In a recent, balance sheet, Delta reported the following accounts receivable (in millions):

	Dec. 31, Year 2	Dec. 31, Year 1
Current Assets:		
⋮		
Accounts receivable, net of an allowance for uncollectible accounts of $36 at December 31 (Year 2) and $33 at December 31 (Year 1)	$1,693	$1,563

Source: Delta Air Lines, Inc., *Form 10-K For the Fiscal Year Ended December 31, 2012.*

At a Glance 9

Describe the common classes of receivables.

Key Points *Receivables* includes all money claims against other entities. Receivables are normally classified as accounts receivable, notes receivable, or other receivables.

Learning Outcomes	Example Exercises	Practice Exercises
• Define the term *receivables*.		
• List some common classifications of receivables.		

Describe the accounting for uncollectible receivables.

Key Points The operating expense recorded from uncollectible receivables is called *bad debt expense*. The two methods of accounting for uncollectible receivables are the direct write-off method and the allowance method.

Learning Outcomes	Example Exercises	Practice Exercises
• Describe how a company may shift the risk of uncollectible receivables to other companies.		
• List factors that indicate an account receivable is uncollectible.		
• Describe two methods of accounting for uncollectible accounts receivable.		

Describe the direct write-off method of accounting for uncollectible receivables.

Key Points Under the direct write-off method, the entry to write off an account debits Bad Debt Expense and credits Accounts Receivable. Neither an allowance account nor an adjusting entry is needed at the end of the period.

Learning Outcomes	Example Exercises	Practice Exercises
• Prepare journal entries to write off an account, using the direct write-off method.	EE9-1	PE9-1A, 9-1B
• Prepare journal entries for the reinstatement and collection of an account previously written off.	EE9-1	PE9-1A, 9-1B

Describe the allowance method of accounting for uncollectible receivables.

Key Points Under the allowance method, an adjusting entry is made for uncollectible accounts. When an account is determined to be uncollectible, it is written off against the allowance account. The allowance account is a contra asset account that normally has a credit balance after the adjusting entry has been posted.

The estimate of uncollectibles may be based on a percent of sales or an analysis of receivables. Exhibit 3 compares and contrasts these two methods.

Learning Outcomes	Example Exercises	Practice Exercises
• Prepare journal entries to write off an account, using the allowance method.	EE9-2	PE9-2A, 9-2B
• Prepare journal entries for the reinstatement and collection of an account previously written off.	EE9-2	PE9-2A, 9-2B
• Determine the adjustment, bad debt expense, and net realizable value of accounts receivable, using the percent of sales method.	EE9-3	PE9-3A, 9-3B
• Determine the adjustment, bad debt expense, and net realizable value of accounts receivable, using the analysis of receivables method.	EE9-4	PE9-4A, 9-4B

Compare the direct write-off and allowance methods of accounting for uncollectible accounts.

Key Points Exhibit 4 illustrates the differences between the direct write-off and allowance methods of accounting for uncollectible accounts.

Learning Outcomes	Example Exercises	Practice Exercises
• Describe the differences in accounting for uncollectible accounts under the direct write-off and allowance methods.		
• Record journal entries, using the direct write-off and allowance methods.		

Describe the accounting for notes receivable.

Key Points A note received to settle an account receivable is recorded as a debit to Notes Receivable and a credit to Accounts Receivable. When a note is paid at maturity, Cash is debited, Notes Receivable is credited, and Interest Revenue is credited. If the maker of a note fails to pay, the dishonored note is recorded by debiting an account receivable for the amount due from the maker of the note.

Learning Outcomes	Example Exercises	Practice Exercises
• Describe the characteristics of a note receivable.		
• Determine the due date and maturity value of a note receivable.	EE9-5	PE9-5A, 9-5B
• Prepare journal entries for the receipt of the payment of a note receivable.	EE9-5	PE9-5A, 9-5B
• Prepare a journal entry for the dishonored note receivable.		

Describe the reporting of receivables on the balance sheet.

Key Points All receivables that are expected to be realized in cash within a year are reported in the Current Assets section of the balance sheet. In addition to the allowance for doubtful accounts, additional receivable disclosures include the market (fair) value and unusual credit risks.

Learning Outcomes	Example Exercises	Practice Exercises
• Describe how receivables are reported in the Current Assets section of the balance sheet.		
• Describe the disclosures related to receivables that should be reported in the financial statements.		

Describe and illustrate the use of accounts receivable turnover and number of days' sales in receivables to evaluate a company's efficiency in collecting its receivables.

Key Points Two financial measures that are especially useful in evaluating efficiency in collecting receivables are (1) the accounts receivable turnover and (2) the number of days' sales in receivables. Generally, the efficiency in collecting accounts receivable has improved when the accounts receivable turnover increases or there is a decrease in the number of days' sales in receivables.

Learning Outcomes	Example Exercises	Practice Exercises
• Describe two measures of the efficiency of managing receivables.		
• Compute and interpret the accounts receivable turnover and the number of days' sales in receivables.	EE9-6	PE9-6A, 9-6B

Key Terms

accounts receivable (416)
accounts receivable turnover (431)
aging the receivables (423)
Allowance for Doubtful Accounts (419)
allowance method (417)
bad debt expense (417)
direct write-off method (417)
dishonored note receivable (429)
maturity value (428)
net realizable value (419)
notes receivable (416)
number of days' sales in receivables (431)
receivables (416)

Illustrative Problem

Ditzler Company, a construction supply company, uses the allowance method of accounting for uncollectible accounts receivable. Selected transactions completed by Ditzler Company are as follows:

Feb. 1. Sold merchandise on account to Ames Co., $8,000. The cost of the merchandise sold was $4,500.

Mar. 15. Accepted a 60-day, 12% note for $8,000 from Ames Co. on account.

Apr. 9. Wrote off a $2,500 account from Dorset Co. as uncollectible.

21. Loaned $7,500 cash to Jill Klein, receiving a 90-day, 14% note.

May 14. Received the interest due from Ames Co. and a new 90-day, 14% note as a renewal of the loan. (Record both the debit and the credit to the notes receivable account.)

June 13. Reinstated the account of Dorset Co., written off on April 9, and received $2,500 in full payment.

July 20. Jill Klein dishonored her note.

Aug. 12. Received from Ames Co. the amount due on its note of May 14.

19. Received from Jill Klein the amount owed on the dishonored note, plus interest for 30 days at 15%, computed on the maturity value of the note.

Dec. 16. Accepted a 60-day, 12% note for $12,000 from Global Company on account.

31. It is estimated that 3% of the credit sales of $1,375,000 for the year ended December 31 will be uncollectible.

Instructions

1. Journalize the transactions.
2. Journalize the adjusting entry to record the accrued interest on December 31 on the Global Company note.

Solution

1.

Feb.	1	Accounts Receivable—Ames Co.		8,000.00	
		Sales			8,000.00
	1	Cost of Merchandise Sold		4,500.00	
		Merchandise Inventory			4,500.00
Mar.	15	Notes Receivable—Ames Co.		8,000.00	
		Accounts Receivable—Ames Co.			8,000.00
Apr.	9	Allowance for Doubtful Accounts		2,500.00	
		Accounts Receivable—Dorset Co.			2,500.00
	21	Notes Receivable—Jill Klein		7,500.00	
		Cash			7,500.00
May	14	Notes Receivable—Ames Co.		8,000.00	
		Cash		160.00	
		Notes Receivable—Ames Co.			8,000.00
		Interest Revenue			160.00
June	13	Accounts Receivable—Dorset Co.		2,500.00	
		Allowance for Doubtful Accounts			2,500.00
	13	Cash		2,500.00	
		Accounts Receivable—Dorset Co.			2,500.00
July	20	Accounts Receivable—Jill Klein		7,762.50	
		Notes Receivable—Jill Klein			7,500.00
		Interest Revenue			262.50
Aug.	12	Cash		8,280.00	
		Notes Receivable—Ames Co.			8,000.00
		Interest Revenue			280.00
	19	Cash		7,859.53	
		Accounts Receivable—Jill Klein			7,762.50
		Interest Revenue			97.03
		($7,762.50 × 15% × 30 ÷ 360).			
Dec.	16	Notes Receivable—Global Company		12,000.00	
		Accounts Receivable—Global Company			12,000.00
	31	Bad Debt Expense		41,250.00	
		Allowance for Doubtful Accounts			41,250.00
		Uncollectible accounts estimate			
		($1,375,000 × 3%).			

2.

Dec.	31	Interest Receivable		60.00	
		Interest Revenue			60.00
		Accrued interest			
		($12,000 × 12% × 15 ÷ 360).			

Discussion Questions

1. What are the three classifications of receivables?
2. Dan's Hardware is a small hardware store in the rural township of Twin Bridges. It rarely extends credit to its customers in the form of an account receivable. The few customers who are allowed to carry accounts receivable are long-time residents of Twin Bridges with a history of doing business at Dan's Hardware. What method of accounting for uncollectible receivables should Dan's Hardware use? Why?
3. What kind of an account (asset, liability, etc.) is Allowance for Doubtful Accounts, and is its normal balance a debit or a credit?
4. After the accounts are adjusted and closed at the end of the fiscal year, Accounts Receivable has a balance of $673,400, and Allowance for Doubtful Accounts has a balance of $11,900. Describe how the accounts receivable and the allowance for doubtful accounts are reported on the balance sheet.
5. A firm has consistently adjusted its allowance account at the end of the fiscal year by adding a fixed percent of the period's sales on account. After seven years, the balance in Allowance for Doubtful Accounts has become very large in relationship to the balance in Accounts Receivable. Give two possible explanations.
6. Which of the two methods of estimating uncollectibles provides for the most accurate estimate of the current net realizable value of the receivables?
7. Neptune Company issued a note receivable to Sailfish Company. (a) Who is the payee? (b) What is the title of the account used by Sailfish Company in recording the note?
8. If a note provides for payment of principal of $85,000 and interest at the rate of 6%, will the interest amount to $5,100? Explain.
9. The maker of a $240,000, 6%, 90-day note receivable failed to pay the note on the due date of November 30. What accounts should be debited and credited by the payee to record the dishonored note receivable?
10. The note receivable dishonored in Discussion Question 9 is paid on December 30 by the maker, plus interest for 30 days at 9%. What entry should be made to record the receipt of the payment?

Practice Exercises

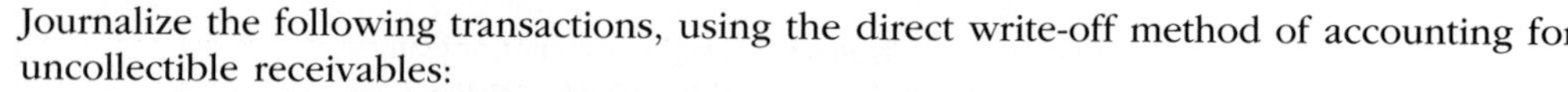

EE 9-1 *p. 418*

PE 9-1A Direct write-off method **OBJ. 3**

SHOW ME HOW

Journalize the following transactions, using the direct write-off method of accounting for uncollectible receivables:

June 2. Received $1,200 from Melissa Crone and wrote off the remainder owed of $4,000 as uncollectible.

Oct. 9. Reinstated the account of Melissa Crone and received $4,000 cash in full payment.

EE 9-1 *p. 418*

PE 9-1B Direct write-off method **OBJ. 3**

SHOW ME HOW

Journalize the following transactions, using the direct write-off method of accounting for uncollectible receivables:

Oct. 2. Received $600 from Rachel Elpel and wrote off the remainder owed of $1,350 as uncollectible.

Dec. 20. Reinstated the account of Rachel Elpel and received $1,350 cash in full payment.

EE 9-2 p. 421

PE 9-2A Allowance method **OBJ. 4**

SHOW ME HOW

Journalize the following transactions, using the allowance method of accounting for uncollectible receivables:

June 2. Received $1,200 from Melissa Crone and wrote off the remainder owed of $4,000 as uncollectible.

Oct. 9. Reinstated the account of Melissa Crone and received $4,000 cash in full payment.

EE 9-2 p. 421

PE 9-2B Allowance method **OBJ. 4**

SHOW ME HOW

Journalize the following transactions, using the allowance method of accounting for uncollectible receivables:

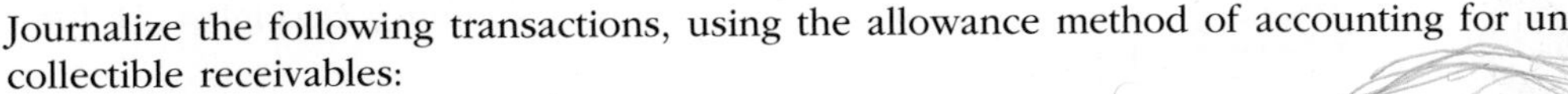

Oct. 2. Received $600 from Rachel Elpel and wrote off the remainder owed of $1,350 as uncollectible.

Dec. 20. Reinstated the account of Rachel Elpel and received $1,350 cash in full payment.

EE 9-3 p. 422

PE 9-3A Percent of sales method **OBJ. 4**

SHOW ME HOW

At the end of the current year, Accounts Receivable has a balance of $1,975,000; Allowance for Doubtful Accounts has a credit balance of $19,670; and sales for the year total $28,550,000. Bad debt expense is estimated at ¾ of 1% of sales.

Determine (a) the amount of the adjusting entry for uncollectible accounts; (b) the adjusted balances of Accounts Receivable, Allowance for Doubtful Accounts, and Bad Debt Expense; and (c) the net realizable value of accounts receivable.

EE 9-3 p. 422

PE 9-3B Percent of sales method **OBJ. 4**

SHOW ME HOW

At the end of the current year, Accounts Receivable has a balance of $3,460,000; Allowance for Doubtful Accounts has a debit balance of $12,500; and sales for the year total $46,300,000. Bad debt expense is estimated at ½ of 1% of sales.

Determine (a) the amount of the adjusting entry for uncollectible accounts; (b) the adjusted balances of Accounts Receivable, Allowance for Doubtful Accounts, and Bad Debt Expense; and (c) the net realizable value of accounts receivable.

EE 9-4 p. 425

PE 9-4A Analysis of receivables method **OBJ. 4**

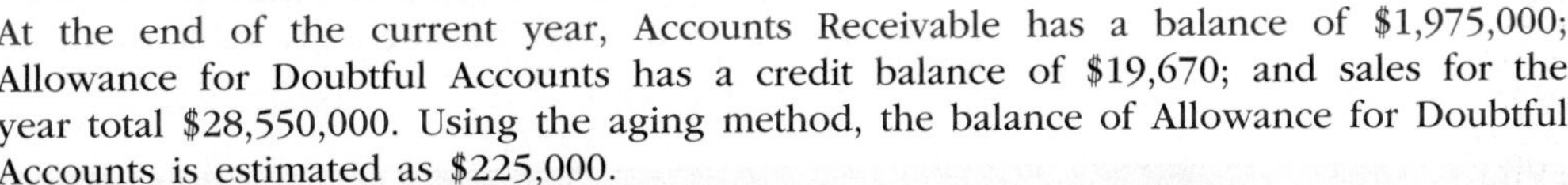

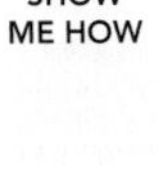
SHOW ME HOW

At the end of the current year, Accounts Receivable has a balance of $1,975,000; Allowance for Doubtful Accounts has a credit balance of $19,670; and sales for the year total $28,550,000. Using the aging method, the balance of Allowance for Doubtful Accounts is estimated as $225,000.

Determine (a) the amount of the adjusting entry for uncollectible accounts; (b) the adjusted balances of Accounts Receivable, Allowance for Doubtful Accounts, and Bad Debt Expense; and (c) the net realizable value of accounts receivable.

EE 9-4 p. 425

PE 9-4B Analysis of receivables method **OBJ. 4**

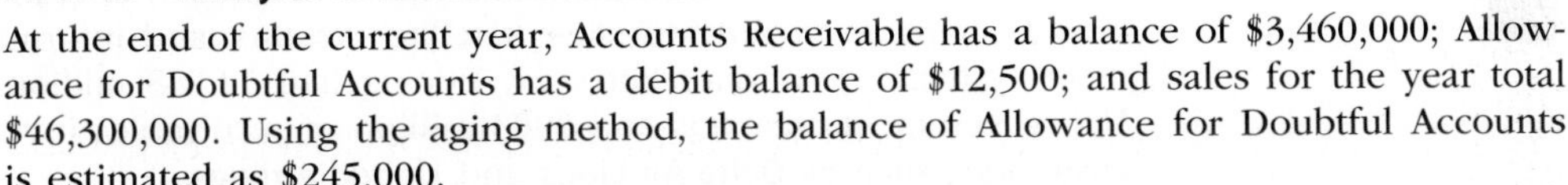

SHOW ME HOW

At the end of the current year, Accounts Receivable has a balance of $3,460,000; Allowance for Doubtful Accounts has a debit balance of $12,500; and sales for the year total $46,300,000. Using the aging method, the balance of Allowance for Doubtful Accounts is estimated as $245,000.

Determine (a) the amount of the adjusting entry for uncollectible accounts; (b) the adjusted balances of Accounts Receivable, Allowance for Doubtful Accounts, and Bad Debt Expense; and (c) the net realizable value of accounts receivable.

EE 9-5 p. 429

PE 9-5A Note receivable **OBJ. 6**

SHOW ME HOW

Guzman Company received a 60-day, 5% note for $54,000 dated July 12 from a customer on account.

a. Determine the due date of the note.
b. Determine the maturity value of the note.
c. Journalize the entry to record the receipt of the payment of the note at maturity.

EE 9-5 p. 429

PE 9-5B Note receivable

OBJ. 6

SHOW ME HOW

Prefix Supply Company received a 120-day, 8% note for $450,000, dated April 9 from a customer on account.

a. Determine the due date of the note.

b. Determine the maturity value of the note.

c. Journalize the entry to record the receipt of the payment of the note at maturity.

EE 9-6 p. 431

PE 9-6A Accounts receivable turnover and number of days' sales in receivables

OBJ. 8

SHOW ME HOW

Financial statement data for years ending December 31 for Chiro-Solutions Company follows:

	2016	2015
Sales	$2,912,000	$2,958,000
Accounts receivable:		
Beginning of year	300,000	280,000
End of year	340,000	300,000

a. Determine the accounts receivable turnover for 2016 and 2015.

b. Determine the number of days' sales in receivables for 2016 and 2015. Use 365 days and round to one decimal place.

c. Does the change in accounts receivable turnover and the number of days' sales in receivables from 2015 to 2016 indicate a favorable or an unfavorable trend?

EE 9-6 p. 431

PE 9-6B Accounts receivable turnover and number of days' sales in receivables

OBJ. 8

SHOW ME HOW

Financial statement data for years ending December 31 for Robinhood Company follows:

	2016	2015
Sales	$7,906,000	$6,726,000
Accounts receivable:		
Beginning of year	600,000	540,000
End of year	580,000	600,000

a. Determine the accounts receivable turnover for 2016 and 2015.

b. Determine the number of days' sales in receivables for 2016 and 2015. Use 365 days and round to one decimal place.

c. Does the change in accounts receivable turnover and the number of days' sales in receivables from 2015 to 2016 indicate a favorable or an unfavorable trend?

Exercises

EX 9-1 Classifications of receivables

OBJ. 1

Boeing is one of the world's major aerospace firms with operations involving commercial aircraft, military aircraft, missiles, satellite systems, and information and battle management systems. As of a recent year, Boeing had $2,788 million of receivables involving U.S. government contracts and $903 million of receivables involving commercial aircraft customers, such as Delta Air Lines and United Airlines.

Should Boeing report these receivables separately in the financial statements or combine them into one overall accounts receivable amount? Explain.

EX 9-2 Nature of uncollectible accounts **OBJ. 2**

✔ a. 17.1%

SHOW ME HOW

MGM Resorts International owns and operates hotels and casinos including the MGM Grand and the Bellagio in Las Vegas, Nevada. As of a recent year, MGM reported accounts receivable of $592,937,000 and allowance for doubtful accounts of $101,207,000 Johnson & Johnson manufactures and sells a wide range of healthcare products including Band-Aids and Tylenol. As of a recent year, Johnson & Johnson reported accounts receivable of $11,775,000,000 and allowance for doubtful accounts of $466,000,000.

a. Compute the percentage of the allowance for doubtful accounts to the accounts receivable for MGM Resorts International. Round to one decimal place.

b. Compute the percentage of the allowance for doubtful accounts to the accounts receivable for Johnson & Johnson. Round to one decimal place.

c. Discuss possible reasons for the difference in the two ratios computed in (a) and (b).

EX 9-3 Entries for uncollectible accounts, using direct write-off method **OBJ. 3**

SHOW ME HOW

Journalize the following transactions in the accounts of Midwest Medical Co., a medical equipment company that uses the direct write-off method of accounting for uncollectible receivables:

Feb. 3. Sold merchandise on account to Dr. Jill Hall, $17,340. The cost of the merchandise sold was $9,500.

Sept. 10. Received $5,000 from Dr. Jill Hall and wrote off the remainder owed on the sale of February 3 as uncollectible.

Dec. 21. Reinstated the account of Dr. Jill Hall that had been written off on September 10 and received $12,340 cash in full payment.

EX 9-4 Entries for uncollectible receivables, using allowance method **OBJ. 4**

SHOW ME HOW

Journalize the following transactions in the accounts of Dining Interiors Company, a restaurant supply company that uses the allowance method of accounting for uncollectible receivables:

Apr. 2. Sold merchandise on account to Peking Palace Co., $41,900. The cost of the merchandise sold was $24,850.

June 9. Received $10,000 from Peking Palace Co. and wrote off the remainder owed on the sale of April 2 as uncollectible.

Oct. 31. Reinstated the account of Peking Palace Co. that had been written off on June 9 and received $31,900 cash in full payment.

EX 9-5 Entries to write off accounts receivable **OBJ. 3, 4**

Creative Solutions Company, a computer consulting firm, has decided to write off the $11,750 balance of an account owed by a customer, Wil Treadwell. Journalize the entry to record the write-off, assuming that (a) the direct write-off method is used and (b) the allowance method is used.

EX 9-6 Providing for doubtful accounts **OBJ. 4**

✔ a. $115,125

✔ b. $148,000

SHOW ME HOW

At the end of the current year, the accounts receivable account has a debit balance of $1,400,000 and sales for the year total $15,350,000. Determine the amount of the adjusting entry to provide for doubtful accounts under each of the following assumptions:

a. The allowance account before adjustment has a debit balance of $23,000. Bad debt expense is estimated at ¾ of 1% of sales.

b. The allowance account before adjustment has a debit balance of $23,000. An aging of the accounts in the customer ledger indicates estimated doubtful accounts of $125,000.

c. The allowance account before adjustment has a credit balance of $14,500. Bad debt expense is estimated at ½ of 1% of sales.

d. The allowance account before adjustment has a credit balance of $14,500. An aging of the accounts in the customer ledger indicates estimated doubtful accounts of $180,000.

✔ Avalanche Auto, 84 days

EX 9-7 Number of days past due

OBJ. 4

Toot Auto Supply distributes new and used automobile parts to local dealers throughout the Midwest. Toot's credit terms are n/30. As of the end of business on October 31, the following accounts receivable were past due:

Account	Due Date	Amount
Avalanche Auto	August 8	$12,000
Bales Auto	October 11	2,400
Derby Auto Repair	June 23	3,900
Lucky's Auto Repair	September 2	6,600
Pit Stop Auto	September 19	1,100
Reliable Auto Repair	July 15	9,750
Trident Auto	August 24	1,800
Valley Repair & Tow	May 17	4,000

Determine the number of days each account is past due as of October 31.

EX 9-8 Aging of receivables schedule

OBJ. 4

SHOW ME HOW

The accounts receivable clerk for Waddell Industries prepared the following partially completed aging of receivables schedule as of the end of business on August 31:

	A	B	C	D	E	F	G
1			Not	Days Past Due			
2			Past				Over
3	Customer	Balance	Due	1–30	31–60	61–90	90
4	Acme Industries Inc.	3,000	3,000				
5	Alliance Company	4,500		4,500			
21	Zollinger Company	5,000			5,000		
22	Subtotals	1,050,000	600,000	220,000	115,000	85,000	30,000

The following accounts were unintentionally omitted from the aging schedule and not included in the preceding subtotals:

Customer	Balance	Due Date
Builders Industries	$44,500	May 1
Elkhorn Company	21,000	June 20
Granite Creek Inc.	7,500	July 13
Lockwood Company	14,000	September 9
Teton Company	13,000	August 7

a. Determine the number of days past due for each of the preceding accounts as of August 31.

b. Complete the aging of receivables schedule by adding the omitted accounts to the bottom of the schedule and updating the totals.

✔ Allowance for doubtful accounts, $142,815

SHOW ME HOW

EX 9-9 Estimating allowance for doubtful accounts

OBJ. 4

Waddell Industries has a past history of uncollectible accounts, as follows. Estimate the allowance for doubtful accounts, based on the aging of receivables schedule you completed in Exercise 9-8.

Age Class	Percent Uncollectible
Not past due	3%
1–30 days past due	4
31–60 days past due	15
61–90 days past due	35
Over 90 days past due	80

SHOW ME HOW

EX 9-10 Adjustment for uncollectible accounts **OBJ. 4**

Using data in Exercise 9-9, assume that the allowance for doubtful accounts for Waddell Industries has a credit balance of $6,350 before adjustment on August 31. Journalize the adjusting entry for uncollectible accounts as of August 31.

SHOW ME HOW

EX 9-11 Estimating doubtful accounts **OBJ. 4**

Selby's Bike Co. is a wholesaler of motorcycle supplies. An aging of the company's accounts receivable on December 31, 2016, and a historical analysis of the percentage of uncollectible accounts in each age category are as follows:

Age Interval	Balance	Percent Uncollectible
Not past due	$1,250,000	¾%
1–30 days past due	500,000	3
31–60 days past due	190,000	5
61–90 days past due	60,000	15
91–180 days past due	36,000	40
Over 180 days past due	24,000	80
	$2,060,000	

Estimate what the proper balance of the allowance for doubtful accounts should be as of December 31, 2016.

SHOW ME HOW

EX 9-12 Entry for uncollectible accounts **OBJ. 4**

Using the data in Exercise 9-11, assume that the allowance for doubtful accounts for Selby's Bike Co. had a debit balance of $7,200 as of December 31, 2016.

Journalize the adjusting entry for uncollectible accounts as of December 31, 2016.

✔ c. $8,225 higher

SHOW ME HOW

EX 9-13 Entries for bad debt expense under the direct write-off and allowance methods **OBJ. 5**

The following selected transactions were taken from the records of Shipway Company for the first year of its operations ending December 31, 2016:

Apr. 13. Wrote off account of Dean Sheppard, $8,450.

May 15. Received $500 as partial payment on the $7,100 account of Dan Pyle. Wrote off the remaining balance as uncollectible.

July 27. Received $8,450 from Dean Sheppard, whose account had been written off on April 13. Reinstated the account and recorded the cash receipt.

Dec. 31. Wrote off the following accounts as uncollectible (record as one journal entry):

Paul Chapman	$2,225
Duane DeRosa	3,550
Teresa Galloway	4,770
Ernie Klatt	1,275
Marty Richey	1,690

31. If necessary, record the year-end adjusting entry for uncollectible accounts.

a. Journalize the transactions for 2016 under the direct write-off method.

b. Journalize the transactions for 2016 under the allowance method. Shipway Company uses the percent of credit sales method of estimating uncollectible accounts expense. Based on past history and industry averages, ¾% of credit sales are expected to be uncollectible. Shipway Company recorded $3,778,000 of credit sales during 2016.

c. How much higher (lower) would Shipway Company's net income have been under the direct write-off method than under the allowance method?

EX 9-14 Entries for bad debt expense under the direct write-off and allowance methods

OBJ. 5

✔ c. $11,090 higher

SHOW ME HOW

The following selected transactions were taken from the records of Rustic Tables Company for the year ending December 31, 2016:

June 8. Wrote off account of Kathy Quantel, $8,440.

Aug. 14. Received $3,000 as partial payment on the $12,500 account of Rosalie Oakes. Wrote off the remaining balance as uncollectible.

Oct. 16. Received the $8,440 from Kathy Quantel, whose account had been written off on June 8. Reinstated the account and recorded the cash receipt.

Dec. 31. Wrote off the following accounts as uncollectible (record as one journal entry):

Wade Dolan	$4,600
Greg Gagne	3,600
Amber Kisko	7,150
Shannon Poole	2,975
Niki Spence	6,630

31. If necessary, record the year-end adjusting entry for uncollectible accounts.

a. Journalize the transactions for 2016 under the direct write-off method.

b. Journalize the transactions for 2016 under the allowance method, assuming that the allowance account had a beginning balance of $36,000 on January 1, 2016, and the company uses the analysis of receivables method. Rustic Tables Company prepared the following aging schedule for its accounts receivable:

Aging Class (Number of Days Past Due)	Receivables Balance on December 31	Estimated Percent of Uncollectible Accounts
0–30 days	$320,000	1%
31–60 days	110,000	3
61–90 days	24,000	10
91–120 days	18,000	33
More than 120 days	43,000	75
Total receivables	$515,000	

c. How much higher (lower) would Rustic Tables' 2016 net income have been under the direct write-off method than under the allowance method?

EX 9-15 Effect of doubtful accounts on net income

OBJ. 5

During its first year of operations, Mack's Plumbing Supply Co. had sales of $3,250,000, wrote off $27,800 of accounts as uncollectible using the direct write-off method, and reported net income of $487,500. Determine what the net income would have been if the allowance method had been used, and the company estimated that 1% of sales would be uncollectible.

EX 9-16 Effect of doubtful accounts on net income

OBJ. 5

✔ b. $11,700 credit balance

Using the data in Exercise 9-15, assume that during the second year of operations Mack's Plumbing Supply Co. had sales of $4,100,000, wrote off $34,000 of accounts as uncollectible using the direct write-off method, and reported net income of $600,000.

a. Determine what net income would have been in the second year if the allowance method (using 1% of sales) had been used in both the first and second years.

b. Determine what the balance of the allowance for doubtful accounts would have been at the end of the second year if the allowance method had been used in both the first and second years.

EX 9-17 Entries for bad debt expense under the direct write-off and allowance methods **OBJ. 5**

✔ c. $9,375 higher

Casebolt Company wrote off the following accounts receivable as uncollectible for the first year of its operations ending December 31, 2016:

Customer	Amount
Shawn Brooke	$ 4,650
Eve Denton	5,180
Art Malloy	11,050
Cassie Yost	9,120
Total	$30,000

a. Journalize the write-offs for 2016 under the direct write-off method.

b. Journalize the write-offs for 2016 under the allowance method. Also, journalize the adjusting entry for uncollectible accounts. The company recorded $5,250,000 of credit sales during 2016. Based on past history and industry averages, ¾% of credit sales are expected to be uncollectible.

c. How much higher (lower) would Casebolt Company's 2016 net income have been under the direct write-off method than under the allowance method?

EX 9-18 Entries for bad debt expense under the direct write-off and allowance methods **OBJ. 5**

Seaforth International wrote off the following accounts receivable as uncollectible for the year ending December 31, 2016:

Customer	Amount
Kim Abel	$ 21,550
Lee Drake	33,925
Jenny Green	27,565
Mike Lamb	19,460
Total	$102,500

The company prepared the following aging schedule for its accounts receivable on December 31, 2016:

Aging Class (Number of Days Past Due)	Receivables Balance on December 31	Estimated Percent of Uncollectible Accounts
0–30 days	$ 715,000	1%
31–60 days	310,000	2
61–90 days	102,000	15
91–120 days	76,000	30
More than 120 days	97,000	60
Total receivables	$1,300,000	

a. Journalize the write-offs for 2016 under the direct write-off method.

b. Journalize the write-offs and the year-end adjusting entry for 2016 under the allowance method, assuming that the allowance account had a beginning balance of $95,000 on January 1, 2016, and the company uses the analysis of receivables method.

c. How much higher (lower) would Seaforth International's 2016 net income have been under the allowance method than under the direct write-off method?

EX 9-19 Determine due date and interest on notes — OBJ. 6

✔ a. May 2, $1,600

SHOW ME HOW

Determine the due date and the amount of interest due at maturity on the following notes dated in 2016:

	Date of Note	Face Amount	Interest Rate	Term of Note
a.	January 3*	$80,000	6%	120 days
b.	February 20*	27,000	4	30 days
c.	May 24	62,500	8	45 days
d.	August 30	30,000	5	90 days
e.	October 4	40,000	7	90 days

* February 2016 has 29 days.

EX 9-20 Entries for notes receivable — OBJ. 6

✔ b. $77,250

SHOW ME HOW

Master Designs Decorators issued a 180-day, 6% note for $75,000, dated May 14, 2016, to Morgan Furniture Company on account.

a. Determine the due date of the note.

b. Determine the maturity value of the note.

c. Journalize the entries to record the following: (1) receipt of the note by Morgan Furniture and (2) receipt of payment of the note at maturity.

EX 9-21 Entries for notes receivable — OBJ. 6

The series of seven transactions recorded in the following T accounts were related to a sale to a customer on account and the receipt of the amount owed. Briefly describe each transaction.

CASH

	Debit		Credit
(7)	61,509		

NOTES RECEIVABLE

	Debit		Credit
(5)	60,000	(6)	60,000

ACCOUNTS RECEIVABLE

	Debit		Credit
(1)	75,000	(3)	15,000
(6)	60,600	(5)	60,000
		(7)	60,600

SALES RETURNS AND ALLOWANCES

	Debit		Credit
(3)	15,000		

MERCHANDISE INVENTORY

	Debit		Credit
(4)	9,000	(2)	45,000

COST OF MERCHANDISE SOLD

	Debit		Credit
(2)	45,000	(4)	9,000

SALES

	Debit		Credit
		(1)	75,000

INTEREST REVENUE

	Debit		Credit
		(6)	600
		(7)	909

EX 9-22 Entries for notes receivable, including year-end entries — OBJ. 6

SHOW ME HOW

The following selected transactions were completed by Zippy Do Co., a supplier of zippers for clothing:

2015

Dec. 3. Received from Chicago Clothing & Bags Co., on account, a $36,000, 90-day, 6% note dated December 3.

31. Recorded an adjusting entry for accrued interest on the note of December 3.

31. Recorded the closing entry for interest revenue.

2016

Mar. 2. Received payment of note and interest from Chicago Clothing & Bags Co.

Journalize the entries to record the transactions.

EX 9-23 Entries for receipt and dishonor of note receivable OBJ. 6

Journalize the following transactions of Trapper Jon's Productions:

June 23 Received a $48,000, 90-day, 8% note dated June 23 from Radon Express Co. on account.

Sept. 21 The note is dishonored by Radon Express Co.

Oct. 21 Received the amount due on the dishonored note plus interest for 30 days at 10% on the total amount charged to Radon Express Co. on September 21.

EX 9-24 Entries for receipt and dishonor of notes receivable OBJ. 4, 6

SHOW ME HOW

Journalize the following transactions in the accounts of Safari Games Co., which operates a riverboat casino:

Apr. 18. Received a $60,000, 30-day, 7% note dated April 18 from Glenn Cross on account.

30. Received a $42,000, 60-day, 8% note dated April 30 from Rhoni Melville on account.

May 18. The note dated April 18 from Glenn Cross is dishonored, and the customer's account is charged for the note, including interest.

June 29. The note dated April 30 from Rhoni Melville is dishonored, and the customer's account is charged for the note, including interest.

Aug. 16. Cash is received for the amount due on the dishonored note dated April 18 plus interest for 90 days at 8% on the total amount debited to Glenn Cross on May 18.

Oct. 22. Wrote off against the allowance account the amount charged to Rhoni Melville on June 29 for the dishonored note dated April 30.

EX 9-25 Receivables on the balance sheet OBJ. 7

List any errors you can find in the following partial balance sheet:

Napa Vino Company
Balance Sheet
December 31, 2016

Assets		
Current assets:		
Cash		$ 78,500
Notes receivable	$ 300,000	
Less interest receivable	4,500	295,500
Accounts receivable	$1,200,000	
Plus allowance for doubtful accounts	11,500	1,211,500

EX 9-26 Accounts receivable turnover and days' sales in receivables OBJ. 8

✔ a. Year 2: 10.7

Polo Ralph Lauren Corporation designs, markets, and distributes a variety of apparel, home decor, accessory, and fragrance products. The company's products include such brands as Polo by Ralph Lauren, Ralph Lauren Purple Label, Ralph Lauren, Polo Jeans Co., and Chaps. Polo Ralph Lauren reported the following (in thousands) for two recent years:

	For the Period Ending	
	Year 2	**Year 1**
Sales	$6,859,500	$5,660,300
Accounts receivable	690,000	592,700

(Continued)

Assume that accounts receivable (in millions) were $486,200 at the beginning of Year 1.

a. Compute the accounts receivable turnover for Year 2 and Year 1. Round to one decimal place.

b. Compute the days' sales in receivables for Year 2 and Year 1. Use 365 days and round to one decimal place.

c. What conclusions can be drawn from these analyses regarding Ralph Lauren's efficiency in collecting receivables?

EX 9-27 Accounts receivable turnover and days' sales in receivables **OBJ. 8**

✔ a. Year 2: 10.3

H.J. Heinz Company was founded in 1869 at Sharpsburg, Pennsylvania, by Henry J. Heinz. The company manufactures and markets food products throughout the world, including ketchup, condiments and sauces, frozen food, pet food, soups, and tuna. For two recent years, H.J. Heinz reported the following (in thousands):

	Year 2	Year 1
Sales	$11,649,079	$10,706,588
Accounts receivable	993,510	1,265,032

Assume that the accounts receivable (in thousands) were $1,045,338 at the beginning of Year 1.

a. Compute the accounts receivable turnover for Year 2 and Year 1. Round to one decimal place.

b. Compute the days' sales in receivables at the end of Year 2 and Year 1. Use 365 days and round to one decimal place.

c. What conclusions can be drawn from these analyses regarding Heinz's efficiency in collecting receivables?

EX 9-28 Accounts receivable turnover and days' sales in receivables 

The Limited Brands Inc. sells women's clothing and personal health care products through specialty retail stores including Victoria's Secret and Bath & Body Works stores. The Limited Brands reported the following (in millions) for two recent years:

	Year 2	Year 1
Sales	$10,364	$9,613
Accounts receivable	269	267

Assume that accounts receivable (in millions) were $249 at the beginning of Year 1.

a. Compute the accounts receivable turnover for Year 2 and Year 1. Round to one decimal place.

b. Compute the day's sales in receivables for Year 2 and Year 1. Use 365 days and round to one decimal place.

c. What conclusions can be drawn from these analyses regarding The Limited Brands' efficiency in collecting receivables?

EX 9-29 Accounts receivable turnover **OBJ. 8**

Use the data in Exercises 9-27 and 9-28 to analyze the accounts receivable turnover ratios of **H.J. Heinz Company** and **The Limited Brands Inc.**

a. Compute the average accounts receivable turnover ratio for The Limited Brands Inc. and H.J. Heinz Company for the years shown in Exercises 9-27 and 9-28.

b. Does The Limited Brands or H.J. Heinz Company have the higher average accounts receivable turnover ratio?

c. Explain the logic underlying your answer in (b).

Problems: Series A

PR 9-1A Entries related to uncollectible accounts — OBJ. 4

✔ 3. $1,749,300

General Ledger

SHOW ME HOW

The following transactions were completed by The Irvine Company during the current fiscal year ended December 31:

Feb. 8. Received 40% of the $18,000 balance owed by DeCoy Co., a bankrupt business, and wrote off the remainder as uncollectible.

May 27. Reinstated the account of Seth Nelsen, which had been written off in the preceding year as uncollectible. Journalized the receipt of $7,350 cash in full payment of Seth's account.

Aug. 13. Wrote off the $6,400 balance owed by Kat Tracks Co., which has no assets.

Oct. 31. Reinstated the account of Crawford Co., which had been written off in the preceding year as uncollectible. Journalized the receipt of $3,880 cash in full payment of the account.

Dec. 31. Wrote off the following accounts as uncollectible (compound entry): Newbauer Co., $7,190; Bonneville Co., $5,500; Crow Distributors, $9,400; Fiber Optics, $1,110.

31. Based on an analysis of the $1,785,000 of accounts receivable, it was estimated that $35,700 will be uncollectible. Journalized the adjusting entry.

Instructions

1. Record the January 1 credit balance of $26,000 in a T account for Allowance for Doubtful Accounts.
2. Journalize the transactions. Post each entry that affects the following selected T accounts and determine the new balances:

   Allowance for Doubtful Accounts
   Bad Debt Expense
3. Determine the expected net realizable value of the accounts receivable as of December 31.
4. Assuming that instead of basing the provision for uncollectible accounts on an analysis of receivables, the adjusting entry on December 31 had been based on an estimated expense of ¼ of 1% of the sales of $18,200,000 for the year, determine the following:
   a. Bad debt expense for the year.
   b. Balance in the allowance account after the adjustment of December 31.
   c. Expected net realizable value of the accounts receivable as of December 31.

PR 9-2A Aging of receivables; estimating allowance for doubtful accounts — OBJ. 4

✔ 3. $121,000

Trophy Fish Company supplies flies and fishing gear to sporting goods stores and outfitters throughout the western United States. The accounts receivable clerk for Trophy Fish prepared the following partially completed aging of receivables schedule as of the end of business on December 31, 2015:

	A	B	C	D	E	F	G	H
1			Not	Days Past Due				
2			Past					
3	Customer	Balance	Due	1–30	31–60	61–90	91–120	Over 120
4	AAA Outfitters	20,000	20,000					
5	Brown Trout Fly Shop	7,500			7,500			
30	Zigs Fish Adventures	4,000		4,000				
31	Subtotals	1,300,000	750,000	290,000	120,000	40,000	20,000	80,000

(Continued)

The following accounts were unintentionally omitted from the aging schedule:

Customer	Due Date	Balance
Adams Sports & Flies	May 22, 2015	$5,000
Blue Dun Flies	Oct. 10, 2015	4,900
Cicada Fish Co.	Sept. 29, 2015	8,400
Deschutes Sports	Oct. 20, 2015	7,000
Green River Sports	Nov. 7, 2015	3,500
Smith River Co.	Nov. 28, 2015	2,400
Western Trout Company	Dec. 7, 2015	6,800
Wolfe Sports	Jan. 20, 2016	4,400

Trophy Fish has a past history of uncollectible accounts by age category, as follows:

Age Class	Percent Uncollectible
Not past due	1%
1–30 days past due	2
31–60 days past due	10
61–90 days past due	30
91–120 days past due	40
Over 120 days past due	80

Instructions

1. Determine the number of days past due for each of the preceding accounts.
2. Complete the aging of receivables schedule by adding the omitted accounts to the bottom of the schedule and updating the totals.
3. Estimate the allowance for doubtful accounts, based on the aging of receivables schedule.
4. Assume that the allowance for doubtful accounts for Trophy Fish Company has a debit balance of $3,600 before adjustment on December 31, 2015. Journalize the adjusting entry for uncollectible accounts.
5. Assume that the adjusting entry in (4) was inadvertently omitted, how would the omission affect the balance sheet and income statement?

PR 9-3A Compare two methods of accounting for uncollectible receivables OBJ. 3, 4, 5

✔ 1. Year 4: Balance of allowance account, end of year, $15,050

Call Systems Company, a telephone service and supply company, has just completed its fourth year of operations. The direct write-off method of recording bad debt expense has been used during the entire period. Because of substantial increases in sales volume and the amount of uncollectible accounts, the company is considering changing to the allowance method. Information is requested as to the effect that an annual provision of 1% of sales would have had on the amount of bad debt expense reported for each of the past four years. It is also considered desirable to know what the balance of Allowance for Doubtful Accounts would have been at the end of each year. The following data have been obtained from the accounts:

			Year of Origin of Accounts Receivable Written Off as Uncollectible			
Year	Sales	Uncollectible Accounts Written Off	1st	2nd	3rd	4th
1st	$ 900,000	$ 4,500	$4,500			
2nd	1,250,000	9,600	3,000	$6,600		
3rd	1,500,000	12,800	1,000	3,700	$8,100	
4th	2,200,000	16,550		1,500	4,300	$10,750

Instructions

1. Assemble the desired data, using the following column headings:

	Bad Debt Expense			
Year	**Expense Actually Reported**	**Expense Based on Estimate**	**Increase (Decrease) in Amount of Expense**	**Balance of Allowance Account, End of Year**

2. Experience during the first four years of operations indicated that the receivables were either collected within two years or had to be written off as uncollectible. Does the estimate of 1% of sales appear to be reasonably close to the actual experience with uncollectible accounts originating during the first two years? Explain.

PR 9-4A Details of notes receivable and related entries

OBJ. 6

✔ 1. Note 2: Due date, June 22; Interest due at maturity, $360

SHOW ME HOW

Flush Mate Co. wholesales bathroom fixtures. During the current fiscal year, Flush Mate Co. received the following notes:

	Date	Face Amount	Term	Interest Rate
1.	Mar. 6	$80,000	45 days	5%
2.	Apr. 23	24,000	60 days	9
3.	July 20	42,000	120 days	6
4.	Sept. 6	54,000	90 days	7
5.	Nov. 29	27,000	60 days	6
6.	Dec. 30	72,000	30 days	5

Instructions

1. Determine for each note (a) the due date and (b) the amount of interest due at maturity, identifying each note by number.
2. Journalize the entry to record the dishonor of Note (3) on its due date.
3. Journalize the adjusting entry to record the accrued interest on Notes (5) and (6) on December 31.
4. Journalize the entries to record the receipt of the amounts due on Notes (5) and (6) in January.

PR 9-5A Notes receivable entries

OBJ. 6

The following data relate to notes receivable and interest for CGH Cable Co., a cable manufacturer and supplier. (All notes are dated as of the day they are received.)

Apr. 10. Received a $144,000, 5%, 60-day note on account.
May 15. Received a $270,000, 7%, 120-day note on account.
June 9. Received $145,200 on note of April 10.
Aug. 22. Received a $150,000, 4%, 45-day note on account.
Sept. 12. Received $276,300 on note of May 15.
30. Received a $210,000, 8%, 60-day note on account.
Oct. 6. Received $150,750 on note of August 22.
18. Received a 120,000, 5%, 60-day note on account.
Nov. 29. Received $212,800 on note of September 30.
Dec. 17. Received $121,000 on note of October 18.

Instructions

Journalize the entries to record the transactions.

General Ledger

PR 9-6A Sales and notes receivable transactions **OBJ. 6**

The following were selected from among the transactions completed by Caldemeyer Co. during the current year. Caldemeyer Co. sells and installs home and business security systems.

Jan. 3. Loaned $18,000 cash to Trina Gelhaus, receiving a 90-day, 8% note.

Feb. 10. Sold merchandise on account to Bradford & Co., $24,000. The cost of the merchandise sold was $14,400.

13. Sold merchandise on account to Dry Creek Co., $60,000. The cost of merchandise sold was $54,000.

Mar. 12. Accepted a 60-day, 7% note for $24,000 from Bradford & Co. on account.

14. Accepted a 60-day, 9% note for $60,000 from Dry Creek Co. on account.

Apr. 3. Received the interest due from Trina Gelhaus and a new 120-day, 9% note as a renewal of the loan of January 3. (Record both the debit and the credit to the notes receivable account.)

May 11. Received from Bradford & Co. the amount due on the note of March 12.

13. Dry Creek Co. dishonored its note dated March 14.

July 12. Received from Dry Creek Co. the amount owed on the dishonored note, plus interest for 60 days at 12% computed on the maturity value of the note.

Aug. 1. Received from Trina Gelhaus the amount due on her note of April 3.

Oct. 5. Sold merchandise on account to Halloran Co., $13,500. The cost of the merchandise sold was $8,100.

15. Received from Halloran Co. the amount of the invoice of October 5, less 2% discount.

Instructions

Journalize the entries to record the transactions.

Problems: Series B

✔ 3. $2,290,000

General Ledger

SHOW ME HOW

PR 9-1B Entries related to uncollectible accounts **OBJ. 4**

The following transactions were completed by The Wild Trout Gallery during the current fiscal year ended December 31:

Jan. 19. Reinstated the account of Arlene Gurley, which had been written off in the preceding year as uncollectible. Journalized the receipt of $2,660 cash in full payment of Arlene's account.

Apr. 3. Wrote off the $12,750 balance owed by Premier GS Co., which is bankrupt.

July 16. Received 25% of the $22,000 balance owed by Hayden Co., a bankrupt business, and wrote off the remainder as uncollectible.

Nov. 23. Reinstated the account of Harry Carr, which had been written off two years earlier as uncollectible. Recorded the receipt of $4,000 cash in full payment.

Dec. 31. Wrote off the following accounts as uncollectible (compound entry): Cavey Co., $3,300; Fogle Co., $8,100; Lake Furniture, $11,400; Melinda Shryer, $1,200.

31. Based on an analysis of the $2,350,000 of accounts receivable, it was estimated that $60,000 will be uncollectible. Journalized the adjusting entry.

Instructions

1. Record the January 1 credit balance of $50,000 in a T account for Allowance for Doubtful Accounts.

2. Journalize the transactions. Post each entry that affects the following T accounts and determine the new balances:

   Allowance for Doubtful Accounts
   Bad Debt Expense

3. Determine the expected net realizable value of the accounts receivable as of December 31.
4. Assuming that instead of basing the provision for uncollectible accounts on an analysis of receivables, the adjusting entry on December 31 had been based on an estimated expense of ½ of 1% of the sales of $15,800,000 for the year, determine the following:
   a. Bad debt expense for the year.
   b. Balance in the allowance account after the adjustment of December 31.
   c. Expected net realizable value of the accounts receivable as of December 31.

PR 9-2B Aging of receivables; estimating allowance for doubtful accounts OBJ. 4

✓ 3. $123,235

Wig Creations Company supplies wigs and hair care products to beauty salons throughout Texas and the Southwest. The accounts receivable clerk for Wig Creations prepared the following partially completed aging of receivables schedule as of the end of business on December 31, 2015:

	A	B	C	D	E	F	G	H
1			Not	Days Past Due				
2			Past					
3	Customer	Balance	Due	1–30	31–60	61–90	91–120	Over 120
4	ABC Beauty	15,000	15,000					
5	Angel Wigs	8,000			8,000			
30	Zodiac Beauty	3,000		3,000				
31	Subtotals	875,000	415,000	210,000	112,000	55,000	18,000	65,000

The following accounts were unintentionally omitted from the aging schedule:

Customer	Due Date	Balance
Arcade Beauty	Aug. 17, 2015	$10,000
Creative Images	Oct. 30, 2015	8,500
Excel Hair Products	July 3, 2015	7,500
First Class Hair Care	Sept. 8, 2015	6,600
Golden Images	Nov. 23, 2015	3,600
Oh That Hair	Nov. 29, 2015	1,400
One Stop Hair Designs	Dec. 7, 2015	4,000
Visions Hair & Nail	Jan. 11, 2016	9,000

Wig Creations has a past history of uncollectible accounts by age category, as follows:

Age Class	Percent Uncollectible
Not past due	1%
1–30 days past due	4
31–60 days past due	16
61–90 days past due	25
91–120 days past due	40
Over 120 days past due	80

Instructions

1. Determine the number of days past due for each of the preceding accounts.
2. Complete the aging of receivables schedule by adding the omitted accounts to the bottom of the schedule and updating the totals.

(Continued)

3. Estimate the allowance for doubtful accounts, based on the aging of receivables schedule.
4. Assume that the allowance for doubtful accounts for Wig Creations has a credit balance of $7,375 before adjustment on December 31, 2015. Journalize the adjustment for uncollectible accounts.
5. Assume that the adjusting entry in (4) was inadvertently omitted, how would the omission affect the balance sheet and income statement?

PR 9-3B Compare two methods of accounting for uncollectible receivables OBJ. 3, 4, 5

✔ 1. Year 4: Balance of allowance account, end of year, $32,550

Digital Depot Company, which operates a chain of 40 electronics supply stores, has just completed its fourth year of operations. The direct write-off method of recording bad debt expense has been used during the entire period. Because of substantial increases in sales volume and the amount of uncollectible accounts, the firm is considering changing to the allowance method. Information is requested as to the effect that an annual provision of ¼% of sales would have had on the amount of bad debt expense reported for each of the past four years. It is also considered desirable to know what the balance of Allowance for Doubtful Accounts would have been at the end of each year. The following data have been obtained from the accounts:

			Year of Origin of Accounts Receivable Written Off as Uncollectible			
Year	Sales	Uncollectible Accounts Written Off	1st	2nd	3rd	4th
1st	$12,500,000	$18,000	$18,000			
2nd	14,800,000	30,200	9,000	$21,200		
3rd	18,000,000	39,900	3,600	9,300	$27,000	
4th	24,000,000	52,600		5,100	12,500	$35,000

Instructions

1. Assemble the desired data, using the following column headings:

	Bad Debt Expense			
Year	Expense Actually Reported	Expense Based on Estimate	Increase (Decrease) in Amount of Expense	Balance of Allowance Account, End of Year

2. Experience during the first four years of operations indicated that the receivables were either collected within two years or had to be written off as uncollectible. Does the estimate of ¼% of sales appear to be reasonably close to the actual experience with uncollectible accounts originating during the first two years? Explain.

PR 9-4B Details of notes receivable and related entries OBJ. 6

✔ 1. Note 1: Due date, Feb. 13; Interest due at maturity, $110

SHOW ME HOW

Gen-X Ads Co. produces advertising videos. During the current fiscal year, Gen-X Ads Co. received the following notes:

	Date	Face Amount	Term	Interest Rate
1.	Jan. 14	$33,000	30 days	4%
2.	Mar. 9	60,000	45 days	7
3.	July 12	48,000	90 days	5
4.	Aug. 23	16,000	75 days	6
5.	Nov. 15	36,000	60 days	8
6.	Dec. 10	24,000	60 days	6

Instructions

1. Determine for each note (a) the due date and (b) the amount of interest due at maturity, identifying each note by number.

2. Journalize the entry to record the dishonor of Note (3) on its due date.
3. Journalize the adjusting entry to record the accrued interest on Notes (5) and (6) on December 31.
4. Journalize the entries to record the receipt of the amounts due on Notes (5) and (6) in January and February.

PR 9-5B Notes receivable entries

OBJ. 6

The following data relate to notes receivable and interest for Owens Co., a financial services company. (All notes are dated as of the day they are received.)

Mar. 8. Received a $33,000, 5%, 60-day note on account.
31. Received an $80,000, 7%, 90-day note on account.
May 7. Received $33,275 on note of March 8.
16. Received a $72,000, 7%, 90-day note on account.
June 11. Received a $36,000, 6%, 45-day note on account.
29. Received $81,400 on note of March 31.
July 26. Received $36,270 on note of June 11.
Aug. 4. Received a $48,000, 9%, 120-day note on account.
14. Received $73,260 on note of May 16.
Dec. 2. Received $49,440 on note of August 4.

Instructions

Journalize the entries to record the transactions.

PR 9-6B Sales and notes receivable transactions

OBJ. 6

General Ledger

The following were selected from among the transactions completed during the current year by Danix Co., an appliance wholesale company:

Jan. 21. Sold merchandise on account to Black Tie Co., $28,000. The cost of merchandise sold was $16,800.
Mar. 18. Accepted a 60-day, 6% note for $28,000 from Black Tie Co. on account.
May 17. Received from Black Tie Co. the amount due on the note of March 18.
June 15. Sold merchandise on account to Pioneer Co. for $17,700. The cost of merchandise sold was $10,600.
21. Loaned $18,000 cash to JR Stutts, receiving a 30-day, 8% note.
25. Received from Pioneer Co. the amount due on the invoice of June 15, less 1% discount.
July 21. Received the interest due from JR Stutts and a new 60-day, 9% note as a renewal of the loan of June 21. (Record both the debit and the credit to the notes receivable account.)
Sept. 19. Received from JR Stutts the amount due on her note of July 21.
22. Sold merchandise on account to Wycoff Co., $20,000. The cost of merchandise sold was $12,000.
Oct. 14. Accepted a 30-day, 6% note for $20,000 from Wycoff Co. on account.
Nov. 13. Wycoff Co. dishonored the note dated October 14.
Dec. 28. Received from Wycoff Co. the amount owed on the dishonored note, plus interest for 45 days at 8% computed on the maturity value of the note.

Instructions

Journalize the entries to record the transactions.

Cases & Projects

CP 9-1 Ethics and professional conduct in business

Bev Wynn, vice president of operations for Dillon County Bank, has instructed the bank's computer programmer to use a 365-day year to compute interest on depository accounts (liabilities). Bev also instructed the programmer to use a 360-day year to compute interest on loans (assets).

Discuss whether Bev is behaving in a professional manner.

CP 9-2 Estimate uncollectible accounts

For several years, Xtreme Co.'s sales have been on a "cash only" basis. On January 1, 2013, however, Xtreme Co. began offering credit on terms of n/30. The amount of the adjusting entry to record the estimated uncollectible receivables at the end of each year has been ½ of 1% of credit sales, which is the rate reported as the average for the industry. Credit sales and the year-end credit balances in Allowance for Doubtful Accounts for the past four years are as follows:

Year	Credit Sales	Allowance for Doubtful Accounts
2013	$4,000,000	$ 5,000
2014	4,400,000	8,250
2015	4,800,000	10,200
2016	5,100,000	14,400

Laurie Jones, president of Xtreme Co., is concerned that the method used to account for and write off uncollectible receivables is unsatisfactory. She has asked for your advice in the analysis of past operations in this area and for recommendations for change.

1. Determine the amount of (a) the addition to Allowance for Doubtful Accounts and (b) the accounts written off for each of the four years.
2. a. Advise Laurie Jones as to whether the estimate of ½ of 1% of credit sales appears reasonable.

   b. Assume that after discussing (a) with Laurie Jones, she asked you what action might be taken to determine what the balance of Allowance for Doubtful Accounts should be at December 31, 2016, and what possible changes, if any, you might recommend in accounting for uncollectible receivables. How would you respond?

CP 9-3 Accounts receivable turnover and days' sales in receivables

Best Buy is a specialty retailer of consumer electronics, including personal computers, entertainment software, and appliances. Best Buy operates retail stores in addition to the Best Buy, Media Play, On Cue, and Magnolia Hi-Fi Web sites. For two recent years, Best Buy reported the following (in millions):

	Year 2	Year 1
Sales	$50,705	$49,747
Accounts receivable at end of year	2,288	2,348

Assume that the accounts receivable (in millions) were $2,020 at the beginning of fiscal Year 1.

1. Compute the accounts receivable turnover for Year 2 and Year 1. Round to one decimal place.
2. Compute the days' sales in receivables at the end of Year 2 and Year 1. Use 365 days and round to one decimal place.

3. What conclusions can be drawn from (1) and (2) regarding Best Buy's efficiency in collecting receivables?
4. What assumption did we make about sales for the Best Buy ratio computations that might distort the ratios and therefore cause the ratios not to be comparable for Year 2 and Year 1?

CP 9-4 Accounts receivable turnover and days' sales in receivables

Apple Inc. designs, manufactures, and markets personal computers and related personal computing and communicating solutions for sale primarily to education, creative, consumer, and business customers. Substantially all of the company's sales over the last five years are from sales of its Macs, iPods, iPads, and related software and peripherals. For two recent fiscal years, Apple reported the following (in millions):

	Year 2	Year 1
Sales	$156,508	$108,249
Accounts receivable at end of year	21,275	13,731

Assume that the accounts receivable (in millions) were $11,560 at the beginning of fiscal Year 1.

1. Compute the accounts receivable turnover for Year 2 and Year 1. Round to one decimal place.
2. Compute the days' sales in receivables at the end of Year 2 and Year 1. Use 365 days and round to one decimal place.
3. What conclusions can be drawn from (1) and (2) regarding Apple's efficiency in collecting receivables?

CP 9-5 Accounts receivable turnover and days' sales in receivables

Costco Wholesale Corporation operates membership warehouses that sell a variety of branded and private label products. Headquartered in Issaquah, Washington, it also sells merchandise online in the United States (Costco.com) and in Canada (Costco.ca). For two recent years, Costco reported the following (in millions):

	Year 2	Year 1
Sales	$99,137	$88,915
Accounts receivable at end of year	1,576	1,455

Assume that the accounts receivable (in thousands) were $1,321 at the beginning of Year 1.

1. Compute the accounts receivable turnover for Year 2 and Year 1. Round to one decimal place.
2. Compute the days' sales in receivables at the end of Year 2 and Year 1. Use 365 days and round to one decimal place.
3. What conclusions can be drawn from (1) and (2) regarding Costco's efficiency in collecting receivables?
4. Given the nature of Costco's operations, do you believe Costco's accounts receivable turnover ratio would be higher or lower than a typical manufacturing company, such as **H.J. Heinz Company**? Explain.

CP 9-6 Accounts receivable turnover

The accounts receivable turnover ratio will vary across companies, depending on the nature of the company's operations. For example, an accounts receivable turnover of 6 for a retailer is unacceptable but might be excellent for a manufacturer of specialty milling equipment. A list of well-known companies follows:

Alcoa Inc.	The Coca-Cola Company	Kroger
AutoZone, Inc.	Delta Air Lines	Procter & Gamble
Barnes & Noble, Inc.	The Home Depot	Walmart
Caterpillar	IBM	Whirlpool Corporation

1. Categorize each of the preceding companies as to whether its turnover ratio is likely to be above or below 15.
2. Based on (1), identify a characteristic of companies with accounts receivable turnover ratios above 15.

CHAPTER 10

Fixed Assets and Intangible Assets

McDonald's

McDonald's began in 1940 in San Bernardino, California, as a Bar-B-Q restaurant operated by two brothers, Dick and Mac McDonald. In 1954, Ray Kroc visited the restaurant and convinced the McDonald brothers to let him franchise its operations nationwide. Ray Kroc opened his first McDonald's in Des Plaines, Illinois, in 1955, with its distinguishing, newly designed Golden Arches. Today, McDonald's operates in 119 countries, has more than 34,000 restaurants, employs more than 400,000 people, has sold more than 250 billion hamburgers, and generates yearly revenues in excess of $27.5 billion.

Would you like to own and operate a McDonald's restaurant? McDonald's grants twenty-year franchises to individuals who want to become owner/operators of a restaurant. Individuals may purchase either an existing or a new restaurant. When opening a new restaurant, the owner must invest in the store equipment, signs, seating, and décor. The company normally owns the land and the building. McDonald's also provides training for its owner/operators. In return, the company is paid a monthly service charge, which is either a fixed amount or a percent of sales. The total cost of opening a new restaurant may exceed several million dollars.

Obviously, the decision to open a McDonald's restaurant is a major commitment with long-lasting implications. This chapter discusses the accounting for investments in long-term, fixed assets such as a new restaurant. This accounting addresses such issues as how much of the investment should be recorded as an asset, how much should be written off as an expense each year, and how the disposal of a fixed asset should be recorded. Finally, accounting for natural resources, such as mineral deposits, and intangible assets, such as patents and copyrights, are discussed.

Source: http://www.aboutmcdonalds.com

Learning Objectives

After studying this chapter, you should be able to:

At a Glance 10 Page 484

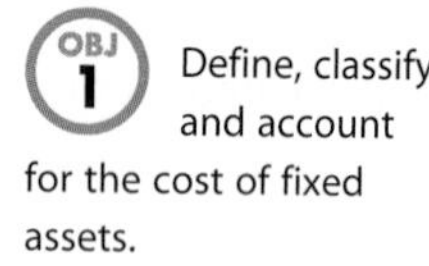

Define, classify, and account for the cost of fixed assets.

Nature of Fixed Assets

Fixed assets are long-term or relatively permanent assets such as equipment, machinery, buildings, and land. Other descriptive titles for fixed assets are *plant assets* or *property, plant, and equipment*. Fixed assets have the following characteristics:

- They exist physically and, thus, are *tangible* assets.
- They are owned and used by the company in its normal operations.
- They are not offered for sale as part of normal operations.

Exhibit 1 shows the percent of fixed assets to total assets for some select companies. As shown in Exhibit 1, fixed assets are often a significant portion of the total assets of a company.

EXHIBIT 1

Fixed Assets as a Percent of Total Assets—Selected Companies

	Fixed Assets as a Percent of Total Assets
Alcoa Inc.	47%
Exxon Mobil Corporation	68
Ford Motor Company	22
Kroger	62
Office Depot Inc.	21
United Parcel Service, Inc.	46
Verizon Communications	39
Walgreen Co.	36
Walmart	58

Classifying Costs

A cost that has been incurred may be classified as a fixed asset, an investment, or an expense. Exhibit 2 shows how to determine the proper classification of a cost and how it should be recorded.

IFRS See Appendix D for more information.

EXHIBIT 2

Classifying Costs

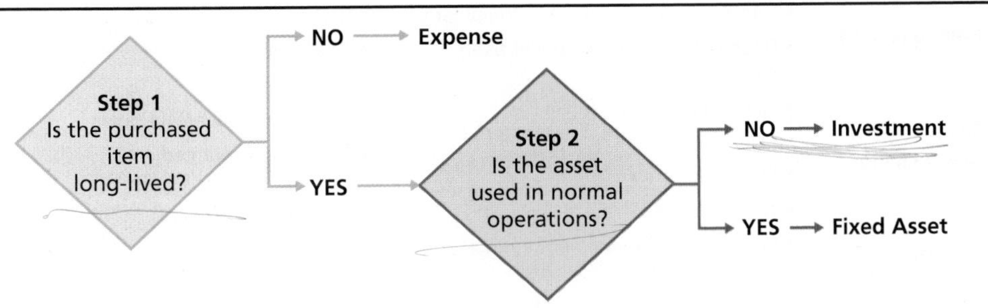

As shown in Exhibit 2, classifying a cost involves the following steps:

- Step 1. Is the purchased item long-lived?
  If *yes*, the item is recorded as an asset on the balance sheet, either as a fixed asset or an investment. Proceed to Step 2.
  If *no*, the item is classified and recorded as an *expense*.
- Step 2. Is the asset used in normal operations?
  If *yes*, the asset is classified and recorded as a *fixed asset*.
  If *no*, the asset is classified and recorded as an *investment*.

Items that are classified and recorded as fixed assets include land, buildings, or equipment. Such assets normally last more than a year and are used in the normal operations. However, standby equipment for use during peak periods or when other equipment breaks down is still classified as a fixed asset, even though it is not used very often. In contrast, fixed assets that have been abandoned or are no longer used in operations are not classified as fixed assets.

Although fixed assets may be sold, they should not be offered for sale as part of normal operations. For example, cars and trucks offered for sale by an automotive dealership are not fixed assets of the dealership. On the other hand, a tow truck used in the normal operations of the dealership is a fixed asset of the dealership.

Investments are long-lived assets that are not used in the normal operations and are held for future resale. Such assets are reported on the balance sheet in a section entitled *Investments*. For example, undeveloped land acquired for future resale would be classified and reported as an investment, not land.

The Cost of Fixed Assets

In addition to purchase price, the costs of acquiring fixed assets include all amounts spent getting the asset in place and ready for use. For example, freight costs and the costs of installing equipment are part of the asset's total cost.

Exhibit 3 summarizes some of the common costs of acquiring fixed assets. These costs are recorded by debiting the related fixed asset account, such as Land,[1] Building, Land Improvements, or Machinery and Equipment.

EXHIBIT 3 **Costs of Acquiring Fixed Assets**

Building

- Architects' fees
- Engineers' fees
- Insurance costs incurred during construction
- Interest on money borrowed to finance construction
- Sales taxes
- Repairs (purchase of existing building)
- Reconditioning (purchase of existing building)
- Modifying for use
- Permits from government agencies

Machinery & Equipment

- Sales taxes
- Freight
- Installation
- Repairs (purchase of used equipment)
- Reconditioning (purchase of used equipment)
- Insurance while in transit
- Assembly
- Modifying for use
- Testing for use
- Permits from government agencies

Land

- Purchase price
- Sales taxes
- Permits from government agencies
- Broker's commissions
- Title fees
- Surveying fees
- Delinquent real estate taxes
- Removing unwanted building less any salvage
- Grading and leveling

Land Improvements
• Trees and shrubs
• Fences
• Outdoor lighting
• Paved parking areas or walkways

Only costs necessary for preparing the fixed asset for use are included as a cost of the asset. Unnecessary costs that do not increase the asset's usefulness are recorded as an expense. For example, the following costs are included as an expense:

- Vandalism
- Mistakes in installation
- Uninsured theft
- Damage during unpacking and installing
- Fines for not obtaining proper permits from governmental agencies

A company may incur costs associated with constructing a fixed asset such as a new building. The direct costs incurred in the construction, such as labor and

[1] As discussed here, land is assumed to be used only as a location or site and not for its mineral deposits or other natural resources.

materials, should be capitalized as a debit to an account entitled *Construction in Progress*. When the construction is complete, the costs are reclassified by crediting Construction in Progress and debiting the proper fixed asset account such as Building. For some companies, construction in progress can be significant.

Intel Corporation reported in a recent annual report construction in progress of $8.2 billion, which was 29% of its total fixed assets.

See Appendix D for more information.

Capital and Revenue Expenditures

Once a fixed asset has been acquired and placed into service, costs may be incurred for ordinary maintenance and repairs. In addition, costs may be incurred for improving an asset or for extraordinary repairs that extend the asset's useful life. Costs that benefit only the current period are called **revenue expenditures**. Costs that improve the asset or extend its useful life are **capital expenditures**.

Ordinary Maintenance and Repairs Costs related to the ordinary maintenance and repairs of a fixed asset are recorded as an expense of the current period. Such expenditures are *revenue expenditures* and are recorded as increases to Repairs and Maintenance Expense. For example, $300 paid for a tune-up of a delivery truck is recorded as follows:

		Repairs and Maintenance Expense		300	
		Cash			300

Asset Improvements After a fixed asset has been placed into service, costs may be incurred to improve the asset. For example, the service value of a delivery truck might be improved by adding a $5,500 hydraulic lift to allow for easier and quicker loading of cargo. Such costs are *capital expenditures* and are recorded as increases to the fixed asset account. In the case of the hydraulic lift, the expenditure is recorded as follows:

		Delivery Truck		5,500	
		Cash			5,500

Because the cost of the delivery truck has increased, depreciation for the truck will also change over its remaining useful life.

Extraordinary Repairs After a fixed asset has been placed into service, costs may be incurred to extend the asset's useful life. For example, the engine of a forklift that is near the end of its useful life may be overhauled at a cost of $4,500, extending its useful life by eight years. Such costs are *capital expenditures* and are recorded as a decrease in an accumulated depreciation account. In the case of the forklift, the expenditure is recorded as follows:

		Accumulated Depreciation—Forklift		4,500	
		Cash			4,500

Because the forklift's remaining useful life has changed, depreciation for the forklift will also change based on the new book value of the forklift.

Integrity, Objectivity, and Ethics in Business

CAPITAL CRIME

One of the largest alleged accounting frauds in history involved the improper accounting for capital expenditures. **WorldCom**, the second largest telecommunications company in the United States at the time, improperly treated maintenance expenditures on its telecommunications network as capital expenditures. As a result, the company had to restate its prior years' earnings downward by nearly $4 billion to correct this error. The company declared bankruptcy within months of disclosing the error, and the CEO was sentenced to 25 years in prison.

The accounting for revenue and capital expenditures is summarized in Exhibit 4.

EXHIBIT 4 **Revenue and Capital Expenditures**

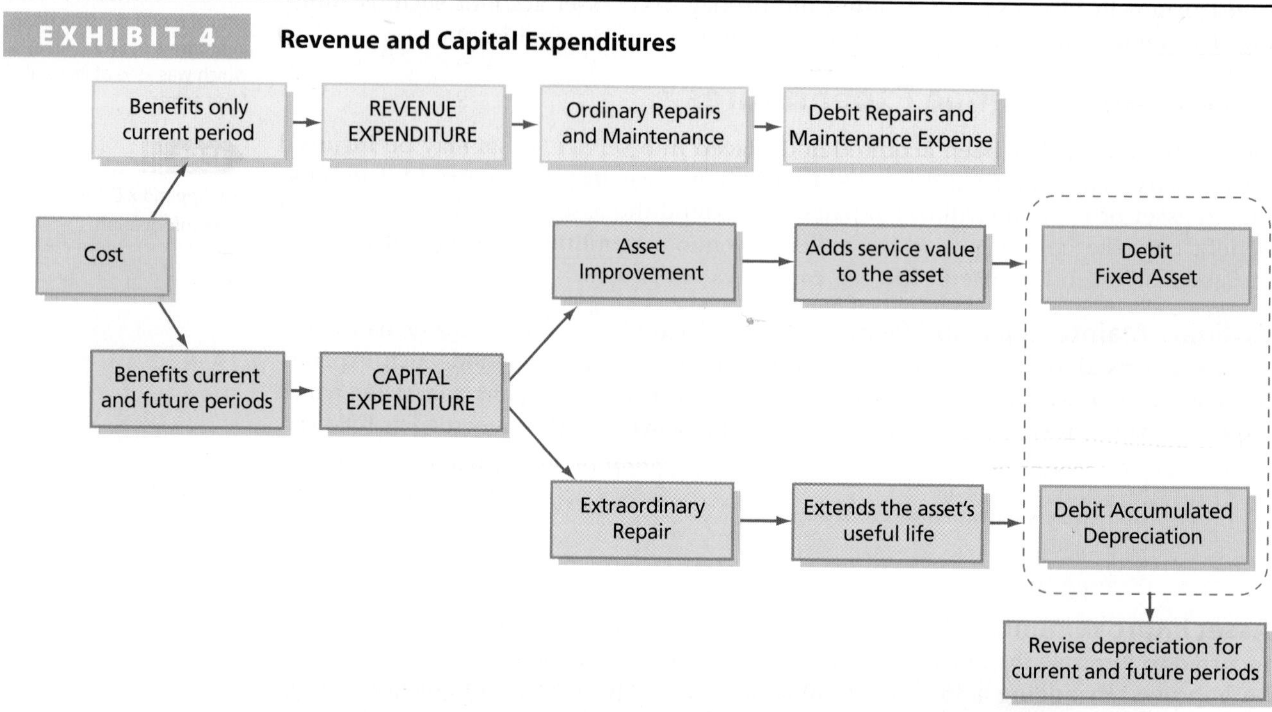

Example Exercise 10-1 Capital and Revenue Expenditures OBJ 1

On June 18, GTS Co. paid $1,200 to upgrade a hydraulic lift and $45 for an oil change for one of its delivery trucks. Journalize the entries for the hydraulic lift upgrade and oil change expenditures.

Follow My Example 10-1

June 18	Delivery Truck	1,200	
	Cash		1,200
18	Repairs and Maintenance Expense	45	
	Cash		45

Practice Exercises: PE 10-1A, PE 10-1B

Leasing Fixed Assets

A *lease* is a contract for the use of an asset for a period of time. Leases are often used in business. For example, automobiles, computers, medical equipment, buildings, and airplanes are often leased.

The two parties to a lease contract are as follows:

- The *lessor* is the party who owns the asset.
- The *lessee* is the party to whom the rights to use the asset are granted by the lessor.

Delta Air Lines leases facilities, aircraft, and equipment.

See Appendix D for more information.

Under a lease contract, the lessee pays rent on a periodic basis for the lease term. An advantage of leasing an asset is that the lessee has access to an asset without having to spend funds or obtain financing to buy the asset. In addition, expenses such as maintenance and repair costs may be the responsibility of the lessor. Finally, the risk of incurring additional cost because the asset becomes obsolete before the end of its useful life can be mitigated by leasing an asset.

The accounting for leases is currently the focus of a joint project by the Financial Accounting Standards (FASB) and the International Accounting Standards Board (IASB) to merge U.S. and international standards.[2] Under the proposed standard lessors and lessees would be required to record assets and liabilities related to certain long-term lease contracts.

For purposes of this text, we assume that leases are short-term and not extending beyond one year. Thus, lease payments are recorded as rent by debiting Rent Expense and crediting Cash. The lease terms, such as a renewal option, may be disclosed in the notes to the financial statements. The asset rentals described in the earlier chapters of this text were accounted for in this manner.

Accounting for Depreciation

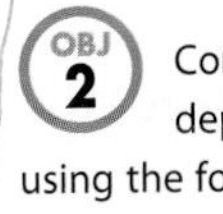

Compute depreciation, using the following methods: straight-line method, units-of-output method, and double-declining-balance method.

Note:
The adjusting entry to record depreciation debits Depreciation Expense and credits Accumulated Depreciation.

Over time, fixed assets, with the exception of land, lose their ability to provide services. Thus, the costs of fixed assets such as equipment and buildings should be recorded as an expense over their useful lives. This periodic recording of the cost of fixed assets as an expense is called **depreciation**. Because land has an unlimited life, it is not depreciated.

The adjusting entry to record depreciation debits Depreciation Expense and credits a contra asset account entitled *Accumulated Depreciation* or *Allowance for Depreciation*. The use of a contra asset account allows the original cost to remain unchanged in the fixed asset account.

Depreciation can be caused by physical or functional factors.

- *Physical depreciation* factors include wear and tear during use or from exposure to weather.
- *Functional depreciation* factors include obsolescence and changes in customer needs that cause the asset to no longer provide services for which it was intended. For example, equipment may become obsolete due to changing technology.

Two common misunderstandings that exist about depreciation as used in accounting include:

- Depreciation does not measure a decline in the market value of a fixed asset. Instead, depreciation is an allocation of a fixed asset's cost to expense over the asset's useful life. Thus, the book value of a fixed asset (cost less accumulated depreciation) usually does not agree with the asset's market value. This is justified in accounting because a fixed asset is for use in a company's operations rather than for resale.
- Depreciation does not provide cash to replace fixed assets as they wear out. This misunderstanding may occur because depreciation, unlike most expenses, does not require an outlay of cash when it is recorded.

Factors in Computing Depreciation Expense

Three factors determine the depreciation expense for a fixed asset. These three factors are as follows:

- The asset's initial cost
- The asset's expected useful life
- The asset's estimated residual value

The initial *cost* of a fixed asset is determined using the concepts discussed and illustrated earlier in this chapter.

The *expected useful life* of a fixed asset is estimated at the time the asset is placed into service. Estimates of expected useful lives are available from industry trade associations. The Internal Revenue Service also publishes guidelines for useful lives, which may be helpful for financial reporting purposes. However, it is not uncommon for different companies to use a different useful life for similar assets.

The **residual value** of a fixed asset at the end of its useful life is estimated at the time the asset is placed into service. Residual value is sometimes referred to as *scrap value, salvage value*, or *trade-in value*. The difference between a fixed asset's initial cost

[2] Proposed Accounting Standards Update, *Leases (Topic 842)*, Financial Accounting Standards Board, May 16, 2013.

and its residual value is called the asset's *depreciable cost*. The depreciable cost is the amount of the asset's cost that is allocated over its useful life as depreciation expense. If a fixed asset has no residual value, then its entire cost should be allocated to depreciation.

Exhibit 5 shows the relationship between depreciation expense and a fixed asset's initial cost, expected useful life, and estimated residual value.

EXHIBIT 5

Depreciation Expense Factors

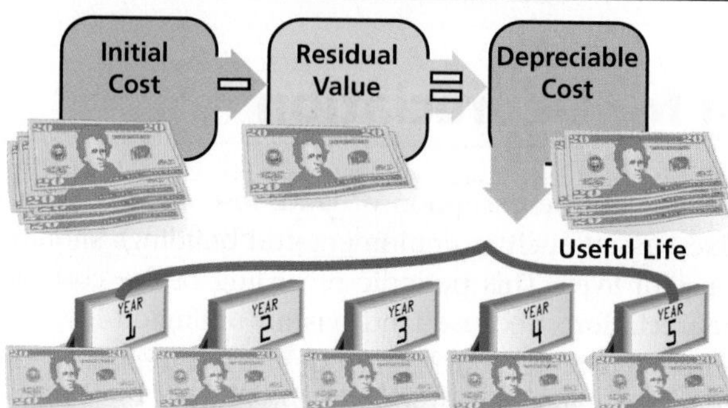

For an asset placed into or taken out of service during the first half of a month, many companies compute depreciation on the asset for the entire month. That is, the asset is treated as having been purchased or sold on the first day of *that* month. Likewise, purchases and sales during the second half of a month are treated as having occurred on the first day of the *next* month. To simplify, this practice is used in this chapter.

The three depreciation methods used most often are as follows:[3]

- Straight-line depreciation
- Units-of-output depreciation
- Double-declining-balance depreciation

Exhibit 6 shows how often these methods are used in financial statements.

EXHIBIT 6

Use of Depreciation Methods

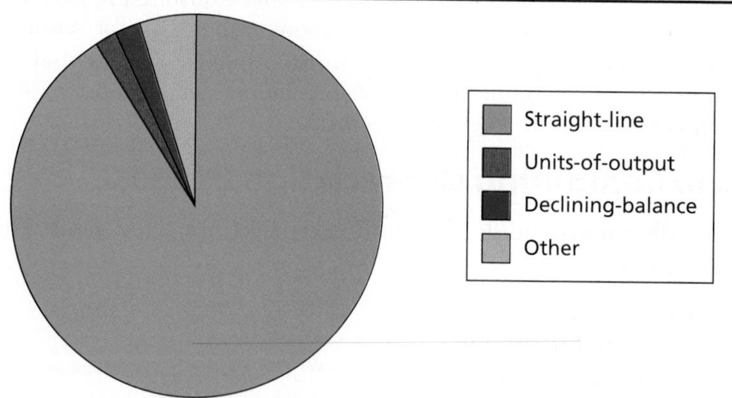

Source: *Accounting Trends & Techniques*, 66th ed., American Institute of Certified Public Accountants, New York, 2012.

It is not necessary for a company to use only one method of computing depreciation for all of its fixed assets. For example, a company may use one method for depreciating equipment and another method for depreciating buildings. A company may also use different depreciation methods for determining income taxes and property taxes.

[3] Another method not often used today, called the *sum-of-the-years-digits method*, is described and illustrated in an online appendix located at www.cengagebrain.com.

Straight-Line Method

The **straight-line method** provides for the same amount of depreciation expense for each year of the asset's useful life. As shown in Exhibit 6, the straight-line method is by far the most widely used depreciation method.

To illustrate, assume that equipment was purchased on January 1 as follows:

Initial cost	$24,000
Expected useful life	5 years
Estimated residual value	$2,000

The annual straight-line depreciation of $4,400 is computed as follows:

$$\text{Annual Depreciation} = \frac{\text{Cost} - \text{Residual Value}}{\text{Useful Life}} = \frac{\$24{,}000 - \$2{,}000}{5 \text{ Years}} = \$4{,}400$$

If an asset is used for only part of a year, the annual depreciation is prorated. For example, assume that the preceding equipment was purchased and placed into service on October 1. The depreciation for the year ending December 31 would be $1,100, computed as follows:

$$\text{First-Year Partial Depreciation} = \$4{,}400 \times 3 \div 12 = \$1{,}100$$

The computation of straight-line depreciation may be simplified by converting the annual depreciation to a percentage of depreciable cost.[4] The straight-line percentage is determined by dividing 100% by the number of years of expected useful life, computed as follows:

Expected Years of Useful Life	Straight-Line Percentage
5 years	20% (100% ÷ 5)
8 years	12.5% (100% ÷ 8)
10 years	10% (100% ÷ 10)
20 years	5% (100% ÷ 20)
25 years	4% (100% ÷ 25)

For the preceding equipment, the annual depreciation of $4,400 can be computed by multiplying the depreciable cost of $22,000 by 20% (100% ÷ 5).

The straight-line method is simple to use. When an asset's revenues are about the same from period to period, straight-line depreciation provides a good matching of depreciation expense with the asset's revenues.

Example Exercise 10-2 Straight-Line Depreciation

OBJ 2

Equipment acquired at the beginning of the year at a cost of $125,000 has an estimated residual value of $5,000 and an estimated useful life of 10 years. Determine (a) the depreciable cost, (b) the straight-line rate, and (c) the annual straight-line depreciation.

Follow My Example 10-2

a. $120,000 ($125,000 – $5,000)

b. 10% = 1 ÷ 10

c. $12,000 ($120,000 × 10%), or ($120,000 ÷ 10 years)

Practice Exercises: PE 10-2A, PE 10-2B

[4] The depreciation rate may also be expressed as a fraction. For example, the annual straight-line rate for an asset with a three-year useful life is 1/3.

Units-of-Output Method

The **units-of-output method** provides the same amount of depreciation expense for each unit of output of the asset. Depending on the asset, the units of output can be expressed in terms of hours, miles driven, or quantity produced. For example, the unit of output for a truck is normally expressed in miles driven. For manufacturing assets, the units of output are often expressed as units of product. In this case, the units-of-output method may be called the *units-of-production method*.

Norfolk Southern Corporation depreciates its train engines based on hours of operation.

The units-of-output method is applied in the following two steps:

- Step 1. Determine the depreciation per unit as follows:

$$\text{Depreciation per Unit} = \frac{\text{Cost} - \text{Residual Value}}{\text{Total Units of Output}}$$

- Step 2. Compute the depreciation expense as follows:

$$\text{Depreciation Expense} = \text{Depreciation per Unit} \times \text{Total Units of Output Used}$$

To illustrate, assume that the equipment in the preceding example is expected to have a useful life of 10,000 operating hours. During the year, the equipment was operated 2,100 hours. The units-of-output depreciation for the year is $4,620, computed as follows:

- Step 1. Determine the depreciation per hour as follows:

$$\text{Depreciation per Hour} = \frac{\text{Cost} - \text{Residual Value}}{\text{Total Units of Output}} = \frac{\$24{,}000 - \$2{,}000}{10{,}000 \text{ Hours}} = \$2.20 \text{ per Hour}$$

- Step 2. Compute the depreciation expense as follows:

$$\text{Depreciation Expense} = \text{Depreciation per Unit} \times \text{Total Units of Output Used}$$
$$\text{Depreciation Expense} = \$2.20 \text{ per Hour} \times 2{,}100 \text{ Hours} = \$4{,}620$$

The units-of-output method is often used when a fixed asset's in-service time (or use) varies from year to year. In such cases, the units-of-output method matches depreciation expense with the asset's revenues.

Example Exercise 10-3 Units-of-Output Depreciation

OBJ 2

Equipment acquired at the beginning of the year at a cost of $180,000 has an estimated residual value of $10,000, has an estimated useful life of 40,000 hours, and was operated 3,600 hours during the year. Determine (a) the depreciable cost, (b) the depreciation rate, and (c) the unit-of-output depreciation for the year.

Follow My Example 10-3

a. $170,000 ($180,000 – $10,000)

b. $4.25 per hour ($170,000 ÷ 40,000 hours)

c. $15,300 (3,600 hours × $4.25)

Practice Exercises: PE 10-3A, PE 10-3B

Double-Declining-Balance Method

The **double-declining-balance method** provides for a declining periodic expense over the expected useful life of the asset. The double-declining-balance method is applied in the following three steps:

- Step 1. Determine the straight-line percentage, using the expected useful life.
- Step 2. Determine the double-declining-balance rate by multiplying the straight-line rate from Step 1 by 2.
- Step 3. Compute the depreciation expense by multiplying the double-declining-balance rate from Step 2 times the book value of the asset.

To illustrate, the equipment purchased in the preceding example is used to compute double-declining-balance depreciation. For the first year, the depreciation is $9,600, computed as follows:

- Step 1. Straight-line percentage = 20% (100% ÷ 5)
- Step 2. Double-declining-balance rate = 40% (20% × 2)
- Step 3. Depreciation expense = $9,600 ($24,000 × 40%)

For the first year, the book value of the equipment is its initial cost of $24,000. After the first year, the **book value** (cost minus accumulated depreciation) declines, and thus, the depreciation also declines. The double-declining-balance depreciation for the full five-year life of the equipment is as follows:

Year	Cost	Acc. Dep. at Beginning of Year	Book Value at Beginning of Year		Double-Declining-Balance Rate	Depreciation for Year	Book Value at End of Year
1	$24,000		$24,000.00	×	40%	$9,600.00	$14,400.00
2	24,000	$ 9,600.00	14,400.00	×	40%	5,760.00	8,640.00
3	24,000	15,360.00	8,640.00	×	40%	3,456.00	5,184.00
4	24,000	18,816.00	5,184.00	×	40%	2,073.60	3,110.40
5	24,000	20,889.60	3,110.40		—	1,110.40	2,000.00

When the double-declining-balance method is used, the estimated residual value is *not* considered. However, the asset should not be depreciated below its estimated residual value. In the preceding example, the estimated residual value was $2,000. Therefore, the depreciation for the fifth year is $1,110.40 ($3,110.40 − $2,000.00) instead of $1,244.16 (40% × $3,110.40).

Like straight-line depreciation, if an asset is used for only part of a year, the annual depreciation is prorated. For example, assume that the preceding equipment was purchased and placed into service on October 1. The depreciation for the year ending December 31 would be $2,400, computed as follows:

First-Year Partial Depreciation = $9,600 × 3 ÷ 12 = $2,400

The depreciation for the second year would then be $8,640, computed as follows:

Second-Year Depreciation = $8,640 = [40% × ($24,000 − $2,400)]

The double-declining-balance method provides a higher depreciation in the first year of the asset's use, followed by declining depreciation amounts. For this reason, the double-declining-balance method is called an **accelerated depreciation method**.

An asset's revenues are often greater in the early years of its use than in later years. In such cases, the double-declining-balance method provides a good matching of depreciation expense with the asset's revenues.

Example Exercise 10-4 Double-Declining-Balance Depreciation

OBJ 2

Equipment acquired at the beginning of the year at a cost of $125,000 has an estimated residual value of $5,000 and an estimated useful life of 10 years. Determine (a) the double-declining-balance rate and (b) the double-declining-balance depreciation for the first year.

Follow My Example 10-4

a. 20% [(1 ÷ 10) × 2]
b. $25,000 ($125,000 × 20%)

Practice Exercises: PE 10-4A, PE 10-4B

Comparing Depreciation Methods

The three depreciation methods are summarized in Exhibit 7. All three methods allocate a portion of the total cost of an asset to an accounting period, while never depreciating an asset below its residual value.

EXHIBIT 7

Summary of Depreciation Methods

Method	Useful Life	Depreciable Cost	Depreciation Rate	Depreciation Expense
Straight-line	Years	Cost less residual value	Straight-line rate*	Constant
Units-of-output	Total units of output	Cost less residual value	$\frac{\text{Cost} - \text{Residual value}}{\text{Total units of output}}$	Variable
Double-declining-balance	Years	Declining book value, but not below residual value	Straight-line rate* × 2	Declining

*Straight-line rate = (100% ÷ Useful life)

The straight-line method provides for the same periodic amounts of depreciation expense over the life of the asset. The units-of-output method provides for periodic amounts of depreciation expense that vary, depending on the amount the asset is used. The double-declining-balance method provides for a higher depreciation amount in the first year of the asset's use, followed by declining amounts.

The depreciation for the straight-line, units-of-output, and double-declining-balance methods is shown in Exhibit 8. The depreciation in Exhibit 8 is based on the equipment purchased in our prior illustrations. For the units-of-output method, we assume that the equipment was used as follows:

Year 1	2,100 hours
Year 2	1,500
Year 3	2,600
Year 4	1,800
Year 5	2,000
Total	10,000 hours

EXHIBIT 8

Comparing Depreciation Methods

	Depreciation Expense		
Year	**Straight-Line Method**	**Units-of-Output Method**	**Double-Declining-Balance Method**
1	$ 4,400*	$ 4,620 ($2.20 × 2,100 hrs.)	$ 9,600.00 ($24,000 × 40%)
2	4,400	3,300 ($2.20 × 1,500 hrs.)	5,760.00 ($14,400 × 40%)
3	4,400	5,720 ($2.20 × 2,600 hrs.)	3,456.00 ($8,640 × 40%)
4	4,400	3,960 ($2.20 × 1,800 hrs.)	2,073.60 ($5,184 × 40%)
5	4,400	4,400 ($2.20 × 2,000 hrs.)	1,110.40**
Total	$22,000	$22,000	$22,000.00

*$4,400 = ($24,000 – $2,000) ÷ 5 years

**$3,110.40 – $2,000.00 because the equipment cannot be depreciated below its residual value of $2,000.

Depreciation for Federal Income Tax

The Internal Revenue Code uses the *Modified Accelerated Cost Recovery System (MACRS)* to compute depreciation for tax purposes. MACRS has eight classes of useful life and depreciation rates for each class. Two of the most common classes are the five-year class and the seven-year class.[5] The five-year class includes automobiles and light-duty trucks. The seven-year class includes most machinery and equipment. Depreciation for these two classes is similar to that computed using the double-declining-balance method.

In using the MACRS rates, residual value is ignored. Also, all fixed assets are assumed to be put in and taken out of service in the middle of the year. For the five-year-class assets, depreciation is spread over six years, as illustrated in Exhibit 9.

EXHIBIT 9

MACRS Depreciation Rates for 5-Year-Class Assets

Year	MACRS Five-Year-Class Depreciation Rates
1	20.0%
2	32.0
3	19.2
4	11.5
5	11.5
6	5.8
	100.0%

To simplify, a company will sometimes use MACRS for both financial statement and tax purposes. This is acceptable if MACRS does not result in significantly different amounts than would have been reported using one of the three depreciation methods discussed in this chapter.

Business Connection

DEPRECIATING ANIMALS?

Under MACRS, various farm animals may be depreciated. The period (years) over which some common classes of farm animals may be depreciated are shown in the table that follows.

Depreciation for farm animals begins when the animal reaches the age of maturity, which is normally when it can be worked, milked, or bred. For race horses, depreciation begins when a horse is put into training.

Class of Animal	Years
Dairy or breeding cattle	7–10
Goats and sheep	5
Hogs	3
Horses	3–12

[5] Real estate is in either a 27½-year or a 31½-year class and is depreciated by the straight-line method.

Revising Depreciation Estimates

Estimates of residual values and useful lives of fixed assets may change due to abnormal wear and tear or obsolescence. When new estimates are determined, they are used to determine the depreciation expense in future periods. The depreciation expense recorded in earlier years is not affected.[6]

To illustrate, assume the following data for a machine that was purchased on January 1, 2015:

Initial machine cost	$140,000
Expected useful life	5 years
Estimated residual value	$10,000
Annual depreciation using the straight-line method	
[($140,000 – $10,000) ÷ 5 years]	$26,000

At the end of 2016, the machine's book value (undepreciated cost) is $88,000, computed as follows:

Initial machine cost	$140,000
Less accumulated depreciation ($26,000 per year × 2 years)	52,000
Book value (undepreciated cost), end of second year	$ 88,000

At the beginning of 2017, the company estimates that the machine's remaining useful life is eight years (instead of three) and that its residual value is $8,000 (instead of $10,000). The depreciation expense for each of the remaining eight years is $10,000, computed as follows:

Book value (undepreciated cost), end of second year	$88,000
Less revised estimated residual value	8,000
Revised remaining depreciable cost	$80,000
Revised annual depreciation expense	
[($88,000 – $8,000) ÷ 8 years]	$10,000

Exhibit 10 shows the book value of the asset over its original and revised lives. After the depreciation is revised at the end of 2016, book value declines at a slower rate. At the end of year 2024, the book value reaches the revised residual value of $8,000.

EXHIBIT 10

Book Value of Asset with Change in Estimate

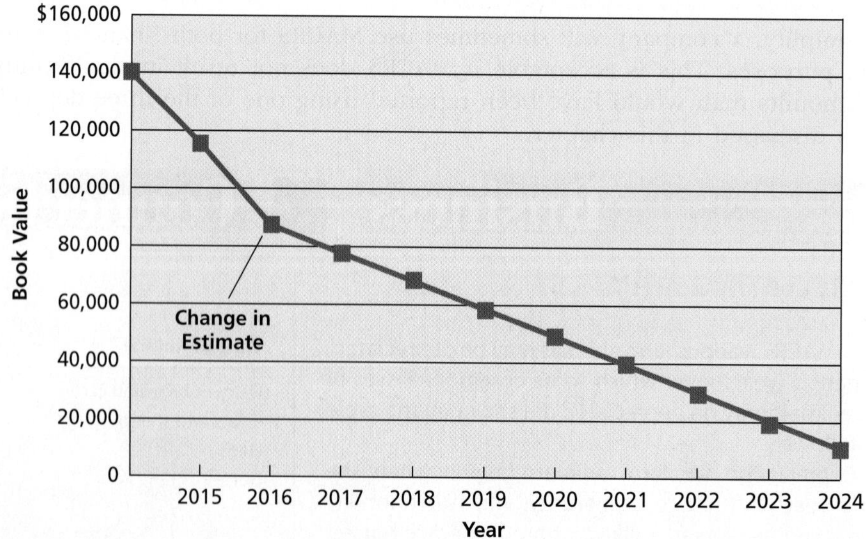

[6] *FASB Accounting Standards Codification*, Section 250-10-05.

Example Exercise 10-5 Revision of Depreciation

A warehouse with a cost of $500,000 has an estimated residual value of $120,000, has an estimated useful life of 40 years, and is depreciated by the straight-line method. (a) Determine the amount of the annual depreciation. (b) Determine the book value at the end of the twentieth year of use. (c) Assuming that at the start of the twenty-first year the remaining life is estimated to be 25 years and the residual value is estimated to be $150,000, determine the depreciation expense for each of the remaining 25 years.

Follow My Example 10-5

a. $9,500 [($500,000 – $120,000) ÷ 40]

b. $310,000 [$500,000 – ($9,500 × 20)]

c. $6,400 [($310,000 – $150,000) ÷ 25]

Practice Exercises: PE 10-5A, PE 10-5B

Disposal of Fixed Assets

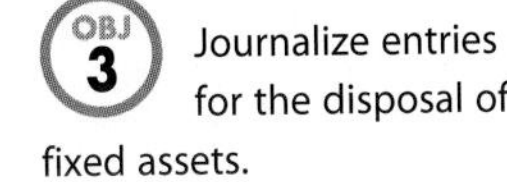

Journalize entries for the disposal of fixed assets.

Fixed assets that are no longer useful may be discarded or sold.[7] In such cases, the fixed asset is removed from the accounts. Just because a fixed asset is fully depreciated, however, does not mean that it should be removed from the accounts.

If a fixed asset is still being used, its cost and accumulated depreciation should remain in the ledger even if the asset is fully depreciated. This maintains accountability for the asset in the ledger. If the asset was removed from the ledger, the accounts would contain no evidence of the continued existence of the asset. In addition, cost and accumulated depreciation data on such assets are often needed for property tax and income tax reports.

Discarding Fixed Assets

If a fixed asset is no longer used and has no residual value, it is discarded. For example, assume that a fixed asset that is fully depreciated and has no residual value is discarded. The entry to record the discarding removes the asset and its related accumulated depreciation from the ledger.

Note:
The entry to record the disposal of a fixed asset removes the cost of the asset and its accumulated depreciation from the accounts.

To illustrate, assume that equipment acquired at a cost of $25,000 is fully depreciated at December 31, 2015. On February 14, 2016, the equipment is discarded. The entry to record the discard is as follows:

Feb.	14	Accumulated Depreciation—Equipment		25,000	
		Equipment			25,000
		To write off equipment discarded.			

If an asset has not been fully depreciated, depreciation should be recorded before removing the asset from the accounting records. To illustrate, assume that equipment costing $6,000 with no estimated residual value is depreciated at a straight-line rate of 10%. On December 31, 2015, the accumulated depreciation balance, after adjusting entries, is $4,650. On March 24, 2016, the asset is removed from service and discarded. The entry to record the depreciation for the three months of 2016 before the asset is discarded is as follows:

Mar.	24	Depreciation Expense—Equipment		150	
		Accumulated Depreciation—Equipment			150
		To record current depreciation on equipment discarded ($600 × 3/12).			

[7] The accounting for the exchange of fixed assets is described and illustrated in the appendix at the end of this chapter.

The discarding of the equipment is then recorded as follows:

Mar.	24	Accumulated Depreciation—Equipment	4,800	
		Loss on Disposal of Equipment	1,200	
		Equipment		6,000
		To write off equipment discarded.		

The loss of $1,200 is recorded because the balance of the accumulated depreciation account ($4,800) is less than the balance in the equipment account ($6,000). Losses on the discarding of fixed assets are reported in the income statement.

Selling Fixed Assets

The entry to record the sale of a fixed asset is similar to the entry for discarding an asset. The only difference is that the receipt of cash is also recorded. If the selling price is more than the book value of the asset, a gain is recorded. If the selling price is less than the book value, a loss is recorded.

To illustrate, assume that equipment is purchased at a cost of $10,000 with no estimated residual value and is depreciated at a straight-line rate of 10%. The equipment is sold for cash on October 12 of the eighth year of its use. The balance of the accumulated depreciation account as of the preceding December 31 is $7,000. The entry to update the depreciation for the nine months of the current year is as follows:

Oct.	12	Depreciation Expense—Equipment	750	
		Accumulated Depreciation—Equipment		750
		To record current depreciation on equipment sold ($10,000 × $\frac{9}{12}$ × 10%).		

After the current depreciation is recorded, the book value of the asset is $2,250 ($10,000 – $7,750). The entries to record the sale, assuming three different selling prices, are as follows:

Sold at book value, for $2,250. No gain or loss.

Oct.	12	Cash	2,250	
		Accumulated Depreciation—Equipment	7,750	
		Equipment		10,000

Sold below book value, for $1,000. Loss of $1,250.

Oct.	12	Cash	1,000	
		Accumulated Depreciation—Equipment	7,750	
		Loss on Sale of Equipment	1,250	
		Equipment		10,000

Sold above book value, for $2,800. Gain of $550.

Oct.	12	Cash	2,800	
		Accumulated Depreciation—Equipment	7,750	
		Equipment		10,000
		Gain on Sale of Equipment		550

Example Exercise 10-6 Sale of Equipment

OBJ 3

Equipment was acquired at the beginning of the year at a cost of $91,000. The equipment was depreciated using the straight-line method based on an estimated useful life of nine years and an estimated residual value of $10,000.

a. What was the depreciation for the first year?

b. Assuming the equipment was sold at the end of the second year for $78,000, determine the gain or loss on the sale of the equipment.

c. Journalize the entry to record the sale.

Dynamic Exhibit

Follow My Example 10-6

a. $9,000 [($91,000 – $10,000) ÷ 9]

b. $5,000 gain {$78,000 – [$91,000 – ($9,000 × 2)]}

c.

Account	Debit	Credit
Cash	78,000	
Accumulated Depreciation—Equipment	18,000	
Equipment		91,000
Gain on Sale of Equipment		5,000

Practice Exercises: PE 10-6A, PE 10-6B

Natural Resources

OBJ 4 Compute depletion and journalize the entry for depletion.

The fixed assets of some companies include timber, metal ores, minerals, or other natural resources. As these resources are harvested or mined and then sold, a portion of their cost is debited to an expense account. This process of transferring the cost of natural resources to an expense account is called **depletion**.

Depletion is determined as follows:[8]

- Step 1. Determine the depletion rate as follows:

$$\text{Depletion Rate} = \frac{\text{Cost of Resource}}{\text{Estimated Total Units of Resource}}$$

- Step 2. Multiply the depletion rate by the quantity extracted from the resource during the period.

$$\text{Depletion Expense} = \text{Depletion Rate} \times \text{Quantity Extracted}$$

To illustrate, assume that Karst Company purchased mining rights as follows:

Cost of mineral deposit	$400,000
Estimated total units of resource	1,000,000 tons
Tons mined during year	90,000 tons

The depletion expense of $36,000 for the year is computed as follows:

$$\text{Step 1. Depletion Rate} = \frac{\text{Cost of Resource}}{\text{Estimated Total Units of Resource}} = \frac{\$400{,}000}{1{,}000{,}000 \text{ Tons}} = \$0.40 \text{ per Ton}$$

Step 2. Depletion Expense = $0.40 per Ton × 90,000 Tons = $36,000

The adjusting entry to record the depletion is as follows:

					Debit	Credit
	Dec.	31	Depletion Expense		36,000	
			Accumulated Depletion			36,000
			Depletion of mineral deposit.			

[8] We assume that there is no significant residual value after all the natural resource is extracted.

Like the accumulated depreciation account, Accumulated Depletion is a contra asset account. It is reported on the balance sheet as a deduction from the cost of the mineral deposit.

Example Exercise 10-7 Depletion

Earth's Treasures Mining Co. acquired mineral rights for $45,000,000. The mineral deposit is estimated at 50,000,000 tons. During the current year, 12,600,000 tons were mined and sold.

a. Determine the depletion rate.

b. Determine the amount of depletion expense for the current year.

c. Journalize the adjusting entry on December 31 to recognize the depletion expense.

Follow My Example 10-7

a. $0.90 per ton ($45,000,000 ÷ 50,000,000 tons)

b. $11,340,000 (12,600,000 tons × $0.90 per ton)

c.

Dec. 31	Depletion Expense	11,340,000	
	Accumulated Depletion		11,340,000
	Depletion of mineral deposit.		

Practice Exercises: PE 10-7A, PE 10-7B

OBJ 5 Describe the accounting for intangible assets, such as patents, copyrights, and goodwill.

Intangible Assets

Patents, copyrights, trademarks, and goodwill are long-lived assets that are used in the operations of a business and are not held for sale. These assets are called **intangible assets** because they do not exist physically.

The accounting for intangible assets is similar to that for fixed assets. The major issues are:

See Appendix D for more information.

- Determining the initial cost.
- Determining the **amortization**, which is the amount of cost to transfer to expense.

Amortization results from the passage of time or a decline in the usefulness of the intangible asset.

Patents

Manufacturers may acquire exclusive rights to produce and sell goods with one or more unique features. Such rights are granted by **patents**, which the federal government issues to inventors. These rights continue in effect for 20 years. A business may purchase patent rights from others, or it may obtain patents developed by its own research and development.

The initial cost of a purchased patent, including any legal fees, is debited to an asset account. This cost is written off, or amortized, over the years of the patent's expected useful life. The expected useful life of a patent may be less than its legal life. For example, a patent may become worthless due to changing technology or consumer tastes.

Patent amortization is normally computed using the straight-line method. The amortization is recorded by debiting an amortization expense account and crediting the patents account. A separate contra asset account is usually *not* used for intangible assets.

To illustrate, assume that at the beginning of its fiscal year, a company acquires patent rights for $100,000. Although the patent will not expire for 14 years, its remaining useful life is estimated as five years. The adjusting entry to amortize the patent at the end of the year is as follows:

Dec.	31	Amortization Expense—Patents		20,000	
		Patents			20,000
		Patent amortization ($100,000 ÷ 5).			

Some companies develop their own patents through research and development. In such cases, any *research and development costs* are usually recorded as current operating expenses in the period in which they are incurred. This accounting for research and development costs is justified on the basis that any future benefits from research and development are highly uncertain.

International  Connection

IFRS INTERNATIONAL FINANCIAL REPORTING STANDARDS (IFRS)

IFRS allow certain research and development (R&D) costs to be recorded as assets when incurred. Typically, R&D costs are classified as either research costs or development costs. If certain criteria are met, research costs can be recorded as an expense, while development costs can be recorded as an asset. This criterion includes such considerations as the company's intent to use or to sell the intangible asset. For example, **Nokia Corporation** (Finland) reported capitalized development costs of €40 million in a recent statement of financial position (balance sheet), where € represents the euro, the common currency of the European Economic Union.*

*Differences between U.S. GAAP and IFRS are further discussed and illustrated in Appendix D.

Copyrights and Trademarks

The exclusive right to publish and sell a literary, artistic, or musical composition is granted by a **copyright**. Copyrights are issued by the federal government and extend for 70 years beyond the author's death. The costs of a copyright include all costs of creating the work plus any other costs of obtaining the copyright. A copyright that is purchased is recorded at the price paid for it. Copyrights are amortized over their estimated useful lives.

A **trademark** is a name, term, or symbol used to identify a business and its products. Most businesses identify their trademarks with ® in their advertisements and on their products.

Under federal law, businesses can protect their trademarks by registering them for 10 years and renewing the registration for 10-year periods. Like a copyright, the legal costs of registering a trademark are recorded as an asset.

If a trademark is purchased from another business, its cost is recorded as an asset. In such cases, the cost of the trademark is considered to have an indefinite useful life. Thus, trademarks are not amortized. Instead, trademarks are reviewed periodically for impaired value. When a trademark is impaired, the trademark should be written down and a loss recognized.

Goodwill

Goodwill refers to an intangible asset of a business that is created from such favorable factors as location, product quality, reputation, and managerial skill. Goodwill allows a business to earn a greater rate of return than normal.

Generally accepted accounting principles (GAAP) allow goodwill to be recorded only if it is objectively determined by a transaction. An example of such a transaction is the purchase of a business at a price in excess of the fair value of its net assets (assets − liabilities). The excess is recorded as goodwill and reported as an intangible asset.

Unlike patents and copyrights, goodwill is not amortized. However, a loss should be recorded if the future prospects of the purchased firm become impaired. This loss would normally be disclosed in the Other Expense section of the income statement.

To illustrate, assume that on December 31 FaceCard Company has determined that $250,000 of the goodwill created from the purchase of Electronic Systems is impaired. The entry to record the impairment is as follows:

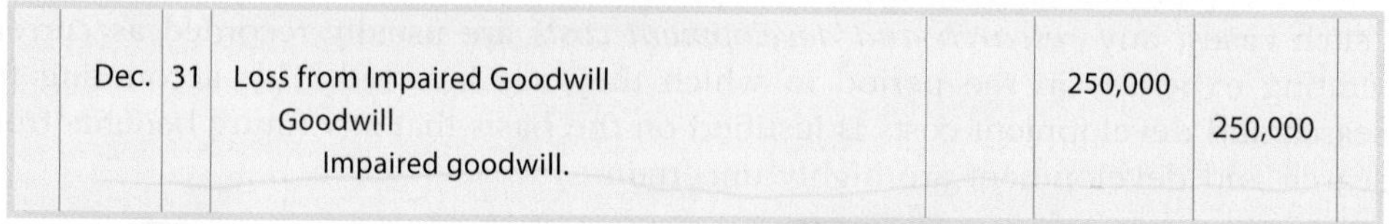

Dec.	31	Loss from Impaired Goodwill		250,000	
		Goodwill			250,000
		Impaired goodwill.			

Exhibit 11 shows common intangible asset disclosures for 500 large firms. Goodwill is the most often reported intangible asset. This is because goodwill arises from merger transactions, which are common.

EXHIBIT 11

Frequency of Intangible Asset Disclosures for 500 Firms

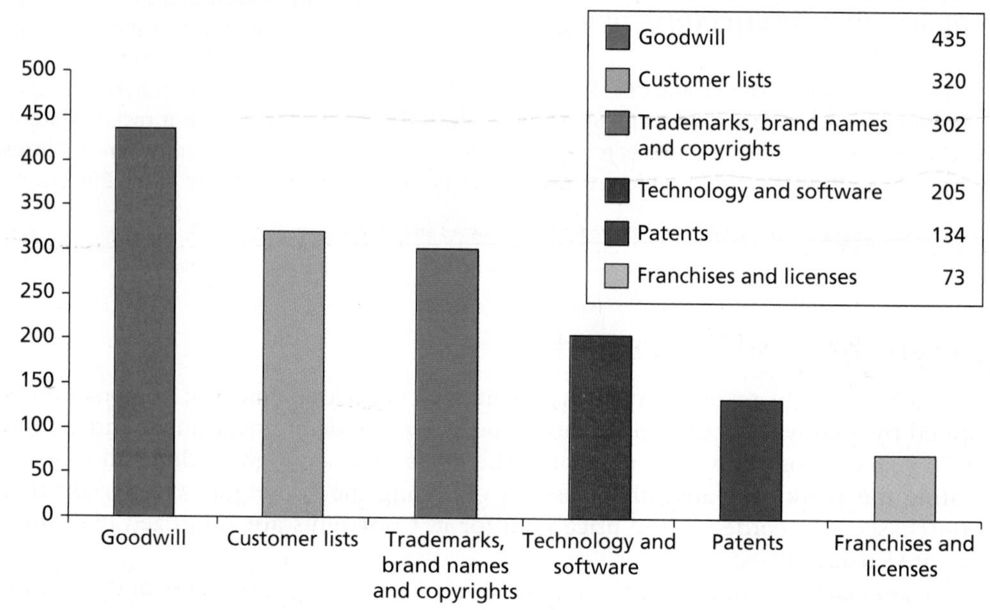

Note: Some firms have multiple disclosures.
Source: *Accounting Trends & Techniques*, 66th ed., American Institute of Certified Public Accountants, New York, 2012.

Exhibit 12 summarizes the characteristics of intangible assets.

EXHIBIT 12

Comparison of Intangible Assets

Intangible Asset	Description	Amortization Period	Periodic Expense
Patent	Exclusive right to benefit from an innovation	Estimated useful life not to exceed legal life	Amortization expense
Copyright	Exclusive right to benefit from a literary, artistic, or musical composition	Estimated useful life not to exceed legal life	Amortization expense
Trademark	Exclusive use of a name, term, or symbol	None	Impairment loss if fair value less than carrying value (impaired)
Goodwill	Excess of purchase price of a business over the fair value of its net assets (assets − liabilities)	None	Impairment loss if fair value less than carrying value (impaired)

Example Exercise 10-8 Impaired Goodwill and Amortization of Patent

On December 31, it was estimated that goodwill of $40,000 was impaired. In addition, a patent with an estimated useful economic life of 12 years was acquired for $84,000 on July 1.

a. Journalize the adjusting entry on December 31 for the impaired goodwill.

b. Journalize the adjusting entry on December 31 for the amortization of the patent rights.

Follow My Example 10-8

a.	Dec. 31	Loss from Impaired Goodwill	40,000	
		Goodwill		40,000
		Impaired goodwill.		
b.	Dec. 31	Amortization Expense—Patents	3,500	
		Patents		3,500
		Amortized patent rights [($84,000 ÷ 12) × (6 ÷ 12)].		

Practice Exercises: PE 10-8A, PE 10-8B

Financial Reporting for Fixed Assets and Intangible Assets

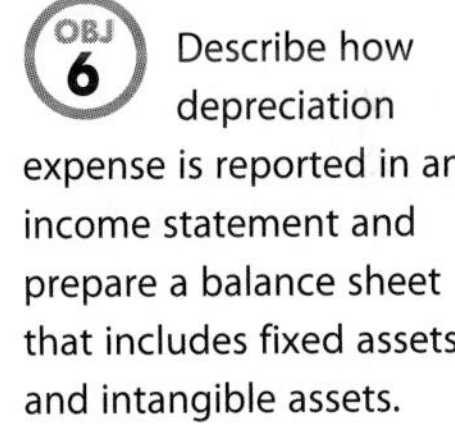

OBJ 6 Describe how depreciation expense is reported in an income statement and prepare a balance sheet that includes fixed assets and intangible assets.

In the income statement, depreciation and amortization expense should be reported separately or disclosed in a note. A description of the methods used in computing depreciation should also be reported.

In the balance sheet, each class of fixed assets should be disclosed on the face of the statement or in the notes. The related accumulated depreciation should also be disclosed, either by class or in total. The fixed assets may be shown at their *book value* (cost less accumulated depreciation), which can also be described as their *net* amount.

If there are many classes of fixed assets, a single amount may be presented in the balance sheet, supported by a note with a separate listing. Fixed assets may be reported under the more descriptive caption of property, plant, and equipment.

Intangible assets are usually reported in the balance sheet in a separate section following fixed assets. The balance of each class of intangible assets should be disclosed net of any amortization.

The balance sheet presentation for **Mornin' Joe**'s fixed and intangible assets follows:

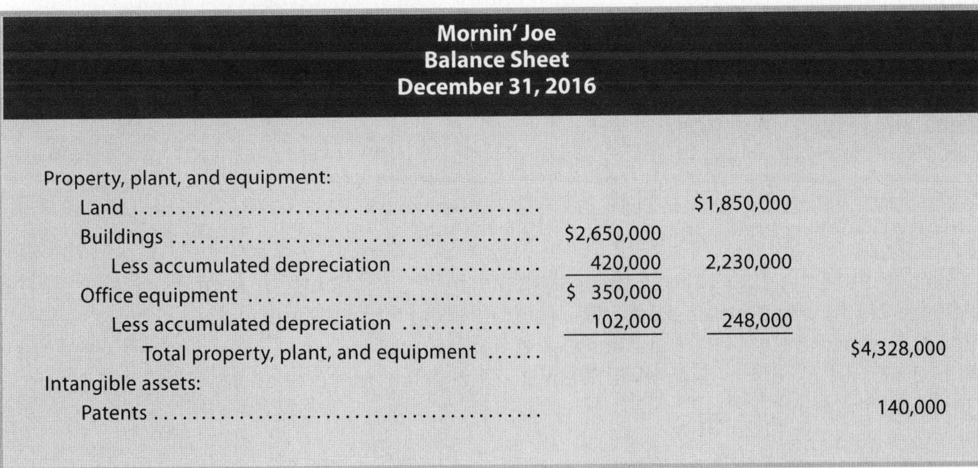

Mornin' Joe
Balance Sheet
December 31, 2016

Property, plant, and equipment:			
Land		$1,850,000	
Buildings	$2,650,000		
Less accumulated depreciation	420,000	2,230,000	
Office equipment	$ 350,000		
Less accumulated depreciation	102,000	248,000	
Total property, plant, and equipment			$4,328,000
Intangible assets:			
Patents			140,000

The cost and related accumulated depletion of mineral rights are normally shown as part of the Fixed Assets section of the balance sheet. The mineral rights may be shown net of depletion on the face of the balance sheet. In such cases, a supporting note discloses the accumulated depletion.

OBJ 7 Describe and illustrate the fixed asset turnover ratio to assess the efficiency of a company's use of its fixed assets.

F·A·I

Financial Analysis and Interpretation: Fixed Asset Turnover Ratio

A measure of a company's efficiency in using its fixed assets to generate revenue is the fixed asset turnover ratio. The **fixed asset turnover ratio** measures the number of dollars of sales earned per dollar of fixed assets. It is computed as follows:

$$\text{Fixed Asset Turnover Ratio} = \frac{\text{Sales}}{\text{Average Book Value of Fixed Assets}}$$

To illustrate, the following data (in millions) were taken from recent financial statements of Starbucks Corporation:

	Year 2	Year 1
Sales	$13,300	$11,700
Fixed assets (net):		
Beginning of year	2,355	2,417
End of year	2,659	2,355

Starbucks' fixed asset turnover ratios for Year 2 and Year 1 are computed as follows:

	Year 2	Year 1
Sales	$13,300	$11,700
Average fixed assets	$2,507	$2,386
	[($2,355 + $2,659) ÷ 2]	[($2,417 + $2,355) ÷ 2]
Fixed asset turnover ratio*	5.31	4.90
	($13,300 ÷ $2,507)	($11,700 ÷ $2,386)

*Rounded to two decimal places.

Business  Connection

HUB-AND-SPOKE OR POINT-TO-POINT?

Southwest Airlines Co. uses a simple fare structure, featuring low, unrestricted, unlimited, everyday coach fares. These fares are made possible by Southwest's use of a point-to-point, rather than a hub-and-spoke, business approach.

United Airlines, Inc., Delta Air Lines, and American Airlines employ a hub-and-spoke approach in which an airline establishes major hubs that serve as connecting links to other cities. For example, Delta has major connecting hubs in Atlanta and Salt Lake City.

In contrast, Southwest focuses on nonstop, point-to-point service between selected cities. As a result, Southwest minimizes connections, delays, and total trip time. This operating approach permits Southwest to achieve high utilization of its fixed assets, such as its 737 aircraft.

The higher the fixed asset turnover, the more efficiently a company is using its fixed assets in generating sales. For example, in Year 2 Starbucks earned $5.31 of sales for every dollar of fixed assets, which is more than $4.90 of sales for every dollar of fixed assets it earned in Year 1. Thus, Starbucks used its fixed assets more efficiently in Year 2.

As illustrated for Starbucks, the fixed asset turnover ratio can be compared across time for a single company. In addition, the ratio can be compared across companies. For example, the fixed asset turnover ratio for a number of different companies and industries is shown in Exhibit 13.

EXHIBIT 13

Fixed Asset Turnover Ratio Examples

Company (industry)	Fixed Asset Turnover Ratio
Comcast Corporation (cable)	2.38
Google (Internet)	4.68
Manpower Inc. (temporary employment)	115.10
Norfolk Southern Corporation (railroad)	0.44
Ruby Tuesday, Inc. (restaurant)	1.33
Southwest Airlines Co. (airline)	1.37

The smaller ratios are associated with companies that require large fixed asset investments. The larger fixed asset turnover ratios are associated with firms that are more labor intensive and require smaller fixed asset investments.

Example Exercise 10-9 Fixed Asset Turnover Ratio

OBJ 7

Financial statement data for years ending December 31 for Broadwater Company follows:

	2016	2015
Sales	$2,862,000	$2,025,000
Fixed assets:		
Beginning of year	750,000	600,000
End of year	840,000	750,000

a. Determine the fixed asset turnover ratio for 2016 and 2015.

b. Does the change in the fixed asset turnover ratio from 2015 to 2016 indicate a favorable or an unfavorable trend?

Follow My Example 10-9

a. Fixed asset turnover:

	2016	2015
Sales	$2,862,000	$2,025,000
Fixed assets:		
Beginning of year	$750,000	$600,000
End of year	$840,000	$750,000
Average fixed assets	$795,000	$675,000
	[($750,000 + $840,000) ÷ 2]	[($600,000 + $750,000) ÷ 2]
Fixed asset turnover	3.6	3.0
	($2,862,000 ÷ $795,000)	($2,025,000 ÷ $675,000)

b. The increase in the fixed asset turnover ratio from 3.0 to 3.6 indicates a favorable trend in the efficiency of using fixed assets to generate sales.

Practice Exercises: PE 10-9A, PE 10-9B

APPENDIX

Exchanging Similar Fixed Assets

Old equipment is often traded in for new equipment having a similar use. In such cases, the seller allows the buyer an amount for the old equipment traded in. This amount, called the **trade-in allowance**, may be either greater or less than the book value of the old equipment. The remaining balance—the amount owed—is either paid in cash or recorded as a liability. It is normally called **boot**, which is its tax name.

Accounting for the exchange of similar assets depends on whether the transaction has *commercial substance*.[9] An exchange has commercial substance if future cash flows change as a result of the exchange. If an exchange of similar assets has commercial substance, a gain or loss is recognized. In such cases, the exchange is accounted for similar to that of a sale of a fixed asset. The gain or loss is determined as the difference between the fair market value (trade-in allowance) of the asset given up (exchanged) and its book value. Alternatively, the gain or loss can be determined as the difference between the fair market value of the new asset received and the assets given up in the exchange (cash and book value of the old asset).

Gain on Exchange

To illustrate a gain on an exchange of similar assets, assume the following:

Similar equipment acquired (new):	
Price (fair market value) of new equipment	$5,000
Trade-in allowance on old equipment	1,100
Cash paid at June 19, date of exchange	$3,900

Equipment traded in (old):	
Cost of old equipment	$4,000
Accumulated depreciation at date of exchange	3,200
Book value at June 19, date of exchange	$ 800

The entry to record this exchange and payment of cash is as follows:

June 19	Accumulated Depreciation—Equipment	3,200	
	Equipment (new equipment)	5,000	
	Equipment (old equipment)		4,000
	Cash		3,900
	Gain on Exchange of Equipment		300

The gain on the exchange, $300, is the difference between the fair market value (trade-in allowance) of the asset given up (exchanged) of $1,100 and its book value of $800, computed as follows:

Fair market value (trade-in allowance) of old equipment	$1,100
Less book value of old equipment	800
Gain on exchange of assets	$ 300

[9] *FASB Accounting Standards Codification*, Section 360-10-30.

The gain on the exchange, $300, can also be determined as the difference between the fair market value of the new asset of $5,000 and the book value of the old asset traded in of $800 plus the cash paid of $3,900, computed as follows:

Price (fair market value) of new equipment		$5,000
Less assets given up in exchange:		
Book value of old equipment ($4,000 – $3,200)	$ 800	
Cash paid on the exchange	3,900	4,700
Gain on exchange of assets		$ 300

Loss on Exchange

To illustrate a loss on an exchange of similar assets, assume that instead of a trade-in allowance of $1,100, a trade-in allowance of only $675 was allowed in the preceding example. In this case, the cash paid on the exchange is $4,325, computed as follows:

Price (fair market value) of new equipment	$5,000
Trade-in allowance of old equipment	675
Cash paid at June 19, date of exchange	$4,325

The entry to record this exchange and payment of cash is as follows:

June 19	Accumulated Depreciation—Equipment	3,200	
	Equipment (new equipment)	5,000	
	Loss on Exchange of Equipment	125	
	Equipment (old equipment)		4,000
	Cash		4,325

The loss on the exchange, $125, is the difference between the fair market value (trade-in allowance) of the asset given up (exchanged) of $675 and its book value of $800, computed as follows:

Fair market value (trade-in allowance) of old equipment	$ 675
Less book value of old equipment	800
Loss on exchange of assets	$(125)

The loss on the exchange, $125, can also be determined as the difference between the fair market value of the new asset of $5,000 and the book value of the old asset traded in of $800 plus the cash paid of $4,325, computed as follows:

Price (fair market value) of new equipment		$5,000
Less assets given up in exchange:		
Book value of old equipment ($4,000 – $3,200)	$ 800	
Cash paid on the exchange	4,325	5,125
Loss on exchange of assets		$ (125)

In those cases where an asset exchange *lacks commercial substance*, no gain is recognized on the exchange. Instead, the cost of the new asset is adjusted for any gain. For example, in the first illustration, the gain of $300 would be subtracted from the purchase price of $5,000 and the new asset would be recorded at $4,700. Accounting for the exchange of assets that lack commercial substance is discussed in more advanced accounting texts.[10]

[10] The exchange of similar assets also involves complex tax issues which are discussed in advanced accounting courses.

At a Glance 10

Define, classify, and account for the cost of fixed assets.

Key Points Fixed assets are long-term tangible assets used in the normal operations of the business such as equipment, buildings, and land. The initial cost of a fixed asset includes all amounts spent to get the asset in place and ready for use. Revenue expenditures include ordinary repairs and maintenance. Capital expenditures include asset improvements and extraordinary repairs.

Learning Outcomes	Example Exercises	Practice Exercises
• Define *fixed assets.*		
• List the types of costs that should be included in the cost of a fixed asset.		
• Provide examples of ordinary repairs, asset improvements, and extraordinary repairs.		
• Prepare journal entries for ordinary repairs, asset improvements, and extraordinary repairs.	**EE10-1**	**PE10-1A, 10-1B**

Compute depreciation, using the following methods: straight-line method, units-of-output method, and double-declining-balance method.

Key Points All fixed assets except land should be depreciated over time. Three factors are considered in determining depreciation: (1) the fixed asset's initial cost, (2) the useful life of the asset, and (3) the residual value of the asset.

Depreciation may be determined using the straight-line, units-of-output, and double-declining-balance methods. Depreciation may be revised into the future for changes in an asset's useful life or residual value.

Learning Outcomes	Example Exercises	Practice Exercises
• Define and describe *depreciation.*		
• List the factors used in determining depreciation.		
• Compute straight-line depreciation.	**EE10-2**	**PE10-2A, 10-2B**
• Compute units-of-output depreciation.	**EE10-3**	**PE10-3A, 10-3B**
• Compute double-declining-balance depreciation.	**EE10-4**	**PE10-4A, 10-4B**
• Compute revised depreciation for a change in an asset's useful life and residual value.	**EE10-5**	**PE10-5A, 10-5B**

Journalize entries for the disposal of fixed assets.

Key Points When discarding a fixed asset, any depreciation for the current period should be recorded, and the book value of the asset is then removed from the accounts.

When a fixed asset is sold, the book value is removed, and the cash or other asset received is recorded. If the selling price is more than the book value of the asset, the transaction results in a gain. If the selling price is less than the book value, there is a loss.

Learning Outcomes	Example Exercises	Practice Exercises
• Prepare the journal entry for discarding a fixed asset.		
• Prepare journal entries for the sale of a fixed asset.	**EE10-6**	**PE10-6A, 10-6B**

Compute depletion and journalize the entry for depletion.

Key Points The amount of periodic depletion is computed by multiplying the quantity of minerals extracted during the period by a depletion rate. The depletion rate is computed by dividing the cost of the mineral deposit by its estimated total units of resource. The entry to record depletion debits a depletion expense account and credits an accumulated depletion account.

Learning Outcomes	Example Exercises	Practice Exercises
• Define and describe *depletion*.		
• Compute a depletion rate.	EE10-7	PE10-7A, 10-7B
• Prepare the journal entry to record depletion.	EE10-7	PE10-7A, 10-7B

Describe the accounting for intangible assets, such as patents, copyrights, and goodwill.

Key Points Long-term assets such as patents, copyrights, trademarks, and goodwill are intangible assets. The cost of patents and copyrights should be amortized over the years of the asset's expected usefulness by debiting an expense account and crediting the intangible asset account. Trademarks and goodwill are not amortized but are written down only upon impairment.

Learning Outcomes	Example Exercises	Practice Exercises
• Define, describe, and provide examples of *intangible assets*.		
• Prepare a journal entry for the purchase of an intangible asset.		
• Prepare a journal entry to amortize the costs of patents and copyrights.	EE10-8	PE10-8A, 10-8B
• Prepare the journal entry to record the impairment of goodwill.	EE10-8	PE10-8A, 10-8B

Describe how depreciation expense is reported in an income statement and prepare a balance sheet that includes fixed assets and intangible assets.

Key Points The amount of depreciation expense and the depreciation methods used should be disclosed in the financial statements. Each major class of fixed assets should be disclosed, along with the related accumulated depreciation. Intangible assets are usually presented in a separate section following fixed assets. Each major class of intangible assets should be disclosed net of the amortization recorded to date.

Learning Outcomes	Example Exercises	Practice Exercises
• Describe and illustrate how fixed assets are reported on the income statement and balance sheet.		
• Describe and illustrate how intangible assets are reported on the income statement and balance sheet.		

Describe and illustrate the fixed asset turnover ratio to assess the efficiency of a company's use of its fixed assets.

Key Points A measure of a company's efficiency in using its fixed assets to generate sales is the fixed asset turnover ratio. The fixed asset turnover ratio measures the number of dollars of sales earned per dollar of fixed assets and is computed by dividing sales by the average book value of fixed assets.

Learning Outcomes	Example Exercises	Practice Exercises
• Describe a measure of the efficiency of a company's use of fixed assets to generate revenue.	EE10-9	PE10-9A, 10-9B
• Compute and interpret the fixed asset turnover ratio.		

Key Terms

accelerated depreciation method (469)
amortization (476)
book value (469)
boot (482)
capital expenditures (463)
capital lease (464)
copyright (477)
depletion (475)
depreciation (465)
double-declining-balance method (469)
fixed asset turnover ratio (480)
fixed assets (460)
goodwill (477)
intangible assets (476)
operating lease (465)
patents (476)
residual value (465)
revenue expenditures (463)
straight-line method (467)
trade-in allowance (482)
trademark (477)
units-of-output method (468)

Illustrative Problem

McCollum Company, a furniture wholesaler, acquired new equipment at a cost of $150,000 at the beginning of the fiscal year. The equipment has an estimated life of five years and an estimated residual value of $12,000. Ellen McCollum, the president, has requested information regarding alternative depreciation methods.

Instructions

1. Determine the annual depreciation for each of the five years of estimated useful life of the equipment, the accumulated depreciation at the end of each year, and the book value of the equipment at the end of each year by (a) the straight-line method and (b) the double-declining-balance method.
2. Assume that the equipment was depreciated under the double-declining-balance method. In the first week of the fifth year, the equipment was sold for $10,000. Journalize the entry to record the sale.

Solution

1.

	Year	Depreciation Expense	Accumulated Depreciation, End of Year	Book Value, End of Year
a.	1	$27,600*	$ 27,600	$122,400
	2	27,600	55,200	94,800
	3	27,600	82,800	67,200
	4	27,600	110,400	39,600
	5	27,600	138,000	12,000

*$27,600 = ($150,000 – $12,000) ÷ 5

b.				
	1	$60,000**	$ 60,000	$90,000
	2	36,000	96,000	54,000
	3	21,600	117,600	32,400
	4	12,960	130,560	19,440
	5	7,440***	138,000	12,000

**$60,000 = $150,000 × 40%

***The asset is not depreciated below the estimated residual value of $12,000.
$7,440 = $150,000 – $130,560 – $12,000

2.

Cash		10,000	
Accumulated Depreciation—Equipment		130,560	
Loss on Sale of Equipment		9,440	
Equipment			150,000

Discussion Questions

1. O'Neil Office Supplies has a fleet of automobiles and trucks for use by salespersons and for delivery of office supplies and equipment. Collins Auto Sales Co. has automobiles and trucks for sale. Under what caption would the automobiles and trucks be reported in the balance sheet of (a) O'Neil Office Supplies and (b) Collins Auto Sales Co.?
2. Bullwinkle Co. acquired an adjacent vacant lot with the hope of selling it in the future at a gain. The lot is not intended to be used in Bullwinkle business operations. Where should such real estate be listed in the balance sheet?
3. Alpine Company solicited bids from several contractors to construct an addition to its office building. The lowest bid received was for $1,200,000. Alpine Company decided to construct the addition itself at a cost of $1,100,000. What amount should be recorded in the building account?
4. Distinguish between the accounting for capital expenditures and revenue expenditures.
5. Immediately after a used truck is acquired, a new motor is installed at a total cost of $3,850. Is this a capital expenditure or a revenue expenditure?
6. Keyser Company purchased a machine that has a manufacturer's suggested life of 20 years. The company plans to use the machine on a special project that will last 12 years. At the completion of the project, the machine will be sold. Over how many years should the machine be depreciated?
7. Is it necessary for a business to use the same method of computing depreciation (a) for all classes of its depreciable assets and (b) for financial statement purposes and in determining income taxes?
8. a. Under what conditions is the use of an accelerated depreciation method most appropriate?
   b. Why is an accelerated depreciation method often used for income tax purposes?
   c. What is the Modified Accelerated Cost Recovery System (MACRS), and under what conditions is it used?
9. For some of the fixed assets of a business, the balance in Accumulated Depreciation is exactly equal to the cost of the asset. (a) Is it permissible to record additional depreciation on the assets if they are still useful to the business? Explain. (b) When should an entry be made to remove the cost and the accumulated depreciation from the accounts?
10. a. Over what period of time should the cost of a patent acquired by purchase be amortized?
    b. In general, what is the required accounting treatment for research and development costs?
    c. How should goodwill be amortized?

Practice Exercises

EE 10-1 p. 464

PE 10-1A Capital and revenue expenditures **OBJ. 1**

SHOW ME HOW

On August 7, Green River Inflatables Co. paid $1,675 to install a hydraulic lift and $40 for an air filter for one of its delivery trucks. Journalize the entries for the new lift and air filter expenditures.

EE 10-1 p. 464

PE 10-1B Capital and revenue expenditures **OBJ. 1**

SHOW ME HOW

On February 14, Garcia Associates Co. paid $2,300 to repair the transmission on one of its delivery vans. In addition, Garcia Associates paid $450 to install a GPS system in its van. Journalize the entries for the transmission and GPS system expenditures.

EE 10-2 p. 467

PE 10-2A Straight-line depreciation **OBJ. 2**

SHOW ME HOW

Equipment acquired at the beginning of the year at a cost of $340,000 has an estimated residual value of $45,000 and an estimated useful life of 10 years. Determine (a) the depreciable cost, (b) the straight-line rate, and (c) the annual straight-line depreciation.

EE 10-2 p. 467

PE 10-2B Straight-line depreciation **OBJ. 2**

SHOW ME HOW

A building acquired at the beginning of the year at a cost of $1,450,000 has an estimated residual value of $300,000 and an estimated useful life of 10 years. Determine (a) the depreciable cost, (b) the straight-line rate, and (c) the annual straight-line depreciation.

EE 10-3 p. 468

PE 10-3A Units-of-output depreciation **OBJ. 2**

SHOW ME HOW

A tractor acquired at a cost of $420,000 has an estimated residual value of $30,000, has an estimated useful life of 25,000 hours, and was operated 1,850 hours during the year. Determine (a) the depreciable cost, (b) the depreciation rate, and (c) the units-of-output depreciation for the year.

EE 10-3 p. 468

PE 10-3B Units-of-output depreciation **OBJ. 2**

SHOW ME HOW

A truck acquired at a cost of $69,000 has an estimated residual value of $12,000, has an estimated useful life of 300,000 miles, and was driven 77,000 miles during the year. Determine (a) the depreciable cost, (b) the depreciation rate, and (c) the units-of-output depreciation for the year.

EE 10-4 p. 470

PE 10-4A Double-declining-balance depreciation **OBJ. 2**

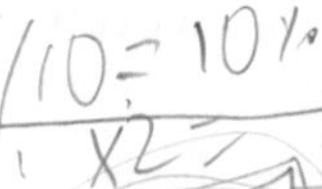
SHOW ME HOW

Equipment acquired at the beginning of the year at a cost of $175,000 has an estimated residual value of $12,000 and an estimated useful life of 10 years. Determine (a) the double-declining-balance rate and (b) the double-declining-balance depreciation for the first year.

EE 10-4 p. 470

PE 10-4B Double-declining-balance depreciation **OBJ. 2**

SHOW ME HOW

A building acquired at the beginning of the year at a cost of $1,375,000 has an estimated residual value of $250,000 and an estimated useful life of 40 years. Determine (a) the double-declining-balance rate and (b) the double-declining-balance depreciation for the first year.

EE 10-5 p. 473

SHOW ME HOW

PE 10-5A Revision of depreciation OBJ. 2

A truck with a cost of $82,000 has an estimated residual value of $16,000, has an estimated useful life of 12 years, and is depreciated by the straight-line method. (a) Determine the amount of the annual depreciation. (b) Determine the book value at the end of the seventh year of use. (c) Assuming that at the start of the eighth year the remaining life is estimated to be six years and the residual value is estimated to be $12,000, determine the depreciation expense for each of the remaining six years.

EE 10-5 p. 473

SHOW ME HOW

PE 10-5B Revision of depreciation OBJ. 2

Equipment with a cost of $180,000 has an estimated residual value of $14,400, has an estimated useful life of 16 years, and is depreciated by the straight-line method. (a) Determine the amount of the annual depreciation. (b) Determine the book value at the end of the tenth year of use. (c) Assuming that at the start of the eleventh year the remaining life is estimated to be eight years and the residual value is estimated to be $10,500, determine the depreciation expense for each of the remaining eight years.

EE 10-6 p. 475

SHOW ME HOW

PE 10-6A Sale of equipment OBJ. 3

Equipment was acquired at the beginning of the year at a cost of $465,000. The equipment was depreciated using the straight-line method based on an estimated useful life of 15 years and an estimated residual value of $45,000.

a. What was the depreciation for the first year?

b. Assuming the equipment was sold at the end of the eighth year for $235,000, determine the gain or loss on the sale of the equipment.

c. Journalize the entry to record the sale.

EE 10-6 p. 475

SHOW ME HOW

PE 10-6B Sale of equipment OBJ. 3

Equipment was acquired at the beginning of the year at a cost of $600,000. The equipment was depreciated using the double-declining-balance method based on an estimated useful life of 16 years and an estimated residual value of $60,000.

a. What was the depreciation for the first year?

b. Assuming the equipment was sold at the end of the second year for $480,000, determine the gain or loss on the sale of the equipment.

c. Journalize the entry to record the sale.

EE 10-7 p. 476

SHOW ME HOW

PE 10-7A Depletion OBJ. 4

Caldwell Mining Co. acquired mineral rights for $127,500,000. The mineral deposit is estimated at 425,000,000 tons. During the current year, 42,000,000 tons were mined and sold.

a. Determine the depletion rate.

b. Determine the amount of depletion expense for the current year.

c. Journalize the adjusting entry on December 31 to recognize the depletion expense.

EE 10-7 p. 476

SHOW ME HOW

PE 10-7B Depletion OBJ. 4

Glacier Mining Co. acquired mineral rights for $494,000,000. The mineral deposit is estimated at 475,000,000 tons. During the current year, 31,500,000 tons were mined and sold.

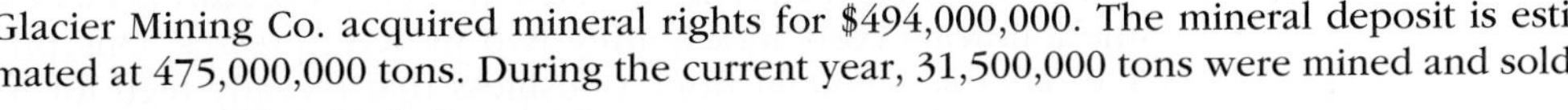

a. Determine the depletion rate.

b. Determine the amount of depletion expense for the current year.

c. Journalize the adjusting entry on December 31 to recognize the depletion expense.

EE 10-8 p. 479

PE 10-8A Impaired goodwill and amortization of patent OBJ. 5

SHOW ME HOW

On December 31, it was estimated that goodwill of $4,000,000 was impaired. In addition, a patent with an estimated useful economic life of 15 years was acquired for $900,000 on August 1.

a. Journalize the adjusting entry on December 31 for the impaired goodwill.

b. Journalize the adjusting entry on December 31 for the amortization of the patent rights.

EE 10-8 p. 479

PE 10-8B Impaired goodwill and amortization of patent OBJ. 5

SHOW ME HOW

On December 31, it was estimated that goodwill of $6,000,000 was impaired. In addition, a patent with an estimated useful economic life of 12 years was acquired for $1,500,000 on April 1.

a. Journalize the adjusting entry on December 31 for the impaired goodwill.

b. Journalize the adjusting entry on December 31 for the amortization of the patent rights.

EE 10-9 p. 481

PE 10-9A Fixed asset turnover ratio OBJ. 7

SHOW ME HOW

Financial statement data for years ending December 31 for DePuy Company follows:

	2016	2015
Sales	$5,510,000	$4,880,000
Fixed assets:		
Beginning of year	1,600,000	1,450,000
End of year	2,200,000	1,600,000

a. Determine the fixed asset turnover ratio for 2016 and 2015.

b. Does the change in the fixed asset turnover ratio from 2015 to 2016 indicate a favorable or an unfavorable trend?

EE 10-9 p. 481

PE 10-9B Fixed asset turnover ratio OBJ. 7

SHOW ME HOW

Financial statement data for years ending December 31 for Davenport Company follows:

	2016	2015
Sales	$1,668,000	$1,125,000
Fixed assets:		
Beginning of year	670,000	580,000
End of year	720,000	670,000

a. Determine the fixed asset turnover ratio for 2016 and 2015.

b. Does the change in the fixed asset turnover ratio from 2015 to 2016 indicate a favorable or an unfavorable trend?

Exercises

EX 10-1 Costs of acquiring fixed assets OBJ. 1

Melinda Stoffers owns and operates ABC Print Co. During February, ABC Print Co. incurred the following costs in acquiring two printing presses. One printing press was new, and the other was bought from a business that recently filed for bankruptcy.

Costs related to new printing press:

1. Fee paid to factory representative for installation
2. Freight
3. Insurance while in transit
4. New parts to replace those damaged in unloading

5. Sales tax on purchase price
6. Special foundation

Costs related to used printing press:

7. Fees paid to attorney to review purchase agreement
8. Freight
9. Installation
10. Repair of damage incurred in reconditioning the press
11. Replacement of worn-out parts
12. Vandalism repairs during installation

a. Indicate which costs incurred in acquiring the new printing press should be debited to the asset account.

b. Indicate which costs incurred in acquiring the used printing press should be debited to the asset account.

EX 10-2 Determining cost of land **OBJ. 1**

Bridger Ski Co. has developed a tract of land into a ski resort. The company has cut the trees, cleared and graded the land and hills, and constructed ski lifts. (a) Should the tree cutting, land clearing, and grading costs of constructing the ski slopes be debited to the land account? (b) If such costs are debited to Land, should they be depreciated?

EX 10-3 Determining cost of land **OBJ. 1**

✔ $196,900

SHOW ME HOW

Northwest Delivery Company acquired an adjacent lot to construct a new warehouse, paying $75,000 and giving a short-term note for $90,000. Legal fees paid were $2,500, delinquent taxes assumed were $22,400, and fees paid to remove an old building from the land were $14,500. Materials salvaged from the demolition of the building were sold for $7,500. A contractor was paid $660,000 to construct a new warehouse. Determine the cost of the land to be reported on the balance sheet.

EX 10-4 Capital and revenue expenditures **OBJ. 1**

Warner Freight Lines Co. incurred the following costs related to trucks and vans used in operating its delivery service:

1. Changed the oil and greased the joints of all the trucks and vans.
2. Changed the radiator fluid on a truck that had been in service for the past four years.
3. Installed a hydraulic lift to a van.
4. Installed security systems on four of the newer trucks.
5. Overhauled the engine on one of the trucks purchased three years ago.
6. Rebuilt the transmission on one of the vans that had been driven 40,000 miles. The van was no longer under warranty.
7. Removed a two-way radio from one of the trucks and installed a new radio with a greater range of communication.
8. Repaired a flat tire on one of the vans.
9. Replaced a truck's suspension system with a new suspension system that allows for the delivery of heavier loads.
10. Tinted the back and side windows of one of the vans to discourage theft of contents.

Classify each of the costs as a capital expenditure or a revenue expenditure.

EX 10-5 Capital and revenue expenditures **OBJ. 1**

Jackie Fox owns and operates Platinum Transport Co. During the past year, Jackie incurred the following costs related to an 18-wheel truck:

1. Changed engine oil.
2. Installed a television in the sleeping compartment of the truck.
3. Installed a wind deflector on top of the cab to increase fuel mileage.
4. Modified the factory-installed turbo charger with a special-order kit designed to add 50 more horsepower to the engine performance.
5. Replaced a headlight that had burned out.
6. Replaced a shock absorber that had worn out.
7. Replaced fog and cab light bulbs.
8. Replaced the hydraulic brake system that had begun to fail during his latest trip through the Rocky Mountains.
9. Removed the old CB radio and replaced it with a newer model with a greater range.
10. Replaced the old radar detector with a newer model that is fastened to the truck with a locking device that prevents its removal.

Classify each of the costs as a capital expenditure or a revenue expenditure.

EX 10-6 Capital and revenue expenditures **OBJ. 1**

SHOW ME HOW

Quality Move Company made the following expenditures on one of its delivery trucks:

Mar. 20. Replaced the transmission at a cost of $1,890.

June 11. Paid $1,350 for installation of a hydraulic lift.

Nov. 30. Paid $55 to change the oil and air filter.

Prepare journal entries for each expenditure.

EX 10-7 Nature of depreciation **OBJ. 2**

Tri-City Ironworks Co. reported $44,500,000 for equipment and $29,800,000 for accumulated depreciation—equipment on its balance sheet.

Does this mean (a) that the replacement cost of the equipment is $44,500,000 and (b) that $29,800,000 is set aside in a special fund for the replacement of the equipment? Explain.

EX 10-8 Straight-line depreciation rates **OBJ. 2**

✔ c. 10%

Convert each of the following estimates of useful life to a straight-line depreciation rate, stated as a percentage: (a) 4 years, (b) 8 years, (c) 10 years, (d) 16 years, (e) 25 years, (f) 40 years, (g) 50 years.

EX 10-9 Straight-line depreciation **OBJ. 2**

✔ $2,600

SHOW ME HOW

A refrigerator used by a meat processor has a cost of $48,000, an estimated residual value of $9,000, and an estimated useful life of 15 years. What is the amount of the annual depreciation computed by the straight-line method?

EX 10-10 Depreciation by units-of-output method **OBJ. 2**

✔ $702

SHOW ME HOW

A diesel-powered tractor with a cost of $180,000 and estimated residual value of $18,000 is expected to have a useful operating life of 36,000 hours. During February, the tractor was operated 156 hours. Determine the depreciation for the month.

✔ a. Truck #1, credit to Accumulated Depreciation, $5,460

SHOW ME HOW

EX 10-11 Depreciation by units-of-output method OBJ. 2

Prior to adjustment at the end of the year, the balance in Trucks is $296,900 and the balance in Accumulated Depreciation—Trucks is $99,740. Details of the subsidiary ledger are as follows:

Truck No.	Cost	Estimated Residual Value	Estimated Useful Life	Accumulated Depreciation at Beginning of Year	Miles Operated During Year
1	$80,000	$15,000	250,000 miles	—	21,000 miles
2	54,000	6,000	300,000	$14,400	33,500
3	72,900	10,900	200,000	60,140	8,000
4	90,000	22,800	240,000	25,200	22,500

a. Determine the depreciation rates per mile and the amount to be credited to the accumulated depreciation section of each of the subsidiary accounts for the miles operated during the current year.

b. Journalize the entry to record depreciation for the year.

✔ a. $4,800

SHOW ME HOW

EX 10-12 Depreciation by two methods OBJ. 2

A John Deere tractor acquired on January 4 at a cost of $120,000 has an estimated useful life of 25 years. Assuming that it will have no residual value, determine the depreciation for each of the first two years (a) by the straight-line method and (b) by the double-declining-balance method.

✔ a. $3,250

SHOW ME HOW

EX 10-13 Depreciation by two methods OBJ. 2

A storage tank acquired at the beginning of the fiscal year at a cost of $75,000 has an estimated residual value of $10,000 and an estimated useful life of 20 years. Determine the following: (a) the amount of annual depreciation by the straight-line method and (b) the amount of depreciation for the first and second years computed by the double-declining-balance method.

✔ a. First year, $3,000

SHOW ME HOW

EX 10-14 Partial-year depreciation OBJ. 2

Sandblasting equipment acquired at a cost of $40,000 has an estimated residual value of $8,000 and an estimated useful life of eight years. It was placed into service on April 1 of the current fiscal year, which ends on December 31. Determine the depreciation for the current fiscal year and for the following fiscal year by (a) the straight-line method and (b) the double-declining-balance method.

✔ a. $23,750

SHOW ME HOW

EX 10-15 Revision of depreciation OBJ. 2

A building with a cost of $1,200,000 has an estimated residual value of $250,000, has an estimated useful life of 40 years, and is depreciated by the straight-line method. (a) What is the amount of the annual depreciation? (b) What is the book value at the end of the twenty-eighth year of use? (c) If at the start of the twenty-ninth year it is estimated that the remaining life is 10 years and that the residual value is $180,000 what is the depreciation expense for each of the remaining 10 years?

✔ b. Depreciation Expense, $800

EX 10-16 Capital expenditure and depreciation OBJ. 1, 2

Willow Creek Company purchased and installed carpet in its new general offices on April 30 for a total cost of $18,000. The carpet is estimated to have a 15-year useful life and no residual value.

a. Prepare the journal entry necessary for recording the purchase of the new carpet.

b. Record the December 31 adjusting entry for the partial-year depreciation expense for the carpet, assuming that Willow Creek Company uses the straight-line method.

SHOW ME HOW

EX 10-17 Entries for sale of fixed asset **OBJ. 3**

Equipment acquired on January 8, 2013, at a cost of $140,000, has an estimated useful life of 16 years, has an estimated residual value of $8,000, and is depreciated by the straight-line method.

a. What was the book value of the equipment at December 31, 2016, the end of the year?

b. Assuming that the equipment was sold on July 1, 2017, for $96,700, journalize the entries to record (1) depreciation for the six months until the sale date, and (2) the sale of the equipment.

✔ b. $357,500

SHOW ME HOW

EX 10-18 Disposal of fixed asset **OBJ. 3**

Equipment acquired on January 6, 2013, at a cost of $425,000, has an estimated useful life of 16 years and an estimated residual value of $65,000

a. What was the annual amount of depreciation for the years 2013, 2014, and 2015 using the straight-line method of depreciation?

b. What was the book value of the equipment on January 1, 2016?

c. Assuming that the equipment was sold on January 3, 2016, for $340,000, journalize the entry to record the sale.

d. Assuming that the equipment had been sold on January 3, 2016, for $372,500 instead of $340,000, journalize the entry to record the sale.

✔ a. $3,885,000

SHOW ME HOW

EX 10-19 Depletion entries **OBJ. 4**

Big Sky Mining Co. acquired mineral rights for $42,000,000. The mineral deposit is estimated at 20,000,000 tons. During the current year, 1,850,000 tons were mined and sold.

a. Determine the amount of depletion expense for the current year.

b. Journalize the adjusting entry to recognize the depletion expense.

✔ a. $105,500

SHOW ME HOW

EX 10-20 Amortization entries **OBJ. 5**

Smith Company acquired patent rights on January 6, 2013, for $882,000. The patent has a useful life equal to its legal life of nine years. On January 3, 2016, Smith successfully defended the patent in a lawsuit at a cost of $45,000.

a. Determine the patent amortization expense for the year ended December 31, 2016.

b. Journalize the adjusting entry to recognize the amortization.

EX 10-21 Book value of fixed assets **OBJ. 6**

Apple Inc. designs, manufactures, and markets personal computers and related software. Apple also manufactures and distributes music players (iPod) and mobile phones (iPhone) along with related accessories and services, including online distribution of third-party music, videos, and applications. The following information was taken from a recent annual report of Apple:

Property, Plant, and Equipment (in millions):

	Current Year	Preceding Year
Land and buildings	$ 2,439	$2,059
Machinery, equipment, and internal-use software	15,743	6,926
Office furniture and equipment	241	184
Other fixed assets related to leases	3,464	2,599
Accumulated depreciation and amortization	6,435	3,991

a. Compute the book value of the fixed assets for the current year and the preceding year and explain the differences, if any.

b. Would you normally expect Apple's book value of fixed assets to increase or decrease during the year?

EX 10-22 Balance sheet presentation

OBJ. 6

List the errors you find in the following partial balance sheet:

Burnt Red Company
Balance Sheet
December 31, 2016

Assets

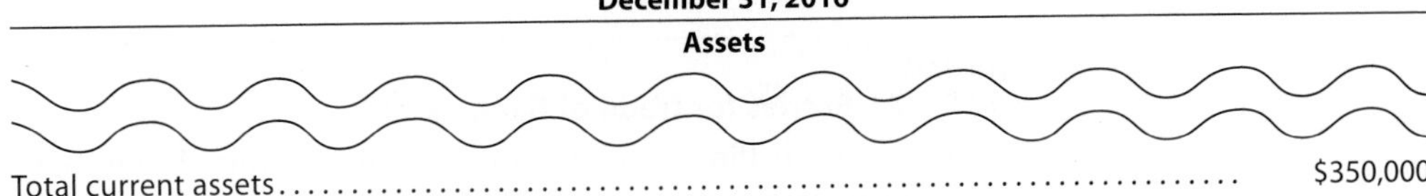

Total current assets			$350,000

	Replacement Cost	Accumulated Depreciation	Book Value
Property, plant, and equipment:			
Land	$ 250,000	$ 50,000	$200,000
Buildings	450,000	160,000	290,000
Factory equipment	375,000	140,000	235,000
Office equipment	125,000	60,000	65,000
Patents	90,000	—	90,000
Goodwill	60,000	10,000	50,000
Total property, plant, and equipment	$1,350,000	$420,000	$930,000

EX 10-23 Fixed asset turnover ratio

OBJ. 7

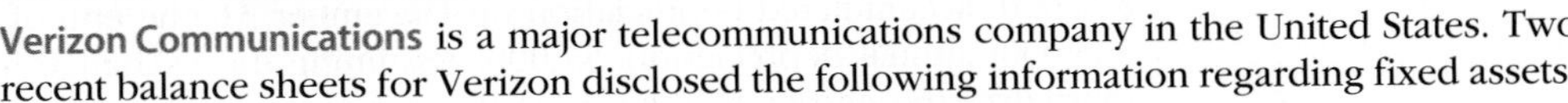

Verizon Communications is a major telecommunications company in the United States. Two recent balance sheets for Verizon disclosed the following information regarding fixed assets:

	Year 2 (in millions)	Year 1 (in millions)
Plant, property, and equipment	$209,575	$215,626
Less accumulated depreciation	120,933	127,192
	$ 88,642	$ 88,434

Verizon's revenue for Year 2 was $115,846 million. Assume the fixed asset turnover for the telecommunications industry averages approximately 1.10.

a. Determine Verizon's fixed asset turnover ratio for Year 2. Round to two decimal places.

b. Interpret Verizon's fixed asset turnover ratio.

EX 10-24 Fixed asset turnover ratio

OBJ. 7

The following table shows the revenue and average net fixed assets (in millions) for a recent fiscal year for **Best Buy** and **RadioShack**:

	Revenue	Average Net Fixed Assets
Best Buy	$50,705	$3,647
RadioShack	4,258	255

a. Compute the fixed asset turnover for each company. Round to two decimal places.

b. Which company uses its fixed assets more efficiently? Explain.

Appendix
EX 10-25 Asset traded for similar asset

✔ a. $185,000

A printing press priced at a fair market value of $275,000 is acquired in a transaction that has commercial substance by trading in a similar press and paying cash for the difference between the trade-in allowance and the price of the new press.

a. Assuming that the trade-in allowance is $90,000, what is the amount of cash given?

b. Assuming that the book value of the press traded in is $68,000, what is the gain or loss on the exchange?

Appendix
EX 10-26 Asset traded for similar asset

✔ b. $18,500 loss

Assume the same facts as in Exercise 10-25, except that the book value of the press traded in is $108,500. (a) What is the amount of cash given? (b) What is the gain or loss on the exchange?

Appendix
EX 10-27 Entries for trade of fixed asset

On July 1, Twin Pines Co., a water distiller, acquired new bottling equipment with a list price (fair market value) of $220,000. Twin Pines received a trade-in allowance (fair market value) of $45,000 on the old equipment of a similar type and paid cash of $175,000. The following information about the old equipment is obtained from the account in the equipment ledger: cost, $180,000; accumulated depreciation on December 31, the end of the preceding fiscal year, $120,000; annual depreciation, $12,000. Assuming the exchange has commercial substance, journalize the entries to record (a) the current depreciation of the old equipment to the date of trade-in and (b) the exchange transaction on July 1.

Appendix
EX 10-28 Entries for trade of fixed asset

On October 1, Bentley Delivery Services acquired a new truck with a list price (fair market value) of $75,000. Bentley Delivery received a trade-in allowance (fair market value) of $24,000 on an old truck of similar type and paid cash of $51,000. The following information about the old truck is obtained from the account in the equipment ledger: cost, $56,000; accumulated depreciation on December 31, the end of the preceding fiscal year, $35,000; annual depreciation, $7,000. Assuming the exchange has commercial substance, journalize the entries to record (a) the current depreciation of the old truck to the date of trade-in and (b) the transaction on October 1.

Problems: Series A

PR 10-1A Allocating payments and receipts to fixed asset accounts **OBJ. 1**

✔ Land, $400,000

The following payments and receipts are related to land, land improvements, and buildings acquired for use in a wholesale ceramic business. The receipts are identified by an asterisk.

a.	Fee paid to attorney for title search	$ 2,500
b.	Cost of real estate acquired as a plant site: Land	285,000
	Building	55,000
c.	Delinquent real estate taxes on property, assumed by purchaser	15,500
d.	Cost of razing and removing building	5,000
e.	Proceeds from sale of salvage materials from old building	4,000*
f.	Special assessment paid to city for extension of water main to the property	29,000
g.	Architect's and engineer's fees for plans and supervision	60,000
h.	Premium on one-year insurance policy during construction	6,000
i.	Cost of filling and grading land	12,000
j.	Money borrowed to pay building contractor	900,000*
k.	Cost of repairing windstorm damage during construction	5,500
l.	Cost of paving parking lot to be used by customers	32,000
m.	Cost of trees and shrubbery planted	11,000
n.	Cost of floodlights installed on parking lot	2,000
o.	Cost of repairing vandalism damage during construction	2,500
p.	Proceeds from insurance company for windstorm and vandalism damage	7,500*
q.	Payment to building contractor for new building	800,000
r.	Interest incurred on building loan during construction	34,500
s.	Refund of premium on insurance policy (h) canceled after 11 months	500*

Instructions

1. Assign each payment and receipt to Land (unlimited life), Land Improvements (limited life), Building, or Other Accounts. Indicate receipts by an asterisk. Identify each item by letter and list the amounts in columnar form, as follows:

Item	Land	Land Improvements	Building	Other Accounts

2. Determine the amount debited to Land, Land Improvements, and Building.
3. The costs assigned to the land, which is used as a plant site, will not be depreciated, while the costs assigned to land improvements will be depreciated. Explain this seemingly contradictory application of the concept of depreciation.
4. What would be the effect on the income statement and balance sheet if the cost of filling and grading land of $12,000 [payment (i)] was incorrectly classified as Land Improvements rather than Land? Assume Land Improvements are depreciated over a 20-year life using the double-declining-balance method.

PR 10-2A Comparing three depreciation methods — OBJ. 2

✔ 1. a. 2014: straight-line depreciation, $28,000

SHOW ME HOW

Monte's Coffee Company purchased packaging equipment on January 5, 2014, for $90,000. The equipment was expected to have a useful life of three years, or 20,000 operating hours, and a residual value of $6,000. The equipment was used for 8,900 hours during 2014, 7,100 hours in 2015, and 4,000 hours in 2016.

Instructions

1. Determine the amount of depreciation expense for the years ended December 31, 2014, 2015, and 2016 by (a) the straight-line method, (b) the units-of-output method, and (c) the double-declining-balance method. Also determine the total depreciation expense for the three years by each method. The following columnar headings are suggested for recording the depreciation expense amounts:

	Depreciation Expense		
Year	Straight-Line Method	Units-of-Output Method	Double-Declining-Balance Method

2. What method yields the highest depreciation expense for 2014?
3. What method yields the most depreciation over the three-year life of the equipment?

PR 10-3A Depreciation by three methods; partial years — OBJ. 2

✔ a. 2014: $65,250

Perdue Company purchased equipment on April 1, 2014, for $270,000. The equipment was expected to have a useful life of three years, or 18,000 operating hours, and a residual value of $9,000. The equipment was used for 7,500 hours during 2014, 5,500 hours in 2015, 4,000 hours in 2016, and 1,000 hours in 2017.

Instructions

Determine the amount of depreciation expense for the years ended December 31, 2014, 2015, 2016, and 2017, by (a) the straight-line method, (b) the units-of-output method, and (c) the double-declining-balance method.

PR 10-4A Depreciation by two methods; sale of fixed asset — OBJ. 2, 3

✔ 1. b. Year 1: $320,000 depreciation expense

General Ledger

New lithographic equipment, acquired at a cost of $800,000 at the beginning of a fiscal year, has an estimated useful life of five years and an estimated residual value of $90,000. The manager requested information regarding the effect of alternative methods on the amount of depreciation expense each year. On the basis of the data presented to the manager, the double-declining-balance method was selected.

In the first week of the fifth year, the equipment was sold for $135,000.

Instructions

1. Determine the annual depreciation expense for each of the estimated five years of use, the accumulated depreciation at the end of each year, and the book value of the equipment at the end of each year by (a) the straight-line method and (b) the

(Continued)

double-declining-balance method. The following columnar headings are suggested for each schedule:

Year	Depreciation Expense	Accumulated Depreciation, End of Year	Book Value, End of Year

2. Journalize the entry to record the sale.
3. Journalize the entry to record the sale, assuming that the equipment was sold for $88,750 instead of $135,000.

General Ledger

PR 10-5A Transactions for fixed assets, including sale

OBJ. 1, 2, 3

The following transactions, adjusting entries, and closing entries were completed by Legacy Furniture Co. during a three-year period. All are related to the use of delivery equipment. The double-declining-balance method of depreciation is used.

2014

Jan. 4. Purchased a used delivery truck for $28,000, paying cash.

Nov. 2. Paid garage $675 for miscellaneous repairs to the truck.

Dec. 31. Recorded depreciation on the truck for the year. The estimated useful life of the truck is four years, with a residual value of $5,000 for the truck.

2015

Jan. 6. Purchased a new truck for $48,000, paying cash.

Apr. 1. Sold the used truck for $15,000. (Record depreciation to date in 2015 for the truck.)

June 11. Paid garage $450 for miscellaneous repairs to the truck.

Dec. 31. Record depreciation for the new truck. It has an estimated residual value of $9,000 and an estimated life of five years.

2016

July 1. Purchased a new truck for $54,000, paying cash.

Oct. 2. Sold the truck purchased January 6, 2015, for $16,750. (Record depreciation to date for 2016 for the truck.)

Dec. 31. Recorded depreciation on the remaining truck. It has an estimated residual value of $12,000 and an estimated useful life of eight years.

Instructions

Journalize the transactions and the adjusting entries.

✓ 1. a. $352,000

PR 10-6A Amortization and depletion entries

OBJ. 4, 5

Data related to the acquisition of timber rights and intangible assets during the current year ended December 31 are as follows:

a. Timber rights on a tract of land were purchased for $1,600,000 on February 22. The stand of timber is estimated at 5,000,000 board feet. During the current year, 1,100,000 board feet of timber were cut and sold.

b. On December 31, the company determined that $3,750,000 of goodwill was impaired.

c. Governmental and legal costs of $6,600,000 were incurred on April 3 in obtaining a patent with an estimated economic life of 12 years. Amortization is to be for three-fourths of a year.

Instructions

1. Determine the amount of the amortization, depletion, or impairment for the current year for each of the foregoing items.
2. Journalize the adjusting entries required to record the amortization, depletion, or impairment for each item.

Problems: Series B

PR 10-1B Allocating payments and receipts to fixed asset accounts

OBJ. 1

✔ Land, $860,000

The following payments and receipts are related to land, land improvements, and buildings acquired for use in a wholesale apparel business. The receipts are identified by an asterisk.

a.	Fee paid to attorney for title search	$ 3,600
b.	Cost of real estate acquired as a plant site: Land	720,000
	Building	60,000
c.	Finder's fee paid to real estate agency	23,400
d.	Delinquent real estate taxes on property, assumed by purchaser	15,000
e.	Architect's and engineer's fees for plans and supervision	75,000
f.	Cost of removing building purchased with land in (b)	10,000
g.	Proceeds from sale of salvage materials from old building	3,400*
h.	Cost of filling and grading land	18,000
i.	Premium on one-year insurance policy during construction	8,400
j.	Money borrowed to pay building contractor	800,000*
k.	Special assessment paid to city for extension of water main to the property	13,400
l.	Cost of repairing windstorm damage during construction	3,000
m.	Cost of repairing vandalism damage during construction	2,000
n.	Cost of trees and shrubbery planted	14,000
o.	Cost of paving parking lot to be used by customers	21,600
p.	Interest incurred on building loan during construction	40,000
q.	Proceeds from insurance company for windstorm and vandalism damage	4,500*
r.	Payment to building contractor for new building	800,000
s.	Refund of premium on insurance policy (i) canceled after 10 months	1,400*

Instructions

1. Assign each payment and receipt to Land (unlimited life), Land Improvements (limited life), Building, or Other Accounts. Indicate receipts by an asterisk. Identify each item by letter and list the amounts in columnar form, as follows:

Item	Land	Land Improvements	Building	Other Accounts

2. Determine the amount debited to Land, Land Improvements, and Building.
3. The costs assigned to the land, which is used as a plant site, will not be depreciated, while the costs assigned to land improvements will be depreciated. Explain this seemingly contradictory application of the concept of depreciation.
4. What would be the effect on the income statement and balance sheet if the cost of paving the parking lot of $21,600 [payment (o)] was incorrectly classified as Land rather than Land Improvements? Assume Land Improvements are depreciated over a 10-year life using the double-declining-balance method.

PR 10-2B Comparing three depreciation methods

OBJ. 2

✔ 1. a. 2015: straight-line depreciation, $71,250

SHOW ME HOW

Waylander Coatings Company purchased waterproofing equipment on January 6, 2015, for $320,000. The equipment was expected to have a useful life of four years, or 20,000 operating hours, and a residual value of $35,000. The equipment was used for 7,200 hours during 2015, 6,400 hours in 2016, 4,400 hours in 2017, and 2,000 hours in 2018.

Instructions

1. Determine the amount of depreciation expense for the years ended December 31, 2015, 2016, 2017, and 2018, by (a) the straight-line method, (b) the units-of-output method, and (c) the double-declining-balance method. Also determine the total depreciation expense for the four years by each method. The following columnar headings are suggested for recording the depreciation expense amounts:

	Depreciation Expense		
Year	Straight-Line Method	Units-of-Output Method	Double-Declining-Balance Method

(Continued)

2. What method yields the highest depreciation expense for 2015?
3. What method yields the most depreciation over the four-year life of the equipment?

✔ a. 2014, $8,400

PR 10-3B Depreciation by three methods; partial years **OBJ. 2**

Layton Company purchased tool sharpening equipment on October 1, 2014, for $108,000. The equipment was expected to have a useful life of three years, or 12,000 operating hours, and a residual value of $7,200. The equipment was used for 1,350 hours during 2014, 4,200 hours in 2015, 3,650 hours in 2016, and 2,800 hours in 2017.

Instructions

Determine the amount of depreciation expense for the years ended December 31, 2014, 2015, 2016, and 2017, by (a) the straight-line method, (b) the units-of-output method, and (c) the double-declining-balance method.

✔ 1. b. Year 1, $55,000 depreciation expense

General Ledger

PR 10-4B Depreciation by two methods; sale of fixed asset **OBJ. 2, 3**

New tire retreading equipment, acquired at a cost of $110,000 at the beginning of a fiscal year, has an estimated useful life of four years and an estimated residual value of $7,500. The manager requested information regarding the effect of alternative methods on the amount of depreciation expense each year. On the basis of the data presented to the manager, the double-declining-balance method was selected.

In the first week of the fourth year, the equipment was sold for $18,000.

Instructions

1. Determine the annual depreciation expense for each of the estimated four years of use, the accumulated depreciation at the end of each year, and the book value of the equipment at the end of each year by (a) the straight-line method and (b) the double-declining-balance method. The following columnar headings are suggested for each schedule:

Year	Depreciation Expense	Accumulated Depreciation, End of Year	Book Value, End of Year

2. Journalize the entry to record the sale.
3. Journalize the entry to record the sale, assuming that the equipment sold for $10,500 instead of $18,000.

General Ledger

PR 10-5B Transactions for fixed assets, including sale **OBJ. 1, 2, 3**

The following transactions, adjusting entries, and closing entries were completed by Robinson Furniture Co. during a three-year period. All are related to the use of delivery equipment. The double-declining-balance method of depreciation is used.

2014

Jan. 8. Purchased a used delivery truck for $24,000, paying cash.

Mar. 7. Paid garage $900 for changing the oil, replacing the oil filter, and tuning the engine on the delivery truck.

Dec. 31. Recorded depreciation on the truck for the fiscal year. The estimated useful life of the truck is four years, with a residual value of $4,000 for the truck.

2015

Jan. 9. Purchased a new truck for $50,000, paying cash.

Feb. 28. Paid garage $250 to tune the engine and make other minor repairs on the used truck.

Apr. 30. Sold the used truck for $9,500. (Record depreciation to date in 2015 for the truck.)

Dec. 31. Record depreciation for the new truck. It has an estimated residual value of $12,000 and an estimated life of eight years.

2016

Sept. 1. Purchased a new truck for $58,500, paying cash.

4. Sold the truck purchased January 9, 2015, for $36,000. (Record depreciation to date for 2016 for the truck.)

Dec. 31. Recorded depreciation on the remaining truck. It has an estimated residual value of $16,000 and an estimated useful life of 10 years.

Instructions

Journalize the transactions and the adjusting entries.

PR 10-6B Amortization and depletion entries OBJ. 4, 5

✔ b. $150,000

Data related to the acquisition of timber rights and intangible assets during the current year ended December 31 are as follows:

a. On December 31, the company determined that $3,400,000 of goodwill was impaired.

b. Governmental and legal costs of $4,800,000 were incurred on September 30 in obtaining a patent with an estimated economic life of eight years. Amortization is to be for one-fourth year.

c. Timber rights on a tract of land were purchased for $2,975,000 on February 4. The stand of timber is estimated at 12,500,000 board feet. During the current year, 4,150,000 board feet of timber were cut and sold.

Instructions

1. Determine the amount of the amortization, depletion, or impairment for the current year for each of the foregoing items.
2. Journalize the adjusting entries to record the amortization, depletion, or impairment for each item.

Cases & Projects

CP 10-1 Ethics and professional conduct in business

Dave Elliott, CPA, is an assistant to the controller of Lyric Consulting Co. In his spare time, Dave also prepares tax returns and performs general accounting services for clients. Frequently, Dave performs these services after his normal working hours, using Lyric Consulting Co.'s computers and laser printers. Occasionally, Dave's clients will call him at the office during regular working hours.

Discuss whether Dave is performing in a professional manner.

CP 10-2 Financial vs. tax depreciation

The following is an excerpt from a conversation between two employees of WXT Technologies, Nolan Sears and Stacy Mays. Nolan is the accounts payable clerk, and Stacy is the cashier.

Nolan: Stacy, could I get your opinion on something?

Stacy: Sure, Nolan.

Nolan: Do you know Rita, the fixed assets clerk?

Stacy: I know who she is, but I don't know her real well. Why?

Nolan: Well, I was talking to her at lunch last Monday about how she liked her job, etc. You know, the usual . . . and she mentioned something about having to keep two sets of books . . . one for taxes and one for the financial statements. That can't be good accounting, can it? What do you think?

Stacy: Two sets of books? It doesn't sound right.

Nolan: It doesn't seem right to me either. I was always taught that you had to use generally accepted accounting principles. How can there be two sets of books? What can be the difference between the two?

How would you respond to Nolan and Stacy if you were Rita?

CP 10-3 Effect of depreciation on net income

Tuttle Construction Co. specializes in building replicas of historic houses. Tim Newman, president of Tuttle Construction, is considering the purchase of various items of equipment on July 1, 2014, for $400,000. The equipment would have a useful life of five years and no residual value. In the past, all equipment has been leased. For tax purposes, Tim is considering depreciating the equipment by the straight-line method. He discussed the matter with his CPA and learned that, although the straight-line method could be elected, it was to his advantage to use the Modified Accelerated Cost Recovery System (MACRS) for tax purposes. He asked for your advice as to which method to use for tax purposes.

1. Compute depreciation for each of the years (2014, 2015, 2016, 2017, 2018, and 2019) of useful life by (a) the straight-line method and (b) MACRS. In using the straight-line method, one-half year's depreciation should be computed for 2014 and 2019. Use the MACRS rates presented in Exhibit 9.
2. Assuming that income before depreciation and income tax is estimated to be $750,000 uniformly per year and that the income tax rate is 40%, compute the net income for each of the years 2014, 2015, 2016, 2017, 2018, and 2019 if (a) the straight-line method is used and (b) MACRS is used.
3. What factors would you present for Tim's consideration in the selection of a depreciation method?

CP 10-4 Applying for patents, copyrights, and trademarks

Internet Project

Group Project

Go to the Internet and review the procedures for applying for a patent, a copyright, and a trademark. You may find information available on Wikipedia (Wikipedia.org) useful for this purpose. Prepare a brief written summary of these procedures.

CP 10-5 Fixed asset turnover: three industries

F·A·I

The following table shows the revenues and average net fixed assets for a recent fiscal year for three different companies from three different industries: retailing, manufacturing, and communications.

	Revenues (in millions)	Average Net Fixed Assets (in millions)
Walmart	$446,950	$110,101
Occidental Petroleum Corporation	24,172	48,874
Comcast Corporation	62,570	27,396

a. For each company, determine the fixed asset turnover ratio. Round to two decimal places.

b. Explain Walmart's ratio relative to the other two companies.

Current Liabilities and Payroll

Starbucks

Buying goods on credit is essential for businesses to run efficiently. The use of credit makes transactions more convenient and improves buying power. For *individuals*, the most common form of short-term credit is a credit card. Credit cards allow individuals to purchase items before they are paid for, while removing the need for individuals to carry large amounts of cash. They also provide documentation of purchases through a monthly credit card statement.

Short-term credit is also used by *businesses* to make purchasing items for manufacture or resale more convenient. It also gives the business control over the payment for goods and services. When **Starbucks** opened its first coffee shop in 1971, it relied on short-term trade credit, or accounts payable, to purchase ingredients for its coffee shop in Seattle's historic Pike Place Market. Today, Starbucks still relies on accounts payable and short-term trade credit, which also gives them control over cash payments by separating the purchase function from the payment function. Thus, the employee responsible for purchasing the ingredients is separated from the employee responsible for paying for the purchase. This separation of duties can help prevent unauthorized purchases or payments.

In addition to accounts payable, a business like Starbucks can also have current liabilities related to payroll, payroll taxes, employee benefits, short-term notes, unearned revenue, and contingencies. This chapter discusses each of these types of current liabilities.

Learning Objectives

After studying this chapter, you should be able to: *Example Exercises*

OBJ 1 **Describe and illustrate current liabilities related to accounts payable, current portion of long-term debt, and notes payable.**
Current Liabilities
- Accounts Payable
- Current Portion of Long-Term Debt
- Short-Term Notes Payable — EE 11-1

OBJ 2 **Determine employer liabilities for payroll, including liabilities arising from employee earnings and deductions from earnings.**
Payroll and Payroll Taxes
- Liability for Employee Earnings
- Deductions from Employee Earnings
- Computing Employee Net Pay — EE 11-2
- Liability for Employer's Payroll Taxes — EE 11-3

OBJ 3 **Describe payroll accounting systems that use a payroll register, employee earnings records, and a general journal.**
Accounting Systems for Payroll and Payroll Taxes
- Payroll Register — EE 11-4, 11-5
- Employee's Earnings Record
- Payroll Checks
- Computerized Payroll System
- Internal Controls for Payroll Systems

OBJ 4 **Journalize entries for employee fringe benefits, including vacation pay and pensions.**
Employees' Fringe Benefits
- Vacation Pay
- Pensions — EE 11-6
- Postretirement Benefits Other than Pensions
- Current Liabilities on the Balance Sheet

OBJ 5 **Describe the accounting treatment for contingent liabilities and journalize entries for product warranties.**
Contingent Liabilities
- Probable and Estimable — EE 11-7
- Probable and Not Estimable
- Reasonably Possible
- Remote

OBJ 6 **Describe and illustrate the use of the quick ratio in analyzing a company's ability to pay its current liabilities.**
Financial Analysis and Interpretation: Quick Ratio — EE 11-8

At a Glance 11 Page 526

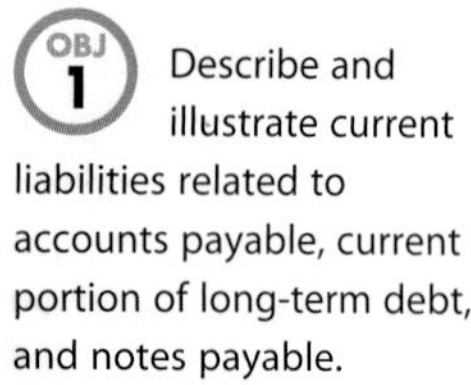
OBJ 1 Describe and illustrate current liabilities related to accounts payable, current portion of long-term debt, and notes payable.

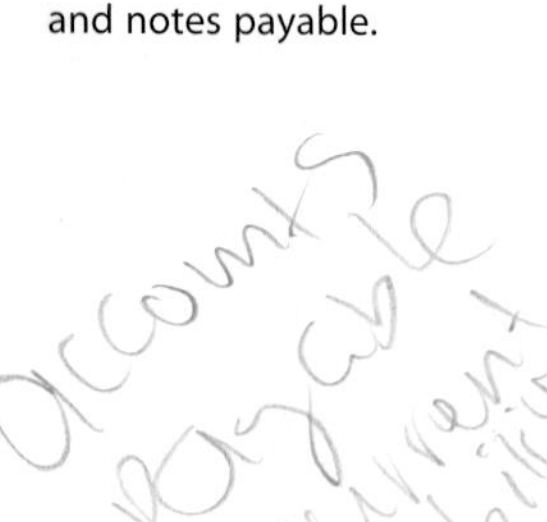

Current Liabilities

When a company or a bank advances *credit,* it is making a loan. The company or bank is called a *creditor* (or *lender*). The individuals or companies receiving the loan are called *debtors* (or *borrowers*).

Debt is recorded as a liability by the debtor. *Long-term liabilities* are debts due beyond one year. Thus, a 30-year mortgage used to purchase property is a long-term liability. *Current liabilities* are debts that will be paid out of current assets and are due within one year.

Three types of current liabilities are discussed in this section—accounts payable, the current portion of long-term debt, and short-term notes payable.

Accounts Payable

Accounts payable transactions have been described and illustrated in earlier chapters. These transactions involve a variety of purchases on account, including the purchase of merchandise and supplies. For most companies, accounts payable is the largest current liability. Exhibit 1 shows the accounts payable balance as a percent of total current liabilities for a number of companies.

EXHIBIT 1

Accounts Payable as a Percent of Total Current Liabilities

Company	Accounts Payable as a Percent of Total Current Liabilities
Alcoa Inc.	45%
Chevron Corp	67
Gap Inc.	50
IBM	18
Verizon Communications, Inc.	60
Walgreen Corp.	50

Current Portion of Long-Term Debt

Long-term liabilities are often paid back in periodic payments, called *installments*. Such installments that are due *within* the coming year are classified as a current liability. The installments due *after* the coming year are classified as a long-term liability.

To illustrate, The Coca-Cola Company reported the following debt payments schedule (in millions):[1]

Fiscal year ending	
2013	$ 1,577
2014	2,633
2015	2,451
2016	1,705
2017	1,439
Thereafter	6,508
Total principal payments	$16,313

The debt of $1,577 due in 2013 would be reported as a current liability on the December 31, 2012 balance sheet. The remaining debt of $14,736 ($16,313 – $1,577) would be reported as a long-term liability on the balance sheet.

Short-Term Notes Payable

Notes may be issued to purchase merchandise or other assets. Notes may also be issued to creditors to satisfy an account payable created earlier.[2]

To illustrate, assume that Nature's Sunshine Company issued a 90-day, 12% note for $1,000, dated August 1, 2015, to Murray Co. for a $1,000 overdue account. The entry to record the issuance of the note is as follows:

Aug.	1	Accounts Payable—Murray Co.		1,000	
		Notes Payable			1,000
		Issued a 90-day, 12% note on account.			

When the note matures, the entry to record the payment of $1,000 plus $30 interest ($1,000 × 12% × 90 ÷ 360) is as follows:

Oct.	30	Notes Payable		1,000	
		Interest Expense		30	
		Cash			1,030
		Paid principal and interest due on note.			

[1] The Coca-Cola Company, *Form 10-K For the Fiscal Year Ended December 31, 2012.*

[2] The accounting for notes received to satisfy an account receivable was described and illustrated in Chapter 9, *Receivables*.

The interest expense is reported in the Other Expense section of the income statement for the year ended December 31, 2015. The interest expense account is closed at December 31.

Each note transaction affects a debtor (borrower) and creditor (lender). The following illustration shows how the same transactions are recorded by the debtor and creditor. In this illustration, the debtor (borrower) is Bowden Co., and the creditor (lender) is Coker Co.

	Bowden Co. (Borrower)			**Coker Co. (Creditor)**		

May 1. Bowden Co. purchased merchandise on account from Coker Co., $10,000, 2/10, n/30. The merchandise cost Coker Co. $7,500.	Merchandise Inventory
	  Accounts Payable
		10,000	
			10,000
				Accounts Receivable
				  Sales
				
				Cost of Merchandise Sold
				  Merchandise Inventory
					10,000
					
					7,500
						
						10,000
						
						7,500

May 31. Bowden Co. issued a 60-day, 12% note for $10,000 to Coker Co. on account.	Accounts Payable
	  Notes Payable
		10,000	
			10,000
				Notes Receivable
				  Accounts Receivable
					10,000	
						10,000

July 30. Bowden Co. paid Coker Co. the amount due on the note of May 31. Interest: $10,000 × 12% × 60 ÷ 360.	Notes Payable
	Interest Expense
	  Cash
		10,000
		200
			
			10,200
				Cash
				  Interest Revenue
				  Notes Receivable
					10,200	
						200
						10,000

A company may also borrow from a bank by issuing a note. To illustrate, assume that on September 19 Iceburg Company borrowed cash from First National Bank by issuing a $4,000, 90-day, 15% note to the bank. The entry to record the issuance of the note and the cash proceeds is as follows:

Sept.	19	Cash		4,000	
		Notes Payable			4,000
		Issued a 90-day, 15% note to First National Bank.			

On the due date of the note (December 18), Iceburg Company owes First National Bank $4,000 plus interest of $150 ($4,000 × 15% × 90 ÷ 360). The entry to record the payment of the note is as follows:

Dec.	18	Notes Payable		4,000	
		Interest Expense		150	
		Cash			4,150
		Paid principal and interest due on note.			

In some cases, a *discounted note* may be issued rather than an interest-bearing note. A discounted note has the following characteristics:

- The interest rate on the note is called the *discount rate*.
- The amount of interest on the note, called the *discount*, is computed by multiplying the discount rate times the face amount of the note.
- The debtor (borrower) receives the face amount of the note less the discount, called the *proceeds*.
- The debtor must repay the face amount of the note on the due date.

To illustrate, assume that on August 10, Cary Company issues a $20,000, 90-day discounted note to Western National Bank. The discount rate is 15%, and the amount of the discount is $750 ($20,000 × 15% × 90 ÷ 360). Thus, the proceeds received by Cary Company are $19,250. The entry by Cary Company is as follows:

Aug.	10	Cash		19,250	
		Interest Expense		750	
		Notes Payable			20,000
		Issued a 90-day discounted note to Western National Bank at a 15% discount rate.			

The entry when Cary Company pays the discounted note on November 8 is as follows:[3]

Nov.	8	Notes Payable		20,000	
		Cash			20,000
		Paid note due.			

Other current liabilities that have been discussed in earlier chapters include accrued expenses, unearned revenue, and interest payable. The accounting for wages and salaries, termed *payroll accounting*, is discussed next.

Example Exercise 11-1 Proceeds from Notes Payable OBJ 1

On July 1, Bella Salon Company borrowed cash from Best Bank by issuing a 60-day note with a face amount of $60,000.

a. Determine the proceeds of the note, assuming the note carries an interest rate of 6%.

b. Determine the proceeds of the note, assuming the note is discounted at 6%.

Dynamic Exhibit

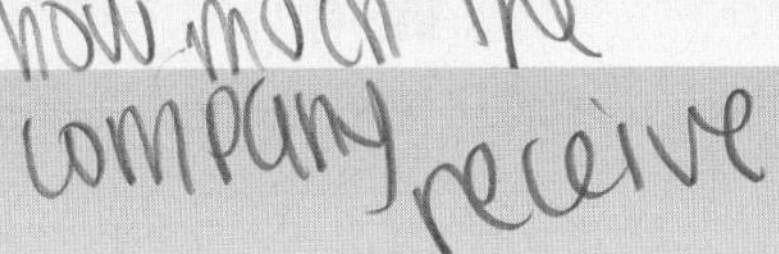

Follow My Example 11-1

a. $60,000

b. $59,400 [$60,000 – ($60,000 × 6% × 60 ÷ 360)]

Practice Exercises: PE 11-1A, PE 11-1B

Payroll and Payroll Taxes

OBJ 2 Determine employer liabilities for payroll, including liabilities arising from employee earnings and deductions from earnings.

In accounting, **payroll** refers to the amount paid to employees for services they provided during the period. A company's payroll is important for the following reasons:

- Payroll and related payroll taxes significantly affect the net income of most companies.
- Payroll is subject to federal and state regulations.
- Good employee morale requires payroll to be paid timely and accurately.

Liability for Employee Earnings

Note: **Employee salaries and wages are expenses to an employer.**

Salary usually refers to payment for managerial and administrative services. Salary is normally expressed in terms of a month or a year. *Wages* usually refers to payment for employee manual labor. The rate of wages is normally stated on an hourly or a weekly basis. The salary or wage of an employee may be increased by bonuses, commissions, profit sharing, or cost-of-living adjustments.

Companies engaged in interstate commerce must follow the Fair Labor Standards Act. This act, sometimes called the Federal Wage and Hour Law, requires employers to pay a minimum rate of 1½ times the regular rate for all hours worked in excess of 40 hours per week. Exemptions are provided for executive, administrative, and some supervisory positions. Increased rates for working overtime, nights, or holidays are common, even when not required by law. These rates may be as much as twice the regular rate.

[3] If the accounting period ends before a discounted note is paid, an adjusting entry should record the prepaid (deferred) interest that is not yet an expense. This deferred interest would be deducted from Notes Payable in the Current Liabilities section of the balance sheet.

To illustrate computing an employee's earnings, assume that **John T. McGrath** is a salesperson employed by **McDermott Supply Co.** McGrath's regular rate is $34 per hour, and any hours worked in excess of 40 hours per week are paid at 1½ times the regular rate. McGrath worked 42 hours for the week ended December 27. His earnings of $1,462 for the week are computed as follows:

Earnings at regular rate (40 hrs. × $34)	$1,360
Earnings at overtime rate [2 hrs. × ($34 × 1½)]	102
Total earnings	$1,462

Deductions from Employee Earnings

The total earnings of an employee for a payroll period, including any overtime pay, are called **gross pay**. From this amount is subtracted one or more *deductions* to arrive at the **net pay**. Net pay is the amount paid the employee. The deductions normally include federal, state, and local income taxes, medical insurance, and pension contributions.

Income Taxes Employers normally withhold a portion of employee earnings for payment of the employees' federal income tax. Each employee authorizes the amount to be withheld by completing an "Employee's Withholding Allowance Certificate," called a W-4. Exhibit 2 is the W-4 form submitted by **John T. McGrath**.

EXHIBIT 2

Employee's Withholding Allowance Certificate (W-4 Form)

Separate here and give Form W-4 to your employer. Keep the top part for your records.

Form **W-4** Department of the Treasury Internal Revenue Service

Employee's Withholding Allowance Certificate

▶ Whether you are entitled to claim a certain number of allowances or exemption from withholding is subject to review by the IRS. Your employer may be required to send a copy of this form to the IRS.

OMB No. 1545-0074 **2014**

1 Your first name and middle initial: John T. | Last name: McGrath | 2 Your social security number: 381 48 9120

Home address (number and street or rural route): 1830 4th Street

3 ☒ Single ☐ Married ☐ Married, but withhold at higher Single rate.
Note. If married, but legally separated, or spouse is a nonresident alien, check the "Single" box.

City or town, state, and ZIP code: Clinton, Iowa 52732-6142

4 If your last name differs from that shown on your social security card, check here. You must call 1-800-772-1213 for a replacement card. ▶ ☐

5 Total number of allowances you are claiming (from line **H** above **or** from the applicable worksheet on page 2) | 5 |

6 Additional amount, if any, you want withheld from each paycheck . . . . | 6 | $

7 I claim exemption from withholding for 2013, and I certify that I meet **both** of the following conditions for exemption.
• Last year I had a right to a refund of **all** federal income tax withheld because I had **no** tax liability, **and**
• This year I expect a refund of **all** federal income tax withheld because I expect to have **no** tax liability.
If you meet both conditions, write "Exempt" here . . . . ▶ | 7 |

Under penalties of perjury, I declare that I have examined this certificate and, to the best of my knowledge and belief, it is true, correct, and complete.

Employee's signature (This form is not valid unless you sign it.) ▶ *John T. McGrath* Date ▶ June 2, 2013

8 Employer's name and address (Employer: Complete lines 8 and 10 only if sending to the IRS.) | 9 Office code (optional) | 10 Employer identification number (EIN)

For Privacy Act and Paperwork Reduction Act Notice, see page 2. Cat. No. 10220Q Form **W-4** (2013)

On the W-4, an employee indicates marital status and the number of withholding allowances. A single employee may claim one withholding allowance. A married employee may claim an additional allowance for a spouse. An employee may also claim an allowance for each dependent other than a spouse. Each allowance reduces the federal income tax withheld from the employee's pay. Exhibit 2 indicates that McGrath is single and, thus, claimed one withholding allowance.

The federal income tax withheld depends on each employee's gross pay and W-4 allowance. Withholding tables issued by the Internal Revenue Service (IRS) are used to determine amounts to withhold. Exhibit 3 is an example of an IRS wage withholding table for a single person who is paid weekly.[4]

In Exhibit 3, each row is the employee's wages after deducting the employee's withholding allowances. Each year, the amount of the standard withholding allowance is determined by the IRS. For ease of computation and because this amount changes each year, we assume that the standard withholding allowance to be deducted in Exhibit 3 for a single person paid weekly is $75.[5] Thus, if two withholding allowances are claimed, $150 ($75 × 2) is deducted.

[4] IRS withholding tables are also available for married employees and for pay periods other than weekly.

[5] The actual IRS standard withholding allowance changes every year and was $75.00 for 2013.

EXHIBIT 3

Wage Bracket Withholding Table

Table for Percentage Method of Withholding WEEKLY Payroll Period

(a) SINGLE person (including head of household)—

If the amount of wages (after subtracting withholding allowances) is:		The amount of income tax to withhold is:	
Not over $42		$0	
Over—	**But not over—**		**of excess over—**
$42	—$214	$0.00 plus 10%	—$42
$214	—$739	$17.20 plus 15%	—$214
$739	—$1,732	$95.95 plus 25%	—$739 ← McGrath wage bracket
$1,732	—$3,566	$344.20 plus 28%	—$1,732
$3,566	—$7,703	$857.72 plus 33%	—$3,566
$7,703	—$7,735	$2,222.93 plus 35%	—$7,703
$7,735		$2,234.13 plus 39.6%	—$7,735

Source: Publication 15, Employer's Tax Guide, Internal Revenue Service, 2013.

To illustrate, **John T. McGrath** made $1,462 for the week ended December 27. McGrath's W-4 claims one withholding allowance of $75. Thus, the wages used in determining McGrath's withholding bracket in Exhibit 3 are $1,387 ($1,462 – $75).

After the person's withholding wage bracket has been computed, the federal income tax to be withheld is determined as follows:

- Step 1. Locate the proper withholding wage bracket in Exhibit 3.
  McGrath's wages after deducting one standard IRS withholding allowance are $1,387 ($1,462 – $75). Therefore, the wage bracket for McGrath is $739–$1,732.
- Step 2. Compute the withholding for the proper wage bracket using the directions in the two right-hand columns in Exhibit 3.
  For McGrath's wage bracket, the withholding is computed as "$95.95 plus 25% of the excess over $739." Hence, McGrath's withholding is $257.95, computed as follows:

Initial withholding from wage bracket	*$ 95.95*
Plus [25% × ($1,387 – $739)]	*162.00*
Total withholding	*$257.95*

Residents of certain cities including Detroit, the District of Columbia, and New York City must pay a city income tax in addition to their federal and state income taxes.

Employers may also be required to withhold state or city income taxes. The amounts to be withheld are determined on state-by-state and city-by-city bases.

Example Exercise 11-2 Federal Income Tax Withholding

OBJ 2

Karen Dunn's weekly gross earnings for the present week were $2,250. Dunn has two exemptions. Using the wage bracket withholding table in Exhibit 3 with a $75 standard withholding allowance for each exemption, what is Dunn's federal income tax withholding?

Follow My Example 11-2

Total wage payment		$ 2,250
One allowance (provided by IRS)	$75	
Multiplied by allowances claimed on Form W-4	× 2	150
Amount subject to withholding		$ 2,100
Initial withholding from wage bracket in Exhibit 3		$344.20
Plus additional withholding: 28% of excess over $1,732		103.04*
Federal income tax withholding		$447.24

*28% × ($2,100 – $1,732)

Practice Exercises: PE 11-2A, PE 11-2B

FICA Tax Employers are required by the Federal Insurance Contributions Act (FICA) to withhold a portion of the earnings of each employee. The **FICA tax** withheld contributes to the following two federal programs:

- *Social security*, which provides payments for retirees, survivors, and disability insurance.
- *Medicare*, which provides health insurance for senior citizens.

The amount withheld from each employee is based on the employee's earnings *paid* in the *calendar* year. The withholding tax rates and maximum earnings subject to tax are often revised by Congress.[6] To simplify, this chapter assumes the following rates and earnings subject to tax:

- Social security: 6% on all earnings
- Medicare: 1.5% on all earnings

To illustrate, assume that **John T. McGrath**'s earnings for the week ending December 27 are $1,462 and the total FICA tax to be withheld is $109.65, computed as follows:

Earnings subject to 6% social security tax	$1,462	
Social security tax rate	× 6%	
Social security tax		$ 87.72
Earnings subject to 1.5% Medicare tax	$1,462	
Medicare tax rate	× 1.5%	
Medicare tax		21.93
Total FICA tax		$109.65

Other Deductions Employees may choose to have additional amounts deducted from their gross pay. For example, an employee may authorize deductions for retirement savings, for charitable contributions, or life insurance. A union contract may also require the deduction of union dues.

Computing Employee Net Pay

Gross earnings less payroll deductions equals *net pay*, sometimes called *take-home pay*. Assuming that **John T. McGrath** authorized deductions for retirement savings and for a United Fund contribution, McGrath's net pay for the week ended December 27 is $1,069.40, computed as follows:

Gross earnings for the week		$1,462.00
Deductions:		
Social security tax	$ 87.72	
Medicare tax	21.93	
Federal income tax	257.95	
Retirement savings	20.00	
United Fund	5.00	
Total deductions		392.60
Net pay		$1,069.40

Example Exercise 11-3 Employee Net Pay

OBJ 2

Karen Dunn's weekly gross earnings for the week ending December 3 were $2,250, and her federal income tax withholding was $447.24. Assuming the social security rate is 6% and Medicare is 1.5%, what is Dunn's net pay?

Follow My Example 11-3

Total wage payment		$2,250.00
Less: Federal income tax withholding	$447.24	
Social security tax ($2,250 × 6%)	135.00	
Medicare tax ($2,250 × 1.5%)	33.75	615.99
Net pay		$1,634.01

Practice Exercises: PE 11-3A, PE 11-3B

[6] For 2013, the social security tax rate was 6.2% and the Medicare tax rate was 1.45%. Earnings subject to the social security tax are limited to an annual threshold amount, but for text examples and problems, assume all accumulated annual earnings are below this threshold and subject to the tax.

Liability for Employer's Payroll Taxes

Employers are subject to the following payroll taxes for amounts paid their employees:

- *FICA Tax:* Employers must match the employee's FICA tax contribution.
- *Federal Unemployment Compensation Tax (FUTA):* This employer tax provides for temporary payments to those who become unemployed. The tax collected by the federal government is allocated among the states for use in state programs rather than paid directly to employees. Congress often revises the FUTA tax rate and maximum earnings subject to tax.
- *State Unemployment Compensation Tax (SUTA):* This employer tax also provides temporary payments to those who become unemployed. The FUTA and SUTA programs are closely coordinated, with the states distributing the unemployment checks.[7] SUTA tax rates and earnings subject to tax vary by state.[8]

The preceding employer taxes are an operating expense of the company. Exhibit 4 summarizes the responsibility for employee and employer payroll taxes.

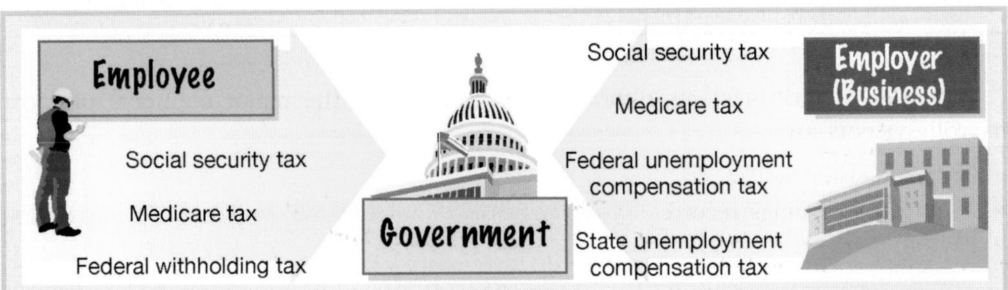

EXHIBIT 4

Responsibility for Tax Payments

Business  Connection

THE MOST YOU WILL EVER PAY

In 1936, the Social Security Board described how the tax was expected to affect a worker's pay, as follows:

The taxes called for in this law will be paid both by your employer and by you. For the next 3 years you will pay maybe 15 cents a week, maybe 25 cents a week, maybe 30 cents or more, according to what you earn. That is to say, during the next 3 years, beginning January 1, 1937, you will pay 1 cent for every dollar you earn, and at the same time your employer will pay 1 cent for every dollar you earn, up to $3,000 a year. . . .

. . . Beginning in 1940 you will pay, and your employer will pay, 1½ cents for each dollar you earn, up to $3,000 a year . . . and then beginning in 1943, you will pay 2 cents, and so will your employer, for every dollar you earn for the next three years. After that, you and your employer will each pay half a cent more for 3 years, and finally, beginning in 1949, . . . you and your employer will each pay 3 cents on each dollar you earn, up to $3,000 a year. That is the most you will ever pay.

The rate on January 1, 2013, was 7.65 cents per dollar earned (7.65%). The social security portion was 6.20% on the first $110,100 of earnings. The Medicare portion was 1.45% on all earnings.

Source: Arthur Lodge, "That Is the Most You Will Ever Pay," *Journal of Accountancy*, October 1985, p. 44.

Accounting Systems for Payroll and Payroll Taxes

 Describe payroll accounting systems that use a payroll register, employee earnings records, and a general journal.

Payroll systems should be designed to:

- Pay employees accurately and timely.
- Meet regulatory requirements of federal, state, and local agencies.
- Provide useful data for management decision-making needs.

[7] This rate may be reduced to 0.8% for credits for state unemployment compensation tax.

[8] For 2013, the maximum state rate credited against the federal unemployment rate was 5.4% of the first $7,000 of each employee's earnings during a calendar year.

EXHIBIT 5 **Payroll Register**

Employee Name	Total Hours	Earnings		
		Regular	**Overtime**	**Total**
Abrams, Julie S.	40	500.00		500.00
Elrod, Fred G.	44	392.00	58.80	450.80
Gomez, Jose C.	40	840.00		840.00
McGrath, John T.	**42**	**1,360.00**	**102.00**	**1,462.00**
Wilkes, Glenn K.	40	480.00		480.00
Zumpano, Michael W.	40	600.00		600.00
Total		13,328.00	574.00	13,902.00

Although payroll systems differ among companies, the major elements of most payroll systems are:

- Payroll register
- Employee's earnings record
- Payroll checks

Payroll Register

The **payroll register** is a multicolumn report used for summarizing the data for each payroll period. Although payroll registers vary by company, a payroll register normally includes the following columns:

- Employee name
- Total hours worked
- Regular earnings
- Overtime earnings
- Total gross earnings
- Social security tax withheld
- Medicare tax withheld
- Federal income tax withheld
- Retirement savings withheld
- Miscellaneous items withheld
- Total withholdings
- Net pay
- Check number of payroll check issued
- Accounts debited for payroll expense

Exhibit 5 illustrates a payroll register for **McDermott Supply Co.** The two right-hand columns of the payroll register indicate the accounts debited for the payroll expense. These columns are often referred to as the *payroll distribution.*

Recording Employees' Earnings The column totals of the payroll register provide the basis for recording the journal entry for payroll. The entry based on the payroll register in Exhibit 5 follows:

Dec.	27	Sales Salaries Expense	11,122.00	
		Office Salaries Expense	2,780.00	
		Social Security Tax Payable		834.12
		Medicare Tax Payable		208.53
		Employees Federal Income Tax Payable		3,332.00
		Retirement Savings Deductions Payable		680.00
		United Fund Deductions Payable		520.00
		Salaries Payable		8,327.35
		Payroll for week ended December 27.		

EXHIBIT 5 **(Concluded)**

	Deductions Withheld						Paid		Accounts Debited		
	Social Security Tax	Medicare Tax	Federal Income Tax	Retirement Savings	Misc.	Total	Net Pay	Check No.	Sales Salaries Expense	Office Salaries Expense	
1	30.00	7.50	48.85	20.00	UF 10.00	116.35	383.65	6857	500.00		1
2	27.05	6.76	30.22		UF 50.00	114.03	336.77	6858		450.80	2
3	50.40	12.60	83.70	25.00	UF 10.00	181.70	658.30	6859	840.00		3
4	**87.72**	**21.93**	**257.95**	**20.00**	**UF 5.00**	**392.60**	**1,069.40**	**6860**	**1,462.00**		4
25	28.80	7.20	45.85	10.00		91.85	388.15	6880	480.00		25
26	36.00	9.00	63.85	5.00	UF 2.00	115.85	484.15	6881		600.00	26
27	834.12	208.53	3,332.00	680.00	UF 520.00	5,574.65	8,327.35		11,122.00	2,780.00	27
28											28

Miscellaneous Deductions: UF—United Fund

Recording and Paying Payroll Taxes Payroll taxes are recorded as liabilities when the payroll is *paid* to employees. In addition, employers compute and report payroll taxes on a *calendar-year* basis, which may differ from the company's fiscal year.

Note:
Payroll taxes become a liability to the employer when the payroll is paid.

Example Exercise 11-4 Journalize Period Payroll

OBJ 3

The payroll register of Chen Engineering Services indicates $900 of social security withheld and $225 of Medicare tax withheld on total salaries of $15,000 for the period. Federal withholding for the period totaled $2,925.

Provide the journal entry for the period's payroll.

Follow My Example 11-4

Salaries Expense	15,000	
Social Security Tax Payable		900
Medicare Tax Payable		225
Employees Federal Income Tax Payable		2,925
Salaries Payable		10,950

Practice Exercises: PE 11-4A, PE 11-4B

On December 27, McDermott Supply has the following payroll data:

Sales salaries	$11,122
Office salaries owed	2,780
Wages owed employees on December 27	$13,902
Wages subject to payroll taxes:	
Social security tax (6%)	$13,902
Medicare tax (1.5%)	13,902
State (5.4%) and federal (0.8%) unemployment compensation tax	2,710

Employers must match the employees' social security and Medicare tax contributions. In addition, the employer must pay state unemployment compensation tax (SUTA) of 5.4% and federal unemployment compensation tax (FUTA) of 0.8%. When payroll is paid on December 27, these payroll taxes are computed as follows:

Social security tax	$ 834.12 ($13,902 × 6%, and from Social Security Tax column of Exhibit 5)
Medicare tax	208.53 ($13,902 × 1.5%, and from Medicare Tax column of Exhibit 5)
SUTA	146.34 ($2,710 × 5.4%)
FUTA	21.68 ($2,710 × 0.8%)
Total payroll taxes	$1,210.67

The entry to journalize the payroll tax expense for Exhibit 5 follows:

Dec.	27	Payroll Tax Expense	1,210.67	
		Social Security Tax Payable		834.12
		Medicare Tax Payable		208.53
		State Unemployment Tax Payable		146.34
		Federal Unemployment Tax Payable		21.68
		Payroll taxes for week ended December 27.		

The preceding entry records a liability for each payroll tax. When the payroll taxes are paid, an entry is recorded debiting the payroll tax liability accounts and crediting Cash.

Example Exercise 11-5 Journalize Payroll Tax

The payroll register of Chen Engineering Services indicates $900 of social security withheld and $225 of Medicare tax withheld on total salaries of $15,000 for the period. Earnings of $5,250 are subject to state and federal unemployment compensation taxes at the federal rate of 0.8% and the state rate of 5.4%.

Provide the journal entry to record the payroll tax expense for the period.

(Continued)

EXHIBIT 6

Employee's Earnings Record

John T. McGrath
1830 4th St.
Clinton, IA 52732-6142 **PHONE: 555-3148**

SINGLE **NUMBER OF WITHHOLDING ALLOWANCES: 1** **PAY RATE: $1,360.00 Per Week**

OCCUPATION: Salesperson **EQUIVALENT HOURLY RATE: $34**

			Earnings				
	Period Ending	**Total Hours**	**Regular Earnings**	**Overtime Earnings**	**Total Earnings**	**Total**	
42	SEPT. 27	53	1,360.00	663.00	2,023.00	75,565.00	42
43	THIRD QUARTER		17,680.00	7,605.00	25,285.00		43
44	OCT. 4	51	1,360.00	561.00	1,921.00	77,486.00	44
50	NOV. 15	50	1,360.00	510.00	1,870.00	89,382.00	50
51	NOV. 22	53	1,360.00	663.00	2,023.00	91,405.00	51
52	NOV. 29	47	1,360.00	357.00	1,717.00	93,122.00	52
53	DEC. 6	53	1,360.00	663.00	2,023.00	95,145.00	53
54	DEC.13	52	1,360.00	612.00	1,972.00	97,117.00	54
55	DEC. 20	51	1,360.00	561.00	1,921.00	99,038.00	55
56	DEC. 27	42	1,360.00	102.00	1,462.00	100,500.00	56
57	FOURTH QUARTER		17,680.00	7,255.00	24,935.00		57
58	YEARLY TOTAL		70,720.00	29,780.00	100,500.00		58

Follow My Example 11-5

Payroll Tax Expense	1,450.50	
Social Security Tax Payable		900.00
Medicare Tax Payable		225.00
State Unemployment Tax Payable		283.50*
Federal Unemployment Tax Payable		42.00**

*$5,250 × 5.4%
**$5,250 × 0.8%

Practice Exercises: PE 11-5A, PE 11-5B

Employee's Earnings Record

Each employee's earnings to date must be determined at the end of each payroll period. This total is necessary for computing the employee's social security tax withholding and the employer's payroll taxes. Thus, detailed payroll records must be kept for each employee. This record is called an **employee's earnings record**.

Exhibit 6 shows a portion of **John T. McGrath**'s employee's earnings record. An employee's earnings record and the payroll register are interrelated. For example, McGrath's earnings record for December 27 can be traced to the fourth line of the payroll register in Exhibit 5.

EXHIBIT 6 **(Concluded)**

SOC. SEC. NO.: 381-48-9120 **EMPLOYEE NO.: 814**

DATE OF BIRTH: February 15, 1982

DATE EMPLOYMENT TERMINATED:

	Deductions							Paid		
	Social Security Tax	Medicare Tax	Federal Income Tax	Retirement Savings	Other		Total	Net Amount	Check No.	
42	121.38	30.35	404.68	20.00			576.41	1,446.59	6175	42
43	1,517.10	379.28	5,391.71	260.00	UF	40.00	7,588.09	17,696.91		43
44	115.26	28.82	376.12	20.00			540.20	1,380.80	6225	44
50	112.20	28.05	361.84	20.00			522.09	1,347.91	6530	50
51	121.38	30.35	404.68	20.00			576.41	1,446.59	6582	51
52	103.02	25.76	321.70	20.00			470.48	1,246.52	6640	52
53	121.38	30.35	404.68	20.00	UF	5.00	581.41	1,441.59	6688	53
54	118.32	29.58	390.40	20.00			558.30	1,413.70	6743	54
55	115.26	28.82	376.12	20.00			540.20	1,380.80	6801	55
56	87.72	21.93	257.95	20.00	UF	5.00	392.60	1,069.40	6860	56
57	1,496.10	374.03	5,293.71	260.00	UF	15.00	7,438.84	17,496.16		57
58	6,030.00	1,507.50	21,387.65	1,040.00	UF	100.00	30,065.15	70,434.85		58

As shown in Exhibit 6, an employee's earnings record has quarterly and yearly totals. These totals are used for tax, insurance, and other reports. For example, one such report is the Wage and Tax Statement, commonly called a *W-2*. This form is provided annually to each employee as well as to the Social Security Administration. The W-2 shown in Exhibit 7 is based on **John T. McGrath**'s employee's earnings record shown in Exhibit 6.

EXHIBIT 7 **Employee's Wage and Tax Statement (W-2 Form)**

22222 | Void ☐ | a Employee's social security number: 381-48-9120 | For Official Use Only ► OMB No. 1545-0008

b Employer identification number (EIN): 61-8436524	1 Wages, tips, other compensation: 100,500.00	2 Federal income tax withheld: 21,387.65
c Employer's name, address, and ZIP code: McDermott Supply Co. 415 5th Ave. So. Dubuque, IA 52736-0142	3 Social security wages: 100,500.00	4 Social security tax withheld: 6,030.00
	5 Medicare wages and tips: 100,500.00	6 Medicare tax withheld: 1,507.50
	7 Social security tips	8 Allocated tips
d Control number	9	10 Dependent care benefits
e Employee's first name and initial: John T. / Last name: McGrath / Suff.	11 Nonqualified plans	12a See instructions for box 12 (Code)
1830 4th St. Clinton, IA 52732-6142	13 Statutory employee ☐ Retirement plan ☐ Third-party sick pay ☐	12b (Code)
	14 Other	12c (Code)
		12d (Code)
f Employee's address and ZIP code		

15 State	Employer's state ID number	16 State wages, tips, etc.	17 State income tax	18 Local wages, tips, etc.	19 Local income tax	20 Locality name
IA						Dubuque

Form **W-2** **Wage and Tax Statement** 2014

Department of the Treasury—Internal Revenue Service

For Privacy Act and Paperwork Reduction Act Notice, see the separate instructions.

Cat. No. 10134D

Copy A For Social Security Administration — Send this entire page with Form W-3 to the Social Security Administration; photocopies are **not** acceptable.

Do Not Cut, Fold, or Staple Forms on This Page

Payroll Checks

Companies pay employees either by electronic funds transfer or by issuing *payroll checks*. With electronic funds transfers, the employee's net pay is electronically deposited into their bank account each period. Later, the employees receive a payroll statement summarizing how the net pay was computed. A payroll statement for the electronic funds transfer of **John T. McGrath**'s pay is shown in Exhibit 8. Each payroll check includes a detachable statement showing how the net pay was computed, which is typically identical to the payroll statement accompanying electronic funds transfers (EFTs).

Most companies use a special payroll bank account to disburse payroll. In such cases, payroll is processed as follows:

1. The total net pay for the period is determined from the payroll register.
2. The company authorizes an electronic funds transfer (EFT) from its regular bank account to the special payroll bank account for the total net pay.
3. Individual EFTs or payroll checks are disbursed from the payroll account.
4. The numbers of the individual payroll disbursements are inserted in the payroll register.

EXHIBIT 8

Payroll Statement

McDermott Supply Co. 415 5th Ave. So. Dubuque, IA 52736-0142	John T. McGrath 1830 4th St. Clinton, IA 52732-6142	**Check Number:** 6860 **Pay Period Ending:** 12/27/14		
HOURS & EARNINGS		**TAXES & DEDUCTIONS**		
DESCRIPTION	AMOUNT	DESCRIPTION	CURRENT AMOUNT	Y-T-D AMOUNT
Rate of Pay Reg.	34	Social Security Tax	87.72	6,030.00
Rate of Pay O.T.	51	Medicare Tax	21.93	1,507.50
Hours Worked Reg.	40	Fed. Income Tax	257.95	21,387.65
Hours Worked O.T.	2	U.S. Savings Bonds	20.00	1,040.00
		United Fund	5.00	100.00
Net Pay	1,069.40			
Total Gross Pay	1,462.00	Total	392.60	30,365.15
Total Gross Y-T-D	100,500.00			

An advantage of using a separate payroll bank account is that reconciling the bank statements is simplified. In addition, a payroll bank account establishes control over payroll checks and, thus, prevents their theft or misuse.

Computerized Payroll System

The inputs into a payroll system may be classified as:

- *Constants:* Data that remain unchanged from payroll to payroll

  Examples: Employee names, social security numbers, marital status, number of income tax withholding allowances, rates of pay, tax rates, and withholding tables
- *Variables:* Data that change from payroll to payroll

  Examples: Number of hours or days worked for each employee, accrued days of sick leave, vacation credits, total earnings to date, and total taxes withheld

In a computerized accounting system, constants are stored within a payroll file. The variables are input each pay period by a payroll clerk. In some systems, employees swipe their identification (ID) cards when they report for and leave from work. In such cases, the hours worked by each employee are automatically updated.

A computerized payroll system also maintains electronic versions of the payroll register and employee earnings records. Payroll system outputs, such as payroll checks, electronic funds transfers, and tax records, are automatically produced each pay period.

Internal Controls for Payroll Systems

The cash payment controls described in Chapter 8 also apply to payrolls. Some examples of payroll controls include the following:

- If a check-signing machine is used, blank payroll checks and access to the machine should be restricted to prevent their theft or misuse.
- The hiring and firing of employees should be properly authorized and approved in writing.
- All changes in pay rates should be properly authorized and approved in writing.
- Employees should be observed when arriving for work to verify that employees are "checking in" for work only once and only for themselves. Employees may "check in" for work by using a time card or by swiping their employee ID card.
- Payroll checks should be distributed by someone other than employee supervisors.
- A special payroll bank account should be used.

Integrity, Objectivity, and Ethics in Business

$8 MILLION FOR 18 MINUTES OF WORK

Computer system controls can be very important in issuing payroll checks. In one case, a Detroit schoolteacher was paid $4,015,625 after deducting $3,884,375 in payroll deductions for 18 minutes of overtime work. The error was caused by a computer glitch when the teacher's employee identification number was substituted incorrectly in the "hourly wage" field and wasn't caught by the payroll software. After six days, the error was discovered, and the money was returned. "One of the things that came with (the software) is a fail-safe that prevents that. It doesn't work," a financial officer said. The district has since installed a program to flag any paycheck exceeding $10,000.

Source: Associated Press, September 27, 2002.

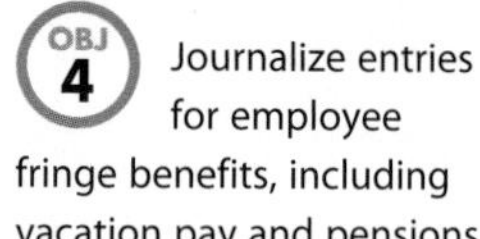

OBJ 4 Journalize entries for employee fringe benefits, including vacation pay and pensions.

Employees' Fringe Benefits

Many companies provide their employees benefits in addition to salary and wages earned. Such **fringe benefits** may include vacation, medical, and retirement benefits.

The cost of employee fringe benefits is recorded as an expense by the employer. To match revenues and expenses, the estimated cost of fringe benefits is recorded as an expense during the period in which the employees earn the benefits.

Vacation Pay

Note:
Vacation pay becomes the employer's liability as the employee earns vacation rights.

Most employers provide employees vacations, sometimes called *compensated absences*. The liability to pay for employee vacations could be accrued as a liability at the end of each pay period. However, many companies wait and record an adjusting entry for accrued vacation at the end of the year.

To illustrate, assume that employees earn one day of vacation for each month worked. The estimated vacation pay for the year ending December 31 is $325,000. The adjusting entry for the accrued vacation is as follows:

Dec.	31	Vacation Pay Expense		325,000	
		Vacation Pay Payable			325,000
		Accrued vacation pay for the year.			

Employees may be required to take all their vacation time within one year. In such cases, any accrued vacation pay will be paid within one year. Thus, the vacation pay payable is reported as a current liability on the balance sheet. If employees are allowed to accumulate their vacation pay, the estimated vacation pay payable that will *not* be taken within a year is reported as a long-term liability.

When employees take vacations, the liability for vacation pay is decreased by debiting Vacation Pay Payable. Salaries or Wages Payable and the other related payroll accounts for taxes and withholdings are credited.

Pensions

A **pension** is a cash payment to retired employees. Pension rights are accrued by employees as they work, based on the employer's pension plan. Two basic types of pension plans are defined contribution and defined benefit plans.[9]

Defined Contribution Plans In a **defined contribution plan**, the company invests contributions on behalf of the employee during the employee's working years. Normally, the employee and employer contribute to the plan. The employee's pension depends on the total contributions and the investment returns earned on those contributions.

One of the more popular defined contribution plans is the 401k plan. Under this plan, employees contribute a portion of their gross pay to investments, such as mutual funds. A 401k plan offers employees two advantages.

- The employee contribution is deducted before taxes.
- The contributions and related earnings are not taxed until withdrawn at retirement.

In most cases, the employer matches some portion of the employee's contribution. The employer's cost is debited to *Pension Expense*. To illustrate, assume that Heaven Scent Perfumes Company contributes 10% of employee monthly salaries to an employee 401k plan. Assuming $500,000 of monthly salaries, the journal entry to record the monthly contribution is as follows:

Dec.	31	Pension Expense		50,000	
		Cash			50,000
		Contributed 10% of monthly salaries to pension plan.			

Defined Benefit Plans In a **defined benefit plan**, the company pays the employee a fixed annual pension based on a formula. The formula is normally based on such factors as the employee's years of service, age, and past salary.

In a defined benefit plan, the employer is obligated to pay for (fund) the employee's future pension benefits. As a result, many companies are replacing their defined benefit plans with defined contribution plans.

The pension cost of a defined benefit plan is debited to *Pension Expense*. Cash is credited for the amount contributed (funded) by the employer. Any unfunded amount is credited to *Unfunded Pension Liability*.

To illustrate, assume that the defined benefit plan of Hinkle Co. requires an annual pension cost of $80,000. This annual contribution is based on estimates of Hinkle's future pension liabilities. On December 31, Hinkle Co. pays $60,000 to the pension fund. The entry to record the payment and the unfunded liability is as follows:

Dec.	31	Pension Expense		80,000	
		Cash			60,000
		Unfunded Pension Liability			20,000
		Annual pension cost and contribution.			

If the unfunded pension liability is to be paid within one year, it is reported as a current liability on the balance sheet. Any portion of the unfunded pension liability that will be paid beyond one year is a long-term liability.

[9] The accounting for pensions is complex due to the uncertainties of estimating future pension liabilities. These estimates depend on such factors as employee life expectancies, employee turnover, expected employee compensation levels, and investment income on pension contributions. Additional accounting and disclosures related to pensions are covered in advanced accounting courses.

Example Exercise 11-6 Vacation Pay and Pension Benefits

OBJ 4

Manfield Services Company provides its employees vacation benefits and a defined contribution pension plan. Employees earned vacation pay of $44,000 for the period. The pension plan requires a contribution to the plan administrator equal to 8% of employee salaries. Salaries were $450,000 during the period.

Provide the journal entry for the (a) vacation pay and (b) pension benefit.

Follow My Example 11-6

a.	Vacation Pay Expense	44,000	
	Vacation Pay Payable		44,000
	Vacation pay accrued for the period.		
b.	Pension Expense	36,000	
	Cash		36,000
	Pension contribution, 8% of $450,000 salary.		

Practice Exercises: PE 11-6A, PE 11-6B

Postretirement Benefits Other than Pensions

Employees may earn rights to other postretirement benefits from their employer. Such benefits may include dental care, eye care, medical care, life insurance, tuition assistance, tax services, and legal services.

The accounting for other postretirement benefits is similar to that of defined benefit pension plans. The estimate of the annual benefits expense is recorded by debiting *Postretirement Benefits Expense*. If the benefits are fully funded, Cash is credited for the same amount. If the benefits are not fully funded, a postretirement benefits plan liability account is also credited.

The financial statements should disclose the nature of the postretirement benefit liabilities. These disclosures are usually included as notes to the financial statements. Additional accounting and disclosures for postretirement benefits are covered in advanced accounting courses.

Current Liabilities on the Balance Sheet

Accounts payable, the current portion of long-term debt, notes payable, and any other debts that are due within one year are reported as current liabilities on the balance sheet. The balance sheet presentation of current liabilities for **Mornin' Joe** follows:

Mornin' Joe
Balance Sheet
December 31, 2016

Liabilities		
Current liabilities:		
Accounts payable	$133,000	
Notes payable (current portion)	200,000	
Salaries and wages payable	42,000	
Payroll taxes payable	16,400	
Interest payable	40,000	
Total current liabilities		$431,400

Business  **Connection**

CITY PENSION PROBLEMS

In June 2013, the city of Detroit, Michigan entered the record books as the largest municipal bankruptcy in history. While the city's financial problems stemmed from a number of factors, including a shrinking population and deteriorating economy, the city's $10 billion in pension-related liabilities were a major contributing factor. Detroit, however, is not alone. A number of other cities, including Charleston, West Virginia, Chicago, Illinois, and Providence, Rhode Island, face similar pension burdens. To overcome these challenges, these cities are restructuring their employee pension plans to reduce the strain that pension obligations place on their financial condition.

Source: "A Look at Pension Problems, Solutions in U.S. Cities," *The Wall Street Journal*, October 6, 2013.

Contingent Liabilities

OBJ 5 Describe the accounting treatment for contingent liabilities and journalize entries for product warranties.

Some liabilities may arise from past transactions only if certain events occur in the future. These *potential* liabilities are called **contingent liabilities.**

The accounting for contingent liabilities depends on the following two factors:

- *Likelihood of occurring:* Probable, reasonably possible, or remote
- *Measurement:* Estimable or not estimable

The likelihood that the event creating the liability occurring is classified as *probable, reasonably possible*, or *remote*. The ability to estimate the potential liability is classified as *estimable* or *not estimable*.

Probable and Estimable

If a contingent liability is *probable* and the amount of the liability can be *reasonably estimated*, it is recorded and disclosed. The liability is recorded by debiting an expense and crediting a liability.

To illustrate, assume that during June a company sold a product for $60,000 that includes a 36-month warranty for repairs.[10] The average cost of repairs over the warranty period is estimated at 5% of the sales price. The entry to record the estimated product warranty expense for June is as follows:

June	30	Product Warranty Expense		3,000	
		Product Warranty Payable			3,000
		Warranty expense for June, 5% × $60,000.			

The preceding entry records warranty expense in the same period in which the sale is recorded. In this way, warranty expense is matched with the related revenue (sales).

If the product is repaired under warranty, the repair costs are recorded by debiting *Product Warranty Payable* and crediting *Cash, Supplies, Wages Payable*, or other appropriate accounts. Thus, if a $200 part is replaced under warranty on August 16, the entry is as follows:

The estimated costs of warranty work on new car sales are a contingent liability for **Ford Motor Company.**

Aug.	16	Product Warranty Payable		200	
		Supplies			200
		Replaced defective part under warranty.			

[10] This discussion is limited to a discussion of assurance type warranties. A more detailed discussion of the types of warranties and their accounting is covered in intermediate and advanced accounting texts.

Example Exercise 11-7 Estimated Warranty Liability

Cook-Rite Co. sold $140,000 of kitchen appliances during August under a six-month warranty. The cost to repair defects under the warranty is estimated at 6% of the sales price. On September 12, a customer required a $200 part replacement plus $90 of labor under the warranty.

Provide the journal entry for (a) the estimated warranty expense on August 31 for August sales, and (b) the September 12 warranty work.

Follow My Example 11-7

		Debit	Credit
a.	Product Warranty Expense	8,400	
	Product Warranty Payable		8,400
	To record warranty expense for August, 6% × $140,000.		
b.	Product Warranty Payable	290	
	Supplies		200
	Wages Payable		90
	Replaced defective part under warranty.		

Practice Exercises: PE 11-7A, PE 11-7B

Probable and Not Estimable

A contingent liability may be probable, but cannot be estimated. In this case, the contingent liability is disclosed in the notes to the financial statements. For example, a company may have accidentally polluted a local river by dumping waste products. At the end of the period, the cost of the cleanup and any fines may not be able to be estimated.

Reasonably Possible

A contingent liability may be only possible. For example, a company may have lost a lawsuit for infringing on another company's patent rights. However, the verdict is under appeal and the company's lawyers feel that the verdict will be reversed or significantly reduced. In this case, the contingent liability is disclosed in the notes to the financial statements.

Remote

A contingent liability may be remote. For example, a ski resort may be sued for injuries incurred by skiers. In most cases, the courts have found that a skier accepts the risk of injury when participating in the activity. Thus, unless the ski resort is grossly negligent, the resort will not incur a liability for ski injuries. In such cases, no disclosure needs to be made in the notes to the financial statements. The accounting treatment of contingent liabilities is summarized in Exhibit 9.

Common examples of contingent liabilities disclosed in notes to the financial statements are litigation, environmental matters, guarantees, and contingencies from the sale of receivables.

An example of a recent contingent liability disclosure from **Google Inc.** follows:[11]

We have had patent, copyright, and trademark infringement lawsuits filed against us claiming that certain of our products, services, and technologies, including Android, Google Search, Google AdWords, Google AdSense, Google Books, Google News, Google Image Search, Google Chrome, Google Talk, Google Voice, Motorola devices and YouTube, infringe the intellectual property rights of others. Adverse results in these lawsuits may include awards of substantial monetary damages, costly royalty or licensing agreements, or orders preventing us from offering certain

[11] Google Inc., *Form 10-K For the Fiscal Year Ended December 31, 2012.*

EXHIBIT 9 **Accounting Treatment of Contingent Liabilities**

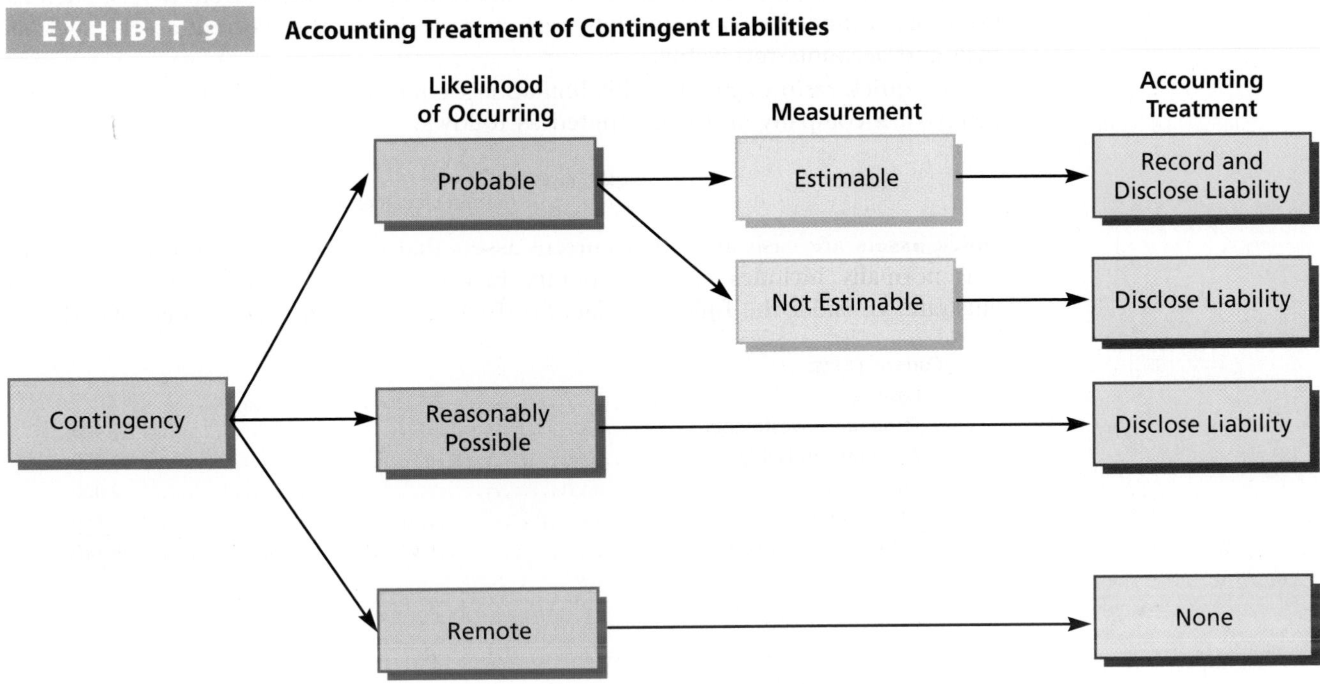

features, functionalities, products, or services, and may also cause us to change our business practices, and require development of non-infringing products or technologies, which could result in a loss of revenues for us and otherwise harm our business. . . .

With respect to our outstanding legal matters, based on our current knowledge, we believe that the amount or range of reasonably possible loss will not, either individually or in the aggregate, have a material adverse effect on our business, consolidated financial position, results of operations, or cash flows. However, the outcome of such legal matters is inherently unpredictable and subject to significant uncertainties. . . .

Professional judgment is necessary in distinguishing between classes of contingent liabilities. This is especially the case when distinguishing between probable and reasonably possible contingent liabilities.

Financial Analysis and Interpretation: Quick Ratio

OBJ 6 Describe and illustrate the use of the quick ratio in analyzing a company's ability to pay its current liabilities.

Current position analysis helps creditors evaluate a company's ability to pay its current liabilities. This analysis is based on the following three measures:

- Working capital
- Current ratio
- Quick ratio

Working capital and the current ratio were discussed in Chapter 4 and are computed as follows:

$$\text{Working Capital} = \text{Current Assets} - \text{Current Liabilities}$$

$$\text{Current Ratio} = \frac{\text{Current Assets}}{\text{Current Liabilities}}$$

While these two measures can be used to evaluate a company's ability to pay its current liabilities, they do not provide insight into the company's ability to pay these liabilities within a short period of time. This is because some current assets, such as inventory, cannot be converted into cash as quickly as other current assets, such as cash and accounts receivable.

The **quick ratio** overcomes this limitation by measuring the "instant" debt-paying ability of a company and is computed as follows:

$$\text{Quick Ratio} = \frac{\text{Quick Assets}}{\text{Current Liabilities}}$$

Quick assets are cash and other current assets that can be easily converted to cash. This normally includes cash, temporary investments, and accounts receivable. To illustrate, consider the following data for TechSolutions, Inc., at the end of 2015:

Current assets:	
Cash	$2,020
Temporary investments	3,400
Accounts receivable	1,600
Inventory	2,000
Other current assets	160
Total current assets	$9,180
Current liabilities:	
Accounts payable	$3,000
Other current liabilities	2,400
Total current liabilities	$5,400
Working capital (current assets – current liabilities)	$3,780
Current ratio (current assets ÷ current liabilities)	1.7

The quick ratio for TechSolutions, Inc., is computed as follows:

$$\text{Quick Ratio} = \frac{\$2,020 + \$3,400 + \$1,600}{\$5,400} = 1.3$$

The quick ratio of 1.3 indicates that the company has more than enough quick assets to pay its current liabilities in a short period of time. A quick ratio below 1.0 would indicate that the company does not have enough quick assets to cover its current liabilities.

Like the current ratio, the quick ratio is particularly useful in making comparisons across companies. To illustrate, the following selected balance sheet data (excluding ratios) were taken from recent financial statements of **Panera Bread Company** and **Starbucks Corporation** (in thousands):

	Panera Bread	Starbucks
Current assets:		
Cash and cash equivalents	$297,141	$1,188,600
Temporary investments	—	848,400
Accounts receivable	86,262	485,900
Inventory	19,714	1,241,500
Other current assets	75,725	435,200
Total current assets	$478,842	$4,199,600
Current liabilities:		
Accounts payable	$ 9,371	$ 389,100
Other current liabilities	268,169	1,820,700
Total current liabilities	$277,540	$2,209,800
Working capital (current assets – current liabilities)	$201,302	$1,989,800
Current ratio (current assets ÷ current liabilities)	1.7	1.9
Quick ratio (quick assets ÷ current liabilities)*	1.4	1.1

*The quick ratio for each company is computed as follows:
Panera Bread: ($297,141 + $86,262) ÷ $277,540 = 1.4
Starbucks: ($1,188,600 + $848,400 + $485,900) ÷ $2,209,800 = 1.1

Starbucks is larger than Panera Bread and has more than nine times the amount of working capital. Such size differences make working capital comparisons between companies difficult. In contrast, the current and quick ratios provide better comparisons across companies. In this example, Starbucks has a slightly higher current ratio than Panera Bread. However, Starbucks' 1.1 quick ratio reveals that it has just enough quick assets to cover its current liabilities, while Panera Bread's quick ratio of 1.4 indicates that the company has more than enough quick assets to meet its current liabilities.

Example Exercise 11-8 Quick Ratio

Sayer Company reported the following current assets and current liabilities for the years ended December 31, 2016 and 2015:

	2016	2015
Cash	$1,250	$1,000
Temporary investments	1,925	1,650
Accounts receivable	1,775	1,350
Inventory	1,900	1,700
Accounts payable	2,750	2,500

a. Compute the quick ratio for 2016 and 2015.

b. Interpret the company's quick ratio across the two time periods.

Follow My Example 11-8

a. December 31, 2016:
Quick Ratio = Quick Assets ÷ Current Liabilities
= ($1,250 + $1,925 + $1,775) ÷ $2,750
= 1.8

December 31, 2015:
Quick Ratio = Quick Assets ÷ Current Liabilities
= ($1,000 + $1,650 + $1,350) ÷ $2,500
= 1.6

b. The quick ratio of Sayer Company has improved from 1.6 in 2015 to 1.8 in 2016. This increase is the result of a large increase in the three types of quick assets (cash, temporary investments, and accounts receivable) compared to a relatively smaller increase in the current liability, accounts payable.

Practice Exercises: PE 11-8A, PE 11-8B

At a Glance 11

Describe and illustrate current liabilities related to accounts payable, current portion of long-term debt, and notes payable.

Key Points Current liabilities are obligations that are to be paid out of current assets and are due within a short time, usually within one year. The three primary types of current liabilities are accounts payable, notes payable, and the current portion of long-term debt.

Learning Outcomes	Example Exercises	Practice Exercises
• Identify and define the most frequently reported current liabilities on the balance sheet.		
• Determine the interest from interest-bearing and discounted notes payable.	**EE11-1**	**PE11-1A, 11-1B**

Determine employer liabilities for payroll, including liabilities arising from employee earnings and deductions from earnings.

Key Points An employer's liability for payroll is determined from employee total earnings, including overtime pay. From this amount, employee deductions are subtracted to arrive at the net pay to be paid to each employee. Most employers also incur liabilities for payroll taxes, such as social security tax, Medicare tax, federal unemployment compensation tax, and state unemployment compensation tax.

Learning Outcomes	Example Exercises	Practice Exercises
• Compute the federal withholding tax from a wage bracket withholding table.	**EE11-2**	**PE11-2A, 11-2B**
• Compute employee net pay, including deductions for social security and Medicare tax.	**EE11-3**	**PE11-3A, 11-3B**

Describe payroll accounting systems that use a payroll register, employee earnings records, and a general journal.

Key Points The payroll register is used in assembling and summarizing the data needed for each payroll period. The payroll register is supported by a detailed payroll record for each employee, called an *employee's earnings record*.

Learning Outcomes	Example Exercises	Practice Exercises
• Journalize the employee's earnings, net pay, and payroll liabilities from the payroll register.	**EE11-4**	**PE11-4A, 11-4B**
• Journalize the payroll tax expense.		
• Describe elements of a payroll system, including the employee's earnings record, payroll checks, and internal controls.	**EE11-5**	**PE11-5A, 11-5B**

Journalize entries for employee fringe benefits, including vacation pay and pensions.

Key Points Fringe benefits are expenses of the period in which the employees earn the benefits. Fringe benefits are recorded by debiting an expense account and crediting a liability account.

Learning Outcomes	Example Exercises	Practice Exercises
• Journalize vacation pay.	EE11-6	PE11-6A, 11-6B
• Distinguish and journalize defined contribution and defined benefit pension plans.	EE11-6	PE11-6A, 11-6B

Describe the accounting treatment for contingent liabilities and journalize entries for product warranties.

Key Points A contingent liability is a potential obligation that results from a past transaction but depends on a future event. The accounting for contingent liabilities is summarized in Exhibit 9.

Learning Outcomes	Example Exercises	Practice Exercises
• Describe the accounting for contingent liabilities.		
• Journalize estimated warranty obligations and services granted under warranty.	EE11-7	PE11-7A, 11-7B

Describe and illustrate the use of the quick ratio in analyzing a company's ability to pay its current liabilities.

Key Points The quick ratio is a measure of a company's ability to pay current liabilities within a short period of time. The quick ratio is computed by dividing quick assets by current liabilities. Quick assets include cash, temporary investments, accounts receivable, and other current assets that can be easily converted into cash. A quick ratio exceeding 1.0 is usually desirable.

Learning Outcomes	Example Exercises	Practice Exercises
• Describe the quick ratio.		
• Compute and evaluate the quick ratio.	EE11-8	PE11-8A, 11-8B

Key Terms

contingent liabilities (521)
current position analysis (523)
defined benefit plan (519)
defined contribution plan (519)
employee's earnings record (515)
FICA tax (510)
fringe benefits (518)
gross pay (508)
net pay (508)
payroll (507)
payroll register (512)
pension (518)
quick assets (524)
quick ratio (524)

Illustrative Problem

Selected transactions of Taylor Company, completed during the fiscal year ended December 31, are as follows:

Mar. 1. Purchased merchandise on account from Kelvin Co., $20,000.

Apr. 10. Issued a 60-day, 12% note for $20,000 to Kelvin Co. on account.

June 9. Paid Kelvin Co. the amount owed on the note of April 10.

Aug. 1. Issued a $50,000, 90-day note to Harold Co. in exchange for a building. Harold Co. discounted the note at 15%.

Oct. 30. Paid Harold Co. the amount due on the note of August 1.

Dec. 27. Journalized the entry to record the biweekly payroll. A summary of the payroll record follows:

Salary distribution:		
Sales	$63,400	
Officers	36,600	
Office	10,000	$110,000
Deductions:		
Social security tax	$ 6,600	
Medicare tax	1,650	
Federal income tax withheld	17,600	
State income tax withheld	4,950	
Savings bond deductions	850	
Medical insurance deductions	1,120	32,770
Net amount		$ 77,230

27. Journalized the entry to record payroll taxes for social security and Medicare from the biweekly payroll.

30. Issued a check in payment of liabilities for employees' federal income tax of $17,600, social security tax of $13,200, and Medicare tax of $3,300.

31. Issued a check for $9,500 to the pension fund trustee to fully fund the pension cost for December.

31. Journalized an entry to record the employees' accrued vacation pay, $36,100.

31. Journalized an entry to record the estimated accrued product warranty liability, $37,240.

Instructions

Journalize the preceding transactions.

Solution

Mar.	1	Merchandise Inventory	20,000	
		Accounts Payable—Kelvin Co.		20,000
Apr.	10	Accounts Payable—Kelvin Co.	20,000	
		Notes Payable		20,000
June	9	Notes Payable	20,000	
		Interest Expense	400	
		Cash		20,400
Aug.	1	Building	48,125	
		Interest Expense	1,875	
		Notes Payable		50,000
Oct.	30	Notes Payable	50,000	
		Cash		50,000
Dec.	27	Sales Salaries Expense	63,400	
		Officers Salaries Expense	36,600	
		Office Salaries Expense	10,000	
		Social Security Tax Payable		6,600
		Medicare Tax Payable		1,650
		Employees Federal Income Tax Payable		17,600
		Employees State Income Tax Payable		4,950
		Bond Deductions Payable		850
		Medical Insurance Payable		1,120
		Salaries Payable		77,230
	27	Payroll Tax Expense	8,250	
		Social Security Tax Payable		6,600
		Medicare Tax Payable		1,650
	30	Employees Federal Income Tax Payable	17,600	
		Social Security Tax Payable	13,200	
		Medicare Tax Payable	3,300	
		Cash		34,100
	31	Pension Expense	9,500	
		Cash		9,500
		Fund pension cost.		
	31	Vacation Pay Expense	36,100	
		Vacation Pay Payable		36,100
		Accrue vacation pay.		
	31	Product Warranty Expense	37,240	
		Product Warranty Payable		37,240
		Accrue warranty expense.		

Discussion Questions

1. Does a discounted note payable provide credit without interest? Discuss.
2. Employees are subject to taxes withheld from their paychecks.
   a. List the federal taxes withheld from most employee paychecks.
   b. Give the title of the accounts credited by amounts withheld.
3. Why are deductions from employees' earnings classified as liabilities for the employer?
4. For each of the following payroll-related taxes, indicate whether they generally apply to (a) employees only, (b) employers only, or (c) both employees and employers:
   1. Federal income tax
   2. Medicare tax
   3. Social security tax
   4. Federal unemployment compensation tax
   5. State unemployment compensation tax
5. What are the principal reasons for using a special payroll bank account?
6. In a payroll system, what types of input data are referred to as (a) constants and (b) variables?
7. To match revenues and expenses properly, should the expense for employee vacation pay be recorded in the period during which the vacation privilege is earned or during the period in which the vacation is taken? Discuss.
8. Explain how a defined contribution pension plan works.
9. When should the liability associated with a product warranty be recorded? Discuss.
10. **General Motors Corporation** reported $2.6 billion of product warranties in the Current Liabilities section of a recent balance sheet. How would costs of repairing a defective product be recorded?

Practice Exercises

SHOW ME HOW

EE 11-1 *p. 507*

PE 11-1A Proceeds from notes payable

OBJ. 1

On October 12, Belleville Co. borrowed cash from Texas Bank by issuing a 30-day note with a face amount of $70,000.

a. Determine the proceeds of the note, assuming the note carries an interest rate of 6%.

b. Determine the proceeds of the note, assuming the note is discounted at 6%.

SHOW ME HOW

EE 11-1 *p. 507*

PE 11-1B Proceeds from notes payable

OBJ. 1

On January 26, Nyree Co. borrowed cash from Conrad Bank by issuing a 45-day note with a face amount of $150,000.

a. Determine the proceeds of the note, assuming the note carries an interest rate of 10%.

b. Determine the proceeds of the note, assuming the note is discounted at 10%.

SHOW ME HOW

EE 11-2 *p. 509*

PE 11-2A Federal income tax withholding

OBJ. 2

Lily Flower's weekly gross earnings for the present week were $2,500. Flower has two exemptions. Using the wage bracket withholding table in Exhibit 3 with a $75 standard withholding allowance for each exemption, what is Flower's federal income tax withholding?

EE 11-2 p. 509

PE 11-2B Federal income tax withholding **OBJ. 2**

Marsha Mellow's weekly gross earnings for the present week were $1,250. Mellow has one exemption. Using the wage bracket withholding table in Exhibit 3 with a $75 standard withholding allowance for each exemption, what is Mellow's federal income tax withholding?

EE 11-3 p. 510

PE 11-3A Employee net pay **OBJ. 2**

Lily Flower's weekly gross earnings for the week ended October 20 were $2,500, and her federal income tax withholding was $517.24. Assuming the social security rate is 6% and Medicare is 1.5% of all earnings, what is Flower's net pay?

EE 11-3 p. 510

PE 11-3B Employee net pay **OBJ. 2**

Marsha Mellow's weekly gross earnings for the week ended May 23 were $1,250, and her federal income tax withholding was $204.95. Assuming the social security rate is 6% and Medicare is 1.5% of all earnings, what is Mellow's net pay?

EE 11-4 p. 513

PE 11-4A Journalize period payroll **OBJ. 3**

The payroll register of Konrath Co. indicates $13,200 of social security withheld and $3,300 of Medicare tax withheld on total salaries of $220,000 for the period. Federal withholding for the period totaled $43,560.

Provide the journal entry for the period's payroll.

SHOW
ME HOW

EE 11-4 p. 513

PE 11-4B Journalize period payroll **OBJ. 3**

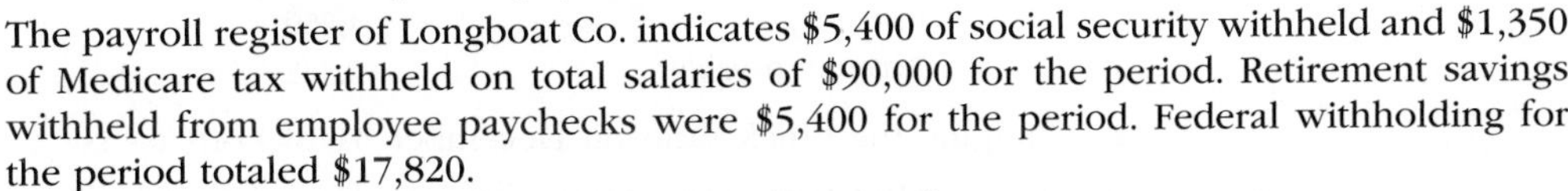

The payroll register of Longboat Co. indicates $5,400 of social security withheld and $1,350 of Medicare tax withheld on total salaries of $90,000 for the period. Retirement savings withheld from employee paychecks were $5,400 for the period. Federal withholding for the period totaled $17,820.

Provide the journal entry for the period's payroll.

EE 11-5 p. 514

PE 11-5A Journalize payroll tax **OBJ. 3**

The payroll register of Konrath Co. indicates $13,200 of social security withheld and $3,300 of Medicare tax withheld on total salaries of $220,000 for the period. Earnings of $35,000 are subject to state and federal unemployment compensation taxes at the federal rate of 0.8% and the state rate of 5.4%.

Provide the journal entry to record the payroll tax expense for the period.

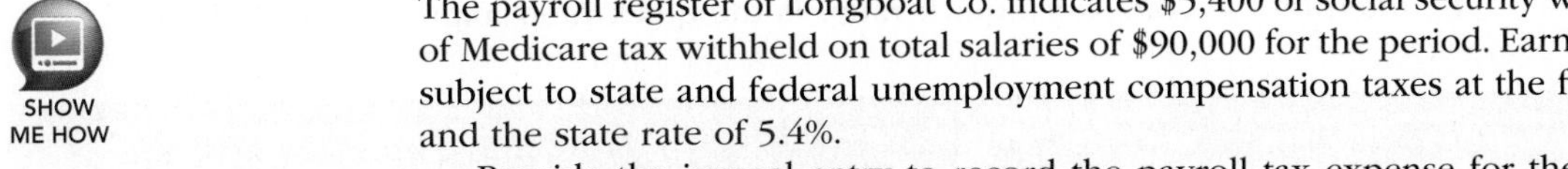

SHOW
ME HOW

EE 11-5 p. 514

PE 11-5B Journalize payroll tax **OBJ. 3**

The payroll register of Longboat Co. indicates $5,400 of social security withheld and $1,350 of Medicare tax withheld on total salaries of $90,000 for the period. Earnings of $10,000 are subject to state and federal unemployment compensation taxes at the federal rate of 0.8% and the state rate of 5.4%.

Provide the journal entry to record the payroll tax expense for the period.

EE 11-6 p. 520

PE 11-6A Vacation pay and pension benefits **OBJ. 4**

Fukushima Company provides its employees with vacation benefits and a defined contribution pension plan. Employees earned vacation pay of $19,500 for the period. The pension plan requires a contribution to the plan administrator equal to 6% of employee salaries. Salaries were $260,000 during the period, and the full amount due was contributed to the pension plan administrator.

Provide the journal entry for the (a) vacation pay and (b) pension benefit.

EE 11-6 p. 520

PE 11-6B Vacation pay and pension benefits

OBJ. 4

SHOW ME HOW

Regling Company provides its employees vacation benefits and a defined benefit pension plan. Employees earned vacation pay of $35,000 for the period. The pension formula calculated a pension cost of $201,250. Only $175,000 was contributed to the pension plan administrator.

Provide the journal entry for the (a) vacation pay and (b) pension benefit.

EE 11-7 p. 522

PE 11-7A Estimated warranty liability

OBJ. 5

SHOW ME HOW

Chloe Co. sold $300,000 of equipment during January under a one-year warranty. The cost to repair defects under the warranty is estimated at 5% of the sales price. On June 20, a customer required a $90 part replacement, plus $42 of labor under the warranty.

Provide the journal entry for (a) the estimated warranty expense on January 31 for January sales, and (b) the June 20 warranty work.

EE 11-7 p. 522

PE 11-7B Estimated warranty liability

OBJ. 5

SHOW ME HOW

Quantas Industries sold $325,000 of consumer electronics during July under a nine-month warranty. The cost to repair defects under the warranty is estimated at 4.5% of the sales price. On November 11, a customer was given $220 cash under terms of the warranty.

Provide the journal entry for (a) the estimated warranty expense on July 31 for July sales, and (b) the November 11 cash payment.

EE 11-8 p. 525

PE 11-8A Quick ratio

OBJ. 6

F·A·I

SHOW ME HOW

Nabors Company reported the following current assets and liabilities for December 31 for two recent years:

	Dec. 31, Current Year	Dec. 31, Previous Year
Cash	$ 650	$ 680
Temporary investments	1,500	1,550
Accounts receivable	700	770
Inventory	1,250	1,400
Accounts payable	2,375	2,000

a. Compute the quick ratio on December 31 of both years.

b. Interpret the company's quick ratio. Is the quick ratio improving or declining?

EE 11-8 p. 525

PE 11-8B Quick ratio

OBJ. 6

F·A·I

SHOW ME HOW

Adieu Company reported the following current assets and liabilities for December 31 for two recent years:

	Dec. 31, Current Year	Dec. 31, Previous Year
Cash	$1,000	$1,140
Temporary investments	1,200	1,400
Accounts receivable	800	910
Inventory	2,200	2,300
Accounts payable	1,875	2,300

a. Compute the quick ratio on December 31 of both years.

b. Interpret the company's quick ratio. Is the quick ratio improving or declining?

Exercises

EX 11-1 Current liabilities

OBJ. 1

✔ Total current liabilities, $1,929,750

SHOW ME HOW

Bon Nebo Co. sold 25,000 annual subscriptions of *Bjorn 20XX* for $85 during December 2016. These new subscribers will receive monthly issues, beginning in January 2017. In addition, the business had taxable income of $840,000 during the first calendar quarter of 2017. The federal tax rate is 40%. A quarterly tax payment will be made on April 12, 2017.

Prepare the Current Liabilities section of the balance sheet for Bon Nebo Co. on March 31, 2017.

EX 11-2 Entries for discounting notes payable — OBJ. 1

SHOW ME HOW

Griffin Enterprises issues a $660,000, 45-day, 4% note to Romo Industries for merchandise inventory.

a. Journalize Griffin Enterprises' entries to record:
   1. the issuance of the note.
   2. the payment of the note at maturity.

b. Journalize Romo Industries' entries to record:
   1. the receipt of the note.
   2. the receipt of the payment of the note at maturity.

EX 11-3 Evaluating alternative notes — OBJ. 1

SHOW ME HOW

A borrower has two alternatives for a loan: (1) issue a $360,000, 60-day, 5% note or (2) issue a $360,000, 60-day note that the creditor discounts at 5%.

a. Calculate the amount of the interest expense for each option.

b. Determine the proceeds received by the borrower in each situation.

c. Which alternative is more favorable to the borrower? Explain.

EX 11-4 Entries for notes payable — OBJ. 1

SHOW ME HOW

A business issued a 45-day, 6% note for $210,000 to a creditor on account. Journalize the entries to record (a) the issuance of the note and (b) the payment of the note at maturity, including interest.

EX 11-5 Entries for discounted note payable — OBJ. 1

SHOW ME HOW

A business issued a 60-day note for $75,000 to a creditor on account. The note was discounted at 7%. Journalize the entries to record (a) the issuance of the note and (b) the payment of the note at maturity.

EX 11-6 Fixed asset purchases with note — OBJ. 1

SHOW ME HOW

On June 30, Collins Management Company purchased land for $400,000 and a building for $560,000, paying $360,000 cash and issuing a 5% note for the balance, secured by a mortgage on the property. The terms of the note provide for 20 semiannual payments of $30,000 on the principal plus the interest accrued from the date of the preceding payment. Journalize the entry to record (a) the transaction on June 30, (b) the payment of the first installment on December 31, and (c) the payment of the second installment the following June 30.

EX 11-7 Current portion of long-term debt — OBJ. 1

PepsiCo, Inc., reported the following information about its long-term debt in the notes to a recent financial statement (in millions):

Long-term debt is comprised of the following:

	December 31	
	Current Year	Previous Year
Total long term-debt	$28,359	$26,773
Less current portion	(4,815)	(6,205)
Long-term debt	$23,544	$20,568

a. How much of the long-term debt was disclosed as a current liability on the current year's December 31 balance sheet?

b. How much did the total current liabilities change between the preceding year and the current year as a result of the current portion of long-term debt?

c. If PepsiCo did not issue additional long-term debt next year, what would be the total long-term debt on December 31 of the upcoming year?

✔ b. Net pay, $1,452

SHOW ME HOW

EX 11-8 Calculate payroll **OBJ. 2**

An employee earns $32 per hour and 1.5 times that rate for all hours in excess of 40 hours per week. Assume that the employee worked 55 hours during the week. Assume further that the social security tax rate was 6.0%, the Medicare tax rate was 1.5%, and federal income tax to be withheld was $398.

a. Determine the gross pay for the week.

b. Determine the net pay for the week.

✔ Administrator net pay, $1,753.98

SHOW ME HOW

EX 11-9 Calculate payroll **OBJ. 2**

Diego Company has three employees—a consultant, a computer programmer, and an administrator. The following payroll information is available for each employee:

	Consultant	Computer Programmer	Administrator
Regular earnings rate	$3,800 per week	$38 per hour	$42 per hour
Overtime earnings rate*	Not applicable	2 times hourly rate	1.5 times hourly rate
Number of withholding allowances	1	2	2

* For hourly employees, overtime is paid for hours worked in excess of 40 hours per week.

For the current pay period, the computer programmer worked 55 hours and the administrator worked 52 hours. The federal income tax withheld for all three employees, who are single, can be determined from the wage bracket withholding table in Exhibit 3 in the chapter. Assume further that the social security tax rate was 6.0%, the Medicare tax rate was 1.5%, and one withholding allowance is $75.

Determine the gross pay and the net pay for each of the three employees for the current pay period.

✔ a. (3) Total earnings, $540,000

EX 11-10 Summary payroll data **OBJ. 2, 3**

In the following summary of data for a payroll period, some amounts have been intentionally omitted:

Earnings:	
1. At regular rate	?
2. At overtime rate	$80,000
3. Total earnings	?
Deductions:	
4. Social security tax	32,400
5. Medicare tax	8,100
6. Income tax withheld	135,000
7. Medical insurance	18,900
8. Union dues	?
9. Total deductions	201,150
10. Net amount paid	338,850
Accounts debited:	
11. Factory Wages	285,000
12. Sales Salaries	?
13. Office Salaries	120,000

a. Calculate the amounts omitted in lines (1), (3), (8), and (12).

b. Journalize the entry to record the payroll accrual.

c. Journalize the entry to record the payment of the payroll.

✔ a. $59,350

SHOW ME HOW

EX 11-11 Payroll tax entries **OBJ. 3**

According to a summary of the payroll of Murtagh Co., $750,000 was subject to the 6.0% social security tax and the 1.5% Medicare tax. Also, $50,000 was subject to state and federal unemployment taxes.

a. Calculate the employer's payroll taxes, using the following rates: state unemployment, 5.4%; federal unemployment, 0.8%.

b. Journalize the entry to record the accrual of payroll taxes.

EX 11-12 Payroll entries

OBJ. 3

SHOW ME HOW

The payroll register for Proctor Company for the week ended February 14 indicated the following:

Salaries	$1,500,000
Social security tax withheld	90,000
Medicare tax withheld	22,500
Federal income tax withheld	300,000

In addition, state and federal unemployment taxes were calculated at the rate of 5.4% and 0.8%, respectively, on $270,000 of salaries.

a. Journalize the entry to record the payroll for the week of February 14.

b. Journalize the entry to record the payroll tax expense incurred for the week of February 14.

EX 11-13 Payroll entries

OBJ. 3

SHOW ME HOW

Widmer Company had gross wages of $240,000 during the week ended June 17. The amount of wages subject to social security tax was $240,000, while the amount of wages subject to federal and state unemployment taxes was $35,000. Tax rates are as follows:

Social security	6.0%
Medicare	1.5%
State unemployment	5.4%
Federal unemployment	0.8%

The total amount withheld from employee wages for federal taxes was $48,000.

a. Journalize the entry to record the payroll for the week of June 17.

b. Journalize the entry to record the payroll tax expense incurred for the week of June 17.

EX 11-14 Payroll internal control procedures

OBJ. 3

Big Howie's Hot Dog Stand is a fast-food restaurant specializing in hot dogs and hamburgers. The store employs 8 full-time and 12 part-time workers. The store's weekly payroll averages $5,600 for all 20 workers.

Big Howie's Hot Dog Stand uses a personal computer to assist in preparing paychecks. Each week, the store's accountant collects employee time cards and enters the hours worked into the payroll program. The payroll program calculates each employee's pay and prints a paycheck. The accountant uses a check-signing machine to sign the paychecks. Next, the restaurant's owner authorizes the transfer of funds from the restaurant's regular bank account to the payroll account.

For the week of May 12, the accountant accidentally recorded 100 hours worked instead of 40 hours for one of the full-time employees.

Does Big Howie's Hot Dog Stand have internal controls in place to catch this error? If so, how will this error be detected?

EX 11-15 Internal control procedures

OBJ. 3

Dave's Scooters is a small manufacturer of specialty scooters. The company employs 14 production workers and four administrative persons. The following procedures are used to process the company's weekly payroll:

a. Whenever an employee receives a pay raise, the supervisor must fill out a wage adjustment form, which is signed by the company president. This form is used to change the employee's wage rate in the payroll system.

b. All employees are required to record their hours worked by clocking in and out on a time clock. Employees must clock out for lunch break. Due to congestion around the time clock area at lunch time, management has not objected to having one employee clock in and out for an entire department.

(Continued)

c. Whenever a salaried employee is terminated, Personnel authorizes Payroll to remove the employee from the payroll system. However, this procedure is not required when an hourly worker is fired. Hourly employees only receive a paycheck if their time cards show hours worked. The computer automatically drops an employee from the payroll system when that employee has six consecutive weeks with no hours worked.

d. Paychecks are signed by using a check-signing machine. This machine is located in the main office so that it can be easily accessed by anyone needing a check signed.

e. Dave's Scooters maintains a separate checking account for payroll checks. Each week, the total net pay for all employees is transferred from the company's regular bank account to the payroll account.

State whether each of the procedures is appropriate or inappropriate, after considering the principles of internal control. If a procedure is inappropriate, describe the appropriate procedure.

EX 11-16 Accrued vacation pay **OBJ. 4**

A business provides its employees with varying amounts of vacation per year, depending on the length of employment. The estimated amount of the current year's vacation pay is $42,000.

a. Journalize the adjusting entry required on January 31, the end of the first month of the current year, to record the accrued vacation pay.

b. How is the vacation pay reported on the company's balance sheet? When is this amount removed from the company's balance sheet?

EX 11-17 Pension plan entries **OBJ. 4**

Yuri Co. operates a chain of gift shops. The company maintains a defined contribution pension plan for its employees. The plan requires quarterly installments to be paid to the funding agent, Whims Funds, by the fifteenth of the month following the end of each quarter. Assume that the pension cost is $365,000 for the quarter ended December 31.

a. Journalize the entries to record the accrued pension liability on December 31 and the payment to the funding agent on January 15.

b. How does a defined contribution plan differ from a defined benefit plan?

EX 11-18 Defined benefit pension plan terms **OBJ. 4**

In a recent year's financial statements, **Procter & Gamble** showed an unfunded pension liability of $5,599 million and a periodic pension cost of $434 million.

Explain the meaning of the $5,599 million unfunded pension liability and the $434 million periodic pension cost.

EX 11-19 Accrued product warranty **OBJ. 5**

Lowe Manufacturing Co. warrants its products for one year. The estimated product warranty is 4% of sales. Assume that sales were $560,000 for January. In February, a customer received warranty repairs requiring $140 of parts and $95 of labor.

a. Journalize the adjusting entry required at January 31, the end of the first month of the current fiscal year, to record the accrued product warranty.

b. Journalize the entry to record the warranty work provided in February.

EX 11-20 Accrued product warranty **OBJ. 5**

General Motors Corporation (GM) disclosed estimated product warranty payable for comparative years as follows:

	(in millions)	
	Year 2	**Year 1**
Current estimated product warranty payable	$3,059	$2,884
Noncurrent estimated product warranty payable	4,327	4,147
Total	$7,386	$7,031

Presume that GM's sales were $135,592 million in Year 2 and that the total paid on warranty claims during Year 2 was $3,000 million.

a. Why are short- and long-term estimated warranty liabilities separately disclosed?

b. Provide the journal entry for the Year 2 product warranty expense.

c. What two conditions must be met in order for a product warranty liability to be reported in the financial statements?

EX 11-21 Contingent liabilities **OBJ. 5**

Several months ago, Ayers Industries Inc. experienced a hazardous materials spill at one of its plants. As a result, the Environmental Protection Agency (EPA) fined the company $240,000. The company is contesting the fine. In addition, an employee is seeking $220,000 in damages related to the spill. Lastly, a homeowner has sued the company for $310,000. The homeowner lives 35 miles from the plant but believes that the incident has reduced the home's resale value by $310,000.

Ayers' legal counsel believes that it is probable that the EPA fine will stand. In addition, counsel indicates that an out-of-court settlement of $125,000 has recently been reached with the employee. The final papers will be signed next week. Counsel believes that the homeowner's case is much weaker and will be decided in favor of Ayers. Other litigation related to the spill is possible, but the damage amounts are uncertain.

a. Journalize the contingent liabilities associated with the hazardous materials spill. Use the account "Damage Awards and Fines" to recognize the expense for the period.

b. Prepare a note disclosure relating to this incident.

EX 11-22 Quick ratio **OBJ. 6**

✔ a. Current year: 1.2

F·A·I

Gmeiner Co. had the following current assets and liabilities on December 31 of two recent years:

	Current Year	Previous Year
Current assets:		
Cash	$ 486,000	$ 500,000
Accounts receivable	210,000	200,000
Inventory	375,000	350,000
Total current assets	$1,071,000	$1,050,000
Current liabilities:		
Current portion of long-term debt	$ 145,000	$ 110,000
Accounts payable	175,000	150,000
Accrued and other current liabilities	260,000	240,000
Total current liabilities	$ 580,000	$ 500,000

a. Determine the quick ratio for December 31 of both years.

b. Interpret the change in the quick ratio between the two balance sheet dates.

EX 11-23 Quick ratio **OBJ. 6**

✔ a. Apple, 1.3

The current assets and current liabilities for **Apple Inc.** and **Dell, Inc.**, are as follows at the end of a recent fiscal period:

	Apple Inc. (in millions)	Dell, Inc. (in millions)
Current assets:		
Cash and cash equivalents	$10,746	$12,569
Short-term investments	18,383	208
Accounts receivable	21,275	9,842
Inventories	791	1,382
Other current assets*	6,458	3,967
Total current assets	$57,653	$27,968
Current liabilities:		
Accounts payable	$32,589	$15,223
Accrued and other current liabilities	5,953	8,216
Total current liabilities	$38,542	$23,439

*These represent prepaid expense and other nonquick current assets.

(*Continued*)

a. Determine the quick ratio for both companies. (Round to one decimal place.)
b. Interpret the quick ratio difference between the two companies.

Problems: Series A

PR 11-1A Liability transactions **OBJ. 1, 5**

General Ledger

SHOW ME HOW

The following items were selected from among the transactions completed by Pioneer Co. during the current year:

Mar. 1. Purchased merchandise on account from Galston Co., $360,000, terms n/30.
31. Issued a 30-day, 5% note for $360,000 to Galston Co., on account.
Apr. 30. Paid Galston Co. the amount owed on the note of March 31.
June 1. Borrowed $180,000 from Pilati Bank, issuing a 45-day, 4% note.
July 1. Purchased tools by issuing a $210,000, 60-day note to Zegna Co., which discounted the note at the rate of 7%.
16. Paid Pilati Bank the interest due on the note of June 1 and renewed the loan by issuing a new 30-day, 6.5% note for $180,000. (Journalize both the debit and credit to the notes payable account.)
Aug. 15. Paid Pilati Bank the amount due on the note of July 16.
30. Paid Zegna Co. the amount due on the note of July 1.
Dec. 1. Purchased office equipment from Taylor Co. for $500,000, paying $120,000 and issuing a series of ten 6% notes for $38,000 each, coming due at 30-day intervals.
22. Settled a product liability lawsuit with a customer for $310,000, payable in January. Pioneer accrued the loss in a litigation claims payable account.
31. Paid the amount due Taylor Co. on the first note in the series issued on December 1.

Instructions

1. Journalize the transactions.
2. Journalize the adjusting entry for each of the following accrued expenses at the end of the current year:
   a. Product warranty cost, $27,500.
   b. Interest on the nine remaining notes owed to Taylor Co.

PR 11-2A Entries for payroll and payroll taxes **OBJ. 2, 3**

✔ 1. (b) Dr. Payroll Tax Expense, $52,795

General Ledger

The following information about the payroll for the week ended December 30 was obtained from the records of Qualitech Co.:

Salaries:		Deductions:	
Sales salaries	$350,000	Income tax withheld	$118,800
Warehouse salaries	180,000	Social security tax withheld	40,500
Office salaries	145,000	Medicare tax withheld	10,125
	$675,000	U.S. savings bonds	14,850
		Group insurance	12,150
			$196,425

Tax rates assumed:

Social security, 6%
Medicare, 1.5%
State unemployment (employer only), 5.4%
Federal unemployment (employer only), 0.8%

Instructions

1. Assuming that the payroll for the last week of the year is to be paid on December 31, journalize the following entries:
   a. December 30, to record the payroll.
   b. December 30, to record the employer's payroll taxes on the payroll to be paid on December 31. Of the total payroll for the last week of the year, $35,000 is subject to unemployment compensation taxes.
2. Assuming that the payroll for the last week of the year is to be paid on January 5 of the following fiscal year, journalize the following entries:
   a. December 30, to record the payroll.
   b. January 5, to record the employer's payroll taxes on the payroll to be paid on January 5. Because it is a new fiscal year, all $675,000 in salaries is subject to unemployment compensation taxes.

PR 11-3A Wage and tax statement data on employer FICA tax

OBJ. 2, 3

✓ 2. (e) $28,574.96

Ehrlich Co. began business on January 2, 2015. Salaries were paid to employees on the last day of each month, and social security tax, Medicare tax, and federal income tax were withheld in the required amounts. An employee who is hired in the middle of the month receives half the monthly salary for that month. All required payroll tax reports were filed, and the correct amount of payroll taxes was remitted by the company for the calendar year. Early in 2016, before the Wage and Tax Statements (Form W-2) could be prepared for distribution to employees and for filing with the Social Security Administration, the employees' earnings records were inadvertently destroyed.

None of the employees resigned or were discharged during the year, and there were no changes in salary rates. The social security tax was withheld at the rate of 6.0% and Medicare tax at the rate of 1.5%. Data on dates of employment, salary rates, and employees' income taxes withheld, which are summarized as follows, were obtained from personnel records and payroll records:

Employee	Date First Employed	Monthly Salary	Monthly Income Tax Withheld
Arnett	Nov. 16	$ 5,500	$ 944
Cruz	Jan. 2	4,800	833
Edwards	Oct. 1	8,000	1,592
Harvin	Dec. 1	6,000	1,070
Nicks	Feb. 1	10,000	2,350
Shiancoe	Mar. 1	11,600	2,600
Ward	Nov. 16	5,220	876

Instructions

1. Calculate the amounts to be reported on each employee's Wage and Tax Statement (Form W-2) for 2015, arranging the data in the following form:

Employee	Gross Earnings	Federal Income Tax Withheld	Social Security Tax Withheld	Medicare Tax Withheld

2. Calculate the following employer payroll taxes for the year: (a) social security; (b) Medicare; (c) state unemployment compensation at 5.4% on the first $10,000 of each employee's earnings; (d) federal unemployment compensation at 0.8% on the first $10,000 of each employee's earnings; (e) total.

✔ 1. Total net pay $15,424.12

PR 11-4A Payroll register

OBJ. 2, 3

The following data for Throwback Industries Inc. relate to the payroll for the week ended December 9, 2016:

Employee	Hours Worked	Hourly Rate	Weekly Salary	Federal Income Tax	U.S. Savings Bonds
Aaron	46	$68.00		$750.20	$100
Cobb	41	62.00		537.68	110
Clemente	48	70.00		832.64	120
DiMaggio	35	56.00		366.04	0
Griffey, Jr.	45	62.00		641.84	130
Mantle			$1,800	342.45	120
Robinson	36	54.00		382.56	130
Williams			2,000	398.24	125
Vaughn	42	62.00		584.72	50

Employees Mantle and Williams are office staff, and all of the other employees are sales personnel. All sales personnel are paid 1½ times the regular rate for all hours in excess of 40 hours per week. The social security tax rate is 6.0%, and Medicare tax is 1.5% of each employee's annual earnings. The next payroll check to be used is No. 901.

Instructions

1. Prepare a payroll register for Throwback Industries Inc. for the week ended December 9, 2016. Use the following columns for the payroll register: Employee, Total Hours, Regular Earnings, Overtime Earnings, Total Earnings, Social Security Tax, Medicare Tax, Federal Income Tax, U.S. Savings Bonds, Total Deductions, Net Pay, Ck. No., Sales Salaries Expense, and Office Salaries Expense.
2. Journalize the entry to record the payroll for the week.

General Ledger

PR 11-5A Payroll accounts and year-end entries

OBJ. 2, 3, 4

The following accounts, with the balances indicated, appear in the ledger of Garcon Co. on December 1 of the current year:

Account	Balance	Account	Balance
211 Salaries Payable	—	218 Bond Deductions Payable	$ 3,400
212 Social Security Tax Payable	$ 9,273	219 Medical Insurance Payable	27,000
213 Medicare Tax Payable	2,318	411 Operations Salaries Expense	950,000
214 Employees Federal Income Tax Payable	15,455	511 Officers Salaries Expense	600,000
215 Employees State Income Tax Payable	13,909	512 Office Salaries Expense	150,000
216 State Unemployment Tax Payable	1,400	519 Payroll Tax Expense	137,951
217 Federal Unemployment Tax Payable	500		

The following transactions relating to payroll, payroll deductions, and payroll taxes occurred during December:

Dec. 2. Issued Check No. 410 for $3,400 to Jay Bank to purchase U.S. savings bonds for employees.

2. Issued Check No. 411 to Jay Bank for $27,046 in payment of $9,273 of social security tax, $2,318 of Medicare tax, and $15,455 of employees' federal income tax due.

13. Journalized the entry to record the biweekly payroll. A summary of the payroll record follows:

Salary distribution:		
Operations	$43,200	
Officers	27,200	
Office	6,800	$77,200
Deductions:		
Social security tax	$ 4,632	
Medicare tax	1,158	
Federal income tax withheld	15,440	
State income tax withheld	3,474	
Savings bond deductions	1,700	
Medical insurance deductions	4,500	30,904
Net amount		$46,296

Dec. 13. Issued Check No. 420 in payment of the net amount of the biweekly payroll.

13. Journalized the entry to record payroll taxes on employees' earnings of December 13: social security tax, $4,632; Medicare tax, $1,158; state unemployment tax, $350; federal unemployment tax, $125.

16. Issued Check No. 424 to Jay Bank for $27,020, in payment of $9,264 of social security tax, $2,316 of Medicare tax, and $15,440 of employees' federal income tax due.

19. Issued Check No. 429 to Sims-Walker Insurance Company for $31,500 in payment of the semiannual premium on the group medical insurance policy.

27. Journalized the entry to record the biweekly payroll. A summary of the payroll record follows:

Salary distribution:		
Operations	$42,800	
Officers	28,000	
Office	7,000	$77,800
Deductions:		
Social security tax	$ 4,668	
Medicare tax	1,167	
Federal income tax withheld	15,404	
State income tax withheld	3,501	
Savings bond deductions	1,700	26,440
Net amount		$51,360

27. Issued Check No. 541 in payment of the net amount of the biweekly payroll.

27. Journalized the entry to record payroll taxes on employees' earnings of December 27: social security tax, $4,668; Medicare tax, $1,167; state unemployment tax, $225; federal unemployment tax, $75.

27. Issued Check No. 543 for $20,884 to State Department of Revenue in payment of employees' state income tax due on December 31.

31. Issued Check No. 545 to Jay Bank for $3,400 to purchase U.S. savings bonds for employees.

31. Paid $45,000 to the employee pension plan. The annual pension cost is $60,000. (Record both the payment and unfunded pension liability.)

Instructions

1. Journalize the transactions.
2. Journalize the following adjusting entries on December 31:
   a. Salaries accrued: operations salaries, $8,560; officers salaries, $5,600; office salaries, $1,400. The payroll taxes are immaterial and are not accrued.
   b. Vacation pay, $15,000.

Problems: Series B

PR 11-1B Liability transactions **OBJ. 1, 5**

The following items were selected from among the transactions completed by Aston Martin Inc. during the current year:

Apr. 15. Borrowed $225,000 from Audi Company, issuing a 30-day, 6% note for that amount.

May 1. Purchased equipment by issuing a $320,000, 180-day note to Spyder Manufacturing Co., which discounted the note at the rate of 6%.

15. Paid Audi Company the interest due on the note of April 15 and renewed the loan by issuing a new 60-day, 8% note for $225,000. (Record both the debit and credit to the notes payable account.)

July 14. Paid Audi Company the amount due on the note of May 15.

(Continued)

Aug. 16. Purchased merchandise on account from Exige Co., $90,000, terms, n/30.

Sept. 15. Issued a 45-day, 6% note for $90,000 to Exige Co., on account.

Oct. 28. Paid Spyder Manufacturing Co. the amount due on the note of May 1.

30. Paid Exige Co. the amount owed on the note of September 15.

Nov. 16. Purchased store equipment from Gallardo Co. for $450,000, paying $50,000 and issuing a series of twenty 9% notes for $20,000 each, coming due at 30-day intervals.

Dec. 16. Paid the amount due Gallardo Co. on the first note in the series issued on November 16.

28. Settled a personal injury lawsuit with a customer for $87,500, to be paid in January. Aston Martin Inc. accrued the loss in a litigation claims payable account.

Instructions

1. Journalize the transactions.
2. Journalize the adjusting entry for each of the following accrued expenses at the end of the current year:
   a. Product warranty cost, $26,800.
   b. Interest on the 19 remaining notes owed to Gallardo Co.

PR 11-2B Entries for payroll and payroll taxes — OBJ. 2, 3

✔ 1. (b) Dr. Payroll Tax Expense, $90,735

General Ledger

The following information about the payroll for the week ended December 30 was obtained from the records of Saine Co.:

Salaries:		Deductions:	
Sales salaries	$ 625,000	Income tax withheld	$232,260
Warehouse salaries	240,000	Social security tax withheld	71,100
Office salaries	320,000	Medicare tax withheld	17,775
	$1,185,000	U.S. savings bonds	35,500
		Group insurance	53,325
			$409,960

Tax rates assumed:
- Social security, 6%
- Medicare, 1.5%
- State unemployment (employer only), 5.4%
- Federal unemployment (employer only), 0.8%

Instructions

1. Assuming that the payroll for the last week of the year is to be paid on December 31, journalize the following entries:
   a. December 30, to record the payroll.
   b. December 30, to record the employer's payroll taxes on the payroll to be paid on December 31. Of the total payroll for the last week of the year, $30,000 is subject to unemployment compensation taxes.
2. Assuming that the payroll for the last week of the year is to be paid on January 4 of the following fiscal year, journalize the following entries:
   a. December 30, to record the payroll.
   b. January 4, to record the employer's payroll taxes on the payroll to be paid on January 4. Because it is a new fiscal year, all $1,185,000 in salaries is subject to unemployment compensation taxes.

PR 11-3B Wage and tax statement data and employer FICA tax — OBJ. 2, 3

✔ 2. (e) $25,136.13

Jocame Inc. began business on January 2, 2015. Salaries were paid to employees on the last day of each month, and social security tax, Medicare tax, and federal income tax were withheld in the required amounts. An employee who is hired in the middle of the month receives half the monthly salary for that month. All required payroll tax reports were filed, and the correct amount of payroll taxes was remitted by the company for the calendar year. Early in 2016, before the Wage and Tax Statements (Form W-2) could be prepared for distribution to employees and for filing with the Social Security Administration, the employees' earnings records were inadvertently destroyed.

None of the employees resigned or were discharged during the year, and there were no changes in salary rates. The social security tax was withheld at the rate of 6.0% and Medicare tax at the rate of 1.5% on salary. Data on dates of employment, salary rates, and employees' income taxes withheld, which are summarized as follows, were obtained from personnel records and payroll records:

Employee	Date First Employed	Monthly Salary	Monthly Income Tax Withheld
Addai	July 16	$ 8,160	$1,704
Kasay	June 1	3,600	533
McGahee	Feb. 16	6,420	1,238
Moss	Jan. 1	4,600	783
Stewart	Dec. 1	4,500	758
Tolbert	Nov. 16	3,250	446
Wells	May 1	10,500	2,359

Instructions

1. Calculate the amounts to be reported on each employee's Wage and Tax Statement (Form W-2) for 2015, arranging the data in the following form:

Employee	Gross Earnings	Federal Income Tax Withheld	Social Security Tax Withheld	Medicare Tax Withheld

2. Calculate the following employer payroll taxes for the year: (a) social security; (b) Medicare; (c) state unemployment compensation at 5.4% on the first $10,000 of each employee's earnings; (d) federal unemployment compensation at 0.8% on the first $10,000 of each employee's earnings; (e) total.

PR 11-4B Payroll register

OBJ. 2, 3

✔ 1. Total net pay, $16,592.58

The following data for Flexco Inc. relate to the payroll for the week ended December 9, 2016:

Employee	Hours Worked	Hourly Rate	Weekly Salary	Federal Income Tax	U.S. Savings Bonds
Carlton	52	$50.00		$667.00	$ 60
Grove			$4,000	860.00	100
Johnson	36	52.00		355.68	0
Koufax	45	58.00		578.55	44
Maddux	37	45.00		349.65	62
Seaver			3,200	768.00	120
Spahn	46	52.00		382.20	0
Winn	48	50.00		572.00	75
Young	43	54.00		480.60	80

Employees Grove and Seaver are office staff, and all of the other employees are sales personnel. All sales personnel are paid 1½ times the regular rate for all hours in excess of 40 hours per week. The social security tax rate is 6.0% of each employee's annual earnings, and Medicare tax is 1.5% of each employee's annual earnings. The next payroll check to be used is No. 328.

Instructions

1. Prepare a payroll register for Flexco Inc. for the week ended December 9, 2016. Use the following columns for the payroll register: Employee, Total Hours, Regular Earnings, Overtime Earnings, Total Earnings, Social Security Tax, Medicare Tax, Federal Income Tax, U.S. Savings Bonds, Total Deductions, Net Pay, Ck. No., Sales Salaries Expense, and Office Salaries Expense.
2. Journalize the entry to record the payroll for the week.

PR 11-5B Payroll accounts and year-end entries

OBJ. 2, 3, 4

General Ledger

The following accounts, with the balances indicated, appear in the ledger of Codigo Co. on December 1 of the current year:

101 Salaries Payable	—	108 Bond Deductions Payable	$ 2,300
102 Social Security Tax Payable	$2,913	109 Medical Insurance Payable	2,520
103 Medicare Tax Payable	728	201 Sales Salaries Expense	700,000
104 Employees Federal Income Tax Payable	4,490	301 Officers Salaries Expense	340,000
105 Employees State Income Tax Payable	4,078	401 Office Salaries Expense	125,000
106 State Unemployment Tax Payable	1,260	408 Payroll Tax Expense	59,491
107 Federal Unemployment Tax Payable	360		

The following transactions relating to payroll, payroll deductions, and payroll taxes occurred during December:

Dec. 1. Issued Check No. 815 to Aberderas Insurance Company for $2,520, in payment of the semiannual premium on the group medical insurance policy.

1. Issued Check No. 816 to Alvarez Bank for $8,131, in payment for $2,913 of social security tax, $728 of Medicare tax, and $4,490 of employees' federal income tax due.

2. Issued Check No. 817 for $2,300 to Alvarez Bank to purchase U.S. savings bonds for employees.

12. Journalized the entry to record the biweekly payroll. A summary of the payroll record follows:

Salary distribution:		
Sales	$14,500	
Officers	7,100	
Office	2,600	$24,200
Deductions:		
Social security tax	$ 1,452	
Medicare tax	363	
Federal income tax withheld	4,308	
State income tax withheld	1,089	
Savings bond deductions	1,150	
Medical insurance deductions	420	8,782
Net amount		$15,418

12. Issued Check No. 822 in payment of the net amount of the biweekly payroll.

12. Journalized the entry to record payroll taxes on employees' earnings of December 12: social security tax, $1,452; Medicare tax, $363; state unemployment tax, $315; federal unemployment tax, $90.

15. Issued Check No. 830 to Alvarez Bank for $7,938, in payment of $2,904 of social security tax, $726 of Medicare tax, and $4,308 of employees' federal income tax due.

26. Journalized the entry to record the biweekly payroll. A summary of the payroll record follows:

Salary distribution:		
Sales	$14,250	
Officers	7,250	
Office	2,750	$24,250
Deductions:		
Social security tax	$ 1,455	
Medicare tax	364	
Federal income tax withheld	4,317	
State income tax withheld	1,091	
Savings bond deductions	1,150	8,377
Net amount		$15,873

26. Issued Check No. 840 for the net amount of the biweekly payroll.

Dec. 26. Journalized the entry to record payroll taxes on employees' earnings of December 26: social security tax, $1,455; Medicare tax, $364; state unemployment tax, $150; federal unemployment tax, $40.

30. Issued Check No. 851 for $6,258 to State Department of Revenue, in payment of employees' state income tax due on December 31.

30. Issued Check No. 852 to Alvarez Bank for $2,300 to purchase U.S. savings bonds for employees.

31. Paid $55,400 to the employee pension plan. The annual pension cost is $65,500. (Record both the payment and the unfunded pension liability.)

Instructions

1. Journalize the transactions.
2. Journalize the following adjusting entries on December 31:
   a. Salaries accrued: sales salaries, $4,275; officers salaries, $2,175; office salaries, $825. The payroll taxes are immaterial and are not accrued.
   b. Vacation pay, $13,350.

Comprehensive Problem 3

✔ 5. Total assets, $3,569,300

General Ledger

Selected transactions completed by Kornett Company during its first fiscal year ended December 31, 2016, were as follows:

Jan. 3. Issued a check to establish a petty cash fund of $4,500.

Feb. 26. Replenished the petty cash fund, based on the following summary of petty cash receipts: office supplies, $1,680; miscellaneous selling expense, $570; miscellaneous administrative expense, $880.

Apr. 14. Purchased $31,300 of merchandise on account, terms 1/10, n/30. The perpetual inventory system is used to account for inventory.

May 13. Paid the invoice of April 14 after the discount period had passed.

17. Received cash from daily cash sales for $21,200. The amount indicated by the cash register was $21,240.

June 2. Received a 60-day, 8% note for $180,000 on the Ryanair account.

Aug. 1. Received amount owed on June 2 note, plus interest at the maturity date.

24. Received $7,600 on the Finley account and wrote off the remainder owed on a $9,000 accounts receivable balance. (The allowance method is used in accounting for uncollectible receivables.)

Sept. 15. Reinstated the Finley account written off on August 24 and received $1,400 cash in full payment.

15. Purchased land by issuing a $670,000, 90-day note to Zahorik Co., which discounted it at 9%.

Oct. 17. Sold office equipment in exchange for $135,000 cash plus receipt of a $100,000, 90-day, 9% note. The equipment had a cost of $320,000 and accumulated depreciation of $64,000 as of October 17.

(Continued)

Nov. 30. Journalized the monthly payroll for November, based on the following data:

Salaries		**Deductions**	
Sales salaries	$135,000	Income tax withheld	$39,266
Office salaries	77,250	Social security tax withheld	12,735
	$212,250	Medicare tax withheld	3,184

Unemployment tax rates:	
State unemployment	5.4%
Federal unemployment	0.8%
Amount subject to unemployment taxes:	
State unemployment	$5,000
Federal unemployment	5,000

30. Journalized the employer's payroll taxes on the payroll.

Dec. 14. Journalized the payment of the September 15 note at maturity.

31. The pension cost for the year was $190,400, of which $139,700 was paid to the pension plan trustee.

Instructions

1. Journalize the selected transactions.
2. Based on the following data, prepare a bank reconciliation for December of the current year:
   a. Balance according to the bank statement at December 31, $283,000.
   b. Balance according to the ledger at December 31, $245,410.
   c. Checks outstanding at December 31, $68,540.
   d. Deposit in transit, not recorded by bank, $29,500.
   e. Bank debit memo for service charges, $750.
   f. A check for $12,700 in payment of an invoice was incorrectly recorded in the accounts as $12,000.
3. Based on the bank reconciliation prepared in (2), journalize the entry or entries to be made by Kornett Company.
4. Based on the following selected data, journalize the adjusting entries as of December 31 of the current year:
   a. Estimated uncollectible accounts at December 31, $16,000, based on an aging of accounts receivable. The balance of Allowance for Doubtful Accounts at December 31 was $2,000 (debit).
   b. The physical inventory on December 31 indicated an inventory shrinkage of $3,300.
   c. Prepaid insurance expired during the year, $22,820.
   d. Office supplies used during the year, $3,920.
   e. Depreciation is computed as follows:

Asset	Cost	Residual Value	Acquisition Date	Useful Life in Years	Depreciation Method Used
Buildings	$900,000	$ 0	January 2	50	Double-declining-balance
Office Equip.	246,000	26,000	January 3	5	Straight-line
Store Equip.	112,000	12,000	July 1	10	Straight-line

   f. A patent costing $48,000 when acquired on January 2 has a remaining legal life of 10 years and is expected to have value for eight years.
   g. The cost of mineral rights was $546,000. Of the estimated deposit of 910,000 tons of ore, 50,000 tons were mined and sold during the year.
   h. Vacation pay expense for December, $10,500.
   i. A product warranty was granted beginning December 1 and covering a one-year period. The estimated cost is 4% of sales, which totaled $1,900,000 in December.
   j. Interest was accrued on the note receivable received on October 17.

5. Based on the following information and the post-closing trial balance that follows, prepare a balance sheet in report form at December 31 of the current year:

The merchandise inventory is stated at cost by the LIFO method.
The product warranty payable is a current liability.

Vacation pay payable:

Current liability	$7,140
Long-term liability	3,360

The unfunded pension liability is a long-term liability.

Notes payable:

Current liability	$ 70,000
Long-term liability	630,000

Kornett Company
Post-Closing Trial Balance
December 31, 2016

	Debit Balances	Credit Balances
Petty Cash	4,500	
Cash	243,960	
Notes Receivable	100,000	
Accounts Receivable	470,000	
Allowance for Doubtful Accounts		16,000
Merchandise Inventory	320,000	
Interest Receivable	1,875	
Prepaid Insurance	45,640	
Office Supplies	13,400	
Land	654,925	
Buildings	900,000	
Accumulated Depreciation—Buildings		36,000
Office Equipment	246,000	
Accumulated Depreciation—Office Equipment		44,000
Store Equipment	112,000	
Accumulated Depreciation—Store Equipment		5,000
Mineral Rights	546,000	
Accumulated Depletion		30,000
Patents	42,000	
Social Security Tax Payable		25,470
Medicare Tax Payable		4,710
Employees Federal Income Tax Payable		40,000
State Unemployment Tax Payable		270
Federal Unemployment Tax Payable		40
Salaries Payable		157,000
Accounts Payable		131,600
Interest Payable		28,000
Product Warranty Payable		76,000
Vacation Pay Payable		10,500
Unfunded Pension Liability		50,700
Notes Payable		700,000
J. Kornett, Capital		2,345,010
	3,700,300	3,700,300

Cases & Projects

CP 11-1 Ethics and professional conduct in business

General Ledger

Tonya Latirno is a certified public accountant (CPA) and staff accountant for Kennedy and Kennedy, a local CPA firm. It had been the policy of the firm to provide a holiday bonus equal to two weeks' salary to all employees. The firm's new management team announced on November 15 that a bonus equal to only one week's salary would be made available to employees this year. Tonya thought that this policy was unfair because she and her co-workers planned on the full two-week bonus. The two-week bonus had been given for 10 straight years, so it seemed as though the firm had breached an implied commitment. Thus, Tonya decided that she would make up the lost bonus week by working an extra six hours of overtime per week over the next five weeks until the end of the year. Kennedy and Kennedy's policy is to pay overtime at 150% of straight time.

Tonya's supervisor was surprised to see overtime being reported, because there is generally very little additional or unusual client service demands at the end of the calendar year. However, the overtime was not questioned, because firm employees are on the "honor system" in reporting their overtime.

Discuss whether the firm is acting in an ethical manner by changing the bonus. Is Tonya behaving in an ethical manner?

CP 11-2 Recognizing pension expense

The annual examination of Felton Company's financial statements by its external public accounting firm (auditors) is nearing completion. The following conversation took place between the controller of Felton Company (Francie) and the audit manager from the public accounting firm (Sumana):

Sumana: You know, Francie, we are about to wrap up our audit for this fiscal year. Yet, there is one item still to be resolved.

Francie: What's that?

Sumana: Well, as you know, at the beginning of the year, Felton began a defined benefit pension plan. This plan promises your employees an annual payment when they retire, using a formula based on their salaries at retirement and their years of service. I believe that a pension expense should be recognized this year, equal to the amount of pension earned by your employees.

Francie: Wait a minute. I think you have it all wrong. The company doesn't have a pension expense until it actually pays the pension in cash when the employee retires. After all, some of these employees may not reach retirement, and if they don't, the company doesn't owe them anything.

Sumana: You're not really seeing this the right way. The pension is earned by your employees during their working years. You actually make the payment much later—when they retire. It's like one long accrual—much like incurring wages in one period and paying them in the next. Thus, I think that you should recognize the expense in the period the pension is earned by the employees.

Francie: Let me see if I've got this straight. I should recognize an expense this period for something that may or may not be paid to the employees in 20 or 30 years, when they finally retire. How am I supposed to determine what the expense is for the current year? The amount of the final retirement depends on many uncertainties: salary levels, employee longevity, mortality rates, and interest earned on investments to fund the pension. I don't think that an amount can be determined, even if I accepted your arguments.

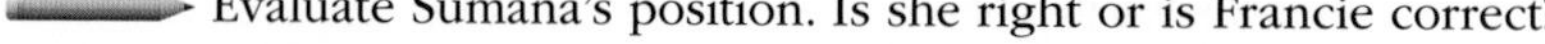

Evaluate Sumana's position. Is she right or is Francie correct?

CP 11-3 Ethics and professional conduct in business

Marvin Turner was discussing summer employment with Tina Song, president of Motown Construction Service:

Tina: I'm glad that you're thinking about joining us for the summer. We could certainly use the help.

Marvin: Sounds good. I enjoy outdoor work, and I could use the money to help with next year's school expenses.

Tina: I've got a plan that can help you out on that. As you know, I'll pay you $14 per hour, but in addition, I'd like to pay you with cash. Since you're only working for the summer, it really doesn't make sense for me to go to the trouble of formally putting you on our payroll system. In fact, I do some jobs for my clients on a strictly cash basis, so it would be easy to just pay you that way.

Marvin: Well, that's a bit unusual, but I guess money is money.

Tina: Yeah, not only that, it's tax-free!

Marvin: What do you mean?

Tina: Didn't you know? Any money that you receive in cash is not reported to the IRS on a W-2 form; therefore, the IRS doesn't know about the income—hence, it's the same as tax-free earnings.

a. Why does Tina Song want to conduct business transactions using cash (not check or credit card)?

b. How should Marvin respond to Tina's suggestion?

CP 11-4 Payroll forms

Group Project

Internet Project

Payroll accounting involves the use of government-supplied forms to account for payroll taxes. Three common forms are the W-2, Form 940, and Form 941. Form a team with three of your classmates and retrieve copies of each of these forms. They may be obtained from a local IRS office, a library, or downloaded from the Internet at www.irs.gov (go to forms and publications). Briefly describe the purpose of each of the three forms.

CP 11-5 Contingent liabilities

Internet Project

Altria Group, Inc., has more than 12 pages dedicated to describing contingent liabilities in the notes to recent financial statements. These pages include extensive descriptions of multiple contingent liabilities. Use the Internet to research Altria Group, Inc., at www.altria.com.

a. What are the major business units of Altria Group?

b. Based on your understanding of this company, why would Altria Group require more than 12 pages of contingency disclosure?

CHAPTER

12

Accounting for Partnerships and Limited Liability Companies

Boston Basketball Partners LLC

Boston Basketball Partners (BBP) LLC are the owners of the Boston Celtics NBA basketball franchise. The letters "LLC" stand for *limited liability company*. Unlike sole proprietorships illustrated in prior chapters, an LLC is a business form that normally has multiple owners. BBP LLC is led by Wic Grousbeck, a former venture fund manager from Boston, with the assistance of more than 15 other owners. Grousbeck called investing in the Celtics "a chance of a lifetime." Surprisingly, Grousbeck claims "money would not be the first priority." Even so, *Forbes* estimates the team is now worth $730 million, which is more than twice what BBP LLC originally paid, while ranking the Celtics as the fourth most valuable team in the NBA. So, Grousbeck must be doing something right. Grousbeck and his team have turned their venture capital skills toward the Celtics. Some of their innovations off the court include building a cable partnership, using technology to evaluate seat usage, and adding advertising sponsors. On the court, they pioneered the "three superstars to win" strategy with Rondo, Garnett, and Allen.

So why would BBP LLC choose the LLC form of organization?

The entity form chosen by a business has an important impact on the owners' legal liability, taxation, and ability to raise money. The four major forms of business entities discussed in this text are the proprietorship, partnership, limited liability company, and corporation. Proprietorships have been discussed in prior chapters. Partnerships and limited liability companies will be discussed in this chapter, and corporations will be introduced in the next chapter.

Learning Objectives

After studying this chapter, you should be able to: *Example Exercises*

At a Glance 12 Page 573

OBJ 1 Describe the characteristics of proprietorships, partnerships, and limited liability companies.

Proprietorships, Partnerships, and Limited Liability Companies

The four most common legal forms for organizing and operating a business are as follows:

- Proprietorship
- Corporation
- Partnership
- Limited liability company

In this section, the characteristics of proprietorships, partnerships, and limited liability companies are described. The characteristics of corporations are described in Chapter 13.

Proprietorships

A *proprietorship* is a company owned by a single individual. The most common proprietorships are professional service providers, such as lawyers, architects, realtors, and physicians.

Characteristics of proprietorships include the following:

- *Simple to form.* There are no legal restrictions or forms to file.
- *No limitation on legal liability.* The owner is personally liable for any debts or legal claims against the business. Thus, creditors can take the personal assets of the owner if the business debts exceed the owner's investment in the company.

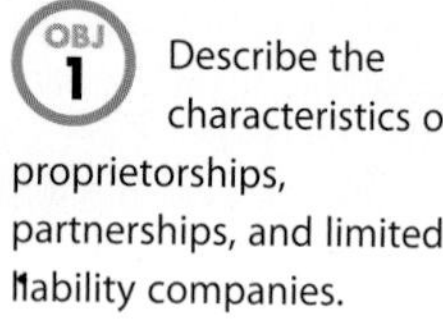

The **Internal Revenue Service (IRS)** estimates that proprietorships file 70% of business tax returns, but earn only 5% of all business revenues.

- *Not taxable.* For federal income tax purposes, a proprietorship is not taxed. Instead, the proprietorship's income or loss is "passed through" to the owner's individual income tax return.[1]
- *Limited life.* When the owner dies or retires, the proprietorship ceases to exist.
- *Limited ability to raise capital (funds).* The ability to raise capital (funds) is limited to what the owner can provide from personal resources or through borrowing.

Partnerships

A **partnership** is an association of two or more persons who own and manage a business for profit.[2] Partnerships are less widely used than proprietorships.

Characteristics of a partnership include the following:

Note:
A partnership is a nontaxable entity that has a limited life and unlimited liability.

- *Moderately complex to form.* A partnership is often formed with a partnership agreement. A **partnership agreement** includes matters such as amounts to be invested, limits on withdrawals, distributions of income and losses, and admission and withdrawal of partners. Thus, an attorney is often used in forming a partnership.
- *No limitation on legal liability.* The partners are personally liable for any debts or legal claims against the partnership. Therefore, creditors can take the personal assets of the partners if the business debts exceed the partners' investment in the business.
- *Not taxable.* For federal income tax purposes, a partnership is not taxed. Instead, the partnership's income or loss is "passed through" to the partners' individual income tax returns. However, partnerships must still report revenues, expenses, and income or loss annually to the Internal Revenue Service.
- *Limited life.* When a partner dies or retires, the partnership ceases to exist. Likewise, the admission of a new partner dissolves the old partnership, and a new partnership must be formed if operations are to continue.
- *Limited ability to raise capital (funds).* The ability to raise capital (funds) for the partnership is limited to what the partners can provide from personal resources or through borrowing.

In addition to those characteristics, some unique aspects of partnerships are:

- *Co-ownership of partnership property.* The property invested in a partnership by a partner becomes the joint property of all the partners. When a partnership is dissolved, each partner's share of the partnership assets is the balance in their capital account.
- *Mutual agency.* Each partner is an agent of the partnership and may act on behalf of the entire partnership. Thus, any liabilities created by one partner become liabilities of all the partners.
- *Participation in income.* Net income and net loss are distributed among the partners according to their partnership agreement. If the partnership agreement does not provide for distribution of income and losses, then income and losses are divided equally among the partners.

Business Connection

BREAKING UP IS HARD TO DO

Former partners of Adam Carolla filed court papers accusing the star of The Adam Carolla Show (adamcarolla.com) of a breach of their partnership agreement. They claimed the partnership agreement gave 30% ownership to Donny Misraje, 10% to Sandy Ganz, and 60% to Carolla. The suit alleges that Carolla began his popular podcast with the help of his partners at a time when future success of the venture was risky and unknown.

The former partners claim to have given up jobs, invested money and equipment, and provided expertise to launch the show. Once the show achieved success, the former partners claim Carolla unfairly kicked them out of the partnership. The court will, in part, use the partnership agreement to help settle this dispute. A partnership agreement helps protect the interests of all parties to a business venture.

Source: Radar Staff, "Best Friend Sues Adam Carolla Over Hit Podcast Show," January 18, 2013.

[1] The proprietor's statement of income is included on Schedule C of the individual 1040 tax return.

[2] The definition of a partnership is included in the Uniform Partnership Act, which has been adopted by most states.

Limited Liability Companies

Many companies have joint ventures organized as LLCs. For example, **Walt Disney Company** has a 42% interest in **A&E Television Networks, LLC.**

A **limited liability company (LLC)** is a form of legal entity that provides limited liability to its owners but is treated as a partnership for tax purposes. Thus, the LLC organizational form is popular for small businesses.

Characteristics of an LLC include the following:

- *Moderately complex to form.* An LLC requires an agreement among the owners, who are called members. The *operating agreement* includes matters such as amounts to be invested, limits on withdrawals, distributions of income and losses, and admission and withdrawal of members. An attorney is normally used in forming an LCC.
- *Limited legal liability.* The members have *limited liability* even if they are active in the company. Thus, the members' personal assets are legally protected against creditor claims made against the LLC. That is, only the members' investments in the company are subject to claims of creditors.
- *Not taxable.* An LLC may elect to be treated as a partnership for tax purposes. In this way, income passes through the LLC and is taxed on the individual members' tax returns.[3]
- *Unlimited life.* Most LLC operating agreements specify continuity of life for the LLC, even when a member withdraws or new members join the LLC.
- *Moderate ability to raise capital (funds).* Because of their limited liability, LLCs are attractive to many investors, thus allowing for greater access to capital (funds) than is normally the case in a partnership.

An LLC may elect to operate as a *member-managed* or a *manager-managed* company. In a member-managed LLC, individual members may legally bind the LLC, like partners bind a partnership. In a manager-managed LLC, only authorized members may legally bind the LLC. Thus, in a manager-managed LLC, members may share in the income of the LLC without concern for managing the company.

Comparing Proprietorships, Partnerships, and Limited Liability Companies

Exhibit 1 summarizes the characteristics of proprietorships, partnerships, and limited liability companies.

EXHIBIT 1 **Characteristics of Proprietorships, Partnerships, and Limited Liability Companies**

Organizational Form	Complexity of Formation	Legal Liability	Taxation	Limitation on Life of Entity	Access to Capital
Proprietorship	Simple	No limitation	Nontaxable (pass-through) entity	Limited	Limited
Partnership	Moderate	No limitation	Nontaxable (pass-through) entity	Limited	Limited
Limited Liability Company	Moderate	Limited liability	Nontaxable (pass-through) entity by election	Unlimited	Moderate

Business Connection

ORGANIZATIONAL FORMS IN THE ACCOUNTING INDUSTRY

The four major accounting firms, KPMG LLP, Ernst & Young, PricewaterhouseCoopers, and Deloitte & Touche, all began as partnerships. This form was legally required due to the theory of mutual agency. That is, the partnership form was thought to create public trust by requiring all partners to be jointly liable and responsible for each other's judgments. In addition, investment in the partnerships was limited to practicing accountants. This prevented any pressures from outside investors affecting professional decisions.

As these firms grew and the risk increased, all of these firms were allowed to change, by law, to limited liability partnerships (LLPs). Thus, while remaining a partnership, the liability of the partners was limited to their investment in the firm. The LLP form is very similar to an LLC, except that investment is restricted to professionals.

[3] An LLC may also be taxed as a separate entity. However, doing so would remove these tax benefits, making this a less common election.

Forming a Partnership and Dividing Income

OBJ 2 Describe and illustrate the accounting for forming a partnership and for dividing the net income and net loss of a partnership.

Most of the day-to-day accounting for a partnership or an LLC is similar to that illustrated in earlier chapters. However, the formation, division of net income or net loss, dissolution, and liquidation of partnerships and LLCs give rise to unique transactions.

In the remainder of this chapter, the unique transactions for partnerships and LLCs are described and illustrated. The accounting for an LLC is the same as a partnership, except that the terms *member* and *members' equity* are used rather than *partner* or *owners' capital*. For this reason, the journal entries for an LLC are shown alongside the partnership entries.

Forming a Partnership

In forming a partnership, the investments of each partner are recorded in separate entries. The assets contributed by a partner are debited to the partnership asset accounts. If any liabilities are assumed by the partnership, the partnership liability accounts are credited. The partner's capital account is credited for the net amount.

To illustrate, assume that Joseph Stevens and Earl Foster, owners of competing hardware stores, agree to combine their businesses in a partnership. Stevens agrees to contribute the following:

Cash	$ 7,200	Office equipment	$2,500
Accounts receivable	16,300	Allowance for doubtful accounts	1,500
Merchandise inventory	28,700	Accounts payable	2,600
Store equipment	5,400		

The entry to record the assets and liabilities contributed by Stevens is as follows:

LLC		
Cash	*7,200*	
Accounts Receivable	*16,300*	
Merchandise Inventory	*28,700*	
Store Equipment	*5,400*	
Office Equipment	*2,500*	
Allowance for Doubtful Accounts		*1,500*
Accounts Payable		*2,600*
Joseph Stevens, Member Equity		*56,000*

Apr.	1	Cash	7,200	
		Accounts Receivable	16,300	
		Merchandise Inventory	28,700	
		Store Equipment	5,400	
		Office Equipment	2,500	
		Allowance for Doubtful Accounts		1,500
		Accounts Payable		2,600
		Joseph Stevens, Capital		56,000

In the preceding entry, the noncash assets are recorded at values agreed upon by the partners. These values are normally based on current market values. As a result, the book value of the assets contributed by the partners normally differs from that recorded by the new partnership.

To illustrate, the store equipment contributed by Stevens may have had a book value of $3,500 in Stevens' ledger (cost of $10,000 less accumulated depreciation of $6,500). However, the store equipment is recorded at its current market value of $5,400 in the preceding entry. The contributions of Foster would be recorded in an entry similar to the entry for Stevens.

Example Exercise 12-1 Journalize Partner's Original Investment

OBJ 1

Reese Howell contributed equipment, inventory, and $34,000 cash to a partnership. The equipment had a book value of $23,000 and a market value of $29,000. The inventory had a book value of $60,000, but only had a market value of $15,000, due to obsolescence. The partnership also assumed a $12,000 note payable owed by Howell that was used originally to purchase the equipment.

Provide the journal entry for Howell's contribution to the partnership.

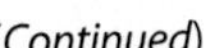
(*Continued*)

Follow My Example 12-1

Cash	34,000	
Inventory	15,000	
Equipment	29,000	
Notes Payable		12,000
Reese Howell, Capital		66,000

Practice Exercises: PE 12-1A, PE 12-1B

Dividing Income

Income or losses of the partnership are divided as specified in the partnership agreement. If there is no specification or agreement, income and losses are divided equally.

Common methods of dividing partnership income are based on:

- Services of the partners
- Services and investments of the partners

Services of Partners One method of dividing partnership income is based on the services provided by each partner to the partnership. These services are often recognized by partner salary allowances. Such allowances reflect differences in partners' abilities and time devoted to the partnership. Since partners are not employees, such allowances are recorded as divisions of net income and are credited to the partners' capital accounts.

To illustrate, assume that the partnership agreement of Jennifer Stone and Crystal Mills provides for the following:

	Monthly Salary Allowance
Jennifer Stone	$5,000
Crystal Mills	4,000
Remaining net income:	Divided Equally

The division of income may be reported at the bottom of the partnership income statement. Using this format, the division of $150,000 of net income would be reported on the bottom of the partnership income statement as follows:

Net income $150,000

Division of net income:

	J. Stone	C. Mills	Total
Annual salary allowance (mo. × 12)	$60,000	$48,000	$108,000
Remaining income	21,000	21,000	42,000
Net income	$81,000	$69,000	$150,000

A closing entry is used to record the division of net income, even if the partners do not withdraw the amounts of their salary allowances. The entry for closing Income Summary and dividing net income is as follows:

LLC

Income Summary	*150,000*	
Jennifer Stone, Member Equity		*81,000*
Crystal Mills, Member Equity		*69,000*

Dec.	31	Income Summary		150,000	
		Jennifer Stone, Capital			81,000
		Crystal Mills, Capital			69,000

If Stone and Mills withdraw their salary allowances monthly, the withdrawals are debited to their drawing accounts. At the end of the year, the drawing account debit balances of $60,000 and $48,000 are then closed to the partners' capital accounts.

Services of Partners and Investments A partnership agreement may divide income based upon salary allowances, as discussed, and also based upon interest on capital balances of each partner. In this way, partners with more invested in the partnership are rewarded by receiving more of the partnership income. One such method of dividing partnership income would be as follows:

1. Partner salary allowances
2. Interest on capital investments
3. Any remaining income equally

To illustrate, assume that the partnership agreement for Stone and Mills provides for the following:

1.

	Monthly Salary Allowance
Jennifer Stone	$5,000
Crystal Mills	4,000

2. Interest of 12% on each partner's capital balance as of January 1.

Capital, Jennifer Stone, January 1	$160,000
Capital, Crystal Mills, January 1	120,000

3. Remaining income: Divided Equally

The $150,000 net income for the year is divided as follows:

Net income	$150,000
Division of net income:	

	J. Stone	C. Mills	Total
Annual salary allowance	$60,000	$48,000	$108,000
Interest allowance	19,200[1]	14,400[2]	33,600
Total	$79,200	$62,400	$141,600
Remaining income	4,200	4,200	8,400
Net income	$83,400	$66,600	$150,000

[1]12% × $160,000
[2]12% × $120,000

The entry for closing Income Summary and dividing net income is as follows:

LLC

Income Summary	*150,000*	
Jennifer Stone, Member Equity		*83,400*
Crystal Mills, Member Equity		*66,600*

Dec.	31	Income Summary	150,000	
		Jennifer Stone, Capital		83,400
		Crystal Mills, Capital		66,600

Integrity, Objectivity, and Ethics in Business

TYRANNY OF THE MAJORITY

Some partnerships involve the contribution of money by one partner and the contribution of effort and expertise by another. This can create a conflict between the two partners, because one works and the other doesn't. Without a properly developed partnership agreement, the working partner could take income in the form of a salary allowance, leaving little for the investor partner. Thus, partnership agreements often require all partners to agree on salary allowances provided to working partners.

Allowances Exceed Net Income In the preceding example, the net income is $150,000. The total of the salary ($108,000) and interest ($33,600) allowances is $141,600. Thus, the net income exceeds the salary and interest allowances. In some cases, however, the net income may be less than the total of the allowances. In this case, the remaining net income to divide is a *negative* amount. This negative amount is divided among the partners as though it were a net loss.

To illustrate, assume the same salary and interest allowances as in the preceding example, but that the net income is $100,000. In this case, the total of the allowances of $141,600 exceeds the net income by $41,600 ($100,000 − $141,600). This amount is divided equally between Stone and Mills. Thus, $20,800 ($41,600 ÷ 2) is deducted from each partner's share of the allowances. The final division of net income between Stone and Mills is as follows:

Net income			$100,000
Division of net income:			

	J. Stone	C. Mills	Total
Annual salary allowance	$ 60,000	$48,000	$108,000
Interest allowance	19,200	14,400	33,600
Total	$ 79,200	$62,400	$141,600
Deduct excess of allowances over income	20,800	20,800	41,600
Net income[4]	$58,400	$41,600	$100,000

The entry for closing Income Summary and dividing net income is as follows:

LLC		
Income Summary	*100,000*	
Jennifer Stone, Member Equity		*58,400*
Crystal Mills, Member Equity		*41,600*

Dec.	31	Income Summary		100,000	
		Jennifer Stone, Capital			58,400
		Crystal Mills, Capital			41,600

Example Exercise 12-2 Dividing Partnership Net Income

OBJ 2

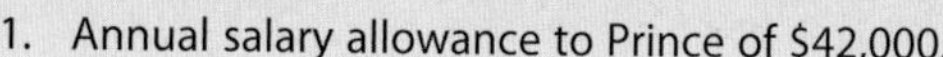

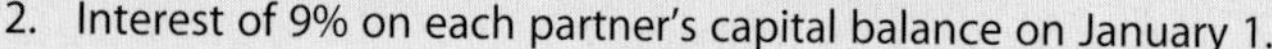

Dynamic Exhibit

Steve Prince and Chelsy Bernard formed a partnership, dividing income as follows:

1. Annual salary allowance to Prince of $42,000.
2. Interest of 9% on each partner's capital balance on January 1.
3. Any remaining net income divided equally.

Prince and Bernard had $20,000 and $150,000 in their January 1 capital balances, respectively. Net income for the year was $240,000.

How much net income should be distributed to Prince and Bernard?

Follow My Example 12-2

	S. Prince	C. Bernard	Total
Annual salary allowance	$ 42,000	$ 0	$ 42,000
Interest allowance	1,800[1]	13,500[2]	15,300
Total	$ 43,800	$ 13,500	$ 57,300
Remaining income	91,350[3]	91,350	182,700
Net income	$135,150	$104,850	$240,000

[1] $20,000 × 9%
[2] $150,000 × 9%
[3] ($240,000 – $42,000 – $15,300) × 50%

Practice Exercises: PE 12-2A, PE 12-2B

[4] In the event of a net loss, the amount deducted from the total allowances would be the "excess of allowances over loss" or the sum of the net loss and the allowances, divided according to the sharing ratio.

Partner Admission and Withdrawal

OBJ 3 Describe and illustrate the accounting for partner admission and withdrawal.

Many partnerships provide for admitting new partners and for partner withdrawals by amending the existing partnership agreement. In this way, the company may continue operating without having to form a new partnership and prepare a new partnership agreement.

Admitting a Partner

As shown in Exhibit 2, a person may be admitted to a partnership by either of the following:

- Purchasing an interest from one or more of the existing partners
- Contributing assets to the partnership

EXHIBIT 2

Two Methods for Admitting a Partner

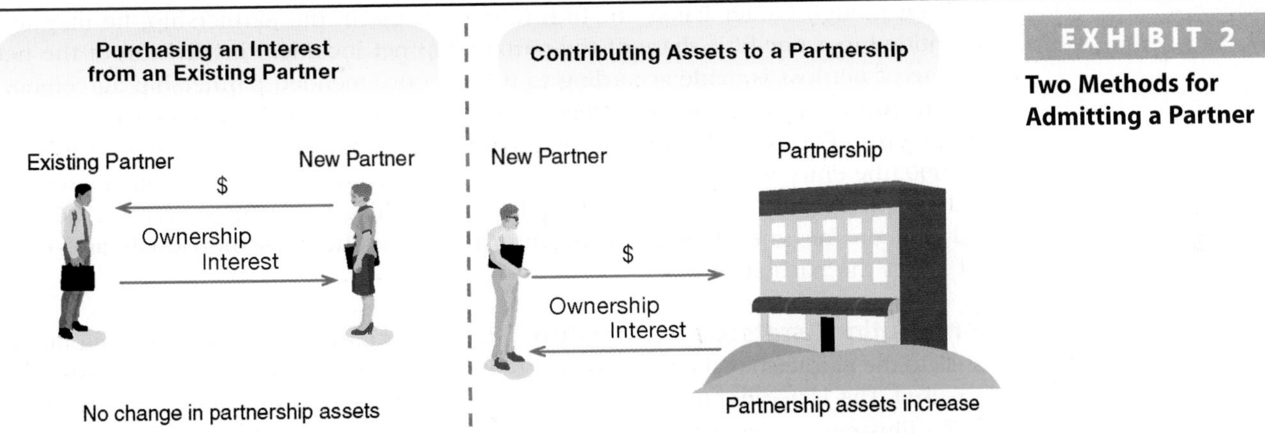

When a new partner is admitted by *purchasing an interest* from one or more of the existing partners, the total assets and the total owners' equity of the partnership are not affected. The capital (equity) of the new partner is recorded by transferring capital (equity) from the existing partners.

When a new partner is admitted by *contributing assets* to the partnership, the total assets and the total owners' equity of the partnership are increased. The capital (equity) of the new partner is recorded as the amount of assets contributed to the partnership by the new partner.

Purchasing an Interest from Existing Partners When a new partner is admitted by purchasing an interest from one or more of the existing partners, the transaction is between the new and existing partners acting as individuals. The admission of the new partner is recorded by transferring owners' equity amounts from the capital accounts of the selling partners to the capital account of the new partner.

To illustrate, assume that on June 1 Tom Andrews and Nathan Bell each sell one-fifth of their partnership equity of Bring It Consulting to Joe Canter for $10,000 in cash. On June 1, the partnership has net assets of $100,000 and both existing partners have capital balances of $50,000 each. This transaction is between Andrews, Bell, and Canter. The only entry required by Bring It Consulting is to record the transfer of capital (equity) from Andrews and Bell to Canter, as follows:

LLC		
Tom Andrews, Member Equity	*10,000*	
Nathan Bell, Member Equity	*10,000*	
Joe Canter, Member Equity		*20,000*

June	1	Tom Andrews, Capital		10,000	
		Nathan Bell, Capital		10,000	
		Joe Canter, Capital			20,000

The effect of the transaction on the partnership accounts is as follows:

BRING IT CONSULTING

Partnership Accounts

Net Assets	
100,000	

Tom Andrews, Capital	
10,000	50,000

Joe Canter, Capital	
	20,000

Nathan Bell, Capital	
10,000	50,000

After Canter is admitted to Bring It Consulting, the total owners' equity is still $100,000. Canter has a one-fifth (20%) interest and a capital balance of $20,000. Andrews and Bell each own two-fifths (40%) interest and have capital balances of $40,000 each.

Even though Canter has a one-fifth (20%) interest in the partnership, he may not be entitled to a one-fifth share of the partnership net income. The division of the net income or net loss is made according to the new or amended partnership agreement.

The preceding entry is not affected by the amount paid by Canter for the one-fifth interest. For example, if Canter had paid $15,000 to Andrews and Bell instead of $10,000, the entry would still be the same. This is because the transaction is between Andrews, Bell, and Canter, rather than the partnership. Any gain or loss by Andrews and Bell on the sale of their partnership interest is theirs as individuals and does not affect the partnership.

Contributing Assets to a Partnership When a new partner is admitted by contributing assets to the partnership, the total assets and the total owners' equity of the partnership are increased. This is because the transaction is between the new partner and the partnership.

To illustrate, assume that instead of purchasing a one-fifth ownership in Bring It Consulting directly from Tom Andrews and Nathan Bell, Joe Canter contributes $20,000 cash to Bring It Consulting for ownership equity of $20,000. The entry to record this transaction is as follows:

LLC

Cash	*20,000*	
Joe Canter, Member Equity		*20,000*

June	1	Cash		20,000	
		Joe Canter, Capital			20,000

The effect of the transaction on the partnership accounts is as follows:

BRING IT CONSULTING

Partnership Accounts

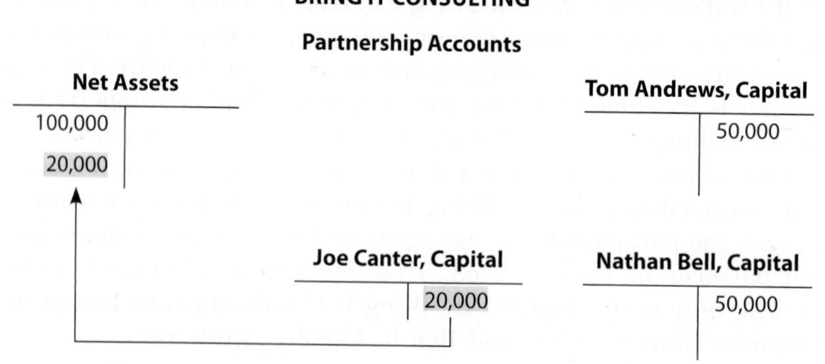

After the admission of Canter, the net assets and total owners' equity of Bring It Consulting increase to $120,000, of which Joe Canter has a $20,000 interest. In contrast, in the prior example, the net assets and total owners' equity of Bring It Consulting did not change from $100,000.

Revaluation of Assets Before a new partner is admitted, the balances of a partnership's asset accounts should be stated at current values. If necessary, the accounts should be adjusted. Any net adjustment (increase or decrease) in asset values is divided among the capital accounts of the existing partners, similar to the division of income.

To illustrate, assume that in the preceding example the balance of the merchandise inventory account is $14,000 and the current replacement value is $17,000. If Andrews and Bell share net income equally, the revaluation is recorded as follows:

LLC		
Merchandise Inventory	*3,000*	
Tom Andrews, Member Equity		*1,500*
Nathan Bell, Member Equity		*1,500*

June	1	Merchandise Inventory		3,000	
		Tom Andrews, Capital			1,500
		Nathan Bell, Capital			1,500

Failure to adjust the partnership accounts for current values before admission of a new partner may result in the new partner sharing in asset gains or losses that arose in prior periods.

Example Exercise 12-3 Revaluing and Contributing Assets to a Partnership

OBJ 3

Blake Nelson invested $45,000 in the Lawrence & Kerry partnership for ownership equity of $45,000. Prior to the investment, land was revalued to a market value of $260,000 from a book value of $200,000. Lynne Lawrence and Tim Kerry share net income in a 1:2 ratio.

a. Provide the journal entry for the revaluation of land.
b. Provide the journal entry to admit Nelson.

Follow My Example 12-3

a. Land	60,000	
Lynne Lawrence, Capital		20,000
Tim Kerry, Capital		40,000
[1] $60,000 × 1/3		
[2] $60,000 × 2/3		
b. Cash	45,000	
Blake Nelson, Capital		45,000

Practice Exercises: PE 12-3A, PE 12-3B

Partner Bonuses A new partner may pay existing partners a bonus to join a partnership. In other cases, existing partners may pay a new partner a bonus to join the partnership.

Bonuses are usually paid because of higher than normal profits the new or existing partners are expected to contribute in the future. For example, a new partner may bring special qualities or skills to the partnership. Celebrities such as actors, musicians, or sports figures often provide name recognition that is expected to increase a partnership's profits.

Partner bonuses are illustrated in Exhibit 3. Existing partners receive a bonus when the ownership interest received by the new partner is less than the amount paid. In

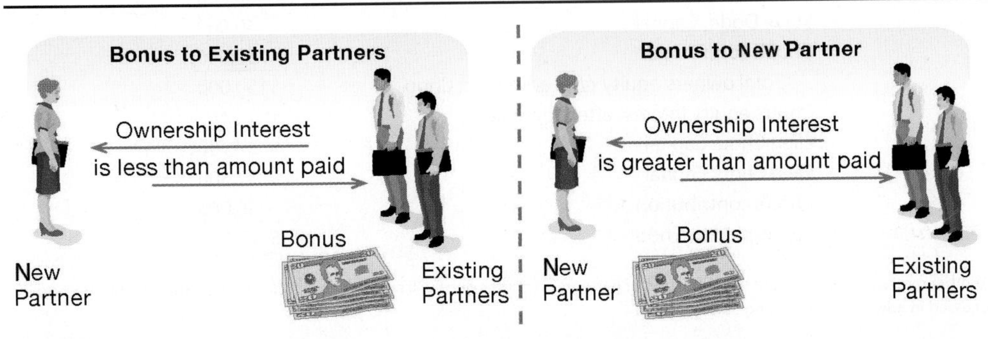

EXHIBIT 3

Partner Bonuses

contrast, the new partner receives a bonus when the ownership interest received by the new partner is greater than the amount paid.

To illustrate, assume that on March 1 the partnership of Marsha Jenkins and Helen Kramer is considering a new partner, Alex Diaz. After the assets of the partnership have been adjusted to current market values, the capital balances of Jenkins and Kramer are as follows:

Marsha Jenkins, Capital	$20,000
Helen Kramer, Capital	24,000
Total owners' equity *before* admitting Diaz	$44,000

Jenkins and Kramer agree to admit Diaz to the partnership for $31,000. In return, Diaz will receive a one-third equity in the partnership and will share equally with Jenkins and Kramer in partnership income or losses. In this case, Diaz is paying Jenkins and Kramer a $6,000 bonus to join the partnership, computed as follows:

Marsha Jenkins, Capital	$20,000
Helen Kramer, Capital	24,000
Diaz's contribution	31,000
Total owners' equity *after* admitting Diaz	$75,000
Diaz's equity interest after admission	× 1/3
Alex Diaz, Capital	$25,000
Diaz's contribution	$31,000
Alex Diaz, Capital	25,000
Bonus paid to Jenkins and Kramer	$ 6,000

The $6,000 bonus paid by Diaz increases Jenkins's and Kramer's capital accounts. It is distributed to the capital accounts of Jenkins and Kramer according to their income-sharing ratio.[5] Assuming that Jenkins and Kramer share profits and losses equally, the entry to record the admission of Diaz to the partnership is as follows:

LLC

Cash	*31,000*	
Alex Diaz, Member Equity		*25,000*
Marsha Jenkins, Member Equity		*3,000*
Helen Kramer, Member Equity		*3,000*

Mar.	1	Cash		31,000	
		Alex Diaz, Capital			25,000
		Marsha Jenkins, Capital			3,000
		Helen Kramer, Capital			3,000

Existing partners may agree to pay the new partner a bonus to join a partnership. To illustrate, assume that after adjusting assets to market values, the capital balances of Janice Cowen and Steve Dodd are as follows:

Janice Cowen, Capital	$ 80,000
Steve Dodd, Capital	40,000
Total owners' equity *before* admitting Chou	$120,000

Cowen and Dodd agree to admit Ellen Chou to the partnership on June 1 for an investment of $30,000. In return, Chou will receive a one-fourth equity interest in the partnership and will share in one-fourth of the profits and losses. In this case, Cowen and Dodd are paying Chou a $7,500 bonus to join the partnership, computed as follows:

Janice Cowen, Capital	$ 80,000
Steve Dodd, Capital	40,000
Chou's contribution	30,000
Total owners' equity *after* admitting Chou	$150,000
Chou's equity interest after admission	× 1/4
Ellen Chou, Capital	$ 37,500
Ellen Chou, Capital	$ 37,500
Chou's contribution	30,000
Bonus paid to Chou	$ 7,500

[5] Another method used to record the admission of partners attributes goodwill rather than a bonus to the partners. This method is discussed in advanced accounting textbooks.

The $7,500 bonus paid to Chou decreases Cowen's and Dodd's capital accounts. It is distributed to the capital accounts of Cowen and Dodd according to their income-sharing ratio. Assuming that the income-sharing ratio of Cowen and Dodd was 2:1 before the admission of Chou, the entry to record the admission of Chou to the partnership is as follows:

LLC		
Cash	*30,000*	
Janice Cowen, Member Equity	*5,000*[1]	
Steve Dodd, Member Equity	*2,500*[2]	
Ellen Chou, Member Equity		*37,500*

June	1	Cash		30,000	
		Janice Cowen, Capital		5,000[1]	
		Steve Dodd, Capital		2,500[2]	
		Ellen Chou, Capital			37,500

[1] $7,500 × 2/3
[2] $7,500 × 1/3

Example Exercise 12-4 Partner Bonus

OBJ 3

Lowman has a capital balance of $51,000 after adjusting assets to fair market value. Conrad contributes $24,000 to receive a 30% interest in a new partnership with Lowman.

Determine the amount and recipient of the partner bonus.

Follow My Example 12-4

Equity of Lowman	$51,000
Conrad's contribution	24,000
Total equity after admitting Conrad	$75,000
Conrad's equity interest	× 30%
Conrad's equity after admission	$22,500
Conrad's contribution	$24,000
Conrad's equity after admission	22,500
Bonus paid to Lowman	$ 1,500

Practice Exercises: PE 12-4A, PE 12-4B

Withdrawal of a Partner

A partner may retire or withdraw from a partnership. In such cases, the withdrawing partner's interest is normally sold to the:

- Existing partners or
- Partnership

A partner generally cannot withdraw without permission of the remaining partners, nor can a partner be forced to withdraw by the other partners. In this sense, a partnership is like a marriage, "for better or for worse."

If the *existing partners* purchase the withdrawing partner's interest, the purchase and sale of the partnership interest is between the partners as individuals. The only entry on the partnership's records is to debit the capital account of the partner withdrawing and to credit the capital account of the partner or partners buying the additional interest.

If the *partnership purchases* the withdrawing partner's interest, the assets and the owners' equity of the partnership are reduced by the purchase price. Before the purchase, the asset accounts should be adjusted to current values. The net amount of any adjustment should be divided among the capital accounts of the partners according to their income-sharing ratio.

The entry to record the purchase debits the capital account of the withdrawing partner and credits Cash for the amount of the purchase. If not enough partnership cash is available to pay the withdrawing partner, a liability may be created (credited) for the amount owed the withdrawing partner.

Death of a Partner

When a partner dies, the partnership accounts should be closed as of the date of death. The net income for the current period should then be determined and divided among the partners' capital accounts. The asset accounts should also be adjusted to current values and the amount of any adjustment divided among the capital accounts of the partners.

After the income is divided and any assets revalued, an entry is recorded to close the deceased partner's capital account. The entry debits the deceased partner's capital account for its balance and credits a liability account, which is payable to the deceased's estate. The remaining partner or partners may then decide to continue the business or liquidate it.

OBJ 4 Describe and illustrate the accounting for liquidating a partnership.

Liquidating Partnerships

When a partnership goes out of business, it sells the assets, pays the creditors, and distributes the remaining cash or other assets to the partners. This winding-up process is called the **liquidation** of the partnership. Although *liquidating* refers to the payment of liabilities, it includes the entire winding-up process.

When the partnership goes out of business and the normal operations are discontinued, the accounts should be adjusted and closed. The only accounts remaining open will be the asset, contra asset, liability, and owners' equity accounts.

The liquidation process is illustrated in Exhibit 4. The steps in the liquidation process are as follows:

Note:
In liquidation, cash is distributed to partners according to their capital balances.

- Step 1. Sell the partnership assets. This step is called **realization.**
- Step 2. Distribute any gains or losses from realization to the partners based on their income-sharing ratio.
- Step 3. Pay the claims of creditors, using the cash from the step 1 realization.
- Step 4. Distribute the remaining cash to the partners based on the balances in their capital accounts.

EXHIBIT 4

Steps in Liquidating a Partnership

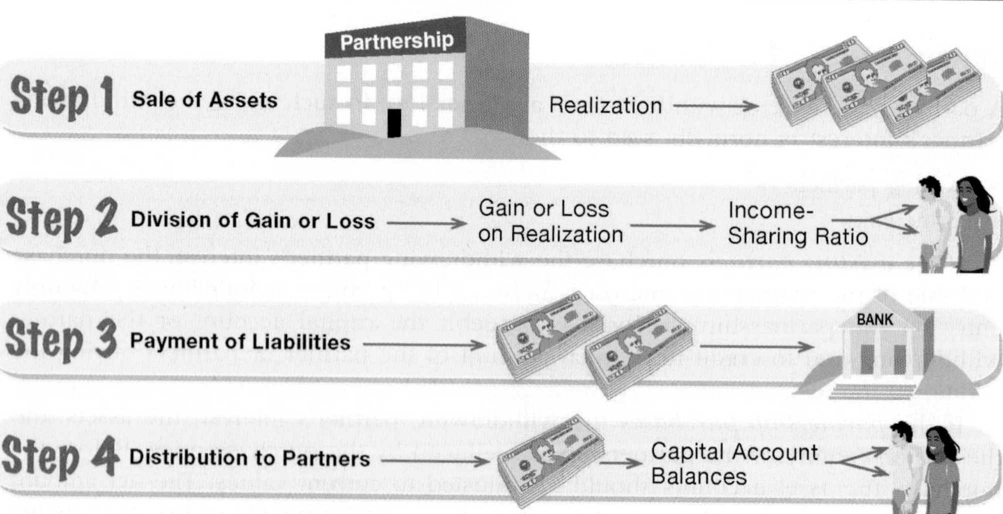

To illustrate, assume that Farley, Green, and Hall decide to liquidate their partnership. On April 9, after discontinuing business operations of the partnership and closing the accounts, the following trial balance is prepared:

Farley, Green, and Hall Post-Closing Trial Balance April 9, 2016	Debit Balances	Credit Balances
Cash	11,000	
Noncash Assets	64,000	
Liabilities		9,000
Jean Farley, Capital		22,000
Brad Green, Capital		22,000
Alice Hall, Capital		22,000
	75,000	75,000

Farley, Green, and Hall share income and losses in a ratio of 5:3:2 (50%, 30%, 20%). To simplify, assume that all noncash assets are sold in a single transaction and that all liabilities are paid at one time. In addition, Noncash Assets and Liabilities will be used as account titles in place of the various asset, contra asset, and liability accounts.

Gain on Realization

Assume that Farley, Green, and Hall sell all noncash assets for $72,000. Thus, a gain of $8,000 ($72,000 – $64,000) is realized. The partnership is liquidated during April as follows:

- Step 1. Sale of assets: $72,000 is realized from sale of all the noncash assets.
- Step 2. Division of gain: The gain of $8,000 is distributed to Farley, Green, and Hall in the income-sharing ratio of 5:3:2. Thus, the partner capital accounts are credited as follows:

Farley	$4,000 ($8,000 × 50%)
Green	2,400 ($8,000 × 30%)
Hall	1,600 ($8,000 × 20%)

- Step 3. Payment of liabilities: Creditors are paid $9,000.
- Step 4. Distribution of cash to partners: The remaining cash of $74,000 is distributed to the partners according to their capital balances as follows:

Farley	$26,000
Green	24,400
Hall	23,600

A **statement of partnership liquidation**, which summarizes the liquidation process, is shown in Exhibit 5.

EXHIBIT 5 **Statement of Partnership Liquidation: Gain on Realization**

Farley, Green, and Hall
Statement of Partnership Liquidation
For Period April 10–30, 2016

		Cash	+ Noncash Assets	= Liabilities	+ Capital Farley (50%)	+ Capital Green (30%)	+ Capital Hall (20%)
	Balances before realization	$11,000	$64,000	$9,000	$22,000	$22,000	$22,000
Steps 1–2 →	Sale of assets and division of gain	+72,000	–64,000		+ 4,000	+ 2,400	+ 1,600
	Balances after realization	$83,000	$ 0	$9,000	$26,000	$24,400	$23,600
Step 3 →	Payment of liabilities	– 9,000		–9,000			
	Balances after payment of liabilities	$74,000	$ 0	$ 0	$26,000	$24,400	$23,600
Step 4 →	Cash distributed to partners	–74,000			–26,000	–24,400	–23,600
	Final balances	$ 0	$ 0	$ 0	$ 0	$ 0	$ 0

The entries to record the steps in the liquidating process are as follows:

Sale of assets (Step 1):

LLC		
Cash	*72,000*	
Noncash Assets		*64,000*
Gain on Realization		*8,000*

		Cash		72,000	
		Noncash Assets			64,000
		Gain on Realization			8,000

Division of gain (Step 2):

LLC		
Gain on Realization	*8,000*	
Jean Farley, Member Equity		*4,000*
Brad Green, Member Equity		*2,400*
Alice Hall, Member Equity		*1,600*

		Gain on Realization		8,000	
		Jean Farley, Capital			4,000
		Brad Green, Capital			2,400
		Alice Hall, Capital			1,600

Payment of liabilities (Step 3):

LLC		
Liabilities	*9,000*	
Cash		*9,000*

		Liabilities		9,000	
		Cash			9,000

Distribution of cash to partners (Step 4):

LLC		
Jean Farley, Member Equity	*26,000*	
Brad Green, Member Equity	*24,400*	
Alice Hall, Member Equity	*23,600*	
Cash		*74,000*

		Jean Farley, Capital		26,000	
		Brad Green, Capital		24,400	
		Alice Hall, Capital		23,600	
		Cash			74,000

As shown in Exhibit 5, *the cash is distributed to the partners based on the balances of their capital accounts.* These balances are determined after the gain on realization has been divided among the partners and the liabilities paid. *The income-sharing ratio should not be used as a basis for distributing the cash to partners.*

Loss on Realization

Assume that Farley, Green, and Hall sell all noncash assets for $44,000. Thus, a loss of $20,000 ($64,000 – $44,000) is realized. The liquidation of the partnership is as follows:

- Step 1. Sale of assets: $44,000 is realized from the sale of all the noncash assets.
- Step 2. Division of loss: The loss of $20,000 is distributed to Farley, Green, and Hall in the income-sharing ratio of 5:3:2. Thus, the partner capital accounts are debited as follows:

Farley	$10,000 ($20,000 × 50%)
Green	6,000 ($20,000 × 30%)
Hall	4,000 ($20,000 × 20%)

- Step 3. Payment of liabilities: Creditors are paid $9,000.

- Step 4. Distribution of cash to partners: The remaining cash of $46,000 is distributed to the partners according to their capital balances as follows:

Farley	$12,000
Green	16,000
Hall	18,000

The steps in liquidating the partnership are summarized in the statement of partnership liquidation shown in Exhibit 6.

EXHIBIT 6 **Statement of Partnership Liquidation: Loss on Realization**

Farley, Green, and Hall
Statement of Partnership Liquidation
For Period April 10–30, 2016

										Capital				
		Cash	+	**Noncash Assets**	=	**Liabilities**	+	**Farley (50%)**	+	**Green (30%)**	+	**Hall (20%)**
	Balances before realization	$11,000		$64,000		$9,000		$22,000		$22,000		$22,000
Steps 1–2 →	Sale of assets and division of loss	+44,000		−64,000				−10,000		− 6,000		− 4,000
	Balances after realization	$55,000		$ 0		$9,000		$12,000		$16,000		$18,000
Step 3 →	Payment of liabilities	− 9,000				−9,000						
	Balances after payment of liabilities	$46,000		$ 0		$ 0		$12,000		$16,000		$18,000
Step 4 →	Cash distributed to partners	−46,000						−12,000		−16,000		−18,000
	Final balances	$ 0		$ 0		$ 0		$ 0		$ 0		$ 0

The entries to liquidate the partnership are as follows:

Sale of assets (Step 1):

LLC		
Cash	*44,000*	
Loss on Realization	*20,000*	
Noncash Assets		*64,000*

		Cash		44,000	
		Loss on Realization		20,000	
		Noncash Assets			64,000

Division of loss (Step 2):

LLC		
Jean Farley, Member Equity	*10,000*	
Brad Green, Member Equity	*6,000*	
Alice Hall, Member Equity	*4,000*	
Loss on Realization		*20,000*

		Jean Farley, Capital		10,000	
		Brad Green, Capital		6,000	
		Alice Hall, Capital		4,000	
		Loss on Realization			20,000

Payment of liabilities (Step 3):

LLC		
Liabilities	*9,000*	
Cash		*9,000*

		Liabilities		9,000	
		Cash			9,000

Distribution of cash to partners (Step 4):

LLC		
Jean Farley, Member Equity	*12,000*	
Brad Green, Member Equity	*16,000*	
Alice Hall, Member Equity	*18,000*	
Cash		*46,000*

		Jean Farley, Capital		12,000	
		Brad Green, Capital		16,000	
		Alice Hall, Capital		18,000	
		Cash			46,000

Example Exercise 12-5 Liquidating Partnerships

OBJ 4

Prior to liquidating their partnership, Todd and Gentry had capital accounts of $50,000 and $100,000, respectively. Prior to liquidation, the partnership had no other cash assets than what was realized from the sale of assets. These assets were sold for $220,000. The partnership had $20,000 of liabilities. Todd and Gentry share income and losses equally. Determine the amount received by Gentry as a final distribution from the liquidation of the partnership.

Follow My Example 12-5

Gentry's equity prior to liquidation		$100,000
Realization of asset sale	$220,000	
Book value of assets ($50,000 + $100,000 + $20,000)	170,000	
Gain on liquidation	$ 50,000	
Gentry's share of gain (50% × $50,000)		25,000
Gentry's cash distribution		$125,000

Practice Exercises: PE 12-5A, PE 12-5B

Loss on Realization—Capital Deficiency

The share of a loss on realization may be greater than the balance in a partner's capital account. The resulting debit balance in the capital account is called a **deficiency**. It represents a claim of the partnership against the partner.

To illustrate, assume that Farley, Green, and Hall sell all noncash assets for $10,000. Thus, a loss of $54,000 ($64,000 – $10,000) is realized. The liquidation of the partnership is as follows:

- Step 1. Sale of assets: $10,000 is realized from the sale of all the noncash assets.
- Step 2. Division of loss: The loss of $54,000 is distributed to Farley, Green, and Hall in the income-sharing ratio of 5:3:2. The partner capital accounts are debited as follows:

Farley	$27,000 ($54,000 × 50%)
Green	16,200 ($54,000 × 30%)
Hall	10,800 ($54,000 × 20%)

- Step 3. Payment of liabilities: Creditors are paid $9,000.
- Step 4. Distribution of cash to partners: The share of the loss allocated to Farley, $27,000 (50% x $54,000), exceeds the $22,000 balance in her capital account. This $5,000 deficiency represents an amount that Farley owes the partnership. Assuming that Farley pays the deficiency, the cash of $17,000 is distributed to the partners according to their capital balances as follows:

Farley	$ 0
Green	5,800
Hall	11,200

The steps in liquidating the partnership are summarized in the statement of partnership liquidation shown in Exhibit 7.

EXHIBIT 7 **Statement of Partnership Liquidation: Loss on Realization—Capital Deficiency**

Farley, Green, and Hall
Statement of Partnership Liquidation
For Period April 10–30, 2016

						Capital	
		Cash +	**Noncash Assets** =	**Liabilities** +	**Farley (50%)** +	**Green (30%)** +	**Hall (20%)**
	Balances before realization	$11,000	$64,000	$9,000	$22,000	$22,000	$22,000
Steps 1–2 →	Sale of assets and division of loss	+10,000	−64,000		−27,000	−16,200	−10,800
	Balances after realization	$21,000	$ 0	$9,000	$(5,000)	$ 5,800	$11,200
Step 3 →	Payment of liabilities	− 9,000		−9,000			
	Balances after payment of liabilities	$12,000	$ 0	$ 0	$(5,000)	$ 5,800	$11,200
Step 4 →	Receipt of deficiency	+ 5,000			+ 5,000		
	Balances	$17,000	$ 0	$ 0	$ 0	$ 5,800	$11,200
Step 4 →	Cash distributed to partners	−17,000				− 5,800	−11,200
	Final balances	$ 0	$ 0	$ 0	$ 0	$ 0	$ 0

The entries to liquidate the partnership are as follows:

Sale of assets (Step 1):

LLC		
Cash	*10,000*	
Loss on Realization	*54,000*	
Noncash Assets		*64,000*

Cash	10,000	
Loss on Realization	54,000	
Noncash Assets		64,000

Division of loss (Step 2):

LLC		
Jean Farley, Member Equity	*27,000*	
Brad Green, Member Equity	*16,200*	
Alice Hall, Member Equity	*10,800*	
Loss on Realization		*54,000*

Jean Farley, Capital	27,000	
Brad Green, Capital	16,200	
Alice Hall, Capital	10,800	
Loss on Realization		54,000

Payment of liabilities (Step 3):

LLC		
Liabilities	*9,000*	
Cash		*9,000*

Liabilities	9,000	
Cash		9,000

Receipt of deficiency (Step 4):

LLC		
Cash	*5,000*	
Jean Farley, Member Equity		*5,000*

Cash	5,000	
Jean Farley, Capital		5,000

Distribution of cash to partners (Step 4):

LLC		
Brad Green, Member Equity	*5,800*	
Alice Hall, Member Equity	*11,200*	
Cash		*17,000*

		Brad Green, Capital		5,800	
		Alice Hall, Capital		11,200	
		Cash			17,000

If the deficient partner does not pay the partnership the deficiency, there will not be sufficient partnership cash to pay the remaining partners in full. Any uncollected deficiency becomes a loss to the partnership and is divided among the remaining partners' capital balances based on their income-sharing ratio. The cash balance will then equal the sum of the capital account balances. The cash can then be distributed to the remaining partners, based on the balances of their capital accounts.

To illustrate, assume that in the preceding example Farley could not pay her deficiency. The deficiency would be allocated to Green and Hall based on their income-sharing ratio of 3:2. The remaining cash of $12,000 would then be distributed to Green ($2,800) and Hall ($9,200), computed as follows:

	Capital Balances *Before* Deficiency	**Allocated (Deficiency)**	**Capital Balances *After* Deficiency**
Farley	$ (5,000)	$ 5,000	$ 0
Green	5,800	(3,000)*	2,800
Hall	11,200	(2,000)**	9,200
Total	$12,000		$12,000

*$3,000 = ($5,000 × 3/5) or ($5,000 × 60%)

**$2,000 = ($5,000 × 2/5) or ($5,000 × 40%)

The entries to allocate Farley's deficiency and distribute the cash are as follows:

Allocation of deficiency (Step 4):

LLC		
Brad Green, Member Equity	*3,000*	
Alice Hall, Member Equity	*2,000*	
Jean Farley, Member Equity		*5,000*

		Brad Green, Capital		3,000	
		Alice Hall, Capital		2,000	
		Jean Farley, Capital			5,000

Distribution of cash to partners (Step 4):

LLC		
Brad Green, Member Equity	*2,800*	
Alice Hall, Member Equity	*9,200*	
Cash		*12,000*

		Brad Green, Capital		2,800	
		Alice Hall, Capital		9,200	
		Cash			12,000

Example Exercise 12-6 Liquidating Partnerships—Deficiency

OBJ 4

Prior to liquidating their partnership, Short and Bain had capital accounts of $20,000 and $80,000, respectively. The partnership assets were sold for $40,000. The partnership had no liabilities. Short and Bain share income and losses equally.

a. Determine the amount of Short's deficiency.
b. Determine the amount distributed to Bain, assuming Short is unable to satisfy the deficiency.

Follow My Example 12-6

a. Short's equity prior to liquidation		$ 20,000
Realization of asset sale	$ 40,000	
Book value of assets ($20,000 + $80,000)	100,000	
Loss on liquidation	$ 60,000	
Short's share of loss (50% × $60,000)		30,000
Short's deficiency		$(10,000)

b. $40,000 ($80,000 – $30,000 share of loss – $10,000 Short deficiency)

Practice Exercises: PE 12-6A, PE 12-6B

Statement of Partnership Equity

OBJ 5 Prepare the statement of partnership equity.

Reporting changes in partnership capital accounts is similar to that for a proprietorship. The primary difference is that there is a capital account for each partner. The changes in partner capital accounts for a period of time are reported in a **statement of partnership equity**.

Exhibit 8 illustrates a statement of partnership equity for Investors Associates, a partnership of Dan Cross and Kelly Baker. Each partner's capital account is shown as a separate column. The partner capital accounts may change due to capital additions, net income, or withdrawals.

EXHIBIT 8

Statement of Partnership Equity

Investors Associates
Statement of Partnership Equity
For the Year Ended December 31, 2016

	Dan Cross, Capital	Kelly Baker, Capital	Total Partnership Capital
Balance, January 1, 2016	$245,000	$365,000	$610,000
Capital additions	50,000		50,000
Net income for the year	40,000	80,000	120,000
Less partner withdrawals	(5,000)	(45,000)	(50,000)
Balance, December 31, 2016	$330,000	$400,000	$730,000

The equity reporting for an LLC is similar to that of a partnership. Instead of a statement of partnership capital, a statement of members' equity is prepared. The **statement of members' equity** reports the changes in member equity for a period. The statement is similar to Exhibit 8, except that the columns represent member equity rather than partner equity.

Financial Analysis and Interpretation: Revenue per Employee

Analyze and interpret employee efficiency.

Many partnerships and LLCs operate as service-oriented enterprises. This is the case for many professions, such as medical, advertising, and accounting. The performance of such firms can be measured by the amount of net income per partner, as illustrated in this chapter. Another measure used to assess the performance of a service-oriented business is revenue per employee.

Revenue per employee is a measure of the efficiency of the business in generating revenues. It is computed as follows:

$$\text{Revenue per Employee} = \frac{\text{Revenue}}{\text{Number of Employees}}$$

In a partnership, the number of partners may be included with employees, or partners may be evaluated separately. Generally, the higher the revenue per employee, the more efficient the company is in generating revenue from its employees. In evaluating revenue per employee, changes over time as well as comparisons with industry peers or averages are often used.

To illustrate comparisons over time, assume Washburn & Lovett, CPAs, has the following information for two years:

	2017	2016
Revenues	$220,000,000	$180,000,000
Number of employees	1,600	1,500

For Washburn & Lovett, the revenue per employee ratio is computed for 2017 and 2016 as follows:

$$\text{Revenue per employee, 2017: } \frac{\$220{,}000{,}000}{1{,}600 \text{ employees}} = \$137{,}500 \text{ per employee}$$

$$\text{Revenue per employee, 2016: } \frac{\$180{,}000{,}000}{1{,}500 \text{ employees}} = \$120{,}000 \text{ per employee}$$

Washburn & Lovett increased revenues by $40,000,000 ($220,000,000 – $180,000,000), or 22.2% ($40,000,000 ÷ $180,000,000) from 2016 to 2017. The number of employees increased by 100, or 6.7% (100 employees ÷ 1,500 employees) between the two years. Thus, the firm increased revenues at a rate faster than the increase in employees. As a result, the revenue per employee improved from $120,000 to $137,500 between the two years, suggesting improved efficiency in generating revenues.

To illustrate comparison within an industry, the revenue per employee for **Starbucks** and **McDonald's** for a recent year are as computed as follows:

$$\text{Starbucks: } \frac{\$13{,}299{,}500{,}000}{160{,}000 \text{ employees}} = \$83{,}122 \text{ per employee}$$

$$\text{McDonald's: } \frac{\$27{,}567{,}000{,}000}{440{,}000 \text{ employees}} = \$62{,}652 \text{ per employee}$$

Starbucks is able to generate more revenues per employee than is McDonald's. Many factors may explain this difference, including relative employee efficiency, extent of part-time workforce, and product pricing.

Example Exercise 12-7 Revenue per Employee

AccuTax, CPAs earned $4,200,000 during 2016 using 20 employees. During 2017, the firm grew revenues to $4,560,000 and expanded the staff to 24 employees.

a. Determine the revenue per employee for each year.
b. Interpret the results.

Follow My Example 12-7

a. 2016: $\frac{\$4{,}200{,}000}{20 \text{ employees}} = \$210{,}000 \text{ per employee}$

2017: $\frac{\$4{,}560{,}000}{24 \text{ employees}} = \$190{,}000 \text{ per employee}$

b. While AccuTax grew revenues by $360,000 ($4,560,000 – $4,200,000), or 8.6% ($360,000 ÷ $4,200,000), the number of employees expanded by 4, or 20% (4/20). The growth in revenue was less than the growth in the number of employees; thus, the revenue per employee declined between the two years. The firm was less efficient in generating revenues from its employees in 2017.

Practice Exercises: PE 12-7A, PE 12-7B

At a Glance 12

Describe the characteristics of proprietorships, partnerships, and limited liability companies.

Key Points The advantages and disadvantages of proprietorships, partnerships, and limited liability companies are summarized in Exhibit 1.

Learning Outcomes	Example Exercises	Practice Exercises
• Identify the advantages and disadvantages of proprietorships, partnerships, and limited liability companies.		

Describe and illustrate the accounting for forming a partnership and for dividing the net income and net loss of a partnership.

Key Points When a partnership is formed, accounts are debited for contributed assets and credited for assumed liabilities, and the partner's capital account is credited for the net amount. The net income of a partnership may be divided among the partners on the basis of services rendered, interest earned on the capital account balance, and the income-sharing ratio.

Learning Outcomes	Example Exercises	Practice Exercises
• Journalize the initial formation of a partnership and establish partner capital.	EE12-1	PE12-1A, 12-1B
• Determine and journalize the income distributed to each partner.	EE12-2	PE12-2A, 12-2B

Describe and illustrate the accounting for partner admission and withdrawal.

Key Points Partnership assets should be restated to current values prior to the admission or withdrawal of a partner. A new partner may be admitted into a partnership by either purchasing an interest from an existing partner or by purchasing an interest directly from the partnership.

Learning Outcomes	Example Exercises	Practice Exercises
• Prepare for partner admission by revaluing assets to approximate current values.	EE12-3	PE12-3A, 12-3B
• Distinguish between partner admission through purchase from an existing partner or purchase from the partnership.	EE12-3	PE12-3A, 12-3B
• Determine partner bonuses.	EE12-4	PE12-4A, 12-4B

Describe and illustrate the accounting for liquidating a partnership.

Key Points A partnership is liquidated by the (1) sale of partnership assets (realization), (2) distribution of gain or loss on realization to the partners, (3) payments to creditors, and (4) distribution of the remaining cash to partners according to their capital account balances. A partner may be deficient when the amount of loss distribution exceeds the capital balance.

Learning Outcomes	Example Exercises	Practice Exercises
• Apply the four steps of liquidating a partnership for either gain or loss on realization.	EE12-5	PE12-5A, 12-5B
• Apply the four steps of partnership liquidation when there is a partner deficiency.	EE12-6	PE12-6A, 12-6B

Prepare the statement of partnership equity.

Key Points A statement of partnership equity reports the changes in partnership equity from capital additions, net income, and withdrawals.

Learning Outcomes	Example Exercises	Practice Exercises
• Prepare a statement of partnership equity.		

Analyze and interpret employee efficiency.

Key Points The revenue per employee ratio is calculated as the total annual revenues divided by the total employees. This ratio measures the total revenue earned by each employee and, thus, is a measure of the efficiency of each employee in revenue terms. The ratio is often used to measure efficiency trends over time and across similar firms.

Learning Outcomes	Example Exercises	Practice Exercises
• Analyze and interpret the revenue per employee ratio.	EE12-7	PE12-7A, 12-7B

Key Terms

deficiency (568)
limited liability company (LLC) (554)
liquidation (564)
partnership (553)
partnership agreement (553)
realization (564)
revenue per employee (571)
statement of members' equity (571)
statement of partnership equity (571)
statement of partnership liquidation (565)

Illustrative Problem

Radcliffe, Sonders, and Towers, who share in income and losses in the ratio of 2:3:5, decided to discontinue operations as of April 30, 2016, and liquidate their partnership. After the accounts were closed on April 30, 2016, the following trial balance was prepared:

Radcliffe, Sonders, and Towers
Post-Closing Trial Balance
April 30, 2016

	Debit Balances	Credit Balances
Cash	5,900	
Noncash Assets	109,900	
Liabilities		26,800
Radcliffe, Capital		14,600
Sonders, Capital		27,900
Towers, Capital		46,500
	115,800	115,800

Between May 1 and May 18, the noncash assets were sold for $27,400, and the liabilities were paid.

Instructions

1. Assuming that the partner with the capital deficiency pays the entire amount owed to the partnership, prepare a statement of partnership liquidation.
2. Journalize the entries to record (a) the sale of the assets, (b) the division of loss on the sale of the assets, (c) the payment of the liabilities, (d) the receipt of the deficiency, and (e) the distribution of cash to the partners.

Solution

1.

Radcliffe, Sonders, and Towers
Statement of Partnership Liquidation
For Period May 1–18, 2016

							Capital				
	Cash	+	Noncash Assets	=	Liabilities	+	Radcliffe (20%)	+	Sonders (30%)	+	Towers (50%)
Balances before realization	$ 5,900		$109,900		$26,800		$14,600		$27,900		$46,500
Sale of assets and division of loss	+27,400		−109,900				−16,500		−24,750		−41,250
Balances after realization	$33,300		$ 0		$26,800		$ (1,900)		$ 3,150		$ 5,250
Payment of liabilities	−26,800				−26,800						
Balances after payment of liabilities	$ 6,500		$ 0		$ 0		$ (1,900)		$ 3,150		$ 5,250
Receipt of deficiency	+ 1,900						+ 1,900				
Balances	$ 8,400		$ 0		$ 0		$ 0		$ 3,150		$ 5,250
Cash distributed to partners	− 8,400								− 3,150		− 5,250
Final balances	$ 0		$ 0		$ 0		$ 0		$ 0		$ 0

2.a.

	Cash		27,400	
	Loss on Realization		82,500	
	Noncash Assets			109,900

b.

	Radcliffe, Capital		16,500	
	Sonders, Capital		24,750	
	Towers, Capital		41,250	
	Loss on Realization			82,500

c.

	Liabilities		26,800	
	Cash			26,800

d.

	Cash		1,900	
	Radcliffe, Capital			1,900

e.

	Sonders, Capital		3,150	
	Towers, Capital		5,250	
	Cash			8,400

Discussion Questions

1. What are the main advantages of (a) proprietorships, (b) partnerships, and (c) limited liability companies?

2. What are the disadvantages of a partnership over a limited liability company form of organization for a profit-making business?

3. Emilio Alvarez and Graciela Zavala joined together to form a partnership. Is it possible for them to lose a greater amount than the amount of their investment in the partnership? Explain.

4. What are the major features of a partnership agreement for a partnership, or an operating agreement for a limited liability company?

5. Josiah Barlow, Patty DuMont, and Owen Maholic are contemplating the formation of a partnership. According to the partnership agreement, Barlow is to invest $60,000 and devote one-half time, DuMont is to invest $40,000 and devote three-fourths time, and Maholic is to make no investment and devote full time. Would Maholic be correct in assuming

that, since he is not contributing any assets to the firm, he is risking nothing? Explain.

6. During the current year, Marsha Engles withdrew $4,000 monthly from the partnership of Engles and Cox Water Management Consultants. Is it possible that her share of partnership net income for the current year might be more or less than $48,000? Explain.
7. a. What accounts are debited and credited to record a partner's cash withdrawal in lieu of salary?

   b. The articles of partnership provide for a salary allowance of $6,000 per month to partner C. If C withdrew only $4,000 per month, would this affect the division of the partnership net income?

   c. At the end of the fiscal year, what accounts are debited and credited to record the division of net income among partners?
8. Explain the difference between the admission of a new partner to a partnership (a) by purchase of an interest from another partner and (b) by contribution of assets to the partnership.
9. Why is it important to state all partnership assets in terms of current prices at the time of the admission of a new partner?
10. Why might a partnership pay a bonus to a newly admitted partner?

Practice Exercises

EE 12-1 p. 555

PE 12-1A Journalizing partner's original investment OBJ. 2

SHOW ME HOW

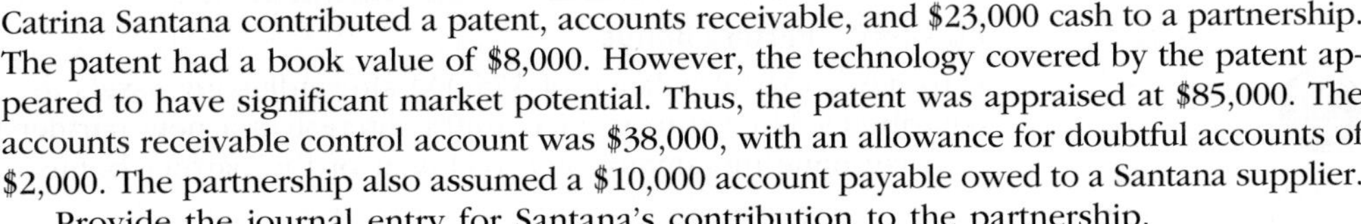

Catrina Santana contributed a patent, accounts receivable, and $23,000 cash to a partnership. The patent had a book value of $8,000. However, the technology covered by the patent appeared to have significant market potential. Thus, the patent was appraised at $85,000. The accounts receivable control account was $38,000, with an allowance for doubtful accounts of $2,000. The partnership also assumed a $10,000 account payable owed to a Santana supplier.

Provide the journal entry for Santana's contribution to the partnership.

EE 12-1 p. 555

PE 12-1B Journalizing partner's original investment OBJ. 2

SHOW ME HOW

Austin Fisher contributed land, inventory, and $36,000 cash to a partnership. The land had a book value of $120,000 and a market value of $175,000. The inventory had a book value of $50,000 and a market value of $42,000. The partnership also assumed a $35,000 note payable owed by Fisher that was used originally to purchase the land.

Provide the journal entry for Fisher's contribution to the partnership.

EE 12-2 p. 558

PE 12-2A Dividing partnership net income OBJ. 2

SHOW ME HOW

Han Lee and Monica Andrews formed a partnership, dividing income as follows:

1. Annual salary allowance to Lee of $32,000.
2. Interest of 4% on each partner's capital balance on January 1.
3. Any remaining net income divided to Lee and Andrews, 2:1.

Lee and Andrews had $80,000 and $150,000, respectively, in their January 1 capital balances. Net income for the year was $64,000.

How much net income should be distributed to Lee and Andrews?

EE 12-2 p. 558

PE 12-2B Dividing partnership net income OBJ. 2

SHOW ME HOW

John Prado and Ayana Nicks formed a partnership, dividing income as follows:

1. Annual salary allowance to Prado, $10,000 and Nicks, $28,000.
2. Interest of 5% on each partner's capital balance on January 1.
3. Any remaining net income divided equally.

(Continued)

Prado and Nicks had $20,000 and $50,000, respectively, in their January 1 capital balances. Net income for the year was $30,000.

How much net income should be distributed to Prado and Nicks?

EE 12-3 p. 561

PE 12-3A Revaluing and contributing assets to a partnership **OBJ. 3**

SHOW ME HOW

Aasif Safar purchased one-half of Michael Thorton's interest in the Vale and Thorton partnership for $34,000. Prior to the investment, land was revalued to a market value of $150,000 from a book value of $80,000. Tony Vale and Michael Thorton share net income equally. Thorton had a capital balance of $28,000 prior to these transactions.

a. Provide the journal entry for the revaluation of land.

b. Provide the journal entry to admit Safar.

EE 12-3 p. 561

PE 12-3B Revaluing and contributing assets to a partnership **OBJ. 3**

SHOW ME HOW

Demarco Lee invested $60,000 in the Camden and Sayler partnership for ownership equity of $60,000. Prior to the investment, equipment was revalued to a market value of $39,000 from a book value of $30,000. Kevin Camden and Chloe Sayler share net income in a 2:1 ratio.

a. Provide the journal entry for the revaluation of equipment.

b. Provide the journal entry to admit Lee.

EE 12-4 p. 563

PE 12-4A Partner bonus **OBJ. 3**

SHOW ME HOW

Bellows has a capital balance of $200,000 after adjusting assets to fair market value. Rodriguez contributes $340,000 to receive a 60% interest in a new partnership with Bellows.

Determine the amount and recipient of the partner bonus.

EE 12-4 p. 563

PE 12-4B Partner bonus **OBJ. 3**

SHOW ME HOW

Hiro has a capital balance of $75,000 after adjusting assets to fair market value. Marone contributes $20,000 to receive a 40% interest in a new partnership with Hiro.

Determine the amount and recipient of the partner bonus.

EE 12-5 p. 568

PE 12-5A Liquidating partnerships **OBJ. 4**

SHOW ME HOW

Prior to liquidating their partnership, Parker and Xi had capital accounts of $40,000 and $75,000, respectively. Prior to liquidation, the partnership had no cash assets other than what was realized from the sale of assets. These partnership assets were sold for $155,000. The partnership had $10,000 of liabilities. Parker and Xi share income and losses equally. Determine the amount received by Parker as a final distribution from liquidation of the partnership.

EE 12-5 p. 568

PE 12-5B Liquidating partnerships **OBJ. 4**

SHOW ME HOW

Prior to liquidating their partnership, Manning and Adamo had capital accounts of $240,000 and $150,000, respectively. Prior to liquidation, the partnership had no cash assets other than what was realized from the sale of assets. These partnership assets were sold for $410,000. The partnership had $80,000 of liabilities. Manning and Adamo share income and losses equally. Determine the amount received by Manning as a final distribution from liquidation of the partnership.

EE 12-6 p. 570

PE 12-6A Liquidating partnerships—deficiency **OBJ. 4**

SHOW ME HOW

Prior to liquidating their partnership, Wakefield and Barns had capital accounts of $105,000 and $55,000, respectively. The partnership assets were sold for $40,000. The partnership had no liabilities. Wakefield and Barns share income and losses equally.

a. Determine the amount of Barns' deficiency.

b. Determine the amount distributed to Wakefield, assuming Barns is unable to satisfy the deficiency.

SHOW ME HOW

EE 12-6 *p. 570*

PE 12-6B Liquidating partnerships—deficiency **OBJ. 4**

Prior to liquidating their partnership, Bonilla and Perez had capital accounts of $185,000 and $245,000, respectively. The partnership assets were sold for $30,000. The partnership had no liabilities. Bonilla and Perez share income and losses equally.

a. Determine the amount of Bonilla's deficiency.

b. Determine the amount distributed to Perez, assuming Bonilla is unable to satisfy the deficiency.

SHOW ME HOW

EE 12-7 *p. 572*

PE 12-7A Revenue per employee **OBJ. 6**

Niles and Cohen, CPAs earned $12,375,000 during 2016 using 75 employees. During 2017, the firm grew revenues to $15,400,000 and expanded the staff to 88 employees.

a. Determine the revenue per employee for each year.

b. Interpret the results.

SHOW ME HOW

EE 12-7 *p. 572*

PE 12-7B Revenue per employee **OBJ. 6**

Eclipse Architects earned $1,800,000 during 2016 using 12 employees. During 2017, the firm reduced revenues to $1,440,000 and reduced the staff to nine employees.

a. Determine the revenue per employee for each year.

b. Interpret the results.

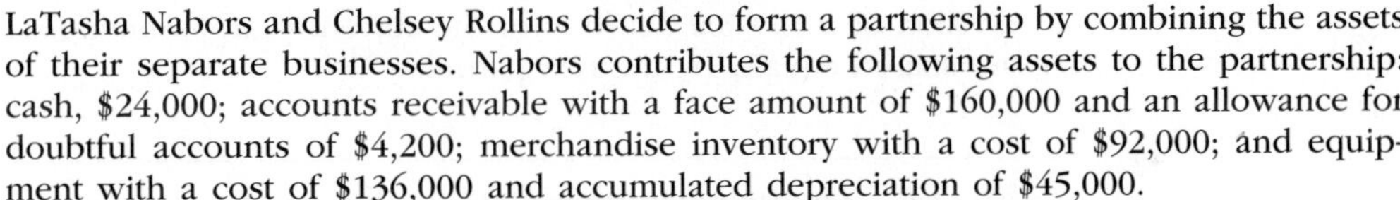

Exercises

SHOW ME HOW

EX 12-1 Recording partner's original investment **OBJ. 2**

LaTasha Nabors and Chelsey Rollins decide to form a partnership by combining the assets of their separate businesses. Nabors contributes the following assets to the partnership: cash, $24,000; accounts receivable with a face amount of $160,000 and an allowance for doubtful accounts of $4,200; merchandise inventory with a cost of $92,000; and equipment with a cost of $136,000 and accumulated depreciation of $45,000.

The partners agree that $6,000 of the accounts receivable are completely worthless and are not to be accepted by the partnership, that $4,800 is a reasonable allowance for the uncollectibility of the remaining accounts, that the merchandise inventory is to be recorded at the current market price of $104,300, and that the equipment is to be valued at $84,500.

Journalize the partnership's entry to record Nabor's investment.

SHOW ME HOW

EX 12-2 Recording partner's original investment **OBJ. 2**

Melissa Myers and Hugo Hernandez form a partnership by combining assets of their former businesses. The following balance sheet information is provided by Myers, sole proprietorship:

Cash		$ 75,000
Accounts receivable	$135,000	
Less: Allowance for doubtful accounts	7,200	127,800
Land		215,000
Equipment	$ 78,000	
Less: Accumulated depreciation—equipment	41,000	37,000
Total assets		$454,800
Accounts payable		$ 24,800
Notes payable		84,000
Melissa Myers, capital		346,000
Total liabilities and owner's equity		$454,800

(Continued)

Myers obtained appraised values for the land and equipment as follows:

Land	$300,000
Equipment	32,700

An analysis of the accounts receivable indicated that the allowance for doubtful accounts should be increased to $9,200.

Journalize the partnership's entry for Myers' investment.

EX 12-3 Dividing partnership income **OBJ. 2**

✔ b. Taylor, $187,500

SHOW ME HOW

Brittany Taylor and Piper Albright formed a partnership, investing $210,000 and $70,000, respectively. Determine their participation in the year's net income of $250,000 under each of the following independent assumptions: (a) no agreement concerning division of net income; (b) divided in the ratio of original capital investment; (c) interest at the rate of 5% allowed on original investments and the remainder divided in the ratio of 2:3; (d) salary allowances of $30,000 and $40,000, respectively, and the balance divided equally; (e) allowance of interest at the rate of 5% on original investments, salary allowances of $30,000 and $40,000, respectively, and the remainder divided equally.

EX 12-4 Dividing partnership income **OBJ. 2**

✔ c. Taylor, $43,300

SHOW ME HOW

Determine the income participation of Taylor and Albright, according to each of the five assumptions as to income division listed in Exercise 12-3, if the year's net income is $96,000.

EX 12-5 Dividing partnership net loss **OBJ. 2**

Leigh Meadows and Luke Kowalski formed a partnership in which the partnership agreement provided for salary allowances of $35,000 and $25,000, respectively. Determine the division of a $30,000 net loss for the current year, assuming remaining income or losses are shared equally by the two partners.

EX 12-6 Negotiating income-sharing ratio **OBJ. 2**

Sixty-year-old Wanda Davis retired from her computer consulting business in Boston and moved to Florida. There she met 27-year-old Ava Jain, who had just graduated from Eldon Community College with an associate degree in computer science. Wanda and Ava formed a partnership called D&J Computer Consultants. Wanda contributed $50,000 for startup costs and devoted one-half time to the business. Ava devoted full time to the business. The monthly drawings were $2,500 for Wanda and $5,000 for Ava.

At the end of the first year of operations, the two partners disagreed on the division of net income. Wanda reasoned that the division should be equal. Although she devoted only one-half time to the business, she contributed all of the startup funds. Ava reasoned that the income-sharing ratio should be 2:1 in her favor because she devoted full time to the business and her monthly drawings were twice those of Wanda.

a. Can you identify any flaws in the partners' reasoning regarding the income-sharing ratio?

b. How could an income-sharing agreement resolve this dispute?

EX 12-7 Dividing LLC income **OBJ. 2**

✔ a. Farley, $86,800

Martin Farley and Ashley Clark formed a limited liability company with an operating agreement that provided a salary allowance of $40,000 and $30,000 to each member, respectively. In addition, the operating agreement specified an income-sharing ratio of 3:2. The two members withdrew amounts equal to their salary allowances.

a. Determine the division of $148,000 net income for the year.

b. Provide journal entries to close the (1) income summary and (2) drawing accounts for the two members.

c. If the net income were less than the sum of the salary allowances, how would income be divided between the two members of the LLC?

EX 12-8 LLC net income and statement of members' equity — OBJ. 2, 5

✔ a. Sanders, $138,500

Marvel Media, LLC, has three members: WLKT Partners, Madison Sanders, and Observer Newspaper, LLC. On January 1, 2016, the three members had equity of $200,000, $40,000, and $160,000, respectively. WLKT Partners contributed an additional $50,000 to Marvel Media, LLC, on June 1, 2016. Madison Sanders received an annual salary allowance of $55,000 during 2016. The members' equity accounts are also credited with 10% interest on each member's January 1 capital balance. Any remaining income is to be shared in the ratio of 4:3:3 among the three members. The net income for Marvel Media, LLC, for 2016 was $360,000. Amounts equal to the salary and interest allowances were withdrawn by the members.

a. Determine the division of income among the three members.

b. Prepare the journal entry to close the net income and withdrawals to the individual member equity accounts.

c. Prepare a statement of members' equity for 2016.

d. What are the advantages of an income-sharing agreement for the members of this LLC?

EX 12-9 Partner income and withdrawal journal entries — OBJ. 2

The notes to the annual report for KPMG LLP (U.K.) indicated the following policies regarding the partners' capital:

> The allocation of profits to those who were partners during the financial year occurs following the finalization of the annual financial statements. During the year, partners receive monthly drawings and, from time to time, additional profit distributions. Both the monthly drawings and profit distributions represent payments on account of current-year profits and are reclaimable from partners until profits have been allocated.

Assume that the partners draw £50 million per month for 2016 and the net income for the year is £740 million. Journalize the partner capital and partner drawing control accounts in the following requirements:

a. Provide the journal entry for the monthly partner drawing for January.

b. Provide the journal entry to close the income summary account at the end of the year.

c. Provide the journal entry to close the drawing account at the end of the year.

d. Why would partner drawings be considered "reclaimable" until profits have been allocated?

EX 12-10 Admitting new partners — OBJ. 3

SHOW ME HOW

Hope Abrams and Crystal Santori are partners who share in the income equally and have capital balances of $180,000 and $62,500, respectively. Abrams, with the consent of Santori, sells one-third of her interest to David Cruz. What entry is required by the partnership if the sales price is (a) $60,000? (b) $80,000?

EX 12-11 Admitting new partners who buy an interest and contribute assets — OBJ. 3

✔ b. Henry, $112,000

SHOW ME HOW

The capital accounts of Trent Henry and Paul Chavez have balances of $140,000 and $90,000, respectively. LeAnne Gilbert and Jen Faber are to be admitted to the partnership. Gilbert buys one-fifth of Henry's interest for $30,000 and one-fourth of Chavez's interest for $20,000. Faber contributes $75,000 cash to the partnership, for which she is to receive an ownership equity of $75,000.

a. Journalize the entries to record the admission of (1) Gilbert and (2) Faber.

b. What are the capital balances of each partner after the admission of the new partners?

EX 12-12 Admitting new partner who contributes assets — OBJ. 3

✔ b. Neel, $35,000

After the tangible assets have been adjusted to current market prices, the capital accounts of Brad Paulson and Drew Webster have balances of $45,000 and $60,000, respectively.

(Continued)

Austin Neel is to be admitted to the partnership, contributing $30,000 cash to the partnership, for which he is to receive an ownership equity of $35,000. All partners share equally in income.

a. Journalize the entry to record the admission of Neel, who is to receive a bonus of $5,000.

b. What are the capital balances of each partner after the admission of the new partner?

c. Why are tangible assets adjusted to current market prices, prior to admitting a new partner?

EX 12-13 Admitting new partner with bonus **OBJ. 3**

Cody Jenkins and Jun Ito formed a partnership to provide landscaping services. Jenkins and Ito shared profits and losses equally. After all the tangible assets have been adjusted to current market prices, the capital accounts of Cody Jenkins and Jun Ito have balances of $72,000 and $38,000, respectively. Valeria Solano has expertise with using the computer to prepare landscape designs, cost estimates, and renderings. Jenkins and Ito deem these skills useful; thus, Solano is admitted to the partnership at a 30% interest for a purchase price of $30,000.

a. Determine the recipient and amount of the partner bonus.

b. Provide the journal entry to admit Solano into the partnership.

c. Why would a bonus be paid in this situation?

EX 12-14 Admitting a new LLC member with bonus **OBJ. 3**

✔ b. (2) Bonus paid to Lin, $7,500

Alert Medical, LLC, consists of two doctors, Abrams and Lipscomb, who share in all income and losses according to a 2:3 income-sharing ratio. Dr. Lin has been asked to join the LLC. Prior to admitting Lin, the assets of Alert Medical were revalued to reflect their current market values. The revaluation resulted in medical equipment being increased by $40,000. Prior to the revaluation, the equity balances for Abrams and Lipscomb were $154,000 and $208,000, respectively.

a. Provide the journal entry for the asset revaluation.

b. Provide the journal entry for the bonus under the following independent situations:

   1. Lin purchased a 30% interest in Alert Medical, LLC, for $228,000.
   2. Lin purchased a 25% interest in Alert Medical, LLC, for $124,000.

EX 12-15 Admitting new partner with bonus **OBJ. 3**

✔ b. (1) Bonus paid to Ortiz, $9,600

L. Bowers and V. Lipscomb are partners in Elegant Event Consultants. Bowers and Lipscomb share income equally. M. Ortiz will be admitted to the partnership. Prior to the admission, equipment was revalued downward by $8,000. The capital balances of each partner are $96,000 and $40,000, respectively, prior to the revaluation.

a. Provide the journal entry for the asset revaluation.

b. Provide the journal entry for Ortiz's admission under the following independent situations:

   1. Ortiz purchased a 20% interest for $20,000.
   2. Ortiz purchased a 30% interest for $60,000.

EX 12-16 Partner bonuses, statement of partners' equity **OBJ. 2, 3, 5**

✔ Dennis Overton, Capital, Dec. 31, 2016, $226,400

The partnership of Angel Investor Associates began operations on January 1, 2016, with contributions from two partners as follows:

Dennis Overton	$180,000
Ben Testerman	120,000

The following additional partner transactions took place during the year:

1. In early January, Randy Campbell is admitted to the partnership by contributing $75,000 cash for a 20% interest.

2. Net income of $150,000 was earned in 2016. In addition, Dennis Overton received a salary allowance of $40,000 for the year. The three partners agree to an income-sharing ratio equal to their capital balances after admitting Campbell.
3. The partners' withdrawals are equal to half of the increase in their capital balances from salary allowance and income.

Prepare a statement of partnership equity for the year ended December 31, 2016.

EX 12-17 Withdrawal of partner **OBJ. 3**

SHOW ME HOW

Justin Marley is to retire from the partnership of Marley and Associates as of March 31, the end of the current fiscal year. After closing the accounts, the capital balances of the partners are as follows: Justin Marley, $140,000; Cherrie Ford, $70,000; and LaMarcus Rollins, $60,000. They have shared net income and net losses in the ratio of 3:2:2. The partners agree that the merchandise inventory should be increased by $15,500, and the allowance for doubtful accounts should be increased by $1,500. Marley agrees to accept a note for $100,000 in partial settlement of his ownership equity. The remainder of his claim is to be paid in cash. Ford and Rollins are to share equally in the net income or net loss of the new partnership.

Journalize the entries to record (a) the adjustment of the assets to bring them into agreement with current market prices and (b) the withdrawal of Marley from the partnership.

EX 12-18 Statement of members' equity, admitting new member **OBJ. 2, 3, 5**

✔ a. 3:7

The statement of members' equity for Bonanza, LLC, follows:

Bonanza, LLC
Statement of Members' Equity
For the Years Ended December 31, 2016 and 2017

	Idaho Properties, LLC, Member Equity	Silver Streams, LLC, Member Equity	Thomas Dunn, Member Equity	Total Members' Equity
Members' equity, January 1, 2016	$273,000	$307,000		$ 580,000
Net income	57,000	133,000		190,000
Members' equity, December 31, 2016	$330,000	$440,000		$ 770,000
Dunn contribution, January 1, 2017	3,000	7,000	$220,000	230,000
Net income	62,500	137,500	50,000	250,000
Less member withdrawals	(32,000)	(48,000)	(40,000)	(120,000)
Members' equity, December 31, 2017	$363,500	$536,500	$230,000	$1,130,000

a. What was the income-sharing ratio in 2016?
b. What was the income-sharing ratio in 2017?
c. How much cash did Thomas Dunn contribute to Bonanza, LLC, for his interest?
d. Why do the member equity accounts of Idaho Properties, LLC, and Silver Streams, LLC, have positive entries for Thomas Dunn's contribution?
e. What percentage interest of Bonanza did Thomas Dunn acquire?
f. Why are withdrawals less than net income?

EX 12-19 Distribution of cash upon liquidation **OBJ. 4**

✔ a. $11,000 loss

Hewitt and Patel are partners, sharing gains and losses equally. They decide to terminate their partnership. Prior to realization, their capital balances are $28,000 and $18,000, respectively. After all noncash assets are sold and all liabilities are paid, there is a cash balance of $35,000.

a. What is the amount of a gain or loss on realization?
b. How should the gain or loss be divided between Hewitt and Patel?
c. How should the cash be divided between Hewitt and Patel?

EX 12-20 Distribution of cash upon liquidation

OBJ. 4

✔ Oliver, $30,000

David Oliver and Umar Ansari, with capital balances of $28,000 and $35,000, respectively, decide to liquidate their partnership. After selling the noncash assets and paying the liabilities, there is $67,000 of cash remaining. If the partners share income and losses equally, how should the cash be distributed?

EX 12-21 Liquidating partnerships—capital deficiency

OBJ. 4

✔ b. $97,500

Lewis, Zapata, and Fowler share equally in net income and net losses. After the partnership sells all assets for cash, divides the losses on realization, and pays the liabilities, the balances in the capital accounts are as follows: Lewis, $73,500 Cr.; Zapata, $41,000 Cr.; Fowler, $17,000 Dr.

a. What term is applied to the debit balance in Fowler's capital account?

b. What is the amount of cash on hand?

c. Journalize the transaction that must take place for Lewis and Zapata to receive cash in the liquidation process equal to their capital account balances.

EX 12-22 Distribution of cash upon liquidation

OBJ. 4

✔ a. Bray, $550

Bray, Lincoln, and Mapes arranged to import and sell orchid corsages for a university dance. They agreed to share equally the net income or net loss of the venture. Bray and Lincoln advanced $225 and $300 of their own respective funds to pay for advertising and other expenses. After collecting for all sales and paying creditors, the partnership has $1,500 in cash.

a. How should the money be distributed?

b. Assuming that the partnership has only $300 instead of $1,500, do any of the three partners have a capital deficiency? If so, how much?

EX 12-23 Liquidating partnerships—capital deficiency

OBJ. 4

Nettles, King, and Tanaka are partners sharing income 3:2:1. After the firm's loss from liquidation is distributed, the capital account balances were: Nettles, $15,000 Dr.; King, $46,000 Cr.; and Tanaka, $71,000 Cr. If Nettles is personally bankrupt and unable to pay any of the $15,000, what will be the amount of cash received by King and Tanaka upon liquidation?

EX 12-24 Statement of partnership liquidation

OBJ. 4, 5

SHOW ME HOW

After closing the accounts on July 1, prior to liquidating the partnership, the capital account balances of Gold, Porter, and Sims are $55,000, $45,000, and $20,000, respectively. Cash, noncash assets, and liabilities total $56,000, $96,000, and $32,000, respectively. Between July 1 and July 29, the noncash assets are sold for $90,000, the liabilities are paid, and the remaining cash is distributed to the partners. The partners share net income and loss in the ratio of 3:2:1. Prepare a statement of partnership liquidation for the period July 1–29, 2016.

EX 12-25 Statement of LLC liquidation

OBJ. 4, 5

Lester, Torres, and Hearst are members of Arcadia Sales, LLC, sharing income and losses in the ratio of 2:2:1, respectively. The members decide to liquidate the limited liability company. The members' equity prior to liquidation and asset realization on August 1, 2016, are as follows:

Lester	$ 49,000
Torres	61,000
Hearst	27,000
Total	$137,000

In winding up operations during the month of August, noncash assets with a book value of $146,000 are sold for $158,000, and liabilities of $35,000 are satisfied. Prior to realization, Arcadia Sales has a cash balance of $26,000.

a. Prepare a statement of LLC liquidation.

b. Provide the journal entry for the final cash distribution to members.

c. What is the role of the income- and loss-sharing ratio in liquidating a LLC?

✔ b. Alvarez, Capital, Dec. 31, $54,000

EX 12-26 Partnership entries and statement of partners' equity — OBJ. 2, 5

The capital accounts of Angel Alvarez and Emma Allison have balances of $47,000 and $73,000, respectively, on January 1, 2016, the beginning of the fiscal year. On March 10, Alvarez invested an additional $8,000. During the year, Alvarez and Allison withdrew $32,000 and $39,000, respectively, and net income for the year was $62,000. The articles of partnership make no reference to the division of net income.

a. Journalize the entries to close (1) the income summary account and (2) the drawing accounts.

b. Prepare a statement of partnership equity for the current year for the partnership of Alvarez and Allison.

EX 12-27 Revenue per professional staff — OBJ. 6

The accounting firm of **Deloitte & Touche** is the largest international accounting firm in the world as ranked by total revenues. For two recent years, Deloitte & Touche reported the following for its U.S. operations:

	Current Year	Previous Year
Revenue (in billions)	$13.1	$11.9
Number of professional staff (including partners)	46,243	41,187

a. For the current and previous years, determine the revenue per professional staff.

b. Interpret the trend between the two years.

F·A·I

EX 12-28 Revenue per employee — OBJ. 6

Superior Cleaning Services, LLC, provides cleaning services for office buildings. The firm has 10 members in the LLC, which did not change between 2016 and 2017. During 2017, the business terminated two commercial contracts. The following revenue and employee information is provided:

	2017	2016
Revenues (in thousands)	$16,200	$18,400
Number of employees (excluding members)	150	200

a. For 2017 and 2016, determine the revenue per employee (excluding members).

b. Interpret the trend between the two years.

Problems: Series A

✔ 3. Keene net income, $41,900

General Ledger

SHOW ME HOW

PR 12-1A Entries and balance sheet for partnership — OBJ. 2

On March 1, 2016, Eric Keene and Abigail McKee form a partnership. Keene agrees to invest $21,100 in cash and merchandise inventory valued at $55,900. McKee invests certain business assets at valuations agreed upon, transfers business liabilities, and contributes sufficient cash to bring her total capital to $60,000. Details regarding the book values of the business assets and liabilities, and the agreed valuations, follow:

(Continued)

	McKee's Ledger Balance	Agreed-Upon Valuation
Accounts Receivable	$18,900	$18,000
Allowance for Doubtful Accounts	1,200	1,500
Equipment	83,500	54,900
Accumulated Depreciation—Equipment	29,800	
Accounts Payable	15,000	15,000
Notes Payable (current)	36,000	36,000

The partnership agreement includes the following provisions regarding the division of net income: interest on original investments at 10%, salary allowances of $22,500 (Keene) and $30,400 (McKee), and the remainder equally.

Instructions

1. Journalize the entries to record the investments of Keene and McKee in the partnership accounts.
2. Prepare a balance sheet as of March 1, 2016, the date of formation of the partnership of Keene and McKee.
3. After adjustments and the closing of revenue and expense accounts at February 28, 2017, the end of the first full year of operations, the income summary account has a credit balance of $90,000, and the drawing accounts have debit balances of $28,000 (Keene) and $30,400 (McKee). Journalize the entries to close the income summary account and the drawing accounts at February 28, 2017.

✔ 1. f. Morrison net income, $40,400

SHOW ME HOW

PR 12-2A Dividing partnership income

OBJ. 2

Morrison and Amato have decided to form a partnership. They have agreed that Morrison is to invest $150,000 and that Amato is to invest $50,000. Morrison is to devote one-half time to the business and Amato is to devote full time. The following plans for the division of income are being considered:

a. Equal division.
b. In the ratio of original investments.
c. In the ratio of time devoted to the business.
d. Interest of 12% on original investments and the remainder equally.
e. Interest of 12% on original investments, salary allowances of $30,000 to Morrison and $64,000 to Amato, and the remainder equally.
f. Plan (e), except that Amato is also to be allowed a bonus equal to 20% of the amount by which net income exceeds the total salary allowances.

Instructions

For each plan, determine the division of the net income under each of the following assumptions: (1) net income of $105,000 and (2) net income of $180,000. Present the data in tabular form, using the following columnar headings:

	$105,000		$180,000	
Plan	Morrison	Amato	Morrison	Amato

✔ 2. Dec. 31 capital—Yost, $125,000

PR 12-3A Financial statements for partnership

OBJ. 2, 5

The ledger of Tyler Lambert and Jayla Yost, attorneys-at-law, contains the following accounts and balances after adjustments have been recorded on December 31, 2016:

Lambert and Yost
Trial Balance
December 31, 2016

	Debit Balances	Credit Balances
Cash	34,000	
Accounts Receivable	47,800	
Supplies	2,000	
Land	120,000	
Building	157,500	
Accumulated Depreciation—Building		67,200
Office Equipment	63,600	
Accumulated Depreciation—Office Equipment		21,700
Accounts Payable		27,900
Salaries Payable		5,100
Tyler Lambert, Capital		135,000
Tyler Lambert, Drawing	50,000	
Jayla Yost, Capital		88,000
Jayla Yost, Drawing	60,000	
Professional Fees		395,300
Salary Expense	154,500	
Depreciation Expense—Building	15,700	
Property Tax Expense	12,000	
Heating and Lighting Expense	8,500	
Supplies Expense	6,000	
Depreciation Expense—Office Equipment	5,000	
Miscellaneous Expense	3,600	
	740,200	740,200

The balance in Yost's capital account includes an additional investment of $10,000 made on April 10, 2016.

Instructions

1. Prepare an income statement for 2016, indicating the division of net income. The partnership agreement provides for salary allowances of $45,000 to Lambert and $54,700 to Yost, allowances of 10% on each partner's capital balance at the beginning of the fiscal year, and equal division of the remaining net income or net loss.
2. Prepare a statement of partnership equity for 2016.
3. Prepare a balance sheet as of the end of 2016.

✓ 3. Total assets, $326,300

PR 12-4A Admitting new partner

OBJ. 3

Musa Moshref and Shaniqua Hollins have operated a successful firm for many years, sharing net income and net losses equally. Taylor Anderson is to be admitted to the partnership on July 1 of the current year, in accordance with the following agreement:

a. Assets and liabilities of the old partnership are to be valued at their book values as of June 30, except for the following:
   - Accounts receivable amounting to $2,500 are to be written off, and the allowance for doubtful accounts is to be increased to 5% of the remaining accounts.
   - Merchandise inventory is to be valued at $76,600.
   - Equipment is to be valued at $155,700.

b. Anderson is to purchase $70,000 of the ownership interest of Hollins for $75,000 cash and to contribute another $45,000 cash to the partnership for a total ownership equity of $115,000.

(Continued)

The post-closing trial balance of Moshref and Hollins as of June 30 is as follows:

Moshref and Hollins
Post-Closing Trial Balance
June 30, 2016

	Debit Balances	Credit Balances
Cash	8,000	
Accounts Receivable	42,500	
Allowance for Doubtful Accounts		1,600
Merchandise Inventory	72,000	
Prepaid Insurance	3,000	
Equipment	180,500	
Accumulated Depreciation—Equipment		43,100
Accounts Payable		21,300
Notes Payable (current)		35,000
Musa Moshref, Capital		120,000
Shaniqua Hollins, Capital		85,000
	306,000	306,000

Instructions

1. Journalize the entries as of June 30 to record the revaluations, using a temporary account entitled Asset Revaluations. The balance in the accumulated depreciation account is to be eliminated. After journalizing the revaluations, close the balance of the asset revaluations account to the capital accounts of Musa Moshref and Shaniqua Hollins.
2. Journalize the additional entries to record Anderson's entrance to the partnership on July 1, 2016.
3. Present a balance sheet for the new partnership as of July 1, 2016.

PR 12-5A Statement of partnership liquidation

OBJ. 4

After the accounts are closed on February 3, 2016, prior to liquidating the partnership, the capital accounts of William Gerloff, Joshua Chu, and Courtney Jewett are $19,300, $4,500, and $22,300, respectively. Cash and noncash assets total $5,200 and $55,900, respectively. Amounts owed to creditors total $15,000. The partners share income and losses in the ratio of 2:1:1. Between February 3 and February 28, the noncash assets are sold for $34,300, the partner with the capital deficiency pays the deficiency to the partnership, and the liabilities are paid.

Instructions

1. Prepare a statement of partnership liquidation, indicating (a) the sale of assets and division of loss, (b) the payment of liabilities, (c) the receipt of the deficiency (from the appropriate partner), and (d) the distribution of cash.
2. Assume the partner with the capital deficiency declares bankruptcy and is unable to pay the deficiency. Journalize the entries to (a) allocate the partner's deficiency and (b) distribute the remaining cash.

PR 12-6A Statement of partnership liquidation

OBJ. 4

On November 1, 2016, the firm of Sails, Welch, and Greenberg decided to liquidate their partnership. The partners have capital balances of $58,000, $72,000, and $10,000, respectively. The cash balance is $32,000, the book values of noncash assets total $128,000, and liabilities total $20,000. The partners share income and losses in the ratio of 2:2:1.

Instructions

1. Prepare a statement of partnership liquidation, covering the period November 1–30, 2016, for each of the following independent assumptions:
   a. All of the noncash assets are sold for $156,000 in cash, the creditors are paid, and the remaining cash is distributed to the partners.

b. All of the noncash assets are sold for $55,000 in cash, the creditors are paid, the partner with the debit capital balance pays the amount owed to the firm, and the remaining cash is distributed to the partners.

2. Assume the partner with the capital deficiency in part (b) declares bankruptcy and is unable to pay the deficiency. Journalize the entries to (a) allocate the partner's deficiency and (b) distribute the remaining cash.

Problems: Series B

PR 12-1B Entries and balance sheet for partnership

OBJ. 2

✔ 3. Lang net income, $63,400

General Ledger

SHOW ME HOW

On April 1, 2015, Whitney Lang and Eli Capri form a partnership. Lang agrees to invest $18,000 cash and merchandise inventory valued at $50,000. Capri invests certain business assets at valuations agreed upon, transfers business liabilities, and contributes sufficient cash to bring his total capital to $120,000. Details regarding the book values of the business assets and liabilities, and the agreed valuations, follow:

	Capri's Ledger Balance	Agreed-Upon Balance
Accounts Receivable	$45,700	$43,400
Allowance for Doubtful Accounts	3,200	3,500
Merchandise Inventory	31,500	28,900
Equipment	89,500	63,400
Accumulated Depreciation—Equipment	19,000	
Accounts Payable	23,400	23,400
Notes Payable (current)	15,000	15,000

The partnership agreement includes the following provisions regarding the division of net income: interest of 10% on original investments, salary allowances of $36,000 (Lang) and $22,000 (Capri), and the remainder equally.

Instructions

1. Journalize the entries to record the investments of Lang and Capri in the partnership accounts.
2. Prepare a balance sheet as of April 1, 2015, the date of formation of the partnership of Lang and Capri.
3. After adjustments and the closing of revenue and expense accounts at March 31, 2016, the end of the first full year of operations, the income summary account has a credit balance of $118,000, and the drawing accounts have debit balances of $40,000 (Lang) and $30,000 (Capri). Journalize the entries to close the income summary account and the drawing accounts at March 31, 2016.

PR 12-2B Dividing partnership income

OBJ. 2

✔ 1. f. Howell net income, $254,550

SHOW ME HOW

Dylan Howell and Demond Nickles have decided to form a partnership. They have agreed that Howell is to invest $50,000 and that Nickles is to invest $75,000. Howell is to devote full time to the business, and Nickles is to devote one-half time. The following plans for the division of income are being considered:

a. Equal division.
b. In the ratio of original investments.
c. In the ratio of time devoted to the business.
d. Interest of 10% on original investments and the remainder in the ratio of 3:2.
e. Interest of 10% on original investments, salary allowances of $38,000 to Howell and $19,000 to Nickles, and the remainder equally.
f. Plan (e), except that Howell is also to be allowed a bonus equal to 20% of the amount by which net income exceeds the total salary allowances.

(Continued)

Instructions

For each plan, determine the division of the net income under each of the following assumptions: (1) net income of $420,000 and (2) net income of $150,000. Present the data in tabular form, using the following columnar headings:

	$420,000		$150,000	
Plan	**Howell**	**Nickles**	**Howell**	**Nickles**

PR 12-3B Financial statements for partnerships

OBJ. 2, 5

✔ 2. Dec. 31 capital—Xue, $179,100

✔ 3. Total assets, $173,900

The ledger of Camila Ramirez and Ping Xue, attorneys-at-law, contains the following accounts and balances after adjustments have been recorded on December 31, 2016:

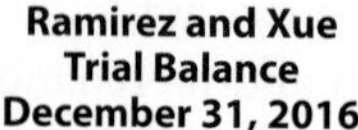

Ramirez and Xue
Trial Balance
December 31, 2016

	Debit Balances	Credit Balances
Cash	70,300	
Accounts Receivable	33,600	
Supplies	5,800	
Land	128,000	
Building	175,000	
Accumulated Depreciation—Building		80,000
Office Equipment	42,000	
Accumulated Depreciation—Office Equipment		25,300
Accounts Payable		12,400
Salaries Payable		10,000
Camila Ramirez, Capital		125,000
Camila Ramirez, Drawing	35,000	
Ping Xue, Capital		155,000
Ping Xue, Drawing	50,000	
Professional Fees		555,300
Salary Expense	384,900	
Depreciation Expense—Building	12,900	
Heating and Lighting Expense	10,500	
Depreciation Expense—Office Equipment	6,300	
Property Tax Expense	3,200	
Supplies Expense	3,000	
Miscellaneous Expense	2,500	
	963,000	963,000

The balance in Xue's capital account includes an additional investment of $20,000 made on May 5, 2016.

Instructions

1. Prepare an income statement for the current fiscal year, indicating the division of net income. The partnership agreement provides for salary allowances of $50,000 to Ramirez and $65,000 to Xue, allowances of 12% on each partner's capital balance at the beginning of the fiscal year, and equal division of the remaining net income or net loss.
2. Prepare a statement of partnership equity for 2016.
3. Prepare a balance sheet as of the end of 2016.

PR 12-4B Admitting new partner

OBJ. 3

Brian Caldwell and Adriana Estrada have operated a successful firm for many years, sharing net income and net losses equally. Kris Mays is to be admitted to the partnership on September 1 of the current year, in accordance with the following agreement:

a. Assets and liabilities of the old partnership are to be valued at their book values as of August 31, except for the following:
   - Accounts receivable amounting to $1,500 are to be written off, and the allowance for doubtful accounts is to be increased to 5% of the remaining accounts.
   - Merchandise inventory is to be valued at $46,800.
   - Equipment is to be valued at $64,500.

b. Mays is to purchase $26,000 of the ownership interest of Estrada for $30,000 cash and to contribute $32,000 cash to the partnership for a total ownership equity of $58,000.

The post-closing trial balance of Caldwell and Estrada as of August 31 follows:

Caldwell and Estrada
Post-Closing Trial Balance
August 31, 2016

	Debit Balances	Credit Balances
Cash	12,300	
Accounts Receivable	19,500	
Allowance for Doubtful Accounts		600
Merchandise Inventory	42,500	
Prepaid Insurance	1,200	
Equipment	67,500	
Accumulated Depreciation—Equipment		15,500
Accounts Payable		8,900
Notes Payable (current)		15,000
Brian Caldwell, Capital		55,000
Adriana Estrada, Capital		48,000
	143,000	143,000

Instructions

1. Journalize the entries as of August 31 to record the revaluations, using a temporary account entitled Asset Revaluations. The balance in the accumulated depreciation account is to be eliminated. After journalizing the revaluations, close the balance of the asset revaluations account to the capital accounts of Brian Caldwell and Adriana Estrada.
2. Journalize the additional entries to record Mays' entrance to the partnership on September 1, 2016.
3. Present a balance sheet for the new partnership as of September 1, 2016.

PR 12-5B Statement of partnership liquidation

OBJ. 4

After the accounts are closed on April 10, 2016, prior to liquidating the partnership, the capital accounts of Zach Fairchild, Austin Lowes, and Amber Howard are $42,000, $7,500, and $36,500, respectively. Cash and noncash assets total $23,500 and $84,500, respectively. Amounts owed to creditors total $22,000. The partners share income and losses in the ratio of 1:1:2. Between April 10 and April 30, the noncash assets are sold for $48,500, the partner with the capital deficiency pays the deficiency to the partnership, and the liabilities are paid.

Instructions

1. Prepare a statement of partnership liquidation, indicating (a) the sale of assets and division of loss, (b) the payment of liabilities, (c) the receipt of the deficiency (from the appropriate partner), and (d) the distribution of cash.
2. Assume the partner with the capital deficiency declares bankruptcy and is unable to pay the deficiency. Journalize the entries to (a) allocate the partner's deficiency and (b) distribute the remaining cash.

PR 12-6B Statement of partnership liquidation

OBJ. 4

On August 3, 2016, the firm of Chapelle, Rock, and Pryor decided to liquidate their partnership. The partners have capital balances of $14,000, $102,000, and $86,000, respectively. The cash balance is $65,000, the book values of noncash assets total $167,000, and liabilities total $30,000. The partners share income and losses in the ratio of 1:2:2.

Instructions

1. Prepare a statement of partnership liquidation, covering the period August 3–29, 2016, for each of the following independent assumptions:
   a. All of the noncash assets are sold for $217,000 in cash, the creditors are paid, and the remaining cash is distributed to the partners.
   b. All of the noncash assets are sold for $72,000 in cash, the creditors are paid, the partner with the debit capital balance pays the amount owed to the firm, and the remaining cash is distributed to the partners.
2. Assume the partner with the capital deficiency in part (b) declares bankruptcy and is unable to pay the deficiency. Journalize the entries to (a) allocate the partner's deficiency and (b) distribute the remaining cash.

Cases & Projects

CP 12-1 Partnership agreement

Taye Barrow, M.D., and James Robbins, M.D., are sole owners of two medical practices that operate in the same medical building. The two doctors agree to combine assets and liabilities of the two businesses to form a partnership. The partnership agreement calls for dividing income equally between the two doctors. After several months, the following conversation takes place between the two doctors:

Barrow: I've noticed that your patient load has dropped over the last couple of months. When we formed our partnership, we were seeing about the same number of patients per week. However, now our patient records show that you have been seeing about half as many patients as I have. Are there any issues that I should be aware of?

Robbins: There's nothing going on. When I was working on my own, I was really putting in the hours. One of the reasons I formed this partnership was to enjoy life a little more and scale back a little bit.

Barrow: I see. Well, I find that I'm working as hard as I did when I was on my own, yet making less than I did previously. Essentially, you're sharing in half of my billings and I'm sharing in half of yours. Since you are working much less than I am, I end up on the short end of the bargain.

Robbins: Well, I don't know what to say. An agreement is an agreement. The partnership is based on a 50/50 split. That's what a partnership is all about.

Barrow: If that's so, then it applies equally well on the effort end of the equation as on the income end.

Discuss whether Robbins is acting in an ethical manner. How could Barrow renegotiate the partnership agreement to avoid this dispute?

CP 12-2 Dividing partnership income

Terry Willard and Jasmine Hill decide to form a partnership. Willard will contribute $300,000 to the partnership, while Hill will contribute only $30,000. However, Hill will be responsible for running the day-to-day operations of the partnership, which are anticipated to require about 45 hours per week. In contrast, Willard will only work five hours per week for the partnership. The two partners are attempting to determine a formula for dividing partnership net income. Willard believes the partners should divide income in the ratio of 7:3, favoring Willard, since Willard provides the majority of the capital. Hill believes the income should be divided 7:3, favoring Hill, since Hill provides the majority of effort in running the partnership business.

How would you advise the partners in developing a method for dividing income?

CP 12-3 Revenue per employee

The following table shows key operating statistics for the four largest public accounting firms:

	U.S. Net Revenues (in millions)	No. of Partners
Deloitte & Touche	$13,067	2,949
PwC	9,552	2,350
Ernst & Young	8,200	2,500
KPMG	5,753	1,775

Source: The 2013 *Accounting Today* Top 100 Firms.

a. Determine the revenue per partner for each firm. Round to the nearest dollar.

b. Interpret the differences between the firms in terms of your answer in (a) and the table information.

CP 12-4 Partnership agreement

General Ledger

Lindsey Wilson has agreed to invest $200,000 into an LLC with Lacy Lovett and Justin Lassiter. Lovett and Lassiter will not invest any money but will provide effort and expertise to the LLC. Lovett and Lassiter have agreed that the net income of the LLC should be divided so that Wilson is to receive a 10% preferred return on her capital investment prior to any remaining income being divided equally among the partners. In addition, Lovett and Lassiter have suggested that the operating agreement be written so that all matters are settled by majority vote, with each partner having a one-third voting interest in the LLC.

If you were providing Lindsey Wilson counsel, what might you suggest in forming the final agreement?

GOOG
Google
GOOGLE INC.
INCORPORATED UNDER THE LAWS OF THE STATE OF DELAWARE
CUSIP
SEE REVERSE SI
GGLAV
THIS CERTIFICATE IS TRANSFERABLE IN CANTON, MA, JERSEY CITY, NJ OR NEW YORK, NY
THIS CERTIFIES THAT
One
IS THE OWNER OF
FULLY PAID AND NON-ASSESSABLE SHARES OF CLASS A COMMON STOCK, PAR VALUE $0.001 PER SHARE, OF
GOOGLE INC.
transferable only on the books of the Corporation by the holder hereof in person or by duly authorized Attorney upon surrender of this certificate properly endorsed. This certificate is not valid until countersigned and registered by the Transfer Agent and Registrar.
WITNESS the facsimile seal of the Corporation and the facsimile signatures of its duly authorized officers.
Dated:
September 13
PRESIDENT AND ASSISTANT SECRETARY
GOOGLE INC. CORPORATE SEAL OCT. 22, 2002 DELAWARE
PRESIDENT AND ASSISTANT SECRETARY
WWW.GIVEASHARE.COM
COUNTERSIGNED AND REGISTERED:
EQUISERVE TRUST COMPANY, N.A.
TRANSFER AGENT AND REGISTRAR
BY:
AUTHORIZED SIGNATURE

CHAPTER 13

Corporations: Organization, Stock Transactions, and Dividends

Google

If you purchase a share of stock from **Google**, you own a small interest in the company. You may request a Google stock certificate as an indication of your ownership.

Google is one of the most visible companies on the Internet. Many of us cannot visit the Web without using Google to power a search or to retrieve our e-mail using Google's gmail. Yet Google's Internet tools are free to online browsers. Google generates most of its revenue through online advertising.

Purchasing a share of stock from Google may be a great gift idea for the "hard-to-shop-for person." However, a stock certificate represents more than just a picture that you can frame. In fact, the stock certificate is a document that reflects legal ownership of the future financial prospects of Google. In addition, as a shareholder, it represents your claim against the assets and earnings of the corporation.

If you are purchasing Google stock as an investment, you should analyze Google's financial statements and management's plans for the future. For example, Google first offered its stock to the public on August 19, 2004, for $100 per share. Google's stock recently sold for more than $1,000 per share, even though it pays no dividends. In addition, Google recently expanded into developing and offering free software platforms for mobile devices such as cell phones. For example, your cell phone may use Google's Android™ operating system. So, should you purchase Google stock?

This chapter describes and illustrates the nature of corporations, including the accounting for stock and dividends. This discussion will aid you in making decisions such as whether or not to buy stock in a company.

Learning Objectives

After studying this chapter, you should be able to:

Objective	Example Exercises
OBJ 1 Describe the nature of the corporate form of organization.	
Nature of a Corporation	
Characteristics of a Corporation	
Forming a Corporation	
OBJ 2 Describe the two main sources of stockholders' equity.	
Stockholders' Equity	
OBJ 3 Describe and illustrate the characteristics of stock, classes of stock, and entries for issuing stock.	
Paid-In Capital from Issuing Stock	
Characteristics of Stock	
Classes of Stock	EE 13-1
Issuing Stock	EE 13-2
Premium on Stock	EE 13-2
No-Par Stock	EE 13-2
OBJ 4 Describe and illustrate the accounting for cash dividends and stock dividends.	
Accounting for Dividends	
Cash Dividends	EE 13-3
Stock Dividends	EE 13-4
OBJ 5 Describe and illustrate the accounting for treasury stock transactions.	
Treasury Stock Transactions	EE 13-5
OBJ 6 Describe and illustrate the reporting of stockholders' equity.	
Reporting Stockholders' Equity	
Stockholders' Equity on the Balance Sheet	EE 13-6
Reporting Retained Earnings	EE 13-7
Statement of Stockholders' Equity	
Reporting Stockholders' Equity for Mornin' Joe	
OBJ 7 Describe the effect of stock splits on corporate financial statements.	
Stock Splits	
OBJ 8 Describe and illustrate the use of earnings per share in evaluating a company's profitability.	
Financial Analysis and Interpretation: Earnings per Share	EE 13-8

At a Glance 13 Page 617

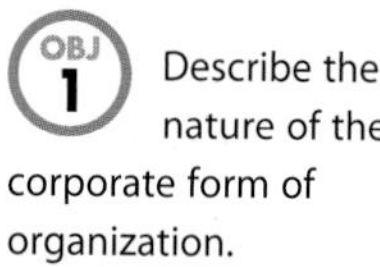

OBJ 1 Describe the nature of the corporate form of organization.

Nature of a Corporation

Most large businesses are organized as corporations. As a result, corporations generate more than 90% of the total business dollars in the United States. In contrast, most small businesses are organized as proprietorships, partnerships, or limited liability companies.

Characteristics of a Corporation

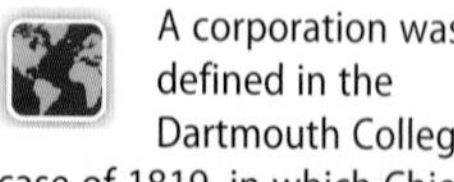

A corporation was defined in the Dartmouth College case of 1819, in which Chief Justice Marshall of the U.S. Supreme Court stated: "A corporation is an artificial being, invisible, intangible, and existing only in contemplation of the law."

A *corporation* is a legal entity, distinct and separate from the individuals who create and operate it. As a legal entity, a corporation may acquire, own, and dispose of property in its own name. It may also incur liabilities and enter into contracts. Most importantly, it can sell shares of ownership, called **stock**. This characteristic gives corporations the ability to raise large amounts of capital.

The **stockholders** or *shareholders* who own the stock own the corporation. They can buy and sell stock without affecting the corporation's operations or continued existence. Corporations whose shares of stock are traded in public markets are called *public corporations*. Corporations whose shares are not traded publicly are usually owned by a small group of investors and are called *nonpublic* or *private corporations*.

The stockholders of a corporation have *limited liability*. This means that creditors usually may not go beyond the assets of the corporation to satisfy their claims. Thus, the financial loss that a stockholder may suffer is limited to the amount invested.

The stockholders control a corporation by electing a *board of directors*. This board meets periodically to establish corporate policies. It also selects the chief executive officer (CEO) and other major officers to manage the corporation's day-to-day affairs. Exhibit 1 shows the organizational structure of a corporation.

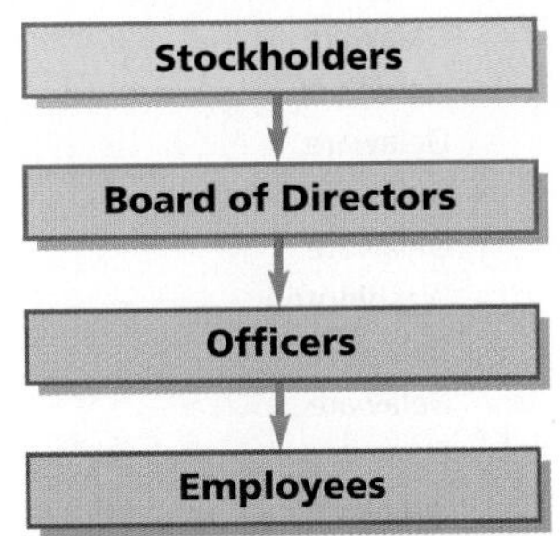

EXHIBIT 1

Organizational Structure of a Corporation

As a separate entity, a corporation is subject to taxes. For example, corporations must pay federal income taxes on their income.[1] Thus, corporate income that is distributed to stockholders in the form of *dividends* has already been taxed. In turn, stockholders must pay income taxes on the dividends they receive. This *double taxation* of corporate earnings is a major disadvantage of the corporate form. The advantages and disadvantages of the corporate form are listed in Exhibit 2.

Note:
Corporations have a separate legal existence, transferable units of ownership, and limited stockholder liability.

EXHIBIT 2 **Advantages and Disadvantages of the Corporate Form**

Advantages	**Explanation**
Separate legal existence	A corporation exists separately from its owners.
Continuous life	A corporation's life is separate from its owners; therefore, it exists indefinitely.
Raising large amounts of capital	The corporate form is suited for raising large amounts of money from shareholders.
Ownership rights are easily transferable	A corporation sells shares of ownership, called *stock*. The stockholders of a public company can transfer their shares of stock to other stockholders through stock markets, such as the New York Stock Exchange.
Limited liability	A corporation's creditors usually may not go beyond the assets of the corporation to satisfy their claims. Thus, the financial loss that a stockholder may suffer is limited to the amount invested.
Disadvantages	**Explanation**
Owner is separate from management	Stockholders control management through a board of directors. The board of directors should represent shareholder interests; however, the board is often more closely tied to management than to shareholders. As a result, the board of directors and management may not always behave in the best interests of stockholders.
Double taxation of dividends	As a separate legal entity, a corporation is subject to taxation. Thus, net income distributed as dividends will be taxed once at the corporation level, and then again at the individual level.
Regulatory costs	Corporations must satisfy many requirements, such as those required by the Sarbanes-Oxley Act.

Forming a Corporation

The first step in forming a corporation is to file an *application of incorporation* with the state. State incorporation laws differ, and corporations often organize in those states with the more favorable laws. For this reason, more than half of the largest companies are incorporated in Delaware. Exhibit 3 lists some corporations, their states of incorporation, and the location of their headquarters.

After the application of incorporation has been approved, the state grants a *charter* or *articles of incorporation*. The articles of incorporation formally create the corporation.[2] The corporate management and board of directors then prepare a set of *bylaws*, which are the rules and procedures for conducting the corporation's affairs.

[1] A majority of states also require corporations to pay income taxes.

[2] The articles of incorporation may also restrict a corporation's activities in certain areas, such as owning certain types of real estate, conducting certain types of business activities, or purchasing its own stock.

EXHIBIT 3

Examples of Corporations and their States of Incorporation

Corporation	State of Incorporation	Headquarters
Caterpillar	Delaware	Peoria, IL
Delta Air Lines	Delaware	Atlanta, GA
The Dow Chemical Company	Delaware	Midland, MI
Google	Delaware	Mountain View, CA
General Electric Company	New York	Fairfield, CT
The Home Depot	Delaware	Atlanta, GA
Kellogg Company	Delaware	Battle Creek, MI
R.J. Reynolds Tobacco Company	Delaware	Winston-Salem, NC
Starbucks Corporation	Washington	Seattle, WA
Sun Microsystems, Inc.	Delaware	Palo Alto, CA
3M	Delaware	St. Paul, MN
The Washington Post Company	Delaware	Washington, D.C.
Whirlpool Corporation	Delaware	Benton Harbor, MI

Costs may be incurred in organizing a corporation. These costs include legal fees, taxes, state incorporation fees, license fees, and promotional costs. Such costs are debited to an expense account entitled *Organizational Expenses*.

To illustrate, a corporation's organizing costs of $8,500 on January 5 are recorded as follows:

Jan.	5	Organizational Expenses	8,500	
		Cash		8,500
		Paid costs of organizing the corporation.		

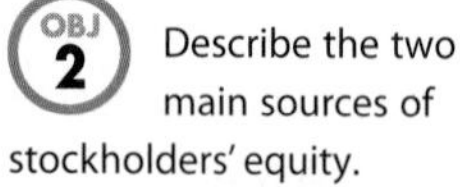

OBJ 2 Describe the two main sources of stockholders' equity.

Stockholders' Equity

The owners' equity in a corporation is called **stockholders' equity**, *shareholders' equity, shareholders' investment,* or *capital.* On the balance sheet, stockholders' equity is reported by its following two main sources, as shown in Exhibit 4:

- Capital contributed to the corporation by the stockholders, called **paid-in capital** or *contributed capital.*
- Net income retained in the business, called **retained earnings**.

EXHIBIT 4

Sources of Stockholders' Equity

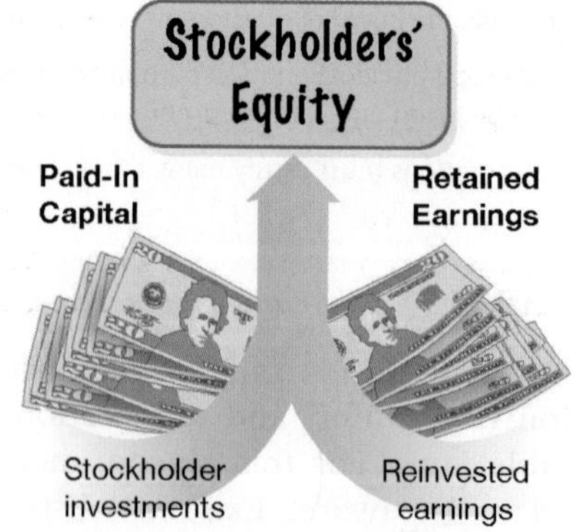

A Stockholders' Equity section of a balance sheet follows:[3]

Stockholders' Equity

Paid-in capital:		
Common stock	$330,000	
Retained earnings	80,000	
Total stockholders' equity		$410,000

[3] The reporting of stockholders' equity is further discussed and illustrated later in this chapter.

The paid-in capital contributed by the stockholders is recorded in separate accounts for each class of stock. If there is only one class of stock, the account is entitled *Common Stock* or *Capital Stock*.

Retained earnings is a corporation's cumulative net income that has not been distributed as dividends. **Dividends** are distributions of a corporation's earnings to stockholders. Sometimes retained earnings that are not distributed as dividends are referred to in the financial statements as *earnings retained for use in the business* and *earnings reinvested in the business*.

Net income increases retained earnings, while a net loss and dividends decrease retained earnings. The net increase or decrease in retained earnings for a period is recorded by the following closing entries:

1. The balance of Income Summary (the net income or net loss) is transferred to Retained Earnings. For net income, Income Summary is debited and Retained Earnings is credited. For a net loss, Retained Earnings is debited and Income Summary is credited.
2. The balance of the dividends account, which is similar to the drawing account for a proprietorship, is transferred to Retained Earnings. Retained Earnings is debited and Dividends is credited for the balance of the dividends account.

Most companies generate net income. In addition, most companies do not pay out all of their net income in dividends. As a result, Retained Earnings normally has a credit balance. However, in some cases, a debit balance in Retained Earnings may occur. A debit balance in Retained Earnings is called a **deficit**. Such a balance results from accumulated net losses. In the Stockholders' Equity section, a deficit is deducted from paid-in capital in determining total stockholders' equity.

The balance of Retained Earnings does not represent surplus cash or cash left over for dividends. This is because cash generated from operations is normally used to improve or expand operations. As cash is used, its balance decreases; however, the balance of the retained earnings account is unaffected. As a result, over time the balance in Retained Earnings becomes less and less related to the balance of Cash.

Paid-In Capital from Issuing Stock

OBJ 3 Describe and illustrate the characteristics of stock, classes of stock, and entries for issuing stock.

The two main sources of stockholders' equity are paid-in capital (or contributed capital) and retained earnings. The main source of paid-in capital is from issuing stock.

Characteristics of Stock

The number of shares of stock that a corporation is *authorized* to issue is stated in its charter. The term *issued* refers to the shares issued to the stockholders. A corporation may reacquire some of the stock that it has issued. The stock remaining in the hands of stockholders is then called **outstanding stock**. The relationship between authorized, issued, and outstanding stock is shown in Exhibit 5.

Upon request, corporations may issue stock certificates to stockholders to document their ownership. Printed on a stock certificate is the name of the company, the name of

EXHIBIT 5

Authorized, Issued, and Outstanding Stock

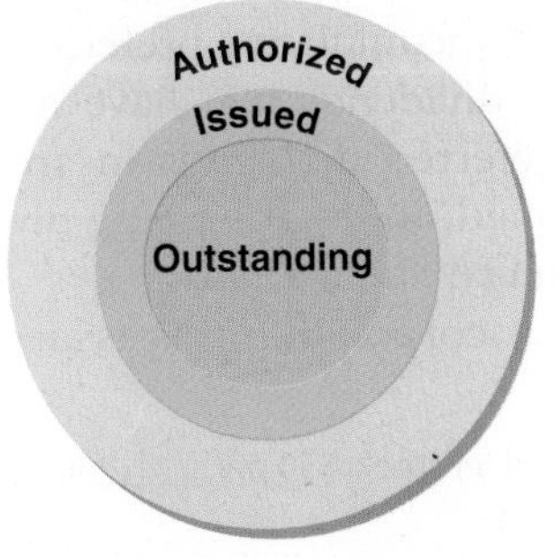

Number of shares authorized, issued, and outstanding

the stockholder, and the number of shares owned. The stock certificate may also indicate a dollar amount assigned to each share of stock, called **par value**. Stock may be issued without par, in which case it is called *no-par stock*. In some states, the board of directors of a corporation is required to assign a *stated value* to no-par stock.

Corporations have limited liability, and thus, creditors have no claim against stockholders' personal assets. To protect creditors, however, some states require corporations to maintain a minimum amount of paid-in capital. This minimum amount, called *legal capital*, usually includes the par or stated value of the shares issued.

The major rights that accompany ownership of a share of stock are as follows:

- The right to vote in matters concerning the corporation.
- The right to share in distributions of earnings.
- The right to share in assets upon liquidation.

These stock rights normally vary with the class of stock.

Classes of Stock

Note:
The two primary classes of paid-in capital are common stock and preferred stock.

When only one class of stock is issued, it is called **common stock**. Each share of common stock has equal rights.

A corporation may also issue one or more classes of stock with various preference rights such as a preference to dividends. Such a stock is called a **preferred stock**. The dividend rights of preferred stock are stated either as dollars per share or as a percent of par. For example, a $50 par value preferred stock with a $4 per share dividend may be described as either:[4]

preferred $4 stock, $50 par
or
preferred 8% stock, $50 par

As shown in Exhibit 6, preferred stockholders have first rights (preference) to any dividends, and thus, they have a greater chance of receiving dividends than common stockholders. However, since dividends are normally based on earnings, a corporation cannot guarantee dividends even to preferred stockholders.

EXHIBIT 6
Dividend Preferences

The payment of dividends is authorized by the corporation's board of directors. When authorized, the directors are said to have *declared* a dividend.

Cumulative preferred stock has a right to receive regular dividends that were not declared (paid) in prior years. Noncumulative preferred stock does not have this right.

Cumulative preferred stock dividends that have not been paid in prior years are said to be **in arrears**. Any preferred dividends in arrears must be paid before any common stock dividends are paid. In addition, any dividends in arrears are normally disclosed in notes to the financial statements.

To illustrate, assume that a corporation has issued the following preferred and common stock:

1,000 shares of cumulative preferred $4 stock, $50 par
4,000 shares of common stock, $15 par

[4] In some cases, preferred stock may receive additional dividends if certain conditions are met. Such stock, called *participating preferred stock*, is not often issued.

The corporation was organized on January 1, 2014, and paid no dividends in 2014 and 2015. In 2016, the corporation paid $22,000 in dividends, of which $12,000 was paid to preferred stockholders and $10,000 was paid to common stockholders, computed as follows:

Total dividends paid		$22,000
Preferred stockholders:		
2014 dividends in arrears (1,000 shares × $4)	$4,000	
2015 dividends in arrears (1,000 shares × $4)	4,000	
2016 dividend (1,000 shares × $4)	4,000	
Total preferred dividends paid		(12,000)
Dividends available to common stockholders		$10,000

As a result, preferred stockholders received $12.00 per share ($12,000 ÷ 1,000 shares) in dividends, while common stockholders received $2.50 per share ($10,000 ÷ 4,000 shares).

In addition to dividend preference, preferred stock may be given preferences to assets if the corporation goes out of business and is liquidated. However, claims of creditors must be satisfied first. Preferred stockholders are next in line to receive any remaining assets, followed by the common stockholders.

Example Exercise 13-1 Dividends per Share

OBJ 3

Sandpiper Company has 20,000 shares of cumulative preferred 1% stock of $100 par and 100,000 shares of $50 par common stock. The following amounts were distributed as dividends:

Year 1	$10,000
Year 2	45,000
Year 3	80,000

Determine the dividends per share for preferred and common stock for each year.

Follow My Example 13-1

	Year 1	Year 2	Year 3
Amount distributed	$10,000	$45,000	$80,000
Preferred dividend (20,000 shares)	10,000	30,000*	20,000
Common dividend (100,000 shares)	$ 0	$15,000	$60,000
*($10,000 + $20,000)			
Dividends per share:			
Preferred stock	$0.50	$1.50	$1.00
Common stock	None	$0.15	$0.60

Practice Exercises: PE 13-1A, PE 13-1B

Issuing Stock

A separate account is used for recording the amount of each class of stock issued to investors in a corporation. For example, assume that a corporation is authorized to issue 10,000 shares of $100 par preferred stock and 100,000 shares of $20 par common stock. The corporation issued 5,000 shares of preferred stock and 50,000 shares of common stock at par for cash. The corporation's entry to record the stock issue is as follows:[5]

Account	Debit	Credit
Cash	1,500,000	
Preferred Stock		500,000
Common Stock		1,000,000
Issued preferred stock and common stock at par for cash.		

Stock is often issued by a corporation at a price other than its par. The price at which stock is sold depends on a variety of factors, such as the following:

- The financial condition, earnings record, and dividend record of the corporation.
- Investor expectations of the corporation's potential earning power.
- General business and economic conditions and expectations.

If stock is issued (sold) for a price that is more than its par, the stock has been sold at a **premium**. For example, if common stock with a par of $50 is sold for $60 per share, the stock has sold at a premium of $10.

If stock is issued (sold) for a price that is less than its par, the stock has been sold at a **discount**. For example, if common stock with a par of $50 is sold for $45 per share, the stock has sold at a discount of $5. Many states do not permit stock to be sold at a discount. In other states, stock may be sold at a discount in only unusual cases. Because stock is rarely sold at a discount, it is not illustrated.

In order to distribute dividends, financial statements, and other reports, a corporation must keep track of its stockholders. Large public corporations normally use a financial institution, such as a bank, for this purpose.[6] In such cases, the financial institution is referred to as a *transfer agent* or *registrar.*

Premium on Stock

When stock is issued at a premium, Cash is debited for the amount received. Common Stock or Preferred Stock is credited for the par amount. The excess of the amount paid over par is part of the paid-in capital. An account entitled *Paid-In Capital in Excess of Par* is credited for this amount.

To illustrate, assume that Caldwell Company issues 2,000 shares of $50 par preferred stock for cash at $55. The entry to record this transaction is as follows:

Account	Debit	Credit
Cash	110,000	
Preferred Stock		100,000
Paid-In Capital in Excess of Par—Preferred Stock		10,000
Issued $50 par preferred stock at $55.		

When stock is issued in exchange for assets other than cash, such as land, buildings, and equipment, the assets acquired are recorded at their fair market value. If this value cannot be determined, the fair market price of the stock issued is used.

To illustrate, assume that a corporation acquired land with a fair market value that cannot be determined. In exchange, the corporation issued 10,000 shares of its

[5] The accounting for investments in stocks from the point of view of the investor is discussed in Chapter 15.

[6] Small corporations may use a subsidiary ledger, called a *stockholders ledger.* in this case, the stock accounts (Preferred Stock and Common Stock) are controlling accounts for the subsidiary ledger.

$10 par common stock. If the stock has a market price of $12 per share, the transaction is recorded as follows:

		Land		120,000	
		Common Stock			100,000
		Paid-In Capital in Excess of Par			20,000
		Issued $10 par common stock, valued at $12 per share, for land.			

No-Par Stock

In most states, no-par preferred and common stock may be issued. When no-par stock is issued, Cash is debited and Common Stock is credited for the proceeds. As no-par stock is issued over time, this entry is the same even if the issuing price varies.

To illustrate, assume that on January 9, a corporation issues 10,000 shares of no-par common stock at $40 a share. On June 27, the corporation issues an additional 1,000 shares at $36. The entries to record these issuances of the no-par stock are as follows:

Jan.	9	Cash		400,000	
		Common Stock			400,000
		Issued 10,000 shares of no-par common stock at $40.			
June	27	Cash		36,000	
		Common Stock			36,000
		Issued 1,000 shares of no-par common stock at $36.			

In some states, no-par stock may be assigned a *stated value per share*. The stated value is recorded like a par value. Any excess of the proceeds over the stated value is credited to *Paid-In Capital in Excess of Stated Value.*

To illustrate, assume that in the preceding example the no-par common stock is assigned a stated value of $25. The issuance of the stock on January 9 and June 27 is recorded as follows:

Jan.	9	Cash		400,000	
		Common Stock			250,000
		Paid-In Capital in Excess of Stated Value			150,000
		Issued 10,000 shares of no-par common stock at $40; stated value, $25.			
June	27	Cash		36,000	
		Common Stock			25,000
		Paid-In Capital in Excess of Stated Value			11,000
		Issued 1,000 shares of no-par common stock at $36; stated value, $25.			

Business  Connection

GOOGLE INC.

Some excepts from Google's bylaws follow:

ARTICLE I—CORPORATE OFFICES

1.1 REGISTERED OFFICE.

The registered office of Google Inc. shall be fixed in the corporation's certificate of incorporation. ...

1.2 OTHER OFFICES.
The corporation's Board of Directors (the "Board") may at any time establish other offices at any place or places where the corporation is qualified to do business.

ARTICLE II—MEETINGS OF STOCKHOLDERS

2.2 ANNUAL MEETING.
The annual meeting of stockholders shall be held each year on a date and at a time designated by the Board. At the annual meeting, directors shall be elected and any other proper business may be transacted.

2.4 NOTICE OF STOCKHOLDERS' MEETINGS.
All notices of meetings of stockholders shall be sent ... not less than ten (10) nor more than sixty (60) days before the date of the meeting to each stockholder entitled to vote at such meeting. ... The notice shall specify the place, if any, date and hour of the meeting, the means of remote communication, if any, by which stockholders and proxy holders may be deemed to be present in person and vote at such meeting. ...

2.8 ADMINISTRATION OF THE MEETING.
Meetings of stockholders shall be presided over by the chairman of the Board. ...

ARTICLE V—OFFICERS

5.1 OFFICERS.
The officers of the corporation shall be a chief executive officer, one or more presidents (at the discretion of the Board), a chairman of the Board and a secretary. The corporation may also have, at the discretion of the Board, a vice chairman of the Board, a chief financial officer, a treasurer, one or more vice presidents, one or more assistant vice presidents, one or more assistant treasurers, one or more assistant secretaries, and any such other officers as may be appointed in accordance with the provisions of these bylaws.

5.6 CHAIRMAN OF THE BOARD.
The chairman of the Board shall be a member of the Board and, if present, preside at meetings of the Board. ...

5.7 CHIEF EXECUTIVE OFFICER.
Subject to the control of the Board, ... the chief executive officer shall, together with the president or presidents of the corporation, have general supervision, direction, and control of the business and affairs of the corporation. ... The chief executive officer shall ... preside at all meetings of the stockholders.

5.11 CHIEF FINANCIAL OFFICER.
The chief financial officer shall keep and maintain ... adequate and correct books and records of accounts of the properties and business transactions of the corporation, including accounts of its assets, liabilities, receipts, disbursements, gains, losses, capital, retained earnings and shares. ...

5.12 TREASURER.
The treasurer shall deposit all moneys and other valuables in the name and to the credit of the corporation. ...

Source: http://investor.google.com/corporate/bylaws.html

Example Exercise 13-2 Entries for Issuing Stock

On March 6, Limerick Corporation issued for cash 15,000 shares of no-par common stock at $30. On April 13, Limerick issued at par 1,000 shares of preferred 4% stock, $40 par for cash. On May 19, Limerick issued for cash 15,000 shares of 4%, $40 par preferred stock at $42.

Journalize the entries to record the March 6, April 13, and May 19 transactions.

Follow My Example 13-2

Mar. 6	Cash	450,000	
	Common Stock		450,000
	(15,000 shares × $30).		
Apr. 13	Cash	40,000	
	Preferred Stock		40,000
	(1,000 shares × $40).		
May 19	Cash	630,000	
	Preferred Stock		600,000
	Paid-In Capital in Excess of Par		30,000
	(15,000 shares × $42).		

Practice Exercises: PE 13-2A, PE 13-2B

Accounting for Dividends

Describe and illustrate the accounting for cash dividends and stock dividends.

When a board of directors declares a cash dividend, it authorizes the distribution of cash to stockholders. When a board of directors declares a stock dividend, it authorizes the distribution of its stock. In both cases, declaring a dividend reduces the retained earnings of the corporation.[7]

Cash Dividends

A cash distribution of earnings by a corporation to its shareholders is a **cash dividend**. Although dividends may be paid in other assets, cash dividends are the most common.

Three conditions for a cash dividend are as follows:

- Sufficient retained earnings
- Sufficient cash
- Formal action by the board of directors

International  Connection

IFRS FOR SMEs

In 2010, the International Accounting Standards Board (IASB) issued a set of accounting standards specifically designed for small- and medium-sized enterprises (SMEs) called International Financial Reporting Standards (IFRS) for SMEs. SMEs in the United States are private companies and such small corporations that they do not report to the Securities and Exchange Commission (SEC). IFRS for SMEs consist of only 230 pages, compared to 2,700 pages for full IFRS. These standards are designed to be cost effective for SMEs. Thus, IFRS for SMEs require fewer disclosures and contain no industry-specific standards or exceptions.

The American Institute of CPAs (AICPA) has accepted IFRS for SMEs as part of U.S. generally accepted accounting principles (GAAP) for private companies not reporting to the SEC. If users, such as bankers and investors, accept these financial statements, IFRS for SMEs may become popular in the United States.*

*Differences between U.S. GAAP and IFRS are further discussed and illustrated in Appendix D.

There must be a sufficient (large enough) balance in Retained Earnings to declare a cash dividend. That is, the balance of Retained Earnings must be large enough so that the dividend does not create a debit balance in the retained earnings account. However, a large Retained Earnings balance does not mean that there is cash available to pay dividends. This is because the balances of Cash and Retained Earnings are often unrelated.

Even if there are sufficient retained earnings and cash, a corporation's board of directors is not required to pay dividends. Nevertheless, many corporations pay quarterly cash dividends to make their stock more attractive to investors. *Special* or *extra dividends* may also be paid when a corporation experiences higher than normal profits.

Three dates included in a dividend announcement are as follows:

1. Date of declaration
2. Date of record
3. Date of payment

Microsoft Corporation declared a dividend of $0.28 per share on November 19, 2013, to common stockholders of record as of February 20, 2014, payable on March 13, 2014.

The *date of declaration* is the date the board of directors formally authorizes the payment of the dividend. On this date, the corporation incurs the liability to pay the amount of the dividend.

The *date of record* is the date the corporation uses to determine which stockholders will receive the dividend. During the period of time between the date of declaration and

[7] In rare cases, when a corporation is reducing its operations or going out of business, a dividend may be a distribution of paid-in capital. Such a dividend is called a *liquidating dividend.*

the date of record, the stock price is quoted as selling *with-dividends*. This means that any investors purchasing the stock before the date of record will receive the dividend.

The *date of payment* is the date the corporation will pay the dividend to the stockholders who owned the stock on the date of record. During the period of time between the record date and the payment date, the stock price is quoted as selling *ex-dividends*. This means that since the date of record has passed, any new investors will not receive the dividend.

To illustrate, assume that on October 1, Hiber Corporation declares the following cash dividends with a date of record of November 10 and a date of payment of December 2:

	Dividend per Share	Total Dividends
Preferred stock, $100 par, 5,000 shares outstanding....................	$2.50	$12,500
Common stock, $10 par, 100,000 shares outstanding	$0.30	30,000
Total		$42,500

On October 1, the declaration date, Hiber Corporation records the following entry:

Declaration Date

Oct.	1	Cash Dividends		42,500	
		Cash Dividends Payable			42,500
		Declared cash dividends.			

Date of Record

On November 10, the date of record, no entry is necessary. This date merely determines which stockholders will receive the dividends.

On December 2, the date of payment, Hiber Corporation records the payment of the dividends as follows:

Date of Payment

Dec.	2	Cash Dividends Payable		42,500	
		Cash			42,500
		Paid cash dividends.			

At the end of the accounting period, the balance in Cash Dividends will be transferred to Retained Earnings as part of the closing process. This closing entry debits Retained Earnings and credits Cash Dividends for the balance of the cash dividends account. If the cash dividends have not been paid by the end of the period, Cash Dividends Payable will be reported on the balance sheet as a current liability.

Example Exercise 13-3 Entries for Cash Dividends

The important dates in connection with a cash dividend of $75,000 on a corporation's common stock are February 26, March 30, and April 2. Journalize the entries required on each date.

Follow My Example 13-3

Feb. 26	Cash Dividends..	75,000	
	Cash Dividends Payable..................................		75,000
Mar. 30	No entry required.		
Apr. 2	Cash Dividends Payable	75,000	
	Cash		75,000

Practice Exercises: PE 13-3A, PE 13-3B

Integrity, Objectivity, and Ethics in Business

THE PROFESSOR WHO KNEW TOO MUCH

A major Midwestern university released a quarterly "American Customer Satisfaction Index" based on its research of customers of popular U.S. products and services. Before the release of the index to the public, the professor in charge of the research bought and sold stocks of some of the companies in the report. The professor was quoted as saying that he thought it was important to test his theories of customer satisfaction with "real" [his own] money.

Is this proper or ethical? Apparently, the dean of the Business School didn't think so. In a statement to the press, the dean stated: "I have instructed anyone affiliated with the (index) not to make personal use of information gathered in the course of producing the quarterly index, prior to the index's release to the general public, and they [the researchers] have agreed."

Sources: Jon E. Hilsenrath and Dan Morse, "Researcher Uses Index to Buy, Short Stocks," *The Wall Street Journal*, February 18, 2003; and Jon E. Hilsenrath, "Satisfaction Theory: Mixed Results," *The Wall Street Journal*, February 19, 2003.

Stock Dividends

A **stock dividend** is a distribution of shares of stock to stockholders. Stock dividends are normally declared only on common stock and issued to common stockholders.

A stock dividend affects only stockholders' equity. Specifically, the amount of the stock dividend is transferred from Retained Earnings to Paid-In Capital. The amount transferred is normally the fair value (market price) of the shares issued in the stock dividend.[8]

To illustrate, assume that the stockholders' equity accounts of Hendrix Corporation as of December 15 are as follows:

Common Stock, $20 par (2,000,000 shares issued)	$40,000,000
Paid-In Capital in Excess of Par—Common Stock	9,000,000
Retained Earnings	26,600,000

On December 15, Hendrix Corporation declares a stock dividend of 5% or 100,000 shares (2,000,000 shares × 5%) to be issued on January 10 to stockholders of record on December 31. The market price of the stock on December 15 (the date of declaration) is $31 per share.

The entry to record the stock dividend is as follows:

Dec.	15	Stock Dividends		3,100,000	
		Stock Dividends Distributable			2,000,000
		Paid-In Capital in Excess of Par—Common Stock			1,100,000
		Declared 5% (100,000 shares) stock dividend on $20 par common stock with a market price of $31 per share.			

After the preceding entry is recorded, Stock Dividends will have a debit balance of $3,100,000. Like cash dividends, the stock dividends account is closed to Retained Earnings at the end of the accounting period. This closing entry debits Retained Earnings and credits Stock Dividends.

At the end of the period, the *stock dividends distributable* and *paid-in capital in excess of par—common stock* accounts are reported in the Paid-In Capital section of the balance sheet. Thus, the effect of the preceding stock dividend is to transfer $3,100,000 of retained earnings to paid-in capital.

[8] The use of fair market value is justified as long as the number of shares issued for the stock dividend is small (less than 25% of the shares outstanding).

On January 10, the stock dividend is distributed to stockholders by issuing 100,000 shares of common stock. The issuance of the stock is recorded by the following entry:

Jan.	10	Stock Dividends Distributable		2,000,000	
		Common Stock			2,000,000
		Issued stock as stock dividend.			

A stock dividend does not change the assets, liabilities, or total stockholders' equity of a corporation. Likewise, a stock dividend does not change an individual stockholder's proportionate interest (equity) in the corporation.

To illustrate, assume a stockholder owns 1,000 of a corporation's 10,000 shares outstanding. If the corporation declares a 6% stock dividend, the stockholder's proportionate interest will not change, computed as follows:

	***Before* Stock Dividend**	***After* Stock Dividend**
Total shares issued	10,000	10,600 [10,000 + (10,000 × 6%)]
Number of shares owned	1,000	1,060 [1,000 + (1,000 × 6%)]
Proportionate ownership	10% (1,000 ÷ 10,000)	10% (1,060 ÷ 10,600)

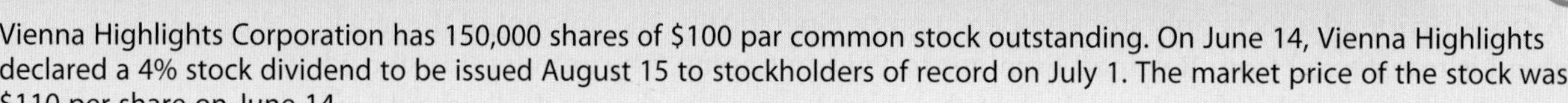

Example Exercise 13-4 Entries for Stock Dividends OBJ 4

Vienna Highlights Corporation has 150,000 shares of $100 par common stock outstanding. On June 14, Vienna Highlights declared a 4% stock dividend to be issued August 15 to stockholders of record on July 1. The market price of the stock was $110 per share on June 14.

Journalize the entries required on June 14, July 1, and August 15.

Follow My Example 13-4

June 14	Stock Dividends (150,000 × 4% × $110)	660,000	
	Stock Dividends Distributable (6,000 × $100)		600,000
	Paid-In Capital in Excess of Par—Common Stock ($660,000 – $600,000)		60,000
July 1	No entry required.		
Aug. 15	Stock Dividends Distributable	600,000	
	Common Stock		600,000

Practice Exercises: PE 13-4A, PE 13-4B

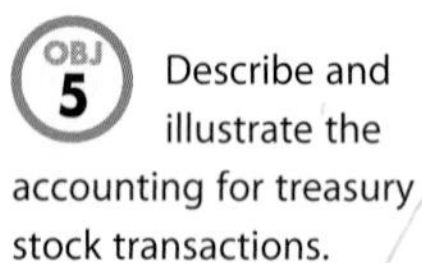

OBJ 5 Describe and illustrate the accounting for treasury stock transactions.

Treasury Stock Transactions

Treasury stock is stock that a corporation has issued and then reacquired. A corporation may reacquire (purchase) its own stock for a variety of reasons, including the following:

- To provide shares for resale to employees
- To reissue as bonuses to employees, or
- To support the market price of the stock

The 2012 edition of *Accounting Trends & Techniques* indicated that 68.2% of the companies surveyed reported treasury stock.

Dynamic Exhibit

The *cost method* is normally used for recording the purchase and resale of treasury stock.[9] Using the cost method, *Treasury Stock* is debited for the cost (purchase price) of the stock. When the stock is resold, Treasury Stock is credited for its cost. Any difference between the cost and the selling price is debited or credited to *Paid-In Capital from Sale of Treasury Stock.*

[9] Another method that is infrequently used, called the *par value method*, is discussed in advanced accounting texts.

To illustrate, assume that a corporation has the following paid-in capital on January 1:

Common stock, $25 par (20,000 shares authorized and issued)	$500,000
Excess of issue price over par	150,000
	$650,000

On February 13, the corporation purchases 1,000 shares of its common stock at $45 per share. The entry to record the purchase of the treasury stock is as follows:

Feb.	13	Treasury Stock		45,000	
		Cash			45,000
		Purchased 1,000 shares of treasury stock at $45.			

On April 29, the corporation sells 600 shares of the treasury stock for $60. The entry to record the sale is as follows:

Apr.	29	Cash		36,000	
		Treasury Stock			27,000
		Paid-In Capital from Sale of Treasury Stock			9,000
		Sold 600 shares of treasury stock at $60.			

A sale of treasury stock may result in a decrease in paid-in capital. To the extent that Paid-In Capital from Sale of Treasury Stock has a credit balance, it is debited for any such decrease. Any remaining decrease is then debited to the retained earnings account.

To illustrate, assume that on October 4, the corporation sells the remaining 400 shares of treasury stock for $40 per share. The entry to record the sale is as follows:

Oct.	4	Cash		16,000	
		Paid-In Capital from Sale of Treasury Stock		2,000	
		Treasury Stock			18,000
		Sold 400 shares of treasury stock at $40.			

The preceding October 4 entry decreases paid-in capital by $2,000. Because Paid-In Capital from Sale of Treasury Stock has a credit balance of $9,000, the entire $2,000 was debited to Paid-In Capital from Sale of Treasury Stock.

No dividends (cash or stock) are paid on the shares of treasury stock. To do so would result in the corporation earning dividend revenue from itself.

Example Exercise 13-5 Entries for Treasury Stock

OBJ 5

On May 3, Buzz Off Corporation reacquired 3,200 shares of its common stock at $42 per share. On July 22, Buzz Off sold 2,000 of the reacquired shares at $47 per share. On August 30, Buzz Off sold the remaining shares at $40 per share.

Journalize the transactions of May 3, July 22, and August 30.

Follow My Example 13-5

May 3	Treasury Stock (3,200 × $42)	134,400	
	Cash		134,400
July 22	Cash (2,000 × $47)	94,000	
	Treasury Stock (2,000 × $42)		84,000
	Paid-In Capital from Sale of Treasury Stock [2,000 × ($47 – $42)]		10,000
Aug. 30	Cash (1,200 × $40)	48,000	
	Paid-In Capital from Sale of Treasury Stock [1,200 × ($42 – $40)]	2,400	
	Treasury Stock (1,200 × $42)		50,400

Practice Exercises: PE 13-5A, PE 13-5B

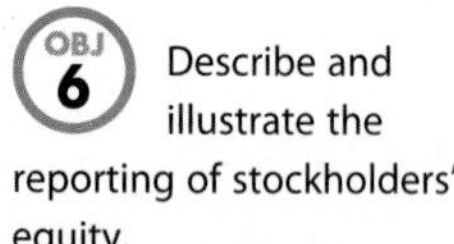
Describe and illustrate the reporting of stockholders' equity.

Reporting Stockholders' Equity

As with other sections of the balance sheet, alternative terms and formats may be used in reporting stockholders' equity. Also, changes in retained earnings and paid-in capital may be reported in separate statements or notes to the financial statements.

Stockholders' Equity on the Balance Sheet

Exhibit 7 shows two methods for reporting stockholders' equity for the December 31, 2016, balance sheet for Telex Inc.

- Method 1. Each class of stock is reported, followed by its related paid-in capital accounts. Retained earnings is then reported followed by a deduction for treasury stock.
- Method 2. The stock accounts are reported, followed by the paid-in capital reported as a single item, Additional paid-in capital. Retained earnings is then reported followed by a deduction for treasury stock.

EXHIBIT 7 **Stockholders' Equity Section of a Balance Sheet**

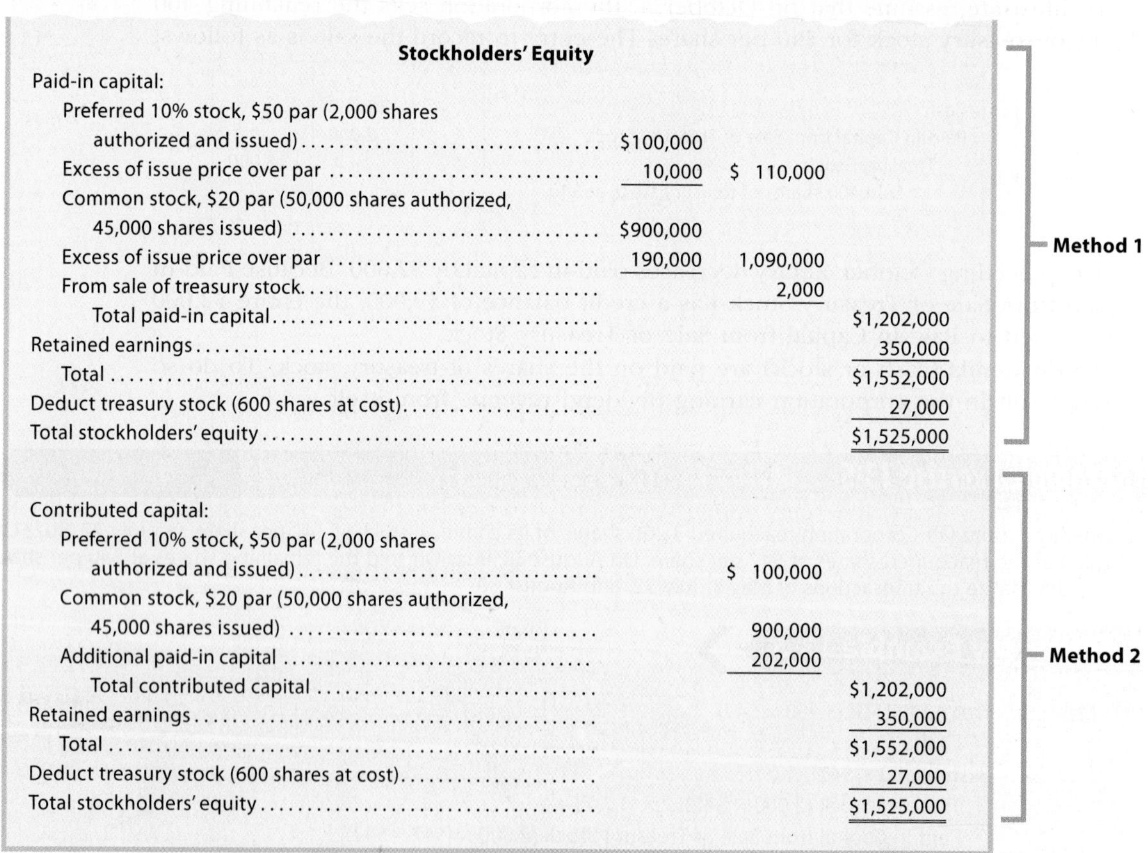

Telex Inc.
Balance Sheet
December 31, 2016

Stockholders' Equity

Paid-in capital:				Method 1
Preferred 10% stock, $50 par (2,000 shares authorized and issued)	$100,000			
Excess of issue price over par	10,000	$ 110,000		
Common stock, $20 par (50,000 shares authorized, 45,000 shares issued)	$900,000			
Excess of issue price over par	190,000	1,090,000		
From sale of treasury stock		2,000		
Total paid-in capital			$1,202,000	
Retained earnings			350,000	
Total			$1,552,000	
Deduct treasury stock (600 shares at cost)			27,000	
Total stockholders' equity			$1,525,000	
Contributed capital:				Method 2
Preferred 10% stock, $50 par (2,000 shares authorized and issued)		$ 100,000		
Common stock, $20 par (50,000 shares authorized, 45,000 shares issued)		900,000		
Additional paid-in capital		202,000		
Total contributed capital			$1,202,000	
Retained earnings			350,000	
Total			$1,552,000	
Deduct treasury stock (600 shares at cost)			27,000	
Total stockholders' equity			$1,525,000	

Significant changes in stockholders' equity during a period may also be presented in a statement of stockholders' equity or in the notes to the financial statements. The statement of stockholders' equity is illustrated later in this section.

Relevant rights and privileges of the various classes of stock outstanding should also be reported.[10] Examples include dividend and liquidation preferences, conversion rights, and redemption rights. Such information may be disclosed on the face of the balance sheet or in the notes to the financial statements.

Example Exercise 13-6 Reporting Stockholders' Equity

OBJ 6

Using the following accounts and balances, prepare the Stockholders' Equity section of the balance sheet. Forty thousand shares of common stock are authorized, and 5,000 shares have been reacquired.

Common Stock, $50 par	$1,500,000
Paid-In Capital from Sale of Treasury Stock	44,000
Paid-In Capital in Excess of Par	160,000
Retained Earnings	4,395,000
Treasury Stock	120,000

Follow My Example 13-6

Stockholders' Equity

Paid-in capital:		
Common stock, $50 par		
(40,000 shares authorized, 30,000 shares issued)	$1,500,000	
Excess of issue price over par	160,000	$1,660,000
From sale of treasury stock		44,000
Total paid-in capital		$1,704,000
Retained earnings		4,395,000
Total		$6,099,000
Deduct treasury stock (5,000 shares at cost)		120,000
Total stockholders' equity		$5,979,000

Practice Exercises: PE 13-6A, PE 13-6B

Reporting Retained Earnings

Changes in retained earnings may be reported using one of the following:

- Separate retained earnings statement
- Combined income and retained earnings statement
- Statement of stockholders' equity

Changes in retained earnings may be reported in a separate retained earnings statement. When a separate **retained earnings statement** is prepared, the beginning balance of retained earnings is reported. The net income is then added (or net loss is subtracted) and any dividends are subtracted to arrive at the ending retained earnings for the period.

To illustrate, a retained earnings statement for Telex Inc. is shown in Exhibit 8.

EXHIBIT 8

Retained Earnings Statement

Telex Inc.
Retained Earnings Statement
For the Year Ended December 31, 2016

Retained earnings, January 1, 2016			$245,000
Net income		$180,000	
Less dividends:			
Preferred stock dividends	$10,000		
Common stock dividends	65,000	75,000	
Increase in retained earnings			105,000
Retained earnings, December 31, 2016			$350,000

[10] *FASB Accounting Standards Codification*, Section 505-10-50.

Changes in retained earnings may also be reported in combination with the income statement. This format emphasizes net income as the connecting link between the income statement and ending retained earnings. Because this format is not often used, we do not illustrate it.

Changes in retained earnings may also be reported in a statement of stockholders' equity. An example of reporting changes in retained earnings in a statement of stockholders' equity for Telex Inc. is shown in Exhibit 9.

Example Exercise 13-7 Retained Earnings Statement

OBJ 6

Dry Creek Cameras Inc. reported the following results for the year ending March 31, 2016:

Retained earnings, April 1, 2015	$3,338,500
Net income	461,500
Cash dividends declared	80,000
Stock dividends declared	120,000

Prepare a retained earnings statement for the fiscal year ended March 31, 2016.

Follow My Example 13-7

Dry Creek Cameras Inc.
Retained Earnings Statement
For the Year Ended March 31, 2016

Retained earnings, April 1, 2015		$3,338,500
Net income	$461,500	
Less dividends declared	200,000	
Increase in retained earnings		261,500
Retained earnings, March 31, 2016		$3,600,000

Practice Exercises: PE 13-7A, PE 13-7B

Restrictions The use of retained earnings for payment of dividends may be restricted by action of a corporation's board of directors. Such **restrictions**, sometimes called *appropriations,* remain part of the retained earnings.

Restrictions of retained earnings are classified as:

- *Legal.* State laws may require a restriction of retained earnings.

  Example: States may restrict retained earnings by the amount of treasury stock purchased. In this way, legal capital cannot be used for dividends.

- *Contractual.* A corporation may enter into contracts that require restrictions of retained earnings.

  Example: A bank loan may restrict retained earnings so that money for repaying the loan cannot be used for dividends.

- *Discretionary.* A corporation's board of directors may restrict retained earnings voluntarily.

  Example: The board may restrict retained earnings and, thus, limit dividend distributions so that more money is available for expanding the business.

Restrictions of retained earnings must be disclosed in the financial statements. Such disclosures are usually included in the notes to the financial statements.

Prior Period Adjustments An error may arise from a mathematical mistake or from a mistake in applying accounting principles. Such errors may not be discovered within the same period in which they occur. In such cases, the effect of the error should not affect the current period's net income. Instead, the correction of the error, called a **prior period adjustment**, is reported in the retained earnings statement. Such corrections are reported as an adjustment to the beginning balance of retained earnings.[11]

[11] Prior period adjustments are illustrated in advanced texts.

Statement of Stockholders' Equity

When the only change in stockholders' equity is due to net income or net loss and dividends, a retained earnings statement is sufficient. However, when a corporation also has changes in stock and paid-in capital accounts, a **statement of stockholders' equity** is normally prepared.

A statement of stockholders' equity is normally prepared in a columnar format. Each column is a major stockholders' equity classification. Changes in each classification are then described in the left-hand column. Exhibit 9 illustrates a statement of stockholders' equity for Telex Inc.

EXHIBIT 9 **Statement of Stockholders' Equity**

Telex Inc.
Statement of Stockholders' Equity
For the Year Ended December 31, 2016

	Preferred Stock	Common Stock	Additional Paid-In Capital	Retained Earnings	Treasury Stock	Total
Balance, January 1, 2016	$100,000	$850,000	$177,000	$245,000	$(17,000)	$1,355,000
Net income				180,000		180,000
Dividends on preferred stock				(10,000)		(10,000)
Dividends on common stock				(65,000)		(65,000)
Issuance of additional common stock		50,000	25,000			75,000
Purchase of treasury stock					(10,000)	(10,000)
Balance, December 31, 2016	$100,000	$900,000	$202,000	$350,000	$(27,000)	$1,525,000

Reporting Stockholders' Equity for Mornin' Joe

Mornin' Joe reports stockholders' equity in its balance sheet. Mornin' Joe also includes a retained earnings statement and statement of stockholders' equity in its financial statements.

The Stockholders' Equity section of Mornin' Joe's balance sheet as of December 31, 2016, follows:

Mornin' Joe
Balance Sheet
December 31, 2016

Stockholders' Equity

Paid-in capital:		
Preferred 10% stock, $50 par (6,000 shares authorized and issued)	$ 300,000	
Excess of issue price over par	50,000	$ 350,000
Common stock, $20 par (50,000 shares authorized, 45,000 shares issued)	$ 900,000	
Excess of issue price over par	1,450,000	2,350,000
Total paid-in capital		$2,700,000
Retained earnings		1,200,300
Total		$3,900,300
Deduct treasury stock (1,000 shares at cost)		46,000
Total stockholders' equity		$3,854,300
Total liabilities and stockholders' equity		$6,169,700

Mornin' Joe's retained earnings statement for the year ended December 31, 2016, is as follows:

Mornin' Joe Retained Earnings Statment For the Year Ended December 31, 2016			
Retained earnings, January 1, 2016			$ 852,700
Net income		$421,600	
Less dividends:			
Preferred stock	$30,000		
Common stock	44,000	74,000	
Increase in retained earnings			347,600
Retained earnings, December 31, 2016			$1,200,300

The statement of stockholders' equity for Mornin' Joe follows:

Mornin' Joe Statement of Stockholders' Equity For the Year Ended December 31, 2016	Preferred Stock	Common Stock	Additional Paid-In Capital	Retained Earnings	Treasury Stock	Total
Balance, January 1, 2016	$300,000	$800,000	$1,325,000	$ 852,700	$(36,000)	$3,241,700
Net income				421,600		421,600
Dividends on preferred stock				(30,000)		(30,000)
Dividends on common stock				(44,000)		(44,000)
Issuance of additional common stock		100,000	175,000			275,000
Purchase of treasury stock					(10,000)	(10,000)
Balance, December 31, 2016	$300,000	$900,000	$1,500,000	$1,200,300	$(46,000)	$3,854,300

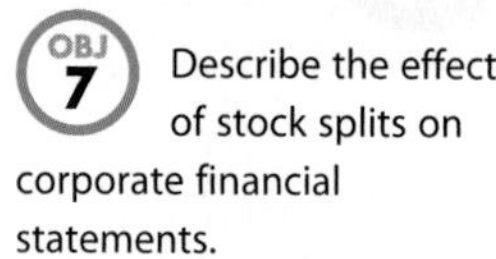

Describe the effect of stock splits on corporate financial statements.

Stock Splits

A **stock split** is a process by which a corporation reduces the par or stated value of its common stock and issues a proportionate number of additional shares. A stock split applies to all common shares including the unissued, issued, and treasury shares.

A major objective of a stock split is to reduce the market price per share of the stock. This attracts more investors and broadens the types and numbers of stockholders.

To illustrate, assume that Rojek Corporation has 10,000 shares of $100 par common stock outstanding with a current market price of $150 per share. The board of directors declares the following stock split:

1. Each common shareholder will receive 5 shares for each share held. This is called a 5-for-1 stock split. As a result, 50,000 shares (10,000 shares × 5) will be outstanding.
2. The par of each share of common stock will be reduced to $20 ($100÷5).

The par value of the common stock outstanding is $1,000,000 both before and after the stock split as shown in Exhibit 10 and computed as follows:

	Before Split	After Split
Number of shares	10,000	50,000
Par value per share	× $100	× $20
Total	$1,000,000	$1,000,000

In addition, each Rojek Corporation shareholder owns the same total par amount of stock before and after the stock split. For example, a stockholder who owned 4 shares of $100 par stock before the split (total par of $400) would own 20 shares of

EXHIBIT 10

Stock Split: Before and After

Before Stock Split	After 5:1 Stock Split
4 shares @ $100 par value per share	20 shares @ $20 par value per share
$400 total par value	**$400 total par value**

$20 par stock after the split (total par of $400). Only the number of shares and the par value per share have changed.

Because there are more shares outstanding after the stock split, the market price of the stock should decrease. For example, in the preceding example, there would be 5 times as many shares outstanding after the split. Thus, the market price of the stock would be expected to fall from $150 to about $30 ($150 ÷ 5).

Stock splits do not require a journal entry because only the par (or stated) value and number of shares outstanding have changed. However, the details of stock splits are normally disclosed in the notes to the financial statements.

Note:
A stock split does not require a journal entry.

Business  Connection

BUFFETT ON STOCK SPLITS

Warren E. Buffett, chairman and chief executive officer of Berkshire Hathaway Inc., opposes stock splits on the basis that they add no value to the company. Since its inception, Berkshire Hathaway has never declared a stock split on its primary (Class A) common stock. As a result, Berkshire Hathaway's Class A common stock sells well above $170,000 per share, which is the most expensive stock on the New York Stock Exchange. Such a high price doesn't bother Buffet because he believes that high stock prices attract more sophisticated and long-term investors and discourage stock speculators and short-term investors.

In contrast, Microsoft Corporation has split its stock nine times since it went public in 1986. As a result, one share of Microsoft purchased in 1986 is equivalent to 288 shares today, which would be worth more than $10,000.

Financial Analysis and Interpretation: Earnings per Share

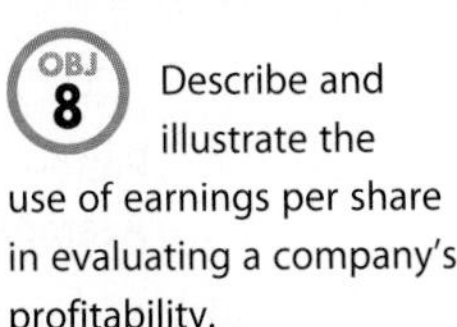

OBJ 8
Describe and illustrate the use of earnings per share in evaluating a company's profitability.

Net income is often used by investors and creditors in evaluating a company's profitability. However, net income by itself is difficult to use in comparing companies of different sizes. Also, trends in net income may be difficult to evaluate if there have been significant changes in a company's stockholders' equity. Thus, the profitability of companies is often expressed as earnings per share.

Earnings per common share (EPS), sometimes called *basic earnings per share*, is the net income per share of common stock outstanding during a period.[12] Corporations whose stock is traded in a public market must report earnings per common share on their income statements.

Earnings per share is computed as follows:

$$\text{Earnings per Share} = \frac{\text{Net Income} - \text{Preferred Dividends}}{\text{Average Number of Common Shares Outstanding}}$$

If a company has preferred stock outstanding, any preferred dividends are subtracted from net income. This is because the numerator represents only those earnings available to the common shareholders.

[12] For complex capital structures, earnings per share assuming dilution may also be reported as described in Chapter 17.

To illustrate, the following data (in thousands) were taken from recent financial statements of Google:

	Year 2	Year 1
Net income	$10,737,000	$9,737,000
Average number of common shares outstanding	327,213 shares	322,778 shares
Earnings per share	$32.81 ($10,737,000 ÷ 327,213 shares)	$30.17 ($9,737,000 ÷ 322,778 shares)

Google had no preferred stock outstanding; thus, no preferred dividends were subtracted in computing earnings per share. As illustrated, Google's earnings per share increased from $30.17 in Year 1 to $32.81 in Year 2. An increase in earnings per share is generally considered a favorable trend.

Earnings per share can be used to compare two companies with different net incomes. For example, the following data (in millions) were taken from a recent year's financial statements for Goldman Sachs Group, Inc., and Wells Fargo & Company:

	Goldman Sachs	Wells Fargo
Net income	$7,475	$18,897
Preferred dividends	$183	$898
Average number of common shares outstanding	516.1 shares	5,287.6 shares

Goldman Sachs:

$$\text{Earnings per Share} = \frac{\text{Net Income} - \text{Preferred Dividends}}{\text{Average Number of Common Shares Outstanding}} = \frac{\$7{,}475 - \$183}{516.1 \text{ shares}} = \frac{\$7{,}292}{516.1 \text{ shares}} = \$14.13$$

Wells Fargo:

$$\text{Earnings per Share} = \frac{\text{Net Income} - \text{Preferred Dividends}}{\text{Average Number of Common Shares Outstanding}} = \frac{\$18{,}897 - \$898}{5{,}287.6 \text{ shares}} = \frac{\$17{,}999}{5{,}287.6 \text{ shares}} = \$3.40$$

Based on earnings per share, Goldman Sachs is more profitable than Wells Fargo.

Example Exercise 13-8 Earnings per Share

OBJ 8

Financial statement data for years ending December 31 for Finnegan Company follows:

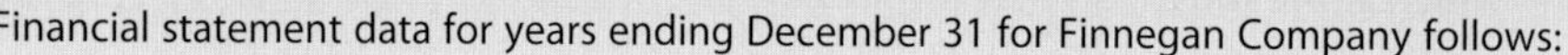

	2016	2015
Net income	$350,000	$195,000
Preferred dividends	$20,000	$15,000
Average number of common shares outstanding	75,000 shares	50,000 shares

a. Determine earnings per share for 2016 and 2015.

b. Does the change in the earnings per share from 2015 to 2016 indicate a favorable or an unfavorable trend?

Follow My Example 13-8

a.

2016:

$$\text{Earnings per Share} = \frac{\text{Net Income} - \text{Preferred Dividends}}{\text{Average Number of Common Shares Outstanding}} = \frac{\$350{,}000 - \$20{,}000}{75{,}000 \text{ shares}} = \frac{\$330{,}000}{75{,}000 \text{ shares}} = \$4.40$$

2015:

$$\text{Earnings per Share} = \frac{\text{Net Income} - \text{Preferred Dividends}}{\text{Average Number of Common Shares Outstanding}} = \frac{\$195{,}000 - \$15{,}000}{50{,}000 \text{ shares}} = \frac{\$180{,}000}{50{,}000 \text{ shares}} = \$3.60$$

b. The increase in the earnings per share from $3.60 to $4.40 indicates a favorable trend in the company's profitability.

Practice Exercises: PE 13-8A, PE 13-8B

At a Glance 13

Describe the nature of the corporate form of organization.

Key Points Corporations have a separate legal existence, transferable units of stock, unlimited life, and limited stockholders' liability. The advantages and disadvantages of the corporate form are summarized in Exhibit 2. Costs incurred in organizing a corporation are debited to Organizational Expenses.

Learning Outcomes	Example Exercises	Practice Exercises
• Describe the characteristics of corporations.		
• List the advantages and disadvantages of the corporate form.		
• Prepare a journal entry for the costs of organizing a corporation.		

Describe the two main sources of stockholders' equity.

Key Points The two main sources of stockholders' equity are (1) capital contributed by the stockholders and others, called *paid-in capital*, and (2) net income retained in the business, called *retained earnings*. Stockholders' equity is reported in a corporation balance sheet according to these two sources.

Learning Outcomes	Example Exercises	Practice Exercises
• Describe what is meant by paid-in capital.		
• Describe what is meant by net income retained in the business.		
• Prepare a simple Stockholders' Equity section of the balance sheet.		

Describe and illustrate the characteristics of stock, classes of stock, and entries for issuing stock.

Key Points The main source of paid-in capital is from issuing common and preferred stock. Stock issued at par is recorded by debiting Cash and crediting the class of stock issued for its par amount. Stock issued for more than par is recorded by debiting Cash, crediting the class of stock for its par, and crediting Paid-In Capital in Excess of Par for the difference. When no-par stock is issued, the entire proceeds are credited to the stock account. No-par stock may be assigned a stated value per share, and the excess of the proceeds over the stated value may be credited to Paid-In Capital in Excess of Stated Value.

Learning Outcomes	Example Exercises	Practice Exercises
• Describe the characteristics of common and preferred stock including rights to dividends.	**EE13-1**	**PE13-1A, 13-1B**
• Journalize the entry for common and preferred stock issued at par.	**EE13-2**	**PE13-2A, 13-2B**
• Journalize the entry for common and preferred stock issued at more than par.	**EE13-2**	**PE13-2A, 13-2B**
• Journalize the entry for issuing no-par stock.	**EE13-2**	**PE13-2A, 13-2B**

Describe and illustrate the accounting for cash dividends and stock dividends.

Key Points The entry to record a declaration of cash dividends debits Dividends and credits Dividends Payable. When a stock dividend is declared, Stock Dividends is debited for the fair value of the stock to be issued. Stock Dividends Distributable is credited for the par or stated value of the common stock to be issued. The difference between the fair value of the stock and its par or stated value is credited to Paid-In Capital in Excess of Par—Common Stock. When the stock is issued on the date of payment, Stock Dividends Distributable is debited and Common Stock is credited for the par or stated value of the stock issued.

Learning Outcomes	Example Exercises	Practice Exercises
• Journalize the entries for the declaration and payment of cash dividends.	EE13-3	PE13-3A, 13-3B
• Journalize the entries for the declaration and payment of stock dividends.	EE13-4	PE13-4A, 13-4B

Describe and illustrate the accounting for treasury stock transactions.

Key Points When a corporation buys its own stock, the cost method of accounting is normally used. Treasury Stock is debited for its cost, and Cash is credited. If the stock is resold, Treasury Stock is credited for its cost and any difference between the cost and the selling price is normally debited or credited to Paid-In Capital from Sale of Treasury Stock.

Learning Outcomes	Example Exercises	Practice Exercises
• Define treasury stock.		
• Describe the accounting for treasury stock.		
• Journalize entries for the purchase and sale of treasury stock.	EE13-5	PE13-5A, 13-5B

Describe and illustrate the reporting of stockholders' equity.

Key Points Two alternatives for reporting stockholders' equity are shown in Exhibit 7. Changes in retained earnings are reported in a retained earnings statement, as shown in Exhibit 8. Restrictions to retained earnings should be disclosed. Any prior period adjustments are reported in the retained earnings statement. Changes in stockholders' equity may be reported on a statement of stockholders' equity, as shown in Exhibit 9.

Learning Outcomes	Example Exercises	Practice Exercises
• Prepare the Stockholders' Equity section of the balance sheet.	EE13-6	PE13-6A, 13-6B
• Prepare a retained earnings statement.	EE13-7	PE13-7A, 13-7B
• Describe retained earnings restrictions and prior period adjustments.		
• Prepare a statement of stockholders' equity.		

Describe the effect of stock splits on corporate financial statements.

Key Points When a corporation reduces the par or stated value of its common stock and issues a proportionate number of additional shares, a stock split has occurred. There are no changes in the balances of any accounts, and no entry is required for a stock split.

Learning Outcomes	Example Exercises	Practice Exercises
• Define and give an example of a stock split.		
• Describe the accounting for and effects of a stock split on the financial statements.		

Describe and illustrate the use of earnings per share in evaluating a company's profitability.

Key Points The profitability of companies is often expressed as earnings per share. Earnings per share is computed by subtracting preferred dividends from net income and dividing by the average number of common shares outstanding.

Learning Outcomes	Example Exercises	Practice Exercises
• Describe the use of earnings per share in evaluating a company's profitability.		
• Compute and interpret earnings per share.	EE13-8	PE13-8A, 13-8B

Key Terms

cash dividend (605)
common stock (600)
cumulative preferred stock (600)
deficit (599)
discount (602)
dividends (599)
earnings per common share (EPS) (615)
in arrears (600)
outstanding stock (599)
paid-in capital (598)
par value (600)
preferred stock (600)
premium (602)
prior period adjustments (612)
restrictions (612)
retained earnings (598)
retained earnings statement (611)
statement of stockholders' equity (613)
stock (596)
stock dividend (607)
stock split (614)
stockholders (596)
stockholders' equity (598)
treasury stock (608)

Illustrative Problem

Altenburg Inc. is a lighting fixture wholesaler located in Arizona. During its current fiscal year, ended December 31, 2016, Altenburg Inc. completed the following selected transactions:

Feb. 3. Purchased 2,500 shares of its own common stock at $26, recording the stock at cost. (Prior to the purchase, there were 40,000 shares of $20 par common stock outstanding.)

May 1. Declared a semiannual dividend of $1 on the 10,000 shares of preferred stock and a $0.30 dividend on the common stock to stockholders of record on May 31, payable on June 15.

June 15. Paid the cash dividends.

Sept. 23. Sold 1,000 shares of treasury stock at $28, receiving cash.

Nov. 1. Declared semiannual dividends of $1 on the preferred stock and $0.30 on the common stock. In addition, a 5% common stock dividend was declared on the common stock outstanding, to be capitalized at the fair market value of the common stock, which is estimated at $30.

Dec. 1. Paid the cash dividends and issued the certificates for the common stock dividend.

Instructions

Journalize the entries to record the transactions for Altenburg Inc.

Solution

Date		Description	Post. Ref.	Debit	Credit
2016 Feb.	3	Treasury Stock		65,000	
		Cash			65,000
May	1	Cash Dividends		21,250	
		Cash Dividends Payable			21,250
		(10,000 × $1) + [(40,000 – 2,500) × $0.30].			
June	15	Cash Dividends Payable		21,250	
		Cash			21,250
Sept.	23	Cash		28,000	
		Treasury Stock			26,000
		Paid-In Capital from Sale of Treasury Stock			2,000
Nov.	1	Cash Dividends		21,550	
		Cash Dividends Payable			21,550
		(10,000 × $1) + [(40,000 – 1,500) × $0.30].			
	1	Stock Dividends		57,750*	
		Stock Dividends Distributable			38,500
		Paid-In Capital in Excess of Par—Common Stock			19,250
		*(40,000 – 1,500) × 5% × $30.			
Dec.	1	Cash Dividends Payable		21,550	
		Stock Dividends Distributable		38,500	
		Cash			21,550
		Common Stock			38,500

Discussion Questions

1. Of two corporations organized at approximately the same time and engaged in competing businesses, one issued $80 par common stock, and the other issued $1 par common stock. Do the par designations provide any indication as to which stock is preferable as an investment? Explain.
2. A stockbroker advises a client to "buy preferred stock. ... With that type of stock, ... [you] will never have to worry about losing the dividends." Is the broker right?
3. A corporation with both preferred stock and common stock outstanding has a substantial credit balance in its retained earnings account at the beginning of the current fiscal year. Although net income for the current year is sufficient to pay the preferred dividend of $150,000 each quarter and a common dividend of $90,000 each quarter, the board of directors declares dividends only on the preferred stock. Suggest possible reasons for passing the dividends on the common stock.
4. An owner of 2,500 shares of Simmons Company common stock receives a stock dividend of 50 shares.
   a. What is the effect of the stock dividend on the stockholder's proportionate interest (equity) in the corporation?
   b. How does the total equity of 2,550 shares compare with the total equity of 2,500 shares before the stock dividend?
5. a. Where should a declared but unpaid cash dividend be reported on the balance sheet?
   b. Where should a declared but unissued stock dividend be reported on the balance sheet?
6. A corporation reacquires 60,000 shares of its own $10 par common stock for $3,000,000, recording it at cost.
   a. What effect does this transaction have on revenue or expense of the period?
   b. What effect does it have on stockholders' equity?
7. The treasury stock in Discussion Question 6 is resold for $3,750,000.
   a. What is the effect on the corporation's revenue of the period?
   b. What is the effect on stockholders' equity?
8. What are the three classifications of restrictions of retained earnings, and how are such restrictions normally reported on the financial statements?
9. Indicate how prior period adjustments would be reported on the financial statements presented only for the current period.
10. What is the primary purpose of a stock split?

Practice Exercises

EE 13-1 p. 601

SHOW ME HOW

PE 13-1A Dividends per share **OBJ. 3**

National Furniture Company has 25,000 shares of cumulative preferred 2% stock, $75 par and 200,000 shares of $10 par common stock. The following amounts were distributed as dividends:

Year 1	$25,000
Year 2	88,000
Year 3	95,500

Determine the dividends per share for preferred and common stock for each year.

EE 13-1 p. 601

PE 13-1B Dividends per share **OBJ. 3**

Zero Calories Company has 16,000 shares of cumulative preferred 1% stock, $40 par and 80,000 shares of $150 par common stock. The following amounts were distributed as dividends:

Year 1	$ 21,600
Year 2	4,000
Year 3	100,800

Determine the dividends per share for preferred and common stock for each year.

EE 13-2 p. 604

PE 13-2A Entries for issuing stock **OBJ. 3**

On August 26, Mountain Realty Inc. issued for cash 120,000 shares of no-par common stock (with a stated value of $5) at $8. On October 1, Mountain Realty Inc. issued at par value 40,000 shares of preferred 1% stock, $10 par for cash. On November 30, Mountain Realty Inc. issued for cash 18,000 shares of preferred 1% stock, $10 par at $13.

Journalize the entries to record the August 26, October 1, and November 30 transactions.

EE 13-2 p. 604

PE 13-2B Entries for issuing stock **OBJ. 3**

On January 22, Zentric Corporation issued for cash 180,000 shares of no-par common stock at $4. On February 14, Zentric Corporation issued at par value 44,000 shares of preferred 2% stock, $55 par for cash. On August 30, Zentric Corporation issued for cash 9,000 shares of preferred 2% stock, $55 par at $60.

Journalize the entries to record the January 22, February 14, and August 30 transactions.

EE 13-3 p. 606

PE 13-3A Entries for cash dividends **OBJ. 4**

The declaration, record, and payment dates in connection with a cash dividend of $710,000 on a corporation's common stock are June 15, August 10, and September 15. Journalize the entries required on each date.

EE 13-3 p. 606

PE 13-3B Entries for cash dividends **OBJ. 4**

The declaration, record, and payment dates in connection with a cash dividend of $480,000 on a corporation's common stock are February 1, March 18, and May 1. Journalize the entries required on each date.

EE 13-4 p. 608

PE 13-4A Entries for stock dividends **OBJ. 4**

Olde Wine Corporation has 250,000 shares of $40 par common stock outstanding. On February 15, Olde Wine Corporation declared a 2% stock dividend to be issued May 2 to stockholders of record on March 27. The market price of the stock was $52 per share on February 15.

Journalize the entries required on February 15, March 27, and May 2.

EE 13-4 p. 608

PE 13-4B Entries for stock dividends **OBJ. 4**

Antique Buggy Corporation has 820,000 shares of $35 par common stock outstanding. On June 8, Antique Buggy Corporation declared a 5% stock dividend to be issued August 12 to stockholders of record on July 13. The market price of the stock was $63 per share on June 8.

Journalize the entries required on June 8, July 13, and August 12.

EE 13-5 p. 609

PE 13-5A Entries for treasury stock **OBJ. 5**

On January 31, Wilderness Resorts Inc. reacquired 22,500 shares of its common stock at $31 per share. On April 20, Wilderness Resorts sold 12,800 of the reacquired shares at $40 per share. On October 4, Wilderness Resorts sold the remaining shares at $28 per share.

Journalize the transactions of January 31, April 20, and October 4.

SHOW ME HOW

EE 13-5 *p. 609*

PE 13-5B Entries for treasury stock **OBJ. 5**

On May 27, Hydro Clothing Inc. reacquired 75,000 shares of its common stock at $8 per share. On August 3, Hydro Clothing sold 54,000 of the reacquired shares at $11 per share. On November 14, Hydro Clothing sold the remaining shares at $7 per share.

Journalize the transactions of May 27, August 3, and November 14.

SHOW ME HOW

EE 13-6 *p. 611*

PE 13-6A Reporting stockholders' equity **OBJ. 6**

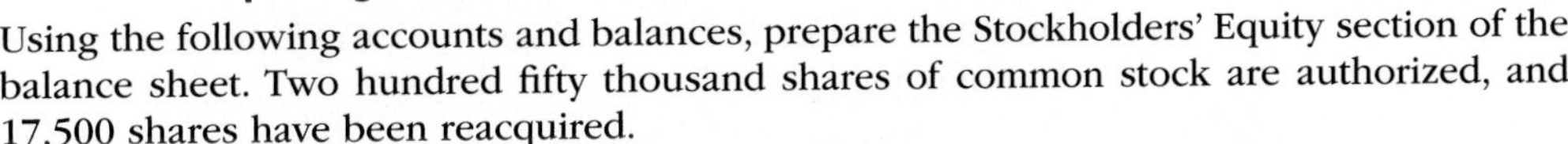

Using the following accounts and balances, prepare the Stockholders' Equity section of the balance sheet. Two hundred fifty thousand shares of common stock are authorized, and 17,500 shares have been reacquired.

Common Stock, $60 par	$12,000,0000
Paid-In Capital from Sale of Treasury Stock	320,000
Paid-In Capital in Excess of Par—Common Stock	3,200,000
Retained Earnings	18,500,000
Treasury Stock	1,137,500

SHOW ME HOW

EE 13-6 *p. 611*

PE 13-6B Reporting stockholders' equity **OBJ. 6**

Using the following accounts and balances, prepare the Stockholders' Equity section of the balance sheet. Five-hundred thousand shares of common stock are authorized, and 40,000 shares have been reacquired.

Common Stock, $120 par	$48,000,000
Paid-In Capital from Sale of Treasury Stock	4,500,000
Paid-In Capital in Excess of Par—Common Stock	6,400,000
Retained Earnings	63,680,000
Treasury Stock	5,200,000

SHOW ME HOW

EE 13-7 *p. 612*

PE 13-7A Retained earnings statement **OBJ. 6**

Rockwell Inc. reported the following results for the year ended June 30, 2016:

Retained earnings, July 1, 2015	$3,900,000
Net income	714,000
Cash dividends declared	100,000
Stock dividends declared	50,000

Prepare a retained earnings statement for the fiscal year ended June 30, 2016.

SHOW ME HOW

EE 13-7 *p. 612*

PE 13-7B Retained earnings statement **OBJ. 6**

Noric Cruises Inc. reported the following results for the year ended October 31, 2016:

Retained earnings, November 1, 2015	$12,400,000
Net income	2,350,000
Cash dividends declared	175,000
Stock dividends declared	300,000

Prepare a retained earnings statement for the fiscal year ended October 31, 2016.

SHOW ME HOW

EE 13-8 *p. 616*

PE 13-8A Earnings per share **OBJ. 8**

Financial statement data for the years ended December 31 for Dovetail Corporation follows:

	2016	2015
Net income	$448,750	$376,000
Preferred dividends	$40,000	$40,000
Average number of common shares outstanding	75,000 shares	60,000 shares

a. Determine the earnings per share for 2016 and 2015.

b. Does the change in the earnings per share from 2015 to 2016 indicate a favorable or an unfavorable trend?

SHOW ME HOW

EE 13-8 *p. 616*

PE 13-8B Earnings per share **OBJ. 8**

Financial statement data for the years ended December 31 for Black Bull Inc. follows:

	2016	2015
Net income	$2,485,700	$1,538,000
Preferred dividends	$50,000	$50,000
Average number of common shares outstanding	115,000 shares	80,000 shares

a. Determine the earnings per share for 2016 and 2015.

b. Does the change in the earnings per share from 2015 to 2016 indicate a favorable or an unfavorable trend?

Exercises

✔ Preferred stock, 1st year: $2.25

SHOW ME HOW

EX 13-1 Dividends per share **OBJ. 3**

Triple Z Inc., a developer of radiology equipment, has stock outstanding as follows: 12,000 shares of cumulative preferred 2% stock, $150 par and 50,000 shares of $10 par common. During its first four years of operations, the following amounts were distributed as dividends: first year, $27,000; second year, $60,000; third year, $80,000; fourth year, $90,000. Calculate the dividends per share on each class of stock for each of the four years.

✔ Preferred stock, 1st year: $0.90

EX 13-2 Dividends per share **OBJ. 3**

Lightfoot Inc., a software development firm, has stock outstanding as follows: 40,000 shares of cumulative preferred 1% stock, $125 par, and 100,000 shares of $150 par common. During its first four years of operations, the following amounts were distributed as dividends: first year, $36,000; second year, $58,000; third year, $75,000; fourth year, $124,000. Calculate the dividends per share on each class of stock for each of the four years.

SHOW ME HOW

EX 13-3 Entries for issuing par stock **OBJ. 3**

On April 20, Gallatin County Rocks Inc., a marble contractor, issued for cash 75,000 shares of $45 par common stock at $54, and on August 7, it issued for cash 20,000 shares of preferred stock, $10 par at $12.

a. Journalize the entries for April 20 and August 7.

b. What is the total amount invested (total paid-in capital) by all stockholders as of August 7?

SHOW ME HOW

EX 13-4 Entries for issuing no-par stock **OBJ. 3**

On May 15, Helena Carpet Inc., a carpet wholesaler, issued for cash 750,000 shares of no-par common stock (with a stated value of $1.50) at $4, and on June 30, it issued for cash 17,500 shares of preferred stock, $50 par at $60.

a. Journalize the entries for May 15 and June 30, assuming that the common stock is to be credited with the stated value.

b. What is the total amount invested (total paid-in capital) by all stockholders as of June 30?

SHOW ME HOW

EX 13-5 Issuing stock for assets other than cash **OBJ. 3**

On July 11, American Lift Corporation, a wholesaler of hydraulic lifts, acquired land in exchange for 5,000 shares of $5 par common stock with a current market price of $32. Journalize the entry to record the transaction.

EX 13-6 Selected stock transactions **OBJ. 3**

Alpha Sounds Corp., an electric guitar retailer, was organized by Michele Kirby, Paul Glenn, and Gretchen Northway. The charter authorized 1,000,000 shares of common stock with a par of $1. The following transactions affecting stockholders' equity were completed during the first year of operations:

a. Issued 100,000 shares of stock at par to Paul Glenn for cash.

b. Issued 3,000 shares of stock at par to Michele Kirby for promotional services provided in connection with the organization of the corporation, and issued 45,000 shares of stock at par to Michele Kirby for cash.

c. Purchased land and a building from Gretchen Northway in exchange for stock issued at par. The building is mortgaged for $180,000 for 20 years at 6%, and there is accrued interest of $5,200 on the mortgage note at the time of the purchase. It is agreed that the land is to be priced at $60,000 and the building at $225,000 and that Gretchen Northway's equity will be exchanged for stock at par. The corporation agreed to assume responsibility for paying the mortgage note and the accrued interest.

Journalize the entries to record the transactions.

EX 13-7 Issuing stock

OBJ. 3

Willow Creek Nursery, with an authorization of 75,000 shares of preferred stock and 200,000 shares of common stock, completed several transactions involving its stock on October 1, the first day of operations. The trial balance at the close of the day follows:

Cash	3,780,000	
Land	840,000	
Buildings	2,380,000	
Preferred 1% Stock, $80 par		2,800,000
Paid-In Capital in Excess of Par—Preferred Stock		420,000
Common Stock, $30 par		3,600,000
Paid-In Capital in Excess of Par—Common Stock		180,000
	7,000,000	7,000,000

All shares within each class of stock were sold at the same price. The preferred stock was issued in exchange for the land and buildings.

Journalize the two entries to record the transactions summarized in the trial balance.

EX 13-8 Issuing stock

OBJ. 3

SHOW ME HOW

Occupational Products Inc., a wholesaler of office products, was organized on March 1 of the current year, with an authorization of 25,000 shares of preferred 2% stock, $100 par and 500,000 shares of $10 par common stock. The following selected transactions were completed during the first year of operations:

Mar. 1. Issued 220,000 shares of common stock at par for cash.

1. Issued 500 shares of common stock at par to an attorney in payment of legal fees for organizing the corporation.

May 31. Issued 70,000 shares of common stock in exchange for land, buildings, and equipment with fair market prices of $150,000, $560,000 and $165,000 respectively.

July 1. Issued 18,000 shares of preferred stock at $110 for cash.

Journalize the transactions.

EX 13-9 Entries for cash dividends

OBJ. 4

SHOW ME HOW

The declaration, record, and payment dates in connection with a cash dividend of $135,000 on a corporation's common stock are January 12, March 13, and April 12. Journalize the entries required on each date.

EX 13-10 Entries for stock dividends

OBJ. 4

✓ b. (1) $3,000,000
(3) $36,500,000

SHOW ME HOW

Senior Life Co. is an HMO for businesses in the Portland area. The following account balances appear on the balance sheet of Senior Life Co.: Common stock (800,000 shares authorized; 500,000 shares issued), $4 par, $2,000,000; Paid-in capital in excess of par—common stock, $1,000,000; and Retained earnings, $33,500,000. The board of directors declared a 2% stock dividend when the market price of the stock was $13 a share. Senior Life Co. reported no income or loss for the current year.

a. Journalize the entries to record (1) the declaration of the dividend, capitalizing an amount equal to market value, and (2) the issuance of the stock certificates.

b. Determine the following amounts before the stock dividend was declared: (1) total paid-in capital, (2) total retained earnings, and (3) total stockholders' equity.

c. Determine the following amounts after the stock dividend was declared and closing entries were recorded at the end of the year: (1) total paid-in capital, (2) total retained earnings, and (3) total stockholders' equity.

EX 13-11 Treasury stock transactions

OBJ. 5

✔ b. $170,000 credit

SHOW ME HOW

Mystic Lake Inc. bottles and distributes spring water. On July 9 of the current year, Mystic Lake reacquired 40,000 shares of its common stock at $44 per share. On September 22, Mystic Lake Inc. sold 30,000 of the reacquired shares at $50 per share. The remaining 10,000 shares were sold at $43 per share on November 23.

a. Journalize the transactions of July 9, September 22, and November 23.

b. What is the balance in Paid-In Capital from Sale of Treasury Stock on December 31 of the current year?

c. For what reasons might Mystic Lake have purchased the treasury stock?

EX 13-12 Treasury stock transactions

OBJ. 5, 6

✔ b. $57,000 credit

SHOW ME HOW

Lawn Smart Inc. develops and produces spraying equipment for lawn maintenance and industrial uses. On May 29 of the current year, Lawn Smart Inc. reacquired 18,000 shares of its common stock at $20 per share. On August 11, 13,500 of the reacquired shares were sold at $24 per share, and on October 30, 3,000 of the reacquired shares were sold at $21.

a. Journalize the transactions of May 29, August 11, and October 30.

b. What is the balance in Paid-In Capital from Sale of Treasury Stock on December 31 of the current year?

c. What is the balance in Treasury Stock on December 31 of the current year?

d. How will the balance in Treasury Stock be reported on the balance sheet?

EX 13-13 Treasury stock transactions

OBJ. 5, 6

✔ b. $55,500 credit

Biscayne Bay Water Inc. bottles and distributes spring water. On May 14 of the current year, Biscayne Bay Water Inc. reacquired 23,500 shares of its common stock at $75 per share. On September 6, Biscayne Bay Water Inc. sold 14,000 of the reacquired shares at $81 per share. The remaining 9,500 shares were sold at $72 per share on November 30.

a. Journalize the transactions of May 14, September 6, and November 30.

b. What is the balance in Paid-In Capital from Sale of Treasury Stock on December 31 of the current year?

c. Where will the balance in Paid-In Capital from Sale of Treasury Stock be reported on the balance sheet?

d. For what reasons might Biscayne Bay Water Inc. have purchased the treasury stock?

EX 13-14 Reporting paid-in capital

OBJ. 6

✔ Total paid-in capital, $13,615,000

The following accounts and their balances were selected from the unadjusted trial balance of Point Loma Group Inc., a freight forwarder, at October 31, the end of the current fiscal year:

Common Stock, no par, $14 stated value	$ 4,480,000
Paid-In Capital from Sale of Treasury Stock	45,000
Paid-In Capital in Excess of Par—Preferred Stock	210,000
Paid-In Capital in Excess of Stated Value—Common Stock	480,000
Preferred 2% Stock, $120 par	8,400,000
Retained Earnings	39,500,000

Prepare the Paid-In Capital portion of the Stockholders' Equity section of the balance sheet using Method 1 of Exhibit 7. There are 375,000 shares of common stock authorized and 85,000 shares of preferred stock authorized.

EX 13-15 Stockholders' Equity section of balance sheet **OBJ. 6**

✔ Total stockholders' equity, $23,676,000

The following accounts and their balances appear in the ledger of Goodale Properties Inc. on June 30 of the current year:

Common Stock, $45 par	$ 3,060,000
Paid-In Capital from Sale of Treasury Stock	115,000
Paid-In Capital in Excess of Par—Common Stock	272,000
Retained Earnings	20,553,000
Treasury Stock	324,000

Prepare the Stockholders' Equity section of the balance sheet as of June 30. Eighty thousand shares of common stock are authorized, and 9,000 shares have been reacquired.

EX 13-16 Stockholders' Equity section of balance sheet **OBJ. 6**

✔ Total stockholders' equity, $89,100,000

Specialty Auto Racing Inc. retails racing products for BMWs, Porsches, and Ferraris. The following accounts and their balances appear in the ledger of Specialty Auto Racing Inc. on July 31, the end of the current year:

Common Stock, $36 par	$10,080,000
Paid-In Capital from Sale of Treasury Stock—Common	340,000
Paid-In Capital in Excess of Par—Common Stock	420,000
Paid-In Capital in Excess of Par—Preferred Stock	384,000
Preferred 1% Stock, $150 par	7,200,000
Retained Earnings	71,684,000
Treasury Stock—Common	1,008,000

Fifty thousand shares of preferred and 300,000 shares of common stock are authorized. There are 24,000 shares of common stock held as treasury stock.

Prepare the Stockholders' Equity section of the balance sheet as of July 31, the end of the current year using Method 1 of Exhibit 7.

EX 13-17 Retained earnings statement **OBJ. 6**

✔ Retained earnings, January 31, $64,210,000

SHOW ME HOW

Sumter Pumps Corporation, a manufacturer of industrial pumps, reports the following results for the year ended January 31, 2016:

Retained earnings, February 1, 2015	$59,650,000
Net income	8,160,000
Cash dividends declared	1,000,000
Stock dividends declared	2,600,000

Prepare a retained earnings statement for the fiscal year ended January 31, 2016.

EX 13-18 Stockholders' Equity section of balance sheet **OBJ. 6**

✔ Corrected total stockholders' equity, $122,800,000

List the errors in the following Stockholders' Equity section of the balance sheet prepared as of the end of the current year:

Stockholders' Equity

Paid-in capital:		
Preferred 2% stock, $80 par		
(125,000 shares authorized and issued)	$10,000,000	
Excess of issue price over par	500,000	$ 10,500,000
Retained earnings		96,700,000
Treasury stock (75,000 shares at cost)		1,755,000
Dividends payable		430,000
Total paid-in capital		$ 109,385,000
Common stock, $20 par (1,000,000 shares authorized, 825,000 shares issued)		17,655,000
Organizing costs		300,000
Total stockholders' equity		$127,340,000

✔ Total stockholders' equity, Dec. 31, $21,587,000

EX 13-19 Statement of stockholders' equity

OBJ. 6

The stockholders' equity T accounts of I-Cards Inc. for the fiscal year ended December 31, 2016, are as follows. Prepare a statement of stockholders' equity for the fiscal year ended December 31, 2016.

COMMON STOCK

			Jan. 1	Balance	4,800,000
			Apr. 14	Issued	
				30,000 shares	1,200,000
			Dec. 31	Balance	6,000,000

PAID-IN CAPITAL IN EXCESS OF PAR

			Jan. 1	Balance	960,000
			Apr. 14	Issued	
				30,000 shares	300,000
			Dec. 31	Balance	1,260,000

TREASURY STOCK

Aug. 7	Purchased				
	12,000 shares	552,000			

RETAINED EARNINGS

Mar. 31	Dividend	69,000	Jan. 1	Balance	11,375,000
June 30	Dividend	69,000	Dec. 31	Closing	
Sept. 30	Dividend	69,000		(net income)	3,780,000
Dec. 31	Dividend	69,000	Dec. 31	Balance	14,879,000

EX 13-20 Effect of stock split

OBJ. 7

SHOW ME HOW

Copper Grill Restaurant Corporation wholesales ovens and ranges to restaurants throughout the Southwest. Copper Grill Restaurant Corporation, which had 50,000 shares of common stock outstanding, declared a 3-for-1 stock split.

a. What will be the number of shares outstanding after the split?

b. If the common stock had a market price of $210 per share before the stock split, what would be an approximate market price per share after the split?

EX 13-21 Effect of cash dividend and stock split

OBJ. 4, 7

Indicate whether the following actions would (+) increase, (–) decrease, or (0) not affect Indigo Inc.'s total assets, liabilities, and stockholders' equity:

	Assets	Liabilities	Stockholders' Equity
(1) Authorizing and issuing stock certificates in a stock split	______	______	______
(2) Declaring a stock dividend	______	______	______
(3) Issuing stock certificates for the stock dividend declared in (2)	______	______	______
(4) Declaring a cash dividend	______	______	______
(5) Paying the cash dividend declared in (4)	______	______	______

EX 13-22 Selected dividend transactions, stock split

OBJ. 4, 7

Selected transactions completed by Canyon Ferry Boating Corporation during the current fiscal year are as follows:

Jan. 8. Split the common stock 2 for 1 and reduced the par from $80 to $40 per share. After the split, there were 150,000 common shares outstanding.

Apr. 30. Declared semiannual dividends of $0.75 on 18,000 shares of preferred stock and $0.28 on the common stock payable on July 1.

July 1. Paid the cash dividends.

Oct. 31. Declared semiannual dividends of $0.75 on the preferred stock and $0.14 on the common stock (before the stock dividend). In addition, a 5% common stock dividend was declared on the common stock outstanding. The fair market value of the common stock is estimated at $52.

Dec. 31. Paid the cash dividends and issued the certificates for the common stock dividend.

Journalize the transactions.

EX 13-23 EPS **OBJ. 8**

F·A·I

Junkyard Arts, Inc., had earnings of $316,000 for 2016. The company had 40,000 shares of common stock outstanding during the year. In addition, the company issued 15,000 shares of $50 par value preferred stock on January 9, 2016. The preferred stock has a dividend of $1.60 per share. There were no transactions in either common or preferred stock during 2016.

Determine the basic earnings per share for Junkyard Arts.

EX 13-24 EPS **OBJ. 8**

Pacific Gas and Electric Company is a large gas and electric utility operating in northern and central California. Three recent years of financial data for Pacific Gas and Electric Company are as follows:

	Fiscal Years Ended (in millions)		
	Year 3	**Year 2**	**Year 1**
Net income	$830	$858	$1,113
Preferred dividends	$14	$14	$14
Average number of common shares outstanding	424	401	382

a. Determine the earnings per share for fiscal Year 3, Year 2, and Year 1. Round to the nearest cent.

b. Evaluate the growth in earnings per share for the three years in comparison to the growth in net income for the three years.

EX 13-25 EPS **OBJ. 8**

For a recent year, **OfficeMax** and **Staples** are two companies competing in the retail office supply business. OfficeMax had a net income of $34,894,000, while Staples had a net loss of $210,706,000. OfficeMax had preferred stock of $28,726,000 with preferred dividends of $2,123,000. Staples had no preferred stock. The average outstanding common shares for each company were as follows:

	Average Number of Common Shares Outstanding
OfficeMax	85,881,000
Staples	669,479,000

a. Determine the earnings per share for each company. Round to the nearest cent.

b. Evaluate the relative profitability of the two companies.

Problems: Series A

PR 13-1A Dividends on preferred and common stock

OBJ. 3

✔ 1. Common dividends in 2013: $36,000

SHOW ME HOW

Sunbird Theatre Inc. owns and operates movie theaters throughout Florida and Georgia. Sunbird Theatre Inc. has declared the following annual dividends over a six-year period: 2011, $20,000; 2012, $36,000; 2013, $70,000; 2014, $90,000; 2015, $100,000 and 2016, $150,000. During the entire period ended December 31 of each year, the outstanding stock of the company was composed of 100,000 shares of cumulative, preferred 1% stock, $30 par, and 400,000 shares of common stock, $20 par.

Instructions

1. Calculate the total dividends and the per-share dividends declared on each class of stock for each of the six years. There were no dividends in arrears on January 1, 2011. Summarize the data in tabular form, using the following column headings:

Year	Total Dividends	Preferred Dividends		Common Dividends	
		Total	Per Share	Total	Per Share
2011	$ 20,000				
2012	36,000				
2013	70,000				
2014	90,000				
2015	102,000				
2016	150,000				

2. Calculate the average annual dividend per share for each class of stock for the six-year period.
3. Assuming a market price per share of $37.50 for the preferred stock and $30.00 for the common stock, calculate the average annual percentage return on initial shareholders' investment, based on the average annual dividend per share (a) for preferred stock and (b) for common stock.

PR 13-2A Stock transactions for corporate expansion

OBJ. 3

General Ledger

On December 1 of the current year, the following accounts and their balances appear in the ledger of Latte Corp., a coffee processor:

Preferred 2% Stock, $50 par (250,000 shares authorized, 80,000 shares issued)	$ 4,000,000
Paid-In Capital in Excess of Par—Preferred Stock	560,000
Common Stock, $35 par (1,000,000 shares authorized, 400,000 shares issued)	14,000,000
Paid-In Capital in Excess of Par—Common Stock	1,200,000
Retained Earnings	180,000,000

At the annual stockholders' meeting on March 31, the board of directors presented a plan for modernizing and expanding plant operations at a cost of approximately $11,000,000. The plan provided (a) that a building, valued at $3,375,000, and the land on which it is located, valued at $1,500,000, be acquired in accordance with preliminary negotiations by the issuance of 125,000 shares of common stock, (b) that 40,000 shares of the unissued preferred stock be issued through an underwriter, and (c) that the corporation borrow $4,000,000. The plan was approved by the stockholders and accomplished by the following transactions:

May 11. Issued 125,000 shares of common stock in exchange for land and a building, according to the plan.

20. Issued 40,000 shares of preferred stock, receiving $52 per share in cash.

31. Borrowed $4,000,000 from Laurel National, giving a 5% mortgage note.

Instructions

Journalize the entries to record the May transactions.

✔ f. Cash dividends, $243,000

General Ledger

SHOW ME HOW

PR 13-3A Selected stock transactions

OBJ. 3, 4, 5

The following selected accounts appear in the ledger of EJ Construction Inc. at the beginning of the current fiscal year:

Preferred 1% Stock, $50 par (100,000 shares authorized, 80,000 shares issued)	$ 4,000,000
Paid-In Capital in Excess of Par—Preferred Stock	175,000
Common Stock, $3 par (5,000,000 shares authorized, 2,000,000 shares issued)	6,000,000
Paid-In Capital in Excess of Par—Common Stock	1,500,000
Retained Earnings	32,350,000

During the year, the corporation completed a number of transactions affecting the stockholders' equity. They are summarized as follows:

a. Issued 500,000 shares of common stock at $8, receiving cash.

b. Issued 10,000 shares of preferred 1% stock at $60.

c. Purchased 50,000 shares of treasury common for $7 per share.

d. Sold 20,000 shares of treasury common for $9 per share.

e. Sold 5,000 shares of treasury common for $6 per share.

f. Declared cash dividends of $0.50 per share on preferred stock and $0.08 per share on common stock.

g. Paid the cash dividends.

Instructions

Journalize the entries to record the transactions. Identify each entry by letter.

✔ 4. Total stockholders' equity, $44,436,200

General Ledger

PR 13-4A Entries for selected corporate transactions

OBJ. 3, 4, 5, 6

Morrow Enterprises Inc. manufactures bathroom fixtures. The stockholders' equity accounts of Morrow Enterprises Inc., with balances on January 1, 2016, are as follows:

Common Stock, $20 stated value (500,000 shares authorized, 375,000 shares issued)	$ 7,500,000
Paid-In Capital in Excess of Stated Value—Common Stock	825,000
Retained Earnings	33,600,000
Treasury Stock (25,000 shares, at cost)	450,000

The following selected transactions occurred during the year:

Jan. 22. Paid cash dividends of $0.08 per share on the common stock. The dividend had been properly recorded when declared on December 1 of the preceding fiscal year for $28,000.

Apr. 10. Issued 75,000 shares of common stock for $24 per share.

June 6. Sold all of the treasury stock for $26 per share.

July 5. Declared a 4% stock dividend on common stock, to be capitalized at the market price of the stock, which is $25 per share.

Aug. 15. Issued the certificates for the dividend declared on July 5.

Nov. 23. Purchased 30,000 shares of treasury stock for $19 per share.

Dec. 28. Declared a $0.10-per-share dividend on common stock.

31. Closed the credit balance of the income summary account, $1,125,000.

31. Closed the two dividends accounts to Retained Earnings.

(Continued)

Instructions

1. Enter the January 1 balances in T accounts for the stockholders' equity accounts listed. Also prepare T accounts for the following: Paid-In Capital from Sale of Treasury Stock; Stock Dividends Distributable; Stock Dividends; Cash Dividends.
2. Journalize the entries to record the transactions, and post to the eight selected accounts.
3. Prepare a retained earnings statement for the year ended December 31, 2016.
4. Prepare the Stockholders' Equity section of the December 31, 2016, balance sheet.

PR 13-5A Entries for selected corporate transactions **OBJ. 3, 4, 5, 7**

✔ Oct. 1, cash dividends, $202,800

General Ledger

Selected transactions completed by Primo Discount Corporation during the current fiscal year are as follows:

Jan. 9. Split the common stock 3 for 1 and reduced the par from $75 to $25 per share. After the split, there were 1,200,000 common shares outstanding.

Feb. 28. Purchased 40,000 shares of the corporation's own common stock at $28, recording the stock at cost.

May 1. Declared semiannual dividends of $0.80 on 75,000 shares of preferred stock and $0.12 on the common stock to stockholders of record on June 1, payable on July 10.

July 10. Paid the cash dividends.

Sept. 7. Sold 30,000 shares of treasury stock at $34, receiving cash.

Oct. 1. Declared semiannual dividends of $0.80 on the preferred stock and $0.12 on the common stock (before the stock dividend). In addition, a 2% common stock dividend was declared on the common stock outstanding. The fair market value of the common stock is estimated at $36.

Dec. 1. Paid the cash dividends and issued the certificates for the common stock dividend.

Instructions

Journalize the transactions.

Problems: Series B

PR 13-1B Dividends on preferred and common stock **OBJ. 3**

✔ 1. Common dividends in 2013: $25,000

SHOW ME HOW

Yosemite Bike Corp. manufactures mountain bikes and distributes them through retail outlets in California, Oregon, and Washington. Yosemite Bike Corp. has declared the following annual dividends over a six-year period ended December 31 of each year: 2011, $24,000; 2012, $10,000; 2013, $126,000; 2014, $100,000; 2015, $125,000; and 2016, $125,000. During the entire period, the outstanding stock of the company was composed of 25,000 shares of cumulative preferred 2% stock, $90 par, and 100,000 shares of common stock, $4 par.

Instructions

1. Determine the total dividends and the per-share dividends declared on each class of stock for each of the six years. There were no dividends in arrears on January 1, 2011. Summarize the data in tabular form, using the following column headings:

		Preferred Dividends		Common Dividends	
Year	**Total Dividends**	**Total**	**Per Share**	**Total**	**Per Share**
2011	$ 24,000				
2012	10,000				
2013	126,000				
2014	100,000				
2015	125,000				
2016	125,000				

2. Determine the average annual dividend per share for each class of stock for the six-year period.
3. Assuming a market price of $100 for the preferred stock and $5 for the common stock, calculate the average annual percentage return on initial shareholders' investment, based on the average annual dividend per share (a) for preferred stock and (b) for common stock.

PR 13-2B Stock transaction for corporate expansion — OBJ. 3

General Ledger

Pulsar Optics produces medical lasers for use in hospitals. The accounts and their balances appear in the ledger of Pulsar Optics on April 30 of the current year as follows:

Preferred 1% Stock, $120 par (300,000 shares authorized, 36,000 shares issued)	$ 4,320,000
Paid-In Capital in Excess of Par—Preferred Stock	180,000
Common Stock, $15 par (2,000,000 shares authorized, 1,400,000 shares issued)	21,000,000
Paid-In Capital in Excess of Par—Common Stock	3,500,000
Retained Earnings	78,000,000

At the annual stockholders' meeting on August 5, the board of directors presented a plan for modernizing and expanding plant operations at a cost of approximately $9,000,000. The plan provided (a) that the corporation borrow $1,500,000, (b) that 20,000 shares of the unissued preferred stock be issued through an underwriter, and (c) that a building, valued at $4,150,000, and the land on which it is located, valued at $800,000, be acquired in accordance with preliminary negotiations by the issuance of 300,000 shares of common stock. The plan was approved by the stockholders and accomplished by the following transactions:

Oct. 9. Borrowed $1,500,000 from St. Peter City Bank, giving a 4% mortgage note.

17. Issued 20,000 shares of preferred stock, receiving $126 per share in cash.

28. Issued 300,000 shares of common stock in exchange for land and a building, according to the plan.

Instructions

Journalize the entries to record the October transactions.

PR 13-3B Selected stock transactions — OBJ. 3, 4, 5

✔ f. Cash dividends, $234,775

General Ledger

SHOW ME HOW

Diamondback Welding & Fabrication Corporation sells and services pipe welding equipment in Illinois. The following selected accounts appear in the ledger of Diamondback Welding & Fabrication Corporation at the beginning of the current fiscal year:

Preferred 2% Stock, $80 par (100,000 shares authorized, 60,000 shares issued)	$ 4,800,000
Paid-In Capital in Excess of Par—Preferred Stock	210,000
Common Stock, $9 par (3,000,000 shares authorized, 1,750,000 shares issued)	15,750,000
Paid-In Capital in Excess of Par—Common Stock	1,400,000
Retained Earnings	52,840,000

During the year, the corporation completed a number of transactions affecting the stockholders' equity. They are summarized as follows:

a. Purchased 87,500 shares of treasury common for $8 per share.

b. Sold 55,000 shares of treasury common for $11 per share.

c. Issued 20,000 shares of preferred 2% stock at $84.

d. Issued 400,000 shares of common stock at $13, receiving cash.

(Continued)

e. Sold 18,000 shares of treasury common for $7.50 per share.

f. Declared cash dividends of $1.60 per share on preferred stock and $0.05 per share on common stock.

g. Paid the cash dividends.

Instructions

Journalize the entries to record the transactions. Identify each entry by letter.

PR 13-4B Entries for selected corporate transactions **OBJ. 3, 4, 5, 6**

✔ 4. Total stockholders' equity, $11,262,432

General Ledger

Nav-Go Enterprises Inc. produces aeronautical navigation equipment. The stockholders' equity accounts of Nav-Go Enterprises Inc., with balances on January 1, 2016, are as follows:

Common Stock, $5 stated value (900,000 shares authorized, 620,000 shares issued)	$3,100,000
Paid-In Capital in Excess of Stated Value—Common Stock	1,240,000
Retained Earnings	4,875,000
Treasury Stock (48,000 shares, at cost)	288,000

The following selected transactions occurred during the year:

Jan. 15. Paid cash dividends of $0.06 per share on the common stock. The dividend had been properly recorded when declared on December 1 of the preceding fiscal year for $34,320.

Mar. 15. Sold all of the treasury stock for $6.75 per share.

Apr. 13. Issued 200,000 shares of common stock for $8 per share.

June 14. Declared a 3% stock dividend on common stock, to be capitalized at the market price of the stock, which is $7.50 per share.

July 16. Issued the certificates for the dividend declared on June 14.

Oct. 30. Purchased 50,000 shares of treasury stock for $6 per share.

Dec. 30. Declared a $0.08-per-share dividend on common stock.

31. Closed the credit balance of the income summary account, $775,000.

31. Closed the two dividends accounts to Retained Earnings.

Instructions

1. Enter the January 1 balances in T accounts for the stockholders' equity accounts listed. Also prepare T accounts for the following: Paid-In Capital from Sale of Treasury Stock; Stock Dividends Distributable; Stock Dividends; Cash Dividends.
2. Journalize the entries to record the transactions, and post to the eight selected accounts.
3. Prepare a retained earnings statement for the year ended December 31, 2016.
4. Prepare the Stockholders' Equity section of the December 31, 2016, balance sheet.

PR 13-5B Entries for selected corporate transactions **OBJ. 3, 4, 5, 7**

✔ Sept. 1, Cash dividends, $95,200

General Ledger

West Yellowstone Outfitters Corporation manufactures and distributes leisure clothing. Selected transactions completed by West Yellowstone Outfitters during the current fiscal year are as follows:

Jan. 15. Split the common stock 4 for 1 and reduced the par from $120 to $30 per share. After the split, there were 800,000 common shares outstanding.

Mar. 1. Declared semiannual dividends of $0.25 on 100,000 shares of preferred stock and $0.07 on the 800,000 shares of $30 par common stock to stockholders of record on March 31, payable on April 30.

Apr. 30. Paid the cash dividends.

May 31. Purchased 60,000 shares of the corporation's own common stock at $32, recording the stock at cost.

Aug. 17. Sold 40,000 shares of treasury stock at $38, receiving cash.

Sept. 1. Declared semiannual dividends of $0.25 on the preferred stock and $0.09 on the common stock (before the stock dividend). In addition, a 1% common stock dividend was declared on the common stock outstanding, to be capitalized at the fair market value of the common stock, which is estimated at $40.

Oct. 31. Paid the cash dividends and issued the certificates for the common stock dividend.

Instructions

Journalize the transactions.

Cases & Projects

CP 13-1 Board of directors' actions

Bernie Ebbers, the CEO of **WorldCom**, a major telecommunications company, was having personal financial troubles. Ebbers pledged a large stake of his WorldCom stock as security for some personal loans. As the price of WorldCom stock sank, Ebbers' bankers threatened to sell his stock in order to protect their loans. To avoid having his stock sold, Ebbers asked the board of directors of WorldCom to loan him nearly $400 million of corporate assets at 2.5% interest to pay off his bankers. The board agreed to lend him the money.

Comment on the decision of the board of directors in this situation.

CP 13-2 Ethics and professional conduct in business

Lou Hoskins and Shirley Crothers are organizing Red Lodge Metals Unlimited Inc. to undertake a high-risk gold-mining venture in Canada. Lou and Shirley tentatively plan to request authorization for 400,000,000 shares of common stock to be sold to the general public. Lou and Shirley have decided to establish par of $0.03 per share in order to appeal to a wide variety of potential investors. Lou and Shirley feel that investors would be more willing to invest in the company if they received a large quantity of shares for what might appear to be a "bargain" price.

Discuss whether Lou and Shirley are behaving in a professional manner.

CP 13-3 Issuing stock

Epstein Engineering Inc. began operations on January 5, 2016, with the issuance of 500,000 shares of $80 par common stock. The sole stockholders of Epstein Engineering Inc. are Barb Abrams and Dr. Amber Epstein, who organized Epstein Engineering Inc.

(Continued)

with the objective of developing a new flu vaccine. Dr. Epstein claims that the flu vaccine, which is nearing the final development stage, will protect individuals against 90% of the flu types that have been medically identified. To complete the project, Epstein Engineering Inc. needs $25,000,000 of additional funds. The local banks have been unwilling to loan the funds because of the lack of sufficient collateral and the riskiness of the business.

The following is a conversation between Barb Abrams, the chief executive officer of Epstein Engineering Inc., and Amber Epstein, the leading researcher:

Barb: What are we going to do? The banks won't loan us any more money, and we've got to have $25 million to complete the project. We are so close! It would be a disaster to quit now. The only thing I can think of is to issue additional stock. Do you have any suggestions?

Amber: I guess you're right. But if the banks won't loan us any more money, how do you think we can find any investors to buy stock?

Barb: I've been thinking about that. What if we promise the investors that we will pay them 5% of sales until they have received an amount equal to what they paid for the stock?

Amber: What happens when we pay back the $25 million? Do the investors get to keep the stock? If they do, it'll dilute our ownership.

Barb: How about, if after we pay back the $25 million, we make them turn in their stock for $120 per share? That's one and one-half times what they paid for it, plus they would have already gotten all their money back. That's a $120 profit per share for the investors.

Amber: It could work. We get our money, but don't have to pay any interest, dividends, or the $80 per share until we start generating sales. At the same time, the investors could get their money back plus $120 per share profit.

Barb: We'll need current financial statements for the new investors. I'll get our accountant working on them and contact our attorney to draw up a legally binding contract for the new investors. Yes, this could work.

In late 2016, the attorney and the various regulatory authorities approved the new stock offering, and 312,500 shares of common stock were privately sold to new investors at the stock's par of $80.

In preparing financial statements for 2016, Barb Abrams and Dan Fisher, the controller for Epstein Engineering Inc., have the following conversation:

Dan: Barb, I've got a problem.

Barb: What's that, Dan?

Dan: Issuing common stock to raise that additional $25 million was a great idea. But . . .

Barb: But what?

Dan: I've got to prepare the 2016 annual financial statements, and I am not sure how to classify the common stock.

Barb: What do you mean? It's common stock.

Dan: I'm not so sure. I called the auditor and explained how we are contractually obligated to pay the new stockholders 5% of sales until $80 per share is paid. Then, we may be obligated to pay them $120 per share.

Barb: So . . .

Dan: So the auditor thinks that we should classify the additional issuance of $25 million as debt, not stock! And, if we put the $25 million on the balance sheet as debt, we will violate our other loan agreements with the banks. And, if these agreements are violated, the banks may call in all our debt immediately. If they do that, we are in deep trouble. We'll probably have to file for bankruptcy. We just don't have the cash to pay off the banks.

1. Discuss the arguments for and against classifying the issuance of the $25 million of stock as debt.
2. What do you think might be a practical solution to this classification problem?

CP 13-4 Interpret stock exchange listing

The following stock exchange data for **Microsoft Corporation** were taken from the **Yahoo!** Finance Web site on November 29, 2013:

Microsoft Corporation (MSFT)			
Last Trade:	38.13	Prev. Clos:	37.60
Trade Time:	1:00 PM EST	1y Target Est:	36.32
		Day's Range:	37.82–38.29
		52wk Range:	26.26–38.29
		Volume:	22,090,428
		Div & Yield:	1.12 (3.00%)

a. If you owned 500 shares of Mircosoft, what amount would you receive as a quarterly dividend?

b. Compute the percentage increase in price from the Previous Close to the Last Trade. Round to two decimal places.

c. What is Microsoft's percentage change in market price from the 52-week low to the Last Trade on November 29, 2013? Round to one decimal place.

d. If you bought 500 shares of Microsoft at the Last Trade price on November 29, 2013, how much would it cost, and who gets the money?

CP 13-5 Dividends

Motion Designs Inc. has paid quarterly cash dividends since 2005. These dividends have steadily increased from $0.05 per share to the latest dividend declaration of $0.50 per share. The board of directors would like to continue this trend and is hesitant to suspend or decrease the amount of quarterly dividends. Unfortunately, sales dropped sharply in the fourth quarter of 2016 because of worsening economic conditions and increased competition. As a result, the board is uncertain as to whether it should declare a dividend for the last quarter of 2016.

On October 1, 2016, Motion Designs Inc. borrowed $4,000,000 from Valley National Bank to use in modernizing its retail stores and to expand its product line in reaction to its competition. The terms of the 10-year, 6% loan require Motion Designs Inc. to:

a. Pay monthly interest on the last day of the month.

b. Pay $400,000 of the principal each October 1, beginning in 2017.

c. Maintain a current ratio (current assets ÷ current liabilities) of 2.

d. Maintain a minimum balance (a compensating balance) of $100,000 in its Valley National Bank account.

(Continued)

On December 31, 2016, $1,000,000 of the $4,000,000 loan had been disbursed in modernization of the retail stores and in expansion of the product line. Motion Designs Inc.'s balance sheet as of December 31, 2016, follows:

Motion Designs Inc.
Balance Sheet
December 31, 2016

Assets			
Current assets:			
Cash		$ 250,000	
Marketable securities		3,000,000	
Accounts receivable	$ 800,000		
Less allowance for doubtful accounts	50,000	750,000	
Merchandise inventory		2,980,000	
Prepaid expenses		20,000	
Total current assets			$ 7,000,000
Property, plant, and equipment:			
Land		$1,500,000	
Buildings	$5,050,000		
Less accumulated depreciation	1,140,000	3,910,000	
Equipment	$3,320,000		
Less accumulated depreciation	730,000	2,590,000	
Total property, plant, and equipment			8,000,000
Total assets			$15,000,000
Liabilities			
Current liabilities:			
Accounts payable	$ 1,590,000		
Notes payable (Valley National Bank)	400,000		
Salaries payable	10,000		
Total current liabilities		$2,000,000	
Long-term liabilities:			
Notes payable (Valley National Bank)		3,600,000	
Total liabilities			$ 5,600,000
Stockholders' Equity			
Paid-in capital:			
Common stock, $25 par (200,000 shares authorized, 180,000 shares issued)	$ 4,500,000		
Excess of issue price over par	270,000		
Total paid-in capital		$4,770,000	
Retained earnings		4,630,000	
Total stockholders' equity			9,400,000
Total liabilities and stockholders' equity			$15,000,000

The board of directors is scheduled to meet January 10, 2017, to discuss the results of operations for 2016 and to consider the declaration of dividends for the fourth quarter of 2016. The chairman of the board has asked for your advice on the declaration of dividends.

1. What factors should the board consider in deciding whether to declare a cash dividend?

2. The board is considering the declaration of a stock dividend instead of a cash dividend. Discuss the issuance of a stock dividend from the point of view of (a) a stockholder and (b) the board of directors.

CP 13-6 Profiling a corporation

Group Project

Internet Project

Select a public corporation you are familiar with or which interests you. Using the Internet, develop a short (1 to 2 pages) profile of the corporation. Include in your profile the following information:

1. Name of the corporation.
2. State of incorporation.
3. Nature of its operations.
4. Total assets for the most recent balance sheet.
5. Total revenues for the most recent income statement.
6. Net income for the most recent income statement.
7. Classes of stock outstanding.
8. Market price of the stock outstanding.
9. High and low price of the stock for the past year.
10. Cash dividends paid for each share of stock during the past year.

In groups of three or four, discuss each corporate profile. Select one of the corporations, assuming that your group has $100,000 to invest in its stock. Summarize why your group selected the corporation it did and how financial accounting information may have affected your decision. Keep track of the performance of your corporation's stock for the remainder of the term.

Note: Most major corporations maintain "home pages" on the Internet. This home page provides a variety of information on the corporation and often includes the corporation's financial statements. In addition, the New York Stock Exchange Web site (www.nyse.com) includes links to the home pages of many listed companies that can be assessed by clicking on "Listings Directory." Financial statements can also be accessed using EDGAR, the electronic archives of financial statements filed with the Securities and Exchange Commission (SEC).

SEC documents can also be retrieved using the EdgarScan™ service at www.sec.gov/edgar/searchedgar/companysearch.html. To obtain annual report information, key in a company name in the appropriate space. Edgar will list the reports available to you for the company you've selected. Select the most recent annual report filing, identified as a 10-K or 10-K405.

ZUMA PRESS, INC./ALAMY

CHAPTER 14

Long-Term Liabilities: Bonds and Notes

Dick's Sporting Goods

Most of us don't have enough money in our bank accounts to buy a house or a car by simply writing a check. Just imagine if you had to save the entire purchase price of a house before you could buy it! To help us make these types of purchases, banks will typically lend us the money, as long as we agree to repay the loan with interest in smaller future payments. Loans such as this, or long-term debt, allow us to purchase assets such as houses and cars today, which benefit us over the long term.

The use of debt can also help a business reach its objectives. Most businesses have to borrow money in order to acquire assets that they will use to generate income. For example, in 1948 Dick Stack borrowed $300 from his grandmother to start a sporting goods store in Binghamton, New York. Over the years the business grew, and in the early 1990s, **Dick's Sporting Goods** used long-term debt to transform itself from a small business to a Fortune 500 company with more than 450 stores across the United States.

While debt can help companies like Dick's Sporting Goods grow to achieve financial success, too much debt can be a financial burden that may even lead to bankruptcy. Just like individuals, businesses must manage debt wisely. In this chapter, we will discuss the nature of, accounting for, and analysis of, long-term debt.

Learning Objectives

After studying this chapter, you should be able to: | *Example Exercises*

At a Glance 14 Page 664

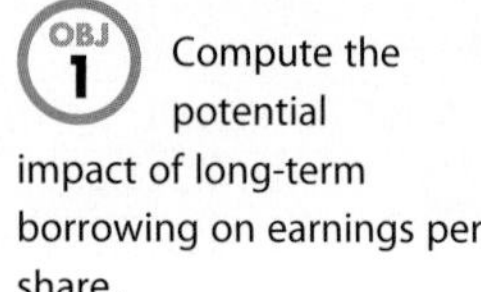

Compute the potential impact of long-term borrowing on earnings per share.

Financing Corporations

Corporations finance their operations using the following sources:

- Short-term debt, such as purchasing goods or services on account.
- Long-term debt, such as issuing bonds or notes payable.
- Equity, such as issuing common or preferred stock.

Short-term debt, including the purchase of goods and services on account and the issuance of short-term notes payable, was discussed in Chapter 11. Issuing equity in the form of common or preferred stock was discussed in Chapter 13. This chapter focuses on the use of long-term debt such as bonds and notes payable to finance a company's operations.

A **bond** is a form of an interest-bearing note. Like a note, a bond requires periodic interest payments, with the face amount to be repaid at the maturity date. For example, a 12% bond requires the company issuing the bond to pay 12% interest on the face amount of the bonds every year. As creditors of the corporation, bondholder claims on the corporation's assets rank ahead of stockholders.

One of the main factors that influences the decision to issue debt or equity is the effect that various financing alternatives will have on earnings per share. **Earnings per share (EPS)** measures the income earned by each share of common stock. It is computed as follows:[1]

$$\text{Earnings per Share} = \frac{\text{Net Income} - \text{Preferred Dividends}}{\text{Number of Common Shares Outstanding}}$$

[1] Earnings per share is also discussed in the *Financial Analysis and Interpretation* section of Chapter 13 and in Chapter 17.

To illustrate the effects that issuing debt can have on earnings per share, consider the following alternative plans for financing Boz Corporation, a $4,000,000 company:

	Plan 1		Plan 2		Plan 3	
	Amount	**Percent**	**Amount**	**Percent**	**Amount**	**Percent**
Issue 12% bonds	—	0%	—	0%	$2,000,000	50%
Issue preferred 9% stock, $50 par value	—	0	$2,000,000	50	1,000,000	25
Issue common stock, $10 par value	$4,000,000	100	2,000,000	50	1,000,000	25
Total amount of financing	$4,000,000	100%	$4,000,000	100%	$4,000,000	100%

The company must choose one of these plans. Each plan finances some of the corporation's operations by issuing common stock. However, the percentage financed by common stock varies from 100% (Plan 1) to 25% (Plan 3).

Assume the following data for Boz Corporation:

- Earnings before interest and income taxes are $800,000.
- The tax rate is 40%.
- All bonds or stocks are issued at their par or face amount.

The effect of the preceding financing plans on Boz's net income and earnings per share is shown in Exhibit 1.

EXHIBIT 1

Effect of Alternative Financing Plans—$800,000 Earnings

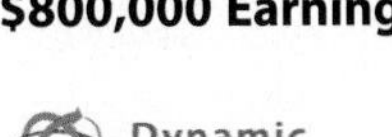

	Plan 1	Plan 2	Plan 3
12% bonds	—	—	$2,000,000
Preferred 9% stock, $50 par	—	$2,000,000	1,000,000
Common stock, $10 par	$4,000,000	2,000,000	1,000,000
Total	$4,000,000	$4,000,000	$4,000,000
Earnings before interest and income tax	$ 800,000	$ 800,000	$ 800,000
Deduct interest on bonds	—	—	240,000[a]
Income before income tax	$ 800,000	$ 800,000	$ 560,000
Deduct income tax	320,000[b]	320,000[b]	224,000[b]
Net income	$ 480,000	$ 480,000	$ 336,000
Dividends on preferred stock	—	180,000[c]	90,000[c]
Available for dividends on common stock	$ 480,000	$ 300,000	$ 246,000
Shares of common stock outstanding	÷ 400,000[d]	÷ 200,000[d]	÷ 100,000[d]
Earnings per share on common stock	$ 1.20	$ 1.50	$ 2.46

[a] $2,000,000 bonds × 12%
[b] Income before income tax × 40%
[c] Preferred stock × 9%
[d] Common stock ÷ $10 par value per share

Exhibit 1 indicates that when earnings are strong, Plan 3 has the highest earnings per share, making it the most attractive for common shareholders. This is because the company is generating more than enough net income to cover the bond interest. If the estimated earnings are more than $800,000, the difference between the earnings per share to common stockholders under Plans 1 and 3 is even greater.[2]

Lower earnings, however, have the opposite effect. If earnings are reduced to $440,000, as illustrated in Exhibit 2, Plans 1 and 2 become more attractive to common stockholders. This is because more of the company's earnings are being used to pay bond interest, leaving less net income attributable to common stockholders.

[2] The higher earnings per share under Plan 3 is due to a finance concept known as *leverage*. This concept is discussed further in Chapter 17.

EXHIBIT 2

Effect of Alternative Financing Plans—$440,000 Earnings

	Plan 1	Plan 2	Plan 3
12% bonds	—	—	$2,000,000
Preferred 9% stock, $50 par	—	$2,000,000	1,000,000
Common stock, $10 par	$4,000,000	2,000,000	1,000,000
Total	$4,000,000	$4,000,000	$4,000,000
Earnings before interest and income tax	$ 440,000	$ 440,000	$ 440,000
Deduct interest on bonds	—	—	240,000
Income before income tax	$ 440,000	$ 440,000	$ 200,000
Deduct income tax	176,000	176,000	80,000
Net income	$ 264,000	$ 264,000	$ 120,000
Dividends on preferred stock	—	180,000	90,000
Available for dividends on common stock	$ 264,000	$ 84,000	$ 30,000
Shares of common stock outstanding	÷ 400,000	÷ 200,000	÷ 100,000
Earnings per share on common stock	$ 0.66	$ 0.42	$ 0.30

In addition to earnings per share, the corporation should consider other factors in deciding among the financing plans. For example, if bonds are issued, the interest and the face value of the bonds at maturity must be paid. If these payments are not made, the bondholders could seek court action and force the company into bankruptcy. In contrast, a corporation is not legally obligated to pay dividends on preferred or common stock.

Example Exercise 14-1 Alternative Financing Plans

OBJ 1

Gonzales Co. is considering the following alternative plans for financing its company:

	Plan 1	Plan 2
Issue 10% bonds (at face value)	—	$2,000,000
Issue common stock, $10 par	$3,000,000	1,000,000

Income tax is estimated at 40% of income.

Determine the earnings per share of common stock under the two alternative financing plans, assuming income before bond interest and income tax is $750,000.

Follow My Example 14-1

	Plan 1	Plan 2
Earnings before bond interest and income tax	$750,000	$750,000
Deduct interest on bonds	0	200,000[2]
Income before income tax	$750,000	$550,000
Deduct income tax	300,000[1]	220,000[3]
Net income	$450,000	$330,000
Dividends on preferred stock	0	0
Available for dividends on common stock	$450,000	$330,000
Shares of common stock outstanding	÷300,000	÷100,000
Earnings per share on common stock	$ 1.50	$ 3.30

[1]$750,000 × 40% [2]$2,000,000 × 10% [3]$550,000 × 40%

Practice Exercises: PE 14-1A, PE 14-1B

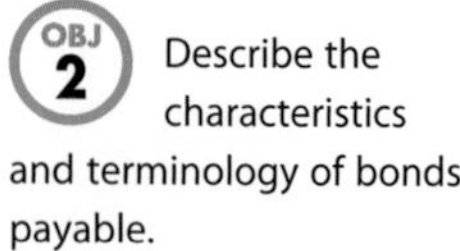

OBJ 2 Describe the characteristics and terminology of bonds payable.

Nature of Bonds Payable

Corporate bonds normally differ in face amount, interest rates, interest payment dates, and maturity dates. Bonds also differ in other ways such as whether corporate assets are pledged in support of the bonds.

Bond Characteristics and Terminology

A bond issue is normally divided into a number of individual bonds. The face amount of each bond is called the *principal*. This is the amount that must be repaid on the dates the bonds mature. The principal is usually $1,000, or a multiple of $1,000. The interest on bonds may be payable annually, semiannually, or quarterly. Most bonds pay interest semiannually.

The underlying contract between the company issuing bonds and the bondholders is called a **bond indenture**. This contract can be written in different ways, depending on the financing needs of the company. The two most common types of bonds are term bonds and serial bonds. When all bonds of an issue mature at the same time, they are called *term bonds*. If the bonds mature over several dates, they are called *serial bonds*. For example, one-tenth of an issue of $1,000,000 bonds, or $100,000, may mature 16 years from the issue date, another $100,000 in the 17th year, and so on.

There are also a variety of more complicated bond structures. For example, *convertible bonds* may be exchanged for shares of common stock, and *callable bonds* may be redeemed by the corporation prior to maturity. These bonds are discussed in intermediate and advanced accounting texts.

Proceeds from Issuing Bonds

When a corporation issues bonds, the proceeds received for the bonds depend on:

- The face amount of the bonds, which is the amount due at the maturity date.
- The interest rate on the bonds.
- The market rate of interest for similar bonds.

The face amount and the interest rate on the bonds are identified in the bond indenture. The interest rate to be paid on the face amount of the bond is called the **contract rate** or *coupon rate*.

The **market rate of interest**, sometimes called the **effective rate of interest**, is the rate determined from sales and purchases of similar bonds. The market rate of interest is affected by a variety of factors, including investors' expectations of current and future economic conditions.

By comparing the market and contract rates of interest, it can be determined whether the bonds will sell for more than, less than, or at their face amount, as shown in Exhibit 3.

EXHIBIT 3 **Issuing Bonds at a Discount, at Face Amount, and at a Premium**

If: Market Rate > Contract Rate

< $1,000 Bond

Less than $1,000

Then: Selling Price < Face Amount

Sold at a DISCOUNT

If: Market Rate = Contract Rate

= $1,000 Bond

$1,000

Then: Selling Price = Face Amount

Sold at FACE AMOUNT

If: Market Rate < Contract Rate

> $1,000 Bond

More than $1,000

Then: Selling Price > Face Amount

Sold at a PREMIUM

If the market rate equals the contract rate, bonds will sell at the **face amount**.

If the market rate is greater than the contract rate, the bonds will sell for less than their face value. The face amount of the bonds less the selling price is called a **discount**. A bond sells at a discount because buyers are not willing to pay the full face amount for bonds with a contract rate that is lower than the market rate.

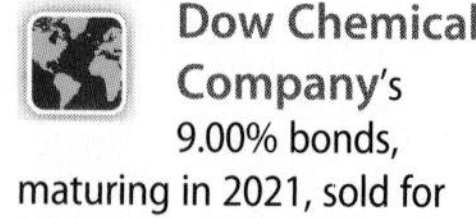
Dow Chemical Company's 9.00% bonds, maturing in 2021, sold for 129.97 on February 26, 2013.

If the market rate is less than the contract rate, the bonds will sell for more than their face value. The selling price of the bonds less the face amount is called a **premium**. A bond sells at a premium because buyers are willing to pay more than the face amount for bonds with a contract rate that is higher than the market rate.

The price of a bond is quoted as a percentage of the bond's face value. For example, a $1,000 bond quoted at 98 could be purchased or sold for $980 ($1,000 × 0.98). Likewise, bonds quoted at 109 could be purchased or sold for $1,090 ($1,000 × 1.09).

Business  Connection

U.S. GOVERNMENT DEBT

Like many corporations, the U.S. government issues debt to finance its operations. The debt is issued by the U.S. Treasury Department in the form of U.S. Treasury bills, notes, and bonds, which have the following characteristics:

	Issued at	Interest Paid	Maturity
U.S. Treasury bills	Discount	None	1 year or less
U.S. Treasury notes	Face value	Semiannual	1 to 10 years
U.S. Treasury bonds	Face value	Semiannual	10 years or more

At the end of 2013, total U.S. government debt issued by the federal government was estimated to be $17,548 billion. The Congressional Budget Office estimated that this amount would grow to $21,325 billion by 2017.

Source: Historical Tables: Budget of the U.S. Government, Fiscal Year 2013, U.S. Office of Management and Budget.

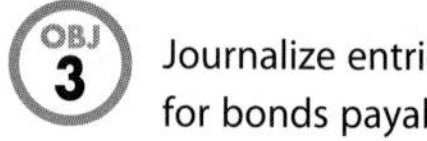
OBJ 3 Journalize entries for bonds payable.

Accounting for Bonds Payable

Bonds may be issued at their face amount, a discount, or a premium. When bonds are issued at less or more than their face amount, the discount or premium must be amortized over the life of the bonds. At the maturity date, the face amount must be repaid. In some situations, a corporation may redeem bonds before their maturity date by repurchasing them from investors.

Bonds Issued at Face Amount

If the market rate of interest is equal to the contract rate of interest, the bonds will sell for their face amount or at a price of 100. To illustrate, assume that on January 1, 2015, Eastern Montana Communications Inc. issued the following bonds:

Face amount	$100,000
Contract rate of interest	12%
Interest paid semiannually on June 30 and December 31.	
Term of bonds	5 years
Market rate of interest	12%

Since the contract rate of interest and the market rate of interest are the same, the bonds will sell at their face amount. The entry to record the issuance of the bonds is as follows:

2015					
Jan.	1	Cash		100,000	
		Bonds Payable			100,000
		Issued $100,000 bonds payable at face amount.			

Every six months (on June 30 and December 31) after the bonds are issued, interest of $6,000 ($100,000 × 12% × ½ year) is paid. The first interest payment on June 30, 2015, is recorded as follows:

2015				
June	30	Interest Expense	6,000	
		Cash		6,000
		Paid six months' interest on bonds.		

At the maturity date, the payment of the principal of $100,000 is recorded as follows:

2019				
Dec.	31	Bonds Payable	100,000	
		Cash		100,000
		Paid bond principal at maturity date.		

Example Exercise 14-2 Issuing Bonds at Face Amount

OBJ 3

On January 1, the first day of the fiscal year, a company issues a $1,000,000, 6%, five-year bond that pays semiannual interest of $30,000 ($1,000,000 × 6% × ½ year), receiving cash of $1,000,000. Journalize the entries to record (a) the issuance of the bonds at their face amount, (b) the first interest payment on June 30, and (c) the payment of the principal on the maturity date.

Follow My Example 14-2

a.		
Cash	1,000,000	
Bonds Payable		1,000,000
b.		
Interest Expense	30,000	
Cash		30,000
c.		
Bonds Payable	1,000,000	
Cash		1,000,000

Practice Exercises: PE 14-2A, PE 14-2B

Bonds Issued at a Discount

If the market rate of interest is greater than the contract rate of interest, the bonds will sell for less than their face amount. This is because investors are not willing to pay the full face amount for bonds that pay a lower contract rate of interest than the rate they could earn on similar bonds (market rate). The difference between the face amount and the selling price of the bonds is the bond discount.[3]

Note:
Bonds will sell at a discount when the market rate of interest is higher than the contract rate.

To illustrate, assume that on January 1, 2015, Western Wyoming Distribution Inc. issued the following bonds:

Face amount	$100,000
Contract rate of interest	12%
Interest paid semiannually on June 30 and December 31.	
Term of bonds	5 years
Market rate of interest	13%

[3] The price that investors are willing to pay for the bonds depends on present value concepts. Present value concepts, including the computation of bond prices, are described and illustrated in Appendix 1 at the end of this chapter.

Because the contract rate of interest is less than the market rate of interest, the bonds will sell at less than their face amount. Assuming the bonds sell for $96,406, the entry to record the issuance of the bonds is as follows:

2015				
Jan.	1	Cash	96,406	
		Discount on Bonds Payable	3,594	
		Bonds Payable		100,000
		Issued $100,000 bonds at discount.		

The $96,406 is the amount investors are willing to pay for bonds that have a lower contract rate of interest (12%) than the market rate (13%). The discount is the market's way of adjusting the contract rate of interest to the higher market rate of interest.

The account, Discount on Bonds Payable, is a contra account to Bonds Payable and has a normal debit balance. It is subtracted from Bonds Payable to determine the carrying amount (or book value) of the bonds payable. The **carrying amount** of bonds payable is the face amount of the bonds less any unamortized discount or plus any unamortized premium. Thus, after the preceding entry, the carrying amount of the bonds payable is $96,406 ($100,000 − $3,594).

Example Exercise 14-3 Issuing Bonds at a Discount

OBJ 3

On the first day of the fiscal year, a company issues a $1,000,000, 6%, five-year bond that pays semiannual interest of $30,000 ($1,000,000 × 6% × ½), receiving cash of $936,420. Journalize the entry to record the issuance of the bonds.

Follow My Example 14-3

Cash	936,420	
Discount on Bonds Payable	63,580	
Bonds Payable		1,000,000

Practice Exercises: PE 14-3A, PE 14-3B

Amortizing a Bond Discount

Every period, a portion of the bond discount must be reduced and added to interest expense to reflect the passage of time. This process, called **amortization**, increases the contract rate of interest on a bond to the market rate of interest that existed on the date the bonds were issued. The entry to amortize a bond discount is as follows:

Interest Expense	XXX	
Discount on Bonds Payable		XXX

The preceding entry may be made annually as an adjusting entry, or it may be combined with the semiannual interest payment. In the latter case, the entry would be as follows:

Interest Expense	XXX	
Discount on Bonds Payable		XXX
Cash (amount of semiannual interest)		XXX

The two methods of computing the amortization of a bond discount are:

- *Straight-line method*
- *Effective interest rate method,* sometimes called the *interest method*

The **effective interest rate method** is required by generally accepted accounting principles. However, the straight-line method may be used if the results do not differ significantly from the interest method. The straight-line method is used in this chapter. The effective interest rate method is described and illustrated in Appendix 2 at the end of this chapter.

The straight-line method provides equal amounts of amortization each period. To illustrate, amortization of the Western Wyoming Distribution bond discount of $3,594 is computed as follows:

Discount on bonds payable	$3,594
Term of bonds	5 years
Semiannual amortization	$359.40 ($3,594 ÷ 10 periods)

The combined entry to record the first interest payment and the amortization of the discount is as follows:

2015					
June	30	Interest Expense		6,359.40	
		Discount on Bonds Payable			359.40
		Cash			6,000.00
		Paid semiannual interest and amortized 1/10 of bond discount.			

The preceding entry is made on each interest payment date. Thus, the amount of the semiannual interest expense on the bonds ($6,359.40) remains the same over the life of the bonds.

The effect of the discount amortization is to increase the interest expense from $6,000.00 to $6,359.40 on every semiannual interest payment date. In effect, this increases the contract rate of interest from 12% to a rate of interest that approximates the market rate of 13%. In addition, as the discount is amortized, the carrying amount of the bonds increases until it equals the face amount of the bonds on the maturity date.

Example Exercise 14-4 Discount Amortization

OBJ 3

Using the bond from Example Exercise 14-3, journalize the first interest payment and the amortization of the related bond discount.

Follow My Example 14-4

Interest Expense	36,358	
Discount on Bonds Payable		6,358
Cash		30,000
Paid interest and amortized the bond discount ($63,580 ÷ 10).		

Practice Exercises: PE 14-4A, PE 14-4B

Bonds Issued at a Premium

If the market rate of interest is less than the contract rate of interest, the bonds will sell for more than their face amount. This is because investors are willing to pay more for bonds that pay a higher contract rate of interest than the rate they could earn on similar bonds (market rate).

Note: **Bonds will sell at a premium when the market rate of interest is less than the contract rate.**

To illustrate, assume that on January 1, 2015, Northern Idaho Transportation Inc. issued the following bonds:

Face amount	$100,000
Contract rate of interest	12%
Interest paid semiannually on June 30 and December 31.	
Term of bonds	5 years
Market rate of interest	11%

Because the contract rate of interest is more than the market rate of interest, the bonds will sell for more than their face amount. Assuming the bonds sell for $103,769, the entry to record the issuance of the bonds is as follows:

2015				
Jan.	1	Cash	103,769	
		Bonds Payable		100,000
		Premium on Bonds Payable		3,769
		Issued $100,000 bonds at a premium.		

The $3,769 premium is the extra amount investors are willing to pay for bonds that have a higher contract rate of interest (12%) than the market rate (11%). The premium is the market's way of adjusting the contract rate of interest to the lower market rate of interest.

The account, Premium on Bonds Payable, has a normal credit balance. It is added to Bonds Payable to determine the carrying amount (or book value) of the bonds payable. Thus, after the preceding entry, the carrying amount of the bonds payable is $103,769 ($100,000 + $3,769).

Example Exercise 14-5 Issuing Bonds at a Premium

OBJ 3

On the first day of the fiscal year, a company issues a $2,000,000, 12%, five-year bond that pays semiannual interest of $120,000 ($2,000,000 × 12% × ½), receiving cash of $2,154,440. Journalize the bond issuance.

Follow My Example 14-5

Cash	2,154,440	
Premium on Bonds Payable		154,440
Bonds Payable		2,000,000

Practice Exercises: PE 14-5A, PE 14-5B

Amortizing a Bond Premium

Like bond discounts, a bond premium must be amortized over the life of the bond. The amortization of a bond premium decreases the contract rate of interest on a bond to the market rate of interest that existed on the date the bonds were issued. The amortization can be computed using either the straight-line or the effective interest rate method. The entry to amortize a bond premium is as follows:

Premium on Bonds Payable	XXX	
Interest Expense		XXX

The preceding entry may be made annually as an adjusting entry, or it may be combined with the semiannual interest payment. In the latter case, it would be:

Interest Expense	XXX	
Premium on Bonds Payable	XXX	
Cash (amount of semiannual interest)		XXX

To illustrate, amortization of the preceding premium of $3,769 is computed as follows using the straight-line method:

Premium on bonds payable..................	$3,769
Term of bonds................................	5 years
Semiannual amortization.....................	$376.90 ($3,769 ÷ 10 periods)

The combined entry to record the first interest payment and the amortization of the premium is as follows:

2015 June	30	Interest Expense		5,623.10	
		Premium on Bonds Payable		376.90	
		Cash			6,000.00
		Paid semiannual interest and amortized 1/10 of bond premium.			

The preceding entry is made on each interest payment date. Thus, the amount of the semiannual interest expense ($5,623.10) on the bonds remains the same over the life of the bonds.

The effect of the premium amortization is to decrease the interest expense from $6,000.00 to $5,623.10. In effect, this decreases the rate of interest from 12% to a rate of interest that approximates the market rate of 11%. In addition, as the premium is amortized, the carrying amount of the bonds decreases until it equals the face amount of bonds on the maturity date.

Example Exercise 14-6 Premium Amortization

OBJ 3

Using the bond from Example Exercise 14-5, journalize the first interest payment and the amortization of the related bond premium.

Follow My Example 14-6

Interest Expense	104,556	
Premium on Bonds Payable	15,444	
Cash..		120,000
Paid interest and amortized the bond premium ($154,440 ÷ 10).		

Practice Exercises: PE 14-6A, PE 14-6B

Business  Connection

BOND RATINGS

When purchasing bonds, investors are very interested in understanding how likely it is that the bond issuer will be able to repay the bond principal and associated interest. To help them assess this likelihood, independent rating agencies review and grade the financial condition of companies that issue bonds. For example, the Standard & Poor's rating agency rates bonds on a scale from D (lowest) to AAA (highest). Bonds with a rating of BBB- or higher are called *investment grade* because they are issued by companies in sound financial condition and are considered to be reasonably safe investments. Bonds issued by companies in relatively weak financial condition receive ratings below BBB-, reflecting the higher potential for default or nonpayment. These lesser quality bonds are referred to as *non-investment grade* or *junk* bonds. The market rate of interest on junk bonds is much higher than the market rate on investment grade bonds, which compensates bond investors for junk bonds' higher risk of default.

Bond Redemption

A corporation may redeem or call bonds before they mature. This is often done when the market rate of interest declines below the contract rate of interest. In such cases, the corporation may issue new bonds at a lower interest rate and use the proceeds to redeem the original bond issue.

Callable bonds can be redeemed by the issuing corporation within the period of time and at the price stated in the bond indenture. Normally, the call price is above the face value. A corporation may also redeem its bonds by purchasing them on the open market.[4]

A corporation usually redeems its bonds at a price different from the carrying amount (or book value) of the bonds. A gain or loss may be realized on a bond redemption as follows:

- A *gain* is recorded if the price paid for redemption is below the bond carrying amount.
- A *loss* is recorded if the price paid for the redemption is above the carrying amount.

Gains and losses on the redemption of bonds are reported in the *Other income (loss)* section of the income statement.

To illustrate, assume that on June 30, 2015, a corporation has the following bond issue:

Face amount of bonds	$100,000
Premium on bonds payable	4,000

On June 30, 2015, the corporation redeemed one-fourth ($25,000) of these bonds in the market for $24,000. The entry to record the redemption is as follows:

2015 June	30	Bonds Payable		25,000	
		Premium on Bonds Payable		1,000	
		Cash			24,000
		Gain on Redemption of Bonds			2,000
		Redeemed $25,000 bonds for $24,000.			

In the preceding entry, only the portion of the premium related to the redeemed bonds ($4,000 × 25% = $1,000) is written off. The difference between the carrying amount of the bonds redeemed, $26,000 ($25,000 + $1,000), and the redemption price, $24,000, is recorded as a gain.

Assume that the corporation calls the remaining $75,000 of outstanding bonds, which are held by a private investor, for $79,500 on July 1, 2015. The entry to record the redemption is as follows:

2015 July	1	Bonds Payable		75,000	
		Premium on Bonds Payable		3,000	
		Loss on Redemption of Bonds		1,500	
		Cash			79,500
		Redeemed $75,000 bonds for $79,500.			

Example Exercise 14-7 Redemption of Bonds Payable OBJ 3

A $500,000 bond issue on which there is an unamortized discount of $40,000 is redeemed for $475,000. Journalize the redemption of the bonds.

[4] Some bond indentures require the corporation issuing the bonds to transfer cash to a special cash fund, called a *sinking fund,* over the life of the bond. Such funds help assure investors that there will be adequate cash to pay the bonds at their maturity date.

Follow My Example 14-7

Bonds Payable	500,000	
Loss on Redemption of Bonds	15,000	
Discount on Bonds Payable		40,000
Cash		475,000

Practice Exercises: PE 14-7A, PE 14-7B

Installment Notes

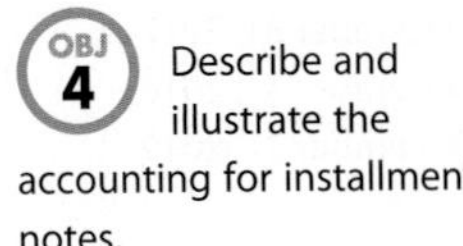
Describe and illustrate the accounting for installment notes.

Corporations often finance their operations by issuing bonds payable. As an alternative, corporations may issue a different kind of notes payable called installment notes. An **installment note** is a debt that requires the borrower to make equal periodic payments to the lender for the term of the note. Unlike bonds, each note payment includes the following:

- Payment of a portion of the amount initially borrowed, called the *principal*
- Payment of interest on the outstanding balance

At the end of the note's term, the principal will have been repaid in full.

Installment notes are often used to purchase specific assets such as equipment, and are often secured by the purchased asset. When a note is secured by an asset, it is called a **mortgage note**. If the borrower fails to pay a mortgage note, the lender has the right to take possession of the pledged asset and sell it to pay off the debt. Mortgage notes are typically issued by an individual bank.

Individuals typically use mortgage notes when buying a house or car.

Issuing an Installment Note

When an installment note is issued, an entry is recorded debiting Cash and crediting Notes Payable. To illustrate, assume that Lewis Company issues the following installment note to City National Bank on January 1, 2015:

Principal amount of note	$24,000
Interest rate	6%
Term of note	5 years
Annual payments	$5,698[5]

The entry to record the issuance of the note is as follows:

2015 Jan.	1	Cash		24,000	
		Notes Payable			24,000
		Issued installment note for cash.			

Annual Payments

The preceding note payable requires Lewis Company to repay the principal and interest in equal payments of $5,698 beginning December 31, 2015, for each of the next five years. Unlike bonds, however, each installment note payment includes an interest and principal component.

The interest portion of an installment note payment is computed by multiplying the interest rate by the carrying amount (book value) of the note at the beginning of the period. The principal portion of the payment is then computed as the difference between the total installment note payment (cash paid) and the interest component. These computations are illustrated in Exhibit 4 (rounded to the nearest dollar).

[5] The amount of the annual payment is calculated by using the present value concepts discussed in Appendix 1 at the end of this chapter. The annual payment of $5,698 is computed by dividing the $24,000 loan amount by the present value of an annuity of $1 for five periods at 6% (4.21236) from Exhibit 10 (rounded to the nearest dollar).

EXHIBIT 4 **Amortization of Installment Notes**

	A	B	C	D	E
For the Year Ending	**January 1 Carrying Amount**	**Note Payment (cash paid)**	**Interest Expense (6% of January 1 Note Carrying Amount)**	**Decrease in Notes Payable (B – C)**	**December 31 Carrying Amount (A – D)**
December 31, 2015	$24,000	$ 5,698	$ 1,440 (6% of $24,000)	$ 4,258	$19,742
December 31, 2016	19,742	5,698	1,185 (6% of $19,742)	4,513	15,229
December 31, 2017	15,229	5,698	914 (6% of $15,229)	4,784	10,445
December 31, 2018	10,445	5,698	627 (6% of $10,445)	5,071	5,374
December 31, 2019	5,374	5,698	324* (6% of $5,374)	5,374	0
		$28,490	**$4,490**	**$24,000**	

*Rounded ($5,374 – $5,698).

1. The January 1, 2015, carrying value (Column A) equals the amount borrowed from the bank. The January 1 balance in the following years equals the December 31 balance from the prior year.
2. The note payment (Column B) remains constant at $5,698, the annual cash payment required by the bank.
3. The interest expense (Column C) is computed at 6% of the installment note carrying amount at the beginning of each year. As a result, the interest expense decreases each year.
4. Notes payable decreases each year by the amount of the principal repayment (Column D). The principal repayment is computed by subtracting the interest expense (Column C) from the total payment (Column B). The principal repayment (Column D) increases each year as the interest expense decreases (Column C).
5. The carrying amount on December 31 (Column E) of the note decreases from $24,000, the initial amount borrowed, to $0 at the end of the five years.

The entry to record the first payment on December 31, 2015, is as follows:

2015				
Dec.	31	Interest Expense	1,440	
		Notes Payable	4,258	
		Cash		5,698
		Paid principal and interest on installment note.		

The entry to record the second payment on December 31, 2016, is as follows:

2016				
Dec.	31	Interest Expense	1,185	
		Notes Payable	4,513	
		Cash		5,698
		Paid principal and interest on installment note.		

As the prior entries show, the cash payment is the same in each year. The interest and principal repayment, however, change each year. This is because the carrying amount (book value) of the note decreases each year as principal is repaid, which decreases the interest component the next period.

The entry to record the final payment on December 31, 2019, is as follows:

2019				
Dec.	31	Interest Expense	324	
		Notes Payable	5,374	
		Cash		5,698
		Paid principal and interest on installment note.		

After the final payment, the carrying amount on the note is zero, indicating that the note has been paid in full. Any assets that secure the note would then be released by the bank.

Example Exercise 14-8 Journalizing Installment Notes

On the first day of the fiscal year, a company issues a $30,000, 10%, five-year installment note that has annual payments of $7,914. The first note payment consists of $3,000 of interest and $4,914 of principal repayment.

a. Journalize the entry to record the issuance of the installment note.

b. Journalize the first annual note payment.

Follow My Example 14-8

a.		
Cash	30,000	
Notes Payable		30,000
b.		
Interest Expense	3,000	
Notes Payable	4,914	
Cash		7,914

Practice Exercises: PE 14-8A, PE 14-8B

Integrity, Objectivity, and Ethics in Business

THE RATINGS GAME

In February 2013, the United States Justice Department filed a lawsuit against the three main credit rating agencies (**Moody's, Standard & Poor's,** and **Fitch**) for inflating their ratings on highly risk bond issuances between 2004 and 2007. During this time period, the three ratings agencies gave their highest rating (AAA) to debt securities that were, in fact, highly risky. During the financial crisis of 2008, most of these bonds experienced significant drops in value, leaving investors with huge losses. The Justice Department lawsuit alleges that the ratings agencies were aware of the high risks associated with these bonds but inflated their ratings because of the large fee they received for providing a rating on these bonds. At the time of this writing, the lawsuit was pending.

Source: "U.S. vs. S&P: The Rating Game," *The Chicago Tribune,* February 6, 2013.

Reporting Long-Term Liabilities

OBJ 5 Describe and illustrate the reporting of long-term liabilities, including bonds and notes payable.

Bonds payable and notes payable are reported as liabilities on the balance sheet. Any portion of the bonds or notes that is due within one year is reported as a current liability. Any remaining bonds or notes are reported as a long-term liability.

Any unamortized premium is reported as an addition to the face amount of the bonds. Any unamortized discount is reported as a deduction from the face amount of the bonds. A description of the bonds and notes should also be reported either on the face of the financial statements or in the accompanying notes.

The reporting of bonds and notes payable for **Mornin' Joe** follows:

Mornin' Joe
Balance Sheet
December 31, 2016

Current liabilities:		
Accounts payable	$133,000	
Notes payable (current portion)	200,000	
Salaries and wages payable	42,000	
Payroll taxes payable	16,400	
Interest payable	40,000	
Total current liabilities		$ 431,400
Long-term liabilities:		
Bonds payable, 8%, due December 31, 2030	$500,000	
Less unamortized discount	16,000	$ 484,000
Notes payable		1,400,000
Total long-term liabilities		$1,884,000
Total liabilities		$2,315,400

OBJ 6 Describe and illustrate how the number of times interest charges are earned is used to evaluate a company's financial condition.

Financial Analysis and Interpretation: Number of Times Interest Charges Are Earned

As we have discussed, the assets of a company are subject to the (1) claims of creditors and (2) the rights of owners. As creditors, bondholders are primarily concerned with the company's ability to make its periodic interest payments and repay the face amount of the bonds at maturity.

Analysts assess the risk that bondholders will not receive their interest payments by computing the **number of times interest charges are earned** during the year as follows:

$$\text{Number of Times Interest Charges Are Earned} = \frac{\text{Income Before Income Tax} + \text{Interest Expense}}{\text{Interest Expense}}$$

This ratio computes the number of times interest payments could be paid out of current period earnings, measuring the company's ability to make its interest payments. Because interest payments reduce income tax expense, the ratio is computed using income before tax.

To illustrate, the following data were taken from a recent annual report of The Coca-Cola Company (in thousands):

Interest expense	$ 733,000
Income before income tax	14,243,000

The number of times interest charges are earned for The Coca-Cola Company is computed as follows:

$$\text{Number of Times Interest Charges Are Earned} = \frac{\$14{,}243{,}000 + \$733{,}000}{\$733{,}000} = 20.43$$

Compare this to the number of times interest charges are earned for United Continental Holdings (an airline), and Verizon Communications (a telecommunications company) which follow (in thousands):

	Coca-Cola	United Continental	Verizon Communications
Interest expense	$733,000	$783,000	$2,523,000
Income before income tax expense	$14,243,000	$250,000	$12,684,000
Number of times interest charges are earned	20.43	1.32	6.03

Coca-Cola's number of times interest charges are earned is 20.43, indicating that the company generates enough income before taxes to pay (cover) its interest payments 20.43 times. As a result, debtholders have extremely good protection in the event of an earnings decline. Compare this to United Continental, which only generates enough income before taxes to pay (cover) its interest payments 1.32 times. A small decrease in United Continental's earnings could jeopardize the payment of interest. Verizon Communications falls in between, with a ratio of 6.03.

Example Exercise 14-9 Number of Times Interest Charges Are Earned

Harris Industries reported the following on the company's income statement in 2016 and 2015:

	2016	2015
Interest expense	$ 200,000	$180,000
Income before income tax expense	1,000,000	720,000

a. Determine the number of times interest charges were earned for 2016 and 2015.
b. Is the number of times interest charges are earned improving or declining?

Follow My Example 14-9

a. 2016:

Number of times interest charges are earned: $\dfrac{\$1{,}000{,}000 + \$200{,}000}{\$200{,}000} = 6.0$

2015:

Number of times interest charges are earned: $\dfrac{\$720{,}000 + \$180{,}000}{\$180{,}000} = 5.0$

b. The number of times interest charges are earned has increased from 5.0 in 2015 to 6.0 in 2016. Thus, the debtholders have improved confidence in the company's ability to make its interest payments.

Practice Exercises: PE 14-9A, PE 14-9B

APPENDIX 1

Present Value Concepts and Pricing Bonds Payable

When a corporation issues bonds, the price that investors are willing to pay for the bonds depends on the following:

- The face amount of the bonds, which is the amount due at the maturity date.
- The periodic interest to be paid on the bonds.
- The market rate of interest.

An investor determines how much to pay for the bonds by computing the present value of the bond's future cash receipts, using the market rate of interest. A bond's future cash receipts include its face value at maturity and the periodic interest payments.

Present Value Concepts

The concept of present value is based on the time value of money. The *time value of money concept* recognizes that cash received today is worth more than the same amount of cash to be received in the future.

To illustrate, what would you rather have: $1,000 today or $1,000 one year from now? You would rather have the $1,000 today because it could be invested to earn interest. For example, if the $1,000 could be invested to earn 10% per year, the $1,000 will accumulate to $1,100 ($1,000 plus $100 interest) in one year. In this sense, you can think of the $1,000 in hand today as the **present value** of $1,100 to be received a year from today. This present value is illustrated in Exhibit 5.

EXHIBIT 5 **Present Value and Future Value**

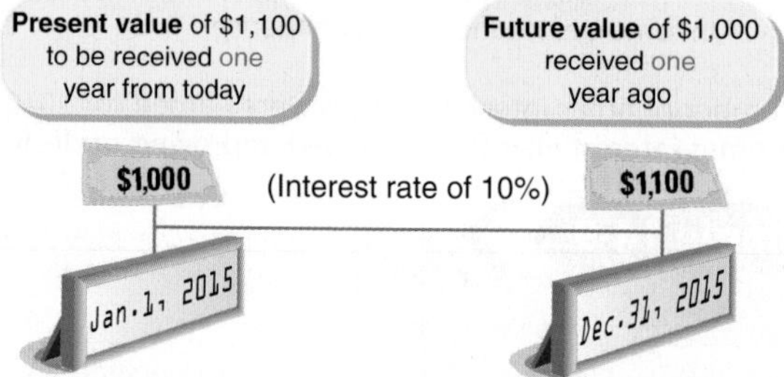

A related concept to present value is **future value**. To illustrate, using the preceding example illustrated in Exhibit 5, the $1,100 to be received on December 31, 2015, is the *future value* of $1,000 on January 1, 2015, assuming an interest rate of 10%.

Present Value of an Amount To illustrate the present value of an amount, assume that $1,000 is to be received in one year. If the market rate of interest is 10%, the present value of the $1,000 is $909.09 ($1,000 ÷ 1.10). This present value is illustrated in Exhibit 6.

EXHIBIT 6 **Present Value of an Amount to Be Received in One Year**

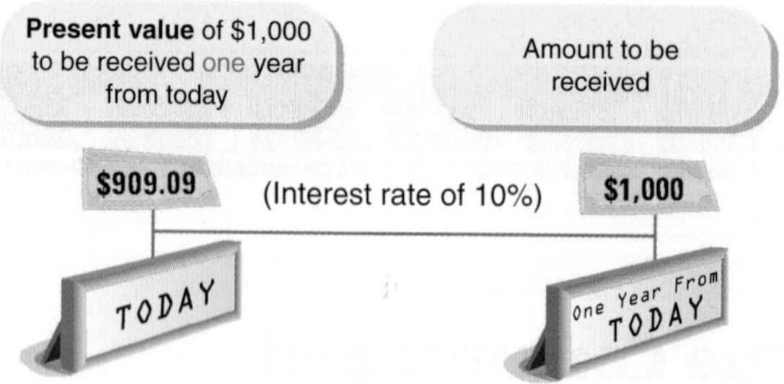

If the $1,000 is to be received in two years, with interest of 10% compounded at the end of the first year, the present value is $826.45 ($909.09 ÷ 1.10).[6] This present value is illustrated in Exhibit 7.

[6] Note that the future value of $826.45 in two years, at an interest rate of 10% compounded annually, is $1,000.

EXHIBIT 7 **Present Value of an Amount to Be Received in Two Years**

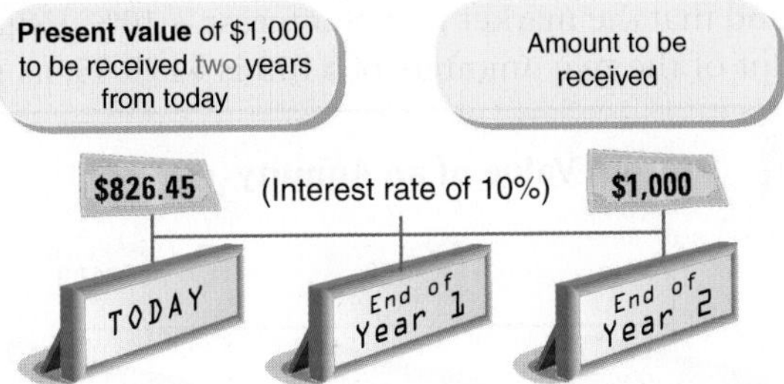

Spreadsheet software and business calculators have built-in present value functions that can also be used to calculate present values.

The present value of an amount to be received in the future can be determined by a series of divisions as illustrated in Exhibits 5, 6, and 7. In practice, however, it is easier to use a table of present values.

The *present value of $1* table is used to find the present value factor for $1 to be received after a number of periods in the future. The amount to be received is then multiplied by this factor to determine its present value.

To illustrate, Exhibit 8 is a partial table of the present value of $1.[7] Exhibit 8 indicates that the present value of $1 to be received in two years with a market rate of interest of 10% a year is 0.82645. Multiplying $1,000 to be received in two years by 0.82645 yields $826.45 ($1,000 × 0.82645). This amount is the same amount computed earlier. In Exhibit 8, the Periods column represents the number of compounding periods, and the percentage columns represent the compound interest rate per period. Thus, the present value factor from Exhibit 8 for 12% for five years is 0.56743. If the interest is compounded semiannually, the interest rate is 6% (12% ÷ 2), and the number of periods is 10 (5 years × 2 times per year). Thus, the present value factor from Exhibit 8 for 6% and 10 periods is 0.55839.

EXHIBIT 8 **Present Value of $1 at Compound Interest**

Periods	4%	4½%	5%	5½%	6%	6½%	7%	10%	11%	12%	13%
1	0.96154	0.956940	0.95238	0.94787	0.94340	0.93897	0.93458	0.90909	0.90090	0.89286	0.88496
2	0.92456	0.915730	0.90703	0.89845	0.89000	0.88166	0.87344	0.82645	0.81162	0.79719	0.78315
3	0.88900	0.876300	0.86384	0.85161	0.83962	0.82785	0.81630	0.75131	0.73119	0.71178	0.69305
4	0.85480	0.838560	0.82270	0.80722	0.79209	0.77732	0.76290	0.68301	0.65873	0.63552	0.61332
5	0.82193	0.802450	0.78353	0.76513	0.74726	0.72988	0.71299	0.62092	0.59345	0.56743	0.54276
6	0.79031	0.767900	0.74622	0.72525	0.70496	0.68533	0.66634	0.56447	0.53464	0.50663	0.48032
7	0.75992	0.734830	0.71068	0.68744	0.66506	0.64351	0.62275	0.51316	0.48166	0.45235	0.42506
8	0.73069	0.703190	0.67684	0.65160	0.62741	0.60423	0.58201	0.46651	0.43393	0.40388	0.37616
9	0.70259	0.672900	0.64461	0.61763	0.59190	0.56735	0.54393	0.42410	0.39092	0.36061	0.33288
10	0.67556	0.643930	0.61391	0.58543	0.55839	0.53273	0.50835	0.38554	0.35218	0.32197	0.29459

Some additional examples using Exhibit 8 follow:

	Number of Periods	Interest Rate	Present Value of $1 Factor from Exhibit 8
10% for *two* years compounded *annually*	2	10%	0.82645
10% for *two* years compounded *semiannually*	4	5%	0.82270
10% for *three* years compounded *semiannually*	6	5%	0.74622
12% for *five* years compounded *semiannually*	10	6%	0.55839

[7] To simplify the illustrations and homework assignments, the tables presented in this chapter are limited to 10 periods for a small number of interest rates, and the amounts are carried to only five decimal places. Computer programs and business function calculators can be used to determine present values for any number of interest rates, decimal places, or periods. More complete interest tables are presented in Appendix A of the text.

Present Value of the Periodic Receipts A series of equal cash receipts spaced equally in time is called an **annuity**. The **present value of an annuity** is the sum of the present values of each cash receipt. To illustrate, assume that $100 is to be received annually for two years and that the market rate of interest is 10%. Using Exhibit 8, the present value of the receipt of the two amounts of $100 is $173.55, as shown in Exhibit 9.

EXHIBIT 9 **Present Value of an Annuity**

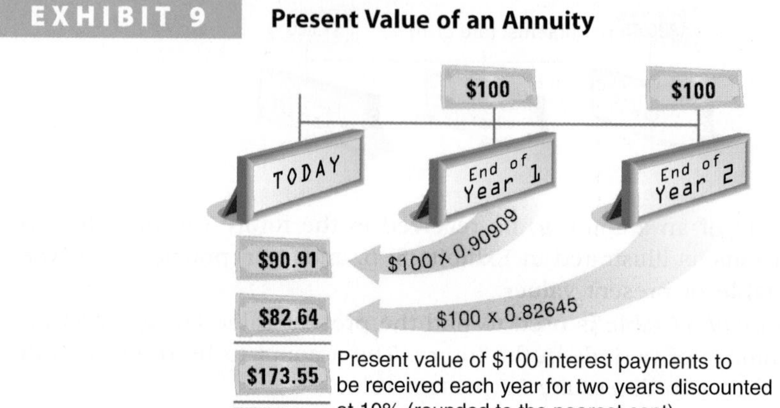

Instead of using present value of $1 tables to determine the present value of each cash flow separately, such as in Exhibit 8, the present value of an annuity can be computed in a single step. Using a value from the *present value of an annuity of $1* table in Exhibit 10, the present value of the entire annuity can be calculated by multiplying the equal cash payment times the appropriate present value of an annuity of $1.

EXHIBIT 10 **Present Value of an Annuity of $1 at Compound Interest**

Periods	4%	4½%	5%	5½%	6%	6½%	7%	10%	11%	12%	13%
1	0.96154	0.95694	0.95238	0.94787	0.94340	0.93897	0.93458	0.90909	0.90090	0.89286	0.88496
2	1.88609	1.87267	1.85941	1.84632	1.83339	1.82063	1.80802	1.73554	1.71252	1.69005	1.66810
3	2.77509	2.74896	2.72325	2.69793	2.67301	2.64848	2.62432	2.48685	2.44371	2.40183	2.36115
4	3.62990	3.58753	3.54595	3.50515	3.46511	3.42580	3.38721	3.16987	3.10245	3.03735	2.97447
5	4.45182	4.38998	4.32948	4.27028	4.21236	4.15568	4.10020	3.79079	3.69590	3.60478	3.51723
6	5.24214	5.15787	5.07569	4.99553	4.91732	4.84101	4.76654	4.35526	4.23054	4.11141	3.99755
7	6.00205	5.89270	5.78637	5.68297	5.58238	5.48452	5.38929	4.86842	4.71220	4.56376	4.42261
8	6.73274	6.59589	6.46321	6.33457	6.20979	6.08875	5.97130	5.33493	5.14612	4.96764	4.79677
9	7.43533	7.26879	7.10782	6.95220	6.80169	6.65610	6.51523	5.75902	5.53705	5.32825	5.13166
10	8.11090	7.91272	7.72173	7.53763	7.36009	7.18883	7.02358	6.14457	5.88923	5.65022	5.42624

To illustrate, the present value of $100 to be received at the end of each of the next two years at 10% compound interest per period is $173.55 ($100 × 1.73554). This amount is the same amount computed previously using the present value of $1.

Pricing Bonds

The selling price of a bond is the sum of the present values of:

- The face amount of the bonds due at the maturity date
- The periodic interest to be paid on the bonds

The market rate of interest is used to compute the present value of both the face amount and the periodic interest.

To illustrate the pricing of bonds, assume that Southern Utah Communications Inc. issued the following bond on January 1, 2015:

Face amount	$100,000
Contract rate of interest	12%
Interest paid semiannually on June 30 and December 31.	
Term of bonds	5 years

Market Rate of Interest of 12% Assuming a market rate of interest of 12%, the bonds would sell for their face amount. As shown by the following present value computations, the bonds would sell for $100,000:

Present value of face amount of $100,000 due in five years, at 12% compounded semiannually: $100,000 × 0.55839 (present value of $1 for 10 periods at 6% from Exhibit 8)	$ 55,839
Present value of 10 semiannual interest payments of $6,000, at 12% compounded semiannually: $6,000 × 7.36009 (present value of an annuity of $1 for 10 periods at 6% from Exhibit 10)	44,161
Total present value of bonds	$100,000

Market Rate of Interest of 13% Assuming a market rate of interest of 13%, the bonds would sell at a discount. As shown by the following present value computations, the bonds would sell for $96,406:[8]

Present value of face amount of $100,000 due in five years, at 13% compounded semiannually: $100,000 × 0.53273 (present value of $1 for 10 periods at 6½% from Exhibit 8)	$53,273
Present value of 10 semiannual interest payments of $6,000, at 13% compounded semiannually: $6,000 × 7.18883 (present value of an annuity of $1 for 10 periods at 6½% from Exhibit 10)	43,133
Total present value of bonds	$96,406

Market Rate of Interest of 11% Assuming a market rate of interest of 11%, the bonds would sell at a premium. As shown by the following present value computations, the bonds would sell for $103,769:

Present value of face amount of $100,000 due in five years, at 11% compounded semiannually: $100,000 × 0.58543 (present value of $1 for 10 periods at 5½% from Exhibit 8)	$ 58,543
Present value of 10 semiannual interest payments of $6,000, at 11% compounded semiannually: $6,000 × 7.53763 (present value of an annuity of $1 for 10 periods at 5½% from Exhibit 10)	45,226
Total present value of bonds	$103,769

As shown, the selling price of the bond varies with the present value of the bond's face amount at maturity, interest payments, and the market rate of interest.

APPENDIX 2

Effective Interest Rate Method of Amortization

The effective interest rate method of amortization provides for a constant *rate* of interest over the life of the bonds. As the discount or premium is amortized, the carrying amount of the bonds changes. As a result, interest expense also changes each period. This is in contrast to the straight-line method, which provides for a constant *amount* of interest expense each period.

[8] Some corporations issue bonds called *zero-coupon bonds* that provide for only the payment of the face amount at maturity. Such bonds sell for large discounts. In this example, such a bond would sell for $53,273, which is the present value of the face amount.

The interest rate used in the effective interest rate method of amortization, sometimes called the *interest method*, is the market rate on the date the bonds are issued. The carrying amount of the bonds is multiplied by this interest rate to determine the interest expense for the period. The difference between the interest expense and the interest payment is the amount of discount or premium to be amortized for the period.

Amortization of Discount by the Interest Method

To illustrate, the following data taken from the chapter illustration of issuing bonds at a discount are used:

Face value of 12%, five-year bonds, interest compounded semiannually....................	$100,000
Present value of bonds at effective (market) rate of interest of 13%	96,406
Discount on bonds payable..	$ 3,594

Exhibit 11 illustrates the interest method for the preceding bonds. Exhibit 11 begins with six columns. The first column is not lettered. The remaining columns are lettered A through E. The exhibit was then prepared as follows:

- Step 1. List the interest payments dates in the first column, which for the preceding bond are 10 interest payment dates (semiannual interest over five years). Also, list on the first line the initial amount of discount in Column D and the initial carrying amount (selling price) of the bonds in Column E.
- Step 2. List in Column A the semiannual interest payments, which for the preceding bond are $6,000 ($100,000 × 6%).
- Step 3. Compute the interest expense in Column B by multiplying the bond carrying amount at the beginning of each period times 6½%, which is the semiannual effective interest (market) rate (13% ÷ 2).
- Step 4. In Column C, compute the discount to be amortized each period by subtracting the interest payment in Column A ($6,000) from the interest expense for the period shown in Column B.
- Step 5. Compute the remaining unamortized discount by subtracting the amortized discount in Column C for the period from the unamortized discount at the beginning of the period in Column D.
- Step 6. Compute the bond carrying amount at the end of the period by subtracting the unamortized discount at the end of the period in Column D from the face amount of the bonds ($100,000).

Steps 3–6 are repeated for each interest payment.

EXHIBIT 11 **Amortization of Discount on Bonds Payable**

	A	B	C	D	E
Interest Payment Date	Interest Paid (6% of Face Amount)	Interest Expense (6½% of Bond Carrying Amount)	Discount Amortization (B – A)	Unamortized Discount (D – C)	Bond Carrying Amount ($100,000 – D)
				$3,594	$ 96,406
June 30, 2015	$6,000	$6,266 (6½% of $96,406)	$266	3,328	96,672
Dec. 31, 2015	6,000	6,284 (6½% of $96,672)	284	3,044	96,956
June 30, 2016	6,000	6,302 (6½% of $96,956)	302	2,742	97,258
Dec. 31, 2016	6,000	6,322 (6½% of $97,258)	322	2,420	97,580
June 30, 2017	6,000	6,343 (6½% of $97,580)	343	2,077	97,923
Dec. 31, 2017	6,000	6,365 (6½% of $97,923)	365	1,712	98,288
June 30, 2018	6,000	6,389 (6½% of $98,288)	389	1,323	98,677
Dec. 31, 2018	6,000	6,414 (6½% of $98,677)	414	909	99,091
June 30, 2019	6,000	6,441 (6½% of $99,091)	441	468	99,532
Dec. 31, 2019	6,000	6,470 (6½% of $99,532)	468*	—	100,000

*Cannot exceed unamortized discount.

As shown in Exhibit 11, the interest expense increases each period as the carrying amount of the bond increases. Also, the unamortized discount decreases each period to zero at the maturity date. Finally, the carrying amount of the bonds increases from $96,406 to $100,000 (the face amount) at maturity.

The entry to record the first interest payment on June 30, 2015, and the related discount amortization is as follows:

2015				
June	30	Interest Expense	6,266	
		Discount on Bonds Payable		266
		Cash		6,000
		Paid semiannual interest and amortized bond discount for 1/2 year.		

If the amortization is recorded only at the end of the year, the amount of the discount amortized on December 31, 2015, would be $550. This is the sum of the first two semiannual amortization amounts ($266 and $284) from Exhibit 11.

Amortization of Premium by the Interest Method

To illustrate, the following data taken from the chapter illustration of issuing bonds at a premium are used:

Present value of bonds at effective (market) rate of interest of 11%	$103,769
Face value of 12%, five-year bonds, interest compounded semiannually	100,000
Premium on bonds payable	$ 3,769

Exhibit 12 illustrates the interest method for the preceding bonds. Exhibit 12 begins with six columns. The first column is not lettered. The remaining columns are lettered A through E. The exhibit was then prepared as follows:

- Step 1. List the number of interest payments in the first column, which for the preceding bond are 10 interest payments (semiannual interest over five years). Also, list on the first line the initial amount of premium in Column D and the initial carrying amount of the bonds in Column E.
- Step 2. List in Column A the semiannual interest payments, which for the preceding bond are $6,000 ($100,000 × 6%).

EXHIBIT 12 Amortization of Premium on Bonds Payable

Interest Payment Date	A Interest Paid (6% of Face Amount)	B Interest Expense (5½% of Bond Carrying Amount)	C Premium Amortization (A – B)	D Unamortized Premium (D – C)	E Bond Carrying Amount ($100,000 + D)
				$3,769	$103,769
June 30, 2015	$6,000	$5,707 (5½% of $103,769)	$293	3,476	103,476
Dec. 31, 2015	6,000	5,691 (5½% of $103,476)	309	3,167	103,167
June 30, 2016	6,000	5,674 (5½% of $103,167)	326	2,841	102,841
Dec. 31, 2016	6,000	5,656 (5½% of $102,841)	344	2,497	102,497
June 30, 2017	6,000	5,637 (5½% of $102,497)	363	2,134	102,134
Dec. 31, 2017	6,000	5,617 (5½% of $102,134)	383	1,751	101,751
June 30, 2018	6,000	5,596 (5½% of $101,751)	404	1,347	101,347
Dec. 31, 2018	6,000	5,574 (5½% of $101,347)	426	921	100,921
June 30, 2019	6,000	5,551 (5½% of $100,921)	449	472	100,472
Dec. 31, 2019	6,000	5,526 (5½% of $100,472)	472*	—	100,000

*Cannot exceed unamortized premium.

- Step 3. Compute the interest expense in Column B by multiplying the bond carrying amount at the beginning of each period times 5½%, which is the semiannual effective interest (market) rate (11% ÷ 2).
- Step 4. In Column C, compute the premium to be amortized each period by subtracting the interest expense for the period shown in Column B from the interest payment in Column A ($6,000).
- Step 5. Compute the remaining unamortized premium by subtracting the amortized premium in Column C for the period from the unamortized premium at the beginning of the period in Column D.
- Step 6. Compute the bond carrying amount at the end of the period by adding the unamortized premium at the end of the period in Column D to the face amount of the bonds ($100,000).

Steps 3–6 are repeated for each interest payment.

As shown in Exhibit 12, the interest expense decreases each period as the carrying amount of the bond decreases. Also, the unamortized premium decreases each period to zero at the maturity date. Finally, the carrying amount of the bonds decreases from $103,769 to $100,000 (the face amount) at maturity.

The entry to record the first interest payment on June 30, 2015, and the related premium amortization is as follows:

2015					
June	30	Interest Expense		5,707	
		Premium on Bonds Payable		293	
		Cash			6,000
		Paid semiannual interest and amortized bond premium for ½ year.			

If the amortization is recorded only at the end of the year, the amount of the premium amortized on December 31, 2015, would be $602. This is the sum of the first two semiannual amortization amounts ($293 and $309) from Exhibit 12.

At a Glance 14

Compute the potential impact of long-term borrowing on earnings per share.

Key Points Corporations can finance their operations by issuing short-term debt, long-term debt, or equity. One of the many factors that influence a corporation's decision on whether it should issue long-term debt or equity is the effect each alternative has on earnings per share.

Learning Outcomes	Example Exercises	Practice Exercises
• Define the concept of a bond.		
• Calculate and compare the effect of alternative long-term financing plans on earnings per share.	EE14-1	PE14-1A, 14-1B

Describe the characteristics and terminology of bonds payable.

Key Points A corporation that issues bonds enters into a contract, or bond indenture.

When a corporation issues bonds, the price that buyers are willing to pay for the bonds depends on (1) the face amount of the bonds, (2) the periodic interest to be paid on the bonds, and (3) the market rate of interest.

Learning Outcomes	Example Exercises	Practice Exercises
• Define the characteristics of a bond.		
• Describe the various types of bonds.		
• Describe the factors that determine the price of a bond.		

Journalize entries for bonds payable.

Key Points The journal entry for issuing bonds payable debits Cash and credits Bonds Payable. Any difference between the face amount of the bonds and the selling price is debited to Discount on Bonds Payable or credited to Premium on Bonds Payable when the bonds are issued. The discount or premium on bonds payable is amortized to interest expense over the life of the bonds.

At the maturity date, the entry to record the repayment of the face value of a bond is a debit to Bonds Payable and a credit to Cash.

When a corporation redeems bonds before they mature, Bonds Payable is debited for the face amount of the bonds, the premium (discount) on bonds payable account is debited (credited) for its unamoritized balance, Cash is credited, and any gain or loss on the redemption is recorded.

Learning Outcomes	Example Exercises	Practice Exercises
• Journalize the issuance of bonds at face value and the payment of periodic interest.	**EE14-2**	**PE14-2A, 14-2B**
• Journalize the issuance of bonds at a discount.	**EE14-3**	**PE14-3A, 14-3B**
• Journalize the amortization of a bond discount.	**EE14-4**	**PE14-4A, 14-4B**
• Journalize the issuance of bonds at a premium.	**EE14-5**	**PE14-5A, 14-5B**
• Journalize the amortization of a bond premium.	**EE14-6**	**PE14-6A, 14-6B**
• Describe bond redemptions.		
• Journalize the redemption of bonds payable	**EE14-7**	**PE14-7A, 14-7B**

Describe and illustrate the accounting for installment notes.

Key Points An installment note requires the borrower to make equal periodic payments to the lender for the term of the note. Unlike bonds, the annual payment in an installment note consists of both principal and interest. The journal entry for the annual payment debits Interest Expense and Notes Payable and credits Cash for the amount of the payment. After the final payment, the carrying amount on the note is zero.

Learning Outcomes	Example Exercises	Practice Exercises
• Define the characteristics of an installment note.		
• Journalize the issuance of installment notes.	**EE14-8**	**PE14-8A, 14-8B**
• Journalize the annual payment for an installment note.		

Describe and illustrate the reporting of long-term liabilities, including bonds and notes payable.

Key Points Bonds payable and notes payable are usually reported as long-term liabilities. If the balance sheet date is within one year, they are reported as current liabilities. A discount on bonds should be reported as a deduction from the related bonds payable. A premium on bonds should be reported as an addition to related bonds payable.

Learning Outcome	Example Exercises	Practice Exercises
• Illustrate the balance sheet presentation of bonds payable and notes payable.		

Describe and illustrate how the number of times interest charges are earned is used to evaluate a company's financial condition.

Key Points The number of times interest charges are earned measures the risk to bondholders that a company will not be able to make its interest payments. It is computed by dividing income before income tax plus interest expense by interest expense. This ratio measures the number of times interest payments could be paid (covered) by current period earnings.

Learning Outcomes	Example Exercises	Practice Exercises
• Describe and compute the number of times interest charges are earned.	EE14-9	PE14-9A, 14-9B
• Interpret the number of times interest charges are earned.		

Key Terms

amortization (648)
annuity (660)
bond (642)
bond indenture (645)
carrying amount (648)
contract rate (645)
discount (645)
earnings per share (EPS) (642)
effective interest rate method (648)
effective rate of interest (645)
face amount (645)
future value (658)
installment note (653)
market rate of interest (645)
mortgage notes (653)
number of times interest charges are earned (656)
premium (646)
present value (658)
present value of annuity (660)

Illustrative Problem

The fiscal year of Russell Inc., a manufacturer of acoustical supplies, ends December 31. Selected transactions for the period 2015 through 2022, involving bonds payable issued by Russell Inc., are as follows:

2015

June 30. Issued $2,000,000 of 25-year, 7% callable bonds dated June 30, 2015, for cash of $1,920,000. Interest is payable semiannually on June 30 and December 31.

Dec. 31. Paid the semiannual interest on the bonds. The bond discount is amortized annually in a separate journal entry.

31. Recorded straight-line amortization of $1,600 of discount on the bonds.

31. Closed the interest expense account.

2016

June 30. Paid the semiannual interest on the bonds. The bond discount is amortized annually in a separate journal entry.

Dec. 31. Paid the semiannual interest on the bonds. The bond discount is amortized annually in a separate journal entry.

31. Recorded straight-line amortization of $3,200 of discount on the bonds.

31. Closed the interest expense account.

2022

June 30. Recorded the redemption of the bonds, which were called at 101.5. The balance in the bond discount account is $57,600 after the payment of interest and amortization of discount have been recorded. (Record the redemption only.)

Instructions

1. Journalize entries to record the preceding transactions.
2. Determine the amount of interest expense for 2015 and 2016.
3. Determine the carrying amount of the bonds as of December 31, 2016.

Solution

1.

2015				
June	30	Cash	1,920,000	
		Discount on Bonds Payable	80,000	
		Bonds Payable		2,000,000
Dec.	31	Interest Expense	70,000	
		Cash		70,000
	31	Interest Expense	1,600	
		Discount on Bonds Payable		1,600
		Amortization of discount from July 1 to December 31.		
	31	Income Summary	71,600	
		Interest Expense		71,600
2016				
June	30	Interest Expense	70,000	
		Cash		70,000
Dec.	31	Interest Expense	70,000	
		Cash		70,000
	31	Interest Expense	3,200	
		Discount on Bonds Payable		3,200
		Amortization of discount from January 1 to December 31.		
	31	Income Summary	143,200	
		Interest Expense		143,200
2022				
June	30	Bonds Payable	2,000,000	
		Loss on Redemption of Bonds Payable	87,600	
		Discount on Bonds Payable		57,600
		Cash		2,030,000

2. a. 2015: $71,600 = $70,000 + $1,600

b. 2016: $143,200 = $70,000 + $70,000 + $3,200

3.

Initial carrying amount of bonds	$1,920,000
Discount amortized on December 31, 2015	1,600
Discount amortized on December 31, 2016	3,200
Carrying amount of bonds, December 31, 2016	$1,924,800

Discussion Questions

1. Describe the two distinct obligations incurred by a corporation when issuing bonds.
2. Explain the meaning of each of the following terms as they relate to a bond issue: (a) convertible, and (b) callable.
3. If you asked your broker to purchase for you a 12% bond when the market interest rate for such bonds was 11%, would you expect to pay more or less than the face amount for the bond? Explain.
4. A corporation issues $26,000,000 of 9% bonds to yield interest at the rate of 7%. (a) Was the amount of cash received from the sale of the bonds greater or less than $26,000,000? (b) Identify the following amounts as they relate to the bond issue: (1) face amount, (2) market or effective rate of interest, (3) contract rate of interest, and (4) maturity amount.
5. If bonds issued by a corporation are sold at a discount, is the market rate of interest greater or less than the contract rate?
6. The following data relate to a $2,000,000, 8% bond issued for a selected semiannual interest period:

Bond carrying amount at beginning of period	$2,125,000
Interest paid during period	160,000
Interest expense allocable to the period	148,750

(a) Were the bonds issued at a discount or at a premium? (b) What is the unamortized amount of the discount or premium account at the beginning of the period? (c) What account was debited to amortize the discount or premium?

7. Bonds Payable has a balance of $5,000,000 and Discount on Bonds Payable has a balance of $150,000. If the issuing corporation redeems the bonds at 98, is there a gain or loss on the bond redemption?
8. What is a mortgage note?
9. Fleeson Company needs additional funds to purchase equipment for a new production facility and is considering either issuing bonds payable or borrowing the money from a local bank in the form of an installment note. How does an installment note differ from a bond payable?
10. In what section of the balance sheet would a bond payable be reported if: (a) it is payable within one year and (b) it is payable beyond one year?

Practice Exercises

EE 14-1 p. 644

PE 14-1A Alternative financing plans **OBJ. 1**

Owen Co. is considering the following alternative financing plans:

	Plan 1	Plan 2
Issue 7% bonds (at face value)	$5,000,000	$3,400,000
Issue preferred $1 stock, $20 par	—	3,600,000
Issue common stock, $25 par	5,000,000	3,000,000

Income tax is estimated at 40% of income.

Determine the earnings per share of common stock, assuming income before bond interest and income tax is $750,000.

SHOW ME HOW

EE 14-1 p. 644

PE 14-1B Alternative financing plans **OBJ. 1**

Brower Co. is considering the following alternative financing plans:

	Plan 1	Plan 2
Issue 10% bonds (at face value)	$4,000,000	$2,500,000
Issue preferred $2.50 stock, $25 par	—	3,000,000
Issue common stock, $10 par	4,000,000	2,500,000

Income tax is estimated at 40% of income.

Determine the earnings per share of common stock, assuming income before bond interest and income tax is $2,000,000.

SHOW ME HOW

EE 14-2 p. 647

PE 14-2A Issuing bonds at face amount **OBJ. 3**

On January 1, the first day of the fiscal year, a company issues a $500,000, 5%, 10-year bond that pays semiannual interest of $12,500 ($500,000 × 5% × ½ year), receiving cash of $500,000. Journalize the entries to record (a) the issuance of the bonds, (b) the first interest payment on June 30, and (c) the payment of the principal on the maturity date.

SHOW ME HOW

EE 14-2 p. 647

PE 14-2B Issuing bonds at face amount **OBJ. 3**

On January 1, the first day of the fiscal year, a company issues a $800,000, 4%, 10-year bond that pays semiannual interest of $16,000 ($800,000 × 4% × ½ year), receiving cash of $800,000. Journalize the entries to record (a) the issuance of the bonds, (b) the first interest payment on June 30, and (c) the payment of the principal on the maturity date.

SHOW ME HOW

EE 14-3 p. 648

PE 14-3A Issuing bonds at a discount **OBJ. 3**

On the first day of the fiscal year, a company issues a $1,200,000, 9%, five-year bond that pays semiannual interest of $54,000 ($1,200,000 × 9% × ½), receiving cash of $1,153,670. Journalize the bond issuance.

SHOW ME HOW

EE 14-3 p. 648

PE 14-3B Issuing bonds at a discount **OBJ. 3**

On the first day of the fiscal year, a company issues a $3,000,000, 11%, five-year bond that pays semiannual interest of $165,000 ($3,000,000 × 11% × ½), receiving cash of $2,889,599. Journalize the bond issuance.

SHOW ME HOW

EE 14-4 p. 649

PE 14-4A Discount amortization **OBJ. 3**

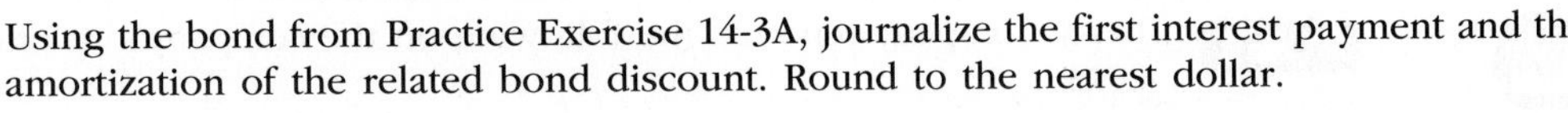

Using the bond from Practice Exercise 14-3A, journalize the first interest payment and the amortization of the related bond discount. Round to the nearest dollar.

SHOW ME HOW

EE 14-4 p. 649

PE 14-4B Discount amortization **OBJ. 3**

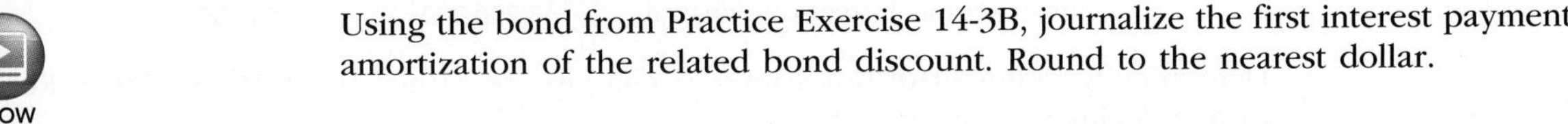

Using the bond from Practice Exercise 14-3B, journalize the first interest payment and the amortization of the related bond discount. Round to the nearest dollar.

SHOW ME HOW

EE 14-5 p. 650

PE 14-5A Issuing bonds at a premium **OBJ. 3**

On the first day of the fiscal year, a company issues a $2,000,000, 8%, five-year bond that pays semiannual interest of $80,000 ($2,000,000 × 8% × ½), receiving cash of $2,170,604. Journalize the bond issuance.

SHOW ME HOW

EE 14-5 p. 650

PE 14-5B Issuing bonds at a premium **OBJ. 3**

On the first day of the fiscal year, a company issues an $8,000,000, 11%, five-year bond that pays semiannual interest of $440,000 ($8,000,000 × 11% × ½), receiving cash of $8,308,869. Journalize the bond issuance.

EE 14-6 p. 651

PE 14-6A Premium amortization **OBJ. 3**

SHOW ME HOW

Using the bond from Practice Exercise 14-5A, journalize the first interest payment and the amortization of the related bond premium. Round to the nearest dollar.

SHOW ME HOW

EE 14-6 p. 651

PE 14-6B Premium amortization **OBJ. 3**

Using the bond from Practice Exercise 14-5B, journalize the first interest payment and the amortization of the related bond premium. Round to the nearest dollar.

SHOW ME HOW

EE 14-7 p. 652

PE 14-7A Redemption of bonds payable **OBJ. 3**

A $1,500,000 bond issue on which there is an unamortized discount of $70,100 is redeemed for $1,455,000. Journalize the redemption of the bonds.

SHOW ME HOW

EE 14-7 p. 652

PE 14-7B Redemption of bonds payable **OBJ. 3**

A $500,000 bond issue on which there is an unamortized premium of $67,000 is redeemed for $490,000. Journalize the redemption of the bonds.

SHOW ME HOW

EE 14-8 p. 655

PE 14-8A Journalizing installment notes **OBJ. 4**

On the first day of the fiscal year, a company issues $65,000, 6%, five-year installment notes that have annual payments of $15,431. The first note payment consists of $3,900 of interest and $11,531 of principal repayment.

a. Journalize the entry to record the issuance of the installment notes.

b. Journalize the first annual note payment.

SHOW ME HOW

EE 14-8 p. 655

PE 14-8B Journalizing installment notes **OBJ. 4**

On the first day of the fiscal year, a company issues $45,000, 8%, six-year installment notes that have annual payments of $9,734. The first note payment consists of $3,600 of interest and $6,134 of principal repayment.

a. Journalize the entry to record the issuance of the installment notes.

b. Journalize the first annual note payment.

EE 14-9 p. 657

F·A·I

SHOW ME HOW

PE 14-9A Number of times interest charges are earned **OBJ. 6**

Berry Company reported the following on the company's income statement in 2016 and 2015:

	2016	2015
Interest expense	$ 320,000	$ 300,000
Income before income tax expense	3,200,000	3,600,000

a. Determine the number of times interest charges are earned for 2016 and 2015. Round to one decimal place.

b. Is the number of times interest charges are earned improving or declining?

EE 14-9 p. 657

F·A·I

SHOW ME HOW

PE 14-9B Number of times interest charges are earned **OBJ. 6**

Averill Products Inc. reported the following on the company's income statement in 2016 and 2015:

	2016	2015
Interest expense	$ 440,000	$ 400,000
Income before income tax expense	5,544,000	4,400,000

a. Determine the number of times interest charges are earned for 2016 and 2015. Round to one decimal place.

b. Is the number of times interest charges are earned improving or declining?

Exercises

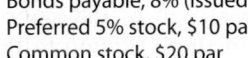

EX 14-1 Effect of financing on earnings per share — OBJ. 1

✔ a. $1.64

SHOW ME HOW

Domanico Co., which produces and sells biking equipment, is financed as follows:

Bonds payable, 8% (issued at face amount)	$10,000,000
Preferred 5% stock, $10 par	10,000,000
Common stock, $20 par	10,000,000

Income tax is estimated at 40% of income.

Determine the earnings per share of common stock, assuming that the income before bond interest and income tax is (a) $10,500,000, (b) $11,800,000, and (c) $13,000,000.

EX 14-2 Evaluate alternative financing plans — OBJ. 1

Based on the data in Exercise 14-1, what factors other than earnings per share should be considered in evaluating these alternative financing plans?

EX 14-3 Corporate financing — OBJ. 1

The financial statements for **Nike, Inc.**, are presented in Appendix C at the end of the text. What is the major source of financing for Nike?

EX 14-4 Bond price — OBJ. 3

United States Steel's 7.375% bonds due in 2020 were reported as selling for 103.00.

Were the bonds selling at a premium or at a discount? Why is United States Steel able to sell its bonds at this price?

EX 14-5 Entries for issuing bonds — OBJ. 3

SHOW ME HOW

Gabriel Co. produces and distributes semiconductors for use by computer manufacturers. Gabriel Co. issued $600,000 of 10-year, 8% bonds on May 1 of the current year at face value, with interest payable on May 1 and November 1. The fiscal year of the company is the calendar year. Journalize the entries to record the following selected transactions for the current year:

May 1. Issued the bonds for cash at their face amount.

Nov. 1. Paid the interest on the bonds.

Dec. 31. Recorded accrued interest for two months.

EX 14-6 Entries for issuing bonds and amortizing discount by straight-line method — OBJ. 2, 3

✔ b. $2,122,340

SHOW ME HOW

On the first day of its fiscal year, Pretender Company issued $18,500,000 of five-year, 10% bonds to finance its operations of producing and selling home improvement products. Interest is payable semiannually. The bonds were issued at a market (effective) interest rate of 12%, resulting in Pretender Company receiving cash of $17,138,298.

a. Journalize the entries to record the following:
   1. Issuance of the bonds.
   2. First semiannual interest payment. The bond discount is combined with the semiannual interest payment. (Round your answer to the nearest dollar.)
   3. Second semiannual interest payment. The bond discount is combined with the semiannual interest payment. (Round your answer to the nearest dollar.)

b. Determine the amount of the bond interest expense for the first year.

c. Explain why the company was able to issue the bonds for only $17,138,298 rather than for the face amount of $18,500,000.

EX 14-7 Entries for issuing bonds and amortizing premium by straight-line method **OBJ. 2, 3**

Lerner Corporation wholesales repair products to equipment manufacturers. On April 1, 2016, Lerner Corporation issued $12,000,000 of five-year, 8% bonds at a market (effective) interest rate of 6%, receiving cash of $13,023,576. Interest is payable semiannually on April 1 and October 1. Journalize the entries to record the following:

a. Issuance of bonds on April 1, 2016.

b. First interest payment on October 1, 2016, and amortization of bond premium for six months, using the straight-line method. (Round to the nearest dollar.)

c. Explain why the company was able to issue the bonds for $13,023,576 rather than for the face amount of $12,000,000.

EX 14-8 Entries for issuing and calling bonds; loss **OBJ. 3**

Adele Corp., a wholesaler of music equipment, issued $22,000,000 of 20-year, 7% callable bonds on March 1, 2016 at their face amount, with interest payable on March 1 and September 1. The fiscal year of the company is the calendar year. Journalize the entries to record the following selected transactions:

2016

Mar. 1. Issued the bonds for cash at their face amount.

Sept. 1. Paid the interest on the bonds.

2020

Sept. 1. Called the bond issue at 102, the rate provided in the bond indenture. (Omit entry for payment of interest.)

EX 14-9 Entries for issuing and calling bonds; gain **OBJ. 3**

Emil Corp. produces and sells wind-energy-driven engines. To finance its operations, Emil Corp. issued $15,000,000 of 20-year, 9% callable bonds on May 1, 2016 at their face amount, with interest payable on May 1 and November 1. The fiscal year of the company is the calendar year. Journalize the entries to record the following selected transactions:

2016

May 1. Issued the bonds for cash at their face amount.

Nov. 1. Paid the interest on the bonds.

2022

Nov. 1. Called the bond issue at 96, the rate provided in the bond indenture. (Omit entry for payment of interest.)

EX 14-10 Entries for installment note transactions **OBJ. 4**

On the first day of the fiscal year, Shiller Company borrowed $85,000 by giving a seven-year, 7% installment note to Soros Bank. The note requires annual payments of $15,772, with the first payment occurring on the last day of the fiscal year. The first payment consists of interest of $5,950 and principal repayment of $9,822.

a. Journalize the entries to record the following:

   1. Issued the installment note for cash on the first day of the fiscal year.
   2. Paid the first annual payment on the note.

b. Explain how the notes payable would be reported on the balance sheet at the end of the first year.

EX 14-11 Entries for installment note transactions OBJ. 4

SHOW ME HOW

On January 1, 2016, Hebron Company issued a $175,000, five-year, 8% installment note to Ventsam Bank. The note requires annual payments of $43,380, beginning on December 31, 2016. Journalize the entries to record the following:

2016

Jan. 1. Issued the note for cash at its face amount.

Dec. 31. Paid the annual payment on the note, which consisted of interest of $14,000 and principal of $29,830.

2019

Dec. 31. Paid the annual payment on the note, included $6,253 of interest. The remainder of the payment reduced the principal balance on the note.

EX 14-12 Entries for installment note transactions OBJ. 4

SHOW ME HOW

On January 1, 2016, Bryson Company obtained a $147,750, four-year, 7% installment note from Campbell Bank. The note requires annual payments of $43,620, beginning on December 31, 2016.

a. Prepare an amortization table for this installment note, similar to the one presented in Exhibit 4.

b. Journalize the entries for the issuance of the note and the four annual note payments.

c. Describe how the annual note payment would be reported in the 2016 income statement.

EX 14-13 Reporting bonds OBJ. 5

At the beginning of the current year, two bond issues (Simmons Industries 7% 20-year bonds and Hunter Corporation 8% 10-year bonds) were outstanding. During the year, the Simmons Industries bonds were redeemed and a significant loss on the redemption of bonds was reported as an extraordinary item on the income statement. At the end of the year, the Hunter Corporation bonds were reported as a noncurrent liability. The maturity date on the Hunter Corporation bonds was early in the following year.

Identify the flaws in the reporting practices related to the two bond issues.

EX 14-14 Number of times interest charges are earned OBJ. 6

The following data were taken from recent annual reports of Southwest Airlines, which operates a low-fare airline service to more than 50 cities in the United States:

	Current Year	Preceding Year
Interest expense	$147,000,000	$194,000,000
Income before income tax	685,000,000	323,000,000

a. Determine the number of times interest charges are earned for the current and preceding years. Round to one decimal place.

b. What conclusions can you draw?

EX 14-15 Number of times interest charges are earned OBJ. 6

F·A·I

Loomis, Inc. reported the following on the company's income statement in 2016 and 2015:

	2016	2015
Interest expense	$ 13,500,000	$ 16,000,000
Income before income tax expense	310,500,000	432,000,000

a. Determine the number of times interest charges were earned for 2016 and 2015. Round to one decimal place.

b. Is the number of times interest charges are earned improving or declining?

EX 14-16 Number of times interest charges are earned OBJ. 6

Iacouva Company reported the following on the company's income statement for 2016 and 2015:

	2016	2015
Interest expense	$5,000,000	$5,000,000
Income before income tax	3,500,000	6,000,000

a. Determine the number of times interest charges are earned for 2016 and 2015. Round to one decimal place.

b. What conclusions can you draw?

Appendix 1
EX 14-17 Present value of amounts due

Tommy John is going to receive $1,000,000 in three years. The current market rate of interest is 10%.

a. Using the present value of $1 table in Exhibit 8, determine the present value of this amount compounded annually.

b. Why is the present value less than the $1,000,000 to be received in the future?

Appendix 1
EX 14-18 Present value of an annuity

Determine the present value of $200,000 to be received at the end of each of four years, using an interest rate of 7%, compounded annually, as follows:

a. By successive computations, using the present value table in Exhibit 8.

b. By using the present value table in Exhibit 10.

c. Why is the present value of the four $200,000 cash receipts less than the $800,000 to be received in the future?

Appendix 1
EX 14-19 Present value of an annuity

✔ $40,395,063

On January 1, 2016, you win $50,000,000 in the state lottery. The $50,000,000 prize will be paid in equal installments of $6,250,000 over eight years. The payments will be made on December 31 of each year, beginning on December 31, 2016. If the current interest rate is 5%, determine the present value of your winnings. Use the present value tables in Appendix A.

Appendix 1
EX 14-20 Present value of an annuity

Assume the same data as in Exercise 14–19, except that the current interest rate is 12%. Will the present value of your winnings using an interest rate of 12% be more than the present value of your winnings using an interest rate of 5%? Why or why not?

Appendix 1
EX 14-21 Present value of bonds payable; discount

Pinder Co. produces and sells high-quality video equipment. To finance its operations, Pinder Co. issued $25,000,000 of five-year, 7% bonds, with interest payable semiannually, at a market (effective) interest rate of 9%. Determine the present value of the bonds payable, using the present value tables in Exhibits 8 and 10. Round to the nearest dollar.

Appendix 1
EX 14-22 Present value of bonds payable; premium

✔ $45,323,443

Moss Co. issued $42,000,000 of five-year, 11% bonds, with interest payable semiannually, at a market (effective) interest rate of 9%. Determine the present value of the bonds payable using the present value tables in Exhibits 8 and 10. Round to the nearest dollar.

Appendix 2
EX 14-23 Amortize discount by interest method

✔ b. $3,923,959

On the first day of its fiscal year, Ebert Company issued $50,000,000 of 10-year, 7% bonds to finance its operations. Interest is payable semiannually. The bonds were issued at a market (effective) interest rate of 9%, resulting in Ebert Company receiving cash of $43,495,895. The company uses the interest method.

a. Journalize the entries to record the following:
   1. Sale of the bonds.
   2. First semiannual interest payment, including amortization of discount. Round to the nearest dollar.
   3. Second semiannual interest payment, including amortization of discount. Round to the nearest dollar.
b. Compute the amount of the bond interest expense for the first year.
c. Explain why the company was able to issue the bonds for only $43,495,895 rather than for the face amount of $50,000,000.

Appendix 2
EX 14-24 Amortize premium by interest method

✔ b. $1,662,619

Shunda Corporation wholesales parts to appliance manufacturers. On January 1, 2016, Shunda Corporation issued $22,000,000 of five-year, 9% bonds at a market (effective) interest rate of 7%, receiving cash of $23,829,684. Interest is payable semiannually. Shunda Corporation's fiscal year begins on January 1. The company uses the interest method.

a. Journalize the entries to record the following:
   1. Sale of the bonds.
   2. First semiannual interest payment, including amortization of premium. Round to the nearest dollar.
   3. Second semiannual interest payment, including amortization of premium. Round to the nearest dollar.
b. Determine the bond interest expense for the first year.
c. Explain why the company was able to issue the bonds for $23,829,684 rather than for the face amount of $22,000,000.

Appendix 1 and Appendix 2
EX 14-25 Compute bond proceeds, amortizing premium by interest method, and interest expense

✔ a. $37,702,483
✔ c. $225,620

Ware Co. produces and sells motorcycle parts. On the first day of its fiscal year, Ware Co. issued $35,000,000 of five-year, 12% bonds at a market (effective) interest rate of 10%, with interest payable semiannually. Compute the following, presenting figures used in your computations:

a. The amount of cash proceeds from the sale of the bonds. Use the tables of present values in Exhibits 8 and 10. Round to the nearest dollar.
b. The amount of premium to be amortized for the first semiannual interest payment period, using the interest method. Round to the nearest dollar.
c. The amount of premium to be amortized for the second semiannual interest payment period, using the interest method. Round to the nearest dollar.
d. The amount of the bond interest expense for the first year.

Appendix 1 and Appendix 2
EX 14-26 Compute bond proceeds, amortizing discount by interest method, and interest expense

✔ a. $71,167,524
✔ b. $670,051

Boyd Co. produces and sells aviation equipment. On the first day of its fiscal year, Boyd Co. issued $80,000,000 of five-year, 9% bonds at a market (effective) interest rate of 12%, with interest payable semiannually. Compute the following, presenting figures used in your computations:

(Continued)

a. The amount of cash proceeds from the sale of the bonds. Use the tables of present values in Exhibits 8 and 10. Round to the nearest dollar.

b. The amount of discount to be amortized for the first semiannual interest payment period, using the interest method. Round to the nearest dollar.

c. The amount of discount to be amortized for the second semiannual interest payment period, using the interest method. Round to the nearest dollar.

d. The amount of the bond interest expense for the first year.

Problems: Series A

PR 14-1A Effect of financing on earnings per share — OBJ. 1

✔ 1. Plan 3: $1.44

Three different plans for financing an $18,000,000 corporation are under consideration by its organizers. Under each of the following plans, the securities will be issued at their par or face amount, and the income tax rate is estimated at 40% of income:

	Plan 1	Plan 2	Plan 3
8% Bonds	—	—	$ 9,000,000
Preferred 4% stock, $20 par	—	$ 9,000,000	4,500,000
Common stock, $10 par	$18,000,000	9,000,000	4,500,000
Total	$18,000,000	$18,000,000	$18,000,000

Instructions

1. Determine the earnings per share of common stock for each plan, assuming that the income before bond interest and income tax is $2,100,000.
2. Determine the earnings per share of common stock for each plan, assuming that the income before bond interest and income tax is $1,050,000.
3. Discuss the advantages and disadvantages of each plan.

PR 14-2A Bond discount, entries for bonds payable transactions — OBJ. 2, 3

✔ 3. $1,232,685

General Ledger

SHOW ME HOW

On July 1, 2016, Merideth Industries Inc. issued $28,500,000 of 10-year, 8% bonds at a market (effective) interest rate of 9%, receiving cash of $26,646,292. Interest on the bonds is payable semiannually on December 31 and June 30. The fiscal year of the company is the calendar year.

Instructions

1. Journalize the entry to record the amount of cash proceeds from the issuance of the bonds on July 1, 2016.
2. Journalize the entries to record the following:
   a. The first semiannual interest payment on December 31, 2016, and the amortization of the bond discount, using the straight-line method. (Round to the nearest dollar.)
   b. The interest payment on June 30, 2017, and the amortization of the bond discount, using the straight-line method. (Round to the nearest dollar.)
3. Determine the total interest expense for 2016.
4. Will the bond proceeds always be less than the face amount of the bonds when the contract rate is less than the market rate of interest?
5. (Appendix 1) Compute the price of $26,646,292 received for the bonds by using the present value tables in Appendix A at the end of the text. (Round to the nearest dollar.)

PR 14-3A Bond premium, entries for bonds payable transactions — OBJ. 2, 3

✔ 3. $2,600,141

General Ledger

Saverin Inc. produces and sells outdoor equipment. On July 1, 2016, Saverin Inc. issued $62,500,000 of 10-year, 9% bonds at a market (effective) interest rate of 8%, receiving cash of $66,747,178. Interest on the bonds is payable semiannually on December 31 and June 30. The fiscal year of the company is the calendar year.

Instructions

1. Journalize the entry to record the amount of cash proceeds from the issuance of the bonds on July 1, 2016.
2. Journalize the entries to record the following:
   a. The first semiannual interest payment on December 31, 2016, and the amortization of the bond premium, using the straight-line method. (Round to the nearest dollar.)
   b. The interest payment on June 30, 2017, and the amortization of the bond premium, using the straight-line method. (Round to the nearest dollar.)
3. Determine the total interest expense for 2016.
4. Will the bond proceeds always be greater than the face amount of the bonds when the contract rate is greater than the market rate of interest?
5. (Appendix 1) Compute the price of 66,747,178 received for the bonds by using the present value tables in Appendix A at the end of the text. (Round to the nearest dollar.)

PR 14-4A Entries for bonds payable and installment note transactions — OBJ. 3, 4

✔ 3. $64,317,346

General Ledger

SHOW ME HOW

The following transactions were completed by Winklevoss Inc., whose fiscal year is the calendar year:

2016

July 1. Issued $74,000,000 of 20-year, 11% callable bonds dated July 1, 2016, at a market (effective) rate of 13%, receiving cash of $63,532,267. Interest is payable semiannually on December 31 and June 30.

Oct. 1. Borrowed $200,000 by issuing a six-year, 6% installment note to Nicks Bank. The note requires annual payments of $40,673, with the first payment occurring on September 30, 2017.

Dec. 31. Accrued $3,000 of interest on the installment note. The interest is payable on the date of the next installment note payment.

31. Paid the semiannual interest on the bonds. The bond discount amortization of $261,693 is combined with the semiannual interest payment.

31. Closed the interest expense account.

2017

June 30. Paid the semiannual interest on the bonds. The bond discount amortization of $261,693 is combined with the semiannual interest payment.

Sept. 30. Paid the annual payment on the note, which consisted of interest of $12,000 and principal of $28,673.

Dec. 31. Accrued $2,570 of interest on the installment note. The interest is payable on the date of the next installment note payment.

31. Paid the semiannual interest on the bonds. The bond discount amortization of $261,693 is combined with the semiannual interest payment.

31. Closed the interest expense account.

2018

June 30. Recorded the redemption of the bonds, which were called at 98. The balance in the bond discount account is $9,420,961 after payment of interest and amortization of discount have been recorded. (Record the redemption only.)

Sept. 30. Paid the second annual payment on the note, which consisted of interest of $10,280 and principal of $30,393.

Instructions

1. Journalize the entries to record the foregoing transactions. Round all amounts to the nearest dollar.
2. Indicate the amount of the interest expense in (a) 2016 and (b) 2017.
3. Determine the carrying amount of the bonds as of December 31, 2017.

Appendix 1 and Appendix 2

PR 14-5A Bond discount, entries for bonds payable transactions, interest method of amortizing bond discount

✓ 3. $1,199,083

On July 1, 2016, Merideth Industries Inc. issued $28,500,000 of 10-year, 8% bonds at a market (effective) interest rate of 9%, receiving cash of $26,646,292. Interest on the bonds is payable semiannually on December 31 and June 30. The fiscal year of the company is the calendar year.

Instructions

1. Journalize the entry to record the amount of cash proceeds from the issuance of the bonds.
2. Journalize the entries to record the following:
   a. The first semiannual interest payment on December 31, 2016, and the amortization of the bond discount, using the interest method. (Round to the nearest dollar.)
   b. The interest payment on June 30, 2017, and the amortization of the bond discount, using the interest method. (Round to the nearest dollar.)
3. Determine the total interest expense for 2016.

Appendix 1 and Appendix 2

PR 14-6A Bond premium, entries for bonds payable transactions, interest method of amortizing bond premium

✓ 3. $2,669,887

Saverin, Inc. produces and sells outdoor equipment. On July 1, 2016, Saverin, Inc. issued $62,500,000 of 10-year, 9% bonds at a market (effective) interest rate of 8%, receiving cash of $66,747,178. Interest on the bonds is payable semiannually on December 31 and June 30. The fiscal year of the company is the calendar year.

Instructions

1. Journalize the entry to record the amount of cash proceeds from the issuance of the bonds.
2. Journalize the entries to record the following:
   a. The first semiannual interest payment on December 31, 2016, and the amortization of the bond premium, using the interest method. (Round to the nearest dollar.)
   b. The interest payment on June 30, 2017, and the amortization of the bond premium, using the interest method. (Round to the nearest dollar.)
3. Determine the total interest expense for 2016.

Problems: Series B

PR 14-1B Effect of financing on earnings per share OBJ. 1

✓ 1. Plan 3: $2.84

Three different plans for financing an $80,000,000 corporation are under consideration by its organizers. Under each of the following plans, the securities will be issued at their par or face amount, and the income tax rate is estimated at 40% of income:

	Plan 1	Plan 2	Plan 3
9% Bonds	—	—	$40,000,000
Preferred 5% stock, $25 par	—	$40,000,000	20,000,000
Common stock, $20 par	$80,000,000	40,000,000	20,000,000
Total	$80,000,000	$80,000,000	$80,000,000

Instructions

1. Determine for each plan the earnings per share of common stock, assuming that the income before bond interest and income tax is $10,000,000.
2. Determine for each plan the earnings per share of common stock, assuming that the income before bond interest and income tax is $6,000,000.
3.  Discuss the advantages and disadvantages of each plan.

PR 14-2B Bond discount, entries for bonds payable transactions — OBJ. 2, 3

✔ 3. $2,392,269

General Ledger

SHOW ME HOW

On July 1, 2016, Livingston Corporation, a wholesaler of manufacturing equipment, issued $46,000,000 of 20-year, 10% bonds at a market (effective) interest rate of 11%, receiving cash of $42,309,236. Interest on the bonds is payable semiannually on December 31 and June 30. The fiscal year of the company is the calendar year.

Instructions

1. Journalize the entry to record the amount of cash proceeds from the issuance of the bonds on July 1, 2016.
2. Journalize the entries to record the following:
   a. The first semiannual interest payment on December 31, 2016, and the amortization of the bond discount, using the straight-line method. (Round to the nearest dollar.)
   b. The interest payment on June 30, 2017, and the amortization of the bond discount, using the straight-line method. (Round to the nearest dollar.)
3. Determine the total interest expense for 2016.
4. Will the bond proceeds always be less than the face amount of the bonds when the contract rate is less than the market rate of interest?
5. *(Appendix 1)* Compute the price of $42,309,236 received for the bonds by using the present value tables in Appendix A at the end of the text. (Round to the nearest dollar.)

PR 14-3B Bond premium, entries for bonds payable transactions — OBJ. 2, 3

✔ 3. $3,494,977

General Ledger

Rodgers Corporation produces and sells football equipment. On July 1, 2016, Rodgers Corporation issued $65,000,000 of 10-year, 12% bonds at a market (effective) interest rate of 10%, receiving cash of $73,100,469. Interest on the bonds is payable semiannually on December 31 and June 30. The fiscal year of the company is the calendar year.

Instructions

1. Journalize the entry to record the amount of cash proceeds from the issuance of the bonds on July 1, 2016.
2. Journalize the entries to record the following:
   a. The first semiannual interest payment on December 31, 2016, and the amortization of the bond premium, using the straight-line method. (Round to the nearest dollar.)
   b. The interest payment on June 30, 2017, and the amortization of the bond premium, using the straight-line method. (Round to the nearest dollar.)
3. Determine the total interest expense for 2016.
4. Will the bond proceeds always be greater than the face amount of the bonds when the contract rate is greater than the market rate of interest?
5. *(Appendix 1)* Compute the price of $73,100,469 received for the bonds by using the present value tables in Appendix A at the end of the text. (Round to the nearest dollar.)

PR 14-4B Entries for bonds payable and installment note transactions — OBJ. 3, 4

✔ 3. $61,644,484

General Ledger

SHOW ME HOW

The following transactions were completed by Montague Inc., whose fiscal year is the calendar year:

2016

July 1. Issued $55,000,000 of 10-year, 9% callable bonds dated July 1, 2016, at a market (effective) rate of 7%, receiving cash of $62,817,040. Interest is payable semiannually on December 31 and June 30.

Oct. 1. Borrowed $450,000 by issuing a six-year, 8% installment note to Intexicon Bank. The note requires annual payments of $97,342, with the first payment occurring on September 30, 2017.

Dec. 31. Accrued $9,000 of interest on the installment note. The interest is payable on the date of the next installment note payment.

31. Paid the semiannual interest on the bonds. The bond discount amortization of $390,852 is combined with the semiannual interest payment.

31. Closed the interest expense account.

(Continued)

2017

June 30. Paid the semiannual interest on the bonds. The bond discount amortization of $390,852 is combined with the semiannual interest payment.

Sept. 30. Paid the annual payment on the note, which consisted of interest of $36,000 and principal of $61,342.

Dec. 31. Accrued $7,773 of interest on the installment note. The interest is payable on the date of the next installment note payment.

31. Paid the semiannual interest on the bonds. The bond discount amortization of $390,852 is combined with the semiannual interest payment.

31. Closed the interest expense account.

2018

June 30. Recorded the redemption of the bonds, which were called at 103. The balance in the bond premium account is $6,253,632 after payment of interest and amortization of premium have been recorded. (Record the redemption only.)

Sept. 30. Paid the second annual payment on the note, which consisted of interest of $31,093 and principal of $66,249.

Instructions

1. Journalize the entries to record the foregoing transactions.
2. Indicate the amount of the interest expense in (a) 2016 and (b) 2017.
3. Determine the carrying amount of the bonds as of December 31, 2017.

Appendix 1 and Appendix 2

PR 14-5B Bond discount, entries for bonds payable transactions, interest method of amortizing bond discount

✔ 3. $2,327,008

On July 1, 2016, Livingston Corporation, a wholesaler of manufacturing equipment, issued $46,000,000 of 20-year, 10% bonds at a market (effective) interest rate of 11%, receiving cash of $42,309,236. Interest on the bonds is payable semiannually on December 31 and June 30. The fiscal year of the company is the calendar year.

Instructions

1. Journalize the entry to record the amount of cash proceeds from the issuance of the bonds.
2. Journalize the entries to record the following:
   a. The first semiannual interest payment on December 31, 2016, and the amortization of the bond discount, using the interest method. (Round to the nearest dollar.)
   b. The interest payment on June 30, 2017, and the amortization of the bond discount, using the interest method. (Round to the nearest dollar.)
3. Determine the total interest expense for 2016.

Appendix 1 and Appendix 2

PR 14-6B Bond premium, entries for bonds payable transactions, interest method of amortizing bond premium

✔ 3. $3,655,023

Rodgers Corporation produces and sells football equipment. On July 1, 2016, Rodgers Corporation issued $65,000,000 of 10-year, 12% bonds at a market (effective) interest rate of 10%, receiving cash of $73,100,469. Interest on the bonds is payable semiannually on December 31 and June 30. The fiscal year of the company is the calendar year.

Instructions

1. Journalize the entry to record the amount of cash proceeds from the issuance of the bonds.
2. Journalize the entries to record the following:
   a. The first semiannual interest payment on December 31, 2016, and the amortization of the bond premium, using the interest method. (Round to the nearest dollar.)
   b. The interest payment on June 30, 2017, and the amortization of the bond premium, using the interest method. (Round to the nearest dollar.)
3. Determine the total interest expense for 2016.

Cases & Projects

CP 14-1 General Electric bond issuance

General Electric Capital, a division of General Electric, uses long-term debt extensively. In a recent year, GE Capital issued $11 billion in long-term debt to investors, then within days filed legal documents to prepare for another $50 billion long-term debt issue. As a result of the $50 billion filing, the price of the initial $11 billion offering declined (due to higher risk of more debt).

> *Bill Gross, a manager of a bond investment fund, "denounced a 'lack in candor' related to GE's recent debt deal. 'It was the most recent and most egregious example of how bondholders are mistreated.' Gross argued that GE was not forthright when GE Capital recently issued $11 billion in bonds, one of the largest issues ever from a U.S. corporation. What bothered Gross is that three days after the issue the company announced its intention to sell as much as $50 billion in additional debt, warrants, preferred stock, guarantees, letters of credit and promissory notes at some future date."*

In your opinion, did GE Capital act unethically by selling $11 billion of long-term debt without telling those investors that a few days later it would be filing documents to prepare for another $50 billion debt offering?

Source: Jennifer Ablan, "Gross Shakes the Bond Market; GE Calms It, a Bit," *Barron's*, March 25, 2002.

CP 14-2 Ethics and professional conduct in business

Solar Industries develops and produces high-efficiency solar panels. The company has an outstanding $10,000,000, 30-year, 10% bond issue dated July 1, 2011. The bond issue is due June 30, 2040. Some bond indentures require the corporation issuing the bonds to transfer cash to a special cash fund, called a sinking fund, over the life of the bond. Such funds help assure investors that there will be adequate cash to pay the bonds at their maturity date.

The bond indenture requires a bond sinking fund, which has a balance of $1,200,000 as of July 1, 2016. The company is currently experiencing a shortage of funds due to a recent acquisition. Bob Lachgar, the company's treasurer, is considering using the funds from the bond sinking fund to cover payroll and other bills that are coming due at the end of the month. Bob's brother-in-law, a trustee of Solar's sinking fund, has indicated a willingness to allow Bob to use the funds from the sinking fund to temporarily meet the company's cash needs.

Discuss whether Bob's proposal is appropriate.

CP 14-3 Present values

Alex Kelton recently won the jackpot in the Colorado lottery while he was visiting his parents. When he arrived at the lottery office to collect his winnings, he was offered the following three payout options:

a. Receive $100,000,000 in cash today.

b. Receive $25,000,000 today and $9,000,000 per year for eight years, with the first payment being received one year from today.

c. Receive $15,000,000 per year for 10 years, with the first payment being received one year from today.

Assuming that the effective rate of interest is 7%, which payout option should Alex select? Use the present value tables in Appendix A. Explain your answer and provide any necessary supporting calculations.

CP 14-4 Preferred stock vs. bonds

Xentec Inc. has decided to expand its operations to owning and operating golf courses. The following is an excerpt from a conversation between the chief executive officer, Peter Kilgallon, and the vice president of finance, Dan Baron:

Peter: Dan, have you given any thought to how we're going to manage the acquisition of Sweeping Bluff Golf Course?

Dan: Well, the two basic options, as I see it, are to issue either preferred stock or bonds. The equity market is a little depressed right now. The rumor is that the Federal Reserve Bank's going to increase the interest rates either this month or next.

Peter: Yes, I've heard the rumor. The problem is that we can't wait around to see what's going to happen. We'll have to move on this next week if we want any chance to complete the acquisition of Sweeping Bluff Golf Course.

Dan: Well, the bond market is strong right now. Maybe we should issue debt this time around.

Peter: That's what I would have guessed as well. Sweeping Bluff Golf Course's financial statements look pretty good, except for the volatility of its income and cash flows. But that's characteristic of the industry.

Discuss the advantages and disadvantages of issuing preferred stock versus bonds.

CP 14-5 Financing business expansion

You hold a 25% common stock interest in YouOwnIt, a family-owned construction equipment company. Your sister, who is the manager, has proposed an expansion of plant facilities at an expected cost of $26,000,000. Two alternative plans have been suggested as methods of financing the expansion. Each plan is briefly described as follows:

Plan 1. Issue $26,000,000 of 20-year, 8% notes at face amount.

Plan 2. Issue an additional 550,000 shares of $10 par common stock at $20 per share, and $15,000,000 of 20-year, 8% notes at face amount.

The balance sheet as of the end of the previous fiscal year is as follows:

YouOwnIt, Inc.
Balance Sheet
December 31, 2016

Assets	
Current assets	$15,000,000
Property, plant, and equipment	22,500,000
Total assets	$37,500,000
Liabilities and Stockholders' Equity	
Liabilities	$11,250,000
Common stock, $10	4,000,000
Paid-in capital in excess of par	500,000
Retained earnings	21,750,000
Total liabilities and stockholders' equity	$37,500,000

Net income has remained relatively constant over the past several years. The expansion program is expected to increase yearly income before bond interest and income tax from $2,667,000 in the previous year to $5,000,000 for this year. Your sister has asked you, as the company treasurer, to prepare an analysis of each financing plan.

1. Prepare a table indicating the expected earnings per share on the common stock under each plan. Assume an income tax rate of 40%. Round to the nearest cent.
2. a. Discuss the factors that should be considered in evaluating the two plans.
   b. Which plan offers the greater benefit to the present stockholders? Give reasons for your opinion.

CP 14-6 Number of times interest charges are earned

The following financial data (in thousands) were taken from recent financial statements of Staples, Inc.:

	Year 3	Year 2	Year 1
Interest expense	$ 173,751	$ 214,824	$ 237,025
Earnings before taxes	1,459,141	1,356,595	1,155,894

1. What is the number of times interest charges are earned for Staples in Year 3, Year 2, and Year 1? (Round your answers to one decimal place.)
2. Evaluate this ratio for Staples.

STAFF/AFP/GETTY IMAGES/NEWSCOM

CHAPTER 15

Investments and Fair Value Accounting

The Coca-Cola Company

You invest cash to earn more cash. For example, you could deposit cash in a bank account to earn interest. You could also invest cash in preferred or common stocks and in corporate or U.S. government notes and bonds.

Preferred and common stock can be purchased through a stock exchange, such as the **New York Stock Exchange (NYSE)**. Preferred stock is purchased primarily with the expectation of earning dividends. Common stock is purchased with the expectation of earning dividends or realizing gains from a price increase in the stock.

Corporate and U.S. government bonds can also be purchased through a bond exchange. Bonds are purchased with the primary expectation of earning interest revenue.

Companies make investments for many of the same reasons that you would as an individual. For example, **The Coca-Cola Company** has invested approximately $3.1 billion of available cash in stocks and bonds. These investments are held by The Coca-Cola Company for interest, dividends, and expected price increases.

Unlike most individuals, however, companies also purchase significant amounts of the outstanding common stock of other companies for strategic reasons. For example, The Coca-Cola Company has more than $9 billion invested in companies where they own between 20% and 50% of the outstanding shares. The vast majority of these investments are in independent bottlers, who bottle and distribute Coca-Cola products.

Investments in debt and equity securities give rise to a number of accounting issues. These issues are described and illustrated in this chapter.

Learning Objectives

After studying this chapter, you should be able to: *Example Exercises*

OBJ 1 **Describe why companies invest in debt and equity securities.**
Why Companies Invest
- Investing Cash in Current Operations
- Investing Cash in Temporary Investments
- Investing Cash in Long-Term Investments

OBJ 2 **Describe and illustrate the accounting for debt investments.**
Accounting for Debt Investments
- Purchase of Bonds
- Interest Revenue
- Sale of Bonds — EE 15-1

OBJ 3 **Describe and illustrate the accounting for equity investments.**
Accounting for Equity Investments
- Cost Method: Less Than 20% Ownership — EE 15-2
- Equity Method: Between 20%–50% Ownership — EE 15-3
- Consolidation: More Than 50% Ownership

OBJ 4 **Describe and illustrate valuing and reporting investments in the financial statements.**
Valuing and Reporting Investments
- Trading Securities — EE 15-4
- Available-for-Sale Securities — EE 15-5
- Held-to-Maturity Securities
- Summary

OBJ 5 **Describe fair value accounting and its effects on the financial statements.**
Fair Value Accounting
- Effect of Fair Value Accounting on the Financial Statements

OBJ 6 **Describe and illustrate the computation of dividend yield.**
Financial Analysis and Interpretation: Dividend Yield — EE 15-6

At a Glance 15 Page 703

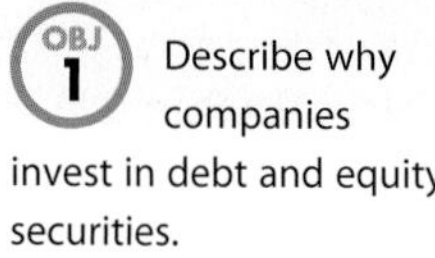
Describe why companies invest in debt and equity securities.

Why Companies Invest

Most companies generate cash from their operations. This cash can be used for the following purposes:

- Investing in current operations
- Investing in temporary investments to earn additional revenue
- Investing in long-term investments in stock of other companies for strategic reasons

Investing Cash in Current Operations

Cash is often used to support the current operating activities of a company. For example, cash may be used to replace worn-out equipment or to purchase new, more efficient and productive equipment. In addition, cash may be reinvested in the company to expand its current operations. For example, a retailer based in the northwest United States might decide to expand by opening stores in the Midwest.

To support its current level of operations, a company also uses cash to pay:

- expenses.
- suppliers of merchandise and other assets.
- interest to creditors.
- dividends to stockholders.

The accounting for the use of cash in current operations has been described and illustrated in earlier chapters. For example, Chapter 10, “Fixed Assets and Intangible Assets,” illustrated the use of cash for purchasing property, plant, and equipment.

In this chapter, we describe and illustrate the use of cash for investing in temporary investments and the stock of other companies.

Investing Cash in Temporary Investments

A company may temporarily have excess cash that is not needed for use in its current operations. This is often the case when a company has a seasonal operating cycle. For example, a significant portion of the annual merchandise sales of a retailer occurs during the fall holiday season. As a result, retailers often experience a large increase in cash during this period, which is not needed until the spring buying season.

Instead of letting excess cash remain idle in a checking account, most companies invest their excess cash in temporary investments. In doing so, companies invest in securities such as:

- **Debt securities**, which are notes and bonds that pay interest and have a fixed maturity date.
- **Equity securities**, which are preferred and common stock that represent ownership in a company and do not have a fixed maturity date.

Investments in debt and equity securities, termed **investments** or *temporary investments*, are reported in the Current Assets section of the balance sheet.

The primary objective of investing in temporary investments is to:

- earn interest revenue.
- receive dividends.
- realize gains from increases in the market price of the securities.

Investments in certificates of deposit and other securities that do not normally change in value are disclosed on the balance sheet as *cash and cash equivalents*. Such investments are held primarily for their interest revenue.

Investing Cash in Long-Term Investments

A company may invest cash in the debt or equity of another company as a long-term investment. Long-term investments may be held for the same investment objectives as temporary investments. However, long-term investments often involve the purchase of a significant portion of the stock of another company. Such investments usually have a strategic purpose, such as:

In 2012, **Dell Computer** purchased **Quest Software** for $2.4 billion. The acquisition allowed Dell to competitively expand into the software sector.

- *Reduction of costs*: When one company buys another company, the combined company may be able to reduce administrative expenses. For example, a combined company does not need two chief executive officers (CEOs) or chief financial officers (CFOs).
- *Replacement of management*: If the purchased company has been mismanaged, the acquiring company may replace the company's management and, thus, improve operations and profits.
- *Expansion*: The acquiring company may purchase a company because it has a complementary product line, territory, or customer base. The new combined company may be able to serve customers better than the two companies could separately.
- *Integration*: A company may integrate operations by acquiring a supplier or customer. Acquiring a supplier may provide a more stable or uninterrupted supply of resources. Acquiring a customer may also provide a market for the company's products or services.

Accounting for Debt Investments

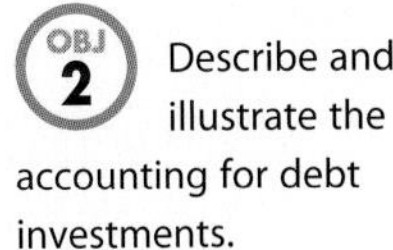

Describe and illustrate the accounting for debt investments.

Debt securities include notes and bonds issued by corporations and governmental organizations. Most companies invest excess cash in bonds as investments to earn interest revenue.

The accounting for bond investments[1] includes recording the following:

- Purchase of bonds
- Interest revenue
- Sale of bonds

Purchase of Bonds

The purchase of bonds is recorded by debiting an investments account for the purchase price of the bonds, including any brokerage commissions. (A *brokerage commission* is the fee charged by the agent who arranges the transaction between the buyer and seller.) If the bonds are purchased between interest dates, the purchase price includes accrued interest since the last interest payment. This is because the seller has earned the accrued interest, but the buyer will receive the accrued interest when it is paid.

To illustrate, assume that Homer Company purchases $18,000 of U.S. Treasury bonds at their face amount on March 17, 2016, plus accrued interest for 45 days. The bonds have an interest rate of 6%, payable on July 31 and January 31.

The entry to record the purchase of the U.S. Treasury bonds is as follows:

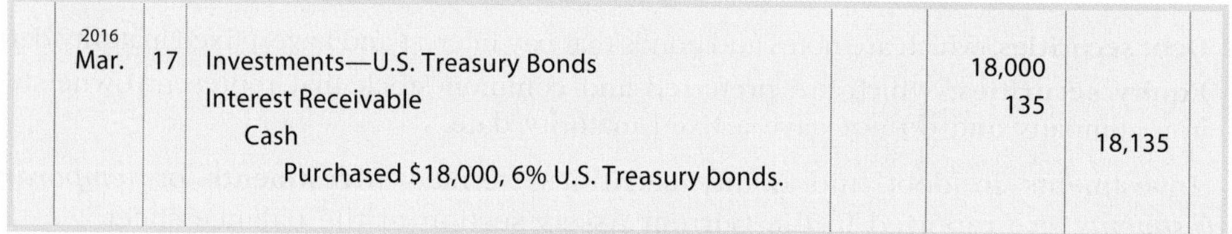

2016					
Mar.	17	Investments—U.S. Treasury Bonds		18,000	
		Interest Receivable		135	
		Cash			18,135
		Purchased $18,000, 6% U.S. Treasury bonds.			

Because Homer Company purchased the bonds on March 17, it is also purchasing the accrued interest for 45 days (January 31 to March 17), as shown in Exhibit 1. The accrued interest of $135 is computed as follows:[2]

$$\text{Accrued Interest} = \$18{,}000 \times 6\% \times (45 \div 360) = \$135$$

The accrued interest is recorded by debiting Interest Receivable for $135. Investments is debited for the purchase price of the bonds of $18,000.

EXHIBIT 1

Interest Timeline

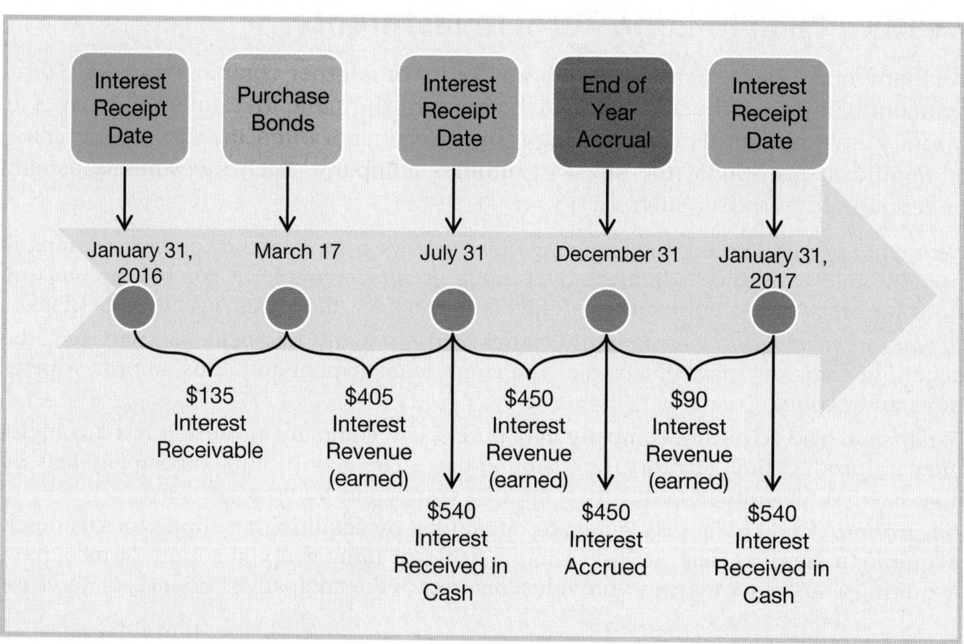

Interest Revenue

On July 31, Homer Company receives a semiannual interest payment of $540 ($18,000 × 6% × ½). The $540 interest includes the $135 accrued interest that Homer Company purchased with the bonds on March 17. Thus, Homer has earned $405 ($540 − $135) of interest revenue since purchasing the bonds, as shown in Exhibit 1.

[1] Debt investments may also include installment notes and short-term notes. The accounting for these debt investments is covered in intermediate and advanced accounting courses.

[2] To simplify, a 360-day year is used to compute interest.

The receipt of the interest on July 31 is recorded as follows:

2016 July	31	Cash		540	
		Interest Receivable			135
		Interest Revenue			405
		Received semiannual interest.			

Homer Company's accounting period ends on December 31. Thus, an adjusting entry must be made to accrue interest for five months (August 1 to December 31) of \$450 (\$18,000 × 6% × 5/12), as shown in Exhibit 1. The adjusting entry to record the accrued interest is as follows:

2016 Dec.	31	Interest Receivable		450	
		Interest Revenue			450
		Accrued 5 months of interest.			

For the year ended December 31, 2016, Homer Company would report Interest Revenue of \$855 (\$405 + \$450) as part of Other Income on its income statement.

The receipt of the semiannual interest of \$540 on January 31, 2017, is recorded as follows:

2017 Jan.	31	Cash		540	
		Interest Revenue			90
		Interest Receivable			450
		Received semiannual interest			

Sale of Bonds

The sale of a bond investment normally results in a gain or loss. If the proceeds from the sale exceed the book value (cost) of the bonds, then a gain is recorded. If the proceeds are less than the book value (cost) of the bonds, a loss is recorded.

To illustrate, on January 31, 2017, Homer Company sells the Treasury bonds at 98, which is a price equal to 98% of their face amount. The sale results in a loss of \$360, computed as follows:

Proceeds from sale	\$17,640*
Less book value (cost) of the bonds	18,000
Loss on sale of bonds	\$ (360)

*\$18,000 × 98%

The entry to record the sale is as follows:

2017 Jan.	31	Cash		17,640	
		Loss on Sale of Investment		360	
		Investments—U.S. Treasury Bonds			18,000
		Sold U.S. Treasury bonds.			

There is no accrued interest upon the sale because the interest payment date is also January 31. If the sale were between interest dates, interest accrued since the last interest payment date would be added to the sale proceeds and credited to Interest Revenue. The loss on the sale of bond investments is reported as part of Other Income (Loss) on Homer Company's income statement.

Example Exercise 15-1 Bond Investment Transactions

Journalize the entries to record the following selected bond investment transactions for Fly Company:

1. Purchased for cash $40,000 of Tyler Company 10% bonds at 100 plus accrued interest of $320.
2. Received the first semiannual interest.
3. Sold $30,000 of the bonds at 102 plus accrued interest of $110.

Follow My Example 15-1

1. Investments—Tyler Company Bonds	40,000	
Interest Receivable	320	
Cash		40,320
2. Cash	2,000*	
Interest Receivable		320
Interest Revenue		1,680
*$40,000 × 10% × ½		
3. Cash	30,710*	
Interest Revenue		110
Gain on Sale of Investments		600
Investments—Tyler Company Bonds		30,000
*Sale proceeds ($30,000 × 102%)	$30,600	
Accrued interest	110	
Total proceeds from sale	$30,710	

Practice Exercises: PE 15-1A, PE 15-1B

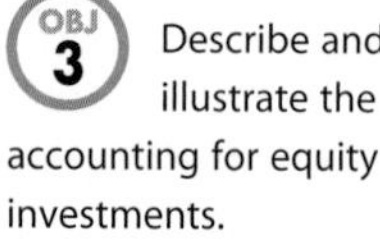

Describe and illustrate the accounting for equity investments.

Accounting for Equity Investments

A company may invest in the preferred or common stock of another company. The company investing in another company's stock is the **investor**. The company whose stock is purchased is the **investee**.

The percent of the investee's outstanding stock purchased by the investor determines the degree of control that the investor has over the investee. This, in turn, determines the accounting method used to record the stock investment, as shown in Exhibit 2.

EXHIBIT 2

Stock Investments

Percent of Outstanding Stock Owned by Investor	Degree of Control of Investor over Investee	Accounting Method
Less than 20%	No control	Cost method
Between 20% and 50%	Significant influence	Equity method
Greater than 50%	Control	Consolidation

Cost Method: Less Than 20% Ownership

If the investor purchases less than 20% of the outstanding stock of the investee, the investor is considered to have no control over the investee. In this case, it is assumed that the investor purchased the stock primarily to earn dividends or to realize gains on price increases of the stock.

Investments of less than 20% of the investee's outstanding stock are accounted for using the **cost method**. Under the cost method, entries are recorded for the following transactions:

- Purchase of stock
- Receipt of dividends
- Sale of stock

Purchase of Stock The purchase of stock is recorded at its cost. Any brokerage commissions are included as part of the cost.

To illustrate, assume that on May 1, Bart Company purchases 2,000 shares of Lisa Company common stock at $49.90 per share plus a brokerage commission of $200. The entry to record the purchase of the stock is as follows:

May	1	Investments—Lisa Company Stock		100,000		
		Cash			100,000	
		Purchased 2,000 shares of Lisa Company common stock [($49.90 × 2,000 shares) + $200].				

Receipt of Dividends On July 31, Bart Company receives a dividend of $0.40 per share from Lisa Company. The entry to record the receipt of the dividend is as follows:

July	31	Cash		800		
		Dividend Revenue			800	
		Received dividend on Lisa Company common stock (2,000 shares × $0.40).				

Dividend Revenue is reported as part of Other Income on Bart Company's income statement.

Sale of Stock The sale of a stock investment normally results in a gain or loss. A gain is recorded if the proceeds from the sale exceed the book value (cost) of the stock. A loss is recorded if the proceeds from the sale are less than the book value (cost).

To illustrate, on September 1, Bart Company sells 1,500 shares of Lisa Company stock for $54.50 per share, less a $160 commission. The sale results in a gain of $6,590, computed as follows:

Proceeds from sale	$81,590*
Book value (cost) of the stock	75,000**
Gain on sale	$ 6,590

*($54.50 × 1,500 shares) – $160
**($100,000 ÷ 2,000 shares) × 1,500 shares

The entry to record the sale is as follows:

Sept.	1	Cash		81,590		
		Gain on Sale of Investments			6,590	
		Investments—Lisa Company Stock			75,000	
		Sold 1,500 shares of Lisa Company common stock.				

The gain on the sale of investments is reported as part of Other Income on Bart Company's income statement.

Example Exercise 15-2 Stock Investment Transactions

On September 1, 1,500 shares of Monroe Company are acquired at a price of $24 per share plus a $40 brokerage commission. On October 14, a $0.60-per-share dividend was received on the Monroe Company stock. On November 11, 750 shares (half) of Monroe Company stock were sold for $20 per share, less a $45 brokerage commission. Prepare the journal entries for the original purchase, dividend, and sale.

Follow My Example 15-2

Sept. 1	Investments—Monroe Company Stock	36,040*	
	Cash		36,040
	*(1,500 shares × $24 per share) + $40		
Oct. 14	Cash	900*	
	Dividend Revenue		900
	*$0.60 per share × 1,500 shares		
Nov. 11	Cash	14,955*	
	Loss on Sale of Investments	3,065	
	Investments—Monroe Company Stock		18,020**
	*(750 shares × $20) – $45		
	**$36,040 × ½		

Practice Exercises: PE 15-2A, PE 15-2B

Equity Method: Between 20%–50% Ownership

If the investor purchases between 20% and 50% of the outstanding stock of the investee, the investor is considered to have a *significant influence* over the investee. In this case, it is assumed that the investor purchased the stock primarily for strategic reasons, such as developing a supplier relationship.

Investments of between 20% and 50% of the investee's outstanding stock are accounted for using the **equity method**. Under the equity method, the stock is recorded initially at its cost, including any brokerage commissions. This is the same as under the cost method.

Under the equity method, the investment account is adjusted for the investor's share of the net income and dividends of the investee. These adjustments are as follows:

- *Net Income:* The investor records its share of the net income of the investee as an increase in the investment account. Its share of any net loss is recorded as a decrease in the investment account.
- *Dividends:* The investor's share of cash dividends received from the investee decreases the investment account.

Purchase of Stock To illustrate, assume that Simpson Inc. purchased its 40% interest in Flanders Corporation's common stock on January 2, 2016, for $350,000. The entry to record the purchase is as follows:

2016 Jan.	2	Investment in Flanders Corporation Stock		350,000	
		Cash			350,000
		Purchased 40% of Flanders			
		Corporation stock.			

Recording Investee Net Income For the year ended December 31, 2016, Flanders Corporation reported net income of $105,000. Under the equity method, Simpson Inc. (the investor) records its share of Flanders net income, as follows:

2016 Dec.	31	Investment in Flanders Corporation Stock	42,000	
		Income of Flanders Corporation		42,000
		Recorded 40% share of Flanders Corporation net income, $105,000 × 40%.		

Income of Flanders Corporation is reported on Simpson Inc.'s income statement. Depending on its significance, it may be reported separately or as part of *Other Income*. If Flanders had a loss during the period, then the journal entry would be a debit to Loss of Flanders Corporation and a credit to the investment account.

Recording Investee Dividends During the year, Flanders Corporation declared and paid cash dividends of $45,000. Under the equity method, Simpson Inc. (the investor) records its share of Flanders dividends as follows:

2016 Dec.	31	Cash	18,000	
		Investment in Flanders Corporation Stock		18,000
		Recorded 40% share of Flanders Corporation dividends, $45,000 × 40%.		

The effect of recording 40% of Flanders Corporation's net income and dividends is to increase the investment account by $24,000 ($42,000 − $18,000). Thus, Investment in Flanders Corporation Stock increases from $350,000 to $374,000, as shown in Exhibit 3.

EXHIBIT 3

Investment and Dividends

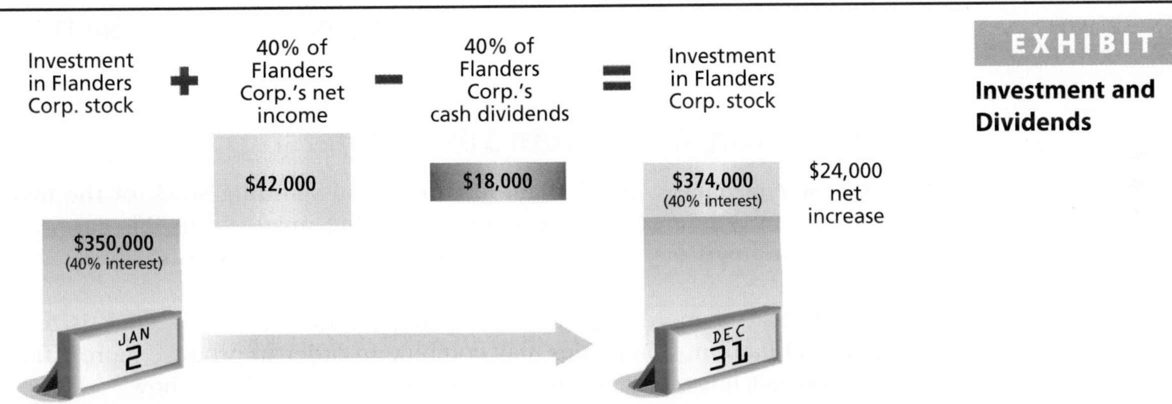

Under the equity method, the investment account reflects the investor's proportional changes in the net book value of the investee. For example, Flanders Corporation's net book value increased by $60,000 (net income of $105,000 less dividends of $45,000) during the year. As a result, Simpson Inc.'s share of Flanders' net book value increased by $24,000 ($60,000 × 40%). Investments accounted for under the equity method are classified on the balance sheet as noncurrent assets.

Sale of Stock Under the equity method, a gain or loss is normally recorded from the sale of an investment. A gain is recorded if the proceeds exceed the *book value* of the investment. A loss is recorded if the proceeds are less than the *book value* of the investment.

To illustrate, if Simpson Inc. sold Flanders Corporation's stock on January 1, 2017, for $400,000, a gain of $26,000 would be reported, computed as follows:

Proceeds from sale	$400,000
Book value of stock investment	374,000
Gain on sale	$ 26,000

The entry to record the sale is as follows:

2017 Jan.	1	Cash		400,000	
		Investment in Flanders Corporation Stock			374,000
		Gain on Sale of Flanders Corporation Stock			26,000
		Sold Flanders Corporation stock.			

Example Exercise 15-3 Equity Method

OBJ 3

On January 2, Olson Company acquired 35% of the outstanding stock of Bryant Company for $140,000. For the year ended December 31, Bryant Company earned income of $44,000 and paid dividends of $20,000. Prepare the entries for Olson Company for the purchase of the stock, the share of Bryant income, and the dividends received from Bryant Company.

Follow My Example 15-3

Jan. 2	Investment in Bryant Company Stock	140,000	
	Cash		140,000
Dec. 31	Investment in Bryant Company Stock	15,400*	
	Income of Bryant Company		15,400
	*Recorded 35% of Bryant income, 35% × $44,000		
Dec. 31	Cash	7,000*	
	Investment in Bryant Company Stock		7,000
	*Recorded 35% of Bryant's $20,000 dividend, 35% × $20,000		

Practice Exercises: PE 15-3A, PE 15-3B

Consolidation: More Than 50% Ownership

If the investor purchases more than 50% of the outstanding stock of the investee, the investor is considered to have *control* over the investee. In this case, it is assumed that the investor purchased the stock of the investee primarily for strategic reasons.

The purchase of more than 50% ownership of the investee's stock is termed a **business combination**. Companies may combine in order to produce more efficiently, diversify product lines, expand geographically, or acquire know-how.

A corporation owning all or a majority of the voting stock of another corporation is called a **parent company**. The corporation that is controlled is called the **subsidiary company**.

Parent and subsidiary corporations often continue to maintain separate accounting records and prepare their own financial statements. In such cases, at the end of the year, the financial statements of the parent and subsidiary are combined and reported as a single company. These combined financial statements are called **consolidated financial statements**. Such statements are normally identified by adding *and Subsidiary(ies)* to the name of the parent corporation or by adding *Consolidated* to the statement title.

To the external stakeholders of the parent company, consolidated financial statements are more meaningful than separate statements for each corporation. This is because the parent company, in substance, controls the subsidiaries. The accounting for business combinations, including preparing consolidated financial statements, is described and illustrated in advanced accounting courses and textbooks.

Business  Connection

MORE CASH MEANS MORE INVESTMENTS FOR DRUG COMPANIES

Patented drugs are the life blood of the pharmaceutical industry. Drug companies with extensive portfolios of patented drugs generate huge cash flows from operating activities. As a result, these companies often have vast amounts of cash on hand to invest in other companies.

Near the end of 2012, the five biggest drug makers had in excess of $70 billion in cash and investments. Many analysts anticipated that these companies would use this excess cash to acquire smaller biotechnology and drug companies for their patented drugs and their ongoing research activities.

Source: "Mergers and Acquisitions on the Rise in 2013 as Big Pharma Companies Hold Record Amounts of Cash on Hand," *Five Star Equities Market Research Report*. Feb. 7, 2013.

Valuing and Reporting Investments

OBJ 4 Describe and illustrate valuing and reporting investments in the financial statements.

Debt and equity securities are *financial assets* that are often traded on public exchanges such as the New York Stock Exchange. As a result, their market value can be observed and, thus, objectively determined. For this reason, generally accepted accounting principles (GAAP) allows some debt securities, and requires equity securities where there is less than a 20% ownership interest to be valued in the accounting records and financial statements at their fair market values.

These securities are classified as follows:

- Trading securities
- Available-for-sale securities
- Held-to-maturity securities

Trading Securities

Trading securities are debt and equity securities that are purchased to earn short-term profits from changes in their market prices. Trading securities are often held by banks, mutual funds, insurance companies, and other financial institutions.

SunTrust Banks Inc. holds over $6 billion in trading securities as current assets.

Because trading securities are held as a short-term investment, they are reported as a current asset on the balance sheet. Trading securities are valued as a portfolio (group) of securities using the securities' fair values. **Fair value** is the market price that the company would receive for a security if it were sold. A change in the fair value of the portfolio (group) of trading securities is recognized as an **unrealized gain or loss** for the period.

To illustrate, assume Maggie Company purchased a portfolio of trading securities during 2016. On December 31, 2016, the cost and fair values of the securities were as follows:

Name	Number of Shares	Total Cost	Total Fair Value
Armour Company	400	$ 5,000	$ 7,200
Maven, Inc.	500	11,000	7,500
Polaris Co.	200	8,000	10,600
Total		$24,000	$25,300

The portfolio of trading securities is reported at its fair value of $25,300. An adjusting entry is made to record the increase in the fair value of $1,300 ($25,300 – $24,000). In order to maintain a record of the original cost of the securities, a valuation account, called *Valuation Allowance for Trading Investments*, is debited for $1,300, and Unrealized Gain on Trading Investments is credited for $1,300.[3] The adjusting entry on

December 31, 2016, to record the fair value of the portfolio of trading securities is as follows:

2016 Dec.	31	Valuation Allowance for Trading Investments	1,300	
		Unrealized Gain on Trading Investments		1,300
		To record increase in fair value of trading securities.		

Unrealized Gain on Trading Investments is reported on the income statement. Depending on its significance, it may be reported separately or as Other Income on the income statement. The valuation allowance is reported on the December 31, 2016, balance sheet as follows:

Maggie Company
Balance Sheet (selected items)
December 31, 2016

Current assets:		
Cash		$120,000
Trading investments (at cost)	$24,000	
Plus valuation allowance for trading investments	1,300	
Trading investments (at fair value)		25,300

If the fair value of the portfolio of trading securities was less than the cost, then the adjustment would debit Unrealized Loss on Trading Investments and credit Valuation Allowance for Trading Investments for the difference. Unrealized Loss on Trading Investments would be reported on the income statement as Other Expenses. Valuation Allowance for Trading Investments would be shown on the balance sheet as a *deduction* from Trading Investments (at cost).

Over time, the valuation allowance account is adjusted to reflect the difference between the cost and the fair value of the portfolio. Thus, increases in the valuation allowance account from the beginning of the period will result in an adjustment to record an unrealized gain, similar to the preceding journal entry. Likewise, decreases in the valuation allowance account from the beginning of the period will result in an adjustment to record an unrealized loss.

Example Exercise 15-4 Valuing Trading Securities at Fair Value

On January 1, 2016, Valuation Allowance for Trading Investments had a zero balance. On December 31, 2016, the cost of the trading securities portfolio was $79,200, and the fair value was $76,800. Prepare the December 31, 2016, adjusting journal entry to record the unrealized gain or loss on trading investments.

Follow My Example 15-4

2016			
Dec. 31	Unrealized Loss on Trading Investments	2,400	
	Valuation Allowance for Trading Investments		2,400*
	To record decrease in fair value of trading investments.		

*Trading investments at fair value, December 31, 2016	$ 76,800
Less trading investments at cost, December 31, 2016	79,200
Unrealized loss on trading investments	$ (2,400)

Practice Exercises: PE 15-4A, PE 15-4B

[3] We assume that the valuation allowance account has a beginning balance of zero to simplify our illustrations.

Integrity, Objectivity, and Ethics in Business

SOCIALLY RESPONSIBLE INVESTING

Socially responsible investing is a growing trend in the United States and Europe that focuses on making investments to improve society. Socially responsible investors attempt to balance investment return with social good by seeking out investments in companies that (1) are environmentally friendly, (2) do not infringe on human rights in the production of a product or provision of a service, and (3) are anti-discriminatory. In some situations, socially responsible investors target emerging markets to both generate a return and help overcome social challenges. In addition, some socially responsible investors refuse to invest in companies that produce alcohol, tobacco, or weapons.

Available-for-Sale Securities

Available-for-sale securities are debt and equity securities that are neither held for trading, held to maturity, nor held for strategic reasons. The accounting for available-for-sale securities is similar to the accounting for trading securities, except for the reporting of changes in fair values. Specifically, changes in the fair values of *trading securities* are reported as an unrealized gain or loss on the income statement. In contrast, changes in the fair values of *available-for-sale securities* are reported as part of stockholders' equity and, thus, excluded from the income statement.

Google, Inc. holds over $34 billion in available-for-sale securities as current assets.

To illustrate, assume that Maggie Company purchased the three securities during 2016 as available-for-sale securities instead of trading securities. On December 31, 2016, the cost and fair values of the securities were as follows:

Name	Number of Shares	Total Cost	Total Fair Value
Armour Company	400	$ 5,000	$ 7,200
Maven, Inc.	500	11,000	7,500
Polaris Co.	200	8,000	10,600
Total		$24,000	$25,300

The portfolio of available-for-sale securities is reported at its fair value of $25,300. An adjusting entry is made to record the increase in fair value of $1,300 ($25,300 – $24,000). In order to maintain a record of the original cost of the securities, a valuation account, called *Valuation Allowance for Available-for-Sale Investments*, is debited for $1,300. This account is similar to the valuation account used for trading securities.

Unlike trading securities, the December 31, 2016, adjusting entry credits a stockholders' equity account instead of an income statement account.[4] The $1,300 increase in fair value is credited to Unrealized Gain (Loss) on Available-for-Sale Investments.

The adjusting entry on December 31, 2016, to record the fair value of the portfolio of available-for-sale securities is as follows:

Date		Description	Post. Ref.	Debit	Credit
2016 Dec.	31	Valuation Allowance for Available-for-Sale Investments		1,300	
		Unrealized Gain (Loss) on Available-for-Sale Investments			1,300
		To record increase in fair value of available-for-sale investments.			

[4] This is a rare exception to the rule that every adjusting entry must affect an income statement and a balance sheet account.

A credit balance in Unrealized Gain (Loss) on Available-for-Sale Investments is added to stockholders' equity, while a debit balance is subtracted from stockholders' equity.

The valuation allowance and the unrealized gain are reported on the December 31, 2016, balance sheet as follows:

Maggie Company
Balance Sheet
December 31, 2016

Current assets:		
Cash		$120,000
Available-for-sale investments (at cost)	$24,000	
Plus valuation allowance for available-for-sale investments	1,300	
Available-for-sale investments (at fair value)		25,300
Stockholders' equity:		
Common stock		$ 10,000
Paid-in capital in excess of par		150,000
Retained earnings		250,000
Unrealized gain (loss) on available-for-sale investments		1,300
Total stockholders' equity		$411,300

Equal

As shown, Unrealized Gain (Loss) on Available-for-Sale Investments is reported as an addition to stockholders' equity. In future years, the cumulative effects of unrealized gains and losses are reported in this account. Because 2014 was the first year that Maggie Company purchased available-for-sale securities, the unrealized gain is reported as the balance of Unrealized Gain (Loss) on Available-for-Sale Investments. This treatment is supported under the theory that available-for-sale securities will be held longer than trading securities, so changes in fair value over time have a greater opportunity to cancel out. Thus, these changes are not reported on the income statement, as is the case with trading securities.

If the fair value was less than the cost, then the adjustment would debit Unrealized Gain (Loss) on Available-for-Sale Investments and credit Valuation Allowance for Available-for-Sale Investments for the difference. Unrealized Gain (Loss) on Trading Investments would be reported in the Stockholders' Equity section as a negative item. Valuation Allowance for Available-for-Sale Investments would be shown on the balance sheet as a deduction from Available-for-Sale Investments (at cost).

Over time, the valuation allowance account is adjusted to reflect the difference between the cost and the fair value of the portfolio. Thus, increases in the valuation allowance from the beginning of the period will result in an adjustment to record an increase in the valuation and unrealized gain (loss) accounts, similar to the journal entry illustrated earlier. Likewise, decreases in the valuation allowance from the beginning of the period will result in an adjustment to record decreases in the valuation and unrealized gain (loss) accounts.

Example Exercise 15-5 Valuing Available-for-Sale Securities at Fair Value

On January 1, 2016, Valuation Allowance for Available-for-Sale Investments had a zero balance. On December 31, 2016, the cost of the available-for-sale securities was $45,700, and the fair value was $50,000.

Prepare the adjusting entry to record the unrealized gain or loss for available-for-sale investments on December 31, 2016.

Follow My Example 15-5

2016			
Dec. 31	Valuation Allowance for Available-for-Sale Investments	4,300*	
	Unrealized Gain (Loss) on Available-for-Sale Investments		4,300
	To record increase in fair value of available-for-sale securities.		

*Available-for-sale investments at fair value, December 31, 2016	$50,000
Less available-for-sale investments at cost, December 31, 2016	45,700
Unrealized gain (loss) on available-for-sale investments	$ 4,300

Practice Exercises: PE 15-5A, PE 15-5B

Held-to-Maturity Securities

Held-to-maturity securities are debt investments, such as notes or bonds, that a company intends to hold until their maturity date. Held-to-maturity securities are primarily purchased to earn interest revenue.

If a held-to-maturity security will mature within a year, it is reported as a current asset on the balance sheet. Held-to-maturity securities maturing beyond a year are reported as noncurrent assets.

Only securities with maturity dates, such as corporate notes and bonds, are classified as held-to-maturity securities. Equity securities are not held-to-maturity securities because they have no maturity date.

Held-to-maturity bond investments are recorded at their cost, including any brokerage commissions, as illustrated earlier in this chapter. If the interest rate on the bonds differs from the market rate of interest, the bonds may be purchased at a premium or discount. In such cases, the premium or discount is amortized over the life of the bonds.

Held-to-maturity bond investments are reported on the balance sheet at their amortized cost. The accounting for held-to-maturity investments, including premium and discount amortization, is described in advanced accounting texts.

Summary

Exhibit 4 summarizes the valuation and balance sheet reporting of trading, available-for-sale, and held-to-maturity securities.

EXHIBIT 4

Summary of Valuing and Reporting of Investments

	Trading Securities	**Available-for-Sale Securities**	**Held-to-Maturity Securities**
Valued at:	**Fair Value**	**Fair Value**	**Amortized Cost**
Changes in valuation are reported as:	Unrealized gain or loss in the income statement as Other income (loss).	Accumulated unrealized gain or loss is reported in stockholders' equity on the balance sheet.	Not applicable. Held-to-Maturity Securities are reported at cost.*
Reported on the balance sheet as:	Cost of investments plus or minus valuation allowance.	Cost of investments plus or minus valuation allowance.	Amortized cost of investment.
Classified on balance sheet as:	A current asset.	Either as a current or noncurrent asset, depending on management's intent.	Either as a current or noncurrent asset, depending on remaining term to maturity.

*Premium or discount amortization is reported as part of interest revenue on the income statement.

Common stock investments in trading and available-for-sale securities are normally less than 20% of the outstanding common stock of the investee. The portfolios are reported at fair value using the valuation allowance account, while the individual securities are accounted for using the cost method. Investments between 20% and 50% of the outstanding common stock of the investee are accounted for using the equity method illustrated earlier in this chapter. Equity method investments are classified as noncurrent assets on the balance sheet.

The balance sheet reporting for the investments of **Mornin' Joe** follows:

Mornin' Joe
Balance Sheet
December 31, 2016

Assets			
Current assets:			
Cash and cash equivalents		$235,000	
Trading investments (at cost)	$420,000		
Plus valuation allowance for trading investments	45,000	465,000	
Accounts receivable	$305,000		
Less allowance for doubtful accounts	12,300	292,700	
Merchandise inventory—at lower of cost (first-in, first-out method) or market		120,000	
Prepaid insurance		24,000	
Total current assets			$1,136,700
Investments:			
Investment in AM Coffee (equity method)			565,000
Property, plant, and equipment:			

Mornin' Joe invests in trading securities and does not have investments in held-to-maturity or available-for-sale securities. Mornin' Joe also owns 40% of AM Coffee Corporation, which is accounted for using the equity method. Mornin' Joe intends to keep its investment in AM Coffee indefinitely for strategic reasons; thus, its investment in AM Coffee is classified as a noncurrent asset. Such investments are normally reported before property, plant, and equipment.

Mornin' Joe reported an Unrealized Gain on Trading Investments of $5,000 and Equity Income in AM Coffee of $57,000 in the Other Income and Expense section of its income statement, as follows:

Mornin' Joe
Income Statement
For the Year Ended December 31, 2016

Revenue from sales:			
Sales		$5,450,000	
Less: Sales returns and allowances	$26,500		
Sales discounts	21,400	47,900	
Sales			$5,402,100
Cost of merchandise sold			2,160,000
Gross profit			$3,242,100
Total operating expenses			2,608,700
Income from operations			$ 633,400
Other income and expense:			
Interest revenue		$ 18,000	
Interest expense		(136,000)	
Loss on disposal of fixed asset		(23,000)	
Unrealized gain on trading investments		5,000	
Equity income in AM Coffee		57,000	(79,000)
Income before income taxes			$ 554,400
Income tax expense			132,800
Net income			$ 421,600

Business  Connection

WARREN BUFFETT: THE SAGE OF OMAHA

Beginning in 1962, Warren Buffett, one of the world's wealthiest and most successful investors, began buying shares of Berkshire Hathaway. He eventually took control of the company and transformed it from a textile manufacturing company into an investment holding company. Today, Berkshire Hathaway holds more than $125 billion in cash and cash equivalents, equity securities, and debt securities. Berkshire's largest holdings include The Coca-Cola Company, American Express, Wells Fargo, and Procter & Gamble. Berkshire Class A common stock trades near $155,000 per share, the highest priced share on the New York Stock Exchange. These shares would have given an investor more than a 1,800% return since 1990.

Buffett compares his investment style to hitting a baseball: "Ted Williams, one of the greatest hitters in the game, stated, 'my argument is, to be a good hitter, you've got to get a good ball to hit. It's the first rule of the book. If I have to bite at stuff that is out of my happy zone, I'm not a .344 hitter. I might only be a .250 hitter.'" Buffett states, "Charlie (Buffett's partner) and I agree and will try to wait for (investment) opportunities that are well within our 'happy zone.'" One of Buffet's recent "happy zone" investments was the acquisition of Burlington Northern Santa Fe Railroad for $34 billion.

Warren Buffett as the CEO of Berkshire Hathaway earns a salary of only $100,000 per year, which is the lowest CEO salary for a company of its size in the United States. However, he personally owns approximately 38% of the company, making him worth more than $40 billion. What will Buffett do with this wealth? He has decided to give nearly all of it to philanthropic causes through the Bill and Melinda Gates Foundation.

Source: Warren E. Buffett, *The Essays of Warren Buffett: Lessons for Corporate America*, edited by Lawrence A. Cunningham, p. 234.

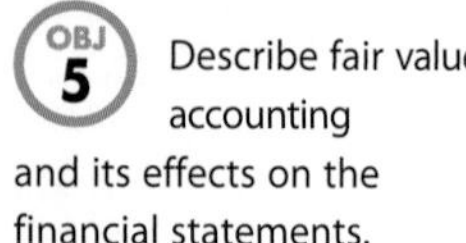

Describe fair value accounting and its effects on the financial statements.

Fair Value Accounting

Fair value is the price that would be received from selling an asset. Fair value assumes that this transaction occurs under *normal* business conditions.

As illustrated earlier, generally accepted accounting principles require trading and available-for-sale investments to be recorded at their fair value. This differs from the traditional historical cost measurement basis, which records assets such as inventory and property, plant, and equipment at their purchase price. As a result, financial statements include some assets that are reported at their historical cost (inventory, property, plant, and equipment), and other assets that are reported at their fair value (trading, and available-for-sale securities).

Over the past several decades, the financial statements of companies in most industries have included more fair value measures. This is partially due to the Financial Accounting Standards Board's increased willingness to apply fair value to certain assets and transactions. As the ability to measure fair value becomes more reliable, a greater number of assets and transactions are likely to be reported at fair value. A more detailed discussion of fair value is provided in intermediate and advanced financial accounting courses.

Effect of Fair Value Accounting on the Financial Statements

The use of fair values for valuing assets and liabilities affects the financial statements. Specifically, the balance sheet and income statement could be affected.

Balance Sheet When an asset is reported at its fair value, any difference between the asset's original cost or prior period's fair value must be recorded. As we illustrated for trading and available-for-sale securities, this difference is reported in a valuation allowance. The account, Valuation Allowance for Trading Investments, was used earlier in this chapter to adjust trading securities to their fair values.

Available-for-sale securities are reported at fair value in the balance sheet. Changes in their fair values are not recognized on the income statement, but are included as part of stockholders' equity through the comprehensive income and accumulated other comprehensive income accounts. These accounts are described in the appendix to this chapter.

Income Statement Trading securities are also reported at fair value in the balance sheet. However, instead of recording the changes in the fair values of trading securities as part of stockholders' equity, the unrealized gains or losses are reported on the income statement.

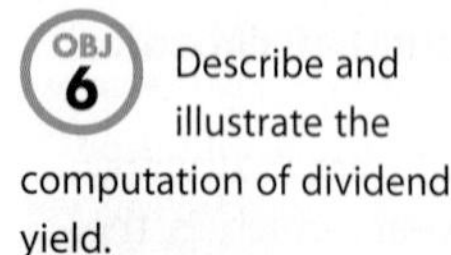

Describe and illustrate the computation of dividend yield.

Financial Analysis and Interpretation: Dividend Yield

The **dividend yield** measures the rate of return to stockholders, based on cash dividends. Dividend yield is most often computed for common stock because preferred stock has a stated dividend rate. In contrast, the cash dividends paid on common stock normally vary with the profitability of the corporation.

The dividend yield is computed as follows:

$$\text{Dividend Yield} = \frac{\text{Dividends per Share of Common Stock}}{\text{Market Price per Share of Common Stock}}$$

To illustrate, the market price of **The Coca-Cola Company** was \$40.69 on March 26, 2013. During the preceding year, The Coca-Cola Company had paid dividends of \$1.05 per share. Thus, the dividend yield of The Coca-Cola Company's common stock is computed as follows:

$$\text{Dividend Yield} = \frac{\text{Dividends per Share of Common Stock}}{\text{Market Price per Share of Common Stock}} = \frac{\$1.05}{\$40.69} = 2.6\%$$

The Coca-Cola Company pays a dividend yield of slightly less than 2.6%. The dividend yield is first a function of a company's profitability, or ability to pay a dividend. For example, many banks nearly eliminated their dividends during the banking crisis of 2008 because they had significant losses. The Coca-Cola Company has sufficient profitability to pay a dividend. Secondly, a company's dividend yield is a function of management's alternative use of funds. If a company has sufficient growth opportunities, funds may be directed toward internal investment, rather than toward paying dividends.

The dividend yield will vary from day to day because the market price of a corporation's stock varies day to day. Current dividend yields are provided with news service quotations of market prices, such as **The Wall Street Journal** or **Yahoo! Finance**.

Recent dividend yields for some selected companies are as follows:

Company	Dividend Yield (%)
Facebook	None
Best Buy	2.20
Coca-Cola Company	2.60
Duke Energy	4.30
Google	None
Hewlett-Packard	2.10
Microsoft	2.80
Verizon Communications	4.10

As can be seen, the dividend yield varies widely across firms. Growth firms tend to retain their earnings to fund future growth. Thus, **Facebook** and **Google** pay no dividends, and **Hewlett-Packard** has a relatively small dividend. Common stockholders of these companies expect to earn most of their return from stock price appreciation. In contrast, **Duke Energy** and **Verizon Communications** are regulated utilities that provide a return to common stockholders mostly through dividends. **Best Buy**, **Coca-Cola**, and **Microsoft** provide a mix of dividends and expected stock price appreciation to their common stockholders.

Example Exercise 15-6 Dividend Yield

On March 11, 2016, Sheldon Corporation had a market price of \$58 per share of common stock. For the previous year, Sheldon paid an annual dividend of \$2.90 per share. Compute the dividend yield for Sheldon Corporation.

Follow My Example 15-6

$$\text{Dividend Yield} = \frac{\text{Dividends per Share of Common Stock}}{\text{Market Price per Share of Common Stock}}$$

$$\text{Dividend Yield} = \frac{\$2.90}{\$58} = 0.05\text{, or }5\%$$

Practice Exercises: PE 15-6A, PE 15-6B

APPENDIX

Comprehensive Income

Comprehensive income is defined as all changes in stockholders' equity during a period, except those resulting from dividends and stockholders' investments. Comprehensive income is computed by adding or subtracting *other comprehensive income* to (from) net income, as follows:

Net income	$XXX
Other comprehensive income	XXX
Comprehensive income	$XXX

Other comprehensive income items include unrealized gains and losses on available-for-sale securities as well as other items such as foreign currency and pension liability adjustments. The *cumulative* effect of other comprehensive income is reported on the balance sheet, as **accumulated other comprehensive income.**

Companies are required to report comprehensive income in the financial statements in one of the following two ways:

- On the income statement, or
- In a separate statement of comprehensive income that immediately follows the income statement.

In the earlier illustration, Maggie Company had reported an unrealized gain of $1,300 on available-for-sale investments. This unrealized gain would be reported in the Stockholders' Equity section of Maggie's 2016 balance sheet, as follows:

Maggie Company
Balance Sheet
December 31, 2016

Stockholders' equity:	
Common stock	$ 10,000
Paid-in capital in excess of par	150,000
Retained earnings	250,000
Unrealized gain (loss) on available-for-sale investments	1,300
Total stockholders' equity	$411,300

Alternatively, Maggie Company could have reported the unrealized gain as part of accumulated other comprehensive income as follows:

Maggie Company Balance Sheet December 31, 2016	
Stockholders' equity:	
Common stock	$ 10,000
Paid-in capital in excess of par	150,000
Retained earnings	250,000
Accumulated other comprehensive income:	
Unrealized gain on available-for-sale investments	1,300
Total stockholders' equity	$411,300

At a Glance 15

Describe why companies invest in debt and equity securities.

Key Points Cash can be used to (1) invest in current operations, (2) invest to earn additional revenue in marketable securities, or (3) invest in marketable securities for strategic reasons.

Learning Outcomes	Example Exercises	Practice Exercises
• Describe the ways excess cash is used by a business. • Describe the purpose of temporary investments. • Describe the strategic purpose of long-term investments.		

Describe and illustrate the accounting for debt investments.

Key Points The accounting for debt investments includes recording the purchase, interest revenue, and sale of the debt. Both the purchase and sale date may include accrued interest.

Learning Outcomes	Example Exercises	Practice Exercises
• Prepare journal entries to record the purchase of a debt investment, including accrued interest.	EE15-1	PE15-1A, 15-1B
• Prepare journal entries for interest revenue from debt investments.	EE15-1	PE15-1A, 15-1B
• Prepare journal entries to record the sale of a debt investment at a gain or loss.	EE15-1	PE15-1A, 15-1B

Describe and illustrate the accounting for equity investments.

Key Points The accounting for equity investments differs, depending on the degree of control. Accounting for investments of less than 20% of the outstanding stock (no control) of the investee includes recording the purchase of stock, the receipt of dividends, and the sale of stock at a gain or loss. Investments of 20%–50% of the outstanding stock of an investee are considered to have significant influence and accounted for under the *equity method*. An investment for more than 50% of the outstanding stock of an investee is treated as a *business combination* and accounted for using *consolidated financial statements*.

Learning Outcomes	Example Exercises	Practice Exercises
• Describe the accounting for less than 20%, 20%–50%, and greater than 50% investments.		
• Prepare journal entries to record the purchase of a stock investment.	**EE15-2**	**PE15-2A, 15-2B**
• Prepare journal entries for the receipt of dividends.	**EE15-2**	**PE15-2A, 15-2B**
• Prepare journal entries for the sale of a stock investment at a gain or loss.	**EE15-2**	**PE15-2A, 15-2B**
• Prepare journal entries for the equity earnings of an equity method investee.	**EE15-3**	**PE15-3A, 15-3B**
• Prepare journal entries for the dividends received from an equity method investee.	**EE15-3**	**PE15-3A, 15-3B**
• Describe a business combination, parent company, and subsidiary company.		
• Describe consolidated financial statements.		

Describe and illustrate valuing and reporting investments in the financial statements.

Key Points Debt and equity security investments of 20%–50% of the outstanding stock (not control) are classified as either (1) trading securities, (2) available-for-sale securities, or (3) held-to-maturity securities for reporting and valuation purposes. *Trading securities* are valued at *fair value*, with unrealized gains and losses reported on the income statement. *Available-for-sale securities* are reported at fair value with unrealized gains or losses reported in the Stockholders' Equity section of the balance sheet. *Held-to-maturity* investments are valued at amortized cost.

Learning Outcomes	Example Exercises	Practice Exercises
• Describe trading securities, held-to-maturity securities, and available-for-sale securities.		
• Prepare journal entries to record the change in the fair value of a trading security portfolio.	**EE15-4**	**PE15-4A, 15-4B**
• Describe and illustrate the reporting of trading securities on the balance sheet.		
• Prepare journal entries to record the change in fair value of an available-for-sale security portfolio.	**EE15-5**	**PE15-5A, 15-5B**
• Describe and illustrate the reporting of available-for-sale securities on the balance sheet.		
• Describe the accounting for held-to-maturity debt securities.		

Describe fair value accounting and its effects on the financial statements.

Key Points There is a trend toward fair value accounting in generally accepted accounting principles. Fair value is the price that would be received to sell an asset.

Learning Outcomes	Example Exercises	Practice Exercises
• Describe fair value accounting.		
• Describe how fair value accounting impacts the balance sheet and income statement.		

Describe and illustrate the computation of dividend yield.

Key Points The dividend yield measures the cash return from common dividends as a percent of the market price of the common stock. The ratio is computed as dividends per share of common stock divided by the market price per share of common stock.

Learning Outcomes	Example Exercises	Practice Exercises
• Compute dividend yield.	**EE15-6**	**PE15-6A, 15-6B**
• Describe how dividend yield measures the return to stockholders from dividends.		

Key Terms

accumulated other comprehensive income (702)
available-for-sale securities (695)
business combination (692)
comprehensive income (702)
consolidated financial statements (692)
cost method (689)
debt securities (685)
dividend yield (700)
equity method (690)
equity securities (685)
fair value (693)
held-to-maturity securities (697)
investee (688)
investments (685)
investor (688)
other comprehensive income (702)
parent company (692)
subsidiary company (692)
trading securities (693)
unrealized gain or loss (693)

Illustrative Problem

The following selected investment transactions were completed by Rosewell Company during 2016, its first year of operations:

2016

Jan. 11. Purchased 800 shares of Bryan Company stock as an available-for-sale security at $23 per share plus an $80 brokerage commission.

Feb. 6. Purchased $40,000 of 8% U.S. Treasury bonds at their face amount plus accrued interest for 36 days. The bonds pay interest on January 1 and July 1. The bonds were classified as held-to-maturity securities.

2016

Mar. 3. Purchased 1,900 shares of Cohen Company stock as a trading security at $48 per share plus a $152 brokerage commission.

Apr. 5. Purchased 2,400 shares of Lyons Inc. stock as an available-for-sale security at $68 per share plus a $120 brokerage commission.

May 12. Purchased 200,000 shares of Myers Company at $37 per share plus an $8,000 brokerage commission. Myers Company has 800,000 common shares issued and outstanding. The equity method was used for this investment.

July 1. Received semiannual interest on bonds purchased on February 6.

Aug. 29. Sold 1,200 shares of Cohen Company stock at $61 per share less a $90 brokerage commission.

Oct. 5. Received an $0.80-per-share dividend on Bryan Company stock.

Nov. 11. Received a $1.10-per-share dividend on Myers Company stock.

16. Purchased 3,000 shares of Morningside Company stock as a trading security for $52 per share plus a $150 brokerage commission.

Dec. 31. Accrued interest on U.S. Treasury bonds.

31. Myers Company earned $1,200,000 during the year. Rosewell recorded its share of Myers Company earnings, using the equity method.

31. Prepared adjusting entries for the portfolios of trading and available-for-sale securities, based upon the following fair values (stock prices):

Bryan Company	$21
Cohen Company	43
Lyons Inc.	88
Myers Company	40
Morningside Company	45

Instructions

1. Journalize the preceding transactions.
2. Prepare the balance sheet disclosure for Rosewell Company's investments on December 31, 2016. Assume held-to-maturity investments are classified as noncurrent assets.

Solution

1.

				Debit	Credit
2016 Jan.	11	Investments—Bryan Company		18,480*	
		Cash			18,480
		*(800 shares × $23 per share) + $80			

				Debit	Credit
Feb.	6	Investments—U.S. Treasury Bonds		40,000	
		Interest Receivable		320*	
		Cash			40,320
		*$40,000 × 8% × (36 days ÷ 360 days)			

				Debit	Credit
Mar.	3	Investments—Cohen Company		91,352*	
		Cash			91,352
		*(1,900 shares × $48 per share) + $152			

Date		Description	Post. Ref.	Debit	Credit
2016 Apr.	5	Investments—Lyons Inc.		163,320*	
		Cash			163,320
		*(2,400 shares × $68 per share) + $120			

Date		Description	Post. Ref.	Debit	Credit
May	12	Investment in Myers Company		7,408,000*	
		Cash			7,408,000
		*(200,000 shares × $37 per share) + $8,000			

Date		Description	Post. Ref.	Debit	Credit
July	1	Cash		1,600*	
		Interest Receivable			320
		Interest Revenue			1,280
		*$40,000 × 8% × ½			

Date		Description	Post. Ref.	Debit	Credit
Aug.	29	Cash		73,110*	
		Investments—Cohen Company			57,696**
		Gain on Sale of Investments			15,414
		*(1,200 shares × $61 per share) – $90			
		**1,200 shares × ($91,352 ÷ 1,900 shares)			

Date		Description	Post. Ref.	Debit	Credit
Oct.	5	Cash		640	
		Dividend Revenue			640
		*800 shares × $0.80 per share			

Date		Description	Post. Ref.	Debit	Credit
Nov.	11	Cash		220,000	
		Investment in Myers Company Stock			220,000
		*200,000 shares × $1.10 per share			

Date		Description	Post. Ref.	Debit	Credit
Nov.	16	Investments—Morningside Company		156,150*	
		Cash			156,150
		*(3,000 shares × $52 per share) + $150			

Date		Description	Post. Ref.	Debit	Credit
Dec.	31	Interest Receivable		1,600	
		Interest Revenue			1,600
		Accrued interest, $40,000 × 8% × ½.			

Date		Description	Post. Ref.	Debit	Credit
Dec.	31	Investment in Myers Company Stock		300,000	
		Income of Myers Company			300,000
		Recorded equity income,			
		$1,200,000 × (200,000 shares ÷ 800,000 shares).			

2016				
Dec.	31	Unrealized Loss on Trading Investments	24,706	
		Valuation Allowance for Trading Investments		24,706
		Recorded decease in fair value of trading investments, $165,100 – $189,806.		

Name	Number of Shares	Total Cost	Total Fair Value
Cohen Company	700	$ 33,656	$ 30,100*
Morningside Company	3,000	156,150	135,000**
Total		$189,806	$165,100

*700 shares × $43 per share
**3,000 shares × $45 per share

Note: Myers Company is valued using the equity method; thus, the fair value is not used.

Dec.	31	Valuation Allowance for Available-for-Sale Investments	46,200	
		Unrealized Gain (Loss) on Available-for-Sale Investments		46,200
		Recorded increase in fair value of available-for-sale investments, $228,000 – $181,800.		

Name	Number of Shares	Total Cost	Total Fair Value
Bryan Company	800	$ 18,480	$ 16,800*
Lyons Inc.	2,400	163,320	211,200**
Total		$181,800	$228,000

*800 shares × $21 per share
**2,400 shares × $88 per share

2.

Rosewell Company
Balance Sheet (Selected)
December 31, 2016

Current assets:		
Cash		$ XXX,XXX
Trading investments (at cost)	$189,806	
Less valuation allowance for trading investments	24,706	
Trading investments at fair value		165,100
Available-for-sale investments (at cost)	$181,800	
Plus valuation allowance for available-for-sale investments	46,200	
Available-for-sale investments at fair value		228,000
Investments:		
Held-to-maturity investments		40,000
Investment in Myers Company (equity method)		7,488,000
Stockholders' equity:		
Common stock		$ XX,XXX
Paid-in capital in excess of par		XXX,XXX
Retained earnings		XXX,XXX
Plus unrealized gain (loss) on available-for-sale investments		46,200
Total stockholders' equity		$ XXX,XXX

Discussion Questions

1. Why might a business invest cash in temporary investments?
2. What causes a gain or loss on the sale of a bond investment?
3. When is the equity method the appropriate accounting for equity investments?
4. How does the accounting for a dividend received differ between the cost method and the equity method?
5. If an investor owns more than 50% of an investee, how is the investment treated on the investor's financial statements?
6. What is the major difference in the accounting for a portfolio of trading securities and a portfolio of available-for-sale securities?
7. If Valuation Allowance for Available-for-Sale Investments has a credit balance, how is it treated on the balance sheet?
8. How would a debit balance in Unrealized Gain (Loss) on Available-for-Sale Investments be reported in the financial statements?
9. What are the factors contributing to the trend toward fair value accounting?
10. How are the balance sheet and income statement affected by fair value accounting?

Practice Exercises

EE 15-1 p. 688

SHOW ME HOW

PE 15-1A Bond investment transactions **OBJ. 2**

Journalize the entries to record the following selected bond investment transactions for Hall Trust:

a. Purchased for cash $300,000 of Oates City 4% bonds at 100 plus accrued interest of $3,000.
b. Received first semiannual interest payment.
c. Sold $150,000 of the bonds at 97 plus accrued interest of $500.

EE 15-1 p. 688

SHOW ME HOW

PE 15-1B Bond investment transactions **OBJ. 2**

Journalize the entries to record the following selected bond investment transactions for Starks Products:

a. Purchased for cash $120,000 of Iceline, Inc. 5% bonds at 100 plus accrued interest of $1,000.
b. Received first semiannual interest payment.
c. Sold $60,000 of the bonds at 101 plus accrued interest of $500.

EE 15-2 p. 690

SHOW ME HOW

PE 15-2A Stock investment transactions **OBJ. 3**

On February 10, 15,000 shares of Sting Company are acquired at a price of $25 per share plus a $150 brokerage commission. On April 12, a $0.40-per-share dividend was received on the Sting Company stock. On May 29, 6,000 shares of the Sting Company stock were sold for $32 per share less a $120 brokerage commission. Prepare the journal entries for the original purchase, the dividend, and the sale under the cost method.

EE 15-2 p. 690

SHOW ME HOW

PE 15-2B Stock investment transactions **OBJ. 3**

On September 12, 2,000 shares of Aspen Company are acquired at a price of $50 per share plus a $200 brokerage commission. On October 15, a $0.50-per-share dividend was received on the Aspen Company stock. On November 10, 1,200 shares of the Aspen Company stock were sold for $42 per share less a $150 brokerage commission. Prepare the journal entries for the original purchase, the dividend, and the sale under the cost method.

EE 15-3 p. 692

SHOW ME HOW

PE 15-3A Equity method OBJ. 3

On January 2, Peyroux Company acquired 35% of the outstanding stock of Gruden Company for $625,000. For the year ended December 31, Gruden Company earned income of $110,000 and paid dividends of $26,000. Prepare the entries for Peyroux Company for the purchase of the stock, the share of Gruden income, and the dividends received from Gruden Company.

EE 15-3 p. 692

SHOW ME HOW

PE 15-3B Equity method OBJ. 3

On January 2, Yorkshire Company acquired 40% of the outstanding stock of Fain Company for $500,000. For the year ended December 31, Fain Company earned income of $140,000 and paid dividends of $50,000. Prepare the entries for Yorkshire Company for the purchase of the stock, the share of Fain income, and the dividends received from Fain Company.

EE 15-4 p. 694

SHOW ME HOW

PE 15-4A Valuing trading securities at fair value OBJ. 4

On January 1, 2016, Valuation Allowance for Trading Investments had a zero balance. On December 31, 2016, the cost of the trading securities portfolio was $385,000, and the fair value was $357,400. Prepare the December 31, 2016, adjusting journal entry to record the unrealized gain or loss on trading investments.

EE 15-4 p. 694

SHOW ME HOW

PE 15-4B Valuing trading securities at fair value OBJ. 4

On January 1, 2016, Valuation Allowance for Trading Investments had a zero balance. On December 31, 2016, the cost of the trading securities portfolio was $41,500, and the fair value was $46,300. Prepare the December 31, 2016, adjusting journal entry to record the unrealized gain or loss on trading investments.

EE 15-5 p. 697

SHOW ME HOW

PE 15-5A Valuing available-for-sale securities at fair value OBJ. 4

On January 1, 2016, Valuation Allowance for Available-for-Sale Investments had a zero balance. On December 31, 2016, the cost of the available-for-sale securities was $78,400, and the fair value was $72,600. Prepare the adjusting entry to record the unrealized gain or loss on available-for-sale investments on December 31, 2016.

EE 15-5 p. 697

SHOW ME HOW

PE 15-5B Valuing available-for-sale securities at fair value OBJ. 4

On January 1, 2016, Valuation Allowance for Available-for-Sale Investments had a zero balance. On December 31, 2016, the cost of the available-for-sale securities was $24,260, and the fair value was $26,350. Prepare the adjusting entry to record the unrealized gain or loss on available-for-sale investments on December 31, 2016.

EE 15-6 p. 701

SHOW ME HOW

PE 15-6A Dividend yield OBJ. 6

On June 30, 2016, Setzer Corporation had a market price of $100 per share of common stock. For the previous year, Setzer paid an annual dividend of $4.00. Compute the dividend yield for Setzer Corporation.

EE 15-6 p. 701

SHOW ME HOW

PE 15-6B Dividend yield OBJ. 6

On October 23, 2016, Wilkerson Company had a market price of $40 per share of common stock. For the previous year, Wilkerson paid an annual dividend of $1.20. Compute the dividend yield for Wilkerson Company.

Exercises

SHOW ME HOW

EX 15-1 Entries for investment in bonds, interest, and sale of bonds OBJ. 2

Parilo Company acquired $170,000 of Makofske Co., 5% bonds on May 1, 2016, at their face amount. Interest is paid semiannually on May 1 and November 1. On November 1, 2016, Parilo Company sold $50,000 of the bonds for 96.

Journalize entries to record the following:

a. The initial acquisition of the bonds on May 1.

b. The semiannual interest received on November 1.

c. The sale of the bonds on November 1.

d. The accrual of $1,000 interest on December 31, 2016.

EX 15-2 Entries for investments in bonds, interest, and sale of bonds OBJ. 2

SHOW ME HOW

Kalyagin Investments acquired $220,000 of Jerris Corp., 7% bonds at their face amount on October 1, 2016. The bonds pay interest on October 1 and April 1. On April 1, 2017, Kalyagin sold $80,000 of Jerris Corp. bonds at 103.

Journalize the entries to record the following:

a. The initial acquisition of the Jerris Corp. bonds on October 1, 2016.

b. The adjusting entry for three months of accrued interest earned on the Jerris Corp. bonds on December 31, 2016.

c. The receipt of semiannual interest on April 1, 2017.

d. The sale of $80,000 of Jerris Corp. bonds on April 1, 2017, at 103.

EX 15-3 Entries for investment in bonds, interest, and sale of bonds OBJ. 2

✔ Oct. 31, Loss on sale of investments, $400

SHOW ME HOW

Bocelli Co. purchased $120,000 of 6%, 20-year Sanz County bonds on May 11, 2016, directly from the county, at their face amount plus accrued interest. The bonds pay semiannual interest on April 1 and October 1. On October 31, 2016, Bocelli Co. sold $30,000 of the Sanz County bonds at 99 plus $150 accrued interest, less a $100 brokerage commission.

Provide journal entries for the following:

a. The purchase of the bonds on May 11, plus 40 days of accrued interest.

b. Semiannual interest on October 1.

c. Sale of the bonds on October 31.

d. Adjusting entry for accrued interest of $1,365 on December 31, 2016.

EX 15-4 Entries for investment in bonds, interest, and sale of bonds OBJ. 2

✔ Aug. 29, Loss on sale of investments, $700

SHOW ME HOW

The following bond investment transactions were completed during 2016 by Starks Company:

Jan. 31. Purchased 75, $1,000 government bonds at 100 plus 30 days' accrued interest. The bonds pay 6% annual interest on July 1 and January 1.

July 1. Received semiannual interest on bond investment.

Aug. 29. Sold 35, $1,000 bonds at 98 plus $350 accrued interest.

a. Journalize the entries for these transactions.

b. Provide the December 31, 2016, adjusting journal entry for semiannual interest earned on the bonds.

EX 15-5 Interest on bond investments OBJ. 2

On April 1, 2016, Rizzo Company purchased $80,000 of 4.5%, 20-year Energizer Company bonds at their face amount plus one month's accrued interest. The bonds pay interest on March 1 and September 1. On November 1, 2016, Rizzo Company sold $30,000 of the Energizer Company bonds acquired on April 1, plus two months' accrued interest. On December 31, 2016, four months' interest was accrued for the remaining bonds.

Determine the interest earned by Rizzo Company on Energizer Company bonds for 2016.

EX 15-6 Entries for investment in stock, receipt of dividends, and sale of shares OBJ. 3

✔ c. Gain on sale of investments, $17,755

SHOW ME HOW

On March 4, Breen Corporation acquired 7,500 shares of the 200,000 outstanding shares of Melton Co. common stock at $40 plus commission charges of $175. On June 15, a cash dividend of $2.10 per share was received. On October 12, 3,000 shares were sold at $46, less commission charges of $175.

Using the cost method, journalize the entries for (a) the purchase of stock, (b) the receipt of dividends, and (c) the sale of 3,000 shares.

EX 15-7 Entries for investment in stock, receipt of dividends, and sale of shares OBJ. 3

✔ June 17, Loss on sale of investments, $8,515

SHOW ME HOW

The following equity investment transactions were completed by Chung Company in 2016:

Mar. 4. Purchased 4,000 shares of Jas Company for a price of $50 per share plus a brokerage commission of $100.

May 12. Received a quarterly dividend of $0.75 per share on the Jas Company investment.

June 17. Sold 1,400 shares for a price of $44 per share less a brokerage commission of $80.

Journalize the entries for these transactions.

EX 15-8 Entries for stock investments, dividends, and sale of stock OBJ. 3

✔ Sept. 25, Dividend revenue, $520

SHOW ME HOW

Yerbury Corp. manufactures construction equipment. Journalize the entries to record the following selected equity investment transactions completed by Yerbury during 2016:

Feb. 2. Purchased for cash 5,300 shares of Wong Inc. stock for $20 per share plus a $110 brokerage commission.

Mar. 6. Received dividends of $0.30 per share on Wong Inc. stock.

June 7. Purchased 2,000 shares of Wong Inc. stock for $26 per share plus a $125 brokerage commission.

July 26. Sold 6,000 shares of Wong Inc. stock for $35 per share less a $100 brokerage commission. Yerbury assumes that the first investments purchased are the first investments sold.

Sept. 25. Received dividends of $0.40 per share on Wong Inc. stock.

EX 15-9 Entries for stock investments, dividends, and sale of stock OBJ. 3

SHOW ME HOW

Seamus Industries Inc. buys and sells investments as part of its ongoing cash management. The following investment transactions were completed during the year:

Feb. 24. Acquired 1,000 shares of Tett Co. stock for $85 per share plus a $150 brokerage commission.

May 16. Acquired 2,500 shares of Issacson Co. stock for $36 per share plus a $100 commission.

July 14. Sold 400 shares of Tett Co. stock for $100 per share less a $75 brokerage commission.

Aug. 12. Sold 750 shares of Issacson Co. stock for $32.50 per share less an $80 brokerage commission.

Oct. 31. Received dividends of $0.40 per share on Tett Co. stock.

Journalize the entries for these transactions.

EX 15-10 Equity method for stock investment OBJ. 3

SHOW ME HOW

At a total cost of $6,300,000, Veravo Corporation acquired 210,000 shares of Strado Corp. common stock as a long-term investment. Veravo Corporation uses the equity method of accounting for this investment. Strado Corp. has 700,000 shares of common stock outstanding, including the shares acquired by Veravo Corporation.

a. Journalize the entries by Veravo Corporation to record the following information:
   1. Strado Corp. reports net income of $860,000 for the current period.
   2. A cash dividend of $0.32 per common share is paid by Strado Corp. during the current period.

b. Why is the equity method appropriate for the Strado Corp. investment?

EX 15-11 Equity method for stock investment OBJ. 3

✔ b. $5,400,500

On January 4, 2016, Spandella Company purchased 175,000 shares of Filington Company directly from one of the founders for a price of $30 per share. Filington has 500,000 shares outstanding, including the Penman shares. On July 2, 2016, Filington paid $620,000 in total dividends to its shareholders. On December 31, 2016, Filington reported a net income of $1,050,000 for the year. Spandella uses the equity method in accounting for its investment in Filington.

a. Provide the Spandella Inc. journal entries for the transactions involving its investment in Filington Inc. during 2016.

b. Determine the December 31, 2016, balance of the Investment in Filington Company. Stock account.

EX 15-12 Equity method for stock investment with loss OBJ. 3

On January 6, 2016, Bulldog Co. purchased 34% of the outstanding stock of Gator Co. for $212,000. Gator Co. paid total dividends of $24,000 to all shareholders on June 30. Gator had a net loss of $56,000 for 2016.

a. Journalize Bulldog's purchase of the stock, receipt of the dividends, and the adjusting entry for the equity loss in Gator Co. stock.

b. Compute the balance of Investment in Gator Co. Stock on December 31, 2016.

c. How does valuing an investment under the equity method differ from valuing an investment at fair value?

EX 15-13 Equity method for stock investment OBJ. 3

Hawkeye Company's balance sheet reported, under the equity method, its long-term investment in Raven Company for comparative years as follows:

	Dec. 31, 2017	Dec. 31, 2016
Investment in Raven Company stock (in millions)	$281	$264

In addition, the 2017 Hawkeye Company income statement disclosed equity earnings in the Raven Company investment as $25 million. Hawkeye Company neither purchased nor sold Raven Company stock during 2017. The fair value of the Raven Company stock investment on December 31, 2017, was $310 million.

Explain the change in Investment in Raven Company Stock from December 31, 2016, to December 31, 2017.

EX 15-14 Missing statement items, trading investments OBJ. 4

✔ g. $6,000

JED Capital Inc. makes investments in trading securities. Selected income statement items for the years ended December 31, 2016 and 2017, plus selected items from comparative balance sheets, are as follows:

JED Capital Inc.
Selected Income Statement Items
For the Years Ended December 31, 2016 and 2017

	2016	2017
Operating income	a.	e.
Unrealized gain (loss)	b.	$(11,000)
Net income	c.	28,000

JED Capital Inc.
Selected Balance Sheet Items
December 31, 2015, 2016, and 2017

	Dec. 31, 2015	Dec. 31, 2016	Dec. 31, 2017
Trading investments, at cost	$144,000	$168,000	$205,000
Valuation allowance for trading investments	(12,000)	17,000	g.
Trading investments, at fair value	d.	f.	h.
Retained earnings	$210,000	$245,000	i.

There were no dividends.

Determine the missing lettered items.

EX 15-15 Fair value journal entries, trading investments **OBJ. 3, 4**

SHOW ME HOW

The investments of Charger Inc. include a single investment: 14,500 shares of Raiders Inc. common stock purchased on February 24, 2016, for $38 per share including brokerage commission. These shares were classified as trading securities. As of the December 31, 2016, balance sheet date, the share price had increased to $42 per share.

a. Journalize the entries to acquire the investment on February 24, and record the adjustment to fair value on December 31, 2016.

b. How is the unrealized gain or loss for trading investments reported on the financial statements?

EX 15-16 Fair value journal entries, trading investments **OBJ. 3, 4**

SHOW ME HOW

Jets Bancorp Inc. purchased a portfolio of trading securities during 2016. The cost and fair value of this portfolio on December 31, 2016, was as follows:

Name	Number of Shares	Total Cost	Total Fair Value
Dolphins Inc.	1,400	$28,000	$30,800
Marino Company	1,200	30,000	27,600
Namath Company	800	28,000	26,400
Total		$86,000	$84,800

On May 10, 2017, Jets Bancorp Inc. purchased 1,000 shares of Giants Inc. at $24 per share plus a $150 brokerage commission.

Provide the journal entries to record the following:

a. The adjustment of the trading security portfolio to fair value on December 31, 2016.

b. The May 10, 2017, purchase of Giants Inc. stock.

EX 15-17 Fair value journal entries, trading investments **OBJ. 3, 4**

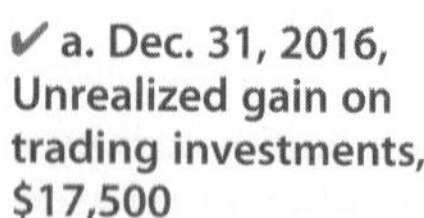

✔ a. Dec. 31, 2016, Unrealized gain on trading investments, $17,500

Last Unguaranteed Financial Inc. purchased the following trading securities during 2016, its first year of operations:

Name	Number of Shares	Cost
Arden Enterprises Inc.	5,000	$150,000
French Broad Industries Inc.	2,750	66,000
Pisgah Construction Inc.	1,600	104,000
Total		$320,000

The market price per share for the trading security portfolio on December 31, 2016, was as follows:

	Market Price per Share, Dec. 31, 2016
Arden Enterprises Inc.	$34
French Broad Industries Inc.	26
Pisgah Construction Inc.	60

a. Provide the journal entry to adjust the trading security portfolio to fair value on December 31, 2016.

b. Assume the market prices of the portfolio were the same on December 31, 2017, as they were on December 31, 2016. What would be the journal entry to adjust the portfolio to fair value?

EX 15-18 Balance sheet presentation, trading investments **OBJ. 4**

The income statement for Delta-tec Inc. for the year ended December 31, 2016, was as follows:

Delta-tec Inc. Income Statement (selected items) For the Year Ended December 31, 2016	
Income from operations	$299,700
Gain on sale of investments	17,800
Less unrealized loss on trading investments	72,500
Net income	$245,000

The balance sheet dated December 31, 2015, showed a Retained Earnings balance of $825,000. During 2016, the company purchased trading investments for the first time at a cost of $346,000. In addition, trading investments with a cost of $66,000 were sold at a gain during 2016. The company paid $65,000 in dividends during 2016.

a. Determine the December 31, 2016, Retained Earnings balance.

b. Provide the December 31, 2016, balance sheet presentation for Trading Investments.

✔ f. $(11,000)

EX 15-19 Missing statement items, available-for-sale securities — OBJ. 4

Highland Industries Inc. makes investments in available-for-sale securities. Selected income statement items for the years ended December 31, 2016 and 2017, plus selected items from comparative balance sheets, are as follows:

Highland Industries Inc.
Selected Income Statement Items
For the Years Ended December 31, 2016 and 2017

	2016	2017
Operating income	a.	g.
Gain (loss) from sale of investments	$7,500	$(12,000)
Net income (loss)	b.	(21,000)

Highland Industries Inc.
Selected Balance Sheet Items
December 31, 2015, 2016, and 2017

	Dec. 31, 2015	Dec. 31, 2016	Dec. 31, 2017
Assets			
Available-for-sale investments, at cost	$ 90,000	$ 86,000	$102,000
Valuation allowance for available-for-sale investments	12,000	(11,000)	h.
Available-for-sale investments, at fair value	c.	e.	i.
Stockholders' Equity			
Unrealized gain (loss) on available-for-sale investments	d.	f.	(16,400)
Retained earnings	$175,400	$220,000	j.

There were no dividends.

Determine the missing lettered items.

EX 15-20 Fair value journal entries, available-for-sale investments — OBJ. 3, 4

The investments of Steelers Inc. include a single investment: 33,100 shares of Bengals Inc. common stock purchased on September 12, 2016, for $13 per share including brokerage commission. These shares were classified as available-for-sale securities. As of the December 31, 2016, balance sheet date, the share price declined to $11 per share.

a. Journalize the entries to acquire the investment on September 12 and record the adjustment to fair value on December 31, 2016.

b. How is the unrealized gain or loss for available-for-sale investments disclosed on the financial statements?

EX 15-21 Fair value journal entries, available-for-sale investments — OBJ. 3, 4

Hurricane Inc. purchased a portfolio of available-for-sale securities in 2016, its first year of operations. The cost and fair value of this portfolio on December 31, 2016, was as follows:

Name	Number of Shares	Total Cost	Total Fair Value
Tornado Inc.	800	$14,000	$15,600
Tsunami Corp.	1,250	31,250	35,000
Typhoon Corp.	2,140	43,870	42,800
Total		$89,120	$93,400

(Continued)

On June 12, 2017, Hurricane purchased 1,450 shares of Rogue Wave Inc. at $45 per share plus a $100 brokerage commission.

a. Provide the journal entries to record the following:
   1. The adjustment of the available-for-sale security portfolio to fair value on December 31, 2016.
   2. The June 12, 2017, purchase of Rogue Wave Inc. stock.

b. How are unrealized gains and losses treated differently for available-for-sale securities than for trading securities?

EX 15-22 Fair value journal entries, available-for-sale investments **OBJ. 3, 4**

Storm, Inc. purchased the following available-for-sale securities during 2016, its first year of operations:

Name	Number of Shares	Cost
Dust Devil, Inc.	1,900	$ 81,700
Gale Co.	850	68,000
Whirlwind Co.	2,850	114,000
Total		$263,700

The market price per share for the available-for-sale security portfolio on December 31, 2016, was as follows:

	Market Price per Share, Dec. 31, 2016
Dust Devil, Inc.	$40
Gale Co.	75
Whirlwind Co.	42

a. Provide the journal entry to adjust the available-for-sale security portfolio to fair value on December 31, 2016.

b. Describe the income statement impact from the December 31, 2016, journal entry.

EX 15-23 Balance sheet presentation of available-for-sale investments **OBJ. 4**

During 2016, its first year of operations, Galileo Company purchased two available-for-sale investments as follows:

Security	Shares Purchased	Cost
Hawking Inc.	900	$44,000
Pavlov Co.	1,780	38,000

Assume that as of December 31, 2016, the Hawking Inc. stock had a market value of $50 per share, and the Pavlov Co. stock had a market value of $24 per share. Galileo Company had net income of $300,000, and paid no dividends for the year ended December 31, 2016. All of the available-for-sale investments are classified as current assets.

a. Prepare the Current Assets section of the balance sheet presentation for the available-for-sale investments.

b. Prepare the Stockholders' Equity section of the balance sheet to reflect the earnings and unrealized gain (loss) for the available-for-sale investments.

EX 15-24 Balance sheet presentation of available-for-sale investments **OBJ. 4**

During 2016, Copernicus Corporation held a portfolio of available-for-sale securities having a cost of $185,000. There were no purchases or sales of investments during the year. The market values at the beginning and end of the year were $225,000 and $160,000, respectively. The net income for 2016 was $180,000, and no dividends were paid during the year. The Stockholders' Equity section of the balance sheet was as follows on December 31, 2015:

Copernicus Corporation
Stockholders' Equity
December 31, 2015

Common stock	$ 50,000
Paid-in capital in excess of par	250,000
Retained earnings	340,000
Unrealized gain (loss) on available-for-sale investments	40,000
Total	$680,000

Prepare the Stockholders' Equity section of the balance sheet for December 31, 2016.

EX 15-25 Dividend yield **OBJ. 6**

At the market close on March 28 of a recent year, **McDonald's Corporation** had a closing stock price of $99.69. In addition, McDonald's Corporation had a dividend per share of $2.87 during the previous year.

Determine McDonald's Corporation's dividend yield. (Round to one decimal place.)

EX 15-26 Dividend yield **OBJ. 6**

✔ a. Dec. 31, current year, 3.00%

The market price for **Microsoft Corporation** closed at $26.71 and $25.96 on December 31, current year, and previous year, respectively. The dividends per share were $0.80 for current year and $0.64 for previous year.

a. Determine the dividend yield for Microsoft on December 31, current year, and previous year. (Round percentages to two decimal places.)

b. Interpret these measures.

EX 15-27 Dividend yield **OBJ. 6**

eBay Inc. developed a Web-based marketplace at www.ebay.com, in which individuals can buy and sell a variety of items. eBay also acquired **PayPal**, an online payments system that allows businesses and individuals to send and receive online payments securely. In a recent annual report, eBay published the following dividend policy:

We have never paid cash dividends on our stock and currently anticipate that we will continue to retain any future earnings for the foreseeable future.

Given eBay's dividend policy, why would an investor be attracted to its stock?

Appendix
EX 15-28 Comprehensive income

On May 12, 2016, Chewco Co. purchased 2,000 shares of Jedi Inc. for $112 per share, including the brokerage commission. The Jedi investment was classified as an available-for-sale security. On December 31, 2016, the fair value of Jedi Inc. was $124 per share. The net income of Chewco Co. was $50,000 for 2016.

Compute the comprehensive income for Chewco Co. for the year ended December 31, 2016.

Appendix
EX 15-29 Comprehensive income

On December 31, 2015, Valur Co. had the following available-for-sale investment disclosure within the Current Assets section of the balance sheet:

Available-for-sale investments (at cost)	$145,000
Plus valuation allowance for available-for-sale investments	40,000
Available-for-sale investments (at fair value)	$185,000

There were no purchases or sales of available-for-sale investments during 2016. On December 31, 2016, the fair value of the available-for-sale investment portfolio was $200,000. The net income of Valur Co. was $210,000 for 2016.

Compute the comprehensive income for Valur Co. for the year ended December 31, 2016.

Problems: Series A

PR 15-1A Debt investment transactions, available-for-sale valuation — OBJ. 2, 4

General Ledger

SHOW ME HOW

Gaelic Industries Inc. is an athletic footware company that began operations on January 1, 2016. The following transactions relate to debt investments acquired by Gaelic Industries Inc., which has a fiscal year ending on December 31:

2016

May 1. Purchased $75,000 of Avery Co. 7%, 15-year bonds at their face amount plus accrued interest of $875. The bonds pay interest semiannually on March 1 and September 1.

16. Purchased $60,000 of Clawhammer 6%, 10-year bonds at their face amount plus accrued interest of $150. The bonds pay interest semiannually on May 1 and November 1.

Sept. 1. Received semiannual interest on the Avery Co. bonds.

30. Sold $30,000 of Avery Co. bonds at 98 plus accrued interest of $175.

Nov. 1. Received semiannual interest on the Clawhammer bonds.

Dec. 31. Accrued $1,050 interest on the Avery Co. bonds.

31. Accrued $600 interest on the Clawhammer bonds.

2017

Mar. 1. Received semiannual interest on the Avery Co. bonds.

May 1. Received semiannual interest on the Clawhammer bonds.

Instructions

1. Journalize the entries to record these transactions.
2. If the bond portfolio is classified as available for sale, what impact would this have on financial statement disclosure?

PR 15-2A Stock investment transactions, trading securities — OBJ. 3, 4

Scofield Financial Co. is a regional insurance company that began operations on January 1, 2016. The following transactions relate to trading securities acquired by Scofield Financial Co., which has a fiscal year ending on December 31:

2016

Mar. 14. Purchased 5,000 shares of Wilkomm Inc. as a trading security at $40 per share plus a brokerage commission of $500.

Apr. 24. Purchased 1,800 shares of McMarsh Inc. as a trading security at $50 plus a brokerage commission of $198.

June 1. Sold 2,600 shares of Wilkomm Inc. for $38 per share less a $100 brokerage commission.

30. Received an annual dividend of $0.35 per share on Wilkomm Inc. stock.

Dec. 31. The portfolio of trading securities was adjusted to fair values of $38 and $49 per share for Wilkomm Inc. and McMarsh Inc., respectively.

2017

Apr. 4. Purchased 3,500 shares of Daley Inc. as a trading security at $30 per share plus a $175 brokerage commission.

June 28. Received an annual dividend of $0.40 per share on Wilkomm Inc. stock.

Sept. 9. Sold 700 shares of Daley Inc. for $32 per share less a $50 brokerage commission.

Dec. 31. The portfolio of trading securities had a cost of $270,578 and a fair value of $350,000, requiring a debit balance in Valuation Allowance for Trading Investments of $79,422 ($350,000 − $270,578). Thus, the credit balance from December 31, 2016, is to be adjusted to the new balance.

Instructions

1. Journalize the entries to record these transactions.
2. Prepare the investment-related current asset balance sheet presentation for Scofield Financial Co. on December 31, 2017.
3. How are unrealized gains or losses on trading investments presented in the financial statements of Scofield Financial Co.?

PR 15-3A Stock investment transactions, equity method and available-for-sale securities

OBJ. 3, 4

Forte Inc. produces and sells theater set designs and costumes. The company began operations on January 1, 2016. The following transactions relate to securities acquired by Forte Inc., which has a fiscal year ending on December 31:

2016

Jan. 22. Purchased 22,000 shares of Sankal Inc. as an available-for-sale security at $18 per share, including the brokerage commission.

Mar. 8. Received a cash dividend of $0.22 per share on Sankal Inc. stock.

Sept. 8. A cash dividend of $0.25 per share was received on the Sankal stock.

Oct. 17. Sold 3,000 shares of Sankal Inc. stock at $16 per share, less a brokerage commission of $75.

Dec. 31. Sankal Inc. is classified as an available-for-sale investment and is adjusted to a fair value of $25 per share. Use the valuation allowance for available-for-sale investments account in making the adjustment.

2017

Jan. 10. Purchased an influential interest in Imboden Inc. for $720,000 by purchasing 96,000 shares directly from the estate of the founder of Imboden Inc. There are 300,000 shares of Imboden Inc. stock outstanding.

Mar. 10. Received a cash dividend of $0.30 per share on Sankal Inc. stock.

Sept. 12. Received a cash dividend of $0.25 per share plus an extra dividend of $0.05 per share on Sankal Inc. stock.

Dec. 31. Received $57,600 of cash dividends on Imboden Inc. stock. Imboden Inc. reported net income of $450,000 in 2017. Forte Inc. uses the equity method of accounting for its investment in Imboden Inc.

31. Sankal Inc. is classified as an available-for-sale investment and is adjusted to a fair value of $22 per share. Use the valuation allowance for available-for-sale investments account in making the adjustment for the decrease in fair value from $25 to $22 per share.

Instructions

1. Journalize the entries to record these transactions.
2. Prepare the investment-related asset and stockholders' equity balance sheet presentation for Forte Inc. on December 31, 2017, assuming the Retained Earnings balance on December 31, 2017, is $389,000.

PR 15-4A Investment reporting

OBJ. 2, 3, 4

✔ h. $(5,800)

O'Brien Industries Inc. is a book publisher. The comparative unclassified balance sheets for December 31, 2017 and 2016 follow. Selected missing balances are shown by letters.

(Continued)

O'Brien Industries Inc.
Balance Sheet
December 31, 2017 and 2016

	Dec. 31, 2017	Dec. 31, 2016
Cash	$233,000	$220,000
Accounts receivable (net)	136,530	138,000
Available-for-sale investments (at cost)—Note 1	a.	103,770
Less valuation allowance for available-for-sale investments	b.	2,500
Available-for-sale investments (fair value)	$ c.	$101,270
Interest receivable	$ d.	—
Investment in Jolly Roger Co. stock—Note 2	e.	$ 77,000
Office equipment (net)	115,000	130,000
Total assets	$ f.	$666,270
Accounts payable	$ 69,400	$ 65,000
Common stock	70,000	70,000
Excess of issue price over par	225,000	225,000
Retained earnings	g.	308,770
Unrealized gain (loss) on available-for-sale investments	h.	(2,500)
Total liabilities and stockholders' equity	$ i.	$666,270

Note 1. Investments are classified as available for sale. The investments at cost and fair value on December 31, 2016, are as follows:

	No. of Shares	Cost per Share	Total Cost	Total Fair Value
Bernard Co. stock	2,250	$17	$ 38,250	$ 37,500
Chadwick Co. stock	1,260	52	65,520	63,770
			$103,770	$101,270

Note 2. The investment in Jolly Roger Co. stock is an equity method investment representing 30% of the outstanding shares of Jolly Roger Co.

The following selected investment transactions occurred during 2017:

May 5. Purchased 3,080 shares of Gozar Inc. at $30 per share including brokerage commission. Gozar Inc. is classified as an available-for-sale security.

Oct. 1. Purchased $40,000 of Nightline Co. 6%, 10-year bonds at 100. The bonds are classified as available for sale. The bonds pay interest on October 1 and April 1.

9. Dividends of $12,500 are received on the Jolly Roger Co. investment.

Dec. 31. Jolly Roger Co. reported a total net income of $112,000 for 2017. O'Brien Industries Inc. recorded equity earnings for its share of Jolly Roger Co. net income.

31. Accrued three months of interest on the Nightline bonds.

31. Adjusted the available-for-sale investment portfolio to fair value, using the following fair value per-share amounts:

Available-for-Sale Investments	Fair Value
Bernard Co. stock	$15.40 per share
Chadwick Co. stock	$46.00 per share
Gozar Inc. stock	$32.00 per share
Nightline Co. bonds	$98 per $100 of face amount

31. Closed the O'Brien Industries Inc. net income of $146,230. O'Brien Industries Inc. paid no dividends during the year.

Instructions

Determine the missing letters in the unclassified balance sheet. Provide appropriate supporting calculations.

Problems: Series B

General Ledger

SHOW ME HOW

PR 15-1B Debt investment transactions, available-for-sale valuation

OBJ. 2, 4

Rekya Mart Inc. is a general merchandise retail company that began operations on January 1, 2016. The following transactions relate to debt investments acquired by Rekya Mart Inc., which has a fiscal year ending on December 31:

2016

Apr. 1. Purchased $90,000 of Smoke Bay 6%, 10-year bonds at their face amount plus accrued interest of $900. The bonds pay interest semiannually on February 1 and August 1.

May 16. Purchased $42,000 of Geotherma Co. 4%, 12-year bonds at their face amount plus accrued interest of $70. The bonds pay interest semiannually on May 1 and November 1.

Aug. 1. Received semiannual interest on the Smoke Bay bonds.

Sept. 1. Sold $12,000 of Smoke Bay bonds at 101 plus accrued interest of $60.

Nov. 1. Received semiannual interest on the Geotherma Co. bonds.

Dec. 31. Accrued $1,950 interest on the Smoke Bay bonds.

31. Accrued $280 interest on the Geotherma Co. bonds.

2017

Feb. 1. Received semiannual interest on the Smoke Bay bonds.

May 1. Received semiannual interest on the Geotherma Co. bonds.

Instructions

1. Journalize the entries to record these transactions.
2. If the bond portfolio is classified as available for sale, what impact would this have on financial statement disclosure?

PR 15-2B Stock investment transactions, trading securities **OBJ. 3, 4**

Zeus Investments Inc. is a regional investment company that began operations on January 1, 2016. The following transactions relate to trading securities acquired by Zeus Investments Inc., which has a fiscal year ending on December 31:

2016

Feb. 14. Purchased 4,800 shares of Apollo Inc. as a trading security at $26 per share plus a brokerage commission of $192.

Apr. 1. Purchased 2,300 shares of Ares Inc. as a trading security at $19 per share plus a brokerage commission of $92.

June 1. Sold 600 shares of Apollo Inc. for $32 per share less a $100 brokerage commission.

27. Received an annual dividend of $0.20 per share on Apollo Inc. stock.

Dec. 31. The portfolio of trading securities was adjusted to fair values of $33 and $18.50 per share for Apollo Inc. and Ares Inc., respectively.

2017

Mar. 14. Purchased 1,200 shares of Athena Inc. as a trading security at $65 per share plus a $120 brokerage commission.

June 26. Received an annual dividend of $0.21 per share on Apollo Inc. stock.

July 30. Sold 480 shares of Athena Inc. for $60 per share less a $50 brokerage commission.

Dec. 31. The portfolio of trading securities had a cost of $200,032 and a fair value of $188,000, requiring a credit balance in Valuation Allowance for Trading Investments of $12,032 ($200,032 − $188,000). Thus, the debit balance from December 31, 2014, is to be adjusted to the new balance.

Instructions

1. Journalize the entries to record these transactions.
2. Prepare the investment-related current asset balance sheet presentation for Zeus Investments Inc. on December 31, 2017.
3. How are unrealized gains or losses on trading investments presented in the financial statements of Zeus Investments Inc.?

PR 15-3B Stock investment transactions, equity method and available-for-sale securities OBJ. 3, 4

Glacier Products Inc. is a wholesaler of rock climbing gear. The company began operations on January 1, 2016. The following transactions relate to securities acquired by Glacier Products Inc., which has a fiscal year ending on December 31:

2016

Jan. 18. Purchased 9,000 shares of Malmo Inc. as an available-for-sale investment at $40 per share, including the brokerage commission.

July 22. A cash dividend of $3.00 per share was received on the Malmo stock.

Oct. 5. Sold 500 shares of Malmo Inc. stock at $58.00 per share, less a brokerage commission of $100.

Dec. 18. Received a regular cash dividend of $3.00 per share on Malmo Inc. stock.

31. Malmo Inc. is classified as an available-for-sale investment and is adjusted to a fair value of $36.00 per share. Use the valuation allowance for available-for-sale investments account in making the adjustment.

2017

Jan. 25. Purchased an influential interest in Helsi Co. for $800,000 by purchasing 75,000 shares directly from the estate of the founder of Helsi. There are 250,000 shares of Helsi Co. stock outstanding.

July 16. Received a cash dividend of $3.00 per share on Malmo Inc. stock.

Dec. 16. Received a cash dividend of $3.00 per share plus an extra dividend of $0.20 per share on Malmo Inc. stock.

31. Received $38,000 of cash dividends on Helsi Co. stock. Helsi Co. reported net income of $170,000 in 2015. Glacier Products Inc. uses the equity method of accounting for its investment in Helsi Co.

31. Malmo Inc. is classified as an available-for-sale investment and is adjusted to a fair value of $44 per share. Use the valuation allowance for available-for-sale investments account in making the adjustment for the increase in fair value from $36 to $44 per share.

Instructions

1. Journalize the entries to record the preceding transactions.
2. Prepare the investment-related asset and stockholders' equity balance sheet presentation for Glacier Products Inc. on December 31, 2017, assuming the Retained Earnings balance on December 31, 2017, is $700,000.

PR 15-4B Investment reporting OBJ. 2, 3, 4

✔ b. $4,680

Teasdale Inc. manufactures and sells commercial and residential security equipment. The comparative unclassified balance sheets for December 31, 2017 and 2016 are provided below. Selected missing balances are shown by letters.

Teasdale Inc.
Balance Sheet
December 31, 2017 and 2016

	Dec. 31, 2017	Dec. 31, 2016
Cash	$160,000	$156,000
Accounts receivable (net)	115,000	108,000
Available-for-sale investments (at cost)—Note 1	a.	91,200
Plus valuation allowance for available-for-sale investments	b.	8,776
Available-for-sale investments (fair value)	$ c.	$ 99,976
Interest receivable	$ d.	—
Investment in Wright Co. stock—Note 2	e.	$ 69,200
Office equipment (net)	96,000	105,000
Total assets	$ f.	$538,176
Accounts payable	$ 91,000	$ 72,000
Common stock	80,000	80,000
Excess of issue price over par	250,000	250,000
Retained earnings	g.	127,400
Unrealized gain (loss) on available-for-sale investments	h.	8,776
Total liabilities and stockholders' equity	$ i.	$538,176

Note 1. Investments are classified as available for sale. The investments at cost and fair value on December 31, 2016, are as follows:

	No. of Shares	Cost per Share	Total Cost	Total Fair Value
Alvarez Inc. stock	960	$38.00	$36,480	$39,936
Hirsch Inc. stock	1,900	28.80	54,720	60,040
			$91,200	$99,976

Note 2. The Investment in Wright Co. stock is an equity method investment representing 30% of the outstanding shares of Wright Co.

The following selected investment transactions occurred during 2017:

Mar. 18. Purchased 800 shares of Richter Inc. at $40 including brokerage commission. Richter is classified as an available-for-sale security.

July 12. Dividends of $12,000 are received on the Wright Co. investment.

Oct. 1. Purchased $24,000 of Toon Co. 4%, 10-year bonds at 100. The bonds are classified as available for sale. The bonds pay interest on October 1 and April 1.

Dec. 31. Wright Co. reported a total net income of $80,000 for 2017. Teasdale recorded equity earnings for its share of Wright Co. net income.

31. Accrued interest for three months on the Toon Co. bonds purchased on October 1.

31. Adjusted the available-for-sale investment portfolio to fair value, using the following fair value per-share amounts:

Available-for-Sale Investments	Fair Value
Alvarez Inc. stock	$41.50 per share
Hirsch Inc. stock	$26.00 per share
Richter Inc. stock	$48.00 per share
Toon Co. bonds	101 per $100 of face amount

31. Closed the Teasdale Inc. net income of $51,240. Teasdale Inc. paid no dividends during the year.

Instructions

Determine the missing letters in the unclassified balance sheet. Provide appropriate supporting calculations.

Comprehensive Problem 4

General Ledger

Selected transactions completed by Equinox Products Inc. during the fiscal year ended December 31, 2016, were as follows:

a. Issued 15,000 shares of $20 par common stock at $30, receiving cash.

b. Issued 4,000 shares of $80 par preferred 5% stock at $100, receiving cash.

c. Issued $500,000 of 10-year, 5% bonds at 104, with interest payable semiannually.

d. Declared a quarterly dividend of $0.50 per share on common stock and $1.00 per share on preferred stock. On the date of record, 100,000 shares of common stock were outstanding, no treasury shares were held, and 20,000 shares of preferred stock were outstanding.

e. Paid the cash dividends declared in (d).

f. Purchased 7,500 shares of Solstice Corp. at $40 per share, plus a $150 brokerage commission. The investment is classified as an available-for-sale investment.

g. Purchased 8,000 shares of treasury common stock at $33 per share.

h. Purchased 40,000 shares of Pinkberry Co. stock directly from the founders for $24 per share. Pinkberry has 125,000 shares issued and outstanding. Equinox Products Inc. treated the investment as an equity method investment.

i. Declared a $1.00 quarterly cash dividend per share on preferred stock. On the date of record, 20,000 shares of preferred stock had been issued.

(Continued)

j. Paid the cash dividends to the preferred stockholders.

k. Received $27,500 dividend from Pinkberry Co. investment in (h).

l. Purchased $90,000 of Dream Inc. 10-year, 5% bonds, directly from the issuing company, at their face amount plus accrued interest of $375. The bonds are classified as a held-to-maturity long-term investment.

m. Sold, at $38 per share, 2,600 shares of treasury common stock purchased in (g).

n. Received a dividend of $0.60 per share from the Solstice Corp. investment in (f).

o. Sold 1,000 shares of Solstice Corp. at $45, including commission.

p. Recorded the payment of semiannual interest on the bonds issued in (c) and the amortization of the premium for six months. The amortization is determined using the straight-line method.

q. Accrued interest for three months on the Dream Inc. bonds purchased in (l).

r. Pinkberry Co. recorded total earnings of $240,000. Equinox Products recorded equity earnings for its share of Pinkberry Co. net income.

s. The fair value for Solstice Corp. stock was $39.02 per share on December 31, 2016. The investment is adjusted to fair value, using a valuation allowance account. Assume Valuation Allowance for Available-for-Sale Investments had a beginning balance of zero.

Instructions

1. Journalize the selected transactions.
2. After all of the transactions for the year ended December 31, 2016, had been posted [including the transactions recorded in part (1) and all adjusting entries], the data that follows were taken from the records of Equinox Products Inc.
   a. Prepare a multiple-step income statement for the year ended December 31, 2016, concluding with earnings per share. In computing earnings per share, assume that the average number of common shares outstanding was 100,000 and preferred dividends were $100,000. (Round earnings per share to the nearest cent.)
   b. Prepare a retained earnings statement for the year ended December 31, 2016.
   c. Prepare a balance sheet in report form as of December 31, 2016.

Income statement data:	
Advertising expense	$ 150,000
Cost of merchandise sold	3,700,000
Delivery expense	30,000
Depreciation expense—office buildings and equipment	30,000
Depreciation expense—store buildings and equipment	100,000
Dividend revenue	4,500
Gain on sale of investment	4,980
Income from Pinkberry Co. investment	76,800
Income tax expense	140,500
Interest expense	21,000
Interest revenue	2,720
Miscellaneous administrative expense	7,500
Miscellaneous selling expense	14,000
Office rent expense	50,000
Office salaries expense	170,000
Office supplies expense	10,000
Sales	5,254,000
Sales commissions	185,000
Sales salaries expense	385,000
Store supplies expense	21,000

Retained earnings and balance sheet data:	
Accounts payable	$ 194,300
Accounts receivable	545,000
Accumulated depreciation—office buildings and equipment	1,580,000
Accumulated depreciation—store buildings and equipment	4,126,000
Allowance for doubtful accounts	8,450

Available-for-sale investments (at cost)	$ 260,130
Bonds payable, 5%, due 2024	500,000
Cash	246,000
Common stock, $20 par (400,000 shares authorized; 100,000 shares issued, 94,600 outstanding)	2,000,000
Dividends:	
Cash dividends for common stock	155,120
Cash dividends for preferred stock	100,000
Goodwill	500,000
Income tax payable	44,000
Interest receivable	1,125
Investment in Pinkberry Co. stock (equity method)	1,009,300
Investment in Dream Inc. bonds (long term)	90,000
Merchandise inventory (December 31, 2016), at lower of cost (FIFO) or market	778,000
Office buildings and equipment	4,320,000
Paid-in capital from sale of treasury stock	13,000
Excess of issue price over par—common stock	886,800
Excess of issue price over par—preferred stock	150,000
Preferred 5% stock, $80 par (30,000 shares authorized; 20,000 shares issued)	1,600,000
Premium on bonds payable	19,000
Prepaid expenses	27,400
Retained earnings, January 1, 2016	9,319,725
Store buildings and equipment	12,560,000
Treasury stock (5,400 shares of common stock at cost of $33 per share)	178,200
Unrealized gain (loss) on available-for-sale investments	(6,500)
Valuation allowance for available-for-sale investments	(6,500)

Cases & Projects

CP 15-1 Benefits of fair value

On July 16, 1998, Wyatt Corp. purchased 40 acres of land for $350,000. The land has been held for a future plant site until the current date, December 31, 2016. On December 18, 2016, TexoPete Inc. purchased 40 acres of land for $2,000,000 to be used for a distribution center. The TexoPete land is located next to the Wyatt Corp. land. Thus, both Wyatt Corp. and TexoPete Inc. own nearly identical pieces of land.

1. What are the valuations of land on the balance sheets of Wyatt Corp. and TexoPete Inc. using generally accepted accounting principles?
2. How might fair value accounting aid comparability when evaluating these two companies?

IFRS

CP 15-2 International fair value accounting

International Financial Reporting Standard No. 16 provides companies the option of valuing property, plant, and equipment at either historical cost or fair value. If fair value is selected, then the property, plant, and equipment must be revalued periodically to fair value. Under fair value, if there is an increase in the value of the property, plant, and equipment during the reporting period, then the increase is credited to stockholders' equity. However, if there is a decrease in fair value, then the decrease is reported as an expense for the period.

How is the international accounting treatment for changes in fair value for property, plant, and equipment similar to investments?

CP 15-3 Ethics and fair value measurement

Financial assets include stocks and bonds. These are fairly simple securities that can often be valued using quoted market prices. However, there are more complex financial instruments that do not have quoted market prices. These complex securities must still be valued on the balance sheet at fair value. Generally accepted accounting principles require that the reporting entity use assumptions in valuing investments when market prices or critical valuation inputs are unobservable.

What are the ethical considerations in making subjective valuations of these complex financial instruments?

CP 15-4 Warren Buffett and "look-through" earnings

Berkshire Hathaway, the investment holding company of Warren Buffett, reports its "less than 20% ownership" investments according to generally accepted accounting principles. However, it also provides additional disclosures that it terms "look-through" earnings.

Warren Buffett states,

Many of these companies (in the less than 20%-owned category) pay out relatively small proportions of their earnings in dividends. This means that only a small proportion of their earning power is recorded in our own current operating earnings. But, while our reported operating earnings reflect only the dividends received from such companies, our economic well-being is determined by their earnings, not their dividends.

The value to Berkshire Hathaway of retained earnings (of our investees) is not determined by whether we own 100%, 50%, 20%, or 1% of the businesses in which they reside.... Our perspective on such "forgotten-but-not-gone" earnings is simple: the way they are accounted for is of no importance, but their ownership and subsequent utilization is all-important. We care not whether the auditors hear a tree fall in the forest; we do care who owns the tree and what's next done with it.

I believe the best way to think about our earnings is in terms of "look-through" results, calculated as follows: Take $250 million, which is roughly our share of the operating earnings retained by our investees (<20% ownership holdings); subtract... incremental taxes we would have owed had that $250 million been paid to us in dividends; then add the remainder, $220 million, to our reported earnings of $371 million. Thus, our "look-through" earnings were about $590 million.

Source: Warren Buffett, *The Essays of Warren Buffett: Lessons for Corporate America*, edited by Lawrence A. Cunningham, pp. 180–183 (excerpted).

1. What are look-through earnings?
2. Why does Warren Buffett favor look-through earnings?

CP 15-5 Reporting investments

Group Project

In groups of three or four, find the latest annual report for **Microsoft Corporation**. The annual report can be found on the company's Web site at www.microsoft.com/msft/default.mspx.

The notes to the financial statements include details of Microsoft's investments. Find the notes that provide details of its investments (Note 4) and the income from its investments (Note 3).

From these disclosures, answer the following questions:

1. What is the total cost of investments?
2. What is the fair value (recorded value) of investments?
3. What is the total unrealized gain from investments?
4. What is the total unrealized loss from investments?
5. What percent of total investments (at fair value) are:
   a. Cash and equivalents
   b. Short-term investments
   c. Equity and other investments (long term)
6. What was the total combined dividend and interest revenue?
7. What was the recognized net gain or loss from sale of investments?

Mornin' Joe

Financial Statements for Mornin' Joe

Financial Statements for Mornin' Joe International

Financial Statements for Mornin' Joe

The financial statements of **Mornin' Joe** follow. Mornin' Joe is a fictitious coffeehouse chain featuring drip and espresso coffee in a café setting. The financial statements of Mornin' Joe are provided to illustrate the complete financial statements of a corporation, using the terms, formats, and reporting illustrated throughout this text. In addition, excerpts of the Mornin' Joe financial statements are used to illustrate the financial reporting presentation for the topics discussed in Chapters 7–15. Thus, you can refer to the complete financial statements in Exhibits 1, 2, 3, and 4 here or the excerpts in Chapters 7–15.

EXHIBIT 1

Income Statement for Mornin' Joe

Mornin' Joe Income Statement For the Year Ended December 31, 2016			
Revenue from sales:			
Sales		$5,450,000	
Less: Sales returns and allowances	$ 26,500		
Sales discounts	21,400	47,900	
Sales			$5,402,100
Cost of merchandise sold			2,160,000
Gross profit			$3,242,100
Operating expenses			
Selling expenses:			
Wages expense	$825,000		
Advertising expense	678,900		
Depreciation expense—buildings	124,300		
Miscellaneous selling expense	26,500		
Total selling expense		$ 1,654,700	
Administrative expenses:			
Office salaries expense	$325,000		
Rent expense	425,600		
Payroll tax expense	110,000		
Depreciation expense—office equipment	68,900		
Bad debt expense	14,000		
Amortization expense	10,500		
Total administrative expenses		954,000	
Total operating expenses			2,608,700
Income from operations			$ 633,400
Other income and expense:			
Interest revenue		$ 18,000	
Interest expense		(136,000)	
Loss on disposal of fixed asset		(23,000)	
Unrealized gain on trading investments		5,000	
Equity income in AM Coffee		57,000	(79,000)
Income before income taxes			$ 554,400
Income tax expense			132,800
Net income			$ 421,600
Basic earnings per share [($421,600 – $30,000) ÷ 44,000 shares issued and outstanding]			$ 8.90

EXHIBIT 2

Balance Sheet for Mornin' Joe

Mornin' Joe **Balance Sheet** **December 31, 2016**			
Assets			
Current assets:			
Cash and cash equivalents		$ 235,000	
Trading investments (at cost)	$ 420,000		
Plus valuation allowance for trading investments	45,000	465,000	
Accounts receivable	$ 305,000		
Less allowance for doubtful accounts	12,300	292,700	
Merchandise inventory—at lower of cost (first-in, first-out method) or market		120,000	
Prepaid insurance		24,000	
Total current assets			$1,136,700
Investments:			
Investment in AM Coffee (equity method)			565,000
Property, plant, and equipment:			
Land		$1,850,000	
Buildings	$2,650,000		
Less accumulated depreciation	420,000	2,230,000	
Office equipment	$ 350,000		
Less accumulated depreciation	102,000	248,000	
Total property, plant, and equipment			4,328,000
Intangible assets:			
Patents			140,000
Total assets			$6,169,700
Liabilities			
Current liabilities:			
Accounts payable		$ 133,000	
Notes payable (current portion)		200,000	
Salaries and wages payable		42,000	
Payroll taxes payable		16,400	
Interest payable		40,000	
Total current liabilities			$ 431,400
Long-term liabilities:			
Bonds payable, 8%, due December 31, 2032		$ 500,000	
Less unamortized discount		16,000	$ 484,000
Notes payable			1,400,000
Total long-term liabilities			$1,884,000
Total liabilities			$2,315,400
Stockholders' Equity			
Paid-in capital:			
Preferred 10% stock, $50 par (6,000 shares authorized and issued)		$ 300,000	
Excess of issue price over par		50,000	$ 350,000
Common stock, $20 par (50,000 shares authorized, 45,000 shares issued)		$ 900,000	
Excess of issue price over par		1,450,000	2,350,000
Total paid-in capital			$2,700,000
Retained earnings			1,200,300
Total			$3,900,300
Deduct treasury stock (1,000 shares at cost)			46,000
Total stockholders' equity			$3,854,300
Total liabilities and stockholders' equity			$6,169,700

EXHIBIT 3

Retained Earnings Statement for Mornin' Joe

Mornin' Joe Retained Earnings Statement For the Year Ended December 31, 2016			
Retained earnings, January 1, 2016			$ 852,700
Net income		$421,600	
Less dividends:			
Preferred stock	$30,000		
Common stock	44,000	74,000	
Increase in retained earnings			347,600
Retained earnings, December 31, 2016			$1,200,300

EXHIBIT 4

Statement of Stockholders' Equity for Mornin' Joe

Mornin' Joe
Statement of Stockholders' Equity
For the Year Ended December 31, 2016

	Preferred Stock	Common Stock	Additional Paid-In Capital	Retained Earnings	Treasury Stock	Total
Balance, January 1, 2016	$300,000	$800,000	$1,325,000	$852,700	$(36,000)	$3,241,700
Net income				421,600		421,600
Dividends on preferred stock				(30,000)		(30,000)
Dividends on common stock				(44,000)		(44,000)
Issuance of additional common stock		100,000	175,000			275,000
Purchase of treasury stock					(10,000)	(10,000)
Balance, December 31, 2016	$300,000	$900,000	$1,500,000	$1,200,300	$(46,000)	$3,854,300

Financial Statements for Mornin' Joe International

Mornin' Joe is planning to expand operations to various places around the world. Financing for this expansion will come from foreign banks. While financial statements prepared under U.S. GAAP may be appropriate for U.S. operations, financial statements prepared for foreign bankers should be prepared using international accounting standards.

The European Union (EU) has developed accounting standards similar in structure to U.S. standards. Its accounting standards board is called the International Accounting Standards Board (IASB). The IASB issues accounting standards that are termed *International Financial Reporting Standards (IFRS)*. The intent of the IASB is to create a set of financial standards that can be used by public companies worldwide, not just in the EU.

Currently, the EU countries and more than 100 other countries around the world have adopted or are planning to adopt IFRS. As a result, there are efforts under way to converge U.S. GAAP with IFRS so as to harmonize accounting standards around the world.

Key Reporting Differences between IFRS and U.S. GAAP

The financial statements of **Mornin' Joe International** using IFRS are presented in Exhibits 1, 2, and 3. This illustration highlights reporting and terminology differences between IFRS and U.S. GAAP. Differences in recording transactions under IFRS and U.S. GAAP are discussed in Appendix D and in various International Connection boxes throughout the text.

The Mornin' Joe International financial statements in Exhibits 5, 6, and 7 are simplified and illustrate only portions of IFRS that are appropriate for introductory accounting. The financial statements are presented in euros (€) for demonstration purposes only. The euro is the standard currency of the European Union. The euro is translated at a 1:1 ratio from the dollar to simplify comparisons. Throughout the illustration, call-outs and end notes to each statement are used to highlight the differences between financial statements prepared under IFRS and under U.S. GAAP.

Statements of Comprehensive Income versus Income Statements

Exhibit 5 illustrates the statement of comprehensive income for **Mornin' Joe International** and shows key differences from the income statements prepared under U.S. GAAP.

EXHIBIT 5 **Statement of Comprehensive Income for Mornin' Joe International**

Title includes the word "Comprehensive."

This is a common term for an equity method investment.

The term "Finance costs" is used, rather than "Interest expense."

The term "Profit for the year" is used, rather than "Net income."

Mornin' Joe International Statement of Comprehensive Income For the Year Ended December 31, 2016	
Sales (net)*	€ 5,402,100
Cost of merchandise sold	(2,160,000)
Gross profit	€ 3,242,100
Selling expenses	(1,654,700)
Administrative expenses	(954,000)
Loss on disposal of fixed asset	(23,000)
Other income (expenses)	23,000
Share in profit (loss) of associates*	57,000
Operating profit	€ 690,400
Finance costs*	(136,000)
Profit before income tax	€ 554,400
Tax expense*	(132,800)
Profit for the year*	€ 421,600
Other comprehensive income	
Gain on revaluation of properties*	44,800
Total comprehensive income for the year, net of tax*	€ 466,400
Earnings per share basic* (€421,600 ÷ 44,000 shares)	€ 9.58

*A required disclosure on the face of the statement of comprehensive income

Expenses are organized by their nature. See Note 2.

Diversity allowed with regard to subtotal definitions. See Note 3.

Other comprehensive income is a required disclosure. See Note 4.

IFRS allows latitude on how statements are organized but does list minimum disclosure requirements that are less restrictive than required by the SEC. See Note 1.

1. IFRS statements are often more summarized than U.S. GAAP statements. To compensate, IFRS requires specific disclosures on the face of the financial statements (denoted *) and additional disclosures in the footnotes to the financial statements. Because additions and subtractions are grouped together in sections of IFRS statements, parentheses are used to indicate subtractions.
2. Expenses in an IFRS income statement are classified by either their nature or function. The nature of an expense is how the expense would naturally be recorded in a journal entry reflecting the economic benefit received for that expense. Examples include salaries, depreciation, advertising, and utilities. The function of an expense identifies the purpose of the expense, such as a selling expense or an administrative expense.

   IFRS does not permit the natural and functional classifications to be mixed together on the same statement. That is, all expenses must be classified by either nature or function. However, if a functional classification of expenses is used, a footnote to the income statement must show the natural classification of expenses. To illustrate, because **Mornin' Joe International** uses the functional classification of expenses in its income statement, it must also show the following natural classification of expenses in a footnote:

Cost of product	€2,100,000	The cost of product purchased for resale
Employee benefits expense	1,260,000	Required natural disclosure
Depreciation and amortization expense	203,700	Required natural disclosure
Rent expense	425,600	
Advertising expense	678,900	
Other expenses	58,500	
Total natural expenses	€4,726,700	

3. IFRS provides flexibility with regard to line items, headings, and subtotals on the income statement. There is less flexibility under U.S. GAAP for public companies.
4. IFRS requires the reporting of other comprehensive income (see appendix to Chapter 15) either on the income statement (see Exhibit 5) or in a separate statement. U.S. GAAP has a similar disclosure treatment. For **Mornin' Joe International**, other comprehensive income consists of the restatement of café locations to fair value (see Note 6 for more details).
5. Under IFRS, there is no standard format for the balance sheet (statement of financial position, see Exhibit 6). A typical format for European Union companies is to begin the asset section of the balance sheet with noncurrent assets. This is followed by current assets listed in reverse order of liquidity. That is, the asset side of the balance sheet is reported in reverse order of liquidity from least liquid to most liquid. Listing noncurrent assets first emphasizes the going concern nature of the entity.

   The liability and owners' equity side of the balance sheet is also reported differently than under U.S. GAAP. Specifically, owners' equity is reported first followed by noncurrent liabilities and current liabilities. Listing equity first emphasizes the going concern nature of the entity and the long-term financial interest of the owners in the business.
6. Under IFRS, property, plant, and equipment (PP&E) may be measured at historical cost or fair value. If fair value is used, the revaluation must be for similar classifications of PP&E but need not be for all PP&E. This departs from U.S. GAAP, which requires PP&E to be measured at historical cost. **Mornin' Joe International** restated its Land and Buildings to fair value because the café sites have readily available real estate market prices. Land and buildings are included together because their fair values are not separable. The office equipment remains at historical cost because it does not have a readily available market price. The increase in fair value is recorded by reducing accumulated depreciation and recognizing the gain as other comprehensive income. This element of other comprehensive income is accumulated in stockholders' equity under the heading Property revaluation reserve.* This treatment is similar (with different titles) to the U.S. GAAP treatment of unrealized gains (losses) from available-for-sale securities. For Mornin' Joe International, there is an increase in the property revaluation reserve of €44,800. This amount is the only difference between Mornin' Joe's U.S. GAAP net income, total assets, and total stockholders' equity and Mornin' Joe International's IFRS total comprehensive income, total assets, and total stockholders' equity.
7. **Mornin' Joe International** recently acquired a coffee plantation. This is an example of a biological asset. IFRS requires separate reporting of biological assets (principally agricultural assets) at fair value.
8. Inventories are valued at lower of cost or market; however, "market" is defined as net realizable value under IFRS. U.S. GAAP defines "market" as replacement cost under most conditions. In addition, IFRS prohibits LIFO cost valuation.
9. Under IFRS, some elements of other comprehensive income and owner's equity are often aggregated under the term "reserves." In contrast, under U.S. GAAP, "reserve" is used to identify a liability. IFRS also does not require separate disclosure of treasury stock as does U.S. GAAP. Specifically, treasury stock may be reported as a reduction of a reserve, a reduction of a stock premium, or as a separate item.
10. The term *provision* is used to denote a liability under IFRS, whereas this term often indicates an expense under U.S. GAAP. For example, *Provision for income taxes* means *Income tax expense* under U.S. GAAP, whereas it would mean *Income taxes payable* under IFRS.
11. Under U.S. GAAP, other comprehensive income items must be included as changes in accumulated other comprehensive income in the statement of changes in stockholders' equity (see Exhibit 7). IFRS allows for similar treatment, with wider latitude for terminology, such as *Property Revaluation Reserve* illustrated by the column title here. In this illustration, treasury stock is included as part of a reserve (Reserve for Own Shares). As discussed in Note 9, under U.S. GAAP the term *reserve* denotes a liability.

Statements of Financial Position versus Balance Sheets

Exhibit 6 illustrates the statement of financial position for **Mornin' Joe International** and shows key differences from the balance sheets prepared under U.S. GAAP.

EXHIBIT 6 **Statement of Financial Position for Mornin' Joe International**

Mornin' Joe International
Statement of Financial Position
December 31, 2016

Assets			
Noncurrent assets			
Property, plant, and equipment*			
Land and buildings at fair value	€4,180,000		
Less: Accumulated depreciation	375,200	€3,804,800	
Office equipment at cost	€ 350,000		
Less: Accumulated depreciation	102,000	248,000	
Biological assets at fair value*		320,000	
Patents at amortized cost*		140,000	
Investment in AM Coffee (equity method)*		565,000	
Total noncurrent assets			€5,077,800
Current assets			
Prepaid insurance		€ 24,000	
Merchandise inventory—**at lower of cost (first-in, first-out) or realizable value***		120,000	
Accounts receivable (net of allowance for doubtful accounts)*		292,700	
Financial assets at fair value through profit or loss*		465,000	
Cash and cash equivalents*		235,000	
Total current assets			1,136,700
Total assets*			€6,214,500
Equity attributable to owners			
Preferred 10% stock, €50 par (6,000 shares authorized and issued)*		€ 300,000	
Common stock, €20 par (50,000 shares authorized, 45,000 shares issued)*		900,000	
Share premium*		1,500,000	
Reserves*		(1,200)	
Retained earnings*		1,200,300	
Total equity attributable to owners*			€3,899,100
Liabilities			
Noncurrent liabilities*			
Bonds payable, 8%, due December 31, 2032 (net of discount)		€ 484,000	
Notes payable		1,400,000	
Total noncurrent liabilities			€1,884,000
Current liabilities			
Accounts payable*		€ 133,000	
Loans*		200,000	
Employee provisions*		58,400	
Interest payable		40,000	
Total current liabilities			431,400
Total liabilities*			€2,315,400
Total equity and liabilities*			€6,214,500

*Required disclosures. Footnotes provide additional subclassification detail.

Preferred title for the "Balance Sheet."

"Biological assets" are a required disclosure at fair value. See Note 7.

Inventory valuation. See Note 8.

International terminology for "Trading investments." Same accounting treatment.

International terminology for "Excess of issue price over par."

Other comprehensive items and treasury stock. See Note 9.

Employee provisions are wages, salaries, and payroll taxes payable. See Note 10.

Sub-classifications of PP&E may be valued at fair value. See Note 6.

Reverse liquidity account order. See Note 5.

Equities listed first, then liabilities. See Note 5.

Noncurrent liabilities listed prior to current liabilities.

Statements of Changes in Equity versus Statements of Stockholders' Equity

Exhibit 7 illustrates the statement of changes in equity for **Mornin' Joe International** and shows key differences from the statements of stockholders' equity prepared under U.S. GAAP.

EXHIBIT 7 **Statement of Changes in Equity for Mornin' Joe International**

Mornin' Joe International
Statement of Changes in Equity
For the Year Ended December 31, 2016

	Preferred Stock	Common Stock	Share Premium	Reserves: Property Revaluation Reserve	Reserves: Reserve for Own Shares	Retained Earnings	Total Equity Attributable to Owners
Balance, January 1, 2016	€300,000	€800,000	€1,325,000	€ 0	(€36,000)	€ 852,700	€3,241,700
Profit for the year						421,600	421,600
Other comprehensive income							
Property revaluation (gain)				44,800			44,800
Total comprehensive income				€44,800		€ 421,600	€ 466,400
Contributions by and distributions to owners							
Dividends on preferred stock						(30,000)	(30,000)
Dividends on common stock						(44,000)	(44,000)
Issuance of additional common stock		100,000	175,000				275,000
Purchase of own shares					(10,000)		(10,000)
Total contributions and distributions to owners	€ 0	€100,000	€ 175,000	€ 0	(€10,000)	(€ 74,000)	€ 191,000
Balance, December 31, 2016	€300,000	€900,000	€1,500,000	€44,800	(€46,000)	€1,200,300	€3,899,100

"Reserves," see Notes 9 and 11.

Discussion Questions

1. Contrast U.S. GAAP financial statement terms with their differing IFRS terms.
2. What is the difference between classifying an expense by nature or function?
3. If a functional expense classification is used for the statement of comprehensive income, what must also be disclosed?
4. How is the term "provision" used differently under IFRS than under U.S. GAAP?
5. What are two main differences in inventory valuation under IFRS compared to U.S. GAAP?
6. What is a "biological asset"?
7. What is the most significant IFRS departure from U.S. GAAP for valuing property, plant, and equipment?
8. What is a "share premium"?
9. How is the term "reserve" used under IFRS, and how does it differ from its meaning under U.S. GAAP?
10. How is treasury stock reported under IFRS? How does this differ from its treatment under U.S. GAAP?

IFRS IFRS Activity 1

Unilever Group is a global company that markets a wide variety of products, including Lever® soap, Breyer's® ice cream, and Hellman's® mayonnaise. A recent income statement and statement of comprehensive income for the Dutch company, Unilever Group, follow:

Unilever Group Consolidated Income Statement For the Year Ended December 31 (in millions of euros)	
Turnover	€51,324
Operating profit	6,989
After (charging)/crediting:	
Non-core items	(73)
Net finance costs	(397)
Finance income	136
Finance costs	(526)
Pensions and similar obligations	(7)
Share of net profit/(loss) of joint ventures and associations	105
Other income from non-current investments	(14)
Profit before taxation	€ 6,683
Taxation	(1,735)
Net profit	€ 4,948
Earnings per share—basic	€ 1.58
Earnings per share—diluted	€ 1.54

Consolidated Statement of Comprehensive Income For the Year Ended December 31	
Fair value gains (losses), net of tax	€ (125)
Actuarial gains (losses) on pensions, net of tax	(644)
Currency retranslation gains (losses), net of tax	(316)
Net income (expense) recognized directly into equity	€(1,085)
Net profit	4,948
Total comprehensive income	€3,863

a. What do you think is meant by "turnover"?

b. How does Unilever's income statement presentation differ significantly from that of Mornin' Joe?

c. How is the total for net finance costs presented differently than would be typically found under U.S. GAAP?

IFRS Activity 2

The following is a recent consolidated statement of financial position on December 31 of a recent year for LVMH, a French company that markets the Louis Vuitton® and Moët Hennessy® brands:

LVMH
Statement of Financial Position
December 31
(in millions of euros)

Assets	
Brands and other intangible assets—net	€11,510
Goodwill—net	7,806
Property, plant, and equipment—net	8,769
Investment in associates	163
Non-current available for sale financial assets	6,004
Other non-current assets	524
Deferred tax	881
Non-current assets	€35,657
Inventories	€ 8,080
Trade accounts receivable	1,985
Income taxes	201
Other current assets	1,811
Cash and cash equivalents	2,196
Current assets	€14,273
TOTAL ASSETS	€49,930
Liabilities and Equity	
Share capital	€ 152
Share premium	3,848
Treasury shares	(414)
Revaluation reserves	2,819
Other reserves	14,393
Cumulative translation adjustment	342
Net profit, group share	3,424
Equity, group share	€24,564
Minority interests	1,102
Total equity	€25,666
Long-term borrowings	€ 3,836
Provisions	1,530
Deferred tax	3,960
Other non-current liabilities	5,456
Total non-current liabilities	€14,782
Short-term borrowings	€ 2,976
Trade accounts payable	3,134
Income taxes payable	442
Provisions	335
Other current liabilities	2,595
Total current liabilities	€ 9,482
TOTAL LIABILITIES AND EQUITY	€49,930

a. Identify presentation differences between the balance sheet of LVMH and a balance sheet prepared under U.S. GAAP. Use the Mornin' Joe balance sheet (Exhibit 2) as an example of a U.S. GAAP balance sheet. (Ignore minority interests and cumulative translation adjustment.)

b. Compare the terms used in this balance sheet with the terms used by Mornin' Joe (Exhibit 2), using the table that follows:

LVMH Term	Mornin' Joe U.S. GAAP Term
Statement of financial position	
Share capital	
Share premium	
Other reserves	
Provisions	

c. What does the "Revaluation reserves" in the Equity section of the balance sheet represent?

IFRS IFRS Activity 3

Under U.S. GAAP, LIFO is an acceptable inventory method. Financial statement information for three companies that use LIFO follows. All table numbers are in millions of dollars.

	LIFO Inventory	FIFO Inventory (from notes)	Impact on Net Income from Using LIFO Rather than FIFO (from notes)	Total Current Assets	Net Income as Reported
Exxon	$9,852	$31,200	$317	$58,984	$30,460
Kroger	4,966	5,793	(57)	7,621	1,116
Ford Motor*	5,917	6,782	4	34,368	4,690

*Autos and trucks only

Assume these companies adopted IFRS, and thus were required to use FIFO, rather than LIFO.

a. Prepare a table with the following columns:

(1)	(2)	(3)	(4)
FIFO less LIFO	IFRS Net Income	$\frac{\text{(FIFO less LIFO)}}{\text{Total Current Assets}}$	$\frac{\text{IFRS Net Income (Col. 2)}}{\text{Reported Net Income}}$

(1) Difference between FIFO and LIFO inventory valuation.

(2) Revised IFRS net income using FIFO.

(3) Difference between FIFO and LIFO inventory valuation as a percent of total current assets.

(4) Revised IFRS net income as a percent of the reported net income.

b. Complete the table for the three companies.

c. For which company would a change to IFRS for inventory valuation have the largest percentage impact on total current assets (Col. 3)?

d. For which company would a change to IFRS for inventory valuation have the largest percentage impact on net income (Col. 4)?

e. Why might Kroger have a negative impact on net income from using LIFO, while the other two companies have a positive impact on net income from using LIFO?

CHAPTER

16

Statement of Cash Flows

National Beverage Co.

Suppose you were to receive $100 from an event. Would it make a difference what the event was? Yes, it would! If you received $100 for your birthday, then it's a gift. If you received $100 as a result of working part time for a week, then it's the result of your effort. If you received $100 as a loan, then it's money that you will have to pay back in the future. If you received $100 as a result of selling your iPod, then it's the result of selling an asset. Thus, $100 received can be associated with different types of events, and these events have different meanings to you, and different implications for your future. You would much rather receive a $100 gift than take out a $100 loan. Likewise, company stakeholders view inflows and outflows of cash differently, depending on their source.

Companies are required to report information about the events causing a change in cash over a period of time. This information is reported in the statement of cash flows. One such company is **National Beverage**, which is an alternative beverage company, known for its innovative soft drinks, enhanced juices and waters, and fortified powders and supplements. You have probably seen the company's **Shasta** and **Faygo** soft drinks, or **LaCroix**, **Everfresh**, and **Crystal Bay** drinks at your local grocery or convenience store. As with any company, cash is important to National Beverage. Without cash, National Beverage would be unable to expand its brands, distribute its product, support extreme sports, or provide a return for its owners. Thus, its managers are concerned about the sources and uses of cash.

In previous chapters, we have used the income statement, balance sheet, statement of retained earnings, and other information to analyze the effects of management decisions on a business's financial position and operating performance. In this chapter, we focus on the events causing a change in cash by presenting the preparation and use of the statement of cash flows.

Learning Objectives

After studying this chapter, you should be able to: | Example Exercises

At a Glance 16 Page 764

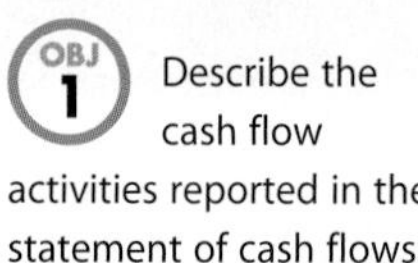

Describe the cash flow activities reported in the statement of cash flows.

Reporting Cash Flows

The **statement of cash flows** reports a company's cash inflows and outflows for a period.[1] The statement of cash flows provides useful information about a company's ability to do the following:

- Generate cash from operations
- Maintain and expand its operating capacity
- Meet its financial obligations
- Pay dividends

The statement of cash flows is used by managers in evaluating past operations and in planning future investing and financing activities. It is also used by external users such as investors and creditors to assess a company's profit potential and ability to pay its debt and pay dividends.

Note:
The statement of cash flows reports cash flows from operating, investing, and financing activities.

The statement of cash flows reports three types of cash flow activities, as follows:

1. **Cash flows from operating activities** are the cash flows from transactions that affect the net income of the company.

   Example: Purchase and sale of merchandise by a retailer.

2. **Cash flows from investing activities** are the cash flows from transactions that affect investments in the noncurrent assets of the company.

   Example: Purchase and sale of fixed assets, such as equipment and buildings.

[1] As used in this chapter, *cash* refers to cash and cash equivalents. Examples of cash equivalents include short-term, highly liquid investments, such as money market accounts, bank certificates of deposit, and U.S. Treasury bills.

3. **Cash flows from financing activities** are the cash flows from transactions that affect the debt and equity of the company.

   Example: Issuing or retiring equity and debt securities.

The cash flows are reported in the statement of cash flows as follows:

Cash flows from operating activities	$XXX
Cash flows from investing activities	XXX
Cash flows from financing activities	XXX
Net increase or decrease in cash for the period	$XXX
Cash at the beginning of the period	XXX
Cash at the end of the period	$XXX

The ending cash on the statement of cash flows equals the cash reported on the company's balance sheet at the end of the year.

Exhibit 1 illustrates the sources (increases) and uses (decreases) of cash by each of the three cash flow activities. A *source* of cash causes the cash flow to increase and is called a *cash inflow*. A *use* of cash causes cash flow to decrease and is called *cash outflow*.

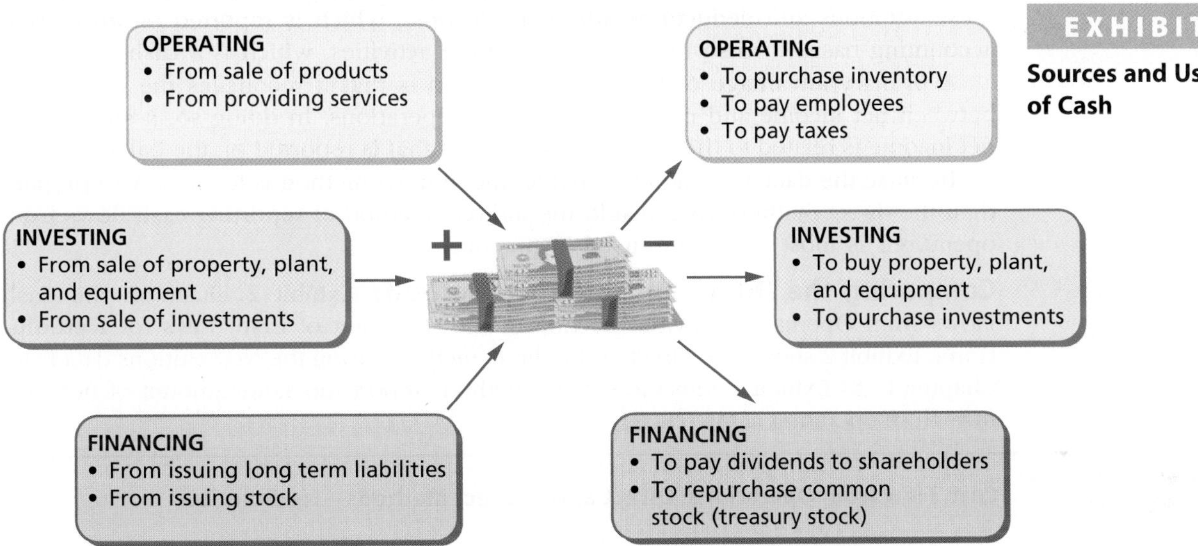

EXHIBIT 1

Sources and Uses of Cash

Cash Flows from Operating Activities

Cash flows from operating activities reports the cash inflows and outflows from a company's day-to-day operations. Companies may select one of two alternative methods for reporting cash flows from operating activities in the statement of cash flows:

- The direct method
- The indirect method

Both methods result in the same amount of cash flows from operating activities. They differ in the way they report cash flows from operating activities.

In fiscal 2012, **Google Inc.** generated $16.6 billion in net cash flow from operating activities.

The Direct Method The **direct method** reports operating cash inflows (receipts) and cash outflows (payments) as follows:

Cash flows from operating activities:		
Cash received from customers		$XXX
Less: Cash payments for merchandise	$XXX	
Cash payments for operating expenses	XXX	
Cash payments for interest	XXX	
Cash payments for income taxes	XXX	XXX
Net cash flow from operating activities		$XXX

The primary operating cash inflow is cash received from customers. The primary operating cash outflows are cash payments for merchandise, operating expenses, interest, and income tax payments. The cash received from operating activities less the cash payments for operating activities is the net cash flow from operating activities.

The primary advantage of the direct method is that it *directly* reports cash receipts and cash payments in the statement of cash flows. Its primary disadvantage is that these data may not be readily available in the accounting records. Thus, the direct method is normally more costly to prepare and, as a result, is used infrequently in practice.

The Indirect Method The **indirect method** reports cash flows from operating activities by beginning with net income and adjusting it for revenues and expenses that do not involve the receipt or payment of cash, as follows:

Cash flows from operating activities:		
Net income	$XXX	
Adjustments to reconcile net income to net cash flow from operating activities	XXX	
Net cash flow from operating activities		$XXX

The adjustments to reconcile net income to net cash flow from operating activities include such items as depreciation and gains or losses on fixed assets. Changes in current operating assets and liabilities such as accounts receivable or accounts payable are also added or deducted, depending on their effect on cash flows. In effect, these additions and deductions adjust net income, which is reported on an accrual accounting basis, to cash flows from operating activities, which is a cash basis.

A primary advantage of the indirect method is that it reconciles the differences between net income and net cash flows from operations. In doing so, it shows how net income is related to the ending cash balance that is reported on the balance sheet.

Because the data are readily available, the indirect method is less costly to prepare than the direct method. As a result, the indirect method of reporting cash flows from operations is most commonly used in practice.

Comparing the Direct and Indirect Methods Exhibit 2 illustrates the Cash Flows from Operating Activities section of the statement of cash flows for **NetSolutions**. Exhibit 2 shows the direct and indirect methods using the NetSolutions data from Chapter 1. As Exhibit 2 illustrates, both methods report the same amount of net cash flow from operating activities, $2,900.

EXHIBIT 2 **Cash Flow from Operations: Direct and Indirect Methods—NetSolutions**

Direct Method

Cash flows from operating activities:	
Cash received from customers	$7,500
Deduct cash payments for expenses and payments to creditors	4,600
Net cash flow from operating activities	$2,900

Indirect Method

Cash flows from operating activities:	
Net income	$3,050
Add increase in accounts payable	400
	$3,450
Deduct increase in supplies	550
Net cash flow from operating activities	$2,900

the same

Business  Connection

CASH CRUNCH!

In late 2011, **American Airlines**' deteriorating cash flow situation forced the company to file for bankruptcy. At the time, the airline had generated $235 million in net cash flow from operating activities for the nine-month period ending September 31, 2011, while spending $1.1 billion on additional property, plant, and equipment. The property, plant, and equipment purchases were paid for by issuing additional debt. By Thanksgiving 2011, it became clear that the company's weak net cash flow from operating activities would not be sufficient to pay off the airline's massive debt. On November 29, 2011, the airline filed for bankruptcy. In February 2013, American and **U.S. Airways** announced plans to merge, creating the largest airline in the world.

Source: M. Curriden and N. Posgate, "American Airlines bankruptcy, merger deals were complex, expensive," *Dallas Morning News*, February 17, 2013.

Cash Flows from Investing Activities

Cash flows from investing activities show the cash inflows and outflows related to changes in a company's long-term assets. Cash flows from investing activities are reported on the statement of cash flows as follows:

Cash flows from investing activities:		
Cash inflows from investing activities	$XXX	
Less cash used for investing activities	XXX	
Net cash flows from investing activities		$XXX

Cash inflows from investing activities normally arise from selling fixed assets, investments, and intangible assets. Cash outflows normally include payments to purchase fixed assets, investments, and intangible assets.

Cash Flows from Financing Activities

Cash flows from financing activities show the cash inflows and outflows related to changes in a company's long-term liabilities and stockholders' equity. Cash flows from financing activities are reported on the statement of cash flows as follows:

In March 2013, U.S. companies in the S&P 500 index were expected to pay $300 billion in dividends to investors during 2013.

Cash flows from financing activities:		
Cash inflows from financing activities	$XXX	
Less cash used for financing activities	XXX	
Net cash flow from financing activities		$XXX

Cash inflows from financing activities normally arise from issuing long-term debt or equity securities. For example, issuing bonds, notes payable, preferred stock, and common stock creates cash inflows from financing activities. Cash outflows from financing activities include paying cash dividends, repaying long-term debt, and acquiring treasury stock.

Noncash Investing and Financing Activities

A company may enter into transactions involving investing and financing activities that do not *directly* affect cash. For example, a company may issue common stock to retire long-term debt. Although this transaction does not directly affect cash, it does eliminate future cash payments for interest and for paying the bonds when they mature. Because such transactions *indirectly* affect cash flows, they are reported in a separate section of the statement of cash flows. This section usually appears at the bottom of the statement of cash flows.

Format of the Statement of Cash Flows

The statement of cash flows presents the cash flows generated by, or used for, the three activities previously discussed: operating, investing, and financing. These three activities are always reported in the same order, following the format illustrated in Exhibit 3.

EXHIBIT 3

Format of the Statement of Cash Flows

COMPANY NAME
Statement of Cash Flows
For the Year Ended xxxx

Cash flows from operating activities		
(List of individual items, as illustrated in Exhibit 1)	XXX	
Net cash flows from operating activities		$XXX
Cash flows from investing activities		
(List of individual items, as illustrated in Exhibit 1)	XXX	
Net cash flows from (used for) investing activities		XXX
Cash flows from financing activities		
(List of individual items, as illustrated in Exhibit 1)	XXX	
Net cash flows from (used for) financing activities		XXX
Increase (decrease) in cash		$XXX
Cash at the beginning of the period		XXX
Cash at the end of the period		$XXX
Noncash investing and financing activites		$XXX

Example Exercise 16-1 Classifying Cash Flows

Identify whether each of the following would be reported as an operating, investing, or financing activity in the statement of cash flows:

a. Purchase of patent
b. Payment of cash dividend
c. Disposal of equipment
d. Cash sales
e. Purchase of treasury stock
f. Payment of wages expense

Follow My Example 16-1

a. Investing
b. Financing
c. Investing
d. Operating
e. Financing
f. Operating

Practice Exercises: PE 16-1A, PE 16-1B

No Cash Flow per Share

Cash flow per share is sometimes reported in the financial press. As reported, cash flow per share is normally computed as *cash flow from operations divided by the number of common shares outstanding*. However, such reporting may be misleading because of the following:

- Users may misinterpret cash flow per share as the per-share amount available for dividends. This would not be the case if the cash generated by operations is required for repaying loans or for reinvesting in the business.
- Users may misinterpret cash flow per share as equivalent to (or better than) earnings per share.

For these reasons, the financial statements, including the statement of cash flows, should not report cash flow per share.

OBJ 2 Prepare a statement of cash flows, using the indirect method.

Preparing the Statement of Cash Flows—The Indirect Method

The indirect method of reporting cash flows from operating activities uses the logic that a change in any balance sheet account (including cash) can be analyzed in terms of changes in the other balance sheet accounts. Thus, by analyzing changes in noncash balance sheet accounts, any change in the cash account can be *indirectly* determined.

To illustrate, the accounting equation can be solved for cash as follows:

Assets = Liabilities + Stockholders' Equity
Cash + Noncash Assets = Liabilities + Stockholders' Equity
Cash = Liabilities + Stockholders' Equity − Noncash Assets

Therefore, any change in the cash account can be determined by analyzing changes in the liability, stockholders' equity, and noncash asset accounts as follows:

Change in Cash = *Change* in Liabilities + *Change* in Stockholders' Equity − *Change* in Noncash Assets

Under the indirect method, there is no order in which the balance sheet accounts must be analyzed. However, net income (or net loss) is the first amount reported on the statement of cash flows. Because net income (or net loss) is a component of any change in Retained Earnings, the first account normally analyzed is Retained Earnings.

To illustrate the indirect method, the income statement and comparative balance sheets for **Rundell Inc.**, shown in Exhibit 4, are used. Ledger accounts and other data supporting the income statement and balance sheet are presented as needed.[2]

EXHIBIT 4

Income Statement and Comparative Balance Sheet

Rundell Inc.
Income Statement
For the Year Ended December 31, 2016

Sales		$1,180,000
Cost of merchandise sold		790,000
Gross profit		$ 390,000
Operating expenses:		
Depreciation expense	$ 7,000	
Other operating expenses	196,000	
Total operating expenses		203,000
Income from operations		$ 187,000
Other income:		
Gain on sale of land	$ 12,000	
Other expense:		
Interest expense	8,000	4,000
Income before income tax		$ 191,000
Income tax expense		83,000
Net income		$ 108,000

Rundell Inc.
Comparative Balance Sheet
December 31, 2016 and 2015

	2016	2015	Increase Decrease*
Assets			
Cash	$ 97,500	$ 26,000	$ 71,500
Accounts receivable (net)	74,000	65,000	9,000
Inventories	172,000	180,000	8,000*
Land	80,000	125,000	45,000*
Building	260,000	200,000	60,000
Accumulated depreciation—building	(65,300)	(58,300)	7,000**
Total assets	$618,200	$537,700	$ 80,500
Liabilities			
Accounts payable (merchandise creditors)	$ 43,500	$ 46,700	$ 3,200*
Accrued expenses payable (operating expenses)	26,500	24,300	2,200
Income taxes payable	7,900	8,400	500*
Dividends payable	14,000	10,000	4,000
Bonds payable	100,000	150,000	50,000*
Total liabilities	$191,900	$239,400	$ 47,500*
Stockholders' Equity			
Common stock ($2 par)	$ 24,000	$ 16,000	$ 8,000
Paid-in capital in excess of par	120,000	80,000	40,000
Retained earnings	282,300	202,300	80,000
Total stockholders' equity	$426,300	$298,300	$128,000
Total liabilities and stockholders' equity	$618,200	$537,700	$ 80,500

**There is a $7,000 increase to Accumulated Depreciation—Building, which is a contra asset account. As a result, the $7,000 increase in this account must be subtracted in summing to the increase in Total assets of $80,500.

[2] An appendix that discusses using a spreadsheet (work sheet) as an aid in assembling data for the statement of cash flows is presented at the end of this chapter. This appendix illustrates the use of this spreadsheet in reporting cash flows from operating activities using the indirect method.

Retained Earnings

The comparative balance sheet for **Rundell Inc.** shows that retained earnings increased $80,000 during the year. The retained earnings account that follows indicates how this change occurred:

Account *Retained Earnings* Account No.

Date		Item	Debit	Credit	Balance Debit	Balance Credit
2016 Jan.	1	Balance				202,300
Dec.	31	Net income		108,000		310,300
	31	Cash dividends	28,000			282,300

The retained earnings account indicates that the $80,000 ($108,000 − $28,000) change resulted from net income of $108,000 and cash dividends of $28,000. The net income of $108,000 is the first amount reported in the Cash Flows from Operating Activities section.

Adjustments to Net Income

The net income of $108,000 reported by **Rundell Inc.** does not equal the cash flows from operating activities for the period. This is because net income is determined using the accrual method of accounting.

Under the accrual method of accounting, revenues and expenses are recorded at different times from when cash is received or paid. For example, merchandise may be sold on account and the cash received at a later date. Likewise, insurance premiums may be paid in the current period but expensed in a following period.

Thus, under the indirect method, adjustments to net income must be made to determine cash flows from operating activities. The typical adjustments to net income are shown in Exhibit 5.[3]

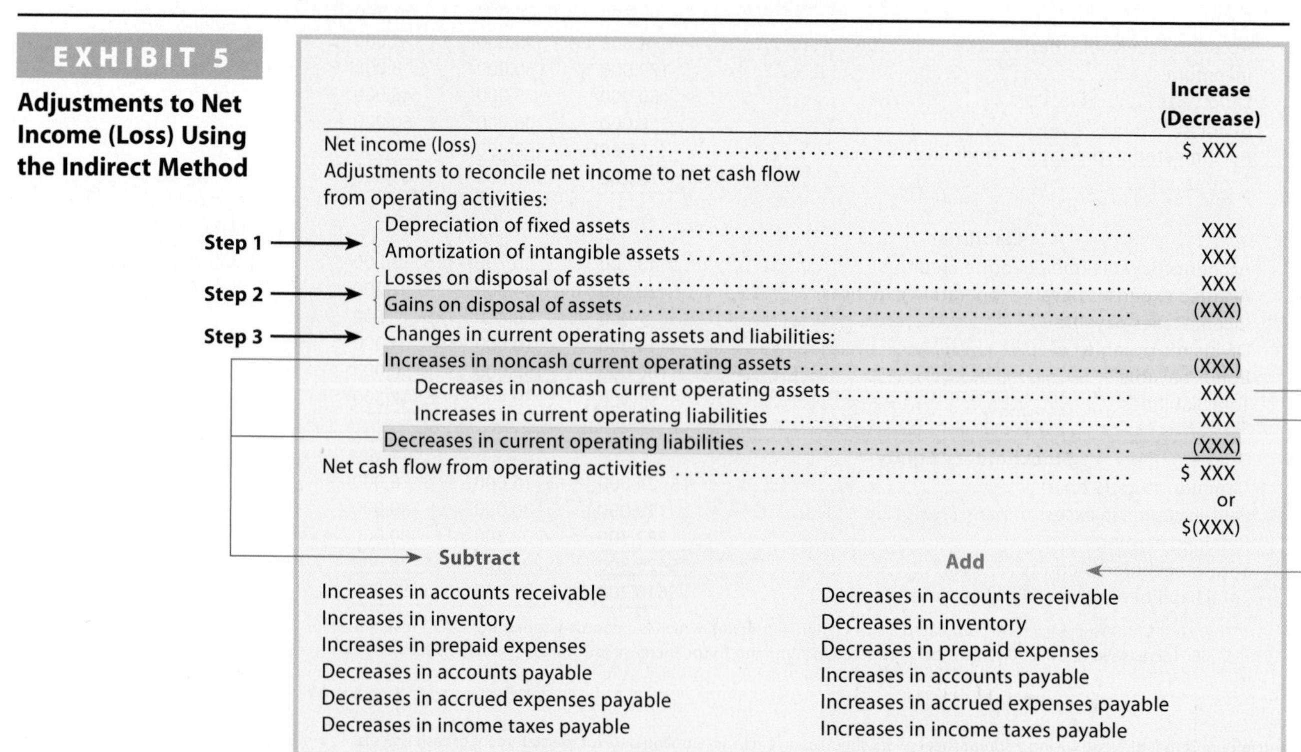

EXHIBIT 5

Adjustments to Net Income (Loss) Using the Indirect Method

		Increase (Decrease)
	Net income (loss)	$ XXX
	Adjustments to reconcile net income to net cash flow from operating activities:	
Step 1	Depreciation of fixed assets	XXX
	Amortization of intangible assets	XXX
Step 2	Losses on disposal of assets	XXX
	Gains on disposal of assets	(XXX)
Step 3	Changes in current operating assets and liabilities:	
	Increases in noncash current operating assets	(XXX)
	Decreases in noncash current operating assets	XXX
	Increases in current operating liabilities	XXX
	Decreases in current operating liabilities	(XXX)
	Net cash flow from operating activities	$ XXX or $(XXX)

Subtract	Add
Increases in accounts receivable	Decreases in accounts receivable
Increases in inventory	Decreases in inventory
Increases in prepaid expenses	Decreases in prepaid expenses
Decreases in accounts payable	Increases in accounts payable
Decreases in accrued expenses payable	Increases in accrued expenses payable
Decreases in income taxes payable	Increases in income taxes payable

[3] Other items that also require adjustments to net income to obtain cash flows from operating activities include amortization of bonds payable discounts (add), losses on debt retirement (add), amortization of bonds payable premiums (deduct), and gains on retirement of debt (deduct).

Net income is normally adjusted to cash flows from operating activities, using the following steps:

- Step 1. Expenses that do not affect cash are added. Such expenses decrease net income but do not involve cash payments and, thus, are added to net income.

  Example: Depreciation of fixed assets and amortization of intangible assets are added to net income.

- Step 2. Losses on the disposal of assets are added and gains on the disposal of assets are deducted. The disposal (sale) of assets is an investing activity rather than an operating activity. However, such losses and gains are reported as part of net income. As a result, any *losses* on disposal of assets are *added* back to net income. Likewise, any *gains* on disposal of assets are *deducted* from net income.

  Example: Land costing $100,000 is sold for $90,000. The loss of $10,000 is added back to net income.

- Step 3. Changes in current operating assets and liabilities are added or deducted as follows:

  - Increases in noncash current operating assets are deducted.
  - Decreases in noncash current operating assets are added.
  - Increases in current operating liabilities are added.
  - Decreases in current operating liabilities are deducted.

  Example: A sale of $10,000 on account increases sales, accounts receivable, and net income by $10,000. However, cash is not affected. Thus, the $10,000 increase in accounts receivable is deducted. Similar adjustments are required for the changes in the other current asset and liability accounts, such as inventory, prepaid expenses, accounts payable, accrued expenses payable, and income taxes payable, as shown in Exhibit 5.

Example Exercise 16-2 Adjustments to Net Income—Indirect Method

OBJ 2

Omni Corporation's accumulated depreciation increased by $12,000, while $3,400 of patent amortization was recognized between balance sheet dates. There were no purchases or sales of depreciable or intangible assets during the year. In addition, the income statement showed a gain of $4,100 from the sale of land. Reconcile Omni's net income of $50,000 to net cash flow from operating activities.

Follow My Example 16-2

Net income	$50,000
Adjustments to reconcile net income to net cash flow from operating activities:	
Depreciation	12,000
Amortization of patents	3,400
Gain from sale of land	(4,100)
Net cash flow from operating activities	$61,300

Practice Exercises: PE 16-2A, PE 16-2B

The Cash Flows from Operating Activities section of **Rundell Inc.'s** statement of cash flows is shown in Exhibit 6.

Rundell's net income of $108,000 is converted to cash flows from operating activities of $100,500 as follows:

Step 1. Add depreciation of $7,000.

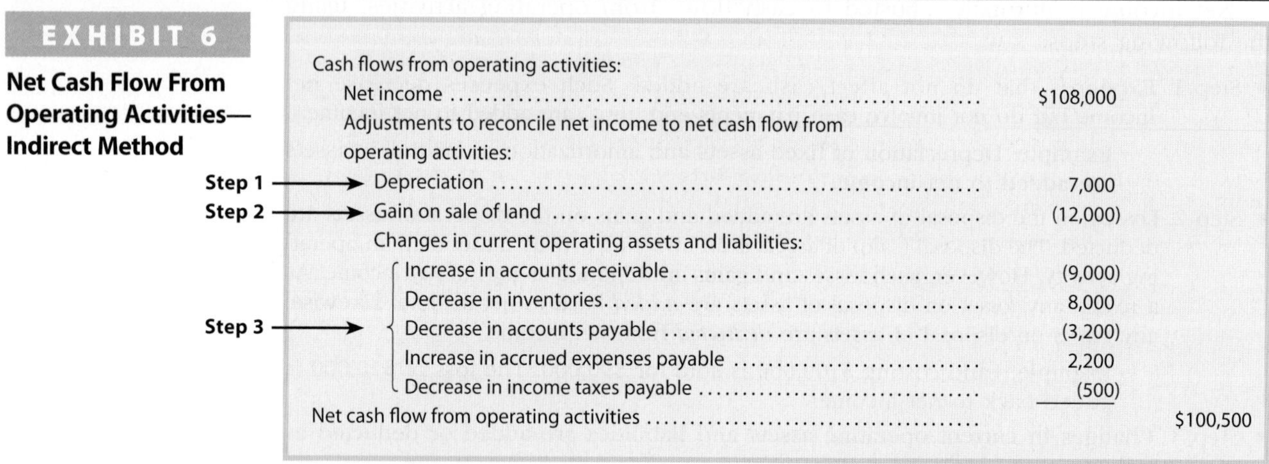

EXHIBIT 6

Net Cash Flow From Operating Activities—Indirect Method

Cash flows from operating activities:		
Net income		$108,000
Adjustments to reconcile net income to net cash flow from operating activities:		
Step 1 → Depreciation	7,000	
Step 2 → Gain on sale of land	(12,000)	
Changes in current operating assets and liabilities:		
Step 3 → Increase in accounts receivable	(9,000)	
Decrease in inventories	8,000	
Decrease in accounts payable	(3,200)	
Increase in accrued expenses payable	2,200	
Decrease in income taxes payable	(500)	
Net cash flow from operating activities		$100,500

Analysis: The comparative balance sheet in Exhibit 4 indicates that Accumulated Depreciation—Building increased by $7,000. The following account indicates that depreciation for the year was $7,000 for the building:

Account *Accumulated Depreciation—Building* — Account No.

Date		Item	Debit	Credit	Balance Debit	Balance Credit
2016						
Jan.	1	Balance				58,300
Dec.	31	Depreciation for year		7,000		65,300

Step 2. Deduct the gain on the sale of land of $12,000.
Analysis: The income statement in Exhibit 4 reports a gain of $12,000 from the sale of land. The proceeds, which include the gain, are reported in the Investing section of the statement of cash flows.[4] Thus, the gain of $12,000 is deducted from net income in determining cash flows from operating activities.

Step 3. Add and deduct changes in current operating assets and liabilities excluding cash.
Analysis: The increases and decreases in the current operating asset and current liability accounts excluding cash are as follows:

Accounts	December 31 2016	December 31 2015	Increase Decrease*
Accounts Receivable (net)	$ 74,000	$ 65,000	$9,000
Inventories	172,000	180,000	8,000*
Accounts Payable (merchandise creditors)	43,500	46,700	3,200*
Accrued Expenses Payable (operating expenses)	26,500	24,300	2,200
Income Taxes Payable	7,900	8,400	500*

Accounts receivable (net): The $9,000 increase is deducted from net income. This is because the $9,000 increase in accounts receivable indicates that sales on account were $9,000 more than the cash received from customers. Thus, sales (and net income) includes $9,000 that was not received in cash during the year.

Inventories: The $8,000 decrease is added to net income. This is because the $8,000 decrease in inventories indicates that the cost of merchandise *sold* exceeds the cost of the merchandise *purchased* during the year by $8,000. In other words, the cost of merchandise sold includes $8,000 of goods from inventory that were not purchased (used cash) during the year.

Accounts payable (merchandise creditors): The $3,200 decrease is deducted from net income. This is because a decrease in accounts payable indicates that the cash

[4] The reporting of the proceeds (cash flows) from the sale of land as part of investing activities is discussed later in this chapter.

payments to merchandise creditors exceed the merchandise *purchased on account* by \$3,200. Therefore, the cost of merchandise sold is \$3,200 less than the cash paid to merchandise creditors during the year.

Accrued expenses payable (operating expenses): The \$2,200 increase is added to net income. This is because an increase in accrued expenses payable indicates that operating expenses exceed the cash payments for operating expenses by \$2,200. In other words, operating expenses reported on the income statement include \$2,200 that did not require a cash outflow during the year.

Income taxes payable: The \$500 decrease is deducted from net income. This is because a decrease in income taxes payable indicates that taxes paid exceed the amount of taxes incurred during the year by \$500. In other words, the amount reported on the income statement for income tax expense is less than the amount paid by \$500.

Example Exercise 16-3 Changes in Current Operating Assets and Liabilities—Indirect Method

Victor Corporation's current operating assets and liabilities from the company's comparative balance sheet were as follows:

	Dec. 31, 2016	Dec. 31, 2015
Accounts receivable	\$ 6,500	\$ 4,900
Inventory	12,300	15,000
Accounts payable	4,800	5,200
Dividends payable	5,000	4,000

Adjust Victor's net income of \$70,000 for changes in operating assets and liabilities to arrive at cash flows from operating activities.

Follow My Example 16-3

Net income	\$70,000
Adjustments to reconcile net income to net cash flow from operating activities:	
Changes in current operating assets and liabilities:	
Increase in accounts receivable	(1,600)
Decrease in inventory	2,700
Decrease in accounts payable	(400)
Net cash flow from operating activities	\$70,700

Note: The change in dividends payable impacts the cash paid for dividends, which is disclosed under financing activities.

Practice Exercises: PE 16-3A, PE 16-3B

Using the preceding analyses, Rundell's net income of \$108,000 is converted to cash flows from operating activities of \$100,500 as shown in Exhibit 6.

Integrity, Objectivity, and Ethics in Business

CREDIT POLICY AND CASH FLOW

Investors frequently use net cash flow from operating activities to assess a company's financial health. If a company is financially healthy, net cash flow from operating activities should be roughly consistent with accrual basis net income. Questions arise, however, when a company's net cash flow from operating activities significantly lags net income. There are two scenarios which can cause this to happen:

- Sales on account are never collected in cash.
- Large cash purchases for inventory are never sold, or sell at a very slow pace.

Both of these scenarios increase net income, without a corresponding increase in net cash flow from operating activities. Prudent investors are often skeptical when they observe these scenarios and tend to avoid these types of investments until the cash flows become clear.

Source: Argersinger, M., "How Companies Fake It (With Cash Flow)," *Daily Finance Investor Center*, July 17, 2011.

Example Exercise 16-4 Cash Flows from Operating Activities—Indirect Method

OBJ 2

Omicron Inc. reported the following data:

Net income	$120,000
Depreciation expense	12,000
Loss on disposal of equipment	15,000
Increase in accounts receivable	5,000
Decrease in accounts payable	2,000

Prepare the Cash Flows from Operating Activities section of the statement of cash flows, using the indirect method.

Follow My Example 16-4

Cash flows from operating activities:		
Net income	$120,000	
Adjustments to reconcile net income to net cash flow from operating activities:		
Depreciation expense	12,000	
Loss on disposal of equipment	15,000	
Changes in current operating assets and liabilities:		
Increase in accounts receivable	(5,000)	
Decrease in accounts payable	(2,000)	
Net cash flow from operating activities		$140,000

Practice Exercises: PE 16-4A, PE 16-4B

Dividends

The retained earnings account of **Rundell Inc.** indicates cash dividends of $28,000 were declared during the year. However, the following dividends payable account indicates that only $24,000 of dividends were paid during the year:

Account *Dividends Payable* — Account No.

Date		Item	Debit	Credit	Balance Debit	Balance Credit
2016 Jan.	1	Balance				10,000
	10	Cash paid	10,000		—	—
June	20	Dividends declared		14,000		14,000
July	10	Cash paid	14,000		—	—
Dec.	20	Dividends declared		14,000		14,000

Because dividend payments are a financing activity, the dividend payment of $24,000 is reported in the Financing Activities section of the statement of cash flows, as follows:

Cash flows from financing activities:	
Cash paid for dividends	$24,000

Common Stock

The common stock account of **Rundell Inc.** increased by $8,000, and the paid-in capital in excess of par—common stock account increased by $40,000, as follows:

Account *Common Stock*						Account No.
					Balance	
Date		Item	Debit	Credit	Debit	Credit
2016 Jan.	1	Balance				16,000
Nov.	1	4,000 shares issued for cash		8,000		24,000

Account *Paid-In Capital in Excess of Par—Common Stock*						Account No.
					Balance	
Date		Item	Debit	Credit	Debit	Credit
2016 Jan.	1	Balance				80,000
Nov.	1	4,000 shares issued for cash		40,000		120,000

These increases were from issuing 4,000 shares of common stock for $12 per share. This cash inflow is reported in the Financing Activities section as follows:

Cash flows from financing activities:	
Cash received from sale of common stock	$48,000

Bonds Payable

The bonds payable account of **Rundell Inc.** decreased by $50,000, as follows:

Account *Bonds Payable*						Account No.
					Balance	
Date		Item	Debit	Credit	Debit	Credit
2016 Jan.	1	Balance				150,000
June	1	Retired by payment of cash at face amount	50,000			100,000

This decrease is from retiring the bonds by a cash payment for their face amount. This cash outflow is reported in the Financing Activities section as follows:

Cash flows from financing activities:	
Cash paid to retire bonds payable	$50,000

Building

The building account of **Rundell Inc.** increased by $60,000, and the accumulated depreciation—building account increased by $7,000, as follows:

Account *Building*						Account No.
					Balance	
Date		Item	Debit	Credit	Debit	Credit
2016 Jan.	1	Balance			200,000	
Dec.	27	Purchased for cash	60,000		260,000	

Account *Accumulated Depreciation—Building*						Account No.
					Balance	
Date		Item	Debit	Credit	Debit	Credit
2016 Jan.	1	Balance				58,300
Dec.	31	Depreciation for the year		7,000		65,300

The purchase of a building for cash of $60,000 is reported as an outflow of cash in the Investing Activities section as follows:

Cash flows from investing activities:	
Cash paid for purchase of building	$60,000

The credit in the accumulated depreciation—building account represents depreciation expense for the year. This depreciation expense of $7,000 on the building was added to net income in determining cash flows from operating activities, as reported in Exhibit 6.

Land

The $45,000 decline in the land account of **Rundell Inc.** was from two transactions, as follows:

Account *Land*						Account No.
					Balance	
Date		Item	Debit	Credit	Debit	Credit
2016 Jan.	1	Balance			125,000	
June	8	Sold for $72,000 cash		60,000	65,000	
Oct.	12	Purchased for $15,000 cash	15,000		80,000	

The June 8 transaction is the sale of land with a cost of $60,000 for $72,000 in cash. The $72,000 proceeds from the sale are reported in the Investing Activities section as follows:

Cash flows from investing activities:	
Cash received from sale of land	$72,000

The proceeds of $72,000 include the $12,000 gain on the sale of land and the $60,000 cost (book value) of the land. As shown in Exhibit 6, the $12,000 gain is deducted from net income in the Cash Flows from Operating Activities section. This is so that the $12,000 cash inflow related to the gain is not included twice as a cash inflow.

The October 12 transaction is the purchase of land for cash of $15,000. This transaction is reported as an outflow of cash in the Investing Activities section as follows:

Cash flows from investing activities:	
Cash paid for purchase of land	$15,000

Example Exercise 16-5 Land Transactions on the Statement of Cash Flows

Alpha Corporation purchased land for $125,000. Later in the year, the company sold a different piece of land with a book value of $165,000 for $200,000. How are the effects of these transactions reported on the statement of cash flows?

Follow My Example 16-5

The gain on the sale of the land is deducted from net income, as follows:

Gain on sale of land	$ (35,000)

The purchase and sale of land is reported as part of cash flows from investing activities, as follows:

Cash received from sale of land	$200,000
Cash paid for purchase of land	(125,000)

Practice Exercises: PE 16-5A, PE 16-5B

Preparing the Statement of Cash Flows

The statement of cash flows for **Rundell Inc.**, using the indirect method, is shown in Exhibit 7. The statement of cash flows indicates that cash increased by $71,500 during the year. The most significant increase in net cash flows ($100,500) was from operating activities. The most significant use of cash ($26,000) was for financing activities. The ending balance of cash on December 31, 2016, is $97,500. This ending cash balance is also reported on the December 31, 2016, balance sheet shown in Exhibit 4.

EXHIBIT 7

Statement of Cash Flows—Indirect Method

Rundell Inc.
Statement of Cash Flows
For the Year Ended December 31, 2016

Cash flows from operating activities:			
Net income		$108,000	
Adjustments to reconcile net income to net cash flow from operating activities:			
Depreciation		7,000	
Gain on sale of land		(12,000)	
Changes in current operating assets and liabilities:			
Increase in accounts receivable		(9,000)	
Decrease in inventories		8,000	
Decrease in accounts payable		(3,200)	
Increase in accrued expenses payable		2,200	
Decrease in income taxes payable		(500)	
Net cash flow from operating activities			$100,500
Cash flows from investing activities:			
Cash received from sale of land		$ 72,000	
Less: Cash paid for purchase of land	$15,000		
Cash paid for purchase of building	60,000	75,000	
Net cash flow used for investing activities			(3,000)
Cash flows from financing activities:			
Cash received from sale of common stock		$ 48,000	
Less: Cash paid to retire bonds payable	$50,000		
Cash paid for dividends	24,000	74,000	
Net cash flow used for financing activities			(26,000)
Increase in cash			$ 71,500
Cash at the beginning of the year			26,000
Cash at the end of the year			$ 97,500

OBJ 3 Prepare a statement of cash flows, using the direct method.

Preparing the Statement of Cash Flows—The Direct Method

The direct method reports cash flows from operating activities as follows:

Cash flows from operating activities:		
Cash received from customers		$ XXX
Less: Cash payments for merchandise	$ XXX	
Cash payments for operating expenses	XXX	
Cash payments for interest	XXX	
Cash payments for income taxes	XXX	XXX
Net cash flow from operating activities		$ XXX

The Cash Flows from Investing and Financing Activities sections of the statement of cash flows are exactly the same under both the direct and indirect methods. The amount of net cash flow from operating activities is also the same, but the manner in which it is reported is different.

Under the direct method, the income statement is adjusted to cash flows from operating activities as shown in Exhibit 8.

EXHIBIT 8

Converting Income Statement to Cash Flows from Operating Activities using the Direct Method

Income Statement	Adjusted to	Cash Flows from Operating Activities
Sales	→	Cash received from customers
Cost of merchandise sold	→	Cash payments for merchandise
Operating expenses:		
Depreciation expense	N/A	N/A
Other operating expenses	→	Cash payments for operating expenses
Gain on sale of land	N/A	N/A
Interest expense	→	Cash payments for interest
Income tax expense	→	Cash payments for income taxes
Net income	→	Net cash flow from operating activities

N/A—Not applicable

As shown in Exhibit 8, depreciation expense is not adjusted or reported as part of cash flows from operating activities. This is because deprecation expense does not involve a cash outflow. The gain on the sale of the land is also not adjusted and is not reported as part of cash flows from operating activities. This is because the cash flow from operating activities is determined directly, rather than by reconciling net income. The cash proceeds from the sale of the land are reported as an investing activity.

To illustrate the direct method, the income statement and comparative balance sheet for Rundell Inc., shown in Exhibit 4, are used.

Cash Received from Customers

The income statement (shown in Exhibit 4) of **Rundell Inc.** reports sales of $1,180,000. To determine the cash received from customers, the $1,180,000 is adjusted for any increase or decrease in accounts receivable. The adjustment is summarized in Exhibit 9.

EXHIBIT 9

Determining the Cash Received from Customers

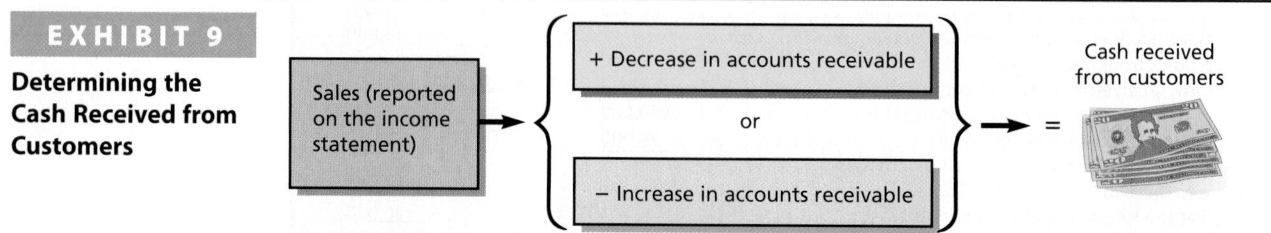

The cash received from customers is $1,171,000, computed as follows:

Sales	$1,180,000
Less increase in accounts receivable	9,000
Cash received from customers	$1,171,000

The increase of $9,000 in accounts receivable (shown in Exhibit 4) during 2016 indicates that sales on account exceeded cash received from customers by $9,000. In other words, sales include $9,000 that did not result in a cash inflow during the year. Thus, $9,000 is deducted from sales to determine the cash received from customers.

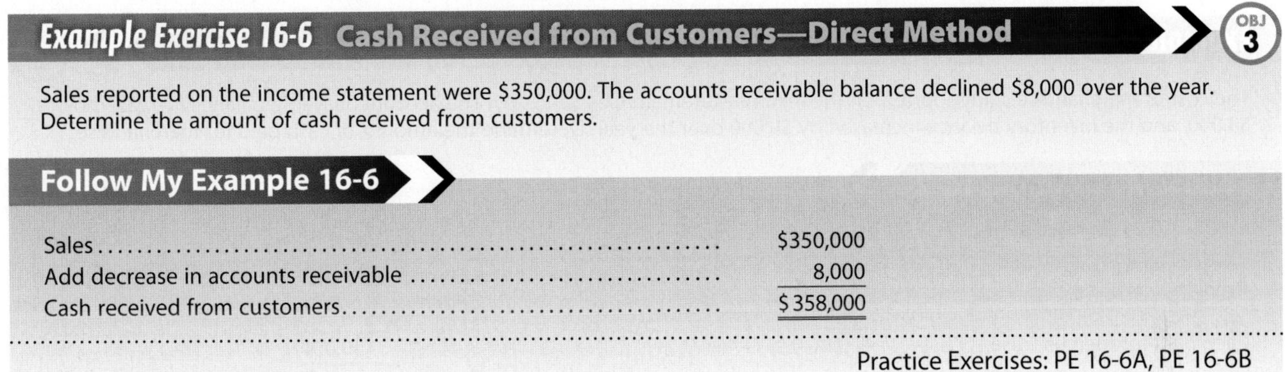

Example Exercise 16-6 Cash Received from Customers—Direct Method

OBJ 3

Sales reported on the income statement were $350,000. The accounts receivable balance declined $8,000 over the year. Determine the amount of cash received from customers.

Follow My Example 16-6

Sales	$350,000
Add decrease in accounts receivable	8,000
Cash received from customers	$358,000

Practice Exercises: PE 16-6A, PE 16-6B

Cash Payments for Merchandise

The income statement (shown in Exhibit 4) for **Rundell Inc.** reports cost of merchandise sold of $790,000. To determine the cash payments for merchandise, the $790,000 is adjusted for any increases or decreases in inventories and accounts payable. Assuming the accounts payable are owed to merchandise suppliers, the adjustment is summarized in Exhibit 10.

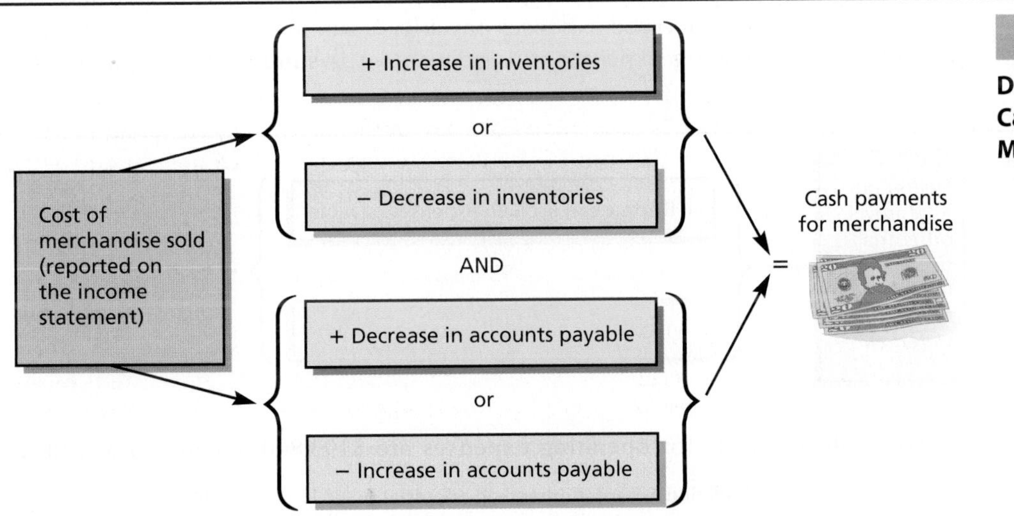

EXHIBIT 10

Determining the Cash Payments for Merchandise

The cash payments for merchandise are $785,200, computed as follows:

Cost of merchandise sold	$790,000
Deduct decrease in inventories	(8,000)
Add decrease in accounts payable	3,200
Cash payments for merchandise	$785,200

The $8,000 decrease in inventories (from Exhibit 4) indicates that the merchandise sold exceeded the cost of the merchandise purchased by $8,000. In other words, the cost of merchandise sold includes $8,000 of goods sold from inventory that did not require a cash outflow during the year. Thus, $8,000 is deducted from the cost of merchandise sold in determining the cash payments for merchandise.

The $3,200 decrease in accounts payable (from Exhibit 4) indicates that cash payments for merchandise were $3,200 more than the purchases on account during 2016. Therefore, $3,200 is added to the cost of merchandise sold in determining the cash payments for merchandise.

Example Exercise 16-7 Cash Payments for Merchandise—Direct Method

The cost of merchandise sold reported on the income statement was $145,000. The accounts payable balance increased by $4,000, and the inventory balance increased by $9,000 over the year. Determine the amount of cash paid for merchandise.

Follow My Example 16-7

Cost of merchandise sold	$145,000
Add increase in inventories	9,000
Deduct increase in accounts payable	(4,000)
Cash paid for merchandise	$150,000

Practice Exercises: PE 16-7A, PE 16-7B

Cash Payments for Operating Expenses

The income statement for **Rundell Inc.** (from Exhibit 4) reports total operating expenses of $203,000, which includes depreciation expense of $7,000. Because depreciation expense does not require a cash outflow, it is omitted from cash payments for operating expenses.

To determine the cash payments for operating expenses, the other operating expenses (excluding depreciation) of $196,000 ($203,000 − $7,000) are adjusted for any increase or decrease in accrued expenses payable. Assuming that the accrued expenses payable are all operating expenses, this adjustment is summarized in Exhibit 11.

EXHIBIT 11

Determining the Cash Payments for Operating Expenses

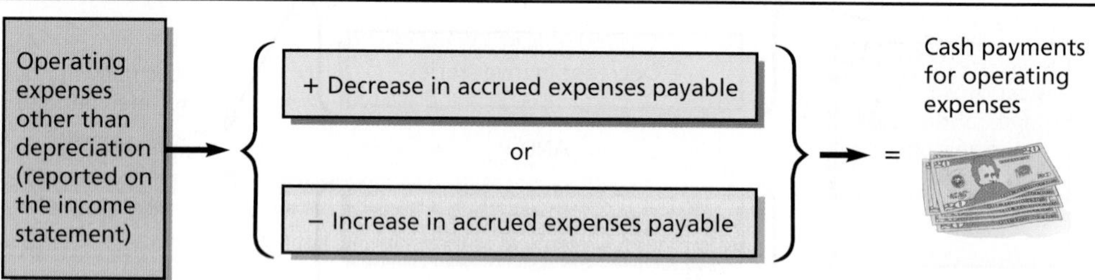

The cash payments for operating expenses are $193,800, computed as follows:

Operating expenses other than depreciation	$196,000
Deduct increase in accrued expenses payable	(2,200)
Cash payments for operating expenses	$193,800

The increase in accrued expenses payable (from Exhibit 4) indicates that the cash payments for operating expenses were $2,200 less than the amount reported for operating expenses during the year. Thus, $2,200 is deducted from the operating expenses in determining the cash payments for operating expenses.

Gain on Sale of Land

The income statement for **Rundell Inc.** (from Exhibit 4) reports a gain of $12,000 on the sale of land. The sale of land is an investing activity. Thus, the proceeds from the sale, which include the gain, are reported as part of the cash flows from investing activities.

Interest Expense

The income statement for **Rundell Inc.** (from Exhibit 4) reports interest expense of $8,000. To determine the cash payments for interest, the $8,000 is adjusted for any increases or decreases in interest payable. The adjustment is summarized in Exhibit 12.

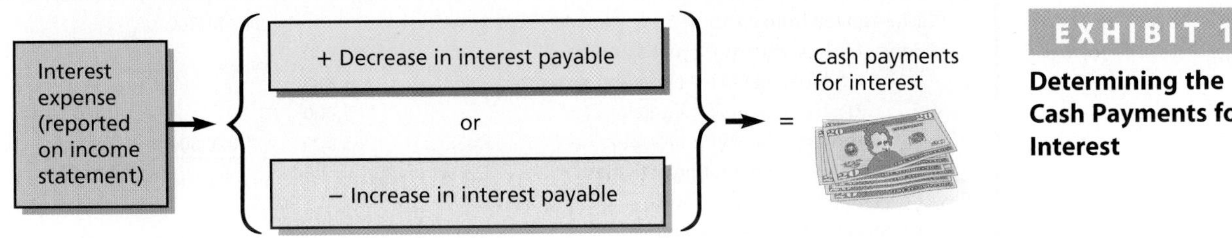

EXHIBIT 12

Determining the Cash Payments for Interest

The comparative balance sheet of Rundell in Exhibit 4 indicates no interest payable. This is because the interest expense on the bonds payable is paid on June 1 and December 31. Because there is no interest payable, no adjustment of the interest expense of $8,000 is necessary.

Cash Payments for Income Taxes

The income statement for **Rundell Inc.** (from Exhibit 3) reports income tax expense of $83,000. To determine the cash payments for income taxes, the $83,000 is adjusted for any increases or decreases in income taxes payable. The adjustment is summarized in Exhibit 13.

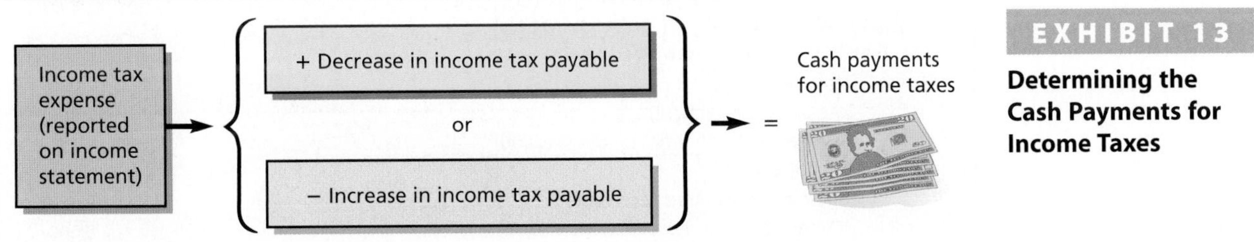

EXHIBIT 13

Determining the Cash Payments for Income Taxes

The cash payments for income taxes are $83,500, computed as follows:

Income tax expense	$83,000
Add decrease in income taxes payable	500
Cash payments for income taxes	$83,500

The $500 decrease in income taxes payable (from Exhibit 4) indicates that the cash payments for income taxes were $500 more than the amount reported for income tax expense during 2016. Thus, $500 is added to the income tax expense in determining the cash payments for income taxes.

Reporting Cash Flows from Operating Activities—Direct Method

The statement of cash flows for **Rundell Inc.**, using the direct method for reporting cash flows from operating activities, is shown in Exhibit 14. The portions of the statement that differ from those prepared under the indirect method are highlighted.

EXHIBIT 14

Statement of Cash Flows—Direct Method

Rundell Inc.
Statement of Cash Flows
For the Year Ended December 31, 2016

Cash flows from operating activities:			
Cash received from customers		$1,171,000	
Deduct: Cash payments for merchandise	$785,200		
Cash payments for operating expenses	193,800		
Cash payments for interest	8,000		
Cash payments for income taxes	83,500	1,070,500	
Net cash flow from operating activities			$100,500
Cash flows from investing activities:			
Cash received from sale of land		$ 72,000	
Less: Cash paid for purchase of land	$ 15,000		
Cash paid for purchase of building	60,000	75,000	
Net cash flow used for investing activities			(3,000)
Cash flows from financing activities:			
Cash received from sale of common stock		$ 48,000	
Less: Cash paid to retire bonds payable	$ 50,000		
Cash paid for dividends	24,000	74,000	
Net cash flow used for financing activities			(26,000)
Increase in cash			$ 71,500
Cash at the beginning of the year			26,000
Cash at the end of the year			$ 97,500
Schedule Reconciling Net Income with Cash Flows from Operating Activities:			
Cash flows from operating activities:			
Net income			$108,000
Adjustments to reconcile net income to net cash flow from operating activities:			
Depreciation			7,000
Gain on sale of land			(12,000)
Changes in current operating assets and liabilities:			
Increase in accounts receivable			(9,000)
Decrease in inventory			8,000
Decrease in accounts payable			(3,200)
Increase in accrued expenses payable			2,200
Decrease in income taxes payable			(500)
Net cash flow from operating activities			$100,500

Exhibit 14 also includes the separate schedule reconciling net income and net cash flow from operating activities. This schedule is included in the statement of cash flows when the direct method is used. This schedule is similar to the Cash Flows from Operating Activities section prepared under the indirect method.

International Connection

IFRS FOR STATEMENT OF CASH FLOWS

The statement of cash flows is required under International Financial Reporting Standards (IFRS). The statement of cash flows under IFRS is similar to that reported under U.S. GAAP in that the statement has separate sections for operating, investing, and financing activities. Like U.S. GAAP, IFRS also allow the use of either the indirect or direct method of reporting cash flows from operating activities. IFRS differ from U.S. GAAP in some minor areas, including:

- Interest paid can be reported as either an operating or a financing activity, while interest received can be reported as either an operating or an investing activity. In contrast, U.S. GAAP reports interest paid or received as an operating activity.
- Dividends paid can be reported as either an operating or a financing activity, while dividends received can be reported as either an operating or an investing activity. In contrast, U.S. GAAP reports dividends paid as a financing activity and dividends received as an operating activity.
- Cash flows to pay taxes are reported as a separate line in the operating activities, in contrast to U.S. GAAP, which does not require a separate line disclosure.

* IFRS are further discussed and illustrated in this chapter and in Appendix D.

Financial Analysis and Interpretation: Free Cash Flow

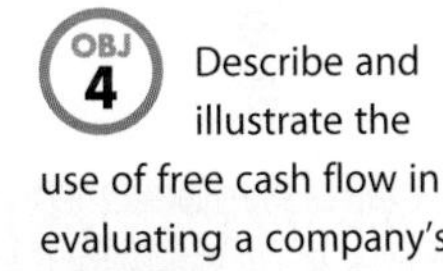

Describe and illustrate the use of free cash flow in evaluating a company's cash flow.

A valuable tool for evaluating the cash flows of a business is free cash flow. **Free cash flow** measures the operating cash flow available to a company to use after purchasing the property, plant, and equipment (PP&E) necessary to maintain current productive capacity.[5] It is computed as follows:

Cash flow from operating activities	$XXX
Less: Investments in PP&E needed to maintain current production	XXX
Free cash flow	$XXX

Analysts often use free cash flow, rather than cash flows from operating activities, to measure the financial strength of a business. Industries such as airlines, railroads, and telecommunications companies must invest heavily in new equipment to remain competitive. Such investments can significantly reduce free cash flow. For example, Verizon Communications Inc.'s free cash flow is approximately 51% of the cash flow from operating activities. In contrast, Apple Inc.'s free cash flow is approximately 89% of the cash flow from operating activities.

To illustrate, the cash flow from operating activities for Research in Motion, Inc., maker of BlackBerry® smartphones, was $2,912 million in a recent fiscal year. The statement of cash flows indicated that the cash invested in property, plant, and equipment was $902 million. Assuming that the amount invested in property, plant, and equipment is necessary to maintain productive capacity, free cash flow would be computed as follows (in millions):

Cash flow from operating activities	$2,912
Less: Investments in PP&E needed to maintain current production	902
Free cash flow	$2,010

Research in Motion's free cash flow was 69% of cash flow from operations and more than 10% of sales. Compare this to the calculation of free cash flows for Apple Inc.

[5] Productive capacity is the number of goods the company is currently producing and selling.

(a computer company), **The Coca-Cola Company** (a beverage company), and Verizon Communications, Inc. (a telecommunications company), that follows (in millions):

	Apple Inc.	The Coca-Cola Company	Verizon Communications, Inc.
Sales	$156,508	$48,017	$115,846
Cash flow from operating activities	50,856	10,645	31,486
Less: Investments in PP&E needed to maintain current production	8,295	2,870	16,175
Free cash flow	$ 42,561	$ 7,775	$ 15,311
Free cash flow as a percentage of cash flow from operations	84%	73%	49%
Free cash flow as a percentage of sales	27%	16%	13%

Positive free cash flow is considered favorable. A company that has free cash flow is able to fund internal growth, retire debt, pay dividends, and benefit from financial flexibility. A company with no free cash flow is unable to maintain current productive capacity. Lack of free cash flow can be an early indicator of liquidity problems. As one analyst notes, "Free cash flow gives the company firepower to reduce debt and ultimately generate consistent, actual income."[6]

Example Exercise 16-8 Free Cash Flow

Omnicron Inc. reported the following on the company's cash flow statement in 2016 and 2015:

	2016	2015
Net cash flow from operating activities	$140,000	$120,000
Net cash flow used for investing activities	(120,000)	(80,000)
Net cash flow used for financing activities	(20,000)	(32,000)

Seventy-five percent of the net cash flow used for investing activities was used to replace existing capacity.

a. Determine Omnicron's free cash flow.

b. Has Omnicron's free cash flow improved or declined from 2015 to 2016?

Follow My Example 16-8

a.

	2016	2015
Net cash flow from operating activities	$140,000	$120,000
Less: Investments in fixed assets to maintain current production	90,000[1]	60,000[2]
Free cash flow	$ 50,000	$ 60,000

[1] $120,000 × 75%
[2] $80,000 × 75%

b. The change from $60,000 to $50,000 indicates an unfavorable trend.

Practice Exercises: PE 16-8A, PE 16-8B

[6] Jill Krutick, *Fortune*, March 30, 1998, p. 106.

APPENDIX

Spreadsheet (Work Sheet) for Statement of Cash Flows—The Indirect Method

A spreadsheet (work sheet) may be used in preparing the statement of cash flows. However, whether or not a spreadsheet (work sheet) is used, the concepts presented in this chapter are not affected.

The data for **Rundell Inc.**, presented in Exhibit 4 are used as a basis for illustrating the spreadsheet (work sheet) for the indirect method. The steps in preparing this spreadsheet (work sheet), shown in Exhibit 15, are as follows:

- Step 1. List the title of each balance sheet account in the Accounts column.
- Step 2. For each balance sheet account, enter its balance as of December 31, 2015, in the first column and its balance as of December 31, 2016, in the last column. Place the credit balances in parentheses.
- Step 3. Add the December 31, 2015 and 2016 column totals, which should total to zero.
- Step 4. Analyze the change during the year in each noncash account to determine its net increase (decrease) and classify the change as affecting cash flows from operating activities, investing activities, financing activities, or noncash investing and financing activities.
- Step 5. Indicate the effect of the change on cash flows by making entries in the Transactions columns.
- Step 6. After all noncash accounts have been analyzed, enter the net increase (decrease) in cash during the period.
- Step 7. Add the Debit and Credit Transactions columns. The totals should be equal.

Analyzing Accounts

In analyzing the noncash accounts (Step 4), try to determine the type of cash flow activity (operating, investing, or financing) that led to the change in the account. As each noncash account is analyzed, an entry (Step 5) is made on the spreadsheet (work sheet) for the type of cash flow activity that caused the change. After all noncash accounts have been analyzed, an entry (Step 6) is made for the increase (decrease) in cash during the period.

The entries made on the spreadsheet are not posted to the ledger. They are only used in preparing and summarizing the data on the spreadsheet.

The order in which the accounts are analyzed is not important. However, it is more efficient to begin with Retained Earnings and proceed upward in the account listing.

Retained Earnings

The spreadsheet (work sheet) shows a Retained Earnings balance of $202,300 at December 31, 2015, and $282,300 at December 31, 2016. Thus, Retained Earnings increased $80,000 during the year. This increase is from the following:

- Net income of $108,000
- Declaring cash dividends of $28,000

To identify the cash flows from these activities, two entries are made on the spreadsheet.

EXHIBIT 15 **End-of-Period Spreadsheet (Work Sheet) for Statement of Cash Flows—Indirect Method**

Step 2 (columns C–F); Step 1 (rows 6–20); Step 3 (row 20 totals, columns B and G); Steps 4–7 (rows 21–40, columns C–F)

	A	B	C	D	E	F	G
1	Rundell Inc.						
2	End-of-Period Spreadsheet (Work Sheet) for Statement of Cash Flows						
3	For the Year Ended December 31, 2016						
4	Accounts	Balance,	Transactions				Balance,
5		Dec. 31, 2015	Debit		Credit		Dec. 31, 2016
6	Cash	26,000	(o)	71,500			97,500
7	Accounts receivable (net)	65,000	(n)	9,000			74,000
8	Inventories	180,000			(m)	8,000	172,000
9	Land	125,000	(k)	15,000	(l)	60,000	80,000
10	Building	200,000	(j)	60,000			260,000
11	Accumulated depreciation—building	(58,300)			(i)	7,000	(65,300)
12	Accounts payable (merchandise creditors)	(46,700)	(h)	3,200			(43,500)
13	Accrued expenses payable (operating expenses)	(24,300)			(g)	2,200	(26,500)
14	Income taxes payable	(8,400)	(f)	500			(7,900)
15	Dividends payable	(10,000)			(e)	4,000	(14,000)
16	Bonds payable	(150,000)	(d)	50,000			(100,000)
17	Common stock	(16,000)			(c)	8,000	(24,000)
18	Paid-in capital in excess of par	(80,000)			(c)	40,000	(120,000)
19	Retained earnings	(202,300)	(b)	28,000	(a)	108,000	(282,300)
20	Totals	0		237,200		237,200	0
21	Operating activities:						
22	Net income		(a)	108,000			
23	Depreciation of building		(i)	7,000			
24	Gain on sale of land				(l)	12,000	
25	Increase in accounts receivable				(n)	9,000	
26	Decrease in inventories		(m)	8,000			
27	Decrease in accounts payable				(h)	3,200	
28	Increase in accrued expenses payable		(g)	2,200			
29	Decrease in income taxes payable				(f)	500	
30	Investing activities:						
31	Sale of land		(l)	72,000			
32	Purchase of land				(k)	15,000	
33	Purchase of building				(j)	60,000	
34	Financing activities:						
35	Issued common stock		(c)	48,000			
36	Retired bonds payable				(d)	50,000	
37	Declared cash dividends				(b)	28,000	
38	Increase in dividends payable		(e)	4,000			
39	Net increase in cash				(o)	71,500	
40	Totals			249,200		249,200	

The $108,000 is reported on the statement of cash flows as part of cash flows from operating activities. Thus, an entry is made in the Transactions columns on the spreadsheet, as follows:

		Debit	Credit
(a)	Operating Activities—Net Income	108,000	
	Retained Earnings		108,000

The preceding entry accounts for the net income portion of the change to Retained Earnings. It also identifies the cash flow in the bottom portion of the spreadsheet as related to operating activities.

The $28,000 of dividends is reported as a financing activity on the statement of cash flows. Thus, an entry is made in the Transactions columns on the spreadsheet, as follows:

(b)	Retained Earnings	28,000	
	Financing Activities—Declared Cash Dividends		28,000

The preceding entry accounts for the dividends portion of the change to Retained Earnings. It also identifies the cash flow in the bottom portion of the spreadsheet as related to financing activities. The $28,000 of declared dividends will be adjusted later for the actual amount of cash dividends paid during the year.

Other Accounts

The entries for the other noncash accounts are made in the spreadsheet in a manner similar to entries (a) and (b). A summary of these entries follows:

(c)	Financing Activities—Issued Common Stock	48,000	
	Common Stock		8,000
	Paid-In Capital in Excess of Par—Common Stock		40,000
(d)	Bonds Payable	50,000	
	Financing Activities—Retired Bonds Payable		50,000
(e)	Financing Activities—Increase in Dividends Payable	4,000	
	Dividends Payable		4,000
(f)	Income Taxes Payable	500	
	Operating Activities—Decrease in Income Taxes Payable		500
(g)	Operating Activities—Increase in Accrued Expenses Payable	2,200	
	Accrued Expenses Payable		2,200
(h)	Accounts Payable	3,200	
	Operating Activities—Decrease in Accounts Payable		3,200
(i)	Operating Activities—Depreciation of Building	7,000	
	Accumulated Depreciation—Building		7,000
(j)	Building	60,000	
	Investing Activities—Purchase of Building		60,000
(k)	Land	15,000	
	Investing Activities—Purchase of Land		15,000
(l)	Investing Activities—Sale of Land	72,000	
	Operating Activities—Gain on Sale of Land		12,000
	Land		60,000
(m)	Operating Activities—Decrease in Inventories	8,000	
	Inventories		8,000
(n)	Accounts Receivable	9,000	
	Operating Activities—Increase in Accounts Receivable		9,000
(o)	Cash	71,500	
	Net Increase in Cash		71,500

After all the balance sheet accounts are analyzed and the entries made on the spreadsheet (work sheet), all the operating, investing, and financing activities are identified in the bottom portion of the spreadsheet. The accuracy of the entries is verified by totaling the Debit and Credit Transactions columns. The totals of the columns should be equal.

Preparing the Statement of Cash Flows

The statement of cash flows prepared from the spreadsheet is identical to the statement in Exhibit 7. The data for the three sections of the statement are obtained from the bottom portion of the spreadsheet.

At a Glance 16

Describe the cash flow activities reported in the statement of cash flows.

Key Points The statement of cash flows reports cash receipts and cash payments by three types of activities: operating activities, investing activities, and financing activities. Cash flows from operating activities reports the cash inflows and outflows from a company's day-to-day operations. Cash flows from investing activities reports the cash inflows and outflows related to changes in a company's long-term assets. Cash flows from financing activities reports the cash inflows and outflows related to changes in a company's long-term liabilities and stockholders' equity. Investing and financing for a business may be affected by transactions that do not involve cash. The effect of such transactions should be reported in a separate schedule accompanying the statement of cash flows.

Learning Outcome	*Example Exercises*	*Practice Exercises*
• Classify transactions that either provide or use cash into either operating, investing, or financing activities.	**EE16-1**	**PE16-1A, 16-1B**

Prepare a statement of cash flows, using the indirect method.

Key Points The indirect method reports cash flows from operating activities by adjusting net income for revenues and expenses that do not involve the receipt or payment of cash. Noncash expenses such as depreciation are added back to net income. Gains and losses on the disposal of assets are added to or deducted from net income. Changes in current operating assets and liabilities are added to or subtracted from net income, depending on their effect on cash. Cash flows from investing activities and cash flows from financing activities are reported below cash flows from operating activities in the statement of cash flows.

Learning Outcomes	*Example Exercises*	*Practice Exercises*
• Determine cash flows from operating activities under the indirect method by adjusting net income for noncash expenses and gains and losses from asset disposals.	**EE16-2**	**PE16-2A, 16-2B**
• Determine cash flows from operating activities under the indirect method by adjusting net income for changes in current operating assets and liabilities.	**EE16-3**	**PE16-3A, 16-3B**
• Prepare the Cash Flows from Operating Activities section of the statement of cash flows, using the indirect method.	**EE16-4**	**PE16-4A, 16-4B**
• Prepare the Cash Flows from Investing Activities and Cash Flows from Financing Activities sections of the statement of cash flows.	**EE16-5**	**PE16-5A, 16-5B**

Prepare a statement of cash flows, using the direct method.

Key Points The amount of cash flows from operating activities is the same under both the direct and indirect methods, but the manner in which cash flows operating activities is reported is different. The direct method reports cash flows from operating activities by major classes of operating cash receipts and cash payments. The difference between the major classes of total operating cash receipts and total operating cash payments is the net cash flow from operating activities. The Cash Flows from Investing and Financing Activities sections of the statement are the same under both the direct and indirect methods.

Learning Outcome	Example Exercises	Practice Exercises
• Prepare the cash flows from operating activities section of the statement of cash flows under the direct method.	**EE16-6** **EE16-7**	**PE16-6A, 16-6B** **PE16-7A, 16-7B**

Describe and illustrate the use of free cash flow in evaluating a company's cash flow.

Key Points Free cash flow measures the operating cash flow available for company use after purchasing the fixed assets that are necessary to maintain current productive capacity. It is calculated by subtracting these fixed asset purchases from net cash flow from operating activities. A company with strong free cash flow is able to fund internal growth, retire debt, pay dividends, and enjoy financial flexibility. A company with weak free cash flow has much less financial flexibility.

Learning Outcomes	Example Exercises	Practice Exercises
• Describe free cash flow.		
• Calculate and evaluate free cash flow.	**EE16-8**	**PE16-8A, 16-8B**

Key Terms

cash flow per share (744)
cash flows from financing activities (741)
cash flows from investing activities (740)
cash flows from operating activities (740)
direct method (741)
free cash flow (759)
indirect method (742)
statement of cash flows (740)

Illustrative Problem

The comparative balance sheet of Dowling Company for December 31, 2016 and 2015, is as follows:

Dowling Company
Comparative Balance Sheet
December 31, 2016 and 2015

	2016	2015
Assets		
Cash	$ 140,350	$ 95,900
Accounts receivable (net)	95,300	102,300
Inventories	165,200	157,900
Prepaid expenses	6,240	5,860
Investments (long-term)	35,700	84,700
Land	75,000	90,000
Buildings	375,000	260,000
Accumulated depreciation—buildings	(71,300)	(58,300)
Machinery and equipment	428,300	428,300
Accumulated depreciation—machinery and equipment	(148,500)	(138,000)
Patents	58,000	65,000
Total assets	$1,159,290	$1,093,660
Liabilities and Stockholders' Equity		
Accounts payable (merchandise creditors)	$ 43,500	$ 46,700
Accrued expenses payable (operating expenses)	14,000	12,500
Income taxes payable	7,900	8,400
Dividends payable	14,000	10,000
Mortgage note payable, due 2023	40,000	0
Bonds payable	150,000	250,000
Common stock, $30 par	450,000	375,000
Excess of issue price over par—common stock	66,250	41,250
Retained earnings	373,640	349,810
Total liabilities and stockholders' equity	$1,159,290	$1,093,660

The income statement for Dowling Company follows:

Dowling Company
Income Statement
For the Year Ended December 31, 2016

Sales		$1,100,000
Cost of merchandise sold		710,000
Gross profit		$ 390,000
Operating expenses:		
Depreciation expense	$ 23,500	
Patent amortization	7,000	
Other operating expenses	196,000	
Total operating expenses		226,500
Income from operations		$ 163,500
Other income:		
Gain on sale of investments	$ 11,000	
Other expense:		
Interest expense	26,000	(15,000)
Income before income tax		$ 148,500
Income tax expense		50,000
Net income		$ 98,500

An examination of the accounting records revealed the following additional information applicable to 2016:

a. Land costing $15,000 was sold for $15,000.

b. A mortgage note was issued for $40,000.

c. A building costing $115,000 was constructed.

d. 2,500 shares of common stock were issued at $40 in exchange for the bonds payable.

e. Cash dividends declared were $74,670.

Instructions

1. Prepare a statement of cash flows, using the indirect method of reporting cash flows from operating activities.
2. Prepare a statement of cash flows, using the direct method of reporting cash flows from operating activities.

Solution

1.

Dowling Company
Statement of Cash Flows—Indirect Method
For the Year Ended December 31, 2016

Cash flows from operating activities:			
Net income		$ 98,500	
Adjustments to reconcile net income to net cash flow from operating activities:			
Depreciation		23,500	
Amortization of patents		7,000	
Gain on sale of investments		(11,000)	
Changes in current operating assets and liabilities:			
Decrease in accounts receivable		7,000	
Increase in inventories		(7,300)	
Increase in prepaid expenses		(380)	
Decrease in accounts payable		(3,200)	
Increase in accrued expenses payable		1,500	
Decrease in income taxes payable		(500)	
Net cash flow from operating activities			$115,120
Cash flows from investing activities:			
Cash received from sale of:			
Investments	$60,000[1]		
Land	15,000	$ 75,000	
Less: Cash paid for construction of building		115,000	
Net cash flow used for investing activities			(40,000)
Cash flows from financing activities:			
Cash received from issuing mortgage note payable		$ 40,000	
Less: Cash paid for dividends		70,670[2]	
Net cash flow used for financing activities			(30,670)
Increase in cash			$ 44,450
Cash at the beginning of the year			95,900
Cash at the end of the year			$140,350

Schedule of Noncash Investing and Financing Activities:

Issued common stock to retire bonds payable	$100,000

[1] $60,000 = $11,000 gain + $49,000 (decrease in investments)

[2] $70,670 = $74,670 – $4,000 (increase in dividends)

2.

Dowling Company
Statement of Cash Flows—Direct Method
For the Year Ended December 31, 2016

Cash flows from operating activities:			
Cash received from customers[1]		$1,107,000	
Deduct: Cash paid for merchandise[2]	$720,500		
Cash paid for operating expenses[3]	194,880		
Cash paid for interest expense	26,000		
Cash paid for income tax[4]	50,500	991,880	
Net cash flow from operating activities			$115,120
Cash flows from investing activities:			
Cash received from sale of:			
Investments	$ 60,000[5]		
Land	15,000	$ 75,000	
Less: Cash paid for construction of building		115,000	
Net cash flow used for investing activities			(40,000)
Cash flows from financing activities:			
Cash received from issuing mortgage note payable		$ 40,000	
Less: Cash paid for dividends[6]		70,670	
Net cash flow used for financing activities			(30,670)
Increase in cash			$ 44,450
Cash at the beginning of the year			95,900
Cash at the end of the year			$140,350
Schedule of Noncash Investing and Financing Activities:			
Issued common stock to retire bonds payable			$100,000
Schedule Reconciling Net Income with Cash Flows from Operating Activities[7]			

Computations:

[1]$1,100,000 + $7,000 = $1,107,000
[2]$710,000 + $3,200 + $7,300 = $720,500
[3]$196,000 + $380 – $1,500 = $194,880
[4]$50,000 + $500 = $50,500
[5]$60,000 = $11,000 gain + $49,000 (decrease in investments)
[6]$74,670 + $10,000 – $14,000 = $70,670
[7]The content of this schedule is the same as the Operating Activities section of part (1) of this solution and is not reproduced here for the sake of brevity.

Discussion Questions

1. What is the principal disadvantage of the direct method of reporting cash flows from operating activities?
2. What are the major advantages of the indirect method of reporting cash flows from operating activities?
3. A corporation issued $2,000,000 of common stock in exchange for $2,000,000 of fixed assets. Where would this transaction be reported on the statement of cash flows?
4. A retail business, using the accrual method of accounting, owed merchandise creditors (accounts payable) $320,000 at the beginning of the year and $350,000 at the end of the year. How would the $30,000 increase be used to adjust net income in determining the amount of cash flows from operating activities by the indirect method? Explain.

5. If salaries payable was $100,000 at the beginning of the year and $75,000 at the end of the year, should $25,000 decrease be added to or deducted from income to determine the amount of cash flows from operating activities by the indirect method? Explain.

6. A long-term investment in bonds with a cost of $500,000 was sold for $600,000 cash. (a) What was the gain or loss on the sale? (b) What was the effect of the transaction on cash flows? (c) How should the transaction be reported on the statement of cash flows if cash flows from operating activities are reported by the indirect method?

7. A corporation issued $2,000,000 of 20-year bonds for cash at 98. How would the transaction be reported on the statement of cash flows?

8. Fully depreciated equipment costing $50,000 was discarded. What was the effect of the transaction on cash flows if (a) $15,000 cash is received for the equipment, (b) no cash is received for the equipment?

9. For the current year, Packers Company decided to switch from the indirect method to the direct method for reporting cash flows from operating activities on the statement of cash flows. Will the change cause the amount of net cash flow from operating activities to be larger, smaller, or the same as if the indirect method had been used? Explain.

10. Name five common major classes of operating cash receipts or operating cash payments presented on the statement of cash flows when the cash flows from operating activities are reported by the direct method.

Practice Exercises

EE 16-1 p. 744

SHOW ME HOW

PE 16-1A Classifying cash flows

OBJ. 1

Identify whether each of the following would be reported as an operating, investing, or financing activity on the statement of cash flows:

a. Repurchase of common stock
b. Cash received from customers
c. Payment of accounts payable
d. Retirement of bonds payable
e. Purchase of equipment
f. Purchase of inventory for cash

EE 16-1 p. 744

SHOW ME HOW

PE 16-1B Classifying cash flows

OBJ. 1

Identify whether each of the following would be reported as an operating, investing, or financing activity on the statement of cash flows:

a. Purchase of investments
b. Disposal of equipment
c. Payment for selling expenses
d. Collection of accounts receivable
e. Cash sales
f. Issuance of bonds payable

EE 16-2 p. 747

SHOW ME HOW

PE 16-2A Adjustments to net income—indirect method

OBJ. 2

Pearl Corporation's accumulated depreciation—furniture account increased by $8,400, while $3,080 of patent amortization was recognized between balance sheet dates. There were no purchases or sales of depreciable or intangible assets during the year. In addition, the income statement showed a loss of $4,480 from the sale of land. Reconcile a net income of $120,400 to net cash flow from operating activities.

EE 16-2 p. 747

SHOW ME HOW

PE 16-2B Adjustments to net income—indirect method

OBJ. 2

Ya Wen Corporation's accumulated depreciation—equipment account increased by $8,750, while $3,250 of patent amortization was recognized between balance sheet dates. There were no purchases or sales of depreciable or intangible assets during the year. In addition, the income statement showed a gain of $18,750 from the sale of investments. Reconcile a net income of $175,000 to net cash flow from operating activities.

EE 16-3 p. 749

PE 16-3A Changes in current operating assets and liabilities—indirect method **OBJ. 2**

Alpenrose Corporation's comparative balance sheet for current assets and liabilities was as follows:

	Dec. 31, 2016	Dec. 31, 2015
Accounts receivable	$27,000	$32,400
Inventory	18,000	15,480
Accounts payable	16,200	14,220
Dividends payable	49,500	53,100

Adjust net income of $207,000 for changes in operating assets and liabilities to arrive at net cash flow from operating activities.

EE 16-3 p. 749

PE 16-3B Changes in current operating assets and liabilities—indirect method **OBJ. 2**

Huluduey Corporation's comparative balance sheet for current assets and liabilities was as follows:

	Dec. 31, 2016	Dec. 31, 2015
Accounts receivable	$18,000	$14,400
Inventory	34,800	29,700
Accounts payable	27,600	20,700
Dividends payable	8,400	10,800

Adjust net income of $160,000 for changes in operating assets and liabilities to arrive at net cash flow from operating activities.

EE 16-4 p. 750

PE 16-4A Cash flows from operating activities—indirect method **OBJ. 2**

Pettygrove Inc. reported the following data:

Net income	$405,000
Depreciation expense	45,000
Gain on disposal of equipment	36,900
Decrease in accounts receivable	25,200
Decrease in accounts payable	6,480

Prepare the Cash Flows from Operating Activities section of the statement of cash flows, using the indirect method.

EE 16-4 p. 750

SHOW
ME HOW

PE 16-4B Cash flows from operating activities—indirect method **OBJ. 2**

Staley Inc. reported the following data:

Net income	$280,000
Depreciation expense	48,000
Loss on disposal of equipment	19,520
Increase in accounts receivable	17,280
Increase in accounts payable	8,960

Prepare the Cash Flows from Operating Activities section of the statement of cash flows, using the indirect method.

EE 16-5 p. 753

PE 16-5A Land transactions on the statement of cash flows **OBJ. 2**

Milo Corporation purchased land for $540,000. Later in the year, the company sold a different piece of land with a book value of $270,000 for $180,000. How are the effects of these transactions reported on the statement of cash flows?

EE 16-5 p. 753

SHOW ME HOW

PE 16-5B Land transactions on the statement of cash flows **OBJ. 2**

IZ Corporation purchased land for $400,000. Later in the year, the company sold a different piece of land with a book value of $200,000 for $240,000. How are the effects of these transactions reported on the statement of cash flows?

EE 16-6 p. 755

SHOW ME HOW

PE 16-6A Cash received from customers—direct method **OBJ. 3**

Sales reported on the income statement were $480,000. The accounts receivable balance increased $54,000 over the year. Determine the amount of cash received from customers.

EE 16-6 p. 755

SHOW ME HOW

PE 16-6B Cash received from customers—direct method **OBJ. 3**

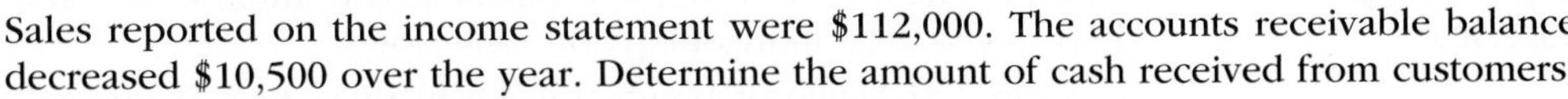

Sales reported on the income statement were $112,000. The accounts receivable balance decreased $10,500 over the year. Determine the amount of cash received from customers.

EE 16-7 p. 756

SHOW ME HOW

PE 16-7A Cash payments for merchandise—direct method **OBJ. 3**

The cost of merchandise sold reported on the income statement was $770,000. The accounts payable balance decreased $44,000, and the inventory balance decreased by $66,000 over the year. Determine the amount of cash paid for merchandise.

EE 16-7 p. 756

SHOW ME HOW

PE 16-7B Cash payments for merchandise—direct method **OBJ. 3**

The cost of merchandise sold reported on the income statement was $240,000. The accounts payable balance increased $12,000, and the inventory balance increased by $19,200 over the year. Determine the amount of cash paid for merchandise.

EE 16-8 p. 760

SHOW ME HOW

PE 16-8A Free cash flow **OBJ. 4**

McMahon Inc. reported the following on the company's statement of cash flows in 2016 and 2015:

	2016	2015
Net cash flow from operating activities	$ 294,000	$ 280,000
Net cash flow used for investing activities	(224,000)	(252,000)
Net cash flow used for financing activities	(63,000)	(42,000)

Seventy percent of the net cash flow used for investing activities was used to replace existing capacity.

a. Determine McMahon's free cash flow for both years.

b. Has McMahon's free cash flow improved or declined from 2015 to 2016?

EE 16-8 p. 760

SHOW ME HOW

PE 16-8B Free cash flow **OBJ. 4**

Dillin Inc. reported the following on the company's statement of cash flows in 2016 and 2015:

	2016	2015
Net cash flow from operating activities	$476,000	$455,000
Net cash flow used for investing activities	(427,000)	(378,000)
Net cash flow used for financing activities	(42,000)	(58,800)

Eighty percent of the net cash flow used for investing activities was used to replace existing capacity.

a. Determine Dillin's free cash flow for both years.

b. Has Dillin's free cash flow improved or declined from 2015 to 2016?

Exercises

EX 16-1 Cash flows from operating activities—net loss OBJ. 1

On its income statement for a recent year, United Continental Holdings, Inc., the parent company of United Airlines, reported a net *loss* of $723 million from operations. On its statement of cash flows, it reported $935 million of cash flows from operating activities.

Explain this apparent contradiction between the loss and the positive cash flows.

EX 16-2 Effect of transactions on cash flows OBJ. 1

✔ a. Cash payment, $525,000

State the effect (cash receipt or payment and amount) of each of the following transactions, considered individually, on cash flows:

a. Retired $500,000 of bonds, on which there was $5,000 of unamortized discount, for $525,000.
b. Sold 6,000 shares of $20 par common stock for $30 per share.
c. Sold equipment with a book value of $98,200 for $117,500.
d. Purchased land for $322,000 cash.
e. Purchased a building by paying $75,000 cash and issuing a $62,500 mortgage note payable.
f. Sold a new issue of $300,000 of bonds at 101.
g. Purchased 2,500 shares of $40 par common stock as treasury stock at $50 per share.
h. Paid dividends of $2.00 per share. There were 50,000 shares issued and 10,000 shares of treasury stock.

EX 16-3 Classifying cash flows OBJ. 1

Identify the type of cash flow activity for each of the following events (operating, investing, or financing):

a. Net income
b. Paid cash dividends
c. Issued common stock
d. Issued bonds
e. Redeemed bonds
f. Sold long-term investments
g. Purchased treasury stock
h. Sold equipment
i. Issued preferred stock
j. Purchased buildings
k. Purchased patents

EX 16-4 Cash flows from operating activities—indirect method OBJ. 2

Indicate whether each of the following would be added to or deducted from net income in determining net cash flow from operating activities by the indirect method:

a. Decrease in merchandise inventory
b. Increase in accounts receivable
c. Increase in accounts payable
d. Loss on retirement of long-term debt
e. Depreciation of fixed assets
f. Decrease in notes receivable due in 60 days from customers
g. Increase in salaries payable
h. Decrease in prepaid expenses
i. Amortization of patent
j. Increase in notes payable due in 120 days to vendors
k. Gain on disposal of fixed assets

EX 16-5 Cash flows from operating activities—indirect method **OBJ. 1, 2**

✔ Net cash flow from operating activities, $417,600

The net income reported on the income statement for the current year was $400,000. Depreciation recorded on store equipment for the year amounted to $16,000. Balances of the current asset and current liability accounts at the beginning and end of the year are as follows:

	End of Year	Beginning of Year
Cash	$41,600	$38,400
Accounts receivable (net)	30,400	28,000
Merchandise inventory	40,000	44,000
Prepaid expenses	4,800	3,600
Accounts payable (merchandise creditors)	40,000	36,000
Wages payable	21,200	24,000

a. Prepare the Cash Flows from Operating Activities section of the statement of cash flows, using the indirect method.

b. Briefly explain why net cash flow from operating activities is different than net income.

EX 16-6 Cash flows from operating activities—indirect method **OBJ. 1, 2**

✔ Net cash flow from operating activities, $394,400

The net income reported on the income statement for the current year was $320,000. Depreciation recorded on equipment and a building amounted to $96,000 for the year. Balances of the current asset and current liability accounts at the beginning and end of the year are as follows:

	End of Year	Beginning of Year
Cash	$ 89,600	$ 96,000
Accounts receivable (net)	112,000	118,400
Inventories	224,000	200,000
Prepaid expenses	12,800	14,400
Accounts payable (merchandise creditors)	96,000	104,000
Salaries payable	16,000	13,600

a. Prepare the Cash Flows from Operating Activities section of the statement of cash flows, using the indirect method.

b. If the direct method had been used, would the net cash flow from operating activities have been the same? Explain.

EX 16-7 Cash flows from operating activities—indirect method **OBJ. 1, 2**

✔ Net cash flow from operating activities, $525,410

The income statement disclosed the following items for 2016:

Depreciation expense	$ 57,600
Gain on disposal of equipment	33,600
Net income	508,000

Balances of the current assets and current liability accounts changed between December 31, 2015, and December 31, 2016, as follows:

	Increase (Decrease)
Accounts receivable	$8,960
Inventory	(5,120)
Prepaid insurance	(1,920)
Accounts payable	(6,080)
Income taxes payable	1,410
Dividends payable	2,200

a. Prepare the Cash Flows from Operating Activities section of the statement of cash flows, using the indirect method.

b. Briefly explain why net cash flows from operating activities is different than net income.

EX 16-8 Determining cash payments to stockholders — OBJ. 2

SHOW ME HOW

The board of directors declared cash dividends totaling $585,000 during the current year. The comparative balance sheet indicates dividends payable of $167,625 at the beginning of the year and $146,250 at the end of the year. What was the amount of cash payments to stockholders during the year?

EX 16-9 Reporting changes in equipment on statement of cash flows — OBJ. 2

An analysis of the general ledger accounts indicates that office equipment, which cost $202,500 and on which accumulated depreciation totaled $84,375 on the date of sale, was sold for $101,250 during the year. Using this information, indicate the items to be reported on the statement of cash flows.

EX 16-10 Reporting changes in equipment on statement of cash flows — OBJ. 2

An analysis of the general ledger accounts indicates that delivery equipment, which cost $80,000 and on which accumulated depreciation totaled $36,000 on the date of sale, was sold for $37,200 during the year. Using this information, indicate the items to be reported on the statement of cash flows.

EX 16-11 Reporting land transactions on statement of cash flows — OBJ. 2

On the basis of the details of the following fixed asset account, indicate the items to be reported on the statement of cash flows:

ACCOUNT *Land* **ACCOUNT NO.**

Date		Item	Debit	Credit	Balance Debit	Balance Credit
2016						
Jan.	1	Balance			868,000	
Mar.	12	Purchased for cash	104,300		972,300	
Oct.	4	Sold for $95,550		63,840	908,460	

EX 16-12 Reporting stockholders' equity items on statement of cash flows — OBJ. 2

On the basis of the following stockholders' equity accounts, indicate the items, exclusive of net income, to be reported on the statement of cash flows. There were no unpaid dividends at either the beginning or the end of the year.

ACCOUNT *Common Stock, $40 par* **ACCOUNT NO.**

Date		Item	Debit	Credit	Balance Debit	Balance Credit
2016						
Jan.	1	Balance, 120,000 shares				4,800,000
Apr.	2	30,000 shares issued for cash		1,200,000		6,000,000
June	30	4,400-share stock dividend		176,000		6,176,000

ACCOUNT *Paid-In Capital in Excess of Par—Common Stock* **ACCOUNT NO.**

Date		Item	Debit	Credit	Balance Debit	Balance Credit
2016						
Jan.	1	Balance				360,000
Apr.	2	30,000 shares issued for cash		720,000		1,080,000
June	30	Stock dividend		114,400		1,194,400

ACCOUNT *Retained Earnings* ACCOUNT NO.

Date		Item	Debit	Credit	Balance	
					Debit	Credit
2016						
Jan.	1	Balance				2,000,000
June	30	Stock dividend	290,440			1,709,560
Dec.	30	Cash dividend	463,200			1,246,360
	31	Net income		1,440,000		2,686,360

EX 16-13 Reporting land acquisition for cash and mortgage note on statement of cash flows **OBJ. 2**

On the basis of the details of the following fixed asset account, indicate the items to be reported on the statement of cash flows:

ACCOUNT *Land* ACCOUNT NO.

Date		Item	Debit	Credit	Balance	
					Debit	Credit
2016						
Jan.	1	Balance			156,000	
Feb.	10	Purchased for cash	246,000		402,000	
Nov.	20	Purchased with long-term mortgage note	324,000		726,000	

EX 16-14 Reporting issuance and retirement of long-term debt **OBJ. 2**

On the basis of the details of the following bonds payable and related discount accounts, indicate the items to be reported in the Financing Activities section of the statement of cash flows, assuming no gain or loss on retiring the bonds:

ACCOUNT *Bonds Payable* ACCOUNT NO.

Date		Item	Debit	Credit	Balance	
					Debit	Credit
2016						
Jan.	1	Balance				750,000
	2	Retire bonds	150,000			600,000
June	30	Issue bonds		450,000		1,050,000

ACCOUNT *Discount on Bonds Payable* ACCOUNT NO.

Date		Item	Debit	Credit	Balance	
					Debit	Credit
2016						
Jan.	1	Balance			33,750	
	2	Retire bonds		12,000	21,750	
June	30	Issue bonds	30,000		51,750	
Dec.	31	Amortize discount		2,625	49,125	

EX 16-15 Determining net income from net cash flow from operating activities OBJ. 2

✔ Net income, $341,770

SHOW ME HOW

Curwen Inc. reported net cash flow from operating activities of $357,500 on its statement of cash flows for the year ended December 31, 2016. The following information was reported in the Cash Flows from Operating Activities section of the statement of cash flows, using the indirect method:

Decrease in income taxes payable	$ 7,700
Decrease in inventories	19,140
Depreciation	29,480
Gain on sale of investments	13,200
Increase in accounts payable	5,280
Increase in prepaid expenses	2,970
Increase in accounts receivable	14,300

a. Determine the net income reported by Curwen Inc. for the year ended December 31, 2016.

b. Briefly explain why Curwen's net income is different than net cash flow from operating activities.

EX 16-16 Cash flows from operating activities—indirect method OBJ. 2

✔ Net cash flow from operating activities, $42,174

Selected data derived from the income statement and balance sheet of National Beverage Co. for a recent year are as follows:

Income statement data (in thousands):	
Net earnings (loss)	$43,993
Losses on inventory write-down and fixed assets	7
Depreciation expense	10,174
Stock-based compensation expense (noncash)	290
Balance sheet data (in thousands):	
Increase in accounts receivable	5,679
Increase in inventory	7,509
Decrease in prepaid expenses	2,239
Decrease in accounts payable and other current liabilities	1,341

a. Prepare the Cash Flows from Operating Activities section of the statement of cash flows, using the indirect method for National Beverage Co.

b. Interpret your results in part (a).

EX 16-17 Statement of cash flows—indirect method OBJ. 2

✔ Net cash flow from operating activities, $150

SHOW ME HOW

The comparative balance sheet of Pelican Joe Industries Inc. for December 31, 2016 and 2015, is as follows:

	Dec. 31, 2016	Dec. 31, 2015
Assets		
Cash	$ 490	$ 160
Accounts receivable (net)	280	200
Inventories	175	110
Land	400	450
Equipment	225	175
Accumulated depreciation—equipment	(60)	(30)
Total assets	$1,510	$1,065
Liabilities and Stockholders' Equity		
Accounts payable (merchandise creditors)	$ 175	$ 160
Dividends payable	30	—
Common stock, $10 par	100	50
Paid-in capital: Excess of issue price over par—common stock	250	125
Retained earnings	955	730
Total liabilities and stockholders' equity	$1,510	$1,065

The following additional information is taken from the records:

1. Land was sold for $125.
2. Equipment was acquired for cash.
3. There were no disposals of equipment during the year.
4. The common stock was issued for cash.
5. There was a $325 credit to Retained Earnings for net income.
6. There was an $100 debit to Retained Earnings for cash dividends declared.

a. Prepare a statement of cash flows, using the indirect method of presenting cash flows from operating activities.

b. Was Pelican Joe Industries Inc. net cash flow from operations more or less than net income? What is the source of this difference?

EX 16-18 Statement of cash flows—indirect method OBJ. 2

List the errors you find in the following statement of cash flows. The cash balance at the beginning of the year was $240,000. All other amounts are correct, except the cash balance at the end of the year.

Shasta Inc.
Statement of Cash Flows
For the Year Ended December 31, 2016

Cash flows from operating activities:			
Net income		$360,000	
Adjustments to reconcile net income to net cash flow from operating activities:			
Depreciation		100,800	
Gain on sale of investments		17,280	
Changes in current operating assets and liabilities:			
Increase in accounts receivable		27,360	
Increase in inventories		(36,000)	
Increase in accounts payable		(3,600)	
Decrease in accrued expenses payable		(2,400)	
Net cash flow from operating activities			$ 463,440
Cash flows from investing activities:			
Cash received from sale of investments		$240,000	
Less: Cash paid for purchase of land	$259,200		
Cash paid for purchase of equipment	432,000	691,200	
Net cash flow used for investing activities			(415,200)
Cash flows from financing activities:			
Cash received from sale of common stock		$312,000	
Cash paid for dividends		132,000	
Net cash flow from financing activities			180,000
Increase in cash			$ 47,760
Cash at the end of the year			192,240
Cash at the beginning of the year			$ 240,000

EX 16-19 Cash flows from operating activities—direct method OBJ. 3

✔ a. $801,900

The cash flows from operating activities are reported by the direct method on the statement of cash flows. Determine the following:

a. If sales for the current year were $753,500 and accounts receivable decreased by $48,400 during the year, what was the amount of cash received from customers?

b. If income tax expense for the current year was $50,600 and income tax payable decreased by $5,500 during the year, what was the amount of cash payments for income taxes?

c. Briefly explain why the cash received from customers in (a) is different than sales.

EX 16-20 Cash paid for merchandise purchases OBJ. 3

The cost of merchandise sold for Kohl's Corporation for a recent year was $11,625 million. The balance sheet showed the following current account balances (in millions):

	Balance, End of Year	Balance, Beginning of Year
Merchandise inventories	$3,199	$3,036
Accounts payable	1,233	1,138

Determine the amount of cash payments for merchandise.

EX 16-21 Determining selected amounts for cash flows from operating activities—direct method OBJ. 3

✔ a. $1,025,800

Selected data taken from the accounting records of Ginis Inc. for the current year ended December 31 are as follows:

	Balance, December 31	Balance, January 1
Accrued expenses payable (operating expenses)	$ 12,650	$ 14,030
Accounts payable (merchandise creditors)	96,140	105,800
Inventories	178,020	193,430
Prepaid expenses	7,360	8,970

During the current year, the cost of merchandise sold was $1,031,550, and the operating expenses other than depreciation were $179,400. The direct method is used for presenting the cash flows from operating activities on the statement of cash flows.

Determine the amount reported on the statement of cash flows for (a) cash payments for merchandise and (b) cash payments for operating expenses.

EX 16-22 Cash flows from operating activities—direct method OBJ. 3

✔ Net cash flow from operating activities, $96,040

The income statement of Booker T Industries Inc. for the current year ended June 30 is as follows:

Sales		$511,000
Cost of merchandise sold		290,500
Gross profit		$220,500
Operating expenses:		
Depreciation expense	$ 39,200	
Other operating expenses	105,000	
Total operating expenses		144,200
Income before income tax		$ 76,300
Income tax expense		21,700
Net income		$ 54,600

Changes in the balances of selected accounts from the beginning to the end of the current year are as follows:

	Increase (Decrease)
Accounts receivable (net)	($11,760)
Inventories	3,920
Prepaid expenses	(3,780)
Accounts payable (merchandise creditors)	(7,980)
Accrued expenses payable (operating expenses)	1,260
Income tax payable	(2,660)

a. Prepare the Cash Flows from Operating Activities section of the statement of cash flows, using the direct method.

b. What does the direct method show about a company's cash flows from operating activities that is not shown using the indirect method?

EX 16-23 Cash flows from operating activities—direct method

OBJ. 3

✔ Net cash flow from operating activities, $123,860

The income statement for Rhino Company for the current year ended June 30 and balances of selected accounts at the beginning and the end of the year are as follows:

Sales		$445,500
Cost of merchandise sold		154,000
Gross profit		$291,500
Operating expenses:		
Depreciation expense	$ 38,500	
Other operating expenses	115,280	
Total operating expenses		153,780
Income before income tax		$137,720
Income tax expense		39,600
Net income		$ 98,120

	End of Year	Beginning of Year
Accounts receivable (net)	$36,300	$31,240
Inventories	92,400	80,300
Prepaid expenses	14,520	15,840
Accounts payable (merchandise creditors)	67,540	62,700
Accrued expenses payable (operating expenses)	19,140	20,900
Income tax payable	4,400	4,400

Prepare the Cash Flows from Operating Activities section of the statement of cash flows, using the direct method.

EX 16-24 Free cash flow

OBJ. 4

SHOW ME HOW

Sweeter Enterprises Inc. has cash flows from operating activities of $539,000. Cash flows used for investments in property, plant, and equipment totaled $210,000, of which 75% of this investment was used to replace existing capacity.

a. Determine the free cash flow for Sweeter Enterprises Inc.

b. How might a lender use free cash flow to determine whether or not to give Sweeter Enterprises Inc. a loan?

EX 16-25 Free cash flow

OBJ. 4

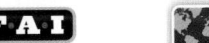

The financial statements for **Nike, Inc.**, are provided in Appendix C at the end of the text.

a. Determine the free cash flow for the most recent fiscal year. Assume that 90% of the additions to property, plant, and equipment were used to maintain productive capacity. Round to the nearest thousand dollars.

b. How might a lender use free cash flow to determine whether or not to give Nike, Inc., a loan?

c. Would you feel comfortable giving Nike a loan, based on the free cash flow calculated in (a)?

EX 16-26 Free cash flow

OBJ. 4

Lovato Motors Inc. has cash flows from operating activities of $720,000. Cash flows used for investments in property, plant, and equipment totaled $440,000, of which 85% of this investment was used to replace existing capacity.

Determine the free cash flow for Lovato Motors Inc.

Problems: Series A

PR 16-1A Statement of cash flows—indirect method

OBJ. 2

✔ Net cash flow from operating activities, $143,540

SHOW ME HOW

The comparative balance sheet of Cromme Inc. for December 31, 2016 and 2015, is shown as follows:

	Dec. 31, 2016	Dec. 31, 2015
Assets		
Cash	$ 625,760	$ 585,920
Accounts receivable (net)	227,840	208,960
Inventories	641,760	617,120
Investments	0	240,000
Land	328,000	0
Equipment	705,120	553,120
Accumulated depreciation—equipment	(166,400)	(148,000)
Total assets	$2,362,080	$2,057,120
Liabilities and Stockholders' Equity		
Accounts payable (merchandise creditors)	$ 424,480	$ 404,960
Accrued expenses payable (operating expenses)	42,240	52,640
Dividends payable	24,000	19,200
Common stock, $4 par	150,000	100,000
Paid-in capital: Excess of issue price over par—common stock	417,500	280,000
Retained earnings	1,303,860	1,200,320
Total liabilities and stockholders' equity	$2,362,080	$2,057,120

Additional data obtained from an examination of the accounts in the ledger for 2016 are as follows:

a. The investments were sold for $280,000 cash.

b. Equipment and land were acquired for cash.

c. There were no disposals of equipment during the year.

d. The common stock was issued for cash.

e. There was a $199,540 credit to Retained Earnings for net income.

f. There was a $96,000 debit to Retained Earnings for cash dividends declared.

Instructions

Prepare a statement of cash flows, using the indirect method of presenting cash flows from operating activities.

PR 16-2A Statement of cash flows—indirect method

OBJ. 2

✔ Net cash flow from operating activities, $419,200

SHOW ME HOW

The comparative balance sheet of Del Ray Enterprises Inc. at December 31, 2016 and 2015, is as follows:

	Dec. 31, 2016	Dec. 31, 2015
Assets		
Cash	$ 146,600	$ 179,800
Accounts receivable (net)	224,600	242,000
Merchandise inventory	321,600	299,200
Prepaid expenses	13,400	9,600
Equipment	655,000	537,000
Accumulated depreciation—equipment	(170,800)	(132,200)
Total assets	$1,190,400	$1,135,400
Liabilities and Stockholders' Equity		
Accounts payable (merchandise creditors)	$ 250,200	$ 237,600
Mortgage note payable	0	336,000
Common stock, $10 par	74,000	24,000
Paid-in capital: Excess of issue price over par—common stock	470,000	320,000
Retained earnings	396,200	217,800
Total liabilities and stockholders' equity	$1,190,400	$1,135,400

Additional data obtained from the income statement and from an examination of the accounts in the ledger for 2016 are as follows:

a. Net income, $332,000
b. Depreciation reported on the income statement, $83,400
c. Equipment was purchased at a cost of $162,800 and fully depreciated equipment costing $44,800 was discarded, with no salvage realized.
d. The mortgage note payable was not due until 2018 but the terms permitted earlier payment without penalty.
e. 10,000 shares of common stock were issued at $20 for cash.
f. Cash dividends declared and paid, $153,600

Instructions

Prepare a statement of cash flows, using the indirect method of presenting cash flows from operating activities.

PR 16-3A Statement of cash flows—indirect method

OBJ. 2

✔ Net cash flow from operating activities, $(169,600)

The comparative balance sheet of Whitman Co. at December 31, 2016 and 2015, is as follows:

	Dec. 31, 2016	Dec. 31, 2015
Assets		
Cash	$ 918,000	$ 964,800
Accounts receivable (net)	828,900	761,940
Inventories	1,268,460	1,162,980
Prepaid expenses	29,340	35,100
Land	315,900	479,700
Buildings	1,462,500	900,900
Accumulated depreciation—buildings	(408,600)	(382,320)
Equipment	512,280	454,680
Accumulated depreciation—equipment	(141,300)	(158,760)
Total assets	$4,785,480	$4,219,020
Liabilities and Stockholders' Equity		
Accounts payable (merchandise creditors)	$ 922,500	$ 958,320
Bonds payable	270,000	0
Common stock, $25 par	317,000	117,000
Paid-in capital: Excess of issue price over par—common stock	758,000	558,000
Retained earnings	2,517,980	2,585,700
Total liabilities and stockholders' equity	$4,785,480	$4,219,020

The noncurrent asset, noncurrent liability, and stockholders' equity accounts for 2016 are as follows:

ACCOUNT *Land* ACCOUNT NO.

Date		Item	Debit	Credit	Balance Debit	Balance Credit
2016						
Jan.	1	Balance			479,700	
Apr.	20	Realized $151,200 cash from sale		163,800	315,900	

ACCOUNT *Buildings* ACCOUNT NO.

Date		Item	Debit	Credit	Balance Debit	Balance Credit
2016						
Jan.	1	Balance			900,900	
Apr.	20	Acquired for cash	561,600		1,462,500	

(Continued)

ACCOUNT ***Accumulated Depreciation—Buildings*** **ACCOUNT NO.**

Date		Item	Debit	Credit	Balance	
					Debit	Credit
2016						
Jan.	1	Balance				382,320
Dec.	31	Depreciation for year		26,280		408,600

ACCOUNT ***Equipment*** **ACCOUNT NO.**

Date		Item	Debit	Credit	Balance	
					Debit	Credit
2016						
Jan.	1	Balance			454,680	
	26	Discarded, no salvage		46,800	407,880	
Aug.	11	Purchased for cash	104,400		512,280	

ACCOUNT ***Accumulated Depreciation—Equipment*** **ACCOUNT NO.**

Date		Item	Debit	Credit	Balance	
					Debit	Credit
2016						
Jan.	1	Balance				158,760
	26	Equipment discarded	46,800			111,960
Dec.	31	Depreciation for year		29,340		141,300

ACCOUNT ***Bonds Payable*** **ACCOUNT NO.**

Date		Item	Debit	Credit	Balance	
					Debit	Credit
2016						
May	1	Issued 20-year bonds		270,000		270,000

ACCOUNT ***Common Stock, $25 par*** **ACCOUNT NO.**

Date		Item	Debit	Credit	Balance	
					Debit	Credit
2016						
Jan.	1	Balance				117,000
Dec.	7	Issued 8,000 shares of common stock for $50 per share		200,000		317,000

ACCOUNT ***Paid-In Capital in Excess of Par—Common Stock*** **ACCOUNT NO.**

Date		Item	Debit	Credit	Balance	
					Debit	Credit
2016						
Jan.	1	Balance				558,000
Dec.	7	Issued 8,000 shares of common stock for $50 per share		200,000		758,000

ACCOUNT *Retained Earnings* ACCOUNT NO.

Date		Item	Debit	Credit	Balance Debit	Balance Credit
2016						
Jan.	1	Balance				2,585,700
Dec.	31	Net loss	35,320			2,550,380
	31	Cash dividends	32,400			2,517,980

Instructions

Prepare a statement of cash flows, using the indirect method of presenting cash flows from operating activities.

PR 16-4A Statement of cash flows—direct method

OBJ. 3

✔ Net cash flow from operating activities, $293,600

General Ledger

SHOW ME HOW

The comparative balance sheet of Canace Products Inc. for December 31, 2016 and 2015, is as follows:

	Dec. 31, 2016	Dec. 31, 2015
Assets		
Cash	$ 643,400	$ 679,400
Accounts receivable (net)	566,800	547,400
Inventories	1,011,000	982,800
Investments	0	240,000
Land	520,000	0
Equipment	880,000	680,000
Accumulated depreciation	(244,400)	(200,400)
Total assets	$3,376,800	$2,929,200
Liabilities and Stockholders' Equity		
Accounts payable (merchandise creditors)	$ 771,800	$ 748,400
Accrued expenses payable (operating expenses)	63,400	70,800
Dividends payable	8,800	6,400
Common stock, $2 par	56,000	32,000
Paid-in capital: Excess of issue price over par—common stock	408,000	192,000
Retained earnings	2,068,800	1,879,600
Total liabilities and stockholders' equity	$3,376,800	$2,929,200

The income statement for the year ended December 31, 2016, is as follows:

Sales		$5,980,000
Cost of merchandise sold		2,452,000
Gross profit		$3,528,000
Operating expenses:		
Depreciation expense	$ 44,000	
Other operating expenses	3,100,000	
Total operating expenses		3,144,000
Operating income		$ 384,000
Other expense:		
Loss on sale of investments		(64,000)
Income before income tax		$ 320,000
Income tax expense		102,800
Net income		$ 217,200

Additional data obtained from an examination of the accounts in the ledger for 2016 are as follows:

a. Equipment and land were acquired for cash.

b. There were no disposals of equipment during the year.

(Continued)

c. The investments were sold for $176,000 cash.

d. The common stock was issued for cash.

e. There was a $28,000 debit to Retained Earnings for cash dividends declared.

Instructions

Prepare a statement of cash flows, using the direct method of presenting cash flows from operating activities.

PR 16-5A Statement of cash flows—direct method applied to PR 16-1A **OBJ. 3**

✔ Net cash flow from operating activities, $143,540

The comparative balance sheet of Cromme Inc. for December 31, 2016 and 2015, is as follows:

	Dec. 31, 2016	Dec. 31, 2015
Assets		
Cash	$ 625,760	$ 585,920
Accounts receivable (net)	227,840	208,960
Inventories	641,760	617,120
Investments	0	240,000
Land	328,000	0
Equipment	705,120	553,120
Accumulated depreciation—equipment	(166,400)	(148,000)
Total assets	$2,362,080	$2,057,120
Liabilities and Stockholders' Equity		
Accounts payable (merchandise creditors)	$ 424,480	$ 404,960
Accrued expenses payable (operating expenses)	42,240	52,640
Dividends payable	24,000	19,200
Common stock, $2 par	150,000	100,000
Paid-in capital: Excess of issue price over par—common stock	417,500	280,000
Retained earnings	1,303,860	1,200,320
Total liabilities and stockholders' equity	$2,362,080	$2,057,120

The income statement for the year ended December 31, 2016, is as follows:

Sales		$5,372,559
Cost of merchandise sold		3,306,190
Gross profit		$2,066,369
Operating expenses:		
Depreciation expense	$ 18,400	
Other operating expenses	1,755,402	
Total operating expenses		1,773,802
Operating income		$ 292,567
Other income:		
Gain on sale of investments		40,000
Income before income tax		$ 332,567
Income tax expense		133,027
Net income		$ 199,540

Additional data obtained from an examination of the accounts in the ledger for 2016 are as follows:

a. The investments were sold for $280,000 cash.

b. Equipment and land were acquired for cash.

c. There were no disposals of equipment during the year.

d. The common stock was issued for cash.

e. There was a $96,000 debit to Retained Earnings for cash dividends declared.

Instructions

Prepare a statement of cash flows, using the direct method of presenting cash flows from operating activities.

Problems: Series B

PR 16-1B Statement of cash flows—indirect method

OBJ. 2

✔ Net cash flow from operating activities, $154,260

SHOW ME HOW

The comparative balance sheet of Merrick Equipment Co. for December 31, 2016 and 2015, is as follows:

	Dec. 31, 2016	Dec. 31, 2015
Assets		
Cash	$ 70,720	$ 47,940
Accounts receivable (net)	207,230	188,190
Inventories	298,520	289,850
Investments	0	102,000
Land	295,800	0
Equipment	438,600	358,020
Accumulated depreciation—equipment	(99,110)	(84,320)
Total assets	$1,211,760	$901,680
Liabilities and Stockholders' Equity		
Accounts payable (merchandise creditors)	$ 205,700	$194,140
Accrued expenses payable (operating expenses)	30,600	26,860
Dividends payable	25,500	20,400
Common stock, $1 par	202,000	102,000
Paid-in capital: Excess of issue price over par—common stock	354,000	204,000
Retained earnings	393,960	354,280
Total liabilities and stockholders' equity	$1,211,760	$901,680

Additional data obtained from an examination of the accounts in the ledger for 2016 are as follows:

a. Equipment and land were acquired for cash.

b. There were no disposals of equipment during the year.

c. The investments were sold for $91,800 cash.

d. The common stock was issued for cash.

e. There was a $141,680 credit to Retained Earnings for net income.

f. There was a $102,000 debit to Retained Earnings for cash dividends declared.

Instructions

Prepare a statement of cash flows, using the indirect method of presenting cash flows from operating activities.

PR 16-2B Statement of cash flows—indirect method

OBJ. 2

✔ Net cash flow from operating activities, $561,400

SHOW ME HOW

The comparative balance sheet of Harris Industries Inc. at December 31, 2016 and 2015, is as follows:

	Dec. 31, 2016	Dec. 31, 2015
Assets		
Cash	$ 443,240	$ 360,920
Accounts receivable (net)	665,280	592,200
Inventories	887,880	1,022,560
Prepaid expenses	31,640	25,200
Land	302,400	302,400
Buildings	1,713,600	1,134,000
Accumulated depreciation—buildings	(466,200)	(414,540)
Machinery and equipment	781,200	781,200
Accumulated depreciation—machinery and equipment	(214,200)	(191,520)
Patents	106,960	112,000
Total assets	$4,251,800	$3,724,420

(Continued)

Liabilities and Stockholders' Equity		
Accounts payable (merchandise creditors)	$ 837,480	$ 927,080
Dividends payable	32,760	25,200
Salaries payable	78,960	87,080
Mortgage note payable, due 2017	224,000	0
Bonds payable	0	390,000
Common stock, $5 par	200,400	50,400
Paid-in capital: Excess of issue price over par—common stock	366,000	126,000
Retained earnings	2,512,200	2,118,660
Total liabilities and stockholders' equity	$4,251,800	$3,724,420

An examination of the income statement and the accounting records revealed the following additional information applicable to 2016:

a. Net income, $524,580.

b. Depreciation expense reported on the income statement: buildings, $51,660; machinery and equipment, $22,680.

c. Patent amortization reported on the income statement, $5,040.

d. A building was constructed for $579,600.

e. A mortgage note for $224,000 was issued for cash.

f. 30,000 shares of common stock were issued at $13 in exchange for the bonds payable.

g. Cash dividends declared, $131,040.

Instructions

Prepare a statement of cash flows, using the indirect method of presenting cash flows from operating activities.

PR 16-3B Statement of cash flows—indirect method

OBJ. 2

✔ Net cash flow from operating activities, $162,800

The comparative balance sheet of Coulson, Inc. at December 31, 2016 and 2015, is as follows:

	Dec. 31, 2016	Dec. 31, 2015
Assets		
Cash	$ 300,600	$ 337,800
Accounts receivable (net)	704,400	609,600
Inventories	918,600	865,800
Prepaid expenses	18,600	26,400
Land	990,000	1,386,000
Buildings	1,980,000	990,000
Accumulated depreciation—buildings	(397,200)	(366,000)
Equipment	660,600	529,800
Accumulated depreciation—equipment	(133,200)	(162,000)
Total assets	$5,042,400	$4,217,400
Liabilities and Stockholders' Equity		
Accounts payable (merchandise creditors)	$ 594,000	$ 631,200
Income taxes payable	26,400	21,600
Bonds payable	330,000	0
Common stock, $20 par	320,000	180,000
Paid-in capital: Excess of issue price over par—common stock	950,000	810,000
Retained earnings	2,822,000	2,574,600
Total liabilities and stockholders' equity	$5,042,400	$4,217,400

The noncurrent asset, noncurrent liability, and stockholders' equity accounts for 2016 are as follows:

ACCOUNT *Land* ACCOUNT NO.

Date		Item	Debit	Credit	Balance Debit	Balance Credit
2016						
Jan.	1	Balance			1,386,000	
Apr.	20	Realized $456,000 cash from sale		396,000	990,000	

ACCOUNT *Buildings* ACCOUNT NO.

Date		Item	Debit	Credit	Balance Debit	Balance Credit
2016						
Jan.	1	Balance			990,000	
Apr.	20	Acquired for cash	990,000		1,980,000	

ACCOUNT *Accumulated Depreciation—Buildings* ACCOUNT NO.

Date		Item	Debit	Credit	Balance Debit	Balance Credit
2016						
Jan.	1	Balance				366,000
Dec.	31	Depreciation for year		31,200		397,200

ACCOUNT *Equipment* ACCOUNT NO.

Date		Item	Debit	Credit	Balance Debit	Balance Credit
2016						
Jan.	1	Balance			529,800	
	26	Discarded, no salvage		66,000	463,800	
Aug.	11	Purchased for cash	196,800		660,600	

ACCOUNT *Accumulated Depreciation—Equipment* ACCOUNT NO.

Date		Item	Debit	Credit	Balance Debit	Balance Credit
2016						
Jan.	1	Balance				162,000
	26	Equipment discarded	66,000			96,000
Dec.	31	Depreciation for year		37,200		133,200

ACCOUNT *Bonds Payable* ACCOUNT NO.

Date		Item	Debit	Credit	Balance Debit	Balance Credit
2016						
May	1	Issued 20-year bonds		330,000		330,000

(Continued)

ACCOUNT *Common Stock, $20 par* ACCOUNT NO.

Date		Item	Debit	Credit	Balance Debit	Balance Credit
2016						
Jan.	1	Balance				180,000
Dec.	7	Issued 7,000 shares of common stock for $40 per share		140,000		320,000

ACCOUNT *Paid-In Capital in Excess of Par—Common Stock* ACCOUNT NO.

Date		Item	Debit	Credit	Balance Debit	Balance Credit
2016						
Jan.	1	Balance				810,000
Dec.	7	Issued 7,000 shares of common stock for $40 per share		140,000		950,000

ACCOUNT *Retained Earnings* ACCOUNT NO.

Date		Item	Debit	Credit	Balance Debit	Balance Credit
2016						
Jan.	1	Balance				2,574,600
Dec.	31	Net income		326,600		2,901,200
	31	Cash dividends	79,200			2,822,000

Instructions

Prepare a statement of cash flows, using the indirect method of presenting cash flows from operating activities.

PR 16-4B Statement of cash flows—direct method

OBJ. 3

✔ Net cash flow from operating activities, $509,220

General Ledger

SHOW ME HOW

The comparative balance sheet of Martinez Inc. for December 31, 2016 and 2015, is as follows:

	Dec. 31, 2016	Dec. 31, 2015
Assets		
Cash	$ 661,920	$ 683,100
Accounts receivable (net)	992,640	914,400
Inventories	1,394,400	1,363,800
Investments	0	432,000
Land	960,000	0
Equipment	1,224,000	984,000
Accumulated depreciation—equipment	(481,500)	(368,400)
Total assets	$4,751,460	$4,008,900
Liabilities and Stockholders' Equity		
Accounts payable (merchandise creditors)	$1,080,000	$ 966,600
Accrued expenses payable (operating expenses)	67,800	79,200
Dividends payable	100,800	91,200
Common stock, $5 par	130,000	30,000
Paid-in capital: Excess of issue price over par—common stock	950,000	450,000
Retained earnings	2,422,860	2,391,900
Total liabilities and stockholders' equity	$4,751,460	$4,008,900

The income statement for the year ended December 31, 2016, is as follows:

Sales		$4,512,000
Cost of merchandise sold		2,352,000
Gross profit		$2,160,000
Operating expenses:		
Depreciation expense	$ 113,100	
Other operating expenses	1,344,840	
Total operating expenses		1,457,940
Operating income		$ 702,060
Other income:		
Gain on sale of investments		156,000
Income before income tax		$ 858,060
Income tax expense		299,100
Net income		$ 558,960

Additional data obtained from an examination of the accounts in the ledger for 2016 are as follows:

a. Equipment and land were acquired for cash.

b. There were no disposals of equipment during the year.

c. The investments were sold for $588,000 cash.

d. The common stock was issued for cash.

e. There was a $528,000 debit to Retained Earnings for cash dividends declared.

Instructions

Prepare a statement of cash flows, using the direct method of presenting cash flows from operating activities.

PR 16-5B Statement of cash flows—direct method applied to PR 16-1B **OBJ. 3**

✔ Net cash flow from operating activities, $154,260

The comparative balance sheet of Merrick Equipment Co. for Dec. 31, 2016 and 2015, is:

	Dec. 31, 2016	Dec. 31, 2015
Assets		
Cash	$ 70,720	$ 47,940
Accounts receivable (net)	207,230	188,190
Inventories	298,520	289,850
Investments	0	102,000
Land	295,800	0
Equipment	438,600	358,020
Accumulated depreciation—equipment	(99,110)	(84,320)
Total assets	$1,211,760	$ 901,680
Liabilities and Stockholders' Equity		
Accounts payable (merchandise creditors)	$ 205,700	$ 194,140
Accrued expenses payable (operating expenses)	30,600	26,860
Dividends payable	25,500	20,400
Common stock, $1 par	202,000	102,000
Paid-in capital: Excess of issue price over par—common stock	354,000	204,000
Retained earnings	393,960	354,280
Total liabilities and stockholders' equity	$1,211,760	$ 901,680

(Continued)

The income statement for the year ended December 31, 2016, is as follows:

Sales		$2,023,898
Cost of merchandise sold		1,245,476
Gross profit		$ 778,422
Operating expenses:		
Depreciation expense	$ 14,790	
Other operating expenses	517,299	
Total operating expenses		532,089
Operating income		$ 246,333
Other expenses:		
Loss on sale of investments		(10,200)
Income before income tax		$ 236,133
Income tax expense		94,453
Net income		$ 141,680

Additional data obtained from an examination of the accounts in the ledger for 2016 are as follows:

a. Equipment and land were acquired for cash.
b. There were no disposals of equipment during the year.
c. The investments were sold for $91,800 cash.
d. The common stock was issued for cash.
e. There was a $102,000 debit to Retained Earnings for cash dividends declared.

Instructions

Prepare a statement of cash flows, using the direct method of presenting cash flows from operating activities.

Cases & Projects

CP 16-1 Ethics and professional conduct in business

Lucas Hunter, president of Simmons Industries Inc., believes that reporting operating cash flow per share on the income statement would be a useful addition to the company's just completed financial statements. The following discussion took place between Lucas Hunter and Simmons' controller, John Jameson, in January, after the close of the fiscal year:

Lucas: I've been reviewing our financial statements for the last year. I am disappointed that our net income per share has dropped by 10% from last year. This won't look good to our shareholders. Is there anything we can do about this?

John: What do you mean? The past is the past, and the numbers are in. There isn't much that can be done about it. Our financial statements were prepared according to generally accepted accounting principles, and I don't see much leeway for significant change at this point.

Lucas: No, no. I'm not suggesting that we "cook the books." But look at the cash flow from operating activities on the statement of cash flows. The cash flow from operating activities has increased by 20%. This is very good news—and, I might add, useful information. The higher cash flow from operating activities will give our creditors comfort.

John: Well, the cash flow from operating activities is on the statement of cash flows, so I guess users will be able to see the improved cash flow figures there.

Lucas: This is true, but somehow I feel that this information should be given a much higher profile. I don't like this information being "buried" in the statement of cash flows. You know as well as I do that many users will focus on the income statement. Therefore, I think we ought to include an operating cash flow per share number on the face of the income statement—someplace under the earnings per share number. In this way, users will get the complete picture of our operating performance. Yes, our earnings per share dropped this year, but our cash flow from operating activities improved! And all the information is in one place where users can see and compare the figures. What do you think?

John: I've never really thought about it like that before. I guess we could put the operating cash flow per share on the income statement, under the earnings per share. Users would really benefit from this disclosure. Thanks for the idea—I'll start working on it.

Lucas: Glad to be of service.

How would you interpret this situation? Is John behaving in an ethical and professional manner?

CP 16-2 Using the statement of cash flows

You are considering an investment in a new start-up company, Giraffe Inc., an Internet service provider. A review of the company's financial statements reveals a negative retained earnings. In addition, it appears as though the company has been running a negative cash flow from operating activities since the company's inception.

How is the company staying in business under these circumstances? Could this be a good investment?

CP 16-3 Analysis of statement of cash flows

Dillip Lachgar is the president and majority shareholder of Argon Inc., a small retail store chain. Recently, Dillip submitted a loan application for Argon Inc. to Compound Bank. It called for a $600,000, 9%, 10-year loan to help finance the construction of a building and the purchase of store equipment, costing a total of $750,000. This will enable Argon Inc. to open a store in the town of Compound. Land for this purpose was acquired last year. The bank's loan officer requested a statement of cash flows in addition to the most recent income statement, balance sheet, and retained earnings statement that Dillip had submitted with the loan application.

As a close family friend, Dillip asked you to prepare a statement of cash flows. From the records provided, you prepared the following statement:

Argon Inc.
Statement of Cash Flows
For the Year Ended December 31, 2016

Cash flows from operating activities:		
Net income	$ 300,000	
Adjustments to reconcile net income to net cash flow from operating activities:		
Depreciation	84,000	
Gain on sale of investments	(30,000)	
Changes in current operating assets and liabilities:		
Decrease in accounts receivable	21,000	
Increase in inventories	(42,000)	
Increase in accounts payable	30,000	
Decrease in accrued expenses payable	(6,000)	
Net cash flow from operating activities		$ 357,000
Cash flows from investing activities:		
Cash received from investments sold	$ 180,000	
Less: Cash paid for purchase of store equipment	(120,000)	
Net cash flow from investing activities		60,000
Cash flows from financing activities:		
Cash paid for dividends	$ (126,000)	
Net cash flow used for financing activities		(126,000)
Increase in cash		$ 291,000
Cash at the beginning of the year		108,000
Cash at the end of the year		$ 399,000
Schedule of Noncash Financing and Investing Activities:		
Issued common stock for land		$ 240,000

(Continued)

After reviewing the statement, Dillip telephoned you and commented, "Are you sure this statement is right?" Dillip then raised the following questions:

1. "How can depreciation be a cash flow?"
2. "Issuing common stock for the land is listed in a separate schedule. This transaction has nothing to do with cash! Shouldn't this transaction be eliminated from the statement?"
3. "How can the gain on the sale of investments be a deduction from net income in determining the cash flow from operating activities?"
4. "Why does the bank need this statement anyway? They can compute the increase in cash from the balance sheets for the last two years."

After jotting down Dillip's questions, you assured him that this statement was "right." But to alleviate Dillip's concern, you arranged a meeting for the following day.

a. How would you respond to each of Dillip's questions?

b. Do you think that the statement of cash flows enhances the chances of Argon Inc. receiving the loan? Discuss.

CP 16-4 Analysis of cash flow from operations

The Commercial Division of Tidewater Inc. provided the following information on its cash flow from operations:

Net income	$ 945,000
Increase in accounts receivable	(1,134,000)
Increase in inventory	(1,260,000)
Decrease in accounts payable	(189,000)
Depreciation	210,000
Cash flow from operating activities	$(1,428,000)

The manager of the Commercial Division provided the accompanying memo with this report:

From: Senior Vice President, Commercial Division

I am pleased to report that we had earnings of $945,000 over the last period. This resulted in a return on invested capital of 8%, which is near our targets for this division. I have been aggressive in building the revenue volume in the division. As a result, I am happy to report that we have increased the number of new credit card customers as a result of an aggressive marketing campaign. In addition, we have found some excellent merchandise opportunities. Some of our suppliers have made some of their apparel merchandise available at a deep discount. We have purchased as much of these goods as possible in order to improve profitability. I'm also happy to report that our vendor payment problems have improved. We are nearly caught up on our overdue payables balances.

Comment on the senior vice president's memo in light of the cash flow information.

CP 16-5 Statement of cash flows

Internet Project

Group Project

This activity will require two teams to retrieve cash flow statement information from the Internet. One team is to obtain the most recent year's statement of cash flows for **Johnson & Johnson**, and the other team the most recent year's statement of cash flows for **JetBlue Airways Corp.**

The statement of cash flows is included as part of the annual report information that is a required disclosure to the Securities and Exchange Commission (SEC). SEC documents can be retrieved using the EdgarScan™ service at www.sec.gov/edgar/searchedgar/companysearch.html.

To obtain annual report information, key in a company name in the appropriate space. EdgarScan will list the reports available to you for the company you've selected. Select the most recent annual report filing, identified as a 10-K or 10-K405. EdgarScan provides an outline of the report, including the separate financial statements. You can double-click the income statement and balance sheet for the selected company into an Excel™ spreadsheet for further analysis.

As a group, compare the two statements of cash flows.

a. How are Johnson & Johnson and JetBlue Airways Corp. similar or different regarding cash flows?

b. Compute and compare the free cash flow for each company, assuming additions to property, plant, and equipment replace current capacity.

MICHAEL WEBER/IMAGEBROKER/GLOW IMAGES

Financial Statement Analysis

Nike, Inc.

"Just do it." These three words identify one of the most recognizable brands in the world, **Nike**. While this phrase inspires athletes to "compete and achieve their potential," it also defines the company.

Nike began in 1964 as a partnership between University of Oregon track coach Bill Bowerman and one of his former student-athletes, Phil Knight. The two began by selling shoes imported from Japan out of the back of Knight's car to athletes at track and field events. As sales grew, the company opened retail outlets, calling itself **Blue Ribbon Sports**. The company also began to develop its own shoes. In 1971, the company commissioned a graphic design student at Portland State University to develop the swoosh logo for a fee of $35. In 1978, the company changed its name to Nike, and in 1980, it sold its first shares of stock to the public.

Nike would have been a great company to invest in at the time. If you had invested in Nike's common stock back in 1990, you would have paid $5.00 per share. As of April 2011, Nike's stock was worth $109.23 per share. Unfortunately, you can't invest using hindsight.

How can you select companies in which to invest? Like any significant purchase, you should do some research to guide your investment decision. If you were buying a car, for example, you might go to **Edmunds.com** to obtain reviews, ratings, prices, specifications, options, and fuel economies to evaluate different vehicles. In selecting companies to invest in, you can use financial analysis to gain insight into a company's past performance and future prospects. This chapter describes and illustrates common financial data that can be analyzed to assist you in making investment decisions such as whether or not to invest in Nike's stock.

Source: www.nikebiz.com/.

Learning Objectives

After studying this chapter, you should be able to: | *Example Exercises*

OBJ 1 **Describe basic financial statement analytical methods.**

Basic Analytical Methods

- Horizontal Analysis — EE 17-1
- Vertical Analysis — EE 17-2
- Common-Sized Statements
- Other Analytical Measures

OBJ 2 **Use financial statement analysis to assess the solvency of a business.**

Liquidity and Solvency Analysis

- Current Position Analysis — EE 17-3
- Accounts Receivable Analysis — EE 17-4
- Inventory Analysis — EE 17-5
- Ratio of Fixed Assets to Long-Term Liabilities
- Ratio of Liabilities to Stockholders' Equity — EE 17-6
- Number of Times Interest Charges Are Earned — EE 17-7

OBJ 3 **Use financial statement analysis to assess the profitability of a business.**

Profitability Analysis

- Ratio of Sales to Assets — EE 17-8
- Rate Earned on Total Assets — EE 17-9
- Rate Earned on Stockholders' Equity
- Rate Earned on Common Stockholders' Equity — EE 17-10
- Earnings per Share on Common Stock
- Price-Earnings Ratio — EE 17-11
- Divdends per Share
- Divdend Yield
- Summary of Analytical Measures

OBJ 4 **Describe the contents of corporate annual reports.**

Corporate Annual Reports

- Management Discussion and Analysis
- Report on Internal Control
- Report on Fairness of the Financial Statements

At a Glance 17 Page 821

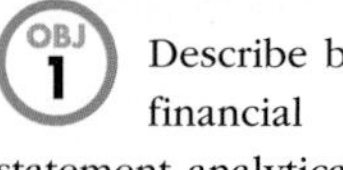
Describe basic financial statement analytical methods.

Basic Analytical Methods

Users analyze a company's financial statements using a variety of analytical methods. Three such methods are:

- Horizontal analysis
- Vertical analysis
- Common-sized statements

Horizontal Analysis

The analysis of increases and decreases in the amount and percentage of comparative financial statement items is called **horizontal analysis**. Each item on the most recent statement is compared with the same item on one or more earlier statements in terms of the following:

- *Amount* of increase or decrease
- *Percent* of increase or decrease

When comparing statements, the earlier statement is normally used as the base year for computing increases and decreases.

Exhibit 1 illustrates horizontal analysis for the December 31, 2016 and 2015, balance sheets of **Lincoln Company**. In Exhibit 1, the December 31, 2015, balance sheet (the earliest year presented) is used as the base year.

Exhibit 1 indicates that total assets decreased by $91,000 (7.4%), liabilities decreased by $133,000 (30.0%), and stockholders' equity increased by $42,000 (5.3%). Since the long-term investments account decreased by $82,500, it appears that most of the decrease in long-term liabilities of $100,000 was achieved through the sale of long-term investments.

EXHIBIT 1

Comparative Balance Sheet—Horizontal Analysis

Lincoln Company
Comparative Balance Sheet
December 31, 2016 and 2015

	Dec. 31, 2016	Dec. 31, 2015	Increase (Decrease) Amount	Increase (Decrease) Percent
Assets				
Current assets	$ 550,000	$ 533,000	$ 17,000	3.2%
Long-term investments	95,000	177,500	(82,500)	(46.5%)
Property, plant, and equipment (net)	444,500	470,000	(25,500)	(5.4%)
Intangible assets	50,000	50,000	—	—
Total assets	$1,139,500	$1,230,500	$ (91,000)	(7.4%)
Liabilities				
Current liabilities	$ 210,000	$ 243,000	$ (33,000)	(13.6%)
Long-term liabilities	100,000	200,000	(100,000)	(50.0%)
Total liabilities	$ 310,000	$ 443,000	$(133,000)	(30.0%)
Stockholders' Equity				
Preferred 6% stock, $100 par	$ 150,000	$ 150,000	—	—
Common stock, $10 par	500,000	500,000	—	—
Retained earnings	179,500	137,500	$ 42,000	30.5%
Total stockholders' equity	$ 829,500	$ 787,500	$ 42,000	5.3%
Total liabilities and stockholders' equity	$1,139,500	$1,230,500	$ (91,000)	(7.4%)

The balance sheets in Exhibit 1 may be expanded or supported by a separate schedule that includes the individual asset and liability accounts. For example, Exhibit 2 is a supporting schedule of **Lincoln Company**'s current asset accounts.

EXHIBIT 2

Comparative Schedule of Current Assets—Horizontal Analysis

Lincoln Company
Comparative Schedule of Current Assets
December 31, 2016 and 2015

	Dec. 31, 2016	Dec. 31, 2015	Increase (Decrease) Amount	Increase (Decrease) Percent
Cash	$ 90,500	$ 64,700	$ 25,800	39.9%
Temporary investments	75,000	60,000	15,000	25.0%
Accounts receivable (net)	115,000	120,000	(5,000)	(4.2%)
Inventories	264,000	283,000	(19,000)	(6.7%)
Prepaid expenses	5,500	5,300	200	3.8%
Total current assets	$550,000	$533,000	$ 17,000	3.2%

Exhibit 2 indicates that while cash and temporary investments increased, accounts receivable and inventories decreased. The decrease in accounts receivable could be caused by improved collection policies, which would increase cash. The decrease in inventories could be caused by increased sales.

Exhibit 3 illustrates horizontal analysis for the 2016 and 2015 income statements of **Lincoln Company**. Exhibit 3 indicates an increase in sales of $298,000, or 24.8%. However, the percentage increase in sales of 24.8% was accompanied by an even greater percentage increase in the cost of goods (merchandise) sold of 27.2%.[1] Thus, gross profit increased by only 19.7% rather than by the 24.0% increase in sales.

EXHIBIT 3

Comparative Income Statement— Horizontal Analysis

Lincoln Company
Comparative Income Statement
For the Years Ended December 31, 2016 and 2015

			Increase (Decrease)	
	2016	**2015**	**Amount**	**Percent**
Sales	$1,498,000	$1,200,000	$298,000	24.8%
Cost of goods sold	1,043,000	820,000	223,000	27.2%
Gross profit	$ 455,000	$ 380,000	$ 75,000	19.7%
Selling expenses	$ 191,000	$ 147,000	$ 44,000	29.9%
Administrative expenses	104,000	97,400	6,600	6.8%
Total operating expenses	$ 295,000	$ 244,400	$ 50,600	20.7%
Income from operations	$ 160,000	$ 135,600	$ 24,400	18.0%
Other income	8,500	11,000	(2,500)	(22.7%)
	$ 168,500	$ 146,600	$ 21,900	14.9%
Other expense (interest)	6,000	12,000	(6,000)	(50.0%)
Income before income tax	$ 162,500	$ 134,600	$ 27,900	20.7%
Income tax expense	71,500	58,100	13,400	23.1%
Net income	$ 91,000	$ 76,500	$ 14,500	19.0%

Exhibit 3 also indicates that selling expenses increased by 29.9%. Thus, the 24.8% increases in sales could have been caused by an advertising campaign, which increased selling expenses. Administrative expenses increased by only 6.8%, total operating expenses increased by 20.7%, and income from operations increased by 18.0%. Interest expense decreased by 50.0%. This decrease was probably caused by the 50.0% decrease in long-term liabilities (Exhibit 1). Overall, net income increased by 19.0%, a favorable result.

Exhibit 4 illustrates horizontal analysis for the 2016 and 2015 retained earnings statements of **Lincoln Company**. Exhibit 4 indicates that retained earnings increased by 30.5% for the year. The increase is due to net income of $91,000 for the year, less dividends of $49,000.

EXHIBIT 4

Comparative Retained Earnings Statement— Horizontal Analysis

Lincoln Company
Comparative Retained Earnings Statement
For the Years Ended December 31, 2016 and 2015

			Increase (Decrease)	
	2016	**2015**	**Amount**	**Percent**
Retained earnings, January 1	$137,500	$100,000	$37,500	37.5%
Net income for the year	91,000	76,500	14,500	19.0%
Total	$228,500	$176,500	$52,000	29.5%
Dividends:				
On preferred stock	$ 9,000	$ 9,000	—	—
On common stock	40,000	30,000	$10,000	33.3%
Total	$ 49,000	$ 39,000	$10,000	25.6%
Retained earnings, December 31	$179,500	$137,500	$42,000	30.5%

[1] The term *cost of goods sold* is often used in practice in place of *cost of merchandise sold*. Such usage is followed in this chapter.

Example Exercise 17-1 Horizontal Analysis

OBJ 1

The comparative cash and accounts receivable balances for a company follow:

	Dec. 31, 2016	Dec. 31, 2015
Cash	$62,500	$50,000
Accounts receivable (net)	74,400	80,000

Based on this information, what is the amount and percentage of increase or decrease that would be shown on a balance sheet with horizontal analysis?

Follow My Example 17-1

Cash	$12,500 increase ($62,500 – $50,000), or 25%
Accounts receivable	$5,600 decrease ($74,400 – $80,000), or (7%)

Practice Exercises: PE 17-1A, PE 17-1B

Vertical Analysis

The percentage analysis of the relationship of each component in a financial statement to a total within the statement is called **vertical analysis.** Although vertical analysis is applied to a single statement, it may be applied on the same statement over time. This enhances the analysis by showing how the percentages of each item have changed over time.

In vertical analysis of the balance sheet, the percentages are computed as follows:

- Each asset item is stated as a percent of the total assets.
- Each liability and stockholders' equity item is stated as a percent of the total liabilities and stockholders' equity.

Exhibit 5 illustrates the vertical analysis of the December 31, 2016 and 2015, balance sheets of **Lincoln Company**. Exhibit 5 indicates that current assets have increased from 43.3% to 48.3% of total assets. Long-term investments decreased from 14.4% to 8.3% of total assets. Stockholders' equity increased from 64.0% to 72.8%, with a comparable decrease in liabilities.

EXHIBIT 5

Comparative Balance Sheet—Vertical Analysis

Lincoln Company
Comparative Balance Sheet
December 31, 2016 and 2015

	Dec. 31, 2016		Dec. 31, 2015	
	Amount	**Percent**	**Amount**	**Percent**
Assets				
Current assets	$ 550,000	48.3%	$ 533,000	43.3%
Long-term investments	95,000	8.3	177,500	14.4
Property, plant, and equipment (net)	444,500	39.0	470,000	38.2
Intangible assets	50,000	4.4	50,000	4.1
Total assets	$1,139,500	100.0%	$1,230,500	100.0%
Liabilities				
Current liabilities	$ 210,000	18.4%	$ 243,000	19.7%
Long-term liabilities	100,000	8.8	200,000	16.3
Total liabilities	$ 310,000	27.2%	$ 443,000	36.0%
Stockholders' Equity				
Preferred 6% stock, $100 par	$ 150,000	13.2%	$ 150,000	12.2%
Common stock, $10 par	500,000	43.9	500,000	40.6
Retained earnings	179,500	15.7	137,500	11.2
Total stockholders' equity	$ 829,500	72.8%	$ 787,500	64.0%
Total liabilities and stockholders' equity	$1,139,500	100.0%	$1,230,500	100.0%

In a vertical analysis of the income statement, each item is stated as a percent of sales. Exhibit 6 illustrates the vertical analysis of the 2016 and 2015 income statements of **Lincoln Company**.

EXHIBIT 6

Comparative Income Statement—Vertical Analysis

Lincoln Company
Comparative Income Statement
For the Years Ended December 31, 2016 and 2015

	2016		2015	
	Amount	**Percent**	**Amount**	**Percent**
Sales	$1,498,000	100.0%	$1,200,000	100.0%
Cost of goods sold	1,043,000	69.6	820,000	68.3
Gross profit	$ 455,000	30.4%	$ 380,000	31.7%
Selling expenses	$ 191,000	12.8%	$ 147,000	12.3%
Administrative expenses	104,000	6.9	97,400	8.1
Total operating expenses	$ 295,000	19.7%	$ 244,400	20.4%
Income from operations	$ 160,000	10.7%	$ 135,600	11.3%
Other income	8,500	0.6	11,000	0.9
	$ 168,500	11.3%	$ 146,600	12.2%
Other expense (interest)	6,000	0.4	12,000	1.0
Income before income tax	$ 162,500	10.9%	$ 134,600	11.2%
Income tax expense	71,500	4.8	58,100	4.8
Net income	$ 91,000	6.1%	$ 76,500	6.4%

Exhibit 6 indicates a decrease in the gross profit rate from 31.7% in 2015 to 30.4% in 2016. Although this is only a 1.3 percentage point (31.7% – 30.4%) decrease, in dollars of potential gross profit, it represents a decrease of $19,474 (1.3% × $1,498,000) based on 2016 sales. Thus, a small percentage decrease can have a large dollar effect.

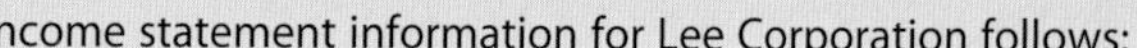

Example Exercise 17-2 Vertical Analysis

OBJ 1

Income statement information for Lee Corporation follows:

Sales	$100,000
Cost of goods sold	65,000
Gross profit	$ 35,000

Prepare a vertical analysis of the income statement for Lee Corporation.

Follow My Example 17-2

	Amount	Percentage	
Sales	$100,000	100%	($100,000 ÷ $100,000)
Cost of goods sold	65,000	65	($65,000 ÷ $100,000)
Gross profit	$ 35,000	35%	($35,000 ÷ $100,000)

Practice Exercises: PE 17-2A, PE 17-2B

Common-Sized Statements

In a **common-sized statement**, all items are expressed as percentages, with no dollar amounts shown. Common-sized statements are often useful for comparing one company with another or for comparing a company with industry averages.

Exhibit 7 illustrates common-sized income statements for **Lincoln Company** and Madison Corporation. Exhibit 7 indicates that Lincoln has a slightly higher rate of gross profit (30.4%) than Madison (30.0%). However, Lincoln has a higher percentage of selling expenses (12.8%) and administrative expenses (6.9%) than does Madison (11.5% and 4.1%). As a result, the income from operations of Lincoln (10.7%) is less than that of Madison (14.4%).

EXHIBIT 7

Common-Sized Income Statements

	Lincoln Company	Madison Corporation
Sales	100.0%	100.0%
Cost of goods sold	69.6	70.0
Gross profit	30.4%	30.0%
Selling expenses	12.8%	11.5%
Administrative expenses	6.9	4.1
Total operating expenses	19.7%	15.6%
Income from operations	10.7%	14.4%
Other income	0.6	0.6
	11.3%	15.0%
Other expense (interest)	0.4	0.5
Income before income tax	10.9%	14.5%
Income tax expense	4.8	5.5
Net income	6.1%	9.0%

The unfavorable difference of 3.7 (14.4% – 10.7%) percentage points in income from operations would concern the managers and other stakeholders of Lincoln. The underlying causes of the difference should be investigated and possibly corrected. For example, Lincoln may decide to outsource some of its administrative duties so that its administrative expenses are more comparative to that of Madison.

Other Analytical Measures

Other relationships may be expressed in ratios and percentages. Often, these relationships are compared within the same statement and, thus, are a type of vertical analysis. Comparing these items with items from earlier periods is a type of horizontal analysis.

Analytical measures are not a definitive conclusion. They are only guides in evaluating financial and operating data. Many other factors, such as trends in the industry and general economic conditions, should also be considered when analyzing a company.

Liquidity and Solvency Analysis

Use financial statement analysis to assess the solvency of a business.

All users of financial statements are interested in the ability of a company to do the following:

- Maintain liquidity and solvency
- Earn income, called **profitability**

The ability of a company to convert assets into cash is called **liquidity**, while the ability of a company to pay its debts is called **solvency**. Liquidity, solvency, and profitability are interrelated. For example, a company that cannot convert assets into cash may have difficulty taking advantage of profitable courses of action requiring immediate cash outlays. Likewise, a company that cannot pay its debts will have difficulty obtaining credit. A lack of credit will, in turn, limit the company's ability to purchase merchandise or expand operations, which decreases its profitability.

Liquidity and solvency are normally assessed using the following:

- Current position analysis
  - Working capital
  - Current ratio
  - Quick ratio
- Accounts receivable analysis
  - Accounts receivable turnover
  - Number of days' sales in receivables
- Inventory analysis
  - Inventory turnover
  - Number of days' sales in inventory
- The ratio of fixed assets to long-term liabilities
- The ratio of liabilities to stockholders' equity
- The number of times interest charges are earned

One popular printed source for industry ratios is *Annual Statement Studies* from Risk Management Association. Online analysis is available from Zacks Investment Research site at www.zacks.com.

The Lincoln Company financial statements presented earlier are used to illustrate the preceding analyses.

Current Position Analysis

A company's ability to pay its current liabilities is called **current position analysis.** It is a solvency measure of special interest to short-term creditors and includes the computation and analysis of the following:

- Working capital
- Current ratio
- Quick ratio

Working Capital A company's **working capital** is computed as follows:

Working Capital = Current Assets – Current Liabilities

To illustrate, the working capital for **Lincoln Company** for 2016 and 2015 is computed as follows:

	2016	2015
Current assets	$550,000	$533,000
Less current liabilities	210,000	243,000
Working capital	$340,000	$290,000

The working capital is used to evaluate a company's ability to pay current liabilities. A company's working capital is often monitored monthly, quarterly, or yearly by creditors and other debtors. However, it is difficult to use working capital to compare companies of different sizes. For example, working capital of $250,000 may be adequate for a local hardware store, but it would be inadequate for **The Home Depot**.

Current Ratio The **current ratio**, sometimes called the *working capital ratio*, is computed as follows:

$$\text{Current Ratio} = \frac{\text{Current Assets}}{\text{Current Liabilities}}$$

To illustrate, the current ratio for **Lincoln Company** is computed as follows:

	2016	2015
Current assets	$550,000	$533,000
Current liabilities	$210,000	$243,000
Current ratio	2.6 ($550,000 ÷ $210,000)	2.2 ($533,000 ÷ $243,000)

The current ratio is a more reliable indicator of a company's ability to pay its current liabilities than is working capital, and it is much easier to compare across companies. To illustrate, assume that as of December 31, 2016, the working capital of a competitor is much greater than $340,000, but its current ratio is only 1.3. Considering these facts alone, Lincoln, with its current ratio of 2.6, is in a more favorable position to obtain short-term credit than the competitor, which has the greater amount of working capital.

Quick Ratio One limitation of working capital and the current ratio is that they do not consider the types of current assets a company has and how easily they can be turned in to cash. Because of this, two companies may have the same working capital and current ratios but differ significantly in their ability to pay their current liabilities.

To illustrate, the current assets and liabilities for **Lincoln Company** and Jefferson Corporation as of December 31, 2016, are as follows:

	Lincoln Company	Jefferson Corporation
Current assets:		
Cash	$ 90,500	$ 45,500
Temporary investments	75,000	25,000
Accounts receivable (net)	115,000	90,000
Inventories	264,000	380,000
Prepaid expenses	5,500	9,500
Total current assets	$550,000	$550,000
Total current assets	$550,000	$550,000
Less current liabilities	210,000	210,000
Working capital	$340,000	$340,000
Current ratio ($550,000 ÷ $210,000)	2.6	2.6

Lincoln and Jefferson both have a working capital of $340,000 and current ratios of 2.6. Jefferson, however, has more of its current assets in inventories. These inventories must be sold and the receivables collected before all the current liabilities can be paid. This takes time. In addition, if the market for its product declines, Jefferson may have difficulty selling its inventory. This, in turn, could impair its ability to pay its current liabilities.

In contrast, Lincoln's current assets contain more cash, temporary investments, and accounts receivable, which can easily be converted to cash. Thus, Lincoln is in a stronger current position than Jefferson to pay its current liabilities.

A ratio that measures the "instant" debt-paying ability of a company is the **quick ratio**, sometimes called the *acid-test ratio*. The quick ratio is computed as follows:

$$\text{Quick Ratio} = \frac{\text{Quick Assets}}{\text{Current Liabilities}}$$

Quick assets are cash and other current assets that can be easily converted to cash. Quick assets normally include cash, temporary investments, and receivables but exclude inventories and prepaid assets.

To illustrate, the quick ratio for **Lincoln Company** is computed as follows:

	2016	2015
Quick assets:		
Cash	$ 90,500	$ 64,700
Temporary investments	75,000	60,000
Accounts receivable (net)	115,000	120,000
Total quick assets	$280,500	$244,700
Current liabilities	$210,000	$243,000
Quick ratio	1.3 ($280,500 ÷ $210,000)	1.0 ($244,700 ÷ $243,000)

Example Exercise 17-3 Current Position Analysis

OBJ 2

The following items are reported on a company's balance sheet:

Cash	$300,000
Temporary investments	100,000
Accounts receivable (net)	200,000
Inventory	200,000
Accounts payable	400,000

Determine (a) the current ratio and (b) the quick ratio.

Follow My Example 17-3

a. Current Ratio = Current Assets ÷ Current Liabilities
= ($300,000 + $100,000 + $200,000 + $200,000) ÷ $400,000
= 2.0

b. Quick Ratio = Quick Assets ÷ Current Liabilities
= ($300,000 + $100,000 + $200,000) ÷ $400,000
= 1.5

Practice Exercises: PE 17-3A, PE 17-3B

Accounts Receivable Analysis

A company's ability to collect its accounts receivable is called **accounts receivable analysis**. It includes the computation and analysis of the following:

- Accounts receivable turnover
- Number of days' sales in receivables

Collecting accounts receivable as quickly as possible improves a company's liquidity. In addition, the cash collected from receivables may be used to improve or expand operations. Quick collection of receivables also reduces the risk of uncollectible accounts.

Accounts Receivable Turnover The **accounts receivable turnover** is computed as follows:

$$\text{Accounts Receivable Turnover} = \frac{\text{Sales}^2}{\text{Average Accounts Receivable}}$$

To illustrate, the accounts receivable turnover for **Lincoln Company** for 2016 and 2015 is computed as follows. Lincoln's accounts receivable balance at the beginning of 2015 is $140,000.

	2016	2015
Sales	$1,498,000	$1,200,000
Accounts receivable (net):		
Beginning of year	$ 120,000	$ 140,000
End of year	115,000	120,000
Total	$ 235,000	$ 260,000
Average accounts receivable	$117,500 ($235,000 ÷ 2)	$130,000 ($260,000 ÷ 2)
Accounts receivable turnover	12.7 ($1,498,000 ÷ $117,500)	9.2 ($1,200,000 ÷ $130,000)

The increase in Lincoln's accounts receivable turnover from 9.2 to 12.7 indicates that the collection of receivables has improved during 2016. This may be due to a change in how credit is granted, collection practices, or both.

[2] If known, *credit* sales should be used in the numerator. Because credit sales are not normally known by external users, we use sales in the numerator.

For Lincoln, the average accounts receivable was computed using the accounts receivable balance at the beginning and the end of the year. When sales are seasonal and, thus, vary throughout the year, monthly balances of receivables are often used. Also, if sales on account include notes receivable as well as accounts receivable, notes and accounts receivable are normally combined for analysis.

Number of Days' Sales in Receivables The **number of days' sales in receivables** is computed as follows:

$$\text{Number of Days' Sales in Receivables} = \frac{\text{Average Accounts Receivable}}{\text{Average Daily Sales}}$$

where

$$\text{Average Daily Sales} = \frac{\text{Sales}}{\text{365 days}}$$

To illustrate, the number of days' sales in receivables for **Lincoln Company** is computed as follows:

	2016	2015
Average accounts receivable	$117,500 ($235,000 ÷ 2)	$130,000 ($260,000 ÷ 2)
Average daily sales	$4,104 ($1,498,000 ÷ 365)	$3,288 ($1,200,000 ÷ 365)
Number of days' sales in receivables	28.6 ($117,500 ÷ $4,104)	39.5 ($130,000 ÷ $3,288)

The number of days' sales in receivables is an estimate of the time (in days) that the accounts receivable have been outstanding. The number of days' sales in receivables is often compared with a company's credit terms to evaluate the efficiency of the collection of receivables.

To illustrate, if Lincoln's credit terms are 2/10, n/30, then Lincoln was very *inefficient* in collecting receivables in 2015. In other words, receivables should have been collected in 30 days or less but were being collected in 39.5 days. Although collections improved during 2016 to 28.6 days, there is probably still room for improvement. On the other hand, if Lincoln's credit terms are n/45, then there is probably little room for improving collections.

Example Exercise 17-4 Accounts Receivable Analysis

OBJ 2

A company reports the following:

Sales	$960,000
Average accounts receivable (net)	48,000

Determine (a) the accounts receivable turnover and (b) the number of days' sales in receivables. Round to one decimal place.

Follow My Example 17-4

a. Accounts Receivable Turnover = Sales ÷ Average Accounts Receivable
= $960,000 ÷ $48,000
= 20.0

b. Number of Days' Sales in Receivables = Average Accounts Receivable ÷ Average Daily Sales
= $48,000 ÷ ($960,000 ÷ 365) = $48,000 ÷ $2,630
= 18.3 days

Practice Exercises: PE 17-4A, PE 17-4B

Inventory Analysis

A company's ability to manage its inventory effectively is evaluated using **inventory analysis**. It includes the computation and analysis of the following:

- Inventory turnover
- Number of days' sales in inventory

Excess inventory decreases liquidity by tying up funds (cash) in inventory. In addition, excess inventory increases insurance expense, property taxes, storage costs, and other related expenses. These expenses further reduce funds that could be used elsewhere to improve or expand operations.

Excess inventory also increases the risk of losses because of price declines or obsolescence of the inventory. On the other hand, a company should keep enough inventory in stock so that it doesn't lose sales because of lack of inventory.

Inventory Turnover The **inventory turnover** is computed as follows:

$$\text{Inventory Turnover} = \frac{\text{Cost of Goods Sold}}{\text{Average Inventory}}$$

To illustrate, the inventory turnover for **Lincoln Company** for 2016 and 2015 is computed as follows. Lincoln's inventory balance at the beginning of 2015 is $311,000.

	2016	2015
Cost of goods sold	$1,043,000	$820,000
Inventories:		
Beginning of year	$ 283,000	$311,000
End of year	264,000	283,000
Total	$ 547,000	$594,000
Average inventory	$273,500 ($547,000 ÷ 2)	$297,000 ($594,000 ÷ 2)
Inventory turnover	3.8 ($1,043,000 ÷ $273,500)	2.8 ($820,000 ÷ $297,000)

The increase in Lincoln's inventory turnover from 2.8 to 3.8 indicates that the management of inventory has improved in 2016. The inventory turnover improved because of an increase in the cost of goods sold, which indicates more sales and a decrease in the average inventories.

What is considered a good inventory turnover varies by type of inventory, companies, and industries. For example, grocery stores have a higher inventory turnover than jewelers or furniture stores. Likewise, within a grocery store, perishable foods have a higher turnover than the soaps and cleansers.

Number of Days' Sales in Inventory The **number of days' sales in inventory** is computed as follows:

$$\text{Number of Days' Sales in Inventory} = \frac{\text{Average Inventory}}{\text{Average Daily Cost of Goods Sold}}$$

where

$$\text{Average Daily Cost of Goods Sold} = \frac{\text{Cost of Goods Sold}}{\text{365 days}}$$

To illustrate, the number of days' sales in inventory for **Lincoln Company** is computed as follows:

	2016	2015
Average inventory	$273,500 ($547,000 ÷ 2)	$297,000 ($594,000 ÷ 2)
Average daily cost of goods sold	$2,858 ($1,043,000 ÷ 365)	$2,247 ($820,000 ÷ 365)
Number of days' sales in inventory	95.7 ($273,500 ÷ $2,858)	132.2 ($297,000 ÷ $2,247)

The number of days' sales in inventory is a rough measure of the length of time it takes to purchase, sell, and replace the inventory. Lincoln's number of days' sales in inventory improved from 132.2 days to 95.7 days during 2016. This is a major improvement in managing inventory.

Example Exercise 17-5 Inventory Analysis

OBJ 2

A company reports the following:

Cost of goods sold	$560,000
Average inventory	112,000

Determine (a) the inventory turnover and (b) the number of days' sales in inventory. Round to one decimal place.

Follow My Example 17-5

a. Inventory Turnover = Cost of Goods Sold ÷ Average Inventory
= $560,000 ÷ $112,000
= 5.0

b. Number of Days' Sales in Inventory = Average Inventory ÷ Average Daily Cost of Goods Sold
= $112,000 ÷ ($560,000 ÷ 365) = $112,000 ÷ $1,534
= 73.0 days

Practice Exercises: PE 17-5A, PE 17-5B

Ratio of Fixed Assets to Long-Term Liabilities

The **ratio of fixed assets to long-term liabilities** provides a measure of whether noteholders or bondholders will be paid. Because fixed assets are often pledged as security for long-term notes and bonds, it is computed as follows:

$$\text{Ratio of Fixed Assets to Long-Term Liabilities} = \frac{\text{Fixed Assets (net)}}{\text{Long-Term Liabilities}}$$

To illustrate, the ratio of fixed assets to long-term liabilities for **Lincoln Company** is computed as follows:

	2016	2015
Fixed assets (net)	$444,500	$470,000
Long-term liabilities	$100,000	$200,000
Ratio of fixed assets to long-term liabilities	4.4 ($444,500 ÷ $100,000)	2.4 ($470,000 ÷ $200,000)

During 2016, Lincoln's ratio of fixed assets to long-term liabilities increased from 2.4 to 4.4. This increase was due primarily to Lincoln paying off one-half of its long-term liabilities in 2016.

Ratio of Liabilities to Stockholders' Equity

The **ratio of liabilities to stockholders' equity** measures how much of the company is financed by debt and equity. It is computed as follows:

$$\text{Ratio of Liabilities to Stockholders' Equity} = \frac{\text{Total Liabilities}}{\text{Total Stockholders' Equity}}$$

To illustrate, the ratio of liabilities to stockholders' equity for **Lincoln Company** is computed as follows:

	2016	2015
Total liabilities	$310,000	$443,000
Total stockholders' equity	$829,500	$787,500
Ratio of liabilities to stockholders' equity	0.4 ($310,000 ÷ $829,500)	0.6 ($443,000 ÷ $787,500)

Lincoln's ratio of liabilities to stockholders' equity decreased from 0.6 to 0.4 during 2016. This is an improvement and indicates that Lincoln's creditors have an adequate margin of safety.

Example Exercise 17-6 Long-Term Solvency Analysis

OBJ 2

The following information was taken from Acme Company's balance sheet:

Fixed assets (net)	$1,400,000
Long-term liabilities	400,000
Total liabilities	560,000
Total stockholders' equity	1,400,000

Determine the company's (a) ratio of fixed assets to long-term liabilities and (b) ratio of liabilities to total stockholders' equity.

Follow My Example 17-6

a. Ratio of Fixed Assets to Long-Term Liabilities = Fixed Assets ÷ Long-Term Liabilities
= $1,400,000 ÷ $400,000
= 3.5

b. Ratio of Liabilities to Total Stockholders' Equity = Total Liabilities ÷ Total Stockholders' Equity
= $560,000 ÷ $1,400,000
= 0.4

Practice Exercises: PE 17-6A, PE 17-6B

Number of Times Interest Charges Are Earned

The **number of times interest charges are earned**, sometimes called the *fixed charge coverage ratio*, measures the risk that interest payments will not be made if earnings decrease. It is computed as follows:

$$\text{Number of Times Interest Charges Are Earned} = \frac{\text{Income Before Income Tax} + \text{Interest Expense}}{\text{Interest Expense}}$$

Interest expense is paid before income taxes. In other words, interest expense is deducted in determining taxable income and, thus, income tax. For this reason, income *before taxes* is used in computing the number of times interest charges are earned.

The *higher* the ratio the more likely interest payments will be paid if earnings decrease. To illustrate, the number of times interest charges are earned for **Lincoln Company** is computed as follows:

	2016	2015
Income before income tax	$162,500	$134,600
Add interest expense	6,000	12,000
Amount available to pay interest	$168,500	$146,600
Number of times interest charges are earned	28.1 ($168,500 ÷ $6,000)	12.2 ($146,600 ÷ $12,000)

The number of times interest charges are earned improved from 12.2 to 28.1 during 2016. This indicates that Lincoln has sufficient earnings to pay interest expense.

The number of times interest charges are earned can be adapted for use with dividends on preferred stock. In this case, the *number of times preferred dividends are earned* is computed as follows:

$$\text{Number of Times Preferred Dividends Are Earned} = \frac{\text{Net Income}}{\text{Preferred Dividends}}$$

Since dividends are paid after taxes, net income is used in computing the number of times preferred dividends are earned. The *higher* the ratio, the more likely preferred dividend payments will be paid if earnings decrease.

Example Exercise 17-7 Times Interest Charges Are Earned OBJ 2

A company reports the following:

Income before income tax	$250,000
Interest expense	100,000

Determine the number of times interest charges are earned.

Follow My Example 17-7

Number of Times Interest Charges Are Earned = (Income Before Income Tax + Interest Expense) ÷ Interest Expense
= ($250,000 + $100,000) ÷ $100,000
= 3.5

Practice Exercises: PE 17-7A, PE 17-7B

Profitability Analysis

Use financial statement analysis to assess the profitability of a business.

Profitability analysis focuses on the ability of a company to earn profits. This ability is reflected in the company's operating results, as reported in its income statement. The ability to earn profits also depends on the assets the company has available for use in its operations, as reported in its balance sheet. Thus, income statement and balance sheet relationships are often used in evaluating profitability.

Note: **Profitability analysis focuses on the relationship between operating results and the resources available to a business.**

Common profitability analyses include the following:

- Ratio of sales to assets
- Rate earned on total assets
- Rate earned on stockholders' equity
- Rate earned on common stockholders' equity
- Earnings per share on common stock
- Price-earnings ratio
- Dividends per share
- Dividend yield

Ratio of Sales to Assets

The **ratio of sales to assets** measures how effectively a company uses its assets. It is computed as follows:

$$\text{Ratio of Sales to Assets} = \frac{\text{Sales}}{\text{Average Total Assets (excluding long-term investments)}}$$

Note that any long-term investments are excluded in computing the ratio of sales to assets. This is because long-term investments are unrelated to normal operations and sales.

To illustrate, the ratio of sales to assets for **Lincoln Company** is computed as follows. Total assets (excluding long-term investments) are $1,010,000 at the beginning of 2015.

	2016	2015
Sales	$1,498,000	$1,200,000
Total assets (excluding long-term investments):		
Beginning of year	$1,053,000*	$1,010,000
End of year	1,044,500**	1,053,000*
Total	$2,097,500	$2,063,000
Average total assets	$1,048,750 ($2,097,500 ÷ 2)	$1,031,500 ($2,063,000 ÷ 2)
Ratio of sales to assets	1.4 ($1,498,000 ÷ $1,048,750)	1.2 ($1,200,000 ÷ $1,031,500)

*($1,230,500 – $177,500)
**($1,139,500 – $95,000)

For Lincoln, the average total assets was computed using total assets (excluding long-term investments) at the beginning and end of the year. The average total assets could also be based on monthly or quarterly averages.

The ratio of sales to assets indicates that Lincoln's use of its operating assets has improved in 2016. This was primarily due to the increase in sales in 2016.

Example Exercise 17-8 Sales to Assets

OBJ 3

A company reports the following:

Sales	$2,250,000
Average total assets	1,500,000

Determine the ratio of sales to assets.

Follow My Example 17-8

Ratio of Sales to Assets = Sales ÷ Average Total Assets
= $2,250,000 ÷ $1,500,000
= 1.5

Practice Exercises: PE 17-8A, PE 17-8B

Rate Earned on Total Assets

The **rate earned on total assets** measures the profitability of total assets, without considering how the assets are financed. In other words, this rate is not affected by the portion of assets financed by creditors or stockholders. It is computed as follows:

$$\text{Rate Earned on Total Assets} = \frac{\text{Net Income} + \text{Interest Expense}}{\text{Average Total Assets}}$$

The rate earned on total assets is computed by adding interest expense to net income. By adding interest expense to net income, the effect of whether the assets are financed by creditors (debt) or stockholders (equity) is eliminated. Because net income includes any income earned from long-term investments, the average total assets includes long-term investments as well as the net operating assets.

To illustrate, the rate earned on total assets by **Lincoln Company** is computed as follows. Total assets are $1,187,500 at the beginning of 2015.

	2016	2015
Net income	$ 91,000	$ 76,500
Plus interest expense	6,000	12,000
Total	$ 97,000	$ 88,500
Total assets:		
Beginning of year	$1,230,500	$1,187,500
End of year	1,139,500	1,230,500
Total	$2,370,000	$2,418,000
Average total assets	$1,185,000 ($2,370,000 ÷ 2)	$1,209,000 ($2,418,000 ÷ 2)
Rate earned on total assets	8.2% ($97,000 ÷ $1,185,000)	7.3% ($88,500 ÷ $1,209,000)

The rate earned on total assets improved from 7.3% to 8.2% during 2016.

The *rate earned on operating assets* is sometimes computed when there are large amounts of nonoperating income and expense. It is computed as follows:

$$\text{Rate Earned on Operating Assets} = \frac{\text{Income from Operations}}{\text{Average Operating Assets}}$$

Because Lincoln Company does not have a significant amount of nonoperating income and expense, the rate earned on operating assets is not illustrated.

Example Exercise 17-9 Rate Earned on Total Assets

OBJ 3

A company reports the following income statement and balance sheet information for the current year:

Net income	$ 125,000
Interest expense	25,000
Average total assets	2,000,000

Determine the rate earned on total assets.

Follow My Example 17-9

Rate Earned on Total Assets = (Net Income + Interest Expense) ÷ Average Total Assets
= ($125,000 + $25,000) ÷ $2,000,000
= $150,000 ÷ $2,000,000
= 7.5%

Practice Exercises: PE 17-9A, PE 17-9B

Rate Earned on Stockholders' Equity

The **rate earned on stockholders' equity** measures the rate of income earned on the amount invested by the stockholders. It is computed as follows:

$$\text{Rate Earned on Stockholders' Equity} = \frac{\text{Net Income}}{\text{Average Total Stockholders' Equity}}$$

To illustrate, the rate earned on stockholders' equity for **Lincoln Company** is computed as follows. Total stockholders' equity is $750,000 at the beginning of 2015.

	2016	2015
Net income	$ 91,000	$ 76,500
Stockholders' equity:		
Beginning of year	$ 787,500	$ 750,000
End of year	829,500	787,500
Total	$1,617,000	$1,537,500
Average stockholders' equity	$808,500 ($1,617,000 ÷ 2)	$768,750 ($1,537,500 ÷ 2)
Rate earned on stockholders' equity	11.3% ($91,000 ÷ $808,500)	10.0% ($76,500 ÷ $768,750)

The rate earned on stockholders' equity improved from 10.0% to 11.3% during 2016.

Leverage involves using debt to increase the return on an investment. The rate earned on stockholders' equity is normally higher than the rate earned on total assets. This is because of the effect of leverage.

For **Lincoln Company**, the effect of leverage for 2016 is 3.1% and for 2015 is 2.7% computed as follows:

	2016	2015
Rate earned on stockholders' equity	11.3%	10.0%
Less rate earned on total assets	8.2	7.3
Effect of leverage	3.1%	2.7%

Exhibit 8 shows the 2016 and 2015 effects of leverage for Lincoln.

Rate Earned on Common Stockholders' Equity

The **rate earned on common stockholders' equity** measures the rate of profits earned on the amount invested by the common stockholders. It is computed as follows:

$$\text{Rate Earned on Common Stockholders' Equity} = \frac{\text{Net Income} - \text{Preferred Dividends}}{\text{Average Common Stockholders' Equity}}$$

EXHIBIT 8

Effect of Leverage

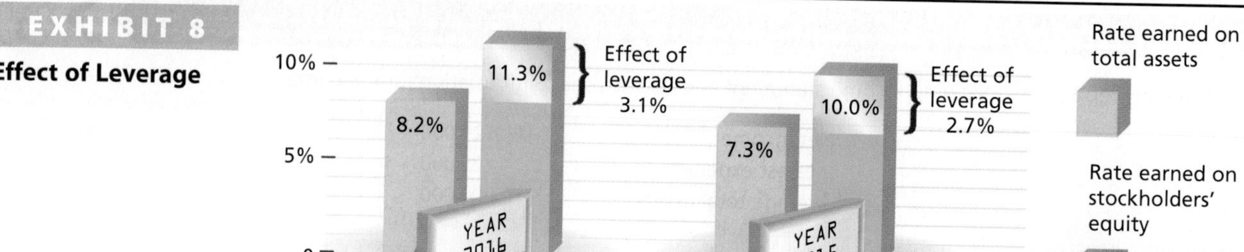

Because preferred stockholders rank ahead of the common stockholders in their claim on earnings, any preferred dividends are subtracted from net income in computing the rate earned on common stockholders' equity.

Lincoln Company had $150,000 of 6% preferred stock outstanding on December 31, 2016 and 2015. Thus, preferred dividends of $9,000 ($150,000 × 6%) are deducted from net income. Lincoln's common stockholders' equity is determined as follows:

	December 31		
	2016	**2015**	**2014**
Common stock, $10 par	$500,000	$500,000	$500,000
Retained earnings	179,500	137,500	100,000
Common stockholders' equity	$679,500	$637,500	$600,000

The retained earnings on December 31, 2014, of $100,000 is the same as the retained earnings on January 1, 2015, as shown in Lincoln's retained earnings statement in Exhibit 4.

Using this information, the rate earned on common stockholders' equity for Lincoln is computed as follows:

	2016	**2015**
Net income	$ 91,000	$ 76,500
Less preferred dividends	9,000	9,000
Total	$ 82,000	$ 67,500
Common stockholders' equity:		
Beginning of year	$ 637,500	$ 600,000
End of year	679,500*	637,500**
Total	$1,317,000	$1,237,500
Average common stockholders' equity	$658,500 ($1,317,000 ÷ 2)	$618,750 ($1,237,500 ÷ 2)
Rate earned on common stockholders' equity	12.5% ($82,000 ÷ $658,500)	10.9% ($67,500 ÷ $618,750)

*($829,500 – $150,000)
**($787,500 – $150,000)

Lincoln's rate earned on common stockholders' equity improved from 10.9% to 12.5% in 2016. This rate differs from the rates earned by Lincoln on total assets and stockholders' equity, which follow:

	2016	**2015**
Rate earned on total assets	8.2%	7.3%
Rate earned on stockholders' equity	11.3%	10.0%
Rate earned on common stockholders' equity	12.5%	10.9%

These rates differ because of leverage, as discussed in the preceding section.

Example Exercise 17-10 Common Stockholders' Profitability Analysis

OBJ 3

A company reports the following:

Net income	$ 125,000
Preferred dividends	5,000
Average stockholders' equity	1,000,000
Average common stockholders' equity	800,000

Determine (a) the rate earned on stockholders' equity and (b) the rate earned on common stockholders' equity.

Follow My Example 17-10

a. Rate Earned on Stockholders' Equity = Net Income ÷ Average Stockholders' Equity
= $125,000 ÷ $1,000,000
= 12.5%

b. Rate Earned on Common Stockholders' Equity = (Net Income – Preferred Dividends) ÷ Average Common Stockholders' Equity
= ($125,000 – $5,000) ÷ $800,000
= 15%

Practice Exercises: PE 17-10A, PE 17-10B

Earnings per Share on Common Stock

Earnings per share (EPS) on common stock measures the share of profits that are earned by a share of common stock. Earnings per share must be reported in the income statement. As a result, earnings per share (EPS) is often reported in the financial press. It is computed as follows:

$$\text{Earnings per Share (EPS) on Common Stock} = \frac{\text{Net Income} - \text{Preferred Dividends}}{\text{Shares of Common Stock Outstanding}}$$

When preferred and common stock are outstanding, preferred dividends are subtracted from net income to determine the income related to the common shares.

To illustrate, the earnings per share (EPS) of common stock for **Lincoln Company** is computed as follows:

	2016	2015
Net income	$91,000	$76,500
Preferred dividends	9,000	9,000
Total	$82,000	$67,500
Shares of common stock outstanding	50,000	50,000
Earnings per share on common stock	$1.64 ($82,000 ÷ 50,000)	$1.35 ($67,500 ÷ 50,000)

Lincoln had $150,000 of 6% preferred stock outstanding on December 31, 2016 and 2015. Thus, preferred dividends of $9,000 ($150,000 × 6%) are deducted from net income in computing earnings per share on common stock.

Lincoln did not issue any additional shares of common stock in 2016. If Lincoln had issued additional shares in 2016, a weighted average of common shares outstanding during the year would have been used.

Lincoln's earnings per share (EPS) on common stock improved from $1.35 to $1.64 during 2016.

Lincoln Company has a simple capital structure with only common stock and preferred stock outstanding. Many corporations, however, have complex capital structures with various types of equity securities outstanding, such as convertible preferred stock,

stock options, and stock warrants. In such cases, the possible effects of such securities on the shares of common stock outstanding are considered in reporting earnings per share. These possible effects are reported separately as *earnings per common share assuming dilution* or *diluted earnings per share*. This topic is described and illustrated in advanced accounting courses and textbooks.

Price-Earnings Ratio

The **price-earnings (P/E) ratio** on common stock measures a company's future earnings prospects. It is often quoted in the financial press and is computed as follows:

$$\text{Price-Earnings (P/E) Ratio} = \frac{\text{Market Price per Share of Common Stock}}{\text{Earnings per Share on Common Stock}}$$

To illustrate, the price-earnings (P/E) ratio for **Lincoln Company** is computed as follows:

	2016	2015
Market price per share of common stock	$41.00	$27.00
Earnings per share on common stock	$1.64	$1.35
Price-earnings ratio on common stock	25 ($41 ÷ $1.64)	20 ($27 ÷ $1.35)

The price-earnings ratio improved from 20 to 25 during 2016. In other words, a share of common stock of Lincoln was selling for 20 times earnings per share at the end of 2015. At the end of 2016, the common stock was selling for 25 times earnings per share. This indicates that the market expects Lincoln to experience favorable earnings in the future.

Example Exercise 17-11 Earnings per Share and Price-Earnings Ratio

A company reports the following:

Net income	$250,000
Preferred dividends	$15,000
Shares of common stock outstanding	20,000
Market price per share of common stock	$35.25

a. Determine the company's earnings per share on common stock.

b. Determine the company's price-earnings ratio. Round to one decimal place.

Follow My Example 17-11

a. Earnings per Share on Common Stock = (Net Income − Preferred Dividends) ÷ Shares of Common Stock Outstanding
= ($250,000 − $15,000) ÷ 20,000
= $11.75

b. Price-Earnings Ratio = Market Price per Share of Common Stock ÷ Earnings per Share on Common Stock
= $35.25 ÷ $11.75
= 3.0

Practice Exercises: PE 17-11A, PE 17-11B

Dividends per Share

Dividends per share measures the extent to which earnings are being distributed to common shareholders. It is computed as follows:

$$\text{Dividends per Share} = \frac{\text{Dividends on Common Stock}}{\text{Shares of Common Stock Outstanding}}$$

To illustrate, the dividends per share for **Lincoln Company** are computed as follows:

	2016	2015
Dividends on common stock	$40,000	$30,000
Shares of common stock outstanding	50,000	50,000
Dividends per share of common stock	$0.80 ($40,000 ÷ 50,000)	$0.60 ($30,000 ÷ 50,000)

The dividends per share of common stock increased from $0.60 to $0.80 during 2016.

Dividends per share are often reported with earnings per share. Comparing the two per-share amounts indicates the extent to which earnings are being retained for use in operations. To illustrate, the dividends and earnings per share for **Lincoln Company** are shown in Exhibit 9.

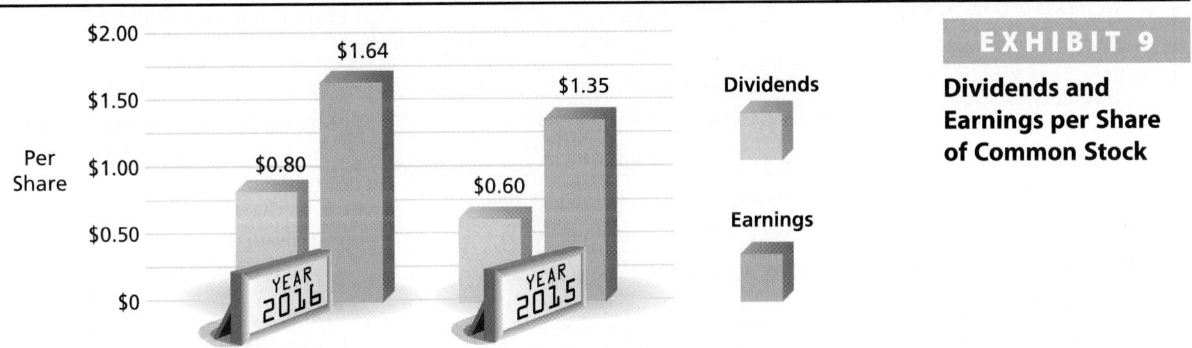

EXHIBIT 9

Dividends and Earnings per Share of Common Stock

Dividend Yield

The **dividend yield** on common stock measures the rate of return to common stockholders from cash dividends. It is of special interest to investors whose objective is to earn revenue (dividends) from their investment. It is computed as follows:

$$\text{Dividend Yield} = \frac{\text{Dividends per Share of Common Stock}}{\text{Market Price per Share of Common Stock}}$$

The dividends per share, dividend yield, and P/E ratio of a common stock are normally quoted on the daily listing of stock prices in *The Wall Street Journal* and on Yahoo!'s finance Web site.

To illustrate, the dividend yield for **Lincoln Company** is computed as follows:

	2016	2015
Dividends per share of common stock	$0.80	$0.60
Market price per share of common stock	$41.00	$27.00
Dividend yield on common stock	2.0% ($0.80 ÷ $41)	2.2% ($0.60 ÷ $27)

The dividend yield declined slightly from 2.2% to 2.0% in 2016. This decline was primarily due to the increase in the market price of Lincoln's common stock.

Summary of Analytical Measures

Exhibit 10 shows a summary of the solvency and profitability measures discussed in this chapter. The type of industry and the company's operations usually affect which measures are used. In many cases, additional measures are used for a specific industry. For example, airlines use *revenue per passenger mile* and *cost per available seat* as profitability measures. Likewise, hotels use *occupancy rates* as a profitability measure.

The analytical measures shown in Exhibit 10 are a useful starting point for analyzing a company's solvency and profitability. However, they are not a substitute for sound judgment. For example, the general economic and business environment should always be considered in analyzing a company's future prospects. In addition, any trends and interrelationships among the measures should be carefully studied.

EXHIBIT 10 **Summary of Analytical Measures**

	Measure	Method of Computation	Use
Liquidity and Solvency Measures	Working Capital	Current Assets – Current Liabilities	To indicate the ability to meet currently maturing obligations (measures solvency)
	Current Ratio	Current Assets / Current Liabilities	
	Quick Ratio	Quick Assets / Current Liabilities	To indicate instant debt-paying ability (measures solvency)
	Accounts Receivable Turnover	Sales / Average Accounts Receivable	To assess the efficiency in collecting receivables and in the management of credit (measures liquidity)
	Numbers of Days' Sales in Receivables	Average Accounts Receivable / Average Daily Sales	
	Inventory Turnover	Cost of Goods Sold / Average Inventory	To assess the efficiency in the management of inventory (measures liquidity)
	Number of Days' Sales in Inventory	Average Inventory / Average Daily Cost of Goods Sold	
	Ratio of Fixed Assets to Long-Term Liabilities	Fixed Assets (net) / Long-Term Liabilities	To indicate the margin of safety to long-term creditors (measures solvency)
	Ratio of Liabilities to Stockholders' Equity	Total Liabilities / Total Stockholders' Equity	To indicate the margin of safety to creditors (measures solvency)
	Number of Times Interest Charges Are Earned	Income Before Income Tax + Interest Expense / Interest Expense	To assess the risk to debtholders in terms of number of times interest charges were earned (measures solvency)
	Number of Times Preferred Dividends Are Earned	Net Income / Preferred Dividends	To assess the risk to preferred stockholders in terms of the number of times preferred dividends were earned (measures solvency)
Profitability Measures	Ratio of Sales to Assets	Sales / Average Total Assets (excluding long-term investments)	To assess the effectiveness in the use of assets
	Rate Earned on Total Assets	Net Income + Interest Expense / Average Total Assets	To assess the profitability of the assets
	Rate Earned on Stockholders' Equity	Net Income / Average Total Stockholders' Equity	To assess the profitability of the investment by stockholders
	Rate Earned on Common Stockholders' Equity	Net Income – Preferred Dividends / Average Common Stockholders' Equity	To assess the profitability of the investment by common stockholders
	Earnings per Share (EPS) on Common Stock	Net Income – Preferred Dividends / Shares of Common Stock Outstanding	
	Price-Earnings (P/E) Ratio	Market Price per Share of Common Stock / Earnings per Share on Common Stock	To indicate future earnings prospects, based on the relationship between market value of common stock and earnings
	Dividends per Share	Dividends on Common Stock / Shares of Common Stock Outstanding	To indicate the extent to which earnings are being distributed to common stockholders
	Dividend Yield	Dividends per Share of Common Stock / Market Price per Share of Common Stock	To indicate the rate of return to common stockholders in terms of dividends

Integrity, Objectivity, and Ethics in Business

CHARACTERISTICS OF FINANCIAL STATEMENT FRAUD

Each year the Association of Certified Fraud Examiners conducts a worldwide survey examining the characteristics of corporate fraud. The most recent study found that:

- 43.3% of frauds were detected by a tip from an employee or someone close to the company;
- Frauds committed by owners and executives tended to be much larger than those caused by employees;
- Most people who are caught committing fraud are first time offenders with clean employment histories; and
- In 81% of the cases, the person committing the fraud displayed one or more behavioral red flags such as living beyond their means, financial difficulties, and excessive control issues.

Fraud examiners can use these trends to help them narrow their focus when searching for fraud.

Source: 2012 Report to the Nations, Association of Certified Fraud Examiners, 2012.

Corporate Annual Reports

OBJ 4 Describe the contents of corporate annual reports.

Public corporations issue annual reports summarizing their operating activities for the past year and plans for the future. Such annual reports include the financial statements and the accompanying notes. In addition, annual reports normally include the following sections:

- Management discussion and analysis
- Report on internal control
- Report on fairness of the financial statements

See Appendix D for more information.

Management Discussion and Analysis

Management's Discussion and Analysis (MD&A) is required in annual reports filed with the Securities and Exchange Commission. It includes management's analysis of current operations and its plans for the future. Typical items included in the MD&A are as follows:

- Management's analysis and explanations of any significant changes between the current and prior years' financial statements.
- Important accounting principles or policies that could affect interpretation of the financial statements, including the effect of changes in accounting principles or the adoption of new accounting principles.
- Management's assessment of the company's liquidity and the availability of capital to the company.
- Significant risk exposures that might affect the company.
- Any "off-balance-sheet" arrangements such as leases not included directly in the financial statements. Such arrangements are discussed in advanced accounting courses and textbooks.

Report on Internal Control

The Sarbanes-Oxley Act of 2002 requires a report on internal control by management. The report states management's responsibility for establishing and maintaining internal control. In addition, management's assessment of the effectiveness of internal controls over financial reporting is included in the report.

Sarbanes-Oxley also requires a public accounting firm to verify management's conclusions on internal control. Thus, two reports on internal control, one by management and one by a public accounting firm, are included in the annual report. In some situations, these may be combined into a single report on internal control.

Report on Fairness of the Financial Statements

All publicly held corporations are required to have an independent audit (examination) of their financial statements. The Certified Public Accounting (CPA) firm that conducts the audit renders an opinion, called the *Report of Independent Registered Public Accounting Firm*, on the fairness of the statements.

An opinion stating that the financial statements present fairly the financial position, results of operations, and cash flows of the company is said to be an *unqualified opinion*, sometimes called a *clean opinion*. Any report other than an unqualified opinion raises a "red flag" for financial statement users and requires further investigation as to its cause.

The annual report of Nike Inc. is shown in Appendix C. The Nike report includes the financial statements as well as the MD&A Report on Internal Control and the Report on Fairness of the Financial Statements.

Integrity, Objectivity, and Ethics in Business

BUY LOW, SELL HIGH

Research analysts work for banks, brokerages, or other financial institutions. Their job is to estimate the value of a company's common stock by reviewing and evaluating the company's business model, strategic plan, and financial performance. Based on this analysis, the analyst develops an estimate of a stock's value, which is called its *fundamental value*. Analysts then advise their clients to "buy" or "sell" a company's stock based on the following guidelines:

Current market price is greater than fundamental value	Sell
Current market price is lower than fundamental value	Buy

If analysts are doing their job well, their clients will enjoy large returns by buying stocks at low prices and selling them at high prices.

APPENDIX

Unusual Items on the Income Statement

Generally accepted accounting principles require that unusual items be reported separately on the income statement. This is because such items do not occur frequently and are typically unrelated to current operations. Without separate reporting of these items, users of the financial statements might be misled about current and future operations.

Unusual items on the income statement are classified as one of the following:

- Affecting the *current period* income statement
- Affecting a *prior period* income statement

Unusual Items Affecting the Current Period's Income Statement

Unusual items affecting the current period's income statement include the following:

- Discontinued operations
- Extraordinary items

These items are reported separately on the income statement for any period in which they occur.

Discontinued Operations A company may discontinue a component of its operations by selling or abandoning the component's operations. For example, a retailer might decide to sell its product only online and, thus, discontinue selling its merchandise at its retail outlets (stores).

If the discontinued component is (1) the result of a strategic shift and (2) has a major effect on the entity's operations and financial results, any gain or loss on discontinued operations is reported on the income statement as a *Gain (or loss) from discontinued operations.* It is reported immediately following *Income from continuing operations.*

To illustrate, assume that Jones Corporation produces and sells electrical products, hardware supplies, and lawn equipment. Because of a lack of profits, Jones discontinues its electrical products operation and sells the remaining inventory and other assets at a loss of $100,000. Exhibit 11 illustrates the reporting of the loss on discontinued operations.[3]

EXHIBIT 11

Unusual Items in the Income Statement

Jones Corporation Income Statement For the Year Ended December 31, 2016	
Sales	$12,350,000
Cost of merchandise sold	5,800,000
Gross profit	$ 6,550,000
Selling and administrative expenses	5,240,000
Income from continuing operations before income tax	$ 1,310,000
Income tax expense	620,000
Income from continuing operations	$ 690,000
Loss on discontinued operations	100,000
Income before extraordinary items	$ 590,000
Extraordinary items:	
Gain on condemnation of land	150,000
Net income	$ 740,000

In addition, a note to the financial statements should describe the operations sold, including the date operations were discontinued, and details about the assets, liabilities, income, and expenses of the discontinued component.

Extraordinary Items An **extraordinary item** is defined as an event or a transaction that has both of the following characteristics:

- Unusual in nature
- Infrequent in occurrence

Gains and losses from natural disasters such as floods, earthquakes, and fires are normally reported as extraordinary items, provided that they occur infrequently. Gains or losses from land or buildings taken (condemned) for public use are also reported as extraordinary items.

Any gain or loss from extraordinary items is reported on the income statement as *Gain (or loss) from extraordinary item.* It is reported immediately following *Income from continuing operations* and any *Gain (or loss) on discontinued operations.*

To illustrate, assume that land owned by Jones Corporation was taken for public use (condemned) by the local government. The condemnation of the land resulted in a gain of $150,000. Exhibit 11 illustrates the reporting of the extraordinary gain.[4,5]

[3] The gain or loss on discontinued operations is reported net of any tax effects. To simplify, the tax effects are not specifically identified in Exhibit 11.

[4] The gain or loss on extraordinary operations is reported net of any tax effects.

[5] At the time of this writing, the Financial Accounting Standards Board had released an exposure draft, which proposes eliminating extraordinary items as a separate line item on the income statement. The outcome of this proposal was uncertain at the time of this writing.

Reporting Earnings per Share Earnings per common share should be reported separately for discontinued operations and extraordinary items. To illustrate, a partial income statement for Jones Corporation is shown in Exhibit 12. The company has 200,000 shares of common stock outstanding.

Exhibit 12 reports earnings per common share for income from continuing operations, discontinued operations, and extraordinary items. However, only earnings per share for income from continuing operations and net income are required by generally accepted accounting principles. The other per-share amounts may be presented in the notes to the financial statements.

EXHIBIT 12

Income Statement with Earnings per Share

Jones Corporation Income Statement For the Year Ended December 31, 2016	
Earnings per common share:	
Income from continuing operations	$3.45
Loss on discontinued operations	0.50
Income before extraordinary items	$2.95
Extraordinary items:	
Gain on condemnation of land	0.75
Net income	$3.70

Unusual Items Affecting the Prior Period's Income Statement

An unusual item may occur that affects a prior period's income statement. Two such items are as follows:

- Errors in applying generally accepted accounting principles
- Changes from one generally accepted accounting principle to another

If an error is discovered in a prior period's financial statement, the prior-period statement and all following statements are restated and thus corrected.

A company may change from one generally accepted accounting principle to another. In this case, the prior-period financial statements are restated as if the new accounting principle had always been used.[5]

For both of the preceding items, the current-period earnings are not affected. That is, only the earnings reported in prior periods are restated. However, because the prior earnings are restated, the beginning balance of Retained Earnings may also have to be restated. This, in turn, may cause the restatement of other balance sheet accounts. Illustrations of these types of adjustments and restatements are provided in advanced accounting courses.

[5] Changes from one acceptable depreciation method to another acceptable depreciation method are an exception to this general rule and are to be treated prospectively as a change in estimate, as discussed in Chapter 10.

At a Glance 17

Describe basic financial statement analytical methods.

Key Points The basic financial statements provide much of the information users need to make economic decisions. Analytical procedures are used to compare items on a current financial statement with related items on earlier statements, or to examine relationships within a financial statement.

Learning Outcomes	*Example Exercises*	*Practice Exercises*
• Prepare a vertical analysis from a company's financial statements.	**EE17-1**	**PE17-1A, 17-1B**
• Prepare a horizontal analysis from a company's financial statements.	**EE17-2**	**PE17-2A, 17-2B**
• Prepare common-sized financial statements.		

Use financial statement analysis to assess the solvency of a business.

Key Points All users of financial statements are interested in the ability of a business to convert assets into cash (liquidity), pay its debts (solvency), and earn income (profitability). Liquidity, solvency, and profitability are interrelated. Liquidity and solvency are normally assessed by examining the following: current position analysis, accounts receivable analysis, inventory analysis, the ratio of fixed assets to long-term liabilities, the ratio of liabilities to stockholders' equity, and the number of times interest charges are earned.

Learning Outcomes	*Example Exercises*	*Practice Exercises*
• Determine working capital.		
• Compute and interpret the current ratio.	**EE17-3**	**PE17-3A, 17-3B**
• Compute and interpret the quick ratio.	**EE17-3**	**PE17-3A, 17-3B**
• Compute and interpret accounts receivable turnover.	**EE17-4**	**PE17-4A, 17-4B**
• Compute and interpret the number of days' sales in receivables.	**EE17-4**	**PE17-4A, 17-4B**
• Compute and interpret inventory turnover.	**EE17-5**	**PE17-5A, 17-5B**
• Compute and interpret the number of days' sales in inventory.	**EE17-5**	**PE17-5A, 17-5B**
• Compute and interpret the ratio of fixed assets to long-term liabilities.	**EE17-6**	**PE17-6A, 17-6B**
• Compute and interpret the ratio of liabilities to stockholders' equity.	**EE17-6**	**PE17-6A, 17-6B**
• Compute and interpret the number of times interest charges are earned.	**EE17-7**	**PE17-7A, 17-7B**

Use financial statement analysis to assess the profitability of a business.

Key Points Profitability analysis focuses on the ability of a company to earn profits. This ability is reflected in the company's operating results as reported on the income statement and resources available as reported on the balance sheet. Major analyses include the ratio of sales to assets, the rate earned on total assets, the rate earned on stockholders' equity, the rate earned on common stockholders' equity, earnings per share on common stock, the price-earnings ratio, dividends per share, and dividend yield.

Learning Outcomes	Example Exercises	Practice Exercises
• Compute and interpret the ratio of sales to assets.	EE17-8	PE17-8A, 17-8B
• Compute and interpret the rate earned on total assets.	EE17-9	PE17-9A, 17-9B
• Compute and interpret the rate earned on stockholders' equity.	EE17-10	PE17-10A, 17-10B
• Compute and interpret the rate earned on common stockholders' equity.	EE17-10	PE17-10A, 17-10B
• Compute and interpret the earnings per share on common stock.	EE17-11	PE17-11A, 17-11B
• Compute and interpret the price-earnings ratio.	EE17-11	PE17-11A, 17-11B
• Compute and interpret the dividends per share and dividend yield.		
• Describe the uses and limitations of analytical measures.		

Describe the contents of corporate annual reports.

Key Points Corporations normally issue annual reports to their stockholders and other interested parties. Such reports summarize the corporation's operating activities for the past year and plans for the future.

Learning Outcome	Example Exercises	Practice Exercises
• Describe the elements of a corporate annual report.		

Key Terms

accounts receivable analysis (804)
accounts receivable turnover (804)
common-sized statement (800)
current position analysis (802)
current ratio (802)
dividend yield (815)
dividends per share (814)
earnings per share (EPS) on common stock (813)
extraordinary item (819)
horizontal analysis (796)
inventory analysis (806)
inventory turnover (806)
leverage (811)
liquidity (801)
Management's Discussion and Analysis (MD&A) (817)
number of days' sales in inventory (806)
number of days' sales in receivables (805)
number of times interest charges are earned (808)
price-earnings (P/E) ratio (814)
profitability (801)
quick assets (803)
quick ratio (803)
rate earned on common stockholders' equity (811)
rate earned on stockholders' equity (811)
rate earned on total assets (810)
ratio of fixed assets to long-term liabilities (807)
ratio of liabilities to stockholders' equity (807)
ratio of sales to assets (809)
solvency (801)
vertical analysis (799)
working capital (802)

Illustrative Problem

Rainbow Paint Co.'s comparative financial statements for the years ending December 31, 2016 and 2015, are as follows. The market price of Rainbow Paint Co.'s common stock was $25 on December 31, 2016, and $30 on December 31, 2015.

Rainbow Paint Co.
Comparative Income Statement
For the Years Ended December 31, 2016 and 2015

	2016	2015
Sales	$5,000,000	$3,200,000
Cost of goods sold	3,400,000	2,080,000
Gross profit	$1,600,000	$1,120,000
Selling expenses	$ 650,000	$ 464,000
Administrative expenses	325,000	224,000
Total operating expenses	$ 975,000	$ 688,000
Income from operations	$ 625,000	$ 432,000
Other income	25,000	19,200
	$ 650,000	$ 451,200
Other expense (interest)	105,000	64,000
Income before income tax	$ 545,000	$ 387,200
Income tax expense	300,000	176,000
Net income	$ 245,000	$ 211,200

Rainbow Paint Co.
Comparative Retained Earnings Statement
For the Years Ended December 31, 2016 and 2015

	2016	2015
Retained earnings, January 1	$723,000	$581,800
Add net income for year	245,000	211,200
Total	$968,000	$793,000
Deduct dividends:		
On preferred stock	$ 40,000	$ 40,000
On common stock	45,000	30,000
Total	$ 85,000	$ 70,000
Retained earnings, December 31	$883,000	$723,000

Rainbow Paint Co. **Comparative Balance Sheet** **December 31, 2016 and 2015**		
	Dec. 31, 2016	**Dec. 31, 2015**
Assets		
Current assets:		
Cash	$ 175,000	$ 125,000
Temporary investments	150,000	50,000
Accounts receivable (net)	425,000	325,000
Inventories	720,000	480,000
Prepaid expenses	30,000	20,000
Total current assets	$1,500,000	$1,000,000
Long-term investments	250,000	225,000
Property, plant, and equipment (net)	2,093,000	1,948,000
Total assets	$3,843,000	$3,173,000
Liabilities		
Current liabilities	$ 750,000	$ 650,000
Long-term liabilities:		
Mortgage note payable, 10%, due 2017	$ 410,000	—
Bonds payable, 8%, due 2020	800,000	$ 800,000
Total long-term liabilities	$1,210,000	$ 800,000
Total liabilities	$1,960,000	$1,450,000
Stockholders' Equity		
Preferred 8% stock, $100 par	$ 500,000	$ 500,000
Common stock, $10 par	500,000	500,000
Retained earnings	883,000	723,000
Total stockholders' equity	$1,883,000	$1,723,000
Total liabilities and stockholders' equity	$3,843,000	$3,173,000

Instructions

Determine the following measures for 2016:

1. Working capital
2. Current ratio
3. Quick ratio
4. Accounts receivable turnover
5. Number of days' sales in receivables
6. Inventory turnover
7. Number of days' sales in inventory
8. Ratio of fixed assets to long-term liabilities
9. Ratio of liabilities to stockholders' equity
10. Number of times interest charges are earned
11. Number of times preferred dividends are earned
12. Ratio of sales to assets
13. Rate earned on total assets
14. Rate earned on stockholders' equity

15. Rate earned on common stockholders' equity
16. Earnings per share on common stock
17. Price-earnings ratio
18. Dividends per share
19. Dividend yield

Solution

(Ratios are rounded to the nearest single digit after the decimal point.)

1. Working capital: $750,000
   $1,500,000 – $750,000
2. Current ratio: 2.0
   $1,500,000 ÷ $750,000
3. Quick ratio: 1.0
   $750,000 ÷ $750,000
4. Accounts receivable turnover: 13.3
   $5,000,000 ÷ [($425,000 + $325,000) ÷ 2]
5. Number of days' sales in receivables: 27.4 days
   $5,000,000 ÷ 365 days = $13,699
   $375,000 ÷ $13,699
6. Inventory turnover: 5.7
   $3,400,000 ÷ [($720,000 + $480,000) ÷ 2]
7. Number of days' sales in inventory: 64.4 days
   $3,400,000 ÷ 365 days = $9,315
   $600,000 ÷ $9,315
8. Ratio of fixed assets to long-term liabilities: 1.7
   $2,093,000 ÷ $1,210,000
9. Ratio of liabilities to stockholders' equity: 1.0
   $1,960,000 ÷ $1,883,000
10. Number of times interest charges are earned: 6.2
    ($545,000 + $105,000) ÷ $105,000
11. Number of times preferred dividends are earned: 6.1
    $245,000 ÷ $40,000
12. Ratio of sales to assets: 1.5
    $5,000,000 ÷ [($3,593,000 + $2,948,000) ÷ 2]
13. Rate earned on total assets: 10.0%
    ($245,000 + $105,000) ÷ [($3,843,000 + $3,173,000) ÷ 2]
14. Rate earned on stockholders' equity: 13.6%
    $245,000 ÷ [($1,883,000 + $1,723,000) ÷ 2]
15. Rate earned on common stockholders' equity: 15.7%
    ($245,000 – $40,000) ÷ [($1,383,000 + $1,223,000) ÷ 2]
16. Earnings per share on common stock: $4.10
    ($245,000 – $40,000) ÷ 50,000 shares
17. Price-earnings ratio: 6.1
    $25 ÷ $4.10
18. Dividends per share: $0.90
    $45,000 ÷ 50,000 shares
19. Dividend yield: 3.6%
    $0.90 ÷ $25

Discussion Questions

1. What is the difference between horizontal and vertical analysis of financial statements?
2. What is the advantage of using comparative statements for financial analysis rather than statements for a single date or period?
3. The current year's amount of net income (after income tax) is 25% larger than that of the preceding year. Does this indicate an improved operating performance? Discuss.
4. How would the current and quick ratios of a service business compare?
5. a. Why is it advantageous to have a high inventory turnover?
   b. Is it possible to have a high inventory turnover and a high number of days' sales in inventory? Discuss.
6. What do the following data taken from a comparative balance sheet indicate about the company's ability to borrow additional funds on a long-term basis in the current year as compared to the preceding year?

	Current Year	Preceding Year
Fixed assets (net)	$1,260,000	$1,360,000
Total long-term liabilities	300,000	400,000

7. a. How does the rate earned on total assets differ from the rate earned on stockholders' equity?
   b. Which ratio is normally higher? Explain.
8. **Kroger**, a grocery store, recently had a price-earnings ratio of 13.7, while the average price-earnings ratio in the grocery store industry was 22.5. What might explain this difference?
9. The dividend yield of **Suburban Propane** was 7.7% in a recent year, and the dividend yield of **Google** was 0% in the same year. What might explain the difference between these ratios?
10. Describe two reports provided by independent auditors in the annual report to shareholders.

Practice Exercises

EE 17-1 p. 799

SHOW ME HOW

PE 17-1A Horizontal analysis — OBJ. 1

The comparative temporary investments and inventory balances of a company follow.

	Current Year	Previous Year
Temporary investments	$59,280	$52,000
Inventory	70,680	76,000

Based on this information, what is the amount and percentage of increase or decrease that would be shown in a balance sheet with horizontal analysis?

EE 17-1 p. 799

SHOW ME HOW

PE 17-1B Horizontal analysis — OBJ. 1

The comparative accounts payable and long-term debt balances for a company follow.

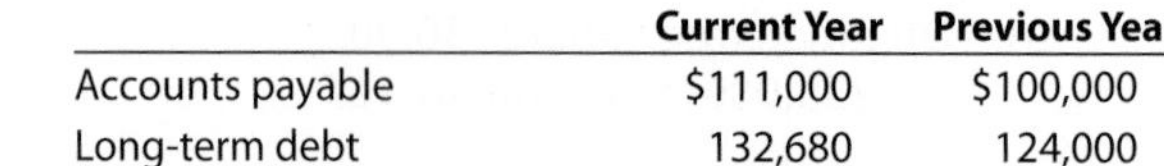

	Current Year	Previous Year
Accounts payable	$111,000	$100,000
Long-term debt	132,680	124,000

Based on this information, what is the amount and percentage of increase or decrease that would be shown in a balance sheet with horizontal analysis?

EE 17-2 p. 800

PE 17-2A Vertical analysis **OBJ. 1**

SHOW ME HOW

Income statement information for Axiom Corporation follows:

Sales	$725,000
Cost of goods sold	391,500
Gross profit	333,500

Prepare a vertical analysis of the income statement for Axiom Corporation.

EE 17-2 p. 800

PE 17-2B Vertical analysis **OBJ. 1**

SHOW ME HOW

Income statement information for Einsworth Corporation follows:

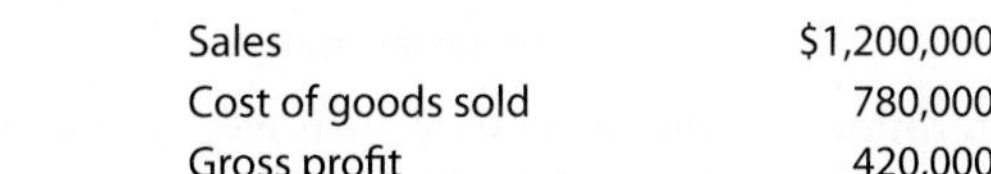

Sales	$1,200,000
Cost of goods sold	780,000
Gross profit	420,000

Prepare a vertical analysis of the income statement for Einsworth Corporation.

EE 17-3 p. 804

PE 17-3A Current position analysis **OBJ. 2**

SHOW ME HOW

The following items are reported on a company's balance sheet:

Cash	$160,000
Marketable securities	75,000
Accounts receivable (net)	65,000
Inventory	140,000
Accounts payable	200,000

Determine (a) the current ratio and (b) the quick ratio. Round to one decimal place.

EE 17-3 p. 804

PE 17-3B Current position analysis **OBJ. 2**

SHOW ME HOW

The following items are reported on a company's balance sheet:

Cash	$210,000
Marketable securities	120,000
Accounts receivable (net)	110,000
Inventory	160,000
Accounts payable	200,000

Determine (a) the current ratio and (b) the quick ratio. Round to one decimal place.

EE 17-4 p. 805

PE 17-4A Accounts receivable analysis **OBJ. 2**

SHOW ME HOW

A company reports the following:

Sales	$832,000
Average accounts receivable (net)	80,000

Determine (a) the accounts receivable turnover and (b) the number of days' sales in receivables. Round to one decimal place.

EE 17-4 p. 805

PE 17-4B Accounts receivable analysis **OBJ. 2**

SHOW ME HOW

A company reports the following:

Sales	$3,150,000
Average accounts receivable (net)	210,000

Determine (a) the accounts receivable turnover and (b) the number of days' sales in receivables. Round to one decimal place.

EE 17-5 p. 807 SHOW ME HOW

PE 17-5A Inventory analysis **OBJ. 2**

A company reports the following:

Cost of goods sold	$630,000
Average inventory	90,000

Determine (a) the inventory turnover and (b) the number of days' sales in inventory. Round to one decimal place.

EE 17-5 p. 807 SHOW ME HOW

PE 17-5B Inventory analysis **OBJ. 2**

A company reports the following:

Cost of goods sold	$435,000
Average inventory	72,500

Determine (a) the inventory turnover and (b) the number of days' sales in inventory. Round to one decimal place.

EE 17-6 p. 808 SHOW ME HOW

PE 17-6A Long-term solvency analysis **OBJ. 2**

The following information was taken from Kellman Company's balance sheet:

Fixed assets (net)	$2,000,000
Long-term liabilities	800,000
Total liabilities	1,000,000
Total stockholders' equity	625,000

Determine the company's (a) ratio of fixed assets to long-term liabilities and (b) ratio of liabilities to stockholders' equity.

EE 17-6 p. 808 SHOW ME HOW

PE 17-6B Long-term solvency analysis **OBJ. 2**

The following information was taken from Charu Company's balance sheet:

Fixed assets (net)	$860,000
Long-term liabilities	200,000
Total liabilities	600,000
Total stockholders' equity	250,000

Determine the company's (a) ratio of fixed assets to long-term liabilities and (b) ratio of liabilities to stockholders' equity.

EE 17-7 p. 809 SHOW ME HOW

PE 17-7A Times interest charges are earned **OBJ. 2**

A company reports the following:

Income before income tax	$4,000,000
Interest expense	400,000

Determine the number of times interest charges are earned.

EE17-7 p. 809 SHOW ME HOW

PE 17-7B Times interest charges are earned **OBJ. 2**

A company reports the following:

Income before income tax	$8,000,000
Interest expense	500,000

Determine the number of times interest charges are earned.

EE 17-8 p. 810

SHOW ME HOW

PE 17-8A Sales to assets **OBJ. 3**

A company reports the following:

Sales	$1,800,000
Average total assets (excluding long-term investments)	1,125,000

Determine the ratio of sales to assets.

SHOW ME HOW

EE 17-8 *p. 810*

PE 17-8B Sales to assets — OBJ. 3

A company reports the following:

Sales	$4,400,000
Average total assets (excluding long-term investments)	2,000,000

Determine the ratio of sales to assets.

SHOW ME HOW

EE 17-9 *p. 811*

PE 17-9A Rate earned on total assets — OBJ. 3

A company reports the following income statement and balance sheet information for the current year:

Net income	$ 250,000
Interest expense	100,000
Average total assets	2,500,000

Determine the rate earned on total assets.

SHOW ME HOW

EE 17-9 *p. 811*

PE 17-9B Rate earned on total assets — OBJ. 3

A company reports the following income statement and balance sheet information for the current year:

Net income	$ 410,000
Interest expense	90,000
Average total assets	5,000,000

Determine the rate earned on total assets.

SHOW ME HOW

EE 17-10 *p. 813*

PE 17-10A Common stockholders' profitability analysis — OBJ. 3

A company reports the following:

Net income	$ 375,000
Preferred dividends	75,000
Average stockholders' equity	2,500,000
Average common stockholders' equity	1,875,000

Determine (a) the rate earned on stockholders' equity and (b) the rate earned on common stockholders' equity. Round to one decimal place.

SHOW ME HOW

EE 17-10 *p. 813*

PE 17-10B Common stockholders' profitability analysis — OBJ. 3

A company reports the following:

Net income	$1,000,000
Preferred dividends	50,000
Average stockholders' equity	6,250,000
Average common stockholders' equity	3,800,000

Determine (a) the rate earned on stockholders' equity and (b) the rate earned on common stockholders' equity. Round to one decimal place.

SHOW ME HOW

EE 17-11 *p. 814*

PE 17-11A Earnings per share and price-earnings ratio — OBJ. 3

A company reports the following:

Net income	$185,000
Preferred dividends	$25,000
Shares of common stock outstanding	100,000
Market price per share of common stock	$20

a. Determine the company's earnings per share on common stock.

b. Determine the company's price-earnings ratio.

EE 17-11 p. 814

SHOW ME HOW

PE 17-11B Earnings per share and price-earnings ratio **OBJ. 3**

A company reports the following:

Net income	$410,000
Preferred dividends	$60,000
Shares of common stock outstanding	50,000
Market price per share of common stock	$84

a. Determine the company's earnings per share on common stock.

b. Determine the company's price-earnings ratio.

Exercises

EX 17-1 Vertical analysis of income statement **OBJ. 1**

✔ a. Current year net income: $175,000; 7.0% of sales

SHOW ME HOW

Revenue and expense data for Gresham Inc. for two recent years are as follows:

	Current Year	Previous Year
Sales	$2,500,000	$2,350,000
Cost of goods sold	1,500,000	1,292,500
Selling expenses	300,000	376,000
Administrative expenses	375,000	305,500
Income tax expense	150,000	141,000

a. Prepare an income statement in comparative form, stating each item for both years as a percent of sales. Round to one decimal place.

b. Comment on the significant changes disclosed by the comparative income statement.

EX 17-2 Vertical analysis of income statement **OBJ. 1**

✔ a. Current fiscal year income from continuing operations, 13.0% of revenues

The following comparative income statement (in thousands of dollars) for the two recent fiscal years was adapted from the annual report of **Speedway Motorsports, Inc.**, owner and operator of several major motor speedways, such as the Atlanta, Texas, and Las Vegas Motor Speedways.

	Current Year	Previous Year
Revenues:		
Admissions	$116,034	$130,239
Event-related revenue	151,562	163,621
NASCAR broadcasting revenue	192,662	185,394
Other operating revenue	29,902	26,951
Total revenue	$490,160	$506,205
Expenses and other:		
Direct expense of events	$101,402	$106,204
NASCAR purse and sanction fees	122,950	120,146
Other direct expenses	18,908	20,352
General and administrative	183,215	241,223
Total expenses and other	$426,475	$487,925
Income from continuing operations	$ 63,685	$ 18,280

a. Prepare a comparative income statement for these two years in vertical form, stating each item as a percent of revenues. Round to one decimal place.

b. Comment on the significant changes.

EX 17-3 Common-sized income statement **OBJ. 1**

✔ a. Tannenhill net income: $120,000; 3.0% of sales

SHOW ME HOW

Revenue and expense data for the current calendar year for Tannenhill Company and for the electronics industry are as follows. The Tannenhill Company data are expressed in dollars. The electronics industry averages are expressed in percentages.

	Tannenhill Company	Electronics Industry Average
Sales	$4,000,000	100.0%
Cost of goods sold	2,120,000	60.0
Gross profit	$1,880,000	40.0%
Selling expenses	$1,080,000	24.0%
Administrative expenses	640,000	14.0
Total operating expenses	$1,720,000	38.0%
Operating income	$ 160,000	2.0%
Other income	120,000	3.0
	$ 280,000	5.0%
Other expense	80,000	2.0
Income before income tax	$ 200,000	3.0%
Income tax expense	80,000	2.0
Net income	$ 120,000	1.0%

a. Prepare a common-sized income statement comparing the results of operations for Tannenhill Company with the industry average. Round to one decimal place.

b. As far as the data permit, comment on significant relationships revealed by the comparisons.

EX 17-4 Vertical analysis of balance sheet OBJ. 1

✔ Retained earnings, Current year, 40.0%

Balance sheet data for Novak Company on December 31, the end of two recent fiscal years, follows:

	Current Year	Previous Year
Current assets	$1,300,000	$ 945,000
Property, plant, and equipment	3,000,000	3,150,000
Intangible assets	700,000	405,000
Current liabilities	1,000,000	720,000
Long-term liabilities	1,500,000	1,575,000
Common stock	500,000	495,000
Retained earnings	2,000,000	1,710,000

Prepare a comparative balance sheet for both years, stating each asset as a percent of total assets and each liability and stockholders' equity item as a percent of the total liabilities and stockholders' equity. Round to one decimal place.

EX 17-5 Horizontal analysis of the income statement OBJ. 1

✔ a. Net income increase, 80.0%

Income statement data for Moreno Company for two recent years ended December 31, are as follows:

	Current Year	Previous Year
Sales	$1,120,000	$1,000,000
Cost of goods sold	971,250	875,000
Gross profit	$ 148,750	$ 125,000
Selling expenses	$ 71,250	$ 62,500
Administrative expenses	56,000	50,000
Total operating expenses	$ 127,250	$ 112,500
Income before income tax	$ 21,500	$ 12,500
Income tax expense	8,000	5,000
Net income	$ 13,500	$ 7,500

a. Prepare a comparative income statement with horizontal analysis, indicating the increase (decrease) for the current year when compared with the previous year. Round to one decimal place.

b. What conclusions can be drawn from the horizontal analysis?

EX 17-6 Current position analysis

OBJ. 2

✔ a. Current year working capital, $1,600,000

SHOW ME HOW

The following data were taken from the balance sheet of Gostkowski Company at the end of two recent fiscal years:

	Current Year	Previous Year
Cash	$ 480,000	$ 392,000
Marketable securities	576,000	411,600
Accounts and notes receivable (net)	384,000	316,400
Inventories	408,000	333,200
Prepaid expenses	552,000	506,800
Total current assets	$2,400,000	$1,960,000
Accounts and notes payable (short-term)	$ 600,000	$ 525,000
Accrued liabilities	200,000	175,000
Total current liabilities	$ 800,000	$ 700,000

a. Determine for each year (1) the working capital, (2) the current ratio, and (3) the quick ratio. Round ratios to one decimal place.

b. What conclusions can be drawn from these data as to the company's ability to meet its currently maturing debts?

EX 17-7 Current position analysis

OBJ. 2

✔ a. (1) Current year's current ratio, 1.1

PepsiCo, Inc., the parent company of Frito-Lay snack foods and Pepsi beverages, had the following current assets and current liabilities at the end of two recent years:

	Current Year (in millions)	Previous Year (in millions)
Cash and cash equivalents	$ 6,297	$4,067
Short-term investments, at cost	322	358
Accounts and notes receivable, net	7,041	6,912
Inventories	3,581	3,827
Prepaid expenses and other current assets	1,479	2,277
Short-term obligations	4,815	6,205
Accounts payable	12,274	11,949

a. Determine the (1) current ratio and (2) quick ratio for both years. Round to one decimal place.

b. What conclusions can you draw from these data?

EX 17-8 Current position analysis

OBJ. 2

The bond indenture for the 10-year, 9% debenture bonds issued January 2, 2015, required working capital of $100,000, a current ratio of 1.5, and a quick ratio of 1.0 at the end of each calendar year until the bonds mature. At December 31, 2016, the three measures were computed as follows:

1. Current assets:		
Cash	$102,000	
Temporary investments	48,000	
Accounts and notes receivable (net)	120,000	
Inventories	36,000	
Prepaid expenses	24,000	
Intangible assets	124,800	
Property, plant, and equipment	55,200	
Total current assets (net)		$510,000
Current liabilities:		
Accounts and short-term notes payable	$ 96,000	
Accrued liabilities	204,000	
Total current liabilities		300,000
Working capital		$210,000
2. Current ratio	1.7	$510,000 ÷ $300,000
3. Quick ratio	1.2	$115,200 ÷ $ 96,000

a. List the errors in the determination of the three measures of current position analysis.

b. Is the company satisfying the terms of the bond indenture?

EX 17-9 Accounts receivable analysis — OBJ. 2

✔ a. Accounts receivable turnover, 2016, 7.0

SHOW ME HOW

The following data are taken from the financial statements of Krawcheck Inc. Terms of all sales are 2/10, n/55.

	2016	2015	2014
Accounts receivable, end of year	$ 500,000	$ 475,000	$440,000
Sales on account	3,412,500	2,836,500	

a. For 2015 and 2016, determine (1) the accounts receivable turnover and (2) the number of days' sales in receivables. Round to the nearest dollar and one decimal place.

b. What conclusions can be drawn from these data concerning accounts receivable and credit policies?

EX 17-10 Accounts receivable analysis — OBJ. 2

Xavier Stores Company and Lestrade Stores Inc. are large retail department stores. Both companies offer credit to their customers through their own credit card operations. Information from the financial statements for both companies for two recent years is as follows (all numbers are in millions):

	Xavier	Lestrade
Merchandise sales	$8,500,000	$4,585,000
Credit card receivables—beginning	820,000	600,000
Credit card receviables—ending	880,000	710,000

a. Determine the (1) accounts receivable turnover and (2) the number of days' sales in receivables for both companies. Round to one decimal place.

b. Compare the two companies with regard to their credit card policies.

EX 17-11 Inventory analysis — OBJ. 2

✔ a. Inventory turnover, current year, 7.5

SHOW ME HOW

The following data were extracted from the income statement of Saleh Inc.:

	Current Year	Previous Year
Sales	$12,750,000	$13,284,000
Beginning inventories	840,000	800,000
Cost of goods sold	6,375,000	7,380,000
Ending inventories	860,000	840,000

a. Determine for each year (1) the inventory turnover and (2) the number of days' sales in inventory. Round to the nearest dollar and one decimal place.

b. What conclusions can be drawn from these data concerning the inventories?

EX 17-12 Inventory analysis — OBJ. 2

✔ a. Dell inventory turnover, 32.1

Dell Inc. and **Hewlett-Packard Company (HP)** compete with each other in the personal computer market. Dell's primary strategy is to assemble computers to customer orders, rather than for inventory. Thus, for example, Dell will build and deliver a computer within four days of a customer entering an order on a Web page. Hewlett-Packard, on the other hand, builds some computers prior to receiving an order, then sells from this inventory once an order is received. Selected financial information for both companies from a recent year's financial statements follows (in millions):

	Dell Inc.	Hewlett-Packard Company
Sales	$56,940	$120,357
Cost of goods sold	44,754	92,385
Inventory, beginning of period	1,382	6,317
Inventory, end of period	1,404	7,490

a. Determine for both companies (1) the inventory turnover and (2) the number of days' sales in inventory. Round to one decimal place.

b. Interpret the inventory ratios by considering Dell's and Hewlett-Packard's operating strategies.

EX 17-13 Ratio of liabilities to stockholders' equity and number of times interest charges are earned OBJ. 2

✔ a. Ratio of liabilities to stockholders' equity, current year, 0.9

The following data were taken from the financial statements of Hunter Inc. for December 31 of two recent years:

	Current Year	Previous Year
Accounts payable	$ 924,000	$ 800,000
Current maturities of serial bonds payable	200,000	200,000
Serial bonds payable, 10%, issued 2009, due 2019	1,000,000	1,200,000
Common stock, $10 par value	250,000	250,000
Paid-in capital in excess of par	1,250,000	1,250,000
Retained earnings	860,000	500,000

The income before income tax was $480,000 and $420,000 for the current and previous years, respectively.

a. Determine the ratio of liabilities to stockholders' equity at the end of each year. Round to one decimal place.

b. Determine the number of times the bond interest charges are earned during the year for both years. Round to one decimal place.

c. What conclusions can be drawn from these data as to the company's ability to meet its currently maturing debts?

EX 17-14 Ratio of liabilities to stockholders' equity and number of times interest charges are earned OBJ. 2

✔ a. Hasbro, 1.9

Hasbro and **Mattel, Inc.**, are the two largest toy companies in North America. Condensed liabilities and stockholders' equity from a recent balance sheet are shown for each company as follows (in thousands):

	Hasbro	Mattel
Current liabilities	$ 960,435	$ 1,716,012
Long-term debt	1,396,421	1,100,000
Deferred liabilities	461,152	643,729
Total liabilities	$ 2,818,008	$ 3,459,741
Shareholders' equity:		
Common stock	$ 104,847	$ 441,369
Additional paid in capital	655,943	1,727,682
Retained earnings	3,354,545	3,515,181
Accumulated other comprehensive loss and other equity items	(72,307)	(464,486)
Treasury stock, at cost	(2,535,649)	(2,152,702)
Total stockholders' equity	$ 1,507,379	$ 3,067,044
Total liabilities and stockholders' equity	$ 4,325,387	$ 6,526,785

The income from operations and interest expense from the income statement for each company were as follows (in thousands):

	Hasbro	Mattel
Income from operations (before income tax)	$453,402	$945,045
Interest expense	117,403	88,835

a. Determine the ratio of liabilities to stockholders' equity for both companies. Round to one decimal place.

b. Determine the number of times interest charges are earned for both companies. Round to one decimal place.

c. Interpret the ratio differences between the two companies.

EX 17-15 Ratio of liabilities to stockholders' equity and ratio of fixed assets to long-term liabilities

OBJ. 2

✔ a. Mondelez International, Inc., 1.3

Recent balance sheet information for two companies in the food industry, **Mondelez International, Inc.**, and **The Hershey Company**, is as follows (in thousands of dollars):

	Mondelez	Hershey
Net property, plant, and equipment	$10,010,000	$1,674,071
Current liabilities	14,873,000	1,471,110
Long-term debt	15,574,000	1,530,967
Other long-term liabilities	12,816,000	716,013
Stockholders' equity	32,215,000	1,036,749

a. Determine the ratio of liabilities to stockholders' equity for both companies. Round to one decimal place.

b. Determine the ratio of fixed assets to long-term liabilities for both companies. Round to one decimal place.

c. Interpret the ratio differences between the two companies.

EX 17-16 Ratio of sales to assets

OBJ. 3

✔ a. YRC Worldwide, 1.5

Three major segments of the transportation industry are motor carriers, such as **YRC Worldwide**; railroads, such as **Union Pacific**; and transportation arrangement services, such as **C.H. Robinson Worldwide Inc.** Recent financial statement information for these three companies is shown as follows (in thousands of dollars):

	YRC Worldwide	Union Pacific	C.H. Robinson Worldwide Inc.
Sales	$4,334,640	$16,965,000	$9,274,305
Average total assets	2,812,504	42,636,000	1,914,974

a. Determine the ratio of sales to assets for all three companies. Round to one decimal place.

b. Assume that the ratio of sales to assets for each company represents their respective industry segment. Interpret the differences in the ratio of sales to assets in terms of the operating characteristics of each of the respective segments.

EX 17-17 Profitability ratios

OBJ. 3

✔ a. Rate earned on total assets, 2016, 12.0%

SHOW ME HOW

The following selected data were taken from the financial statements of Robinson Inc. for December 31, 2016, 2015 and 2014:

	December 31		
	2016	2015	2014
Total assets	$4,800,000	$4,400,000	$4,000,000
Notes payable (8% interest)	2,250,000	2,250,000	2,250,000
Common stock	250,000	250,000	250,000
Preferred 4% stock, $100 par (no change during year)	500,000	500,000	500,000
Retained earnings	1,574,000	1,222,000	750,000

The 2016 net income was $372,000, and the 2015 net income was $492,000. No dividends on common stock were declared between 2014 and 2016.

a. Determine the rate earned on total assets, the rate earned on stockholders' equity, and the rate earned on common stockholders' equity for the years 2015 and 2016. Round to one decimal place.

b. What conclusions can be drawn from these data as to the company's profitability?

EX 17-18 Profitability ratios

OBJ. 3

✔a. Year 3 rate earned on total assets, 12.2%

Ralph Lauren Corp. sells men's apparel through company-owned retail stores. Recent financial information for Ralph Lauren follows (all numbers in thousands):

	Fiscal Year 3	Fiscal Year 2	
Net income	$567,600	$479,500	
Interest expense	18,300	22,200	
	Fiscal Year 3	**Fiscal Year 2**	**Fiscal Year 1**
Total assets (at end of fiscal year)	$4,981,100	$4,648,900	$4,356,500
Total stockholders' equity (at end of fiscal year)	3,304,700	3,116,600	2,735,100

Assume the apparel industry average rate earned on total assets is 8.0%, and the average rate earned on stockholders' equity is 10.0% for the year ended April 2, Year 3.

a. Determine the rate earned on total assets for Ralph Lauren for fiscal Years 2 and 3. Round to one digit after the decimal place.

b. Determine the rate earned on stockholders' equity for Ralph Lauren for fiscal Years 2 and 3. Round to one decimal place.

c. Evaluate the two-year trend for the profitability ratios determined in (a) and (b).

d. Evaluate Ralph Lauren's profit performance relative to the industry.

EX 17-19 Six measures of solvency or profitability

OBJ. 2, 3

✔ c. Ratio of sales to assets, 4.2

The following data were taken from the financial statements of Gates Inc. for the current fiscal year. Assuming that long-term investments totaled $3,000,000 throughout the year and that total assets were $7,000,000 at the beginning of the current fiscal year, determine the following: (a) ratio of fixed assets to long-term liabilities, (b) ratio of liabilities to stockholders' equity, (c) ratio of sales to assets, (d) rate earned on total assets, (e) rate earned on stockholders' equity, and (f) rate earned on common stockholders' equity. Round to one decimal place.

Property, plant, and equipment (net)			$ 3,200,000
Liabilities:			
Current liabilities		$1,000,000	
Mortgage note payable, 6%, issued 2005, due 2021		2,000,000	
Total liabilities			$ 3,000,000
Stockholders' equity:			
Preferred $10 stock, $100 par (no change during year)			$ 1,000,000
Common stock, $10 par (no change during year)			2,000,000
Retained earnings:			
Balance, beginning of year	$1,570,000		
Net income	930,000	$2,500,000	
Preferred dividends	$ 100,000		
Common dividends	400,000	500,000	
Balance, end of year			2,000,000
Total stockholders' equity			$ 5,000,000
Sales			$18,900,000
Interest expense			$ 120,000

EX 17-20 Six measures of solvency or profitability

OBJ. 2, 3

✔ d. Price-earnings ratio, 10.0

The balance sheet for Garcon Inc. at the end of the current fiscal year indicated the following:

Bonds payable, 8% (issued in 2006, due in 2026)	$5,000,000
Preferred $4 stock, $50 par	2,500,000
Common stock, $10 par	5,000,000

Income before income tax was \$3,000,000, and income taxes were \$1,200,000 for the current year. Cash dividends paid on common stock during the current year totaled \$1,200,000. The common stock was selling for \$32 per share at the end of the year. Determine each of the following: (a) number of times bond interest charges are earned, (b) number of times preferred dividends are earned, (c) earnings per share on common stock, (d) price-earnings ratio, (e) dividends per share of common stock, and (f) dividend yield. Round to one decimal place, except earnings per share, which should be rounded to two decimal places.

EX 17-21 Earnings per share, price-earnings ratio, dividend yield

OBJ. 3

✔ b. Price-earnings ratio, 15.0

SHOW ME HOW

The following information was taken from the financial statements of Tolbert Inc. for December 31 of the current fiscal year:

Common stock, \$20 par (no change during the year)	\$10,000,000
Preferred \$4 stock, \$40 par (no change during the year)	2,500,000

The net income was \$1,750,000 and the declared dividends on the common stock were \$1,125,000 for the current year. The market price of the common stock is \$45 per share.

For the common stock, determine (a) the earnings per share, (b) the price-earnings ratio, (c) the dividends per share, and (d) the dividend yield. Round to one decimal place, except earnings per share, which should be rounded to two decimal places.

EX 17-22 Price-earnings ratio; dividend yield

OBJ. 3

The table that follows shows the stock price, earnings per share, and dividends per share for three companies for a recent year:

	Price	Earnings per Share	Dividends per Share
Deere & Co.	\$ 86.20	\$ 8.71	\$2.04
Google	873.32	36.75	0.00
The Coca-Cola Company	39.79	1.97	1.02

a. Determine the price-earnings ratio and dividend yield for the three companies. Round to one decimal place.

b. Explain the differences in these ratios across the three companies.

Appendix
EX 17-23 Earnings per share, extraordinary item

✔ b. Earnings per share on common stock, \$7.60

The net income reported on the income statement of Cutler Co. was \$4,000,000. There were 500,000 shares of \$10 par common stock and 100,000 shares of \$2 preferred stock outstanding throughout the current year. The income statement included two extraordinary items: an \$800,000 gain from condemnation of land and a \$400,000 loss arising from flood damage, both after applicable income tax. Determine the per-share figures for common stock for (a) income before extraordinary items and (b) net income.

Appendix
EX 17-24 Extraordinary item

Assume that the amount of each of the following items is material to the financial statements. Classify each item as either normally recurring (NR) or extraordinary (E).

a. Loss on the disposal of equipment considered to be obsolete because of the development of new technology.

b. Uninsured loss on building due to hurricane damage. The building was purchased by the company in 1910 and had not previously incurred hurricane damage.

c. Gain on sale of land condemned by the local government for a public works project.

d. Uninsured flood loss. (Flood insurance is unavailable because of periodic flooding in the area.)

e. Interest revenue on notes receivable.

f. Uncollectible accounts expense.

g. Loss on sale of investments in stocks and bonds.

Appendix

EX 17-25 Income statement and earnings per share for extraordinary items and discontinued operations

Apex Inc. reports the following for a recent year:

Income from continuing operations before income tax	$1,000,000
Extraordinary property loss from hurricane	$140,000*
Loss from discontinued operations	$240,000*
Weighted average number of shares outstanding	20,000
Applicable tax rate	40%

*Net of any tax effect.

a. Prepare a partial income statement for Apex Inc., beginning with income from continuing operations before income tax.

b. Calculate the earnings per common share for Apex Inc., including per-share amounts for unusual items.

Appendix

EX 17-26 Unusual items

Discuss whether Colston Company correctly reported the following items in the financial statements:

a. In a recent year, the company discovered a clerical error in the prior year's accounting records. As a result, the reported net income for the previous year was overstated by $45,000. The company corrected this error by restating the prior-year financial statements.

b. In a recent year, the company voluntarily changed its method of accounting for long-term construction contracts from the percentage of completion method to the completed contract method. Both methods are acceptable under generally acceptable accounting principles. The cumulative effect of this change was reported as a separate component of income in the current period income statement.

Problems: Series A

PR 17-1A Horizontal analysis of income statement **OBJ. 1**

✔ 1. Sales, 12.5% increase

General Ledger

SHOW ME HOW

For 2016, Clapton Company reported a decline in net income. At the end of the year, S. Hand, the president, is presented with the following condensed comparative income statement:

Clapton Company
Comparative Income Statement
For the Years Ended December 31, 2016 and 2015

	2016	2015
Sales	$6,750,000	$6,000,000
Cost of goods sold	2,480,000	2,000,000
Gross profit	$4,270,000	$4,000,000
Selling expenses	$1,260,000	$1,000,000
Administrative expenses	625,000	500,000
Total operating expenses	$1,885,000	$1,500,000
Income from operations	$2,385,000	$2,500,000
Other income	110,000	100,000
Income before income tax	$2,495,000	$2,600,000
Income tax expense	60,000	50,000
Net income	$2,435,000	$2,550,000

Instructions

1. Prepare a comparative income statement with horizontal analysis for the two-year period, using 2015 as the base year. Round to one decimal place.
2. To the extent the data permit, comment on the significant relationships revealed by the horizontal analysis prepared in (1).

✔ 1. Net income, 2016, 13.0%

General Ledger

PR 17-2A Vertical analysis of income statement — OBJ. 1

For 2016, Indigo Company initiated a sales promotion campaign that included the expenditure of an additional $39,000 for advertising. At the end of the year, Lumi Neer, the president, is presented with the following condensed comparative income statement:

Indigo Company
Comparative Income Statement
For the Years Ended December 31, 2016 and 2015

	2016	2015
Sales	$820,000	$600,000
Cost of goods sold	311,600	240,000
Gross profit	$508,400	$360,000
Selling expenses	$164,000	$108,000
Administrative expenses	57,400	54,000
Total operating expenses	$221,400	$162,000
Income from operations	$287,000	$198,000
Other income	65,600	48,000
Income before income tax	$352,600	$246,000
Income tax expense	246,000	180,000
Net income	$106,600	$ 66,000

Instructions

1. Prepare a comparative income statement for the two-year period, presenting an analysis of each item in relationship to sales for each of the years. Round to one decimal place.
2. To the extent the data permit, comment on the significant relationships revealed by the vertical analysis prepared in (1).

✔ 2. c. Current ratio, 2.0

PR 17-3A Effect of transactions on current position analysis — OBJ. 2

Data pertaining to the current position of Forte Company are as follows:

Cash	$412,500
Marketable securities	187,500
Accounts and notes receivable (net)	300,000
Inventories	700,000
Prepaid expenses	50,000
Accounts payable	200,000
Notes payable (short-term)	250,000
Accrued expenses	300,000

Instructions

1. Compute (a) the working capital, (b) the current ratio, and (c) the quick ratio. Round to one decimal place.

2. List the following captions on a sheet of paper:

Transaction	Working Capital	Current Ratio	Quick Ratio

Compute the working capital, the current ratio, and the quick ratio after each of the following transactions, and record the results in the appropriate columns. *Consider each transaction separately* and assume that only that transaction affects the data given. Round to one decimal place.

a. Sold marketable securities at no gain or loss, $70,000.
b. Paid accounts payable, $125,000.
c. Purchased goods on account, $110,000.
d. Paid notes payable, $100,000.
e. Declared a cash dividend, $150,000.
f. Declared a common stock dividend on common stock, $50,000.
g. Borrowed cash from bank on a long-term note, $225,000.
h. Received cash on account, $125,000.
i. Issued additional shares of stock for cash, $600,000.
j. Paid cash for prepaid expenses, $10,000.

PR 17-4A Nineteen measures of solvency and profitability

OBJ. 2, 3

✔ **5. Number of days' sales in receivables, 36.5**

The comparative financial statements of Bettancort Inc. are as follows. The market price of Bettancort Inc. common stock was $71.25 on December 31, 2016.

Bettancort Inc.
Comparative Retained Earnings Statement
For the Years Ended December 31, 2016 and 2015

	2016	2015
Retained earnings, January 1	$2,655,000	$2,400,000
Add net income for year	300,000	280,000
Total	$2,955,000	$2,680,000
Deduct dividends:		
On preferred stock	$ 15,000	$ 15,000
On common stock	10,000	10,000
Total	$ 25,000	$ 25,000
Retained earnings, December 31	$2,930,000	$2,655,000

Bettancort Inc.
Comparative Income Statement
For the Years Ended December 31, 2016 and 2015

	2016	2015
Sales	$1,200,000	$1,000,000
Cost of goods sold	500,000	475,000
Gross profit	$ 700,000	$ 525,000
Selling expenses	$ 240,000	$ 200,000
Administrative expenses	180,000	150,000
Total operating expenses	$ 420,000	$ 350,000
Income from operations	$ 280,000	$ 175,000
Other income	166,000	225,000
	$ 446,000	$ 400,000
Other expense (interest)	66,000	60,000
Income before income tax	$ 380,000	$ 340,000
Income tax expense	80,000	60,000
Net income	$ 300,000	$ 280,000

Bettancort Inc.
Comparative Balance Sheet
December 31, 2016 and 2015

	Dec. 31, 2016	Dec. 31, 2015
Assets		
Current assets:		
Cash	$ 450,000	$ 400,000
Marketable securities	300,000	260,000
Accounts receivable (net)	130,000	110,000
Inventories	67,000	58,000
Prepaid expenses	153,000	139,000
Total current assets	$1,100,000	$ 967,000
Long-term investments	2,350,000	2,200,000
Property, plant, and equipment (net)	1,320,000	1,188,000
Total assets	$4,770,000	$4,355,000
Liabilities		
Current liabilities	$ 440,000	$ 400,000
Long-term liabilities:		
Mortgage note payable, 8%, due 2021	$ 100,000	$ 0
Bonds payable, 5%, due 2017	1,000,000	1,000,000
Total long-term liabilities	$1,100,000	$1,000,000
Total liabilities	$1,540,000	$1,400,000
Stockholders' Equity		
Preferred $0.75 stock, $10 par	$ 200,000	$ 200,000
Common stock, $10 par	100,000	100,000
Retained earnings	2,930,000	2,655,000
Total stockholders' equity	$3,230,000	$2,955,000
Total liabilities and stockholders' equity	$4,770,000	$4,355,000

Instructions

Determine the following measures for 2016, rounding to one decimal place:

1. Working capital
2. Current ratio
3. Quick ratio
4. Accounts receivable turnover
5. Number of days' sales in receivables
6. Inventory turnover
7. Number of days' sales in inventory
8. Ratio of fixed assets to long-term liabilities
9. Ratio of liabilities to stockholders' equity
10. Number of times interest charges are earned
11. Number of times preferred dividends are earned
12. Ratio of sales to assets
13. Rate earned on total assets
14. Rate earned on stockholders' equity
15. Rate earned on common stockholders' equity
16. Earnings per share on common stock
17. Price-earnings ratio
18. Dividends per share of common stock
19. Dividend yield

PR 17-5A Solvency and profitability trend analysis

OBJ. 2, 3

Addai Company has provided the following comparative information:

	2016	2015	2014	2013	2012
Net income	$ 273,406	$ 367,976	$ 631,176	$ 884,000	$ 800,000
Interest expense	616,047	572,003	528,165	495,000	440,000
Income tax expense	31,749	53,560	106,720	160,000	200,000
Total assets (ending balance)	4,417,178	4,124,350	3,732,443	3,338,500	2,750,000
Total stockholders' equity (ending balance)	3,706,557	3,433,152	3,065,176	2,434,000	1,550,000
Average total assets	4,270,764	3,928,396	3,535,472	3,044,250	2,475,000
Average total stockholders' equity	3,569,855	3,249,164	2,749,588	1,992,000	1,150,000

You have been asked to evaluate the historical performance of the company over the last five years.

Selected industry ratios have remained relatively steady at the following levels for the last five years:

	2012–2016
Rate earned on total assets	28%
Rate earned on stockholders' equity	18%
Number of times interest charges are earned	2.7
Ratio of liabilities to stockholders' equity	0.4

Instructions

1. Prepare four line graphs with the ratio on the vertical axis and the years on the horizontal axis for the following four ratios (rounded to one decimal place):
   a. Rate earned on total assets
   b. Rate earned on stockholders' equity
   c. Number of times interest charges are earned
   d. Ratio of liabilities to stockholders' equity

   Display both the company ratio and the industry benchmark on each graph. That is, each graph should have two lines.
2. Prepare an analysis of the graphs in (1).

Problems: Series B

PR 17-1B Horizontal analysis of income statement

OBJ. 1

✔ 1. Sales, 30.0% increase

General Ledger

SHOW ME HOW

For 2016, Macklin Inc. reported a significant increase in net income. At the end of the year, John Mayer, the president, is presented with the following condensed comparative income statement:

Macklin Inc.
Comparative Income Statement
For the Years Ended December 31, 2016 and 2015

	2016	2015
Sales	$910,000	$700,000
Cost of goods sold	441,000	350,000
Gross profit	$469,000	$350,000
Selling expenses	$ 139,150	$115,000
Administrative expenses	99,450	85,000
Total operating expenses	$238,600	$200,000
Income from operations	$230,400	$150,000
Other income	65,000	50,000
Income before income tax	$295,400	$200,000
Income tax expense	65,000	50,000
Net income	$230,400	$150,000

Instructions

1. Prepare a comparative income statement with horizontal analysis for the two-year period, using 2015 as the base year. Round to one decimal place.
2. To the extent the data permit, comment on the significant relationships revealed by the horizontal analysis prepared in (1).

PR 17-2B Vertical analysis of income statement

OBJ. 1

✔ 1. Net income, 2015, 14.0%

General Ledger

For 2016, Fielder Industries Inc. initiated a sales promotion campaign that included the expenditure of an additional $40,000 for advertising. At the end of the year, Leif Grando, the president, is presented with the following condensed comparative income statement:

Fielder Industries Inc.
Comparative Income Statement
For the Years Ended December 31, 2016 and 2015

	2016	2015
Sales	$1,300,000	$1,180,000
Cost of goods sold	682,500	613,600
Gross profit	$ 617,500	$ 566,400
Selling expenses	$ 260,000	$ 188,800
Adminstrative expenses	169,000	177,000
Total operating expenses	$ 429,000	$ 365,800
Income from operations	$ 188,500	$ 200,600
Other income	78,000	70,800
Income before income tax	$ 266,500	$ 271,400
Income tax expense	117,000	106,200
Net income	$ 149,500	$ 165,200

Instructions

1. Prepare a comparative income statement for the two-year period, presenting an analysis of each item in relationship to sales for each of the years. Round to one decimal place.
2. To the extent the data permit, comment on the significant relationships revealed by the vertical analysis prepared in (1).

PR 17-3B Effect of transactions on current position analysis

OBJ. 2

✔ 2. g. Quick ratio, 1.6

Data pertaining to the current position of Lucroy Industries Inc. are as follows:

Cash	$ 800,000
Marketable securities	550,000
Accounts and notes receivable (net)	850,000
Inventories	700,000
Prepaid expenses	300,000
Accounts payable	1,200,000
Notes payable (short-term)	700,000
Accrued expenses	100,000

Instructions

1. Compute (a) the working capital, (b) the current ratio, and (c) the quick ratio. Round to one decimal place.
2. List the following captions on a sheet of paper:

Transaction	Working Capital	Current Ratio	Quick Ratio

Compute the working capital, the current ratio, and the quick ratio after each of the following transactions, and record the results in the appropriate columns. *Consider each transaction separately* and assume that only that transaction affects the data given. Round to one decimal place.

a. Sold marketable securities at no gain or loss, $500,000.
b. Paid accounts payable, $287,500.
c. Purchased goods on account, $400,000.
d. Paid notes payable, $125,000.
e. Declared a cash dividend, $325,000.
f. Declared a common stock dividend on common stock, $150,000.
g. Borrowed cash from bank on a long-term note, $1,000,000.
h. Received cash on account, $75,000.
i. Issued additional shares of stock for cash, $2,000,000.
j. Paid cash for prepaid expenses, $200,000.

PR 17-4B Nineteen measures of solvency and profitability **OBJ. 2, 3**

✔ 9. Ratio of liabilities to stockholders' equity, 0.4

The comparative financial statements of Stargel Inc. are as follows. The market price of Stargel Inc. common stock was $119.70 on December 31, 2016.

Stargel Inc.
Comparative Retained Earnings Statement
For the Years Ended December 31, 2016 and 2015

	2016	2015
Retained earnings, January 1	$5,375,000	$4,545,000
Add net income for year	900,000	925,000
Total	$6,275,000	$5,470,000
Deduct dividends:		
On preferred stock	$ 45,000	$ 45,000
On common stock	50,000	50,000
Total	$ 95,000	$ 95,000
Retained earnings, December 31	$6,180,000	$5,375,000

Stargel Inc.
Comparative Income Statement
For the Years Ended December 31, 2016 and 2015

	2016	2015
Sales	$10,000,000	$9,400,000
Cost of goods sold	5,350,000	4,950,000
Gross profit	$ 4,650,000	$4,450,000
Selling expenses	$ 2,000,000	$1,880,000
Administrative expenses	1,500,000	1,410,000
Total operating expenses	$ 3,500,000	$3,290,000
Income from operations	$ 1,150,000	$1,160,000
Other income	150,000	140,000
	$ 1,300,000	$1,300,000
Other expense (interest)	170,000	150,000
Income before income tax	$ 1,130,000	$1,150,000
Income tax expense	230,000	225,000
Net income	$ 900,000	$ 925,000

Stargel Inc.
Comparative Balance Sheet
December 31, 2016 and 2015

	Dec. 31, 2016	Dec. 31, 2015
Assets		
Current assets:		
Cash	$ 500,000	$ 400,000
Marketable securities	1,010,000	1,000,000
Accounts receivable (net)	740,000	510,000
Inventories	1,190,000	950,000
Prepaid expenses	250,000	229,000
Total current assets	$3,690,000	$3,089,000
Long-term investments	2,350,000	2,300,000
Property, plant, and equipment (net)	3,740,000	3,366,000
Total assets	$9,780,000	$8,755,000
Liabilities		
Current liabilities	$ 900,000	$ 880,000
Long-term liabilities:		
Mortgage note payable, 8.8%, due 2021	$ 200,000	$ 0
Bonds payable, 9%, due 2017	1,500,000	1,500,000
Total long-term liabilities	$1,700,000	$1,500,000
Total liabilities	$2,600,000	$2,380,000
Stockholders' Equity		
Preferred $0.90 stock, $10 par	$ 500,000	$ 500,000
Common stock, $5 par	500,000	500,000
Retained earnings	6,180,000	5,375,000
Total stockholders' equity	$7,180,000	$6,375,000
Total liabilities and stockholders' equity	$9,780,000	$8,755,000

Instructions

Determine the following measures for 2016, rounding to one decimal place, except per-share amounts, which should be rounded to the nearest penny:

1. Working capital
2. Current ratio
3. Quick ratio
4. Accounts receivable turnover
5. Number of days' sales in receivables
6. Inventory turnover
7. Number of days' sales in inventory
8. Ratio of fixed assets to long-term liabilities
9. Ratio of liabilities to stockholders' equity
10. Number of times interest charges are earned
11. Number of times preferred dividends are earned
12. Ratio of sales to assets
13. Rate earned on total assets
14. Rate earned on stockholders' equity
15. Rate earned on common stockholders' equity
16. Earnings per share on common stock
17. Price-earnings ratio
18. Dividends per share of common stock
19. Dividend yield

PR 17-5B Solvency and profitability trend analysis **OBJ. 2, 3**

Crosby Company has provided the following comparative information:

	2016	2015	2014	2013	2012
Net income	$ 5,571,720	$ 3,714,480	$ 2,772,000	$ 1,848,000	$ 1,400,000
Interest expense	1,052,060	891,576	768,600	610,000	500,000
Income tax expense	1,225,572	845,222	640,320	441,600	320,000
Total assets (ending balance)	29,378,491	22,598,839	17,120,333	12,588,480	10,152,000
Total stockholders' equity (ending balance)	18,706,200	13,134,480	9,420,000	6,648,000	4,800,000
Average total assets	25,988,665	19,859,586	14,854,406	11,370,240	8,676,000
Average total stockholders' equity	15,920,340	11,277,240	8,034,000	5,724,000	4,100,000

You have been asked to evaluate the historical performance of the company over the last five years.

Selected industry ratios have remained relatively steady at the following levels for the last five years:

	2012–2016
Rate earned on total assets	19%
Rate earned on stockholders' equity	26%
Number of times interest charges are earned	3.4
Ratio of liabilities to stockholders' equity	1.4

Instructions

1. Prepare four line graphs with the ratio on the vertical axis and the years on the horizontal axis for the following four ratios (rounded to one decimal place):
   a. Rate earned on total assets
   b. Rate earned on stockholders' equity
   c. Number of times interest charges are earned
   d. Ratio of liabilities to stockholders' equity

   Display both the company ratio and the industry benchmark on each graph. That is, each graph should have two lines.
2. Prepare an analysis of the graphs in (1).

Nike, Inc., Problem

Financial Statement Analysis

The financial statements for **Nike, Inc.**, are presented in Appendix C at the end of the text. The following additional information (in thousands) is available:

Accounts receivable at May 31, 2010	$ 3,138
Inventories at May 31, 2010	2,715
Total assets at May 31, 2010	14,998
Stockholders' equity at May 31, 2010	9,843

Instructions

1. Determine the following measures for the fiscal years ended May 31, 2013 (fiscal 2012), and May 31, 2012 (fiscal 2011), rounding to one decimal place.
   a. Working capital
   b. Current ratio
   c. Quick ratio
   d. Accounts receivable turnover
   e. Number of days' sales in receivables
   f. Inventory turnover
   g. Number of days' sales in inventory
   h. Ratio of liabilities to stockholders' equity
   i. Ratio of sales to assets

j. Rate earned on total assets, assuming interest expense is $23 million for the year ending May 31, 2013, and $31 million for the year ending May 31, 2012
k. Rate earned on common stockholders' equity
l. Price-earnings ratio, assuming that the market price was $61.66 per share on May 31, 2013, and $53.10 per share on May 31, 2012
m. Percentage relationship of net income to sales

2. What conclusions can be drawn from these analyses?

Cases & Projects

CP 17-1 Analysis of financing corporate growth

Assume that the president of Freeman Industries Inc. made the following statement in the Annual Report to Shareholders:

"The founding family and majority shareholders of the company do not believe in using debt to finance future growth. The founding family learned from hard experience during Prohibition and the Great Depression that debt can cause loss of flexibility and eventual loss of corporate control. The company will not place itself at such risk. As such, all future growth will be financed either by stock sales to the public or by internally generated resources."

As a public shareholder of this company, how would you respond to this policy?

CP 17-2 Receivables and inventory turnover

Rodgers Industries Inc. has completed its fiscal year on December 31. The auditor, Josh McCoy, has approached the CFO, Aaron Mathews, regarding the year-end receivables and inventory levels of Rodgers Industries. The following conversation takes place:

Josh: We are beginning our audit of Rodgers Industries and have prepared ratio analyses to determine if there have been significant changes in operations or financial position. This helps us guide the audit process. This analysis indicates that the inventory turnover has decreased from 5.1 to 2.7, while the accounts receivable turnover has decreased from 11 to 7. Could you explain this change in operations?

Aaron: There is little need for concern. The inventory represents computers that we were unable to sell during the holiday buying season. We are confident, however, that we will be able to sell these computers as we move into the next fiscal year.

Josh: What gives you this confidence?

Aaron: We will increase our advertising and provide some very attractive price concessions to move these machines. We have no choice. Newer technology is already out there, and we have to unload this inventory.

Josh: ... and the receivables?

Aaron: As you may be aware, the company is under tremendous pressure to expand sales and profits. As a result, we lowered our credit standards to our commercial customers so that we would be able to sell products to a broader customer base. As a result of this policy change, we have been able to expand sales by 35%.

Josh: Your responses have not been reassuring to me.

Aaron: I'm a little confused. Assets are good, right? Why don't you look at our current ratio? It has improved, hasn't it? I would think that you would view that very favorably.

Why is Josh concerned about the inventory and accounts receivable turnover ratios and Aaron's responses to them? What action may Josh need to take? How would you respond to Aaron's last comment?

CP 17-3 Vertical analysis

The condensed income statements through income from operations for **Dell Inc.** and **Apple Inc.** for recent fiscal years follow (numbers in millions of dollars):

	Dell Inc.	Apple Inc.
Sales	$56,940	$156,508
Cost of sales	44,754	87,846
Gross profit	$12,186	$68,662
Selling, general, and administrative expenses	$ 8,102	$10,040
Research and development	1,072	3,381
Operating expenses	$ 9,174	$13,421
Income from operations	$ 3,012	$55,241

Prepare comparative common-sized statements, rounding percents to one decimal place. Interpret the analyses.

CP 17-4 Profitability and stockholder ratios

Deere & Co. manufactures and distributes farm and construction machinery that it sells around the world. In addition to its manufacturing operations, Deere & Co.'s credit division loans money to customers to finance the purchase of their farm and construction equipment.

The following information is available for three recent years (in millions except per-share amounts):

	Year 3	Year 2	Year 1
Net income (loss)	$3,064.7	$2,799.9	$1,865.0
Preferred dividends	$0.00	$0.00	$0.00
Interest expense	$782.8	$759.4	$811.4
Shares outstanding for computing earnings per share	397	417	424
Cash dividend per share	$1.79	$1.52	$1.16
Average total assets	$52,237	$45,737	$42,200
Average stockholders' equity	$6,821	$6,545	$5,555
Average stock price per share	$79.27	$80.48	$61.18

1. Calculate the following ratios for each year (Round percentages to one decimal place):
   a. Rate earned on total assets
   b. Rate earned on stockholders' equity
   c. Earnings per share
   d. Dividend yield
   e. Price-earnings ratio
2. What is the ratio of average liabilities to average stockholders' equity for Year 3?
3. Based on these data, evaluate Deere & Co.'s performance.

CP 17-5 Comprehensive profitability and solvency analysis

Marriott International, Inc., and **Hyatt Hotels Corporation** are two major owners and managers of lodging and resort properties in the United States. Abstracted income statement information for the two companies is as follows for a recent year:

	Marriott (in millions)	Hyatt (in millions)
Operating profit before other expenses and interest	$ 677	$ 39
Other income (expenses)	54	118
Interest expense	(180)	(54)
Income before income taxes	$ 551	$103
Income tax expense	93	37
Net income	$ 458	$ 66

Balance sheet information is as follows:

	Marriott (in millions)	Hyatt (in millions)
Total liabilities	$7,398	$2,125
Total stockholders' equity	1,585	5,118
Total liabilities and stockholders' equity	$8,983	$7,243

The average liabilities, average stockholders' equity, and average total assets were as follows:

	Marriott (in millions)	Hyatt (in millions)
Average total liabilities	$7,095	$2,132
Average total stockholders' equity	1,364	5,067
Average total assets	8,458	7,199

1. Determine the following ratios for both companies (round to one decimal place after the whole percent):
   a. Rate earned on total assets
   b. Rate earned on stockholders' equity
   c. Number of times interest charges are earned
   d. Ratio of liabilities to stockholders' equity
2. Analyze and compare the two companies, using the information in (1).

Appendices

Appendix A

Interest Tables

Present Value of $1 at Compound Interest Due in *n* Periods

Periods	4.0%	4.5%	5%	5.5%	6%	6.5%	7%
1	0.96154	0.95694	0.95238	0.94787	0.94340	0.93897	0.93458
2	0.92456	0.91573	0.90703	0.89845	0.89000	0.88166	0.87344
3	0.88900	0.87630	0.86384	0.85161	0.83962	0.82785	0.81630
4	0.85480	0.83856	0.82270	0.80722	0.79209	0.77732	0.76290
5	0.82193	0.80245	0.78353	0.76513	0.74726	0.72988	0.71299
6	0.79031	0.76790	0.74622	0.72525	0.70496	0.68533	0.66634
7	0.75992	0.73483	0.71068	0.68744	0.66506	0.64351	0.62275
8	0.73069	0.70319	0.67684	0.65160	0.62741	0.60423	0.58201
9	0.70259	0.67290	0.64461	0.61763	0.59190	0.56735	0.54393
10	0.67556	0.64393	0.61391	0.58543	0.55839	0.53273	0.50835
11	0.64958	0.61620	0.58468	0.55491	0.52679	0.50021	0.47509
12	0.62460	0.58966	0.55684	0.52598	0.49697	0.46968	0.44401
13	0.60057	0.56427	0.53032	0.49856	0.46884	0.44102	0.41496
14	0.57748	0.53997	0.50507	0.47257	0.44230	0.41410	0.38782
15	0.55526	0.51672	0.48102	0.44793	0.41727	0.38883	0.36245
16	0.53391	0.49447	0.45811	0.42458	0.39365	0.36510	0.33873
17	0.51337	0.47318	0.43630	0.40245	0.37136	0.34281	0.31657
18	0.49363	0.45280	0.41552	0.38147	0.35034	0.32189	0.29586
19	0.47464	0.43330	0.39573	0.36158	0.33051	0.30224	0.27651
20	0.45639	0.41464	0.37689	0.34273	0.31180	0.28380	0.25842
21	0.43883	0.39679	0.35894	0.32486	0.29416	0.26648	0.24151
22	0.42196	0.37970	0.34185	0.30793	0.27751	0.25021	0.22571
23	0.40573	0.36335	0.32557	0.29187	0.26180	0.23494	0.21095
24	0.39012	0.34770	0.31007	0.27666	0.24698	0.22060	0.19715
25	0.37512	0.33273	0.29530	0.26223	0.23300	0.20714	0.18425
26	0.36069	0.31840	0.28124	0.24856	0.21981	0.19450	0.17220
27	0.34682	0.30469	0.26785	0.23560	0.20737	0.18263	0.16093
28	0.33348	0.29157	0.25509	0.22332	0.19563	0.17148	0.15040
29	0.32065	0.27902	0.24295	0.21168	0.18456	0.16101	0.14056
30	0.30832	0.26700	0.23138	0.20064	0.17411	0.15119	0.13137
31	0.29646	0.25550	0.22036	0.19018	0.16425	0.14196	0.12277
32	0.28506	0.24450	0.20987	0.18027	0.15496	0.13329	0.11474
33	0.27409	0.23397	0.19987	0.17087	0.14619	0.12516	0.10723
34	0.26355	0.22390	0.19035	0.16196	0.13791	0.11752	0.10022
35	0.25342	0.21425	0.18129	0.15352	0.13011	0.11035	0.09366
40	0.20829	0.17193	0.14205	0.11746	0.09722	0.08054	0.06678
45	0.17120	0.13796	0.11130	0.08988	0.07265	0.05879	0.04761
50	0.14071	0.11071	0.08720	0.06877	0.05429	0.04291	0.03395

Present Value of $1 at Compound Interest Due in *n* Periods

Periods	8%	9%	10%	11%	12%	13%	14%
1	0.92593	0.91743	0.90909	0.90090	0.89286	0.88496	0.87719
2	0.85734	0.84168	0.82645	0.81162	0.79719	0.78315	0.76947
3	0.79383	0.77218	0.75131	0.73119	0.71178	0.69305	0.67497
4	0.73503	0.70843	0.68301	0.65873	0.63552	0.61332	0.59208
5	0.68058	0.64993	0.62092	0.59345	0.56743	0.54276	0.51937
6	0.63017	0.59627	0.56447	0.53464	0.50663	0.48032	0.45559
7	0.58349	0.54703	0.51316	0.48166	0.45235	0.42506	0.39964
8	0.54027	0.50187	0.46651	0.43393	0.40388	0.37616	0.35056
9	0.50025	0.46043	0.42410	0.39092	0.36061	0.33288	0.30751
10	0.46319	0.42241	0.38554	0.35218	0.32197	0.29459	0.26974
11	0.42888	0.38753	0.35049	0.31728	0.28748	0.26070	0.23662
12	0.39711	0.35553	0.31863	0.28584	0.25668	0.23071	0.20756
13	0.36770	0.32618	0.28966	0.25751	0.22917	0.20416	0.18207
14	0.34046	0.29925	0.26333	0.23199	0.20462	0.18068	0.15971
15	0.31524	0.27454	0.23939	0.20900	0.18270	0.15989	0.14010
16	0.29189	0.25187	0.21763	0.18829	0.16312	0.14150	0.12289
17	0.27027	0.23107	0.19784	0.16963	0.14564	0.12522	0.10780
18	0.25025	0.21199	0.17986	0.15282	0.13004	0.11081	0.09456
19	0.23171	0.19449	0.16351	0.13768	0.11611	0.09806	0.08295
20	0.21455	0.17843	0.14864	0.12403	0.10367	0.08678	0.07276
21	0.19866	0.16370	0.13513	0.11174	0.09256	0.07680	0.06383
22	0.18394	0.15018	0.12285	0.10067	0.08264	0.06796	0.05599
23	0.17032	0.13778	0.11168	0.09069	0.07379	0.06014	0.04911
24	0.15770	0.12640	0.10153	0.08170	0.06588	0.05323	0.04308
25	0.14602	0.11597	0.09230	0.07361	0.05882	0.04710	0.03779
26	0.13520	0.10639	0.08391	0.06631	0.05252	0.04168	0.03315
27	0.12519	0.09761	0.07628	0.05974	0.04689	0.03689	0.02908
28	0.11591	0.08955	0.06934	0.05382	0.04187	0.03264	0.02551
29	0.10733	0.08215	0.06304	0.04849	0.03738	0.02889	0.02237
30	0.09938	0.07537	0.05731	0.04368	0.03338	0.02557	0.01963
31	0.09202	0.06915	0.05210	0.03935	0.02980	0.02262	0.01722
32	0.08520	0.06344	0.04736	0.03545	0.02661	0.02002	0.01510
33	0.07889	0.05820	0.04306	0.03194	0.02376	0.01772	0.01325
34	0.07305	0.05339	0.03914	0.02878	0.02121	0.01568	0.01162
35	0.06763	0.04899	0.03558	0.02592	0.01894	0.01388	0.01019
40	0.04603	0.03184	0.02209	0.01538	0.01075	0.00753	0.00529
45	0.03133	0.02069	0.01372	0.00913	0.00610	0.00409	0.00275
50	0.02132	0.01345	0.00852	0.00542	0.00346	0.00222	0.00143

Present Value of Ordinary Annuity of $1 per Period

Periods	4.0%	4.5%	5%	5.5%	6%	6.5%	7%
1	0.96154	0.95694	0.95238	0.94787	0.94340	0.93897	0.93458
2	1.88609	1.87267	1.85941	1.84632	1.83339	1.82063	1.80802
3	2.77509	2.74896	2.72325	2.69793	2.67301	2.64848	2.62432
4	3.62990	3.58753	3.54595	3.50515	3.46511	3.42580	3.38721
5	4.45182	4.38998	4.32948	4.27028	4.21236	4.15568	4.10020
6	5.24214	5.15787	5.07569	4.99553	4.91732	4.84101	4.76654
7	6.00205	5.89270	5.78637	5.68297	5.58238	5.48452	5.38929
8	6.73274	6.59589	6.46321	6.33457	6.20979	6.08875	5.97130
9	7.43533	7.26879	7.10782	6.95220	6.80169	6.65610	6.51523
10	8.11090	7.91272	7.72173	7.53763	7.36009	7.18883	7.02358
11	8.76048	8.52892	8.30641	8.09254	7.88687	7.68904	7.49867
12	9.38507	9.11858	8.86325	8.61852	8.38384	8.15873	7.94269
13	9.98565	9.68285	9.39357	9.11708	8.85268	8.59974	8.35765
14	10.56312	10.22283	9.89864	9.58965	9.29498	9.01384	8.74547
15	11.11839	10.73955	10.37966	10.03758	9.71225	9.40267	9.10791
16	11.65230	11.23402	10.83777	10.46216	10.10590	9.76776	9.44665
17	12.16567	11.70719	11.27407	10.86461	10.47726	10.11058	9.76322
18	12.65930	12.15999	11.68959	11.24607	10.82760	10.43247	10.05909
19	13.13394	12.59329	12.08532	11.60765	11.15812	10.73471	10.33560
20	13.59033	13.00794	12.46221	11.95038	11.46992	11.01851	10.59401
21	14.02916	13.40472	12.82115	12.27524	11.76408	11.28498	10.83553
22	14.45112	13.78442	13.16300	12.58317	12.04158	11.53520	11.06124
23	14.85684	14.14777	13.48857	12.87504	12.30338	11.77014	11.27219
24	15.24696	14.49548	13.79864	13.15170	12.55036	11.99074	11.46933
25	15.62208	14.82821	14.09394	13.41393	12.78336	12.19788	11.65358
26	15.98277	15.14661	14.37519	13.66250	13.00317	12.39237	11.82578
27	16.32959	15.45130	14.64303	13.89810	13.21053	12.57500	11.98671
28	16.66306	15.74287	14.89813	14.12142	13.40616	12.74648	12.13711
29	16.98371	16.02189	15.14107	14.33310	13.59072	12.90749	12.27767
30	17.29203	16.28889	15.37245	14.53375	13.76483	13.05868	12.40904
31	17.58849	16.54439	15.59281	14.72393	13.92909	13.20063	12.53181
32	17.87355	16.78889	15.80268	14.90420	14.08404	13.33393	12.64656
33	18.14765	17.02286	16.00255	15.07507	14.23023	13.45909	12.75379
34	18.41120	17.24676	16.19290	15.23703	14.36814	13.57661	12.85401
35	18.66461	17.46101	16.37419	15.39055	14.49825	13.68696	12.94767
40	19.79277	18.40158	17.15909	16.04612	15.04630	14.14553	13.33171
45	20.72004	19.15635	17.77407	16.54773	15.45583	14.48023	13.60552
50	21.48218	19.76201	18.25593	16.93152	15.76186	14.72452	13.80075

Present Value of Ordinary Annuity of $1 per Period

Periods	8%	9%	10%	11%	12%	13%	14%
1	0.92593	0.91743	0.90909	0.90090	0.89286	0.88496	0.87719
2	1.78326	1.75911	1.73554	1.71252	1.69005	1.66810	1.64666
3	2.57710	2.53129	2.48685	2.44371	2.40183	2.36115	2.32163
4	3.31213	3.23972	3.16987	3.10245	3.03735	2.97447	2.91371
5	3.99271	3.88965	3.79079	3.69590	3.60478	3.51723	3.43308
6	4.62288	4.48592	4.35526	4.23054	4.11141	3.99755	3.88867
7	5.20637	5.03295	4.86842	4.71220	4.56376	4.42261	4.28830
8	5.74664	5.53482	5.33493	5.14612	4.96764	4.79677	4.63886
9	6.24689	5.99525	5.75902	5.53705	5.32825	5.13166	4.94637
10	6.71008	6.41766	6.14457	5.88923	5.65022	5.42624	5.21612
11	7.13896	6.80519	6.49506	6.20652	5.93770	5.68694	5.45273
12	7.53608	7.16073	6.81369	6.49236	6.19437	5.91765	5.66029
13	7.90378	7.48690	7.10336	6.74987	6.42355	6.12181	5.84236
14	8.22424	7.78615	7.36669	6.96187	6.62817	6.30249	6.00207
15	8.55948	8.06069	7.60608	7.19087	6.81086	6.46238	6.14217
16	8.85137	8.31256	7.82371	7.37916	6.97399	6.60388	6.26506
17	9.12164	8.54363	8.02155	7.54879	7.11963	6.72909	6.37286
18	9.37189	8.75563	8.20141	7.70162	7.24967	6.83991	6.46742
19	9.60360	8.95011	8.36492	7.83929	7.36578	6.93797	6.55037
20	9.81815	9.12855	8.51356	7.96333	7.46944	7.02475	6.62313
21	10.01680	9.29224	8.64869	8.07507	7.56200	7.10155	6.68696
22	10.20074	9.44243	8.77154	8.17574	7.64465	7.16951	6.74294
23	10.37106	9.58021	8.88322	8.26643	7.71843	7.22966	6.79206
24	10.52876	9.70661	8.98474	8.34814	7.78432	7.28288	6.83514
25	10.67478	9.82258	9.07704	8.42174	7.84314	7.32998	6.87293
26	10.80998	9.92897	9.16095	8.48806	7.89566	7.37167	6.90608
27	10.93516	10.02658	9.23722	8.54780	7.94255	7.40856	6.93515
28	11.05108	10.11613	9.30657	8.60162	7.98442	7.44120	6.96066
29	11.15841	10.19828	9.36961	8.65011	8.02181	7.47009	6.98304
30	11.25778	10.27365	9.42691	8.69379	8.05518	7.49565	7.00266
31	11.34980	10.34280	9.47901	8.73315	8.08499	7.51828	7.01988
32	11.43500	10.40624	9.52638	8.76860	8.11159	7.53830	7.03498
33	11.51389	10.46444	9.56943	8.80054	8.13535	7.55602	7.04823
34	11.58693	10.51784	9.60857	8.82932	8.15656	7.57170	7.05985
35	11.65457	10.56682	9.64416	8.85524	8.17550	7.58557	7.07005
40	11.92461	10.75736	9.77905	8.95105	8.24378	7.63438	7.10504
45	12.10840	10.88120	9.86281	9.00791	8.28252	7.66086	7.12322
50	12.23348	10.96168	9.91481	9.04165	8.30450	7.67524	7.13266

Appendix B

Reversing Entries

Some of the adjusting entries recorded at the end of the accounting period affect transactions that occur in the next period. In such cases, a reversing entry may be used to simplify the recording of the next period's transactions.

To illustrate, an adjusting entry for accrued wages expense affects the first payment of wages in the next period. Without using a reversing entry, Wages Payable must be debited for the accrued wages at the end of the preceding period. In addition, Wages Expense must also be debited for only that portion of the payroll that is an expense of the current period.

Using a reversing entry, however, simplifies the analysis and recording of the first wages payment in the next period. As the term implies, a *reversing entry* is the exact opposite of the related adjusting entry. The amounts and accounts are the same as the adjusting entry, but the debits and credits are reversed.

Reversing entries are illustrated by using the accrued wages for **NetSolutions** presented in Chapter 3. These data are summarized in Exhibit 1.

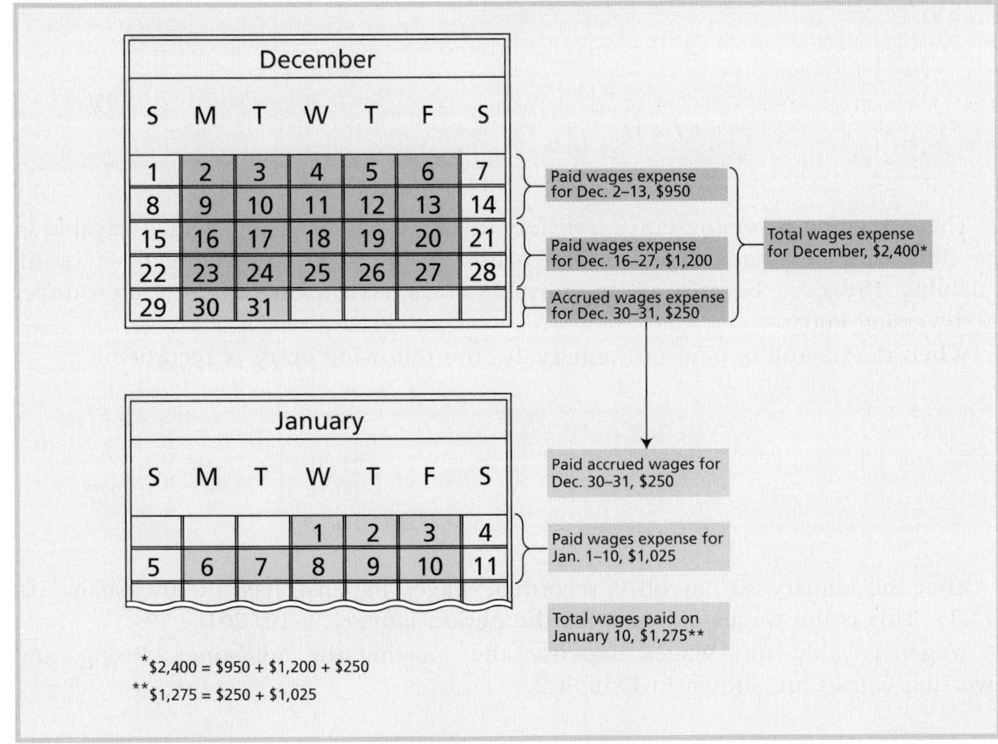

EXHIBIT 1

Accrued Wages

The adjusting entry for the accrued wages of December 30 and 31 is as follows:

Date		Description	Post. Ref.	Debit	Credit
2015 Dec.	31	Wages Expense	51	250	
		Wages Payable	22		250
		Accrued wages.			

After the adjusting entry is recorded, Wages Expense will have a debit balance of $4,525 ($4,275 + $250) and Wages Payable will have a credit balance of $250, as shown in Exhibit 2.

After the closing entries are recorded, Wages Expense will have a zero balance. However, because Wages Payable is a liability account, it is not closed. Thus, Wages Payable will have a credit balance of $250 as of January 1, 2016.

Without recording a reversing entry, the payment of the $1,275 payroll on January 10 would be recorded as follows:

Date		Description	Post. Ref.	Debit	Credit
2016 Jan.	10	Wages Payable	22	250	
		Wages Expense	51	1,025	
		Cash	11		1,275

To record the January 10 payroll correctly, Wages Payable must be debited for $250, as shown in the preceding entry. This means that the employee who records the January 10 payroll must refer to the December 31, 2015, adjusting entry or to the ledger to determine the amount to debit Wages Payable.

Because the January 10 payroll is not recorded in the normal manner, there is a greater chance that an error may occur. This chance of error is reduced by recording a reversing entry as of the first day of the next period. For example, the reversing entry for the accrued wages expense would be recorded on January 1, 2016, as follows:

Date		Description	Post. Ref.	Debit	Credit
2016 Jan.	1	Wages Payable	22	250	
		Wages Expense	51		250
		Reversing entry.			

The preceding reversing entry transfers the $250 liability from Wages Payable to the credit side of Wages Expense. The nature of the $250 is unchanged—it is still a liability. However, because of its unusual nature, an explanation is written under the reversing entry.

When the payroll is paid on January 10, the following entry is recorded:

Date		Description	Post. Ref.	Debit	Credit
Jan.	10	Wages Expense	51	1,275	
		Cash	11		1,275

After the January 10 payroll is recorded, Wages Expense has a debit balance of $1,025. This is the wages expense for the period January 1–10, 2016.

Wages Payable and Wages Expense after posting the adjusting, closing, and reversing entries are shown in Exhibit 2.

EXHIBIT 2

Wages Payable and Wages Expense Accounts

Account *Wages Payable* — *Account No. 22*

Date		Item	Post. Ref.	Debit	Credit	Balance Debit	Balance Credit
2015 Dec.	31	Adjusting	5		250		250
2016 Jan.	1	Reversing	7	250		—	—

Account *Wages Expense* — *Account No. 51*

Date		Item	Post. Ref.	Debit	Credit	Balance Debit	Balance Credit
2015 Nov.	30		1	2,125		2,125	
Dec.	13		3	950		3,075	
	27		3	1,200		4,275	
	31	Adjusting	5	250		4,525	
	31	Closing	6		4,525	—	—
2016 Jan.	1	Reversing	7		250		250
	10		7	1,275		1,025	

In addition to accrued expenses (accrued liabilities), reversing entries are also used for accrued revenues (accrued assets). To illustrate, the reversing entry for NetSolutions' accrued fees earned as of December 31, 2015, is as follows:

Jan.	1	Fees Earned	41	500	
		Accounts Receivable	12		500
		Reversing entry.			

The use of reversing entries is optional. However, in computerized accounting systems, data entry employees often input routine accounting entries. In such cases, reversing entries may be useful in avoiding errors.

Exercises

EX B-1 Adjusting and reversing entries

On the basis of the following data, (a) journalize the adjusting entries at December 31, the end of the current fiscal year, and (b) journalize the reversing entries on January 1, the first day of the following year:

1. Sales salaries are uniformly $11,750 for a five-day workweek, ending on Friday. The last payday of the year was Friday, December 26.
2. Accrued fees earned but not recorded at December 31, $51,300.

EX B-2 Adjusting and reversing entries

On the basis of the following data, (a) journalize the adjusting entries at June 30, the end of the current fiscal year, and (b) journalize the reversing entries on July 1, the first day of the following year:

1. Wages are uniformly $66,000 for a five-day workweek, ending on Friday. The last payday of the year was Friday, June 27.
2. Accrued fees earned but not recorded at June 30, $25,000.

EX B-3 Entries posted to the wages expense account

Portions of the wages expense account of a business follow:

Account ***Wages Expense*** **Account No. 53**

Date	Item	Post. Ref.	Dr.	Cr.	Balance Dr.	Balance Cr.
2015						
Dec. 26	(1)	125	15,400		800,000	
31	(2)	126	9,250		809,250	
31	(3)	127		809,250	—	—
2016						
Jan. 1	(4)	128		9,250		9,250
2	(5)	129	14,800		5,550	

a. Indicate the nature of the entry (payment, adjusting, closing, reversing) from which each numbered posting was made.

b. Journalize the complete entry from which each numbered posting was made.

EX B-4 Entries posted to the salaries expense account

Portions of the salaries expense account of a business follow:

Account ***Salaries Expense*** **Account No. 62**

Date	Item	Post. Ref.	Dr.	Cr.	Balance Dr.	Balance Cr.
2015						
Dec. 27	(1)	29	22,000		1,200,000	
31	(2)	30	13,200		1,213,200	
31	(3)	31		1,213,200	—	—
2016						
Jan. 1	(4)	32		13,200		13,200
2	(5)	33	24,000		10,800	

a. Indicate the nature of the entry (payment, adjusting, closing, reversing) from which each numbered posting was made.

b. Journalize the complete entry from which each numbered posting was made.

Appendix C

Nike Inc., Form 10-K
For the Fiscal Year Ended May 31, 2013

NIKE INC

FORM 10-K
(Annual Report)

Filed 07/23/13 for the Period Ending 05/31/13

Address	ONE BOWERMAN DR BEAVERTON, OR 97005-6453
Telephone	5036713173
CIK	0000320187
Symbol	NKE
SIC Code	3021 - Rubber and Plastics Footwear
Industry	Footwear
Sector	Consumer Cyclical
Fiscal Year	05/31

Source: Nike Inc, *Form 10-K For the Fiscal Year Ended May 31, 2013.*

Management's Annual Report on Internal Control Over Financial Reporting

Management is responsible for establishing and maintaining adequate internal control over financial reporting, as such term is defined in Rule 13a-15(f) and Rule 15d-15(f) of the Securities Exchange Act of 1934, as amended. Internal control over financial reporting is a process designed to provide reasonable assurance regarding the reliability of financial reporting and the preparation of the financial statements for external purposes in accordance with generally accepted accounting principles in the United States of America. Internal control over financial reporting includes those policies and procedures that: (i) pertain to the maintenance of records that, in reasonable detail, accurately and fairly reflect the transactions and dispositions of assets of the Company; (ii) provide reasonable assurance that transactions are recorded as necessary to permit preparation of financial statements in accordance with generally accepted accounting principles, and that receipts and expenditures of the Company are being made only in accordance with authorizations of our management and directors; and (iii) provide reasonable assurance regarding prevention or timely detection of unauthorized acquisition, use or disposition of assets of the Company that could have a material effect on the financial statements.

While "reasonable assurance" is a high level of assurance, it does not mean absolute assurance. Because of its inherent limitations, internal control over financial reporting may not prevent or detect every misstatement and instance

of fraud. Controls are susceptible to manipulation, especially in instances of fraud caused by the collusion of two or more people, including our senior management. Also, projections of any evaluation of effectiveness to future periods are subject to the risk that controls may become inadequate because of changes in conditions, or that the degree of compliance with the policies or procedures may deteriorate.

Under the supervision and with the participation of our Chief Executive Officer and Chief Financial Officer, our management conducted an evaluation of the effectiveness of our internal control over financial reporting based upon the framework in *Internal Control — Integrated Framework* issued by the Committee of Sponsoring Organizations of the Treadway Commission (COSO). Based on the results of our evaluation, our management concluded that our internal control over financial reporting was effective as of May 31, 2013.

PricewaterhouseCoopers LLP, an independent registered public accounting firm, has audited (1) the consolidated financial statements and (2) the effectiveness of our internal control over financial reporting as of May 31, 2013, as stated in their report herein.

Mark G. Parker
President and Chief Executive Officer

Donald W. Blair
Chief Financial Officer

Report of Independent Registered Public Accounting Firm

To the Board of Directors and Shareholders of NIKE, Inc.:

In our opinion, the consolidated financial statements listed in the index appearing under Item 15(a)(1) present fairly, in all material respects, the financial position of NIKE, Inc. and its subsidiaries at May 31, 2013 and 2012, and the results of their operations and their cash flows for each of the three years in the period ended May 31, 2013 in conformity with accounting principles generally accepted in the United States of America. In addition, in our opinion, the financial statement schedule listed in the appendix appearing under Item 15(a)(2) presents fairly, in all material respects, the information set forth therein when read in conjunction with the related consolidated financial statements. Also in our opinion, the Company maintained, in all material respects, effective internal control over financial reporting as of May 31, 2013, based on criteria established in *Internal Control — Integrated Framework* issued by the Committee of Sponsoring Organizations of the Treadway Commission (COSO). The Company's management is responsible for these financial statements and financial statement schedule, for maintaining effective internal control over financial reporting and for its assessment of the effectiveness of internal control over financial reporting, included in Management's Annual Report on Internal Control Over Financial Reporting appearing under Item 8. Our responsibility is to express opinions on these financial statements, on the financial statement schedule, and on the Company's internal control over financial reporting based on our integrated audits. We conducted our audits in accordance with the standards of the Public Company Accounting Oversight Board (United States). Those standards require that we plan and perform the audits to obtain reasonable assurance about whether the financial statements are free of material misstatement and whether effective internal control over financial reporting was maintained in all material respects. Our audits of the financial statements included examining, on a test basis, evidence supporting the amounts and disclosures in the financial statements, assessing the accounting principles used and significant estimates made by management, and evaluating the overall financial statement presentation. Our audit of internal control over financial reporting included obtaining an understanding of internal control over financial reporting, assessing the risk that a material weakness exists, and testing and evaluating the design and operating effectiveness of internal control based on the assessed risk. Our audits also included performing such other procedures as we considered necessary in the circumstances. We believe that our audits provide a reasonable basis for our opinions.

A company's internal control over financial reporting is a process designed to provide reasonable assurance regarding the reliability of financial reporting and the preparation of financial statements for external purposes in accordance with generally accepted accounting principles. A company's internal control over financial reporting includes those policies and procedures that (i) pertain to the maintenance of records that, in reasonable detail, accurately and fairly reflect the transactions and dispositions of the assets of the company; (ii) provide reasonable assurance that transactions are recorded as necessary to permit preparation of financial statements in accordance with generally accepted accounting principles, and that receipts and expenditures of the company are being made only in accordance with authorizations of management and directors of the company; and (iii) provide reasonable assurance regarding prevention or timely detection of unauthorized acquisition, use, or disposition of the company's assets that could have a material effect on the financial statements.

Because of its inherent limitations, internal control over financial reporting may not prevent or detect misstatements. Also, projections of any evaluation of effectiveness to future periods are subject to the risk that controls may become inadequate because of changes in conditions, or that the degree of compliance with the policies or procedures may deteriorate.

/S/ PRICEWATERHOUSECOOPERS LLP

Portland, Oregon July 23, 2013

NIKE, Inc. Consolidated Statements Of Income

(In millions, except per share data)	Year Ended May 31, 2013	2012	2011
Income from continuing operations:			
Revenues	$ 25,313	$ 23,331	$ 20,117
Cost of sales	14,279	13,183	10,915
Gross profit	11,034	10,148	9,202
Demand creation expense	2,745	2,607	2,344
Operating overhead expense	5,035	4,458	4,017
Total selling and administrative expense	7,780	7,065	6,361
Interest (income) expense, net (Notes 6, 7 and 8)	(3)	4	4
Other (income) expense, net (Note 17)	(15)	54	(25)
Income before income taxes	3,272	3,025	2,862
Income tax expense (Note 9)	808	756	690
NET INCOME FROM CONTINUING OPERATIONS	**2,464**	**2,269**	**2,172**
NET INCOME (LOSS) FROM DISCONTINUED OPERATIONS	**21**	**(46)**	**(39)**
NET INCOME	**$ 2,485**	**$ 2,223**	**$ 2,133**
Earnings per share from continuing operations:			
Basic earnings per common share (Notes 1 and 12)	$ 2.75	$ 2.47	$ 2.28
Diluted earnings per common share (Notes 1 and 12)	$ 2.69	$ 2.42	$ 2.24
Earnings per share from discontinued operations:			
Basic earnings per common share (Notes 1 and 12)	$ 0.02	$ (0.05)	$ (0.04)
Diluted earnings per common share (Notes 1 and 12)	$ 0.02	$ (0.05)	$ (0.04)
Dividends declared per common share	$ 0.81	$ 0.70	$ 0.60

The accompanying notes to consolidated financial statements are an integral part of this statement.

NIKE, Inc. Consolidated Statements of Comprehensive Income

	Year Ended May 31,		
(In millions)	2013	2012	2011
Net income	$ 2,485	$ 2,223	$ 2,133
Other comprehensive income (loss), net of tax:			
Foreign currency translation and other[(1)]	30	(295)	263
Net gain (loss) on cash flow hedges[(2)]	117	255	(242)
Net gain (loss) on net investment hedges[(3)]	—	45	(57)
Reclassification to net income of previously deferred (gains) losses related to hedge derivative instruments[(4)]	(105)	49	(84)
Release of cumulative translation loss related to Umbro[(5)] (Notes 14 and 15)	83	—	—
Total other comprehensive income, net of tax	125	54	(120)
TOTAL COMPREHENSIVE INCOME	**$ 2,610**	**$ 2,277**	**$ 2,013**

(1) Net of tax (expense) benefit of $(12) million, $0 million, and $(121) million, respectively.

(2) Net of tax (expense) benefit of $(22) million, $(8) million, and $66 million, respectively.

(3) Net of tax benefit of $0 million, $0 million, and $28 million, respectively.

(4) Net of tax (benefit) expense of $0 million, $(14) million, and $24 million, respectively.

(5) Net of tax (benefit) of $(47) million, $0 million, and $0 million, respectively.

The accompanying notes to consolidated financial statements are an integral part of this statement.

NIKE, Inc. Consolidated Balance Sheets

(In millions)	May 31, 2013	2012
ASSETS		
Current assets:	$ 3,337	
Cash and equivalents		$ 2,317
Short-term investments (Note 6)	2,628	1,440
Accounts receivable, net (Note 1)	3,117	3,132
Inventories (Notes 1 and 2)	3,434	3,222
Deferred income taxes (Note 9)	308	262
Prepaid expenses and other current assets (Notes 6 and 17)	802	857
Assets of discontinued operations (Note 15)	—	615
Total current assets	13,626	11,845
Property, plant and equipment, net (Note 3)	2,452	2,209
Identifiable intangible assets, net (Note 4)	382	370
Goodwill (Note 4)	131	131
Deferred income taxes and other assets (Notes 6, 9 and 17)	993	910
TOTAL ASSETS	**$ 17,584**	**$ 15,465**
LIABILITIES AND SHAREHOLDERS' EQUITY		
Current liabilities:		
Current portion of long-term debt (Note 8)	$ 57	$ 49
Notes payable (Note 7)	121	108
Accounts payable (Note 7)	1,646	1,549
Accrued liabilities (Notes 5, 6 and 17)	1,986	1,941
Income taxes payable (Note 9)	98	65
Liabilities of discontinued operations (Note 15)	18	170
Total current liabilities	3,926	3,882
Long-term debt (Note 8)	1,210	228
Deferred income taxes and other liabilities (Notes 6, 9 and 17)	1,292	974
Commitments and contingencies (Note 16)	—	—
Redeemable Preferred Stock (Note 10)	—	—
Shareholders' equity:		
Common stock at stated value (Note 11):		
Class A convertible — 178 and 180 shares outstanding	—	—
Class B — 716 and 736 shares outstanding	3	3
Capital in excess of stated value	5,184	4,641
Accumulated other comprehensive income (Note 14)	274	149
Retained earnings	5,695	5,588
Total shareholders' equity	11,156	10,381
TOTAL LIABILITIES AND SHAREHOLDERS' EQUITY	**$ 17,584**	**$ 15,465**

The accompanying notes to consolidated financial statements are an integral part of this statement.

NIKE, Inc. Consolidated Statements of Cash Flows

	Year Ended May 31,		
(In millions)	2013	2012	2011
Cash provided by operations:			
Net income	$ 2,485	$ 2,223	$ 2,133
Income charges (credits) not affecting cash:			
Depreciation	438	373	335
Deferred income taxes	21	(60)	(76)
Stock-based compensation (Note 11)	174	130	105
Amortization and other	75	32	23
Net gain on divestitures	(124)	—	—
Changes in certain working capital components and other assets and liabilities:			
Decrease (increase) in accounts receivable	142	(323)	(273)
(Increase) in inventories	(197)	(805)	(551)
(Increase) in prepaid expenses and other current assets	(28)	(141)	(35)
Increase in accounts payable, accrued liabilities and income taxes payable	41	470	151
Cash provided by operations	3,027	1,899	1,812
Cash (used) provided by investing activities:			
Purchases of short-term investments	(3,702)	(2,705)	(7,616)
Maturities of short-term investments	1,501	2,585	4,313
Sales of short-term investments	998	1,244	2,766
Additions to property, plant and equipment	(636)	(597)	(432)
Disposals of property, plant and equipment	14	2	1
Proceeds from divestitures	786	—	—
Increase in other assets, net of other liabilities	(28)	(37)	(30)
Settlement of net investment hedges	—	22	(23)
Cash (used) provided by investing activities	(1,067)	514	(1,021)
Cash used by financing activities:			
Net proceeds from long-term debt issuance	986	—	—
Long-term debt payments, including current portion	(49)	(203)	(8)
Increase (decrease) in notes payable	15	(65)	41
Proceeds from exercise of stock options and other stock issuances	313	468	345
Excess tax benefits from share-based payment arrangements	72	115	64
Repurchase of common stock	(1,674)	(1,814)	(1,859)
Dividends — common and preferred	(703)	(619)	(555)
Cash used by financing activities	(1,040)	(2,118)	(1,972)
Effect of exchange rate changes	100	67	57
Net increase (decrease) in cash and equivalents	1,020	362	(1,124)
Cash and equivalents, beginning of year	2,317	1,955	3,079
CASH AND EQUIVALENTS, END OF YEAR	**$ 3,337**	**$ 2,317**	**$ 1,955**
Supplemental disclosure of cash flow information:			
Cash paid during the year for:			
Interest, net of capitalized interest	$ 20	$ 29	$ 32
Income taxes	702	638	736
Dividends declared and not paid	188	165	145

The accompanying notes to consolidated financial statements are an integral part of this statement.

NIKE, Inc. Consolidated Statements of Shareholders' Equity

	Common Stock				Capital in Excess of Stated Value	Accumulated Other Comprehensive Income	Retained Earnings	Total
	Class A		Class B					
(In millions, except per share data)	Shares	Amount	Shares	Amount				
Balance at May 31, 2010	**180**	**$ —**	**788**	**$ 3**	**$ 3,441**	**$ 215**	**$ 6,095**	**$ 9,754**
Stock options exercised			14		368			368
Repurchase of Class B Common Stock			(48)		(14)		(1,857)	(1,871)
Dividends on Common stock ($0.60 per share)							(569)	(569)
Issuance of shares to employees			2		49			49
Stock-based compensation (Note 11)					105			105
Forfeiture of shares from employees			—		(5)		(1)	(6)
Net income							2,133	2,133
Other Comprehensive Income						(120)		(120)
Balance at May 31, 2011	**180**	**$ —**	**756**	**$ 3**	**$ 3,944**	**$ 95**	**$ 5,801**	**$ 9,843**
Stock options exercised			18		528			528
Repurchase of Class B Common Stock			(40)		(12)		(1,793)	(1,805)
Dividends on Common stock ($0.70 per share)							(639)	(639)
Issuance of shares to employees			2		57			57
Stock-based compensation (Note 11)					130			130
Forfeiture of shares from employees			—		(6)		(4)	(10)
Net income							2,223	2,223
Other comprehensive income						54		54
Balance at May 31, 2012	**180**	**$ —**	**736**	**$ 3**	**$ 4,641**	**$ 149**	**$ 5,588**	**$ 10,381**
Stock options exercised			10		322			322
Conversion to Class B Common Stock	(2)		2					—
Repurchase of Class B Common Stock			(34)		(10)		(1,647)	(1,657)
Dividends on Common stock ($0.81 per share)							(727)	(727)
Issuance of shares to employees			2		65			65
Stock-based compensation (Note 11)					174			174
Forfeiture of shares from employees			—		(8)		(4)	(12)
Net income							2,485	2,485
Other comprehensive income						125		125
Balance at May 31, 2013	**178**	**$ —**	**716**	**$ 3**	**$ 5,184**	**$ 274**	**$ 5,695**	**$ 11,156**

The accompanying notes to consolidated financial statements are an integral part of this statement.

NOTE 1 — Summary of Significant Accounting Policies

Description of Business

NIKE, Inc. is a worldwide leader in the design, development and worldwide marketing and selling of athletic footwear, apparel, equipment, accessories and services. Wholly-owned NIKE, Inc. subsidiaries include Converse Inc., which designs, markets and distributes casual footwear, apparel and accessories and Hurley International LLC, which designs, markets and distributes action sports and youth lifestyle footwear, apparel and accessories.

Basis of Consolidation

The consolidated financial statements include the accounts of NIKE, Inc. and its subsidiaries (the "Company"). All significant intercompany transactions and balances have been eliminated.

The Company completed the sale of Cole Haan during the third quarter ended February 28, 2013 and completed the sale of Umbro during the second quarter ended November 30, 2012. As a result, the Company reports the operating results of Cole Haan and Umbro in the net income (loss) from discontinued operations line in the consolidated statements of income for all periods presented. In addition, the assets and liabilities associated with these businesses are reported as assets of discontinued operations and liabilities of discontinued operations, as appropriate, in the consolidated balance sheets (refer to Note 15 — Discontinued Operations). Unless otherwise indicated, the disclosures accompanying the consolidated financial statements reflect the Company's continuing operations.

On November 15, 2012, the Company announced a two-for-one split of both NIKE Class A and Class B Common shares. The stock split was a 100 percent stock dividend payable on December 24, 2012 to shareholders of record at the close of business December 10, 2012. Common stock began trading at the split-adjusted price on December 26, 2012. All share numbers and per share amounts presented reflect the stock split.

Recognition of Revenues

Wholesale revenues are recognized when title and the risks and rewards of ownership have passed to the customer, based on the terms of sale. This occurs upon shipment or upon receipt by the customer depending on the country of the sale and the agreement with the customer. Retail store revenues are recorded at the time of sale. Provisions for post-invoice sales discounts, returns and miscellaneous claims from customers are estimated and recorded as a reduction to revenue at the time of sale. Post-invoice sales discounts consist of contractual programs with certain customers or discretionary discounts that are expected to be granted to certain customers at a later date. Estimates of discretionary discounts, returns and claims are based on historical rates, specific identification of outstanding claims and outstanding returns not yet received from customers, and estimated discounts, returns and claims expected but not yet finalized with customers. As of May 31, 2013 and 2012, the Company's reserve balances for post-invoice sales discounts, returns and miscellaneous claims were $531 million and $455 million, respectively.

Cost of Sales

Cost of sales consists primarily of inventory costs, as well as warehousing costs (including the cost of warehouse labor), third party royalties, certain foreign currency hedge gains and losses, and research, design and development costs.

Shipping and Handling Costs

Shipping and handling costs are expensed as incurred and included in cost of sales.

Operating Overhead Expense

Operating overhead expense consists primarily of payroll and benefit related costs, rent, depreciation and amortization, professional services, and meetings and travel.

Demand Creation Expense

Demand creation expense consists of advertising and promotion costs, including costs of endorsement contracts, television, digital and print advertising, brand events, and retail brand presentation. Advertising production costs are expensed the first time an advertisement is run. Advertising placement costs are expensed in the month the advertising appears, while costs related to brand events are expensed when the event occurs. Costs related to retail brand presentation are expensed when the presentation is completed and delivered.

A significant amount of the Company's promotional expenses result from payments under endorsement contracts. Accounting for endorsement payments is based upon specific contract provisions. Generally, endorsement payments are expensed on a straight-line basis over the term of the contract after giving recognition to periodic performance compliance provisions of the contracts. Prepayments made under contracts are included in prepaid expenses or other assets depending on the period to which the prepayment applies.

Some of the contracts provide for contingent payments to endorsers based upon specific achievements in their sports (e.g., winning a championship). The Company records selling and administrative expense for these amounts when the endorser achieves the specific goal.

Some of the contracts provide for payments based upon endorsers maintaining a level of performance in their sport over an extended period of time (e.g., maintaining a top ranking in a sport for a year). These amounts are recorded in selling and administrative expense when the Company determines that it is probable that the specified level of performance will be maintained throughout the period. In these instances, to the extent that actual payments to the endorser differ from our estimate due to changes in the endorser's athletic performance, increased or decreased selling and administrative expense may be recorded in a future period.

Some of the contracts provide for royalty payments to endorsers based upon a predetermined percentage of sales of particular products. The Company expenses these payments in cost of sales as the related sales occur. In certain contracts, the Company offers minimum guaranteed royalty payments. For contractual obligations for which the Company estimates it will not meet the minimum guaranteed amount of royalty fees through sales of product, the Company records the amount of the guaranteed payment in excess of that earned through sales of product in selling and administrative expense uniformly over the remaining guarantee period.

Through cooperative advertising programs, the Company reimburses retail customers for certain costs of advertising the Company's products. The Company records these costs in selling and administrative expense at the point in time when it is obligated to its customers for the costs, which is when the related revenues are recognized. This obligation may arise prior to the related advertisement being run.

Total advertising and promotion expenses were $2,745 million, $2,607 million, and $2,344 million for the years ended May 31, 2013, 2012 and 2011, respectively. Prepaid advertising and promotion expenses recorded in prepaid expenses and other current assets totaled $386 million and $281 million at May 31, 2013 and 2012, respectively.

Cash and Equivalents

Cash and equivalents represent cash and short-term, highly liquid investments, including commercial paper, U.S. treasury, U.S. agency, and corporate debt securities with maturities of three months or less at date of purchase.

Short-Term Investments

Short-term investments consist of highly liquid investments, including commercial paper, U.S. treasury, U.S. agency, and corporate debt securities, with maturities over three months from the date of purchase. Debt securities that the Company has the ability and positive intent to hold to maturity are carried at amortized cost. At May 31, 2013 and 2012, the Company did not hold any short-term investments that were classified as trading or held-to- maturity.

At May 31, 2013 and 2012, short-term investments consisted of available- for-sale securities. Available-for-sale securities are recorded at fair value with unrealized gains and losses reported, net of tax, in other comprehensive income, unless unrealized losses are determined to be other than temporary. Realized gains and losses on the sale of securities are determined by specific identification. The Company considers all available-for-sale securities, including those with maturity dates beyond 12 months, as available to support current operational liquidity needs and therefore classifies all securities with maturity dates beyond three months at the date of purchase as current assets within short-term investments on the consolidated balance sheets.

Refer to Note 6 — Fair Value Measurements for more information on the Company's short-term investments.

Allowance for Uncollectible Accounts Receivable

Accounts receivable consists primarily of amounts receivable from customers. The Company makes ongoing estimates relating to the collectability of its accounts receivable and maintains an allowance for estimated losses resulting from the inability of its customers to make required payments. In determining the amount of the allowance, the Company considers historical levels of credit losses and makes judgments about the creditworthiness of significant customers based on ongoing credit evaluations. Accounts receivable with anticipated collection dates greater than 12 months from the balance sheet date and related allowances are considered non-current and recorded in other assets. The allowance for uncollectible accounts receivable was $104 million and $91 million at May 31, 2013 and 2012, respectively, of which $54 million and $45 million, respectively, was classified as long-term and recorded in other assets.

Inventory Valuation

Inventories are stated at lower of cost or market and valued primarily on an average cost basis. Inventory costs primarily consist of product cost from our suppliers, as well as freight, import duties, taxes, insurance and logistics and other handling fees.

Property, Plant and Equipment and Depreciation

Property, plant and equipment are recorded at cost. Depreciation for financial reporting purposes is determined on a straight-line basis for buildings and leasehold improvements over 2 to 40 years and for machinery and equipment over 2 to 15 years.

Depreciation and amortization of assets used in manufacturing, warehousing and product distribution are recorded in cost of sales. Depreciation and amortization of other assets are recorded in selling and administrative expense.

Software Development Costs

Internal Use Software. Expenditures for major software purchases and software developed for internal use are capitalized and amortized over a 2 to 10 year period on a straight-line basis. The Company's policy provides for the capitalization of external direct costs of materials and services associated with developing or obtaining internal use computer software. In addition, the Company also capitalizes certain payroll and payroll-related costs for employees who are directly associated with internal use computer software projects. The amount of capitalizable payroll costs with respect to these employees is limited to the time directly spent on such projects. Costs associated with preliminary project stage activities, training, maintenance and all other post-implementation stage activities are expensed as incurred.

Computer Software to be Sold, Leased or Otherwise Marketed. Development costs of computer software to be sold, leased, or otherwise marketed as an integral part of a product are subject to capitalization beginning when a product's technological feasibility has been established and ending when a product is available for general release to customers. In most instances, the Company's products are released soon after technological feasibility has been established. Therefore, costs incurred subsequent to achievement of technological feasibility are usually not significant, and generally most software development costs have been expensed as incurred.

Impairment of Long-Lived Assets

The Company reviews the carrying value of long-lived assets or asset groups to be used in operations whenever events or changes in circumstances indicate that the carrying amount of the assets might not be recoverable. Factors that would necessitate an impairment assessment include a significant adverse change in the extent or manner in which an asset is used, a significant adverse change in legal factors or the business climate that could affect the value of the asset, or a significant decline in the observable market value of an asset, among others. If such facts indicate a potential impairment, the Company would assess the recoverability of an asset group by determining if the carrying value of the asset group exceeds the sum of the projected undiscounted cash flows expected to result from the use and eventual disposition of the assets over the remaining economic life of the primary asset in the asset group. If the recoverability test indicates that the carrying value of the asset group is not recoverable, the Company will estimate the fair value of the asset group using appropriate valuation methodologies, which would typically include an estimate of discounted cash flows. Any impairment would be measured as the difference between the asset group's carrying amount and its estimated fair value.

Identifiable Intangible Assets and Goodwill

The Company performs annual impairment tests on goodwill and intangible assets with indefinite lives in the fourth quarter of each fiscal year, or when events occur or circumstances change that would, more likely than not, reduce the fair value of a reporting unit or an intangible asset with an indefinite life below its carrying value. Events or changes in circumstances that may trigger interim impairment reviews include significant changes in business climate, operating results, planned investments in the reporting unit, planned divestitures or an expectation that the carrying amount may not be recoverable, among other factors. The Company may first assess qualitative factors to determine whether it is more likely than not that the fair value of a reporting unit is less than its carrying amount. If, after assessing the totality of events and circumstances, the Company determines that it is more likely than not that the fair value of the reporting unit is greater than its carrying amount, the two-step impairment test is unnecessary. The two-step impairment test first requires the Company to estimate the fair value of its reporting units. If the carrying value of a reporting unit exceeds its fair value, the goodwill of that reporting unit is potentially impaired and the Company proceeds to step two of the impairment analysis. In step two of the analysis, the Company measures and records an impairment loss equal to the excess of the carrying value of the reporting unit's goodwill over its implied fair value, if any.

The Company generally bases its measurement of the fair value of a reporting unit on a blended analysis of the present value of future discounted cash flows and the market valuation approach. The discounted cash flows model indicates the fair value of the reporting unit based on the present value of the cash flows that the Company expects the reporting unit to generate in the future. The Company's significant estimates in the discounted cash flows model include: its weighted average cost of capital; long-term rate of growth and profitability of the reporting unit's business; and working capital effects. The market valuation approach indicates the fair value of the business based on a comparison of the reporting unit to comparable publicly traded companies in similar lines of business. Significant estimates in the market valuation approach model include identifying similar companies with comparable business factors such as size, growth, profitability, risk and return on investment, and assessing comparable revenue and operating income multiples in estimating the fair value of the reporting unit.

Indefinite-lived intangible assets primarily consist of acquired trade names and trademarks. The Company may first perform a qualitative assessment to determine whether it is more likely than not that an indefinite-lived intangible asset is impaired. If, after assessing the totality of events and circumstances, the Company determines that it is more likely than not that the indefinite-lived intangible asset is not impaired, no quantitative fair value measurement is necessary. If a quantitative fair value measurement calculation is required for these intangible assets, the Company utilizes the relief-from-royalty method. This method assumes that trade names and trademarks have value to the extent that their owner is relieved of the obligation to pay royalties for the benefits received from them. This method requires the Company to estimate the future revenue for the related brands, the appropriate royalty rate and the weighted average cost of capital.

Operating Leases

The Company leases retail store space, certain distribution and warehouse facilities, office space, and other non-real estate assets under operating leases. Operating lease agreements may contain rent escalation clauses, rent holidays or certain landlord incentives, including tenant improvement allowances. Rent expense for non-cancelable operating leases with scheduled rent increases or landlord incentives are recognized on a straight- line basis over the lease term, beginning with the effective lease commencement date, which is generally the date in which the Company takes possession of or controls the physical use of the property. Certain leases also provide for contingent rents, which are determined as a percentage of sales in excess of specified levels. A contingent rent liability is recognized together with the corresponding rent expense when specified levels have been achieved or when the Company determines that achieving the specified levels during the period is probable.

Fair Value Measurements

The Company measures certain financial assets and liabilities at fair value on a recurring basis, including derivatives and available-for-sale securities. Fair value is the price the Company would receive to sell an asset or pay to transfer a liability in an orderly transaction with a market participant at the measurement date. The Company uses a three-level hierarchy established by the Financial Accounting Standards Board ("FASB") that prioritizes fair value measurements based on the types of inputs used for the various valuation techniques (market approach, income approach, and cost approach).

The levels of hierarchy are described below:

- Level 1: Observable inputs such as quoted prices in active markets for identical assets or liabilities.
- Level 2: Inputs other than quoted prices that are observable for the asset or liability, either directly or indirectly; these include quoted prices for similar assets or liabilities in active markets and quoted prices for identical or similar assets or liabilities in markets that are not active.
- Level 3: Unobservable inputs for which there is little or no market data available, which require the reporting entity to develop its own assumptions.

The Company's assessment of the significance of a particular input to the fair value measurement in its entirety requires judgment and considers factors specific to the asset or liability. Financial assets and liabilities are classified in their entirety based on the most conservative level of input that is significant to the fair value measurement.

Pricing vendors are utilized for certain Level 1 and Level 2 investments. These vendors either provide a quoted market price in an active market or use observable inputs without applying significant adjustments in their pricing. Observable inputs include broker quotes, interest rates and yield curves observable at commonly quoted intervals, volatilities and credit risks. The Company's fair value processes include controls that are designed to ensure appropriate fair values are recorded. These controls include an analysis of period-over-period fluctuations and comparison to another independent pricing vendor.

Refer to Note 6 — Fair Value Measurements for additional information.

Foreign Currency Translation and Foreign Currency Transactions

Adjustments resulting from translating foreign functional currency financial statements into U.S. Dollars are included in the foreign currency translation adjustment, a component of accumulated other comprehensive income in shareholders' equity.

The Company's global subsidiaries have various assets and liabilities, primarily receivables and payables, which are denominated in currencies other than their functional currency. These balance sheet items are subject to remeasurement, the impact of which is recorded in other (income) expense, net, within the consolidated statements of income.

Accounting for Derivatives and Hedging Activities

The Company uses derivative financial instruments to reduce its exposure to changes in foreign currency exchange rates and interest rates. All derivatives are recorded at fair value on the balance sheet and changes in the fair value of derivative financial instruments are either recognized in other comprehensive income (a component of shareholders' equity), debt or net income depending on the nature of the underlying exposure, whether the derivative is formally designated as a hedge, and, if designated, the extent to which the hedge is effective. The Company classifies the cash flows at settlement from derivatives in the same category as the cash flows from the related hedged items. For undesignated hedges and designated cash flow hedges, this is within the cash provided by operations component of the consolidated statements of cash flows. For designated net investment hedges, this is generally within the cash provided or used by investing activities component of the cash flow statement. As our fair value hedges are receive-fixed, pay- variable interest rate swaps, the cash flows associated with these derivative instruments are periodic interest payments while the swaps are outstanding. These cash flows are reflected within the cash provided by operations component of the cash flow statement.

Refer to Note 17 — Risk Management and Derivatives for more information on the Company's risk management program and derivatives.

Stock-Based Compensation

The Company estimates the fair value of options and stock appreciation rights granted under the NIKE, Inc. 1990 Stock Incentive Plan (the "1990 Plan") and employees' purchase rights under the Employee Stock Purchase Plans ("ESPPs") using the Black-Scholes option pricing model. The Company recognizes this fair value, net of estimated forfeitures, as selling and administrative expense in the consolidated statements of income over the vesting period using the straight-line method.

Refer to Note 11 — Common Stock and Stock-Based Compensation for more information on the Company's stock programs.

Income Taxes

The Company accounts for income taxes using the asset and liability method. This approach requires the recognition of deferred tax assets and liabilities for the expected future tax consequences of temporary differences between the carrying amounts and the tax basis of assets and liabilities. The Company records a valuation allowance to reduce deferred tax assets to the amount management believes is more likely than not to be realized. United States income taxes are provided currently on financial statement earnings of non-U.S. subsidiaries that are expected to be repatriated. The Company determines annually the amount of undistributed non-U.S. earnings to invest indefinitely in its non-U.S. operations.

The Company recognizes a tax benefit from uncertain tax positions in the financial statements only when it is more likely than not that the position will be sustained upon examination by relevant tax authorities. The Company recognizes interest and penalties related to income tax matters in income tax expense.

Refer to Note 9 — Income Taxes for further discussion.

Earnings Per Share

Basic earnings per common share is calculated by dividing net income by the weighted average number of common shares outstanding during the year. Diluted earnings per common share is calculated by adjusting weighted average outstanding shares, assuming conversion of all potentially dilutive stock options and awards.

Refer to Note 12 — Earnings Per Share for further discussion.

Management Estimates

The preparation of financial statements in conformity with generally accepted accounting principles requires management to make estimates, including estimates relating to assumptions that affect the reported amounts of assets and liabilities and disclosure of contingent assets and liabilities at the date of financial statements and the reported amounts of revenues and expenses during the reporting period. Actual results could differ from these estimates.

Recently Adopted Accounting Standards

In July 2012, the FASB issued an accounting standards update intended to simplify how an entity tests indefinite-lived intangible assets other than goodwill for impairment by providing entities with an option to perform a qualitative assessment to determine whether further impairment testing is necessary. This accounting standard update will be effective for the Company beginning June 1, 2013, and early adoption is permitted. The Company early adopted this standard and the adoption did not have a material impact on its consolidated financial position or results of operations.

In September 2011, the FASB issued updated guidance on the periodic testing of goodwill for impairment. This guidance will allow companies to assess qualitative factors to determine if it is more-likely-than-not that goodwill might be impaired and whether it is necessary to perform the two-step goodwill impairment test required under current accounting standards. This new guidance was effective for the Company beginning June 1, 2012 and the adoption did not have a material effect on its consolidated financial position or results of operations.

In June 2011, the FASB issued guidance on the presentation of comprehensive income. This new guidance eliminates the current option to report other comprehensive income and its components in the statement of shareholders' equity. Companies are now required to present the components of net income and other comprehensive income in either one continuous statement, referred to as the statement of comprehensive income, or in two separate, but consecutive statements. This requirement was effective for the Company beginning June 1, 2012. As this guidance only amended the presentation of the components of comprehensive income, the adoption did not have an impact on the Company's consolidated financial position or results of operations. Further, this guidance required companies to present reclassification adjustments out of accumulated other comprehensive income by component in both the statement in which net income is presented and the statement in which other comprehensive income is presented. This requirement will be effective for the Company beginning June 1, 2013. As this guidance only amends the presentation of the components of comprehensive income, the Company does not anticipate the adoption will have an impact on the Company's consolidated financial position or results of operations.

Recently Issued Accounting Standards

In December 2011, the FASB issued guidance enhancing disclosure requirements surrounding the nature of an entity's right to offset and related arrangements associated with its financial instruments and derivative instruments. This new guidance requires companies to disclose both gross and net information about instruments and transactions eligible for offset in the statement of financial position and instruments and transactions subject to master netting arrangements. This new guidance is effective for the Company beginning June 1, 2013. As this guidance only requires expanded disclosures, the Company does not anticipate the adoption will have an impact on its consolidated financial position or results of operations.

NOTE 2 — Inventories

Inventory balances of $3,434 million and $3,222 million at May 31, 2013 and 2012, respectively, were substantially all finished goods.

NOTE 3 — Property, Plant and Equipment

Property, plant and equipment included the following:

	As of May 31,	
(In millions)	2013	2012
Land	$ 268	$ 252
Buildings	1,174	1,158
Machinery, equipment and internal-use software	2,985	2,654
Leasehold improvements	945	883
Construction in process	128	110
Total property, plant and equipment, gross	5,500	5,057
Less accumulated depreciation	3,048	2,848
TOTAL PROPERTY, PLANT AND EQUIPMENT, NET	**$ 2,452**	**$ 2,209**

Capitalized interest was not material for the years ended May 31, 2013, 2012, and 2011. The Company had $81 million in capital lease obligations as of May 31, 2013 included in machinery, equipment, and internal-use software; there were no capital lease obligations as of May 31, 2012.

NOTE 4 — Identifiable Intangible Assets and Goodwill

The following table summarizes the Company's identifiable intangible asset balances as of May 31, 2013 and 2012:

	As of May 31, 2013			As of May 31, 2012		
(In millions)	Gross Carrying Amount	Accumulated Amortization	Net Carrying Amount	Gross Carrying Amount	Accumulated Amortization	Net Carrying Amount
Amortized intangible assets:						
Patents	$ 119	$ (35)	$ 84	$ 99	$ (29)	$ 70
Trademarks	43	(32)	11	40	(26)	14
Other	20	(16)	4	19	(16)	3
TOTAL	**$ 182**	**$ (83)**	**$ 99**	**$ 158**	**$ (71)**	**$ 87**
Unamortized intangible assets — Trademarks			283			283
IDENTIFIABLE INTANGIBLE ASSETS, NET			**$ 382**			**$ 370**

Amortization expense, which is included in selling and administrative expense, was $14 million, $14 million, and $13 million for the years ended May 31, 2013, 2012, and 2011, respectively. The estimated amortization expense for intangible assets subject to amortization for each of the years ending May 31, 2014 through May 31, 2018 are as follows: 2014: $13 million; 2015: $9 million; 2016: $9 million; 2017: $7 million; 2018: $6 million.

Goodwill was $131 million at May 31, 2013 and May 31, 2012, respectively, and is included in the Company's "Other" category for segment reporting purposes. There were no accumulated impairment balances for goodwill as of either period end.

NOTE 5 — Accrued Liabilities

Accrued liabilities included the following:

(In millions)	As of May 31, 2013	As of May 31, 2012
Compensation and benefits, excluding taxes	$ 713	$ 691
Endorsement compensation	264	288
Taxes other than income taxes	192	169
Dividends payable	188	165
Import and logistics costs	111	133
Advertising and marketing	77	94
Fair value of derivatives	34	55
Other[(1)]	407	346
TOTAL ACCRUED LIABILITIES	**$ 1,986**	**$ 1,941**

(1) Other consists of various accrued expenses with no individual item accounting for more than 5% of the balance at May 31, 2013 and 2012.

NOTE 6 — Fair Value Measurements

The following table presents information about the Company's financial assets and liabilities measured at fair value on a recurring basis as of May 31, 2013 and 2012, and indicates the fair value hierarchy of the valuation techniques utilized by the Company to determine such fair value. Refer to Note 1 – Summary of Significant Accounting Policies for additional detail regarding the Company's fair value measurement methodology.

	As of May 31, 2013				
	Fair Value Measurements Using				
(In millions)	Level 1	Level 2	Level 3	Assets/Liabilities at Fair Value	Balance Sheet Classification
ASSETS					
Derivatives:					
Foreign exchange forwards and options	$ —	$ 278	$ —	$ 278	Other current assets and other long-term assets
Interest rate swap contracts	—	11	—	11	Other current assets and other long-term assets
Total derivatives	—	289	—	289	
Available-for-sale securities:					
U.S. Treasury securities	425	—	—	425	Cash and equivalents
U.S. Agency securities	—	20	—	20	Cash and equivalents
Commercial paper and bonds	—	1,035	—	1,035	Cash and equivalents
Money market funds	—	836	—	836	Cash and equivalents
U.S. Treasury securities	1,583	—	—	1,583	Short-term investments
U.S. Agency securities	—	401	—	401	Short-term investments
Commercial paper and bonds	—	644	—	644	Short-term investments
Non-marketable preferred stock	—	—	5	5	Other long-term assets
Total available-for-sale securities	2,008	2,936	5	4,949	
TOTAL ASSETS	**$ 2,008**	**$ 3,225**	**$ 5**	**$ 5,238**	
LIABILITIES					
Derivatives:					
Foreign exchange forwards and options	$ —	$ 34	$ —	$ 34	Accrued liabilities and other long-term liabilities
TOTAL LIABILITIES	**$ —**	**$ 34**	**$ —**	**$ 34**	

	As of May 31, 2012				
	Fair Value Measurements Using			Assets / Liabilities at	
(In millions)	Level 1	Level 2	Level 3	Fair Value	Balance Sheet Classification
ASSETS					
Derivatives:					
Foreign exchange forwards and options	$ —	$ 265	$ —	$ 265	Other current assets and other long-term assets
Embedded derivatives	—	1	—	1	Other current assets
Interest rate swap contracts	—	15	—	15	Other current assets and other long-term assets
Total derivatives	—	281	—	281	
Available-for-sale securities:					
U.S. Treasury securities	226	—	—	226	Cash and equivalents
U.S. Agency securities	—	254	—	254	Cash and equivalents
Commercial paper and bonds	—	159	—	159	Cash and equivalents
Money market funds	—	770	—	770	Cash and equivalents
U.S. Treasury securities	927	—	—	927	Short-term investments
U.S. Agency securities	—	230	—	230	Short-term investments
Commercial paper and bonds	—	283	—	283	Short-term investments
Non-marketable preferred stock	—	—	3	3	Other long-term assets
Total available-for-sale securities	1,153	1,696	3	2,852	
TOTAL ASSETS	**$ 1,153**	**$ 1,977**	**$ 3**	**$ 3,133**	
LIABILITIES					
Derivatives:					
Foreign exchange forwards and options	$ —	$ 55	$ —	$ 55	Accrued liabilities and other long-term liabilities
TOTAL LIABILITIES	**$ —**	**$ 55**	**$ —**	**$ 55**	

Derivative financial instruments include foreign exchange forwards and options, embedded derivatives and interest rate swap contracts. The fair value of derivative contracts is determined using observable market inputs such as the daily market foreign currency rates, forward pricing curves, currency volatilities, currency correlations and interest rates, and considers nonperformance risk of the Company and that of its counterparties. Adjustments relating to these nonperformance risks were not material at May 31, 2013 or 2012. Refer to Note 17 — Risk Management and Derivatives for additional detail.

Available-for-sale securities comprise investments in U.S. Treasury and Agency securities, money market funds, corporate commercial paper and bonds. These securities are valued using market prices on both active markets (Level 1) and less active markets (Level 2). Pricing vendors are utilized for certain Level 1 or Level 2 investments. These vendors either provide a quoted market price in an active market or use observable inputs without applying significant adjustments in their pricing. Observable inputs include broker quotes, interest rates and yield curves observable at commonly quoted intervals, volatilities and credit risks. The carrying amounts reflected in the consolidated balance sheets for short-term investments and cash and equivalents approximate fair value.

The Company's Level 3 assets comprise investments in certain non- marketable preferred stock. These investments are valued using internally developed models with unobservable inputs. These Level 3 investments are an immaterial portion of our portfolio. Changes in Level 3 investment assets were immaterial during the years ended May 31, 2013 and 2012.

No transfers among the levels within the fair value hierarchy occurred during the years ended May 31, 2013 or 2012.

As of May 31, 2013 and 2012, the Company had no assets or liabilities that were required to be measured at fair value on a non-recurring basis.

Short-Term Investments

As of May 31, 2013 and 2012, short-term investments consisted of available- for-sale securities. As of May 31, 2013, the Company held $2,229 million of available-for-sale securities with maturity dates within one year from the purchase date and $399 million with maturity dates over one year and less than five years from the purchase date within short-term investments. As of May 31, 2012, the Company held $1,129 million of available-for-sale securities with maturity dates within one year from purchase date and $311 million with maturity dates over one year and less than five years from purchase date within short-term investments.

Short-term investments classified as available-for-sale consist of the following at fair value:

(In millions)	As of May 31, 2013	2012
Available-for-sale investments:		
U.S. treasury and agencies	$ 1,984	$ 1,157
Commercial paper and bonds	644	283
TOTAL ACCRUED LIABILITIES	**$ 2,628**	**$ 1,440**

Included in interest (income) expense, net was interest income related to cash and equivalents and short-term investments of $26 million, $27 million, and $28 million for the years ended May 31, 2013, 2012, and 2011, respectively.

For fair value information regarding notes payable and long-term debt, refer to Note 7 — Short-Term Borrowings and Credit Lines and Note 8 — Long-Term Debt.

NOTE 7 — Short-Term Borrowings and Credit Lines

Notes payable and interest-bearing accounts payable to Sojitz Corporation of America ("Sojitz America") as of May 31, 2013 and 2012, are summarized below:

	As of May 31,			
	2013		2012	
(In millions)	Borrowings	Interest Rate	Borrowings	Interest Rate
Notes payable:				
U.S. operations	$ 20	0.00%[(1)]	$ 30	5.50%[(1)]
Non-U.S. operations	101	4.77%[(1)]	78	9.46%[(1)]
TOTAL NOTES PAYABLE	**$ 121**		**$ 108**	
Interest-Bearing Accounts Payable:				
Sojitz America	$ 55	0.99%	$ 75	1.10%

(1) Weighted average interest rate includes non-interest bearing overdrafts.

The carrying amounts reflected in the consolidated balance sheets for notes payable approximate fair value.

The Company purchases through Sojitz America certain athletic footwear, apparel and equipment it acquires from non-U.S. suppliers. These purchases are for the Company's operations outside of the United States, Europe and Japan. Accounts payable to Sojitz America are generally due up to 60 days after shipment of goods from the foreign port. The interest rate on such accounts payable is the 60-day London Interbank Offered Rate ("LIBOR") as of the beginning of the month of the invoice date, plus 0.75%.

As of May 31, 2013 and 2012, the Company had no amounts outstanding under its commercial paper program.

In November 2011, the Company entered into a committed credit facility agreement with a syndicate of banks which provides for up to $1 billion of borrowings pursuant to a revolving credit facility with the option to increase borrowings to $1.5 billion with lender approval. The facility matures on November 1, 2016, with a one-year extension option prior to both the second and third anniversary of the closing date, provided that extensions shall not extend beyond November 1, 2018. Based on the Company's current long- term senior unsecured debt ratings of A+ and A1 from Standard and Poor's Corporation and Moody's Investor Services, respectively, the interest rate charged on any outstanding borrowings would be the prevailing LIBOR plus 0.56%. The facility fee is 0.065% of the total commitment. Under this committed credit facility, the Company must maintain, among other things, certain minimum specified financial ratios with which the Company was in compliance at May 31, 2013. No amounts were outstanding under this facility as of May 31, 2013 or 2012.

NOTE 8 — Long-Term Debt

Long-term debt, net of unamortized premiums and discounts and swap fair value adjustments, comprises the following:

Scheduled Maturity (Dollars in millions)	Original Principal	Interest Rate	Interest Payments	Book Value Outstanding As of May 31, 2013	2012
Corporate Bond Payables:[4]					
July 23, 2012[1]	$ 25	5.66%	Semi-Annually	$ —	$ 25
August 7, 2012[1]	$ 15	5.40%	Semi-Annually	—	15
October 1, 2013	$ 50	4.70%	Semi-Annually	50	50
October 15, 2015[1]	$ 100	5.15%	Semi-Annually	111	115
May 1, 2023[5]	$ 500	2.25%	Semi-Annually	499	—
May 1, 2043[5]	$ 500	3.63%	Semi-Annually	499	—
Promissory Notes:[2]					
April 1, 2017	$ 40	6.20%	Monthly	40	—
January 1, 2018	$ 19	6.79%	Monthly	19	—
Japanese Yen Notes:				34	
August 20, 2001 through November 20, 2020[3]	¥ 9,000	2.60%	Quarterly		50
August 20, 2001 through November 20, 2020[3]	¥ 4,000	2.00%	Quarterly	15	22
Total				1,267	277
Less current maturities				57	49
TOTAL LONG-TERM DEBT				**$ 1,210**	**$ 228**

(1) The Company has entered into interest rate swap agreements whereby the Company receives fixed interest payments at the same rate as the note and pays variable interest payments based on the six-month LIBOR plus a spread. The swaps have the same notional amount and maturity date as the corresponding note. At May 31, 2013, the interest rates payable on these swap agreements ranged from approximately 0.3% to 0.4%.

(2) The Company assumed a total of $59 million in bonds payable on May 30, 2013 as part of its agreement to purchase certain Corporate properties, which was treated as a non-cash financing transaction. The property serves as collateral for the debt. The purchase of these properties was accounted for as a business combination where the total consideration of $85 million was allocated to the land and buildings acquired; no other tangible or intangible assets or liabilities resulted from the purchase. The bonds mature in 2017 and 2018 and the Company does not have the ability to re-negotiate the terms of the debt agreements and would incur significant financial penalties if the notes are paid off prior to maturity.

(3) NIKE Logistics YK assumed a total of ¥13.0 billion in loans as part of its agreement to purchase a distribution center in Japan, which serves as collateral for the loans. These loans mature in equal quarterly installments during the period August 20, 2001 through November 20, 2020.

(4) Senior unsecured obligations rank equally with our other unsecured and unsubordinated indebtedness.

(5) The bonds carry a make whole call provision and are redeemable at any time prior to maturity. The bonds also feature a par call provision payable 3 months and 6 months prior to the scheduled maturity date for the bonds maturing on May 1, 2023 and May 1, 2043, respectively.

The scheduled maturity of long-term debt in each of the years ending May 31, 2014 through 2018 are $57 million, $7 million, $108 million, $45 million and $25 million, respectively, at face value.

The fair value of the Company's long-term debt, including the current portion, was approximately $1,219 million at May 31, 2013 and $283 million at May 31, 2012. The fair value of long-term debt is estimated based upon quoted prices of similar instruments (level 2).

NOTE 9 — Income Taxes

Income before income taxes is as follows:

(In millions)	Year Ended May 31, 2013	2012	2011
Income before income taxes:			
United States	$ 1,240	$ 804	$ 1,040
Foreign	2,032	2,221	1,822
TOTAL INCOME BEFORE INCOME TAXES	$ 3,272	$ 3,025	$ 2,862

The provision for income taxes is as follows:

	Year Ended May 31,		
(In millions)	2013	2012	2011
Current:			
United States			
Federal	$ 434	$ 289	$ 298
State	69	51	57
Foreign	398	488	435
Total	901	828	790
Deferred:			
United States			
Federal	1	(48)	(62)
State	(4)	5	—
Foreign	(90)	(29)	(38)
Total	(93)	(72)	(100)
TOTAL INCOME TAX EXPENSE	**$ 808**	**$ 756**	**$ 690**

A reconciliation from the U.S. statutory federal income tax rate to the effective income tax rate is as follows:

	Year Ended May 31,		
	2013	2012	2011
Federal income tax rate	35.0%	35.0%	35.0%
State taxes, net of federal benefit	1.4%	1.3%	1.3%
Foreign earnings	-11.8%	-11.9%	-11.4%
Other, net	0.1%	0.6%	-0.8%
EFFECTIVE INCOME TAX RATE	**24.7%**	**25.0%**	**24.1%**

The effective tax rate from continuing operations for the year ended May 31, 2013 was 30 basis points lower than the effective tax rate from continuing operations for the year ended May 31, 2012 primarily due to tax benefits received from the intercompany sale of intellectual property rights outside of the U.S., the retroactive reinstatement of the research and development credit and the intra-period allocation of tax expense between continuing operations, discontinued operations, and other comprehensive income. The decrease in the effective tax rate was partially offset by a higher effective tax rate on operations as a result of an increase in earnings in higher tax jurisdictions. The effective tax rate from continuing operations for the year ended May 31, 2012 was 90 basis points higher than the effective tax rate from continuing operations for the year ended May 31, 2011 primarily due to the changes in uncertain tax positions partially offset by a reduction in the effective rate related to a decrease in earnings in higher tax jurisdictions.

Deferred tax assets and (liabilities) comprise the following:

(In millions)	As of May 31, 2013	As of May 31, 2012
Deferred tax assets:		
Allowance for doubtful accounts	$ 20	$ 17
Inventories	40	37
Sales return reserves	101	84
Deferred compensation	197	186
Stock-based compensation	140	126
Reserves and accrued liabilities	66	66
Foreign loss carry-forwards	19	35
Foreign tax credit carry-forwards	106	216
Undistributed earnings of foreign subsidiaries	162	82
Other	47	62
Total deferred tax assets	898	911
Valuation allowance	(5)	(27)
Total deferred tax assets after valuation allowance	893	884
Deferred tax liabilities:		
Property, plant and equipment	(241)	(191)
Intangibles	(96)	(98)
Other	(20)	(22)
Total deferred tax liability	(357)	(311)
NET DEFERRED TAX ASSET	**$ 536**	**$ 573**

The following is a reconciliation of the changes in the gross balance of unrecognized tax benefits:

(In millions)	As of May 31, 2013	2012	2011
Unrecognized tax benefits, as of the beginning of the period	$ 285	$ 212	$ 282
Gross increases related to prior period tax positions	77	48	13
Gross decreases related to prior period tax positions	(3)	(25)	(98)
Gross increases related to current period tax positions	130	91	59
Gross decreases related to current period tax positions	(9)	(1)	(6)
Settlements	—	(20)	(43)
Lapse of statute of limitations	(21)	(9)	(8)
Changes due to currency translation	(12)	(11)	13
UNRECOGNIZED TAX BENEFITS, AS OF THE END OF THE PERIOD	**$ 447**	**$ 285**	**$ 212**

As of May 31, 2013, the total gross unrecognized tax benefits, excluding related interest and penalties, were $447 million, $281 million of which would affect the Company's effective tax rate if recognized in future periods.

The Company recognizes interest and penalties related to income tax matters in income tax expense. The liability for payment of interest and penalties increased $4 million, $17 million, and $10 million during the years ended May 31, 2013, 2012, and 2011, respectively. As of May 31, 2013 and 2012, accrued interest and penalties related to uncertain tax positions was $112 million and $108 million, respectively (excluding federal benefit).

The Company is subject to taxation primarily in the U.S., China, the Netherlands, and Brazil, as well as various state and other foreign jurisdictions. The Company has concluded substantially all U.S. federal income tax matters through fiscal 2010. The Company is currently under audit by the Internal Revenue Service for the 2011 through 2013 tax years. Many issues are at an advanced stage in the examination process, the most significant of which includes the negotiation of a U.S. Unilateral Advanced Pricing Agreement that covers intercompany transfer pricing issues for fiscal years May 31, 2011 through May 31, 2015. In addition, the Company is in appeals regarding the validation of foreign tax credits taken. The Company's major foreign jurisdictions, China, the Netherlands and Brazil, have concluded substantially all income tax matters through calendar 2005, fiscal 2007 and calendar 2006, respectively. Although the timing of resolution of audits is not certain, the Company evaluates all domestic and foreign audit issues in the aggregate, along with the expiration of applicable statutes of limitations, and estimates that it is reasonably possible the total gross unrecognized tax benefits could decrease by up to $86 million within the next 12 months.

We provide for United States income taxes on the undistributed earnings of foreign subsidiaries unless they are considered indefinitely reinvested outside the United States. At May 31, 2013, the indefinitely reinvested earnings in foreign subsidiaries upon which United States income taxes have not been provided was approximately $6.7 billion. If these undistributed earnings were repatriated to the United States, or if the shares of the relevant foreign subsidiaries were sold or otherwise transferred, they would generate foreign tax credits that would reduce the federal tax liability associated with the foreign dividend or the otherwise taxable transaction. Assuming a full utilization of the foreign tax credits, the potential net deferred tax liability associated with these temporary differences of undistributed earnings would be approximately $2.2 billion at May 31, 2013.

A portion of the Company's foreign operations are benefiting from a tax holiday, which will phase out in 2019. This tax holiday may be extended when certain conditions are met or may be terminated early if certain conditions are not met. The impact of this tax holiday decreased foreign taxes by $108 million, $117 million, and $36 million for the fiscal years ended May 31, 2013, 2012, and 2011, respectively. The benefit of the tax holiday on net income per share (diluted) was $0.12, $0.12, and $0.04 for the fiscal years ended May 31, 2013, 2012, and 2011, respectively.

Deferred tax assets at May 31, 2013 and 2012 were reduced by a valuation allowance relating to tax benefits of certain subsidiaries with operating losses. The net change in the valuation allowance was a decrease of $22 million, an increase of $23 million, and a decrease of $1 million for the years ended May 31, 2013, 2012, and 2011, respectively.

The Company does not anticipate that any foreign tax credit carry-forwards will expire unutilized.

The Company has available domestic and foreign loss carry-forwards of $58 million at May 31, 2013. Such losses will expire as follows:

	Year Ending May 31,						
(In millions)	2014	2015	2016	2017	2018-2032	Indefinite	Total
Net Operating Losses	$ —	—	2	—	52	4	$ 58

During the years ended May 31, 2013, 2012, and 2011, income tax benefits attributable to employee stock-based compensation transactions of $76 million, $120 million, and $68 million, respectively, were allocated to shareholders' equity.

NOTE 10 — Redeemable Preferred Stock

Sojitz America is the sole owner of the Company's authorized Redeemable Preferred Stock, $1 par value, which is redeemable at the option of Sojitz America or the Company at par value aggregating $0.3 million. A cumulative dividend of $0.10 per share is payable annually on May 31 and no dividends may be declared or paid on the common stock of the Company unless dividends on the Redeemable Preferred Stock have been declared and paid in full. There have been no changes in the Redeemable Preferred Stock in the three years ended May 31, 2013, 2012, and 2011. As the holder of the Redeemable Preferred Stock, Sojitz America does not have general voting rights but does have the right to vote as a separate class on the sale of all or substantially all of the assets of the Company and its subsidiaries, on merger, consolidation, liquidation or dissolution of the Company or on the sale or assignment of the NIKE trademark for athletic footwear sold in the United States. The Redeemable Preferred Stock has been fully issued to Sojitz America and is not blank check preferred stock. The Company's articles of incorporation do not permit the issuance of additional preferred stock.

NOTE 11 — Common Stock and Stock-Based Compensation

The authorized number of shares of Class A Common Stock, no par value, and Class B Common Stock, no par value, are 200 million and 1,200 million, respectively. Each share of Class A Common Stock is convertible into one share of Class B Common Stock. Voting rights of Class B Common Stock are limited in certain circumstances with respect to the election of directors. There are no differences in the dividend and liquidation preferences or participation rights of the Class A and Class B common shareholders.

In 1990, the Board of Directors adopted, and the shareholders approved, the NIKE, Inc. 1990 Stock Incentive Plan (the "1990 Plan"). The 1990 Plan provides for the issuance of up to 326 million previously unissued shares of Class B Common Stock in connection with stock options and other awards granted under the plan. The 1990 Plan authorizes the grant of non-statutory stock options, incentive stock options, stock appreciation rights, restricted stock, restricted stock units, and performance-based awards. The exercise price for stock options and stock appreciation rights may not be less than the fair market value of the underlying shares on the date of grant. A committee of the Board of Directors administers the 1990 Plan. The committee has the authority to determine the employees to whom awards will be made, the amount of the awards, and the other terms and conditions of the awards. Substantially all stock option grants outstanding under the 1990 Plan were granted in the first quarter of each fiscal year, vest ratably over four years, and expire 10 years from the date of grant.

The following table summarizes the Company's total stock-based compensation expense recognized in selling and administrative expense:

	Year Ended May 31,		
(In millions)	2013	2012	2011
Stock options[(1)]	$ 123	$ 96	$ 77
ESPPs	19	16	14
Restricted stock	32	18	14
TOTAL STOCK-BASED COMPENSATION EXPENSE	**$ 174**	**$ 130**	**$ 105**

(1) Expense for stock options includes the expense associated with stock appreciation rights. Accelerated stock option expense is recorded for employees eligible for accelerated stock option vesting upon retirement. Accelerated stock option expense for years ended May 31, 2013, 2012, and 2011 was $22 million, $17 million, and $12 million, respectively.

As of May 31, 2013, the Company had $199 million of unrecognized compensation costs from stock options, net of estimated forfeitures, to be recognized as selling and administrative expense over a weighted average period of 2.3 years.

The weighted average fair value per share of the options granted during the years ended May 31, 2013, 2012, and 2011, as computed using the Black-Scholes pricing model, was $12.71, $11.08, and $8.84, respectively. The weighted average assumptions used to estimate these fair values are as follows:

	Year Ended May 31,		
	2013	**2012**	**2011**
Dividend yield	1.5%	1.4%	1.6%
Expected volatility	35.0%	29.5%	31.5%
Weighted average expected life (in years)	5.3	5.0	5.0
Risk-free interest rate	0.6%	1.4%	1.7%

The Company estimates the expected volatility based on the implied volatility in market traded options on the Company's common stock with a term greater than one year, along with other factors. The weighted average expected life of options is based on an analysis of historical and expected future exercise patterns. The interest rate is based on the U.S. Treasury (constant maturity) risk-free rate in effect at the date of grant for periods corresponding with the expected term of the options.

The following summarizes the stock option transactions under the plan discussed above:

	Shares[(1)]	**Weighted Average Option Price**
	(In millions)	
Options outstanding May 31, 2010	72.2	$ 23.30
Exercised	(14.0)	21.35
Forfeited	(1.3)	29.03
Granted	12.7	34.60
Options outstanding May 31, 2011	69.6	$ 25.65
Exercised	(18.0)	22.81
Forfeited	(1.0)	35.61
Granted	13.7	45.87
Options outstanding May 31, 2012	64.3	$ 30.59
Exercised	(9.9)	24.70
Forfeited	(1.3)	40.14
Granted	14.6	46.55
Options outstanding May 31, 2013	67.7	$ 34.72
Options exercisable at May 31,		
2011	40.1	$ 22.03
2012	33.9	24.38
2013	35.9	27.70

(1) Includes stock appreciation rights transactions.

The weighted average contractual life remaining for options outstanding and options exercisable at May 31, 2013 was 6.3 years and 4.7 years, respectively. The aggregate intrinsic value for options outstanding and exercisable at May 31, 2013 was $1,823 million and $1,218 million, respectively. The aggregate intrinsic value was the amount by which the market value of the underlying stock exceeded the exercise price of the options. The total intrinsic value of the options exercised during the years ended May 31, 2013, 2012, and 2011 was $293 million, $453 million, and $267 million, respectively.

In addition to the 1990 Plan, the Company gives employees the right to purchase shares at a discount to the market price under employee stock purchase plans ("ESPPs"). Employees are eligible to participate through payroll deductions of up to 10% of their compensation. At the end of each six- month offering period, shares are purchased by the participants at 85% of the lower of the fair market value at the beginning or the end of the offering period. Employees purchased 1.6 million, 1.7 million, and 1.6 million shares during each of the three years ended May 31, 2013, 2012 and 2011, respectively.

From time to time, the Company grants restricted stock units and restricted stock to key employees under the 1990 Plan. The number of shares underlying such awards granted to employees during the years ended May 31, 2013, 2012, and 2011 were 1.6 million, 0.7 million, and 0.4 million with weighted average values per share of $46.86, $49.49, and $35.11, respectively. Recipients of restricted stock are entitled to cash dividends and to vote their respective shares throughout the period of restriction. Recipients of restricted stock units are entitled to dividend equivalent cash payments upon vesting. The value of all grants of restricted stock and restricted stock units was established by the market price on the date of grant. During the years ended May 31, 2013, 2012, and 2011, the aggregate fair value of restricted stock and restricted stock units vested was $25 million, $22 million, and $15 million, respectively, determined as of the date of vesting.

NOTE 12 — Earnings Per Share

The following is a reconciliation from basic earnings per share to diluted earnings per share. Options to purchase an additional 0.1 million, 0.2 million, and 0.3 million shares of common stock were outstanding at May 31, 2013, 2012, and 2011 respectively, but were not included in the computation of diluted earnings per share because the options were anti-dilutive.

(In millions, except per share data)	Year Ended May 31, 2013	2012	2011
Determination of shares:			
Weighted average common shares outstanding	897.3	920.0	951.1
Assumed conversion of dilutive stock options and awards	19.1	19.6	20.2
DILUTED WEIGHTED AVERAGE COMMON SHARES OUTSTANDING	**916.4**	**939.6**	**971.3**
Earnings per share from continuing operations:			
Basic earnings per common share	$ 2.75	$ 2.47	$ 2.28
Diluted earnings per common share	$ 2.69	$ 2.42	$ 2.24
Earnings per share from discontinued operations:			
Basic earnings per common share	$ 0.02	$ (0.05)	$ (0.04)
Diluted earnings per common share	$ 0.02	$ (0.05)	$ (0.04)
Basic earnings per common share for NIKE, Inc.	$ 2.77	$ 2.42	$ 2.24
Diluted earnings per common share for NIKE, Inc.	$ 2.71	$ 2.37	$ 2.20

NOTE 13 — Benefit Plans

The Company has a profit sharing plan available to most U.S.-based employees. The terms of the plan call for annual contributions by the Company as determined by the Board of Directors. A subsidiary of the Company also had a profit sharing plan available to its U.S.-based employees prior to fiscal 2012. The terms of the plan called for annual contributions as determined by the subsidiary's executive management. Contributions of $47 million, $40 million, and $39 million were made to the plans and are included in selling and administrative expense for the years ended May 31, 2013, 2012, and 2011, respectively. The Company has various 401(k) employee savings plans available to U.S.-based employees. The Company matches a portion of employee contributions. Company contributions to the savings plans were $46 million, $42 million, and $38 million for the years ended May 31, 2013, 2012, and 2011, respectively, and are included in selling and administrative expense.

The Company also has a Long-Term Incentive Plan ("LTIP") that was adopted by the Board of Directors and approved by shareholders in September 1997 and later amended in fiscal 2007. The Company recognized $50 million, $51 million, and $31 million of selling and administrative expense related to cash awards under the LTIP during the years ended May 31, 2013, 2012, and 2011, respectively.

The Company has pension plans in various countries worldwide. The pension plans are only available to local employees and are generally government mandated. The liability related to the unfunded pension liabilities of the plans was $104 million and $113 million at May 31, 2013 and May 31, 2012, respectively, which was primarily classified as long-term in other liabilities.

NOTE 14 — Accumulated Other Comprehensive Income

The components of accumulated other comprehensive income, net of tax, are as follows:

(In millions)	May 31 2013	2012
Cumulative translation adjustment and other	$ (14)	$ (127)
Net deferred gain on cash flow hedge derivatives	193	181
Net deferred gain on net investment hedge derivatives	95	95
ACCUMULATED OTHER COMPREHENSIVE INCOME	**$ 274**	**$ 149**

Refer to Note 17 — Risk Management and Derivatives for more information on the Company's risk management program and derivatives.

NOTE 15 — Discontinued Operations

The Company continually evaluates its existing portfolio of businesses to ensure resources are invested in those businesses that are accretive to the NIKE Brand and represent the largest growth potential and highest returns. During the year, the Company divested of Umbro and Cole Haan, allowing it to focus its resources on driving growth in the NIKE, Jordan, Converse and Hurley brands.

On February 1, 2013, the Company completed the sale of Cole Haan to Apax Partners for an agreed upon purchase price of $570 million and received at closing $561 million, net of $9 million of purchase price adjustments. The transaction resulted in a gain on sale of $231 million, net of $137 million in tax expense; this gain is included in the net income (loss) from discontinued operations line item on the consolidated statements of income. There were no adjustments to these recorded amounts as of May 31, 2013. Beginning November 30, 2012, the Company classified the Cole Haan disposal group as held-for-sale and presented the results of Cole Haan's operations in the net income (loss) from discontinued operations line item on the consolidated statements of income. From this date until the sale, the assets and liabilities of Cole Haan were recorded in the assets of discontinued operations and liabilities of discontinued operations line items on the consolidated balance sheets, respectively. Previously, these amounts were reported in the Company's segment presentation as "Other Businesses."

Under the sale agreement, the Company agreed to provide certain transition services to Cole Haan for an expected period of 3 to 9 months from the date of sale. The Company will also license NIKE proprietary Air and Lunar technologies to Cole Haan for a transition period. The continuing cash flows related to these items are not expected to be significant to Cole Haan and the Company will have no significant continuing involvement with Cole Haan beyond the transition services. Additionally, preexisting guarantees of certain Cole Haan lease payments remain in place after the sale; the maximum exposure under the guarantees is $44 million at May 31, 2013. The fair value of the guarantees is not material.

On November 30, 2012, the Company completed the sale of certain assets of Umbro to Iconix Brand Group ("Iconix") for $225 million. The Umbro disposal group was classified as held-for-sale as of November 30, 2012 and the results of Umbro's operations are presented in the net income (loss) from discontinued operations line item on the consolidated statements of income. The remaining liabilities of Umbro are recorded in the liabilities of discontinued operations line items on the consolidated balance sheets. Previously, these amounts were reported in the Company's segment presentation as "Other Businesses." Upon meeting the held-for-sale criteria, the Company recorded a loss of $107 million, net of tax, on the sale of Umbro and the loss is included in the net income (loss) from discontinued operations line item on the consolidated statements of income. The loss on sale was calculated as the net sales price less Umbro assets of $248 million, including intangibles, goodwill, and fixed assets, other miscellaneous charges of $22 million, and the release of the associated cumulative translation adjustment of $129 million. The tax benefit on the loss was $67 million. There were no adjustments to these recorded amounts as of May 31, 2013.

Under the sale agreement, the Company provided transition services to Iconix while certain markets were transitioned to Iconix-designated licensees. These transition services are complete and the Company has wound down the remaining operations of Umbro.

For the year ended May 31, 2013, net income (loss) from discontinued operations included, for both businesses, the net gain or loss on sale, net operating losses, tax expenses, and approximately $20 million in wind down costs.

Summarized results of the Company's discontinued operations are as follows:

	Year Ended May 31,		
(In millions)	2013	2012	2011
Revenues	$ 523	$ 796	$ 746
Income (loss) before income taxes	108	(43)	(18)
Income tax expense (benefit)	87	3	21
Net income (loss) from discontinued operations	**$ 21**	**$ (46)**	**$ (39)**

As of May 31, 2013 and 2012, the aggregate components of assets and liabilities classified as discontinued operations and included in current assets and current liabilities consisted of the following:

	As of May 31,	
(In millions)	2013	2012
Accounts Receivable, net	$ —	$ 148
Inventories	—	128
Deferred income taxes and other assets	—	35
Property, plant and equipment, net	—	70
Identifiable intangible assets, net	—	234
TOTAL ASSETS	**$ —**	**$ 615**
Accounts payable	$ 1	$ 42
Accrued liabilities	17	112
Deferred income taxes and other liabilities	—	16
TOTAL LIABILITIES	**$ 18**	**$ 170**

NOTE 16 — Commitments and Contingencies

The Company leases space for certain of its offices, warehouses and retail stores under leases expiring from 1 to 21 years after May 31, 2013. Rent expense was $482 million, $431 million, and $386 million for the years ended May 31, 2013, 2012 and 2011, respectively. Amounts of minimum future annual rental commitments under non-cancelable operating leases in each of the five years ending May 31, 2014 through 2018 are $403 million, $340 million, $304 million, $272 million, $225 million, respectively, and $816 million in later years. Amounts of minimum future annual commitments under non- cancelable capital leases in each of the four years ending May 31, 2014 through 2017 are $23 million, $28 million, $21 million, and $9 million, respectively; the Company has no capital lease obligations beyond the year ending May 31, 2017.

As of May 31, 2013 and 2012, the Company had letters of credit outstanding totaling $149 million and $137 million, respectively. These letters of credit were generally issued for the purchase of inventory and guarantees of the Company's performance under certain self-insurance and other programs.

In connection with various contracts and agreements, the Company provides routine indemnifications relating to the enforceability of intellectual property rights, coverage for legal issues that arise and other items where the Company is acting as the guarantor. Currently, the Company has several such agreements in place. However, based on the Company's historical experience and the estimated probability of future loss, the Company has determined that the fair value of such indemnifications is not material to the Company's financial position or results of operations.

In the ordinary course of its business, the Company is involved in various legal proceedings involving contractual and employment relationships, product liability claims, trademark rights, and a variety of other matters. While the Company cannot predict the outcome of its pending legal matters with certainty, the Company does not believe any currently identified claim, proceeding or litigation, either individually or in aggregate, will have a material impact on the Company's results of operations, financial position or cash flows.

NOTE 17 — Risk Management and Derivatives

The Company is exposed to global market risks, including the effect of changes in foreign currency exchange rates and interest rates, and uses derivatives to manage financial exposures that occur in the normal course of business. The Company does not hold or issue derivatives for trading or speculative purposes.

The Company may elect to designate certain derivatives as hedging instruments under the accounting standards for derivatives and hedging. The Company formally documents all relationships between designated hedging instruments and hedged items as well as its risk management objective and strategy for undertaking hedge transactions. This process includes linking all derivatives designated as hedges to either recognized assets or liabilities or forecasted transactions.

The majority of derivatives outstanding as of May 31, 2013 are designated as cash flow or fair value hedges. All derivatives are recognized on the balance sheet at fair value and classified based on the instrument's maturity date. The total notional amount of outstanding derivatives as of May 31, 2013 was approximately $9 billion, which primarily comprises cash flow hedges for Euro/U.S. Dollar, British Pound/Euro, and Japanese Yen/U.S. Dollar currency pairs. As of May 31, 2013, there were outstanding currency forward contracts with maturities up to 24 months.

The following table presents the fair values of derivative instruments included within the consolidated balance sheets as of May 31, 2013 and 2012:

	Asset Derivatives			Liability Derivatives		
(In millions)	Balance Sheet Location	2013	2012	Balance Sheet Location	2013	2012
Derivatives formally designated as hedging instruments:						
Foreign exchange forwards and options	Prepaid expenses and other current assets	$ 141	$ 203	Accrued liabilities	$ 12	$ 35
Foreign exchange forwards and options	Deferred income taxes and other long-term assets	79	7	Deferred income taxes and other long-term liabilities	—	—
Interest rate swap contracts	Deferred income taxes and other long-term assets	11	15	Deferred income taxes and other long-term liabilities	—	—
Total derivatives formally designated as hedging instruments		$ 231	$ 225		$ 12	$ 35
Derivatives not designated as hedging instruments:						
Foreign exchange forwards and options	Prepaid expenses and other current assets	$ 58	$ 55	Accrued liabilities	$ 22	$ 20
Embedded derivatives	Prepaid expenses and other current assets	—	1	Accrued liabilities	—	—
Total derivatives not designated as hedging instruments		58	56		22	20
TOTAL DERIVATIVES		**$ 289**	**$ 281**		**$ 34**	**$ 55**

The following tables present the amounts affecting the consolidated statements of income for years ended May 31, 2013, 2012 and 2011:

	Amount of Gain (Loss) Recognized in Other Comprehensive Income on Derivatives[(1)]			Amount of Gain (Loss) Reclassified From Accumulated Other Comprehensive Income into Income[(1)]			
	Year Ended May 31,			Location of Gain (Loss) Reclassified From Accumulated Other Comprehensive Income Into Income [(1)]	Year Ended May 31,		
(In millions)	2013	2012	2013		2013	2012	2013
Derivatives designated as cash flow hedges:							
Foreign exchange forwards and options	$ 42	$ (29)	$ (87)	Revenue	$ (19)	$ 5	$ (30)
Foreign exchange forwards and options	67	253	(152)	Cost of sales	113	(57)	103
Foreign exchange forwards and options	(3)	3	(4)	Selling and administrative expense	2	(2)	1
Foreign exchange forwards and options	33	36	(65)	Other (income) expense, net	9	(9)	34
Total designated cash flow hedges	$ 139	$ 263	$ (308)		$ 105	$ (63)	$ 108
Derivatives designated as net investment hedges:							
Foreign exchange forwards and options	$ —	$ 45	$ (85)	Other (income) expense, net	$ —	$ —	$ —

(1) *For the years ended May 31, 2013, 2012, and 2011, the amounts recorded in other (income) expense, net as a result of hedge ineffectiveness and the discontinuance of cash flow hedges because the forecasted transactions were no longer probable of occurring were immaterial.*

(In millions)	Amount of Gain (Loss) Recognized in Income on Derivatives Year Ended May 31, 2013	2012	2011	Location of Gain (Loss) Recognized in Income on Derivatives
Derivatives designated as fair value hedges:				
Interest rate swaps[(1)]	$ 5	$ 6	$ 6	Interest (income) expense, net
Derivatives not designated as hedging instruments:				
Foreign exchange forwards and options	51	64	(30)	Other (income) expense, net
Embedded derivatives	$ (4)	$ 1	$ —	Other (income) expense, net

(1) All interest rate swap agreements meet the shortcut method requirements under the accounting standards for derivatives and hedging. Accordingly, changes in the fair values of the interest rate swap agreements are considered to exactly offset changes in the fair value of the underlying long-term debt. Refer to "Fair Value Hedges" in this note for additional detail.

Refer to Note 5 — Accrued Liabilities for derivative instruments recorded in accrued liabilities, Note 6 — Fair Value Measurements for a description of how the above financial instruments are valued, Note 14 — Accumulated Other Comprehensive Income and the consolidated statements of shareholders' equity for additional information on changes in other comprehensive income for the years ended May 31, 2013, 2012 and 2011.

Cash Flow Hedges

The purpose of the Company's foreign currency hedging activities is to protect the Company from the risk that the eventual cash flows resulting from transactions in foreign currencies will be adversely affected by changes in exchange rates. Foreign currency exposures that the Company may elect to hedge in this manner include product cost exposures, non-functional currency denominated external and intercompany revenues, selling and administrative expenses, investments in U.S. Dollar-denominated available- for-sale debt securities and certain other intercompany transactions.

Product cost exposures are primarily generated through non-functional currency denominated product purchases and the foreign currency adjustment program described below. NIKE entities primarily purchase products in two ways: (1) Certain NIKE entities purchase product from the NIKE Trading Company ("NTC"), a wholly-owned sourcing hub that buys NIKE branded products from third party factories, predominantly in U.S. Dollars. The NTC, whose functional currency is the U.S. Dollar, then sells the products to NIKE entities in their respective functional currencies. When the NTC sells to a NIKE entity with a different functional currency, the result is a foreign currency exposure for the NTC; (2) Other NIKE entities purchase product directly from third party factories in U.S. Dollars. These purchases generate a foreign currency exposure for those NIKE entities with a functional currency other than the U.S. Dollar.

In January 2012, the Company implemented a foreign currency adjustment program with certain factories. The program is designed to more effectively manage foreign currency risk by assuming certain of the factories' foreign currency exposures, some of which are natural offsets to our existing foreign currency exposures. Under this program, the Company's payments to these factories are adjusted for rate fluctuations in the basket of currencies ("factory currency exposure index") in which the labor, materials and overhead costs incurred by the factories in the production of NIKE branded products ("factory input costs") are denominated. For the portion of the indices denominated in the local or functional currency of the factory, the Company may elect to place formally designated cash flow hedges. For all currencies within the indices, excluding the U.S. Dollar and the local or functional currency of the factory, an embedded derivative contract is created upon the factory's acceptance of NIKE's purchase order. Embedded derivative contracts are separated from the related purchase order and their accounting treatment is described further below.

The Company's policy permits the utilization of derivatives to reduce its foreign currency exposures where internal netting or other strategies cannot be effectively employed. Hedged transactions are denominated primarily in Euros, British Pounds and Japanese Yen. The Company may enter into hedge contracts typically starting up to 12 to 18 months in advance of the forecasted transaction and may place incremental hedges for up to 100% of the exposure by the time the forecasted transaction occurs.

All changes in fair value of derivatives designated as cash flow hedges, excluding any ineffective portion, are recorded in other comprehensive income until net income is affected by the variability of cash flows of the hedged transaction. In most cases, amounts recorded in other comprehensive income will be released to net income some time after the maturity of the related derivative. Effective hedge results are classified within the consolidated statements of income in the same manner as the underlying exposure, with the results of hedges of non-functional currency denominated revenues and product cost exposures, excluding embedded derivatives as described below, recorded in revenues or cost of sales, when the underlying hedged transaction affects consolidated net income. Results of hedges of selling and administrative expense are recorded together with those costs when the related expense is recorded. Results of hedges of anticipated purchases and sales of U.S. Dollar-denominated available-for-sale securities are recorded in other (income) expense, net when the securities are sold. Results of hedges of certain anticipated intercompany transactions are recorded in other (income) expense, net when the transaction occurs. The Company classifies the cash flows at settlement from these designated cash flow hedge derivatives in the same category as the cash flows from the related hedged items, generally within the cash provided by operations component of the cash flow statement.

Premiums paid on options are initially recorded as deferred charges. The Company assesses the effectiveness of options based on the total cash flows method and records total changes in the options' fair value to other comprehensive income to the degree they are effective.

The Company formally assesses, both at a hedge's inception and on an ongoing basis, whether the derivatives that are used in the hedging transaction have been highly effective in offsetting changes in the cash flows of hedged items and whether those derivatives may be expected to remain highly effective in future periods. Effectiveness for cash flow hedges is assessed based on forward rates. Ineffectiveness was not material for the years ended May 31, 2013, 2012 and 2011.

The Company discontinues hedge accounting prospectively when (1) it determines that the derivative is no longer highly effective in offsetting changes in the cash flows of a hedged item (including hedged items such as firm commitments or forecasted transactions); (2) the derivative expires or is sold, terminated, or exercised; (3) it is no longer probable that the forecasted transaction will occur; or (4) management determines that designating the derivative as a hedging instrument is no longer appropriate.

When the Company discontinues hedge accounting because it is no longer probable that the forecasted transaction will occur in the originally expected period, but is expected to occur within an additional two-month period of time thereafter, the gain or loss on the derivative remains in accumulated other comprehensive income and is reclassified to net income when the forecasted transaction affects consolidated net income. However, if it is probable that a forecasted transaction will not occur by the end of the originally specified time period or within an additional two-month period of time thereafter, the gains and losses that were accumulated in other comprehensive income will be recognized immediately in other (income) expense, net. In all situations in which hedge accounting is discontinued and the derivative remains outstanding, the Company will carry the derivative at its fair value on the balance sheet, recognizing future changes in the fair value in other (income) expense, net. For the years ended May 31, 2013, 2012 and 2011, the amounts recorded in other (income) expense, net as a result of the discontinuance of cash flow hedging because the forecasted transaction was no longer probable of occurring were immaterial.

As of May 31, 2013, $132 million of deferred net gains (net of tax) on both outstanding and matured derivatives accumulated in other comprehensive income are expected to be reclassified to net income during the next 12 months concurrent with the underlying hedged transactions also being recorded in net income. Actual amounts ultimately reclassified to net income are dependent on the exchange rates in effect when derivative contracts that are currently outstanding mature. As of May 31, 2013, the maximum term over which the Company is hedging exposures to the variability of cash flows for its forecasted transactions is 24 months.

Fair Value Hedges

The Company is also exposed to the risk of changes in the fair value of certain fixed-rate debt attributable to changes in interest rates. Derivatives currently used by the Company to hedge this risk are receive-fixed, pay-variable interest rate swaps. As of May 31, 2013, all interest rate swap agreements are designated as fair value hedges of the related long-term debt and meet the shortcut method requirements under the accounting standards for derivatives and hedging. Accordingly, changes in the fair values of the interest rate swap agreements are considered to exactly offset changes in the fair value of the underlying long-term debt. The cash flows associated with the Company's fair value hedges are periodic interest payments while the swaps are outstanding, which are reflected within the cash provided by operations component of the cash flow statement. The Company recorded no ineffectiveness from its interest rate swaps designated as fair value hedges for the years ended May 31, 2013, 2012, or 2011.

Net Investment Hedges

The Company has hedged and may, in the future, hedge the risk of variability in foreign-currency-denominated net investments in wholly-owned international operations. All changes in fair value of the derivatives designated as net investment hedges, except ineffective portions, are reported in the cumulative translation adjustment component of other comprehensive income along with the foreign currency translation adjustments on those investments. The Company classifies the cash flows at settlement of its net investment hedges within the cash provided or used by investing component of the cash flow statement. The Company assesses hedge effectiveness based on changes in forward rates. The Company recorded no ineffectiveness from its net investment hedges for the years ended May 31, 2013, 2012, or 2011.

Embedded Derivatives

As part of the foreign currency adjustment program described above, currencies within the factory currency exposure indices that are neither the Dollar nor the local or functional currency of the factory, an embedded derivative contract is created upon the factory's acceptance of NIKE's purchase order. Embedded derivative contracts are treated as foreign currency forward contracts that are bifurcated from the related purchase order and recorded at fair value as a derivative asset or liability on the balance sheet with their corresponding change in fair value recognized in other (income) expense, net from the date a purchase order is accepted by a factory through the date the purchase price is no longer subject to foreign currency fluctuations. At May 31, 2013, the notional amount of embedded derivatives was approximately $136 million.

Undesignated Derivative Instruments

The Company may elect to enter into foreign exchange forwards to mitigate the change in fair value of specific assets and liabilities on the balance sheet and/or the embedded derivative contracts explained above. These forwards are not designated as hedging instruments under the accounting standards for derivatives and hedging. Accordingly, these undesignated instruments are recorded at fair value as a derivative asset or liability on the balance sheet with their corresponding change in fair value recognized in other (income) expense, net, together with the re-measurement gain or loss from the hedged balance sheet position or embedded derivative contract. The Company classifies the cash flows at settlement from undesignated instruments in the same category as the cash flows from the related hedged items, generally within the cash provided by operations component of the cash flow statement.

Credit Risk

The Company is exposed to credit-related losses in the event of non- performance by counterparties to hedging instruments. The counterparties to all derivative transactions are major financial institutions with investment grade credit ratings. However, this does not eliminate the Company's exposure to credit risk with these institutions. This credit risk is limited to the unrealized gains in such contracts should any of these counterparties fail to perform as contracted. To manage this risk, the Company has established strict counterparty credit guidelines that are continually monitored.

The Company's derivative contracts contain credit risk related contingent features designed to protect against significant deterioration in counterparties' creditworthiness and their ultimate ability to settle outstanding derivative contracts in the normal course of business. The Company's bilateral credit related contingent features generally require the owing entity, either the Company or the derivative counterparty, to post collateral for the portion of the fair value in excess of $50 million should the fair value of outstanding derivatives per counterparty be greater than $50 million. Additionally, a certain level of decline in credit rating of either the Company or the counterparty could also trigger collateral requirements. As of May 31, 2013, the Company was in compliance with all credit risk related contingent features and the fair value of its derivative instruments with credit risk related contingent features in a net liability position was insignificant. Accordingly, the Company was not required to post any collateral as a result of these contingent features. Further, as of May 31, 2013 those counterparties which were required to post collateral complied with such requirements. Given the considerations described above, the Company considers the impact of the risk of counterparty default to be immaterial.

NOTE 18 — Operating Segments and Related Information

Operating Segments. The Company's operating segments are evidence of the structure of the Company's internal organization. The major segments are defined by geographic regions for operations participating in NIKE Brand sales activity excluding NIKE Golf. Each NIKE Brand geographic segment operates predominantly in one industry: the design, development, marketing and selling of athletic footwear, apparel, and equipment. The Company's reportable operating segments for the NIKE Brand are: North America, Western Europe, Central & Eastern Europe, Greater China, Japan, and Emerging Markets. The Company's NIKE Brand Direct to Consumer operations are managed within each geographic segment.

The Company's "Other" category is broken into two components for presentation purposes to align with the way management views the Company. The "Global Brand Divisions" category primarily represents NIKE Brand licensing businesses that are not part of a geographic operating segment, demand creation and operating overhead expenses that are centrally managed for the NIKE Brand, and costs associated with product development and supply chain operations. The "Other Businesses" category consists of the activities of Converse Inc., Hurley International LLC, and NIKE Golf. Activities represented in the "Other" category are considered immaterial for individual disclosure.

Corporate consists largely of unallocated general and administrative expenses, including expenses associated with centrally managed departments, depreciation and amortization related to the Company's headquarters, unallocated insurance and benefit programs, including stock- based compensation, certain foreign currency gains and losses, including certain hedge gains and losses, certain corporate eliminations and other items.

The primary financial measure used by the Company to evaluate performance of individual operating segments is earnings before interest and taxes (commonly referred to as "EBIT"), which represents net income before interest (income) expense, net and income taxes in the consolidated statements of income. Reconciling items for EBIT represent corporate expense items that are not allocated to the operating segments for management reporting.

As part of our centrally managed foreign exchange risk management program, standard foreign currency rates are assigned twice per year to each NIKE Brand entity in our geographic operating segments and certain Other Businesses. These rates are set approximately nine months in advance of the future selling season based on average market spot rates in the calendar month preceding the date they are established. Inventories and cost of sales for geographic operating segments and certain Other Businesses reflect use of these standard rates to record non-functional currency product purchases in the entity's functional currency. Differences between assigned standard foreign currency rates and actual market rates are included in Corporate, together with foreign currency hedge gains and losses generated from our centrally managed foreign exchange risk management program and other conversion gains and losses.

Accounts receivable, inventories and property, plant and equipment for operating segments are regularly reviewed by management and are therefore provided below. Additions to long-lived assets as presented in the following table represent capital expenditures.

Certain prior year amounts have been reclassified to conform to fiscal 2013 presentation.

(In millions)	Year Ended May 31, 2013	2012	2011
REVENUE			
North America	$ 10,387	$ 8,839	$ 7,579
Western Europe	4,128	4,144	3,868
Central & Eastern Europe	1,287	1,200	1,040
Greater China	2,453	2,539	2,060
Japan	791	835	773
Emerging Markets	3,718	3,411	2,737
Global Brand Divisions	117	111	96
Total NIKE Brand	22,881	21,079	18,153
Other Businesses	2,500	2,298	2,041
Corporate	(68)	(46)	(77)
TOTAL NIKE CONSOLIDATED REVENUES	**$ 25,313**	**$ 23,331**	**$ 20,117**
EARNINGS BEFORE INTEREST AND TAXES			
North America	$ 2,534	$ 2,030	$ 1,736
Western Europe	640	597	730
Central & Eastern Europe	259	234	244
Greater China	809	911	777
Japan	133	136	114
Emerging Markets	1,011	853	688
Global Brand Divisions	(1,396)	(1,200)	(971)
Total NIKE Brand	3,990	3,561	3,318
Other Businesses	456	385	353
Corporate	(1,177)	(917)	(805)
Total NIKE Consolidated Earnings Before Interest and Taxes	3,269	3,029	2,866
Interest (income) expense, net	(3)	4	4
TOTAL NIKE CONSOLIDATED EARNINGS BEFORE TAXES	**$ 3,272**	**$ 3,025**	**$ 2,862**
ADDITIONS TO LONG-LIVED ASSETS			
North America	$ 201	$ 131	$ 79
Western Europe	74	93	75
Central & Eastern Europe	22	20	5
Greater China	52	38	43
Japan	6	14	9
Emerging Markets	49	27	21
Global Brand Divisions	216	131	44
Total NIKE Brand	620	454	276
Other Businesses	29	24	27
Corporate	131	109	118
TOTAL ADDITIONS TO LONG-LIVED ASSETS	**$ 780**	**$ 587**	**$ 421**
DEPRECIATION			
North America	$ 85	$ 78	$ 70
Western Europe	68	62	52
Central & Eastern Europe	9	6	4
Greater China	34	25	19
Japan	21	23	22
Emerging Markets	20	15	14
Global Brand Divisions	83	53	39
Total NIKE Brand	320	262	220
Other Businesses	24	25	24
Corporate	74	66	71
TOTAL DEPRECIATION	**$ 418**	**$ 353**	**$ 315**

(In millions)	As of May 31, 2013	2012
ACCOUNTS RECEIVABLE, NET		
North America	$ 1,214	$ 1,149
Western Europe	356	420
Central & Eastern Europe	301	261
Greater China	52	221
Japan	133	152
Emerging Markets	546	476
Global Brand Divisions	28	30
Total NIKE Brand	2,630	2,709
Other Businesses	436	401
Corporate	51	22
TOTAL ACCOUNTS RECEIVABLE, NET	**$ 3,117**	**$ 3,132**
INVENTORIES		
North America	$ 1,435	$ 1,272
Western Europe	539	488
Central & Eastern Europe	207	180
Greater China	204	217
Japan	60	83
Emerging Markets	555	521
Global Brand Divisions	32	35
Total NIKE Brand	3,032	2,796
Other Businesses	400	384
Corporate	2	42
TOTAL INVENTORIES	**$ 3,434**	**$ 3,222**
PROPERTY, PLANT AND EQUIPMENT, NET		
North America	$ 406	$ 378
Western Europe	326	314
Central & Eastern Europe	44	30
Greater China	213	191
Japan	269	359
Emerging Markets	89	59
Global Brand Divisions	353	205
Total NIKE Brand	1,700	1,536
Other Businesses	77	76
Corporate	675	597
TOTAL PROPERTY, PLANT AND EQUIPMENT, NET	**$ 2,452**	**$ 2,209**

Revenues by Major Product Lines. Revenues to external customers for NIKE Brand products are attributable to sales of footwear, apparel and equipment. Other revenues to external customers primarily include external sales by Converse, Hurley, and NIKE Golf.

(In millions)	Year Ended May 31, 2013	2012	2011
Footwear	$ 14,539	$ 13,428	$ 11,519
Apparel	6,820	6,336	5,516
Equipment	1,405	1,204	1,022
Other	2,549	2,363	2,060
TOTAL NIKE CONSOLIDATED REVENUES	**$ 25,313**	**$ 23,331**	**$ 20,117**

Appendix D

International Financial Reporting Standards (IFRS)

IFRS

The Need for Global Accounting Standards

As discussed in Chapter 1, the Financial Accounting Standards Board (FASB) establishes generally accepted accounting principles (GAAP) for public companies in the United States. Of course, there is a world beyond the borders of the United States. In recent years, the removal of trade barriers and the growth in cross-border equity and debt issuances have led to a dramatic increase in international commerce. As a result, often companies are reporting financial results to users outside of the United States.

Historically, accounting standards have varied considerably across countries. These variances have been driven by cultural, legal, and political differences and resulted in financial statements that were not easily comparable and difficult to interpret. These differences caused problems for companies in Europe and Asia, where local economies have become increasingly tied to international commerce.

During the last decade, however, a common set of International Financial Reporting Standards (IFRS) has emerged to reduce cross-country differences in accounting standards, primarily in countries outside of North America. While much of the world has migrated to IFRS, the United States has not. Because of the size of the United States and its significant role in world commerce, U.S. GAAP still has a global impact. As a result, there are currently two major accounting standard-setting efforts in the world, U.S. GAAP and IFRS. These two sets of accounting standards add cost and complexity for companies doing business and obtaining financing internationally.

Overview of IFRS

International Financial Reporting Standards have emerged during the last 10 years to meet the financial reporting needs of an increasingly global business environment.

What Is IFRS? International Financial Reporting Standards are a set of global accounting standards developed by an international standard-setting body called the International Accounting Standards Board (IASB). Like the Financial Accounting Standards Board, the IASB is an independent entity that establishes accounting rules. Unlike the FASB, the IASB does not establish accounting rules for any specific country. Rather, it develops accounting rules that can be used by a variety of countries, with the goal of developing a single set of global accounting standards.

Who Uses IFRS? IFRS applies to companies that issue publicly traded debt or equity securities, called **public companies**, in countries that have adopted IFRS as their accounting standards. Since 2005, all 28 countries in the European Union (EU) have been required to prepare financial statements using IFRS. In addition, more than 100 other countries have adopted IFRS for public companies (see Exhibit 1). In other major economies, Japan is considering mandatory adoption by 2016, India allows limited use of IFRS, and China is converging its standards with IFRS over time. In addition, the G20 (Group of 20) leadership has called for uniform global accounting standards.

EXHIBIT 1

IFRS Adopters

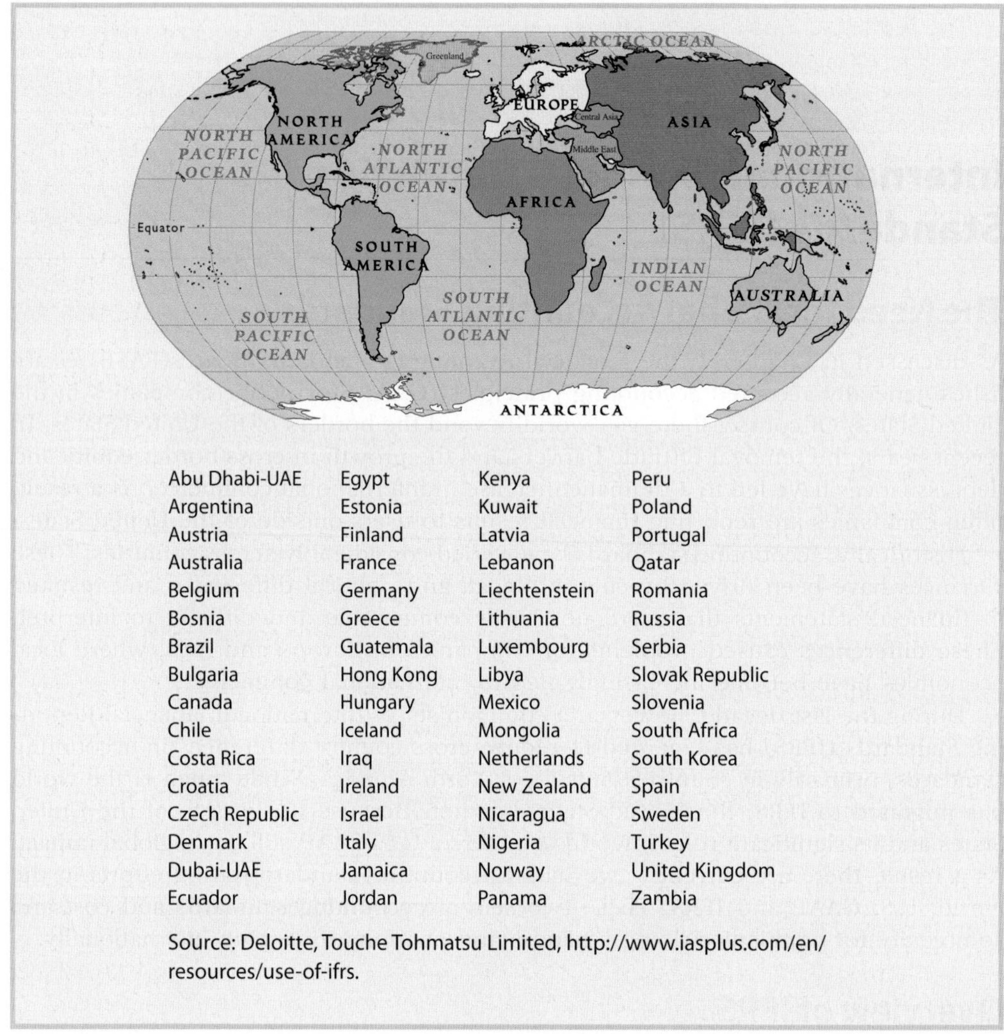

Abu Dhabi-UAE	Egypt	Kenya	Peru
Argentina	Estonia	Kuwait	Poland
Austria	Finland	Latvia	Portugal
Australia	France	Lebanon	Qatar
Belgium	Germany	Liechtenstein	Romania
Bosnia	Greece	Lithuania	Russia
Brazil	Guatemala	Luxembourg	Serbia
Bulgaria	Hong Kong	Libya	Slovak Republic
Canada	Hungary	Mexico	Slovenia
Chile	Iceland	Mongolia	South Africa
Costa Rica	Iraq	Netherlands	South Korea
Croatia	Ireland	New Zealand	Spain
Czech Republic	Israel	Nicaragua	Sweden
Denmark	Italy	Nigeria	Turkey
Dubai-UAE	Jamaica	Norway	United Kingdom
Ecuador	Jordan	Panama	Zambia

Source: Deloitte, Touche Tohmatsu Limited, http://www.iasplus.com/en/resources/use-of-ifrs.

U.S. GAAP and IFRS: The Road Forward

The United States has not formally adopted IFRS for U.S. companies. The wide acceptance being gained by IFRS around the world, however, has placed considerable pressure on the United States to align U.S. GAAP with IFRS. There are two possible paths that the United States could take to achieve this: (1) adoption of IFRS by the U.S. Securities and Exchange Commission or (2) convergence of U.S. GAAP and IFRS. These two options are briefly discussed in this section.

Adoption of IFRS by the SEC The U.S. Securities and Exchange Commission (SEC) is the U.S. governmental agency that has authority over the accounting and financial disclosures for U.S. public companies. Only the SEC has the authority to adopt IFRS for U.S. public companies. After considerable deliberation over a period of nearly five years, the SEC published a Final Report on the issues surrounding IFRS adoption.[1] Notably, this report did not include a final policy decision or recommendation in favor of U.S. public companies adopting IFRS. Indeed, since this report, the SEC has distanced itself from the adoption position, and it is now acknowledged as unsupported. This leaves what remains of the convergence pathway.

Convergence of U.S. GAAP and IFRS Convergence involves aligning IFRS and U.S. GAAP one topic at a time, by slowly merging IFRS and U.S. GAAP into two broadly uniform sets of accounting standards. To this end, the FASB and IASB have agreed to work together on a select number of difficult and high-profile accounting issues. These issues frame a large portion of the disagreement between the two sets of standards and, if accomplished, will significantly reduce the differences between U.S. GAAP and IFRS. The projects selected for the convergence effort represent some of the more technical topics in accounting and are covered in intermediate and advanced accounting courses. As of 2013, there remain a small number of topics as part of the formal convergence effort between the FASB and IASB. Once these topics have been completed, the formal joint convergence effort will end. It is unclear how convergence between the two boards will proceed after these topics are converged.

One of the major limitations of convergence is that both the FASB and IASB continue to operate as the accounting standard-setting bodies for their respective jurisdictions. As such, convergence would not result in a single set of global accounting standards. Only those standards that go through the joint FASB–IASB standard-setting process would be released as uniform. Standards that do not go through a joint standard-setting process may create inconsistencies between U.S. GAAP and IFRS. Thus, convergence does not guarantee complete uniformity between U.S. GAAP and IFRS. Thus, there will remain differences in U.S. GAAP and IFRS in the foreseeable future. Understanding these differences are important because of increased globalization of business.

Differences Between U.S. GAAP and IFRS

U.S. GAAP and IFRS differ both in their approach to standard setting, as well as their financial statement presentation and recording of transactions.

Rules-Based Versus Principles Approach to Standard Setting U.S. GAAP is considered to be a "rules-based" approach to accounting standard setting. The accounting standards provide detailed and specific rules on the accounting for business transactions. There are few exceptions or varying interpretations of the accounting for a business event. This structure is consistent with the U.S. legal and regulatory system, reflecting the social and economic values of the United States.

In contrast, IFRS is designed to meet the needs of many countries. Differences in legal, political, and economic systems create different needs for and uses of financial information in different countries. For example, Germany needs a financial reporting system that reflects the central role of banks in its financial system, while the Netherlands needs a financial reporting system that reflects the significant role of outside equity in its financial system.

To accommodate economic, legal, and social diversity, IFRS must be broad enough to capture these differences while still presenting comparable financial statements. Under IFRS, there is greater opportunity for different interpretations of the accounting treatment of a business event across different business entities. To support this, IFRS often has more extensive disclosures that support alternative assumptions. Thus, IFRS provides more latitude for professional judgment than typically found in comparable U.S. GAAP. Many countries find this feature attractive in reducing regulatory costs associated with using and auditing financial reports. This "principles-based" approach presents one of the most significant challenges to adopting IFRS in the United States.

[1] Work Plan for the Consideration of Incorporating International Financial Accounting Standards into the Financial Reporting System for U.S. Issuers: Final Staff Report, U.S. Securities Exchange Commission, July 13, 2012.

Technical Differences Between IFRS and U.S. GAAP Although U.S. GAAP is similar to IFRS, differences arise in the presentation format, balance sheet valuations, and technical accounting procedures. The Mornin' Joe International financial statements presented after Chapter 15 highlight the financial statement format, presentation, and recording differences between U.S. GAAP and IFRS. In addition, the International Connection boxes in Chapters 1, 4, 7, 10, 13, and 16 discuss some of the significant differences between U.S. GAAP and IFRS. A more comprehensive summary of the key differences between U.S. GAAP and IFRS that are relevant to an introductory accounting course is provided in Exhibit 2.

Discussion Questions

1. Briefly discuss why global accounting standards are needed in today's business environment.
2. What are International Financial Reporting Standards? Who uses these accounting standards?
3. What body is responsible for setting International Financial Reporting Standards?
4. Briefly discuss the differences between (a) adoption of IFRS by the U.S. Securities and Exchange Commission and (b) convergence of U.S. GAAP with IFRS.
5. Briefly discuss the difference between (a) a "rules-based" approach to accounting standard setting and (b) a "principles-based" approach to accounting standard setting.
6. How is property, plant, and equipment measured on the balance sheet under IFRS? How does this differ from the way property, plant, and equipment is measured on the balance sheet under U.S. GAAP?
7. What inventory costing methods are allowed under IFRS? How does this differ from the treatment under U.S. GAAP?

EXHIBIT 2 **Comparison of Accounting for Selected Items Under U.S. GAAP and IFRS**

	U.S. GAAP	IFRS	Text Reference
General:			
Financial statement titles	Balance Sheet Statement of Stockholders' Equity Statement of Cash Flows	Statement of Financial Position Statement of Changes in Equity Statement of Cash Flows	General
Financial periods presented	Public companies must present two years of comparative information for income statement, statement of stockholders' equity, and statement of cash flows	One year of comparative information must be presented	General
Conceptual basis for standard setting	"Rules-based" approach	"Principles-based" approach	General
Internal control requirements	Sarbanes-Oxley Act (SOX) Section 404		Ch 8; LO 1
Balance Sheet:	***Balance Sheet***	***Statement of Financial Position***	
Terminology differences	"Payable" "Stockholders' Equity" "Net Income (Loss)"	"Provision" "Capital and Reserves" "Profit or (Loss)"	Ch 11 Ch 13 General
Inventory—LIFO	LIFO allowed	LIFO prohibited	Ch 7; LO 3, 4, 5
Inventory—valuation	Market is defined as "replacement value" Reversal of lower-of-cost-or-market write-downs not allowed	Market is defined as "fair value" Reversal of write-downs allowed	Ch 7; LO 6 Ch 7; LO 6
Long-lived assets	May NOT be revalued to fair value	May be revalued to fair value on a regular basis	Ch 10; LO 1

(Continued)

EXHIBIT 2 **Comparison of Accounting for Selected Items Under U.S. GAAP and IFRS (*Continued*)**

	U.S. GAAP	IFRS	Text Reference
Land held for investment	Treated as held for use or sale, and recorded at historical cost	May be accounted for on a historical cost basis or on a fair value basis with changes in fair value recognized through profit and loss	Ch 10; LO 1
Property, plant, & equipment—valuation	Historical cost If impaired, impairment loss may NOT be reversed in future periods	May select between historical cost or revalued amount (a form of fair value) If impaired, impairment loss may be reversed in future periods	Ch 10; LO 1
Cost of major overhaul (Capital and revenue expenditures)	Different treatment for ordinary repairs and maintenance, asset improvement, extraordinary repairs	Typically included as part of the cost of the asset or asset component if future economic benefit is probable and can be reliably measured	Ch 10; LO 1
Intangible assets—valuation	Acquisition cost, unless impaired	Fair value permitted if the intangible asset trades in an active market	Ch 10; LO 5
Intangible assets—impairment loss reversal	Prohibited	Prohibited for goodwill but allowed for other intangible assets	Ch 10; LO 5
Deferred tax liability	The amount due within one year classified as current	Always noncurrent	Appendix D
Income Statement:	***Income Statement***	***Statement of Comprehensive Income***	
Revenue recognition	Detailed guidance depending on the transaction	Broad guidance	Ch 3; LO 1
Classification of expenses on income statement	Public companies must present expenses on the income statement by function (e.g., cost of goods sold, selling, administrative)	Expenses may be presented based either by function (e.g., cost of goods sold, selling) or by the nature of expense (e.g., wages expense, interest expense)	Ch 6; LO 1
Research and development costs	Expensed as incurred	Research costs expensed Development costs capitalized once technical and economic feasibility attained	Ch 10; LO 5
Extraordinary items	Allowed for items that are both unusual in nature and infrequent in occurrence	Prohibited	Ch 17; Appendix

(Continued)

EXHIBIT 2 **Comparison of Accounting for Selected Items Under U.S. GAAP and IFRS (*Concluded*)**

	U.S. GAAP	IFRS	Text Reference
Statement of Cash Flows:	***Statement of Cash Flows***	***Statement of Cash Flows***	
Classification of interest paid or received	Treated as an operating activity	Interest paid may be treated as either an operating or a financing activity; interest received may be treated as an operating or investing activity	Ch 16; LO 3
Classification of dividend paid or received	Dividend paid treated as a financing activity, dividend received treated as an operating activity	Dividend paid may be treated as either an operating or a financing activity; dividend received may be treated as an operating or investing activity	Ch 16; LO 3

Appendix E

Revenue Recognition

Companies recognize revenue when services have been performed or products have been delivered to customers. For example, when McDonald's sells a hamburger, the revenue is earned when the hamburger is delivered to the customer. In this example, revenue recognition is simple because the hamburger is delivered and cash is received at a single point in time.

Revenue recognition is more complex, however, when a transaction includes several items that are sold together, items that are delivered over time, or items whose prices depend upon future events. To address these more complex transactions, the Financial Accounting Standards Board (FASB) issued a new accounting standard in May 2014.[1] The new Standard uses a five-step method for determining when revenue should be recognized. The five steps are as follows:

- Step 1. *Identify the contract with the customer.* The new Standard treats every revenue transaction as a contract. A contract is an agreement by the seller to provide a good or service in exchange for payment from the buyer. A contract may be verbal and implicit, such as the purchase of a McDonald's hamburger, or written and explicit, such as a cell phone contract.
- Step 2. *Identify the separate performance obligations in the contract.* Every contract requires the seller and buyer to perform. For example, when you purchase a McDonald's hamburger, you (the buyer) perform by paying and McDonald's (the seller) performs by delivering a hamburger. When you purchase a cell phone from Verizon, the transaction is more complex. You perform by paying cash or charging your credit card and signing a written contract. Verizon performs by delivering you the phone and promising to provide you cellular service in the future. In this case, Verizon has two performance obligations: (1) to provide the phone and (2) to provide cellular service in the future.
- Step 3. *Determine the transaction price.* The transaction price is the amount the seller is entitled to receive in exchange for the goods and services they have provided. In the case of the McDonald's hamburger, the transaction price is the amount paid for the hamburger. In the case of Verizon, the transaction price must be estimated for the phone (the first performance obligation) and cellular service (the second performance obligation).
- Step 4. *Allocate the transaction price to the separate performance obligations.* Since the sale of a McDonald's hamburger involves the sale of a single item that is immediately delivered, the entire transaction price is allocated to the hamburger. In more complex transactions, such as a Verizon cellular service contract, the revenue received from the customer must be allocated among the performance obligations. This allocation is often based on the stand-alone (separate) price of each good or service. For example, Verizon should allocate the revenue from the customer between the phone

[1] Accounting Standards Update, *Revenue from Contracts with Customers (Topic 606)*, Financial Accounting Standards Board, May 2014, Norwalk, CT.

(first performance obligation) and the commitment to provide cellular service (second performance obligation).

- Step 5. *Recognize revenue when each separate performance obligation is satisfied.* The seller should recognize (record) revenue as each performance obligation is satisfied. In the case of McDonald's, the performance obligation is satisfied when the clerk delivers the hamburger to the customer. At this point, the control of the hamburger has passed to the customer. In the case of Verizon, it satisfies its first performance obligation when it delivers you the phone. Verizon satisfies its second performance obligation over time by providing you cellular service. Thus, Verizon should record some revenue at the time you sign the contract and receive your phone and some revenue as you are provided cellular service.

To illustrate, assume that on March 1, 2016, Chandler Evans upgrades (replaces) his cell phone with Star Cellular at no cost by signing a two-year agreement. The new agreement cannot be cancelled and requires a payment of $90 per month. The cell phone selected by Evans cost Star Cellular $250.

The five-step method would be applied by Star Cellular as follows:

- Step 1. *Identify the contract with the customer.* The contract with Chandler Evans is the two-year cellular service agreement that includes delivery of a new cell phone.
- Step 2. *Identify the separate performance obligations in the contract.* Star Cellular has two separate performance obligations to Evans under the contract. First, Star Cellular must deliver a new cell phone at the time that Evans signs the service agreement. Second, Star Cellular must provide Evans cell service for two years.
- Step 3. *Determine the transaction price.* The transaction price is the total amount Star Cellular will receive over the contract period. In this case, Star Cellular will receive $2,160 ($90 × 24 months) over the contract period.[2]
- Step 4. *Allocate the transaction price to the separate performance obligations.* Assume that Star Cellular sells the cell phone and cell service separately at the following prices:

Cell phone	$ 600
Cell service for two years	3,000
Total price if sold separately	$3,600

The transaction price is allocated to each performance obligation based upon what each obligation would sell for separately as a stand-alone product. To illustrate, the cell phone is allocated $360 of the transaction price of $2,160, computed as follows:

$$\text{Cell Phone} = \text{Contract Price} \times \frac{\text{Price of Cell Phone Sold Separately}}{\text{Total Price of Cell Phone and Cell Service Sold Separately}}$$

$$\text{Cell Phone} = \$2{,}160 \times \frac{\$600}{\$3{,}600} = \$360$$

The cell service is allocated $1,800 of the transaction price of $2,160, computed as follows:

$$\text{Cell Service} = \text{Contract Price} \times \frac{\text{Price of Cell Service Sold Separately}}{\text{Total Price of Cell Phone and Cell Service Sold Separate}}$$

$$\text{Cell Service} = \$2{,}160 \times \frac{\$3{,}000}{\$3{,}600} = \$1{,}800$$

[2] An interest component may need to be considered in long-term contracts. To simplify, we ignore interest.

- Step 5. *Recognize revenue when each separate performance obligation is satisfied.* The $360 of revenue from the cell phone is recognized when the customer signs the service agreement and receives the phone. At this point, the first performance obligation has been satisfied by Star Cellular and the control of the phone has passed to the customer. The journal entry to record cell phone revenue on March 1, 2016, is as follows:

2016				
Mar.	1	Accounts Receivable—Chandler Evans	360	
		Sales		360
		Cost of Merchandise Sold	250	
		Merchandise Inventory		250

The $1,800 of cell service revenue is recognized as the performance obligation is satisfied over the two-year term of the contract. For example, $75 ($1,800 ÷ 24 months) of service revenue would be recorded each month. The journal entry to record the service revenue for March is as follows:

2016				
Mar.	31	Cash	90	
		Accounts Receivable ($360 ÷ 24 months)		15
		Cell Service Revenue ($1,800 ÷ 24 months)		75

The preceding journal entries illustrate how over the life of the two-year contract the total revenue from the contract of $2,160 is divided between the sale of the cell phone ($360 of revenue) and providing of cell service ($1,800 of revenue). In addition, the journal entries illustrate when revenue from the phone and service is recorded.

Exhibit 1 summarizes the division of revenue and its recording over the two-year contract.

EXHIBIT 1 **Recording Revenue over Two-Year Contract**

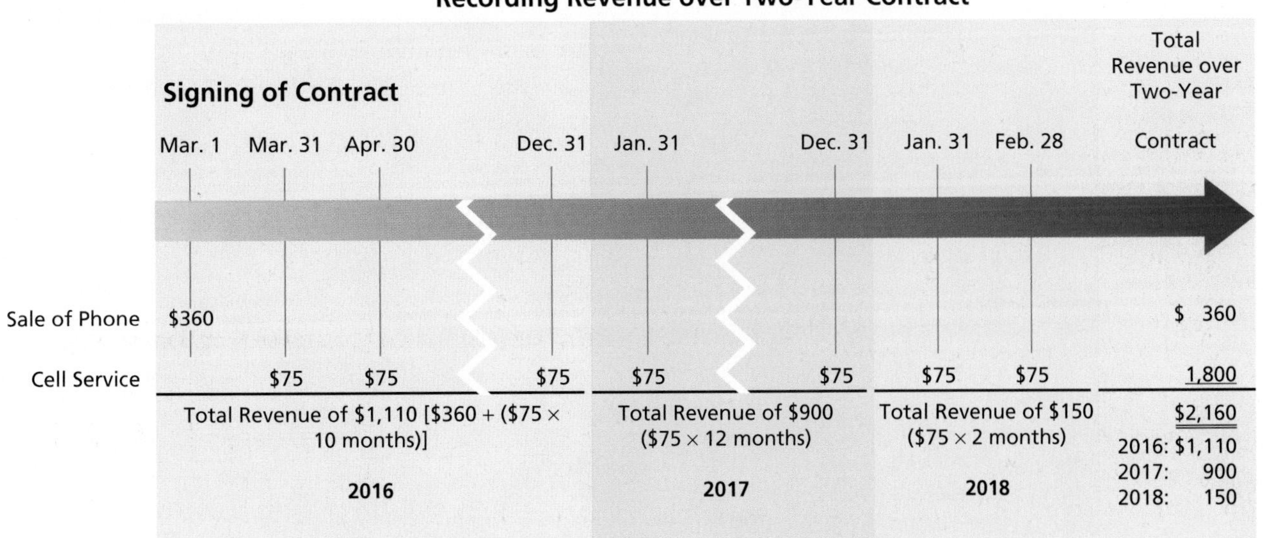

Glossary

A

accelerated depreciation method A depreciation method that provides for a higher depreciation amount in the first year of the asset's use, followed by a gradually declining amount of depreciation. (Ch. 10)

account An accounting form that is used to record the increases and decreases in each financial statement item. (Ch. 2)

account form The form of balance sheet that resembles the basic format of the accounting equation, with assets on the left side and Liabilities and Owner's Equity sections on the right side. (Chs. 1, 6)

account payable The liability created by a purchase on account. (Ch. 1)

account receivable A claim against the customer created by selling merchandise or services on credit. (Chs. 1, 2, 9)

accounting An information system that provides reports to stakeholders about the economic activities and condition of a business. (Ch. 1)

accounting cycle The process that begins with analyzing and journalizing transactions and ends with the post-closing trial balance. (Ch. 4)

accounting equation Assets = Liabilities + Owner's Equity. (Ch. 1)

accounting period concept The accounting concept that assumes that the economic life of the business can be divided into time periods. (Ch. 3)

accounting system The methods and procedures used by a business to collect, classify, summarize, and report financial data for use by management and external users. (Ch. 5)

accounts payable subsidiary ledger The subsidiary ledger containing the individual accounts with suppliers (creditors). (Ch. 5)

accounts receivable analysis A company's ability to collect its accounts receivable. (Ch. 17)

accounts receivable subsidiary ledger The subsidiary ledger containing the individual accounts with customers. (Ch. 5)

accounts receivable turnover The relationship between net sales and accounts receivable, computed by dividing the net sales by the average net accounts receivable; measures how frequently during the year the accounts receivable are being converted to cash. (Chs. 9, 17)

accrual basis of accounting Under this basis of accounting, revenues and expenses are reported in the income statement in the period in which they are earned or incurred. (Ch. 3)

accrued expenses Expenses that have been incurred but not recorded in the accounts. (Ch. 3)

accrued revenues Revenues that have been earned but not recorded in the accounts. (Ch. 3)

Accumulated Depreciation The contra asset account credited when recording the depreciation of a fixed asset. (Ch. 3)

accumulated other comprehensive income The cumulative effects of other comprehensive income items reported separately in the Stockholders' Equity section of the balance sheet. (Ch. 15)

adjusted trial balance The trial balance prepared after all the adjusting entries have been posted. (Ch. 3)

adjusting entries The journal entries that bring the accounts up to date at the end of the accounting period. (Ch. 3)

adjusting process An analysis and updating of the accounts when financial statements are prepared. (Ch. 3)

administrative expenses (general expenses) Expenses incurred in the administration or general operations of the business. (Ch. 6)

aging the receivables The process of analyzing the accounts receivable and classifying them according to various age groupings, with the due date being the base point for determining age. (Ch. 9)

Allowance for Doubtful Accounts The contra asset account for accounts receivable. (Ch. 9)

allowance method The method of accounting for uncollectible accounts that provides an expense for uncollectible receivables in advance of their write-off. (Ch. 9)

amortization The periodic transfer of the cost of an intangible asset to expense. (Chs. 10, 14)

annuity A series of equal cash flows at fixed intervals. (Ch. 14)

assets The resources owned by a business. (Chs. 1, 2)

available-for-sale securities Securities that management expects to sell in the future but which are not actively traded for profit. (Ch. 15)

B

bad debt expense The operating expense incurred because of the failure to collect receivables. (Ch. 9)

balance of the account The amount of the difference between the debits and the credits that have been entered into an account. (Ch. 2)

balance sheet A list of the assets, liabilities, and owner's equity as of a specific date, usually at the close of the last day of a month or a year. (Ch. 1)

bank reconciliation The analysis that details the items responsible for the difference between the cash balance reported in the bank statement and the balance of the cash account in the ledger. (Ch. 8)

bank statement A summary of all transactions mailed to the depositor or made available online by the bank each month. (Ch. 8)

bond A form of an interest-bearing note used by corporations to borrow on a long-term basis. (Ch. 14)

bond indenture The contract between a corporation issuing bonds and the bondholders. (Ch. 14)

book value The cost of a fixed asset minus accumulated depreciation on the asset. (Ch. 10)

book value of the asset (or net book value) The difference between the cost of a fixed asset and its accumulated depreciation. (Ch. 3)

boot The amount a buyer owes a seller when a fixed asset is traded in on a similar asset. (Ch. 10)

business An organization in which basic resources (inputs), such as materials and labor, are assembled and processed to provide goods or services (outputs) to customers. (Ch. 1)

business combination A business making an investment in another business by acquiring a controlling share, often greater than 50%, of the outstanding voting stock of another corporation by paying cash or exchanging stock. (Ch. 15)

business entity concept A concept of accounting that limits the economic data in the accounting system to data related directly to the activities of the business. (Ch. 1)

business transaction An economic event or condition that directly changes an entity's financial condition or directly affects its results of operations. (Ch. 1)

C

capital account An account used for a proprietorship that represents the owner's equity. (Ch. 2)

capital expenditures The costs of acquiring fixed assets, adding to a fixed asset, improving a fixed asset, or extending a fixed asset's useful life. (Ch. 10)

capital lease A lease that includes one or more provisions that result in treating the leased assets as purchased assets in the accounts. (Ch. 10)

carrying amount The balance of the bonds payable account (face amount of the bonds) less any unamortized discount or plus any unamortized premium. (Ch. 14)

cash Coins, currency (paper money), checks, money orders, and money on deposit that is available for unrestricted withdrawal from banks and other financial institutions. (Ch. 8)

cash basis of accounting Under this basis of accounting, revenues and expenses are reported in the income statement in the period in which cash is received or paid. (Ch. 3)

cash dividend A cash distribution of earnings by a corporation to its shareholders. (Ch. 13)

cash equivalents Highly liquid investments that are usually reported with cash on the balance sheet. (Ch. 8)

cash flow per share Normally computed as cash flow from operations per share. (Ch. 16)

cash flows from financing activities The section of the statement of cash flows that reports cash flows from transactions affecting the equity and debt of the business. (Ch. 16)

cash flows from investing activities The section of the statement of cash flows that reports cash flows from transactions affecting investments in noncurrent assets. (Ch. 16)

cash flows from operating activities The section of the statement of cash flows that reports the cash transactions affecting the determination of net income. (Ch. 16)

cash payments journal The special journal in which all cash payments are recorded. (Ch. 5)

cash receipts journal The special journal in which all cash receipts are recorded. (Ch. 5)

cash short and over account An account which has recorded errors in cash sales or errors in making change causing the amount of actual cash on hand to differ from the beginning amount of cash plus the cash sales for the day. (Ch. 8)

Certified Public Accountant (CPA) Public accountants who have met a state's education, experience, and examination requirements. (Ch. 1)

chart of accounts A list of the accounts in the ledger. (Ch. 2)

clearing account Another name for the income summary account because it has the effect of clearing the revenue and expense accounts of their balances. (Ch. 4)

closing entries The entries that transfer the balances of the revenue, expense, and drawing accounts to the owner's capital account. (Ch. 4)

closing process The transfer process of converting temporary account balances to zero by transferring the revenue and expense account balances to Income Summary, transferring the income summary account balance to the owner's capital account, and transferring the owner's drawing account to the owner's capital account. (Ch. 4)

closing the books The process of transferring temporary accounts balances to permanent accounts at the end of the accounting period. (Ch. 4)

common stock The stock outstanding when a corporation has issued only one class of stock. (Ch. 13)

common-sized statement A financial statement in which all items are expressed only in relative terms. (Ch. 17)

compensating balance A requirement by some banks requiring depositors to maintain minimum cash balances in their bank accounts. (Ch. 8)

comprehensive income All changes in stockholders' equity during a period, except those resulting from dividends and stockholders' investments. (Ch. 15)

consigned inventory Merchandise that is shipped by manufacturers to retailers who act as the manufacturer's selling agent. (Ch. 7)

consignee The name for the retailer in a consigned inventory arrangement. (Ch. 7)

consignor The name for the manufacturer in a consigned inventory arrangement. (Ch. 7)

consolidated financial statements Financial statements resulting from combining parent and subsidiary statements. (Ch. 15)

contingent liabilities Liabilities that may arise from past transactions if certain events occur in the future. (Ch. 11)

contra accounts (or contra asset accounts) An account offset against another account. (Ch. 3)

contract rate The periodic interest to be paid on the bonds that is identified in the bond indenture; expressed as a percentage of the face amount of the bond. (Ch. 14)

control environment The overall attitude of management and employees about the importance of controls. (Ch. 8)

controlling account The account in the general ledger that summarizes the balances of the accounts in a subsidiary ledger. (Ch. 5)

copyright An exclusive right to publish and sell a literary, artistic, or musical composition. (Ch. 10)

corporation A business organized under state or federal statutes as a separate legal entity. (Ch. 1)

correcting journal entry An entry that is prepared when an error has already been journalized and posted. (Ch. 2)

cost concept A concept of accounting that determines the amount initially entered into the accounting records for purchases. (Ch. 1)

cost method A method of accounting for equity investments representing less than 20% of the outstanding shares of the investee. The purchase is at original cost, and any gains or losses upon sale are recognized by the difference between the sale proceeds and the original cost. (Ch. 15)

cost of merchandise sold The cost that is reported as an expense when merchandise is sold. (Ch. 6)

credit Amount entered on the right side of an account. (Ch. 2)

credit memorandum (credit memo) A form used by a seller to inform the buyer of the amount the seller proposes to credit to the account receivable due from the buyer. (Ch. 6)

credit period The amount of time the buyer is allowed in which to pay the seller. (Ch. 6)

credit terms Terms for payment on account by the buyer to the seller. (Ch. 6)

cumulative preferred stock Stock that has a right to receive regular dividends that were not declared (paid) in prior years. (Ch. 13)

current assets Cash and other assets that are expected to be converted to cash or sold or used up, usually within one year or less, through the normal operations of the business. (Ch. 4)

current liabilities Liabilities that will be due within a short time (usually one year or less) and that are to be paid out of current assets. (Ch. 4)

current position analysis A company's ability to pay its current liabilities. (Chs. 11, 17)

current ratio A financial ratio that is computed by dividing current assets by current liabilities. (Chs. 4, 17)

D

debit Amount entered on the left side of an account. (Ch. 2)

debit memorandum (debit memo) A form used by a buyer to inform the seller of the amount the buyer proposes to debit to the account payable due the seller. (Ch. 6)

debt securities Notes and bond investments that provide interest revenue over a fixed maturity. (Ch. 15)

deficiency The debit balance in the owner's equity account of a partner. (Ch. 12)

deficit A debit balance in the retained earnings account. (Ch. 13)

defined benefit plan A pension plan that promises employees a fixed annual pension benefit at retirement, based on years of service and compensation levels. (Ch. 11)

defined contribution plan A pension plan that requires a fixed amount of money to be invested on the employee's behalf during the employee's working years. (Ch. 11)

depletion The process of transferring the cost of natural resources to an expense account. (Ch. 10)

depreciate To lose usefulness as all fixed assets except land do. (Ch. 3)

depreciation The systematic periodic transfer of the cost of a fixed asset to an expense account during its expected useful life. (Chs. 3, 10)

depreciation expense The portion of the cost of a fixed asset that is recorded as an expense each year of its useful life. (Ch. 3)

direct method A method of reporting the cash flows from operating activities as the difference between the operating cash receipts and the operating cash payments. (Ch. 16)

direct write-off method The method of accounting for uncollectible accounts that recognizes the expense only when accounts are judged to be worthless. (Ch. 9)

discount The interest deducted from the maturity value of a note or the excess of the face amount of bonds over their issue price. (Chs. 13, 14)

dishonored note receivable A note that the maker fails to pay on the due date. (Ch. 9)

dividend yield A ratio, computed by dividing the annual dividends paid per share of common stock by the market price per share at a specific date, that indicates the rate of return to stockholders in terms of cash dividend distributions. (Chs. 15, 17)

dividends Distribution of a corporation's earnings to stockholders. (Ch. 13)

dividends per share Measures the extent to which earnings are being distributed to common shareholders. (Ch. 17)

double-declining-balance method A method of depreciation that provides periodic depreciation expense based on the declining book value of a fixed asset over its estimated life. (Ch. 10)

double-entry accounting system A system of accounting for recording transactions, based on recording increases and decreases in accounts so that debits equal credits. (Ch. 2)

drawing The account used to record amounts withdrawn by an owner of a proprietorship. (Ch. 2)

E

earnings The amount by which revenues exceed expenses. (Ch. 1)

earnings per common share (EPS) Net income per share of common stock outstanding during a period. (Chs. 13, 14)

earnings per share (EPS) on common stock The profitability ratio of net income available to common shareholders to the number of common shares outstanding. (Ch. 17)

e-commerce The use of the Internet for performing business transactions. (Ch. 5)

effective interest rate method The method of amortizing discounts and premiums that provides for a constant rate of interest on the carrying amount of the bonds at the beginning of each period; often called simply the "interest method." (Ch. 14)

effective rate of interest The market rate of interest at the time bonds are issued. (Ch. 14)

electronic funds transfer (EFT) A system in which computers rather than paper (money, checks, etc.) are used to effect cash transactions. (Ch. 8)

elements of internal control The control environment, risk assessment, control activities, information and communication, and monitoring. (Ch. 8)

employee fraud The intentional act of deceiving an employer for personal gain. (Ch. 8)

employee's earnings record A detailed record of each employee's earnings. (Ch. 11)

equity method A method of accounting for an investment in common stock by which the investment account is adjusted for the investor's share of periodic net income and cash dividends of the investee. (Ch. 15)

equity securities The common and preferred stock of a firm. (Ch. 15)

ethics Moral principles that guide the conduct of individuals. (Ch. 1)

expenses Assets used up or services consumed in the process of generating revenues. (Chs. 1, 2)

extraordinary item An event or a transaction that is both (1) unusual in nature and (2) infrequent in occurrence. (Ch. 17)

F

face amount An amount at which bonds sell if the market rate equals the contract rate. (Ch. 14)

fair value The price that would be received for selling an asset or paying off a liability, often the market price for an equity or debt security. (Ch. 15)

fees earned Revenue from providing services. (Ch. 1)

FICA tax Federal Insurance Contributions Act tax used to finance federal programs for old-age and disability benefits (social security) and health insurance for the aged (Medicare). (Ch. 11)

financial accounting The branch of accounting that is concerned with recording transactions using generally accepted accounting principles (GAAP) for a business or other economic unit and with a periodic preparation of various statements from such records. (Ch. 1)

Financial Accounting Standards Board (FASB) The authoritative body that has the primary responsibility for developing accounting principles. (Ch. 1)

financial statements Financial reports that summarize the effects of events on a business. (Ch. 1)

first-in, first-out (FIFO) inventory cost flow method The method of inventory costing based on the assumption that the costs of merchandise sold should be charged against revenue in the order in which the costs were incurred. (Ch. 7)

fiscal year The annual accounting period adopted by a business. (Ch. 4)

fixed asset turnover ratio The number of dollars of sales that are generated from each dollar of average fixed assets during the year, computed by dividing the net sales by the average net fixed assets. (Ch. 10)

fixed assets (or plant assets) Long-term or relatively permanent tangible assets such as equipment, machinery, and buildings that are used in the normal business operations and that depreciate over time. (Chs. 3, 4, 10)

FOB (free on board) destination Freight terms in which the seller pays the transportation costs from the shipping point to the final destination. (Ch. 6)

FOB (free on board) shipping point Freight terms in which the buyer pays the transportation costs from the shipping point to the final destination. (Ch. 6)

free cash flow The amount of operating cash flow remaining after replacing current productive capacity and maintaining current dividends. (Ch. 16)

fringe benefits Benefits provided to employees in addition to wages and salaries. (Ch. 11)

future value The value of an asset or cash at a specified date in the future that is equivalent in value to a specified sum today. (Ch. 14)

G

general journal The two-column form used for entries that do not "fit" in any of the special journals. (Ch. 5)

general ledger The primary ledger, when used in conjunction with subsidiary ledgers, that contains all of the balance sheet and income statement accounts. (Ch. 5)

general-purpose financial statements A type of financial accounting report that is distributed to external users. The term "general purpose" refers to the wide range of decision-making needs that the reports are designed to serve. (Ch. 1)

generally accepted accounting principles (GAAP) Generally accepted guidelines for the preparation of financial statements. (Ch. 1)

goodwill An intangible asset that is created from such favorable factors as location, product quality, reputation, and managerial skill. (Ch. 10)

gross pay The total earnings of an employee for a payroll period. (Ch. 11)

gross profit Sales minus the cost of merchandise sold. (Ch. 6)

gross profit method A method of estimating inventory cost that is based on the relationship of gross profit to sales. (Ch. 7)

H

held-to-maturity securities Investments in bonds or other debt securities that management intends to hold to their maturity. (Ch. 15)

horizontal analysis Financial analysis that compares an item in a current statement with the same item in prior statements. (Ch. 2)

I

in arrears Cumulative preferred stock dividends that have not been paid in prior years are said to be in arrears. (Ch. 13)

income from operations (operating income) Revenues less operating expenses and service department charges for a profit or an investment center. (Ch. 6)

income statement A summary of the revenue and expenses for a specific period of time, such as a month or a year. (Ch. 1)

Income Summary An account to which the revenue and expense account balances are transferred at the end of a period. (Ch. 4)

indirect method A method of reporting the cash flows from operating activities as the net income from operations adjusted for all deferrals of past cash receipts and payments and all accruals of expected future cash receipts and payments. (Ch. 16)

installment note A debt that requires the borrower to make equal periodic payments to the lender for the term of the note. (Ch. 14)

intangible assets Long-term assets that are useful in the operations of a business, are not held for sale, and are without physical qualities. (Ch. 10)

interest revenue Money received for interest. (Ch. 1)

internal controls The policies and procedures used to safeguard assets, ensure accurate business information, and ensure compliance with laws and regulations. (Chs. 5, 8)

International Accounting Standards Board (IASB) An organization that issues International Financial Reporting Standards for many countries outside the United States. (Ch. 1)

inventory analysis A company's ability to manage its inventory effectively. (Ch. 17)

inventory shrinkage (inventory shortage) The amount by which the merchandise for sale, as indicated by the balance of the merchandise inventory account, is larger than the total amount of merchandise counted during the physical inventory. (Ch. 6)

inventory turnover The relationship between the volume of goods sold and inventory, computed by dividing the cost of goods sold by the average inventory. (Chs. 7, 17)

investee The company whose stock is purchased by the investor. (Ch. 15)

investments The balance sheet caption used to report long-term investments in stocks not intended as a source of cash in the normal operations of the business. (Ch. 15)

investor The company investing in another company's stock. (Ch. 15)

invoice The bill that the seller sends to the buyer. (Chs. 5, 6)

J

journal The initial record in which the effects of a transaction are recorded. (Ch. 2)

journal entry The form of recording a transaction in a journal. (Ch. 2)

journalizing The process of recording a transaction in the journal. (Ch. 2)

L

last-in, first-out (LIFO) inventory cost flow method A method of inventory costing based on the assumption that the most recent merchandise inventory costs should be charged against revenue. (Ch. 7)

ledger A group of accounts for a business. (Ch. 2)

leverage Using debt to increase the return on an investment. (Ch. 17)

liabilities The rights of creditors that represent debts of the business. (Chs. 1, 2)

limited liability company (LLC) A business form consisting of one or more persons or entities filing an operating agreement with a state to conduct business with limited liability to the owners, yet treated as a partnership for tax purposes. (Chs. 1, 12)

liquidation The winding-up process when a partnership goes out of business. (Ch. 12)

liquidity The ability to convert assets into cash. (Chs. 4, 17)

long-term liabilities Liabilities that usually will not be due for more than one year. (Ch. 4)

lower-of-cost-or-market (LCM) method A method of valuing inventory that reports the inventory at the lower of its cost or current market value (replacement cost). (Ch. 7)

M

management (or managerial) accounting The branch of accounting that uses both historical and estimated data in providing information that management uses in conducting daily operations, in planning future operations, and in developing overall business strategies. (Ch. 1)

Management's Discussion and Analysis (MD&A) An annual report disclosure that provides management's analysis of the results of operations and financial condition. (Ch. 17)

manufacturing business A type of business that changes basic inputs into products that are sold to individual customers. (Ch. 1)

market rate of interest The rate determined from sales and purchases of similar bonds. (Ch. 14)

matching concept (or matching principle) A concept of accounting in which expenses are matched with the revenue generated during a period by those expenses. (Chs. 1, 3)

maturity value The amount that is due at the maturity or due date of a note. (Ch. 9)

merchandise inventory Merchandise on hand (not sold) at the end of an accounting period. (Ch. 6)

merchandising business A type of business that purchases products from other businesses and sells them to customers. (Ch. 1)

mortgage notes An installment note that may be secured by a pledge of the borrower's assets. (Ch. 14)

multiple-step income statement A form of income statement that contains several sections, subsections, and subtotals. (Ch. 6)

N

natural business year A fiscal year that ends when business activities have reached the lowest point in an annual operating cycle. (Ch. 4)

net income or net profit The amount by which revenues exceed expenses. (Ch. 1)

net loss The amount by which expenses exceed revenues. (Ch. 1)

net pay Gross pay less payroll deductions; the amount the employer is obligated to pay the employee. (Ch. 11)

net realizable value The estimated selling price of an item of inventory less any direct costs of disposal, such as sales commissions. (Chs. 7, 9)

net sales Revenue received for merchandise sold to customers less any sales returns and allowances and sales discounts. (Ch. 6)

normal balance of an account The normal balance of an account can be either a debit or a credit depending on whether increases in the account are recorded as debits or credits. (Ch. 2)

notes receivable A customer's written promise to pay an amount and possibly interest at an agreed-upon rate. (Chs. 4, 9)

number of days' sales in inventory The relationship between the volume of sales and inventory, computed by dividing the inventory at the end of the year by the average daily cost of goods sold. (Chs. 7, 17)

number of days' sales in receivables The relationship between sales and accounts receivable, computed by dividing the net accounts receivable at the end of the year by the average daily sales. (Chs. 9, 17)

number of times interest charges are earned A ratio that measures creditor margin of safety for interest payments, calculated as income before interest and taxes divided by interest expense. (Chs. 14, 17)

O

objectivity concept A concept of accounting that requires accounting records and the data reported in financial statements to be based on objective evidence. (Ch. 1)

operating cycle The process by which a company spends cash, generates revenues, and receives cash either at the time the revenues are generated or later by collecting an accounts receivable. (Ch. 6)

operating lease A lease that does not meet the criteria for capital leases and thus is accounted for as an operating expense. (Ch. 10)

other comprehensive income Specified items that are reported separately from net income, including foreign currency items, pension liability adjustments, and unrealized gains and losses on investments. (Ch. 15)

other expense Expenses that cannot be traced directly to operations. (Ch. 6)

other income Revenue from sources other than the primary operating activity of a business. (Ch. 6)

outstanding stock The stock in the hands of stockholders. (Ch. 13)

owner's equity The owner's right to the assets of the business. (Chs. 1, 2)

P

paid-in capital Capital contributed to a corporation by the stockholders and others. (Ch. 13)

par The monetary amount printed on a stock certificate. (Ch. 12)

par value A dollar amount assigned to each share of stock. (Ch. 13)

parent company The corporation owning all or a majority of the voting stock of the other corporation. (Ch. 15)

partnership An unincorporated business form consisting of two or more persons conducting business as co-owners for profit. (Chs. 1, 12)

partnership agreement The formal written contract creating a partnership. (Ch. 12)

patents Exclusive rights to produce and sell goods with one or more unique features. (Ch. 10)

payroll The total amount paid to employees for a certain period. (Ch. 11)

payroll register A multicolumn report used to assemble and summarize payroll data at the end of each payroll period. (Ch. 11)

pension A cash payment to retired employees. (Ch. 11)

periodic inventory system The inventory system in which the inventory records do not show the amount available for sale or sold during the period. (Ch. 6)

perpetual inventory system The inventory system in which each purchase and sale of merchandise is recorded in an inventory account. (Ch. 6)

petty cash fund A special cash fund to pay relatively small amounts. (Ch. 8)

physical inventory A detailed listing of merchandise on hand. (Chs. 6, 7)

posting The process of transferring the debits and credits from the journal entries to the accounts. (Ch. 2)

preferred stock A class of stock with preferential rights over common stock. (Ch. 13)

premium The excess of the issue price of a stock over its par value or the excess of the issue price of bonds over their face amount. (Chs. 13, 14)

prepaid expenses Items such as supplies that will be used in the business in the future. (Chs. 1, 3)

present value concept Cash to be received (or paid) in the future is not the equivalent of the same amount of money received at an earlier date. (Ch. 14)

present value of an annuity The sum of the present values of a series of equal cash flows to be received at fixed intervals. (Ch. 14)

price-earnings (P/E) ratio The ratio of the market price per share of common stock, at a specific date, to the annual earnings per share. (Ch. 17)

prior period adjustments Corrections of material errors related to a prior period or periods, excluded from the determination of net income. (Ch. 13)

private accounting The field of accounting whereby accountants are employed by a business firm or a not-for-profit organization. (Ch. 1)

profit The difference between the amounts received from customers for goods or services provided and the amounts paid for the inputs used to provide the goods or services. (Ch. 1)

profitability The ability of a firm to earn income. (Ch. 17)

proprietorship A business owned by one individual. (Ch. 1)

public accounting The field of accounting where accountants and their staff provide services on a fee basis. (Ch. 1)

public companies Companies that issue publicly traded debt or equity securities. (App. D)

Public Company Accounting Oversight Board (PCAOB) A new oversight body for the accounting profession that was established by the Sarbanes-Oxley Act. (Ch. 1)

purchase order The purchase order authorizes the purchase of the inventory from an approved vendor. (Ch. 7)

purchases discounts Discounts taken by the buyer for early payment of an invoice. (Ch. 6)

purchases journal The journal in which all items purchased on account are recorded. (Ch. 5)

purchases returns and allowances From the buyer's perspective, returned merchandise or an adjustment for defective merchandise. (Ch. 6)

Q

quick assets Cash and other current assets that can be quickly converted to cash, such as marketable securities and receivables. (Chs. 11, 17)

quick ratio A financial ratio that measures the ability to pay current liabilities with quick assets (cash, marketable securities, accounts receivable). (Chs. 11, 17)

R

rate earned on common stockholders' equity A measure of profitability computed by dividing net income, reduced by preferred dividend requirements, by common stockholders' equity. (Ch. 17)

rate earned on stockholders' equity A measure of profitability computed by dividing net income by total stockholders' equity. (Ch. 17)

rate earned on total assets A measure of the profitability of assets, without regard to the equity of creditors and stockholders in the assets. (Ch. 17)

ratio of cash to monthly cash expenses Ratio that helps assess how long a company can continue to operate without additional financing or generating positive cash flows from operations. (Ch. 8)

ratio of fixed assets to long-term liabilities A leverage ratio that measures the margin of safety of long-term creditors, calculated as the net fixed assets divided by the long-term liabilities. (Ch. 17)

ratio of liabilities to owner's (stockholders') equity A comprehensive leverage ratio that measures the relationship of the claims of creditors to stockholders' equity. (Chs. 1, 17)

ratio of net sales to assets Ratio that measures how effectively a company uses its assets, computed as net sales divided by average total assets. (Chs. 6, 17)

real (permanent) accounts Term for balance sheet accounts because they are relatively permanent and carried forward from year to year. (Ch. 4)

realization The sale of assets when a partnership is being liquidated. (Ch. 12)

receivables All money claims against other entities, including people, business firms, and other organizations. (Ch. 9)

receiving report The form or electronic transmission used by the receiving personnel to indicate that materials have been received and inspected. (Ch. 7)

rent revenue Money received for rent. (Ch. 1)

report form The form of balance sheet with the Liabilities and Owner's Equity sections presented below the Assets section. (Ch. 6)

residual value The estimated value of a fixed asset at the end of its useful life. (Ch. 10)

restrictions Amounts of retained earnings that have been limited for use as dividends. (Ch. 13)

retail inventory method A method of estimating inventory cost that is based on the relationship of gross profit to sales. (Ch. 7)

retained earnings Net income retained in a corporation. (Ch. 13)

retained earnings statement A summary of the changes in the retained earnings in a corporation for a specific period of time, such as a month or a year. (Ch. 13)

revenue expenditures Costs that benefit only the current period or costs incurred for normal maintenance and repairs of fixed assets. (Ch. 10)

revenue journal The journal in which all sales and services on account are recorded. (Ch. 5)

revenue per employee A measure of the efficiency of the business in generating revenues, which is computed as revenue divided by number of employees. (Ch. 12)

revenue recognition concept The concept that supports recording revenues when services have been performed or products delivered to customers. (Ch. 3)

revenues Increases in assets from performing services or delivering products to customers. (Chs. 1, 2)

rules of debit and credit In the double-entry accounting system, specific rules for recording debits and credits based on the type of account. (Ch. 2)

S

sales The total amount charged customers for merchandise sold, including cash sales and sales on account. (Chs. 1, 6)

sales discounts From the seller's perspective, discounts that a seller may offer the buyer for early payment. (Ch. 6)

sales returns and allowances From the seller's perspective, returned merchandise or an adjustment for defective merchandise. (Ch. 6)

Sarbanes-Oxley Act (SOX) An act passed by Congress to restore public confidence and trust in the financial statements of companies. (Chs. 1, 8)

Securities and Exchange Commission (SEC) An agency of the U.S. government that has authority over the accounting and financial disclosures for companies whose shares of ownership (stock) are traded and sold to the public. (Ch. 1)

selling expenses Expenses that are incurred directly in the selling of merchandise. (Ch. 6)

service business A business providing services rather than products to customers. (Ch. 1)

single-step income statement A form of income statement in which the total of all expenses is deducted from the total of all revenues. (Ch. 6)

slide An error in which the entire number is moved one or more spaces to the right or the left, such as writing $542.00 as $54.20 or $5,420.00. (Ch. 2)

solvency The ability of a firm to pay its debts as they come due. (Chs. 4, 17)

special journals Journals designed to be used for recording a single type of transaction. (Ch. 5)

special-purpose funds Cash funds used for a special business need. (Ch. 8)

specific identification inventory cost flow method Inventory method in which the unit sold is identified with a specific purchase. (Ch. 7)

statement of cash flows A summary of the cash receipts and cash payments for a specific period of time, such as a month or a year. (Chs. 1, 16)

statement of members' equity A summary of the changes in each member's equity in a limited liability corporation that have occurred during a specific period of time. (Ch. 12)

statement of owner's equity A summary of the changes in owner's equity that have occurred during a specific period of time, such as a month or a year. (Ch. 1)

statement of partnership equity A summary of the changes in each partner's capital in a partnership that have occurred during a specific period of time. (Ch. 12)

statement of partnership liquidation A summary of the liquidation process whereby cash is distributed to the partners based on the balances in their capital accounts. (Ch. 12)

statement of stockholders' equity A summary of the changes in the stockholders' equity in a corporation that have occurred during a specific period of time. (Ch. 13)

stock Shares of ownership of a corporation. (Ch. 13)

stock dividend A distribution of shares of stock to its stockholders. (Ch. 13)

stock split A reduction in the par or stated value of a common stock and the issuance of a proportionate number of additional shares. (Ch. 13)

stockholders The owners of a corporation. (Ch. 13)

stockholders' equity The owners' equity in a corporation. (Ch. 13)

straight-line method A method of depreciation that provides for equal periodic depreciation expense over the estimated life of a fixed asset. (Ch. 10)

subsidiary company The corporation that is controlled by a parent company. (Ch. 15)

subsidiary inventory ledger The subsidiary ledger containing individual accounts for items of inventory. (Ch. 7)

subsidiary ledger A ledger containing individual accounts with a common characteristic. (Ch. 5)

T

T account The simplest form of an account. (Ch. 2)

temporary (nominal) accounts Accounts that report amounts for only one period. (Ch. 4)

trade discounts Discounts from the list prices in published catalogs or special discounts offered to certain classes of buyers. (Ch. 6)

trade-in allowance The amount a seller allows a buyer for a fixed asset that is traded in for a similar asset. (Ch. 10)

trademark A name, term, or symbol used to identify a business and its products. (Ch. 10)

trading securities Securities that management intends to actively trade for profit. (Ch. 15)

transposition An error in which the order of the digits is changed, such as writing $542 as $452 or $524. (Ch. 2)

treasury stock Stock that a corporation has once issued and then reacquires. (Ch. 13)

trial balance A summary listing of the titles and balances of accounts in the ledger. (Ch. 2)

U

unadjusted trial balance A summary listing of the titles and balances of accounts in the ledger prior to the posting of adjusting entries. (Ch. 2)

unearned revenue The liability created by receiving revenue in advance. (Chs. 2, 3)

unit of measure concept A concept of accounting requiring that economic data be recorded in dollars. (Ch. 1)

units-of-output method A method of depreciation that provides for depreciation expense based on the expected productive capacity of a fixed asset. (Ch. 10)

unrealized gain or loss Changes in the fair value of equity or debt securities for a period. (Ch. 15)

V

variable costs Costs that vary in total dollar amount as the level of activity changes. (Ch. 21)

vertical analysis An analysis that compares each item in a current statement with a total amount within the same statement. (Chs. 3, 17)

voucher A special form for recording relevant data about a liability and the details of its payment. (Ch. 8)

voucher system A set of procedures for authorizing and recording liabilities and cash payments. (Ch. 8)

W

weighted average inventory cost flow method A method of inventory costing in which the cost of the units sold and in ending inventory is a weighted average of the purchase costs. (Ch. 7)

working capital The excess of the current assets of a business over its current liabilities. (Chs. 4, 17)

Index

B

C

D

E

F

G

H

I

J

O

P

Q

R

X

Y

Z